OECD International Direct Investment Statistics 2021

OECD
BETTER POLICIES FOR BETTER LIVES

Please cite this publication as:
OECD (2022), *OECD International Direct Investment Statistics 2021*, OECD Publishing, Paris, *https://doi.org/10.1787/981db434-en*.

ISBN 978-92-64-81120-1 (print)
ISBN 978-92-64-87249-3 (pdf)

OECD International Direct Investment Statistics
ISSN 2307-4361 (print)
ISSN 2307-437X (online)

Corrigenda to publications may be found on line at: *www.oecd.org/about/publishing/corrigenda.htm*.

Table of contents

Conventional signs and abbreviations

Foreign direct investment (FDI) flows and FDI positions are converted using average exchange rates and end of period exchange rates, respectively.

Data in national currencies are available and are accessible via *OECD International Direct Investment Statistics* (*http:/dx.doi.org/10.1787/idi-data-en*).

Signs and abbreviations

..	Not available
.	Decimal point
|	Break in series
c	Confidential data
d	Secondary confidentiality
-	Nil

Reporting and partner countries

OECD total	The OECD aggregate corresponds to the member country composition of the reporting period: 2010-15: 34 member countries 2016-17: 35 member countries, including Latvia 2018: 36 member countries, including Lithuania 2020: 37 member countries, including Colombia 2021: 38 member countries, including Costa Rica
European Union	EU27 for 2007 to 2012, EU28 for 2013-19 and EU27 (excluding UK) from 2020.
ASEAN	Association of South-East Asian Nations, includes: Brunei Darussalam, Cambodia, Indonesia, Lao People's Democratic Republic, Malaysia, Myanmar, Philippines, Singapore, Thailand, Viet Nam.

International comparisons

INTERNATIONAL COMPARISONS

Table 1. Foreign direct investment inflows, US dollars

Million US dollars

	2012	2013	2014	2015	2016	2017	2018	2019	2020	2021
Australia[1]	59 540	56 273	58 505	29 584	48 397	45 220	68 462	39 218	20 140	29 773
Austria	4 003	5 813	4 800	1 295	-8 401	14 926	5 512	2 913	-14 963	5 855
Belgium[2]	88 627	-5 751	32 082	-24 013	68 178	-3 057	27 119	-9 209	13 881	22 955
Canada	43 118	69 371	59 008	43 853	36 062	22 764	37 654	50 142	23 174	59 694
Chile[2]	31 662	22 020	22 793	20 508	12 249	6 129	7 736	12 499	8 386	15 252
Colombia[1]	15 040	16 210	16 169	11 621	13 858	13 701	11 299	13 990	7 459	9 402
Costa Rica	2 258	2 741	2 927	2 752	2 204	2 778	2 487	2 812	1 757	3 324
Czech Republic[1]	8 000	3 641	5 492	465	9 814	9 518	11 010	10 109	9 411	5 805
Denmark[2]	644	1 045	4 680	3 617	235	3 771	1 716	7 073	3 210	5 540
Estonia	1 566	771	684	36	1 058	1 947	1 516	3 184	3 388	989
Finland	4 156	-106 |	18 548	2 110	8 576	2 858	-2 170	13 455	-1 422	8 927
France[1]	16 069	34 264	2 669	45 355	23 055	24 780	41 807	28 362	4 862	14 159
Germany[1]	28 190	12 771 |	-3 200	30 534	15 618	48 538	72 053	52 664	64 442	31 263
Greece[1]	1 741	2 817	2 683	1 268	2 762	3 477	3 971	5 019	3 205	5 731
Hungary	14 625	3 587	7 967	-14 545	-5 439	3 514	6 460	4 329	6 801	5 459
Iceland[2]	1 025	397	447	709	-427	-41	-382	-225	-933	174
Ireland	48 901 |	50 585	48 186	217 820	39 377	52 722	-12 512	158 489	82 122	15 926
Israel[1]	9 018	11 842	6 049	11 336	11 988	16 893	21 515	17 363	24 283	29 615
Italy[1]	93	24 267 |	23 224	19 631	28 441	23 996	37 659	18 145	-23 568	8 486
Japan	1 732	2 303	10 622	-2 251	19 357	9 354	9 961	13 724	10 255	24 650
Korea	11 117	6 083 |	-917	3 076	7 415	12 699	13 299	12 548	8 765	16 820
Latvia[1]	1 113	903	896	741	253	708	963	902	1 011	5 326
Lithuania	802	574	-133	1 055	302	1 019	976	3 022	3 484	2 053
Luxembourg[2]	2 825 |	23 288	20 034	45 422	17 564	-27 311	-26 029	12 801	102 036	-9 053
Mexico[2]	21 757	48 245	30 531	35 517	31 186	34 131	34 090	34 411	27 934	31 621
Netherlands[2]	20 121	51 096	45 018	163 714	54 369	9 146	86 903	-19 119	-126 528	-81 045
New Zealand[1]	3 502	1 860	2 437	-311	2 979	2 721	2 297	4 279	3 812	3 482
Norway	16 655	-5 916 |	19 504	-2 515	-3 900	-5 922	226	17 354	-3 731	6 737
Poland[1]	12 441	3 626	17 612	13 063	16 596	9 537	16 376	13 326	13 650	24 822
Portugal[2]	8 157	8 216	4 560	9 180	5 684	6 912	7 175	12 251	7 566	7 980
Slovak Republic[1]	2 826	-604	-512	106	805	4 008	1 643	2 511	-1 926	59
Slovenia[1]	339	-151	1 050	1 675	1 245	896	1 383	1 463	205	1 517
Spain	24 667	28 342	22 571	8 557	31 538	41 877	57 427	17 416	12 607	9 776
Sweden	16 349	4 125	4 032	8 449	19 153	12 511	3 807	9 111	18 805	26 972
Switzerland[2]	..	..	11 384	71 228	84 983	119 136	-95 712	-91 207	-42 187	37 210
Turkey[1]	13 743	13 565	12 973	18 978	13 653	10 959	12 535	9 701	7 773	12 177
United Kingdom	55 626	51 673	24 704	39 189	258 570	96 401	87 818	45 445	18 201	27 564
United States[1]	211 467	217 274	211 985	483 849	480 016	325 073	216 014	237 973	164 396	381 933
OECD total	**828 750**	**767 622**	**752 064**	**1 302 656**	**1 349 377**	**958 287**	**774 064**	**768 244**	**461 762**	**808 930**
European Union[3]	**438 691**	**337 779**	**346 509**	**613 416**	**607 121**	**368 664**	**445 027**	**451 168**	**194 583**	**138 290**
G20	**890 956**	**1 013 455**	**866 436**	**1 133 901**	**1 288 724**	**988 025**	**1 023 838**	**917 809**	**713 631**	**1 190 315**
of which:										
Non-OECD G20 countries	**428 504**	**477 367**	**436 332**	**386 589**	**326 953**	**334 110**	**392 487**	**375 475**	**387 258**	**552 176**
Argentina	15 324	9 822	5 065	11 759	3 260	11 517	11 717	6 663	4 019	6 534
Brazil	82 060	59 089	63 846	49 961	53 700	66 585	59 802	65 386	28 318	50 367
China	241 214	290 928	268 097	242 489	174 750	166 084	235 365	187 170	253 096	333 979
India	23 995	28 153	34 577	44 009	44 459	39 966	42 117	50 610	64 362	44 708
Indonesia	19 138	18 817	21 811	16 641	3 921	20 579	20 563	23 883	18 591	20 081
Russian Federation	30 188	53 397	29 152	11 858	37 176	25 954	13 228	32 076	10 410	38 240
Saudi Arabia	12 182	8 865	8 012	8 141	7 453	1 419	4 247	4 563	5 399	..
South Africa	4 403	8 296	5 772	1 729	2 235	2 007	5 447	5 125	3 062	40 889
World	**1 653 811**	**1 582 644**	**1 591 330**	**2 130 898**	**2 046 619**	**1 690 506**	**1 498 604**	**1 514 339**	**1 133 273**	**1 778 916**

.. Not available; | Break in series

Note: Detailed metadata at: *http://metalinks.oecd.org/idi/20220712/ea54.*

1. Resident Special Purpose Entities (SPEs) are not present or not significant.
2. Data excludes Special Purpose Entities (SPEs).
3. EU27 for 2007 to 2012, EU28 for 2013-19 and EU27 (excluding UK) from 2020.

Source: *OECD International Direct Investment Statistics (database): https://doi.org/10.1787/idi-data-en*

INTERNATIONAL COMPARISONS

Table 2. Foreign direct investment outflows, US dollars

Million US dollars

	2012	2013	2014	2015	2016	2017	2018	2019	2020	2021
Australia[1]	7 889	1 441	18 184	-9 340	2 304	6 355	7 797	9 264	9 168	13 915
Austria	13 060	15 598	-665	6 915	-1 323	10 679	5 678	12 655	-2 222	10 925
Belgium[2]	77 031	24 853	26 737	61 561	40 164	29 563	43 554	-9 306	11 745	45 756
Canada	55 875	57 364	60 273	67 467	69 518	76 179	58 036	79 377	46 526	89 901
Chile[2]	21 225	9 315	10 847	15 171	8 070	3 558	1 940	9 904	11 583	14 454
Colombia[1]	-606	7 652	3 899	4 218	4 517	3 690	5 126	3 153	1 656	3 362
Costa Rica	455	340	109	211	77	126	53	117	112	215
Czech Republic[1]	1 794	4 021	1 620	2 488	2 182	7 557	8 663	4 128	2 989	5 582
Denmark[2]	7 349	7 162	8 249	9 424	10 112	10 025	-76	16 844	10 900	22 396
Estonia	1 054	516	42	182	486	888	45	1 966	219	1 547
Finland	7 546	-2 307 |	1 743	-16 080	24 252	-575	11 448	4 864	5 850	3 626
France[1]	35 453	20 365	49 785	53 206	64 785	35 908	101 978	33 817	45 906	-2 842
Germany[1]	62 188	39 512 |	83 968	99 003	63 599	86 333	97 172	137 289	60 486	151 671
Greece[1]	678	-785	3 015	1 578	-1 665	168	477	642	547	926
Hungary	11 802	1 943	3 854	-16 118	-8 272	1 220	3 363	3 211	4 222	2 882
Iceland[2]	-3 205	460	-257	-31	-1 147	-208	76	479	-391	19
Ireland	22 557 |	29 164	41 182	168 443	30 055	-2 043	4 314	34 442	-46 482	62 229
Israel[1]	2 276	3 858	4 526	10 969	14 579	7 624	6 087	8 690	6 375	9 713
Italy[1]	7 992	25 130 |	26 327	21 640	16 165	24 478	31 523	19 786	-1 852	11 757
Japan	122 514	135 745	129 157	128 698	155 923	164 563	144 963	232 723	115 716	146 768
Korea	27 355	31 488 |	19 994	18 490	30 508	51 044	45 232	50 984	34 832	60 820
Latvia[1]	193	412	540	73	160	138	203	-104	269	3 361
Lithuania	541	132	59	377	43	80	704	1 746	2 868	663
Luxembourg[2]	-13 402 |	46 599	43 365	31 912	-1 240	14 987	-25 462	-2 576	102 391	25 395
Mexico[2]	22 313	15 459	7 507	10 672	160	3 988	8 365	10 640	2 710	-717
Netherlands[2]	6 174	69 690	53 951	233 438	185 089	20 856	-47 986	19 892	-177 245	28 858
New Zealand[1]	-433	530	472	-58	196	227	376	-168	523	-1 876
Norway	19 791	6 213 |	32 939	30 947	3 092	-7 415	11 405	12 973	-2 067	16 820
Poland[1]	2 905	-451	4 701	3 172	12 389	1 908	1 239	1 674	1 104	178
Portugal[2]	-8 474	769	-3 260	4 810	879	-928	1 374	4 011	2 566	-1 231
Slovak Republic[1]	-73	-313	43	6	95	1 323	291	43	235	389
Slovenia[1]	-258	-214	275	267	290	338	281	610	508	922
Spain	-2 479	14 294	36 743	41 917	43 902	55 926	37 523	24 826	34 941	-1 625
Sweden	28 977	30 279	9 162	13 045	4 703	27 369	17 834	16 104	23 689	20 347
Switzerland[2]	..	..	730	83 871	97 493	24 295	60 287	-53 034	-27 464	9 122
Turkey[1]	4 106	3 536	6 681	4 813	2 953	2 625	3 655	2 969	3 231	4 987
United Kingdom	20 767	40 483	-151 368	-66 827	-37 587	142 443	82 943	-6 080	-65 388	107 751
United States[1]	338 363	321 937	347 658	274 486	305 441	353 663	-128 316	57 964	264 791	433 613
OECD total	**941 066**	**997 398**	**882 786**	**1 295 015**	**1 142 946**	**1 158 952**	**602 164**	**746 520**	**485 548**	**1 302 577**
European Union[3]	**349 557**	**388 452**	**300 428**	**691 509**	**447 537**	**475 267**	**362 897**	**355 960**	**72 992**	**385 004**
G20	**812 092**	**856 529**	**815 989**	**817 607**	**919 272**	**1 168 033**	**660 381**	**843 322**	**683 515**	**1 272 844**
of which:										
Non-OECD G20 countries	**107 278**	**164 068**	**217 823**	**215 298**	**245 504**	**220 454**	**207 034**	**212 691**	**167 388**	**255 220**
Argentina	1 055	890	1 921	875	1 787	1 156	1 726	1 539	1 294	1 363
Brazil	-8 425	-478	-3 261	-11 643	-5 901	19 040	-16 336	19 031	-12 935	23 083
China	64 963	72 971	123 130	174 391	216 424	138 293	143 027	136 910	153 721	128 037
India	8 553	1 765	11 686	7 514	5 047	11 090	11 418	13 141	11 122	15 520
Indonesia	5 422	6 647	7 077	5 937	-12 215	2 077	8 053	3 352	4 448	3 596
Russian Federation	28 423	70 685	64 203	27 090	26 951	34 153	35 820	22 024	6 778	63 602
Saudi Arabia	4 402	4 943	5 396	5 390	8 936	7 280	19 252	13 547	4 911	..
South Africa	2 886	6 646	7 671	5 744	4 474	7 366	4 074	3 147	-1 951	19
World	**1 298 625**	**1 384 974**	**1 428 842**	**1 726 065**	**1 559 055**	**1 603 082**	**935 356**	**1 125 355**	**795 809**	**1 850 434**

.. Not available; | Break in series

Note: Detailed metadata at: *http://metalinks.oecd.org/idi/20220712/ea54*.

1. Resident Special Purpose Entities (SPEs) are not present or not significant.
2. Data excludes Special Purpose Entities (SPEs).
3. EU27 for 2007 to 2012, EU28 for 2013-19 and EU27 (excluding UK) from 2020.

Source: OECD *International Direct Investment Statistics (database): https://doi.org/10.1787/idi-data-en*

Table 3. Foreign direct investment inflows as a percentage of GDP

Per cent

	2012	2013	2014	2015	2016	2017	2018	2019	2020	2021
Australia[1]	3.7	3.6	4.0	2.4	3.7	3.2	4.7	2.8	1.4	1.8
Austria	1.0	1.4	1.1	0.3	-2.1	3.6	1.2	0.7	-3.5	1.2
Belgium[2]	17.9	-1.1	6.0	-5.2	14.3	-0.6	5.0	-1.7	2.7	3.8
Canada	2.4	3.8	3.3	2.8	2.4	1.4	2.2	2.9	1.4	3.0
Chile[2]	11.9	7.9	8.7	8.4	4.9	2.2	2.6	4.4	3.4	4.6
Colombia[1]	4.1	4.2	4.2	4.0	4.9	4.4	3.4	4.3	2.7	3.1
Costa Rica	4.8	5.4	5.6	4.9	3.7	4.6	4.0	4.4	2.8	5.4
Czech Republic[1]	3.8	1.7	2.6	0.2	5.0	4.4	4.4	4.0	3.8	2.1
Denmark[2]	0.2	0.3	1.3	1.2	0.1	1.1	0.5	2.0	0.9	1.4
Estonia	6.8	3.1	2.6	0.2	4.4	7.2	5.0	10.3	11.1	2.7
Finland	1.6	0.0 |	6.7	0.9	3.6	1.1	-0.8	5.0	-0.5	3.0
France[1]	0.6	1.2	0.1	1.9	0.9	1.0	1.5	1.0	0.2	0.5
Germany[1]	0.8	0.3 |	-0.1	0.9	0.5	1.3	1.8	1.4	1.7	0.7
Greece[1]	0.7	1.2	1.1	0.6	1.4	1.7	1.9	2.4	1.7	2.7
Hungary	11.3	2.6	5.6	-11.6	-4.2	2.5	4.0	2.6	4.4	3.0
Iceland[2]	6.9	2.5	2.5	4.0	-2.1	-0.2	-1.5	-0.9	-4.3	0.7
Ireland	21.7 |	21.2	18.6	74.7	13.1	15.5	-3.2	39.7	19.3	3.2
Israel[1]	3.5	4.0	1.9	3.8	3.8	4.8	5.8	4.4	6.0	6.1
Italy[1]	0.0	1.1 |	1.1	1.1	1.5	1.2	1.8	0.9	-1.2	0.4
Japan	0.0	0.0	0.2	-0.1	0.4	0.2	0.2	0.3	0.2	0.5
Korea	0.9	0.4 |	-0.1	0.2	0.5	0.8	0.8	0.8	0.5	0.9
Latvia[1]	4.0	3.0	2.9	2.7	0.9	2.3	2.8	2.6	3.0	13.7
Lithuania	1.9	1.2	-0.3	2.5	0.7	2.1	1.8	5.5	6.2	3.1
Luxembourg[2]	4.7 |	35.7	29.1	75.6	28.2	-41.6	-36.5	18.2	139.1	-10.4
Mexico[2]	1.8	3.8	2.3	3.0	2.9	2.9	2.8	2.7	2.6	2.5
Netherlands[2]	2.4	5.8	5.0	21.4	6.9	1.1	9.5	-2.1	-13.8	-8.0
New Zealand[1]	2.0	1.0	1.2	-0.2	1.6	1.3	1.1	2.0	1.8	1.4
Norway	3.3	-1.1 |	3.9	-0.7	-1.1	-1.5	0.1	4.3	-1.0	1.4
Poland[1]	2.5	0.7	3.2	2.7	3.5	1.8	2.8	2.2	2.3	3.7
Portugal[2]	3.8	3.6	2.0	4.6	2.8	3.1	3.0	5.1	3.3	3.2
Slovak Republic[1]	3.0	-0.6	-0.5	0.1	0.9	4.2	1.6	2.4	-1.8	0.1
Slovenia[1]	0.7	-0.3	2.1	3.9	2.8	1.8	2.6	2.7	0.4	2.5
Spain	1.9	2.1	1.6	0.7	2.6	3.2	4.0	1.3	1.0	0.7
Sweden	3.0	0.7	0.7	1.7	3.7	2.3	0.7	1.7	3.5	4.3
Switzerland[2]	..	..	1.6	10.1	12.2	16.9	-13.0	-12.5	-5.6	4.6
Turkey[1]	1.6	1.4	1.4	2.2	1.6	1.3	1.6	1.3	1.1	1.5
United Kingdom	2.1	1.9	0.8	1.3	9.6	3.6	3.1	1.6	0.7	0.9
United States[1]	1.3	1.3	1.2	2.7	2.6	1.7	1.0	1.1	0.8	1.7
OECD total	**1.7**	**1.6**	**1.5**	**2.8**	**2.8**	**1.9**	**1.4**	**1.4**	**0.9**	**1.4**
European Union[3]	**2.6**	**1.9**	**1.8**	**3.7**	**3.7**	**2.1**	**2.4**	**2.4**	**1.3**	**0.8**
G20	**1.5**	**1.7**	**1.4**	**1.9**	**2.2**	**1.6**	**1.5**	**1.3**	**1.1**	**1.6**
of which:										
Non-OECD G20 countries	**2.4**	**2.5**	**2.2**	**2.1**	**1.7**	**1.6**	**1.7**	**1.6**	**1.7**	**2.1**
Argentina	2.6	1.6	0.9	1.8	0.6	1.8	2.3	1.5	1.0	1.4
Brazil	3.3	2.4	2.6	2.8	3.0	3.2	3.1	3.5	2.0	3.1
China	2.8	3.0	2.6	2.2	1.6	1.3	1.7	1.3	1.7	2.0
India	1.3	1.5	1.7	2.1	1.9	1.5	1.6	1.8	2.5	1.5
Indonesia	2.1	2.1	2.4	1.9	0.4	2.0	2.0	2.1	1.8	1.7
Russian Federation	1.4	2.3	1.4	0.9	2.9	1.6	0.8	1.9	0.7	2.3
Saudi Arabia	1.7	1.2	1.1	1.2	1.2	0.2	0.5	0.6	0.8	..
South Africa	1.1	2.3	1.6	0.5	0.8	0.6	1.5	1.5	1.0	9.8

.. Not available; | Break in series

Note: Detailed metadata at: *http://metalinks.oecd.org/idi/20220712/ea54.*

1. Resident Special Purpose Entities (SPEs) are not present or not significant.
2. Data excludes Special Purpose Entities (SPEs).
3. EU27 for 2007 to 2012, EU28 for 2013-19 and EU27 (excluding UK) from 2020.

Source: *OECD International Direct Investment Statistics (database): https://doi.org/10.1787/idi-data-en*

INTERNATIONAL COMPARISONS

Table 4. Foreign direct investment outflows as a percentage of GDP

Per cent

	2012	2013	2014	2015	2016	2017	2018	2019	2020	2021
Australia[1]	0.5	0.1	1.2	-0.7	0.2	0.4	0.5	0.7	0.6	0.9
Austria	3.2	3.6	-0.2	1.8	-0.3	2.6	1.2	2.8	-0.5	2.3
Belgium[2]	15.5	4.8	5.0	13.3	8.4	5.9	8.0	-1.7	2.3	7.6
Canada	3.1	3.1	3.3	4.3	4.5	4.6	3.4	4.6	2.8	4.5
Chile[2]	7.9	3.3	4.2	6.2	3.2	1.3	0.7	3.5	4.7	4.4
Colombia[1]	-0.2	2.0	1.0	1.4	1.6	1.2	1.5	1.0	0.6	1.1
Costa Rica	1.0	0.7	0.2	0.4	0.1	0.2	0.1	0.2	0.2	0.3
Czech Republic[1]	0.9	1.9	0.8	1.3	1.1	3.5	3.5	1.6	1.2	2.0
Denmark[2]	2.2	2.1	2.3	3.1	3.2	3.0	0.0	4.8	3.1	5.7
Estonia	4.6	2.1	0.2	0.8	2.0	3.3	0.1	6.3	0.7	4.3
Finland	2.9	-0.9 |	0.6	-6.9	10.1	-0.2	4.2	1.8	2.2	1.2
France[1]	1.3	0.7	1.7	2.2	2.6	1.4	3.7	1.2	1.7	-0.1
Germany[1]	1.8	1.1 |	2.2	2.9	1.8	2.3	2.4	3.5	1.6	3.6
Greece[1]	0.3	-0.3	1.3	0.8	-0.9	0.1	0.2	0.3	0.3	0.4
Hungary	9.2	1.4	2.7	-12.9	-6.4	0.9	2.1	2.0	2.7	1.6
Iceland[2]	-21.7	2.9	-1.4	-0.2	-5.5	-0.8	0.3	1.9	-1.8	0.1
Ireland	10.0 |	12.2	15.9	57.8	10.0	-0.6	1.1	8.6	-10.9	12.5
Israel[1]	0.9	1.3	1.5	3.7	4.6	2.1	1.6	2.2	1.6	2.0
Italy[1]	0.4	1.2 |	1.2	1.2	0.9	1.2	1.5	1.0	-0.1	0.6
Japan	2.0	2.6	2.7	2.9	3.2	3.4	2.9	4.6	2.4	2.9
Korea	2.1	2.3 |	1.3	1.3	2.0	3.1	2.6	3.1	2.1	3.3
Latvia[1]	0.7	1.4	1.7	0.3	0.6	0.5	0.6	-0.3	0.8	8.6
Lithuania	1.3	0.3	0.1	0.9	0.1	0.2	1.3	3.2	5.1	1.0
Luxembourg[2]	-22.4 |	71.5	63.0	53.1	-2.0	22.8	-35.7	-3.7	139.6	29.3
Mexico[2]	1.9	1.2	0.6	0.9	0.0	0.3	0.7	0.8	0.2	-0.1
Netherlands[2]	0.7	7.9	6.0	30.5	23.6	2.5	-5.2	2.2	-19.4	2.8
New Zealand[1]	-0.2	0.3	0.2	0.0	0.1	0.1	0.2	-0.1	0.2	-0.8
Norway	3.9	1.2 |	6.6	8.0	0.8	-1.9	2.6	3.2	-0.6	3.5
Poland[1]	0.6	-0.1	0.9	0.7	2.6	0.4	0.2	0.3	0.2	0.0
Portugal[2]	-3.9	0.3	-1.4	2.4	0.4	-0.4	0.6	1.7	1.1	-0.5
Slovak Republic[1]	-0.1	-0.3	0.0	0.0	0.1	1.4	0.3	0.0	0.2	0.3
Slovenia[1]	-0.6	-0.4	0.6	0.6	0.6	0.7	0.5	1.1	0.9	1.5
Spain	-0.2	1.1	2.7	3.5	3.6	4.3	2.6	1.8	2.7	-0.1
Sweden	5.2	5.2	1.6	2.6	0.9	5.1	3.2	3.0	4.4	3.2
Switzerland[2]	..	..	0.1	11.9	14.0	3.4	8.2	-7.2	-3.7	1.1
Turkey[1]	0.5	0.4	0.7	0.6	0.3	0.3	0.5	0.4	0.4	0.6
United Kingdom	0.8	1.5	-4.9	-2.3	-1.4	5.3	2.9	-0.2	-2.4	3.4
United States[1]	2.1	1.9	2.0	1.5	1.6	1.8	-0.6	0.3	1.3	1.9
OECD total	**1.9**	**2.0**	**1.8**	**2.7**	**2.4**	**2.3**	**1.1**	**1.4**	**0.9**	**2.2**
European Union[3]	**2.0**	**2.1**	**1.6**	**4.2**	**2.7**	**2.7**	**1.9**	**1.9**	**0.5**	**2.3**
G20	**1.4**	**1.4**	**1.3**	**1.4**	**1.5**	**1.8**	**1.0**	**1.2**	**1.0**	**1.7**
of which:										
Non-OECD G20 countries	**0.6**	**0.9**	**1.1**	**1.1**	**1.3**	**1.0**	**0.9**	**0.9**	**0.7**	**1.0**
Argentina	0.2	0.1	0.3	0.1	0.3	0.2	0.3	0.3	0.3	0.3
Brazil	-0.3	0.0	-0.1	-0.6	-0.3	0.9	-0.9	1.0	-0.9	1.4
China	0.8	0.8	1.2	1.6	1.9	1.1	1.0	1.0	1.0	0.8
India	0.5	0.1	0.6	0.4	0.2	0.4	0.4	0.5	0.4	0.5
Indonesia	0.6	0.7	0.8	0.7	-1.3	0.2	0.8	0.3	0.4	0.3
Russian Federation	1.3	3.1	3.1	2.0	2.1	2.2	2.1	1.3	0.5	3.9
Saudi Arabia	0.6	0.7	0.7	0.8	1.4	1.1	2.4	1.7	0.7	..
South Africa	0.7	1.8	2.2	1.8	1.5	2.1	1.1	0.9	-0.6	0.0

.. Not available; | Break in series

Note: Detailed metadata at: *http://metalinks.oecd.org/idi/20220712/ea54.*

1. Resident Special Purpose Entities (SPEs) are not present or not significant.
2. Data excludes Special Purpose Entities (SPEs).
3. EU27 for 2007 to 2012, EU28 for 2013-19 and EU27 (excluding UK) from 2020.

Source: *OECD International Direct Investment Statistics (database): https://doi.org/10.1787/idi-data-en*

Table 5. Foreign direct investment inward positions (stocks), US dollars

At year end

Million US dollars

	2012	2013	2014	2015	2016	2017	2018	2019	2020	2021
Australia[1]	615 116	568 855	582 540	566 437	611 119	699 378	701 331	731 200	790 633	..
Austria[2]	171 697	186 591	182 785	165 845	156 671	198 302	191 850	200 116	207 899	204 922
Belgium[2]	..	557 245	496 519	520 992	517 401	580 190	502 412	581 645	519 514	..
Canada	953 503	982 529	994 712	806 298	903 454	940 279	922 029	1 156 062	1 235 585	1 437 837
Chile[2]	207 298	216 519	224 928	231 213	247 684	270 773	266 028	265 763	269 876	..
Colombia[1]	112 949	128 213	141 810	149 073	164 428	179 334	188 833	204 916	212 299	218 928
Costa Rica	18 811	21 789	24 381	30 647	33 869	36 743	39 393	43 564	46 617	49 941
Czech Republic[1]	136 494	134 085	121 512	116 628	121 855	155 994	164 225	171 334	195 240	200 587
Denmark[2]	98 320	74 943	95 766	91 979	99 403	115 887	117 653	128 998	148 648	133 547
Estonia[2]	.. d	21 780	.. d	18 447	19 119	23 324	24 351	27 449	33 754	33 089
Finland[2]	..	..	..	..	..	87 215	69 534	83 269	88 402	..
France[1]	680 337	761 383	700 027	687 394	694 881	819 328	809 660	854 882	963 836	..
Germany[1]	863 410 |	955 173	862 229	795 471	805 991	996 954	973 458	991 531	1 177 898	1 131 387
Greece[1]	24 763	25 850	24 567	26 951	24 615	33 404	35 737	45 151	41 575	..
Hungary[2]	104 401	109 150	100 411	86 254	82 701	92 556	92 067	94 094	102 633	101 698
Iceland[2]	10 367	7 367	7 889	7 851	9 841	10 130	8 751	8 415	7 611	7 714
Ireland	383 164 |	414 747	429 823	890 126	840 646	1 058 012	1 070 770	1 246 879	1 382 743	1 378 429
Israel[1]	75 805	86 531	89 619	99 313	107 483	127 161	143 971	161 397	185 188	235 592
Italy[1]	363 586	364 965 |	352 482	340 477	352 626	424 743	434 624	443 532	472 703	454 923
Japan	205 754	170 713	171 664	174 146	196 614	202 441	204 524	223 810	232 313	..
Korea[2]	..	166 375	168 827	168 923	174 979	210 864	213 966	218 310	..	..
Latvia[1]	13 488	15 905	15 128	14 733	14 326	17 645	17 512	17 975	20 526	23 744
Lithuania	17 725	19 526	16 888	16 047	16 171	19 622	19 418	23 244	29 376	29 397
Luxembourg[2]	168 336	181 237	111 362	265 670	220 059	208 396	173 465	192 276	1 104 608	1 013 943
Mexico[2]	426 101	469 236	456 569	430 576	432 742	497 297	516 647	567 782	545 612	578 792
Netherlands[2]	628 120	797 556	1 082 512	1 269 589	1 323 743	1 504 859	1 467 717	1 665 255	2 854 781	2 576 295
New Zealand[1]	71 579	75 344	76 622	66 479	70 095	75 722	76 310	81 550	92 487	91 887
Norway[2]	..	190 836	173 127	147 487	147 524	145 488	153 178	169 294	169 441	..
Poland[2]	198 953	229 167	211 951	183 869	186 735	238 990	231 603	241 621	251 778	269 225
Portugal[2]	105 726	132 122	123 728	123 513	122 726	152 168	147 826	157 838	171 325	171 115
Slovak Republic[1]	55 118	58 022	49 738	46 016	47 592	59 510	59 857	60 601	64 239	59 369
Slovenia[1]	12 202	12 269	12 385	12 642	13 672	16 739	17 465	18 174	20 330	20 044
Spain[2]	..	638 731	587 426	553 237	554 200	669 819	704 895	720 761	815 401	777 635
Sweden[2]	..	359 801	293 526	291 338	293 910	337 867	314 353	322 357	385 407	360 757
Switzerland[2]	..	..	720 433	822 116	1 029 891	1 159 471	1 091 084	1 155 340	1 230 531	1 218 359
Turkey[1]	190 125	151 832	183 679	159 435	149 366	196 557	144 904	160 455	228 703	..
United Kingdom	1 440 525	1 512 648	1 581 494	1 530 652	1 460 578	1 881 501	1 996 726	2 045 078	2 219 789	2 634 131
United States[1]	3 915 804	4 948 418	5 456 888	5 731 383	6 502 750	7 806 330	7 346 877	9 362 942	10 813 507	13 619 022
OECD total	**14 853 882**	**16 514 068**	**17 037 031**	**17 718 391**	**18 828 928**	**22 250 992**	**21 655 001**	**24 844 856**	**29 551 116**	**32 554 912**
European Union[3]	**7 743 884**	**8 431 148**	**8 314 947**	**8 863 289**	**8 790 650**	**10 573 233**	**10 484 259**	**11 219 242**	**12 019 869**	**10 553 433**
G20	**13 873 084**	**15 388 334**	**15 929 595**	**15 715 732**	**17 007 700**	**19 538 625**	**19 123 352**	**21 864 534**	**24 354 421**	**28 241 582**
of which:										
Non-OECD G20 countries	**4 068 272**	**4 336 208**	**4 418 485**	**4 324 540**	**4 722 599**	**4 862 954**	**4 858 606**	**5 108 951**	**5 455 532**	**5 951 696**
Argentina	98 706	88 338	89 716	79 773	74 868	80 700	72 589	70 458	84 319	98 928
Brazil	664 208	627 789	601 490	429 843	563 539	623 021	568 741	705 031	595 285	592 761
China	2 068 000	2 331 238	2 599 102	2 696 344	2 755 147	2 725 662	2 827 064	2 796 396	3 231 225	3 623 770
India	224 987	226 549	265 838	282 617	318 320	377 287	386 172	426 940	480 190	..
Indonesia	211 635	230 799	217 487	222 410	249 859	231 492	225 720	235 348	240 564	259 268
Russian Federation	438 195	471 475	290 039	262 748	393 910	441 123	408 097	493 156	449 047	521 876
Saudi Arabia	199 032	207 897	215 909	224 050	231 502	227 566	231 814	236 376	241 775	..
South Africa	163 509	152 123	138 904	126 755	135 453	156 103	138 410	145 247	133 127	..
World	**23 473 725**	**25 785 632**	**26 747 879**	**27 512 295**	**29 272 682**	**33 770 996**	**33 348 031**	**37 117 903**	**42 416 383**	**45 230 745**

.. Not available; d Secondary Confidentiality; | Break in series

Note: Detailed metadata at: *http://metalinks.oecd.org/idi/20220712/ea54.*

1. Resident Special Purpose Entities (SPEs) are not present or not significant.
2. Data excludes Special Purpose Entities (SPEs).
3. EU27 for 2007 to 2012, EU28 for 2013-19 and EU27 (excluding UK) from 2020.

Source: *OECD International Direct Investment Statistics (database): https://doi.org/10.1787/idi-data-en*

Table 6. Foreign direct investment outward positions (stocks), US dollars

At year end

Million US dollars

	2012	2013	2014	2015	2016	2017	2018	2019	2020	2021
Australia[1]	476 541	456 977	467 173	416 606	435 713	503 963	499 193	581 286	627 263	..
Austria[2]	215 786	238 357	224 039	210 510	202 757	240 856	236 491	245 850	244 871	251 394
Belgium[2]	..	565 311	554 624	582 582	599 380	707 828	544 143	585 845	581 682	..
Canada	972 042	1 131 177	1 125 917	1 156 042	1 290 015	1 532 829	1 367 220	1 665 840	1 947 124	2 285 326
Chile[2]	97 193	102 396	107 027	107 589	121 419	126 478	126 343	137 601	143 187	..
Colombia[1]	31 531	39 183	43 082	47 300	51 817	55 507	60 633	63 786	65 443	68 804
Costa Rica	1 545	1 914	2 035	2 813	2 866	3 023	3 219	3 446	4 074	4 289
Czech Republic[1]	17 368	20 627	18 235	18 591	19 426	32 364	41 003	45 135	51 283	53 607
Denmark[2]	183 987	157 753	167 395	164 758	169 708	205 107	208 362	220 724	248 411	256 707
Estonia[2]	.. d	.. d	.. d	5 607	5 843	7 232	7 346	9 466	10 269	12 095
Finland[2]	..	..	..	..	..	124 607	128 744	146 329	143 485	..
France[1]	1 272 327	1 325 443	1 294 151	1 268 228	1 284 859	1 440 434	1 455 821	1 430 471	1 547 860	..
Germany[1]	1 344 222 |	1 448 428	1 388 804	1 362 440	1 380 580	1 671 520	1 688 586	1 789 755	1 986 598	2 056 084
Greece[1]	44 960	36 300	32 431	27 288	18 006	20 104	19 498	19 235	14 015	..
Hungary[2]	39 165	39 929	40 533	35 537	25 019	29 293	28 904	32 269	36 745	38 705
Iceland[2]	12 305	9 503	8 415	7 637	6 058	5 269	5 229	5 346	5 321	5 139
Ireland	412 011 |	534 765	618 800	909 668	856 582	986 846	955 265	1 111 705	1 197 232	1 452 568
Israel[1]	72 565	77 745	79 011	84 696	94 633	101 540	104 879	105 097	110 210	117 645
Italy[1]	534 980	533 906 |	477 456	456 619	456 380	547 578	554 360	558 578	585 177	553 336
Japan	1 037 700	1 118 009	1 152 007	1 228 767	1 315 221	1 497 525	1 568 766	1 780 246	1 837 075	..
Korea[2]	..	237 932	242 792	276 100	296 641	343 089	383 983	433 671	..	..
Latvia[1]	1 113	1 600	1 805	1 838	1 933	2 249	2 343	2 167	2 571	5 927
Lithuania	3 898	4 063	3 659	3 670	3 714	4 330	4 836	7 078	10 588	10 828
Luxembourg[2]	146 096	198 277	177 054	227 416	203 852	275 218	231 861	278 904	1 322 868	1 272 856
Mexico[2]	154 746	145 921	152 103	143 720	149 645	181 664	160 280	175 633	189 536	185 268
Netherlands[2]	1 001 416	1 147 501	1 612 014	1 907 265	2 132 045	2 389 258	2 196 542	2 505 198	3 759 408	3 356 949
New Zealand[1]	19 130	18 385	17 996	17 026	16 888	17 800	17 181	17 008	20 923	18 720
Norway[2]	..	181 736	162 028	172 432	192 013	200 887	200 999	214 390	209 741	..
Poland[2]	26 102	27 725	21 797	22 281	25 388	28 478	26 424	27 457	30 073	27 562
Portugal[2]	57 941	71 462	56 919	58 878	57 777	62 673	52 523	56 177	57 265	55 798
Slovak Republic[1]	4 765	4 830	2 820	2 462	2 631	4 590	4 589	4 732	5 239	5 419
Slovenia[1]	7 533	7 142	6 477	5 997	6 052	7 159	6 993	7 684	8 533	8 390
Spain[2]	..	572 343	519 308	505 765	496 605	575 744	556 147	574 297	589 288	565 360
Sweden[2]	..	414 533	377 441	338 754	.. d	372 465	382 260	398 661	451 422	434 895
Switzerland[2]	..	..	943 605	1 039 201	1 174 818	1 260 217	1 338 582	1 388 218	1 522 604	1 470 468
Turkey[1]	30 936	33 318	39 458	35 546	38 453	45 585	44 607	48 726	50 765	..
United Kingdom	1 693 955	1 796 164	1 681 283	1 605 446	1 567 989	1 849 781	1 844 710	1 965 930	2 137 520	2 166 355
United States[1]	5 222 874	6 254 171	6 320 124	6 059 272	6 395 424	7 865 017	6 370 722	7 579 148	8 240 764	9 813 545
OECD total	**18 293 175**	**20 197 079**	**20 262 491**	**20 610 727**	**21 545 306**	**25 326 105**	**23 429 586**	**26 223 088**	**30 430 102**	**32 142 786**
European Union[3]	**9 109 793**	**9 815 598**	**9 916 694**	**10 341 328**	**10 481 056**	**12 183 675**	**11 739 239**	**12 601 941**	**13 498 566**	**13 223 232**
G20	**14 340 313**	**16 103 602**	**16 191 740**	**16 063 869**	**17 073 256**	**20 574 650**	**19 132 018**	**21 543 042**	**23 523 493**	**25 558 169**
of which:										
Non-OECD G20 countries	**1 398 205**	**1 622 156**	**1 850 473**	**2 055 083**	**2 462 335**	**3 095 666**	**3 193 771**	**3 533 757**	**3 940 139**	**4 001 620**
Argentina	32 919	34 517	36 180	37 843	39 735	40 930	42 228	42 829	40 985	42 452
Brazil	203 897	203 799	209 993	184 909	203 186	242 964	213 261	247 605	277 875	296 185
China	551 941	691 346	922 481	1 156 046	1 423 737	1 844 990	2 001 548	2 236 641	2 580 658	2 581 854
India	118 072	119 838	132 741	139 038	144 086	155 176	166 594	179 734	190 857	206 400
Indonesia	12 401	19 350	25 396	29 351	59 134	65 928	72 765	80 727	88 844	95 636
Russian Federation	332 836	385 322	332 961	290 092	342 849	388 693	346 593	407 318	381 141	399 313
Saudi Arabia	34 359	39 303	44 699	63 121	73 973	84 437	104 613	123 904	128 815	..
South Africa	111 779	128 681	146 023	154 683	175 635	272 548	246 170	214 999	250 964	..
World	**22 437 601**	**24 774 762**	**25 389 782**	**26 319 907**	**27 473 020**	**32 692 192**	**30 862 383**	**34 082 953**	**38 990 514**	**40 962 982**

.. Not available; d Secondary Confidentiality; | Break in series

Note: Detailed metadata at: *http://metalinks.oecd.org/idi/20220712/ea54*.

1. Resident Special Purpose Entities (SPEs) are not present or not significant.
2. Data excludes Special Purpose Entities (SPEs).
3. EU27 for 2007 to 2012, EU28 for 2013-19 and EU27 (excluding UK) from 2020.

Source: *OECD International Direct Investment Statistics (database): https://doi.org/10.1787/idi-data-en*

INTERNATIONAL COMPARISONS

Table 7. Foreign direct investment inward positions (stocks), as a percentage of GDP

At year end

Per cent

	2012	2013	2014	2015	2016	2017	2018	2019	2020	2021
Australia[1]	38.7	36.9	39.8	45.5	46.7	49.5	48.2	53.1	55.6	..
Austria[2]	41.9	43.4	41.3	43.4	39.6	47.5	42.1	45.0	48.0	43.0
Belgium[2]	..	106.8	92.7	112.7	108.7	115.4	92.4	109.1	100.8	..
Canada	52.2	53.2	55.1	51.8	59.1	57.0	53.5	66.4	75.1	72.2
Chile[2]	77.6	77.8	86.3	94.8	98.9	97.7	89.2	94.1	110.0	..
Colombia[1]	30.5	33.6	37.2	50.8	58.1	57.5	56.5	63.4	78.2	72.8
Costa Rica	39.8	42.8	46.9	54.3	57.6	60.7	63.2	68.1	75.5	81.3
Czech Republic[1]	65.4	63.3	58.0	62.0	62.1	71.4	66.0	67.9	79.6	71.0
Denmark[2]	30.1	21.8	27.1	30.4	31.7	34.9	33.0	37.1	41.7	33.7
Estonia[2]	.. d	86.7	.. d	80.6	79.4	86.6	79.9	88.4	110.1	91.2
Finland[2]	..	..	..	..	..	34.1	25.2	31.0	32.5	..
France[1]	25.4	27.1	24.5	28.2	28.1	31.6	29.0	31.3	36.6	..
Germany[1]	24.5 |	25.6	22.2	23.7	23.2	27.1	24.5	25.5	30.6	26.8
Greece[1]	10.2	10.8	10.4	13.8	12.7	16.7	16.9	22.0	22.0	..
Hungary[2]	81.0	80.4	71.2	68.9	64.3	64.7	57.3	57.5	65.9	56.0
Iceland[2]	70.3	45.7	44.2	44.8	47.3	41.0	33.4	33.9	35.0	30.3
Ireland	170.3 |	173.9	165.8	305.2	280.4	311.8	278.1	312.4	324.7	276.5
Israel[1]	29.3	29.4	28.8	33.1	33.7	35.8	38.5	40.6	45.5	48.9
Italy[1]	17.4	17.0 |	16.3	18.5	18.8	21.7	20.8	22.1	25.0	21.6
Japan	3.3	3.3	3.5	4.0	4.0	4.2	4.1	4.4	4.7	..
Korea[2]	..	12.1	11.4	11.5	11.7	13.0	12.4	13.3	..	..
Latvia[1]	47.9	52.7	48.2	54.0	51.0	57.9	50.9	52.4	61.1	61.0
Lithuania	41.3	42.0	34.8	38.7	37.6	41.1	36.1	42.5	52.6	44.9
Luxembourg[2]	281.6	278.0	161.9	442.3	353.7	317.1	243.3	273.9	1 505.9	1 169.3
Mexico[2]	35.5	36.8	34.7	36.7	40.1	42.9	42.3	44.7	50.2	45.0
Netherlands[2]	74.9	90.9	121.3	165.8	168.8	180.5	160.6	183.0	312.4	253.5
New Zealand[1]	40.6	39.5	38.1	37.3	37.1	36.6	36.0	38.4	43.9	37.1
Norway[2]	..	36.5	34.7	38.2	40.0	36.5	35.1	41.8	46.8	..
Poland[2]	39.9	44.0	39.1	38.5	39.5	45.4	39.4	40.5	42.3	39.9
Portugal[2]	48.9	58.3	53.8	61.9	59.5	68.7	61.0	65.8	75.0	68.5
Slovak Republic[1]	58.3	58.7	49.1	52.0	53.0	62.3	56.6	57.6	61.1	51.7
Slovenia[1]	26.2	25.3	24.8	29.3	30.5	34.4	32.2	33.5	37.9	32.6
Spain[2]	..	47.1	42.8	46.3	45.0	51.0	49.6	51.7	63.6	54.7
Sweden[2]	..	61.3	50.4	57.7	57.0	62.5	56.6	60.4	71.2	57.5
Switzerland[2]	..	..	98.1	117.1	148.1	164.6	148.3	157.9	163.6	149.9
Turkey[1]	21.6	15.9	19.6	18.4	17.2	22.9	18.6	21.1	31.8	..
United Kingdom	53.3	54.3	51.6	52.2	54.2	70.7	69.9	72.2	82.0	82.6
United States[1]	24.2	29.5	31.1	31.4	34.7	39.9	35.6	43.7	51.8	59.4
OECD total	**30.5**	**33.5**	**33.9**	**37.4**	**38.9**	**44.0**	**40.5**	**46.1**	**56.4**	**56.0**
European Union[3]	**45.3**	**46.6**	**44.4**	**53.7**	**52.9**	**60.5**	**55.5**	**60.4**	**78.5**	**61.8**
G20	**23.9**	**25.9**	**26.1**	**26.9**	**28.6**	**30.9**	**28.5**	**32.0**	**36.7**	**38.2**
of which:										
Non-OECD G20 countries	**23.0**	**23.0**	**22.5**	**22.9**	**24.8**	**22.9**	**21.2**	**21.8**	**24.0**	**22.9**
Argentina	17.0	14.4	15.8	12.4	13.4	12.6	14.0	15.7	22.0	21.7
Brazil	26.9	25.4	24.5	23.9	31.4	30.2	29.7	37.6	41.2	36.0
China	24.2	24.4	24.8	24.4	24.5	22.1	20.3	19.5	21.9	21.5
India	12.3	12.2	13.0	13.4	13.9	14.2	14.2	14.9	18.5	..
Indonesia	23.1	25.3	24.4	25.8	26.8	22.8	21.7	21.0	22.7	21.9
Russian Federation	19.8	20.6	14.1	19.3	30.9	28.0	24.4	29.0	30.7	31.7
Saudi Arabia	27.0	27.8	28.5	34.2	35.9	33.0	29.5	29.8	34.5	..
South Africa	41.3	41.5	39.6	39.9	45.7	44.7	37.6	41.3	44.1	..

.. Not available; d Secondary Confidentiality; | Break in series

Note: Detailed metadata at: *http://metalinks.oecd.org/idi/20220712/ea54.*

1. Resident Special Purpose Entities (SPEs) are not present or not significant.
2. Data excludes Special Purpose Entities (SPEs).
3. EU27 for 2007 to 2012, EU28 for 2013-19 and EU27 (excluding UK) from 2020.

Source: *OECD International Direct Investment Statistics (database): https://doi.org/10.1787/idi-data-en*

Table 8. Foreign direct investment outward positions (stocks), as a percentage of GDP

At year end

Per cent

	2012	2013	2014	2015	2016	2017	2018	2019	2020	2021
Australia[1]	30.0	29.6	31.9	33.5	33.3	35.7	34.3	42.2	44.1	..
Austria[2]	52.7	55.4	50.6	55.1	51.2	57.7	52.0	55.2	56.5	52.7
Belgium[2]	..	108.3	103.6	126.0	125.9	140.8	100.1	109.9	112.9	..
Canada	53.2	61.3	62.4	74.3	84.4	92.9	79.4	95.7	118.3	114.8
Chile[2]	36.4	36.8	41.1	44.1	48.5	45.7	42.4	48.7	58.3	..
Colombia[1]	8.5	10.3	11.3	16.1	18.3	17.8	18.1	19.7	24.1	22.9
Costa Rica	3.3	3.8	3.9	5.0	4.9	5.0	5.2	5.4	6.6	7.0
Czech Republic[1]	8.3	9.7	8.7	9.9	9.9	14.8	16.5	17.9	20.9	19.0
Denmark[2]	56.2	45.9	47.4	54.4	54.2	61.8	58.4	63.5	69.8	64.9
Estonia[2]	.. d	.. d	.. d	24.5	24.3	26.9	24.1	30.5	33.5	33.4
Finland[2]	..	..	..	..	..	48.7	46.7	54.5	52.8	..
France[1]	47.4	47.1	45.3	52.0	52.0	55.5	52.2	52.4	58.8	..
Germany[1]	38.1 |	38.8	35.7	40.6	39.8	45.4	42.5	46.0	51.6	48.7
Greece[1]	18.6	15.2	13.8	13.9	9.3	10.1	9.2	9.4	7.4	..
Hungary[2]	30.4	29.4	28.7	28.4	19.4	20.5	18.0	19.7	23.6	21.3
Iceland[2]	83.4	58.9	47.1	43.6	29.1	21.3	20.0	21.5	24.5	20.2
Ireland	183.1 |	224.2	238.7	311.9	285.8	290.8	248.1	278.5	281.1	291.4
Israel[1]	28.1	26.4	25.4	28.2	29.7	28.6	28.1	26.4	27.1	24.4
Italy[1]	25.6	24.9 |	22.1	24.9	24.3	27.9	26.5	27.8	30.9	26.3
Japan	16.7	21.7	23.8	28.0	26.7	30.8	31.7	35.0	37.4	..
Korea[2]	..	17.4	16.4	18.8	19.8	21.1	22.3	26.3	..	..
Latvia[1]	4.0	5.3	5.8	6.7	6.9	7.4	6.8	6.3	7.6	15.2
Lithuania	9.1	8.7	7.5	8.9	8.6	9.1	9.0	13.0	18.9	16.5
Luxembourg[2]	244.4	304.1	257.3	378.6	327.6	418.8	325.3	397.3	1 803.4	1 467.9
Mexico[2]	12.9	11.4	11.6	12.3	13.9	15.7	13.1	13.8	17.4	14.4
Netherlands[2]	119.4	130.8	180.7	249.1	271.9	286.5	240.3	275.2	411.4	330.4
New Zealand[1]	10.9	9.6	8.9	9.6	8.9	8.6	8.1	8.0	9.9	7.6
Norway[2]	..	34.8	32.5	44.7	52.1	50.4	46.0	52.9	57.9	..
Poland[2]	5.2	5.3	4.0	4.7	5.4	5.4	4.5	4.6	5.0	4.1
Portugal[2]	26.8	31.6	24.8	29.5	28.0	28.3	21.7	23.4	25.1	22.3
Slovak Republic[1]	5.0	4.9	2.8	2.8	2.9	4.8	4.3	4.5	5.0	4.7
Slovenia[1]	16.2	14.8	13.0	13.9	13.5	14.7	12.9	14.2	15.9	13.6
Spain[2]	..	42.2	37.9	42.3	40.3	43.9	39.1	41.2	46.0	39.7
Sweden[2]	..	70.6	64.9	67.1	.. d	68.8	68.8	74.7	83.4	69.3
Switzerland[2]	..	..	128.5	148.0	168.9	178.9	182.0	189.7	202.4	180.9
Turkey[1]	3.5	3.5	4.2	4.1	4.4	5.3	5.7	6.4	7.0	..
United Kingdom	62.6	64.5	54.8	54.7	58.2	69.5	64.6	69.4	78.9	68.0
United States[1]	32.2	37.3	36.1	33.2	34.1	40.2	30.9	35.4	39.4	42.8
OECD total	**37.6**	**41.0**	**40.3**	**43.5**	**44.5**	**50.1**	**43.9**	**48.7**	**58.0**	**55.3**
European Union[3]	**53.2**	**54.2**	**52.9**	**62.6**	**63.1**	**69.7**	**62.2**	**67.9**	**88.2**	**77.4**
G20	**24.7**	**27.1**	**26.5**	**27.5**	**28.7**	**32.5**	**28.5**	**31.5**	**35.5**	**34.5**
of which:										
Non-OECD G20 countries	**7.9**	**8.6**	**9.4**	**10.9**	**12.9**	**14.6**	**14.0**	**15.0**	**17.3**	**15.4**
Argentina	5.7	5.6	6.4	5.9	7.1	6.4	8.1	9.5	10.7	9.3
Brazil	8.3	8.2	8.6	10.3	11.3	11.8	11.1	13.2	19.2	18.0
China	6.5	7.2	8.8	10.5	12.7	15.0	14.4	15.6	17.5	15.3
India	6.5	6.5	6.5	6.6	6.3	5.8	6.1	6.3	7.4	7.0
Indonesia	1.4	2.1	2.9	3.4	6.3	6.5	7.0	7.2	8.4	8.1
Russian Federation	15.1	16.8	16.2	21.3	26.9	24.7	20.8	24.0	26.0	24.2
Saudi Arabia	4.7	5.3	5.9	9.6	11.5	12.3	13.3	15.6	18.4	..
South Africa	28.2	35.1	41.6	48.7	59.3	78.0	66.8	61.2	83.1	..

.. Not available; d Secondary Confidentiality; | Break in series

Note: Detailed metadata at: *http://metalinks.oecd.org/idi/20220712/ea54*.

1. Resident Special Purpose Entities (SPEs) are not present or not significant.
2. Data excludes Special Purpose Entities (SPEs).
3. EU27 for 2007 to 2012, EU28 for 2013-19 and EU27 (excluding UK) from 2020.

Source: *OECD International Direct Investment Statistics (database): https://doi.org/10.1787/idi-data-en*

Table 9. Income on inward Foreign Direct Investment, US dollars
At year end

Million US dollars

	2012	2013	2014	2015	2016	2017	2018	2019	2020	2021
Australia[1]	35 683	33 996	29 806	23 884	27 454	37 261	44 228	42 674	28 795	50 488
Austria[2]	11 598	9 505	9 459	9 845	12 146	15 987	16 220	15 671	4 982	11 652
Belgium	27 461	26 890	34 389	28 819	33 268	28 057	38 457	38 509	36 329	43 074
Canada	48 209	47 319	47 786	34 640	31 001	37 274	41 885	41 289	24 955	47 172
Chile[2]	18 890	18 899	15 058	10 741	10 982	14 744	17 037	15 160	14 543	22 165
Colombia[1]	14 952	13 691	11 652	5 052	4 795	7 346	10 576	9 228	3 257	7 616
Costa Rica	1 368	1 557	1 786	1 948	1 938	2 590	2 771	3 247	2 782	3 287
Czech Republic[1]	15 115	15 441	16 098	14 474	15 344	19 127	19 260	20 343	15 597	15 886
Denmark[2]	..	6 395	5 452	4 620	5 481	6 134	6 695	7 414	5 374	8 289
Estonia	1 818	1 846	1 916	1 385	1 591	1 737	1 944	1 995	1 615	2 371
Finland	6 267	5 536 |	6 597	4 632	6 492	8 426	7 765	8 323	6 308	6 702
France[1]	30 551 |	26 824	24 900	26 923	29 484	36 341	40 914	38 056	24 197	35 731
Germany[1]	40 166	32 635 |	41 345	28 784	37 942	45 450	46 365	39 365	33 943	40 655
Greece[1]	-3 481	-332	522	1 157	1 150	1 452	1 552	1 868	1 696	2 320
Hungary[2]	7 530	6 828	9 484	8 855	7 682	10 335	10 576	9 251	8 361	9 550
Iceland[2]	751 |	-47 |	-47	31	-29	40	-42	-267	-357	34
Ireland	50 379 |	49 514	52 055	71 582	61 829	75 987	93 028	94 837	105 624	147 738
Israel[1]	6 425	5 362	3 949	5 808	5 846	5 586	6 311	7 894	7 465	11 904
Italy[1]	12 486	10 059 |	11 199	11 685	14 147	19 621	20 410	17 824	2 223	-1 234
Japan	15 278	13 031	26 287 |	23 858	34 242	33 302	34 928	33 504	30 212	29 973
Korea[1]	..	7 580	-1 142	2 261	4 031	3 633	4 447	3 443	12 420	13 887
Latvia[1]	1 004	1 077	1 040	1 154	1 191	1 392	1 856	1 623	1 109	2 014
Lithuania[1]	1 245	1 186	684	1 642	1 678	1 944	2 193	2 318	2 229	3 043
Luxembourg[2]	18 284	21 841	12 222	9 229	13 076	10 672	9 747	11 515	23 568	27 163
Mexico[2]	19 365	30 453	22 654	18 466	17 331	18 920	23 191	25 078	21 792	20 259
Netherlands[2]	25 437	37 471 |	43 658	72 731	69 293	64 204	86 983	81 265	133 926	141 694
New Zealand[1]	6 185	6 758	7 330	5 849	5 534	7 208	7 001	5 801	4 841	7 517
Norway	17 688	15 179 |	7 757	6 038	7 061	10 943	13 012	13 438	6 477	2 625
Poland[1]	16 000	18 620	21 426	18 178	20 939	21 419	23 500	23 372	21 642	29 671
Portugal[2]	4 774	3 211	4 035	4 842	5 699	6 223	8 397	7 261	5 350	6 239
Slovak Republic[1]	4 079	3 297 |	3 949	4 421	4 411	4 330	4 553	5 029	3 852	3 904
Slovenia[1]	265	-1	-49	1 078	1 252	1 255	1 566	1 618	1 182	1 538
Spain	22 199	28 313	24 010	22 030	23 653	28 808	32 971	32 175	26 825	28 496
Sweden	19 443	21 065	23 603	22 053	21 836	22 166	24 955	23 558	21 840	30 329
Switzerland[2]	..	..	.. d	55 470	71 334	88 425	103 380	103 196	72 511	101 510
Turkey[1]	2 655	3 678	2 363	3 589	3 137	3 279	3 193	3 471	1 897	4 873
United Kingdom	72 338	79 526	79 045	73 586	67 864	74 333	100 332	55 925	49 322	82 553
United States[1]	172 761	184 116	187 547	166 149	162 199	192 748	216 466	212 889	165 379	292 353
OECD total	**796 888**	**817 719**	**853 741**	**807 490**	**844 305**	**968 698**	**1 128 623**	**1 059 160**	**934 065**	**1 295 041**
European Union[3]	..	..	..	..	..	..	..	..	..	..
G20	..	..	..	..	..	..	..	..	..	..
of which:										
Non-OECD G20 countries	..	..	..	..	..	..	..	..	..	..
Argentina	..	..	..	..	..	..	..	..	..	..
Brazil	46 366	23 326	27 980	13 915	30 359	41 474	45 740	54 051	39 364	54 626
China	..	..	..	..	..	..	..	..	..	..
India	..	..	..	..	..	..	..	..	..	..
Indonesia	..	..	..	..	..	..	..	..	..	..
Russian Federation	..	..	..	..	..	..	..	..	..	..
Saudi Arabia	..	..	..	..	..	..	..	..	..	..
South Africa	..	..	..	..	..	..	..	..	..	..
World	..	..	..	..	..	..	..	..	..	..

.. Not available; d Secondary Confidentiality; | Break in series

Note: Detailed metadata at: *http://metalinks.oecd.org/idi/20220712/ea54.*

1. Resident Special Purpose Entities (SPEs) are not present or not significant.
2. Data excludes Special Purpose Entities (SPEs).
3. EU27 for 2007 to 2012, EU28 for 2013-19 and EU27 (excluding UK) from 2020.

Source: *OECD International Direct Investment Statistics (database): https://doi.org/10.1787/idi-data-en*

Table 10. Income on outward Foreign Direct Investment, US dollars
At year end

Million US dollars

	2012	2013	2014	2015	2016	2017	2018	2019	2020	2021
Australia[1]	20 772	19 746	19 180	13 785	13 306	14 010	16 505	16 990	15 061	22 840
Austria[2]	13 963	14 106	11 648	10 823	15 536	15 260	15 238	16 984	5 107	13 277
Belgium	23 559	26 157	34 250	29 336	33 352	28 221	37 564	36 326	32 405	39 329
Canada	45 094	44 446	47 130	41 825	40 774	54 143	63 033	63 515	56 396	75 561
Chile[2]	4 163	4 400	5 397	3 824	3 388	4 119	4 043	5 302	4 382	5 539
Colombia[1]	2 844	2 806	3 183	3 562	3 732	3 935	3 986	4 490	2 396	3 887
Costa Rica	112	78	158	114	101	74	107	135	93	71
Czech Republic[1]	2 251	1 320	1 589	1 861	2 015	4 665	4 194	5 619	2 176	4 031
Denmark[2]	..	12 430	13 709	12 126	12 027	13 256	15 499	15 461	14 777	19 662
Estonia	440	652	595	364	492	485	697	713	602	1 054
Finland	10 144	7 865 |	10 942	7 373	7 890	8 836	10 202	13 653	12 867	13 263
France[1]	78 845 |	78 541	78 586	70 308	69 441	77 145	95 033	99 044	59 572	79 067
Germany[1]	81 156	89 600 |	89 541	84 972	98 391	94 299	136 740	128 245	103 484	141 074
Greece[1]	1 169	795	3 114	1 801	627	1 099	694	935	956	1 402
Hungary[2]	1 710	1 437	1 687	988	1 823	2 058	1 894	2 209	1 520	1 796
Iceland[2]	-268 |	300 |	164	283	436	302	364	324	251	215
Ireland	13 905 |	16 389	17 675	11 765	14 640	17 470	19 828	17 406	16 707	31 220
Israel[1]	4 194	4 239	5 188	6 575	6 453	7 202	7 740	6 797	5 250	7 629
Italy[1]	26 239	22 849 |	26 374	12 049	17 895	24 782	29 994	28 628	16 515	15 621
Japan	68 079	68 225	100 236 |	96 359	110 503	120 205	130 295	136 709	134 545	127 679
Korea[1]	..	9 924	6 305	-124	9 055	10 259	9 631	9 063	13 827	24 016
Latvia[1]	82	97	53	156	116	218	152	113	115	307
Lithuania[1]	100	165	120	136	146	166	303	230	319	266
Luxembourg[2]	8 925	8 537	9 107	7 691	8 978	9 888	8 010	5 685	19 474	23 456
Mexico[2]	6 779	8 076	7 332	3 430	2 980	4 764	5 228	6 091	5 081	5 870
Netherlands[2]	65 871	64 468 |	59 981	102 679	87 923	104 243	132 827	113 072	129 558	144 624
New Zealand[1]	679	572	707	511	741	523	392	609	535	994
Norway	11 065	8 667 |	13 770	9 078	6 772	8 408	12 160	5 478	239	4 641
Poland[1]	1 332	406	1 641	719	977	2 288	2 205	2 301	1 474	1 789
Portugal[2]	2 355	2 542	2 045	2 008	2 517	3 694	4 418	2 786	3 079	3 568
Slovak Republic[1]	216	273 |	811	350	206	391	424	356	351	366
Slovenia[1]	-388	-552	-87	55	176	220	357	376	279	351
Spain	33 934	38 884	35 392	31 694	33 709	36 232	43 159	42 330	34 152	35 001
Sweden	32 720	34 882	36 148	26 830	25 633	30 745	34 933	34 514	31 781	42 305
Switzerland[2]	..	..	.. d	82 129	86 079	94 398	99 486	95 760	80 446	110 677
Turkey[1]	98	273	314	224	202	299	958	814	1 101	1 578
United Kingdom	127 585	123 000	112 807	87 381	69 270	113 394	125 920	117 344	65 927	146 674
United States[1]	458 257	467 395	471 765	443 462	451 921	544 536	566 422	549 113	481 906	601 940
OECD total	**1 233 292**	**1 239 895**	**1 311 281**	**1 208 502**	**1 240 224**	**1 456 231**	**1 640 634**	**1 585 522**	**1 354 705**	**1 752 638**
European Union[3]	..	..	..	..	..	..	..	..	..	..
G20	..	..	..	..	..	..	..	..	..	..
of which:										
Non-OECD G20 countries	..	..	..	..	..	..	..	..	..	..
Argentina	..	..	..	..	..	..	..	..	..	..
Brazil	2 457	7 447	2 526	-2 398	7 878	17 332	4 835	16 071	13 199	23 584
China	..	..	..	..	..	..	..	..	..	..
India	..	..	..	..	..	..	..	..	..	..
Indonesia	..	..	..	..	..	..	..	..	..	..
Russian Federation	..	..	..	..	..	..	..	..	..	..
Saudi Arabia	..	..	..	..	..	..	..	..	..	..
South Africa	..	..	..	..	..	..	..	..	..	..
World	..	..	..	..	..	..	..	..	..	..

.. Not available; d Secondary Confidentiality; | Break in series

Note: Detailed metadata at: *http://metalinks.oecd.org/idi/20220712/ea54.*

1. Resident Special Purpose Entities (SPEs) are not present or not significant.
2. Data excludes Special Purpose Entities (SPEs).
3. EU27 for 2007 to 2012, EU28 for 2013-19 and EU27 (excluding UK) from 2020.

Source: OECD *International Direct Investment Statistics (database): https://doi.org/10.1787/idi-data-en*

Table 11. Income on inward Foreign Direct Investment as a percentage of GDP

At year end

Per cent

	2012	2013	2014	2015	2016	2017	2018	2019	2020	2021
Australia[1]	2.2	2.2	2.0	1.9	2.1	2.6	3.0	3.1	2.0	3.1
Austria[2]	2.8	2.2	2.1	2.6	3.1	3.8	3.6	3.5	1.1	2.4
Belgium	5.5	5.2	6.4	6.2	7.0	5.6	7.1	7.2	7.0	7.2
Canada	2.6	2.6	2.6	2.2	2.0	2.3	2.4	2.4	1.5	2.4
Chile[2]	7.1	6.8	5.8	4.4	4.4	5.3	5.7	5.4	5.9	6.7
Colombia[1]	4.0	3.6	3.1	1.7	1.7	2.4	3.2	2.9	1.2	2.5
Costa Rica	2.9	3.1	3.4	3.5	3.3	4.3	4.4	5.1	4.5	5.3
Czech Republic[1]	7.2	7.3	7.7	7.7	7.8	8.7	7.7	8.1	6.4	5.6
Denmark[2]	..	1.9	1.5	1.5	1.8	1.8	1.9	2.1	1.5	2.1
Estonia	7.9	7.4	7.2	6.1	6.6	6.5	6.4	6.4	5.3	6.5
Finland	2.4	2.0 |	2.4	2.0	2.7	3.3	2.8	3.1	2.3	2.2
France[1]	1.1 |	1.0	0.9	1.1	1.2	1.4	1.5	1.4	0.9	1.2
Germany[1]	1.1	0.9 |	1.1	0.9	1.1	1.2	1.2	1.0	0.9	1.0
Greece[1]	-1.4	-0.1	0.2	0.6	0.6	0.7	0.7	0.9	0.9	1.1
Hungary[2]	5.8	5.0	6.7	7.1	6.0	7.2	6.6	5.7	5.4	5.3
Iceland[2]	5.1 |	-0.3 |	-0.3	0.2	-0.1	0.2	-0.2	-1.1	-1.6	0.1
Ireland	22.4 |	20.8	20.1	24.5	20.6	22.4	24.2	23.8	24.8	29.6
Israel[1]	2.5	1.8	1.3	1.9	1.8	1.6	1.7	2.0	1.8	2.5
Italy[1]	0.6	0.5 |	0.5	0.6	0.8	1.0	1.0	0.9	0.1	-0.1
Japan	0.2	0.3	0.5 |	0.5	0.7	0.7	0.7	0.7	0.6	0.6
Korea[1]	..	0.6	-0.1	0.2	0.3	0.2	0.3	0.2	0.8	0.8
Latvia[1]	3.6	3.6	3.3	4.2	4.2	4.6	5.4	4.7	3.3	5.2
Lithuania[1]	2.9	2.5	1.4	4.0	3.9	4.1	4.1	4.2	4.0	4.7
Luxembourg[2]	30.6	33.5	17.8	15.4	21.0	16.2	13.7	16.4	32.1	31.3
Mexico[2]	1.6	2.4	1.7	1.6	1.6	1.6	1.9	2.0	2.0	1.6
Netherlands[2]	3.0	4.3 |	4.9	9.5	8.8	7.7	9.5	8.9	14.7	13.9
New Zealand[1]	3.5	3.5	3.6	3.3	2.9	3.5	3.3	2.7	2.3	3.0
Norway	3.5	2.9 |	1.6	1.6	1.9	2.7	3.0	3.3	1.8	0.5
Poland[1]	3.2	3.6	3.9	3.8	4.4	4.1	4.0	3.9	3.6	4.4
Portugal[2]	2.2	1.4	1.8	2.4	2.8	2.8	3.5	3.0	2.3	2.5
Slovak Republic[1]	4.3	3.3 |	3.9	5.0	4.9	4.5	4.3	4.8	3.7	3.4
Slovenia[1]	0.6	0.0	-0.1	2.5	2.8	2.6	2.9	3.0	2.2	2.5
Spain	1.7	2.1	1.8	1.8	1.9	2.2	2.3	2.3	2.1	2.0
Sweden	3.5	3.6	4.1	4.4	4.2	4.1	4.5	4.4	4.0	4.8
Switzerland[2]	..	..	.. d	7.9	10.3	12.6	14.1	14.1	9.6	12.5
Turkey[1]	0.3	0.4	0.3	0.4	0.4	0.4	0.4	0.5	0.3	0.6
United Kingdom	2.7	2.9	2.6	2.5	2.5	2.8	3.5	2.0	1.8	2.6
United States[1]	1.1	1.1	1.1	0.9	0.9	1.0	1.1	1.0	0.8	1.3
OECD total	**1.6**	**1.7**	**1.7**	**1.7**	**1.7**	**1.9**	**2.1**	**2.0**	**1.8**	**2.2**
European Union[3]	..	..	..	..	..	..	..	..	..	..
G20	..	..	..	..	..	..	..	..	..	..
of which:										
Non-OECD G20 countries	..	..	..	..	..	..	..	..	..	..
Argentina	..	..	..	..	..	..	..	..	..	..
Brazil	1.9	0.9	1.1	0.8	1.7	2.0	2.4	2.9	2.7	3.3
China	..	..	..	..	..	..	..	..	..	..
India	..	..	..	..	..	..	..	..	..	..
Indonesia	..	..	..	..	..	..	..	..	..	..
Russian Federation	..	..	..	..	..	..	..	..	..	..
Saudi Arabia	..	..	..	..	..	..	..	..	..	..
South Africa	..	..	..	..	..	..	..	..	..	..

.. Not available; d Secondary Confidentiality; | Break in series

Note: Detailed metadata at: *http://metalinks.oecd.org/idi/20220712/ea54*.

1. Resident Special Purpose Entities (SPEs) are not present or not significant.
2. Data excludes Special Purpose Entities (SPEs).
3. EU27 for 2007 to 2012, EU28 for 2013-19 and EU27 (excluding UK) from 2020.

Source: *OECD International Direct Investment Statistics (database)*: *https://doi.org/10.1787/idi-data-en*

Table 12. Income on outward Foreign Direct Investment as a percentage of GDP
At year end

Per cent

	2012	2013	2014	2015	2016	2017	2018	2019	2020	2021
Australia[1]	1.3	1.3	1.3	1.1	1.0	1.0	1.1	1.2	1.1	1.4
Austria[2]	3.4	3.3	2.6	2.8	3.9	3.7	3.3	3.8	1.2	2.8
Belgium	4.7	5.0	6.4	6.3	7.0	5.6	6.9	6.8	6.3	6.6
Canada	2.5	2.4	2.6	2.7	2.7	3.3	3.7	3.6	3.4	3.8
Chile[2]	1.6	1.6	2.1	1.6	1.4	1.5	1.4	1.9	1.8	1.7
Colombia[1]	0.8	0.7	0.8	1.2	1.3	1.3	1.2	1.4	0.9	1.3
Costa Rica	0.2	0.2	0.3	0.2	0.2	0.1	0.2	0.2	0.2	0.1
Czech Republic[1]	1.1	0.6	0.8	1.0	1.0	2.1	1.7	2.2	0.9	1.4
Denmark[2]	..	3.6	3.9	4.0	3.8	4.0	4.3	4.4	4.1	5.0
Estonia	1.9	2.6	2.2	1.6	2.0	1.8	2.3	2.3	2.0	2.9
Finland	3.9	2.9 |	4.0	3.1	3.3	3.5	3.7	5.1	4.7	4.4
France[1]	2.9 |	2.8	2.8	2.9	2.8	3.0	3.4	3.6	2.3	2.7
Germany[1]	2.3	2.4 |	2.3	2.5	2.8	2.6	3.4	3.3	2.7	3.3
Greece[1]	0.5	0.3	1.3	0.9	0.3	0.5	0.3	0.5	0.5	0.6
Hungary[2]	1.3	1.1	1.2	0.8	1.4	1.4	1.2	1.4	1.0	1.0
Iceland[2]	-1.8 |	1.9 |	0.9	1.6	2.1	1.2	1.4	1.3	1.2	0.8
Ireland	6.2 |	6.9	6.8	4.0	4.9	5.1	5.1	4.4	3.9	6.3
Israel[1]	1.6	1.4	1.7	2.2	2.0	2.0	2.1	1.7	1.3	1.6
Italy[1]	1.3	1.1 |	1.2	0.7	1.0	1.3	1.4	1.4	0.9	0.7
Japan	1.1	1.3	2.1 |	2.2	2.2	2.5	2.6	2.7	2.7	2.5
Korea[1]	..	0.7	0.4	0.0	0.6	0.6	0.6	0.6	0.8	1.3
Latvia[1]	0.3	0.3	0.2	0.6	0.4	0.7	0.4	0.3	0.3	0.8
Lithuania[1]	0.2	0.4	0.2	0.3	0.3	0.3	0.6	0.4	0.6	0.4
Luxembourg[2]	14.9	13.1	13.2	12.8	14.4	15.0	11.2	8.1	26.5	27.1
Mexico[2]	0.6	0.6	0.6	0.3	0.3	0.4	0.4	0.5	0.5	0.5
Netherlands[2]	7.9	7.3 |	6.7	13.4	11.2	12.5	14.5	12.4	14.2	14.2
New Zealand[1]	0.4	0.3	0.4	0.3	0.4	0.3	0.2	0.3	0.3	0.4
Norway	2.2	1.7 |	2.8	2.4	1.8	2.1	2.8	1.4	0.1	1.0
Poland[1]	0.3	0.1	0.3	0.2	0.2	0.4	0.4	0.4	0.2	0.3
Portugal[2]	1.1	1.1	0.9	1.0	1.2	1.7	1.8	1.2	1.3	1.4
Slovak Republic[1]	0.2	0.3 |	0.8	0.4	0.2	0.4	0.4	0.3	0.3	0.3
Slovenia[1]	-0.8	-1.1	-0.2	0.1	0.4	0.5	0.7	0.7	0.5	0.6
Spain	2.6	2.9	2.6	2.7	2.7	2.8	3.0	3.0	2.7	2.5
Sweden	5.9	5.9	6.2	5.3	5.0	5.7	6.3	6.5	5.9	6.7
Switzerland[2]	..	..	.. d	11.7	12.4	13.4	13.5	13.1	10.7	13.6
Turkey[1]	0.0	0.0	0.0	0.0	0.0	0.0	0.1	0.1	0.2	0.2
United Kingdom	4.7	4.4	3.7	3.0	2.6	4.3	4.4	4.1	2.4	4.6
United States[1]	2.8	2.8	2.7	2.4	2.4	2.8	2.7	2.6	2.3	2.6
OECD total	**2.5**	**2.5**	**2.6**	**2.6**	**2.6**	**2.9**	**3.1**	**2.9**	**2.6**	**3.0**
European Union[3]	..	..	..	..	..	..	..	..	..	..
G20	..	..	..	..	..	..	..	..	..	..
of which:										
Non-OECD G20 countries	..	..	..	..	..	..	..	..	..	..
Argentina	..	..	..	..	..	..	..	..	..	..
Brazil	0.1	0.3	0.1	-0.1	0.4	0.8	0.3	0.9	0.9	1.4
China	..	..	..	..	..	..	..	..	..	..
India	..	..	..	..	..	..	..	..	..	..
Indonesia	..	..	..	..	..	..	..	..	..	..
Russian Federation	..	..	..	..	..	..	..	..	..	..
Saudi Arabia	..	..	..	..	..	..	..	..	..	..
South Africa	..	..	..	..	..	..	..	..	..	..

.. Not available; d Secondary Confidentiality; | Break in series

Note: Detailed metadata at: *http://metalinks.oecd.org/idi/20220712/ea54.*

1. Resident Special Purpose Entities (SPEs) are not present or not significant.
2. Data excludes Special Purpose Entities (SPEs).
3. EU27 for 2007 to 2012, EU28 for 2013-19 and EU27 (excluding UK) from 2020.

Source: *OECD International Direct Investment Statistics (database): https://doi.org/10.1787/idi-data-en*

Country tables

AUSTRALIA

Table 1. Foreign direct investment flows by country

Million US dollars

	Inward					Outward				
	2016	2017	2018	2019	2020	2016	2017	2018	2019	2020
WORLD	**48 291.1**	**45 300.0**	**68 033.2**	**36 151.4**	..	**2 265.7**	**5 932.3**	**6 361.4**	**5 396.5**	..
OECD COUNTRIES	**38 536.4**	**32 815.5**	**52 769.9**	**27 818.2**	..	**10 727.7**	**12 610.9**	**15 852.7**	**14 981.6**	..
Australia	-	-	-	-	..	-	-	-	-	..
Austria	.. c	.. c	.. c	177.2	..	.. c	.. c	.. c	1.4	..
Belgium	98.1	-135.6	316.7	-73.0	..	-3.7	.. c	.. c	.. c	..
Canada	1 296.4	2 481.4	5 243.9	4 527.7	..	199.2	875.2	5 138.6	1 479.8	..
Chile	.. c	.. c	.. c	.. c	..	37.9	95.0	109.8	41.0	..
Colombia	.. c	.. c	.. c	.. c	..	-12.6	.. c	-39.6	.. c	..
Costa Rica	.. c	-	-	.. c	..	.. c	.. c	.. c	.. c	..
Czech Republic	-2.2	-0.8	.. c	.. c	..	.. c	.. c	7.5	.. c	..
Denmark	.. c	.. c	85.2	.. c	..	.. c	.. c	.. c	.. c	..
Estonia	.. c	-	-	-	..	.. c	.. c	.. c	.. c	..
Finland	.. c	.. c	133.7	.. c	..	3.0	.. c	-	.. c	..
France	37.9	286.6	15 587.5	-10 254.4	..	406.6	11.5	469.1	-326.7	..
Germany	579.1	1 225.4	1 547.8	688.8	..	507.7	570.9	632.7	319.0	..
Greece	.. c	.. c	.. c	.. c	..	.. c	.. c	.. c	13.2	..
Hungary	-0.7	.. c	.. c	0.7	..	.. c	.. c	.. c	.. c	..
Iceland	.. c	-	-	-	..	-	-	-	.. c	..
Ireland	-15.6	-1 612.4	404.1	289.2	..	5.9	-223.0	-4.5	.. c	..
Israel	.. c	.. c	3.0	.. c	..	-	.. c	.. c	.. c	..
Italy	-91.4	25.3	-100.1	-36.8	..	1.5	.. c	3.7	.. c	..
Japan	7 047.5	4 949.8	7 031.4	8 319.3	..	.. c	.. c	216.6	.. c	..
Korea	959.6	.. c	1 257.2	1 129.5	..	.. c	.. c	221.1	29.2	..
Latvia	-	-	-	-	..	-	-	-	-	..
Lithuania	.. c	.. c	.. c	-	..	-	-	-	-	..
Luxembourg	2 732.5	2 544.3	-826.2	331.5	..	.. c	.. c	91.9	.. c	..
Mexico	-	.. c	.. c	-1.4	..	.. c	.. c	-68.7	.. c	..
Netherlands	2 100.6	3 019.4	-3 997.2	3 038.2	..	.. c	.. c	492.3	.. c	..
New Zealand	681.6	-39.9	611.8	-526.9	..	893.5	885.9	-648.4	2 448.0	..
Norway	.. c	-90.4	-56.0	.. c	..	.. c	.. c	.. c	.. c	..
Poland	.. c	.. c	-1.5	1.4	..	.. c	.. c	.. c	.. c	..
Portugal	-	.. c	.. c	.. c	..	.. c	.. c	.. c	.. c	..
Slovak Republic	.. c	.. c	-	-	..	.. c	.. c	.. c	.. c	..
Slovenia	-	-	-	-	..	.. c	.. c	.. c	.. c	..
Spain	-4.5	-1.5	2.2	.. c	..	.. c	.. c	8.2	55.6	..
Sweden	85.5	50.6	274.9	125.1	..	.. c	2.3	-20.9	.. c	..
Switzerland	709.9	421.5	776.1	-551.2	..	.. c	.. c	.. c	219.6	..
Turkey	-	.. c	.. c	.. c	..	.. c	.. c	-0.7	.. c	..
United Kingdom	12 557.1	11 924.3	6 197.1	20 111.2	..	859.3	2 690.6	9 528.6	8 458.3	..
United States	9 814.2	7 013.6	18 046.6	397.6	..	6 785.1	4 684.7	1 799.5	1 940.6	..
EUROPE	..	..	..	..	..	..	..	..	..	..
Bulgaria	.. c	.. c	.. c	.. c	..	.. c	.. c	.. c	.. c	..
Croatia	.. c	.. c	.. c	-	..	.. c	.. c	.. c	.. c	..
Cyprus	.. c	-	-	-	..	.. c	-	.. c	.. c	..
Malta	.. c	-	-	-	..	.. c	.. c	.. c	.. c	..
Montenegro	-	-	-	-	..	-	-	-	-	..
Romania	.. c	-	-	-	..	0.7	.. c	.. c	.. c	..
Russian Federation	.. c	.. c	.. c	.. c	..	10.4	.. c	20.2	.. c	..
Ukraine	-	-	-	-	..	.. c	.. c	.. c	.. c	..
AFRICA	..	..	..	..	..	..	..	..	..	..
Northern Africa	..	..	..	..	..	..	..	..	..	..
Algeria	.. c	.. c	.. c	-	..	-	-	-	.. c	..
Egypt	.. c	.. c	.. c	.. c	..	.. c	.. c	.. c	.. c	..
Libya	-	-	-	-	..	.. c	.. c	.. c	-	..
Morocco	.. c	.. c	-	-	..	.. c	.. c	-	.. c	..
Tunisia	.. c	.. c	.. c	-	..	-	-	-	-	..
Other African countries	..	..	..	..	..	..	..	..	..	..
Nigeria	.. c	.. c	.. c	.. c	..	.. c	.. c	.. c	.. c	..
South Africa	.. c	121.1	220.4	-22.9	..	-26.0	39.9	-162.1	13.9	..
AMERICA	..	..	..	..	..	..	..	..	..	..
Northern America	11 110.5	9 495.0	23 290.5	4 925.3	..	6 984.3	5 559.8	6 938.1	3 420.4	..
Central America and Caribbean countries	..	..	..	..	..	..	..	..	..	..
Bahamas	.. c	.. c	.. c	.. c	..	.. c	.. c	.. c	.. c	..
Bermuda	540.4	3 034.7	2 616.0	.. c	..	-356.1	.. c	278.6	.. c	..
Cayman Islands	.. c	49.0	-1 054.8	.. c	..	.. c	.. c	-895.6	.. c	..
El Salvador	-	-	-	-	..	.. c	.. c	.. c	.. c	..
Guatemala	-	-	-	-	..	.. c	.. c	.. c	.. c	..
Honduras	-	-	-	-	..	.. c	.. c	.. c	.. c	..
Nicaragua	-	-	-	-	..	-	.. c	.. c	.. c	..
Panama	.. c	.. c	.. c	-	..	.. c	.. c	.. c	.. c	..
Virgin Islands, U.S.	-	.. c	.. c	-	..	-	-	-	-	..
South America	..	..	..	..	..	..	..	..	..	..
Argentina	.. c	-2.3	.. c	.. c	..	.. c	.. c	0.7	.. c	..
Bolivia	-	-	-	-	..	.. c	.. c	.. c	.. c	..
Brazil	.. c	.. c	.. c	29.9	..	124.1	333.4	-171.8	-37.5	..
Ecuador	-	-	-	-	..	.. c	29.1	.. c	.. c	..
Paraguay	-	-	-	-	..	-	-	-	-	..
Peru	.. c	.. c	.. c	.. c	..	.. c	.. c	5.2	.. c	..
Uruguay	-	-	-	-	..	.. c	.. c	.. c	.. c	..
Venezuela	.. c	.. c	.. c	.. c	..	.. c	.. c	.. c	.. c	..

Table 1. Foreign direct investment flows by country *(cont.)*

Million US dollars

	Inward					Outward				
	2016	2017	2018	2019	2020	2016	2017	2018	2019	2020
ASIA	..	..	..	..	..	..	..	..	..	..
Near and Middle East	..	..	..	..	..	..	..	..	..	..
Gulf Arabian countries	..	..	..	..	..	..	..	..	..	..
Kuwait	.. c	.. c	.. c	.. c	..	.. c	.. c	.. c	.. c	..
Qatar	.. c	.. c	.. c	.. c	..	.. c	-	.. c	.. c	..
Saudi Arabia	-89.9	.. c	.. c	.. c	..	.. c	.. c	4.5	.. c	..
United Arab Emirates	-136.0	95.0	60.5	.. c	..	19.3	.. c	.. c	12.5	..
Other Near and Middle East	..	..	..	..	..	..	..	..	..	..
Jordan	.. c	.. c	.. c	.. c	..	-	-	.. c	-	..
Other Asian countries	..	..	..	..	..	..	..	..	..	..
China	1 266.6	705.0	3 244.9	3 017.3	..	-266.9	-1 526.6	816.5	198.1	..
Hong Kong, China	1 102.4	1 917.4	1 824.9	672.8	..	-487.6	237.6	38.1	-380.2	..
India	44.6	26.8	-17.2	287.1	..	50.5	98.1	38.1	79.2	..
Indonesia	7.4	.. c	1.5	.. c	..	56.5	136.4	.. c	269.0	..
Iran, Islamic Republic of	.. c	.. c	.. c	.. c	..	-	-	-	-	..
Malaysia	142.7	1 102.0	162.8	221.0	..	176.2	68.2	103.8	.. c	..
Philippines	0.7	-4.6	-44.8	-11.1	..	61.0	71.3	-85.9	28.5	..
Singapore	-3 491.4	2 827.8	4 180.9	2 976.3	..	159.8	118.0	265.2	787.5	..
Chinese Taipei	-3.0	39.9	32.9	.. c	..	-7.4	.. c	.. c	.. c	..
Thailand	.. c	508.1	-59.0	-198.8	..	6.7	91.2	-3.0	-52.8	..
Viet Nam	3.0	-1.5	3.7	-2.1	..	6.7	28.4	.. c	63.3	..
AUSTRALIA, OCEANIA AND POLAR REGIONS	..	..	..	..	..	..	..	..	..	..
WORLD unallocated and confidential	**10 414.0**	**3 764.3**	**3 067.2**	**790.3**	..	**-6 669.1**	**-3 387.2**	**-11 068.2**	**-10 325.3**	..
European Union (since 01/02/2020)	..	..	..	..	..	..	..	..	..	..
G20 countries excl. European Union	.. d	.. d	.. d	.. d	..	.. d	.. d	.. d	.. d	..
G20 OECD countries	**32 200.3**	.. d	.. d	.. d	..	.. d	.. d	**17 940.5**	.. d	..
G20 Non-OECD countries	.. d	.. d	.. d	.. d	..	.. d	.. d	.. d	.. d	..
MENA countries	.. d	.. d	.. d	.. d	..	.. d	.. d	.. d	.. d	..
ASEAN countries	**-4 058.6**	**4 428.7**	**4 248.9**	**2 992.3**	..	**596.9**	**875.9**	**-3 070.1**	**1 106.6**	..

- Nil; .. Not available; c Confidential data; d Secondary Confidentiality

Note: Detailed metadata at: *http://metalinks.oecd.org/idi/20220712/6d95.*

Source: *OECD International Direct Investment Statistics (database): https://doi.org/10.1787/idi-data-en*

AUSTRALIA

Table 2. Foreign direct investment positions by country

At year end

Million US dollars

	Inward					Outward				
	2016	2017	2018	2019	2020	2016	2017	2018	2019	2020
WORLD	**611 062.2**	**699 543.7**	**701 809.0**	**714 273.8**	..	**435 767.0**	**503 204.1**	**497 022.2**	**579 278.4**	..
OECD COUNTRIES	**375 223.6**	**426 988.5**	**436 587.4**	**441 921.1**	..	**227 866.9**	**267 834.0**	**272 452.7**	**333 515.0**	..
Australia	-	-	-	-	..	-	-	-	-	..
Austria	.. c	.. c	.. c	.. c	..	.. c	.. c	.. c	.. c	..
Belgium	1 818.4	1 737.8	2 783.7	2 482.3	..	.. c	.. c	.. c	2 972.7	..
Canada	20 142.5	25 415.3	28 521.3	33 008.5	..	5 883.5	8 180.3	23 772.6	24 589.1	..
Chile	.. c	.. c	.. c	.. c	..	1 159.2	1 259.7	1 279.6	1 436.3	..
Colombia	.. c	.. c	.. c	.. c	..	91.9	157.6	150.3	149.2	..
Costa Rica	-	-	-	-	..	.. c	.. c	.. c	18.2	..
Czech Republic	1.4	.. c	.. c	.. c	..	.. c	.. c	.. c	.. c	..
Denmark	.. c	.. c	723.5	751.8	..	.. c	.. c	.. c	.. c	..
Estonia	-	-	-	-	..	.. c	.. c	.. c	.. c	..
Finland	.. c	.. c	253.4	234.0	..	3.6	3.9	.. c	6.3	..
France	4 428.4	4 892.0	19 408.5	8 854.5	..	1 895.8	1 880.5	2 227.6	2 696.0	..
Germany	14 141.1	18 724.0	17 154.2	15 436.1	..	.. c	.. c	.. c	.. c	..
Greece	.. c	.. c	.. c	-	..	.. c	.. c	32.5	.. c	..
Hungary	.. c	.. c	.. c	.. c	..	.. c	.. c	.. c	.. c	..
Iceland	-	-	-	-	..	-	-	-	.. c	..
Ireland	2 925.5	1 514.7	1 487.9	1 623.3	..	.. c	.. c	.. c	536.7	..
Israel	.. c	.. c	.. c	.. c	..	-	.. c	.. c	.. c	..
Italy	433.4	542.1	382.6	372.0	..	112.9	178.6	.. c	100.9	..
Japan	70 806.8	76 388.0	77 025.7	81 343.8	..	.. c	691.1	926.7	1 158.1	..
Korea	3 324.2	4 239.1	4 789.7	5 250.5	..	589.7	669.2	765.1	861.8	..
Latvia	-	-	-	-	..	-	-	-	-	..
Lithuania	.. c	-	-	-	..	-	-	-	-	..
Luxembourg	4 592.6	7 355.9	5 943.0	5 650.5	..	1 191.8	1 783.0	.. c	.. c	..
Mexico	-	1.6	.. c	.. c	..	1 041.2	723.0	600.6	765.1	..
Netherlands	37 278.6	43 626.9	36 699.6	38 385.8	..	5 845.9	5 343.6	5 424.2	3 730.8	..
New Zealand	4 280.8	4 469.2	4 473.5	3 917.2	..	48 034.0	48 760.6	40 024.0	58 577.7	..
Norway	619.4	627.1	452.4	449.1	..	.. c	.. c	.. c	.. c	..
Poland	0.7	3.1	1.4	2.8	..	.. c	33.5	31.8	37.1	..
Portugal	.. c	-	.. c	.. c	..	8.7	9.4	7.1	9.8	..
Slovak Republic	.. c	-	-	-	..	.. c	.. c	.. c	.. c	..
Slovenia	-	-	-	-	..	.. c	.. c	.. c	.. c	..
Spain	.. c	.. c	-	-	..	31.8	28.1	33.9	91.8	..
Sweden	1 516.6	1 625.5	1 651.6	1 647.9	..	266.3	290.9	.. c	334.9	..
Switzerland	7 255.4	7 575.1	7 949.6	7 388.8	..	.. c	.. c	257.6	505.9	..
Turkey	.. c	.. c	.. c	.. c	..	91.2	.. c	.. c	.. c	..
United Kingdom	54 824.9	69 744.2	69 767.1	89 064.0	..	57 693.9	70 470.3	83 219.2	100 512.2	..
United States	143 942.8	155 360.7	154 894.1	143 742.0	..	89 867.6	104 398.3	91 698.9	102 163.5	..
EUROPE	..	..	..	..	..	..	..	..	..	..
Bulgaria	.. c	.. c	.. c	.. c	..	.. c	.. c	.. c	.. c	..
Croatia	-	.. c	-	-	..	.. c	.. c	.. c	.. c	..
Cyprus	-	-	-	-	..	.. c	.. c	.. c	.. c	..
Malta	-	-	-	-	..	.. c	.. c	.. c	.. c	..
Montenegro	-	-	-	-	..	-	-	-	-	..
Romania	.. c	.. c	.. c	.. c	..	.. c	.. c	.. c	4.2	..
Russian Federation	.. c	.. c	.. c	.. c	..	36.2	.. c	179.3	.. c	..
Ukraine	-	-	-	-	..	.. c	.. c	.. c	.. c	..
AFRICA	..	..	..	..	..	..	..	..	..	..
Northern Africa	..	..	..	..	..	..	..	..	..	..
Algeria	.. c	.. c	.. c	.. c	..	-	-	-	.. c	..
Egypt	.. c	.. c	.. c	.. c	..	5.8	.. c	.. c	2.1	..
Libya	-	-	-	-	..	.. c	.. c	.. c	.. c	..
Morocco	.. c	-	-	-	..	.. c	.. c	.. c	.. c	..
Tunisia	.. c	.. c	-	-	..	.. c	.. c	.. c	.. c	..
Other African countries	..	..	..	..	..	..	..	..	..	..
Nigeria	.. c	.. c	.. c	.. c	..	.. c	.. c	.. c	.. c	..
South Africa	2 556.4	2 309.5	2 151.3	2 067.5	..	875.5	2 131.7	758.8	634.1	..
AMERICA	..	..	..	..	..	..	..	..	..	..
Northern America	164 085.4	180 776.1	183 415.4	176 750.5	..	95 751.1	112 578.6	115 471.5	126 752.6	..
Central America and Caribbean countries	..	..	..	..	..	..	..	..	..	..
Bahamas	1 424.0	1 511.6	.. c	.. c	..	.. c	.. c	.. c	.. c	..
Bermuda	27 295.2	32 931.1	31 415.9	29 164.2	..	24 045.6	.. c	.. c	.. c	..
Cayman Islands	4 119.4	4 391.2	2 901.6	3 131.1	..	.. c	.. c	.. c	.. c	..
El Salvador	-	-	-	-	..	.. c	.. c	.. c	25.2	..
Guatemala	-	-	-	-	..	.. c	.. c	.. c	.. c	..
Honduras	-	-	-	-	..	.. c	.. c	.. c	.. c	..
Nicaragua	-	-	-	-	..	-	.. c	.. c	.. c	..
Panama	-	.. c	-	-	..	.. c	.. c	.. c	.. c	..
Virgin Islands, U.S.	-	.. c	-	-	..	-	-	-	-	..
South America	..	..	..	..	..	..	..	..	..	..
Argentina	.. c	.. c	.. c	.. c	..	170.8	287.8	.. c	316.7	..
Bolivia	-	-	-	-	..	.. c	.. c	.. c	.. c	..
Brazil	.. c	.. c	.. c	.. c	..	3 217.8	.. c	3 099.9	3 138.8	..
Ecuador	-	-	-	-	..	.. c	103.0	.. c	43.4	..
Paraguay	-	-	-	-	..	-	-	-	-	..
Peru	.. c	.. c	.. c	.. c	..	200.4	230.9	226.6	255.0	..
Uruguay	-	-	-	-	..	4.3	.. c	.. c	.. c	..
Venezuela	.. c	.. c	.. c	-	..	.. c	.. c	.. c	.. c	..

Table 2. Foreign direct investment positions by country *(cont.)*

At year end

Million US dollars

	Inward					Outward				
	2016	2017	2018	2019	2020	2016	2017	2018	2019	2020
ASIA	..	..	..	..	..	..	..	..	..	..
Near and Middle East	..	..	..	..	..	..	..	..	..	..
Gulf Arabian countries	..	..	..	..	..	..	..	..	..	..
Kuwait	.. c	.. c	.. c	.. c	..	.. c	.. c	.. c	.. c	..
Qatar	.. c	.. c	.. c	.. c	..	-2.9	.. c	.. c	.. c	..
Saudi Arabia	646.9	713.7	662.8	381.8	..	.. c	.. c	.. c	.. c	..
United Arab Emirates	1 186.0	1 708.9	1 197.8	1 860.9	..	.. c	.. c	.. c	.. c	..
Other Near and Middle East	..	..	..	..	..	..	..	..	..	..
Jordan	.. c	.. c	.. c	.. c	..	.. c	.. c	-	-	..
Other Asian countries	..	..	..	..	..	..	..	..	..	..
China	27 997.8	29 941.5	29 493.9	32 223.1	..	9 672.9	10 492.2	9 812.3	10 867.4	..
Hong Kong, China	9 895.8	12 418.7	12 646.8	11 293.4	..	3 230.1	3 350.8	4 047.1	5 346.5	..
India	670.8	701.2	612.6	781.9	..	1 270.6	1 442.9	1 144.8	1 353.6	..
Indonesia	-	.. c	-	11.9	..	4 515.9	5 886.4	1 610.7	2 484.4	..
Iran, Islamic Republic of	.. c	-	.. c	-	..	-	-	-	-	..
Malaysia	8 890.7	10 502.3	9 935.8	10 305.5	..	4 036.9	4 619.0	4 203.8	4 441.3	..
Philippines	3.6	.. c	.. c	.. c	..	695.4	753.5	554.8	641.8	..
Singapore	17 081.0	21 588.8	23 111.9	25 268.0	..	14 549.9	15 749.2	17 852.2	19 695.9	..
Chinese Taipei	80.3	120.9	131.3	401.5	..	.. c	.. c	.. c	946.5	..
Thailand	3 372.6	4 260.2	4 141.7	4 123.2	..	1 265.6	1 363.4	979.0	1 095.8	..
Viet Nam	.. c	.. c	.. c	.. c	..	1 120.8	1 576.3	.. c	1 849.6	..
AUSTRALIA, OCEANIA AND POLAR REGIONS	..	..	..	..	..	..	..	..	..	..
WORLD unallocated and confidential	**115 487.7**	**133 970.0**	**130 304.2**	**132 972.0**	..	**140 559.3**	**196 991.7**	**191 292.3**	**223 713.3**	..
European Union (since 01/02/2020)	..	..	..	..	..	..	..	..	..	..
G20 countries excl. European Union	.. d	.. d	.. d	.. d	..	.. d	.. d	.. d	.. d	..
G20 OECD countries	.. d	.. d	.. d	.. d	..	.. d	.. d	.. d	.. d	..
G20 Non-OECD countries	.. d	.. d	.. d	.. d	..	.. d	.. d	.. d	.. d	..
MENA countries	.. d	.. d	.. d	.. d	..	.. d	.. d	.. d	.. d	..
ASEAN countries	**29 348.0**	**36 346.6**	**37 151.3**	**39 652.5**	..	**27 463.1**	**31 541.2**	**28 377.3**	**31 841.9**	..

- Nil; .. Not available; c Confidential data; d Secondary Confidentiality

Note: Inward FDI positions are allocated according to the ultimate investing country. Data excludes resident Special Purpose Entities (SPEs). Detailed metadata at: *http://metalinks.oecd.org/idi/20220712/6d95*.

Source: OECD *International Direct Investment Statistics (database)*: *https://doi.org/10.1787/idi-data-en*

AUSTRALIA

Table 3. Foreign direct investment income by country

Million US dollars

	Inward					Outward				
	2016	2017	2018	2019	2020	2016	2017	2018	2019	2020
WORLD	**27 454.1**	**37 310.9**	**44 029.3**	**43 575.5**	**..**	**13 315.2**	**14 217.9**	**16 748.3**	**16 859.7**	**..**
OECD COUNTRIES	**15 566.8**	**23 427.8**	**28 555.3**	**29 568.4**	**..**	**7 112.2**	**7 936.2**	**9 686.3**	**9 758.8**	**..**
Australia	-	-	-	-	..	-	-	-	-	..
Austria	.. c	.. c	.. c	.. c	..	.. c	.. c	.. c	.. c	..
Belgium	19.3	111.1	218.9	177.9	..	-	.. c	.. c	.. c	..
Canada	304.8	671.3	632.0	1 007.2	..	.. c	58.2	316.0	.. c	..
Chile	-	-	-	-	..	.. c	92.7	.. c	.. c	..
Colombia	-	-	-	-	..	.. c	.. c	.. c	.. c	..
Costa Rica	-	-	-	-	..	.. c	.. c	.. c	.. c	..
Czech Republic	-	-	-	-	..	.. c	.. c	.. c	.. c	..
Denmark	.. c	.. c	.. c	89.0	..	.. c	.. c	.. c	.. c	..
Estonia	-	-	-	-	..	.. c	.. c	.. c	.. c	..
Finland	.. c	.. c	.. c	.. c	..	.. c	.. c	.. c	.. c	..
France	557.5	505.8	783.6	793.8	..	.. c	101.9	.. c	.. c	..
Germany	.. c	.. c	1 110.8	.. c	..	.. c	.. c	.. c	.. c	..
Greece	-	-	-	-	..	.. c	.. c	.. c	.. c	..
Hungary	-	-	-	-	..	.. c	.. c	.. c	.. c	..
Iceland	-	-	-	-	..	-	-	-	-	..
Ireland	263.1	.. c	.. c	193.2	..	.. c	.. c	.. c	.. c	..
Israel	.. c	.. c	.. c	.. c	..	-	-	-	-	..
Italy	.. c	.. c	.. c	.. c	..	.. c	.. c	.. c	.. c	..
Japan	4 103.2	5 257.9	6 382.3	6 993.1	..	98.9	.. c	.. c	79.9	..
Korea	123.4	.. c	404.1	.. c	..	.. c	5.4	12.0	5.6	..
Latvia	-	-	-	-	..	-	-	-	-	..
Lithuania	-	-	-	-	..	-	-	-	-	..
Luxembourg	180.6	239.9	82.9	79.2	..	.. c	.. c	.. c	.. c	..
Mexico	-	-	-	-	..	.. c	99.6	.. c	.. c	..
Netherlands	726.2	1 273.7	1 862.3	1 788.4	..	.. c	.. c	.. c	.. c	..
New Zealand	459.4	474.4	273.4	.. c	..	3 301.9	3 635.5	3 598.3	2 849.8	..
Norway	.. c	.. c	.. c	.. c	..	.. c	.. c	.. c	.. c	..
Poland	-	-	-	-	..	.. c	.. c	.. c	.. c	..
Portugal	-	-	-	-	..	.. c	.. c	.. c	.. c	..
Slovak Republic	-	-	-	-	..	.. c	.. c	.. c	.. c	..
Slovenia	-	-	-	-	..	.. c	.. c	.. c	.. c	..
Spain	-	-	.. c	.. c	..	.. c	.. c	.. c	2.8	..
Sweden	96.6	.. c	130.7	.. c	..	.. c	.. c	.. c	.. c	..
Switzerland	.. c	.. c	722.3	.. c	..	.. c	.. c	5.2	.. c	..
Turkey	-	-	-	-	..	.. c	.. c	.. c	.. c	..
United Kingdom	991.6	4 152.8	5 691.3	5 759.4	..	1 436.9	1 117.3	1 398.4	2 122.8	..
United States	6 226.1	8 125.5	9 723.6	9 509.3	..	903.9	1 564.9	2 849.0	3 013.8	..
EUROPE	..	..	..	..	..	..	..	..	..	..
Bulgaria	-	-	-	-	..	.. c	.. c	.. c	.. c	..
Croatia	-	-	-	-	..	.. c	.. c	.. c	.. c	..
Cyprus	-	-	-	-	..	.. c	-	.. c	.. c	..
Malta	.. c	-	-	-	..	-	.. c	-	-	..
Montenegro	-	-	-	-	..	-	-	-	-	..
Romania	-	-	-	-	..	-	.. c	.. c	.. c	..
Russian Federation	.. c	.. c	-	-	..	.. c	1.5	.. c	.. c	..
Ukraine	-	-	-	-	..	.. c	.. c	.. c	.. c	..
AFRICA	..	..	..	..	..	..	..	..	..	..
Northern Africa	..	..	..	..	..	..	..	..	..	..
Algeria	-	-	-	-	..	-	-	-	-	..
Egypt	-	-	-	-	..	.. c	.. c	.. c	.. c	..
Libya	-	-	-	-	..	.. c	.. c	-	-	..
Morocco	-	-	-	-	..	-	-	-	.. c	..
Tunisia	-	-	-	-	..	-	-	-	-	..
Other African countries	..	..	..	..	..	..	..	..	..	..
Nigeria	-	-	-	-	..	.. c	.. c	-	-	..
South Africa	168.7	105.8	125.5	189.8	..	14.1	.. c	.. c	.. c	..
AMERICA	..	..	..	..	..	..	..	..	..	..
Northern America	6 530.9	8 796.8	10 355.6	10 516.4	..	..	1 623.1	3 165.0	..	..
Central America and Caribbean countries	..	..	..	..	..	..	..	..	..	..
Bahamas	.. c	.. c	.. c	.. c	..	.. c	-	-	-	..
Bermuda	1 549.1	1 906.7	2 913.3	1 716.8	..	.. c	.. c	.. c	.. c	..
Cayman Islands	.. c	216.9	228.6	241.2	..	.. c	.. c	.. c	.. c	..
El Salvador	-	-	-	-	..	.. c	.. c	.. c	.. c	..
Guatemala	-	-	-	-	..	.. c	.. c	.. c	.. c	..
Honduras	-	-	-	-	..	.. c	.. c	.. c	.. c	..
Nicaragua	-	-	-	-	..	.. c	.. c	.. c	.. c	..
Panama	.. c	-	-	-	..	.. c	.. c	.. c	.. c	..
Virgin Islands, U.S.	-	-	-	-	..	-	-	-	-	..
South America	..	..	..	..	..	..	..	..	..	..
Argentina	.. c	.. c	.. c	.. c	..	.. c	.. c	.. c	.. c	..
Bolivia	-	-	-	-	..	.. c	.. c	.. c	.. c	..
Brazil	.. c	.. c	.. c	.. c	..	.. c	98.9	.. c	.. c	..
Ecuador	-	-	-	-	..	.. c	.. c	.. c	-	..
Paraguay	-	-	-	-	..	-	-	-	-	..
Peru	-	-	-	-	..	.. c	.. c	.. c	.. c	..
Uruguay	-	-	-	-	..	.. c	.. c	.. c	.. c	..
Venezuela	-	-	-	-	..	.. c	.. c	.. c	.. c	..

Table 3. Foreign direct investment income by country *(cont.)*

Million US dollars

	Inward					Outward				
	2016	2017	2018	2019	2020	2016	2017	2018	2019	2020
ASIA	..	..	..	..	..	..	..	..	..	..
Near and Middle East	..	..	..	..	..	..	..	..	..	..
Gulf Arabian countries	..	..	..	..	..	..	..	..	..	..
Kuwait	.. c	11.5	.. c	.. c	..	.. c	.. c	-	-	..
Qatar	.. c	.. c	.. c	.. c	..	.. c	-	-	-	..
Saudi Arabia	.. c	.. c	.. c	.. c	..	.. c	.. c	.. c	.. c	..
United Arab Emirates	94.4	158.6	76.2	7.6	..	2.2	.. c	9.0	.. c	..
Other Near and Middle East	..	..	..	..	..	..	..	..	..	..
Jordan	.. c	.. c	.. c	.. c	..	-	-	-	-	..
Other Asian countries	..	..	..	..	..	..	..	..	..	..
China	136.0	456.7	1 306.5	1 547.9	..	492.8	174.7	239.0	155.7	..
Hong Kong, China	813.2	888.2	1 053.3	.. c	..	208.9	201.5	242.0	.. c	..
India	40.1	.. c	.. c	.. c	..	65.4	70.5	.. c	.. c	..
Indonesia	-	-	-	-	..	61.7	162.5	268.2	.. c	..
Iran, Islamic Republic of	-	-	-	-	..	-	-	-	-	..
Malaysia	84.7	.. c	.. c	.. c	..	.. c	219.2	184.5	209.9	..
Philippines	-	-	-	-	..	54.3	.. c	.. c	29.2	..
Singapore	.. c	799.3	735.0	1 378.3	..	396.2	.. c	673.0	980.7	..
Chinese Taipei	3.0	11.5	.. c	.. c	..	.. c	.. c	.. c	.. c	..
Thailand	.. c	.. c	.. c	.. c	..	29.0	38.3	17.9	.. c	..
Viet Nam	-	-	-	-	..	10.4	.. c	44.1	.. c	..
AUSTRALIA, OCEANIA AND POLAR REGIONS	..	..	..	..	..	..	..	..	..	..
WORLD unallocated and confidential	**10 337.5**	**10 436.0**	**8 417.1**	**12 103.3**	..	**5 910.2**	**6 463.3**	**6 534.7**	**6 933.3**	..
European Union (since 01/02/2020)	..	..	..	..	..	..	..	..	..	..
G20 countries excl. European Union	.. d	.. d	.. d	.. d	..	.. d	.. d	.. d	.. d	..
G20 OECD countries	.. d	.. d	.. d	.. d	..	.. d	.. d	.. d	.. d	..
G20 Non-OECD countries	.. d	.. d	.. d	.. d	..	.. d	.. d	.. d	.. d	..
MENA countries	.. d	.. d	.. d	.. d	..	.. d	.. d	.. d	.. d	..
ASEAN countries	**1 233.2**	**964.1**	**880.7**	**1 527.8**	..	**849.6**	**1 412.4**	**1 410.3**	**1 627.9**	..

- Nil; .. Not available; c Confidential data; d Secondary Confidentiality

Note: Detailed metadata at: *http://metalinks.oecd.org/idi/20220712/6d95.*

Source: *OECD International Direct Investment Statistics (database): https://doi.org/10.1787/idi-data-en*

AUSTRALIA

Table 4. Foreign direct investment flows by industrial sector

Million US dollars

	Inward					Outward				
	2016	2017	2018	2019	2020	2016	2017	2018	2019	2020
All FDI activities	**48 291.1**	**45 300.0**	**68 033.2**	**36 151.4**	..	**2 265.7**	**5 932.3**	**6 361.4**	**5 396.5**	..
Agriculture, forestry and fishing	**.. c**	**308.8**	**-366.8**	**.. c**	..	**.. c**	**.. c**	**.. c**	**.. c**	..
Mining and quarrying	**23 351.7**	**14 658.6**	**13 385.4**	**3 270.3**	..	**300.3**	**-465.2**	**3 232.2**	**5 330.5**	..
Extraction activities	..	..	..	..	..	..	..	..	..	..
Manufacturing	**3 785.0**	**5 859.5**	**7 909.9**	**15 500.1**	..	**3 306.3**	**4 728.3**	**4 728.5**	**7 764.6**	..
of which:										
Food products, beverages and tobacco	..	..	..	..	..	..	..	..	..	..
Textiles, wood and paper products; printing	..	..	..	..	..	..	..	..	..	..
Chemical, rubber, plastic, non-metallic mineral products	..	..	..	..	..	..	..	..	..	..
Metal and machinery products, except electrical equipment	..	..	..	..	..	..	..	..	..	..
Motor vehicles, trailers, semi-trailers, other transport equipment	..	..	..	..	..	..	..	..	..	..
Other manufacturing	..	..	..	..	..	..	..	..	..	..
Electricity, gas, steam and air conditioning supply	**-762.7**	**2 889.9**	**1 111.5**	**.. c**	..	**20.8**	**388.5**	**462.4**	**.. c**	..
Water supply; sewerage, waste management and remediation activities	..	..	..	..	..	..	..	..	..	..
Construction	**102.6**	**951.8**	**570.7**	**1 378.3**	..	**127.1**	**460.6**	**685.7**	**.. c**	..
Services	**25 740.7**	**22 041.5**	**43 594.5**	**9 036.6**	..	**5 933.2**	**8 812.2**	**7 208.5**	**-5 498.0**	..
Wholesale and retail trade; repair of motor vehicles and motorcycles	2 192.8	2 031.6	4 546.9	1 593.8	..	997.5	-296.6	2 813.9	209.2	..
Transportation and storage	3 710.0	630.7	860.5	1 085.0	..	-198.5	-216.1	47.1	59.8	..
Accommodation and food service activities	-25.3	269.8	1 764.4	966.8	..	3.7	90.4	.. c	.. c	..
Information and communication	-305.5	1 378.7	2 711.6	2 562.7	..	-427.4	477.4	258.5	.. c	..
Financial and insurance activities	5 360.1	9 221.4	24 995.1	476.8	..	4 919.3	6 818.9	3 581.1	-5 435.5	..
Activities of holding companies	..	..	..	..	..	..	..	..	..	..
Real estate activities	.. c	.. c	5 505.3	519.2	..	-334.5	2 401.7	374.2	-2 098.4	..
Professional, scientific and technical activities	842.2	968.7	833.6	770.1	..	.. c	-264.4	-150.1	.. c	..
Administrative and support service activities	.. c	360.2	.. c	510.2	..	599.1	611.5	130.7	253.0	..
Public administration; activities of households and of extraterritorial organisations	.. c	.. c	148.7	.. c	..	-	-	-	-	..
Education	.. c	.. c	-485.5	.. c	..	.. c	.. c	.. c	.. c	..
Human health and social work activities	1 449.5	482.8	-72.5	-409.4	..	503.2	.. c	307.8	1 389.4	..
Arts, entertainment and recreation	.. c	.. c	.. c	.. c	..	.. c	.. c	.. c	43.8	..
Other services	.. c	.. c	.. c	38.2	..	-	-	.. c	.. c	..
Not allocated and confidential	**.. c**	**-1 410.1**	**1 827.9**	**.. c**	..	**.. c**	**.. c**	**.. c**	**.. c**	..
Private real estate activities	..	..	..	..	..	..	..	..	..	..

- Nil; .. Not available; c Confidential data

Note: Detailed metadata at: *http://metalinks.oecd.org/idi/20220712/6d95.*

Source: *OECD International Direct Investment Statistics (database): https://doi.org/10.1787/idi-data-en*

AUSTRALIA

Table 5. Foreign direct investment positions by industrial sector

At year end

Million US dollars

	Inward					Outward				
	2016	2017	2018	2019	2020	2016	2017	2018	2019	2020
All FDI activities	**611 062.2**	**699 543.7**	**701 809.0**	**714 273.8**	..	**435 767.0**	**503 204.1**	**497 022.2**	**579 278.4**	..
Agriculture, forestry and fishing	**2 372.6**	**2 783.7**	**2 232.5**	**2 370.2**	..	.. c	.. c	.. c	.. c	..
Mining and quarrying	**245 386.4**	**271 293.2**	**263 284.9**	**252 264.4**	..	**92 374.8**	**102 974.0**	**108 060.4**	**121 657.7**	..
Extraction activities	..	..	..	..	..	..	..	..	..	..
Manufacturing	**68 764.8**	**79 385.4**	**78 193.8**	**92 090.0**	..	**68 969.6**	**88 580.5**	**99 330.2**	**138 332.5**	..
of which:										
Food products, beverages and tobacco	..	..	..	..	..	..	..	..	..	..
Textiles, wood and paper products; printing	..	..	..	..	..	..	..	..	..	..
Chemical, rubber, plastic, non-metallic mineral products	..	..	..	..	..	..	..	..	..	..
Metal and machinery products, except electrical equipment	..	..	..	..	..	..	..	..	..	..
Motor vehicles, trailers, semi-trailers, other transport equipment	..	..	..	..	..	..	..	..	..	..
Other manufacturing	..	..	..	..	..	..	..	..	..	..
Electricity, gas, steam and air conditioning supply	**11 457.3**	**15 913.0**	**15 638.8**	**15 228.8**	..	**3 374.1**	**3 906.1**	**4 211.6**	**4 389.4**	..
Water supply; sewerage, waste management and remediation activities	..	..	..	..	..	..	..	..	..	..
Construction	**14 157.7**	**18 064.9**	**14 323.1**	**12 650.5**	..	**6 360.3**	**7 564.2**	**5 480.7**	**6 231.3**	..
Services	**198 319.8**	**232 652.7**	**252 951.0**	**259 466.1**	..	**158 719.2**	**177 943.2**	**161 785.7**	**174 956.2**	..
Wholesale and retail trade; repair of motor vehicles and motorcycles	39 201.9	44 242.3	42 800.7	42 258.1	..	5 324.9	4 633.0	6 730.7	6 672.0	..
Transportation and storage	18 687.4	17 174.9	16 257.1	16 357.5	..	2 919.7	2 864.1	2 947.5	3 043.5	..
Accommodation and food service activities	5 045.6	5 336.6	6 282.5	6 548.7	..	58.6	128.7	57.2	156.9	..
Information and communication	18 188.9	19 856.5	19 565.2	21 365.5	..	1 360.3	2 176.9	2 204.3	2 017.1	..
Financial and insurance activities	49 826.3	61 665.2	80 555.5	79 286.8	..	125 790.9	141 538.9	124 203.8	135 143.3	..
Activities of holding companies	..	..	..	..	..	..	..	..	..	..
Real estate activities	54 721.4	71 255.8	72 900.9	77 704.1	..	11 984.1	14 897.4	14 176.3	13 374.9	..
Professional, scientific and technical activities	3 909.6	5 234.4	5 186.3	5 628.1	..	2 069.5	2 183.9	2 025.0	2 802.5	..
Administrative and support service activities	2 730.1	3 176.8	5 246.3	5 563.7	..	2 343.7	3 382.0	3 377.3	3 927.7	..
Public administration; activities of households and of extraterritorial organisations	.. c	.. c	.. c	.. c	..	-	-	-	-	..
Education	.. c	.. c	.. c	.. c	..	.. c	.. c	.. c	.. c	..
Human health and social work activities	2 553.5	3 107.4	2 722.3	2 360.4	..	4 591.9	4 682.2	4 743.1	6 956.5	..
Arts, entertainment and recreation	.. c	.. c	.. c	.. c	..	.. c	.. c	.. c	.. c	..
Other services	219.2	.. c	.. c	.. c	..	-	-	.. c	-	..
Not allocated and confidential	**70 603.5**	**79 450.9**	**75 184.9**	**80 203.9**	..	.. c	.. c	.. c	.. c	..
Private real estate activities	..	..	..	..	..	..	..	..	..	..

- Nil; .. Not available; c Confidential data

Note: Detailed metadata at: *http://metalinks.oecd.org/idi/20220712/6d95*.

Source: *OECD International Direct Investment Statistics (database)*: *https://doi.org/10.1787/idi-data-en*

AUSTRALIA

Table 6. Foreign direct investment income by industrial sector

Million US dollars

	Inward					Outward				
	2016	2017	2018	2019	2020	2016	2017	2018	2019	2020
All FDI activities	**27 454.1**	**37 310.9**	**44 029.3**	**43 575.5**	..	**13 315.2**	**14 217.9**	**16 748.3**	**16 859.7**	..
Agriculture, forestry and fishing	**107.8**	**105.8**	**.. c**	**16.0**	..	**-**	**-**	**.. c**	**.. c**	..
Mining and quarrying	**4 842.8**	**12 388.7**	**17 431.8**	**18 523.0**	..	**-164.3**	**2 207.8**	**2 296.3**	**2 818.5**	..
Extraction activities	..	..	..	..	..	..	..	..	..	..
Manufacturing	**4 677.8**	**4 493.8**	**4 815.1**	**3 492.0**	..	**2 993.4**	**3 321.3**	**3 743.9**	**3 904.9**	..
of which:										
Food products, beverages and tobacco	..	..	..	..	..	..	..	..	..	..
Textiles, wood and paper products; printing	..	..	..	..	..	..	..	..	..	..
Chemical, rubber, plastic, non-metallic mineral products	..	..	..	..	..	..	..	..	..	..
Metal and machinery products, except electrical equipment	..	..	..	..	..	..	..	..	..	..
Motor vehicles, trailers, semi-trailers, other transport equipment	..	..	..	..	..	..	..	..	..	..
Other manufacturing	..	..	..	..	..	..	..	..	..	..
Electricity, gas, steam and air conditioning supply	**815.4**	**.. c**	**1 175.8**	**1 295.6**	..	**.. c**	**.. c**	**.. c**	**.. c**	..
Water supply; sewerage, waste management and remediation activities	..	..	..	..	..	..	..	..	..	..
Construction	**.. c**	**1 160.2**	**1 249.7**	**.. c**	..	**.. c**	**422.3**	**.. c**	**.. c**	..
Services	**14 249.6**	**15 772.9**	**17 266.0**	**16 790.2**	..	**6 985.1**	**4 928.3**	**6 643.0**	**6 151.4**	..
Wholesale and retail trade; repair of motor vehicles and motorcycles	2 583.1	1 969.5	3 563.2	3 373.9	..	197.0	-87.4	162.8	.. c	..
Transportation and storage	767.1	627.6	904.6	674.2	..	20.1	108.1	147.9	182.1	..
Accommodation and food service activities	799.8	784.0	660.3	745.1	..	.. c	.. c	.. c	.. c	..
Information and communication	1 064.4	1 246.8	1 054.8	809.1	..	82.5	-76.6	-52.3	73.7	..
Financial and insurance activities	3 734.5	4 831.8	4 995.9	5 122.0	..	5 491.0	3 827.9	5 051.9	4 528.4	..
Activities of holding companies	..	..	..	..	..	..	..	..	..	..
Real estate activities	.. c	.. c	.. c	.. c	..	.. c	.. c	.. c	491.4	..
Professional, scientific and technical activities	161.3	-1.5	132.2	230.1	..	.. c	.. c	.. c	.. c	..
Administrative and support service activities	139.7	153.3	106.1	.. c	..	.. c	.. c	.. c	.. c	..
Public administration; activities of households and of extraterritorial organisations	.. c	.. c	.. c	.. c	..	-	-	.. c	-	..
Education	.. c	.. c	.. c	43.8	..	.. c	.. c	.. c	-	..
Human health and social work activities	191.0	187.8	115.0	2.1	..	.. c	.. c	.. c	.. c	..
Arts, entertainment and recreation	.. c	.. c	.. c	1.4	..	.. c	.. c	.. c	.. c	..
Other services	.. c	.. c	.. c	52.8	..	-	-	-	-	..
Not allocated and confidential	**.. c**	**.. c**	**.. c**	**.. c**	..	**.. c**	**.. c**	**.. c**	**.. c**	..
Private real estate activities	..	..	..	..	..	..	..	..	..	..

- Nil; .. Not available; c Confidential data

Note: Detailed metadata at: *http://metalinks.oecd.org/idi/20220712/6d95*.

Source: *OECD International Direct Investment Statistics (database): https://doi.org/10.1787/idi-data-en*

AUSTRIA

Table 1. Foreign direct investment flows by country

Million US dollars

	Inward					Outward				
	2016	2017	2018	2019	2020	2016	2017	2018	2019	2020
WORLD	**-8 500.5**	**14 921.7**	**5 386.5**	**3 034.8**	**-15 009.7**	**-2 031.4**	**10 228.8**	**5 608.4**	**12 508.7**	**-2 394.3**
OECD COUNTRIES	**-8 340.2**	**7 038.7**	**8 379.6**	**1 460.9**	**-8 850.1**	**8 929.6**	**6 060.2**	**1 645.2**	**6 866.7**	**1 217.1**
Australia	-11.1	-55.2	-70.8	17.9	871.8	119.4	86.8	345.8	92.9	58.1
Austria	-	-	-	-	-	-	-	-	-	-
Belgium	14.4	665.1	-1 352.5	1 955.7	403.4	454.5	-273.9	-291.5	90.7	139.0
Canada	25.4	230.0	-41.3	-303.4	-157.3	-184.7	-391.2	-275.0	-128.7	26.2
Chile	-2.2	-3.4	-15.3	-1.1	-3.4	17.7	-	31.9	12.3	-10.3
Colombia	..	..	..	..	..	..	..	..	..	..
Costa Rica	..	-	..	..	..	..	..	..	..	..
Czech Republic	28.8	3.4	184.1	-54.9	169.8	-1 019.6	554.6	584.2	1 259.4	-405.7
Denmark	-426.8	-	7.1	30.2	34.2	12.2	-78.9	5.9	34.7	13.7
Estonia	-3.3	-	-	-1.1	1.1	18.8	-77.8	113.3	4.5	-70.7
Finland	44.2	57.5	-10.6	25.7	-100.3	91.8	113.9	129.8	305.6	-308.8
France	-315.2	7.9	-186.5	282.1	-409.1	19.9	310.0	101.5	15.7	-143.6
Germany	938.8	4 137.1	6 707.2	-1 256.0	-3 499.7	1 282.8	1 889.3	-2 334.5	1 094.8	1 311.7
Greece	38.7	48.5	-355.2	201.5	-286.0	85.1	3.4	-334.0	31.3	-12.5
Hungary	-8.8	-80.0	-4.7	95.2	-10.3	-832.7	335.9	738.8	607.9	-115.1
Iceland	1.1	13.5	-	-	-	-	-	-4.7	-	-
Ireland	696.7	-811.6	1 628.7	272.0	1.1	86.3	31.6	-296.2	51.5	57.0
Israel	-10.0	-1.1	-2.4	5.6	-22.8	-2.2	4.5	-1.2	41.4	3.4
Italy	-7 566.1	666.2	103.9	-1 230.3	463.8	811.7	-168.0	669.2	-245.2	370.4
Japan	80.7	287.5	-77.9	-137.7	-140.2	31.0	-9.0	38.9	19.0	27.4
Korea	364.9	319.0	1 308.9	111.9	16.0	-43.1	-10.1	86.2	99.6	-5.7
Latvia	..	..	..	..	..	..	..	..	..	..
Lithuania	..	-	..	..	..	..	..	..	..	..
Luxembourg	2 051.3	110.5	1 279.4	-1 364.6	-643.9	800.6	-232.2	172.3	-12 662.0	-1 247.9
Mexico	-33.2	196.1	-11.8	1.1	-36.5	174.7	131.9	142.8	208.2	20.5
Netherlands	-2 337.7	355.1	-5 645.0	670.5	-1 517.9	6 886.0	5 024.2	-1 865.9	13 659.5	-891.2
New Zealand	-	-1.1	-5.9	-22.4	-	-31.0	-34.9	570.0	-199.3	75.2
Norway	-33.2	19.2	-10.6	22.4	80.9	191.3	-804.9	-666.8	-216.1	-80.9
Poland	-5.5	144.3	-216.0	-12.3	52.4	558.4	1 079.9	-9.4	251.9	654.1
Portugal	18.8	7.9	7.1	-15.7	19.4	-1.1	32.7	-59.0	167.9	-18.2
Slovak Republic	-36.5	-379.9	428.4	-25.7	217.7	5.5	-479.1	231.3	166.8	95.7
Slovenia	-117.2	-62.0	-27.1	21.3	164.1	-81.8	320.1	211.3	281.0	207.4
Spain	-97.3	-11.3	291.5	-3.4	35.3	194.6	280.7	577.1	12.3	-242.7
Sweden	70.8	157.8	240.8	-101.9	210.8	21.0	411.5	126.3	-59.3	-164.1
Switzerland	1 237.4	951.4	643.2	1 327.7	250.7	1 237.4	-799.2	1 311.2	868.7	1 089.5
Turkey	180.3	231.1	164.1	126.5	54.7	-2 687.2	-1 252.4	354.1	104.1	57.0
United Kingdom	-808.4	857.9	1 413.9	446.7	-2 312.3	826.1	-210.8	-293.9	672.8	247.3
United States	-2 326.7	-1 028.1	2 007.6	376.1	-2 744.2	-213.4	248.0	1 524.8	202.6	400.0
EUROPE	**-6 914.7**	**13 042.5**	**3 075.7**	**1 177.7**	**-7 521.4**	**4 073.9**	**7 960.8**	**849.8**	**8 842.5**	**-1 030.2**
Bulgaria	195.7	30.4	-9.4	1.1	66.1	-1 933.0	-308.9	-119.2	119.8	23.9
Croatia	16.6	-94.7	53.1	4.5	78.6	-1 803.6	58.6	74.4	42.5	19.4
Cyprus	..	..	..	..	..	..	..	..	..	..
Malta	..	..	..	..	..	..	..	..	..	..
Montenegro	..	-	..	..	..	..	..	..	..	..
Romania	-10.0	-	-20.1	-148.9	-159.5	-1 015.2	756.4	1 207.4	447.8	-87.7
Russian Federation	-25.4	6 417.5	-2 747.6	283.2	-1 112.3	-517.5	1 364.0	594.8	995.2	-1 384.6
Ukraine	14.4	-7.9	7.1	-29.1	42.2	-222.3	-13.5	110.9	341.4	-167.5
AFRICA	**276.5**	**1 288.5**	**16.5**	**578.8**	**20.5**	**-35.4**	**144.3**	**-61.4**	**39.2**	**79.8**
Northern Africa	-3.3	-24.8	-	4.5	2.3	-54.2	28.2	7.1	30.2	28.5
Algeria	..	-	..	..	..	..	-	..	..	..
Egypt	..	..	..	..	..	..	..	..	..	..
Libya	-	-	-	-	-	..	-	..	..	..
Morocco	..	..	..	..	..	..	..	..	..	..
Tunisia	..	..	..	..	..	..	..	..	..	..
Other African countries	..	..	..	..	..	..	..	..	..	..
Nigeria	..	..	..	..	..	..	..	..	..	..
South Africa	..	..	..	..	..	..	..	..	..	..
AMERICA	**-2 345.5**	**-77.8**	**1 583.9**	**755.6**	**-3 569.2**	**-7 431.2**	**351.7**	**1 038.6**	**220.5**	**683.8**
Northern America	-2 301.2	-798.1	1 965.1	72.8	-2 901.4	-398.1	-143.2	1 249.9	73.9	425.1
Central America and Caribbean countries	174.7	1 403.4	376.5	381.7	-879.8	-7 227.7	441.9	-467.4	173.5	-340.7
Bahamas	-	-	..	-	-	..	-	..	..	..
Bermuda	..	..	..	..	..	..	..	..	..	..
Cayman Islands	..	..	..	..	..	..	..	..	..	..
El Salvador	-	-	-	-	-	-	-	-	-	-
Guatemala	..	-	..	..	..	..	-	..	..	..
Honduras	-	-	-	-	-	..	..	..	..	..
Nicaragua	-	-	-	-	-	..	-	..	..	..
Panama	..	..	..	..	..	..	..	..	..	..
Virgin Islands, U.S.	..	..	..	..	..	-	-	-	-	-
South America	-219.0	-684.3	-758.9	301.1	213.1	194.6	53.0	256.1	-26.9	598.3
Argentina	-1.1	7.9	17.7	216.1	-250.7	121.6	18.0	18.9	-	11.4
Bolivia	-	-	..	..	..	..	-	..	..	..
Brazil	-105.1	-688.8	-744.7	107.5	455.8	-39.8	47.3	128.6	-20.2	618.8
Ecuador	-	-	..	..	..	..	-	..	..	..
Paraguay	-	-	-	-	-	..	..	-	-	-
Peru	..	..	..	..	..	..	-	..	..	..
Uruguay	..	-	..	..	..	..	..	..	..	..
Venezuela	..	-	..	..	..	..	..	..	..	..

Table 1. Foreign direct investment flows by country *(cont.)*

Million US dollars

	Inward					Outward				
	2016	2017	2018	2019	2020	2016	2017	2018	2019	2020
ASIA	**492.1**	**724.8**	**781.3**	**526.1**	**-4 813.7**	**1 255.1**	**1 720.2**	**2 865.6**	**3 513.9**	**-2 261.0**
Near and Middle East	-152.6	86.8	-363.5	143.3	-4 713.4	548.5	45.1	1 921.4	1 453.0	-648.4
Gulf Arabian countries	-139.3	86.8	-361.1	138.8	-4 721.4	528.6	55.2	1 921.4	1 416.1	-649.6
Kuwait	..	..	..	..	..	-	-	..	-	..
Qatar	..	..	..	..	..	..	..	..	..	..
Saudi Arabia	..	..	..	..	..	..	..	..	..	..
United Arab Emirates	..	..	..	..	..	..	..	..	..	..
Other Near and Middle East	-13.3	-	-2.4	4.5	8.0	19.9	-10.1	-	36.9	2.3
Jordan	..	..	..	..	..	..	..	..	..	..
Other Asian countries	644.7	638.0	1 144.8	382.9	-100.3	706.6	1 675.1	944.2	2 060.9	-1 612.5
China	2.2	22.5	139.3	35.8	209.7	268.7	592.9	434.3	86.2	-1 954.4
Hong Kong, China	147.1	-134.1	87.3	219.4	-249.6	206.8	242.4	276.2	521.7	165.2
India	-1.1	-	-16.5	-10.1	-8.0	86.3	39.5	114.5	81.7	117.4
Indonesia	-3.3	3.4	-1.2	-	-1.1	21.0	-5.6	20.1	4.5	52.4
Iran, Islamic Republic of	..	-	..	..	..	..	..	..	..	..
Malaysia	..	..	..	..	..	..	..	..	..	..
Philippines	-2.2	-	-	-	1.1	8.8	9.0	5.9	12.3	-3.4
Singapore	-5.5	-19.2	7.1	-135.5	-435.3	7.7	1 030.3	-118.0	228.4	-249.6
Chinese Taipei	..	..	..	..	..	..	..	..	..	..
Thailand	-88.5	-23.7	-421.3	241.8	491.2	28.8	-232.2	34.2	68.3	216.5
Viet Nam	..	-	..	..	..	..	..	..	..	..
AUSTRALIA, OCEANIA AND POLAR REGIONS	**-11.1**	**-56.4**	**-77.9**	**-3.4**	**872.9**	**87.4**	**51.9**	**915.9**	**-107.5**	**133.3**
WORLD unallocated and confidential	**2.2**	**-**	**7.1**	**-**	**1.1**	**18.8**	**-**	**-**	**-**	**-**
European Union (since 01/02/2020)	**..**	**..**	**..**	**..**	**-4 768.1**	**..**	**..**	**..**	**..**	**-948.1**
G20 countries excl. European Union	**-9 319.9**	**12 939.9**	**8 029.0**	**-350.4**	**-8 589.2**	**127.2**	**2 748.3**	**1 624.0**	**3 258.7**	**-274.6**
G20 OECD countries	**-9 470.3**	**5 849.4**	**11 314.8**	**-1 565.0**	**-7 891.7**	**136.0**	**624.5**	**360.0**	**2 135.9**	**2 367.0**
G20 Non-OECD countries	**150.4**	**7 090.5**	**-3 286.9**	**1 214.6**	**-697.4**	**-8.8**	**2 123.8**	**1 264.0**	**1 122.8**	**-2 642.7**
MENA countries	**-146.0**	**62.0**	**-361.1**	**139.9**	**-4 719.1**	**473.3**	**69.9**	**1 927.3**	**1 444.1**	**-622.2**
ASEAN countries	**-45.3**	**-3.4**	**-347.0**	**200.4**	**52.4**	**103.9**	**789.1**	**18.9**	**1 218.0**	**43.3**

- Nil; .. Not available

Note: Data excludes resident Special Purpose Entities (SPEs). Detailed metadata at: *http://metalinks.oecd.org/idi/20220712/6d95*.

Source: *OECD International Direct Investment Statistics (database): https://doi.org/10.1787/idi-data-en*

AUSTRIA

Table 2. Foreign direct investment positions by country

At year end

Million US dollars

	Inward					Outward				
	2016	2017	2018	2019	2020	2016	2017	2018	2019	2020
WORLD	**150 648.3**	**191 442.8**	**185 184.3**	**193 695.8**	**200 835.7**	**196 996.9**	**233 762.3**	**229 977.1**	**239 293.4**	**237 598.5**
OECD COUNTRIES	**113 170.7**	**137 211.6**	**138 007.8**	**143 373.4**	..	**152 926.1**	**181 758.2**	**175 480.9**	**178 169.0**	..
Australia	67.5	87.6	80.1	44.9	50.3	2 130.3	2 551.0	2 742.2	4 183.3	4 661.9
Austria	2 342.2	5 155.9	5 863.3	4 661.9	5 349.1	-	-	-	-	-
Belgium	765.3	891.1	794.6	860.5	863.9	2 004.8	1 921.3	1 576.6	1 619.9	1 891.0
Canada	3 706.1	4 439.9	6 189.6	4 528.2	4 954.0	986.6	512.1	152.3	212.3	246.7
Chile	1.1	1.2	1.1	1.1	1.2	159.2	167.9	176.3	171.9	171.8
Colombia	-	-	-	-	-	..	..	..	..	..
Costa Rica	-	-	-	-	-	..	..	..	..	..
Czech Republic	254.0	206.3	416.8	395.4	574.3	11 573.7	14 570.6	15 115.6	15 223.5	15 934.5
Denmark	179.2	218.3	226.7	237.0	268.7	176.0	277.0	266.8	347.1	396.4
Estonia	-8.4	1.2	1.1	-	-	246.7	203.9	271.4	284.2	234.4
Finland	728.4	838.3	640.0	415.6	347.3	615.6	804.7	891.9	1 188.5	1 153.5
France	3 677.7	5 865.9	4 915.3	4 937.1	5 224.0	4 177.3	4 940.0	3 927.2	2 220.8	2 270.2
Germany	44 714.9	56 338.5	59 998.9	58 280.2	60 166.9	28 231.3	36 575.9	33 133.7	38 910.4	44 506.1
Greece	758.9	899.5	476.3	478.5	390.2	376.3	417.4	138.5	156.1	157.1
Hungary	190.8	207.5	221.0	275.2	244.2	6 870.5	8 163.8	8 229.9	8 611.5	8 717.6
Iceland	-	-	-	-	-	4.2	6.0	2.3	1.1	1.2
Ireland	662.0	722.0	700.7	1 871.5	1 613.7	179.2	251.9	89.3	197.7	227.0
Israel	160.2	266.3	246.2	124.7	142.3	5.3	9.6	3.4	41.6	47.9
Italy	10 314.1	11 662.3	11 117.5	11 281.7	11 670.1	3 163.3	3 788.7	4 485.9	4 452.9	5 304.9
Japan	2 142.9	4 072.9	4 001.6	3 680.1	4 110.9	175.0	171.5	296.5	343.7	390.2
Korea	227.7	255.5	411.0	485.3	595.2	1 105.7	1 166.9	1 205.6	1 291.8	1 367.0
Latvia	..	..	..	..	..	..	..	..	..	..
Lithuania	..	-	-	-	-	..	..	..	..	..
Luxembourg	3 321.4	3 328.1	2 951.7	3 764.3	3 996.8	12 643.6	14 292.4	13 346.7	4 239.5	7 126.0
Mexico	1 660.2	2 729.7	2 200.6	2 519.7	2 688.7	717.8	889.9	1 076.3	1 257.0	1 237.0
Netherlands	4 421.8	-399.4	542.7	6 831.0	9 169.2	25 500.2	36 103.4	36 373.9	39 647.3	21 316.7
New Zealand	-	-	-	-	-	97.0	62.4	612.5	405.5	512.9
Norway	248.8	310.6	128.2	205.6	279.8	2 792.2	2 203.2	1 462.1	1 298.6	1 237.0
Poland	16.9	25.2	17.2	401.0	446.7	5 051.1	7 031.7	5 920.5	6 279.5	7 196.0
Portugal	85.4	88.8	90.5	102.2	115.4	227.7	297.4	258.8	246.0	249.1
Slovak Republic	24.2	28.8	26.3	46.1	338.7	6 250.7	7 266.7	7 071.2	6 621.0	7 535.9
Slovenia	122.3	154.7	20.6	21.3	17.2	2 843.9	3 642.4	3 711.9	3 804.8	4 433.7
Spain	1 242.8	1 452.4	731.6	759.4	1 483.6	1 183.7	1 560.3	1 728.9	1 756.9	1 905.8
Sweden	918.1	1 036.2	1 221.7	1 184.0	1 457.8	1 535.8	1 772.6	1 678.5	1 533.4	1 691.0
Switzerland	9 112.5	13 261.0	12 744.4	14 829.3	15 496.4	9 551.0	8 546.4	8 516.1	9 818.0	12 804.0
Turkey	218.2	247.1	243.9	303.3	368.1	3 580.7	1 790.6	1 386.5	2 062.5	1 219.8
United Kingdom	5 716.2	6 682.7	5 992.7	6 132.3	5 536.9	8 187.0	7 778.8	6 123.2	6 052.6	6 523.5
United States	15 170.2	16 128.6	14 782.5	13 698.0	14 252.1	10 451.1	11 849.4	13 234.5	13 385.8	13 818.9
EUROPE	**113 256.0**	**142 347.1**	**138 714.2**	**146 182.9**	**154 371.1**	**166 382.4**	**198 366.5**	**189 994.3**	**194 263.1**	**191 381.8**
Bulgaria	278.3	317.8	295.4	298.8	222.1	3 152.7	3 238.2	2 973.4	3 037.5	3 344.0
Croatia	1.1	3.6	-2.3	-	-3.7	3 959.1	4 552.7	4 704.6	4 915.7	5 392.1
Cyprus	..	..	..	..	..	..	..	..	..	..
Malta	..	..	..	..	..	..	..	..	..	..
Montenegro	-	-	-	-	-	..	..	..	..	..
Romania	55.9	68.4	60.7	3.4	2.5	8 282.9	10 100.7	10 266.8	11 133.5	11 957.3
Russian Federation	20 206.6	30 197.9	25 330.9	25 676.3	26 270.7	4 966.8	6 103.4	6 861.7	8 164.5	5 702.5
Ukraine	42.2	45.6	52.7	56.2	55.2	331.0	488.1	603.4	1 024.5	692.1
AFRICA	**1 924.7**	**3 004.3**	**2 875.0**	**3 402.6**	**3 774.7**	**820.1**	**993.0**	**1 033.9**	**1 043.6**	**1 095.8**
Northern Africa	-	-	-	-	-	172.9	293.8	360.7	365.1	417.2
Algeria	-	-	-	-	-	..	..	..	..	..
Egypt	-	-	..	-	..	..	..	..	..	..
Libya	-	-	-	-	-	..	..	..	..	..
Morocco	-	-	-	-	-	..	..	..	..	..
Tunisia	-	-	-	-	-	..	..	..	..	..
Other African countries	..	..	..	..	..	..	..	..	..	..
Nigeria	..	-	-	-	-	..	..	..	..	..
South Africa	..	..	..	..	..	..	..	..	..	..
AMERICA	**21 840.4**	**26 765.4**	**25 935.4**	**22 906.1**	**23 699.8**	**15 143.9**	**16 569.9**	**17 841.8**	**18 010.6**	**18 734.8**
Northern America	18 877.4	20 568.5	20 972.1	18 225.1	19 207.3	11 437.8	12 361.5	13 386.8	13 598.1	14 065.5
Central America and Caribbean countries	1 666.5	2 581.0	2 679.2	2 661.2	3 169.7	1 933.2	2 360.3	2 458.2	2 428.7	2 341.4
Bahamas	-	-	..	-	-	..	-	..	..	..
Bermuda	..	..	..	..	..	..	..	..	..	..
Cayman Islands	-	-	..	..	..	..	..	..	..	..
El Salvador	-	-	-	-	-	-	-	-	-	-
Guatemala	-	-	-	-	-	..	..	..	..	..
Honduras	-	-	-	-	-	..	..	..	..	..
Nicaragua	-	-	-	-	-	..	..	..	..	..
Panama	..	..	..	..	..	..	..	..	..	..
Virgin Islands, U.S.	-	-	-	-	-	-	-	-	-	-
South America	1 296.5	3 617.2	2 284.2	2 018.6	1 324.1	1 773.0	1 848.2	1 995.6	1 982.7	2 327.9
Argentina	49.5	62.4	708.7	917.8	94.5	92.8	106.7	130.5	105.6	95.7
Bolivia	-	-	-	-	-	..	..	..	..	..
Brazil	1 239.6	3 552.4	1 574.3	1 099.8	1 228.4	1 173.2	1 334.9	1 356.8	1 379.5	1 773.2
Ecuador	-	-	-	-	-	..	..	..	..	..
Paraguay	-	-	-	-	-	..	-	-	-	-
Peru	-	-	..	-	-	..	..	..	..	..
Uruguay	-	-	..	..	..	..	..	..	..	..
Venezuela	..	-	-	-	-	..	-	..	..	..

AUSTRIA

Table 2. Foreign direct investment positions by country *(cont.)*

At year end

Million US dollars

	Inward					Outward				
	2016	2017	2018	2019	2020	2016	2017	2018	2019	2020
ASIA	**13 276.1**	**18 914.6**	**17 271.6**	**19 490.0**	**17 090.4**	**12 422.3**	**15 217.1**	**17 751.3**	**21 389.6**	**21 212.4**
Near and Middle East	6 269.6	8 725.1	7 033.4	9 614.7	7 187.4	4 986.8	5 805.9	7 618.5	9 551.8	8 964.3
Gulf Arabian countries	6 108.4	8 457.7	6 787.3	9 417.0	6 928.5	4 921.5	5 724.4	7 554.4	9 457.4	8 864.9
Kuwait	..	..	..	..	..	-	-	..	-	..
Qatar	-	-	-	..	..	..	..	..	..	..
Saudi Arabia	..	..	..	..	..	..	..	..	..	..
United Arab Emirates	..	..	..	..	..	..	..	..	..	..
Other Near and Middle East	162.3	267.5	247.3	197.7	258.9	65.4	81.6	64.1	95.5	98.2
Jordan	..	..	..	..	..	..	..	..	..	..
Other Asian countries	7 005.4	10 189.5	10 237.0	9 876.4	9 903.1	7 435.4	9 411.1	10 132.8	11 836.7	12 249.4
China	375.3	903.1	1 126.6	996.4	1 141.2	2 615.2	3 445.7	3 764.6	3 756.5	3 568.5
Hong Kong, China	3 301.4	3 500.8	3 145.2	3 018.4	2 383.1	877.0	1 232.9	1 551.4	1 791.7	2 039.5
India	123.3	328.6	311.4	403.3	446.7	450.1	645.2	717.9	779.6	909.3
Indonesia	-	-	-	-	-	226.6	226.7	240.4	239.3	290.8
Iran, Islamic Republic of	-	-	..	..	..	..	..	..	..	..
Malaysia	..	..	..	..	..	..	..	..	..	..
Philippines	-	-	-	-	-	79.1	79.2	73.3	91.0	92.0
Singapore	610.3	568.5	603.4	540.3	501.9	1 290.2	1 805.0	1 702.5	1 937.8	1 721.7
Chinese Taipei	..	..	..	..	..	..	..	..	..	..
Thailand	-	16.8	5.7	6.7	8.6	331.0	249.5	139.7	214.6	433.2
Viet Nam	-	-	-	-	..	..	..	..	..	..
AUSTRALIA, OCEANIA AND POLAR REGIONS	**67.5**	**87.6**	**80.1**	**44.9**	**50.3**	**2 228.3**	**2 615.7**	**3 357.0**	**4 588.9**	**5 174.9**
WORLD unallocated and confidential	**283.5**	**323.8**	**308.0**	**1 669.3**	**1 849.3**	**-**	**-**	**-1.1**	**-2.2**	**-1.2**
European Union (since 01/02/2020)	..	..	..	..	..	..	..	..	..	**155 128.2**
G20 countries excl. European Union	**111 744.5**	**146 831.4**	**142 111.3**	**138 619.4**	**142 876.4**	**72 912.4**	**84 441.1**	**81 369.4**	**89 260.8**	**94 233.6**
G20 OECD countries	**87 616.7**	**108 510.4**	**109 934.7**	**105 891.9**	**109 619.6**	**62 907.1**	**72 017.3**	**67 765.1**	**74 373.2**	**81 546.2**
G20 Non-OECD countries	**24 127.8**	**38 320.9**	**32 176.6**	**32 727.5**	**33 256.8**	**10 005.3**	**12 425.0**	**13 605.5**	**14 887.7**	**12 687.4**
MENA countries	**6 108.4**	**8 457.7**	**6 787.3**	**9 415.9**	**6 928.5**	**5 118.6**	**6 054.2**	**7 954.0**	**9 859.6**	**9 321.4**
ASEAN countries	**689.4**	**716.0**	**883.9**	**821.2**	**796.4**	**2 139.8**	**2 642.1**	**2 512.0**	**3 780.0**	**3 882.7**

- Nil; .. Not available

Note: Detailed metadata at: *http://metalinks.oecd.org/idi/20220712/6d95*.

Source: *OECD International Direct Investment Statistics (database)*: *https://doi.org/10.1787/idi-data-en*

AUSTRIA

Table 3. Foreign direct investment income by country

Million US dollars

	Inward					Outward				
	2016	2017	2018	2019	2020	2016	2017	2018	2019	2020
WORLD	**11 956.2**	**15 794.2**	**16 014.4**	**15 477.4**	**4 789.7**	**15 376.5**	**15 095.3**	**15 065.5**	**16 821.9**	**4 939.0**
OECD COUNTRIES	**10 632.5**	**13 050.4**	**13 104.0**	**12 347.5**	**4 258.7**	**9 847.4**	**9 533.3**	**8 484.6**	**10 368.3**	**3 569.2**
Australia	10.0	11.3	11.8	4.5	1.1	123.9	147.7	36.6	31.3	82.1
Austria	-	-	-	-	-	-	-	-	-	-
Belgium	130.5	73.3	69.6	62.7	22.8	129.4	137.5	125.1	101.9	53.6
Canada	16.6	-6.8	9.4	16.8	10.3	224.5	-143.2	-393.0	97.4	4.6
Chile	-	-	-11.8	-	-	13.3	-3.4	31.9	-5.6	2.3
Colombia	..	-	..	..	..	..	..	..	..	..
Costa Rica	..	-	-	-	-	..	..	..	..	..
Czech Republic	4.4	22.5	64.9	48.1	27.4	1 712.9	1 924.2	2 079.5	2 205.3	302.0
Denmark	27.6	28.2	34.2	41.4	13.7	21.0	10.1	16.5	36.9	13.7
Estonia	-3.3	-	-	-	-	14.4	20.3	28.3	15.7	5.7
Finland	63.0	55.2	94.4	90.7	5.7	54.2	77.8	138.1	341.4	44.4
France	253.2	200.7	123.9	439.9	82.1	94.0	-128.5	118.0	43.7	42.2
Germany	3 680.2	4 781.9	6 770.9	3 689.7	1 622.8	954.3	2 409.0	2 261.3	1 297.4	610.8
Greece	38.7	47.3	24.8	36.9	3.4	-3.3	-5.6	-4.7	-1.1	1.1
Hungary	44.2	44.0	23.6	62.7	-35.3	680.1	1 050.6	1 154.3	1 016.5	163.0
Iceland	-	-	-	-	-	-	-	-	-	-
Ireland	34.3	-21.4	-157.0	-52.6	60.4	27.6	28.2	-5.9	-4.5	-18.2
Israel	-	-	-	-	-	-	-1.1	-3.5	-7.8	1.1
Italy	412.5	812.8	586.6	414.2	234.8	76.3	11.3	-131.0	-29.1	58.1
Japan	50.9	49.6	35.4	-31.3	12.5	2.2	6.8	38.9	15.7	5.7
Korea	-10.0	3.4	38.9	29.1	6.8	189.1	99.2	135.7	190.3	25.1
Latvia	..	-	..	..	..	..	..	..	..	..
Lithuania	..	-	-	-	-	..	..	..	..	..
Luxembourg	1 402.2	12.4	985.5	602.3	460.4	732.1	-307.7	-1 017.3	220.5	152.7
Mexico	7.7	10.1	7.1	10.1	3.4	152.6	121.7	122.7	128.7	21.7
Netherlands	2 069.0	4 775.1	2 568.2	3 921.4	1 021.1	1 091.5	383.3	511.0	881.0	741.9
New Zealand	-	-	-	-	-	58.6	48.5	30.7	94.0	16.0
Norway	-16.6	-13.5	-1.2	33.6	4.6	19.9	19.2	257.3	86.2	27.4
Poland	-2.2	-12.4	-22.4	-14.6	-2.3	329.5	455.4	411.9	334.7	216.5
Portugal	28.8	15.8	14.2	22.4	2.3	14.4	-	-33.0	98.5	2.3
Slovak Republic	-	3.4	-22.4	-23.5	6.8	755.3	695.5	731.7	733.2	271.2
Slovenia	-	2.3	-	2.2	-	305.2	402.4	407.2	361.6	86.6
Spain	81.8	87.9	47.2	88.4	26.2	232.2	151.1	283.3	117.5	25.1
Sweden	191.3	158.9	245.5	136.6	27.4	160.3	220.9	109.8	111.9	51.3
Switzerland	1 406.6	1 084.4	827.3	1 571.7	423.9	901.3	98.1	234.9	883.2	214.2
Turkey	194.6	193.9	158.1	78.4	41.0	170.3	170.2	138.1	165.7	35.3
United Kingdom	362.7	423.9	385.9	905.6	104.8	-69.7	742.9	5.9	478.0	33.0
United States	150.4	206.3	192.4	157.8	70.7	660.2	664.0	627.9	277.6	261.0
EUROPE	**10 810.6**	**13 110.1**	**13 246.8**	**12 400.1**	**4 712.3**	**12 057.9**	**11 928.8**	**11 974.5**	**13 978.5**	**4 065.0**
Bulgaria	110.6	22.5	4.7	106.3	5.7	291.9	143.2	133.4	304.5	63.8
Croatia	-11.1	-10.1	-10.6	-3.4	-4.6	334.0	223.2	407.2	482.5	96.9
Cyprus	..	..	..	..	..	..	..	..	..	..
Malta	..	..	..	..	..	..	..	..	..	..
Montenegro	..	-	-	-	..	..	..	..	..	..
Romania	-4.4	-2.3	-2.4	-12.3	-9.1	525.3	860.1	1 370.2	1 176.5	437.6
Russian Federation	-102.8	87.9	152.2	110.8	506.0	927.8	1 197.2	1 147.2	1 391.5	141.3
Ukraine	-42.0	-22.5	-2.4	-3.4	-2.3	112.8	152.2	237.2	439.9	14.8
AFRICA	**43.1**	**478.0**	**28.3**	**638.1**	**53.6**	**-43.1**	**59.7**	**64.9**	**21.3**	**22.8**
Northern Africa	-1.1	-1.1	-2.4	-2.2	-2.3	-58.6	-3.4	-1.2	15.7	6.8
Algeria	..	-	-	-	-	..	..	..	..	..
Egypt	..	-	..	..	-	..	-	..	..	..
Libya	..	-	-	-	-	..	-	..	..	..
Morocco	..	..	..	..	..	..	..	..	..	..
Tunisia	..	..	..	..	..	..	..	..	..	..
Other African countries	..	..	..	..	..	..	..	..	..	..
Nigeria	..	-	-	-	-	..	..	..	..	..
South Africa	..	..	..	..	..	..	..	..	..	..
AMERICA	**-171.4**	**846.6**	**1 357.3**	**893.3**	**-131.1**	**1 427.6**	**824.0**	**721.1**	**645.9**	**344.2**
Northern America	167.0	199.5	201.8	174.6	82.1	884.7	520.8	233.7	375.0	265.5
Central America and Caribbean countries	139.3	231.1	102.7	118.7	134.5	457.8	264.9	358.8	183.6	47.9
Bahamas	..	..	-	-	-	..	-	-	..	..
Bermuda	..	..	..	..	..	..	..	..	-	..
Cayman Islands	..	..	..	..	..	..	..	..	..	..
El Salvador	..	-	-	-	-	..	-	-	-	-
Guatemala	..	-	-	-	-	..	-	-	-	-
Honduras	..	-	-	-	-	..	..	..	..	..
Nicaragua	..	-	-	-	-	..	..	..	..	..
Panama	..	..	..	..	..	..	..	..	..	..
Virgin Islands, U.S.	..	..	..	..	..	..	-	-	-	-
South America	-477.7	416.0	1 052.8	600.0	-347.6	85.1	37.2	127.5	87.3	30.8
Argentina	-	37.2	24.8	211.6	9.1	18.8	7.9	1.2	3.4	2.3
Bolivia	..	-	-	-	-	..	-	..	..	..
Brazil	-477.7	378.8	1 039.8	388.4	-357.8	15.5	15.8	41.3	73.9	20.5
Ecuador	..	-	-	-	-	..	-	..	..	..
Paraguay	..	-	-	-	-	..	-	-	-	-
Peru	..	-	..	..	..	..	-	..	..	..
Uruguay	..	-	..	..	..	..	..	..	..	..
Venezuela	..	-	-	-	-	..	-	..	..	..

AUSTRIA

Table 3. Foreign direct investment income by country *(cont.)*

Million US dollars

	Inward					Outward				
	2016	2017	2018	2019	2020	2016	2017	2018	2019	2020
ASIA	**1 261.7**	**1 341.5**	**1 367.9**	**1 540.4**	**155.0**	**1 764.9**	**2 097.8**	**2 244.8**	**2 054.2**	**414.8**
Near and Middle East	875.8	939.0	781.3	1 083.6	86.6	834.9	762.0	858.0	548.5	189.2
Gulf Arabian countries	888.0	945.8	782.5	1 082.5	85.5	831.6	768.8	862.7	557.5	188.0
Kuwait	..	..	..	..	..	..	-	..	-	..
Qatar	..	..	..	..	..	..	..	..	..	..
Saudi Arabia	..	..	..	..	..	..	..	..	..	..
United Arab Emirates	..	..	..	..	..	..	..	..	..	..
Other Near and Middle East	-12.2	-6.8	-	1.1	1.1	2.2	-6.8	-4.7	-9.0	1.1
Jordan	..	..	..	..	..	..	..	..	..	..
Other Asian countries	385.9	402.4	585.4	456.7	68.4	930.0	1 335.8	1 385.6	1 505.7	225.6
China	-1.1	-7.9	5.9	3.4	3.4	504.3	1 148.7	986.7	855.3	79.8
Hong Kong, China	289.7	322.4	433.1	463.5	35.3	23.2	99.2	208.9	276.5	22.8
India	-	-	-	-	-	24.3	38.3	36.6	23.5	11.4
Indonesia	-	-	-	-	-	17.7	14.7	4.7	-32.5	2.3
Iran, Islamic Republic of	..	-	..	..	..	..	..	..	..	..
Malaysia	..	..	..	..	..	..	..	..	..	..
Philippines	-1.1	-	-	-	-	16.6	14.7	14.2	14.6	2.3
Singapore	3.3	-4.5	5.9	-11.2	2.3	79.6	-131.9	-135.7	70.5	35.3
Chinese Taipei	..	..	..	..	..	..	..	..	..	..
Thailand	-4.4	-2.3	-2.4	-2.2	-1.1	29.9	18.0	16.5	15.7	4.6
Viet Nam	..	-	-	-	..	..	..	..	..	..
AUSTRALIA, OCEANIA AND POLAR REGIONS	**8.8**	**11.3**	**11.8**	**4.5**	**1.1**	**183.6**	**196.1**	**67.3**	**125.4**	**98.0**
WORLD unallocated and confidential	**3.3**	**6.8**	**2.4**	**1.1**	**-1.1**	**-14.4**	**-11.3**	**-7.1**	**-3.4**	**-5.7**
European Union (since 01/02/2020)	**..**	**..**	**..**	**..**	**3 594.3**	**..**	**..**	**..**	**..**	**3 454.1**
G20 countries excl. European Union	**4 596.9**	**7 659.8**	**9 566.9**	**7 073.8**	**2 421.7**	**4 102.6**	**6 523.5**	**5 181.2**	**5 030.8**	**1 447.3**
G20 OECD countries	**5 128.8**	**6 687.0**	**8 320.5**	**5 717.0**	**2 190.3**	**2 578.8**	**4 102.1**	**2 962.4**	**2 697.9**	**1 178.3**
G20 Non-OECD countries	**-533.0**	**972.8**	**1 246.3**	**1 356.8**	**230.2**	**1 523.8**	**2 421.4**	**2 218.8**	**2 332.9**	**268.9**
MENA countries	**875.8**	**937.9**	**778.9**	**1 080.3**	**83.2**	**773.0**	**762.0**	**859.2**	**572.0**	**194.9**
ASEAN countries	**54.2**	**30.4**	**62.6**	**-13.4**	**4.6**	**174.7**	**-68.8**	**-24.8**	**111.9**	**79.8**

- Nil; .. Not available

Note: Data excludes resident Special Purpose Entities (SPEs). Detailed metadata at: *http://metalinks.oecd.org/idi/20220712/6d95*.

Source: *OECD International Direct Investment Statistics (database): https://doi.org/10.1787/idi-data-en*

AUSTRIA

Table 4. Foreign direct investment flows by industrial sector

Million US dollars

	Inward					Outward				
	2016	2017	2018	2019	2020	2016	2017	2018	2019	2020
All FDI activities	**-8 500.5**	**14 921.7**	**5 386.5**	**3 034.8**	**-15 009.7**	**-2 031.4**	**10 228.8**	**5 608.4**	**12 508.7**	**-2 394.3**
Agriculture, forestry and fishing	**-1.1**	**-1.1**	**-1.2**	**-1.1**	**-**	**110.6**	**14.7**	**-61.4**	**7.8**	**16.0**
Mining and quarrying	**64.1**	**-189.4**	**166.4**	**103.0**	**167.5**	**-796.2**	**-1 209.6**	**1 725.5**	**2 527.7**	**2 029.6**
Extraction activities	..	..	..	..	..	..	..	..	..	..
Manufacturing	**483.2**	**354.0**	**1 456.4**	**601.1**	**619.9**	**2 566.6**	**2 431.5**	**4 445.9**	**1 783.3**	**-1 623.9**
of which:										
Food products, beverages and tobacco	360.5	-80.0	-16.5	47.0	-137.9	68.6	92.4	-118.0	-14.6	-27.4
Textiles, wood and paper products; printing	-22.1	-	159.3	-77.2	-85.5	831.6	1 481.2	1 307.7	806.0	152.7
Chemical, rubber, plastic, non-metallic mineral products	-19.9	157.8	-139.3	-49.3	420.5	57.5	-370.9	1 023.3	126.5	-910.5
Metal and machinery products, except electrical equipment	-7.7	325.8	863.9	668.3	136.8	-230.0	301.0	1 396.2	-3.4	-828.5
Motor vehicles, trailers, semi-trailers, other transport equipment	434.6	-120.6	514.6	-60.5	-389.7	1 006.3	800.4	374.1	569.8	-174.4
Other manufacturing	-262.1	69.9	74.4	72.8	674.6	833.8	128.5	462.6	300.0	164.1
Electricity, gas, steam and air conditioning supply	**-8.8**	**102.6**	**49.6**	**97.4**	**-1 023.4**	**52.0**	**-1 778.8**	**218.3**	**147.8**	**109.4**
Water supply; sewerage, waste management and remediation activities	**2.2**	**-**	**4.7**	**-4.5**	**-6.8**	**58.6**	**-25.9**	**29.5**	**38.1**	**-17.1**
Construction	**34.3**	**200.7**	**298.6**	**154.5**	**55.8**	**-786.2**	**-206.3**	**-208.9**	**216.1**	**-612.0**
Services	**-9 216.0**	**14 453.8**	**3 412.0**	**2 082.2**	**-14 823.9**	**-3 909.1**	**10 766.5**	**-723.5**	**7 569.7**	**-3 669.5**
Wholesale and retail trade; repair of motor vehicles and motorcycles	2 502.5	2 988.4	341.1	1 922.1	-3 805.1	1 668.7	1 698.8	-388.3	-89.6	-2 419.4
Transportation and storage	409.2	41.7	-22.4	142.2	-28.5	110.6	225.5	-72.0	-385.1	-100.3
Accommodation and food service activities	-87.4	14.7	-10.6	-11.2	4.6	-66.4	-199.5	29.5	52.6	207.4
Information and communication	1 016.3	-720.3	-2 159.8	13.4	418.2	-110.6	590.7	-141.6	-165.7	291.7
Financial and insurance activities	-8 222.9	-1 357.2	436.7	320.2	-1 662.7	-8 549.2	889.4	3 196.0	4 304.3	-17 801.7
Activities of holding companies	-311.8	-1 379.8	3.5	578.8	-206.3	-2 634.1	-7.9	2 428.9	2 094.5	-17 401.7
Real estate activities	-682.3	2 198.2	-225.4	2 955.3	-347.6	-253.2	567.0	-1 874.2	396.3	-158.4
Professional, scientific and technical activities	-4 017.5	10 990.9	4 326.7	-3 226.2	-9 214.8	2 961.4	7 134.5	-1 961.5	2 800.9	17 822.2
Administrative and support service activities	-106.2	273.9	782.5	-116.4	-192.6	275.4	-390.0	310.4	587.7	284.9
Public administration; activities of households and of extraterritorial organisations	-	-	-	-	-	-1.1	5.6	82.6	-96.3	-1 801.7
Education	..	..	..	..	..	..	-	..	..	..
Human health and social work activities	..	..	..	..	..	..	..	..	..	..
Arts, entertainment and recreation	-31.0	22.5	-43.7	48.1	8.0	59.7	245.7	112.1	181.4	-27.4
Other services	-1.1	-5.6	-	-	-	-42.0	7.9	-10.6	36.9	25.1
Not allocated and confidential	**141.5**	**1.1**	**-**	**2.2**	**1.1**	**672.3**	**236.7**	**182.9**	**218.3**	**1 373.2**
Private real estate activities	..	-	..	..	..	..	-	..	..	..

- Nil; .. Not available

Note: Data excludes resident Special Purpose Entities (SPEs). Detailed metadata at: *http://metalinks.oecd.org/idi/20220712/6d95*.

Source: *OECD International Direct Investment Statistics (database)*: *https://doi.org/10.1787/idi-data-en*

AUSTRIA

Table 5. Foreign direct investment positions by industrial sector

At year end

Million US dollars

	Inward					Outward				
	2016	2017	2018	2019	2020	2016	2017	2018	2019	2020
All FDI activities	**150 648.3**	**191 442.8**	**185 184.3**	**193 695.8**	**200 835.7**	**196 996.9**	**233 762.3**	**229 977.1**	**239 293.4**	**237 598.5**
Agriculture, forestry and fishing	**21.1**	**22.8**	**20.6**	**20.2**	**22.1**	**83.3**	**189.5**	**174.0**	**328.0**	**333.8**
Mining and quarrying	**403.7**	**266.3**	**361.8**	**465.1**	**690.9**	**6 124.2**	**4 882.5**	**6 852.5**	**12 454.5**	**14 920.8**
Extraction activities	..	..	..	..	..	..	..	..	..	..
Manufacturing	**14 262.7**	**17 458.6**	**18 518.4**	**17 656.7**	**20 073.6**	**39 284.3**	**46 703.0**	**49 252.3**	**52 714.0**	**50 004.9**
of which:										
Food products, beverages and tobacco	1 696.0	1 745.0	1 715.1	1 609.8	1 641.9	1 559.0	1 953.7	1 836.5	1 832.2	1 737.6
Textiles, wood and paper products; printing	919.2	2 287.1	2 157.1	949.2	947.4	5 516.0	7 232.0	7 971.1	8 670.0	8 873.5
Chemical, rubber, plastic, non-metallic mineral products	4 047.6	4 454.3	4 416.1	4 329.4	5 393.3	13 321.4	14 671.4	14 542.0	12 493.8	13 237.2
Metal and machinery products, except electrical equipment	3 324.5	4 365.6	5 290.8	5 868.3	6 370.1	8 363.0	10 202.7	11 049.9	10 981.8	9 587.7
Motor vehicles, trailers, semi-trailers, other transport equipment	2 492.9	2 764.5	3 227.6	3 145.4	3 054.4	3 760.9	5 030.0	5 132.8	5 639.2	5 788.4
Other manufacturing	1 781.4	1 842.2	1 711.7	1 754.7	2 667.8	6 765.0	7 613.3	8 721.1	13 095.9	10 780.5
Electricity, gas, steam and air conditioning supply	**807.4**	**1 262.9**	**1 098.0**	**1 527.7**	**517.9**	**4 305.9**	**2 299.1**	**1 970.5**	**2 131.0**	**2 762.3**
Water supply; sewerage, waste management and remediation activities	**78.0**	**91.1**	**97.3**	**86.5**	**87.1**	**710.4**	**885.1**	**970.9**	**804.3**	**828.3**
Construction	**387.9**	**466.5**	**679.0**	**715.6**	**846.7**	**2 706.9**	**3 197.4**	**4 380.6**	**5 027.0**	**4 992.0**
Services	**134 557.8**	**171 874.5**	**164 409.2**	**173 224.0**	**178 597.4**	**142 510.8**	**175 605.7**	**166 377.4**	**165 835.8**	**163 347.7**
Wholesale and retail trade; repair of motor vehicles and motorcycles	18 748.8	25 600.9	24 734.4	26 150.3	26 621.7	28 932.2	33 926.6	31 496.5	30 243.8	32 396.6
Transportation and storage	1 531.6	2 223.6	2 213.2	2 328.7	2 158.5	1 292.3	1 634.7	1 706.0	1 624.4	1 616.1
Accommodation and food service activities	303.6	442.6	413.3	495.4	546.1	595.6	379.0	409.9	659.4	921.6
Information and communication	3 649.2	3 112.3	2 552.1	2 228.7	3 140.3	3 100.0	3 451.7	3 347.8	1 973.7	2 635.9
Financial and insurance activities	22 282.1	26 037.4	29 370.3	27 920.7	28 537.2	64 026.6	77 059.2	74 719.5	93 596.9	84 804.3
Activities of holding companies	6 343.4	8 737.1	13 839.0	12 922.9	13 514.5	32 799.6	38 105.1	38 898.6	54 884.3	43 120.6
Real estate activities	3 869.5	7 615.7	6 629.3	8 825.0	9 307.9	6 417.2	7 449.0	7 154.8	7 569.1	7 987.5
Professional, scientific and technical activities	81 512.6	103 522.4	94 682.8	101 553.6	104 374.8	33 278.2	45 436.6	42 310.5	24 104.7	29 165.5
Administrative and support service activities	2 530.8	3 157.8	3 692.5	3 561.0	3 729.3	3 754.6	3 649.6	2 846.3	3 060.0	3 509.6
Public administration; activities of households and of extraterritorial organisations	-	-	-	-	-	17.9	21.6	81.3	-16.9	-1 936.4
Education	..	..	..	..	..	..	-	..	..	..
Human health and social work activities	..	..	..	..	..	..	..	..	..	..
Arts, entertainment and recreation	91.7	122.3	85.9	96.6	114.1	878.0	1 162.1	1 228.5	1 697.4	1 813.7
Other services	14.8	9.6	8.0	5.6	6.1	99.1	113.9	87.0	330.3	366.9
Not allocated and confidential	**129.7**	**..**	**-**	**-**	**-**	**-5.3**	**-**	**-1.1**	**-1.1**	**408.6**
Private real estate activities	..	-	..	..	..	..	-	..	..	..

- Nil; .. Not available

Note: Data excludes resident Special Purpose Entities (SPEs). Detailed metadata at: *http://metalinks.oecd.org/idi/20220712/6d95*.

Source: *OECD International Direct Investment Statistics (database)*: *https://doi.org/10.1787/idi-data-en*

AUSTRIA

Table 6. Foreign direct investment income by industrial sector

Million US dollars

	Inward					Outward				
	2016	2017	2018	2019	2020	2016	2017	2018	2019	2020
All FDI activities	**11 956.2**	**15 794.2**	**16 014.4**	**15 477.4**	**4 789.7**	**15 376.5**	**15 095.3**	**15 065.5**	**16 821.9**	**4 939.0**
Agriculture, forestry and fishing	**-1.1**	**-1.1**	**-1.2**	**-1.1**	**-**	**1.1**	**-**	**2.4**	**3.4**	**6.8**
Mining and quarrying	**67.5**	**87.9**	**90.9**	**50.4**	**22.8**	**-748.6**	**259.3**	**383.6**	**568.7**	**310.0**
Extraction activities	..	..	..	..	..	..	..	..	..	..
Manufacturing	**2 001.5**	**1 869.0**	**2 205.8**	**1 809.0**	**1 079.2**	**5 229.5**	**4 709.7**	**5 725.2**	**4 962.5**	**1 343.6**
of which:										
Food products, beverages and tobacco	382.6	361.9	555.9	569.8	38.7	165.9	180.4	126.3	147.8	33.0
Textiles, wood and paper products; printing	108.4	139.8	174.7	133.2	30.8	1 271.7	1 370.8	1 742.0	1 469.8	649.6
Chemical, rubber, plastic, non-metallic mineral products	527.5	417.1	429.6	309.0	514.0	2 191.8	1 790.1	1 776.2	1 457.5	257.6
Metal and machinery products, except electrical equipment	666.8	783.5	867.5	779.1	353.3	764.1	553.5	1 066.9	366.1	148.1
Motor vehicles, trailers, semi-trailers, other transport equipment	270.9	9.0	-26.0	-67.2	53.6	238.9	281.8	342.3	364.9	86.6
Other manufacturing	45.3	157.8	204.2	85.1	88.9	597.1	533.2	671.5	1 156.4	168.7
Electricity, gas, steam and air conditioning supply	**27.6**	**136.4**	**75.5**	**62.7**	**19.4**	**13.3**	**86.8**	**135.7**	**207.1**	**50.1**
Water supply; sewerage, waste management and remediation activities	**11.1**	**25.9**	**16.5**	**9.0**	**2.3**	**38.7**	**65.4**	**64.9**	**67.2**	**10.3**
Construction	**-2.2**	**18.0**	**21.2**	**51.5**	**13.7**	**267.6**	**128.5**	**253.7**	**332.5**	**92.3**
Services	**9 851.8**	**13 656.9**	**13 808.6**	**13 749.0**	**3 320.8**	**10 573.9**	**9 844.4**	**8 498.8**	**10 680.6**	**3 116.8**
Wholesale and retail trade; repair of motor vehicles and motorcycles	2 177.4	3 261.2	3 659.9	3 057.2	208.5	2 730.3	3 670.4	2 505.6	3 301.2	559.5
Transportation and storage	168.1	139.8	-40.1	66.0	29.6	133.8	162.3	192.4	36.9	29.6
Accommodation and food service activities	29.9	12.4	10.6	24.6	-	66.4	24.8	11.8	54.9	10.3
Information and communication	482.1	411.5	276.2	253.0	292.9	90.7	111.6	131.0	173.5	54.7
Financial and insurance activities	1 604.6	2 356.0	2 404.1	2 271.4	553.8	5 180.8	4 793.1	4 087.1	5 619.6	1 772.1
Activities of holding companies	1 130.2	1 289.6	1 529.6	1 773.2	325.9	2 119.9	496.0	-83.8	1 147.4	1 022.2
Real estate activities	143.8	214.2	520.5	629.1	390.9	186.9	343.8	126.3	358.2	101.4
Professional, scientific and technical activities	4 859.0	7 079.2	6 814.6	7 192.4	2 328.2	1 861.1	1 101.3	1 088.2	864.2	507.1
Administrative and support service activities	385.9	178.1	151.1	204.9	35.3	291.9	-375.4	308.0	129.9	50.1
Public administration; activities of households and of extraterritorial organisations	-	-	-	-	-	-1.1	-1.1	-1.2	-1.1	-1.1
Education	..	..	..	..	..	..	-	..	..	..
Human health and social work activities	..	..	..	..	..	..	..	..	..	..
Arts, entertainment and recreation	-2.2	4.5	2.4	-11.2	8.0	50.9	12.4	57.8	61.6	27.4
Other services	-1.1	-4.5	2.4	-	-	-11.1	9.0	-9.4	41.4	3.4
Not allocated and confidential	**-**	**1.1**	**-203.0**	**-253.0**	**331.6**	**1.1**	**1.1**	**1.2**	**-**	**9.1**
Private real estate activities	..	-	..	..	..	..	-	..	..	..

- Nil; .. Not available

Note: Data excludes resident Special Purpose Entities (SPEs). Detailed metadata at: *http://metalinks.oecd.org/idi/20220712/6d95*.

Source: *OECD International Direct Investment Statistics (database)*: *https://doi.org/10.1787/idi-data-en*

BELGIUM

Table 1. Foreign direct investment flows by country

Million US dollars

	Inward					Outward				
	2016	2017	2018	2019	2020	2016	2017	2018	2019	2020
WORLD	**68 178.7**	**-3 058.3**	**27 120.3**	**-9 206.3**	**13 880.3**	**40 165.9**	**29 563.7**	**43 553.6**	**-9 305.9**	**11 745.9**
OECD COUNTRIES	**65 172.0**	**-2 678.4**	**29 732.1**	**-7 726.4**	**11 609.1**	**41 489.6**	**25 016.3**	**41 038.6**	**-9 510.8**	**9 545.3**
Australia	-259.9	978.5	.. c	.. c	.. c	8.8	.. c	.. c	.. c	.. c
Austria	404.7	-387.8	.. c	-216.1	.. c	17.7	-361.9	.. c	1 037.7	29.6
Belgium	-	-	-	-	-	-	-	-	-	-
Canada	325.1	461.1	.. c	.. c	.. c	317.4	.. c	210.1	574.3	294.0
Chile	-12.2	45.1	.. c	.. c	.. c	-84.0	.. c	.. c	.. c	.. c
Colombia	-3.3	.. c	.. c	.. c	.. c	29.9	.. c	.. c	.. c	.. c
Costa Rica	.. c	.. c	.. c	.. c	.. c	-1.1	.. c	.. c	.. c	.. c
Czech Republic	.. c	.. c	.. c	.. c	.. c	722.1	665.1	.. c	.. c	.. c
Denmark	-151.5	-77.8	193.6	.. c	297.4	27.6	171.3	.. c	.. c	.. c
Estonia	8.8	.. c	.. c	.. c	.. c	11.1	6.8	.. c	.. c	.. c
Finland	-96.2	-940.1	.. c	.. c	.. c	37.6	68.8	.. c	-541.8	.. c
France	11 004.1	-146.5	6 429.8	.. c	10 550.4	5 402.0	3 379.6	7 392.9	1 303.0	-1 046.2
Germany	-1 407.7	-11 309.9	-7 533.3	11 251.5	.. c	-1 307.1	.. c	.. c	234.0	.. c
Greece	-8.8	36.1	.. c	.. c	.. c	.. c	98.1	154.6	.. c	-93.4
Hungary	1 403.3	-2 199.3	.. c	.. c	.. c	76.3	.. c	234.9	.. c	521.9
Iceland	.. c	.. c	.. c	.. c	.. c	.. c	.. c	.. c	.. c	.. c
Ireland	3 518.7	.. c	.. c	12 608.3	.. c	-353.9	148.8	.. c	.. c	.. c
Israel	-76.3	.. c	.. c	.. c	.. c	12.2	30.4	.. c	.. c	.. c
Italy	907.9	346.1	.. c	.. c	-1 636.5	745.3	.. c	1 474.1	.. c	397.7
Japan	2 961.4	.. c	.. c	.. c	.. c	447.9	-347.2	.. c	.. c	.. c
Korea	137.1	173.6	.. c	.. c	.. c	25.4	168.0	.. c	.. c	.. c
Latvia	.. c	.. c	-3.5	.. c	.. c	-14.4	12.4	8.3	.. c	8.0
Lithuania	.. c	.. c	.. c	.. c	.. c	1.1	1.1	.. c	.. c	.. c
Luxembourg	14 935.3	6 442.3	-6 694.2	-15 972.2	419.4	12 966.9	.. c	1 491.8	-18 713.8	-5 157.8
Mexico	-63.0	.. c	.. c	.. c	.. c	-21 045.0	.. c	.. c	145.5	35.3
Netherlands	-19 941.4	-976.2	10 588.9	-8 708.2	615.4	6 772.1	.. c	-3 096.9	.. c	1 986.3
New Zealand	115.0	-41.7	.. c	.. c	.. c	-64.1	140.9	.. c	.. c	.. c
Norway	-8 077.0	-1 323.4	.. c	.. c	.. c	307.4	-21.4	.. c	.. c	.. c
Poland	116.1	390.0	.. c	.. c	.. c	179.1	.. c	803.7	.. c	.. c
Portugal	226.7	.. c	.. c	.. c	.. c	335.1	.. c	48.4	.. c	.. c
Slovak Republic	147.1	.. c	.. c	.. c	.. c	-44.2	135.3	.. c	.. c	.. c
Slovenia	-15.5	.. c	.. c	-31.3	.. c	98.4	10.1	.. c	.. c	.. c
Spain	2 707.1	-545.6	.. c	.. c	.. c	822.7	326.9	.. c	.. c	376.1
Sweden	4 525.0	-3 593.7	.. c	.. c	.. c	61.9	1 270.4	.. c	.. c	.. c
Switzerland	1 842.3	2 314.3	.. c	.. c	-57 791.5	-122.7	.. c	.. c	1 271.7	.. c
Turkey	10.0	.. c	.. c	.. c	.. c	1 300.5	-102.6	.. c	.. c	.. c
United Kingdom	6 184.9	862.4	2 964.7	.. c	.. c	.. c	.. c	-7 600.6	-8 516.7	-1 311.7
United States	43 172.6	2 108.0	.. c	.. c	.. c	-60 143.8	.. c	33 337.7	12 381.1	1 345.9
EUROPE	**19 181.7**	**-5 966.6**	**10 535.8**	**-19 516.4**	**13 392.6**	**122 805.5**	**20 518.5**	**7 806.0**	**-22 470.6**	**7 733.3**
Bulgaria	31.0	.. c	.. c	.. c	.. c	89.6	732.7	.. c	.. c	-33.0
Croatia	5.5	.. c	.. c	.. c	.. c	21.0	7.9	.. c	.. c	.. c
Cyprus	174.7	-57.5	.. c	.. c	.. c	303.0	1 016.8	-1 372.6	.. c	.. c
Malta	39.8	639.2	.. c	.. c	.. c	21.0	12.4	.. c	.. c	.. c
Montenegro	.. c	.. c	-	-	.. c	-	-	-	-	.. c
Romania	-4.4	80.0	.. c	.. c	.. c	140.4	69.9	.. c	.. c	.. c
Russian Federation	128.3	-314.5	.. c	.. c	.. c	211.2	-206.3	.. c	.. c	.. c
Ukraine	6.6	.. c	.. c	.. c	.. c	-3.3	6.8	22.4	.. c	.. c
AFRICA	**-598.3**	**463.3**	**.. c**	**.. c**	**.. c**	**294.2**	**550.1**	**-325.7**	**-109.7**	**968.7**
Northern Africa	-22.1	50.7	-108.6	-64.9	-68.4	394.8	.. c	-46.0	32.5	38.7
Algeria	.. c	.. c	.. c	.. c	.. c	-1.1	-1.1	.. c	.. c	.. c
Egypt	-7.7	45.1	.. c	.. c	.. c	362.7	.. c	.. c	.. c	.. c
Libya	.. c	.. c	.. c	.. c	.. c	.. c	.. c	.. c	.. c	.. c
Morocco	.. c	.. c	.. c	-9.0	.. c	33.2	31.6	.. c	.. c	.. c
Tunisia	.. c	.. c	.. c	.. c	.. c	-	.. c	.. c	.. c	.. c
Other African countries	-577.2	412.6	.. c	.. c	.. c	-100.6	.. c	-280.9	-142.2	928.8
Nigeria	.. c	.. c	.. c	.. c	.. c	32.1	11.3	.. c	.. c	.. c
South Africa	66.4	230.0	.. c	.. c	.. c	28.8	.. c	.. c	.. c	.. c
AMERICA	**43 824.0**	**1 811.5**	**16 237.5**	**7 804.8**	**.. c**	**-80 869.2**	**.. c**	**33 592.6**	**13 779.2**	**2 312.3**
Northern America	43 496.6	2 570.2	16 165.5	.. c	.. c	-59 826.4	578.3	33 547.7	12 955.3	1 639.9
Central America and Caribbean countries	-59.7	-227.7	.. c	.. c	.. c	-21 046.1	.. c	.. c	155.6	85.5
Bahamas	.. c	.. c	.. c	.. c	.. c	.. c	.. c	-	-	-
Bermuda	.. c	.. c	-505.1	-41.4	313.4	-4.4	.. c	.. c	.. c	14.8
Cayman Islands	-77.4	-23.7	.. c	.. c	.. c	-17.7	.. c	.. c	.. c	.. c
El Salvador	.. c	.. c	-	.. c	.. c	.. c	.. c	.. c	.. c	.. c
Guatemala	.. c	.. c	.. c	-	.. c	.. c	.. c	.. c	.. c	.. c
Honduras	-	.. c	-	-	.. c	.. c	.. c	.. c	.. c	.. c
Nicaragua	.. c	.. c	-	.. c	.. c	.. c	.. c	.. c	.. c	.. c
Panama	5.5	.. c	.. c	.. c	.. c	.. c	.. c	.. c	.. c	.. c
Virgin Islands, U.S.	-	.. c	.. c	.. c	.. c	-	-	-	-	-
South America	387.0	-529.8	.. c	.. c	.. c	3.3	570.4	197.1	668.3	586.9
Argentina	.. c	-136.4	.. c	.. c	.. c	52.0	.. c	.. c	.. c	.. c
Bolivia	-	.. c	-1.2	.. c	.. c	-	-	.. c	.. c	.. c
Brazil	677.9	-445.3	.. c	.. c	.. c	-60.8	440.8	.. c	502.6	204.0
Ecuador	-6.6	-	.. c	.. c	.. c	.. c	.. c	.. c	.. c	.. c
Paraguay	-1.1	.. c	-1.2	.. c	.. c	.. c	.. c	.. c	.. c	.. c
Peru	.. c	.. c	.. c	.. c	.. c	.. c	.. c	.. c	.. c	.. c
Uruguay	.. c	.. c	.. c	.. c	.. c	3.3	.. c	.. c	.. c	.. c
Venezuela	.. c	34.9	.. c	.. c	.. c	-77.4	.. c	.. c	.. c	.. c

BELGIUM

Table 1. Foreign direct investment flows by country *(cont.)*

Million US dollars

	Inward					Outward				
	2016	2017	2018	2019	2020	2016	2017	2018	2019	2020
ASIA	**5 912.9**	**-302.1**	**352.9**	**.. c**	**2 376.1**	**-2 014.8**	**1 455.3**	**2 957.6**	**-117.5**	**741.9**
Near and Middle East	-298.6	19.2	-636.1	-123.1	59.3	147.1	.. c	119.2	244.0	.. c
Gulf Arabian countries	-16.6	45.1	.. c	-42.5	87.7	148.2	263.8	87.3	.. c	764.7
Kuwait	.. c	.. c	.. c	.. c	-	-	-	-	-	-
Qatar	6.6	.. c	.. c	.. c	.. c	-10.0	.. c	.. c	.. c	.. c
Saudi Arabia	-28.8	13.5	.. c	.. c	.. c	60.8	5.6	.. c	.. c	.. c
United Arab Emirates	2.2	-101.5	.. c	.. c	.. c	97.3	278.4	.. c	.. c	37.6
Other Near and Middle East	.. c	.. c	.. c	.. c	.. c	-1.1	.. c	31.9	44.8	.. c
Jordan	.. c	.. c	.. c	.. c	.. c	.. c	.. c	.. c	.. c	.. c
Other Asian countries	6 211.4	-321.3	989.0	.. c	2 316.8	-2 161.9	.. c	2 838.4	-361.6	2.3
China	319.6	153.3	.. c	.. c	.. c	-46.4	.. c	-5.9	.. c	570.9
Hong Kong, China	1 872.2	-431.7	.. c	.. c	.. c	-2 960.3	.. c	.. c	.. c	.. c
India	-42.0	.. c	.. c	.. c	.. c	278.7	264.9	.. c	.. c	.. c
Indonesia	-23.2	.. c	.. c	.. c	.. c	164.8	237.9	.. c	.. c	.. c
Iran, Islamic Republic of	.. c	.. c	.. c	.. c	.. c	.. c	.. c	.. c	.. c	.. c
Malaysia	.. c	.. c	.. c	.. c	.. c	67.5	208.5	.. c	.. c	.. c
Philippines	.. c	.. c	.. c	.. c	.. c	19.9	4.5	.. c	.. c	.. c
Singapore	457.8	.. c	.. c	.. c	.. c	-353.9	629.0	.. c	.. c	.. c
Chinese Taipei	39.8	37.2	.. c	.. c	.. c	-6.6	-11.3	.. c	.. c	.. c
Thailand	.. c	.. c	.. c	.. c	.. c	61.9	13.5	.. c	.. c	.. c
Viet Nam	-1.1	.. c	.. c	.. c	.. c	6.6	.. c	-245.5	56.0	.. c
AUSTRALIA, OCEANIA AND POLAR REGIONS	**-139.3**	**933.4**	**128.6**	**.. c**	**.. c**	**-49.8**	**1 320.0**	**-475.6**	**.. c**	**.. c**
WORLD unallocated and confidential	**-2.2**	**2.3**	**.. d**	**.. d**	**.. d**	**-**	**- d**	**-1.2**	**.. d**	**.. d**
European Union (since 01/02/2020)	..	..	..	..	**68 760.1**	..	..	..	..	**-3 740.2**
G20 countries excl. European Union	**63 831.7**	**-7 176.2**	**22 336.8**	**15 751.7**	**13 421.1**	**20 416.9**	**-3 150.7**	**34 977.0**	**9 376.5**	**-9.1**
G20 OECD countries	**62 971.4**	**-6 706.1**	**21 236.9**	**15 063.2**	**12 586.9**	**19 726.9**	**-4 025.5**	**34 650.1**	**7 752.2**	**-2 891.2**
G20 Non-OECD countries	**860.3**	**-470.1**	**.. c**	**688.5**	**.. c**	**690.0**	**874.8**	**326.9**	**1 624.3**	**2 882.1**
MENA countries	**-38.7**	**95.8**	**-684.5**	**-110.8**	**12.5**	**505.4**	**545.6**	**49.6**	**230.6**	**803.4**
ASEAN countries	**931.1**	**-219.8**	**.. c**	**.. c**	**.. c**	**-2.2**	**1 356.1**	**.. c**	**.. c**	**.. c**

- Nil; .. Not available; c Confidential data; d Secondary Confidentiality

Note: Data excludes resident Special Purpose Entities (SPEs). Detailed metadata at: *http://metalinks.oecd.org/idi/20220712/6d95.*

Source: OECD *International Direct Investment Statistics (database): https://doi.org/10.1787/idi-data-en*

BELGIUM

Table 2. Foreign direct investment positions by country

At year end

Million US dollars

	Inward					Outward				
	2016	2017	2018	2019	2020	2016	2017	2018	2019	2020
WORLD	**517 401.7**	**580 190.7**	**502 399.8**	**581 637.8**	**519 509.1**	**599 379.2**	**707 828.0**	**544 143.6**	**585 844.8**	**581 682.4**
OECD COUNTRIES	**507 827.6**	**569 778.1**	**495 602.2**	**576 135.7**	**513 400.4**	**573 158.0**	**675 578.1**	**520 060.7**	**554 438.3**	**549 023.2**
Australia	-1 033.0	-20.4	-77.9	386.4	298.2	2 224.1	2 973.1	1 874.3	1 719.8	1 707.0
Austria	1 412.5	1 183.7	803.8	865.0	1 133.9	635.6	259.1	248.5	1 029.0	1 417.4
Belgium	-	-	-	-	-	-	-	-	-	-
Canada	-144.4	127.1	612.5	657.2	455.3	1 540.0	2 190.0	1 882.3	1 714.2	1 991.7
Chile	24.2	-307.0	-249.6	-197.7	-147.3	1 019.3	1 255.7	1 199.9	1 213.2	1 235.7
Colombia	-40.1	-61.2	-150.0	-182.0	-184.1	128.6	253.1	147.7	130.3	154.6
Costa Rica	.. c	.. c	198.1	982.9	46.6	-	-1.2	2.3	34.8	22.1
Czech Republic	3 388.8	5 169.1	1 202.2	678.5	882.3	6 267.5	6 527.9	6 003.0	6 231.2	6 654.8
Denmark	748.4	832.3	1 647.6	1 335.7	1 926.6	561.8	916.3	761.4	912.2	814.8
Estonia	9.5	6.0	-40.1	-85.4	-17.2	7.4	31.2	36.6	20.2	14.7
Finland	1 345.0	833.5	2 051.8	1 173.9	1 773.2	598.7	485.7	1 031.6	346.0	1 234.5
France	127 166.6	134 665.4	84 202.0	123 712.6	98 493.1	41 659.1	44 699.0	50 503.8	53 509.3	56 048.6
Germany	10 587.1	395.8	4 061.1	16 703.0	16 129.6	9 343.3	12 020.9	11 426.6	11 063.8	14 119.5
Greece	599.8	893.5	176.3	565.0	617.3	774.7	1 596.3	1 117.5	2 273.6	2 456.7
Hungary	4 297.5	2 058.0	-72.1	33.7	50 686.0	1 852.0	2 936.0	2 413.6	1 878.2	2 244.4
Iceland	-	3.6	1.1	2.2	1.2	112.8	145.1	119.1	134.8	128.9
Ireland	1 769.8	5 397.0	32 147.9	44 238.4	53 606.6	6 589.0	6 657.5	4 254.6	2 757.8	3 157.4
Israel	-71.7	-84.0	159.1	83.1	-31.9	64.3	36.0	49.2	57.3	7.4
Italy	1 411.4	2 126.4	1 475.8	705.5	-854.1	9 295.9	11 009.8	10 447.7	11 934.4	13 332.9
Japan	15 879.6	18 331.7	20 415.6	23 393.6	24 475.4	2 631.0	2 421.4	1 341.9	1 337.9	1 581.8
Korea	1 054.1	1 397.2	493.5	317.9	557.1	336.3	615.3	1 068.2	2 377.0	605.0
Latvia	.. c	-2.4	-3.4	2.2	11.0	10.5	37.2	55.0	30.3	82.2
Lithuania	-8.4	1.2	6.9	-14.6	31.9	6.3	7.2	-1.1	12.4	17.2
Luxembourg	127 452.3	155 106.7	108 156.6	113 309.4	104 490.1	140 822.2	203 565.6	147 948.2	139 884.3	142 678.9
Mexico	-660.9	-714.8	-443.1	-834.6	-299.4	-4 890.9	-	-129.4	73.0	-138.7
Netherlands	156 584.8	176 560.3	132 799.4	146 877.1	123 274.0	228 930.1	247 303.9	203 444.0	201 804.1	197 040.1
New Zealand	-6.3	-38.4	-36.6	-18.0	46.6	-14.8	122.3	140.8	135.9	147.3
Norway	-4 635.8	-4 587.4	-358.4	616.7	-173.0	756.8	621.3	421.3	543.7	559.6
Poland	-2 209.3	-2 088.0	-113.4	79.8	-315.4	2 777.5	3 658.0	3 847.0	4 606.8	5 004.3
Portugal	-163.4	-143.9	214.1	262.9	274.9	2 709.0	3 157.8	400.7	1 435.6	2 499.7
Slovak Republic	266.7	284.2	-24.0	42.7	24.5	1 322.9	1 623.9	1 671.6	1 641.2	1 866.5
Slovenia	-21.1	-24.0	19.5	-11.2	40.5	675.7	756.8	161.4	173.0	136.2
Spain	-375.3	181.1	3 482.9	3 279.0	4 247.1	4 341.7	4 926.8	5 392.7	6 973.7	7 954.4
Sweden	11 575.8	8 120.7	4 627.9	4 474.3	4 801.8	748.4	967.9	894.2	1 761.4	2 342.6
Switzerland	43 837.9	53 512.8	54 729.8	42 734.2	-10 671.2	1 569.5	3 986.6	3 707.4	3 776.7	10 079.8
Turkey	-14.8	-51.6	226.7	741.4	137.4	3 767.3	3 653.2	3 200.1	4 473.2	3 132.9
United Kingdom	4 119.3	5 367.0	15 168.3	16 159.3	9 031.8	142 859.7	135 060.0	58 428.0	78 347.6	59 057.6
United States	3 629.2	5 286.6	28 136.0	33 868.8	28 645.2	-38 736.2	-30 638.0	-5 302.3	8 256.6	7 657.4
EUROPE	**490 791.6**	**548 100.3**	**446 715.1**	**519 478.8**	**460 158.3**	**614 905.7**	**705 694.4**	**522 713.5**	**543 541.9**	**540 353.4**
Bulgaria	95.9	125.9	145.4	21.3	49.1	474.3	1 577.1	1 419.7	1 172.8	1 639.5
Croatia	-6.3	-1.2	9.2	1.1	33.1	470.1	668.0	828.9	1 403.1	811.1
Cyprus	845.4	927.1	511.8	1 115.5	1 044.3	2 246.2	3 476.9	-281.7	51.7	217.2
Malta	781.1	1 554.3	-35.5	201.1	-90.8	32.7	49.2	55.0	70.8	101.9
Montenegro	-	-2.4	-	-	-	-	-	-	-	-
Romania	-42.2	-51.6	-201.5	-133.7	-272.4	1 425.1	1 352.8	1 031.6	1 416.5	1 814.9
Russian Federation	44.3	-261.5	-164.9	-133.7	-184.1	1 203.8	1 408.0	1 462.1	1 595.1	1 419.8
Ukraine	-5.3	-3.6	-19.5	-16.9	-18.4	-2.1	-1.2	20.6	78.6	69.9
AFRICA	**-796.9**	**-191.9**	**71.0**	**-92.1**	**-184.1**	**2 049.1**	**2 640.9**	**1 013.3**	**993.0**	**-1 935.2**
Northern Africa	-3.2	.. c	-8.0	-93.2	-186.5	645.1	1 261.7	148.8	170.7	-866.4
Algeria	2.1	3.6	-22.9	-27.0	-31.9	15.8	22.8	10.3	16.9	-1 086.0
Egypt	-34.8	8.4	-98.5	-138.2	-163.2	446.9	792.8	32.1	34.8	50.3
Libya	4.2	1.2	2.3	2.2	2.5	3.2	3.6	3.4	-	-
Morocco	21.1	38.4	89.3	56.2	-7.4	151.8	407.8	91.6	110.1	153.4
Tunisia	.. c	.. c	21.8	13.5	13.5	27.4	34.8	11.5	9.0	16.0
Other African countries	-793.7	-251.9	80.1	1.1	-	1 404.0	1 379.2	864.4	822.3	-1 068.8
Nigeria	.. c	.. c	18.3	29.2	25.8	73.8	78.0	82.4	71.9	-2 234.6
South Africa	-431.1	-225.5	-9.2	-42.7	20.9	320.4	305.8	-6.9	68.5	828.3
AMERICA	**4 536.7**	**5 542.1**	**27 552.1**	**32 309.6**	**26 809.4**	**-37 018.0**	**-22 230.8**	**754.5**	**16 204.2**	**16 942.0**
Northern America	3 485.8	5 413.8	28 752.0	34 528.2	29 101.7	-37 196.2	-28 448.1	-3 420.0	9 970.8	9 649.0
Central America and Caribbean countries	3 413.1	3 729.9	-755.7	-869.5	-1 368.3	-4 766.5	36.0	-304.6	-93.2	-176.7
Bahamas	7.4	7.2	3.4	3.4	-2.5	2.1	-	-	-	-
Bermuda	3 106.4	3 374.9	-1 246.9	-1 112.1	-1 275.0	85.4	142.7	-	-	90.8
Cayman Islands	1 191.1	1 283.3	1 067.1	125.8	9.8	8.4	2.4	3.4	11.2	6.1
El Salvador	-	-	-	1.1	1.2	5.3	6.0	6.9	7.9	6.1
Guatemala	1.1	1.2	3.4	4.5	3.7	1.1	1.2	2.3	1.1	1.2
Honduras	-	-	1.1	1.1	-	4.2	-129.5	-211.8	-252.8	-197.6
Nicaragua	-	-	-	1.1	1.2	11.6	13.2	18.3	24.7	24.5
Panama	-95.9	-116.3	-327.5	-31.5	-9.8	1.1	-6.0	-1.1	1.1	1.2
Virgin Islands, U.S.	-	1.2	2.3	2.2	1.2	-	-	-	-	-
South America	-2 362.2	-3 601.6	-443.1	-1 350.3	-925.3	4 944.7	6 182.5	4 480.2	6 326.7	7 469.6
Argentina	239.3	-513.3	82.4	-732.4	-619.7	1 634.9	1 741.4	142.0	164.0	136.2
Bolivia	-	-2.4	2.3	1.1	1.2	1.1	1.2	1.1	-	3.7
Brazil	-2 540.3	-2 720.1	-56.1	-174.1	99.4	1 562.1	2 313.5	2 193.7	3 886.8	4 925.8
Ecuador	-13.7	-8.4	-28.6	-21.3	-22.1	7.4	12.0	27.5	79.8	116.6
Paraguay	-	-	-1.1	-2.2	-1.2	33.7	60.0	77.9	55.0	69.9
Peru	-10.5	.. c	-11.5	-25.8	-18.4	600.8	621.3	651.5	757.1	811.1
Uruguay	-6.3	1.2	-40.1	-14.6	-19.6	10.5	9.6	8.0	7.9	7.4
Venezuela	-22.1	12.0	16.0	-9.0	-13.5	-53.8	-86.4	32.1	32.6	8.6

BELGIUM

Table 2. Foreign direct investment positions by country *(cont.)*

At year end

Million US dollars

	Inward					Outward				
	2016	2017	2018	2019	2020	2016	2017	2018	2019	2020
ASIA	**23 561.7**	**26 427.2**	**27 649.4**	**29 057.5**	**31 946.3**	**17 215.1**	**18 279.0**	**17 469.7**	**22 838.7**	**23 240.9**
Near and Middle East	91.7	214.7	-96.2	-246.0	-321.5	2 257.8	1 914.1	1 179.3	1 199.7	1 994.1
Gulf Arabian countries	75.9	179.9	-387.0	-457.2	-428.3	1 432.5	1 168.1	1 115.2	1 124.5	1 958.5
Kuwait	-23.2	1.2	-	-1.1	-1.2	-	-	-	-	-
Qatar	3.2	70.8	19.5	14.6	13.5	56.9	54.0	125.9	148.3	141.1
Saudi Arabia	-40.1	-20.4	-222.1	-194.3	-213.5	71.7	73.2	85.9	105.6	948.6
United Arab Emirates	186.6	159.5	-190.1	-275.2	-244.2	1 295.5	1 024.2	904.5	847.0	839.4
Other Near and Middle East	15.8	34.8	289.7	211.2	106.8	825.3	746.0	65.3	76.4	36.8
Jordan	-	3.6	2.3	2.2	2.5	745.2	684.8	-5.7	-4.5	2.5
Other Asian countries	23 470.0	26 211.3	27 745.6	29 302.4	32 267.8	14 957.3	16 364.8	16 290.4	21 639.0	21 246.8
China	-412.1	-295.0	-1 386.5	79.8	257.7	2 094.4	2 529.4	2 002.5	3 784.5	4 205.4
Hong Kong, China	6 592.2	6 617.9	3 270.0	2 973.5	3 640.9	3 639.7	3 346.1	2 794.8	3 349.8	1 524.1
India	52.7	178.7	416.8	325.8	353.4	1 303.9	1 499.2	1 020.2	1 758.0	2 053.0
Indonesia	25.3	34.8	53.8	-12.4	30.7	495.4	761.6	690.4	758.3	773.1
Iran, Islamic Republic of	-	4.8	8.0	6.7	6.1	-	14.4	13.7	18.0	-
Malaysia	163.4	125.9	85.9	40.4	79.8	472.2	735.2	571.3	1 543.5	1 865.3
Philippines	.. c	.. c	-65.3	-119.1	-38.0	311.0	64.8	87.0	66.3	57.7
Singapore	313.1	-171.5	4 429.8	2 309.6	2 859.2	2 779.6	3 486.4	5 991.5	5 446.0	6 911.3
Chinese Taipei	72.7	115.1	21.8	-32.6	-31.9	76.9	57.6	45.8	-70.8	105.5
Thailand	-302.5	-172.7	-6.9	-21.3	23.3	353.1	393.4	428.2	939.1	1 551.1
Viet Nam	-4.2	-2.4	-16.0	-1.1	6.1	21.1	289.0	16.0	70.8	60.1
AUSTRALIA, OCEANIA AND POLAR REGIONS	**-693.6**	**287.8**	**232.4**	**725.7**	**676.2**	**2 227.3**	**3 444.5**	**2 192.6**	**2 266.9**	**2 303.4**
WORLD unallocated and confidential	**2.1**	**25.2**	**179.8**	**158.4**	**103.1**	**-**	**-**	**-**	**-**	**778.0**
European Union (since 01/02/2020)	**..**	**..**	**..**	**..**	**462 024.8**	**..**	**..**	**..**	**..**	**465 756.5**
G20 countries excl. European Union	**158 933.3**	**163 088.3**	**152 984.9**	**214 927.0**	**176 814.3**	**178 715.1**	**194 636.6**	**142 331.1**	**186 927.7**	**174 385.8**
G20 OECD countries	**161 996.4**	**166 910.5**	**154 270.7**	**215 811.1**	**177 069.6**	**170 028.5**	**184 004.6**	**134 741.2**	**174 806.8**	**159 095.6**
G20 Non-OECD countries	**-3 063.1**	**-3 822.3**	**-1 285.8**	**-884.1**	**-255.2**	**8 686.6**	**10 632.0**	**7 589.9**	**12 120.9**	**15 290.2**
MENA countries	**162.3**	**.. d**	**-264.5**	**-422.4**	**-478.6**	**2 824.9**	**3 117.1**	**1 260.6**	**.. d**	**1 094.6**
ASEAN countries	**201.3**	**-176.3**	**4 498.5**	**2 210.7**	**2 969.7**	**4 551.5**	**5 817.9**	**7 821.2**	**8 860.9**	**11 248.0**

- Nil; .. Not available; c Confidential data; d Secondary Confidentiality

Note: Data excludes resident Special Purpose Entities (SPEs). Detailed metadata at: *http://metalinks.oecd.org/idi/20220712/6d95*.

Source: *OECD International Direct Investment Statistics (database)*: *https://doi.org/10.1787/idi-data-en*

Table 3. Foreign direct investment income by country

Million US dollars

	Inward					Outward				
	2016	2017	2018	2019	2020	2016	2017	2018	2019	2020
WORLD	**31 450.8**	**..**	**34 643.0**	**36 077.5**	**35 155.6**	**32 119.9**	**..**	**33 554.8**	**33 134.4**	**30 520.8**
OECD COUNTRIES	**31 321.5**	**..**	**34 483.7**	**36 079.7**	**35 017.7**	**30 771.9**	**..**	**31 410.4**	**30 629.1**	**28 584.6**
Australia	-24.3	..	-	16.8	23.9	4.4	..	-103.9	138.8	153.8
Austria	118.3	..	85.0	57.1	93.4	52.0	..	.. c	.. c	.. c
Belgium	-	..	-	-	-	-	..	-	-	-
Canada	60.8	..	28.3	43.7	63.8	78.5	..	41.3	82.8	88.9
Chile	-16.6	..	.. c	.. c	-12.5	28.8	..	-3.5	128.7	349.9
Colombia	-1.1	..	.. c	.. c	.. c	16.6	..	.. c	.. c	.. c
Costa Rica	.. c	..	2.4	10.1	2.3	-1.1	..	.. c	.. c	.. c
Czech Republic	3.3	..	.. c	.. c	.. c	799.5	..	973.7	1 172.1	671.2
Denmark	67.5	..	.. c	.. c	.. c	27.6	..	.. c	.. c	.. c
Estonia	-	..	.. c	.. c	.. c	3.3	..	4.7	4.5	4.6
Finland	2.2	..	.. c	106.3	136.8	96.2	..	.. c	.. c	.. c
France	7 862.4	..	6 223.3	6 043.9	8 545.9	3 345.1	..	2 914.0	1 823.6	833.0
Germany	1 607.9	..	1 887.2	1 812.4	605.1	290.8	..	.. c	1 254.9	-414.8
Greece	-2.2	..	-11.8	.. c	.. c	-10.0	..	.. c	.. c	.. c
Hungary	46.4	..	.. c	-	714.5	214.5	..	.. c	.. c	.. c
Iceland	.. c	..	-	-	-	3.3	..	3.5	17.9	5.7
Ireland	222.3	..	.. c	.. c	933.3	395.9	..	.. c	.. c	.. c
Israel	-8.8	..	.. c	.. c	.. c	18.8	..	.. c	.. c	.. c
Italy	-73.0	..	22.4	2.2	.. c	662.4	..	686.9	616.8	412.5
Japan	822.7	..	2 365.2	1 254.9	245.0	113.9	..	.. c	.. c	.. c
Korea	57.5	..	101.5	97.4	.. c	57.5	..	154.6	34.7	57.0
Latvia	-	..	.. c	.. c	-	3.3	..	3.5	1.1	3.4
Lithuania	.. c	..	.. c	.. c	-4.6	1.1	..	1.2	1.1	1.1
Luxembourg	9 896.1	..	6 564.4	6 367.4	6 739.6	1 073.8	..	7 329.2	6 131.2	4 529.9
Mexico	-19.9	..	-35.4	-60.5	-72.9	822.7	..	53.1	38.1	125.4
Netherlands	8 477.3	..	10 237.2	10 970.6	9 489.5	11 435.4	..	5 689.8	12 152.7	7 259.3
New Zealand	-2.2	..	-2.4	-3.4	.. c	66.4	..	36.6	33.6	31.9
Norway	-56.4	..	-9.4	2.2	.. c	35.4	..	.. c	.. c	.. c
Poland	-73.0	..	-5.9	-2.2	.. c	320.7	..	276.2	339.2	394.3
Portugal	42.0	..	.. c	-	-	499.8	..	.. c	87.3	124.2
Slovak Republic	-1.1	..	-2.4	-1.1	-	123.9	..	60.2	115.3	63.8
Slovenia	-	..	-1.2	.. c	-	118.3	..	.. c	.. c	.. c
Spain	120.5	..	148.7	144.4	.. c	494.3	..	203.0	.. c	104.8
Sweden	749.8	..	871.0	1 182.1	1 073.5	84.0	..	.. c	.. c	.. c
Switzerland	754.2	..	815.5	.. c	394.3	-245.5	..	266.7	1 016.5	7 764.1
Turkey	4.4	..	.. c	.. c	.. c	217.8	..	.. c	249.6	250.7
United Kingdom	230.0	..	2 246.0	2 635.2	3 090.6	10 470.0	..	.. c	4 270.7	5 108.8
United States	457.8	..	2 596.5	3 741.2	2 787.5	-928.9	..	-1 548.4	-556.4	246.2
EUROPE	**30 000.0**	**..**	**29 370.9**	**30 986.2**	**31 882.6**	**31 049.4**	**..**	**33 129.9**	**31 188.9**	**27 781.2**
Bulgaria	-1.1	..	.. c	-	.. c	26.5	..	.. c	.. c	.. c
Croatia	-	..	.. c	-	-	34.3	..	.. c	.. c	.. c
Cyprus	58.6	..	.. c	.. c	6.8	193.5	..	.. c	.. c	.. c
Malta	-19.9	..	.. c	.. c	.. c	8.8	..	8.3	2.2	6.8
Montenegro	-	..	-	-	-	-	..	-	-	-
Romania	-3.3	..	-1.2	-4.5	-2.3	95.1	..	.. c	.. c	.. c
Russian Federation	-25.4	..	-4.7	.. c	.. c	174.7	..	.. c	.. c	.. c
Ukraine	.. c	..	.. c	.. c	.. c	-6.6	..	14.2	17.9	3.4
AFRICA	**-22.1**	**..**	**-1.2**	**-11.2**	**-18.2**	**-277.6**	**..**	**83.8**	**64.9**	**257.6**
Northern Africa	2.2	..	.. c	.. c	.. c	-32.1	..	11.8	16.8	-13.7
Algeria	-	..	-	-	-	3.3	..	3.5	3.4	-10.3
Egypt	-1.1	..	.. c	.. c	.. c	-153.7	..	-	.. c	.. c
Libya	-	..	-	-	-	-	..	-	-	-
Morocco	.. c	..	.. c	.. c	.. c	105.1	..	.. c	.. c	.. c
Tunisia	-	..	-	-	-	12.2	..	14.2	12.3	14.8
Other African countries	-24.3	..	-4.7	-10.1	-16.0	-245.5	..	.. c	48.1	270.1
Nigeria	.. c	..	.. c	.. c	.. c	13.3	..	22.4	12.3	327.1
South Africa	-8.8	..	-1.2	-	-	29.9	..	16.5	.. c	.. c
AMERICA	**347.2**	**..**	**2 636.6**	**3 702.0**	**2 751.0**	**301.9**	**..**	**-991.4**	**359.3**	**1 103.1**
Northern America	518.6	..	2 623.6	3 784.8	2 852.4	-849.3	..	-1 508.3	-472.4	336.2
Central America and Caribbean countries	32.1	..	-26.0	-72.8	-90.0	828.3	..	61.4	43.7	134.5
Bahamas	-	..	-	-	-	-	..	-	-	-
Bermuda	.. c	..	.. c	.. c	.. c	3.3	..	-	3.4	-
Cayman Islands	14.4	..	.. c	.. c	.. c	-	..	1.2	-	-
El Salvador	-	..	-	-	-	1.1	..	1.2	1.1	1.1
Guatemala	.. c	..	.. c	-	-	-	..	.. c	.. c	.. c
Honduras	-	..	-	-	-	-	..	-2.4	-6.7	-2.3
Nicaragua	-	..	-	-	-	1.1	..	5.9	5.6	8.0
Panama	-	..	.. c	.. c	.. c	.. c	..	.. c	.. c	.. c
Virgin Islands, U.S.	-	..	-	-	-	-	..	-	-	-
South America	-203.5	..	37.8	-12.3	-9.1	324.0	..	456.7	789.2	632.5
Argentina	-	..	.. c	.. c	.. c	40.9	..	13.0	9.0	1.1
Bolivia	-	..	-	-	-	-	..	.. c	.. c	.. c
Brazil	-184.7	..	.. c	15.7	4.6	94.0	..	259.6	585.5	289.5
Ecuador	-	..	-	-	-	1.1	..	.. c	.. c	.. c
Paraguay	-	..	-	-	-	1.1	..	3.5	1.1	1.1
Peru	.. c	..	.. c	.. c	.. c	.. c	..	.. c	.. c	.. c
Uruguay	.. c	..	-	-	-	5.5	..	.. c	.. c	.. c
Venezuela	-	..	.. c	.. c	.. c	-52.0	..	.. c	.. c	.. c

Table 3. Foreign direct investment income by country *(cont.)*

Million US dollars

	Inward					Outward				
	2016	2017	2018	2019	2020	2016	2017	2018	2019	2020
ASIA	**1 152.3**	**..**	**2 639.0**	**1 388.1**	**515.1**	**968.7**	**..**	**1 391.5**	**1 345.6**	**1 194.3**
Near and Middle East	4.4	..	38.9	-	-4.6	170.3	..	57.8	.. c	77.5
Gulf Arabian countries	13.3	..	34.2	.. c	.. c	110.6	..	33.0	213.8	72.9
Kuwait	-	..	-	-	-	-	..	-	-	-
Qatar	.. c	..	1.2	-	-	-6.6	..	-20.1	12.3	9.1
Saudi Arabia	.. c	..	.. c	.. c	.. c	17.7	..	13.0	13.4	18.2
United Arab Emirates	14.4	..	35.4	-2.2	3.4	99.5	..	38.9	185.8	45.6
Other Near and Middle East	-8.8	..	.. c	.. c	.. c	59.7	..	24.8	.. c	4.6
Jordan	-	..	-	-	-	32.1	..	.. c	.. c	.. c
Other Asian countries	1 147.8	..	2 600.0	1 387.0	519.7	798.4	..	1 333.6	1 102.7	1 116.8
China	241.1	..	.. c	.. c	.. c	14.4	..	69.6	357.1	380.6
Hong Kong, China	86.3	..	123.9	23.5	192.6	310.7	..	.. c	.. c	.. c
India	-19.9	..	.. c	.. c	26.2	103.9	..	.. c	.. c	.. c
Indonesia	-1.1	..	-	-	-	28.8	..	.. c	.. c	.. c
Iran, Islamic Republic of	-	..	-	-	-	4.4	..	4.7	2.2	1.1
Malaysia	-2.2	..	.. c	.. c	.. c	59.7	..	.. c	.. c	.. c
Philippines	-	..	-	-	-	11.1	..	.. c	.. c	.. c
Singapore	-24.3	..	53.1	23.5	9.1	-16.6	..	.. c	.. c	27.4
Chinese Taipei	2.2	..	.. c	.. c	.. c	8.8	..	.. c	.. c	.. c
Thailand	-14.4	..	.. c	.. c	.. c	46.4	..	.. c	.. c	.. c
Viet Nam	-	..	.. c	.. c	.. c	-	..	-4.7	12.3	61.5
AUSTRALIA, OCEANIA AND POLAR REGIONS	**-26.5**	**..**	**-2.4**	**13.4**	**22.8**	**76.3**	**..**	**-57.8**	**174.6**	**185.8**
WORLD unallocated and confidential	**-**	**..**	**-**	**-1.1**	**2.3**	**1.1**	**..**	**-1.2**	**1.1**	**-1.1**
European Union (since 01/02/2020)	**..**	**..**	**..**	**..**	**28 439.9**	**..**	**..**	**..**	**..**	**14 683.8**
G20 countries excl. European Union	**10 985.3**	**..**	**15 377.1**	**15 524.5**	**15 334.5**	**15 639.7**	**..**	**15 883.4**	**9 434.7**	**7 716.2**
G20 OECD countries	**10 985.3**	**..**	**15 429.0**	**15 528.9**	**15 320.8**	**15 134.4**	**..**	**15 150.5**	**8 019.7**	**6 860.4**
G20 Non-OECD countries	**1.1**	**..**	**-51.9**	**-5.6**	**16.0**	**505.4**	**..**	**732.9**	**1 413.9**	**857.0**
MENA countries	**16.6**	**..**	**43.7**	**-1.1**	**.. c**	**118.3**	**..**	**46.0**	**229.5**	**59.3**
ASEAN countries	**-42.0**	**..**	**57.8**	**25.7**	**14.8**	**140.4**	**..**	**.. c**	**253.0**	**328.2**

- Nil; .. Not available; c Confidential data

Note: Data excludes resident Special Purpose Entities (SPEs). Detailed metadata at: *http://metalinks.oecd.org/idi/20220712/6d95*.

Source: *OECD International Direct Investment Statistics (database): https://doi.org/10.1787/idi-data-en*

Table 4. Foreign direct investment flows by industrial sector

Million US dollars

	Inward					Outward				
	2016	2017	2018	2019	2020	2016	2017	2018	2019	2020
All FDI activities	**68 178.7**	**-3 058.3**	**27 120.3**	**-9 206.3**	**13 880.3**	**40 165.9**	**29 563.7**	**43 553.6**	**-9 305.9**	**11 745.9**
Agriculture, forestry and fishing	**2.2**	**.. c**	**.. c**	**-**	**-**	**-5.5**	**1.1**	**.. c**	**.. c**	**-**
Mining and quarrying	**-**	**.. c**	**-**	**-**	**-**	**-497.6**	**53.0**	**.. c**	**-164.6**	**-**
Extraction activities	-	-	-	-	-	-	-	-	-	-
Manufacturing	**11 350.2**	**-7 497.5**	**-243.1**	**-5 715.9**	**4 006.8**	**3 827.3**	**1 953.6**	**-5 218.9**	**1 629.9**	**925.4**
of which:										
Food products, beverages and tobacco	2 281.3	-354.0	-152.2	549.6	-	2 085.6	435.1	125.1	-2 685.5	126.5
Textiles, wood and paper products; printing	101.7	189.4	.. c	.. c	.. c	236.6	.. c	.. c	794.8	.. c
Chemical, rubber, plastic, non-metallic mineral products	5 607.7	-8 187.4	4.7	-3 820.7	3 998.9	288.6	199.5	-998.5	1 965.7	279.2
Metal and machinery products, except electrical equipment	74.1	1 096.8	-31.9	.. c	.. c	938.8	657.2	-4 497.8	1 497.8	214.2
Motor vehicles, trailers, semi-trailers, other transport equipment	1 623.4	93.6	.. c	-4.5	-12.5	520.8	112.7	27.1	29.1	51.3
Other manufacturing	1 662.1	-334.8	-87.3	.. c	.. c	-243.3	217.6	-259.6	29.1	4.6
Electricity, gas, steam and air conditioning supply	**-4 599.1**	**3 727.9**	**-30.7**	**.. c**	**.. c**	**1 056.1**	**2 918.5**	**.. c**	**.. c**	**.. c**
Water supply; sewerage, waste management and remediation activities	**-112.8**	**.. c**	**-**	**-**	**.. c**	**-18.8**	**-39.5**	**.. c**	**.. c**	**.. c**
Construction	**-382.6**	**339.3**	**-1 608.6**	**.. c**	**.. c**	**-95.1**	**490.4**	**27.1**	**34.7**	**476.4**
Services	**62 415.1**	**1 432.8**	**14 418.7**	**-1 981.4**	**19 327.6**	**35 780.2**	**26 024.1**	**49 408.7**	**-3 256.5**	**13 969.2**
Wholesale and retail trade; repair of motor vehicles and motorcycles	7 904.5	-5 789.7	.. c	.. c	1 014.2	533.0	1 376.4	-5 551.8	.. c	880.9
Transportation and storage	254.3	-213.1	.. c	568.7	.. c	455.6	.. c	673.9	-506.0	82.1
Accommodation and food service activities	37.6	.. c	.. c	.. c	-	95.1	216.4	.. c	.. c	.. c
Information and communication	3 822.8	696.7	.. c	.. c	.. c	338.4	1 229.9	221.9	.. c	-539.0
Financial and insurance activities	10 456.7	5 407.5	14 140.2	-7 762.2	16 613.1	-13 526.5	30 395.7	42 673.2	3 965.1	15 310.5
Activities of holding companies	-13 570.7	-1 685.3	3 140.6	-9 464.9	-503.7	-30 043.1	11 857.7	15 706.4	4 645.7	800.0
Real estate activities	1 332.5	-92.4	-914.7	-7.8	.. c	899.0	-158.9	.. c	.. c	.. c
Professional, scientific and technical activities	41 210.9	1 172.4	.. c	3 511.7	1 103.1	48 179.8	-6 105.3	11 164.9	16.8	-1 862.1
Administrative and support service activities	-2 416.2	160.1	.. c	.. c	.. c	-1 081.5	993.1	266.7	514.9	100.3
Public administration; activities of households and of extraterritorial organisations	-	-	-	-	-	1.1	.. c	-	-	-
Education	-	-	-	-	-	1.1	.. c	-	-	-
Human health and social work activities	-	.. c	-	.. c	-	-	.. c	.. c	.. c	.. c
Arts, entertainment and recreation	-25.4	-25.9	-	-	.. c	-	.. c	.. c	.. c	-
Other services	-163.7	-71.0	-	-	457.0	-115.0	-444.1	35.4	17.9	.. c
Not allocated and confidential	**-14.4**	**.. c**	**.. c**	**.. c**	**.. c**	**119.4**	**-1 837.4**	**.. c**	**.. c**	**.. c**
Private real estate activities	**-479.9**	**.. c**	**.. c**	**.. c**	**.. c**	**-**	**-**	**-**	**-**	**-**

- Nil; c Confidential data

Note: Data excludes resident Special Purpose Entities (SPEs). Detailed metadata at: *http://metalinks.oecd.org/idi/20220712/6d95*.

Source: *OECD International Direct Investment Statistics (database)*: *https://doi.org/10.1787/idi-data-en*

Table 5. Foreign direct investment positions by industrial sector

At year end

Million US dollars

	Inward					Outward				
	2016	2017	2018	2019	2020	2016	2017	2018	2019	2020
All FDI activities	**517 401.7**	**580 190.7**	**502 399.8**	**581 637.8**	**519 509.1**	**599 379.2**	**707 828.0**	**544 143.6**	**585 844.8**	**581 682.4**
Agriculture, forestry and fishing	**.. d**	**109.1**	**100.8**	**321.3**	**369.4**	**5.3**	**6.0**	**8.0**	**5.6**	**-7.4**
Mining and quarrying	**250.9**	**268.7**	**628.6**	**660.5**	**-**	**4 550.4**	**4 544.3**	**4 800.8**	**4 230.5**	**-**
Extraction activities	-	-	-	-	-	-	-	-	-	-
Manufacturing	**142 889.2**	**158 937.4**	**80 783.1**	**92 393.8**	**97 445.1**	**119 590.0**	**141 909.3**	**139 032.5**	**150 412.3**	**145 352.8**
of which:										
Food products, beverages and tobacco	8 780.4	10 467.7	8 681.0	7 660.1	5 736.9	26 508.9	33 335.3	41 422.0	43 136.4	39 892.0
Textiles, wood and paper products; printing	4 208.9	4 816.5	4 034.8	5 062.9	5 366.3	2 363.2	2 913.2	2 988.3	3 641.9	3 531.7
Chemical, rubber, plastic, non-metallic mineral products	110 265.6	119 929.2	50 929.7	65 158.4	70 193.9	63 177.0	70 122.3	60 990.4	65 111.2	72 977.1
Metal and machinery products, except electrical equipment	11 550.5	14 947.2	9 302.7	7 261.3	8 485.7	19 568.9	26 560.3	25 469.4	31 211.0	20 887.2
Motor vehicles, trailers, semi-trailers, other transport equipment	1 620.1	2 120.4	1 882.3	1 764.8	1 957.3	979.2	1 621.5	2 136.5	2 074.8	2 097.2
Other manufacturing	6 464.6	6 655.1	5 953.7	5 486.4	5 705.0	6 993.8	7 356.7	6 027.0	5 235.9	5 968.8
Electricity, gas, steam and air conditioning supply	**14 817.1**	**18 481.7**	**12 538.4**	**12 428.7**	**19 152.0**	**20 636.7**	**30 477.3**	**30 430.5**	**37 873.5**	**38 429.3**
Water supply; sewerage, waste management and remediation activities	**1 419.8**	**1 713.8**	**858.7**	**973.9**	**-196.3**	**597.7**	**544.5**	**201.5**	**171.9**	**2.5**
Construction	**2 583.5**	**3 713.1**	**2 046.0**	**3 039.8**	**1 995.3**	**1 997.5**	**2 759.7**	**3 299.7**	**3 234.1**	**2 699.7**
Services	**322 023.8**	**378 251.4**	**214 741.2**	**204 277.7**	**181 221.0**	**436 127.3**	**514 180.9**	**337 630.0**	**365 387.6**	**362 742.7**
Wholesale and retail trade; repair of motor vehicles and motorcycles	42 686.8	51 069.8	22 536.1	20 228.0	26 648.7	31 281.8	36 072.2	26 253.7	27 480.3	27 696.7
Transportation and storage	3 602.8	4 202.4	5 209.5	5 644.8	5 685.4	3 177.0	7 950.3	4 303.9	4 455.2	4 179.7
Accommodation and food service activities	2 654.2	2 808.8	2 346.0	1 961.4	2 280.0	1 029.8	1 779.8	878.2	906.5	812.4
Information and communication	8 008.9	10 161.9	4 350.8	4 091.2	5 214.1	11 070.9	12 528.2	12 836.0	5 640.3	4 823.9
Financial and insurance activities	125 992.4	153 926.6	117 704.4	112 083.8	99 080.9	79 222.1	108 631.6	100 138.5	99 418.1	105 210.5
Activities of holding companies	69 405.5	70 684.8	48 322.6	37 954.4	24 605.5	36 950.6	49 890.9	37 010.5	33 102.7	31 595.3
Real estate activities	7 845.5	8 314.9	4 957.6	4 430.5	5 266.9	2 980.9	3 635.2	4 695.4	5 428.0	7 726.1
Professional, scientific and technical activities	114 280.6	131 084.2	46 965.9	49 396.8	31 456.6	297 704.2	336 712.6	185 005.7	217 142.2	208 788.8
Administrative and support service activities	16 215.9	15 068.4	9 388.6	5 506.6	3 665.5	1 757.1	5 919.9	3 114.3	3 363.3	3 097.3
Public administration; activities of households and of extraterritorial organisations	-	-	-	-	-	7 487.1	26.4	-	-	-
Education	84.3	95.9	114.5	112.3	197.6	.. d	6.0	6.9	9.0	4.9
Human health and social work activities	326.8	403.0	411.0	25.8	713.0	.. d	33.6	51.5	79.8	88.4
Arts, entertainment and recreation	253.0	292.6	328.6	356.1	495.8	181.3	211.1	202.7	202.2	139.9
Other services	72.7	822.7	429.4	439.2	517.9	200.3	674.0	142.0	1 261.5	174.3
Not allocated and confidential	**.. d**	**638.0**	**182 570.4**	**259 456.3**	**210 770.6**	**-650.4**	**-121.1**	**15 654.9**	**8 834.0**	**8 340.9**
Private real estate activities	**17 768.5**	**18 077.5**	**8 132.6**	**8 085.8**	**8 752.0**	**11 728.7**	**13 527.2**	**13 085.6**	**15 695.3**	**24 122.0**

- Nil; .. Not available; d Secondary Confidentiality

Note: Data excludes resident Special Purpose Entities (SPEs). Detailed metadata at: *http://metalinks.oecd.org/idi/20220712/6d95*.

Source: *OECD International Direct Investment Statistics (database): https://doi.org/10.1787/idi-data-en*

Table 6. Foreign direct investment income by industrial sector

Million US dollars

	Inward					Outward				
	2016	2017	2018	2019	2020	2016	2017	2018	2019	2020
All FDI activities	**31 450.8**	..	**34 643.0**	**36 077.5**	**35 155.6**	**32 119.9**	..	**33 554.8**	**33 134.4**	**30 520.8**
Agriculture, forestry and fishing	**-13.3**	..	**-5.9**	**1.1**	**1.1**	**-17.7**	..	**2.4**	**-1.1**	**-2.3**
Mining and quarrying	**-64.1**	..	**217.2**	**361.6**	**-**	**85.1**	..	**902.9**	**1 794.5**	**-**
Extraction activities	-	..	-	-	-	-	..	-	-	-
Manufacturing	**11 927.5**	..	**12 653.1**	**14 353.5**	**12 331.6**	**8 360.1**	..	**.. c**	**.. c**	**.. c**
of which:										
Food products, beverages and tobacco	644.7	..	690.4	493.7	803.4	263.2	..	-707.0	619.1	91.2
Textiles, wood and paper products; printing	216.7	..	981.9	647.0	638.2	147.1	..	53.1	278.7	155.0
Chemical, rubber, plastic, non-metallic mineral products	9 062.3	..	6 673.0	10 585.5	9 103.1	6 170.5	..	.. c	.. c	.. c
Metal and machinery products, except electrical equipment	1 373.4	..	2 292.0	1 944.5	1 244.4	1 155.6	..	1 430.4	1 954.6	755.6
Motor vehicles, trailers, semi-trailers, other transport equipment	266.5	..	269.1	235.1	149.3	82.9	..	139.3	-91.8	-104.8
Other manufacturing	362.7	..	1 745.5	446.7	393.2	540.8	..	971.3	564.2	253.0
Electricity, gas, steam and air conditioning supply	**658.0**	..	**292.7**	**-56.0**	**201.7**	**-141.5**	..	**1 418.6**	**529.5**	**480.9**
Water supply; sewerage, waste management and remediation activities	**88.5**	..	**53.1**	**66.0**	**63.8**	**5.5**	..	**5.9**	**31.3**	**26.2**
Construction	**10.0**	..	**179.4**	**222.8**	**116.2**	**-144.9**	..	**229.0**	**-32.5**	**-106.0**
Services	**16 930.2**	..	**20 629.1**	**19 307.1**	**9 597.7**	**22 231.6**	..	**24 509.6**	**20 395.2**	**2 692.9**
Wholesale and retail trade; repair of motor vehicles and motorcycles	4 093.8	..	3 246.8	.. c	.. c	1 836.8	..	1 404.5	.. c	.. c
Transportation and storage	171.4	..	.. c	.. c	.. c	128.3	..	167.6	181.4	63.8
Accommodation and food service activities	68.6	..	.. c	.. c	.. c	-17.7	..	-3.5	11.2	-63.8
Information and communication	376.0	..	82.6	.. c	.. c	499.8	..	.. c	.. c	.. c
Financial and insurance activities	7 905.6	..	10 173.5	8 165.2	5 242.2	6 929.1	..	3 504.1	5 768.5	1 323.1
Activities of holding companies	1 167.8	..	3 672.8	3 508.3	1 785.8	3 248.9	..	384.8	2 677.7	125.4
Real estate activities	-420.2	..	186.5	219.4	59.3	113.9	..	48.4	150.0	93.4
Professional, scientific and technical activities	3 072.0	..	5 124.5	4 708.4	1 275.2	10 903.5	..	17 697.4	11 937.8	420.5
Administrative and support service activities	1 612.3	..	885.2	.. c	.. c	802.8	..	.. c	.. c	.. c
Public administration; activities of households and of extraterritorial organisations	-	..	-	-	-	1 015.2	..	-	-	-
Education	6.6	..	7.1	-	-	3.3	..	2.4	-	-
Human health and social work activities	-4.4	..	-	-2.2	-5.7	4.4	..	7.1	7.8	4.6
Arts, entertainment and recreation	36.5	..	23.6	47.0	21.7	10.0	..	5.9	4.5	-5.7
Other services	11.1	..	85.0	57.1	1.1	3.3	..	72.0	70.5	-
Not allocated and confidential	**1 914.2**	..	**624.3**	**1 821.3**	**12 843.3**	**1 741.7**	..	**.. c**	**.. c**	**.. c**
Private real estate activities	**-**	..	**-**	**-**	**-**	**-**	..	**-**	**-**	**-**

- Nil; .. Not available; c Confidential data

Note: Data excludes resident Special Purpose Entities (SPEs). Detailed metadata at: *http://metalinks.oecd.org/idi/20220712/6d95*.

Source: *OECD International Direct Investment Statistics (database): https://doi.org/10.1787/idi-data-en*

CANADA

Table 1. Foreign direct investment flows by country

Million US dollars

	Inward					Outward				
	2016	2017	2018	2019	2020	2016	2017	2018	2019	2020
WORLD	**36 061.9**	**22 764.2**	**38 231.8**	**47 829.4**	**24 098.3**	**69 518.2**	**76 178.7**	**57 405.3**	**78 886.1**	**46 433.3**
OECD COUNTRIES	..	..	..	..	..	..	..	..	..	..
Australia	-498.5	378.9	1 869.3	1 797.5	-1 366.7	1 469.4	339.3	2 184.6	-1 193.3	1 150.3
Austria	..	..	..	..	..	..	..	..	..	..
Belgium	..	..	..	..	..	..	..	..	..	..
Canada	-	-	-	-	-	-	-	-	-	-
Chile	..	..	..	..	..	..	..	..	..	..
Colombia	..	..	..	..	..	..	..	..	..	..
Costa Rica	..	..	..	..	..	..	..	..	..	..
Czech Republic	..	..	..	..	..	..	..	..	..	..
Denmark	..	..	..	..	..	..	..	..	..	..
Estonia	..	..	..	..	..	..	..	..	..	..
Finland	..	..	..	..	..	..	..	..	..	..
France	427.4	610.3	1 756.1	1 506.0	1 183.3	-98.4	192.3	1 800.4	481.3	141.3
Germany	370.7	514.6	471.2	349.0	608.0	1 381.9	-286.9	952.7	1 218.6	1 344.0
Greece	..	..	..	..	..	..	..	..	..	..
Hungary	..	..	..	..	..	..	..	..	..	..
Iceland	..	..	..	..	..	..	..	..	..	..
Ireland	..	..	..	..	..	..	..	..	..	..
Israel	..	..	..	..	..	..	..	..	..	..
Italy	..	..	..	..	..	..	..	..	..	..
Japan	1 009.7	775.1	666.4	182.2	-203.1	-131.6	1 021.7	1 104.2	-105.0	221.3
Korea	..	..	..	..	..	..	..	..	..	..
Latvia	..	..	..	..	..	..	..	..	..	..
Lithuania	..	..	..	..	..	..	..	..	..	..
Luxembourg	1 617.1	2 598.9	-302.2	1 688.2	-422.6	-2 124.5	-3 602.6	195.1	5 025.6	-639.8
Mexico	-50.8	192.4	23.9	-9.9	130.4	1 458.4	885.9	158.5	757.6	2 998.0
Netherlands	4 824.4	-970.0	4 561.9	5 317.3	2 827.2	1 039.2	1 010.4	1 006.1	1 640.0	681.4
New Zealand	..	..	..	..	..	..	..	..	..	..
Norway	..	..	..	..	..	..	..	..	..	..
Poland	..	..	..	..	..	..	..	..	..	..
Portugal	..	..	..	..	..	..	..	..	..	..
Slovak Republic	..	..	..	..	..	..	..	..	..	..
Slovenia	..	..	..	..	..	..	..	..	..	..
Spain	..	..	..	..	..	..	..	..	..	..
Sweden	..	..	..	..	..	..	..	..	..	..
Switzerland	9 600.3	-3 278.5	-933.5	5 935.0	-3 143.6	-455.7	1 435.9	-7 624.2	5 122.4	-16.1
Turkey	..	..	..	..	..	..	..	..	..	..
United Kingdom	-1 773.1	2 894.5	2 879.0	1 625.4	2 664.9	8 183.6	3 334.2	6 921.3	6 078.3	2 253.9
United States	18 669.4	12 631.9	16 950.1	20 843.1	8 933.5	55 928.3	68 020.6	37 333.1	26 023.8	27 784.9
EUROPE	..	..	..	..	..	..	..	..	..	..
Bulgaria	..	..	..	..	..	..	..	..	..	..
Croatia	..	..	..	..	..	..	..	..	..	..
Cyprus	..	..	..	..	..	..	..	..	..	..
Malta	..	..	..	..	..	..	..	..	..	..
Montenegro	..	..	..	..	..	..	..	..	..	..
Romania	..	..	..	..	..	..	..	..	..	..
Russian Federation	..	..	..	..	..	..	..	..	..	..
Ukraine	..	..	..	..	..	..	..	..	..	..
AFRICA	..	..	..	..	..	..	..	..	..	..
Northern Africa	..	..	..	..	..	..	..	..	..	..
Algeria	..	..	..	..	..	..	..	..	..	..
Egypt	..	..	..	..	..	..	..	..	..	..
Libya	..	..	..	..	..	..	..	..	..	..
Morocco	..	..	..	..	..	..	..	..	..	..
Tunisia	..	..	..	..	..	..	..	..	..	..
Other African countries	..	..	..	..	..	..	..	..	..	..
Nigeria	..	..	..	..	..	..	..	..	..	..
South Africa	..	..	..	..	..	..	..	..	..	..
AMERICA	..	..	..	..	..	..	..	..	..	..
Northern America	..	..	..	..	..	..	..	..	..	..
Central America and Caribbean countries	..	..	..	..	..	..	..	..	..	..
Bahamas	..	..	..	..	..	..	..	..	..	..
Bermuda	..	..	..	..	..	..	..	..	..	..
Cayman Islands	245.5	176.5	217.9	3 049.8	686.0	2 615.7	1 792.6	-3 988.9	2 265.6	202.5
El Salvador	..	..	..	..	..	..	..	..	..	..
Guatemala	..	..	..	..	..	..	..	..	..	..
Honduras	..	..	..	..	..	..	..	..	..	..
Nicaragua	..	..	..	..	..	..	..	..	..	..
Panama	..	..	..	..	..	..	..	..	..	..
Virgin Islands, U.S.	..	..	..	..	..	..	..	..	..	..
South America	..	..	..	..	..	..	..	..	..	..
Argentina	..	..	..	..	..	..	..	..	..	..
Bolivia	..	..	..	..	..	..	..	..	..	..
Brazil	443.6	1 098.5	1 253.9	1 156.3	1 162.6	-90.6	32.4	514.1	476.6	89.3
Ecuador	..	..	..	..	..	..	..	..	..	..
Paraguay	..	..	..	..	..	..	..	..	..	..
Peru	..	..	..	..	..	..	..	..	..	..
Uruguay	..	..	..	..	..	..	..	..	..	..
Venezuela	..	..	..	..	..	..	..	..	..	..

CANADA

Table 1. Foreign direct investment flows by country *(cont.)*

Million US dollars

	Inward					Outward				
	2016	2017	2018	2019	2020	2016	2017	2018	2019	2020
ASIA	..	..	..	..	..	..	..	..	..	..
Near and Middle East	..	..	..	..	..	..	..	..	..	..
Gulf Arabian countries	..	..	..	..	..	..	..	..	..	..
Kuwait	..	..	..	..	..	..	..	..	..	..
Qatar	..	..	..	..	..	..	..	..	..	..
Saudi Arabia	..	..	..	..	..	..	..	..	..	..
United Arab Emirates	..	..	..	..	..	..	..	..	..	..
Other Near and Middle East	..	..	..	..	..	..	..	..	..	..
Jordan	..	..	..	..	..	..	..	..	..	..
Other Asian countries	..	..	..	..	..	..	..	..	..	..
China	5 693.4	1 959.4	2 502.2	849.3	333.0	968.8	1 324.9	429.9	438.8	871.8
Hong Kong, China	1 188.8	-209.8	1 525.6	-438.7	-669.2	666.9	1 824.2	622.1	1 053.6	3 437.2
India	..	..	..	..	..	..	..	..	..	..
Indonesia	..	..	..	..	..	..	..	..	..	..
Iran, Islamic Republic of	..	..	..	..	..	..	..	..	..	..
Malaysia	..	..	..	..	..	..	..	..	..	..
Philippines	..	..	..	..	..	..	..	..	..	..
Singapore	..	..	..	..	..	..	..	..	..	..
Chinese Taipei	..	..	..	..	..	..	..	..	..	..
Thailand	..	..	..	..	..	..	..	..	..	..
Viet Nam	..	..	..	..	..	..	..	..	..	..
AUSTRALIA, OCEANIA AND POLAR REGIONS	..	..	..	..	..	..	..	..	..	..
WORLD unallocated and confidential	**-5 987.4**	**2 932.0**	**4 249.7**	**3 958.6**	**11 184.5**	**-6 017.7**	**4 997.6**	**7 266.1**	**24 112.4**	**2 652.2**
European Union (since 01/02/2020)	..	..	..	..	..	..	..	..	..	..
G20 countries excl. European Union	..	..	..	..	..	..	..	..	..	..
G20 OECD countries	..	..	..	..	..	..	..	..	..	..
G20 Non-OECD countries	..	..	..	..	..	..	..	..	..	..
MENA countries	..	..	..	..	..	..	..	..	..	..
ASEAN countries	..	..	..	..	..	..	..	..	..	..

- Nil; .. Not available

Note: Detailed metadata at: *http://metalinks.oecd.org/idi/20220712/6d95.*

Source: *OECD International Direct Investment Statistics (database)*: *https://doi.org/10.1787/idi-data-en*

CANADA

Table 2. Foreign direct investment positions by country

At year end

Million US dollars

	Inward					Outward				
	2016	2017	2018	2019	2020	2016	2017	2018	2019	2020
WORLD	**603 759.6**	**658 556.6**	**683 705.7**	**779 799.6**	**813 861.9**	**823 099.0**	**938 918.8**	**1 002 299.9**	**1 079 509.9**	**1 142 881.2**
OECD COUNTRIES	**510 685.4**	**554 670.2**	**583 178.6**	**665 329.6**	..	**611 580.4**	**707 399.9**	**765 978.5**	**823 360.9**	**885 724.5**
Australia	7 319.9	6 649.4	7 937.8	12 799.4	..	21 327.9	28 290.4	29 560.2	32 473.6	36 689.8
Austria	1 455.2	1 392.7	876.8	1 000.3	..	1 575.2	2 228.3	1 919.0	4 289.0	4 712.9
Belgium	1 664.1	2 051.0	2 312.0	4 230.9	..	1 043.4	1 078.8	1 696.5	725.1	189.4
Canada	6 439.6	9 977.3	21 789.2	26 943.6	..	-	-	-	-	-
Chile	530.6	243.7	220.1	219.9	..	13 129.5	15 403.6	17 770.4	16 552.2	17 983.7
Colombia	..	..	..	..	..	2 967.9	3 449.3	3 860.0	3 909.6	4 402.8
Costa Rica	..	..	..	..	..	3.0	128.7	252.9	207.7	209.6
Czech Republic	..	..	..	..	..	456.5	9.5	318.2	13.9	88.9
Denmark	706.3	731.8	743.9	798.2	..	592.1	548.1	1 471.2	4 405.8	4 889.1
Estonia	..	..	..	..	..	96.1	133.5	62.9	26.4	26.0
Finland	420.8	833.4	527.9	749.9	..	1 120.9	1 275.8	1 195.3	1 162.9	1 330.5
France	11 681.5	14 076.0	16 865.2	17 468.3	..	4 681.6	8 682.1	7 777.9	8 178.0	9 027.8
Germany	18 610.6	21 256.3	20 453.8	26 011.5	..	8 619.9	7 278.4	7 852.6	8 971.0	11 145.4
Greece	..	..	..	..	..	201.8	235.9	239.5	232.6	166.4
Hungary	..	..	..	..	..	3 633.0	3 995.9	1 750.0	3 880.9	7 359.5
Iceland	..	..	..	..	..	-	138.2	-	-	0.4
Ireland	4 445.1	8 056.6	5 980.9	10 425.4	..	8 295.2	6 989.2	7 296.0	8 645.3	9 328.5
Israel	846.2	992.7	1 308.1	682.6	..	601.8	908.0	-151.5	430.5	400.7
Italy	3 602.0	5 136.1	2 753.5	3 912.5	..	414.8	827.8	636.5	620.9	736.0
Japan	28 801.6	30 856.5	31 828.3	35 720.3	..	3 627.0	5 026.2	6 454.6	6 305.9	6 806.1
Korea	2 262.9	2 895.2	3 543.7	4 885.7	..	1 190.9	1 468.9	1 810.6	1 181.5	1 410.5
Latvia	..	..	..	..	..	5.2	2.4	2.5	1.1	1.2
Lithuania	..	..	..	..	..	344.8	388.5	350.5	351.5	363.0
Luxembourg	14 640.5	18 175.1	16 619.3	11 956.1	..	58 760.7	63 221.3	74 221.2	73 869.6	79 746.1
Mexico	2 255.7	2 258.0	2 018.9	2 013.1	..	13 110.9	16 311.6	19 422.2	20 564.2	22 418.9
Netherlands	20 498.1	15 874.0	17 081.3	21 936.1	..	24 983.2	27 059.1	30 190.9	31 709.9	34 844.0
New Zealand	..	..	..	..	..	440.9	328.1	964.3	1 416.7	1 621.7
Norway	5 644.6	4 955.9	5 251.1	5 712.5	..	1 194.6	1 456.1	1 331.3	1 021.1	996.2
Poland	2 018.0	2 422.0	2 151.7	2 115.1	..	192.2	233.6	257.7	436.8	457.5
Portugal	..	..	..	..	..	35.0	46.9	128.0	49.7	56.8
Slovak Republic	..	..	..	..	..	-13.4	1.6	-3.8	-8.9	-9.2
Slovenia	..	..	..	..	..	-	0.8	0.1	0.5	0.6
Spain	3 900.4	4 007.1	7 481.0	10 291.7	..	4 082.8	4 092.0	5 862.8	5 625.5	6 293.4
Sweden	1 747.5	1 894.2	1 946.2	2 138.6	..	3 151.1	3 377.0	5 372.9	4 993.2	5 954.6
Switzerland	20 058.1	23 425.4	20 598.8	26 754.1	..	-43.9	3 429.5	4 062.8	3 181.7	3 462.2
Turkey	..	..	..	..	..	804.3	1 184.5	995.9	1 122.3	1 553.3
United Kingdom	38 114.8	36 759.1	36 139.6	43 641.2	..	69 159.2	80 122.3	76 366.7	86 250.2	90 822.7
United States	312 802.9	338 727.1	356 746.3	392 240.0	..	365 109.9	422 014.6	458 793.0	494 680.2	520 447.1
EUROPE	**152 762.2**	**166 229.8**	**162 613.4**	**194 122.9**	..	**206 281.4**	**232 646.2**	**244 991.3**	**276 611.9**	**301 659.7**
Bulgaria	..	..	..	..	..	-	22.2	77.8	51.6	58.3
Croatia	..	..	..	..	..	-	-	-0.4	-0.3	-0.4
Cyprus	1 384.7	1 967.9	1 591.5	1 348.1	..	3 320.9	2 789.2	1 152.3	2 296.9	2 352.9
Malta	..	..	..	..	..	569.0	1 010.5	2 101.7	1 229.1	1 311.2
Montenegro	..	..	..	..	..	-	-	-	-	-
Romania	..	..	..	..	..	408.9	539.4	682.1	278.6	237.2
Russian Federation	1 988.1	2 719.6	2 909.0	3 207.3	..	928.0	1 220.2	748.7	741.7	608.1
Ukraine	..	..	..	..	..	234.6	540.2	4.5	45.4	63.1
AFRICA	**1 385.5**	**1 450.2**	**1 046.1**	**965.1**	..	**4 864.8**	**7 113.1**	**7 162.4**	**8 241.9**	**9 028.2**
Northern Africa	..	..	..	..	..	93.1	54.0	-	102.7	-86.5
Algeria	..	..	..	..	..	7.4	7.9	-27.5	-12.0	-150.9
Egypt	..	..	..	..	..	-6.0	-25.4	4.5	2.9	-49.6
Libya	..	..	..	..	..	-	-	-	-	-
Morocco	..	..	..	..	..	5.2	13.5	0.0	59.1	58.7
Tunisia	..	..	..	..	..	86.4	58.0	49.5	52.7	55.4
Other African countries	..	..	..	..	..	4 772.5	7 058.3	-	8 146.4	9 122.2
Nigeria	..	..	..	..	..	404.4	398.0	285.7	339.1	344.4
South Africa	564.9	503.0	917.9	771.6	..	1 471.7	1 621.4	630.5	776.1	697.9
AMERICA	**346 476.1**	**375 883.1**	**399 878.4**	**440 786.6**	..	**552 763.8**	**626 374.3**	**671 060.0**	**713 037.5**	**738 139.5**
Northern America	..	..	..	..	..	365 109.9	422 014.6	-	494 680.2	520 447.1
Central America and Caribbean countries	..	..	..	..	..	147 596.6	158 195.1	-	167 241.7	168 704.1
Bahamas	..	..	..	..	..	16 873.5	19 170.6	19 459.6	18 931.6	15 711.3
Bermuda	596.3	722.5	572.7	751.7	..	31 658.6	36 352.9	44 360.4	51 330.5	49 702.3
Cayman Islands	1 143.0	917.2	614.3	654.6	..	30 575.7	32 423.7	29 144.3	33 555.8	34 575.6
El Salvador	..	..	..	..	..	586.1	498.9	481.0	377.7	217.9
Guatemala	..	..	..	..	..	9.7	-2.4	64.2	40.1	36.7
Honduras	..	..	..	..	..	66.3	352.7	546.8	220.2	235.0
Nicaragua	..	..	..	..	..	353.0	278.0	524.1	2.5	26.0
Panama	..	..	..	..	..	3 498.9	3 832.2	2 810.0	2 325.4	2 678.8
Virgin Islands, U.S.	..	..	..	..	..	-	-	-	-	-
South America	..	..	..	..	..	38 812.8	45 023.8	-	49 599.7	47 102.1
Argentina	..	..	..	..	..	2 478.6	1 688.9	2 010.4	1 444.1	1 091.0
Bolivia	..	..	..	..	..	102.8	107.2	104.3	118.3	119.8
Brazil	22 035.7	22 041.4	17 614.8	17 801.0	..	8 987.1	11 538.0	10 178.4	11 584.2	8 657.1
Ecuador	..	..	..	..	..	1 055.3	965.2	1 767.1	2 250.0	2 250.5
Paraguay	..	..	..	..	..	-	31.8	0.0	15.4	15.7
Peru	..	..	..	..	..	9 615.7	10 804.7	10 239.9	12 904.6	11 683.3
Uruguay	..	..	..	..	..	334.4	779.3	766.8	788.2	815.9
Venezuela	..	..	..	..	..	-35.7	136.6	-0.8	0.1	0.0

Table 2. Foreign direct investment positions by country *(cont.)*

At year end

Million US dollars

	Inward					Outward				
	2016	2017	2018	2019	2020	2016	2017	2018	2019	2020
ASIA	..	..	..	..	..	**36 945.0**	**43 848.9**	**47 851.9**	**47 437.5**	**55 605.6**
Near and Middle East	..	..	..	..	..	886.3	797.6	-	551.8	539.9
Gulf Arabian countries	..	..	..	..	..	285.2	-110.4	-	120.6	138.7
Kuwait	1 483.8	1 732.1	1 606.3	1 743.9	..	-	-	-0.1	81.7	92.1
Qatar	..	..	..	..	..	-	-	-5.1	0.2	0.1
Saudi Arabia	..	..	..	..	..	14.2	81.8	1.4	29.3	33.5
United Arab Emirates	7 672.5	7 104.4	6 689.2	6 178.8	..	257.7	-211.3	25.0	-87.0	-84.3
Other Near and Middle East	..	..	..	..	..	601.0	908.0	-	431.2	401.2
Jordan	..	..	..	..	..	-	-	-	-	-
Other Asian countries	..	..	..	..	..	35 947.7	42 879.7	-	46 884.5	55 061.1
China	18 662.4	21 359.3	20 242.5	28 249.8	..	7 610.0	10 398.0	9 959.9	8 654.4	10 073.8
Hong Kong, China	8 544.3	9 619.4	11 243.9	14 802.1	..	6 338.7	6 871.6	8 070.5	9 598.8	13 987.2
India	3 931.8	4 706.7	4 196.8	4 027.2	..	1 112.7	1 314.0	1 840.4	1 554.4	1 541.7
Indonesia	295.9	306.5	593.9	981.7	..	2 211.2	2 313.3	2 178.3	2 688.4	2 702.0
Iran, Islamic Republic of	..	..	..	..	..	-	-	-	-	-
Malaysia	7 346.8	7 122.8	5 545.6	6 183.8	..	719.4	882.6	-228.8	-267.4	-181.4
Philippines	..	..	..	..	..	1 510.4	1 615.8	2 170.1	1 779.9	1 990.1
Singapore	389.1	393.1	166.5	1 110.8	..	3 349.2	4 335.9	6 907.1	5 594.3	6 092.7
Chinese Taipei	..	..	..	..	..	84.2	70.7	425.3	414.2	433.6
Thailand	..	..	..	..	..	115.4	139.0	191.3	158.2	253.7
Viet Nam	..	..	..	..	..	72.2	525.1	156.6	656.5	681.6
AUSTRALIA, OCEANIA AND POLAR REGIONS	..	..	..	..	..	**22 244.0**	**28 936.3**	**31 182.7**	**34 173.8**	**38 439.7**
WORLD unallocated and confidential	**15 578.6**	**21 255.5**	**25 265.2**	**26 558.9**	..	**-**	**-**	**51.7**	**7.3**	**8.4**
European Union (since 01/02/2020)	..	..	..	..	..	..	..	..	..	**180 667.5**
G20 countries excl. European Union	..	..	..	..	..	**512 859.9**	**601 382.3**	**637 218.2**	**687 820.5**	**726 462.7**
G20 OECD countries	..	..	..	..	..	**488 046.5**	**571 206.7**	**609 670.1**	**660 347.8**	**701 057.6**
G20 Non-OECD countries	..	..	..	..	..	**24 813.4**	**30 175.6**	**27 548.1**	**27 472.7**	**25 405.1**
MENA countries	..	..	..	..	..	**378.3**	**-56.4**	**68.9**	**223.6**	**52.4**
ASEAN countries	..	..	..	..	..	**8 088.2**	**9 992.9**	**11 655.7**	**11 093.1**	**12 336.1**

- Nil; .. Not available

Note: Inward FDI positions are allocated according to the ultimate investing country. Detailed metadata at: *http://metalinks.oecd.org/idi/20220712/6d95.*

Source: *OECD International Direct Investment Statistics (database): https://doi.org/10.1787/idi-data-en*

CANADA

Table 3. Foreign direct investment income by country

Million US dollars

	Inward					Outward				
	2016	2017	2018	2019	2020	2016	2017	2018	2019	2020
WORLD	**31 001.1**	**37 274.4**	**41 599.4**	**42 323.2**	**24 886.0**	**40 774.1**	**54 142.8**	**62 400.7**	**64 145.9**	**56 118.1**
OECD COUNTRIES	..	..	..	..	..	..	..	..	..	..
Australia	..	..	..	..	..	..	..	..	..	..
Austria	..	..	..	..	..	..	..	..	..	..
Belgium	..	..	..	..	..	..	..	..	..	..
Canada	-	-	-	-	-	-	-	-	-	-
Chile	..	..	..	..	..	..	..	..	..	..
Colombia	..	..	..	..	..	..	..	..	..	..
Costa Rica	..	..	..	..	..	..	..	..	..	..
Czech Republic	..	..	..	..	..	..	..	..	..	..
Denmark	..	..	..	..	..	..	..	..	..	..
Estonia	..	..	..	..	..	..	..	..	..	..
Finland	..	..	..	..	..	..	..	..	..	..
France	..	..	..	..	..	..	..	..	..	..
Germany	..	..	..	..	..	..	..	..	..	..
Greece	..	..	..	..	..	..	..	..	..	..
Hungary	..	..	..	..	..	..	..	..	..	..
Iceland	..	..	..	..	..	..	..	..	..	..
Ireland	..	..	..	..	..	..	..	..	..	..
Israel	..	..	..	..	..	..	..	..	..	..
Italy	..	..	..	..	..	..	..	..	..	..
Japan	565.9	629.8	1 382.9	1 286.4	763.8	-123.8	1 010.0	953.7	36.5	248.5
Korea	..	..	..	..	..	..	..	..	..	..
Latvia	..	..	..	..	..	..	..	..	..	..
Lithuania	..	..	..	..	..	..	..	..	..	..
Luxembourg	..	..	..	..	..	..	..	..	..	..
Mexico	..	..	..	..	..	..	..	..	..	..
Netherlands	..	..	..	..	..	..	..	..	..	..
New Zealand	..	..	..	..	..	..	..	..	..	..
Norway	..	..	..	..	..	..	..	..	..	..
Poland	..	..	..	..	..	..	..	..	..	..
Portugal	..	..	..	..	..	..	..	..	..	..
Slovak Republic	..	..	..	..	..	..	..	..	..	..
Slovenia	..	..	..	..	..	..	..	..	..	..
Spain	..	..	..	..	..	..	..	..	..	..
Sweden	..	..	..	..	..	..	..	..	..	..
Switzerland	..	..	..	..	..	..	..	..	..	..
Turkey	..	..	..	..	..	..	..	..	..	..
United Kingdom	3 035.8	2 774.4	3 482.4	3 676.5	3 655.2	6 768.6	4 004.7	6 087.3	6 732.5	5 785.3
United States	15 744.4	17 226.7	18 910.7	18 230.8	11 414.9	13 734.5	23 562.5	27 296.3	24 341.2	23 930.4
EUROPE	..	..	..	..	..	..	..	..	..	..
Bulgaria	..	..	..	..	..	..	..	..	..	..
Croatia	..	..	..	..	..	..	..	..	..	..
Cyprus	..	..	..	..	..	..	..	..	..	..
Malta	..	..	..	..	..	..	..	..	..	..
Montenegro	..	..	..	..	..	..	..	..	..	..
Romania	..	..	..	..	..	..	..	..	..	..
Russian Federation	..	..	..	..	..	..	..	..	..	..
Ukraine	..	..	..	..	..	..	..	..	..	..
AFRICA	..	..	..	..	..	..	..	..	..	..
Northern Africa	..	..	..	..	..	..	..	..	..	..
Algeria	..	..	..	..	..	..	..	..	..	..
Egypt	..	..	..	..	..	..	..	..	..	..
Libya	..	..	..	..	..	..	..	..	..	..
Morocco	..	..	..	..	..	..	..	..	..	..
Tunisia	..	..	..	..	..	..	..	..	..	..
Other African countries	..	..	..	..	..	..	..	..	..	..
Nigeria	..	..	..	..	..	..	..	..	..	..
South Africa	..	..	..	..	..	..	..	..	..	..
AMERICA	..	..	..	..	..	..	..	..	..	..
Northern America	..	..	..	..	..	..	..	..	..	..
Central America and Caribbean countries	..	..	..	..	..	..	..	..	..	..
Bahamas	..	..	..	..	..	..	..	..	..	..
Bermuda	..	..	..	..	..	..	..	..	..	..
Cayman Islands	..	..	..	..	..	..	..	..	..	..
El Salvador	..	..	..	..	..	..	..	..	..	..
Guatemala	..	..	..	..	..	..	..	..	..	..
Honduras	..	..	..	..	..	..	..	..	..	..
Nicaragua	..	..	..	..	..	..	..	..	..	..
Panama	..	..	..	..	..	..	..	..	..	..
Virgin Islands, U.S.	..	..	..	..	..	..	..	..	..	..
South America	..	..	..	..	..	..	..	..	..	..
Argentina	..	..	..	..	..	..	..	..	..	..
Bolivia	..	..	..	..	..	..	..	..	..	..
Brazil	..	..	..	..	..	..	..	..	..	..
Ecuador	..	..	..	..	..	..	..	..	..	..
Paraguay	..	..	..	..	..	..	..	..	..	..
Peru	..	..	..	..	..	..	..	..	..	..
Uruguay	..	..	..	..	..	..	..	..	..	..
Venezuela	..	..	..	..	..	..	..	..	..	..

CANADA

Table 3. Foreign direct investment income by country *(cont.)*

Million US dollars

	Inward					Outward				
	2016	2017	2018	2019	2020	2016	2017	2018	2019	2020
ASIA	..	..	..	..	..	..	..	..	..	..
Near and Middle East	..	..	..	..	..	..	..	..	..	..
Gulf Arabian countries	..	..	..	..	..	..	..	..	..	..
Kuwait	..	..	..	..	..	..	..	..	..	..
Qatar	..	..	..	..	..	..	..	..	..	..
Saudi Arabia	..	..	..	..	..	..	..	..	..	..
United Arab Emirates	..	..	..	..	..	..	..	..	..	..
Other Near and Middle East	..	..	..	..	..	..	..	..	..	..
Jordan	..	..	..	..	..	..	..	..	..	..
Other Asian countries	..	..	..	..	..	..	..	..	..	..
China	..	..	..	..	..	..	..	..	..	..
Hong Kong, China	..	..	..	..	..	..	..	..	..	..
India	..	..	..	..	..	..	..	..	..	..
Indonesia	..	..	..	..	..	..	..	..	..	..
Iran, Islamic Republic of	..	..	..	..	..	..	..	..	..	..
Malaysia	..	..	..	..	..	..	..	..	..	..
Philippines	..	..	..	..	..	..	..	..	..	..
Singapore	..	..	..	..	..	..	..	..	..	..
Chinese Taipei	..	..	..	..	..	..	..	..	..	..
Thailand	..	..	..	..	..	..	..	..	..	..
Viet Nam	..	..	..	..	..	..	..	..	..	..
AUSTRALIA, OCEANIA AND POLAR REGIONS	..	..	..	..	..	..	..	..	..	..
WORLD unallocated and confidential	**11 655.1**	**16 643.4**	**17 823.4**	**19 129.6**	**9 052.1**	**20 394.8**	**25 565.7**	**28 063.5**	**33 035.7**	**26 153.9**
European Union (since 01/02/2020)	..	..	..	..	..	..	..	..	..	..
G20 countries excl. European Union	..	..	..	..	..	..	..	..	..	..
G20 OECD countries	..	..	..	..	..	..	..	..	..	..
G20 Non-OECD countries	..	..	..	..	..	..	..	..	..	..
MENA countries	..	..	..	..	..	..	..	..	..	..
ASEAN countries	..	..	..	..	..	..	..	..	..	..

- Nil; .. Not available

Note: Detailed metadata at: *http://metalinks.oecd.org/idi/20220712/6d95.*

Source: *OECD International Direct Investment Statistics (database)*: *https://doi.org/10.1787/idi-data-en*

CANADA

Table 4. Foreign direct investment flows by industrial sector

Million US dollars

	Inward					Outward				
	2016	2017	2018	2019	2020	2016	2017	2018	2019	2020
All FDI activities	**36 061.9**	**22 764.2**	**38 231.8**	**47 829.4**	**24 098.3**	**69 518.2**	**76 178.7**	**57 405.3**	**78 886.1**	**46 433.3**
Agriculture, forestry and fishing	..	..	..	..	..	..	..	..	..	..
Mining and quarrying	**8 148.0**	**-3 761.5**	**4 360.2**	**15 391.8**	**-5 431.0**	**12 721.0**	**-3 825.8**	**13 373.7**	**13 291.2**	**3 963.7**
Extraction activities	..	..	..	..	..	..	..	..	..	..
Manufacturing	**3 285.9**	**8 230.0**	**12 183.4**	**14 397.3**	**4 793.6**	**4 524.6**	**-1 830.5**	**3 957.5**	**3 623.9**	**3 793.3**
of which:										
Food products, beverages and tobacco	..	..	..	..	..	..	..	..	..	..
Textiles, wood and paper products; printing	..	..	..	..	..	..	..	..	..	..
Chemical, rubber, plastic, non-metallic mineral products	..	..	..	..	..	..	..	..	..	..
Metal and machinery products, except electrical equipment	..	..	..	..	..	..	..	..	..	..
Motor vehicles, trailers, semi-trailers, other transport equipment	..	..	..	..	..	..	..	..	..	..
Other manufacturing	..	..	..	..	..	..	..	..	..	..
Electricity, gas, steam and air conditioning supply	..	..	..	..	..	..	..	..	..	..
Water supply; sewerage, waste management and remediation activities	..	..	..	..	..	..	..	..	..	..
Construction	..	..	..	..	..	..	..	..	..	..
Services	..	..	..	..	..	..	..	..	..	..
Wholesale and retail trade; repair of motor vehicles and motorcycles	..	..	..	..	..	..	..	..	..	..
Transportation and storage	8 787.9	9 227.4	3 400.8	204.3	7 179.6	17 115.3	44 137.7	10 281.6	10 236.1	1 197.4
Accommodation and food service activities	..	..	..	..	..	..	..	..	..	..
Information and communication	..	..	..	..	..	..	..	..	..	..
Financial and insurance activities	6 928.6	3 498.4	1 963.3	5 659.6	3 773.8	17 922.0	21 106.4	23 532.2	22 100.5	21 439.6
Activities of holding companies	..	..	..	..	..	..	..	..	..	..
Real estate activities	..	..	..	..	..	..	..	..	..	..
Professional, scientific and technical activities	3 837.9	-51.1	4 195.8	5 825.2	4 196.1	-1 204.4	5 882.2	7 636.3	25 580.3	5 539.5
Administrative and support service activities	..	..	..	..	..	..	..	..	..	..
Public administration; activities of households and of extraterritorial organisations	..	..	..	..	..	..	..	..	..	..
Education	..	..	..	..	..	..	..	..	..	..
Human health and social work activities	..	..	..	..	..	..	..	..	..	..
Arts, entertainment and recreation	..	..	..	..	..	..	..	..	..	..
Other services	..	..	..	..	..	..	..	..	..	..
Not allocated and confidential	**5 073.6**	**5 621.0**	**12 128.4**	**18 040.4**	**24 735.8**	**18 439.6**	**10 708.6**	**-1 376.0**	**61 970.9**	**38 676.3**
Private real estate activities	..	..	..	..	..	..	..	..	..	..

.. Not available

Note: Detailed metadata at: *http://metalinks.oecd.org/idi/20220712/6d95*.

Source: *OECD International Direct Investment Statistics (database)*: *https://doi.org/10.1787/idi-data-en*

Table 5. Foreign direct investment positions by industrial sector

At year end

Million US dollars

	Inward					Outward				
	2016	2017	2018	2019	2020	2016	2017	2018	2019	2020
All FDI activities	**603 759.6**	**658 556.6**	**683 705.7**	**779 799.6**	**813 861.9**	**823 099.0**	**938 918.8**	**1 002 299.9**	**1 079 509.9**	**1 142 881.2**
Agriculture, forestry and fishing	**107.2**	**144.6**	**4 162.2**	**2 576.2**	**2 610.0**	**2 432.4**	**1 236.9**	**1 314.2**	**1 781.8**	**2 182.6**
Mining and quarrying	**128 794.2**	**137 229.9**	**129 780.8**	**151 995.3**	**145 489.7**	**139 518.1**	**144 041.2**	**120 706.1**	**134 556.5**	**138 554.1**
Extraction activities	110 904.9	117 823.3	112 790.4	121 580.2	115 120.2	76 560.7	77 378.5	62 214.6	65 158.5	67 404.4
Manufacturing	**135 076.3**	**141 055.8**	**134 903.2**	**150 160.6**	**155 014.2**	**67 044.8**	**73 464.4**	**76 629.3**	**72 376.4**	**76 004.3**
of which:										
Food products, beverages and tobacco	20 252.5	20 165.2	23 139.4	28 359.1	30 806.0	11 257.2	13 439.0	14 343.3	16 232.8	17 135.4
Textiles, wood and paper products; printing	9 324.5	9 021.3	7 356.6	7 483.2	6 970.5	5 154.5	5 931.8	6 790.5	5 386.8	6 621.8
Chemical, rubber, plastic, non-metallic mineral products	69 323.8	71 748.5	64 706.3	72 041.2	72 159.3	11 788.2	12 477.0	14 193.9	13 042.3	12 875.3
Metal and machinery products, except electrical equipment	12 814.5	13 717.0	16 363.7	16 691.4	17 127.7	13 876.5	11 178.9	9 133.9	9 460.2	9 459.6
Motor vehicles, trailers, semi-trailers, other transport equipment	14 454.5	16 178.1	14 236.3	16 031.4	18 035.6	14 796.3	16 599.9	19 240.1	17 410.8	18 217.4
Other manufacturing	8 767.4	9 934.1	9 101.0	9 554.4	9 915.2	10 171.3	13 783.8	12 927.6	10 843.6	11 694.8
Electricity, gas, steam and air conditioning supply	**1 557.3**	**1 263.1**	**6 326.3**	**7 682.7**	**8 238.6**	**23 957.7**	**30 637.9**	**53 317.3**	**57 361.3**	**59 622.0**
Water supply; sewerage, waste management and remediation activities	..	..	..	..	..	..	..	..	..	..
Construction	**2 422.7**	**2 948.8**	**4 192.3**	**4 929.0**	**4 945.7**	**926.5**	**2 568.3**	**3 422.0**	**2 601.5**	**2 188.1**
Services	**331 108.2 e**	**369 780.7 e**	**398 027.3 e**	**455 644.6 e**	**490 355.0 e**	**570 010.4 e**	**669 448.7 e**	**732 692.5 e**	**797 093.5 e**	**847 504.7 e**
Wholesale and retail trade; repair of motor vehicles and motorcycles	76 746.9	85 603.0	98 605.1	106 199.9	114 550.7	28 031.6	28 607.4	28 801.3	44 414.3	45 793.8
Transportation and storage	7 906.5	10 888.1	12 139.2	10 648.5	11 703.4	35 114.3	53 816.3	73 799.4	78 878.4	80 806.4
Accommodation and food service activities	3 009.6	3 139.5	4 942.8	5 490.1	5 674.3	2 044.4	3 008.4	2 357.3	2 998.3	2 932.8
Information and communication	4 874.5	4 895.1	7 072.4	10 617.3	12 421.9	34 336.0	35 806.3	35 845.7	42 594.4	50 441.3
Financial and insurance activities	215 556.7	240 722.9	247 696.9	287 739.6	300 347.8	404 099.2	469 118.2	495 519.5	533 439.3	569 696.9
Activities of holding companies	121 448.6	136 620.6	158 939.9	191 082.9	198 197.0	105 888.9	126 549.9	133 496.7	150 208.0	159 836.7
Real estate activities	8 783.0	9 747.4	12 839.4	16 420.6	16 870.3	46 784.8	58 827.5	63 519.7	60 754.2	61 771.8
Professional, scientific and technical activities	14 231.0	14 784.7	14 731.5	18 528.8	28 786.8	19 600.1	20 264.5	32 849.7	34 014.5	36 061.7
Administrative and support service activities	..	..	..	..	..	..	..	..	..	..
Public administration; activities of households and of extraterritorial organisations	..	..	..	..	..	..	..	..	..	..
Education	..	..	..	..	..	..	..	..	..	..
Human health and social work activities	..	..	..	..	..	..	..	..	..	..
Arts, entertainment and recreation	..	..	..	..	..	..	..	..	..	..
Other services	..	..	..	..	..	..	..	..	..	..
Not allocated and confidential	**4 693.5**	**6 133.6**	**6 313.6**	**6 811.1**	**7 208.7**	**19 209.1**	**17 521.4**	**14 218.5**	**13 738.9**	**16 825.4**
Private real estate activities	..	..	..	..	..	..	..	..	..	..

.. Not available; e Estimated value

Note: Detailed metadata at: *http://metalinks.oecd.org/idi/20220712/6d95.*

Source: *OECD International Direct Investment Statistics (database): https://doi.org/10.1787/idi-data-en*

CANADA

Table 6. Foreign direct investment income by industrial sector

Million US dollars

	Inward					Outward				
	2016	2017	2018	2019	2020	2016	2017	2018	2019	2020
All FDI activities	**31 001.1**	**37 274.4**	**41 599.4**	**42 323.2**	**24 886.0**	**40 774.1**	**54 142.8**	**62 400.7**	**64 145.9**	**56 118.1**
Agriculture, forestry and fishing	..	..	..	..	..	..	..	..	..	..
Mining and quarrying	..	..	..	..	..	..	..	..	..	..
Extraction activities	..	..	..	..	..	..	..	..	..	..
Manufacturing	..	..	..	..	..	..	..	..	..	..
of which:										
Food products, beverages and tobacco	..	..	..	..	..	..	..	..	..	..
Textiles, wood and paper products; printing	..	..	..	..	..	..	..	..	..	..
Chemical, rubber, plastic, non-metallic mineral products	..	..	..	..	..	..	..	..	..	..
Metal and machinery products, except electrical equipment	..	..	..	..	..	..	..	..	..	..
Motor vehicles, trailers, semi-trailers, other transport equipment	..	..	..	..	..	..	..	..	..	..
Other manufacturing	..	..	..	..	..	..	..	..	..	..
Electricity, gas, steam and air conditioning supply	..	..	..	..	..	..	..	..	..	..
Water supply; sewerage, waste management and remediation activities	..	..	..	..	..	..	..	..	..	..
Construction	..	..	..	..	..	..	..	..	..	..
Services	..	..	..	..	..	..	..	..	..	..
Wholesale and retail trade; repair of motor vehicles and motorcycles	..	..	..	..	..	..	..	..	..	..
Transportation and storage	..	..	..	..	..	..	..	..	..	..
Accommodation and food service activities	..	..	..	..	..	..	..	..	..	..
Information and communication	..	..	..	..	..	..	..	..	..	..
Financial and insurance activities	..	..	..	..	..	..	..	..	..	..
Activities of holding companies	..	..	..	..	..	..	..	..	..	..
Real estate activities	..	..	..	..	..	..	..	..	..	..
Professional, scientific and technical activities	..	..	..	..	..	..	..	..	..	..
Administrative and support service activities	..	..	..	..	..	..	..	..	..	..
Public administration; activities of households and of extraterritorial organisations	..	..	..	..	..	..	..	..	..	..
Education	..	..	..	..	..	..	..	..	..	..
Human health and social work activities	..	..	..	..	..	..	..	..	..	..
Arts, entertainment and recreation	..	..	..	..	..	..	..	..	..	..
Other services	..	..	..	..	..	..	..	..	..	..
Not allocated and confidential	..	..	..	**42 323.2**	**24 886.0**	..	..	..	**64 145.9**	**56 118.1**
Private real estate activities	..	..	..	..	..	..	..	..	..	..

.. Not available

Note: Detailed metadata at: *http://metalinks.oecd.org/idi/20220712/6d95*.

Source: *OECD International Direct Investment Statistics (database): https://doi.org/10.1787/idi-data-en*

CZECH REPUBLIC

Table 1. Foreign direct investment flows by country

Million US dollars

	Inward					Outward				
	2016	2017	2018	2019	2020	2016	2017	2018	2019	2020
WORLD	**9 814.5**	**9 517.9**	**11 010.4**	**10 108.9**	**6 291.9**	**2 181.7**	**7 557.0**	**8 662.6**	**4 128.4**	**3 142.1**
OECD COUNTRIES	**.. c**	**.. c**	**11 773.8**	**8 820.2**	**5 886.3**	**.. c**	**3 372.3**	**9 873.9**	**4 177.9**	**2 011.0**
Australia	31.3	23.3	-17.7	17.6	1.1	.. c	.. c	.. c	.. c	-0.3
Austria	-188.5	861.0	650.0	2 306.4	735.7	5.5	17.1	10.5	6.4	213.5
Belgium	-484.9	-739.0	2 913.9	699.3	1 688.9	-17.2	0.6	28.2	-119.0	-1.8
Canada	-53.1	8.3	32.7	51.1	5.7	-3.0	7.3	-0.3	8.4	-0.5
Chile	0.0	0.0	0.8	-1.5	0.7	0.1	.. c	.. c	.. c	-13.1
Colombia	0.3	-0.9	0.4	-0.9	0.1	0.5	-0.3	0.5	-0.5	0.0
Costa Rica	.. c	.. c	.. c	.. c	.. c	-0.1	0.0	-	-	-
Czech Republic	-	-	-	-	-	-	-	-	-	-
Denmark	73.0	6.7	-135.4	52.5	41.1	0.4	2.0	-1.7	-1.3	2.0
Estonia	4.0	2.3	1.1	-1.3	2.1	-1.5	0.6	-1.9	0.0	0.0
Finland	13.1	57.6	30.3	29.9	-32.8	20.5	2.2	5.7	19.0	-6.7
France	707.3	416.4	784.0	209.9	-356.1	42.5	8.0	-47.3	2 034.5	133.7
Germany	2 535.1	4 553.2	2 406.4	-1 014.8	198.0	-227.7	234.5	108.2	60.8	-400.6
Greece	-4.4	-10.5	4.5	0.9	2.7	0.2	-937.4	0.5	1.2	269.8
Hungary	20.0	126.4	-123.8	314.2	363.9	-29.8	175.5	247.2	199.9	76.8
Iceland	.. c	.. c	.. c	36.0	0.2	0.0	0.0	0.0	0.0	0.0
Ireland	41.3	-184.2	163.9	140.1	-141.6	-294.8	-368.3	-94.3	-48.5	4.6
Israel	52.2	-0.5	42.5	36.5	-3.3	-	.. c	.. c	.. c	.. c
Italy	739.9	325.4	313.6	304.7	203.0	-89.2	151.3	27.9	-262.7	143.8
Japan	97.1	122.1	171.3	148.3	646.7	0.1	.. c	-3.5	-0.1	11.8
Korea	167.6	478.2	67.6	-140.1	134.8	-0.5	.. c	.. c	.. c	.. c
Latvia	9.1	4.4	2.0	-7.3	4.2	3.7	11.2	-4.4	-1.7	11.3
Lithuania	-6.1	4.5	-10.5	-7.4	5.4	-0.2	5.5	-9.0	5.9	-0.6
Luxembourg	1 015.7	2 493.6	2 631.0	3 490.7	1 001.3	379.0	2 785.0	894.0	-377.1	599.8
Mexico	-19.5	-44.4	36.5	31.5	52.4	-6.0	2.3	0.2	-0.6	18.8
Netherlands	2 044.1	-2 043.9	459.4	715.2	-710.7	464.0	2 330.7	3 324.3	862.2	1 110.7
New Zealand	-1.7	0.6	1.3	-0.9	-3.1	-	-	-	-	-
Norway	99.9	-13.9	46.7	44.6	6.4	50.6	7.8	-84.0	-7.6	-6.0
Poland	450.9	997.5	-305.8	-15.4	451.0	-67.5	240.6	572.3	124.9	518.5
Portugal	-27.6	11.2	-10.4	0.6	-9.2	0.2	-0.2	-0.1	0.8	0.1
Slovak Republic	361.2	-232.3	404.1	158.7	441.4	607.2	-1 148.4	1 169.8	539.7	-333.2
Slovenia	1.1	-0.5	73.1	-37.5	-10.8	233.9	-9.9	-69.6	20.1	-0.5
Spain	215.0	77.3	210.0	89.6	1.2	-1.1	15.1	30.5	65.2	5.1
Sweden	246.2	261.8	332.6	241.4	-28.6	3.7	4.8	-2.7	-27.1	-24.3
Switzerland	426.1	1 190.3	315.5	-512.7	439.2	-45.5	-19.0	1 347.2	263.3	179.6
Turkey	2.8	-9.6	16.2	19.7	7.5	-44.0	56.4	76.9	-118.7	-110.6
United Kingdom	-620.1	-583.0	34.0	1 157.9	529.1	8.6	-283.2	1 840.2	829.7	-302.7
United States	81.4	-303.0	232.4	261.8	218.9	-29.2	48.1	550.8	98.7	-87.9
EUROPE	**8 666.3**	**9 273.3**	**10 729.7**	**9 599.4**	**4 917.4**	**2 182.8**	**7 331.9**	**7 889.4**	**4 222.1**	**2 969.7**
Bulgaria	6.0	4.2	-4.9	6.4	-8.9	77.6	48.8	3.9	-18.2	237.8
Croatia	3.4	3.3	5.3	4.7	-0.1	-63.2	103.0	131.6	-140.2	31.3
Cyprus	1 099.5	1 657.7	-550.4	654.6	352.6	693.2	3 667.1	-1 953.1	534.4	482.7
Malta	-194.5	16.4	-18.0	180.2	42.9	28.3	23.2	-0.9	-12.4	5.9
Montenegro	-0.6	0.5	0.3	.. c	-	-	-	0.0	-0.2	-0.1
Romania	20.5	-14.7	-9.2	-5.4	-205.1	348.5	150.9	296.1	-456.5	122.8
Russian Federation	-1.3	-123.8	103.2	189.3	-77.5	33.4	51.3	-8.7	213.5	-31.9
Ukraine	35.4	13.0	5.2	25.8	7.5	-1.4	3.8	9.6	30.2	4.4
AFRICA	**.. c**	**.. c**	**-32.4**	**35.2**	**437.6**	**.. c**	**.. c**	**66.7**	**-100.7**	**-11.8**
Northern Africa	.. c	.. c	-9.1	-14.5	433.5	.. c	.. c	.. c	.. c	0.6
Algeria	.. c	.. c	-	-	.. c	-	-	-	-	-
Egypt	3.8	-3.8	2.0	-0.5	-0.4	.. c	.. c	.. c	.. c	0.3
Libya	-	-	-	-	-	-	-	-	-	-
Morocco	-0.9	-2.7	-11.2	-16.2	436.8	-	-	-	-	.. c
Tunisia	0.1	0.4	0.2	2.2	-2.9	-0.1	-0.9	1.0	0.0	.. c
Other African countries	-0.6	11.9	-23.4	49.8	4.1	5.6	23.9	21.3	-93.5	-12.4
Nigeria	.. c	-2.4	-4.5	-4.9	.. c	-0.2	0.0	-	-	-
South Africa	2.2	16.7	-15.8	29.5	8.8	5.6	23.9	21.3	-95.0	-12.4
AMERICA	**.. c**	**-405.1**	**216.5**	**199.2**	**180.4**	**-38.0**	**91.7**	**523.7**	**90.4**	**-82.0**
Northern America	28.3	-294.7	265.1	312.9	224.6	-32.2	55.4	550.5	107.2	-88.4
Central America and Caribbean countries	-29.3	-112.3	-53.0	-100.3	-43.2	-7.1	3.4	18.9	-16.7	18.8
Bahamas	28.8	27.1	8.8	-89.6	-11.5	-	-	-	-	-
Bermuda	-0.6	-24.6	0.2	6.3	2.2	-	-	-	-	-
Cayman Islands	-4.3	0.6	-7.2	1.2	2.9	-	-	-	-	-
El Salvador	-	.. c	.. c	7.2	.. c	-	-	-	-	-
Guatemala	-	0.0	-1.0	0.0	-	-	-	-	-	-
Honduras	.. c	.. c	.. c	.. c	-	-	-	-	-	-
Nicaragua	.. c	.. c	.. c	.. c	1.7	-	-	-	-	-
Panama	10.2	-11.4	21.6	-40.4	-11.8	-	-	-	0.1	-
Virgin Islands, U.S.	-	-	-	-	-	-	-	-	-	-
South America	.. c	1.8	4.4	-13.4	-1.0	1.2	32.9	-45.6	-0.1	-12.3
Argentina	0.5	2.7	1.6	-0.5	-0.5	.. c	.. c	.. c	.. c	0.9
Bolivia	-	-	-	-	.. c	-	-	-	-	-
Brazil	5.3	0.3	0.1	-9.9	-0.8	-1.0	0.2	-7.4	-0.4	-0.2
Ecuador	.. c	.. c	.. c	.. c	0.1	-	-	-	-	-
Paraguay	-	-	-	-	-	-	-	-	-	-
Peru	-0.2	.. c	.. c	-0.5	.. c	0.4	-0.1	0.1	-0.1	0.0
Uruguay	-	-	-	-	.. c	-	-	-	-	-
Venezuela	-	-	.. c	.. c	-	-	-	-	-	-

CZECH REPUBLIC

Table 1. Foreign direct investment flows by country *(cont.)*

Million US dollars

	Inward					Outward				
	2016	2017	2018	2019	2020	2016	2017	2018	2019	2020
ASIA	**.. c**	**.. c**	**106.9**	**240.4**	**756.2**	**55.8**	**131.5**	**190.1**	**-81.0**	**266.7**
Near and Middle East	.. c	.. c	27.6	148.5	-42.6	78.3	151.7	64.2	51.8	247.1
Gulf Arabian countries	0.9	-8.9	-14.8	98.7	-42.5	-2.4	.. c	-1.9	6.0	0.1
Kuwait	.. c	.. c	0.4	0.5	-	-	-	-	-	-
Qatar	.. c	.. c	.. c	0.0	-36.4	-	-	-	-	-
Saudi Arabia	2.5	-5.1	2.8	38.3	1.9	-	-	-	.. c	-0.1
United Arab Emirates	-7.8	-4.6	-8.9	58.9	-8.8	-2.4	2.3	-1.9	.. c	0.2
Other Near and Middle East	.. c	.. c	42.5	49.7	0.0	80.7	.. c	.. c	45.8	.. c
Jordan	-1.2	1.3	0.0	0.6	.. c	-	-	-	-	-
Other Asian countries	1 108.1	508.5	79.3	91.9	798.8	-22.5	-20.2	126.0	-132.8	19.6
China	512.0	-59.6	-55.0	39.9	116.2	-45.4	-32.8	14.0	-20.7	-55.9
Hong Kong, China	46.2	-9.0	-11.2	61.1	-42.0	0.3	0.1	-0.1	2.5	12.0
India	-108.9	-23.2	-1.7	20.8	18.0	21.2	8.4	118.4	-118.4	50.7
Indonesia	-0.4	-0.4	-2.0	4.7	0.2	-0.3	-0.1	-	2.5	-2.5
Iran, Islamic Republic of	0.3	-	-	.. c	.. c	-	-	-	-	-
Malaysia	10.9	1.3	-0.7	-1.4	2.8	-	-	-	-	.. c
Philippines	0.0	1.7	2.7	2.7	-0.3	-	-	0.2	2.2	0.8
Singapore	121.5	-9.0	104.8	35.8	-77.3	.. c	.. c	.. c	.. c	-0.2
Chinese Taipei	209.3	-7.5	-198.6	-54.9	0.1	-	0.4	-0.1	-0.4	-0.4
Thailand	-11.5	12.0	1.9	-9.7	2.2	0.1	0.0	.. c	.. c	-0.1
Viet Nam	-1.2	2.8	-0.9	4.4	-0.6	0.8	6.7	-1.4	-9.4	2.1
AUSTRALIA, OCEANIA AND POLAR REGIONS	**31.3**	**117.5**	**-6.3**	**18.1**	**-1.2**	**.. c**	**.. c**	**-5.1**	**-1.9**	**-0.3**
WORLD unallocated and confidential	**.. d**	**.. d**	**-3.9**	**16.7**	**1.5**	**.. d**	**.. d**	**-2.3**	**-0.5**	**-0.2**
European Union (since 01/02/2020)	**..**	**..**	**..**	**..**	**..**	**..**	**..**	**..**	**..**	**..**
G20 countries excl. European Union	**4 081.5**	**4 794.5**	**4 110.2**	**1 360.1**	**1 707.6**	**-334.5**	**.. c**	**2 682.3**	**2 637.9**	**-645.8**
G20 OECD countries	**3 669.9**	**4 986.9**	**4 077.0**	**1 047.8**	**1 641.2**	**.. c**	**224.2**	**2 545.5**	**2 650.5**	**-594.5**
G20 Non-OECD countries	**411.7**	**-192.4**	**33.3**	**312.3**	**66.4**	**.. c**	**.. c**	**136.8**	**-12.5**	**-51.3**
MENA countries	**4.2**	**-13.9**	**-23.1**	**84.3**	**391.6**	**.. c**	**-26.4**	**43.6**	**-1.3**	**0.7**
ASEAN countries	**.. c**	**8.6**	**100.6**	**36.6**	**-72.9**	**.. c**	**.. c**	**-1.6**	**-5.0**	**-0.2**

- Nil; .. Not available; c Confidential data; d Secondary Confidentiality

Note: Detailed metadata at: *http://metalinks.oecd.org/idi/20220712/6d95.*

Source: *OECD International Direct Investment Statistics (database)*: *https://doi.org/10.1787/idi-data-en*

CZECH REPUBLIC

Table 2. Foreign direct investment positions by country

At year end

Million US dollars

	Inward					Outward				
	2016	2017	2018	2019	2020	2016	2017	2018	2019	2020
WORLD	**121 854.6**	**155 994.1**	**164 224.5**	**171 333.7**	**188 771.7**	**19 426.3**	**32 364.1**	**41 003.4**	**45 134.6**	**56 213.0**
OECD COUNTRIES	**113 133.7**	**145 348.9**	**153 452.7**	**158 922.8**	**175 181.1**	**14 557.3**	**22 431.2**	**32 851.7**	**35 829.7**	**44 739.1**
Australia	88.1	103.2	101.2	5.2	5.5	-	.. c	.. c	.. c	-6.4
Austria	11 581.3	13 659.9	13 675.2	14 919.1	16 477.1	41.1	72.7	73.9	81.8	339.2
Belgium	4 974.1	5 314.4	5 524.2	6 164.8	6 514.5	184.5	212.5	225.4	98.6	106.6
Canada	390.3	488.6	570.2	220.3	222.7	.. c	28.3	26.2	35.3	36.1
Chile	1.3	1.6	1.6	-	-	-0.2	.. c	.. c	0.3	0.4
Colombia	-	-	-	-	-	0.4	-	0.4	-	0.0
Costa Rica	-	.. c	-	-	-	-0.1	-	-	-	-
Czech Republic	9 482.4	22 133.1	23 397.5	24 810.1	32 570.1	-	-	-	-	-
Denmark	869.2	927.5	823.0	799.3	845.5	5.8	8.6	6.6	11.9	13.9
Estonia	.. c	3.3	7.0	11.4	12.1	0.7	2.6	0.2	0.4	0.5
Finland	356.8	489.6	480.0	429.0	507.8	5.0	7.0	8.5	20.5	13.8
France	10 620.3	12 579.8	11 780.4	12 135.6	12 837.6	233.8	286.8	233.1	1 043.2	1 318.4
Germany	26 097.5	31 225.7	34 730.2	37 927.1	40 112.1	492.8	857.5	721.6	765.7	463.4
Greece	.. c	4.6	.. c	12.6	13.4	881.3	3.8	4.2	5.1	293.1
Hungary	244.8	382.7	393.8	302.8	321.7	132.0	430.8	403.8	567.1	730.3
Iceland	.. c	.. c	.. c	.. c	.. c	0.0	0.0	0.0	0.0	0.0
Ireland	576.9	586.5	379.0	514.3	534.1	511.2	188.8	89.1	36.2	47.6
Israel	607.5	733.3	693.7	761.9	819.8	-	.. c	.. c	.. c	3.6
Italy	5 676.6	6 222.4	6 239.7	6 911.8	7 311.5	-37.2	119.7	164.8	285.2	3 628.9
Japan	2 519.3	3 284.3	3 328.8	4 163.1	4 408.9	.. c	.. c	0.0	0.6	1.0
Korea	2 294.0	3 174.2	2 892.5	3 971.3	4 268.1	.. c	.. c	.. c	-	0.0
Latvia	15.2	25.3	22.8	.. c	.. c	8.3	26.5	14.5	10.0	23.0
Lithuania	.. c	2.8	.. c	.. c	.. c	1.4	7.3	-1.5	2.2	2.0
Luxembourg	1 838.7	1 978.9	2 286.3	1 967.7	2 274.3	952.7	6 180.9	9 690.6	10 201.0	12 029.2
Mexico	293.2	.. c	.. c	370.6	392.0	4.6	7.0	7.0	7.1	9.4
Netherlands	8 392.4	10 505.4	12 092.7	7 731.2	7 550.5	6 581.6	9 636.3	11 967.4	11 987.7	14 405.4
New Zealand	-	-	2.3	38.9	41.1	-	-	-	-	0.0
Norway	120.7	147.6	151.4	172.9	155.0	.. c	131.7	67.8	0.6	-5.3
Poland	2 038.8	3 869.4	4 200.0	4 238.8	4 486.5	645.1	794.8	1 138.3	1 309.8	1 845.8
Portugal	49.3	67.0	32.2	48.6	47.4	4.3	4.7	4.4	5.2	5.8
Slovak Republic	2 766.9	1 986.1	2 779.2	3 041.6	3 217.9	3 085.1	2 888.4	3 633.7	4 385.0	4 948.4
Slovenia	34.9	34.6	48.3	26.4	27.9	211.1	218.9	103.6	117.9	128.0
Spain	1 102.0	1 325.8	1 276.1	1 377.7	1 501.9	28.6	48.6	82.5	140.7	156.8
Sweden	946.2	1 307.3	1 615.4	1 811.0	1 935.0	22.4	29.8	19.6	-1.9	-3.2
Switzerland	4 657.7	6 157.6	6 758.2	6 157.1	6 766.6	1.0	-19.6	1 274.3	1 298.3	1 614.1
Turkey	.. c	2.6	7.6	7.9	28.1	44.1	83.3	-74.2	-336.1	-567.2
United Kingdom	5 604.1	5 949.8	5 562.8	5 831.9	6 192.9	314.1	58.0	2 283.4	3 035.1	2 461.6
United States	8 867.5	10 321.0	11 251.4	11 998.0	12 735.8	69.7	85.2	685.8	717.7	694.8
EUROPE	**.. c**	**133 052.4**	**140 584.1**	**144 486.5**	**160 264.5**	**.. c**	**31 190.6**	**39 215.8**	**43 113.2**	**54 128.6**
Bulgaria	10.4	9.0	12.2	13.2	14.0	482.7	742.0	583.1	836.5	1 196.0
Croatia	17.1	37.8	35.8	24.6	26.0	1.9	114.5	555.3	394.6	459.7
Cyprus	4 096.8	4 424.5	4 638.4	3 689.4	3 981.1	1 923.5	5 890.9	3 568.5	4 083.5	5 162.2
Malta	363.1	440.8	440.7	439.9	481.8	42.8	53.6	16.6	14.6	239.7
Montenegro	-	-	-	-	-	-	-	-0.3	-0.2	-0.3
Romania	3.8	3.3	4.0	4.1	4.4	1 039.0	1 211.2	1 473.3	1 557.7	1 841.1
Russian Federation	799.6	955.7	793.2	861.7	945.2	192.7	272.5	262.1	507.9	491.3
Ukraine	89.6	117.0	118.8	140.7	150.2	4.2	9.7	12.9	69.0	81.3
AFRICA	**43.2**	**.. c**	**78.1**	**255.8**	**273.7**	**.. c**	**.. c**	**137.8**	**36.0**	**23.9**
Northern Africa	5.7	.. c	.. c	.. c	.. c	.. c	.. c	.. c	.. c	.. c
Algeria	-	-	-	-	-	-	-	-	-	-
Egypt	.. c	.. c	.. c	.. c	.. c	.. c	.. c	.. c	.. c	.. c
Libya	-	-	-	-	-	-	-	-	-	-
Morocco	-	-	-	-	-	-	-	-	-	0.1
Tunisia	.. c	-	-	-	-	0.8	-0.4	0.7	0.7	0.8
Other African countries	37.5	14.6	73.5	251.5	269.2	2.7	28.0	49.3	-45.0	-61.4
Nigeria	-	-	-	-	-	-0.3	-	-	-	-
South Africa	.. c	-	.. c	259.9	274.9	3.1	28.0	49.3	-46.5	-63.4
AMERICA	**.. c**	**12 143.3**	**12 978.6**	**13 241.8**	**14 041.4**	**.. c**	**180.6**	**764.3**	**789.2**	**769.5**
Northern America	9 257.8	10 809.7	11 821.5	12 218.3	12 958.5	.. c	113.5	712.1	753.0	730.9
Central America and Caribbean countries	1 042.3	1 329.7	1 151.2	1 032.7	1 092.6	4.5	24.5	50.0	33.4	35.6
Bahamas	191.9	.. c	.. c	.. c	.. c	-	-	-	-	-
Bermuda	65.3	68.9	66.0	35.1	.. c	-	-	-	-	-
Cayman Islands	290.4	448.9	219.2	195.9	207.2	-	-	-	-	-
El Salvador	-	-	-	-	-	-	-	-	-	-
Guatemala	-	-	-	-	-	-	-	-	-	-
Honduras	-	-	-	-	-	-	-	-	-	-
Nicaragua	-	-	-	-	-	-	-	-	-	-
Panama	-53.3	-65.1	-59.6	54.9	54.6	-	-	-	0.4	0.4
Virgin Islands, U.S.	-	-	-	-	-	-	-	-	-	-
South America	.. c	4.0	5.9	.. c	.. c	9.7	42.6	2.2	2.8	2.9
Argentina	-	-	-	-	-	.. c	.. c	.. c	.. c	2.1
Bolivia	-	-	-	-	-	-	-	-	-	-
Brazil	1.8	2.3	2.8	.. c	.. c	0.1	-0.3	0.0	0.1	-0.9
Ecuador	.. c	-	-	-	-	-	-	-	-	-
Paraguay	-	-	-	-	-	-	-	-	-	-
Peru	-	-	-	-	-	0.0	-	0.1	-	0.0
Uruguay	-	-	-	-	-	-	-	-	-	-
Venezuela	-	-	1.5	1.6	1.7	-	-	-	-	-

Table 2. Foreign direct investment positions by country *(cont.)*

At year end

Million US dollars

	Inward					Outward				
	2016	2017	2018	2019	2020	2016	2017	2018	2019	2020
ASIA	**7 656.0**	**10 526.7**	**10 335.8**	**13 138.5**	**13 968.7**	**.. c**	**858.8**	**852.2**	**1 165.1**	**1 260.2**
Near and Middle East	.. c	.. c	824.2	1 012.6	1 095.4	.. c	713.9	321.6	768.4	809.4
Gulf Arabian countries	.. c	100.7	71.7	121.2	136.4	.. c	.. c	1.5	7.5	8.0
Kuwait	6.9	6.3	.. c	.. c	.. c	-	-	-	-	-
Qatar	-	-	-	-	-	-	-	-	-	-
Saudi Arabia	7.2	.. c	-0.8	34.8	39.9	-	-	-	.. c	6.2
United Arab Emirates	66.2	81.4	58.5	72.4	84.0	.. c	1.3	.. c	.. c	1.7
Other Near and Middle East	632.3	.. c	752.5	891.4	959.0	186.9	.. c	.. c	760.9	801.3
Jordan	-	1.5	1.4	2.0	2.1	-	-	-	-	-
Other Asian countries	.. c	.. c	9 511.6	12 125.9	12 873.3	153.4	144.9	530.6	396.7	450.8
China	794.3	1 100.9	1 012.0	1 500.7	1 591.6	64.0	39.2	424.4	409.1	410.9
Hong Kong, China	191.7	244.8	243.8	251.6	276.0	5.2	5.2	6.0	8.5	25.0
India	97.1	91.6	126.0	103.2	109.2	68.7	80.7	196.7	70.8	98.2
Indonesia	-	-	-	-	-	0.2	-	-	2.5	2.6
Iran, Islamic Republic of	-	-	-	-	-	-	-	-	-	-
Malaysia	.. c	.. c	.. c	15.5	16.4	-	-	-	-	0.0
Philippines	-	-	-	.. c	.. c	-	-	0.2	2.4	2.5
Singapore	392.7	824.7	911.6	1 027.9	1 087.2	.. c	.. c	.. c	.. c	-115.6
Chinese Taipei	554.6	833.7	798.3	917.5	980.3	-	0.4	0.4	0.0	-0.3
Thailand	-	-	92.9	.. c	.. c	0.0	-	.. c	-	0.1
Viet Nam	5.1	6.4	-	-	-	11.5	18.1	16.7	7.3	10.8
AUSTRALIA, OCEANIA AND POLAR REGIONS	**95.9**	**.. c**	**117.0**	**47.3**	**50.0**	**-**	**.. c**	**-4.3**	**-6.3**	**-6.4**
WORLD unallocated and confidential	**.. d**	**.. d**	**130.9**	**146.9**	**155.4**	**.. d**	**.. d**	**37.6**	**37.4**	**37.2**
European Union (since 01/02/2020)	**..**	**..**	**..**	**..**	**143 618.7**	**..**	**..**	**..**	**..**	**49 395.6**
G20 countries excl. European Union	**64 159.4**	**75 830.8**	**78 741.4**	**86 292.4**	**91 464.7**	**.. c**	**.. c**	**4 974.9**	**6 498.5**	**8 987.3**
G20 OECD countries	**.. c**	**.. c**	**76 771.5**	**83 542.7**	**88 515.3**	**1 142.0**	**1 525.0**	**4 041.1**	**5 547.6**	**8 040.2**
G20 Non-OECD countries	**.. c**	**.. c**	**1 969.9**	**2 749.6**	**2 949.5**	**.. c**	**.. c**	**933.8**	**950.9**	**947.2**
MENA countries	**94.9**	**108.6**	**79.8**	**149.3**	**166.1**	**86.2**	**67.5**	**90.0**	**88.4**	**93.3**
ASEAN countries	**.. c**	**.. c**	**1 019.2**	**1 133.3**	**1 144.7**	**.. c**	**.. c**	**-98.2**	**-103.2**	**-99.5**

- Nil; .. Not available; c Confidential data; d Secondary Confidentiality

Note: Inward FDI positions are allocated according to the ultimate investing country. Detailed metadata at: *http://metalinks.oecd.org/idi/20220712/6d95*.

Source: *OECD International Direct Investment Statistics (database): https://doi.org/10.1787/idi-data-en*

CZECH REPUBLIC

Table 3. Foreign direct investment income by country

Million US dollars

	Inward					Outward				
	2016	2017	2018	2019	2020	2016	2017	2018	2019	2020
WORLD	**15 343.8**	**19 127.2**	**19 259.5**	**20 342.6**	**14 203.8**	**2 014.9**	**4 665.4**	**4 194.2**	**5 619.4**	**4 449.0**
OECD COUNTRIES	**.. c**	**.. c**	**18 890.1**	**19 685.1**	**13 902.7**	**1 585.0**	**3 715.0**	**3 754.0**	**4 213.3**	**3 485.6**
Australia	2.6	2.9	4.6	6.5	3.8	-	.. c	.. c	.. c	.. c
Austria	1 982.7	2 029.7	2 292.9	2 477.0	1 214.3	2.2	3.0	12.5	5.0	7.1
Belgium	1 003.2	804.4	1 148.6	1 333.0	631.4	2.8	3.3	-0.1	-0.7	-0.1
Canada	7.7	6.9	14.0	5.6	9.5	.. c	-2.2	-0.2	4.2	0.1
Chile	-	-	-	-	-	0.1	-	.. c	0.0	0.0
Colombia	-	-	-	-	-	0.2	-	0.0	-	0.0
Costa Rica	-	-	-	-	-	-0.1	-	-	-	-
Czech Republic	-	-	-	-	-	-	-	-	-	-
Denmark	99.5	92.0	109.0	86.9	69.8	0.7	1.0	0.8	-0.9	2.5
Estonia	-1.3	1.9	0.5	1.0	0.4	-1.4	0.5	-0.1	0.1	0.1
Finland	54.6	45.6	52.7	40.6	60.4	4.4	2.0	-7.9	-2.8	-6.1
France	1 187.1	1 316.2	1 386.7	1 239.3	682.6	10.7	11.2	21.0	41.8	1.7
Germany	2 666.0	2 984.8	3 450.1	3 259.3	2 410.8	34.3	286.9	-74.5	8.6	86.8
Greece	-0.4	.. c	.. c	.. c	1.7	-	0.1	0.1	-0.4	-0.1
Hungary	102.6	-5.1	23.7	31.4	64.5	-1.0	60.8	51.7	72.1	40.1
Iceland	-	-	-	.. c	.. c	0.0	0.0	0.0	0.0	0.0
Ireland	0.7	-8.9	5.8	61.2	13.6	-1.3	2.0	3.5	3.3	3.2
Israel	4.6	3.2	4.9	5.3	5.3	-	.. c	-	.. c	.. c
Italy	373.8	493.2	553.0	557.5	267.5	-0.1	1.8	24.7	166.0	167.5
Japan	151.9	117.0	91.8	86.5	52.1	.. c	.. c	-0.2	0.0	-0.1
Korea	413.9	351.8	351.7	390.2	-12.4	-0.5	-0.6	-	-	-
Latvia	3.4	4.6	.. c	.. c	4.0	1.3	13.3	9.5	7.0	4.4
Lithuania	.. c	1.7	3.9	.. c	5.6	-0.2	-0.3	-2.7	-1.1	-0.3
Luxembourg	1 786.1	4 721.1	2 958.1	3 797.1	3 452.5	3.9	1 342.0	1 409.1	1 614.3	1 491.3
Mexico	-2.4	-3.4	-3.4	.. c	.. c	1.2	1.1	0.6	0.2	2.3
Netherlands	2 982.4	3 518.3	3 365.1	3 668.3	2 507.5	1 314.7	1 620.3	1 621.8	1 540.5	1 171.8
New Zealand	-	-	-	-	0.1	-	-	-	-	-
Norway	30.3	20.9	29.7	29.0	22.6	1.9	.. c	-8.7	0.0	-6.1
Poland	286.7	209.3	676.2	185.0	417.8	-21.4	66.9	104.9	-19.4	79.9
Portugal	-19.1	-13.4	-3.8	-4.3	-11.4	.. c	0.0	-0.1	0.3	0.1
Slovak Republic	300.5	325.8	431.6	252.9	490.8	213.5	221.5	267.6	395.9	360.4
Slovenia	11.3	8.3	12.8	11.3	27.8	16.5	20.4	6.7	8.0	4.4
Spain	96.2	106.7	111.9	141.4	111.4	2.3	2.2	4.1	7.2	7.8
Sweden	224.5	203.8	366.1	414.2	229.0	.. c	-0.1	-2.4	-0.6	-3.2
Switzerland	483.3	670.7	759.0	973.4	648.0	0.1	0.7	254.2	242.1	176.8
Turkey	.. c	1.1	0.8	0.4	0.5	-26.7	25.8	-68.6	-21.3	-58.7
United Kingdom	297.9	315.6	512.6	450.2	367.2	1.5	2.0	112.1	85.9	0.8
United States	191.0	190.9	175.0	177.3	151.1	7.2	12.7	14.6	58.8	-49.2
EUROPE	**.. c**	**18 552.8**	**18 827.8**	**19 682.4**	**14 131.6**	**1 928.8**	**4 637.3**	**4 095.6**	**5 534.5**	**4 560.0**
Bulgaria	-1.3	.. c	.. c	-0.3	7.4	26.1	44.8	41.7	70.2	90.2
Croatia	2.0	1.0	2.5	4.0	2.6	-0.7	1.5	45.8	37.1	66.3
Cyprus	572.2	710.2	677.4	670.9	497.4	307.4	683.2	23.3	1 038.0	558.7
Malta	28.3	52.4	24.8	41.9	11.4	25.9	.. c	.. c	11.8	18.1
Montenegro	-	-	-	-	-	-	-	-0.1	-0.1	0.0
Romania	0.3	-0.4	0.0	-1.2	4.8	-50.7	95.0	161.3	150.5	206.5
Russian Federation	7.8	8.1	-86.0	-10.0	-57.3	-10.7	44.7	25.6	84.6	49.3
Ukraine	-0.3	-0.3	-3.2	-1.2	-3.1	1.2	1.1	3.3	13.6	8.0
AFRICA	**.. c**	**-3.8**	**-5.1**	**0.9**	**-5.5**	**.. c**	**.. c**	**17.8**	**7.9**	**-4.4**
Northern Africa	0.1	0.3	0.7	-0.2	-2.2	.. c	.. c	.. c	.. c	14.1
Algeria	-	-	-	-	-	-	-	-	-	-
Egypt	.. c	.. c	.. c	.. c	.. c	.. c	.. c	.. c	.. c	.. c
Libya	-	-	-	-	-	-	-	-	-	-
Morocco	-	.. c	.. c	.. c	.. c	-	-	-	-	-
Tunisia	.. c	-	-	-	-	0.0	0.0	0.0	0.0	.. c
Other African countries	.. c	-4.1	-5.8	1.1	-3.3	2.6	1.1	-1.8	-6.3	-18.4
Nigeria	-	-	-	-	-	-0.2	-	-	-	-
South Africa	-	-	-	-	-	2.6	1.2	-1.8	-6.3	-18.4
AMERICA	**200.8**	**.. c**	**177.3**	**146.8**	**100.0**	**.. c**	**13.0**	**33.0**	**46.3**	**-46.7**
Northern America	198.7	197.8	189.0	182.9	160.5	.. c	10.5	14.4	63.0	-49.1
Central America and Caribbean countries	2.2	3.5	-11.6	-36.1	-60.5	1.1	1.4	19.1	-15.9	2.3
Bahamas	11.1	8.0	9.1	.. c	7.7	-	-	-	-	-
Bermuda	0.6	0.7	2.2	.. c	.. c	-	-	-	-	-
Cayman Islands	1.4	1.1	2.4	1.1	2.9	-	-	-	-	-
El Salvador	-	-	-	-	-	-	-	-	-	-
Guatemala	-	-	-	-	-	-	-	-	-	-
Honduras	-	-	-	-	-	-	-	-	-	-
Nicaragua	.. c	.. c	.. c	-	.. c	-	-	-	-	-
Panama	-8.2	1.1	-2.8	-15.0	-2.1	-	-	-	0.1	-
Virgin Islands, U.S.	-	-	-	-	-	-	-	-	-	-
South America	0.0	.. c	.. c	.. c	.. c	-1.0	1.2	-0.4	-0.8	0.1
Argentina	-	-	-	-	-	.. c	-	0.0	-0.2	0.9
Bolivia	-	-	-	-	-	-	-	-	-	-
Brazil	.. c	.. c	.. c	.. c	.. c	-1.3	-0.9	-0.4	-0.3	-0.7
Ecuador	.. c	-	-	-	-	-	-	-	-	-
Paraguay	-	-	-	-	-	-	-	-	-	-
Peru	-	-	-	-	-	0.3	-	0.0	-	0.0
Uruguay	-	-	-	-	-	-	-	-	-	-
Venezuela	-	-	-	-	-	-	-	-	-	-

Table 3. Foreign direct investment income by country *(cont.)*

Million US dollars

	Inward					Outward				
	2016	2017	2018	2019	2020	2016	2017	2018	2019	2020
ASIA	**.. c**	**.. c**	**254.8**	**503.9**	**-26.9**	**.. c**	**2.4**	**47.5**	**30.7**	**-60.1**
Near and Middle East	.. c	.. c	9.0	15.7	8.7	.. c	30.9	40.7	29.6	1.5
Gulf Arabian countries	2.1	.. c	0.5	10.0	0.7	.. c	.. c	-0.1	0.2	0.0
Kuwait	-	-	-	-	-	-	-	-	-	-
Qatar	-	-	-	-	-	-	-	-	-	-
Saudi Arabia	.. c	-	.. c	0.1	0.1	-	-	-	-	-
United Arab Emirates	2.1	-0.9	0.5	9.6	0.4	.. c	0.0	.. c	.. c	0.0
Other Near and Middle East	.. c	4.7	8.6	5.8	8.0	66.5	.. c	40.8	29.4	.. c
Jordan	-	-	-	-	-	-	-	-	-	-
Other Asian countries	572.8	370.7	245.8	488.1	-35.6	-11.9	-28.5	6.8	1.1	-61.7
China	-17.9	-111.8	-252.5	-15.8	-101.9	-11.9	-31.7	3.9	-0.3	-3.6
Hong Kong, China	3.9	5.8	1.7	4.2	0.6	.. c	.. c	0.3	0.2	16.1
India	1.0	-0.8	-0.4	-0.1	0.6	1.2	4.1	3.3	1.7	-75.1
Indonesia	-	-	-	-	-	-0.4	-	-	-	-
Iran, Islamic Republic of	-	-	-	-	-	-	-	-	-	-
Malaysia	.. c	.. c	.. c	-2.8	-0.5	-	-	-	-	-
Philippines	.. c	.. c	.. c	.. c	.. c	-	-	-	-	-
Singapore	9.6	2.6	22.8	13.3	15.0	.. c	.. c	.. c	.. c	.. c
Chinese Taipei	9.1	3.7	29.3	13.5	9.2	-	-0.2	-0.2	-0.2	-0.3
Thailand	0.8	1.0	1.3	-	1.0	0.1	-	.. c	-	.. c
Viet Nam	-	-	-	-	-	-	0.3	-0.3	-0.2	-0.4
AUSTRALIA, OCEANIA AND POLAR REGIONS	**.. c**	**2.5**	**4.7**	**8.6**	**4.6**	**-**	**.. c**	**0.3**	**0.1**	**0.2**
WORLD unallocated and confidential	**.. d**	**.. d**	**0.0**	**0.0**	**-**	**.. d**	**- d**	**-**	**0.0**	**0.0**
European Union (since 01/02/2020)	**..**	**..**	**..**	**..**	**..**	**..**	**..**	**..**	**..**	**..**
G20 countries excl. European Union	**.. c**	**.. c**	**6 197.9**	**6 146.7**	**3 777.1**	**.. c**	**356.1**	**60.3**	**423.3**	**103.8**
G20 OECD countries	**.. c**	**5 776.9**	**6 537.0**	**6 172.5**	**3 935.6**	**45.2**	**338.7**	**29.7**	**344.1**	**151.5**
G20 Non-OECD countries	**-9.1**	**.. c**	**-339.1**	**-25.8**	**-158.5**	**.. c**	**17.4**	**30.6**	**79.2**	**-47.7**
MENA countries	**2.2**	**-0.7**	**1.1**	**9.8**	**-1.5**	**3.6**	**11.5**	**19.5**	**14.3**	**14.1**
ASEAN countries	**11.5**	**4.5**	**24.6**	**10.8**	**15.8**	**.. c**	**.. c**	**-0.4**	**-0.3**	**-0.5**

- Nil; .. Not available; c Confidential data; d Secondary Confidentiality

Note: Detailed metadata at: *http://metalinks.oecd.org/idi/20220712/6d95.*

Source: *OECD International Direct Investment Statistics (database)*: *https://doi.org/10.1787/idi-data-en*

Table 4. Foreign direct investment flows by industrial sector

Million US dollars

	Inward					Outward				
	2016	2017	2018	2019	2020	2016	2017	2018	2019	2020
All FDI activities	**9 814.5**	**9 517.9**	**11 010.4**	**10 108.9**	**6 291.9**	**2 181.7**	**7 557.0**	**8 662.6**	**4 128.4**	**3 142.1**
Agriculture, forestry and fishing	**26.6**	**-19.1**	**25.9**	**-46.5**	**11.2**	**10.7**	**0.5**	**-11.1**	**.. c**	**.. c**
Mining and quarrying	**.. c**	**.. c**	**-8.5**	**-50.6**	**39.3**	**4.9**	**1.6**	**10.6**	**-6.4**	**-0.6**
Extraction activities	3.9	12.9	-7.0	-11.7	35.0	-	-	-	-	-
Manufacturing	**2 310.9**	**1 595.5**	**3 734.1**	**1 545.7**	**671.2**	**260.1**	**444.3**	**170.4**	**137.8**	**55.2**
of which:										
Food products, beverages and tobacco	393.5	-5.3	-512.4	-252.2	-127.6	.. c	.. c	1.0	122.1	-2.9
Textiles, wood and paper products; printing	308.2	.. c	267.8	232.1	166.0	-29.0	29.0	73.7	-125.0	18.5
Chemical, rubber, plastic, non-metallic mineral products	305.0	355.0	-73.4	555.8	-53.7	.. c	177.5	-56.1	104.0	-4.5
Metal and machinery products, except electrical equipment	284.7	210.8	348.2	86.5	-313.4	.. c	-38.1	14.4	-47.3	56.9
Motor vehicles, trailers, semi-trailers, other transport equipment	732.7	.. c	3 033.6	120.2	867.0	.. c	.. c	273.8	137.3	-60.7
Other manufacturing	.. c	.. c	670.2	803.2	132.9	.. c	302.7	-136.3	-53.3	47.8
Electricity, gas, steam and air conditioning supply	**540.2**	**309.5**	**460.9**	**-35.1**	**689.5**	**.. c**	**.. c**	**907.2**	**-165.4**	**28.3**
Water supply; sewerage, waste management and remediation activities	**.. c**	**.. c**	**-204.5**	**10.9**	**-21.9**	**0.2**	**-0.2**	**-0.3**	**5.3**	**3.2**
Construction	**.. c**	**450.2**	**319.2**	**515.6**	**-13.6**	**543.9**	**233.9**	**66.4**	**-325.2**	**37.6**
Services	**6 869.8**	**6 917.1**	**6 086.9**	**7 825.5**	**4 973.4**	**1 071.5**	**6 954.9**	**7 549.1**	**4 521.9**	**3 018.5**
Wholesale and retail trade; repair of motor vehicles and motorcycles	419.1	.. c	377.4	365.8	1 323.6	38.3	.. c	440.3	-92.3	-557.3
Transportation and storage	-240.2	.. c	-58.4	291.6	499.0	.. c	80.6	-14.8	-303.7	-3.2
Accommodation and food service activities	.. c	.. c	35.3	123.7	-13.0	3.2	-0.3	.. c	.. c	.. c
Information and communication	.. c	.. c	30.6	537.8	391.4	-955.5	398.0	94.0	262.5	-216.7
Financial and insurance activities	2 068.7	.. c	6 107.6	6 060.0	2 850.7	.. c	5 931.1	3 970.5	2 439.9	3 421.9
Activities of holding companies	.. c	.. c	3 229.5	3 455.2	1 483.7	1 780.9	.. c	1 639.4	2 176.3	3 381.8
Real estate activities	.. c	1 507.2	-854.1	904.2	-156.9	-48.4	131.3	1 545.1	795.6	57.8
Professional, scientific and technical activities	1 011.5	.. c	911.0	-904.8	-58.7	-0.8	341.3	1 593.6	1 472.0	303.0
Administrative and support service activities	.. c	267.4	-502.7	430.0	128.0	-13.5	.. c	-68.3	-70.7	-5.7
Public administration; activities of households and of extraterritorial organisations	-	-	-	-	-	-	-	-	-	-
Education	-3.1	2.0	8.0	-5.6	-1.7	-	-	-	-	0.1
Human health and social work activities	9.1	.. c	38.1	-7.6	-19.1	-	-	-	-	.. c
Arts, entertainment and recreation	-0.1	33.3	-9.6	29.9	20.8	0.1	5.1	4.9	17.2	.. c
Other services	.. c	.. c	3.8	0.6	9.3	-4.3	.. c	.. c	3.0	.. c
Not allocated and confidential	**.. c**	**.. c**	**0.4**	**0.4**	**32.9**	**.. c**	**.. c**	**-22.1**	**.. c**	**.. c**
Private real estate activities	**299.0**	**139.9**	**596.0**	**342.9**	**-90.0**	**-3.3**	**27.3**	**-7.7**	**2.4**	**-2.3**

- Nil; c Confidential data

Note: Detailed metadata at: *http://metalinks.oecd.org/idi/20220712/6d95.*

Source: *OECD International Direct Investment Statistics (database): https://doi.org/10.1787/idi-data-en*

Table 5. Foreign direct investment positions by industrial sector

At year end

Million US dollars

	Inward					Outward				
	2016	2017	2018	2019	2020	2016	2017	2018	2019	2020
All FDI activities	**121 854.6**	**155 994.1**	**164 224.5**	**171 333.7**	**188 771.7**	**19 426.3**	**32 364.1**	**41 003.4**	**45 134.6**	**56 213.0**
Agriculture, forestry and fishing	**319.4**	**.. c**	**370.7**	**334.7**	**-**	**61.7**	**69.8**	**58.8**	**.. c**	**-**
Mining and quarrying	**.. c**	**672.9**	**637.2**	**585.1**	**-**	**14.9**	**14.7**	**32.3**	**17.9**	**-**
Extraction activities	265.4	353.7	340.5	322.0	-	-	-	-	-	-
Manufacturing	**38 458.9**	**45 505.7**	**46 661.3**	**48 417.5**	**51 740.3**	**1 581.3**	**2 421.3**	**3 143.4**	**3 423.9**	**3 646.0**
of which:										
Food products, beverages and tobacco	.. c	5 032.5	4 467.1	4 307.8	4 746.2	.. c	.. c	611.7	664.0	636.1
Textiles, wood and paper products; printing	2 689.1	3 237.8	3 224.9	3 537.7	3 867.4	98.2	200.9	236.3	137.3	181.8
Chemical, rubber, plastic, non-metallic mineral products	5 724.8	.. c	6 357.6	6 714.2	7 219.9	.. c	955.0	866.6	1 113.1	1 195.6
Metal and machinery products, except electrical equipment	.. c	11 892.9	11 764.3	12 401.9	13 135.4	.. c	276.6	218.3	161.8	180.6
Motor vehicles, trailers, semi-trailers, other transport equipment	9 627.7	.. c	12 684.7	12 643.4	13 372.9	.. c	.. c	934.9	1 064.3	1 042.2
Other manufacturing	6 469.6	7 976.8	8 162.8	8 812.6	9 398.5	85.8	.. c	275.7	283.6	409.7
Electricity, gas, steam and air conditioning supply	**3 859.4**	**4 747.7**	**4 973.3**	**4 759.6**	**5 034.3**	**.. c**	**779.2**	**1 667.7**	**1 348.0**	**1 849.2**
Water supply; sewerage, waste management and remediation activities	**935.9**	**.. c**	**690.6**	**672.6**	**711.4**	**1.9**	**2.1**	**1.7**	**7.1**	**1.6**
Construction	**1 733.0**	**2 551.9**	**2 390.4**	**2 869.9**	**3 037.0**	**832.5**	**1 382.4**	**995.6**	**1 319.4**	**1 052.9**
Services	**73 030.0**	**97 525.3**	**104 435.0**	**109 215.7**	**123 468.4**	**15 146.9**	**26 560.5**	**34 223.1**	**38 137.0**	**48 738.3**
Wholesale and retail trade; repair of motor vehicles and motorcycles	.. c	13 789.2	14 916.5	16 114.7	17 044.5	.. c	867.6	1 217.8	1 034.6	1 098.5
Transportation and storage	.. c	.. c	1 466.7	1 665.4	1 686.8	.. c	275.1	169.1	162.8	171.5
Accommodation and food service activities	.. c	.. c	689.3	837.3	885.7	-22.8	32.4	.. c	.. c	.. c
Information and communication	7 109.2	8 686.1	8 642.0	9 134.6	9 956.6	.. c	-626.9	-539.4	-316.8	-501.2
Financial and insurance activities	32 849.8	.. c	51 185.4	54 040.9	64 523.8	14 545.4	.. c	29 314.9	31 856.9	42 931.3
Activities of holding companies	7 123.5	15 236.4	19 523.4	21 138.0	29 652.6	12 799.5	.. c	25 661.8	28 600.8	39 129.4
Real estate activities	.. c	.. c	13 668.0	14 783.5	15 672.8	-41.1	141.1	1 566.3	2 359.6	2 421.2
Professional, scientific and technical activities	6 730.1	.. c	11 684.9	9 989.7	10 566.1	478.6	.. c	2 360.7	2 949.8	2 528.1
Administrative and support service activities	1 211.0	1 838.4	1 502.0	2 010.7	2 454.8	-6.9	.. c	14.5	-52.7	-51.3
Public administration; activities of households and of extraterritorial organisations	-	-	-	-	-	-	-	-	-	-
Education	33.0	42.9	42.3	35.3	37.3	-	-	-	-	-
Human health and social work activities	217.6	.. c	255.6	232.8	246.2	-	-	0.0	0.0	0.0
Arts, entertainment and recreation	76.7	.. c	210.4	225.8	240.4	70.4	83.7	69.5	92.5	90.0
Other services	.. c	.. c	172.0	144.9	153.3	30.6	.. c	19.7	22.3	20.7
Not allocated and confidential	**.. c**	**.. c**	**-2.1**	**-1.7**	**41.5**	**.. c**	**651.9**	**423.9**	**.. c**	**445.3**
Private real estate activities	**2 822.1**	**3 618.3**	**4 068.3**	**4 480.3**	**4 738.8**	**400.2**	**481.9**	**456.7**	**453.6**	**479.8**

- Nil; c Confidential data

Note: Detailed metadata at: *http://metalinks.oecd.org/idi/20220712/6d95*.

Source: *OECD International Direct Investment Statistics (database): https://doi.org/10.1787/idi-data-en*

CZECH REPUBLIC

Table 6. Foreign direct investment income by industrial sector

Million US dollars

	Inward					Outward				
	2016	2017	2018	2019	2020	2016	2017	2018	2019	2020
All FDI activities	**15 343.8**	**19 127.2**	**19 259.5**	**20 342.6**	**14 203.8**	**2 014.9**	**4 665.4**	**4 194.2**	**5 619.4**	**4 449.0**
Agriculture, forestry and fishing	**8.5**	**.. c**	**8.3**	**4.8**	**9.8**	**2.9**	**2.1**	**-1.2**	**1.3**	**.. c**
Mining and quarrying	**-171.3**	**.. c**	**96.3**	**-4.4**	**31.3**	**0.5**	**0.7**	**1.5**	**0.5**	**1.3**
Extraction activities	.. c	1.7	-7.2	-5.4	8.6	-	-	-	-	-
Manufacturing	**7 025.9**	**6 923.6**	**6 476.7**	**6 357.9**	**3 708.7**	**140.8**	**170.5**	**45.7**	**217.6**	**102.5**
of which:										
Food products, beverages and tobacco	.. c	.. c	363.5	553.1	380.6	.. c	.. c	-22.1	19.1	79.2
Textiles, wood and paper products; printing	461.7	433.5	469.0	513.4	362.2	5.8	29.2	48.3	16.7	16.3
Chemical, rubber, plastic, non-metallic mineral products	1 536.9	1 263.4	1 156.9	1 034.1	825.8	.. c	50.7	-64.8	61.9	8.6
Metal and machinery products, except electrical equipment	942.3	1 096.2	876.4	1 118.3	442.0	31.4	.. c	18.8	5.4	7.6
Motor vehicles, trailers, semi-trailers, other transport equipment	2 484.4	2 612.8	2 487.9	2 159.1	1 014.3	.. c	.. c	27.9	91.7	-19.8
Other manufacturing	1 075.4	.. c	1 123.1	979.8	683.8	.. c	10.1	37.6	22.8	10.6
Electricity, gas, steam and air conditioning supply	**641.1**	**510.0**	**561.8**	**480.3**	**698.4**	**.. c**	**48.4**	**-0.5**	**48.0**	**27.7**
Water supply; sewerage, waste management and remediation activities	**137.3**	**161.9**	**114.3**	**114.0**	**85.1**	**0.7**	**0.9**	**0.7**	**0.4**	**2.5**
Construction	**191.8**	**.. c**	**352.4**	**450.4**	**265.9**	**-23.1**	**92.0**	**72.0**	**117.1**	**65.4**
Services	**7 506.3**	**11 054.3**	**11 649.3**	**12 939.2**	**9 398.7**	**1 671.5**	**4 342.0**	**4 052.5**	**5 216.7**	**4 248.3**
Wholesale and retail trade; repair of motor vehicles and motorcycles	1 709.0	.. c	2 100.5	1 773.6	1 797.4	-10.8	.. c	74.8	31.9	135.5
Transportation and storage	278.7	.. c	244.0	263.1	212.4	.. c	.. c	31.7	19.2	11.1
Accommodation and food service activities	.. c	.. c	72.3	79.2	-6.4	0.8	0.6	.. c	.. c	.. c
Information and communication	879.5	944.8	1 288.2	1 506.7	1 192.1	.. c	61.1	79.0	100.1	66.0
Financial and insurance activities	.. c	6 428.6	6 264.7	7 452.8	4 953.2	1 402.7	.. c	3 594.7	4 771.6	3 829.6
Activities of holding companies	.. c	3 350.4	2 260.8	3 384.5	3 107.1	1 349.1	.. c	3 021.1	4 232.9	3 710.3
Real estate activities	.. c	.. c	281.3	603.7	283.0	28.4	.. c	110.9	173.9	35.7
Professional, scientific and technical activities	332.4	757.9	1 195.3	1 024.2	771.8	63.4	.. c	135.1	215.0	145.2
Administrative and support service activities	97.8	139.9	150.2	160.7	143.1	27.5	.. c	4.6	-121.7	-7.1
Public administration; activities of households and of extraterritorial organisations	-	-	-	-	-	-	-	-	-	-
Education	2.1	4.5	1.7	1.4	-1.7	-	-	-	-	0.1
Human health and social work activities	21.8	.. c	15.1	23.5	8.1	-	-	-	-	.. c
Arts, entertainment and recreation	29.3	.. c	14.2	42.7	22.4	15.7	20.5	21.8	26.6	33.9
Other services	.. c	.. c	21.8	7.8	23.4	0.7	3.8	-0.7	0.0	.. c
Not allocated and confidential	**4.3**	**.. c**	**0.4**	**0.4**	**3.5**	**.. c**	**8.7**	**23.5**	**17.7**	**.. c**
Private real estate activities	-	-	-	-	**2.3**	-	-	-	-	**0.2**

- Nil; c Confidential data

Note: Detailed metadata at: *http://metalinks.oecd.org/idi/20220712/6d95.*

Source: *OECD International Direct Investment Statistics (database): https://doi.org/10.1787/idi-data-en*

DENMARK

Table 1. Foreign direct investment flows by country

Million US dollars

	Inward					Outward				
	2016	2017	2018	2019	2020	2016	2017	2018	2019	2020
WORLD	**235.0**	**3 771.2**	**1 715.5**	**7 073.0**	**3 210.2**	**10 111.9**	**10 024.8**	**-75.2**	**16 843.5**	**10 899.3**
OECD COUNTRIES	**188.7**	**3 963.0**	**916.1**	**6 796.5**	**2 965.3**	**7 635.1**	**9 134.0**	**-3 776.7**	**14 818.9**	**8 506.4**
Australia	-3.4	-11.8	3.2	-15.3	-3.8	-56.9	-113.3	-508.3	-91.9	121.5
Austria	0.1	-2.4	-17.1	3.3	2.9	14.7	-53.6	-21.9	72.9	29.8
Belgium	17.2	218.7	93.0	55.9	206.4	341.0	-294.5	-208.3	145.7	367.5
Canada	-5.5	-1.2	0.5	-5.1	-10.4	89.0	154.8	109.3	-68.7	41.3
Chile	-1.5	-0.2	-	-	-0.6	69.2	35.4	44.5	12.1	21.2
Colombia	-0.7	-	-	-	-	-8.5	5.0	-5.5	19.8	27.2
Costa Rica	-	-	-	-	-	282.4	211.3	.. d	91.0	11.6
Czech Republic	-7.6	0.8	1.4	-0.3	0.8	5.8	68.3	-72.5	46.3	63.1
Denmark	-	-	-	-	-	-	-	-	-	-
Estonia	-28.2	88.8	-49.6	.. d	.. d	59.4	-169.7	2.9	3.1	21.6
Finland	1 270.3	-3 111.0	367.6	74.5	114.6	-337.6	-2 858.5	-469.8	38.5	-177.8
France	-316.9	7 802.6	-1 993.7	.. d	-225.6	340.5	312.8	433.7	197.0	865.2
Germany	-280.8	9.2	-18.4	51.0	-160.0	746.9	5 328.9	-1 655.5	-2 383.8	1 221.5
Greece	-3.0	-0.3	-	-	-	8.0	10.8	32.3	9.6	-0.3
Hungary	87.1	54.1	-17.4	16.2	8.4	235.8	128.6	207.8	-34.3	380.8
Iceland	-2.1	-20.1	-36.9	-	-	10.4	91.8	57.2	7.2	13.0
Ireland	38.8	-40.6	867.0	1 000.3	395.1	227.9	-45.7	-739.5	105.0	659.4
Israel	-1.3	-0.2	-	-	-	-2.7	44.4	-23.4	-40.8	114.0
Italy	22.4	172.4	-59.4	134.0	-15.0	218.5	199.8	79.2	-65.7	52.3
Japan	-109.1	-50.6	.. d	.. d	.. d	82.0	-119.5	88.5	-134.6	-145.7
Korea	-5.9	-1.8	-2.4	13.0	-6.0	20.8	56.8	101.5	-68.8	25.1
Latvia	-2.4	24.1	-0.8	-0.2	1.7	-20.4	-55.4	23.3	8.7	-15.0
Lithuania	-3.3	0.2	-1.0	3.4	0.6	67.5	-58.3	39.6	16.0	-0.8
Luxembourg	-3 052.2	-4 001.8	-4 294.0	3 725.6	-684.3	275.0	-57.7	436.8	.. d	405.7
Mexico	10.8	17.4	-6.2	-8.2	0.2	142.2	46.4	60.3	19.5	53.5
Netherlands	-743.2	2 763.2	1 417.1	63.9	1 261.5	732.8	91.6	-1 603.5	1 235.1	395.4
New Zealand	-2.4	3.2	3.2	-3.4	.. d	15.2	2.9	-3.3	4.6	.. d
Norway	504.2	236.0	4 702.5	566.2	679.3	-136.4	783.4	-4 004.1	646.6	811.2
Poland	-22.3	-5.6	31.8	-7.2	.. d	493.1	31.7	154.6	237.7	85.3
Portugal	-2.2	2.6	-5.1	0.9	-	18.4	26.7	268.8	-27.3	11.9
Slovak Republic	-1.3	-0.2	-0.3	0.5	-	-13.7	14.7	-4.9	17.4	23.1
Slovenia	-0.1	0.9	-1.7	0.3	-	-2.1	-1.1	-0.8	3.1	-3.2
Spain	61.1	447.9	401.0	-679.4	.. d	701.8	218.7	581.1	-108.7	-1 225.3
Sweden	-1 303.9	-862.0	43.4	156.8	330.5	-504.8	165.3	3 281.2	722.1	1 384.9
Switzerland	106.8	-365.1	-702.3	2 516.6	-198.4	-664.7	392.5	-166.8	3 826.7	-1 765.7
Turkey	-6.7	1.5	-11.6	-15.4	21.9	11.9	-37.6	74.6	138.1	114.2
United Kingdom	2 795.1	604.1	417.4	360.9	-232.5	4 227.7	3 963.6	-1 794.7	2 215.7	800.4
United States	1 175.9	-9.7	-304.0	-1 053.9	-312.7	286.4	770.9	1 423.8	3 595.0	2 194.7
EUROPE	**-728.3**	**3 582.8**	**1 352.3**	**6 827.7**	**460.9**	**6 730.0**	**9 133.0**	**-5 460.4**	**12 009.4**	**4 854.6**
Bulgaria	-0.9	-0.2	-	-	-	-10.8	27.6	68.3	61.8	3.7
Croatia	-	-	-	-	-24.2	6.7	18.0	33.1	10.0	36.7
Cyprus	9.5	-29.5	10.5	19.0	5.7	14.3	27.3	-18.1	-13.0	-39.6
Malta	133.1	-327.6	-4.0	0.3	-4.0	-	0.2	2.4	-0.8	-0.6
Montenegro	-	-	-	-	-	44.7	15.1	.. d	-	-
Romania	-2.1	-	-	-	-0.2	2.5	307.0	-118.3	85.2	43.4
Russian Federation	11.7	-77.4	8.7	31.5	19.1	-239.8	321.1	304.9	182.2	122.7
Ukraine	-1.6	-0.2	-	-	-	18.1	87.9	24.9	25.6	19.9
AFRICA	**-4.2**	**91.8**	**-60.7**	**47.1**	**18.0**	**17.4**	**-163.6**	**499.4**	**-553.9**	**325.3**
Northern Africa	-3.7	-0.5	-	-	12.7	101.2	-238.9	.. d	.. d	65.6
Algeria	-1.0	-0.2	-	-	-	43.1	-232.8	.. d	.. d	0.6
Egypt	-1.9	-0.2	-	-	0.2	66.6	-95.0	4.0	-62.5	-59.3
Libya	-	-	-	-	-	-	-	-	-	11.8
Morocco	-0.7	-	-	-	12.7	-8.3	89.2	.. d	40.0	.. d
Tunisia	-	-0.2	-	-	-	-0.1	-0.3	7.4	-0.2	-10.2
Other African countries	-0.4	92.2	-60.7	47.1	5.2	-83.9	75.3	37.2	-75.6	259.7
Nigeria	-1.2	-0.2	-	-	-	-4.5	-42.9	44.7	-58.5	146.7
South Africa	-2.2	92.4	-60.7	47.1	7.6	43.2	254.8	43.2	55.8	-42.2
AMERICA	**1 162.9**	**20.1**	**-378.9**	**-1 083.0**	**-330.9**	**1 863.8**	**750.7**	**1 979.6**	**3 917.3**	**2 220.0**
Northern America	1 162.1	2.4	-330.7	-1 066.4	-320.5	323.0	929.4	1 498.1	3 584.5	2 252.5
Central America and Caribbean countries	9.1	15.1	4.9	-6.1	-0.8	1 727.7	-294.2	265.0	183.7	-235.2
Bahamas	-13.8	-19.1	0.3	13.8	4.4	-	-	-0.6	0.3	0.5
Bermuda	11.9	16.4	10.1	-14.2	-7.6	-5.6	14.2	11.6	10.5	49.5
Cayman Islands	-0.1	0.2	0.2	-	-	-36.1	44.2	.. d	18.7	.. d
El Salvador	-	-	-	-	-1.2	-	-	-	-	1.1
Guatemala	-	-	-	-	-	0.7	0.8	-1.6	-1.2	-6.0
Honduras	-	-	-	-	-	-5.6	10.6	3.2	-0.8	14.8
Nicaragua	-	-	-	-	-	-0.3	-1.2	-0.5	-1.8	5.4
Panama	0.3	0.3	0.3	0.3	-	-57.1	2.9	33.4	-9.9	40.5
Virgin Islands, U.S.	-	-	-	-	-	-	-0.2	-	0.3	-
South America	-8.5	2.7	-53.1	-10.5	-9.5	-187.1	115.6	216.5	149.0	202.7
Argentina	-1.5	5.0	-24.9	-33.1	-	-63.9	-51.4	36.6	-4.0	-193.4
Bolivia	-	-	-	-	-	-0.1	-1.1	-1.7	-0.2	-2.3
Brazil	-3.7	-2.1	-28.2	22.6	-8.7	-161.5	-27.6	131.0	135.7	324.8
Ecuador	-	-	-	-	-	-	167.7	5.7	0.2	-1.2
Paraguay	-	-	-	-	-	-	-	-	-	-
Peru	-0.1	-	-	-	-	-12.9	-3.3	15.0	8.4	49.8
Uruguay	-0.9	-	-	-	-0.2	0.1	-7.6	4.6	-23.1	-25.7
Venezuela	-	-	-	-	-	-9.5	-2.0	-13.5	-	2.6

DENMARK

Table 1. Foreign direct investment flows by country *(cont.)*

Million US dollars

	Inward					Outward				
	2016	2017	2018	2019	2020	2016	2017	2018	2019	2020
ASIA	**-280.2**	**-47.7**	**.. d**	**1 168.1**	**1 578.1**	**1 684.5**	**510.0**	**3 480.8**	**1 553.0**	**1 723.2**
Near and Middle East	-13.4	-1.7	-6.2	11.4	20.5	31.2	-742.7	21.2	-99.6	137.7
Gulf Arabian countries	-10.4	-1.5	-6.2	11.4	20.5	34.9	-788.0	34.7	-9.0	-28.7
Kuwait	-0.4	-0.2	0.3	-0.2	0.8	1.6	0.8	7.4	9.6	4.3
Qatar	-0.9	-0.2	-	-	-	19.3	-689.5	7.8	-59.7	6.0
Saudi Arabia	-4.9	-0.9	-	-	-	14.1	6.5	45.6	11.2	20.0
United Arab Emirates	-3.3	-	-6.5	11.5	19.7	16.9	-88.6	-24.1	130.6	-33.2
Other Near and Middle East	-3.1	-0.2	-	-	-	-3.7	45.3	-13.5	-90.6	166.5
Jordan	-0.7	-	-	-	-	1.5	-3.2	6.3	-8.1	5.8
Other Asian countries	-266.7	-46.0	.. d	1 156.8	1 557.6	1 653.4	1 252.7	3 459.6	1 652.4	1 585.4
China	-29.9	-4.2	-6.7	31.2	52.3	347.7	334.0	342.6	223.6	-181.1
Hong Kong, China	-6.1	-0.3	.. d	.. d	33.3	24.1	-38.2	70.3	97.8	-383.8
India	-3.3	-0.6	-0.5	0.6	-10.1	93.5	98.3	262.6	19.3	-85.6
Indonesia	-1.2	-0.2	-	-	0.2	-6.8	8.5	15.5	34.2	-31.0
Iran, Islamic Republic of	-1.3	-0.2	-	-	-3.5	55.7	30.7	8.4	-49.6	-17.1
Malaysia	-1.5	-0.9	-1.3	7.2	-1.1	72.7	50.9	82.2	76.2	104.2
Philippines	-1.0	-	-	0.3	4.1	-24.8	-8.8	-9.3	1.8	-0.5
Singapore	-84.8	22.4	-33.6	-30.4	30.6	1 107.3	824.9	1 712.7	861.7	1 248.2
Chinese Taipei	-2.5	-0.8	-1.9	7.5	56.3	9.8	31.2	112.6	155.8	845.2
Thailand	-16.9	-8.2	-9.8	-6.6	29.8	-121.4	-153.0	165.7	55.8	-41.9
Viet Nam	-2.8	-0.3	-	-	-1.2	-17.2	17.3	42.6	14.7	-6.3
AUSTRALIA, OCEANIA AND POLAR REGIONS	**-5.8**	**-8.8**	**6.3**	**-18.7**	**.. d**	**-192.5**	**-190.9**	**-543.0**	**-74.2**	**1 773.8**
WORLD unallocated and confidential	**90.6**	**133.0**	**.. d**	**132.0**	**- d**	**8.8**	**-14.4**	**-31.7**	**-7.9**	**2.4**
European Union (since 01/02/2020)	**..**	**..**	**-3 229.6**	**3 325.1**	**144.1**	**..**	**..**	**731.8**	**4 901.3**	**4 584.2**
G20 countries excl. European Union	**3 241.1**	**8 544.0**	**.. d**	**.. d**	**.. d**	**6 135.5**	**11 507.8**	**-405.5**	**4 009.8**	**5 278.2**
G20 OECD countries	**3 276.0**	**8 532.1**	**.. d**	**.. d**	**.. d**	**6 109.1**	**10 563.5**	**-1 587.6**	**3 351.8**	**5 343.9**
G20 Non-OECD countries	**-34.9**	**12.0**	**-112.1**	**99.9**	**60.4**	**26.4**	**944.3**	**1 182.1**	**658.0**	**-65.7**
MENA countries	**-15.6**	**-1.8**	**-6.2**	**11.4**	**33.3**	**139.5**	**-1 029.6**	**.. d**	**.. d**	**.. d**
ASEAN countries	**-108.0**	**12.7**	**-44.7**	**-29.7**	**62.4**	**1 028.6**	**867.3**	**2 493.4**	**1 361.8**	**1 515.7**

- Nil; .. Not available; d Secondary Confidentiality

Note: Data excludes resident Special Purpose Entities (SPEs). Detailed metadata at: *http://metalinks.oecd.org/idi/20220712/6d95*.

Source: *OECD International Direct Investment Statistics (database): https://doi.org/10.1787/idi-data-en*

Table 2. Foreign direct investment positions by country

At year end

Million US dollars

	Inward					Outward				
	2016	2017	2018	2019	2020	2016	2017	2018	2019	2020
WORLD	**99 403.4**	**115 887.4**	**117 652.7**	**128 998.0**	**148 648.1**	**169 708.2**	**205 106.7**	**208 361.7**	**220 724.1**	**248 411.4**
OECD COUNTRIES	**93 622.7**	**109 363.4**	**110 139.6**	**121 319.1**	**140 203.2**	**134 466.7**	**168 343.0**	**169 865.8**	**181 445.5**	**204 857.7**
Australia	9.2	1.0	12.7	-4.2	16.5	2 000.3	2 189.1	1 706.6	1 787.9	2 398.1
Austria	236.5	215.1	253.6	207.3	248.8	219.3	317.0	327.0	352.8	401.5
Belgium	822.1	1 289.2	1 409.5	1 420.0	1 652.8	974.1	753.9	700.7	1 042.3	1 596.7
Canada	30.1	70.4	68.4	50.5	787.4	1 095.6	1 195.9	1 595.9	1 482.9	1 429.8
Chile	0.1	0.5	.. d	.. d	.. d	346.5	381.9	269.7	367.9	423.8
Colombia	-2.8	-0.3	-0.2	-0.2	-0.2	78.7	103.1	80.7	93.3	96.7
Costa Rica	-	-	-	-	-	403.1	612.8	.. d	.. d	.. d
Czech Republic	38.6	24.8	14.7	74.1	86.7	997.8	1 113.5	1 084.8	1 103.4	1 258.3
Denmark	-	-	-	-	-	-	-	-	-	-
Estonia	-17.2	65.9	57.4	.. d	-31.5	272.1	262.9	375.2	357.6	457.1
Finland	4 690.6	2 591.1	7 929.9	7 951.6	6 464.8	6 248.4	3 228.9	3 031.9	2 766.7	2 681.3
France	3 805.2	7 334.6	6 062.1	4 474.9	4 796.9	6 111.3	7 192.8	7 637.8	7 085.9	9 172.3
Germany	5 145.8	6 090.2	6 399.2	7 066.8	8 166.4	15 171.4	26 470.4	26 981.0	23 964.9	27 043.9
Greece	-7.5	-4.2	5.4	2.2	-0.7	219.6	191.7	191.3	192.3	263.0
Hungary	5.5	97.6	.. d	.. d	.. d	852.4	1 117.0	1 192.6	974.7	1 410.8
Iceland	66.9	60.4	30.4	31.5	32.2	871.6	1 042.9	1 261.8	.. d	.. d
Ireland	1 555.6	1 574.0	3 324.4	4 553.2	5 599.6	1 358.9	1 537.6	1 185.4	926.0	844.7
Israel	28.1	33.0	16.1	37.4	43.9	114.1	144.3	124.1	87.3	146.1
Italy	483.2	804.8	626.0	1 024.3	1 141.5	1 352.8	1 527.6	1 535.9	1 451.6	2 025.4
Japan	470.7	468.6	.. d	2 423.0	4 393.5	992.7	770.2	946.3	632.4	1 025.5
Korea	-9.8	33.2	39.0	52.4	2.5	268.4	272.7	350.6	259.4	359.5
Latvia	9.9	153.0	72.7	18.1	20.5	279.6	310.4	597.0	592.6	687.1
Lithuania	15.5	9.5	2.5	.. d	.. d	577.6	629.4	920.9	714.4	690.5
Luxembourg	14 934.5	13 139.0	13 004.7	13 996.5	12 410.7	995.3	1 188.5	1 561.3	5 696.3	6 643.9
Mexico	105.3	139.0	-14.7	-22.8	-21.1	689.2	912.4	1 086.5	1 118.4	1 260.2
Netherlands	10 385.5	16 798.8	17 666.0	15 783.8	18 670.4	11 616.5	14 675.8	11 765.5	14 298.0	16 799.1
New Zealand	43.4	60.9	51.2	38.9	.. d	167.7	122.3	244.0	363.5	2 024.6
Norway	10 008.9	12 381.6	13 211.2	14 533.6	17 239.5	6 282.0	9 095.5	7 935.1	8 774.7	9 860.2
Poland	61.1	28.8	191.7	137.7	29.7	3 839.0	4 379.4	4 645.1	4 821.7	5 178.5
Portugal	15.9	-1.0	2.5	-6.4	4.3	350.5	492.8	590.4	549.3	733.6
Slovak Republic	21.1	15.5	16.7	11.4	12.4	548.4	635.0	857.9	791.8	932.7
Slovenia	7.4	1.1	-0.3	0.4	2.8	36.3	71.0	102.8	80.3	81.6
Spain	1 149.0	734.2	1 359.3	608.5	543.0	3 605.7	4 423.2	4 996.3	4 436.7	5 033.5
Sweden	20 240.3	23 444.1	17 624.8	20 964.2	24 290.5	25 608.3	28 915.9	30 325.6	30 961.4	33 802.8
Switzerland	3 557.7	3 356.8	2 975.0	6 031.7	7 537.0	3 922.3	4 445.3	4 144.4	4 131.4	4 152.1
Turkey	9.5	-6.6	-22.1	-36.1	-26.9	525.5	654.8	825.2	969.5	914.4
United Kingdom	9 431.7	11 806.9	11 357.3	13 892.7	16 180.5	21 918.4	30 084.6	27 139.2	29 882.0	31 167.8
United States	6 287.6	6 560.6	5 518.9	5 611.1	7 959.1	14 613.8	18 225.8	21 630.5	26 513.3	29 953.0
EUROPE	**88 774.2**	**104 024.7**	**105 824.3**	**115 223.7**	**127 601.7**	**117 257.5**	**148 825.0**	**145 524.0**	**152 696.4**	**169 519.6**
Bulgaria	0.7	0.3	1.4	0.7	-0.3	84.1	121.0	215.4	283.0	327.9
Croatia	-	-	-	0.3	-25.6	162.5	262.7	289.4	274.4	328.3
Cyprus	396.6	229.7	431.0	443.1	286.3	117.4	134.7	171.3	226.3	174.8
Malta	435.7	142.7	23.5	21.7	72.6	64.5	92.0	67.6	65.6	75.9
Montenegro	-	-	-	-	-	330.8	119.2	-	-	-
Romania	7.7	1.0	2.9	0.2	1.0	298.7	741.5	1 017.0	972.8	801.3
Russian Federation	1 020.7	1 056.6	.. d	.. d	.. d	277.8	788.5	1 166.1	1 347.7	1 330.7
Ukraine	-0.4	0.2	1.5	0.2	-0.8	192.5	255.3	315.5	390.2	351.5
AFRICA	**-6.8**	**79.4**	**198.9**	**209.6**	**244.0**	**1 851.0**	**2 020.9**	**2 682.9**	**1 882.4**	**2 302.6**
Northern Africa	-9.6	-1.3	19.5	1.2	15.4	1 087.2	784.7	1 191.8	742.2	726.5
Algeria	-3.8	-0.3	-	-	-0.3	687.5	486.2	583.3	139.3	118.5
Egypt	-3.1	-0.6	18.1	-0.2	-0.7	369.5	153.5	173.0	115.2	53.8
Libya	-	-	-	-	-	0.1	0.2	0.5	1.3	4.8
Morocco	-2.7	-0.2	0.9	0.9	15.8	21.3	129.8	.. d	.. d	.. d
Tunisia	-	-	0.5	0.4	0.5	8.8	14.8	25.9	23.2	16.5
Other African countries	2.8	80.7	179.5	208.4	228.6	763.8	1 236.4	1 490.9	1 140.2	1 575.9
Nigeria	4.5	1.1	-	-	0.5	45.2	77.3	153.8	89.4	196.4
South Africa	-4.8	6.9	-30.1	21.9	30.7	348.4	704.9	736.9	720.5	820.3
AMERICA	**7 095.2**	**7 477.8**	**6 445.7**	**6 484.7**	**9 331.3**	**21 295.2**	**25 624.6**	**29 950.8**	**34 932.1**	**38 883.9**
Northern America	6 609.9	6 968.9	5 892.4	5 966.7	9 065.1	15 832.3	19 556.5	23 267.6	28 089.2	31 494.8
Central America and Caribbean countries	478.3	520.6	440.2	408.5	127.4	3 699.5	3 866.2	4 526.8	4 716.2	4 711.9
Bahamas	172.0	159.2	.. d	.. d	.. d	9.5	9.5	21.6	26.7	20.8
Bermuda	86.2	131.0	.. d	.. d	.. d	85.8	107.0	112.1	.. d	.. d
Cayman Islands	-78.8	-82.5	-47.9	-42.4	-52.2	600.5	139.5	.. d	.. d	.. d
El Salvador	-	-	-	-	.. d	1.1	1.1	0.8	0.9	2.0
Guatemala	-	-	-	-	-	0.7	1.0	0.2	-1.3	0.8
Honduras	-	-	-	-	-	26.8	105.8	35.4	36.0	48.4
Nicaragua	-	-	-	-	-	14.5	15.6	26.4	25.6	33.3
Panama	167.6	153.7	.. d	.. d	4.0	-21.0	-28.4	18.9	25.0	66.7
Virgin Islands, U.S.	-	-	-	-	-	-	1.5	1.4	1.6	2.0
South America	7.1	-11.9	113.4	109.3	138.8	1 763.6	2 202.1	2 156.3	2 126.6	2 677.0
Argentina	5.7	-24.5	-58.9	-91.7	-50.7	116.3	452.7	498.7	518.7	498.1
Bolivia	-	-	-	-	-	1.4	3.7	5.2	3.3	9.2
Brazil	4.0	12.1	7.5	27.7	13.2	1 048.4	1 010.5	1 036.1	885.9	1 354.2
Ecuador	-	-	-	-	-	2.1	93.4	.. d	.. d	.. d
Paraguay	-	-	-	-	-	2.0	2.7	2.5	0.2	-
Peru	3.3	0.5	-	-	0.3	73.3	78.5	125.0	132.9	178.6
Uruguay	-3.3	-0.3	-	-	-0.5	54.4	28.8	32.5	24.4	18.0
Venezuela	-	-	-	-	-	40.4	46.7	6.1	1.0	1.2

Table 2. Foreign direct investment positions by country *(cont.)*

At year end

Million US dollars

	Inward					Outward				
	2016	2017	2018	2019	2020	2016	2017	2018	2019	2020
ASIA	**1 402.8**	**1 706.6**	**2 701.0**	**4 685.1**	**7 216.7**	**26 292.0**	**25 489.6**	**27 421.5**	**28 193.4**	**32 171.7**
Near and Middle East	24.8	73.5	120.7	369.1	384.5	1 371.8	773.7	1 039.4	954.0	1 224.4
Gulf Arabian countries	3.0	41.7	102.2	330.7	340.1	1 211.0	599.6	884.0	884.7	1 007.3
Kuwait	6.5	7.2	7.2	6.7	8.4	10.9	13.2	21.6	27.0	19.3
Qatar	5.0	1.1	-	-	0.5	597.1	94.1	73.6	13.2	50.4
Saudi Arabia	-15.0	41.1	42.8	40.7	10.4	197.8	193.5	254.2	255.1	342.1
United Arab Emirates	9.5	-7.2	51.8	.. d	.. d	348.4	274.3	397.4	545.8	509.1
Other Near and Middle East	21.8	31.7	18.6	38.3	44.4	160.6	174.1	155.4	69.4	217.1
Jordan	-2.7	-0.2	-	-	-0.2	18.0	4.8	14.9	8.2	14.4
Other Asian countries	1 378.0	1 633.3	2 580.5	4 316.0	6 832.2	24 920.2	24 715.9	26 382.2	27 239.5	30 947.2
China	310.5	259.2	136.7	160.3	201.9	4 362.4	4 329.9	5 455.7	3 655.1	4 925.9
Hong Kong, China	237.6	410.3	1 132.0	1 044.5	.. d	3 068.3	2 712.1	2 648.6	2 794.8	1 785.7
India	61.7	5.3	7.4	5.5	-5.9	820.8	1 061.4	1 418.7	1 468.4	1 514.5
Indonesia	3.8	1.0	4.9	1.9	-	142.9	118.9	140.5	179.5	198.3
Iran, Islamic Republic of	-5.0	-0.5	0.3	0.2	-6.4	101.1	118.4	117.2	85.8	197.4
Malaysia	30.8	28.0	101.7	43.0	30.5	922.3	988.5	1 201.6	1 613.7	1 407.0
Philippines	-3.8	-0.3	0.2	0.2	4.3	161.4	136.9	136.2	127.8	184.9
Singapore	100.8	194.3	272.6	347.4	753.3	13 205.5	13 370.0	12 932.0	15 189.6	16 180.8
Chinese Taipei	36.9	110.3	95.4	101.3	277.2	47.9	42.9	118.7	204.9	1 825.6
Thailand	143.1	145.6	143.7	134.1	.. d	569.7	419.3	519.1	584.6	603.2
Viet Nam	1.1	0.8	8.9	0.3	2.6	118.8	115.0	215.5	241.6	272.7
AUSTRALIA, OCEANIA AND POLAR REGIONS	**52.9**	**67.5**	**70.9**	**40.0**	**.. d**	**2 124.0**	**2 202.9**	**1 830.8**	**2 045.9**	**4 435.6**
WORLD unallocated and confidential	**2 085.0**	**2 531.4**	**2 411.9**	**2 355.0**	**.. d**	**888.4**	**943.7**	**951.6**	**974.0**	**1 098.1**
European Union (since 01/02/2020)	**..**	**..**	**76 555.2**	**79 020.7**	**84 646.2**	**..**	**..**	**102 366.6**	**104 982.5**	**119 427.2**
G20 countries excl. European Union	**27 155.0**	**34 660.3**	**.. d**	**.. d**	**.. d**	**72 054.1**	**98 156.6**	**102 142.2**	**104 179.1**	**117 733.8**
G20 OECD countries	**25 768.5**	**33 302.7**	**.. d**	**34 532.6**	**43 396.4**	**64 739.4**	**89 496.3**	**91 435.4**	**95 148.2**	**106 749.9**
G20 Non-OECD countries	**1 386.5**	**1 357.7**	**.. d**	**.. d**	**.. d**	**7 314.7**	**8 660.4**	**10 706.8**	**9 030.8**	**10 983.9**
MENA countries	**-12.8**	**39.3**	**124.1**	**.. d**	**.. d**	**2 346.0**	**1 412.6**	**.. d**	**.. d**	**.. d**
ASEAN countries	**252.9**	**343.6**	**532.0**	**526.8**	**958.5**	**15 280.0**	**15 359.6**	**15 261.5**	**18 014.8**	**19 070.6**

- Nil; .. Not available; d Secondary Confidentiality

Note: Data excludes resident Special Purpose Entities (SPEs). Detailed metadata at: *http://metalinks.oecd.org/idi/20220712/6d95*.

Source: *OECD International Direct Investment Statistics (database)*: *https://doi.org/10.1787/idi-data-en*

DENMARK

Table 3. Foreign direct investment income by country

Million US dollars

	Inward					Outward				
	2016	2017	2018	2019	2020	2016	2017	2018	2019	2020
WORLD	**5 481.4**	**6 133.9**	**6 694.9**	**7 414.5**	**5 373.7**	**12 061.1**	**13 256.1**	**15 499.0**	**15 461.4**	**14 777.3**
OECD COUNTRIES	**5 340.7**	**5 999.3**	**6 555.6**	**7 233.4**	**5 092.9**	**9 531.7**	**11 169.1**	**12 596.7**	**12 211.7**	**11 432.9**
Australia	3.3	3.0	3.3	3.6	2.8	104.1	28.8	71.4	205.4	105.8
Austria	15.2	4.7	10.5	16.6	13.8	23.8	28.0	42.3	36.1	30.7
Belgium	36.5	72.1	103.7	80.1	62.4	69.8	112.4	111.8	123.0	-110.5
Canada	4.2	5.5	4.3	5.2	-29.7	75.2	102.1	89.3	102.7	107.8
Chile	-	-	10.8	10.8	9.6	79.6	24.4	25.5	25.0	22.9
Colombia	..	..	..	..	..	..	..	..	..	..
Costa Rica	..	..	..	..	..	..	..	..	..	..
Czech Republic	0.7	0.9	1.0	1.3	4.4	87.8	68.2	124.0	91.9	104.9
Denmark	-	-	-	-	-	-	-	-	-	-
Estonia	0.1	0.2	2.7	1.3	0.2	39.4	61.5	63.5	64.2	56.1
Finland	99.7	217.7	484.7	469.5	359.8	385.8	365.2	322.5	322.1	238.0
France	240.4	549.2	548.0	840.7	607.5	394.2	635.1	503.2	370.1	471.1
Germany	559.4	392.2	597.3	485.8	332.6	444.5	1 050.3	1 169.7	527.9	1 674.0
Greece	-	-	0.5	0.3	0.2	23.6	18.2	26.6	13.0	20.6
Hungary	-	-	-	-	-	76.8	130.0	116.6	85.8	99.4
Iceland	4.2	3.5	2.7	2.2	2.0	12.2	18.6	23.4	18.1	19.9
Ireland	168.3	166.0	77.3	76.5	84.2	83.6	272.8	319.8	.. d	201.5
Israel	..	..	..	..	..	..	..	..	..	..
Italy	23.8	35.4	23.4	50.5	28.0	77.1	133.6	166.3	35.2	116.8
Japan	-78.4	-28.0	7.6	56.5	31.2	94.2	83.2	93.0	43.2	109.4
Korea	-	0.5	1.0	1.1	0.3	32.1	23.2	46.3	27.7	56.3
Latvia	0.1	24.2	2.9	2.2	0.6	23.5	17.6	42.1	34.8	28.6
Lithuania	0.4	0.6	0.3	0.3	0.3	56.0	70.9	154.7	160.0	137.7
Luxembourg	497.3	388.2	179.1	243.7	135.0	94.6	60.0	90.3	91.8	52.4
Mexico	14.3	16.4	-	-	-	63.9	104.1	77.5	49.0	99.5
Netherlands	282.6	457.9	472.2	544.7	615.4	383.6	392.0	418.9	498.0	490.5
New Zealand	-0.9	5.6	6.2	3.0	2.4	21.7	6.7	2.2	25.8	16.5
Norway	573.6	858.3	1 029.4	1 013.3	657.8	588.6	737.1	896.3	715.7	647.8
Poland	-3.1	0.5	40.4	39.6	0.9	291.1	255.7	331.2	378.8	376.5
Portugal	0.6	2.1	0.6	0.3	0.3	21.7	45.6	55.8	53.4	70.0
Slovak Republic	0.9	0.9	1.0	0.9	0.6	45.8	53.0	73.2	71.2	58.9
Slovenia	-	0.2	0.2	0.2	0.2	20.9	13.0	11.4	17.1	17.7
Spain	61.2	306.9	258.0	135.1	254.5	-11.1	198.1	127.2	182.2	222.4
Sweden	1 332.1	946.3	855.9	1 145.7	851.7	1 142.8	1 256.9	1 733.0	1 933.4	1 479.4
Switzerland	232.4	249.6	145.4	75.4	133.0	2 341.2	2 120.9	1 844.3	1 995.7	2 286.8
Turkey	0.1	0.2	0.3	0.3	0.3	43.5	19.8	54.8	41.5	80.3
United Kingdom	706.2	664.1	716.2	1 471.8	602.9	1 547.1	1 481.9	1 524.4	1 712.9	952.8
United States	564.3	653.5	967.5	452.7	325.1	805.7	1 246.5	1 840.8	1 903.2	1 076.4
EUROPE	**4 986.8**	**5 417.0**	**5 650.9**	**6 772.0**	**4 923.9**	**8 579.7**	**9 944.0**	**10 884.6**	**10 233.9**	**10 247.8**
Bulgaria	-	-	-	-	-	2.8	4.8	5.9	4.2	7.2
Croatia	-	-	-	-	-	21.1	25.0	29.5	17.1	21.6
Cyprus	33.1	43.5	40.9	36.4	25.1	19.9	12.9	26.1	33.6	27.7
Malta	88.8	8.6	3.5	3.1	.. d	4.9	4.7	4.1	2.4	2.6
Montenegro	..	..	..	..	..	..	..	..	..	..
Romania	0.3	0.2	0.2	0.2	0.2	14.6	42.3	87.6	90.4	41.9
Russian Federation	32.1	10.1	21.4	17.4	10.2	30.0	50.7	120.9	166.1	220.3
Ukraine	..	..	..	..	..	..	..	..	..	..
AFRICA	**0.6**	**1.2**	**4.6**	**4.2**	**2.8**	**112.3**	**269.3**	**305.4**	**434.8**	**88.4**
Northern Africa	0.1	0.2	1.1	0.5	-	119.9	168.7	.. d	.. d	22.2
Algeria	..	..	..	..	..	..	..	..	..	..
Egypt	0.1	0.2	1.0	0.5	-	28.4	18.8	5.4	4.0	5.2
Libya	..	..	..	..	..	..	..	..	..	..
Morocco	-	-	-	-	-	0.1	3.6	4.8	8.1	11.8
Tunisia	..	..	..	..	..	..	..	..	..	..
Other African countries	0.4	1.1	3.6	3.7	2.6	-7.4	100.4	90.8	40.2	66.2
Nigeria	-	-	-	-	-	5.8	8.5	0.6	3.3	8.9
South Africa	0.3	0.3	1.0	1.6	1.5	15.9	50.1	45.0	13.9	24.3
AMERICA	**602.6**	**688.3**	**1 005.8**	**482.4**	**336.9**	**1 050.1**	**1 645.6**	**2 193.4**	**2 398.0**	**1 483.0**
Northern America	576.5	664.5	973.5	469.6	310.5	872.7	1 356.6	1 908.6	2 041.3	1 190.9
Central America and Caribbean countries	22.0	23.8	22.0	1.6	15.3	49.9	180.3	123.5	214.9	195.2
Bahamas	..	..	..	..	..	..	..	..	..	..
Bermuda	..	..	..	..	..	..	..	..	..	..
Cayman Islands	..	..	..	..	..	..	..	..	..	..
El Salvador	..	..	..	..	..	..	..	..	..	..
Guatemala	..	..	..	..	..	..	..	..	..	..
Honduras	..	..	..	..	..	..	..	..	..	..
Nicaragua	..	..	..	..	..	..	..	..	..	..
Panama	..	..	..	..	..	..	..	..	..	..
Virgin Islands, U.S.	..	..	..	..	..	..	..	..	..	..
South America	4.2	-	10.5	11.1	11.2	127.3	108.8	161.2	141.7	96.9
Argentina	-	-0.2	-	-0.2	-	2.2	-17.6	49.7	32.2	-66.8
Bolivia	..	..	..	..	..	..	..	..	..	..
Brazil	4.3	-0.2	-0.3	0.3	1.5	52.3	107.2	63.5	69.0	93.9
Ecuador	..	..	..	..	..	..	..	..	..	..
Paraguay	..	..	..	..	..	..	..	..	..	..
Peru	..	..	..	..	..	..	..	..	..	..
Uruguay	-	-	-	-	-	-8.2	-5.0	1.9	-2.7	7.0
Venezuela	-	-	-	-	-	0.7	-0.2	-1.4	0.8	2.6

DENMARK

Table 3. Foreign direct investment income by country *(cont.)*

Million US dollars

	Inward					Outward				
	2016	2017	2018	2019	2020	2016	2017	2018	2019	2020
ASIA	**-111.0**	**18.6**	**23.9**	**148.9**	**104.7**	**2 191.6**	**1 358.0**	**2 047.5**	**2 160.8**	**2 846.7**
Near and Middle East	2.5	3.9	5.4	25.8	23.7	208.9	32.0	75.7	119.2	77.3
Gulf Arabian countries	0.9	2.0	4.0	23.7	21.1	202.2	25.0	69.7	120.3	69.6
Kuwait	..	..	..	..	..	..	..	..	..	..
Qatar	..	..	..	..	..	..	..	..	..	..
Saudi Arabia	..	..	..	..	..	..	..	..	..	..
United Arab Emirates	..	..	..	..	..	..	..	..	..	..
Other Near and Middle East	1.8	2.0	1.4	2.1	2.4	6.7	7.1	6.0	-1.2	7.6
Jordan	..	..	..	..	..	..	..	..	..	..
Other Asian countries	-113.5	14.7	18.5	123.1	81.0	1 982.8	1 325.9	1 971.8	2 041.6	2 769.3
China	4.2	3.9	5.1	4.9	5.5	538.7	403.8	631.7	508.3	860.1
Hong Kong, China	3.6	5.3	9.3	4.9	4.4	239.3	70.3	153.0	135.8	175.8
India	1.0	2.4	0.6	13.2	17.3	44.6	29.1	82.8	94.2	10.7
Indonesia	-	-	0.3	0.2	-	11.3	24.8	30.7	21.4	11.9
Iran, Islamic Republic of	..	..	..	..	..	..	..	..	..	..
Malaysia	1.5	1.2	5.9	35.5	2.3	104.3	88.0	99.5	132.3	94.5
Philippines	-	-	-	-	-	1.2	5.8	1.3	2.1	12.2
Singapore	-51.1	19.4	-16.8	1.2	20.2	610.5	281.3	508.3	895.8	1 029.3
Chinese Taipei	1.9	6.5	7.3	6.7	2.0	-6.2	2.7	37.5	.. d	76.3
Thailand	3.9	3.5	-2.1	-1.6	-2.0	205.6	143.7	145.1	109.6	105.5
Viet Nam	..	..	..	..	..	..	..	..	..	..
AUSTRALIA, OCEANIA AND POLAR REGIONS	**2.4**	**8.8**	**9.8**	**6.9**	**5.4**	**126.1**	**36.2**	**74.4**	**232.0**	**122.9**
WORLD unallocated and confidential	**-**	**-**	**-0.2**	**0.2**	**0.2**	**1.3**	**3.0**	**-6.3**	**1.8**	**-11.5**
European Union (since 01/02/2020)	**..**	**..**	**3 704.3**	**4 174.9**	**3 485.6**	**..**	**..**	**6 157.4**	**5 493.5**	**5 937.0**
G20 countries excl. European Union	**..**	**..**	**..**	**..**	**..**	**..**	**..**	**..**	**..**	**..**
G20 OECD countries	**2 037.4**	**2 291.8**	**2 868.9**	**3 368.3**	**1 900.9**	**3 681.6**	**4 908.5**	**5 636.7**	**5 019.0**	**4 850.0**
G20 Non-OECD countries	**..**	**..**	**..**	**..**	**..**	**..**	**..**	**..**	**..**	**..**
MENA countries	**..**	**..**	**..**	**..**	**..**	**..**	**..**	**..**	**..**	**..**
ASEAN countries	**-45.8**	**24.2**	**-12.7**	**35.4**	**20.3**	**1 034.8**	**691.8**	**916.3**	**1 266.7**	**1 486.4**

- Nil; .. Not available; d Secondary Confidentiality

Note: Data excludes resident Special Purpose Entities (SPEs). Detailed metadata at: *http://metalinks.oecd.org/idi/20220712/6d95*.

Source: *OECD International Direct Investment Statistics (database)*: *https://doi.org/10.1787/idi-data-en*

DENMARK

Table 4. Foreign direct investment flows by industrial sector

Million US dollars

	Inward					Outward				
	2016	2017	2018	2019	2020	2016	2017	2018	2019	2020
All FDI activities	**235.0**	**3 771.2**	**1 715.5**	**7 073.0**	**3 210.2**	**10 111.9**	**10 024.8**	**-75.2**	**16 843.5**	**10 899.3**
Agriculture, forestry and fishing	**-**	**-**	**-**	**-**	**-**	**13.5**	**17.0**	**59.4**	**40.2**	**-31.9**
Mining and quarrying	**463.2**	**7 374.1**	**.. d**	**-1 685.8**	**.. d**	**1 905.4**	**-316.1**	**.. d**	**.. d**	**-43.9**
Extraction activities	456.3	7 374.8	.. d	-1 685.4	.. d	1 905.4	-316.1	.. d	.. d	-43.9
Manufacturing	**-648.7**	**959.4**	**400.7**	**4 562.5**	**206.5**	**-642.1**	**1 214.5**	**1 824.8**	**8 653.1**	**421.0**
of which:										
Food products, beverages and tobacco	-16.3	-0.8	469.8	-68.4	115.0	1 400.6	1 067.4	744.6	415.5	267.5
Textiles, wood and paper products; printing	-0.4	-7.0	-7.8	-10.2	12.2	154.4	60.6	-27.9	45.0	68.6
Chemical, rubber, plastic, non-metallic mineral products	-62.3	-171.5	-304.0	-15.3	472.5	-1 698.8	-225.4	1 420.4	2 878.9	472.6
Metal and machinery products, except electrical equipment	-613.2	993.7	248.7	4 845.6	-262.2	-390.3	303.7	-391.4	4 995.5	-490.1
Motor vehicles, trailers, semi-trailers, other transport equipment	9.7	-1.4	65.4	-1.6	-1.5	14.0	9.4	27.7	31.8	-7.3
Other manufacturing	34.2	146.2	-71.4	-187.4	-129.5	-122.0	-1.2	51.2	286.4	109.4
Electricity, gas, steam and air conditioning supply	**-708.8**	**-1 026.4**	**-56.5**	**.. d**	**84.8**	**588.6**	**1 601.5**	**.. d**	**4 475.9**	**306.6**
Water supply; sewerage, waste management and remediation activities	**-5.8**	**6.7**	**0.5**	**-42.7**	**7.6**	**-0.6**	**-**	**0.3**	**-**	**-**
Construction	**34.9**	**13.9**	**-30.4**	**-34.8**	**-69.4**	**-33.1**	**-20.4**	**-32.2**	**39.3**	**-30.0**
Services	**1 028.6**	**-3 257.3**	**4 666.5**	**3 977.8**	**1 637.1**	**8 079.7**	**7 566.7**	**1 491.1**	**6 035.4**	**9 634.5**
Wholesale and retail trade; repair of motor vehicles and motorcycles	79.5	57.1	293.8	696.6	-121.5	620.1	474.6	49.4	277.4	688.0
Transportation and storage	-136.8	-37.3	-29.1	39.7	-178.7	403.8	4 022.5	111.0	-1 896.8	1 083.8
Accommodation and food service activities	-13.5	-39.5	-3.8	-15.0	17.4	-	-	-	-	-
Information and communication	-349.9	-140.0	562.0	1 090.7	447.1	-353.2	-104.1	.. d	328.4	.. d
Financial and insurance activities	2 906.3	-3 886.7	152.8	-441.0	1 598.1	4 602.0	1 040.2	1 163.4	2 406.0	5 071.2
Activities of holding companies	..	..	..	..	..	..	..	..	..	..
Real estate activities	40.9	65.3	289.2	466.2	56.6	165.4	393.5	413.2	174.8	11.8
Professional, scientific and technical activities	-431.4	555.2	434.3	2 469.0	-587.4	2 484.3	1 326.0	2 265.9	4 356.9	-374.2
Administrative and support service activities	-1 105.1	138.6	.. d	-386.0	430.1	194.0	283.4	424.6	.. d	404.6
Public administration; activities of households and of extraterritorial organisations	23.6	-	-	-	-	-83.9	55.0	-8.9	26.1	.. d
Education	-	-	-	-	-	-	-	-	-	-
Human health and social work activities	-20.4	-11.2	35.6	29.1	-6.0	47.2	75.6	20.1	.. d	.. d
Arts, entertainment and recreation	10.3	18.3	-18.8	4.5	1.2	-	-	-	-	-
Other services	25.0	22.7	29.3	24.1	-20.2	-	-	-0.5	-0.8	0.3
Not allocated and confidential	**-23.5**	**-432.3**	**.. d**	**.. d**	**.. d**	**239.3**	**38.3**	**.. d**	**.. d**	**642.9**
Private real estate activities	**95.1**	**133.1**	**.. d**	**.. d**	**..**	**-38.9**	**-76.6**	**.. d**	**.. d**	**..**

- Nil; .. Not available; d Secondary Confidentiality

Note: Data excludes resident Special Purpose Entities (SPEs). Detailed metadata at: *http://metalinks.oecd.org/idi/20220712/6d95*.

Source: *OECD International Direct Investment Statistics (database): https://doi.org/10.1787/idi-data-en*

DENMARK

Table 5. Foreign direct investment positions by industrial sector

At year end

Million US dollars

	Inward					Outward				
	2016	2017	2018	2019	2020	2016	2017	2018	2019	2020
All FDI activities	**99 403.4**	**115 887.4**	**117 652.7**	**128 998.0**	**148 648.1**	**169 708.2**	**205 106.7**	**208 361.7**	**220 724.1**	**248 411.4**
Agriculture, forestry and fishing	**64.4**	**114.2**	**108.9**	**97.5**	**95.4**	**299.5**	**335.7**	**556.2**	**502.0**	**655.2**
Mining and quarrying	**2 101.0**	**3 950.4**	**2 364.3**	**857.0**	**2 139.8**	**14 901.3**	**15 228.0**	**.. d**	**.. d**	**428.2**
Extraction activities	2 062.4	3 913.8	2 325.2	830.3	2 069.0	14 865.0	15 191.6	.. d	.. d	306.9
Manufacturing	**9 980.7**	**11 633.5**	**11 363.3**	**13 802.3**	**19 557.1**	**40 865.8**	**47 836.9**	**46 440.0**	**52 083.2**	**36 697.5**
of which:										
Food products, beverages and tobacco	2 650.9	2 977.9	3 314.7	3 481.2	4 144.5	23 407.7	27 324.6	25 512.9	25 522.1	7 639.3
Textiles, wood and paper products; printing	306.5	405.9	354.6	348.6	422.3	841.8	981.4	1 097.0	965.4	1 287.8
Chemical, rubber, plastic, non-metallic mineral products	3 364.3	3 874.7	3 566.0	3 478.2	6 237.5	7 354.1	8 501.5	8 423.6	10 379.0	11 210.7
Metal and machinery products, except electrical equipment	2 112.4	2 611.6	2 615.7	5 575.7	8 061.8	8 118.2	9 787.8	8 965.1	12 606.4	13 377.6
Motor vehicles, trailers, semi-trailers, other transport equipment	37.4	49.3	40.5	36.1	37.5	200.2	197.8	.. d	.. d	.. d
Other manufacturing	1 509.2	1 714.3	1 471.6	882.4	653.4	943.9	1 043.9	2 260.5	2 390.8	2 962.2
Electricity, gas, steam and air conditioning supply	**2 783.3**	**912.4**	**827.1**	**1 535.1**	**2 068.8**	**7 771.0**	**10 667.1**	**13 413.2**	**18 552.3**	**.. d**
Water supply; sewerage, waste management and remediation activities	**162.6**	**195.4**	**193.7**	**142.6**	**168.5**	**13.0**	**13.0**	**25.8**	**32.2**	**83.4**
Construction	**203.7**	**348.1**	**358.9**	**409.5**	**379.7**	**222.3**	**238.9**	**176.1**	**191.7**	**436.0**
Services	**80 469.2**	**93 684.9**	**97 628.6**	**107 334.7**	**120 728.2**	**98 500.3**	**122 755.6**	**127 410.8**	**132 567.9**	**183 963.9**
Wholesale and retail trade; repair of motor vehicles and motorcycles	12 705.3	13 929.5	13 214.7	11 175.4	12 201.2	12 283.2	13 656.6	13 496.9	12 429.6	33 974.0
Transportation and storage	2 927.6	2 532.5	2 719.7	2 881.6	3 906.3	10 093.7	15 116.7	15 240.8	10 792.0	10 832.7
Accommodation and food service activities	175.3	273.7	328.3	339.7	380.8	33.3	62.7	130.4	132.1	167.4
Information and communication	5 076.4	6 251.8	5 857.0	7 363.7	9 136.6	2 040.3	2 092.4	826.3	1 456.1	2 076.7
Financial and insurance activities	46 764.1	52 818.0	53 537.4	58 177.3	58 978.1	44 971.6	55 601.1	54 141.8	57 220.9	71 314.7
Activities of holding companies	..	..	..	..	..	..	..	..	..	..
Real estate activities	2 359.6	3 762.1	5 303.7	7 008.6	8 271.8	2 525.2	3 160.8	3 663.2	3 752.0	5 115.7
Professional, scientific and technical activities	4 603.4	6 622.9	9 542.7	12 311.4	15 871.8	22 034.4	24 731.4	30 462.9	32 300.7	42 579.1
Administrative and support service activities	5 815.3	7 386.8	6 923.3	7 814.5	11 774.8	2 721.6	6 217.9	7 423.5	12 447.5	13 554.0
Public administration; activities of households and of extraterritorial organisations	-1.0	-1.0	-	-	-	821.2	1 008.1	.. d	.. d	2 992.1
Education	-9.4	-3.7	20.6	19.9	22.0	21.3	19.5	25.6	23.4	29.2
Human health and social work activities	-8.8	21.4	55.1	102.5	63.4	818.1	946.7	.. d	.. d	.. d
Arts, entertainment and recreation	-2.3	14.7	29.0	16.9	0.3	58.0	69.9	8.3	41.2	101.0
Other services	63.5	76.2	.. d	.. d	121.0	78.1	71.8	80.8	66.4	69.3
Not allocated and confidential	**1 537.1**	**2 515.6**	**.. d**	**.. d**	**.. d**	**3 402.6**	**3 726.0**	**.. d**	**.. d**	**.. d**
Private real estate activities	**2 101.3**	**2 532.8**	**.. d**	**.. d**	**.. d**	**3 732.4**	**4 305.5**	**.. d**	**.. d**	**.. d**

- Nil; .. Not available; d Secondary Confidentiality

Note: Data excludes resident Special Purpose Entities (SPEs). Detailed metadata at: *http://metalinks.oecd.org/idi/20220712/6d95*.

Source: *OECD International Direct Investment Statistics (database)*: *https://doi.org/10.1787/idi-data-en*

DENMARK

Table 6. Foreign direct investment income by industrial sector

Million US dollars

	Inward					Outward				
	2016	2017	2018	2019	2020	2016	2017	2018	2019	2020
All FDI activities	**5 481.4**	**6 133.9**	**6 694.9**	**7 414.5**	**5 373.7**	**12 061.1**	**13 256.1**	**15 499.0**	**15 461.4**	**14 777.3**
Agriculture, forestry and fishing	**12.8**	**15.1**	**8.9**	**9.7**	**7.9**	**22.3**	**25.3**	**38.8**	**36.1**	**26.1**
Mining and quarrying	**-234.0**	**-59.2**	**66.8**	**433.3**	**312.6**	**429.4**	**717.1**	**.. d**	**.. d**	**106.4**
Extraction activities	-253.3	-72.7	63.4	.. d	305.4	426.5	714.4	.. d	.. d	101.3
Manufacturing	**1 127.4**	**1 255.1**	**1 212.2**	**1 177.2**	**584.7**	**4 672.0**	**4 617.5**	**5 142.3**	**5 629.3**	**5 315.5**
of which:										
Food products, beverages and tobacco	275.0	249.3	269.3	279.0	229.6	1 021.9	1 045.6	1 219.6	1 588.8	1 391.8
Textiles, wood and paper products; printing	22.7	16.2	8.2	24.1	26.8	70.7	69.5	73.3	71.8	86.8
Chemical, rubber, plastic, non-metallic mineral products	391.5	404.9	265.9	407.1	-91.1	2 705.5	2 734.0	2 970.1	2 888.7	3 061.0
Metal and machinery products, except electrical equipment	204.0	302.8	547.9	378.6	272.4	769.7	612.0	709.1	801.9	552.7
Motor vehicles, trailers, semi-trailers, other transport equipment	3.9	7.3	11.2	8.4	3.5	16.2	19.4	15.2	24.9	16.5
Other manufacturing	230.1	274.8	109.8	80.1	143.5	88.0	137.1	154.9	253.3	206.5
Electricity, gas, steam and air conditioning supply	**69.5**	**53.5**	**73.0**	**129.7**	**166.2**	**296.7**	**382.8**	**585.9**	**678.5**	**.. d**
Water supply; sewerage, waste management and remediation activities	**-4.0**	**5.8**	**2.7**	**-13.5**	**6.0**	**-**	**0.9**	**1.6**	**1.3**	**2.4**
Construction	**72.4**	**63.3**	**53.5**	**74.5**	**93.4**	**2.7**	**6.8**	**12.8**	**1.6**	**15.0**
Services	**4 316.1**	**4 748.9**	**5 220.7**	**5 512.1**	**4 149.6**	**6 570.5**	**7 447.4**	**9 167.2**	**8 423.0**	**8 506.7**
Wholesale and retail trade; repair of motor vehicles and motorcycles	944.2	1 122.1	1 188.9	949.0	491.3	1 006.0	1 136.2	1 158.3	843.1	804.6
Transportation and storage	-192.5	-1.8	-125.9	210.4	135.1	465.0	424.4	1 107.5	1 086.0	1 743.5
Accommodation and food service activities	19.5	0.8	32.2	34.3	30.7	1.9	4.2	6.7	6.6	6.3
Information and communication	115.7	-43.3	103.3	87.7	149.5	125.5	211.6	149.7	150.4	92.0
Financial and insurance activities	2 718.5	2 781.4	2 944.6	3 055.5	2 079.2	3 060.7	3 480.0	3 962.9	3 743.0	2 470.3
Activities of holding companies	..	..	..	..	..	..	..	..	..	..
Real estate activities	119.0	178.7	285.3	316.8	230.5	108.6	126.2	165.4	177.4	163.3
Professional, scientific and technical activities	334.0	267.8	319.3	444.1	546.3	1 549.0	1 650.2	1 839.4	2 028.0	2 618.2
Administrative and support service activities	251.5	431.1	438.4	390.2	467.0	209.0	339.8	768.8	353.9	420.7
Public administration; activities of households and of extraterritorial organisations	-	-	-	1.1	-	-24.5	1.4	-45.0	-8.8	.. d
Education	0.3	0.9	1.4	1.3	1.2	0.9	1.4	1.1	0.9	0.8
Human health and social work activities	-19.8	-12.9	0.8	-5.7	-0.9	61.8	64.2	47.8	37.5	.. d
Arts, entertainment and recreation	0.6	0.8	2.5	2.2	0.9	3.6	3.9	0.5	1.6	3.2
Other services	25.3	23.3	29.9	25.2	19.0	3.0	4.1	4.6	3.3	2.6
Not allocated and confidential	**121.2**	**51.5**	**57.0**	**91.5**	**53.3**	**67.6**	**58.3**	**.. d**	**.. d**	**.. d**
Private real estate activities	-	-	..	..	..	-	-	..	..	..

- Nil; .. Not available; d Secondary Confidentiality

Note: Data excludes resident Special Purpose Entities (SPEs). Detailed metadata at: *http://metalinks.oecd.org/idi/20220712/6d95*.

Source: *OECD International Direct Investment Statistics (database)*: *https://doi.org/10.1787/idi-data-en*

ESTONIA

Table 1. Foreign direct investment flows by country

Million US dollars

	Inward					Outward				
	2016	2017	2018	2019	2020	2016	2017	2018	2019	2020
WORLD	**1 058.4**	**1 946.6**	**1 516.5**	**3 183.9**	**3 387.8**	**486.5**	**887.8**	**44.5**	**1 965.7**	**219.2**
OECD COUNTRIES	**860.3**	**1 578.7**	**1 204.9**	**2 984.9**	**3 273.4**	**415.1**	**894.1**	**-64.4**	**1 920.2**	**.. d**
Australia	1.2	-4.2	0.4	6.5	0.9	0.7	-0.6	0.4	0.6	2.4
Austria	16.0	-54.5	64.9	4.9	-13.9	-0.4	0.0	0.2	0.4	1.4
Belgium	17.3	11.5	14.3	-19.4	-10.6	5.6	3.0	-0.2	0.5	1.2
Canada	-0.7	-6.8	17.9	2.1	1.1	0.0	0.1	0.1	0.1	0.6
Chile	0.0	0.0	0.0	-0.1	0.6	.. c	.. c	.. c	0.0	0.1
Colombia	0.1	0.0	0.0	0.0	0.0	-	-	-	-	-
Costa Rica	0.1	-0.1	0.5	0.0	-0.2	-	-	-	-	-
Czech Republic	4.3	8.3	0.1	3.7	-6.2	4.5	2.9	0.3	-1.7	2.4
Denmark	76.0	0.9	34.6	-108.4	164.6	7.3	-48.3	2.1	0.2	-2.2
Estonia	-	-	-	-	-	-	-	-	-	-
Finland	381.0	141.3	337.5	379.2	133.1	64.2	808.9	129.4	155.5	136.7
France	42.8	49.1	24.3	88.5	20.5	6.3	6.3	21.4	2.4	4.0
Germany	8.0	126.1	176.4	73.6	325.0	17.7	2.0	-7.4	4.5	17.4
Greece	0.4	0.8	1.3	1.8	1.0	0.2	0.0	.. c	0.2	.. c
Hungary	1.4	-0.4	6.2	7.2	4.3	1.0	-0.2	0.7	0.2	0.2
Iceland	4.6	5.7	6.8	8.2	2.0	0.0	0.0	10.1	.. c	.. c
Ireland	-4.5	-108.8	176.2	81.3	61.5	-10.1	-3.2	-0.7	0.2	0.1
Israel	0.3	1.4	4.3	6.6	-0.9	-0.1	0.8	-0.2	0.1	0.3
Italy	19.9	-6.7	-9.8	11.1	7.4	11.9	-0.3	1.8	2.8	1.5
Japan	10.6	5.1	20.1	33.3	27.7	-	-	.. c	-	.. c
Korea	0.2	-1.1	0.0	1.5	1.2	-	.. c	.. c	.. c	.. c
Latvia	117.4	46.0	56.7	85.0	-16.7	106.6	14.8	223.7	732.1	96.9
Lithuania	26.2	100.7	-5.5	290.0	142.3	-69.7	131.9	18.8	985.7	-68.8
Luxembourg	-17.4	109.6	1 105.7	66.4	2 177.4	0.9	-0.2	49.9	-10.8	-9.7
Mexico	0.0	-0.4	-3.0	-2.1	-2.1	0.2	.. c	.. c	-1.2	.. c
Netherlands	15.1	-107.2	-644.2	95.9	31.5	6.9	8.0	-652.2	22.2	-9.1
New Zealand	1.7	0.3	0.0	1.4	1.8	.. c	.. c	.. c	.. c	.. c
Norway	-250.2	37.3	-279.5	34.6	73.4	2.3	14.8	8.1	2.1	5.8
Poland	29.0	3.5	58.2	5.2	41.8	79.2	11.0	16.3	38.5	24.4
Portugal	5.1	9.4	-0.1	0.5	3.0	22.5	-12.9	3.4	-1.1	4.2
Slovak Republic	0.3	3.3	3.5	-17.9	2.5	0.5	-0.6	0.5	2.2	-3.6
Slovenia	0.1	0.1	0.3	0.1	0.4	-	-0.2	0.8	.. c	-0.1
Spain	1.5	-4.0	18.5	0.8	14.3	22.8	21.2	18.5	10.7	10.7
Sweden	293.9	713.4	-166.2	1 586.6	21.4	30.5	-14.2	25.2	-10.1	6.1
Switzerland	20.5	38.4	67.0	33.7	-8.5	-0.4	-0.8	5.6	-3.8	7.6
Turkey	-2.6	11.1	6.3	5.1	18.3	0.2	8.8	0.6	0.5	0.3
United Kingdom	36.4	547.1	70.1	214.1	39.7	28.1	66.0	25.0	-47.8	-69.8
United States	30.9	3.1	41.5	3.8	13.3	5.8	0.3	32.8	35.1	83.6
EUROPE	**958.1**	**1 773.9**	**1 388.3**	**3 150.9**	**3 343.3**	**458.5**	**825.8**	**-29.5**	**1 903.8**	**100.3**
Bulgaria	0.8	0.0	1.8	2.0	1.8	-	4.9	3.4	5.4	0.0
Croatia	1.1	-0.1	-0.2	1.5	-0.6	0.4	1.5	2.1	5.3	-1.1
Cyprus	-51.8	-64.4	119.5	33.5	-84.9	32.6	-182.8	-37.3	6.6	-57.8
Malta	27.1	12.4	5.2	23.7	13.9	11.4	6.3	-7.7	3.5	-0.2
Montenegro	.. c	0.5	0.2	-0.2	-0.2	-	-	.. c	0.2	-
Romania	1.5	2.3	-0.2	3.4	6.1	15.0	-5.0	-0.1	-11.3	2.2
Russian Federation	74.8	54.6	52.6	89.0	41.2	47.0	21.5	10.8	-8.0	13.1
Ukraine	44.6	68.2	54.3	52.2	80.7	-15.8	-18.3	69.2	-5.9	-2.1
AFRICA	**-7.4**	**9.1**	**1.6**	**-1.0**	**-3.1**	**-0.9**	**-1.9**	**11.7**	**6.6**	**12.0**
Northern Africa	0.0	0.4	1.2	0.9	0.6	.. c	0.3	1.6	1.7	.. c
Algeria	.. c	0.0	0.2	0.1	0.0	-	-	-	-	-
Egypt	0.0	0.3	0.7	0.2	0.2	-	0.1	0.5	0.3	.. c
Libya	-	-	.. c	0.0	0.0	-	-	-	-	-
Morocco	-	0.0	0.3	0.2	0.3	.. c	.. c	.. c	.. c	-
Tunisia	0.0	0.0	0.0	0.3	0.2	-	-	-	-	-
Other African countries	-7.5	8.7	0.5	-1.9	-3.7	-1.0	-2.1	10.1	4.9	12.2
Nigeria	.. c	0.0	0.0	0.0	0.2	-	.. c	.. c	.. c	.. c
South Africa	0.2	0.0	-0.8	-0.6	0.2	.. c	.. c	2.5	4.1	1.6
AMERICA	**57.9**	**-87.4**	**34.6**	**-48.3**	**-1.9**	**5.9**	**1.4**	**34.1**	**32.9**	**84.5**
Northern America	30.2	-3.7	59.4	5.9	14.4	5.8	0.4	32.9	35.1	84.3
Central America and Caribbean countries	26.4	-84.6	-25.6	-54.9	-17.1	0.0	0.4	0.7	-1.2	0.1
Bahamas	0.4	-0.2	0.0	0.0	2.9	.. c	-	-	-	-
Bermuda	-	.. c	-	-	-	-	-	-	-	-
Cayman Islands	-5.2	-10.7	4.1	-5.9	-15.3	-	-	-	-	-
El Salvador	-	.. c	.. c	0.0	-	-	-	-	-	-
Guatemala	-	-	-	-	.. c	-	-	-	-	-
Honduras	-	.. c	.. c	.. c	.. c	-	-	-	-	-
Nicaragua	-	.. c	.. c	-	.. c	-	-	-	-	-
Panama	8.2	1.6	-1.4	-0.9	0.3	-0.1	0.1	0.1	0.0	0.0
Virgin Islands, U.S.	-	.. c	.. c	-	-	-	-	-	-	-
South America	1.2	1.0	0.8	0.7	0.8	0.1	0.6	0.5	-1.0	0.1
Argentina	-	0.0	0.0	0.1	0.2	.. c	-	.. c	-	-
Bolivia	0.3	.. c	.. c	0.1	0.1	-	-	-	-	-
Brazil	0.8	0.7	0.6	0.2	-0.4	0.3	0.2	0.6	-1.0	0.1
Ecuador	0.1	0.0	0.1	0.0	0.0	-	-	.. c	-	-
Paraguay	-	.. c	-	.. c	-0.3	-	-	-	-	-
Peru	0.1	0.1	0.1	0.2	0.1	-	-	-	-	-
Uruguay	-	0.0	0.0	0.0	0.4	.. c	.. c	.. c	-	-
Venezuela	-	-	0.0	0.0	0.0	-	-	-	-	-

ESTONIA

Table 1. Foreign direct investment flows by country *(cont.)*

Million US dollars

	Inward					Outward				
	2016	2017	2018	2019	2020	2016	2017	2018	2019	2020
ASIA	**10.3**	**251.6**	**88.4**	**67.8**	**40.4**	**22.3**	**62.9**	**27.8**	**21.2**	**19.0**
Near and Middle East	1.2	209.8	17.4	27.0	-16.7	16.0	59.3	29.4	6.0	19.4
Gulf Arabian countries	0.3	206.0	5.8	-16.1	-24.2	-0.4	2.4	6.0	6.9	8.3
Kuwait	.. c	0.0	0.0	0.0	0.1	-	-	-	-	-
Qatar	.. c	0.0	0.0	0.0	0.0	-	-	-	-	-
Saudi Arabia	0.0	0.0	0.0	0.4	0.7	-	-	-	-	-
United Arab Emirates	0.8	206.0	5.6	-16.7	-25.1	2.7	3.1	4.3	4.3	9.8
Other Near and Middle East	0.9	3.8	11.6	43.1	7.4	16.4	56.9	23.3	-1.0	11.1
Jordan	.. c	0.1	0.0	0.0	0.0	.. c	.. c	.. c	.. c	.. c
Other Asian countries	9.2	41.7	71.0	40.9	57.1	6.2	3.6	-1.6	15.2	-0.3
China	-8.6	5.6	10.1	-1.6	9.3	0.1	0.1	0.7	0.4	0.2
Hong Kong, China	12.6	8.6	9.7	7.3	-8.7	4.8	-4.7	0.4	0.1	0.2
India	-0.9	1.7	-0.3	4.1	1.3	.. c	2.6	.. c	-0.3	0.7
Indonesia	0.0	0.0	-	0.0	0.1	-	0.2	0.1	0.8	0.0
Iran, Islamic Republic of	0.1	0.1	0.1	0.1	0.0	-	-	-	-	-
Malaysia	0.2	0.3	0.1	0.3	0.3	-	.. c	-	.. c	.. c
Philippines	0.1	0.3	-0.1	0.2	0.2	-	0.1	-	0.0	-
Singapore	-4.5	17.8	18.4	-13.2	8.5	-0.1	-2.8	-1.5	0.7	-1.1
Chinese Taipei	0.2	0.6	0.9	-0.4	-0.1	.. c	-	-	-	.. c
Thailand	-0.8	-2.0	3.6	0.8	0.8	0.6	0.3	-0.2	.. c	0.1
Viet Nam	0.1	0.0	0.1	0.0	0.0	.. c	-	-	-	-
AUSTRALIA, OCEANIA AND POLAR REGIONS	**38.9**	**-1.5**	**0.6**	**8.2**	**3.1**	**0.6**	**-0.4**	**0.5**	**1.3**	**3.3**
WORLD unallocated and confidential	**0.7**	**1.0**	**2.9**	**6.3**	**6.0**	**0.0**	**-**	**0.0**	**0.0**	**0.0**
European Union (since 01/02/2020)	..	..	..	..	..	..	..	..	..	..
G20 countries excl. European Union	**213.0**	**785.0**	**406.3**	**529.1**	**505.7**	**119.6**	**114.2**	**89.7**	**-7.1**	**56.0**
G20 OECD countries	**146.7**	**722.4**	**344.1**	**437.5**	**453.0**	**71.1**	**89.1**	**75.5**	**-3.0**	**40.4**
G20 Non-OECD countries	**66.3**	**62.6**	**62.2**	**91.7**	**52.7**	**48.5**	**25.1**	**14.2**	**-4.1**	**15.6**
MENA countries	**0.0**	**206.3**	**7.0**	**-15.1**	**-23.5**	**-0.4**	**41.4**	**11.4**	**13.3**	**13.0**
ASEAN countries	**-4.9**	**16.3**	**22.0**	**-11.8**	**10.0**	**0.4**	**-2.0**	**-1.7**	**1.6**	**-1.0**

- Nil; .. Not available; c Confidential data; d Secondary Confidentiality

Note: Detailed metadata at: *http://metalinks.oecd.org/idi/20220712/6d95*.

Source: OECD *International Direct Investment Statistics (database)*: *https://doi.org/10.1787/idi-data-en*

ESTONIA

Table 2. Foreign direct investment positions by country

At year end

Million US dollars

	Inward					Outward				
	2016	2017	2018	2019	2020	2016	2017	2018	2019	2020
WORLD	**19 658.5**	**24 048.9**	**25 049.2**	**28 156.0**	**34 510.8**	**6 298.5**	**7 812.4**	**7 959.1**	**10 161.3**	**11 058.5**
OECD COUNTRIES	**16 366.1**	**20 032.9**	**22 201.6**	**23 649.1**	**29 035.5**	**2 775.7**	**3 679.9**	**5 504.8**	**7 724.6**	**.. d**
Australia	20.0	39.7	40.9	37.5	58.1	3.1	2.9	4.7	5.2	8.3
Austria	281.8	355.7	322.3	398.1	385.3	3.5	3.9	4.8	5.1	5.4
Belgium	79.8	98.9	128.2	140.0	175.2	45.8	4.0	3.7	3.2	4.8
Canada	113.3	68.2	324.0	420.8	748.0	0.4	0.6	0.7	0.8	1.5
Chile	0.0	0.0	0.0	0.1	0.6	0.1	0.2	0.2	0.2	0.3
Colombia	0.1	0.2	1.9	1.1	1.7	-	-	-	-	-
Costa Rica	0.0	0.0	0.7	1.3	1.7	0.0	0.0	0.0	0.0	0.0
Czech Republic	12.7	13.8	20.2	19.7	29.0	11.2	16.5	21.2	19.0	17.4
Denmark	528.3	670.9	661.1	523.0	533.5	53.4	10.1	11.6	14.5	11.9
Estonia	1 390.4	1 572.1	1 269.7	1 004.7	1 445.1	-	-	-	-	-
Finland	4 421.6	5 356.1	5 937.4	6 543.9	7 181.5	462.0	917.5	733.6	833.0	952.5
France	451.1	571.1	589.5	652.9	713.3	46.2	54.9	71.7	72.7	84.7
Germany	596.6	716.0	740.9	859.9	960.0	71.3	61.2	50.6	53.6	101.6
Greece	29.1	31.9	4.1	5.2	7.4	2.4	2.7	2.5	2.7	3.1
Hungary	5.9	9.1	10.7	10.4	13.7	4.1	4.5	4.9	5.0	5.6
Iceland	27.2	74.1	98.8	84.8	93.0	0.0	0.0	.. c	.. c	.. c
Ireland	56.6	49.3	58.6	82.5	87.1	5.7	2.2	1.4	1.7	2.0
Israel	11.0	12.0	7.3	5.7	7.5	2.3	3.5	3.1	3.1	3.8
Italy	182.2	187.1	177.5	188.0	640.6	119.6	92.4	77.6	76.3	98.2
Japan	141.5	171.5	273.2	330.2	352.7	0.2	0.2	0.2	0.2	0.3
Korea	0.1	0.2	0.4	0.7	1.1	0.0	6.7	11.5	11.5	12.7
Latvia	530.8	535.3	600.7	562.0	631.2	1 102.6	1 385.2	1 635.1	2 366.1	2 605.5
Lithuania	742.0	1 008.7	1 089.4	1 131.4	1 296.6	1 210.1	1 606.1	1 591.5	2 904.7	3 071.0
Luxembourg	536.0	687.4	1 113.6	1 342.1	3 171.8	21.2	24.0	61.6	11.2	2.2
Mexico	0.0	0.1	-1.1	0.5	0.9	0.5	1.0	1.6	0.4	0.5
Netherlands	561.6	674.0	526.4	595.7	634.6	232.4	266.2	286.3	306.6	293.1
New Zealand	1.9	1.9	1.9	3.1	4.1	0.0	4.5	4.4	4.8	6.1
Norway	602.8	1 159.4	430.0	444.7	488.5	44.8	69.6	72.0	73.4	76.6
Poland	94.4	120.6	128.6	207.1	227.7	124.8	152.6	161.2	193.8	230.9
Portugal	0.5	6.6	8.5	12.3	16.7	24.6	14.4	17.0	14.8	29.6
Slovak Republic	21.0	22.3	31.0	29.8	33.4	22.7	25.2	12.3	14.5	11.7
Slovenia	-0.1	0.2	0.4	0.7	0.6	0.1	-0.2	0.5	0.5	0.4
Spain	33.5	43.0	44.7	55.2	64.3	83.5	122.9	130.8	142.8	172.2
Sweden	4 328.0	5 285.8	5 764.1	6 050.3	6 591.4	109.5	145.1	175.7	163.7	184.0
Switzerland	271.3	301.5	368.9	340.5	342.5	28.9	31.4	52.6	33.7	37.8
Turkey	6.0	18.4	24.1	28.8	51.4	2.4	5.6	6.0	6.3	7.1
United Kingdom	380.6	526.1	719.2	767.2	1 019.6	47.2	131.6	136.5	139.2	156.9
United States	648.6	652.6	686.3	769.8	1 025.8	99.0	116.9	145.9	231.5	346.4
EUROPE	**17 858.7**	**21 876.0**	**22 820.8**	**25 356.5**	**30 495.8**	**6 077.2**	**7 457.7**	**7 568.5**	**9 670.6**	**10 440.8**
Bulgaria	2.5	3.3	5.8	5.7	11.7	33.9	42.0	44.6	50.3	55.4
Croatia	0.4	0.7	0.7	1.2	1.7	24.9	28.4	28.5	29.3	29.3
Cyprus	346.7	412.8	396.0	352.3	481.4	1 403.8	1 395.0	1 275.1	1 264.2	1 295.0
Malta	50.9	48.1	51.9	67.0	50.2	33.3	52.9	44.4	50.4	47.9
Montenegro	.. c	0.0	0.4	0.1	-0.3	0.6	0.7	0.8	1.0	1.1
Romania	2.3	4.8	4.0	8.1	8.7	38.1	37.3	33.2	22.6	27.3
Russian Federation	759.0	708.9	816.2	1 065.6	996.4	250.4	330.3	307.2	279.1	358.4
Ukraine	218.0	280.3	339.3	418.4	515.8	251.8	265.6	321.7	311.6	255.6
AFRICA	**18.2**	**42.9**	**30.4**	**27.4**	**43.2**	**15.3**	**15.5**	**29.5**	**36.1**	**36.7**
Northern Africa	0.8	2.1	3.3	5.4	10.1	13.4	15.5	16.4	17.4	3.7
Algeria	0.0	0.1	0.3	0.3	0.3	-	-	-	-	-
Egypt	0.7	1.9	2.6	4.1	8.2	0.7	0.8	1.3	1.4	1.4
Libya	0.0	0.1	0.1	0.1	0.1	-	-	-	-	-
Morocco	0.0	0.0	0.3	0.6	1.0	12.7	14.6	15.0	16.0	2.3
Tunisia	.. c	0.0	0.1	0.3	0.5	0.0	0.1	0.1	0.1	0.1
Other African countries	17.4	40.8	27.1	22.0	33.1	1.9	-0.1	13.1	18.7	33.0
Nigeria	0.6	0.7	0.7	0.6	0.7	-	.. c	.. c	.. c	.. c
South Africa	1.8	1.1	3.4	0.9	-1.4	0.2	0.6	2.9	7.9	9.8
AMERICA	**1 179.1**	**1 105.3**	**1 290.6**	**1 414.9**	**2 017.3**	**115.2**	**136.4**	**165.9**	**248.0**	**353.9**
Northern America	761.9	720.8	1 010.3	1 190.6	1 773.8	99.5	117.5	146.6	232.2	347.9
Central America and Caribbean countries	413.7	379.9	271.1	210.3	218.3	1.7	2.3	2.8	1.6	2.4
Bahamas	1.7	2.0	1.8	0.8	1.0	0.0	0.0	0.0	0.0	0.0
Bermuda	0.3	0.5	0.5	0.7	0.8	-	-	-	-	-
Cayman Islands	.. c	.. c	.. c	-0.1	-0.1	0.2	0.3	0.3	0.3	0.3
El Salvador	0.4	0.8	1.2	2.1	3.4	-	-	-	-	-
Guatemala	-	-	-	-	.. c	-	-	-	-	-
Honduras	-	-	-0.1	-0.2	-0.2	-	-	-	-	-
Nicaragua	-	.. c	0.0	0.0	0.0	-	-	-	-	-
Panama	32.3	21.7	18.4	8.6	6.9	0.2	0.2	0.1	0.2	0.2
Virgin Islands, U.S.	-	.. c	.. c	.. c	.. c	-	-	-	-	-
South America	3.4	4.7	9.2	14.0	25.3	14.1	16.6	16.5	14.3	3.5
Argentina	0.5	0.5	0.6	0.7	1.0	0.1	0.1	0.2	0.1	0.0
Bolivia	0.3	0.3	0.2	0.3	0.3	-	-	-	-	-
Brazil	0.6	0.7	1.0	1.5	2.0	14.0	16.1	16.0	14.0	3.2
Ecuador	1.6	2.4	4.5	9.2	15.4	0.0	0.0	0.1	0.1	0.1
Paraguay	-	.. c	.. c	0.0	0.0	-	-	-	-	-
Peru	.. c	.. c	0.5	0.6	0.8	-	-	-	-	-
Uruguay	0.0	0.0	0.0	0.0	0.0	.. c	.. c	-	-	-
Venezuela	-	-	0.2	0.2	2.7	.. c	.. c	.. c	.. c	.. c

ESTONIA

Table 2. Foreign direct investment positions by country (*cont.*)

At year end

Million US dollars

	Inward					Outward				
	2016	2017	2018	2019	2020	2016	2017	2018	2019	2020
ASIA	**339.4**	**695.8**	**530.7**	**821.4**	**1 432.4**	**87.6**	**195.4**	**186.1**	**196.4**	**212.5**
Near and Middle East	22.1	252.2	43.7	228.6	100.2	34.6	103.8	130.7	127.6	150.0
Gulf Arabian countries	7.0	227.4	13.7	185.3	17.9	-7.3	-6.3	-0.4	7.3	16.3
Kuwait	0.2	0.2	0.2	0.2	0.2	-	-	-	-	-
Qatar	0.6	0.8	1.1	1.3	1.0	-	-	-	-	-
Saudi Arabia	1.5	1.4	1.9	1.5	2.3	-	-	-	-	-
United Arab Emirates	3.4	223.5	8.7	180.5	11.9	-8.5	-6.5	-2.3	2.1	12.4
Other Near and Middle East	15.1	24.8	29.9	43.3	82.3	41.9	110.1	131.1	120.3	133.7
Jordan	0.0	0.0	0.5	0.1	0.1	.. c	.. c	.. c	.. c	.. c
Other Asian countries	317.3	443.6	487.0	592.8	1 332.1	53.0	91.5	55.4	68.8	62.6
China	13.3	14.2	19.1	50.9	55.2	4.5	5.2	6.3	6.7	8.0
Hong Kong, China	46.6	46.1	20.9	19.9	9.1	5.0	24.6	13.1	11.5	12.4
India	0.9	1.7	3.7	5.9	547.0	1.4	4.2	3.3	2.4	3.4
Indonesia	0.1	0.2	0.2	0.2	0.2	0.3	0.6	0.6	1.4	1.6
Iran, Islamic Republic of	0.3	0.5	0.4	0.8	1.0	-	-	-	-	-
Malaysia	0.5	0.7	0.7	1.0	1.3	-	0.1	0.1	0.2	0.2
Philippines	0.4	0.8	1.2	0.7	2.0	0.0	0.2	0.2	0.2	0.2
Singapore	94.1	162.4	117.4	116.5	289.8	1.6	2.5	1.4	3.6	-1.2
Chinese Taipei	0.3	0.9	1.6	1.3	1.2	0.1	0.1	0.0	0.0	0.1
Thailand	0.1	0.4	1.8	2.4	5.8	5.7	6.8	6.3	6.2	6.8
Viet Nam	.. c	0.0	0.1	0.1	0.1	.. c	.. c	-	-	-
AUSTRALIA, OCEANIA AND POLAR REGIONS	**39.5**	**59.6**	**60.2**	**51.5**	**70.4**	**3.2**	**7.4**	**9.1**	**10.2**	**14.7**
WORLD unallocated and confidential	**223.5**	**269.2**	**316.4**	**484.3**	**451.8**	**0.0**	**0.0**	**0.0**	**-**	**0.0**
European Union (since 01/02/2020)	**..**	**18 485.6**	**19 691.3**	**..**	**25 395.5**	**..**	**6 467.1**	**6 481.3**	**..**	**9 342.6**
G20 countries excl. European Union	**3 317.6**	**3 679.6**	**4 421.0**	**5 183.4**	**7 174.1**	**660.9**	**830.9**	**843.5**	**909.0**	**1 202.4**
G20 OECD countries	**2 539.9**	**2 951.0**	**3 574.9**	**4 056.2**	**5 571.5**	**390.0**	**473.9**	**506.9**	**597.5**	**818.0**
G20 Non-OECD countries	**777.6**	**728.7**	**846.1**	**1 127.2**	**1 602.6**	**270.8**	**357.0**	**336.6**	**311.6**	**384.4**
MENA countries	**12.9**	**236.5**	**26.8**	**197.1**	**38.5**	**6.1**	**46.3**	**60.0**	**72.8**	**75.2**
ASEAN countries	**95.2**	**164.6**	**121.6**	**121.0**	**299.3**	**8.1**	**10.6**	**8.8**	**11.9**	**8.0**

- Nil; .. Not available; c Confidential data; d Secondary Confidentiality

Note: Inward FDI positions are allocated according to the ultimate investing country. Detailed metadata at: *http://metalinks.oecd.org/idi/20220712/6d95*.

Source: *OECD International Direct Investment Statistics (database)*: *https://doi.org/10.1787/idi-data-en*

ESTONIA

Table 3. Foreign direct investment income by country

Million US dollars

	Inward					Outward				
	2016	2017	2018	2019	2020	2016	2017	2018	2019	2020
WORLD	**1 591.0**	**1 736.6**	**1 944.5**	**1 994.9**	**1 614.9**	**492.4**	**485.4**	**696.8**	**713.2**	**602.1**
OECD COUNTRIES	**1 348.1**	**1 420.6**	**1 602.0**	**1 765.6**	**1 427.2**	**190.0**	**222.9**	**467.1**	**558.9**	**.. d**
Australia	1.3	0.1	-0.5	-0.7	-0.5	0.2	0.0	0.1	0.1	0.0
Austria	13.9	28.9	30.4	20.3	-4.0	0.1	0.0	0.1	0.2	0.8
Belgium	7.3	14.8	14.9	10.5	12.1	0.6	0.5	2.6	0.0	0.1
Canada	1.7	-0.2	2.3	3.9	3.2	0.0	0.0	0.0	0.0	0.0
Chile	.. c	-	.. c	0.0	0.0	0.0	0.0	0.0	0.0	0.0
Colombia	0.0	0.0	0.0	0.0	0.0	-	-	-	-	-
Costa Rica	-	.. c	0.5	0.0	0.0	0.0	0.0	0.0	0.0	-
Czech Republic	4.0	9.2	4.5	5.0	5.3	0.5	0.3	1.1	0.7	2.2
Denmark	33.5	34.6	28.6	20.4	41.9	4.3	4.0	-0.1	-0.4	-1.7
Estonia	-	-	-	-	-	-	-	-	-	-
Finland	383.1	385.2	397.1	342.7	282.0	5.2	71.4	131.3	164.4	75.9
France	25.4	31.6	41.7	45.1	36.0	0.9	1.6	1.2	1.7	1.4
Germany	27.8	48.0	60.1	58.2	70.8	1.7	0.5	-10.7	-8.0	-4.6
Greece	0.2	0.8	1.7	1.7	1.7	1.4	0.0	0.0	0.0	0.0
Hungary	0.4	1.5	1.9	4.2	2.6	0.2	0.2	0.6	0.4	0.4
Iceland	9.5	7.9	9.8	8.5	14.2	-	-	-	-	-
Ireland	0.4	-1.2	5.2	2.9	4.9	0.5	0.2	-0.1	0.0	0.0
Israel	1.8	1.6	0.4	0.2	0.9	0.0	0.0	0.0	0.0	0.0
Italy	4.7	6.0	12.1	12.5	8.1	-0.4	-0.7	1.6	1.1	0.6
Japan	0.4	0.3	5.5	10.4	14.4	0.0	0.0	0.0	0.0	0.0
Korea	.. c	-	0.2	0.2	0.2	-	-	-	.. c	.. c
Latvia	31.5	57.5	33.3	16.9	11.8	115.7	107.7	120.6	149.3	131.4
Lithuania	41.9	78.8	44.7	71.3	80.6	105.5	126.7	164.3	200.3	219.3
Luxembourg	18.2	30.3	24.4	79.1	55.6	3.3	4.2	2.9	-4.0	-2.1
Mexico	0.0	0.0	-2.8	0.1	0.1	0.0	0.0	0.0	0.0	0.0
Netherlands	133.3	82.8	121.7	152.3	71.3	39.8	0.5	0.1	4.7	10.5
New Zealand	0.0	0.0	0.0	-	0.0	0.0	0.1	0.1	0.1	0.1
Norway	30.6	35.6	42.6	46.1	42.3	0.8	1.0	0.7	2.9	1.3
Poland	16.8	12.0	8.0	9.8	5.4	-0.1	0.8	5.2	-2.2	11.9
Portugal	2.8	5.7	-1.8	4.4	5.3	0.0	0.1	0.9	0.5	0.8
Slovak Republic	0.3	3.2	3.5	3.2	2.2	0.5	0.7	1.6	-0.7	-2.8
Slovenia	0.0	0.3	0.0	0.3	0.3	0.0	-	0.4	0.0	0.1
Spain	4.5	5.0	9.6	10.7	10.7	6.1	4.9	6.1	4.4	3.4
Sweden	536.9	541.7	522.9	649.9	554.2	8.4	13.8	15.3	16.5	8.1
Switzerland	19.7	19.1	25.9	26.0	21.0	0.6	7.9	17.6	22.5	3.0
Turkey	-2.1	0.1	-0.9	1.4	7.7	0.1	0.1	0.1	0.1	0.1
United Kingdom	32.7	53.5	122.4	135.0	50.7	-0.2	3.1	4.3	2.4	8.7
United States	7.4	4.8	32.8	13.2	14.3	-0.3	-0.1	-0.8	1.9	9.4
EUROPE	**1 547.5**	**1 691.7**	**1 837.0**	**1 958.1**	**1 571.7**	**488.1**	**482.9**	**686.0**	**697.3**	**579.5**
Bulgaria	0.3	0.4	0.9	0.5	2.0	0.9	1.0	1.9	5.9	4.1
Croatia	0.3	0.3	0.5	0.5	0.5	0.4	0.0	0.2	0.3	0.2
Cyprus	34.2	35.3	138.3	72.8	-12.9	107.6	96.6	92.6	67.6	47.5
Malta	14.0	4.5	8.2	21.0	16.8	6.5	3.8	15.8	10.3	9.2
Montenegro	-	0.4	0.2	-0.2	-0.1	0.0	0.0	0.0	0.0	0.0
Romania	1.6	2.0	0.3	1.5	1.9	0.1	7.4	0.8	0.2	-0.3
Russian Federation	80.6	75.8	54.8	34.2	44.6	29.5	6.0	12.8	22.0	4.3
Ukraine	30.1	62.3	52.6	56.0	69.6	3.5	3.7	78.9	14.0	5.6
AFRICA	**-0.4**	**-1.9**	**1.5**	**1.3**	**1.2**	**0.6**	**0.2**	**1.3**	**1.8**	**1.4**
Northern Africa	0.1	0.3	1.2	0.8	0.8	0.6	0.2	1.2	1.6	-0.1
Algeria	0.0	0.0	0.2	0.0	0.0	-	-	-	-	-
Egypt	0.0	0.3	0.7	0.3	0.3	0.0	0.0	0.0	0.2	-0.1
Libya	0.0	0.0	0.0	0.0	0.0	-	-	-	-	-
Morocco	-	0.0	0.3	0.3	0.3	0.5	0.2	1.2	1.4	0.0
Tunisia	-	-	0.0	0.2	0.2	0.0	0.0	0.0	0.0	0.0
Other African countries	-0.5	-2.3	0.3	0.5	0.4	0.0	0.0	0.1	0.2	1.5
Nigeria	0.0	0.0	0.0	0.0	0.0	-	-	.. c	.. c	.. c
South Africa	0.1	-0.1	-0.5	0.1	0.1	0.0	0.0	0.0	0.1	0.4
AMERICA	**31.2**	**11.2**	**58.4**	**18.0**	**2.3**	**1.3**	**0.1**	**-0.5**	**2.9**	**9.5**
Northern America	9.1	4.6	35.1	17.1	17.5	-0.3	-0.1	-0.8	1.9	9.4
Central America and Caribbean countries	21.6	6.3	22.8	0.1	-16.0	1.1	0.0	0.0	0.0	0.0
Bahamas	0.0	-0.2	.. c	.. c	0.0	-	0.0	0.0	0.0	0.0
Bermuda	0.0	0.0	0.0	0.0	0.0	-	-	-	-	-
Cayman Islands	9.0	7.6	.. c	8.5	-19.9	0.0	0.0	0.0	0.0	0.0
El Salvador	0.0	0.0	0.0	0.0	0.0	-	-	-	-	-
Guatemala	-	-	-	-	-	-	-	-	-	-
Honduras	-	-	-	.. c	.. c	-	-	-	-	-
Nicaragua	-	-	-	-	-	-	-	-	-	-
Panama	11.5	3.1	-1.2	0.5	0.4	0.0	0.0	0.0	0.0	0.0
Virgin Islands, U.S.	-	-	-	-	-	-	-	-	-	-
South America	0.5	0.3	0.5	0.8	0.9	0.5	0.1	0.3	1.0	0.0
Argentina	0.0	-	0.0	0.1	0.1	0.0	0.0	0.0	0.0	0.0
Bolivia	0.4	0.3	0.2	0.2	0.3	-	-	-	-	-
Brazil	0.0	-0.1	0.2	0.1	0.1	0.5	0.1	0.3	1.0	0.0
Ecuador	0.0	0.0	0.1	0.1	0.2	0.0	0.0	0.0	0.0	0.0
Paraguay	-	-	-	-	-	-	-	-	-	-
Peru	.. c	.. c	0.1	0.1	0.1	-	-	-	-	-
Uruguay	-	0.0	0.0	0.0	-	-	-	-	-	-
Venezuela	-	-	-	0.0	0.0	-	-	-	-	-

ESTONIA

Table 3. Foreign direct investment income by country *(cont.)*

Million US dollars

	Inward					Outward				
	2016	2017	2018	2019	2020	2016	2017	2018	2019	2020
ASIA	**8.7**	**32.0**	**44.5**	**10.2**	**32.4**	**2.2**	**2.2**	**9.7**	**10.7**	**11.4**
Near and Middle East	3.9	7.8	11.1	27.1	11.1	1.6	1.2	8.2	9.4	10.0
Gulf Arabian countries	0.5	3.9	5.2	1.9	1.8	0.0	-1.1	0.6	-0.1	0.9
Kuwait	0.0	0.0	0.0	0.0	-	-	-	-	-	-
Qatar	0.0	0.0	0.0	0.0	0.0	-	-	-	-	-
Saudi Arabia	0.0	0.0	0.0	0.0	0.0	-	-	-	-	-
United Arab Emirates	0.4	3.8	5.1	1.7	1.6	-0.3	-0.4	-0.1	-0.8	0.0
Other Near and Middle East	3.4	3.9	5.9	25.2	9.3	1.6	2.3	7.6	9.5	9.1
Jordan	.. c	.. c	-	-	-	-	-	-	-	.. c
Other Asian countries	4.8	24.2	33.4	-16.8	21.3	0.6	1.0	1.5	1.3	1.4
China	0.2	0.8	3.8	2.4	-4.1	-0.1	0.0	0.0	-0.1	-0.1
Hong Kong, China	1.6	0.5	-19.0	-27.1	-10.3	0.2	0.5	0.2	0.0	0.0
India	0.1	0.4	0.6	1.4	1.5	0.0	0.3	0.0	0.0	0.0
Indonesia	0.0	0.0	-0.1	0.0	0.0	0.0	0.0	0.0	0.0	0.0
Iran, Islamic Republic of	0.1	0.0	0.0	0.0	0.0	-	-	-	-	-
Malaysia	0.0	0.1	0.1	0.4	0.4	-	-	-	.. c	.. c
Philippines	-	0.3	0.0	0.1	0.1	0.0	0.0	0.0	0.0	0.0
Singapore	6.6	15.7	32.9	-13.5	1.3	-0.1	0.0	0.1	0.1	0.1
Chinese Taipei	-0.1	-0.3	0.8	-0.3	-0.2	0.0	0.0	0.0	0.0	0.0
Thailand	0.1	0.1	0.6	0.7	1.1	0.2	0.2	0.2	0.2	0.1
Viet Nam	.. c	.. c	0.0	0.0	0.0	-	-	-	-	-
AUSTRALIA, OCEANIA AND POLAR REGIONS	**2.3**	**2.3**	**0.2**	**0.0**	**-0.1**	**0.2**	**0.1**	**0.2**	**0.4**	**0.2**
WORLD unallocated and confidential	**1.6**	**1.3**	**2.8**	**7.3**	**7.4**	**0.0**	**0.0**	**0.0**	**0.0**	**0.0**
European Union (since 01/02/2020)	..	..	..	..	..	..	..	..	..	..
G20 countries excl. European Union	**180.3**	**221.1**	**331.7**	**317.7**	**247.3**	**32.0**	**11.0**	**8.8**	**22.4**	**20.3**
G20 OECD countries	**99.2**	**144.3**	**272.9**	**279.3**	**205.0**	**2.0**	**4.6**	**-4.3**	**-0.8**	**15.6**
G20 Non-OECD countries	**81.1**	**76.8**	**58.8**	**38.4**	**42.3**	**29.9**	**6.4**	**13.1**	**23.2**	**4.6**
MENA countries	**0.7**	**4.4**	**6.6**	**2.8**	**2.7**	**0.5**	**-0.9**	**1.8**	**1.5**	**2.7**
ASEAN countries	**6.7**	**16.2**	**33.5**	**-12.4**	**2.8**	**0.1**	**0.1**	**0.3**	**0.4**	**0.2**

- Nil; .. Not available; c Confidential data; d Secondary Confidentiality

Note: Detailed metadata at: *http://metalinks.oecd.org/idi/20220712/6d95.*

Source: *OECD International Direct Investment Statistics (database): https://doi.org/10.1787/idi-data-en*

ESTONIA

Table 4. Foreign direct investment flows by industrial sector

Million US dollars

	Inward					Outward				
	2016	2017	2018	2019	2020	2016	2017	2018	2019	2020
All FDI activities	**1 058.4**	**1 946.6**	**1 516.5**	**3 183.9**	**3 387.8**	**486.5**	**887.8**	**44.5**	**1 965.7**	**219.2**
Agriculture, forestry and fishing	**28.1**	**31.5**	**31.5**	**25.0**	**-7.0**	**4.2**	**2.9**	**21.0**	**3.7**	**1.1**
Mining and quarrying	**-3.4**	**-3.2**	**4.1**	**4.5**	**5.9**	**29.6**	**-51.3**	**1.5**	**4.1**	**3.3**
Extraction activities	0.4	0.1	0.1	0.0	0.0	29.6	-49.9	1.6	.. c	.. c
Manufacturing	**215.6**	**858.6**	**240.3**	**277.7**	**36.2**	**164.5**	**586.6**	**224.4**	**94.7**	**218.4**
of which:										
Food products, beverages and tobacco	11.3	62.5	59.8	-8.4	17.6	8.2	-35.7	1.2	-14.6	23.5
Textiles, wood and paper products; printing	96.0	28.1	123.4	37.5	14.2	5.3	-31.8	76.8	22.6	86.3
Chemical, rubber, plastic, non-metallic mineral products	-77.6	-15.1	40.3	26.3	31.1	2.5	-2.4	18.1	-0.3	45.2
Metal and machinery products, except electrical equipment	-0.5	72.3	2.6	138.5	-42.9	10.2	1.5	20.3	-16.4	22.4
Motor vehicles, trailers, semi-trailers, other transport equipment	88.5	705.5	23.6	42.7	10.8	112.0	649.5	50.8	37.8	20.0
Other manufacturing	97.8	5.2	-9.4	41.2	5.4	26.2	5.5	57.4	65.6	21.0
Electricity, gas, steam and air conditioning supply	**-28.4**	**5.0**	**9.5**	**8.0**	**-0.1**	**38.1**	**10.9**	**9.4**	**136.6**	**4.7**
Water supply; sewerage, waste management and remediation activities	**-2.0**	**19.0**	**5.7**	**0.8**	**-6.1**	**.. c**	**.. c**	**.. c**	**0.8**	**.. c**
Construction	**45.2**	**-3.6**	**-56.8**	**73.6**	**-6.9**	**-54.7**	**31.9**	**26.6**	**20.6**	**-28.8**
Services	**803.3**	**1 039.4**	**1 282.1**	**2 794.4**	**3 365.7**	**281.2**	**281.5**	**-272.9**	**1 683.8**	**10.7**
Wholesale and retail trade; repair of motor vehicles and motorcycles	182.3	345.7	210.6	332.9	55.9	39.8	40.0	136.9	10.3	7.1
Transportation and storage	2.0	-2.2	157.4	34.7	-27.5	11.2	-53.6	29.6	7.9	53.4
Accommodation and food service activities	9.0	2.6	0.0	7.9	-11.3	-1.8	25.5	9.5	3.9	-13.3
Information and communication	70.5	143.2	-16.8	247.7	163.3	-15.0	32.6	43.8	-214.2	10.0
Financial and insurance activities	427.6	361.5	1 185.7	1 764.4	509.1	15.4	299.1	112.4	1 663.6	-106.3
Activities of holding companies	82.5	-2.4	462.6	68.4	71.2	-16.1	113.2	-2.0	31.6	39.1
Real estate activities	14.9	-24.9	-30.9	193.1	46.1	93.5	72.4	6.2	194.7	67.9
Professional, scientific and technical activities	-12.7	64.2	404.8	120.0	2 544.2	37.6	-6.5	-617.0	28.2	27.4
Administrative and support service activities	104.9	140.2	-636.5	73.4	27.8	56.5	-114.5	-25.0	-9.8	-45.5
Public administration; activities of households and of extraterritorial organisations	-	-	-	-	-	-	.. c	.. c	.. c	-
Education	1.7	1.5	0.3	5.2	1.0	.. c	0.9	.. c	1.6	1.8
Human health and social work activities	-2.9	-0.1	-0.8	2.0	7.1	-0.1	-0.3	.. c	0.4	.. c
Arts, entertainment and recreation	2.2	4.9	5.5	11.0	47.9	20.6	6.1	19.5	-3.6	8.2
Other services	3.7	2.8	2.9	2.2	2.1	23.5	-19.6	12.3	0.7	0.4
Not allocated and confidential	**0.0**	**0.0**	**0.0**	**0.0**	**0.0**	**.. c**	**.. c**	**.. c**	**21.4**	**.. c**
Private real estate activities	-	-	-	-	-	-	-	-	-	-

- Nil; c Confidential data

Note: Detailed metadata at: *http://metalinks.oecd.org/idi/20220712/6d95.*

Source: *OECD International Direct Investment Statistics (database)*: *https://doi.org/10.1787/idi-data-en*

Table 5. Foreign direct investment positions by industrial sector

At year end

Million US dollars

	Inward					Outward				
	2016	2017	2018	2019	2020	2016	2017	2018	2019	2020
All FDI activities	**19 658.5**	**24 048.9**	**25 049.2**	**28 156.0**	**34 510.8**	**6 298.5**	**7 812.4**	**7 959.1**	**10 161.3**	**11 058.5**
Agriculture, forestry and fishing	**367.2**	**427.4**	**517.9**	**579.9**	**635.7**	**21.6**	**36.8**	**53.3**	**61.2**	**86.3**
Mining and quarrying	**76.6**	**80.9**	**88.8**	**87.1**	**100.2**	**101.6**	**109.5**	**105.7**	**106.8**	**143.8**
Extraction activities	0.5	0.5	0.6	0.9	1.0	97.2	105.9	102.4	103.6	140.4
Manufacturing	**2 662.1**	**3 149.8**	**3 195.6**	**3 437.9**	**3 897.0**	**1 009.0**	**1 217.3**	**1 380.6**	**1 436.8**	**1 847.5**
of which:										
Food products, beverages and tobacco	572.9	690.9	719.3	705.3	790.4	111.9	102.3	93.1	88.9	132.8
Textiles, wood and paper products; printing	688.8	812.6	868.6	930.6	1 077.5	296.3	305.9	365.4	371.3	486.6
Chemical, rubber, plastic, non-metallic mineral products	287.1	331.6	352.7	339.3	448.8	110.3	111.3	119.5	113.0	165.2
Metal and machinery products, except electrical equipment	305.9	396.6	352.8	480.7	500.7	89.5	59.2	87.7	76.1	107.1
Motor vehicles, trailers, semi-trailers, other transport equipment	195.2	230.1	241.2	279.1	315.9	328.1	556.9	413.2	449.0	564.5
Other manufacturing	612.3	687.9	661.0	702.9	763.8	72.9	81.7	301.7	338.5	391.3
Electricity, gas, steam and air conditioning supply	**167.2**	**181.4**	**190.0**	**218.3**	**240.4**	**172.2**	**168.7**	**165.8**	**310.7**	**340.2**
Water supply; sewerage, waste management and remediation activities	**134.9**	**140.2**	**126.2**	**124.9**	**146.8**	**.. c**	**.. c**	**3.0**	**.. c**	**.. c**
Construction	**202.8**	**305.8**	**239.1**	**290.1**	**269.4**	**258.6**	**379.6**	**426.7**	**447.7**	**466.4**
Services	**15 526.1**	**19 154.2**	**19 936.4**	**22 651.5**	**28 488.4**	**4 231.9**	**5 337.1**	**5 200.9**	**7 126.5**	**7 449.6**
Wholesale and retail trade; repair of motor vehicles and motorcycles	2 498.6	3 018.3	2 901.0	3 088.3	3 488.4	504.1	663.5	747.6	793.7	763.3
Transportation and storage	927.4	989.8	1 096.7	919.6	903.8	238.9	201.2	200.6	201.7	205.9
Accommodation and food service activities	108.9	134.5	119.3	125.5	122.5	91.5	84.7	74.9	78.0	82.8
Information and communication	689.9	971.8	1 257.9	1 444.9	1 859.8	87.5	111.8	145.5	236.3	246.1
Financial and insurance activities	5 427.3	6 952.7	7 761.7	9 614.6	10 504.5	845.8	1 428.7	1 171.6	2 792.9	2 794.5
Activities of holding companies	1 058.9	1 076.4	1 075.0	1 350.3	3 146.8	137.3	261.1	177.4	280.7	258.2
Real estate activities	3 514.1	4 315.0	4 505.6	5 149.1	6 096.8	868.2	1 207.2	1 316.3	1 525.9	1 722.3
Professional, scientific and technical activities	1 614.2	1 779.7	1 563.3	1 556.9	4 441.9	149.9	142.6	106.6	99.9	128.3
Administrative and support service activities	674.1	890.6	640.2	641.6	641.9	1 332.8	1 383.1	1 296.7	1 259.7	1 339.8
Public administration; activities of households and of extraterritorial organisations	-	-	-	-	-	-	.. c	.. c	.. c	.. c
Education	3.5	6.2	4.2	9.1	10.2	0.3	1.8	.. c	3.9	6.1
Human health and social work activities	28.9	33.8	32.3	30.5	41.0	.. c	.. c	.. c	.. c	.. c
Arts, entertainment and recreation	25.5	44.1	42.3	50.5	354.0	78.0	94.5	112.4	106.4	125.3
Other services	13.7	17.6	12.0	20.8	23.7	30.9	13.6	24.0	24.8	31.4
Not allocated and confidential	**521.6**	**609.3**	**755.3**	**766.3**	**732.8**	**.. c**	**.. c**	**623.1**	**.. c**	**.. c**
Private real estate activities	-	-	-	-	-	-	-	-	-	-

- Nil; c Confidential data

Note: Detailed metadata at: *http://metalinks.oecd.org/idi/20220712/6d95*.

Source: *OECD International Direct Investment Statistics (database)*: *https://doi.org/10.1787/idi-data-en*

ESTONIA

Table 6. Foreign direct investment income by industrial sector

Million US dollars

	Inward					Outward				
	2016	2017	2018	2019	2020	2016	2017	2018	2019	2020
All FDI activities	**1 591.0**	**1 736.6**	**1 944.5**	**1 994.9**	**1 614.9**	**492.4**	**485.4**	**696.8**	**713.2**	**602.1**
Agriculture, forestry and fishing	**9.3**	**13.3**	**27.8**	**27.7**	**13.0**	**0.3**	**-0.5**	**2.5**	**2.1**	**0.1**
Mining and quarrying	**3.6**	**6.9**	**9.0**	**5.1**	**10.3**	**29.7**	**1.4**	**0.1**	**.. c**	**.. c**
Extraction activities	0.5	0.1	0.1	0.0	0.0	.. c	1.2	0.2	.. c	.. c
Manufacturing	**298.2**	**315.7**	**307.5**	**231.7**	**236.0**	**49.3**	**73.9**	**133.0**	**142.9**	**114.5**
of which:										
Food products, beverages and tobacco	44.0	56.3	54.4	54.5	51.5	1.8	2.7	2.9	-4.2	2.1
Textiles, wood and paper products; printing	80.5	69.6	78.2	39.0	47.1	26.8	23.3	19.4	26.2	48.7
Chemical, rubber, plastic, non-metallic mineral products	42.8	31.0	47.2	9.2	32.1	-2.8	-3.9	-0.4	-2.9	5.4
Metal and machinery products, except electrical equipment	43.2	50.7	38.7	47.1	54.9	-1.0	1.1	7.8	2.2	4.6
Motor vehicles, trailers, semi-trailers, other transport equipment	15.2	47.9	23.7	23.4	11.3	13.9	41.4	47.7	14.1	19.2
Other manufacturing	72.4	60.1	65.2	58.6	39.0	10.5	9.2	55.6	107.5	34.5
Electricity, gas, steam and air conditioning supply	**17.6**	**14.3**	**16.6**	**11.9**	**8.4**	**10.0**	**9.7**	**15.7**	**32.3**	**34.8**
Water supply; sewerage, waste management and remediation activities	**13.7**	**15.4**	**11.1**	**7.3**	**0.9**	**.. c**	**.. c**	**.. c**	**1.1**	**.. c**
Construction	**32.4**	**-3.1**	**5.5**	**29.6**	**12.7**	**18.5**	**16.8**	**13.4**	**22.6**	**35.7**
Services	**1 216.3**	**1 374.2**	**1 567.1**	**1 681.6**	**1 333.8**	**357.8**	**363.5**	**509.6**	**484.9**	**380.7**
Wholesale and retail trade; repair of motor vehicles and motorcycles	284.8	331.2	328.3	309.3	225.0	61.6	43.2	113.5	52.2	47.2
Transportation and storage	59.5	52.9	79.6	100.6	57.5	-19.8	-5.8	2.3	-0.4	12.3
Accommodation and food service activities	14.3	16.4	16.1	14.2	-19.0	-3.6	-3.0	-0.2	-1.0	-7.2
Information and communication	79.6	101.3	103.8	38.3	93.4	2.3	11.7	13.3	9.5	12.9
Financial and insurance activities	522.2	502.6	641.8	811.0	637.6	113.5	112.6	168.7	237.6	168.1
Activities of holding companies	79.0	35.4	97.8	147.5	105.5	29.3	4.6	9.4	4.1	6.4
Real estate activities	140.7	147.6	167.3	188.6	128.5	38.0	64.4	79.5	76.0	78.1
Professional, scientific and technical activities	47.5	124.5	118.9	112.7	96.7	13.9	18.3	2.1	6.9	22.2
Administrative and support service activities	60.0	90.2	105.2	84.4	61.6	106.0	94.8	100.6	73.4	48.1
Public administration; activities of households and of extraterritorial organisations	-	-	-	-	-	-	.. c	.. c	.. c	.. c
Education	1.1	1.4	0.0	0.3	-0.3	.. c	.. c	.. c	0.1	.. c
Human health and social work activities	3.8	3.4	5.8	6.4	33.1	.. c	.. c	.. c	.. c	.. c
Arts, entertainment and recreation	-1.7	-1.9	-1.6	13.9	18.9	45.5	27.4	29.4	30.3	-1.1
Other services	4.5	4.4	1.8	1.8	0.8	0.0	0.1	0.0	.. c	.. c
Not allocated and confidential	**0.0**	**0.0**	**0.0**	**-**	**0.0**	**.. c**	**.. c**	**.. c**	**.. c**	**.. c**
Private real estate activities	**-**	**-**	**-**	**-**	**-**	**-**	**-**	**-**	**-**	**-**

- Nil; c Confidential data

Note: Detailed metadata at: *http://metalinks.oecd.org/idi/20220712/6d95.*

Source: *OECD International Direct Investment Statistics (database): https://doi.org/10.1787/idi-data-en*

FINLAND

Table 1. Foreign direct investment flows by country

Million US dollars

	Inward					Outward				
	2016	2017	2018	2019	2020	2016	2017	2018	2019	2020
WORLD	**8 573.5**	**2 857.6**	**-2 170.4**	**13 455.7**	**-1 423.4**	**24 253.0**	**-572.7**	**11 448.1**	**4 865.1**	**5 849.6**
OECD COUNTRIES	**8 751.5**	**2 567.9**	**-3 982.1**	**8 506.7**	**-877.5**	**22 307.9**	**-3 970.2**	**11 127.1**	**3 159.1**	**5 378.9**
Australia	-	.. d	13.0	.. d	.. d	-88.5	-138.7	147.5	120.9	-58.1
Austria	112.8	-16.9	246.7	414.2	-295.2	-4.4	-65.4	146.3	76.1	-6.8
Belgium	149.3	-208.5	165.2	-225.0	405.7	778.5	-3 039.1	2 022.9	-180.2	-202.8
Canada	-1 133.5	.. d	-33.0	-12.3	95.7	134.9	-359.6	1 025.6	120.9	-84.3
Chile	-	-21.4	20.1	-3.4	5.7	3.3	-11.3	128.6	24.6	-37.6
Colombia	-	-	-	-1.1	-	-	19.2	.. d	-33.6	-43.3
Costa Rica	-	-	-	-	-	-	2.3	-1.2	-1.1	-
Czech Republic	17.7	20.3	-10.6	-3.4	.. d	25.4	58.6	73.2	-4.5	13.7
Denmark	43.1	417.1	500.4	-118.7	128.8	975.3	441.9	-132.2	.. d	289.5
Estonia	-29.9	683.1	100.3	-38.1	.. d	665.7	824.0	566.5	245.2	-100.3
Finland	-	-	-	-	-	-	-	-	-	-
France	-35.4	243.5	-62.6	568.7	-35.3	13 415.9	-11 931.0	-1 036.2	-778.0	-1 033.6
Germany	557.3	372.0	260.8	413.1	-43.3	-767.4	-465.6	-154.6	-100.8	-230.2
Greece	-	1.1	-1.2	.. d	-1.1	.. d	55.2	-4.7	-9.0	-5.7
Hungary	5.5	4.5	-20.1	-22.4	72.9	1.1	10.1	11.8	-43.7	5.7
Iceland	.. c	-	.. c	-6.7	-	.. d	-	-1.2	1.1	-9.1
Ireland	.. d	.. d	-439.0	-1 985.9	192.6	-1 257.3	582.8	1 811.6	996.3	2 893.4
Israel	.. c	.. d	.. d	-49.3	-80.9	.. c	.. d	23.6	31.3	20.5
Italy	174.7	.. d	.. d	60.5	45.6	52.0	-449.8	516.9	38.1	-2.3
Japan	-3 132.8	-4.5	416.6	-24.6	28.5	-7.7	328.0	-82.6	268.7	-143.6
Korea	-	7.9	34.2	.. d	.. d	-19.9	-27.1	21.2	356.0	-254.1
Latvia	-24.3	7.9	11.8	1.1	.. d	7.7	18.0	34.2	48.1	-9.1
Lithuania	-6.6	-3.4	-2.4	3.4	-6.8	61.9	119.5	49.6	-15.7	-43.3
Luxembourg	8 525.9	2 944.4	-180.6	2 303.8	-480.9	1 306.0	-240.1	67.3	312.3	-672.4
Mexico	-7.7	2.3	-1.2	-1.1	5.7	-88.5	108.2	370.6	-202.6	-86.6
Netherlands	638.1	1 940.0	-2 135.0	366.1	245.0	4 201.0	14 293.8	-238.4	52.6	-2 419.4
New Zealand	-	3.4	-3.5	-	-1.1	8.8	-48.5	24.8	25.7	-34.2
Norway	397.0	177.0	420.2	3 446.8	183.5	-70.8	-262.7	548.8	1 400.4	1 417.7
Poland	55.3	-4.5	5.9	.. d	8.0	140.4	102.6	-114.5	-14.6	-2.3
Portugal	6.6	-5.6	-1.2	-32.5	-3.4	3.3	-5.6	72.0	-19.0	17.1
Slovak Republic	47.6	6.8	-49.6	3.4	1.1	7.7	-15.8	-29.5	31.3	70.7
Slovenia	-	-	.. d	.. d	-	-4.4	6.8	2.4	2.2	-1.1
Spain	15.5	-30.4	47.2	22.4	-61.5	82.9	237.9	24.8	48.1	117.4
Sweden	656.9	-2 561.2	-3 461.6	3 192.7	-1 098.6	3 347.3	385.5	2 153.9	1 635.5	1 622.8
Switzerland	606.0	-267.2	400.1	-11.2	-209.7	-1 417.7	-51.9	51.9	107.5	-266.7
Turkey	-	2.3	.. d	-19.0	13.7	.. d	81.2	-57.8	136.6	-461.5
United Kingdom	399.2	-65.4	-771.9	645.9	72.9	-765.2	589.6	139.3	448.9	1 290.0
United States	756.4	-1 205.1	436.7	-358.2	-12.5	1 539.3	-5 008.5	2 941.1	-1 568.3	3 831.3
EUROPE	**12 383.1**	**3 989.4**	**-3 395.5**	**9 553.3**	**-1 200.0**	**21 212.0**	**1 681.9**	**6 526.6**	**3 782.6**	**1 962.4**
Bulgaria	-	-	-	-	.. d	.. d	2.3	9.4	5.6	-11.4
Croatia	-	-	-	-	-1.1	.. d	1.1	5.9	-6.7	-2.3
Cyprus	12.2	.. d	1 345.5	.. d	-535.6	5.5	1.1	1.2	2.2	.. d
Malta	.. c	-3.4	11.8	.. c	.. d	69.7	16.9	-3.5	.. d	-12.5
Montenegro	-	-	-	-	-	-	-	2.4	.. d	-3.4
Romania	.. d	-1.1	-2.4	2.2	-5.7	2.2	-32.7	24.8	30.2	22.8
Russian Federation	376.0	219.8	74.4	104.1	305.4	176.9	239.0	112.1	-84.0	-263.2
Ukraine	-	-	1.2	-	-	-36.5	10.1	3.5	11.2	6.8
AFRICA	**35.4**	**-41.7**	**-3.5**	**24.6**	**12.5**	**-6.6**	**110.5**	**35.4**	**190.3**	**85.5**
Northern Africa	-	-	-2.4	-1.1	-	-2.2	34.9	22.4	106.3	-6.8
Algeria	-	-	-	-	-	-	-	-	-2.2	-
Egypt	-	-	-3.5	1.1	-2.3	-	27.1	16.5	91.8	-12.5
Libya	-	-	-	-	-	-	-	-	-	1.1
Morocco	-	-	-	-1.1	1.1	.. d	4.5	9.4	13.4	9.1
Tunisia	-	-	-	-	-	-	3.4	-3.5	2.2	-3.4
Other African countries	35.4	-41.7	-1.2	25.7	13.7	-5.5	75.5	13.0	84.0	92.3
Nigeria	-	-	-	-	-	-1.1	3.4	22.4	.. d	-9.1
South Africa	.. d	-1.1	-2.4	-6.7	4.6	2.2	53.0	1.2	52.6	58.1
AMERICA	**-629.2**	**-1 135.2**	**734.1**	**-632.5**	**-185.8**	**3 133.9**	**-3 520.5**	**4 357.4**	**-1 201.2**	**4 083.2**
Northern America	-377.1	-1 219.7	403.6	-370.5	84.3	1 674.2	-5 368.1	3 966.7	-1 447.4	3 747.0
Central America and Caribbean countries	-247.7	98.1	310.4	-265.3	-281.5	1 618.9	1 720.2	375.3	-194.8	-36.5
Bahamas	-	.. c	.. c	.. c	.. c	-	.. d	-	-	.. c
Bermuda	.. c	.. c	.. c	.. c	-	.. d	.. d	2.4	-1.1	-
Cayman Islands	.. c	.. c	.. c	32.5	.. d	-	-	-	-	-
El Salvador	-	-	-	-	-	-	-1.1	-	-	-
Guatemala	-	-	-	-	-	-	-3.4	-1.2	2.2	-1.1
Honduras	-	-	-	-	-	4.4	1.1	.. d	-	-
Nicaragua	-	-	-	-	-	-	-	-	-	-
Panama	-	-	-	-	-1.1	-3.3	-1.1	-1.2	4.5	23.9
Virgin Islands, U.S.	-	-	-	-	-	-	-	-	-	-
South America	-4.4	-13.5	20.1	3.4	12.5	-159.2	126.3	15.3	441.1	373.8
Argentina	-10.0	9.0	-1.2	-	-1.1	-2.2	18.0	-1.2	-10.1	9.1
Bolivia	-	-	-	-	-	-	1.1	-	-1.1	-
Brazil	-	3.4	-	2.2	8.0	.. d	98.1	100.3	209.3	-149.3
Ecuador	-	-	-	-	-	.. d	-6.8	.. d	11.2	6.8
Paraguay	-	-	-	-	-	-	2.3	-	-	1.1
Peru	-	-1.1	-1.2	2.2	-1.1	.. d	-6.8	21.2	-14.6	35.3
Uruguay	4.4	-3.4	1.2	3.4	-	133.8	14.7	-305.7	254.1	551.6
Venezuela	-	-	-	-	-	-1.1	-	-1.2	-	.. d

Table 1. Foreign direct investment flows by country *(cont.)*

Million US dollars

	Inward					Outward				
	2016	2017	2018	2019	2020	2016	2017	2018	2019	2020
ASIA	**-3 157.1**	**48.5**	**491.0**	**4 505.8**	**-47.9**	**-7.7**	**1 343.7**	**351.7**	**1 943.4**	**-192.6**
Near and Middle East	.. d	.. d	-16.5	-42.5	-75.2	146.0	136.4	31.9	5.6	53.6
Gulf Arabian countries	.. d	.. d	36.6	5.6	6.8	.. d	118.4	7.1	-29.1	47.9
Kuwait	-	-	1.2	-	-	-	.. c	-1.2	-2.2	2.3
Qatar	-	-2.3	3.5	-	-	.. d	14.7	.. d	.. d	3.4
Saudi Arabia	.. c	21.4	30.7	-	10.3	27.6	86.8	-77.9	-39.2	61.5
United Arab Emirates	.. d	.. d	3.5	5.6	-4.6	14.4	-82.3	62.6	-67.2	-25.1
Other Near and Middle East	.. c	.. d	.. d	-49.3	-80.9	.. d	16.9	24.8	34.7	5.7
Jordan	-	-	-	-	-	-	-	-2.4	2.2	-3.4
Other Asian countries	.. d	-2.3	507.5	4 548.3	27.4	-153.7	1 207.3	319.8	1 938.9	-246.2
China	8.8	-46.2	5.9	4 180.0	152.7	109.5	213.1	68.5	26.9	-653.0
Hong Kong, China	4.4	45.1	28.3	.. d	-216.5	-130.5	10.1	-51.9	469.0	-18.2
India	13.3	11.3	-10.6	21.3	75.2	-2.2	381.0	62.6	-73.9	23.9
Indonesia	-	-1.1	-10.6	-	-	40.9	-15.8	115.7	-73.9	-33.0
Iran, Islamic Republic of	-	-	-	-	-	.. c	19.2	.. d	14.6	5.7
Malaysia	1.1	-2.3	-1.2	2.2	-1.1	-22.1	32.7	5.9	39.2	-29.6
Philippines	-	-1.1	-	-	1.1	-8.8	4.5	-	-5.6	4.6
Singapore	.. d	-13.5	47.2	-30.2	-10.3	-19.9	174.7	2.4	.. d	602.8
Chinese Taipei	-1.1	1.1	-3.5	1.1	-	.. d	7.9	-3.5	-5.6	259.8
Thailand	-	-2.3	1.2	-2.2	1.1	-1.1	95.8	236.0	-206.0	6.8
Viet Nam	-	-	-	-	-	-5.5	.. d	4.7	-9.0	3.4
AUSTRALIA, OCEANIA AND POLAR REGIONS	**-**	**-2.3**	**9.4**	**.. d**	**.. d**	**-77.4**	**-187.1**	**175.9**	**148.9**	**-90.0**
WORLD unallocated and confidential	**-58.6**	**-1.1**	**-5.9**	**.. d**	**.. d**	**-1.1**	**-1.1**	**1.2**	**1.1**	**1.1**
European Union (since 01/02/2020)	**..**	**..**	**..**	**..**	**..**	**..**	**..**	**..**	**..**	**..**
G20 countries excl. European Union	**-2 085.6**	**-429.5**	**540.5**	**5 571.5**	**723.6**	**13 579.6**	**-16 198.9**	**4 211.0**	**-1 151.9**	**1 819.9**
G20 OECD countries	**-2 421.8**	**-645.9**	**453.2**	**1 271.7**	**167.5**	**13 508.8**	**-17 273.1**	**3 831.0**	**-1 159.7**	**2 765.8**
G20 Non-OECD countries	**336.2**	**215.3**	**87.3**	**4 299.8**	**556.1**	**70.8**	**1 074.3**	**380.0**	**7.8**	**-945.9**
MENA countries	**.. d**	**.. d**	**34.2**	**4.5**	**5.7**	**134.9**	**146.5**	**29.5**	**79.5**	**28.5**
ASEAN countries	**.. d**	**-19.2**	**36.6**	**-31.3**	**-10.3**	**-17.7**	**297.6**	**362.3**	**862.0**	**548.1**

- Nil; .. Not available; c Confidential data; d Secondary Confidentiality

Note: Detailed metadata at: *http://metalinks.oecd.org/idi/20220712/6d95*.

Source: *OECD International Direct Investment Statistics (database): https://doi.org/10.1787/idi-data-en*

FINLAND

Table 2. Foreign direct investment positions by country
At year end

Million US dollars

	Inward					Outward				
	2016	2017	2018	2019	2020	2016	2017	2018	2019	2020
WORLD	**79 930.4**	**89 986.8**	**72 068.9**	**85 816.7**	**90 511.7**	**108 938.5**	**124 908.9**	**128 845.9**	**146 462.6**	**143 667.9**
OECD COUNTRIES	**68 168.0**	**76 454.8**	**60 545.0**	**70 861.6**	**74 760.1**	**104 142.5**	**115 754.4**	**119 009.6**	**134 262.0**	**132 757.4**
Australia	.. c	.. c	19.5	.. c	.. c	431.1	411.4	454.5	569.5	520.3
Austria	-50.6	-80.4	40.1	429.1	1 109.3	121.2	-32.4	3.4	120.2	17.2
Belgium	170.8	155.9	131.7	434.7	384.1	3 350.9	1 650.3	3 284.9	1 929.9	1 321.6
Canada	1 085.7	.. d	2 545.2	2 530.9	2 748.8	1 634.9	1 129.8	1 625.8	1 849.0	1 576.9
Chile	-	-	-	-	-	148.6	217.1	282.8	247.1	189.0
Colombia	-	-	-	-	-	2.1	32.4	96.2	61.8	13.5
Costa Rica	-	-	-	-	-	-	1.2	-1.1	-2.2	-2.5
Czech Republic	.. c	.. c	.. c	.. c	.. c	161.3	241.1	301.1	313.4	285.9
Denmark	5 656.2	6 622.7	3 666.1	3 658.7	3 250.7	2 076.5	3 087.1	7 410.1	7 390.5	8 635.4
Estonia	.. d	115.1	87.0	269.6	.. d	2 638.3	3 403.7	4 593.5	4 159.7	4 277.8
Finland	4 711.7	3 192.6	-1 260.6	2 346.7	-1 677.5	-	-	-	-	-
France	1 687.6	2 094.0	2 326.5	3 225.1	2 608.9	14 709.6	3 811.5	2 608.2	1 636.7	686.0
Germany	2 997.8	7 569.0	8 115.4	7 931.9	8 900.5	2 151.4	2 367.5	2 779.9	2 660.1	3 470.4
Greece	-	-	-	-	-	9.5	52.8	46.9	33.7	30.7
Hungary	-	-	-	-	-	36.9	33.6	43.5	-10.1	-8.6
Iceland	.. c	1.2	.. c	.. c	9.8	.. d	2.4	.. c	2.2	.. d
Ireland	.. d	1 737.8	2 066.6	1 858.0	2 059.1	9 971.5	12 187.6	12 812.0	23 588.0	22 750.0
Israel	.. c	.. c	.. c	.. c	.. c	.. c	166.7	179.8	68.5	61.4
Italy	937.1	1 077.0	1 199.9	1 189.6	1 381.8	332.0	-10.8	414.5	606.6	563.3
Japan	1 467.3	2 019.7	950.3	1 159.3	1 407.5	-43.2	311.8	224.4	492.0	375.5
Korea	-	.. c	.. c	.. c	.. c	109.6	195.5	158.0	561.7	281.0
Latvia	-	.. c	-	-	-	258.2	221.9	148.8	217.9	222.1
Lithuania	-	-	-	-	-	286.7	458.1	454.5	474.1	360.8
Luxembourg	2 330.6	2 807.6	2 593.3	2 818.5	4 790.8	2 687.9	2 369.9	2 325.4	2 345.5	4 309.7
Mexico	-	-	-	-	-	74.8	181.1	458.0	150.5	18.4
Netherlands	8 122.7	4 317.6	4 222.6	3 540.8	4 977.3	19 254.8	37 856.8	33 524.2	35 577.4	26 263.3
New Zealand	-	.. c	.. c	-	-	29.5	-21.6	27.5	50.6	34.4
Norway	971.9	1 314.5	1 483.9	5 320.2	5 793.3	2 452.8	2 203.2	5 518.7	7 393.8	8 764.3
Poland	.. c	.. c	.. c	.. c	-	1 098.3	1 593.9	1 384.2	1 390.7	1 504.5
Portugal	3.2	.. c	.. c	.. c	.. c	40.1	19.2	90.5	50.6	36.8
Slovak Republic	-	-	-	-	-	165.5	103.1	38.9	204.4	244.2
Slovenia	-	-	-	-	-	6.3	14.4	.. d	40.4	.. d
Spain	308.8	381.4	420.2	426.9	510.5	940.2	1 290.5	1 229.7	1 239.0	1 461.5
Sweden	29 237.9	27 312.3	17 534.9	17 800.5	18 959.4	29 774.4	32 377.1	25 269.1	28 840.7	31 336.4
Switzerland	879.1	1 156.2	967.5	1 234.6	1 099.5	-483.8	596.1	486.6	694.2	1 044.3
Turkey	.. c	.. c	.. c	-	.. c	1 997.5	2 432.2	1 835.4	1 342.4	360.8
United Kingdom	746.3	1 101.0	2 576.1	3 044.3	3 351.3	818.0	3 334.1	3 740.6	4 162.0	5 163.8
United States	5 332.6	.. d	9 466.5	10 253.9	11 721.7	7 051.8	1 958.5	5 210.7	3 868.8	6 541.9
EUROPE	**63 101.1**	**63 286.2**	**48 961.5**	**58 425.1**	**61 495.9**	**98 504.3**	**115 503.7**	**114 029.1**	**130 730.2**	**126 492.8**
Bulgaria	-	-	-	-	-	6.3	9.6	17.2	22.5	12.3
Croatia	-	-	-	-	-	-	2.4	8.0	1.1	-1.2
Cyprus	8.4	6.0	.. d	.. c	-	1.1	7.2	8.0	9.0	11.0
Malta	.. c	.. c	.. c	-	-	360.5	427.0	405.3	386.4	375.5
Montenegro	-	-	-	-	-	-	-	2.3	4.5	-
Romania	-	-	-	-	-	83.3	58.8	58.4	89.9	108.0
Russian Federation	1 428.3	1 713.8	1 598.4	.. d	2 288.6	2 886.1	2 852.0	2 852.1	3 511.6	2 595.4
Ukraine	-	-	-	-	-	150.7	194.3	63.0	60.7	66.3
AFRICA	**.. c**	**.. d**	**.. d**	**.. d**	**.. c**	**160.2**	**386.2**	**415.6**	**571.8**	**683.5**
Northern Africa	-	-	-	-	-	5.3	42.0	74.4	129.2	101.9
Algeria	-	-	-	-	-	-	1.2	11.5	.. d	.. d
Egypt	-	-	-	-	-	-	26.4	42.4	94.4	67.5
Libya	-	-	-	-	-	-	-	-	-	1.2
Morocco	-	-	-	-	-	5.3	12.0	19.5	20.2	31.9
Tunisia	-	-	-	-	-	-	2.4	2.3	.. c	.. c
Other African countries	.. c	.. d	.. d	137.0	.. c	154.9	343.0	340.1	442.6	582.9
Nigeria	-	-	-	-	-	-1.1	10.8	32.1	40.4	33.1
South Africa	.. c	.. c	.. c	.. c	.. c	69.6	203.9	185.5	255.0	358.3
AMERICA	**6 740.8**	**14 173.7**	**13 813.8**	**15 215.7**	**17 349.4**	**7 618.8**	**3 749.1**	**8 668.4**	**7 400.6**	**10 252.8**
Northern America	6 418.3	11 566.3	12 010.5	12 783.6	14 471.7	8 686.6	3 088.3	6 836.5	5 717.8	8 118.8
Central America and Caribbean countries	322.5	2 607.3	1 803.3	2 432.0	2 878.9	-1 961.6	-466.5	514.1	203.3	213.5
Bahamas	-	-	.. c	.. c	.. c	2.1	1.2	-	-	.. c
Bermuda	.. d	.. d	.. c	.. c	.. c	.. d	.. d	.. c	.. c	.. c
Cayman Islands	.. c	.. d	1 670.5	1 612.0	.. d	-	-	-	-	-
El Salvador	-	-	-	-	-	-	-1.2	-	-	-
Guatemala	-	-	-	-	-	-	-3.6	-4.6	-1.1	-2.5
Honduras	-	-	-	-	-	.. c	4.8	.. d	3.4	-
Nicaragua	-	-	-	-	-	-	-	-	-	-
Panama	-	-	-	-	-	.. c	21.6	9.2	14.6	41.7
Virgin Islands, U.S.	-	-	-	-	-	-	-	-	-	-
South America	-	-	-	-	-	894.9	1 127.4	1 317.8	1 478.3	1 919.3
Argentina	-	-	-	-	-	.. d	36.0	29.8	19.1	31.9
Bolivia	-	-	-	-	-	-	1.2	1.1	-1.1	-1.2
Brazil	-	-	-	-	-	455.4	681.2	863.3	787.5	602.5
Ecuador	-	-	-	-	-	16.9	16.8	20.6	31.5	40.5
Paraguay	-	-	-	-	-	-	1.2	-	-	2.5
Peru	-	-	-	-	-	.. d	64.8	85.9	68.5	79.8
Uruguay	-	-	-	-	-	214.0	78.0	-64.1	259.5	955.9
Venezuela	-	-	-	-	-	.. d	1.2	-1.1	-	-

FINLAND

Table 2. Foreign direct investment positions by country *(cont.)*

At year end

Million US dollars

	Inward					Outward				
	2016	2017	2018	2019	2020	2016	2017	2018	2019	2020
ASIA	**9 828.2**	**12 374.7**	**9 195.1**	**.. d**	**11 629.6**	**2 187.2**	**4 870.5**	**5 239.3**	**7 125.4**	**5 665.7**
Near and Middle East	.. d	2 395.1	1 788.4	1 817.6	.. d	540.7	766.4	746.5	608.9	379.2
Gulf Arabian countries	.. d	.. d	.. d	.. d	.. d	395.3	591.3	556.4	529.1	319.1
Kuwait	-	-	-	-	-	-	-2.4	-3.4	.. c	-4.9
Qatar	-	-	-	-	-	.. d	26.4	26.3	2.2	-14.7
Saudi Arabia	-	-	-	-	-	.. d	353.8	264.5	217.9	69.9
United Arab Emirates	.. d	.. d	.. d	.. d	.. d	94.9	64.8	108.8	51.7	-17.2
Other Near and Middle East	.. c	.. c	.. c	.. c	.. c	145.5	176.3	190.1	79.8	60.1
Jordan	-	-	-	-	-	-	-	-2.3	-	.. d
Other Asian countries	.. d	9 979.6	7 405.5	10 206.7	.. d	1 646.5	4 104.1	4 492.8	6 516.5	5 286.5
China	.. d	.. d	.. d	.. d	.. d	-318.3	190.7	330.9	621.2	-92.0
Hong Kong, China	-	.. c	.. d	.. d	.. d	-296.2	-279.4	-246.2	-11.2	-667.6
India	-	.. c	.. d	.. d	.. d	188.7	435.4	490.0	468.4	342.4
Indonesia	-	-	-	-	-	104.4	189.5	288.5	240.4	195.1
Iran, Islamic Republic of	-	-	-	-	-	.. c	-21.6	-59.5	-44.9	-40.5
Malaysia	-	-	-	-	-	47.4	130.7	119.1	150.5	110.4
Philippines	-	-	-	-	-	1.1	.. d	2.3	1.1	6.1
Singapore	.. c	.. c	99.6	19.1	33.1	1 653.8	2 425.0	2 513.2	3 589.1	3 975.9
Chinese Taipei	-	-	.. c	-	-	.. d	42.0	32.1	22.5	284.7
Thailand	-	-	-	-	-	178.1	334.6	559.9	348.2	443.0
Viet Nam	-	-	-	-	-	33.7	.. d	26.3	14.6	17.2
AUSTRALIA, OCEANIA AND POLAR REGIONS	**.. c**	**.. c**	**.. d**	**.. c**	**.. c**	**468.0**	**399.4**	**493.5**	**634.7**	**571.8**
WORLD unallocated and confidential	**.. d**	**.. d**	**.. d**	**.. d**	**.. d**	**-**	**-**	**-**	**-**	**1.2**
European Union (since 01/02/2020)	..	..	..	..	..	..	..	..	..	..
G20 countries excl. European Union	**23 765.2**	**35 154.7**	**35 216.4**	**35 623.5**	**43 499.8**	**32 853.4**	**21 062.6**	**24 813.4**	**24 020.4**	**23 664.3**
G20 OECD countries	**14 303.8**	**25 561.3**	**27 299.1**	**29 366.4**	**32 208.9**	**29 266.4**	**16 121.4**	**19 508.8**	**17 898.2**	**19 560.7**
G20 Non-OECD countries	**9 461.4**	**9 592.2**	**7 917.3**	**6 257.0**	**11 291.0**	**3 587.0**	**4 941.2**	**5 304.6**	**6 122.2**	**4 104.8**
MENA countries	**.. d**	**.. d**	**.. d**	**.. d**	**.. d**	**413.2**	**640.4**	**636.6**	**666.1**	**416.0**
ASEAN countries	**.. c**	**.. c**	**99.6**	**19.1**	**33.1**	**2 018.6**	**3 153.0**	**3 521.9**	**4 353.0**	**4 750.3**

- Nil; .. Not available; c Confidential data; d Secondary Confidentiality

Note: Inward FDI positions are allocated according to the ultimate investing country. Detailed metadata at: *http://metalinks.oecd.org/idi/20220712/6d95*.

Source: *OECD International Direct Investment Statistics (database): https://doi.org/10.1787/idi-data-en*

FINLAND

Table 3. Foreign direct investment income by country

Million US dollars

	Inward					Outward				
	2016	2017	2018	2019	2020	2016	2017	2018	2019	2020
WORLD	**6 491.2**	**8 425.2**	**7 764.7**	**8 324.2**	**6 307.7**	**7 889.0**	**8 835.5**	**10 201.8**	**13 652.7**	**12 867.2**
OECD COUNTRIES	**6 489.0**	**8 303.5**	**7 676.1**	**8 400.3**	**6 346.4**	**7 260.9**	**7 702.6**	**9 529.1**	**11 876.2**	**11 089.5**
Australia	-	-1.1	-	.. c	.. c	-17.7	40.6	60.2	-4.5	-27.4
Austria	64.1	92.4	109.8	103.0	103.7	50.9	64.3	121.6	118.7	107.1
Belgium	42.0	29.3	-14.2	38.1	57.0	98.4	347.2	-20.1	97.4	83.2
Canada	5.5	16.9	5.9	9.0	5.7	85.1	102.6	98.0	150.0	124.2
Chile	-	.. d	.. d	-	-	26.5	16.9	20.1	20.2	17.1
Colombia	-	-	-	-	-	-	1.1	-	-1.1	-
Costa Rica	-	-	-	-	-	-	-	-	-	.. d
Czech Republic	4.4	2.3	-1.2	-4.5	-5.7	38.7	56.4	44.8	61.6	39.9
Denmark	332.9	520.8	640.9	298.9	217.7	237.8	629.0	315.1	418.7	757.8
Estonia	-40.9	9.0	-20.1	22.4	-36.5	193.5	294.2	322.2	281.0	155.0
Finland	-	-	-	-	-	-	-	-	-	-
France	89.6	85.7	125.1	120.9	155.0	-3.3	42.8	66.1	-1.1	49.0
Germany	321.8	342.7	269.1	87.3	245.0	-261.0	-157.8	-8.3	509.3	71.8
Greece	-	-	-	-	-	4.4	11.3	5.9	12.3	8.0
Hungary	1.1	-	1.2	1.1	1.1	2.2	13.5	15.3	12.3	16.0
Iceland	-	-	-5.9	-6.7	-	.. c	-	.. c	-	1.1
Ireland	13.3	12.4	-5.9	63.8	-61.5	122.7	120.6	92.1	288.8	463.8
Israel	.. c	.. c	.. c	.. c	.. c	.. c	11.3	10.6	4.5	2.3
Italy	121.6	147.7	165.2	150.0	116.2	34.3	-50.7	72.0	77.2	84.3
Japan	180.3	162.3	182.9	60.5	17.1	-	-31.6	16.5	7.8	10.3
Korea	-	4.5	4.7	.. d	.. d	7.7	11.3	15.3	26.9	14.8
Latvia	-	-	2.4	-1.1	-	22.1	40.6	31.9	20.2	22.8
Lithuania	-	-	.. d	-	-	26.5	36.1	66.1	79.5	36.5
Luxembourg	779.6	710.2	257.3	1 172.1	653.0	105.1	102.6	67.3	443.3	49.0
Mexico	-	-	-	-	-	-68.6	12.4	47.2	16.8	4.6
Netherlands	520.8	1 485.7	1 576.8	1 460.9	1 489.5	2 552.3	1 789.0	1 364.3	2 669.9	2 147.0
New Zealand	-	-	-	-	-	1.1	-	.. d	2.2	-11.4
Norway	148.2	112.7	211.3	136.6	297.4	226.7	46.2	328.1	717.6	800.0
Poland	2.2	3.4	3.5	-	-	125.0	202.9	172.3	206.0	243.9
Portugal	-	-	-	-	-	6.6	7.9	9.4	14.6	12.5
Slovak Republic	.. c	7.9	2.4	2.2	-	7.7	9.0	13.0	16.8	14.8
Slovenia	-	-	-	-	-	2.2	2.3	9.4	3.4	2.3
Spain	6.6	4.5	9.4	-1.1	-17.1	74.1	30.4	54.3	45.9	11.4
Sweden	3 435.8	3 948.8	3 541.8	4 260.6	2 471.8	3 079.7	3 181.2	4 766.9	4 448.7	4 569.8
Switzerland	216.7	168.0	178.2	174.6	222.2	97.3	93.6	88.5	97.4	279.2
Turkey	1.1	1.1	1.2	1.1	2.3	118.3	184.9	110.9	122.0	1.1
United Kingdom	146.0	312.3	301.0	154.5	188.0	121.6	130.8	299.8	339.2	68.4
United States	87.4	84.5	125.1	84.0	232.5	154.8	346.1	846.2	551.9	862.7
EUROPE	**6 179.4**	**8 047.6**	**7 463.7**	**8 241.4**	**6 120.8**	**7 379.2**	**7 689.1**	**8 871.7**	**11 567.2**	**10 395.4**
Bulgaria	-	-	-	-	-	-	1.1	-7.1	1.1	2.3
Croatia	-	-	-	-	-	-	-	-	-	1.1
Cyprus	.. c	.. c	42.5	30.2	13.7	1.1	2.3	2.4	5.6	6.8
Malta	.. c	.. c	.. c	.. c	.. c	29.9	10.1	-2.4	-12.3	-26.2
Montenegro	-	-	-	-	-	-	-	-	-	-
Romania	-	-	-	.. d	.. d	2.2	5.6	4.7	12.3	5.7
Russian Federation	-65.2	4.5	61.4	6.7	5.7	231.1	425.0	453.2	431.0	308.8
Ukraine	-	-	-	-	-	23.2	19.2	8.3	17.9	6.8
AFRICA	**-**	**1.1**	**1.2**	**.. c**	**.. d**	**4.4**	**10.1**	**4.7**	**10.1**	**21.7**
Northern Africa	-	-	-	-	-	-	4.5	-4.7	4.5	-11.4
Algeria	-	-	-	-	-	-	-	-1.2	-	-
Egypt	-	-	-	-	-	-	2.3	-2.4	2.2	-10.3
Libya	-	-	-	-	-	-	-	-	-	-
Morocco	-	-	-	-	-	-	2.3	1.2	-	-1.1
Tunisia	-	-	-	-	-	-	-1.1	-2.4	2.2	-
Other African countries	-	1.1	1.2	.. c	4.6	4.4	5.6	9.4	6.7	31.9
Nigeria	-	-	-	-	-	-	-	1.2	1.1	-
South Africa	-	-	-	-	-	4.4	2.3	2.4	6.7	14.8
AMERICA	**120.5**	**170.2**	**107.4**	**176.9**	**266.7**	**-220.1**	**587.3**	**887.5**	**886.6**	**886.6**
Northern America	91.8	101.5	131.0	91.8	238.2	240.0	448.7	944.2	700.8	986.9
Central America and Caribbean countries	.. c	68.8	-23.6	84.0	27.4	-57.5	23.7	53.1	21.3	18.2
Bahamas	-	.. c	.. c	.. c	.. c	-	-	-	-	.. c
Bermuda	8.8	1.1	1.2	-	-	3.3	1.1	1.2	-	-
Cayman Islands	.. c	.. c	.. c	.. c	10.3	-	-	-	-	-
El Salvador	-	-	-	-	-	-	-	-	-	-
Guatemala	-	-	-	-	-	-	-	-	-	-
Honduras	-	-	-	-	-	4.4	1.1	1.2	-	-
Nicaragua	-	-	-	-	-	-	-	-	-	-
Panama	-	-	-	-	-	-1.1	7.9	-	2.2	1.1
Virgin Islands, U.S.	-	-	-	-	-	-	-	-	-	-
South America	.. d	-	-	.. d	-	-402.5	115.0	-109.8	164.6	-118.5
Argentina	-	-	-	-	-	4.4	4.5	-3.5	-5.6	-3.4
Bolivia	-	-	-	-	-	-	-	-	-	-
Brazil	-	-	-	-	-	-319.6	28.2	-7.1	-15.7	-21.7
Ecuador	-	-	-	-	-	-8.8	-1.1	-2.4	4.5	3.4
Paraguay	-	-	-	-	-	-	-	-	-	-
Peru	-	-	-	-	-	10.0	6.8	9.4	5.6	-2.3
Uruguay	.. d	-	-	-	-	-113.9	59.7	-127.5	156.7	-112.8
Venezuela	-	-	-	-	-	-	-	-	-	-

Table 3. Foreign direct investment income by country *(cont.)*

Million US dollars

	Inward					Outward				
	2016	2017	2018	2019	2020	2016	2017	2018	2019	2020
ASIA	**190.2**	**207.4**	**193.6**	**-111.9**	**-91.2**	**743.1**	**508.4**	**370.6**	**1 190.0**	**1 603.4**
Near and Middle East	.. c	40.6	.. c	.. c	.. c	98.4	58.6	27.1	-9.0	19.4
Gulf Arabian countries	-	.. d	-	-	-	87.4	51.9	18.9	-21.3	28.5
Kuwait	-	-	-	-	-	-	-	.. d	.. d	.. d
Qatar	-	-	-	-	-	6.6	6.8	-5.9	-3.4	-4.6
Saudi Arabia	-	-	-	-	-	52.0	28.2	23.6	-33.6	17.1
United Arab Emirates	-	.. d	-	-	-	22.1	11.3	-1.2	6.7	8.0
Other Near and Middle East	.. c	.. c	.. c	.. c	.. c	12.2	7.9	9.4	12.3	-9.1
Jordan	-	-	-	-	-	-	-	-2.4	2.2	-3.4
Other Asian countries	.. d	166.8	.. d	.. d	.. d	643.6	449.8	343.4	1 200.0	1 584.0
China	-	-	.. d	84.0	131.1	127.2	-181.5	-62.6	-202.6	-3.4
Hong Kong, China	-	1.1	-10.6	-270.9	-225.6	-36.5	-37.2	-81.4	244.0	570.9
India	-	-7.9	.. c	-2.2	3.4	-15.5	56.4	24.8	5.6	115.1
Indonesia	-	-	-	-	-	15.5	-7.9	16.5	6.7	3.4
Iran, Islamic Republic of	-	-	-	-	-	-3.3	-4.5	-11.8	1.1	-
Malaysia	-	.. d	-	.. d	-	11.1	-14.7	-3.5	6.7	-9.1
Philippines	-	-	-	-	-	1.1	2.3	-	-	1.1
Singapore	.. c	7.9	20.1	11.2	-	561.8	645.9	429.6	1 094.8	874.1
Chinese Taipei	-	-	-	-	.. d	-33.2	2.3	-	1.1	4.6
Thailand	-	.. d	-	.. d	-	3.3	6.8	16.5	-4.5	10.3
Viet Nam	-	-	-	-	-	-4.4	1.1	2.4	3.4	1.1
AUSTRALIA, OCEANIA AND POLAR REGIONS	-	**-1.1**	-	**.. c**	**.. c**	**-16.6**	**41.7**	**66.1**	**-2.2**	**-39.9**
WORLD unallocated and confidential	**1.1**	-	**-1.2**	**.. d**	**.. d**	**-1.1**	**-1.1**	**1.2**	**1.1**	-
European Union (since 01/02/2020)	..	..	..	..	..	..	..	..	..	..
G20 countries excl. European Union	**886.9**	**1 153.2**	**1 228.6**	**764.6**	**1 110.0**	**268.7**	**986.4**	**2 070.1**	**1 987.0**	**1 693.4**
G20 OECD countries	**952.1**	**1 156.6**	**1 180.2**	**676.1**	**969.8**	**170.3**	**631.3**	**1 621.6**	**1 795.6**	**1 262.7**
G20 Non-OECD countries	**-65.2**	**-3.4**	**48.4**	**88.4**	**140.2**	**98.4**	**355.1**	**448.5**	**192.5**	**430.8**
MENA countries	-	**.. d**	-	-	-	**87.4**	**51.9**	**10.6**	**-13.4**	**5.7**
ASEAN countries	**.. c**	**7.9**	**20.1**	**11.2**	-	**588.3**	**632.4**	**461.5**	**1 107.1**	**880.9**

- Nil; .. Not available; c Confidential data; d Secondary Confidentiality

Note: Detailed metadata at: *http://metalinks.oecd.org/idi/20220712/6d95*.

Source: OECD *International Direct Investment Statistics (database)*: *https://doi.org/10.1787/idi-data-en*

FINLAND

Table 4. Foreign direct investment flows by industrial sector

Million US dollars

	Inward					Outward				
	2016	2017	2018	2019	2020	2016	2017	2018	2019	2020
All FDI activities	**8 573.5**	**2 857.6**	**-2 170.4**	**13 455.7**	**-1 423.4**	**24 253.0**	**-572.7**	**11 448.1**	**4 865.1**	**5 849.6**
Agriculture, forestry and fishing	**-**	**-**	**.. c**	**-**	**-1.1**	**-2.2**	**.. c**	**.. c**	**.. c**	**2.3**
Mining and quarrying	**-1 302.7**	**.. d**	**.. d**	**94.0**	**-235.9**	**167.0**	**.. d**	**.. d**	**.. d**	**.. d**
Extraction activities	-1 302.7	.. d	93.2	94.0	-235.9	167.0	-3.4	60.2	.. d	.. d
Manufacturing	**2 754.6**	**2 058.4**	**-2 126.8**	**841.8**	**-736.2**	**19 691.5**	**-2 345.8**	**5 178.8**	**2 041.9**	**435.3**
of which:										
Food products, beverages and tobacco	-117.2	160.1	128.6	59.3	174.4	-285.3	207.4	343.4	.. d	-34.2
Textiles, wood and paper products; printing	173.6	-16.9	-1 711.3	-39.2	-34.2	426.8	184.9	-694.0	1 874.0	1 039.3
Chemical, rubber, plastic, non-metallic mineral products	882.5	366.4	-514.6	569.8	94.6	846.0	205.2	506.3	536.2	738.5
Metal and machinery products, except electrical equipment	1 291.6	1 595.1	-180.6	-788.1	-174.4	18 451.8	-2 672.8	4 077.7	516.1	-1 106.6
Motor vehicles, trailers, semi-trailers, other transport equipment	366.0	-62.0	68.5	-11.2	147.0	2.2	16.9	31.9	.. d	-57.0
Other manufacturing	157.0	15.8	81.4	1 053.4	-942.5	248.8	-288.6	915.9	-811.6	-143.6
Electricity, gas, steam and air conditioning supply	**.. d**	**195.0**	**79.1**	**418.7**	**66.1**	**1 081.5**	**928.9**	**3 618.6**	**9.0**	**3 230.8**
Water supply; sewerage, waste management and remediation activities	**.. c**	**.. c**	**.. d**	**22.4**	**13.7**	**-136.0**	**184.9**	**17.7**	**.. c**	**2.3**
Construction	**-297.5**	**-127.4**	**-161.7**	**137.7**	**34.2**	**-195.7**	**-74.4**	**616.1**	**895.6**	**-656.4**
Services	**7 212.2**	**528.7**	**-220.7**	**11 750.8**	**-784.0**	**3 088.6**	**445.3**	**1 559.1**	**1 643.3**	**2 821.7**
Wholesale and retail trade; repair of motor vehicles and motorcycles	-380.4	1 677.4	-175.9	-150.0	5.7	227.8	-232.2	28.3	1 130.6	757.8
Transportation and storage	284.2	134.1	249.0	141.1	.. d	16.6	-45.1	48.4	-39.2	-
Accommodation and food service activities	.. d	80.0	.. d	113.1	43.3	-	-	-	-31.3	.. c
Information and communication	9 870.6	-1 737.1	241.9	-1 585.1	-1 151.0	.. d	-1 281.7	.. d	-483.6	-1 201.1
Financial and insurance activities	-2 866.3	-2 558.9	-717.6	9 691.0	550.4	2 236.0	1 614.2	823.8	1 806.8	3 825.6
Activities of holding companies	-2 822.1	86.8	-225.4	7 904.4	.. d	211.2	.. d	85.0	.. d	.. d
Real estate activities	263.2	2 371.8	552.3	869.8	-182.3	12.2	-57.5	572.4	-740.0	-26.2
Professional, scientific and technical activities	27.6	84.5	-31.9	1 833.7	53.6	289.7	-75.5	136.9	169.0	-712.3
Administrative and support service activities	-64.1	343.8	-246.7	961.6	-189.2	136.0	-10.1	355.2	-189.2	-88.9
Public administration; activities of households and of extraterritorial organisations	-	-	-	-	-	127.2	545.6	280.9	10.1	174.4
Education	-	-	-	-	-	-	-	-	-	-
Human health and social work activities	.. d	.. d	-105.0	-126.5	141.3	.. d	2.3	-	-12.3	.. c
Arts, entertainment and recreation	.. c	.. c	.. c	.. d	.. c	.. c	.. c	.. c	.. d	.. c
Other services	-	-	-	.. c	.. c	.. d	.. d	.. d	.. d	.. d
Not allocated and confidential	**.. c**	**.. c**	**.. c**	**1.1**	**-**	**-**	**.. c**	**.. c**	**.. c**	**.. d**
Private real estate activities	**-**	**330.3**	**.. d**	**189.2**	**219.9**	**558.4**	**285.2**	**352.9**	**75.0**	**.. d**

- Nil; .. Not available; c Confidential data; d Secondary Confidentiality

Note: Detailed metadata at: *http://metalinks.oecd.org/idi/20220712/6d95.*

Source: *OECD International Direct Investment Statistics (database): https://doi.org/10.1787/idi-data-en*

Table 5. Foreign direct investment positions by industrial sector
At year end

Million US dollars

	Inward					Outward				
	2016	2017	2018	2019	2020	2016	2017	2018	2019	2020
All FDI activities	**79 930.4**	**89 986.8**	**72 068.9**	**85 816.7**	**90 511.7**	**108 938.5**	**124 908.9**	**128 845.9**	**146 462.6**	**143 667.9**
Agriculture, forestry and fishing	-	-	.. c	.. c	.. c	.. c	.. c	.. c	.. c	.. c
Mining and quarrying	**1 853.1**	**2 401.1**	.. d	.. d	.. d	.. d	.. d	.. d	.. d	.. d
Extraction activities	1 853.1	2 401.1	2 413.6	2 510.7	2 628.5	436.4	458.1	585.1	554.9	.. d
Manufacturing	**23 635.5**	**34 032.1**	**25 588.5**	**27 250.1**	**27 848.8**	**57 161.4**	**64 925.6**	**62 412.4**	**64 106.9**	**63 919.5**
of which:										
Food products, beverages and tobacco	1 256.5	1 527.9	1 623.5	1 530.0	965.8	1 639.1	2 079.6	2 226.9	1 792.9	1 702.0
Textiles, wood and paper products; printing	3 492.1	4 108.9	2 139.9	2 260.2	2 607.7	12 492.9	13 474.5	12 639.1	15 233.7	17 004.5
Chemical, rubber, plastic, non-metallic mineral products	7 982.5	9 425.5	8 717.7	9 706.8	10 079.8	7 279.4	8 732.3	8 448.6	9 377.7	10 239.3
Metal and machinery products, except electrical equipment	9 202.1	16 392.4	10 459.1	10 005.6	10 279.8	34 582.1	38 118.3	35 029.8	34 768.6	32 069.0
Motor vehicles, trailers, semi-trailers, other transport equipment	306.7	435.4	373.3	171.9	364.5	.. d	197.9	211.8	5.6	41.7
Other manufacturing	1 394.5	2 140.8	2 276.2	3 575.6	3 550.1	.. d	2 323.1	3 856.2	2 927.4	2 861.7
Electricity, gas, steam and air conditioning supply	**3.2**	**1 283.3**	**1 227.4**	**1 978.2**	**1 924.2**	**11 238.5**	**14 346.4**	**16 289.2**	**32 429.8**	**22 645.7**
Water supply; sewerage, waste management and remediation activities	.. c	.. c	.. d	**47.2**	**51.5**	**63.2**	**239.9**	.. d	.. c	.. c
Construction	**659.9**	**899.5**	**841.5**	**1 293.0**	**603.8**	**322.5**	**321.4**	**997.3**	**1 983.8**	**392.7**
Services	**52 648.9**	**49 737.3**	**40 263.3**	**50 870.6**	**55 178.6**	**36 933.7**	**41 141.8**	**44 611.9**	**43 582.3**	**51 931.5**
Wholesale and retail trade; repair of motor vehicles and motorcycles	3 593.3	6 110.6	5 374.4	5 355.0	5 060.7	2 422.3	2 619.3	2 829.2	3 820.5	3 831.1
Transportation and storage	874.9	1 113.0	1 187.3	1 234.6	1 260.3	441.7	435.4	385.8	533.6	650.4
Accommodation and food service activities	.. d	549.3	.. d	689.7	774.3	4.2	-	-	85.4	52.8
Information and communication	14 733.8	14 074.1	12 944.8	11 388.5	10 139.9	7 353.2	6 874.6	6 014.4	4 823.6	3 182.0
Financial and insurance activities	25 317.8	14 137.7	6 867.4	16 782.7	19 333.7	21 625.4	25 770.0	28 708.5	28 634.0	35 573.7
Activities of holding companies	.. d	199.1	147.7	8 426.2	9 571.7	1 065.7	.. d	1 448.4	1 285.1	916.7
Real estate activities	3 540.6	8 728.7	8 202.4	8 035.3	8 218.2	1 414.6	1 212.5	1 795.3	1 095.3	1 308.1
Professional, scientific and technical activities	1 848.8	2 356.7	2 040.3	3 750.8	5 401.9	1 196.4	1 279.7	1 130.1	1 233.4	4 098.7
Administrative and support service activities	1 473.6	2 122.8	1 898.3	2 909.5	3 850.8	1 408.2	1 674.3	2 091.8	1 653.6	1 704.5
Public administration; activities of households and of extraterritorial organisations	-	-	-	-	-	626.1	1 147.8	1 353.3	1 391.8	1 349.9
Education	-	-	-	-	-	-	-	-	-	-
Human health and social work activities	.. d	.. d	1 161.0	553.8	948.6	.. d	-	.. d	156.1	.. d
Arts, entertainment and recreation	.. c	.. c	.. c	.. d	.. c	.. c	.. c	.. c	.. d	.. c
Other services	-	-	-	.. c	.. c	.. d	.. d	121.4	.. d	170.6
Not allocated and confidential	.. c	.. c	.. c	.. c	.. c	.. c	.. c	.. c	.. c	.. c
Private real estate activities	.. d	.. d	.. d	**1 837.8**	**2 245.7**	**2 634.1**	**3 300.6**	.. d	.. d	**3 929.3**

- Nil; .. Not available; c Confidential data; d Secondary Confidentiality

Note: Detailed metadata at: *http://metalinks.oecd.org/idi/20220712/6d95*.

Source: *OECD International Direct Investment Statistics (database)*: *https://doi.org/10.1787/idi-data-en*

FINLAND

Table 6. Foreign direct investment income by industrial sector

Million US dollars

	Inward					Outward				
	2016	2017	2018	2019	2020	2016	2017	2018	2019	2020
All FDI activities	**6 491.2**	**8 425.2**	**7 764.7**	**8 324.2**	**6 307.7**	**7 889.0**	**8 835.5**	**10 201.8**	**13 652.7**	**12 867.2**
Agriculture, forestry and fishing	**-**	**-**	**1.2**	**1.1**	**1.1**	**-2.2**	**1.1**	**.. c**	**.. c**	**4.6**
Mining and quarrying	**-63.0**	**36.1**	**116.8**	**126.5**	**167.5**	**21.0**	**13.5**	**.. d**	**.. d**	**-30.8**
Extraction activities	-63.0	36.1	116.8	126.5	167.5	21.0	13.5	33.0	-28.0	-30.8
Manufacturing	**1 819.1**	**3 048.1**	**3 095.7**	**2 337.4**	**2 626.8**	**2 466.0**	**4 566.6**	**4 529.7**	**6 445.8**	**5 106.6**
of which:										
Food products, beverages and tobacco	125.0	217.6	310.4	190.3	184.6	128.3	175.9	131.0	.. d	-10.3
Textiles, wood and paper products; printing	188.0	267.2	231.3	167.9	127.6	1 200.9	1 400.1	1 069.3	2 226.6	1 096.3
Chemical, rubber, plastic, non-metallic mineral products	1 033.9	1 057.4	1 307.7	1 107.1	1 179.5	1 153.4	820.7	1 022.1	1 352.3	1 427.9
Metal and machinery products, except electrical equipment	204.6	1 203.9	735.3	391.8	706.6	-269.8	2 179.0	2 111.4	2 705.7	2 529.9
Motor vehicles, trailers, semi-trailers, other transport equipment	-85.1	7.9	57.8	24.6	9.1	-1.1	2.3	5.9	.. d	-2.3
Other manufacturing	352.8	293.1	453.2	454.5	419.4	254.3	-11.3	190.0	11.2	65.0
Electricity, gas, steam and air conditioning supply	**.. d**	**293.1**	**134.5**	**660.5**	**.. d**	**374.9**	**560.3**	**794.3**	**857.5**	**1 090.6**
Water supply; sewerage, waste management and remediation activities	**.. c**	**2.3**	**.. c**	**-**	**.. c**	**.. c**	**.. c**	**.. c**	**.. c**	**2.3**
Construction	**-18.8**	**47.3**	**.. d**	**58.2**	**155.0**	**559.5**	**280.7**	**279.7**	**588.8**	**680.3**
Services	**4 813.7**	**4 998.3**	**4 345.6**	**5 140.5**	**3 320.8**	**4 460.9**	**3 411.1**	**4 526.1**	**5 742.8**	**6 013.7**
Wholesale and retail trade; repair of motor vehicles and motorcycles	613.7	617.7	636.1	592.2	762.4	310.7	227.7	102.7	495.9	308.8
Transportation and storage	82.9	121.7	139.3	150.0	31.9	49.8	-9.0	8.3	13.4	47.9
Accommodation and food service activities	32.1	.. d	17.7	52.6	-116.2	-	-	-	3.4	1.1
Information and communication	860.3	1 098.0	922.9	2 261.3	703.1	1 387.8	392.3	311.6	391.8	200.6
Financial and insurance activities	2 855.2	2 360.5	1 690.1	1 167.6	1 299.1	2 376.4	2 456.3	3 703.5	4 642.3	5 211.4
Activities of holding companies	504.3	25.9	-56.7	-89.6	61.5	49.8	80.0	206.5	123.1	53.6
Real estate activities	170.3	387.8	504.0	935.9	204.0	103.9	90.2	31.9	-82.8	27.4
Professional, scientific and technical activities	66.4	116.1	164.1	-167.9	306.6	96.2	18.0	116.8	24.6	116.2
Administrative and support service activities	112.8	162.3	253.7	154.5	116.2	100.6	195.0	219.5	174.6	125.4
Public administration; activities of households and of extraterritorial organisations	-	-	-	-	-	35.4	36.1	26.0	76.1	-10.3
Education	-	-	-	-	-	-	-	-	-	-
Human health and social work activities	26.5	100.3	24.8	-19.0	1.1	-	-	-	-	-
Arts, entertainment and recreation	-5.5	.. c	-7.1	.. d	.. d	-3.3	.. c	-4.7	.. c	.. c
Other services	-	-	-	.. c	.. c	4.4	.. c	11.8	.. c	.. c
Not allocated and confidential	**.. c**	**-**	**.. c**	**-**	**.. c**	**.. c**	**.. c**	**.. c**	**.. c**	**-**
Private real estate activities	**-**	**-**	**-**	**-**	**-**	**-**	**-**	**-**	**-**	**-**

- Nil; .. Not available; c Confidential data; d Secondary Confidentiality

Note: Detailed metadata at: *http://metalinks.oecd.org/idi/20220712/6d95*.

Source: *OECD International Direct Investment Statistics (database)*: *https://doi.org/10.1787/idi-data-en*

Table 1. Foreign direct investment flows by country

Million US dollars

	Inward					Outward				
	2016	2017	2018	2019	2020	2016	2017	2018	2019	2020
WORLD	**23 054.3**	**24 779.6**	**41 806.9**	**28 362.3**	**4 861.5**	**64 784.9**	**35 908.0**	**101 978.0**	**33 817.3**	**45 905.4**
OECD COUNTRIES	**22 293.5**	**23 757.2**	**42 163.3**	**23 511.7**	**4 322.5**	**55 650.8**	**33 573.4**	**85 207.1**	**17 415.2**	**37 531.6**
Australia	497.6	-518.5	35.4	155.6	-145.9	-742.0	1 748.4	8 522.4	-2 024.0	148.1
Austria	142.7	121.7	-1 275.8	-340.3	-119.7	181.4	354.0	1 303.0	184.7	-286.0
Belgium	-5 049.2	-822.9	-797.8	1 571.7	1 447.3	8 497.2	-20 665.1	7 068.3	1 890.7	10 478.6
Canada	320.7	954.8	1 753.8	-598.9	185.8	369.3	1 834.1	-2 231.8	125.4	227.9
Chile	74.1	11.3	-461.5	7.8	13.7	-94.0	1 769.8	478.0	14.6	-33.0
Colombia	..	..	..	..	..	68.6	-19.2	-15.3	7.8	129.9
Costa Rica	..	..	..	..	..	..	..	..	..	..
Czech Republic	102.8	-137.5	-185.3	292.2	54.7	421.3	414.8	699.9	462.3	436.5
Denmark	320.7	484.7	1 273.5	67.2	-291.7	424.6	622.3	2 107.9	-5 469.6	-439.9
Estonia	..	..	..	..	..	..	..	..	..	..
Finland	13 714.5	-11 199.4	-2 543.4	-111.9	-365.8	34.3	1 424.9	41.3	818.3	-106.0
France	-	-	-	-	-	-	-	-	-	-
Germany	5 461.7	11 767.6	4 516.7	104.1	1 693.4	10 055.3	9 023.8	-26 962.1	-2 593.8	2 129.9
Greece	-70.8	233.3	-138.1	-66.0	-18.2	77.4	-200.7	-75.5	-16.8	-49.0
Hungary	10.0	15.8	244.3	-305.6	-28.5	-209.0	-261.5	931.2	264.2	389.7
Iceland	..	..	..	..	..	..	..	..	..	..
Ireland	-750.9	1 376.4	-3 108.7	2 523.2	1 286.6	-2 332.2	2 664.9	2 083.1	-10 547.4	-390.9
Israel	59.7	53.0	-43.7	314.6	-209.7	243.3	-170.2	139.3	33.6	80.9
Italy	3 314.2	727.1	2 165.7	2 110.2	-2 202.8	13 788.6	3 496.8	31 836.4	2 555.7	3 324.2
Japan	1 006.3	1 334.7	1 088.2	82.8	-108.3	1 712.9	2 730.2	756.5	-2 844.5	217.7
Korea	237.8	83.4	580.7	188.1	-134.5	-531.9	649.3	854.5	-510.5	11.4
Latvia	..	..	..	..	..	..	..	..	..	..
Lithuania	..	..	..	..	..	-32.1	32.7	55.5	62.7	-1.1
Luxembourg	13 760.9	-7 702.6	26 814.6	-1 458.6	-860.4	-3 212.4	11 172.4	4 771.6	11 638.9	1 539.6
Mexico	161.5	-74.4	-584.2	..	..	127.2	1 273.8	272.6	487.0	-44.4
Netherlands	-4 129.2	4 066.1	16 901.9	-9 477.2	5 525.9	4 009.7	3 121.4	44 032.8	38 684.7	1 755.0
New Zealand	78.5	-5.6	-60.2	32.5	-12.5	36.5	-10.1	27.1	179.1	3.4
Norway	76.3	251.4	212.4	129.9	890.0	-412.5	-1 794.6	-699.9	36.9	-1 012.0
Poland	-806.1	962.7	440.2	2 465.0	1 801.7	1 184.3	-443.0	1 592.1	347.0	-1 125.9
Portugal	123.9	224.3	121.6	-12.3	11.4	-614.8	307.7	913.5	892.2	761.3
Slovak Republic	-18.8	..	101.5	-30.2	45.6	131.6	39.5	441.4	-41.4	-190.3
Slovenia	..	..	..	..	..	34.3	115.0	-2.4	-179.1	-106.0
Spain	-241.1	2 792.2	-1 781.0	5 945.4	137.9	4 780.5	1 961.4	2 197.6	-2 546.7	-1 487.2
Sweden	802.8	75.5	-221.9	-303.4	-388.6	834.9	3 627.6	273.8	-622.4	-612.0
Switzerland	2 109.9	-2 199.3	3 977.3	8 695.8	829.6	3 236.8	169.1	4 770.4	-612.3	514.0
Turkey	-105.1	-94.7	-27.1	-11.2	-10.3	-474.4	369.7	347.0	716.4	-94.6
United Kingdom	-972.0	21 544.4	755.3	3 685.2	-2 589.2	-1 291.6	12 058.4	-2 233.0	3 990.8	9 409.7
United States	-7 935.4	-615.5	-7 644.3	7 996.2	-1 949.9	15 409.7	-3 848.5	849.8	-17 895.4	11 980.6
EUROPE	**27 703.2**	**21 898.3**	**48 766.7**	**16 161.4**	**6 312.3**	**43 957.8**	**29 230.1**	**77 112.0**	**43 252.0**	**26 818.2**
Bulgaria	..	..	44.8	..	5.7	207.9	-72.1	129.8	-660.5	-34.2
Croatia	..	..	..	..	..	28.8	-473.5	-64.9	50.4	-34.2
Cyprus	-149.3	224.3	131.0	320.2	-294.0	653.5	-48.5	509.9	313.4	510.5
Malta	179.1	-653.8	570.0	-	83.2	71.9	-36.1	92.1	-305.6	16.0
Montenegro	..	..	..	..	..	105.1	116.1	-116.8	23.5	65.0
Romania	..	..	..	167.9	-9.1	89.6	264.9	397.7	376.1	129.9
Russian Federation	-94.0	341.6	-338.7	31.3	50.1	3 626.0	1 636.8	193.6	3 693.0	1 594.3
Ukraine	..	..	..	..	..	170.3	60.9	256.1	70.5	-41.0
AFRICA	**-631.4**	**319.0**	**-345.8**	**25.7**	**-155.0**	**303.0**	**-1 580.4**	**509.9**	**3 567.7**	**1 504.3**
Northern Africa	-371.6	-25.9	125.1	122.0	80.9	820.5	-171.3	260.8	118.7	263.2
Algeria	-328.4	45.1	9.4	22.4	21.7	70.8	205.2	363.5	63.8	123.1
Egypt	-8.8	-77.8	118.0	-19.0	22.8	160.3	-649.3	185.3	189.2	44.4
Libya	8.8	6.8	10.6	6.7	1.1	14.4	..	-313.9	345.9	66.1
Morocco	-43.1	-20.3	-43.7	97.4	42.2	505.4	443.0	80.3	-675.0	-29.6
Tunisia	1.1	20.3	30.7	14.6	-6.8	69.7	178.1	-55.5	194.8	59.3
Other African countries	-259.9	344.9	-472.1	-96.3	-235.9	-517.5	-1 409.1	249.0	3 449.0	1 239.9
Nigeria	..	..	..	..	..	235.5	-30.4	-789.6	330.2	-312.3
South Africa	150.4	-217.6	26.0	66.0	28.5	181.4	273.9	164.1	119.8	353.3
AMERICA	**-8 503.8**	**382.1**	**-6 887.8**	**6 814.1**	**614.2**	**22 464.9**	**6 046.7**	**13 852.2**	**-10 886.6**	**14 141.3**
Northern America	-7 614.7	340.4	-5 890.5	7 397.3	-1 763.0	15 779.1	-2 014.4	-1 383.2	-17 770.1	12 207.4
Central America and Caribbean countries	-940.0	-22.5	-403.6	-589.9	2 295.2	3 250.0	2 119.3	13 780.2	3 928.1	918.5
Bahamas	..	..	..	..	..	-53.1	31.6	-	-	3.4
Bermuda	-140.4	5.6	207.7	40.3	1 112.3	1 093.7	108.2	16 106.5	3 386.3	1 308.3
Cayman Islands	-38.7	15.8	132.2	..	926.5	2 190.6	-36.1	-2 873.8	10.1	14.8
El Salvador	..	..	..	..	..	..	..	..	..	..
Guatemala	..	..	..	..	..	..	..	..	..	..
Honduras	..	..	..	..	..	..	..	..	..	..
Nicaragua	..	..	..	..	..	..	..	..	..	..
Panama	-	29.3	-8.3	4.5	2.3	-282.0	166.8	99.1	-53.7	-359.0
Virgin Islands, U.S.	-	-	-	..	..	..	..	..	..	..
South America	50.9	65.4	-593.7	6.7	82.1	3 435.8	5 943.0	1 455.2	2 955.3	1 014.2
Argentina	..	..	..	..	..	-66.4	467.8	24.8	-400.8	123.1
Bolivia	..	..	..	..	..	-23.2	421.6	-51.9	-4.5	-83.2
Brazil	-31.0	172.5	-182.9	..	69.5	2 239.3	2 899.3	1 052.8	3 505.0	679.2
Ecuador	-	..	..	..	..	..	..	..	..	..
Paraguay	..	..	..	..	..	..	..	..	..	..
Peru	..	..	..	..	..	1 427.6	491.5	13.0	-235.1	-200.6
Uruguay	..	..	..	..	..	5.5	-107.1	-15.3	9.0	-10.3
Venezuela	..	..	..	..	..	-96.2	36.1	-180.6	-10.1	19.4

Table 1. Foreign direct investment flows by country *(cont.)*

Million US dollars

	Inward					Outward				
	2016	2017	2018	2019	2020	2016	2017	2018	2019	2020
ASIA	**3 891.4**	**2 799.0**	**-269.1**	**4 378.1**	**-527.6**	**-1 118.0**	**-1 380.9**	**2 420.6**	**-1 150.8**	**3 482.6**
Near and Middle East	612.6	1 592.8	-671.5	1 539.2	638.2	1 089.2	-774.4	348.2	20.2	1 592.0
Gulf Arabian countries	801.7	438.5	-679.8	1 391.5	779.5	884.7	-738.4	-514.6	-335.8	1 516.8
Kuwait	..	..	173.5	47.0	124.2	5.5	..	77.9	..	35.3
Qatar	1 425.4	864.6	-901.7	1 275.0	400.0	353.9	-1 479.0	113.3	70.5	-155.0
Saudi Arabia	38.7	-96.9	-2.4	4.5	99.1	278.7	-815.0	158.1	-999.7	-87.7
United Arab Emirates	-557.3	-308.9	53.1	-40.3	158.4	257.7	1 534.2	-332.8	-2.2	1 548.7
Other Near and Middle East	-189.1	1 155.5	7.1	147.8	-141.3	204.6	-36.1	862.7	356.0	75.2
Jordan	..	..	..	..	..	-7.7	-5.6	436.7	81.7	-185.8
Other Asian countries	3 277.7	1 205.1	402.5	2 838.9	-1 165.8	-2 207.2	-605.3	2 072.5	-1 170.9	1 890.6
China	226.7	130.8	-605.5	251.9	222.2	593.8	851.1	915.9	-2 037.4	1 456.4
Hong Kong, China	1 612.3	899.6	-230.1	1 057.9	158.4	-2 101.1	-412.6	-363.5	-1 034.4	-1 776.6
India	-86.3	-36.1	..	110.8	68.4	-246.6	463.3	692.8	864.2	2 377.2
Indonesia	173.6	436.3	192.4	82.8	..	-632.5	-1 137.4	581.8	701.9	-72.9
Iran, Islamic Republic of	-54.2	166.8	-161.7	7.8	-9.1	-73.0	747.4	-686.9	-147.8	-20.5
Malaysia	-1.1	11.3	10.6	9.0	16.0	-39.8	36.1	190.0	293.3	-62.7
Philippines	-8.8	..	..	..	..	-869.2	25.9	-41.3	-28.0	-61.5
Singapore	94.0	-459.9	-312.8	991.8	-663.2	178.0	-2 138.4	-80.3	3 652.7	-21.7
Chinese Taipei	39.8	21.4	33.0	-30.2	-25.1	36.5	119.5	103.9	-31.3	47.9
Thailand	42.0	-67.6	-63.7	29.1	17.1	200.2	-546.7	-133.4	150.0	-13.7
Viet Nam	..	..	73.2	36.9	-42.2	-75.2	136.4	116.8	86.2	-3.4
AUSTRALIA, OCEANIA AND POLAR REGIONS	**597.1**	**-621.1**	**241.9**	**1 059.0**	**-1 168.1**	**-800.6**	**3 591.5**	**8 694.7**	**-1 588.5**	**8.0**
WORLD unallocated and confidential	**-2.2**	**2.3**	**301.0**	**-76.1**	**-214.2**	**-22.1**	**1.1**	**-611.4**	**623.5**	**-49.0**
European Union (since 01/02/2020)	..	..	..	..	..	..	..	..	..	..
G20 countries excl. European Union	**2 365.4**	**35 866.3**	**1 583.9**	**14 013.2**	**-5 505.4**	**44 397.9**	**33 974.7**	**15 797.2**	**-12 545.6**	**33 733.3**
G20 OECD countries	**1 986.1**	**35 109.9**	**2 639.0**	**13 576.6**	**-5 386.9**	**38 424.2**	**29 336.0**	**12 012.3**	**-17 992.8**	**27 309.4**
G20 Non-OECD countries	**379.3**	**756.4**	**-1 056.3**	**436.6**	**-118.5**	**5 973.7**	**4 638.7**	**3 783.8**	**5 447.2**	**6 422.8**
MENA countries	**165.9**	**1 481.2**	**-448.5**	**1 344.5**	**931.1**	**1 747.2**	**-800.4**	**254.9**	**-107.5**	**1 625.1**
ASEAN countries	**291.9**	**-1 402.3**	**-138.1**	**1 175.4**	**-1 344.7**	**-1 198.7**	**-5 600.3**	**301.0**	**4 980.4**	**-225.6**

- Nil; .. Not available

Note: Detailed metadata at: *http://metalinks.oecd.org/idi/20220712/6d95.*

Source: *OECD International Direct Investment Statistics (database): https://doi.org/10.1787/idi-data-en*

Table 2. Foreign direct investment positions by country
At year end

Million US dollars

	Inward					Outward				
	2016	2017	2018	2019	2020	2016	2017	2018	2019	2020
WORLD	**694 881.4**	**819 327.2**	**809 659.9**	**854 882.0**	**963 836.1**	**1 284 859.3**	**1 440 434.2**	**1 455 820.9**	**1 430 470.7**	**1 547 859.9**
OECD COUNTRIES	**635 961.8**	**762 991.1**	**758 470.3**	**802 307.3**	**909 582.8**	**1 069 930.4**	**1 204 348.8**	**1 214 159.6**	**1 185 753.8**	**1 298 737.3**
Australia	3 484.8	3 209.4	2 887.6	3 996.9	3 780.8	12 319.0	11 922.5	17 608.2	15 998.7	16 999.6
Austria	1 744.5	1 620.3	1 664.8	1 518.8	1 460.3	2 853.4	3 187.8	4 163.0	4 008.1	4 056.9
Belgium	46 226.4	45 617.7	50 824.4	54 922.5	60 346.1	165 440.1	170 187.1	158 421.1	153 293.6	179 111.5
Canada	7 132.9	12 182.8	14 326.8	16 498.5	16 092.8	12 018.6	12 535.4	11 708.3	11 686.1	12 186.8
Chile	765.3	906.7	500.3	787.5	1 115.5	1 767.7	3 830.7	3 989.0	2 198.4	2 172.0
Colombia	..	..	..	167.4	173.0	904.4	909.1	1 179.3	1 078.4	1 168.2
Costa Rica	..	..	..	..	..	..	..	..	..	..
Czech Republic	183.4	249.5	221.0	214.6	757.1	8 511.6	9 847.7	10 267.9	9 958.4	9 839.2
Denmark	4 775.0	6 074.6	6 454.1	6 221.1	6 640.1	7 817.0	9 521.5	17 482.3	10 082.0	10 816.1
Estonia	..	..	..	..	..	..	..	..	..	..
Finland	20 905.5	12 606.1	4 907.3	4 429.3	4 465.6	1 092.0	2 812.4	2 790.2	3 677.8	3 931.8
France	42 307.4	60 784.4	43 327.2	40 792.0	45 065.7	-	-	-	-	-
Germany	72 064.9	91 506.4	94 403.5	99 824.8	123 159.9	62 205.1	87 449.0	67 750.2	61 513.1	69 685.9
Greece	246.7	587.7	261.0	250.5	295.7	1 610.6	1 731.8	1 363.6	1 380.6	1 455.4
Hungary	120.2	347.8	423.6	328.0	374.3	3 210.7	3 600.4	3 536.8	3 247.6	3 637.3
Iceland	154.9	170.3	..	..	127.6	..	..	..	..	..
Ireland	5 303.0	6 505.2	5 753.4	6 038.0	6 362.7	19 622.6	25 185.9	35 873.6	23 668.8	25 293.9
Israel	953.9	1 296.5	1 131.2	1 565.9	1 499.6	3 138.0	3 261.0	3 104.0	3 333.0	3 672.8
Italy	24 305.9	30 239.9	33 951.2	35 780.7	39 088.2	65 369.5	77 132.4	95 604.5	72 330.9	81 749.9
Japan	16 865.2	20 215.9	19 476.8	17 862.3	19 235.5	27 856.0	29 297.2	26 486.1	22 718.5	23 024.9
Korea	331.0	217.1	835.8	1 031.2	971.9	4 202.6	5 087.6	5 406.5	4 514.7	4 781.0
Latvia	..	..	..	..	..	..	..	..	..	..
Lithuania	..	..	..	..	..	157.1	262.7	282.8	330.3	360.8
Luxembourg	33 639.7	50 136.7	66 376.2	76 315.4	91 538.8	46 858.9	59 832.1	54 108.1	59 982.0	67 031.5
Mexico	1 424.1	1 310.9	1 654.5	1 535.6	1 713.1	2 569.8	4 051.3	4 726.4	5 007.9	4 771.1
Netherlands	46 167.4	39 871.7	34 452.7	36 545.7	44 681.6	134 564.1	155 648.8	189 231.7	224 582.1	237 540.8
New Zealand	129.7	253.1	234.7	269.6	288.4	428.0	362.2	456.8	468.4	503.1
Norway	2 187.2	3 721.5	2 263.6	2 325.3	2 688.7	6 882.0	5 441.4	5 058.4	4 740.5	3 843.4
Poland	-1 538.9	-1 099.8	-840.4	..	1 332.7	17 193.0	19 641.4	19 364.6	19 782.1	19 218.3
Portugal	1 704.4	2 583.4	2 878.4	3 031.9	3 410.2	3 742.0	4 712.2	5 259.9	6 157.0	7 545.7
Slovak Republic	..	..	..	..	..	450.1	548.1	990.4	957.1	840.6
Slovenia	..	..	..	..	..	635.6	632.0	349.2	259.5	168.1
Spain	15 922.8	21 017.0	21 917.8	25 413.4	28 080.7	49 303.3	60 416.2	57 175.4	62 472.5	66 286.7
Sweden	6 407.7	9 672.6	9 653.1	9 377.7	9 847.8	5 598.2	9 399.1	8 052.4	6 953.5	6 933.4
Switzerland	85 522.3	95 298.6	96 574.3	108 696.9	127 475.8	44 511.4	49 269.6	47 695.2	44 500.1	50 511.7
Turkey	269.8	238.7	598.8	3 826.1	4 150.2	3 788.3	3 789.9	3 335.2	3 514.9	2 872.7
United Kingdom	74 732.8	102 156.4	90 964.0	93 822.7	102 843.3	116 238.0	136 754.6	123 306.6	132 609.5	147 337.1
United States	121 413.5	143 389.3	150 136.2	148 850.8	160 293.3	238 007.8	237 090.4	229 044.0	209 675.4	229 260.0
EUROPE	**486 007.2**	**581 748.6**	**569 598.1**	**613 236.4**	**706 696.5**	**796 403.5**	**928 930.2**	**944 309.6**	**947 692.7**	**1 036 117.3**
Bulgaria	..	..	..	..	..	994.0	1 079.4	1 041.9	477.4	485.9
Croatia	..	..	..	..	..	748.4	211.1	137.4	200.0	180.4
Cyprus	319.4	359.8	302.3	708.8	517.9	1 408.2	1 427.2	1 859.4	2 054.6	2 795.4
Malta	967.6	375.4	241.6	196.6	229.5	657.7	794.0	719.0	703.2	785.4
Montenegro	..	..	..	..	..	167.6	285.4	155.7	150.5	211.1
Romania	183.4	233.9	273.6	304.4	339.9	4 519.9	5 219.5	5 206.1	5 530.2	5 955.3
Russian Federation	1 073.0	947.5	945.7	966.1	1 046.8	17 820.2	19 896.9	20 801.5	25 917.8	23 227.4
Ukraine	..	..	..	..	..	570.3	766.4	902.2	938.0	797.6
AFRICA	**9 495.1**	**11 605.9**	**8 902.0**	**8 561.0**	**10 229.5**	**60 422.7**	**62 233.1**	**59 735.5**	**56 871.5**	**59 861.3**
Northern Africa	3 072.6	3 462.5	3 558.5	3 454.3	3 931.8	16 715.5	18 714.3	19 037.1	19 027.2	19 738.6
Algeria	496.5	539.7	673.2	718.9	808.7	2 855.5	2 798.0	2 949.4	2 872.4	2 910.8
Egypt	183.4	217.1	233.6	287.6	325.2	1 988.0	1 609.5	2 525.8	2 272.5	2 265.3
Libya	..	..	..	..	..	421.6	..	-204.9	358.3	465.1
Morocco	1 853.1	2 048.5	2 002.5	1 770.4	2 027.2	10 591.3	13 154.2	12 915.0	11 315.4	11 773.2
Tunisia	461.7	562.5	554.2	578.5	659.0	857.0	1 108.2	850.7	2 207.4	2 325.4
Other African countries	6 422.5	8 143.4	5 343.5	5 106.7	6 298.9	43 707.2	43 518.8	40 698.4	37 845.4	40 122.7
Nigeria	..	..	..	..	..	11 545.3	11 444.0	10 361.8	9 530.4	8 819.5
South Africa	2 579.3	3 130.2	320.6	353.9	911.8	2 588.8	2 798.0	3 217.3	3 331.8	3 680.2
AMERICA	**135 828.0**	**163 817.5**	**172 004.8**	**173 251.0**	**184 972.4**	**296 572.2**	**307 705.7**	**311 722.0**	**286 572.7**	**302 287.4**
Northern America	128 544.3	155 572.1	164 463.0	165 350.5	176 387.3	250 026.4	249 625.8	240 752.2	221 362.6	241 446.8
Central America and Caribbean countries	5 524.4	6 189.7	5 885.0	5 944.7	6 179.9	11 229.1	14 297.2	30 327.5	25 141.5	26 395.9
Bahamas	..	..	..	..	..	440.6	488.1	444.2	435.9	450.4
Bermuda	2 346.4	3 500.8	2 704.4	2 962.3	3 464.2	3 757.8	5 124.7	21 166.7	15 779.6	17 600.9
Cayman Islands	591.3	190.7	346.9	592.0	282.2	1 940.6	1 733.0	510.6	488.7	515.4
El Salvador	..	..	..	..	..	..	..	..	..	..
Guatemala	..	..	..	..	..	..	..	..	..	..
Honduras	..	..	..	..	..	..	..	..	..	..
Nicaragua	..	..	..	..	..	..	..	..	..	..
Panama	307.8	371.8	..	..	..	687.3	677.6	739.6	708.8	352.2
Virgin Islands, U.S.	..	..	..	..	..	..	..	..	..	..
South America	1 759.2	2 055.6	1 656.7	1 955.7	2 405.2	35 316.7	43 783.9	40 642.3	40 068.5	34 444.7
Argentina	123.3	148.7	152.3	151.7	173.0	3 032.6	3 586.0	1 742.6	1 118.9	1 077.4
Bolivia	..	..	..	..	..	806.4	831.1	778.6	774.0	701.9
Brazil	528.1	677.6	738.5	677.4	747.3	25 305.2	30 149.9	29 411.5	31 531.1	26 885.5
Ecuador	131.8	..	..	..	..	..	..	..	..	..
Paraguay	..	..	..	..	..	..	..	..	..	..
Peru	..	..	..	..	..	1 247.0	1 120.2	1 071.7	922.3	695.8
Uruguay	..	..	..	..	..	288.8	203.9	171.7	166.3	142.3
Venezuela	..	..	..	..	..	1 813.0	3 024.7	2 028.9	1 955.7	887.2

Table 2. Foreign direct investment positions by country *(cont.)*

At year end

Million US dollars

	Inward					Outward				
	2016	2017	2018	2019	2020	2016	2017	2018	2019	2020
ASIA	**45 882.8**	**58 395.3**	**55 790.0**	**55 373.0**	**57 529.8**	**118 080.5**	**126 623.9**	**119 676.0**	**119 774.2**	**128 995.0**
Near and Middle East	12 174.6	14 427.9	15 359.5	14 993.3	15 692.7	12 576.2	13 747.9	13 086.8	12 678.1	14 741.7
Gulf Arabian countries	10 120.2	9 415.9	10 012.6	11 885.0	12 446.9	7 861.3	8 740.7	7 854.4	6 810.8	8 563.0
Kuwait	139.1	..	433.9	357.2	370.6	108.6	..	136.2	..	131.3
Qatar	5 328.3	6 306.1	6 379.7	7 869.0	8 026.8	3 296.1	2 308.7	1 975.0	1 849.0	1 718.0
Saudi Arabia	527.0	627.2	531.3	667.3	679.8	5 382.1	4 685.8	4 854.6	3 601.4	3 594.3
United Arab Emirates	3 990.7	2 253.5	2 506.3	2 763.4	3 101.0	-797.9	1 693.5	1 640.7	1 476.1	3 130.4
Other Near and Middle East	2 055.4	5 012.0	5 346.9	3 108.3	3 245.8	4 714.9	5 007.2	5 232.4	5 867.2	6 178.7
Jordan	..	..	..	..	..	261.4	278.2	406.5	566.2	369.4
Other Asian countries	33 708.2	43 968.6	40 431.6	40 378.6	41 838.3	105 504.4	112 877.2	106 589.2	107 096.2	114 253.3
China	7 131.9	11 928.5	9 629.0	9 157.5	9 523.9	24 350.2	29 357.2	28 898.6	30 088.7	33 081.4
Hong Kong, China	4 148.8	5 177.5	4 624.5	5 912.2	6 638.9	10 327.8	10 948.7	10 748.8	10 174.1	8 240.3
India	527.0	492.9	411.0	330.3	494.5	5 762.6	6 543.5	6 486.1	6 805.2	11 940.1
Indonesia	870.7	780.8	833.5	635.8	-505.6	2 711.1	1 190.9	1 380.8	1 947.9	1 854.2
Iran, Islamic Republic of	237.2	285.4	308.0	293.2	326.4	728.4	1 544.7	692.7	599.9	624.6
Malaysia	338.4	381.4	380.1	413.4	465.1	744.2	1 091.4	1 214.8	1 485.1	1 433.3
Philippines	..	..	..	..	..	402.7	352.6	271.4	188.7	130.1
Singapore	1 513.7	2 397.5	1 980.8	2 635.4	2 397.8	10 478.6	11 928.5	10 430.5	13 664.3	14 109.7
Chinese Taipei	153.9	322.6	317.2	316.8	331.3	585.0	759.2	877.0	867.2	984.2
Thailand	1 082.5	1 226.9	1 074.0	1 195.2	1 283.6	2 011.2	1 718.6	1 604.1	1 705.2	1 686.1
Viet Nam	148.6	..	190.1	202.2	228.2	593.4	730.4	709.9	768.4	785.4
AUSTRALIA, OCEANIA AND POLAR REGIONS	**3 766.2**	**3 685.5**	**3 338.7**	**4 439.5**	**4 380.9**	**13 409.9**	**14 973.6**	**20 999.5**	**19 546.2**	**20 630.8**
WORLD unallocated and confidential	**13 902.2**	**74.4**	**26.3**	**21.3**	**27.0**	**-29.5**	**-32.4**	**-621.7**	**13.5**	**-31.9**
European Union (since 01/02/2020)	..	..	..	..	**468 382.6**	..	..	..	..	**805 863.3**
G20 countries excl. European Union	**377 689.5**	**484 182.1**	**466 125.5**	**476 763.6**	**529 465.0**	**631 527.4**	**703 318.5**	**681 770.1**	**643 913.7**	**698 008.3**
G20 OECD countries	**364 331.2**	**465 449.7**	**452 563.5**	**463 822.7**	**516 393.4**	**544 575.7**	**605 111.5**	**584 976.0**	**539 570.9**	**592 669.0**
G20 Non-OECD countries	**13 358.3**	**18 732.3**	**13 561.9**	**12 940.9**	**13 071.5**	**86 951.6**	**98 208.2**	**96 795.3**	**104 342.8**	**105 339.3**
MENA countries	**14 362.8**	**16 581.9**	**17 830.3**	**16 944.5**	**18 194.9**	**25 685.7**	**28 702.3**	**28 178.4**	**27 317.5**	**29 611.0**
ASEAN countries	**4 188.9**	**5 194.3**	**4 700.0**	**5 350.5**	**4 172.3**	**19 810.3**	**17 890.4**	**16 198.8**	**20 977.3**	**21 271.3**

- Nil; .. Not available

Note: Inward FDI positions are allocated according to the ultimate investing country. Detailed metadata at: *http://metalinks.oecd.org/idi/20220712/6d95*.

Source: *OECD International Direct Investment Statistics (database)*: *https://doi.org/10.1787/idi-data-en*

FRANCE

Table 3. Foreign direct investment income by country

Million US dollars

	Inward					Outward				
	2016	2017	2018	2019	2020	2016	2017	2018	2019	2020
WORLD	**29 483.6**	**36 340.9**	**40 913.5**	**38 055.5**	**24 197.2**	**69 441.6**	**77 144.6**	**95 033.6**	**99 044.0**	**59 571.5**
OECD COUNTRIES	..	..	..	..	..	..	..	..	..	..
Australia	..	..	..	..	..	..	..	..	..	..
Austria	..	..	..	..	..	..	..	..	..	..
Belgium	3 294.3	3 110.1	3 185.4	2 702.3	1 375.5	7 248.7	5 726.5	12 943.5	15 139.4	7 692.3
Canada	54.2	-315.6	63.7	2.2	188.0	1 036.2	-604.2	521.7	159.0	435.3
Chile	..	..	..	..	..	..	..	..	..	..
Colombia	..	..	..	..	..	..	..	..	..	..
Costa Rica	..	..	..	..	..	..	..	..	..	..
Czech Republic	16.6	-18.0	11.8	3.4	19.4	974.2	1 050.6	1 098.8	813.8	410.3
Denmark	..	..	..	..	..	..	..	..	..	..
Estonia	..	..	..	..	..	..	..	..	..	..
Finland	..	..	..	..	..	..	..	..	..	..
France	-	-	-	-	-	-	-	-	-	-
Germany	2 247.0	4 191.2	3 958.5	3 340.4	2 396.6	5 174.2	7 534.7	5 031.3	5 184.1	2 372.7
Greece	..	..	..	..	..	..	..	..	..	..
Hungary	..	..	..	..	..	..	..	..	..	..
Iceland	..	..	..	..	..	..	..	..	..	..
Ireland	126.1	95.8	75.5	190.3	197.2	1 541.5	1 464.3	4 211.0	1 969.1	1 408.5
Israel	..	..	..	..	..	..	..	..	..	..
Italy	994.1	579.4	965.4	1 268.3	559.5	3 731.1	4 101.0	5 564.7	4 690.5	3 034.8
Japan	535.2	737.2	976.0	444.4	410.3	3 550.8	3 788.8	2 928.1	-1 102.7	981.2
Korea	..	..	..	..	..	..	..	..	..	..
Latvia	..	..	..	..	..	..	..	..	..	..
Lithuania	..	..	..	..	..	..	..	..	..	..
Luxembourg	4 075.0	5 334.2	5 485.7	10 389.6	5 676.4	2 599.8	2 386.4	2 788.9	3 281.1	2 093.4
Mexico	..	..	..	..	..	..	..	..	..	..
Netherlands	6 679.2	8 007.0	12 431.3	7 198.0	3 674.1	6 190.4	5 424.4	10 926.5	8 821.2	9 568.1
New Zealand	..	..	..	..	..	..	..	..	..	..
Norway	118.3	190.5	213.6	178.0	66.1	637.0	445.3	633.8	932.5	161.8
Poland	-107.3	-137.5	-125.1	-26.9	21.7	954.3	1 366.3	1 589.8	1 300.8	735.0
Portugal	103.9	56.4	72.0	52.6	35.3	464.4	529.8	979.6	971.7	210.8
Slovak Republic	..	..	..	..	..	..	..	..	..	..
Slovenia	..	..	..	..	..	..	..	..	..	..
Spain	1 071.5	1 340.3	1 822.3	1 554.9	876.4	3 060.9	4 513.6	3 692.9	3 845.3	2 418.2
Sweden	391.5	714.7	558.2	426.5	164.1	408.1	560.3	505.1	511.6	278.1
Switzerland	2 654.0	1 518.4	3 465.1	2 903.8	2 924.2	5 463.9	6 428.8	3 812.1	5 424.8	1 968.1
Turkey	3.3	1.1	3.5	-	1.1	263.2	441.9	421.3	419.8	118.5
United Kingdom	4 122.5	4 213.7	3 936.0	4 902.0	2 528.8	6 108.6	6 157.1	5 175.3	9 247.7	5 704.8
United States	2 073.4	3 416.8	1 653.5	732.1	1 912.3	5 539.1	5 383.8	10 168.8	12 907.2	8 894.6
EUROPE	..	..	..	..	..	..	..	..	..	..
Bulgaria	..	..	..	..	..	..	..	..	..	..
Croatia	..	..	..	..	..	..	..	..	..	..
Cyprus	..	..	..	..	..	..	..	..	..	..
Malta	..	..	..	..	..	..	..	..	..	..
Montenegro	..	..	-	-	-	..	..	..	..	..
Romania	-1.1	-2.3	-4.7	-	1.1	538.5	724.8	719.9	727.6	237.0
Russian Federation	1.1	31.6	34.2	69.4	9.1	1 119.1	1 289.6	459.1	3 028.1	993.7
Ukraine	..	..	..	..	..	..	..	..	..	..
AFRICA	..	..	..	..	..	..	..	..	..	..
Northern Africa	..	..	..	..	..	..	..	..	..	..
Algeria	..	..	..	..	..	..	..	..	..	..
Egypt	..	..	..	..	..	..	..	..	..	..
Libya	..	..	..	..	..	..	..	..	..	..
Morocco	17.7	1.1	8.3	7.8	9.1	404.7	559.1	670.4	542.9	327.1
Tunisia	..	..	..	..	..	..	..	..	..	..
Other African countries	..	..	..	..	..	..	..	..	..	..
Nigeria	..	..	..	..	..	..	..	..	..	..
South Africa	..	..	..	..	..	..	..	..	..	..
AMERICA	..	..	..	..	..	..	..	..	..	..
Northern America	..	..	..	..	..	..	..	..	..	..
Central America and Caribbean countries	..	..	..	..	..	..	..	..	..	..
Bahamas	..	..	..	..	..	..	..	..	..	..
Bermuda	..	..	..	..	..	..	..	..	..	..
Cayman Islands	..	..	..	..	..	..	..	..	..	..
El Salvador	..	..	..	..	..	..	..	..	..	..
Guatemala	..	..	-	-	-	..	..	..	..	..
Honduras	..	..	-	-	-	..	..	..	..	..
Nicaragua	..	..	..	..	..	..	..	..	..	..
Panama	..	..	..	..	..	..	..	..	..	..
Virgin Islands, U.S.	..	..	-	..	..	..	..	..	..	..
South America	..	..	..	..	..	..	..	..	..	..
Argentina	..	..	..	..	..	..	..	..	..	..
Bolivia	..	..	-	-	-	..	..	..	..	..
Brazil	-5.5	-1.1	-1.2	-1.1	1.1	938.8	874.8	789.6	1 187.7	1 129.3
Ecuador	..	..	..	-	-	..	..	..	..	..
Paraguay	..	..	-	-	-	..	..	..	..	..
Peru	..	..	..	..	..	..	..	..	..	..
Uruguay	..	..	..	..	..	..	..	..	..	..
Venezuela	..	..	..	..	..	..	..	..	..	..

FRANCE

Table 3. Foreign direct investment income by country *(cont.)*

Million US dollars

	Inward					Outward				
	2016	2017	2018	2019	2020	2016	2017	2018	2019	2020
ASIA	..	..	..	..	..	..	..	..	..	..
Near and Middle East	..	..	..	..	..	..	..	..	..	..
Gulf Arabian countries	..	..	..	..	..	..	..	..	..	..
Kuwait	..	..	..	..	..	..	..	..	..	..
Qatar	..	..	..	..	..	..	..	..	..	..
Saudi Arabia	..	..	..	..	..	..	..	..	..	..
United Arab Emirates	..	..	..	..	..	..	..	..	..	..
Other Near and Middle East	..	..	..	..	..	..	..	..	..	..
Jordan	..	..	..	..	..	..	..	..	..	..
Other Asian countries	..	..	..	..	..	..	..	..	..	..
China	1.1	11.3	-15.3	9.0	55.8	988.6	1 636.8	2 170.4	2 157.2	1 293.4
Hong Kong, China	144.9	276.2	-46.0	167.9	189.2	1 071.5	1 643.6	2 171.6	1 996.0	477.5
India	-3.3	-7.9	-8.3	-28.0	1.1	275.4	289.7	326.9	358.2	278.1
Indonesia	-64.1	54.1	49.6	94.0	21.7	374.9	471.2	140.4	134.3	77.5
Iran, Islamic Republic of	..	..	..	..	..	..	..	..	..	..
Malaysia	..	..	..	..	..	..	..	..	..	..
Philippines	..	..	..	..	..	..	..	..	..	..
Singapore	23.2	16.9	23.6	19.0	23.9	270.9	1 463.2	2 450.1	1 949.0	629.1
Chinese Taipei	..	..	..	..	..	..	..	..	..	..
Thailand	..	..	..	..	..	..	..	..	..	..
Viet Nam	..	..	..	..	..	..	..	..	..	..
AUSTRALIA, OCEANIA AND POLAR REGIONS	..	..	..	..	..	..	..	..	..	..
WORLD unallocated and confidential	..	..	..	..	..	..	..	..	..	..
European Union (since 01/02/2020)	..	..	..	..	..	..	..	..	..	..
G20 countries excl. European Union	..	..	..	..	..	..	..	..	..	..
G20 OECD countries	..	..	..	..	..	..	..	..	..	..
G20 Non-OECD countries	..	..	..	..	..	..	..	..	..	..
MENA countries	..	..	..	..	..	..	..	..	..	..
ASEAN countries	..	..	..	..	..	..	..	..	..	..

- Nil; .. Not available

Note: Detailed metadata at: *http://metalinks.oecd.org/idi/20220712/6d95*.

Source: *OECD International Direct Investment Statistics (database)*: *https://doi.org/10.1787/idi-data-en*

FRANCE

Table 4. Foreign direct investment flows by industrial sector

Million US dollars

	Inward					Outward				
	2016	2017	2018	2019	2020	2016	2017	2018	2019	2020
All FDI activities	**23 054.3**	**24 779.6**	**41 806.9**	**28 362.3**	**4 861.5**	**64 784.9**	**35 908.0**	**101 978.0**	**33 817.3**	**45 905.4**
Agriculture, forestry and fishing	**113.9**	**60.9**	**469.7**	**-94.0**	**59.3**	**-131.6**	**81.2**	**67.3**	**-56.0**	**-190.3**
Mining and quarrying	**-134.9**	**4.5**	**971.3**	**581.0**	**-1 537.3**	**4 397.9**	**-4 181.0**	**5 152.8**	**7 153.3**	**2 021.7**
Extraction activities	-136.0	4.5	971.3	581.0	-1 537.3	4 399.0	-4 181.0	5 152.8	7 153.3	2 021.7
Manufacturing	**8 033.8**	**789.1**	**14 356.2**	**-9 255.6**	**2 859.3**	**16 377.3**	**8 349.7**	**38 648.6**	**-823.9**	**8 965.2**
of which:										
Food products, beverages and tobacco	-3 915.7	2 874.5	-110.9	-6 585.7	-980.1	3 229.0	12 540.9	-1 009.1	3 183.7	157.3
Textiles, wood and paper products; printing	513.1	-473.5	-830.9	3 091.9	-264.4	915.6	-2 262.4	830.9	673.9	19 489.5
Chemical, rubber, plastic, non-metallic mineral products	984.2	9 234.6	-3 813.3	2 353.1	114.0	6 261.2	-3 119.2	8 529.4	-3 135.6	-12 348.7
Metal and machinery products, except electrical equipment	12 446.1	-8 089.3	-1 942.6	-698.5	-1 114.5	8 010.6	-6 490.8	-1 606.3	7 179.0	-1 045.0
Motor vehicles, trailers, semi-trailers, other transport equipment	-393.7	-653.8	-1 764.4	-9 797.4	6 651.9	-263.2	8 347.4	861.6	-5 356.5	1 102.0
Other manufacturing	-1 600.1	-2 102.4	22 818.4	2 381.1	-1 548.7	-1 776.0	-667.3	31 043.3	-3 369.5	1 609.1
Electricity, gas, steam and air conditioning supply	**1 255.1**	**-2 361.6**	**-241.9**	**-719.8**	**-93.4**	**803.9**	**-2 678.4**	**3 325.9**	**5 081.2**	**6 412.5**
Water supply; sewerage, waste management and remediation activities	**49.8**	**-312.3**	**-57.8**	**-21.3**	**-45.6**	**2.2**	**-74.4**	**-696.3**	**-973.9**	**3 717.4**
Construction	**1 359.1**	**-5 241.8**	**521.7**	**-686.2**	**-983.5**	**-764.1**	**-5 485.3**	**1 773.9**	**1 925.4**	**753.3**
Services	**-2 208.3**	**28 480.4**	**24 971.1**	**38 489.9**	**-7 997.7**	**40 132.7**	**38 282.0**	**53 396.7**	**21 290.7**	**11 764.1**
Wholesale and retail trade; repair of motor vehicles and motorcycles	212.3	6 206.7	-803.7	7 065.9	-5 508.8	4 821.4	-3 512.6	3 979.7	-12 928.5	1 635.3
Transportation and storage	1 351.3	2 724.6	-122.7	1 047.8	-118.5	-360.5	-1 116.0	1 896.6	2 677.7	3 760.7
Accommodation and food service activities	2 440.6	519.7	-335.2	675.0	-700.9	2 612.0	8 297.8	-5 523.4	1 427.3	-1 084.9
Information and communication	557.3	2 658.1	1 896.6	4 324.4	-1 573.8	116.1	1 024.7	11 533.1	7 843.9	1 463.2
Financial and insurance activities	-11 714.0	15 086.2	24 781.1	17 995.1	-4 877.5	26 855.0	10 438.5	10 948.9	12 941.9	6 413.7
Activities of holding companies	-5 298.0	4 725.5	13 578.4	6 022.6	-3 382.3	819.4	1 199.4	2 552.8	9 838.8	1 537.3
Real estate activities	-2 011.5	-59.7	-1 602.7	792.6	4 013.7	3 758.7	1 533.1	22 760.5	2 329.6	2 128.8
Professional, scientific and technical activities	3 773.1	5.6	1 921.4	5 014.0	613.1	1 586.9	15 394.0	6 986.9	4 808.0	-1 889.5
Administrative and support service activities	2 275.8	-73.3	-1 254.6	1 040.0	118.5	560.7	6 020.7	625.5	1 777.7	-978.9
Public administration; activities of households and of extraterritorial organisations	..	..	-8.3	-	..	201.3	224.3	-13.0	116.4	-205.1
Education	266.5	443.0	-114.5	-184.7	-57.0	..	..	..	..	..
Human health and social work activities	512.0	310.0	33.0	842.9	-754.4	-84.0	64.3	247.8	106.3	683.8
Arts, entertainment and recreation	130.5	651.6	590.1	-68.3	878.6	..	..	48.4	48.1	..
Other services	..	..	-9.4	-56.0	-34.2	50.9	-84.5	-89.7	143.3	-127.6
Not allocated and confidential	**14 585.9**	**3 360.4**	**816.7**	**68.3**	**12 600.6**	**3 966.6**	**1 614.2**	**309.2**	**220.5**	**12 461.5**
Private real estate activities	-	-	-	-	-	-	-	-	-	-

- Nil; .. Not available

Note: Detailed metadata at: *http://metalinks.oecd.org/idi/20220712/6d95.*

Source: *OECD International Direct Investment Statistics (database): https://doi.org/10.1787/idi-data-en*

FRANCE

Table 5. Foreign direct investment positions by industrial sector

At year end

Million US dollars

	Inward					Outward				
	2016	2017	2018	2019	2020	2016	2017	2018	2019	2020
All FDI activities	**694 881.4**	**819 327.2**	**809 659.9**	**854 882.0**	**963 836.1**	**1 284 859.3**	**1 440 434.2**	**1 455 820.9**	**1 430 470.7**	**1 547 859.9**
Agriculture, forestry and fishing	**678.8**	**847.9**	**1 102.6**	**750.4**	**877.4**	**393.2**	**407.8**	**816.4**	**743.7**	**568.2**
Mining and quarrying	**4 899.3**	**3 858.2**	**4 047.4**	**4 314.8**	**2 839.6**	**113 755.7**	**111 445.2**	**121 654.5**	**125 851.5**	**132 567.2**
Extraction activities	4 707.5	3 858.2	4 047.4	4 314.8	2 839.6	113 755.7	111 631.1	121 654.5	125 851.5	132 567.2
Manufacturing	**179 479.3**	**214 549.1**	**221 803.3**	**229 537.2**	**274 471.7**	**380 503.8**	**412 138.4**	**450 558.7**	**422 280.4**	**457 058.5**
of which:										
Food products, beverages and tobacco	26 577.4	31 909.3	34 120.7	29 892.2	31 628.4	61 354.5	87 626.5	84 115.0	91 245.8	95 573.7
Textiles, wood and paper products; printing	7 447.0	8 383.3	9 047.4	12 075.9	12 912.0	15 642.5	14 238.4	14 069.2	14 611.3	36 100.1
Chemical, rubber, plastic, non-metallic mineral products	75 444.3	99 878.9	98 584.8	108 946.3	138 817.0	137 969.9	143 912.2	162 904.7	158 896.9	160 062.6
Metal and machinery products, except electrical equipment	36 895.8	34 863.3	23 695.9	22 593.8	24 929.4	41 073.0	34 918.4	34 277.5	37 415.2	37 723.6
Motor vehicles, trailers, semi-trailers, other transport equipment	14 685.4	24 922.0	18 899.7	9 731.5	17 608.3	62 618.3	71 271.3	65 016.0	63 261.1	66 827.8
Other manufacturing	18 427.3	14 593.4	37 453.6	46 297.5	48 576.5	61 845.7	60 171.5	90 177.5	56 847.9	60 770.6
Electricity, gas, steam and air conditioning supply	**4 382.8**	**5 328.6**	**6 430.0**	**5 443.7**	**5 854.7**	**85 793.2**	**89 033.3**	**87 208.6**	**84 413.6**	**95 925.9**
Water supply; sewerage, waste management and remediation activities	**719.9**	**628.4**	**649.2**	**624.6**	**617.3**	**4 973.1**	**5 095.9**	**5 265.6**	**3 657.6**	**7 769.1**
Construction	**22 863.9**	**21 286.9**	**17 362.0**	**16 073.9**	**16 495.3**	**22 586.7**	**19 066.9**	**18 414.2**	**20 443.7**	**21 965.9**
Services	**454 420.8**	**543 691.5**	**550 983.5**	**590 631.3**	**641 255.4**	**647 115.0**	**769 919.6**	**753 818.4**	**754 071.0**	**798 170.3**
Wholesale and retail trade; repair of motor vehicles and motorcycles	46 885.2	64 986.8	65 827.8	69 338.4	69 717.8	95 101.7	104 246.8	103 178.4	93 989.0	100 623.4
Transportation and storage	9 967.3	12 963.5	12 621.9	13 682.3	15 426.4	8 656.1	11 014.6	12 753.6	13 492.5	18 210.8
Accommodation and food service activities	7 609.4	9 949.6	9 990.8	11 497.4	10 780.5	12 998.8	23 349.7	15 340.1	16 187.4	15 707.4
Information and communication	18 234.4	26 144.2	25 106.5	30 603.2	33 195.5	75 413.7	83 576.4	90 967.5	97 190.5	104 346.5
Financial and insurance activities	172 687.9	199 371.6	209 534.0	226 131.2	241 921.7	322 707.9	362 414.2	345 100.8	340 191.0	359 926.4
Activities of holding companies	74 580.0	92 681.7	102 180.0	108 225.1	114 874.2	34 721.2	42 110.8	44 743.5	53 681.2	54 387.0
Real estate activities	143 840.0	176 452.4	170 791.2	176 622.1	200 805.0	74 232.1	74 326.0	101 426.6	104 365.3	109 382.7
Professional, scientific and technical activities	39 808.2	35 250.7	38 097.1	41 162.7	45 930.8	48 424.2	98 427.7	70 405.3	72 614.0	73 847.1
Administrative and support service activities	9 265.3	10 406.6	9 429.8	10 774.0	11 692.2	5 912.3	8 438.5	10 891.9	11 937.8	11 374.4
Public administration; activities of households and of extraterritorial organisations	..	..	-	-	..	256.1	530.1	458.0	477.4	300.7
Education	1 368.2	2 029.3	1 804.4	1 577.2	1 661.6	..	..	..	..	..
Human health and social work activities	3 723.0	4 646.2	4 506.5	5 740.3	5 383.5	2 757.5	2 924.0	2 967.7	3 161.1	4 128.1
Arts, entertainment and recreation	904.4	1 302.5	2 981.5	3 142.0	4 380.9	..	..	171.7	168.5	..
Other services	..	..	290.8	360.6	358.3	546.0	519.3	153.4	294.3	175.5
Not allocated and confidential	**27 436.5**	**29 136.5**	**7 281.9**	**7 506.2**	**21 424.7**	**29 738.6**	**33 326.9**	**18 084.5**	**19 009.2**	**33 834.8**
Private real estate activities	-	-	-	-	-	-	-	-	-	-

- Nil; .. Not available

Note: Detailed metadata at: *http://metalinks.oecd.org/idi/20220712/6d95*.

Source: *OECD International Direct Investment Statistics (database): https://doi.org/10.1787/idi-data-en*

FRANCE

Table 6. Foreign direct investment income by industrial sector

Million US dollars

	Inward					Outward				
	2016	2017	2018	2019	2020	2016	2017	2018	2019	2020
All FDI activities	**29 483.6**	**36 340.9**	**40 913.5**	**38 055.5**	**24 197.2**	**69 441.6**	**77 144.6**	**95 033.6**	**99 044.0**	**59 571.5**
Agriculture, forestry and fishing	..	..	..	..	..	..	..	..	..	..
Mining and quarrying	..	..	..	..	..	..	..	..	..	..
Extraction activities	..	..	..	..	..	..	..	..	..	..
Manufacturing	..	..	..	..	..	..	..	..	..	..
of which:										
Food products, beverages and tobacco	..	..	..	..	..	..	..	..	..	..
Textiles, wood and paper products; printing	..	..	..	..	..	..	..	..	..	..
Chemical, rubber, plastic, non-metallic mineral products	..	..	..	..	..	..	..	..	..	..
Metal and machinery products, except electrical equipment	..	..	..	..	..	..	..	..	..	..
Motor vehicles, trailers, semi-trailers, other transport equipment	..	..	..	..	..	..	..	..	..	..
Other manufacturing	..	..	..	..	..	..	..	..	..	..
Electricity, gas, steam and air conditioning supply	..	..	..	..	..	..	..	..	..	..
Water supply; sewerage, waste management and remediation activities	..	..	..	..	..	..	..	..	..	..
Construction	..	..	..	..	..	..	..	..	..	..
Services	..	..	..	..	..	..	..	..	..	..
Wholesale and retail trade; repair of motor vehicles and motorcycles	..	..	..	..	..	..	..	..	..	..
Transportation and storage	..	..	..	..	..	..	..	..	..	..
Accommodation and food service activities	..	..	..	..	..	..	..	..	..	..
Information and communication	..	..	..	..	..	..	..	..	..	..
Financial and insurance activities	..	..	..	..	..	..	..	..	..	..
Activities of holding companies	..	..	..	..	..	..	..	..	..	..
Real estate activities	..	..	..	..	..	..	..	..	..	..
Professional, scientific and technical activities	..	..	..	..	..	..	..	..	..	..
Administrative and support service activities	..	..	..	..	..	..	..	..	..	..
Public administration; activities of households and of extraterritorial organisations	-	-	-	-	..	-	..	..	..	..
Education	..	..	..	..	..	..	..	..	..	..
Human health and social work activities	..	..	..	..	..	..	..	..	..	..
Arts, entertainment and recreation	..	..	..	..	..	..	..	..	..	..
Other services	..	..	..	..	..	..	..	..	..	..
Not allocated and confidential	..	..	..	..	**24 197.2**	..	..	..	..	**59 571.5**
Private real estate activities	-	-	-	-	..	-	-	-	-	..

- Nil; .. Not available

Note: Detailed metadata at: *http://metalinks.oecd.org/idi/20220712/6d95.*

Source: *OECD International Direct Investment Statistics (database): https://doi.org/10.1787/idi-data-en*

GERMANY

Table 1. Foreign direct investment flows by country

Million US dollars

	Inward					Outward				
	2016	2017	2018	2019	2020	2016	2017	2018	2019	2020
WORLD	**15 617.9**	**48 537.8**	**62 034.3**	**54 061.5**	**35 570.0**	**63 599.0**	**86 333.2**	**86 190.2**	**139 274.4**	**34 870.5**
OECD COUNTRIES	**16 871.5**	**45 515.4**	**60 854.1**	**52 559.3**	**20 550.3**	**53 929.1**	**69 736.8**	**70 416.6**	**135 231.0**	**40 818.0**
Australia	-159.0	890.8	341.9	668.7	615.7	209.9	1 145.8	1 686.2	-615.9	1 318.0
Austria	-338.5	2 349.4	3 868.8	2 664.1	3 516.7	11 292.7	6 111.7	372.2	2 819.2	493.8
Belgium	316.1	-8 189.8	-3 635.4	-5 793.9	-1 729.7	-4 667.6	-17 567.0	-478.5	15 264.0	8 471.9
Canada	2 436.0	773.6	-913.2	2 536.2	1 085.5	994.4	775.3	1 368.1	1 855.8	-297.6
Chile	9.5	265.4	-125.3	116.0	314.0	-83.7	163.9	-81.6	85.7	-180.4
Colombia	-12.6	3.1	-32.2	8.9	19.6	174.1	133.5	140.2	143.2	-51.0
Costa Rica	-0.3	-1.1	-1.1	-7.1	8.0	16.2	-39.8	15.7	-52.5	238.3
Czech Republic	1 234.9	-47.2	-609.8	328.6	572.7	2 185.1	2 791.5	1 809.7	-370.1	-235.9
Denmark	-1 176.1	5 516.9	-498.8	-60.8	760.0	-165.6	1 346.3	950.1	1 056.4	29.6
Estonia	23.5	11.6	-19.4	6.4	4.3	21.9	112.9	77.2	27.6	72.3
Finland	-248.3	-1 211.0	-5.9	-438.4	725.8	-347.3	791.5	514.4	715.9	759.6
France	5 034.5	6 524.3	-23 915.9	-1 382.1	1 561.0	-402.6	10 113.6	4 134.4	-1 281.8	285.6
Germany	-	-	-	-	-	-	-	-	-	-
Greece	-10.0	31.6	-39.6	57.3	21.6	244.6	897.2	580.3	38.3	103.8
Hungary	-27.1	-225.6	70.8	2 039.2	-712.7	1 432.7	-1 907.6	-502.7	2 204.1	-381.8
Iceland	-9.7	0.6	0.8	3.9	-1.2	26.6	53.9	81.6	19.7	41.3
Ireland	-3 128.6	246.6	46 280.9	3 549.2	2 578.8	-3 038.3	-9.5	14 663.8	-4 622.4	107.0
Israel	113.4	49.7	284.8	67.7	-12.9	288.3	259.6	465.7	1 031.2	-464.6
Italy	644.9	-1 230.3	209.0	-2 232.1	-2 954.1	3 275.7	615.3	2 192.4	7 809.5	2 672.5
Japan	1 872.4	2 548.3	2 294.8	5 057.1	579.0	1 715.0	791.9	295.4	507.8	2 034.9
Korea	712.8	123.5	-20.0	1 056.1	788.4	467.1	1 051.7	-131.9	992.0	1 320.4
Latvia	3.0	-31.1	9.6	-0.6	4.6	23.6	31.3	64.0	312.7	129.1
Lithuania	-12.4	-24.9	-42.1	-1 166.4	-81.8	150.9	-20.3	37.4	375.2	3 444.4
Luxembourg	356.8	3 005.5	2 563.5	35 659.5	17 439.8	11 634.0	24 378.5	12 373.5	33 996.2	981.8
Mexico	91.5	-104.3	204.3	114.5	179.1	1 382.7	3 311.0	1 895.3	972.2	-831.1
Netherlands	2 378.8	9 845.5	33 631.7	-7 092.6	-17 908.7	3 411.0	-4 250.6	-2 804.6	31 957.0	10 353.0
New Zealand	-10.1	5.5	-8.8	-19.1	13.4	-2.7	-25.9	85.1	8.5	-107.1
Norway	-968.6	747.8	-622.3	19.3	-454.8	-746.8	1 038.0	-796.3	580.8	-701.4
Poland	-305.4	-174.5	401.1	-397.8	547.6	2 931.4	2 819.4	2 204.5	2 115.7	780.8
Portugal	58.8	-31.3	-89.2	-49.0	11.3	824.6	203.9	113.3	400.4	-143.0
Slovak Republic	181.7	-228.2	-122.8	-9.2	529.0	71.2	859.0	-124.7	621.0	293.9
Slovenia	-3.4	14.7	-0.3	-23.9	9.3	25.3	-65.9	162.1	42.7	76.5
Spain	1 845.0	-1 177.9	2 150.2	750.2	-49.7	2 558.2	4 270.6	9 116.0	3 235.2	2 846.6
Sweden	-1 034.5	8 517.4	-6 758.7	3 042.7	459.2	1 064.8	36.7	4 462.9	2 495.8	-394.1
Switzerland	6 133.6	2 042.7	10 948.5	-2 545.3	-1 297.3	3 701.1	3 695.6	-1 537.8	-651.8	-362.6
Turkey	-56.6	220.6	-519.1	320.3	75.2	602.3	1 596.4	1 751.8	653.5	1 481.1
United Kingdom	866.4	-5 743.5	806.7	7 072.1	5 626.5	616.1	2 751.4	3 520.3	-8 335.9	1 071.5
United States	33.9	20 178.2	-5 266.7	8 641.4	7 715.2	12 383.5	21 549.3	11 897.0	38 914.4	5 799.2
EUROPE	**8 473.1**	**21 413.5**	**65 344.3**	**37 638.5**	**18 637.6**	**35 830.4**	**42 043.6**	**55 979.7**	**87 627.0**	**32 409.3**
Bulgaria	103.4	23.7	44.7	-13.2	34.6	219.7	252.0	131.3	-251.6	196.2
Croatia	34.0	-40.0	7.2	5.4	-0.8	135.5	291.4	270.1	40.5	-13.4
Cyprus	213.5	329.5	1 547.4	351.1	730.8	79.9	-715.1	-1 696.8	-4 929.6	-1 904.3
Malta	58.2	94.2	-69.2	2 759.5	7 831.3	-4 755.1	126.4	-1 378.6	-156.2	783.6
Montenegro	-0.1	-0.1	0.8	1.0	0.2	17.5	1.1	-7.9	-30.8	5.0
Romania	25.6	47.5	5.1	-86.6	189.3	1 058.4	-56.4	758.2	659.2	190.7
Russian Federation	-231.6	-156.4	-414.9	-429.4	1 212.2	1 643.0	81.7	3 671.4	1 160.0	265.9
Ukraine	-48.0	-6.9	6.1	114.4	-66.6	35.2	224.3	417.3	229.6	226.6
AFRICA	**-65.6**	**296.2**	**-127.2**	**38.5**	**-16.7**	**1 940.2**	**1 578.8**	**2 142.3**	**1 072.5**	**1 054.6**
Northern Africa	-6.4	75.2	-52.5	26.0	-8.9	1 201.1	679.8	1 513.0	434.2	316.7
Algeria	1.2	6.0	-4.9	-1.1	-5.8	328.4	328.6	300.7	-107.1	-28.3
Egypt	-12.6	54.8	-33.8	61.6	-20.5	689.4	-65.4	-345.7	180.0	177.7
Libya	-16.6	-1.3	18.9	0.0	-	-213.4	361.3	1.7	140.2	34.4
Morocco	13.0	-6.3	1.3	-4.6	11.4	385.8	9.8	1 490.6	163.8	26.7
Tunisia	8.5	21.9	-34.1	-29.9	5.9	10.9	45.5	65.8	57.3	106.1
Other African countries	-59.2	221.1	-74.7	12.5	-7.8	739.1	899.0	629.2	638.3	737.9
Nigeria	39.6	-15.5	10.7	16.7	-3.8	42.5	62.0	134.2	41.1	42.3
South Africa	-99.6	266.3	-41.5	-60.7	-78.1	712.3	570.2	360.2	273.5	478.8
AMERICA	**2 624.0**	**23 381.6**	**-7 425.9**	**6 069.6**	**16 003.7**	**13 379.7**	**26 812.8**	**16 367.9**	**42 055.7**	**1 804.5**
Northern America	2 469.9	20 951.8	-6 179.9	11 177.6	8 800.7	13 377.9	22 324.6	13 265.0	40 770.2	5 501.6
Central America and Caribbean countries	66.0	2 059.7	-959.4	-5 104.9	6 777.4	518.8	2 539.2	296.0	-391.9	-3 276.4
Bahamas	5.8	58.7	-2 007.6	-836.8	59.9	4.3	12.8	9.3	7.7	-43.1
Bermuda	-1 084.3	23.3	-226.8	1 713.7	-3 440.2	115.0	-132.3	298.5	-271.5	-1 741.9
Cayman Islands	-77.1	536.1	-2 442.8	-1 308.2	-1 309.6	-987.5	-614.9	-882.1	-144.7	-336.1
El Salvador	-	-1.1	-3.5	-1.1	2.3	-5.5	-1.4	-16.3	1.9	1.6
Guatemala	2.2	1.2	-2.0	-4.4	0.0	-12.9	6.1	0.5	-4.5	-0.1
Honduras	2.2	1.1	-3.5	1.1	-20.5	-7.5	-13.0	-4.2	11.9	55.3
Nicaragua	-	-	-	-	1.1	0.5	-22.9	8.0	-0.6	4.1
Panama	-3.3	33.5	-17.0	-2.1	9.9	-27.8	107.9	-633.3	-686.7	-465.3
Virgin Islands, U.S.	-	-496.5	-67.2	-	-	-	-	-	-	-
South America	88.1	370.0	-286.6	-3.1	425.5	-517.0	1 949.0	2 806.9	1 677.3	-420.7
Argentina	42.7	31.6	-25.1	-8.3	6.5	204.1	707.2	111.4	509.1	9.7
Bolivia	0.0	0.0	1.2	0.0	-	-91.3	1.4	7.5	16.7	-5.8
Brazil	35.7	44.7	-111.4	-113.6	56.3	-991.9	1 173.0	1 397.6	546.5	-528.1
Ecuador	1.8	-2.2	4.6	-1.1	-3.4	21.1	27.8	26.2	40.3	33.3
Paraguay	9.2	0.8	-2.3	-0.3	0.0	0.7	15.4	21.6	25.6	-15.8
Peru	0.4	-5.6	-13.0	-0.4	4.0	72.1	26.3	36.4	86.4	-58.4
Uruguay	-11.0	2.0	-4.6	-2.4	23.5	-4.2	133.1	1 300.7	170.8	236.0
Venezuela	12.3	29.7	21.6	-0.8	4.0	159.1	-444.3	-145.9	48.6	132.9

Table 1. Foreign direct investment flows by country *(cont.)*

Million US dollars

	Inward					Outward				
	2016	2017	2018	2019	2020	2016	2017	2018	2019	2020
ASIA	**4 770.2**	**2 823.5**	**3 881.7**	**9 678.9**	**323.6**	**12 237.2**	**14 770.6**	**9 928.7**	**9 132.3**	**-1 608.7**
Near and Middle East	190.3	626.2	-18.3	-554.1	-2 971.2	947.2	996.9	641.7	1 759.2	-647.3
Gulf Arabian countries	59.1	569.8	-302.1	-619.5	-2 954.7	613.4	835.0	153.5	758.7	-205.5
Kuwait	11.6	9.9	-15.0	-5.6	-2.5	85.0	90.1	-72.7	-52.2	5.9
Qatar	124.3	556.0	-230.1	-554.8	-2 849.9	126.3	29.6	-310.1	42.0	206.6
Saudi Arabia	-132.2	-123.9	-26.0	-24.1	10.4	356.3	3.5	-274.7	-73.8	-82.5
United Arab Emirates	71.1	140.8	-11.8	-16.5	-101.4	-74.7	671.6	872.6	831.9	-304.3
Other Near and Middle East	131.2	56.3	283.8	65.4	-16.5	333.8	161.9	488.3	1 000.5	-441.9
Jordan	7.7	2.3	1.2	1.1	-1.1	0.6	-26.7	-23.2	-36.9	-25.2
Other Asian countries	4 579.9	2 197.3	3 900.0	10 233.0	3 294.8	11 290.0	13 773.7	9 287.0	7 373.1	-961.4
China	527.1	105.2	262.1	1 699.4	516.6	8 429.1	7 247.5	5 486.8	3 828.8	-2 420.4
Hong Kong, China	1 109.9	-590.9	1 712.3	3 052.3	1 342.9	363.6	1 249.5	255.6	1 705.8	-316.8
India	-48.5	-34.7	-151.0	-112.3	-54.7	1 501.2	1 247.3	1 367.9	998.1	-2 105.0
Indonesia	22.2	-11.9	0.1	-22.3	8.1	98.8	157.7	205.2	98.8	270.2
Iran, Islamic Republic of	14.8	31.7	-118.1	-139.9	-205.7	264.6	-548.2	153.4	85.5	-44.3
Malaysia	67.4	-211.0	8.0	-24.1	24.8	580.5	608.7	299.7	70.1	-206.5
Philippines	4.5	2.8	-10.7	-16.7	19.4	-362.8	189.1	228.6	226.5	-150.3
Singapore	171.3	-40.5	-161.5	-136.7	161.8	-2 685.1	678.7	489.2	-607.5	378.5
Chinese Taipei	72.0	20.9	43.1	-27.9	15.3	130.7	178.3	150.6	-657.4	-36.6
Thailand	-109.6	22.6	84.9	-77.9	26.7	389.0	597.5	129.3	-31.8	-10.0
Viet Nam	4.2	4.5	-12.5	1.0	77.5	107.2	94.0	8.5	34.3	-0.1
AUSTRALIA, OCEANIA AND POLAR REGIONS	**-183.7**	**623.0**	**361.4**	**636.0**	**621.8**	**211.6**	**1 127.4**	**1 771.6**	**-613.0**	**1 212.4**
WORLD unallocated and confidential	**0.0**	**0.0**	**-**	**-**	**-**	**0.0**	**-**	**-**	**-**	**-1.7**
European Union (since 01/02/2020)	..	..	..	..	..	..	..	..	..	..
G20 countries excl. European Union	**11 592.5**	**24 302.0**	**-27 286.0**	**22 780.9**	**16 948.8**	**33 197.0**	**54 889.8**	**40 934.8**	**48 812.7**	**10 743.1**
G20 OECD countries	**11 476.7**	**24 181.2**	**-26 778.1**	**21 852.3**	**15 271.5**	**21 244.1**	**43 701.7**	**28 609.0**	**41 471.8**	**14 854.5**
G20 Non-OECD countries	**115.9**	**120.9**	**-507.8**	**928.6**	**1 677.4**	**11 952.9**	**11 188.1**	**12 325.8**	**7 341.0**	**-4 111.4**
MENA countries	**70.3**	**653.5**	**-354.5**	**-594.0**	**-2 965.2**	**1 817.0**	**1 494.8**	**1 650.4**	**1 133.0**	**120.8**
ASEAN countries	**154.5**	**-237.9**	**-92.8**	**-277.5**	**312.7**	**-1 866.9**	**2 342.7**	**1 327.2**	**-59.2**	**477.2**

- Nil; .. Not available

Note: Detailed metadata at: *http://metalinks.oecd.org/idi/20220712/6d95.*

Source: *OECD International Direct Investment Statistics (database): https://doi.org/10.1787/idi-data-en*

Table 2. Foreign direct investment positions by country
At year end

Million US dollars

	Inward					Outward				
	2016	2017	2018	2019	2020	2016	2017	2018	2019	2020
WORLD	**794 510.4**	**963 121.9**	**940 535.8**	**934 693.3**	**1 129 941.1**	**1 367 630.4**	**1 650 292.6**	**1 707 633.4**	**1 775 679.6**	**1 955 453.4**
OECD COUNTRIES	**740 795.8**	**894 279.2**	**876 027.0**	**869 105.8**	..	**1 135 030.0**	**1 372 342.3**	**1 431 585.8**	**1 486 116.6**	**1 672 810.2**
Australia	4 354.4	4 985.6	4 963.4	.. d	..	11 963.7	14 618.6	13 118.8	13 180.2	17 670.9
Austria	23 894.8	30 129.5	27 894.4	28 102.7	..	50 981.3	67 678.1	69 567.2	66 100.9	71 811.3
Belgium	10 011.6	12 332.7	12 003.7	11 954.6	..	35 196.6	23 258.6	20 749.9	30 011.2	45 187.1
Canada	.. d	.. d	.. d	.. d	..	14 705.4	16 977.7	17 339.1	18 638.5	18 506.6
Chile	1 499.9	563.7	.. d	1 996.2	..	.. d	.. d	2 405.5	2 341.0	2 330.3
Colombia	3.2	3.6	3.4	4.5	..	1 342.9	1 573.5	1 567.4	1 647.9	1 494.7
Costa Rica	-	-	1.1	1.1	..	190.8	145.1	172.9	149.4	390.2
Czech Republic	855.9	990.6	1 226.2	1 322.2	..	20 343.6	27 824.4	21 898.3	21 552.5	22 810.2
Denmark	8 241.8	9 631.8	9 426.4	10 308.9	..	6 134.7	7 669.7	7 670.0	8 113.9	8 642.8
Estonia	5.3	.. c	.. c	.. c	..	23.2	135.5	269.1	301.1	427.0
Finland	2 875.5	4 096.9	8 164.6	7 902.7	..	2 937.7	3 693.9	3 780.6	3 927.2	5 527.1
France	53 257.1	71 321.7	66 101.4	63 809.3	..	70 393.2	101 458.4	101 120.9	90 535.8	99 585.2
Germany	71 940.6	92 616.9	72 905.9	81 348.0	..	-	-	-	-	-
Greece	76.9	52.8	55.0	74.1	..	5 065.9	7 118.0	7 122.7	8 022.9	8 117.6
Hungary	99.1	122.3	65.3	106.7	..	13 877.9	18 726.3	17 342.6	17 720.7	17 733.5
Iceland	16.9	18.0	.. d	.. d	..	.. d	.. d	203.8	204.4	258.9
Ireland	5 347.3	5 403.0	40 730.5	30 720.1	..	10 209.8	12 131.2	24 057.7	24 194.6	32 069.0
Israel	5 062.7	6 658.7	5 699.6	5 813.3	..	1 197.4	1 432.0	1 332.7	1 580.5	1 141.2
Italy	33 599.7	35 820.3	33 314.6	33 404.9	..	32 880.8	39 486.7	39 305.0	41 422.2	50 033.1
Japan	37 322.7	42 010.1	45 934.3	45 447.1	..	8 340.9	10 455.7	10 436.2	10 441.5	12 660.4
Korea	5 755.2	6 801.4	6 185.0	5 987.4	..	8 271.3	10 551.7	9 687.4	10 114.6	12 348.8
Latvia	.. c	14.4	14.9	16.9	..	649.3	819.1	751.1	1 084.0	1 329.0
Lithuania	.. c	.. c	.. c	.. c	..	953.9	1 002.6	907.9	1 250.3	4 789.5
Luxembourg	53 514.3	59 018.9	66 671.6	66 726.6	..	136 757.7	179 161.7	185 012.6	206 612.0	228 617.0
Mexico	.. d	.. d	555.3	374.1	..	9 058.7	12 890.4	15 273.6	17 657.8	15 787.2
Netherlands	46 522.6	56 352.8	55 116.8	58 677.8	..	133 641.8	160 338.2	192 933.4	214 939.3	291 422.3
New Zealand	.. d	.. d	.. d	.. c	..	663.0	1 590.3	1 660.2	1 625.5	1 727.8
Norway	2 241.0	3 022.3	.. d	.. d	..	6 929.5	6 646.7	6 578.9	5 404.4	5 296.4
Poland	716.8	946.3	700.7	862.7	..	29 132.5	38 969.8	38 908.9	38 839.6	40 206.2
Portugal	416.4	405.4	388.1	364.0	..	3 359.3	4 188.1	4 248.9	4 472.0	5 400.7
Slovak Republic	1.1	1.2	2.3	2.2	..	3 158.0	4 368.0	3 967.3	4 384.4	5 273.0
Slovenia	76.9	67.2	57.2	51.7	..	1 135.2	1 492.0	1 481.6	1 384.0	1 687.3
Spain	24 900.4	29 051.3	25 503.8	23 536.3	..	48 540.1	66 265.3	67 418.1	68 345.3	90 895.8
Sweden	14 714.9	20 596.1	19 385.2	20 936.9	..	23 485.8	25 335.8	25 122.5	22 690.4	29 841.7
Switzerland	59 685.9	68 648.4	65 539.3	70 249.4	..	38 921.7	45 225.5	45 238.2	44 523.7	44 723.3
Turkey	1 612.7	2 002.9	1 718.6	1 767.0	..	9 351.7	10 593.7	9 717.2	8 993.5	8 947.1
United Kingdom	92 148.2	102 553.4	81 573.2	76 763.6	..	140 717.8	158 648.4	150 833.5	127 023.1	132 023.6
United States	171 626.4	217 855.6	208 369.6	200 069.6	..	254 632.7	289 576.6	314 121.8	348 485.7	336 486.7
EUROPE	**527 565.1**	**628 361.7**	**613 628.3**	**615 563.9**	..	**873 344.6**	**1 079 400.3**	**1 111 278.9**	**1 127 157.9**	**1 312 874.0**
Bulgaria	.. c	.. c	.. d	.. d	..	1 926.8	2 168.4	1 936.1	2 053.5	2 510.7
Croatia	.. c	-	.. c	.. c	..	2 160.9	2 547.4	2 652.9	2 724.1	3 115.7
Cyprus	1 300.7	1 760.6	.. d	.. d	..	215.0	-1 079.4	-2 201.7	-7 077.1	-8 851.4
Malta	721.0	369.4	338.9	352.7	..	9 407.6	21 597.5	20 562.2	22 220.8	22 211.3
Montenegro	-	-	1.1	1.1	..	.. d	.. d	93.9	95.5	62.6
Romania	6.3	.. c	.. c	.. c	..	7 802.3	9 087.3	9 200.8	9 382.2	10 006.1
Russian Federation	8 730.9	11 671.9	11 013.3	11 013.3	..	18 945.9	22 066.4	20 784.3	23 941.8	19 613.5
Ukraine	.. c	.. c	.. c	.. c	..	2 679.5	2 844.8	3 260.8	3 288.0	3 310.8
AFRICA	**1 514.7**	**1 800.2**	**2 267.0**	**2 262.4**	..	**10 170.8**	**11 134.6**	**11 268.6**	**11 137.9**	**14 137.9**
Northern Africa	198.2	104.3	144.3	146.0	..	2 624.6	2 422.6	2 578.4	2 799.4	4 814.1
Algeria	3.2	3.6	3.4	3.4	..	533.4	663.2	746.5	712.2	789.1
Egypt	56.9	.. d	.. d	.. d	..	1 573.7	973.9	588.5	687.5	1 499.6
Libya	134.9	.. c	.. c	.. c	..	-255.1	-26.4	-41.2	51.7	794.0
Morocco	.. c	.. c	.. c	.. c	..	536.5	581.7	1 004.1	1 033.5	1 341.3
Tunisia	.. d	1.2	2.3	2.2	..	237.2	230.3	279.4	314.5	390.2
Other African countries	1 316.5	1 694.7	2 122.7	2 116.4	..	7 546.1	8 713.1	8 690.2	8 338.6	9 323.8
Nigeria	.. c	.. c	.. c	.. c	..	374.2	315.4	624.0	274.1	530.1
South Africa	1 308.1	.. d	2 078.1	2 056.8	..	5 764.7	6 751.0	6 341.9	6 188.5	6 570.1
AMERICA	**185 547.6**	**233 380.9**	**227 672.3**	**220 878.5**	..	**310 884.4**	**352 379.5**	**379 465.3**	**420 076.4**	**397 782.5**
Northern America	179 464.5	227 303.9	219 621.0	212 961.1	..	269 338.0	306 554.3	331 461.0	367 124.2	354 993.3
Central America and Caribbean countries	2 931.4	4 084.9	5 075.6	4 924.7	..	16 394.0	19 362.0	20 287.4	23 795.8	18 145.8
Bahamas	.. c	6.0	.. d	.. d	..	106.5	136.7	305.7	297.7	262.6
Bermuda	1 368.2	1 911.7	2 711.2	2 484.8	..	1 794.0	1 838.6	2 130.8	3 142.0	349.7
Cayman Islands	-546.0	-582.9	-913.7	-625.7	..	1 418.8	887.5	-289.7	-105.6	-432.0
El Salvador	-	-	-	-	..	117.0	36.0	63.0	60.7	63.8
Guatemala	4.2	4.8	5.7	5.6	..	98.0	100.7	99.6	92.1	84.7
Honduras	-	-	-	-	..	84.3	116.3	122.5	149.4	110.4
Nicaragua	-	-	-	-	..	.. d	42.0	43.5	37.1	41.7
Panama	.. c	.. c	.. c	.. c	..	2 534.0	2 465.8	1 683.1	1 631.1	1 116.7
Virgin Islands, U.S.	1.1	1.2	2.3	2.2	..	.. c	.. c	.. c	-	-
South America	3 150.6	1 992.1	2 975.7	2 992.6	..	25 152.3	26 464.4	27 717.0	29 156.4	24 643.5
Argentina	2.1	2.4	3.4	3.4	..	2 286.3	2 597.7	2 334.6	2 931.9	2 361.0
Bolivia	-	-	-	-	..	84.3	84.0	.. d	.. d	.. d
Brazil	1 620.1	1 390.0	1 041.9	.. d	..	14 884.6	15 774.8	14 830.5	15 594.2	12 461.7
Ecuador	-	1.2	1.1	1.1	..	326.8	367.0	401.9	479.7	402.5
Paraguay	-	-	-	-	..	173.9	.. d	235.9	235.9	222.1
Peru	3.2	3.6	3.4	1.1	..	714.7	704.0	811.8	971.7	840.6
Uruguay	13.7	18.0	.. d	.. c	..	770.5	827.5	3 027.3	3 111.7	3 072.8
Venezuela	8.4	9.6	9.2	10.1	..	2 297.9	1 498.0	2 017.4	1 760.3	1 360.9

Table 2. Foreign direct investment positions by country *(cont.)*

At year end

Million US dollars

	Inward					Outward				
	2016	2017	2018	2019	2020	2016	2017	2018	2019	2020
ASIA	**75 274.6**	**94 770.9**	**91 985.3**	**90 808.8**	..	**160 563.9**	**191 111.8**	**190 767.1**	**202 428.7**	**211 434.5**
Near and Middle East	16 689.2	19 673.8	17 215.5	16 217.7	..	8 090.0	10 865.9	11 556.0	12 107.4	12 113.1
Gulf Arabian countries	11 551.6	12 940.8	11 443.8	10 344.9	..	5 991.4	8 801.9	9 300.4	9 638.3	10 073.6
Kuwait	322.5	430.6	.. d	450.5	..	220.3	263.9	321.7	244.9	289.6
Qatar	6 660.7	8 334.1	7 849.8	7 748.8	..	300.4	319.0	353.8	308.9	555.9
Saudi Arabia	378.4	428.2	297.7	250.5	..	1 613.8	1 498.0	2 003.7	2 266.9	1 375.6
United Arab Emirates	2 343.2	2 257.1	1 487.3	.. d	..	3 462.6	6 430.8	6 570.9	6 692.9	7 706.5
Other Near and Middle East	5 136.5	6 734.2	5 771.7	5 872.8	..	2 098.7	2 064.0	2 255.6	2 469.1	2 039.5
Jordan	5.3	.. c	.. c	.. c	..	158.1	134.3	129.4	110.1	61.4
Other Asian countries	58 585.4	75 097.1	74 769.9	74 591.1	..	152 473.9	180 247.1	179 210.0	190 321.3	199 321.4
China	7 611.5	16 408.0	12 348.3	12 510.7	..	77 044.4	92 397.5	92 792.5	95 024.7	98 478.3
Hong Kong, China	1 265.9	1 917.7	2 767.3	3 138.6	..	5 402.1	6 351.6	5 213.0	7 753.3	9 618.4
India	2 874.5	3 271.8	2 632.2	2 755.6	..	25 177.6	28 169.8	26 085.4	29 293.4	26 782.4
Indonesia	3.2	.. c	.. c	.. c	..	2 743.8	3 010.3	2 782.2	2 952.1	3 315.7
Iran, Islamic Republic of	1 710.8	2 140.8	2 303.6	2 126.5	..	406.9	410.2	502.6	362.8	360.8
Malaysia	770.5	911.5	883.9	749.3	..	4 412.4	5 441.4	5 816.4	5 667.3	5 879.2
Philippines	-	.. c	.. c	.. c	..	1 022.5	1 303.7	1 497.6	1 613.1	1 467.7
Singapore	341.5	472.5	638.9	428.0	..	12 935.6	14 070.5	15 877.0	18 148.7	19 046.5
Chinese Taipei	609.3	912.7	804.9	900.9	..	1 922.6	2 312.3	2 246.4	2 381.5	2 488.6
Thailand	186.6	56.4	75.6	279.7	..	2 996.7	3 763.5	4 015.3	4 282.2	4 302.4
Viet Nam	.. c	.. c	.. c	.. c	..	708.3	828.7	902.2	905.4	938.8
AUSTRALIA, OCEANIA AND POLAR REGIONS	**4 609.5**	**4 808.1**	**4 984.0**	**5 179.7**	..	**12 666.8**	**16 265.3**	**14 853.4**	**14 879.8**	**19 469.9**
WORLD unallocated and confidential	**-1.1**	**-**	**-1.1**	**-**	..	**-**	**1.2**	**-**	**-1.1**	**-245.4**
European Union (since 01/02/2020)	..	..	..	..	..	..	..	..	..	**1 090 398.8**
G20 countries excl. European Union	**502 493.9**	**620 960.7**	**562 275.0**	.. d	..	**708 777.3**	**837 523.4**	**848 910.0**	**864 686.6**	**875 008.0**
G20 OECD countries	**479 965.2**	**586 121.4**	.. d	.. d	..	**560 316.2**	**665 257.9**	**680 953.7**	**686 494.0**	**704 049.6**
G20 Non-OECD countries	**22 528.7**	**34 838.1**	.. d	**29 559.7**	..	**148 461.1**	**172 265.5**	**167 956.3**	**178 192.5**	**170 958.4**
MENA countries	**11 805.6**	**13 099.1**	**11 641.9**	**10 531.3**	..	**8 992.3**	**11 597.5**	.. d	**12 773.5**	**15 289.0**
ASEAN countries	**1 332.4**	**1 516.0**	**1 667.0**	.. d	..	**24 840.3**	**28 446.9**	**30 938.9**	**33 720.5**	**35 291.4**

- Nil; .. Not available; c Confidential data; d Secondary Confidentiality

Note: Inward FDI positions are allocated according to the ultimate investing country. Inward FDI positions by immediate counterpart country are available for the most recent year in the OECD FDI database according to BMD4. Detailed metadata at: *http://metalinks.oecd.org/idi/20220712/6d95*.

Source: *OECD International Direct Investment Statistics (database)*: *https://doi.org/10.1787/idi-data-en*

GERMANY

Table 3. Foreign direct investment income by country

Million US dollars

	Inward					Outward				
	2016	2017	2018	2019	2020	2016	2017	2018	2019	2020
WORLD	**37 941.7**	**45 450.1**	**43 217.5**	**36 853.1**	**30 739.8**	**98 391.1**	**94 299.0**	**128 762.7**	**121 627.4**	**93 822.7**
OECD COUNTRIES	**37 472.1**	**44 106.7**	**41 170.8**	**34 831.9**	**28 720.3**	**74 706.3**	**64 802.7**	**99 743.0**	**94 518.0**	**72 791.7**
Australia	70.8	698.7	668.7	547.1	405.3	512.3	93.1	685.8	687.4	573.2
Austria	1 941.1	4 439.1	4 138.3	3 436.8	2 715.6	4 100.8	5 681.0	4 637.1	4 472.1	3 579.1
Belgium	984.8	1 203.2	1 792.9	1 549.1	1 312.4	1 744.5	867.2	4 736.5	4 495.6	3 477.1
Canada	91.1	430.5	8.1	17.7	30.1	884.9	791.0	754.4	714.5	543.6
Chile	-19.7	-19.6	16.4	26.9	44.0	127.5	110.0	44.1	45.3	28.7
Colombia	0.0	-0.1	-1.0	-0.7	0.0	36.8	79.1	104.4	93.2	71.6
Costa Rica	-0.3	0.1	0.0	0.0	-0.1	-11.2	-28.0	-37.2	-33.9	-25.9
Czech Republic	1 458.7	70.0	-20.6	-32.1	-24.3	2 269.4	2 762.8	2 803.4	2 644.1	2 042.2
Denmark	738.9	594.9	601.7	442.8	336.6	544.4	1 167.9	779.1	756.3	607.3
Estonia	0.2	0.1	4.8	0.0	-0.1	18.4	26.7	38.4	32.1	25.2
Finland	119.1	-697.0	302.4	268.5	189.8	351.9	332.4	367.3	363.7	306.0
France	5 865.7	6 063.7	3 461.2	2 799.3	2 139.1	2 975.1	6 540.5	3 415.9	3 197.0	2 561.1
Germany	-	-	-	-	-	-	-	-	-	-
Greece	1.2	23.5	17.3	8.6	2.1	187.9	477.4	358.9	345.7	316.4
Hungary	40.0	35.8	18.0	28.0	28.6	951.7	1 946.8	1 867.6	1 756.3	1 334.1
Iceland	1.1	1.8	1.0	1.1	0.9	0.0	6.9	10.3	13.6	13.3
Ireland	869.7	758.1	747.1	565.4	451.0	687.6	486.7	1 093.7	1 026.1	835.9
Israel	67.9	84.0	207.8	167.0	122.9	78.6	91.4	41.9	44.5	35.5
Italy	2 054.0	4 014.1	3 075.7	2 450.8	1 853.5	2 097.3	2 531.0	2 109.3	2 149.1	1 812.7
Japan	233.6	1 149.5	1 344.5	1 138.6	885.0	1 172.2	1 693.6	1 299.8	1 235.2	954.0
Korea	206.7	188.5	175.2	141.2	104.9	1 097.0	1 491.7	1 500.5	1 411.5	1 074.9
Latvia	0.7	0.1	-0.8	-1.1	-0.8	38.3	50.9	53.5	52.0	39.9
Lithuania	2.5	3.6	-6.8	-30.9	-37.3	31.1	84.1	77.7	97.5	69.5
Luxembourg	855.5	4 840.3	3 182.9	3 376.3	3 762.7	7 997.8	4 252.0	8 097.0	7 896.5	6 028.8
Mexico	-9.1	-53.3	-10.1	-7.2	-4.9	916.5	1 004.7	919.5	902.9	713.9
Netherlands	8 349.7	10 174.6	7 497.8	6 165.1	5 091.7	8 497.8	7 026.2	18 443.0	17 139.0	12 336.2
New Zealand	0.8	2.2	2.2	1.7	1.2	113.6	138.4	59.1	57.8	42.5
Norway	30.7	363.4	-70.8	54.6	116.5	355.3	631.3	446.7	427.8	388.0
Poland	254.1	201.2	276.0	229.1	199.4	2 544.6	2 972.8	3 678.1	3 459.9	2 725.1
Portugal	-15.9	4.9	-28.3	-22.8	-7.1	414.6	501.3	488.4	497.9	398.3
Slovak Republic	8.8	11.0	11.3	15.1	12.8	600.9	631.4	635.7	595.6	458.4
Slovenia	30.1	25.5	22.8	32.1	47.9	152.1	53.7	121.0	115.5	89.6
Spain	2 165.7	-194.8	1 054.5	875.0	641.2	2 404.4	1 989.2	4 170.1	3 946.2	3 085.0
Sweden	-560.5	940.2	960.5	797.1	675.0	4 856.9	1 576.3	2 330.2	2 276.5	1 729.7
Switzerland	6 880.6	1 981.2	5 551.3	4 626.4	3 626.4	5 513.5	5 506.0	3 778.3	3 597.6	2 831.7
Turkey	49.8	99.1	67.7	61.8	45.0	863.4	1 343.4	1 065.3	1 089.8	833.5
United Kingdom	1 858.4	4 551.8	3 712.1	3 142.9	2 538.9	4 808.0	4 214.9	7 932.4	7 660.0	6 090.5
United States	2 847.6	2 120.6	2 387.7	1 960.0	1 414.3	14 827.0	5 812.3	20 903.0	19 315.5	14 739.3
EUROPE	**33 652.4**	**40 551.5**	**37 815.6**	**32 128.2**	**26 773.4**	**60 331.6**	**60 002.5**	**79 486.0**	**75 579.5**	**58 659.6**
Bulgaria	12.4	13.5	1.0	3.1	2.7	152.3	194.6	105.1	110.5	91.4
Croatia	11.1	5.9	12.2	11.7	6.2	235.8	198.1	254.5	189.7	152.7
Cyprus	90.4	352.3	406.8	354.6	271.4	143.7	21.0	-45.3	-83.5	-95.0
Malta	49.9	90.6	1.4	51.7	98.6	410.8	379.9	433.6	381.3	302.7
Montenegro	0.0	0.2	0.0	0.0	0.0	7.8	5.8	2.1	2.5	2.0
Romania	15.1	19.4	20.4	18.3	20.0	987.2	963.2	980.5	944.2	723.3
Russian Federation	-100.0	543.8	605.7	487.2	366.7	3 041.3	3 734.0	3 241.2	2 995.9	2 666.5
Ukraine	1.2	-3.6	-4.7	-4.5	-4.6	22.1	-28.5	462.7	439.9	340.3
AFRICA	**197.3**	**166.2**	**1.1**	**7.5**	**9.0**	**1 270.2**	**1 125.2**	**1 018.5**	**849.9**	**661.5**
Northern Africa	17.7	13.5	7.9	7.8	8.0	387.9	338.1	519.8	351.2	262.3
Algeria	0.2	0.1	0.2	0.2	0.1	210.2	94.7	98.9	107.0	59.7
Egypt	16.6	12.6	7.0	6.8	5.8	251.7	39.7	261.8	109.2	91.3
Libya	0.0	0.0	0.0	0.7	2.0	-140.4	179.4	28.1	2.3	2.7
Morocco	0.1	0.2	0.2	0.1	0.1	50.4	-7.7	93.9	95.6	79.4
Tunisia	0.8	0.7	0.5	0.0	0.0	16.0	32.0	37.0	37.1	29.1
Other African countries	179.6	152.7	-6.8	-0.3	0.9	882.3	787.1	498.7	498.7	399.2
Nigeria	-5.1	1.4	0.9	-0.9	-0.9	-13.8	17.1	29.0	27.5	21.0
South Africa	190.1	136.0	-16.9	-7.1	-4.7	826.1	718.6	419.0	403.6	316.3
AMERICA	**3 492.7**	**3 172.0**	**3 384.8**	**2 995.6**	**2 577.3**	**16 170.5**	**7 501.1**	**21 727.2**	**20 215.7**	**15 458.0**
Northern America	2 938.8	2 551.1	2 395.8	1 977.8	1 444.4	15 711.8	6 603.4	21 657.4	20 030.0	15 282.9
Central America and Caribbean countries	570.8	633.2	955.9	980.4	1 080.2	188.8	981.8	-434.9	-390.8	-279.0
Bahamas	3.3	22.1	91.5	74.2	55.0	1.3	14.4	5.3	5.0	4.0
Bermuda	272.9	372.6	447.2	429.9	332.2	257.3	184.7	240.1	215.0	155.9
Cayman Islands	194.5	183.7	111.3	46.8	3.5	-1 053.8	46.9	-681.3	-649.7	-496.9
El Salvador	-	0.0	-0.1	-0.1	0.0	-1.1	0.6	7.6	6.7	5.1
Guatemala	-	-	0.0	-	0.0	-3.0	7.3	11.4	9.2	7.0
Honduras	0.2	0.2	0.2	-	0.0	18.3	19.9	20.6	19.4	14.8
Nicaragua	-	-	-	-	-	3.0	1.6	2.7	7.0	10.6
Panama	-4.5	-1.9	-0.5	-0.9	-0.7	53.0	19.8	-636.6	-598.8	-458.7
Virgin Islands, U.S.	-	0.0	-	-	-	-	-	-	-	-
South America	-16.8	-12.3	33.1	37.4	52.7	269.8	-84.0	504.7	576.6	454.1
Argentina	-4.4	-3.3	-2.4	0.6	1.1	242.3	184.6	27.4	36.7	27.0
Bolivia	0.0	0.0	0.0	-0.1	-0.1	4.5	9.1	10.4	9.2	7.1
Brazil	8.9	10.2	18.3	10.0	6.5	-825.8	-697.5	72.5	95.3	147.6
Ecuador	0.1	0.0	0.1	0.0	0.8	17.7	24.3	25.9	26.5	17.8
Paraguay	-0.6	-0.3	-0.2	-0.3	-0.3	-2.0	2.2	-0.2	0.1	0.4
Peru	0.6	0.6	0.6	0.0	0.1	90.4	62.5	26.9	99.0	20.2
Uruguay	-2.3	-0.4	1.1	0.9	0.7	26.1	20.1	49.0	47.0	38.9
Venezuela	0.6	0.6	0.4	-	-	560.0	123.9	144.4	124.2	94.9

Table 3. Foreign direct investment income by country *(cont.)*

Million US dollars

	Inward					Outward				
	2016	2017	2018	2019	2020	2016	2017	2018	2019	2020
ASIA	**543.0**	**1 089.1**	**1 343.2**	**1 173.0**	**973.6**	**20 000.6**	**25 445.4**	**25 798.4**	**24 250.9**	**18 440.9**
Near and Middle East	192.7	250.8	264.8	219.3	185.0	1 007.5	615.7	517.1	457.4	354.7
Gulf Arabian countries	121.2	160.3	56.9	56.0	64.7	840.8	455.8	405.3	330.9	266.5
Kuwait	16.0	41.4	9.5	6.7	4.8	51.5	85.9	-38.7	-36.8	-18.6
Qatar	118.7	85.4	74.9	73.7	72.7	29.1	39.0	30.4	24.3	19.5
Saudi Arabia	-19.2	29.4	-31.4	-21.2	-14.4	292.8	80.1	74.2	25.3	16.4
United Arab Emirates	8.0	2.2	3.9	-0.6	3.9	381.3	212.4	310.1	288.8	221.6
Other Near and Middle East	71.5	90.5	207.8	163.3	120.3	166.8	160.0	111.8	126.5	88.2
Jordan	0.7	0.3	1.1	-	-	32.4	11.9	5.2	9.4	2.3
Other Asian countries	350.3	838.3	1 078.4	953.7	788.6	18 993.1	24 829.6	25 281.4	23 793.6	18 086.2
China	11.2	5.2	-84.8	-51.1	-39.6	11 920.5	14 554.7	17 417.7	16 426.2	12 468.3
Hong Kong, China	-143.6	-451.4	49.2	60.9	77.4	1 074.6	2 140.9	1 305.2	1 266.7	987.3
India	-26.5	-15.4	-42.7	-34.9	-23.7	915.4	1 356.6	1 270.1	1 129.8	897.4
Indonesia	0.8	26.2	-0.1	-0.2	-0.1	366.5	363.7	320.8	301.4	230.8
Iran, Islamic Republic of	64.8	27.7	-188.5	-153.8	-111.9	73.5	123.3	94.5	60.9	46.6
Malaysia	45.9	19.5	37.6	29.1	20.8	583.7	566.4	576.8	572.4	412.7
Philippines	0.9	1.0	0.9	0.3	0.3	8.8	181.6	231.6	216.5	167.1
Singapore	-60.8	-155.5	-233.4	-184.4	-130.3	708.5	1 243.1	783.0	743.1	567.0
Chinese Taipei	8.8	17.7	12.0	9.6	7.3	183.7	206.7	-364.8	-345.1	-256.9
Thailand	10.6	23.8	7.7	0.6	0.1	533.5	585.1	548.2	516.3	399.4
Viet Nam	-2.5	0.5	0.2	-0.2	-0.1	179.5	96.1	63.7	104.4	45.5
AUSTRALIA, OCEANIA AND POLAR REGIONS	**56.2**	**471.3**	**672.8**	**548.8**	**406.5**	**627.1**	**234.0**	**742.1**	**740.4**	**612.3**
WORLD unallocated and confidential	**0.1**	**0.1**	**0.0**	**0.1**	**-**	**-8.9**	**-9.1**	**-9.6**	**-9.1**	**-9.7**
European Union (since 01/02/2020)	..	..	..	..	..	..	..	..	..	..
G20 countries excl. European Union	**13 329.5**	**19 995.3**	**15 336.6**	**12 635.7**	**9 702.8**	**46 932.9**	**45 811.2**	**63 428.8**	**59 777.3**	**46 666.8**
G20 OECD countries	**13 268.8**	**19 263.2**	**14 891.0**	**12 252.3**	**9 411.2**	**30 153.8**	**25 516.3**	**40 585.9**	**38 363.0**	**29 896.6**
G20 Non-OECD countries	**60.8**	**732.1**	**445.6**	**383.4**	**291.6**	**16 779.1**	**20 294.9**	**22 842.9**	**21 414.3**	**16 770.2**
MENA countries	**140.9**	**178.5**	**66.3**	**62.9**	**72.0**	**1 270.4**	**818.5**	**944.4**	**708.7**	**539.5**
ASEAN countries	**-4.2**	**-84.0**	**-186.6**	**-154.3**	**-109.0**	**2 391.3**	**3 147.9**	**2 533.8**	**2 463.0**	**1 829.1**

- Nil; .. Not available

Note: Detailed metadata at: *http://metalinks.oecd.org/idi/20220712/6d95.*

Source: *OECD International Direct Investment Statistics (database)*: *https://doi.org/10.1787/idi-data-en*

GERMANY

Table 4. Foreign direct investment flows by industrial sector

Million US dollars

	Inward					Outward				
	2016	2017	2018	2019	2020	2016	2017	2018	2019	2020
All FDI activities	**15 617.9**	**48 537.8**	**62 034.3**	**54 061.5**	**35 570.0**	**63 599.0**	**86 333.2**	**86 190.2**	**139 274.4**	**34 870.5**
Agriculture, forestry and fishing	**3.9**	**31.4**	**38.1**	**-42.5**	..	**-25.1**	**110.2**	**-65.2**	**-3.7**	..
Mining and quarrying	**124.4**	**1.3**	**-33.5**	**-6.4**	..	**1 085.8**	**2 086.6**	**318.6**	**-1 568.3**	..
Extraction activities	10.4	-5.0	-35.7	22.8	..	93.9	1 461.9	308.3	-1 672.7	..
Manufacturing	**-946.5**	**7 898.7**	**4 182.8**	**1 240.7**	..	**2 254.5**	**4 504.3**	**-28 921.6**	**17 490.3**	..
of which:										
Food products, beverages and tobacco	1 002.7	-390.8	207.6	-785.6	..	-299.9	-153.5	2 251.3	367.5	..
Textiles, wood and paper products; printing	-65.0	-101.3	-18.6	713.7	..	-12.7	350.3	146.0	-0.9	..
Chemical, rubber, plastic, non-metallic mineral products	-2 783.6	4 123.4	4 426.2	-941.6	..	-402.1	767.2	4 684.2	-2 675.6	..
Metal and machinery products, except electrical equipment	-1 023.1	1 936.7	-527.8	-1 970.9	..	2 818.5	-3 497.2	2 761.6	-1 249.9	..
Motor vehicles, trailers, semi-trailers, other transport equipment	592.9	887.1	1 842.3	-1 087.4	..	3 352.5	3 617.8	-22 277.3	25 420.6	..
Other manufacturing	1 329.5	1 443.6	-1 746.9	5 312.5	..	-3 201.9	3 419.8	-16 487.5	-4 371.5	..
Electricity, gas, steam and air conditioning supply	**-6 861.0**	**12.9**	**2 676.7**	**-333.2**	..	**-7 335.9**	**372.9**	**-5 427.2**	**331.3**	..
Water supply; sewerage, waste management and remediation activities	**35.0**	**15.0**	**-155.3**	**279.9**	..	**111.1**	**29.3**	**1 093.5**	**-473.7**	..
Construction	**-239.4**	**278.8**	**274.4**	**-66.4**	..	**39.3**	**59.7**	**281.4**	**97.8**	..
Services	**7 303.8**	**40 733.7**	**40 833.2**	**62 504.7**	..	**25 124.1**	**53 575.8**	**68 371.1**	**74 424.9**	..
Wholesale and retail trade; repair of motor vehicles and motorcycles	1 253.2	3 211.3	4 300.6	1 383.9	..	3 452.1	7 365.7	-8 244.1	1 076.0	..
Transportation and storage	564.1	4 078.2	-1 573.8	-1 121.1	..	-3 048.7	389.1	1 008.3	2 232.2	..
Accommodation and food service activities	.. d	540.3	-22.3	119.3	..	70.3	50.9	116.6	-33.5	..
Information and communication	-2 332.6	-2 514.9	-959.9	6 127.4	..	-5 190.8	-3 916.0	-2 471.6	442.1	..
Financial and insurance activities	-1 432.5	-8 200.7	-6 588.8	13 266.9	..	18 767.8	15 121.0	24 117.9	51 213.3	..
Activities of holding companies	-4 015.0	-3 132.1	-9 542.3	-466.5	..	12 759.5	2 256.7	3 414.2	37 250.6	..
Real estate activities	64.3	6 382.7	-417.6	1 840.5	..	-224.6	444.3	10.6	2 046.6	..
Professional, scientific and technical activities	8 204.3	37 282.1	44 650.9	38 710.3	..	9 455.2	35 703.5	53 246.5	16 809.8	..
Administrative and support service activities	860.2	-274.3	995.2	2 390.6	..	1 752.0	-1 298.0	812.0	181.9	..
Public administration; activities of households and of extraterritorial organisations	.. c	7.0	6.6	2.4	..	.. d	-268.8	-276.9	294.2	..
Education	19.0	5.4	0.2	-1.7	..	-9.2	0.4	12.4	3.2	..
Human health and social work activities	18.8	88.2	475.6	-112.1	..	.. c	1.2	1.3	-0.9	..
Arts, entertainment and recreation	33.3	123.0	4.0	-117.1	..	79.8	-10.4	29.7	82.9	..
Other services	30.6	5.5	-37.6	15.5	..	-0.6	-7.0	8.5	77.0	..
Not allocated and confidential	**15 016.0**	**-1 529.4**	**12 851.5**	**-12 779.4**	**35 570.0**	**41 810.2**	**23 628.1**	**48 001.3**	**45 247.9**	**34 870.5**
Private real estate activities	**1 181.7**	**1 095.3**	**1 366.4**	**3 264.1**	..	**535.0**	**1 966.2**	**2 538.3**	**3 728.0**	..

.. Not available; c Confidential data; d Secondary Confidentiality

Note: Detailed metadata at: *http://metalinks.oecd.org/idi/20220712/6d95*.

Source: *OECD International Direct Investment Statistics (database)*: *https://doi.org/10.1787/idi-data-en*

GERMANY

Table 5. Foreign direct investment positions by industrial sector

At year end

Million US dollars

	Inward					Outward				
	2016	2017	2018	2019	2020	2016	2017	2018	2019	2020
All FDI activities	**794 510.4**	**963 121.9**	**940 535.8**	**934 693.3**	**1 129 941.1**	**1 367 630.4**	**1 650 292.6**	**1 707 633.4**	**1 775 679.6**	**1 955 453.4**
Agriculture, forestry and fishing	**335.2**	**317.8**	**289.7**	**266.2**	..	**2 718.5**	**3 446.9**	**3 333.0**	**3 799.1**	..
Mining and quarrying	**2 109.2**	**756.8**	**664.1**	**585.3**	..	**7 578.8**	**6 292.9**	**6 727.7**	**6 441.2**	..
Extraction activities	1 834.1	467.7	477.4	443.7	..	7 142.4	5 674.0	6 391.1	6 038.0	..
Manufacturing	**40 651.4**	**61 803.8**	**59 264.9**	**50 296.6**	..	**207 732.7**	**252 445.4**	**261 750.6**	**276 878.2**	..
of which:										
Food products, beverages and tobacco	3 687.2	5 164.3	6 915.5	4 602.3	..	6 068.3	6 851.8	7 909.3	8 235.2	..
Textiles, wood and paper products; printing	4 339.6	5 170.3	4 696.6	4 474.3	..	5 025.8	6 114.2	6 167.9	6 295.2	..
Chemical, rubber, plastic, non-metallic mineral products	16 038.8	23 623.2	18 758.9	21 240.2	..	47 308.9	58 905.0	63 966.1	78 811.5	..
Metal and machinery products, except electrical equipment	14 714.9	14 385.9	15 144.3	13 501.5	..	55 578.2	62 529.4	66 479.3	70 733.5	..
Motor vehicles, trailers, semi-trailers, other transport equipment	-2 861.8	5 397.0	7 711.2	-158.4	..	52 905.0	71 795.4	73 079.9	66 494.0	..
Other manufacturing	4 732.8	8 063.1	6 039.6	6 636.7	..	40 846.4	46 250.9	44 148.2	46 309.8	..
Electricity, gas, steam and air conditioning supply	**7 424.9**	**7 964.7**	**7 080.4**	**8 069.0**	..	**13 382.5**	**16 228.1**	**15 361.8**	**14 827.0**	..
Water supply; sewerage, waste management and remediation activities	**416.4**	**448.5**	**255.3**	**268.5**	..	**1 545.3**	**1 842.2**	**1 989.9**	**1 956.9**	..
Construction	**792.7**	**2 481.4**	**2 340.3**	**3 031.9**	..	**2 079.7**	**2 293.1**	**2 395.2**	**2 051.2**	..
Services	**717 454.4**	**858 397.7**	**838 777.2**	**836 908.6**	..	**957 855.0**	**1 162 030.5**	**1 209 368.0**	**1 253 408.2**	..
Wholesale and retail trade; repair of motor vehicles and motorcycles	43 973.9	57 640.9	48 328.4	50 678.5	..	113 203.3	140 154.7	131 147.2	152 183.8	..
Transportation and storage	8 046.8	9 555.0	9 009.6	11 677.2	..	7 031.7	11 362.4	12 082.7	12 482.6	..
Accommodation and food service activities	1 534.7	2 091.6	2 283.0	2 335.4	..	1 760.3	2 197.2	2 714.7	2 145.6	..
Information and communication	36 232.7	35 265.1	26 384.2	26 480.6	..	21 608.5	28 622.0	30 160.3	30 786.3	..
Financial and insurance activities	284 748.6	333 929.0	324 616.4	353 336.3	..	507 963.5	604 655.8	619 263.8	626 536.7	..
Activities of holding companies	221 776.1	257 343.5	238 834.4	257 764.5	..	454 265.8	559 715.8	617 844.1	633 712.6	..
Real estate activities	23 540.6	25 747.2	26 809.0	26 346.9	..	27 663.1	34 245.6	40 224.4	40 152.8	..
Professional, scientific and technical activities	317 975.1	391 577.1	396 597.2	359 326.0	..	257 246.8	316 247.3	344 276.4	357 100.7	..
Administrative and support service activities	567.1	1 638.3	3 519.6	5 598.7	..	12 629.9	14 358.4	17 418.1	20 123.6	..
Public administration; activities of households and of extraterritorial organisations	.. c	.. c	.. c	.. c	..	.. c	.. c	.. d	.. d	..
Education	20.0	32.4	36.6	29.2	..	32.7	55.2	69.8	66.3	..
Human health and social work activities	265.6	345.4	259.9	226.9	..	8 298.7	9 624.6	11 432.3	11 228.9	..
Arts, entertainment and recreation	348.9	418.6	334.3	343.7	..	150.7	177.5	.. d	.. d	..
Other services	.. d	.. d	.. d	.. d	..	.. d	.. d	306.8	357.2	..
Not allocated and confidential	**-**	**-2.4**	**-1.1**	**-**	**1 129 941.1**	**-**	**-**	**-1.1**	**-**	**1 955 453.4**
Private real estate activities	**25 326.2**	**30 953.5**	**31 865.1**	**35 267.4**	..	**174 738.1**	**205 713.6**	**206 708.3**	**216 317.7**	..

- Nil; .. Not available; c Confidential data; d Secondary Confidentiality

Note: Detailed metadata at: *http://metalinks.oecd.org/idi/20220712/6d95*.

Source: *OECD International Direct Investment Statistics (database)*: *https://doi.org/10.1787/idi-data-en*

Table 6. Foreign direct investment income by industrial sector

Million US dollars

	Inward					Outward				
	2016	2017	2018	2019	2020	2016	2017	2018	2019	2020
All FDI activities	**37 941.7**	**45 450.1**	**43 217.5**	**36 853.1**	**30 739.8**	**98 391.1**	**94 299.0**	**128 762.7**	**121 627.4**	**93 822.7**
Agriculture, forestry and fishing	**4.0**	**4.1**	**7.4**	**5.7**	..	**6.3**	**17.3**	**3.8**	**1.7**	..
Mining and quarrying	**4.8**	**-2.2**	**-0.6**	**13.8**	..	**624.3**	**197.4**	**181.1**	**241.6**	..
Extraction activities	0.8	-4.7	-1.3	5.1	..	606.9	177.5	155.4	229.9	..
Manufacturing	**2 645.4**	**3 890.9**	**4 651.4**	**3 716.6**	..	**16 594.8**	**22 150.1**	**28 026.8**	**25 432.5**	..
of which:										
Food products, beverages and tobacco	302.5	603.0	622.5	545.8	..	327.9	508.0	659.3	757.3	..
Textiles, wood and paper products; printing	195.6	145.6	329.7	298.9	..	210.1	262.6	233.6	252.2	..
Chemical, rubber, plastic, non-metallic mineral products	507.4	1 496.3	1 680.3	816.6	..	2 243.5	3 187.2	3 493.1	3 527.3	..
Metal and machinery products, except electrical equipment	1 412.7	1 272.5	1 526.9	1 512.4	..	3 546.9	3 574.1	3 619.4	3 044.7	..
Motor vehicles, trailers, semi-trailers, other transport equipment	-16.3	9.1	119.8	107.9	..	7 869.3	11 993.9	17 703.6	12 382.4	..
Other manufacturing	243.6	364.5	372.2	435.0	..	2 397.1	2 624.2	2 317.8	5 468.6	..
Electricity, gas, steam and air conditioning supply	**354.9**	**1 026.9**	**1 213.5**	**211.9**	..	**341.6**	**-28.2**	**448.1**	**613.8**	..
Water supply; sewerage, waste management and remediation activities	**12.0**	**12.9**	**14.7**	**10.5**	..	**15.7**	**10.5**	**14.0**	**11.2**	..
Construction	**864.2**	**676.6**	**794.8**	**851.7**	..	**299.5**	**236.7**	**223.7**	**227.0**	..
Services	**26 775.4**	**24 804.5**	**23 303.5**	**22 170.9**	..	**35 207.9**	**43 954.8**	**48 058.8**	**45 638.7**	..
Wholesale and retail trade; repair of motor vehicles and motorcycles	2 142.9	2 038.5	2 126.9	2 324.0	..	1 541.1	1 125.0	1 821.7	1 575.6	..
Transportation and storage	206.9	532.3	363.4	178.2	..	510.7	1 514.2	819.4	1 471.4	..
Accommodation and food service activities	98.1	23.4	29.3	99.1	..	3.3	2.8	2.6	4.5	..
Information and communication	561.2	1 000.5	879.7	1 558.2	..	44.2	228.7	64.8	302.9	..
Financial and insurance activities	5 736.7	8 694.0	8 807.6	6 615.3	..	19 997.9	28 817.0	29 957.5	26 844.4	..
Activities of holding companies	3 452.3	7 674.2	6 537.8	7 238.0	..	13 470.7	20 733.2	21 156.8	19 576.6	..
Real estate activities	450.1	828.6	537.6	2 111.8	..	253.2	118.1	383.8	281.5	..
Professional, scientific and technical activities	17 238.7	11 458.0	10 288.7	9 069.8	..	12 575.5	11 877.4	14 535.3	14 786.6	..
Administrative and support service activities	205.1	100.4	117.9	87.5	..	127.8	54.5	104.3	102.5	..
Public administration; activities of households and of extraterritorial organisations	88.9	94.0	114.8	99.1	..	152.9	192.7	334.5	216.7	..
Education	.. c	0.1	0.2	0.4	..	-16.6	-12.1	-1.4	-1.1	..
Human health and social work activities	.. d	19.7	22.1	10.8	..	0.0	0.8	0.6	1.0	..
Arts, entertainment and recreation	7.5	14.3	12.8	15.2	..	16.1	25.7	30.6	44.5	..
Other services	39.0	0.8	2.4	1.4	..	1.9	10.0	5.2	8.3	..
Not allocated and confidential	**5 497.6**	**13 323.6**	**11 100.8**	**7 927.5**	**30 739.8**	**41 322.3**	**23 037.4**	**47 406.4**	**44 657.4**	**93 822.7**
Private real estate activities	**1 783.4**	**1 712.7**	**2 132.0**	**1 944.6**	..	**3 978.6**	**4 723.1**	**4 400.0**	**4 803.5**	..

.. Not available; c Confidential data; d Secondary Confidentiality

Note: Detailed metadata at: *http://metalinks.oecd.org/idi/20220712/6d95*.

Source: *OECD International Direct Investment Statistics (database): https://doi.org/10.1787/idi-data-en*

GREECE

Table 1. Foreign direct investment flows by country

Million US dollars

	Inward					Outward				
	2016	2017	2018	2019	2020	2016	2017	2018	2019	2020
WORLD	**2 762.4**	**3 477.4**	**3 970.8**	**5 019.2**	**3 205.2**	**-1 665.4**	**168.0**	**476.6**	**641.6**	**547.4**
OECD COUNTRIES	**1 925.6**	**2 864.7**	**2 371.6**	**3 409.7**	**1 861.1**	**-2 404.6**	**302.6**	**86.2**	**-73.6**	**-12.1**
Australia	5.4	7.9	16.3	18.6	31.9	-0.2	-0.3	-2.0	-0.7	2.1
Austria	7.3	-1.7	2.5	56.1	26.1	-7.2	-7.2	-2.3	-2.3	-3.8
Belgium	-18.1	37.0	163.0	38.4	-63.4	-1.0	-0.6	-0.3	2.9	43.7
Canada	205.6	183.8	176.7	246.1	11.5	0.0	-0.1	0.1	0.0	0.2
Chile	-	-	-	0.1	-	-	-	-	-	-
Colombia	-	-	-	-	-	0.1	0.1	0.1	-	-2.0
Costa Rica	-	-	-	-	0.0	-	-	-	-	-
Czech Republic	6.5	5.2	18.6	4.4	22.2	-6.9	-7.7	-7.1	1.0	2.1
Denmark	-3.8	-3.1	-18.1	1.6	12.3	-	-1.0	-1.9	-1.6	0.0
Estonia	0.6	0.6	0.6	2.1	2.8	-	-	-	-	-
Finland	-2.1	4.8	-15.1	7.2	-15.4	-	-0.6	-0.7	-0.6	-0.2
France	144.2	-46.2	-28.9	154.0	86.5	-3.0	8.2	-10.9	6.4	4.2
Germany	242.3	715.4	541.6	509.0	119.0	12.4	12.5	5.1	2.2	2.9
Greece	-	-	-	-	-	-	-	-	-	-
Hungary	0.6	0.3	8.8	6.0	0.9	0.6	0.6	0.2	0.4	-
Iceland	0.0	-0.3	-1.0	-0.8	-	-	-	-	-	-
Ireland	-15.4	26.2	-66.4	-62.0	-44.6	11.0	-	-	-	2.3
Israel	3.2	32.1	28.3	79.1	36.6	0.7	-	0.9	0.6	-0.6
Italy	84.0	133.4	341.5	72.8	308.5	-2.7	13.1	-44.8	-5.2	-11.9
Japan	-0.6	-4.7	-3.8	-1.7	0.2	-0.3	-0.3	-0.4	0.5	-
Korea	1.3	-0.6	-0.2	1.3	0.5	-	-	-	0.0	1.1
Latvia	1.6	1.1	2.3	1.2	1.0	-	-	-	-	-
Lithuania	0.0	0.1	0.8	1.1	0.4	-	-	-	-	-
Luxembourg	810.7	111.8	406.7	491.5	-243.9	55.1	95.5	55.6	48.1	22.2
Mexico	0.0	0.5	1.9	0.1	0.1	-	0.0	-	-	-
Netherlands	99.5	489.9	-91.7	1 107.6	392.8	-38.3	29.4	-61.7	-69.0	16.7
New Zealand	0.0	0.5	1.5	1.1	0.9	-	-	-	-	-
Norway	-0.3	1.8	4.9	37.7	6.3	0.0	-0.4	-0.8	-0.5	-
Poland	1.7	5.1	2.9	9.7	8.1	5.9	4.8	-7.8	45.1	2.3
Portugal	0.0	6.5	-2.3	2.0	6.4	0.6	0.5	-0.4	1.3	1.6
Slovak Republic	0.4	0.7	1.9	4.0	0.9	-0.3	-0.3	-0.3	-0.3	-
Slovenia	0.7	0.6	-1.4	-0.1	1.2	1.3	2.6	3.0	2.4	5.2
Spain	109.3	47.0	30.7	259.3	57.6	11.6	0.3	0.2	6.4	4.4
Sweden	4.5	1.6	18.9	26.7	10.5	0.7	-5.4	-3.6	-3.1	1.8
Switzerland	152.3	849.3	552.8	220.0	534.0	-0.8	22.6	5.3	-6.4	1.5
Turkey	5.8	44.7	35.6	15.6	15.4	-2 467.4	58.0	57.0	27.8	12.9
United Kingdom	14.6	175.2	159.3	10.3	458.2	-118.1	8.5	31.0	-58.0	-119.5
United States	63.5	38.4	82.3	89.6	75.4	141.8	70.3	72.6	-70.9	1.8
EUROPE	**1 990.1**	**3 082.9**	**3 070.2**	**3 702.2**	**2 649.3**	**-2 084.1**	**-3.2**	**365.6**	**626.2**	**520.5**
Bulgaria	35.7	24.0	33.3	41.6	57.3	259.6	-545.7	42.7	67.6	52.8
Croatia	0.2	0.1	-0.1	-2.1	-	2.6	0.5	0.5	0.4	-0.7
Cyprus	285.2	413.8	810.2	585.6	809.7	51.6	391.3	811.6	489.7	538.9
Malta	4.6	11.1	24.8	5.5	7.7	2.8	-0.1	-0.2	-0.1	1.5
Montenegro	-	-	6.0	2.9	8.3	0.3	0.3	0.3	0.3	-0.2
Romania	2.2	-0.5	6.7	12.4	14.5	52.6	-0.8	-354.3	41.7	-74.3
Russian Federation	14.8	18.9	11.8	28.0	9.4	38.6	39.1	42.7	0.0	1.2
Ukraine	0.3	0.0	0.2	-0.2	-	-3.7	-2.8	-2.2	-3.6	-6.6
AFRICA	**-11.4**	**-4.9**	**-13.2**	**-1.0**	**18.2**	**12.9**	**0.9**	**-12.2**	**-0.6**	**-16.8**
Northern Africa	2.6	7.3	8.7	9.9	12.3	0.1	0.5	0.0	-0.1	-17.1
Algeria	-	-	-	-	1.0	-	0.1	-	0.0	-
Egypt	2.0	7.3	8.7	9.8	11.3	0.3	0.4	0.2	0.0	-6.5
Libya	-	-	-	-	-	-0.2	0.0	-0.3	-0.1	-3.5
Morocco	0.3	-	-	0.1	-	-	-	-	-	-7.1
Tunisia	0.3	-	-	0.0	-	0.0	-	-	-	-
Other African countries	-14.0	-12.2	-22.0	-10.9	5.9	12.8	0.5	-12.1	-0.6	0.4
Nigeria	-	-	0.9	0.4	0.1	-	-	-	-	-
South Africa	0.0	0.5	0.8	1.1	2.2	-	0.2	-11.9	-	0.1
AMERICA	**364.1**	**229.7**	**141.7**	**382.8**	**101.8**	**107.3**	**21.7**	**-92.5**	**-100.9**	**11.8**
Northern America	269.1	222.3	259.0	335.7	86.9	141.8	70.2	72.7	-70.9	2.0
Central America and Caribbean countries	94.9	7.3	-118.9	46.6	13.9	-34.8	-48.4	-164.7	-29.8	9.7
Bahamas	1.6	3.8	2.5	0.1	5.7	-	-	-	-	-
Bermuda	106.3	17.6	7.0	0.3	3.0	-	-13.9	-	-	9.5
Cayman Islands	-0.4	0.1	-0.3	41.7	2.3	-2.4	-30.5	-31.8	-30.1	-0.1
El Salvador	-	-	-	-	-	-	-	-	-	-
Guatemala	-	-	0.0	-	1.0	-	-	-0.1	-0.1	0.0
Honduras	-	-	-	-	-	-	-	-	-	-
Nicaragua	-	-	-	-	-	-	-	-	-	-
Panama	0.5	-0.8	0.1	-1.8	0.2	-0.1	-	-	-	-
Virgin Islands, U.S.	-	-	-	-	-	-	-	-	-	-
South America	0.1	0.2	1.7	0.5	1.0	0.3	0.0	-0.5	-0.2	0.1
Argentina	-	-	0.5	-	-	-	-	-	-	-
Bolivia	-	-	-	-	-	-	-	-	-	-
Brazil	-	0.2	0.4	0.4	-	0.3	-0.1	-0.6	-0.2	0.5
Ecuador	-	-	-	-	-	-	-	-	-	-
Paraguay	-	-	-	-	-	-	-	-	-	-
Peru	-	-	0.4	-	0.6	-	-	-	-	0.5
Uruguay	0.1	-	0.3	-	0.4	-	-	-	-	-
Venezuela	-	-	-	-	-	-	-	-	-	-

Table 1. Foreign direct investment flows by country *(cont.)*

Million US dollars

	Inward					Outward				
	2016	2017	2018	2019	2020	2016	2017	2018	2019	2020
ASIA	**420.0**	**169.7**	**755.3**	**918.4**	**402.2**	**298.8**	**149.0**	**217.7**	**117.6**	**27.5**
Near and Middle East	33.1	85.8	96.1	144.8	121.4	13.2	45.1	42.7	13.3	26.7
Gulf Arabian countries	18.4	25.7	31.5	32.3	65.8	17.2	45.6	44.4	13.2	27.3
Kuwait	1.0	4.9	1.4	2.5	1.8	-	-	-	-	-
Qatar	9.2	2.5	1.9	-3.1	2.9	16.7	44.9	36.6	8.9	-0.1
Saudi Arabia	2.4	1.1	3.9	2.4	2.8	-0.1	-	-	0.0	1.7
United Arab Emirates	2.9	13.6	20.7	29.0	55.5	0.6	0.9	7.8	4.2	-7.8
Other Near and Middle East	14.7	60.1	64.6	112.5	55.6	-4.0	-0.6	-1.7	0.1	-0.6
Jordan	2.9	4.6	4.5	2.8	1.4	-	-	-2.3	-	0.0
Other Asian countries	386.9	84.0	659.2	773.6	280.7	285.5	104.0	175.0	104.4	0.8
China	32.4	53.7	254.2	205.7	33.8	0.4	0.7	10.9	0.2	-0.1
Hong Kong, China	350.6	29.2	370.5	484.9	158.5	285.5	103.6	164.4	100.9	-0.4
India	0.3	0.0	1.3	3.2	32.1	0.0	0.0	0.0	0.5	0.1
Indonesia	0.0	-	-	-	0.1	-	-	-	-	-
Iran, Islamic Republic of	0.0	1.5	2.8	0.7	0.4	-	-	-	-	-
Malaysia	0.2	0.2	0.3	0.5	-	-	-	-	-	-
Philippines	-	-	-	-	0.2	-	-	-	-	-
Singapore	1.3	2.9	28.1	74.3	51.1	-	-	-	-	-0.1
Chinese Taipei	0.1	-	3.0	1.6	0.9	-	-	-	-	0.3
Thailand	0.0	0.2	-	-0.3	0.3	-	-	-	-	-
Viet Nam	-	-	0.3	0.7	0.9	-	-	-	-	0.0
AUSTRALIA, OCEANIA AND POLAR REGIONS	**-0.9**	**-0.6**	**13.8**	**14.6**	**32.8**	**-0.2**	**-0.5**	**-2.0**	**-0.7**	**4.3**
WORLD unallocated and confidential	**0.5**	**0.5**	**3.0**	**2.2**	**1.0**	**0.0**	**0.0**	**0.0**	**-0.1**	**0.0**
European Union (since 01/02/2020)	..	..	..	..	**1 579.1**	..	..	..	..	**611.7**
G20 countries excl. European Union	**816.1**	**1 322.3**	**1 595.3**	**1 356.4**	**1 187.6**	**-2 398.3**	**209.6**	**149.0**	**-97.4**	**-102.9**
G20 OECD countries	**766.2**	**1 247.8**	**1 322.4**	**1 115.7**	**1 107.2**	**-2 437.4**	**169.8**	**107.9**	**-97.9**	**-106.3**
G20 Non-OECD countries	**49.8**	**74.4**	**272.9**	**240.7**	**80.4**	**39.1**	**39.9**	**41.1**	**0.5**	**3.4**
MENA countries	**31.9**	**60.4**	**73.2**	**72.4**	**90.9**	**13.0**	**45.8**	**42.0**	**12.8**	**10.2**
ASEAN countries	**1.5**	**3.4**	**28.8**	**74.6**	**52.5**	**-**	**-**	**-**	**2.3**	**-0.1**

- Nil; .. Not available

Note: Detailed metadata at: *http://metalinks.oecd.org/idi/20220712/6d95*.

Source: *OECD International Direct Investment Statistics (database)*: *https://doi.org/10.1787/idi-data-en*

GREECE

Table 2. Foreign direct investment positions by country

At year end

Million US dollars

	Inward					Outward				
	2016	2017	2018	2019	2020	2016	2017	2018	2019	2020
WORLD	**24 614.9**	**33 404.1**	**35 736.7**	**45 151.2**	**41 574.5**	**18 005.9**	**20 104.3**	**19 497.9**	**19 234.9**	**14 014.5**
OECD COUNTRIES	**24 961.0**	**33 380.5**	**33 761.7**	**40 909.6**	**37 402.6**	**4 570.0**	**5 863.0**	**6 243.4**	**7 240.9**	**3 199.4**
Australia	-4.5	9.8	19.6	33.8	112.4	1.9	11.7	9.2	8.9	42.5
Austria	351.7	507.5	291.6	278.9	144.4	625.6	722.2	416.6	243.2	320.3
Belgium	1 450.0	801.5	1 296.8	2 707.9	2 302.1	47.9	153.1	148.6	153.5	436.8
Canada	591.1	876.3	722.0	1 315.3	51.4	-	17.4	15.7	13.9	16.4
Chile	0.0	0.0	0.0	0.1	0.1	-	0.2	0.2	0.2	1.7
Colombia	-0.2	-0.2	-0.2	-0.2	0.0	-	1.0	1.0	1.0	1.2
Costa Rica	-	-	-	-	0.9	-	0.1	0.1	0.1	0.2
Czech Republic	-0.3	13.6	21.9	335.9	503.1	-0.4	0.2	-0.7	-0.7	18.3
Denmark	86.6	194.2	204.5	212.6	34.4	5.0	2.0	-1.8	-5.5	1.7
Estonia	0.0	5.3	5.6	7.2	10.0	-	0.1	0.1	0.1	0.1
Finland	12.0	50.1	52.5	39.7	31.1	-	1.1	0.6	0.7	0.5
France	1 464.2	1 743.3	1 523.3	1 723.5	3 350.9	26.0	69.0	64.6	66.2	71.6
Germany	5 226.2	7 721.0	7 963.9	9 246.9	6 829.8	232.4	366.7	368.1	374.5	681.5
Greece	-	-	-	-	-	-	-	-	-	-
Hungary	39.0	44.8	14.9	18.8	12.6	0.4	1.9	2.0	2.2	4.4
Iceland	1.1	1.7	1.7	1.7	0.5	-	-	-	-	-
Ireland	410.6	474.4	448.5	387.0	276.5	11.4	13.8	13.3	13.1	3.9
Israel	34.9	46.5	64.0	112.4	118.0	-	0.5	3.6	3.7	1.2
Italy	1 024.3	1 241.4	1 527.5	1 729.7	1 733.6	339.7	568.5	560.5	569.2	420.5
Japan	44.7	47.1	42.0	39.4	32.0	-0.6	12.9	12.3	12.1	0.5
Korea	8.2	20.2	12.4	11.1	19.5	-12.5	-14.9	-14.2	-14.0	0.1
Latvia	0.0	12.8	13.9	15.0	79.3	-	0.3	0.3	0.3	0.3
Lithuania	0.0	3.5	3.9	4.9	5.8	-	0.1	0.1	0.1	0.1
Luxembourg	5 634.6	7 731.4	7 495.4	9 000.2	6 602.4	-192.6	-383.6	-368.6	-113.1	522.5
Mexico	-25.0	-27.9	-25.6	-24.9	1.9	-	-	-	-	0.3
Netherlands	5 014.6	5 763.3	5 734.8	7 156.6	7 236.0	2 034.0	2 185.0	2 023.9	1 773.3	1 418.4
New Zealand	-0.1	0.8	1.6	2.4	3.4	-	0.7	0.7	0.7	0.9
Norway	59.4	37.3	24.1	52.8	43.0	29.0	6.8	7.1	7.4	3.3
Poland	5.1	15.2	10.9	18.5	19.1	51.7	44.5	50.9	41.7	42.0
Portugal	0.6	1.5	2.5	3.5	5.3	4.7	5.4	4.9	4.8	5.1
Slovak Republic	-5.8	-5.4	-3.8	-3.7	3.8	-6.6	-6.5	-4.8	-4.7	4.1
Slovenia	5.7	6.9	22.2	21.6	9.1	11.9	20.0	20.9	21.4	27.3
Spain	818.6	865.6	785.2	789.4	1 210.4	125.9	154.0	110.7	81.7	166.0
Sweden	101.2	143.3	122.5	147.4	126.7	3.9	10.0	8.4	7.7	8.5
Switzerland	1 928.8	3 408.4	3 556.3	3 560.2	3 244.1	0.6	92.9	98.8	102.0	122.0
Turkey	6.7	42.6	59.8	71.0	67.1	143.5	153.5	273.2	264.3	381.0
United Kingdom	106.5	549.3	785.7	649.3	1 705.9	-1 253.0	-784.3	-85.7	48.2	-2 361.4
United States	570.3	1 036.7	959.5	1 243.6	1 476.9	2 340.3	2 438.0	2 504.0	3 563.5	836.0
EUROPE	**21 772.7**	**29 790.5**	**32 077.4**	**39 725.3**	**36 163.7**	**12 646.7**	**13 554.8**	**13 249.9**	**12 402.9**	**11 973.4**
Bulgaria	-8.0	4.9	71.6	92.7	152.4	1 328.0	1 474.7	1 354.3	1 226.5	1 687.2
Croatia	0.0	0.4	0.0	0.2	-0.3	62.7	6.9	5.8	5.9	18.5
Cyprus	-2 040.2	-1 728.8	-112.7	1 189.8	64.2	4 500.8	4 971.6	5 043.1	5 196.4	5 710.3
Malta	1.4	-38.9	-41.6	5.8	-3.2	-4.7	-0.8	-2.3	-2.2	2.9
Montenegro	-	0.7	1.6	-1.8	3.5	50.8	96.1	94.3	102.2	47.7
Romania	-3.2	5.7	10.1	17.0	18.2	2 486.5	1 792.6	1 767.9	1 402.6	687.8
Russian Federation	27.3	102.7	110.6	119.7	139.5	86.1	77.6	11.3	12.4	10.5
Ukraine	-0.2	2.4	2.3	2.1	2.7	37.8	46.8	44.3	44.7	31.4
AFRICA	**62.9**	**64.5**	**45.8**	**69.3**	**84.5**	**91.1**	**302.3**	**340.0**	**53.1**	**85.9**
Northern Africa	-0.2	8.6	13.6	20.8	30.5	18.5	279.7	334.0	46.9	76.5
Algeria	0.0	0.0	0.0	0.0	0.7	-	-	-	-	0.0
Egypt	-0.1	8.3	13.1	20.2	29.1	12.9	278.9	333.4	16.0	99.8
Libya	-	-	-	-	-	0.3	0.3	0.0	30.4	-6.1
Morocco	0.0	0.2	0.2	0.3	0.3	5.4	0.2	0.2	0.2	-17.6
Tunisia	-0.2	0.2	0.3	0.4	0.4	-0.1	0.3	0.3	0.3	0.4
Other African countries	63.2	55.8	32.2	48.5	53.9	72.6	22.5	6.0	6.2	9.4
Nigeria	0.0	0.0	0.5	0.8	1.0	25.2	0.3	0.3	0.3	1.1
South Africa	-0.1	0.7	1.5	2.1	2.4	19.8	16.5	2.7	2.8	3.7
AMERICA	**1 837.9**	**2 239.4**	**2 095.3**	**2 961.0**	**2 464.0**	**3 383.2**	**3 802.5**	**3 574.6**	**4 481.5**	**1 676.9**
Northern America	1 161.4	1 913.0	1 681.5	2 558.9	1 528.3	2 340.3	2 455.4	2 519.7	3 577.4	852.4
Central America and Caribbean countries	679.0	299.7	414.6	402.9	933.8	1 042.8	1 193.1	915.2	901.2	800.7
Bahamas	-	0.9	1.0	1.1	1.4	-	1.0	1.0	1.0	1.1
Bermuda	500.3	1.0	1.5	1.6	349.0	-	-	-	-	395.8
Cayman Islands	23.2	13.2	13.9	65.0	70.5	490.9	131.5	125.6	123.3	2.0
El Salvador	-	-	-	-	-	-	-	-	-	-
Guatemala	0.0	-0.1	0.0	0.0	0.7	-	-	0.3	0.5	0.3
Honduras	-0.3	-0.3	-0.3	-0.3	0.1	-	-	-	-	-
Nicaragua	-	-	-	-	-	-	-	-	-	-
Panama	91.4	147.2	141.8	140.4	113.8	9.5	12.3	1.5	1.5	1.8
Virgin Islands, U.S.	-	-	-	-	-	-	-	-	-	-
South America	-2.5	26.8	-0.8	-0.8	1.9	-	154.0	139.7	2.9	23.8
Argentina	-0.7	-0.8	-0.5	-0.5	0.3	-	0.5	0.5	0.5	0.5
Bolivia	-	-	-	-	-	-	0.0	0.0	0.0	0.0
Brazil	-1.6	27.6	-0.4	-0.5	0.2	-	151.9	137.5	0.7	2.2
Ecuador	-	0.0	-	-	-	-	0.1	0.1	0.1	0.1
Paraguay	-	-	-	-	-	-	-	-	-	-
Peru	-	0.0	0.0	0.0	0.5	-	0.1	0.1	0.1	3.7
Uruguay	0.0	0.1	0.2	0.3	0.3	-	0.3	0.3	0.3	0.4
Venezuela	-	0.0	0.0	0.0	0.0	-	-	-	-	-

Table 2. Foreign direct investment positions by country *(cont.)*

At year end

Million US dollars

	Inward					Outward				
	2016	2017	2018	2019	2020	2016	2017	2018	2019	2020
ASIA	**909.5**	**1 246.0**	**1 441.1**	**2 328.4**	**2 712.9**	**1 883.0**	**2 391.5**	**2 283.0**	**2 246.8**	**187.8**
Near and Middle East	217.4	235.4	277.8	561.1	670.7	33.4	48.0	48.4	50.2	115.7
Gulf Arabian countries	177.9	98.7	108.9	320.6	365.6	25.5	35.0	28.9	38.1	103.3
Kuwait	-	4.0	4.8	6.7	8.7	-	-	-	-	-
Qatar	33.4	63.0	62.3	59.6	70.6	0.0	0.2	0.3	14.2	34.3
Saudi Arabia	-0.4	10.8	12.8	15.2	19.9	-	0.0	0.0	-3.5	3.8
United Arab Emirates	144.9	14.5	20.7	229.2	253.5	14.9	20.5	21.3	18.9	39.6
Other Near and Middle East	39.5	136.7	168.9	240.5	305.1	7.9	13.0	19.5	12.1	12.4
Jordan	1.0	8.1	10.3	12.6	14.2	-	0.9	4.8	0.9	1.0
Other Asian countries	692.0	1 010.6	1 163.3	1 767.3	2 042.2	1 849.6	2 343.5	2 234.5	2 196.6	72.1
China	10.1	128.8	256.0	400.4	745.7	24.1	22.3	21.4	21.2	20.2
Hong Kong, China	574.9	744.3	764.4	1 174.9	1 006.2	1 823.5	2 316.4	2 208.0	2 167.0	24.6
India	0.4	0.8	0.8	1.5	1.8	12.4	0.0	0.0	0.4	-1.6
Indonesia	0.0	0.1	0.1	0.1	0.4	8.6	0.3	0.3	0.3	0.3
Iran, Islamic Republic of	48.6	56.7	56.6	56.6	110.1	-	-	-	-	-
Malaysia	0.3	0.7	0.9	1.3	1.1	-1.1	-1.1	-1.1	-1.0	-
Philippines	0.0	-	-	-	0.0	0.0	0.1	0.1	0.1	0.1
Singapore	1.6	4.3	19.4	67.2	109.9	-0.8	2.4	2.4	2.5	4.2
Chinese Taipei	0.1	0.1	1.8	2.9	3.9	-1.9	-2.1	-2.0	-1.9	8.5
Thailand	0.5	0.7	0.7	0.5	0.2	-2.5	-1.4	-1.3	-1.2	1.4
Viet Nam	0.0	0.0	0.2	0.6	1.4	-	-	-	-	1.0
AUSTRALIA, OCEANIA AND POLAR REGIONS	**31.8**	**47.7**	**61.2**	**49.7**	**129.4**	**1.9**	**13.4**	**10.8**	**10.5**	**44.4**
WORLD unallocated and confidential	**-**	**16.0**	**15.9**	**17.4**	**20.2**	**0.0**	**39.9**	**39.6**	**40.0**	**46.2**
European Union (since 01/02/2020)	..	..	..	..	30 757.7	..	..	..	..	12 260.6
G20 countries excl. European Union	**9 047.7**	**13 530.6**	**13 970.8**	**16 576.7**	**16 291.8**	**1 968.7**	**3 107.6**	**3 881.4**	**4 941.7**	**128.6**
G20 OECD countries	**9 012.7**	**13 259.9**	**13 590.1**	**16 038.6**	**15 381.6**	**1 817.7**	**2 838.6**	**3 707.7**	**4 906.9**	**88.9**
G20 Non-OECD countries	**35.0**	**270.7**	**380.7**	**538.1**	**910.2**	**151.0**	**269.0**	**173.7**	**34.8**	**39.7**
MENA countries	**181.6**	**196.1**	**224.1**	**463.9**	**537.9**	**49.6**	**317.7**	**369.4**	**87.6**	**182.8**
ASEAN countries	**2.3**	**5.9**	**21.4**	**70.0**	**113.2**	**4.2**	**8.2**	**8.4**	**11.2**	**19.2**

- Nil; .. Not available

Note: Detailed metadata at: *http://metalinks.oecd.org/idi/20220712/6d95.*

Source: *OECD International Direct Investment Statistics (database): https://doi.org/10.1787/idi-data-en*

GREECE

Table 3. Foreign direct investment income by country

Million US dollars

	Inward					Outward				
	2016	2017	2018	2019	2020	2016	2017	2018	2019	2020
WORLD	**1 149.8**	**1 451.9**	**1 551.9**	**1 868.3**	**1 696.0**	**627.5**	**1 098.5**	**694.2**	**934.7**	**956.3**
OECD COUNTRIES	**922.0**	**1 325.3**	**1 426.1**	**1 681.8**	**1 471.4**	**200.7**	**360.7**	**472.2**	**469.3**	**403.1**
Australia	0.1	0.1	0.1	5.0	12.4	0.1	0.2	0.2	0.3	3.3
Austria	-10.2	-9.1	-9.2	-3.1	21.0	-6.0	-7.4	-2.2	-2.3	1.0
Belgium	-11.9	61.2	63.3	46.7	69.6	3.2	1.1	3.8	4.8	48.6
Canada	192.4	179.8	172.5	258.8	0.2	2.8	2.5	3.8	3.7	4.9
Chile	0.0	0.0	0.0	0.0	-	0.0	0.0	0.0	0.0	0.0
Colombia	-	-	-	-	-	-	-	-	-	-
Costa Rica	0.0	0.0	0.0	0.0	0.0	0.0	0.0	0.0	0.0	0.0
Czech Republic	1.1	-0.1	0.2	0.8	4.7	-6.4	-5.8	-5.4	1.1	8.5
Denmark	4.8	5.9	6.6	6.2	7.6	0.0	-0.3	0.4	-1.6	1.8
Estonia	0.0	0.0	0.0	0.0	0.0	1.3	1.3	2.6	1.0	0.2
Finland	-2.2	4.2	11.5	8.7	9.0	-	-0.6	-0.7	-0.6	-
France	14.9	27.3	66.5	189.2	36.6	2.5	7.5	1.5	6.2	6.7
Germany	207.0	291.9	231.0	448.8	390.8	32.9	52.1	44.0	44.8	57.2
Greece	-	-	-	-	-	-	-	-	-	-
Hungary	0.0	0.0	0.0	0.0	0.0	0.6	0.6	0.3	0.2	0.1
Iceland	0.0	0.0	-0.1	-0.1	-	0.0	0.0	0.0	0.0	0.0
Ireland	-13.7	20.6	4.9	-62.0	-76.7	0.1	0.2	1.4	2.7	4.9
Israel	0.9	1.1	0.5	0.9	0.5	0.3	0.3	1.0	1.4	0.4
Italy	104.7	45.8	59.1	-0.7	67.5	15.6	27.1	36.1	36.4	-2.0
Japan	-0.3	-4.4	-4.0	-2.7	0.2	-0.3	-0.3	-0.3	-0.3	-
Korea	0.0	-0.6	7.0	2.2	0.4	-	-	0.0	3.2	1.1
Latvia	0.0	0.0	0.0	0.0	-	0.1	0.1	0.1	0.1	0.0
Lithuania	-	0.0	0.0	0.0	0.0	-	-	-	-	-
Luxembourg	116.3	180.0	458.1	113.7	-60.3	56.9	65.7	42.3	51.8	34.3
Mexico	-	0.0	-	0.0	0.0	-	-	-	0.0	-
Netherlands	-18.6	223.8	212.6	407.0	486.7	-70.3	-14.0	43.8	142.6	43.4
New Zealand	-	0.0	0.0	-	-	0.0	0.0	0.0	0.0	0.0
Norway	-1.3	-0.2	0.4	2.6	2.8	0.1	-0.7	-0.4	-0.2	1.2
Poland	0.0	0.3	0.3	0.3	0.3	5.9	3.4	2.9	3.3	3.4
Portugal	0.0	0.1	1.0	0.0	0.0	0.9	0.5	-0.4	1.3	1.8
Slovak Republic	0.1	0.1	0.1	0.2	0.2	-0.2	-0.2	-0.1	-0.2	0.1
Slovenia	-0.1	-0.1	-1.4	0.0	0.5	1.9	3.1	3.1	2.4	5.2
Spain	110.1	73.4	78.9	-3.0	29.8	3.3	2.5	7.2	7.7	6.8
Sweden	5.6	2.8	12.4	15.6	2.9	0.3	-3.8	-2.9	-3.0	2.0
Switzerland	-28.0	83.0	115.9	113.1	144.1	47.0	77.9	88.6	82.1	115.8
Turkey	-1.8	-2.1	-2.2	-2.1	1.5	47.4	61.6	53.6	50.7	5.5
United Kingdom	212.5	115.3	-88.3	90.5	282.8	-100.7	14.0	66.4	-37.9	30.0
United States	39.4	25.3	28.5	45.0	36.3	161.4	72.3	81.5	67.4	17.2
EUROPE	**925.7**	**1 303.6**	**1 386.3**	**1 602.8**	**1 592.9**	**206.7**	**947.7**	**527.3**	**767.8**	**916.0**
Bulgaria	-0.7	-0.5	-0.3	-0.8	-4.2	124.0	330.7	-1.5	138.8	115.7
Croatia	0.0	0.0	0.0	0.0	0.0	0.4	0.4	0.4	0.4	-1.7
Cyprus	249.9	201.8	190.1	265.5	174.8	-77.1	254.4	172.4	174.2	392.6
Malta	0.0	-6.4	-6.7	-17.9	0.5	12.5	0.1	7.6	0.1	2.9
Montenegro	-	-	-	-	-	0.6	0.5	0.5	0.4	-0.1
Romania	0.2	0.4	0.2	0.4	0.1	17.6	-34.9	-63.0	7.7	0.2
Russian Federation	-2.6	-6.7	-6.3	-1.4	-3.8	41.9	40.2	44.0	1.7	3.2
Ukraine	0.0	-	0.0	0.0	-	-3.1	-1.9	-1.2	-3.2	1.7
AFRICA	**-12.9**	**-15.8**	**-25.5**	**-19.8**	**9.2**	**2.1**	**3.1**	**1.4**	**2.2**	**-15.9**
Northern Africa	0.0	0.0	0.0	0.1	1.6	0.1	2.1	-0.1	0.1	-17.0
Algeria	-	-	-	-	-	0.0	0.0	0.0	0.0	0.0
Egypt	0.0	0.0	0.0	0.1	1.6	0.3	0.4	0.2	0.2	-6.3
Libya	0.0	0.0	0.0	-	0.0	-0.2	0.0	-0.3	-0.1	-3.5
Morocco	-	-	0.0	-	-	-	1.7	-	-	-7.1
Tunisia	-	0.0	-	0.0	-	0.0	-	-	-	-
Other African countries	-12.9	-15.8	-25.5	-19.9	7.6	1.9	1.0	1.5	2.1	1.1
Nigeria	-	-	-	-	0.1	-	-	-	-	-
South Africa	0.0	0.0	0.0	0.8	0.0	0.0	0.1	0.0	0.6	0.0
AMERICA	**215.2**	**188.2**	**184.4**	**310.6**	**43.6**	**132.2**	**41.9**	**53.1**	**49.5**	**40.1**
Northern America	231.9	205.0	201.0	303.8	36.5	164.2	74.8	85.2	71.2	22.0
Central America and Caribbean countries	-16.8	-17.1	-17.3	6.2	7.0	-32.0	-33.0	-32.7	-23.2	16.4
Bahamas	-	-	-	-	-	2.6	1.2	2.8	1.2	3.0
Bermuda	-0.1	0.0	-0.2	-0.1	3.0	0.0	0.0	0.0	0.0	12.5
Cayman Islands	-0.4	-0.3	-0.3	3.5	2.3	-2.4	-30.4	-31.5	-29.7	0.2
El Salvador	-	-	-	-	-	0.0	0.0	0.0	0.0	0.0
Guatemala	0.0	0.0	0.0	0.0	0.0	0.0	0.0	-0.1	-0.1	0.0
Honduras	0.0	0.0	0.0	0.0	0.0	-	-	-	-	-
Nicaragua	0.0	-	0.0	0.0	0.0	-	-	-	-	0.0
Panama	-3.7	-2.7	-2.9	-3.0	-	0.1	0.3	0.2	0.1	0.1
Virgin Islands, U.S.	-	-	-	-	-	-	-	-	4.9	-
South America	0.1	0.2	0.7	0.6	0.1	0.0	0.1	0.5	1.6	1.6
Argentina	0.0	0.0	0.0	0.0	0.0	-	-	0.0	-	-
Bolivia	0.0	0.0	0.0	-	0.0	0.0	0.0	0.0	0.0	0.0
Brazil	0.1	0.2	0.7	0.6	0.1	0.0	-0.3	-1.0	-0.2	-
Ecuador	-	-	-	-	-	0.0	0.0	0.0	0.0	0.0
Paraguay	0.0	0.0	0.0	0.0	0.0	0.0	0.0	0.0	0.0	0.0
Peru	0.0	-	-	-	-	0.0	0.5	1.5	1.8	0.5
Uruguay	-	-	-	-	-	-	-	-	-	-
Venezuela	-	0.0	0.0	-	0.0	-	-	-	-	-

Table 3. Foreign direct investment income by country *(cont.)*

Million US dollars

	Inward					Outward				
	2016	2017	2018	2019	2020	2016	2017	2018	2019	2020
ASIA	**28.3**	**-13.8**	**16.0**	**-27.3**	**37.2**	**285.7**	**105.1**	**110.0**	**112.2**	**9.6**
Near and Middle East	-6.0	-5.9	-10.9	-34.0	8.4	0.6	4.1	4.0	4.1	0.3
Gulf Arabian countries	-7.0	-7.0	-11.5	-34.9	5.4	1.3	2.4	3.2	2.8	-0.8
Kuwait	-	-	0.0	-	0.0	-	-	-	-	0.2
Qatar	-0.5	-0.4	-2.6	-9.0	-	-	0.0	0.8	0.0	-0.1
Saudi Arabia	0.0	0.0	0.0	1.1	0.2	0.0	-	-	-	1.8
United Arab Emirates	-6.6	-6.8	-9.0	-27.0	5.1	1.3	2.4	2.4	2.8	-3.8
Other Near and Middle East	1.0	1.2	0.6	0.9	3.1	-0.7	1.7	0.8	1.4	1.0
Jordan	0.0	0.0	0.0	0.0	-	0.0	0.0	0.0	0.0	0.0
Other Asian countries	34.3	-8.0	26.9	6.7	28.8	285.1	101.1	106.0	108.1	9.3
China	1.8	0.2	20.3	0.2	8.3	0.1	0.1	0.3	0.4	0.7
Hong Kong, China	32.7	-3.1	3.5	6.4	17.8	284.7	100.0	105.0	102.8	3.7
India	-	-	0.0	-	0.2	0.0	0.3	0.1	0.5	0.1
Indonesia	-	-	-	-	-	0.0	0.0	0.0	0.0	0.0
Iran, Islamic Republic of	-	0.0	0.0	0.0	0.2	0.0	-	-	-	0.0
Malaysia	0.0	0.0	0.0	0.0	0.0	-	0.1	0.1	0.1	0.1
Philippines	-	-	-	-	-	-	-	0.1	-	-
Singapore	0.0	-	0.0	0.0	1.7	0.5	0.7	0.3	1.2	2.1
Chinese Taipei	-	-	0.0	-	-	0.0	0.2	0.4	0.2	1.6
Thailand	-	-	-	-	0.0	-	-	0.0	-	-
Viet Nam	-	-	0.0	-	-	0.0	0.0	0.0	0.0	0.0
AUSTRALIA, OCEANIA AND POLAR REGIONS	**-6.3**	**-10.2**	**-11.2**	**0.5**	**12.4**	**0.6**	**0.2**	**1.0**	**1.6**	**5.0**
WORLD unallocated and confidential	**0.0**	**-0.1**	**2.0**	**1.5**	**0.7**	**0.2**	**0.4**	**1.5**	**1.4**	**1.4**
European Union (since 01/02/2020)	..	..	..	..	**1 161.5**	..	..	..	..	**733.6**
G20 countries excl. European Union	**768.3**	**672.0**	**485.0**	**1 035.5**	**833.7**	**203.7**	**277.3**	**330.0**	**177.5**	**129.6**
G20 OECD countries	**769.0**	**678.3**	**470.3**	**1 034.2**	**828.6**	**161.7**	**236.9**	**286.6**	**174.6**	**123.8**
G20 Non-OECD countries	**-0.7**	**-6.3**	**14.7**	**1.3**	**5.1**	**42.1**	**40.4**	**43.4**	**2.9**	**5.8**
MENA countries	**-7.0**	**-7.0**	**-11.4**	**-34.7**	**7.1**	**0.7**	**6.1**	**3.1**	**2.8**	**-17.5**
ASEAN countries	**0.0**	**0.0**	**0.0**	**0.0**	**1.7**	**0.5**	**0.8**	**0.6**	**1.3**	**2.2**

- Nil; .. Not available

Note: Detailed metadata at: *http://metalinks.oecd.org/idi/20220712/6d95*.

Source: *OECD International Direct Investment Statistics (database)*: *https://doi.org/10.1787/idi-data-en*

Table 4. Foreign direct investment flows by industrial sector

Million US dollars

	Inward					Outward				
	2016	2017	2018	2019	2020	2016	2017	2018	2019	2020
All FDI activities	**2 762.4**	**3 477.4**	**3 970.8**	**5 019.2**	**3 205.2**	**-1 665.4**	**168.0**	**476.6**	**641.6**	**547.4**
Agriculture, forestry and fishing	**5.2**	**10.3**	**17.2**	**-35.1**	**24.6**	**-0.3**	**7.5**	**0.3**	**1.5**	**-0.1**
Mining and quarrying	**128.6**	**128.0**	**37.9**	**-90.4**	**29.8**	**35.3**	**10.2**	**1.2**	**14.0**	**15.5**
Extraction activities	-6.1	20.8	26.9	-44.3	-54.1	0.1	10.1	6.8	13.7	-
Manufacturing	**50.1**	**311.6**	**364.9**	**375.9**	**272.7**	**188.3**	**126.6**	**74.6**	**-114.7**	**68.8**
of which:										
Food products, beverages and tobacco	54.7	68.2	-5.5	190.8	163.7	28.7	41.8	35.8	9.5	51.8
Textiles, wood and paper products; printing	3.3	-6.2	5.9	7.8	39.1	1.3	2.3	5.1	-3.0	6.0
Chemical, rubber, plastic, non-metallic mineral products	20.3	179.5	350.8	258.3	21.4	22.3	4.8	5.5	-12.1	4.2
Metal and machinery products, except electrical equipment	-3.1	29.0	19.0	-18.2	56.8	-21.8	31.7	-1.0	34.2	38.1
Motor vehicles, trailers, semi-trailers, other transport equipment	4.5	0.7	0.2	-0.2	-0.4	-	0.8	-	-	-
Other manufacturing	-29.6	40.5	-5.6	-62.6	-7.9	157.8	45.0	29.1	-143.2	-31.4
Electricity, gas, steam and air conditioning supply	**19.6**	**465.4**	**85.6**	**55.2**	**76.7**	**7.5**	**27.3**	**47.7**	**13.2**	**-22.0**
Water supply; sewerage, waste management and remediation activities	**0.0**	**1.0**	**1.0**	**1.2**	**0.3**	**4.1**	**0.8**	**-1.6**	**0.0**	**5.6**
Construction	**39.1**	**-15.6**	**-77.0**	**40.9**	**91.0**	**100.2**	**116.5**	**78.5**	**150.8**	**85.0**
Services	**2 308.8**	**2 200.3**	**2 756.4**	**3 832.6**	**2 203.6**	**-2 030.8**	**-125.2**	**272.4**	**575.0**	**379.0**
Wholesale and retail trade; repair of motor vehicles and motorcycles	97.2	100.7	133.1	83.2	66.0	402.6	150.5	301.2	54.5	-28.4
Transportation and storage	600.6	1 455.9	870.4	278.0	-14.5	6.5	8.7	-50.9	7.8	21.3
Accommodation and food service activities	488.6	123.1	137.2	124.6	450.6	6.6	1.0	-0.8	35.4	1.8
Information and communication	-165.5	-132.9	301.6	104.6	382.6	-189.4	-144.5	-147.4	-145.7	40.7
Financial and insurance activities	886.6	516.4	721.9	764.0	398.5	-2 305.7	-334.3	47.9	273.0	255.9
Activities of holding companies	153.8	49.7	300.2	27.0	270.7	-240.5	365.1	291.7	133.2	345.7
Real estate activities	162.6	78.3	844.3	1 989.2	763.0	-7.1	138.6	102.0	207.4	22.9
Professional, scientific and technical activities	10.1	24.0	-123.1	296.1	72.0	-22.0	-2.8	9.3	-33.3	-1.3
Administrative and support service activities	50.6	52.8	56.2	46.3	9.9	-36.8	53.1	5.7	13.7	2.8
Public administration; activities of households and of extraterritorial organisations	-	-	-	-	-	-	-	-	-	-
Education	4.2	-0.1	0.0	0.1	0.1	-	-0.1	-	-	-
Human health and social work activities	30.9	20.6	-89.3	194.6	-120.2	-6.2	-3.8	-4.3	-4.4	0.7
Arts, entertainment and recreation	131.9	-35.7	-100.1	-62.4	197.4	151.7	8.7	9.7	166.1	62.2
Other services	11.0	-2.8	4.2	14.3	-2.0	-31.0	-0.2	0.0	0.4	0.4
Not allocated and confidential	**45.8**	**6.8**	**11.6**	**-0.4**	**40.3**	**31.6**	**0.0**	**-1.3**	**0.1**	**8.2**
Private real estate activities	**165.4**	**369.5**	**773.3**	**839.3**	**466.3**	**-1.2**	**4.2**	**4.7**	**1.8**	**7.4**

- Nil

Note: Detailed metadata at: *http://metalinks.oecd.org/idi/20220712/6d95*.

Source: OECD *International Direct Investment Statistics (database)*: *https://doi.org/10.1787/idi-data-en*

GREECE

Table 5. Foreign direct investment positions by industrial sector

At year end

Million US dollars

	Inward					Outward				
	2016	2017	2018	2019	2020	2016	2017	2018	2019	2020
All FDI activities	**24 614.9**	**33 404.1**	**35 736.7**	**45 151.2**	**41 574.5**	**18 005.9**	**20 104.3**	**19 497.9**	**19 234.9**	**14 014.5**
Agriculture, forestry and fishing	**260.7**	**327.6**	**82.0**	**234.0**	**279.2**	**56.1**	**63.0**	**60.1**	**6.5**	**-**
Mining and quarrying	**1 222.2**	**1 403.1**	**1 578.6**	**1 731.5**	**1 448.3**	**22.4**	**32.5**	**18.2**	**17.8**	**13.6**
Extraction activities	101.2	111.6	314.9	244.3	205.3	10.8	19.3	5.6	5.5	-
Manufacturing	**8 005.2**	**9 072.8**	**9 187.1**	**11 222.8**	**9 045.9**	**2 956.4**	**3 455.2**	**3 726.8**	**4 013.1**	**903.1**
of which:										
Food products, beverages and tobacco	1 867.2	2 097.2	2 565.6	2 864.5	1 929.1	207.1	278.1	279.0	266.7	88.3
Textiles, wood and paper products; printing	119.0	132.2	124.1	192.6	129.8	39.4	63.8	60.3	59.2	1.4
Chemical, rubber, plastic, non-metallic mineral products	3 009.9	4 339.3	3 947.6	4 331.0	2 827.1	136.7	150.1	217.5	230.5	219.6
Metal and machinery products, except electrical equipment	1 526.1	848.1	1 090.3	1 479.7	1 783.6	483.9	372.0	260.7	281.5	520.5
Motor vehicles, trailers, semi-trailers, other transport equipment	11.4	11.3	1.2	11.0	3.0	-	5.3	-	-	-
Other manufacturing	1 471.7	1 644.6	1 458.4	2 344.1	2 373.3	2 089.3	2 585.9	2 909.4	3 175.2	73.3
Electricity, gas, steam and air conditioning supply	**2 529.6**	**3 103.2**	**2 673.3**	**2 479.6**	**1 310.2**	**174.8**	**220.8**	**245.6**	**296.4**	**7.6**
Water supply; sewerage, waste management and remediation activities	**37.0**	**35.4**	**40.0**	**42.7**	**0.9**	**22.4**	**25.5**	**25.3**	**25.0**	**21.4**
Construction	**241.4**	**337.2**	**493.2**	**719.0**	**311.3**	**98.3**	**116.8**	**137.2**	**256.8**	**658.3**
Services	**12 237.3**	**17 180.0**	**18 999.8**	**24 526.9**	**23 256.5**	**14 607.9**	**15 190.6**	**14 244.8**	**13 247.9**	**9 761.3**
Wholesale and retail trade; repair of motor vehicles and motorcycles	5 447.0	5 782.3	5 707.9	6 627.8	4 729.4	3 683.9	4 910.7	4 419.0	4 243.3	1 103.2
Transportation and storage	1 769.0	3 552.6	4 082.2	4 214.8	4 000.0	187.1	212.7	199.1	195.2	20.4
Accommodation and food service activities	874.9	1 039.1	1 021.3	1 099.8	1 015.8	41.8	39.7	31.3	161.0	-
Information and communication	4 137.7	5 926.0	5 969.6	6 756.8	6 402.6	1 768.8	1 420.3	1 571.4	622.2	211.1
Financial and insurance activities	-4 369.9	-4 743.9	-2 935.7	-882.5	1 269.2	8 013.3	7 469.1	6 890.9	6 487.1	6 249.0
Activities of holding companies	716.9	644.8	1 775.5	2 612.0	4 181.4	4 864.3	4 096.5	3 789.7	3 726.8	6 296.0
Real estate activities	2 103.9	2 316.0	2 151.9	2 609.9	2 469.8	382.6	367.4	383.4	767.4	1 686.6
Professional, scientific and technical activities	273.6	333.7	413.1	316.8	501.5	189.4	389.3	327.0	210.2	186.7
Administrative and support service activities	711.4	1 050.0	988.8	1 176.5	227.5	136.9	157.6	134.2	152.0	233.3
Public administration; activities of households and of extraterritorial organisations	1.7	2.0	1.9	1.8	-	-	-	-	-	-
Education	0.9	1.0	0.9	0.9	6.0	-	-	-	-	-
Human health and social work activities	84.1	298.9	368.8	560.2	458.4	15.7	17.4	15.3	15.1	-0.2
Arts, entertainment and recreation	1 194.0	1 612.0	1 213.1	2 027.2	2 174.7	167.8	191.0	260.1	385.4	71.6
Other services	9.0	10.3	16.2	16.9	1.6	20.7	15.5	13.0	8.9	-0.4
Not allocated and confidential	**81.4**	**105.6**	**106.7**	**401.5**	**962.3**	**67.7**	**-421.4**	**-363.4**	**-59.9**	**985.3**
Private real estate activities	**-**	**1 839.2**	**2 576.1**	**3 793.1**	**4 959.9**	**-**	**1 421.2**	**1 403.2**	**1 431.2**	**1 663.9**

- Nil

Note: Detailed metadata at: *http://metalinks.oecd.org/idi/20220712/6d95*.

Source: *OECD International Direct Investment Statistics (database): https://doi.org/10.1787/idi-data-en*

GREECE

Table 6. Foreign direct investment income by industrial sector

Million US dollars

	Inward					Outward				
	2016	2017	2018	2019	2020	2016	2017	2018	2019	2020
All FDI activities	**1 149.8**	**1 451.9**	**1 551.9**	**1 868.3**	**1 696.0**	**627.5**	**1 098.5**	**694.2**	**934.7**	**956.3**
Agriculture, forestry and fishing	**1.6**	**2.7**	**3.4**	**-45.5**	**8.2**	**0.1**	**0.2**	**0.1**	**2.0**	**0.3**
Mining and quarrying	**-6.1**	**74.0**	**10.2**	**-128.5**	**-73.9**	**1.8**	**12.8**	**5.4**	**10.8**	**8.2**
Extraction activities	27.6	108.0	46.4	-34.6	-73.9	0.9	3.7	4.6	1.7	0.2
Manufacturing	**103.9**	**332.8**	**593.3**	**664.5**	**230.9**	**142.1**	**142.1**	**175.3**	**203.2**	**229.0**
of which:										
Food products, beverages and tobacco	65.2	85.3	136.4	235.7	161.1	6.4	44.7	50.0	115.9	21.2
Textiles, wood and paper products; printing	-1.3	-14.1	-7.8	-13.8	3.0	1.2	1.9	2.6	2.9	0.7
Chemical, rubber, plastic, non-metallic mineral products	73.1	233.6	443.7	469.8	-83.1	4.3	3.9	11.1	14.0	44.7
Metal and machinery products, except electrical equipment	-9.5	26.5	3.7	-33.4	61.2	-22.3	-9.9	-9.3	4.6	4.7
Motor vehicles, trailers, semi-trailers, other transport equipment	7.0	0.0	-0.3	0.3	2.9	-	-	0.1	0.2	-
Other manufacturing	-30.6	1.5	17.5	5.9	85.8	152.4	101.4	120.9	65.5	157.8
Electricity, gas, steam and air conditioning supply	**34.2**	**109.9**	**-21.9**	**40.7**	**73.2**	**12.8**	**2.9**	**-8.2**	**3.9**	**10.6**
Water supply; sewerage, waste management and remediation activities	**0.0**	**1.0**	**1.0**	**1.8**	**0.2**	**0.8**	**0.8**	**0.0**	**0.3**	**3.9**
Construction	**17.2**	**34.7**	**34.6**	**40.8**	**31.6**	**50.7**	**59.4**	**76.5**	**40.1**	**4.5**
Services	**931.5**	**841.3**	**858.8**	**1 236.0**	**1 352.9**	**301.0**	**789.5**	**351.1**	**571.0**	**592.5**
Wholesale and retail trade; repair of motor vehicles and motorcycles	206.3	180.4	265.2	301.0	372.9	354.5	165.0	175.3	121.4	30.7
Transportation and storage	174.0	136.9	176.3	197.1	22.7	89.6	129.7	190.7	150.2	220.6
Accommodation and food service activities	-14.9	-15.4	-10.6	-5.0	51.5	1.9	4.4	5.2	9.6	5.7
Information and communication	-64.1	27.7	138.4	188.5	312.2	-187.7	-152.2	-147.6	-144.4	41.1
Financial and insurance activities	448.8	364.5	332.2	325.3	160.6	37.5	207.3	48.6	342.5	208.5
Activities of holding companies	145.8	18.4	98.8	97.2	8.1	-86.4	-183.2	-50.2	151.3	145.8
Real estate activities	58.1	28.5	42.8	165.5	180.0	5.3	39.5	21.8	47.8	21.7
Professional, scientific and technical activities	-8.6	26.1	30.6	30.9	81.6	-20.8	-2.4	16.1	-43.1	18.8
Administrative and support service activities	19.0	31.7	37.5	55.0	18.1	6.7	391.7	17.4	44.5	1.2
Public administration; activities of households and of extraterritorial organisations	-	-	-	-	-	-	-	-	-	-
Education	-0.1	-0.1	5.8	1.0	4.1	-	-	-	0.1	-
Human health and social work activities	29.0	-23.0	-26.4	37.2	6.0	-2.8	-2.9	-3.1	-3.1	2.6
Arts, entertainment and recreation	69.2	82.7	-145.9	-66.1	139.2	16.8	9.4	26.9	45.4	39.1
Other services	14.9	1.3	12.8	5.7	4.1	0.1	0.1	-0.1	0.2	2.5
Not allocated and confidential	**67.2**	**55.2**	**69.7**	**58.0**	**72.2**	**103.5**	**76.1**	**72.0**	**71.9**	**72.7**
Private real estate activities	**0.4**	**0.3**	**2.9**	**0.4**	**0.7**	**14.7**	**14.7**	**21.8**	**31.5**	**34.4**

- Nil

Note: Detailed metadata at: *http://metalinks.oecd.org/idi/20220712/6d95.*

Source: *OECD International Direct Investment Statistics (database): https://doi.org/10.1787/idi-data-en*

HUNGARY

Table 1. Foreign direct investment flows by country

Million US dollars

	Inward					Outward				
	2016	2017	2018	2019	2020	2016	2017	2018	2019	2020
WORLD	**-5 438.6**	**3 527.5**	**6 460.1**	**4 105.1**	**6 721.5**	**-8 272.2**	**1 221.6**	**3 363.5**	**3 238.2**	**4 286.3**
OECD COUNTRIES	**-6 730.6**	**1 662.5**	**6 591.8**	**3 536.5**	**6 517.8**	**1 277.8**	**-947.9**	**1 796.0**	**1 534.7**	.. d
Australia	13.6	-47.1	13.1	-1.2	47.2	9.7	-18.8	10.3	5.4	7.2
Austria	-186.2	264.2	546.5	869.7	862.1	23.8	9.2	28.2	-31.2	-34.2
Belgium	299.5	-278.1	1 818.5	-885.5	1 623.3	77.9	-2 841.3	0.2	-0.9	-0.1
Canada	8.6	-69.4	-77.0	10.6	-119.0	9.4	13.0	11.5	.. c	0.9
Chile	3.5	2.0	1.2	-0.7	0.7	.. c	.. c	.. c	-	.. c
Colombia	0.4	-0.3	-113.3	-6.9	4.3	.. c	.. c	.. c	.. c	.. c
Costa Rica	0.0	-0.1	0.0	0.0	0.0	-	-	-	-	-
Czech Republic	131.8	186.2	63.4	93.2	-381.9	-3.3	297.9	63.4	160.8	811.7
Denmark	147.1	148.3	228.7	70.7	235.8	.. c	.. c	.. c	.. c	.. c
Estonia	-0.1	0.3	0.3	0.0	-0.3	-0.3	0.5	0.0	-1.3	0.1
Finland	1.3	8.5	10.9	11.3	28.6	0.1	0.0	0.0	-1.3	-0.1
France	1 912.5	381.4	610.7	289.2	701.5	3.9	23.4	14.2	12.2	-84.3
Germany	3 707.4	-1 772.3	-733.8	1 405.8	-2 197.0	115.2	21.2	-1.7	-58.1	153.3
Greece	50.7	1.4	-4.2	3.6	-2.8	0.1	0.4	-0.2	-0.2	-0.1
Hungary	-	-	-	-	-	-	-	-	-	-
Iceland	-1.1	-3.7	1.8	-0.6	-1.9	-	.. c	.. c	.. c	.. c
Ireland	-4 021.9	59.9	834.9	-4 797.0	-1 043.5	1.2	440.4	1 361.6	-1 114.4	2.7
Israel	-25.2	-2 104.0	-35.0	-90.8	1 595.6	317.2	330.3	162.9	-157.0	169.2
Italy	1 387.8	7.9	-100.7	204.6	-456.8	371.1	5.1	63.2	-26.6	69.0
Japan	118.2	173.1	223.6	309.3	218.9	3.1	1.0	1.4	1.9	0.5
Korea	185.8	264.3	1 079.6	882.0	855.5	16.5	11.5	1.2	-1.7	-2.0
Latvia	-4.6	-1.3	-0.4	-1.2	-0.3	-0.3	0.3	-0.1	1.5	0.4
Lithuania	3.5	1.9	-2.2	8.7	13.3	1.3	0.7	0.7	-0.6	-0.3
Luxembourg	-164.3	468.8	1 147.9	1 132.6	1 114.2	215.6	-239.8	-101.7	-178.5	1 020.9
Mexico	74.1	-30.5	-68.7	-52.4	8.5	85.5	18.4	18.9	-3.4	18.8
Netherlands	-9 255.4	2 038.7	939.3	137.8	814.4	-62.3	183.2	138.9	1 306.4	2 771.7
New Zealand	-9.9	2.2	-4.9	0.0	0.6	-	-	-	-	-
Norway	-14.2	10.5	-416.6	-15.5	3.3	.. c	.. c	.. c	.. c	.. c
Poland	124.2	764.7	171.6	210.0	-340.1	51.0	395.8	115.6	458.7	12.8
Portugal	-9.5	18.7	6.0	9.1	-4.0	-4.5	-0.3	0.2	0.2	1.6
Slovak Republic	-3.9	-15.5	-5.4	28.8	-5.2	162.4	21.2	-181.6	155.9	-170.9
Slovenia	5.3	-1.8	3.8	5.3	17.3	1.3	4.2	38.9	403.1	77.9
Spain	37.4	3.0	221.3	-182.1	-84.4	118.3	164.1	121.4	122.5	-8.1
Sweden	33.9	-35.1	-20.0	133.3	124.4	0.5	.. c	1.5	137.5	1.7
Switzerland	134.7	2 256.6	-38.0	703.1	979.7	17.4	252.1	-466.9	-254.2	-874.9
Turkey	11.4	11.6	-3.4	19.3	32.7	-23.8	-1.6	-3.8	-2.4	-1.4
United Kingdom	-882.4	-1 398.2	-815.1	1 880.4	1 795.6	21.0	40.9	17.4	73.1	-223.7
United States	-540.6	347.3	994.3	1 145.2	77.6	-249.9	-80.8	378.8	524.8	387.1
EUROPE	**-5 978.5**	**3 607.2**	**4 752.2**	**1 617.1**	**3 258.6**	**1 799.7**	**281.3**	**3 138.8**	**2 886.5**	**3 687.2**
Bulgaria	3.7	3.0	12.6	8.7	4.2	-42.8	-25.3	737.2	212.7	192.2
Croatia	-4.8	-18.7	29.2	-14.4	0.0	163.7	725.4	171.9	48.1	75.6
Cyprus	0.4	20.2	40.0	-349.3	-320.4	354.1	192.5	637.8	318.3	-440.0
Malta	-117.8	48.5	-472.4	67.2	-66.2	-22.0	120.7	64.0	59.7	53.7
Montenegro	0.0	0.0	-0.1	0.1	0.1	2.7	-146.0	66.3	64.7	11.4
Romania	23.2	28.0	11.6	130.3	84.3	-21.7	189.6	115.4	327.0	-35.0
Russian Federation	154.1	63.5	166.5	139.8	-61.6	71.7	199.4	33.9	106.6	-20.9
Ukraine	57.8	51.7	8.0	-74.8	12.4	191.5	61.3	65.8	98.8	98.7
AFRICA	**311.7**	**306.1**	**167.8**	**104.8**	**91.6**	**10.5**	**1.9**	**-6.4**	**-4.4**	**-17.4**
Northern Africa	5.6	4.7	3.7	-20.7	-18.1	-0.4	-0.5	-2.7	-0.1	-0.2
Algeria	0.1	0.6	0.1	-2.3	0.1	-	-	-	-	-
Egypt	1.7	5.3	1.9	2.5	-5.9	.. c	.. c	.. c	.. c	-
Libya	-	-	-	.. c	.. c	-	-	-	-	-
Morocco	3.4	-2.2	1.6	2.2	-8.4	-	.. c	.. c	-0.1	.. c
Tunisia	0.4	1.1	0.2	-23.1	-3.9	-	-	-	-	-
Other African countries	306.1	301.4	164.1	125.5	109.6	.. c	.. c	.. c	-4.3	-17.2
Nigeria	-0.3	0.3	0.1	-0.1	0.2	-	-	-	-	-
South Africa	-2.7	-2.8	2.4	14.1	-12.5	.. c	.. c	.. c	.. c	.. c
AMERICA	**-374.1**	**1 598.6**	**-38.4**	**1 356.4**	**64.4**	**-10 421.6**	**559.6**	**20.2**	**637.9**	**401.6**
Northern America	-532.0	277.9	917.4	1 155.7	-41.4	-240.5	-67.8	390.3	528.1	388.0
Central America and Caribbean countries	145.7	1 314.1	-844.8	199.0	124.9	-10 260.9	566.4	-427.8	0.3	22.6
Bahamas	.. c	6.1	1.9	0.1	.. c	-	-	-	-	-
Bermuda	-1.3	1.5	0.9	-4.5	0.3	-	-	-	.. c	.. c
Cayman Islands	230.0	252.2	132.3	421.9	102.1	-	.. c	.. c	-	-
El Salvador	.. c	-	.. c	-	.. c	-	-	.. c	.. c	.. c
Guatemala	.. c	.. c	0.0	0.0	0.0	-	-	.. c	.. c	.. c
Honduras	-0.5	0.0	0.1	0.1	-0.1	-	-	-	-	-
Nicaragua	-	-	-	-	-	-	-	-	-	-
Panama	-26.5	-2.1	5.7	-4.9	-0.4	.. c	.. c	-	-	-
Virgin Islands, U.S.	-	-	-	-	-	-	-	-	-	-
South America	12.1	6.6	-110.9	1.7	-19.1	79.7	60.9	57.8	109.5	-9.0
Argentina	0.6	0.5	1.5	0.4	-23.8	.. c	.. c	.. c	.. c	.. c
Bolivia	.. c	-	-	-	-	-	-	-	-	-
Brazil	5.0	-4.1	0.5	9.6	-2.9	70.4	76.5	57.3	107.1	-7.6
Ecuador	0.2	-0.1	0.2	0.0	0.0	.. c	-	-	-	-
Paraguay	.. c	.. c	.. c	.. c	-	-	-	-	-	-
Peru	1.9	0.2	-1.1	-0.8	2.6	.. c	.. c	-	-	-
Uruguay	0.3	0.3	0.2	0.0	.. c	-	.. c	.. c	.. c	-
Venezuela	0.1	8.1	0.0	0.1	0.0	-	-	-	-	-

Table 1. Foreign direct investment flows by country *(cont.)*

Million US dollars

	Inward					Outward				
	2016	2017	2018	2019	2020	2016	2017	2018	2019	2020
ASIA	**470.8**	**-2 070.7**	**1 576.1**	**1 102.8**	**3 138.1**	**329.0**	**397.2**	**200.5**	**-287.2**	**207.8**
Near and Middle East	117.4	-2 165.6	-33.7	-242.5	1 513.0	337.4	353.6	179.0	-148.8	172.0
Gulf Arabian countries	146.2	-58.6	-3.1	-153.3	-83.7	20.1	23.3	15.8	7.6	2.8
Kuwait	0.0	.. c	0.0	0.0	0.0	.. c	-	-	-	-
Qatar	-0.5	-0.7	-3.0	51.9	-41.8	-	-	-	-	-
Saudi Arabia	1.2	0.5	0.3	-0.2	0.3	-	-	-	-	-
United Arab Emirates	147.6	-59.2	-2.3	-205.2	-42.2	.. c	.. c	.. c	10.0	13.6
Other Near and Middle East	-28.8	-2 107.0	-30.6	-89.2	1 596.7	317.3	330.2	163.2	-156.4	169.2
Jordan	0.0	.. c	.. c	0.0	0.0	-	-	-	-	-
Other Asian countries	353.5	95.0	1 609.8	1 345.3	1 625.1	-8.4	43.7	21.5	-138.4	35.7
China	80.9	8.7	58.1	152.7	256.8	7.9	3.3	-2.3	-1.6	4.6
Hong Kong, China	9.5	-275.9	277.8	-69.7	272.6	28.8	20.1	-67.2	-26.4	-5.2
India	-64.9	-0.5	8.0	5.5	-11.0	-1.1	0.6	-0.3	-2.4	-3.5
Indonesia	-3.5	4.7	0.7	-1.0	-0.2	-	-	-	.. c	.. c
Iran, Islamic Republic of	.. c	.. c	.. c	.. c	.. c	-	-	-	-	-
Malaysia	-22.1	3.3	24.7	0.7	-1.6	.. c	-	-	.. c	.. c
Philippines	-0.8	23.5	4.9	0.1	-34.7	.. c	.. c	-	.. c	.. c
Singapore	13.6	-63.3	-17.8	19.4	83.1	-71.2	-0.3	49.9	-112.4	22.8
Chinese Taipei	40.8	-54.8	-51.3	50.8	-13.1	.. c	.. c	.. c	0.6	1.1
Thailand	-1.2	-3.1	8.5	-2.4	5.6	-	-	-	-	-
Viet Nam	-0.2	0.7	-3.4	0.9	1.2	-	-	-	-	.. c
AUSTRALIA, OCEANIA AND POLAR REGIONS	**3.8**	**-44.9**	**170.6**	**114.4**	**306.6**	**9.7**	**-18.8**	**10.3**	**5.4**	**7.2**
WORLD unallocated and confidential	**127.7**	**131.0**	**-168.2**	**-190.3**	**-137.7**	**0.5**	**0.3**	**0.0**	**-**	**-**
European Union (since 01/02/2020)	**..**	**..**	**5 357.9**	**..**	**720.4**	**..**	**..**	**3 389.2**	**..**	**4 472.0**
G20 countries excl. European Union	**6 167.3**	**-2 061.3**	**1 360.7**	**6 413.7**	**1 109.7**	**530.6**	**298.4**	**595.8**	**735.1**	**282.4**
G20 OECD countries	**5 996.4**	**-2 131.8**	**1 122.6**	**6 092.7**	**964.7**	**361.8**	**33.2**	**511.5**	**528.5**	**325.4**
G20 Non-OECD countries	**170.9**	**70.5**	**238.1**	**321.0**	**145.0**	**168.8**	**265.3**	**84.3**	**206.6**	**-43.0**
MENA countries	**151.8**	**-57.2**	**3.4**	**-173.4**	**-101.4**	**19.7**	**22.8**	**13.1**	**7.5**	**2.6**
ASEAN countries	**-14.1**	**-34.4**	**17.6**	**17.7**	**53.4**	**-71.2**	**-0.3**	**49.9**	**-112.7**	**29.9**

- Nil; .. Not available; c Confidential data; d Secondary Confidentiality

Note: Data excludes resident Special Purpose Entities (SPEs). Detailed metadata at: *http://metalinks.oecd.org/idi/20220712/6d95*.

Source: OECD *International Direct Investment Statistics (database)*: *https://doi.org/10.1787/idi-data-en*

HUNGARY

Table 2. Foreign direct investment positions by country

At year end

Million US dollars

	Inward					Outward				
	2016	2017	2018	2019	2020	2016	2017	2018	2019	2020
WORLD	**82 701.0**	**93 537.1**	**92 067.2**	**93 448.4**	**101 323.9**	**25 018.8**	**29 846.5**	**28 903.9**	**32 279.7**	**36 992.0**
OECD COUNTRIES	**70 880.2**	**78 905.2**	**79 044.3**	**79 208.5**	..	**14 722.5**	**16 436.5**	**14 339.7**	**15 658.6**	.. d
Australia	28.9	6.6	4.6	15.3	..	33.6	31.9	8.1	17.1	48.7
Austria	6 608.4	8 205.0	9 119.8	9 389.1	..	93.7	104.4	112.2	72.5	33.8
Belgium	1 499.5	1 632.5	1 709.7	1 949.5	..	3 469.1	2 081.7	8.3	4.4	4.5
Canada	352.3	1 960.0	1 825.4	1 692.0	..	18.6	4.3	-17.5	-18.2	-21.4
Chile	-	-	-	-	..	.. c	.. c	.. c	.. c	.. c
Colombia	-	-	-	-	..	.. c	.. c	.. c	.. c	.. c
Costa Rica	-	-	-	-	..	-	-	-	-	-
Czech Republic	384.8	545.5	1 161.7	1 164.4	..	329.9	737.5	761.3	947.6	1 794.4
Denmark	781.3	995.1	953.9	963.0	..	.. c	.. c	.. c	.. c	.. c
Estonia	-	10.3	17.4	16.3	..	0.3	0.8	0.8	-0.4	-0.5
Finland	74.2	103.9	97.3	68.6	..	1.1	1.3	1.2	0.2	-
France	4 711.2	5 830.0	5 788.9	5 723.7	..	41.9	48.5	73.5	66.2	7.8
Germany	24 020.3	22 322.3	20 641.0	21 344.8	..	199.7	225.8	218.7	156.2	437.8
Greece	3.1	3.5	3.4	-	..	0.2	0.7	0.5	0.0	-0.1
Hungary	322.9	738.8	846.8	859.2	..	-	-	-	-	-
Iceland	-	-	-	-	..	-	.. c	.. c	.. c	.. c
Ireland	275.4	370.9	624.0	601.3	..	137.5	592.3	1 282.0	155.6	157.3
Israel	931.1	1 287.5	1 333.5	1 235.8	..	3 177.7	2 983.8	2 455.4	2 553.6	2 172.7
Italy	3 209.0	3 896.3	3 565.9	3 605.5	..	397.3	449.0	764.6	434.0	548.0
Japan	2 563.0	3 186.7	3 300.9	3 606.0	..	5.7	6.7	8.0	9.6	12.7
Korea	1 438.1	3 423.0	4 075.5	5 148.9	..	551.0	645.9	74.5	70.0	10.1
Latvia	-	-	-	-	..	0.8	2.7	2.5	3.7	4.1
Lithuania	3.5	3.6	4.3	4.1	..	4.3	6.9	7.7	7.0	1.7
Luxembourg	1 366.1	1 522.2	1 601.6	1 652.7	..	1 230.6	1 375.6	1 242.7	980.1	1 998.2
Mexico	162.8	182.9	161.4	145.0	..	136.7	164.2	153.7	137.4	118.7
Netherlands	2 285.3	2 722.4	3 217.2	3 169.1	..	-167.0	364.9	790.4	1 985.5	5 508.2
New Zealand	36.7	41.6	36.6	39.4	..	-	-	-	-	-
Norway	514.4	586.3	145.8	146.6	..	.. c	.. c	.. c	.. c	.. c
Poland	237.9	411.8	434.7	415.0	..	429.4	1 396.5	1 391.9	1 725.5	1 265.9
Portugal	76.2	99.1	11.7	17.3	..	-3.8	-4.1	-3.9	-3.3	-1.5
Slovak Republic	81.2	100.3	150.8	161.9	..	2 445.7	2 779.1	2 623.3	2 924.2	2 707.8
Slovenia	4.9	10.1	11.2	12.8	..	16.5	24.4	60.7	439.9	549.1
Spain	701.9	700.8	638.3	602.4	..	994.6	1 337.2	1 382.2	1 467.5	1 448.2
Sweden	463.3	605.8	727.1	860.0	..	0.2	.. c	6.4	14.2	17.6
Switzerland	1 855.0	2 342.6	2 648.6	2 771.1	..	285.9	335.9	-236.7	-337.1	-1 224.4
Turkey	53.5	63.1	58.1	102.8	..	27.1	23.2	12.7	13.9	18.4
United Kingdom	3 046.9	3 842.4	4 107.7	4 340.2	..	70.2	120.8	146.9	241.5	256.9
United States	12 790.4	11 156.0	10 019.6	7 384.9	..	796.8	596.7	1 001.9	1 585.6	1 746.4
EUROPE	**56 534.3**	**62 547.6**	**63 342.4**	**65 788.4**	..	**19 513.7**	**23 990.1**	**24 005.7**	**26 690.3**	**31 574.6**
Bulgaria	9.8	16.5	14.5	12.2	..	897.9	1 031.8	1 659.7	1 789.2	2 136.9
Croatia	12.6	27.3	38.3	30.7	..	2 952.7	4 284.9	4 258.0	4 213.2	4 354.0
Cyprus	973.0	887.5	1 028.1	982.4	..	3 008.0	3 060.5	3 884.7	4 185.0	3 793.7
Malta	402.9	222.3	193.8	234.6	..	128.5	199.6	273.4	347.0	452.5
Montenegro	-	-	-	-	..	172.5	81.9	136.3	202.5	267.4
Romania	146.0	259.4	302.9	398.1	..	1 181.9	1 554.3	1 470.0	1 913.7	2 220.6
Russian Federation	640.6	856.0	1 025.3	1 217.7	..	463.8	783.0	616.0	775.8	640.2
Ukraine	456.3	554.6	562.2	362.1	..	116.2	157.3	216.5	352.0	367.7
AFRICA	**274.7**	**283.5**	**243.4**	**254.6**	..	**6.0**	**6.3**	**7.6**	**6.3**	**-22.2**
Northern Africa	0.1	0.1	0.1	14.1	..	2.7	2.6	-0.3	1.8	1.8
Algeria	-	-	-	-	..	-	-	-	-	-
Egypt	0.1	0.1	0.1	14.1	..	.. c	2.2	.. c	.. c	.. c
Libya	-	-	-	-	..	.. c	.. c	.. c	.. c	-
Morocco	-	-	-	-	..	-	.. c	.. c	.. c	.. c
Tunisia	-	-	-	-	..	-	-	-	-	-
Other African countries	274.6	283.4	243.3	240.5	..	.. c	.. c	.. c	4.5	-24.0
Nigeria	-	-	-	-	..	-	-	-	-	-
South Africa	48.6	65.7	120.5	114.2	..	.. c	.. c	.. c	-	.. c
AMERICA	**13 345.5**	**13 545.1**	**12 255.0**	**9 429.0**	..	**1 100.9**	**1 496.2**	**1 592.9**	**2 259.4**	**2 340.8**
Northern America	13 142.7	13 116.0	11 845.0	9 076.9	..	815.4	601.0	984.4	1 567.4	1 725.0
Central America and Caribbean countries	193.1	418.5	400.0	349.7	..	144.1	690.5	187.6	181.7	170.4
Bahamas	1.9	6.8	30.6	30.6	..	-	-	-	-	-
Bermuda	2.6	0.6	-	-6.1	..	-	-	-	-	.. c
Cayman Islands	39.3	34.5	31.7	35.6	..	-	.. c	.. c	-	-
El Salvador	-	-	-	-	..	-	-	.. c	.. c	.. c
Guatemala	-	-	-	-	..	-	-	.. c	.. c	.. c
Honduras	-	-	-	-	..	-	-	-	-	-
Nicaragua	-	-	-	-	..	-	-	-	-	-
Panama	13.6	13.2	1.0	-1.4	..	.. c	-	-	-	-
Virgin Islands, U.S.	-	-	-	-	..	-	-	-	-	-
South America	9.7	10.6	9.9	2.4	..	141.4	204.7	421.0	510.3	445.4
Argentina	5.6	6.3	6.1	-	..	.. c	.. c	.. c	.. c	.. c
Bolivia	-	-	-	-	..	-	-	-	-	-
Brazil	1.8	1.5	1.3	-	..	109.6	194.1	414.5	502.9	439.0
Ecuador	-	-	-	-	..	.. c	-	-	-	-
Paraguay	-	-	-	-	..	-	-	-	-	-
Peru	-	-	-	-	..	.. c	-	-	-	-
Uruguay	2.3	2.8	2.5	2.4	..	.. c	.. c	.. c	-	-
Venezuela	-	-	-	-	..	-	-	-	-	-

Table 2. Foreign direct investment positions by country *(cont.)*

At year end

Million US dollars

	Inward					Outward				
	2016	2017	2018	2019	2020	2016	2017	2018	2019	2020
ASIA	**10 009.1**	**14 163.1**	**16 065.5**	**17 776.7**	**..**	**4 351.1**	**4 308.6**	**3 277.2**	**3 294.8**	**3 038.4**
Near and Middle East	1 345.0	1 676.5	1 656.4	1 618.2	..	3 481.0	3 315.1	2 766.6	2 873.1	2 476.0
Gulf Arabian countries	411.6	386.4	317.8	364.8	..	294.5	322.6	302.2	310.0	294.9
Kuwait	-	-	-	-	..	-	-	-	-	-
Qatar	-8.0	-9.5	-12.1	31.4	..	-	-	-	-	-
Saudi Arabia	6.3	7.0	8.4	4.5	..	-	-	-	-	-
United Arab Emirates	413.3	388.8	261.3	262.3	..	.. c	90.0	82.7	94.8	91.3
Other Near and Middle East	933.4	1 290.2	1 338.6	1 253.4	..	3 186.5	2 992.6	2 464.4	2 563.1	2 181.2
Jordan	-	-	-	-	..	-	-	-	-	-
Other Asian countries	8 664.1	12 486.5	14 409.1	16 158.5	..	870.0	993.4	510.5	421.7	562.3
China	1 933.8	1 989.3	2 575.7	2 677.2	..	35.8	40.8	38.5	38.6	43.9
Hong Kong, China	177.6	231.1	274.3	276.7	..	-19.9	-2.0	-22.6	-47.3	-44.7
India	2 200.4	2 676.1	3 161.2	2 880.3	..	23.1	25.4	27.0	27.3	24.1
Indonesia	-	-	-	-	..	-	-	-	.. c	.. c
Iran, Islamic Republic of	-	-	-	-	..	-	-	-	-	-
Malaysia	26.0	30.7	36.9	37.7	..	.. c	.. c	.. c	-6.6	-2.9
Philippines	-	-	-	-	..	.. c	-	-	.. c	.. c
Singapore	22.9	-56.1	-231.6	-4.2	..	254.8	245.9	328.3	231.9	413.1
Chinese Taipei	299.7	978.7	1 195.8	1 521.0	..	.. c	.. c	.. c	1.4	2.3
Thailand	5.1	9.1	8.6	8.3	..	-	-	-	-	-
Viet Nam	-	-	-	-	..	.. c	.. c	.. c	.. c	.. c
AUSTRALIA, OCEANIA AND POLAR REGIONS	**65.7**	**48.2**	**41.1**	**62.5**	**..**	**33.6**	**31.9**	**8.1**	**17.1**	**48.7**
WORLD unallocated and confidential	**2 471.8**	**2 949.6**	**119.8**	**137.2**	**..**	**13.6**	**13.3**	**12.4**	**11.8**	**11.7**
European Union (since 01/02/2020)	**..**	**..**	**..**	**..**	**..**	**..**	**..**	**22 273.2**	**..**	**29 440.5**
G20 countries excl. European Union	**57 213.3**	**61 471.2**	**60 447.4**	**60 002.8**	**..**	**2 943.6**	**3 372.5**	**3 545.7**	**4 064.0**	**4 310.7**
G20 OECD countries	**52 376.2**	**55 869.3**	**53 549.0**	**53 108.9**	**..**	**2 278.5**	**2 317.0**	**2 445.1**	**2 713.3**	**3 184.2**
G20 Non-OECD countries	**4 837.1**	**5 601.9**	**6 898.5**	**6 893.9**	**..**	**665.1**	**1 055.5**	**1 100.7**	**1 350.7**	**1 126.6**
MENA countries	**414.0**	**389.1**	**323.1**	**393.4**	**..**	**297.2**	**325.2**	**301.9**	**311.8**	**296.7**
ASEAN countries	**54.1**	**-16.4**	**-186.2**	**41.7**	**..**	**247.7**	**237.3**	**320.2**	**235.9**	**419.1**

- Nil; .. Not available; c Confidential data; d Secondary Confidentiality

Note: Data excludes resident Special Purpose Entities (SPEs). Inward FDI positions are allocated according to the ultimate investing country. Inward FDI positions by immediate counterpart country are available for the most recent year in the OECD FDI database according to BMD4. Detailed metadata at: *http://metalinks.oecd.org/idi/20220712/6d95*.

Source: OECD *International Direct Investment Statistics (database): https://doi.org/10.1787/idi-data-en*

HUNGARY

Table 3. Foreign direct investment income by country

Million US dollars

	Inward					Outward				
	2016	2017	2018	2019	2020	2016	2017	2018	2019	2020
WORLD	**7 682.1**	**10 474.0**	**10 575.6**	**9 250.2**	**8 262.9**	**1 822.6**	**2 149.5**	**1 893.7**	**2 209.1**	**1 429.7**
OECD COUNTRIES	**6 183.6**	**8 876.2**	**9 266.8**	**8 298.9**	**.. d**	**1 019.5**	**1 143.5**	**798.8**	**977.3**	**.. d**
Australia	21.3	1.1	-0.2	1.9	0.2	.. c	0.8	9.2	8.8	2.6
Austria	855.8	981.2	1 248.4	1 389.5	1 192.5	-0.5	9.9	17.5	9.6	-6.6
Belgium	17.0	137.4	193.3	190.1	170.8	52.3	1.5	1.5	0.6	0.5
Canada	29.9	38.6	10.0	-0.6	-1.1	.. c	.. c	.. c	.. c	.. c
Chile	.. c	.. c	.. c	-	-	-	.. c	.. c	-	.. c
Colombia	-	-	.. c	.. c	.. c	.. c	.. c	.. c	.. c	.. c
Costa Rica	-	-	-	-	-	-	-	-	-	-
Czech Republic	45.6	42.8	53.4	86.5	51.9	24.2	23.9	-21.3	48.7	84.3
Denmark	118.2	155.7	211.3	125.0	148.1	.. c	.. c	.. c	.. c	.. c
Estonia	-	-	-	-	-	-0.3	0.0	-0.1	-0.1	0.0
Finland	7.7	17.5	27.8	31.3	27.5	0.0	0.1	-0.1	-0.2	-
France	535.1	597.1	548.4	459.2	532.0	5.6	12.4	12.5	11.5	1.5
Germany	1 229.8	1 889.2	2 117.9	1 656.4	1 848.5	9.7	23.1	12.9	6.5	127.1
Greece	-0.9	-	0.0	0.0	0.3	0.0	0.0	-0.4	-0.2	-0.1
Hungary	-	-	-	-	-	-	-	-	-	-
Iceland	-	-	-	-	-	-	.. c	.. c	.. c	-
Ireland	188.6	158.5	328.6	42.9	-23.9	1.4	-1.7	140.9	2.7	5.9
Israel	8.3	7.1	-64.0	-83.3	-22.5	320.6	267.3	142.0	176.2	157.5
Italy	287.7	183.8	159.9	225.7	195.6	-7.6	-6.9	23.6	3.6	-10.8
Japan	98.5	122.0	122.6	75.7	6.2	3.0	1.5	1.8	2.0	-0.7
Korea	158.3	178.9	153.4	163.3	337.6	108.2	102.1	1.2	0.0	-3.0
Latvia	-	-	-	-	-	-1.1	-1.5	-2.3	-2.0	-1.4
Lithuania	5.0	3.2	6.6	7.0	8.9	-3.1	-4.1	-5.3	-6.4	-4.5
Luxembourg	348.1	845.9	1 000.9	763.0	717.5	79.3	85.4	41.0	95.4	52.0
Mexico	-24.2	-17.2	-18.7	-20.2	.. c	82.6	14.3	14.0	-7.2	23.2
Netherlands	1 250.1	1 625.2	1 718.9	1 767.9	1 728.9	-21.0	173.9	123.9	384.6	22.9
New Zealand	.. c	.. c	.. c	.. c	.. c	-	-	-	-	-
Norway	96.5	117.5	1.1	1.5	5.0	-	-	-	-	-
Poland	45.5	45.4	146.4	222.5	-15.6	32.6	76.5	46.4	139.8	-99.0
Portugal	58.4	62.8	0.8	7.0	3.9	3.0	0.1	0.1	0.1	0.1
Slovak Republic	29.2	19.2	37.1	45.4	48.8	275.8	212.1	199.8	96.9	-107.0
Slovenia	5.3	6.2	7.6	8.0	8.5	7.4	11.4	9.6	63.6	79.1
Spain	165.4	230.7	169.9	84.6	27.7	-0.4	19.5	5.4	-2.2	-6.3
Sweden	68.9	73.0	96.8	79.0	150.6	.. c	.. c	0.5	2.7	62.4
Switzerland	164.5	834.4	596.7	424.5	326.4	58.4	127.3	84.7	-44.5	-71.9
Turkey	7.1	6.2	9.6	0.2	0.9	-7.2	-2.8	-3.1	-1.1	3.3
United Kingdom	410.7	516.7	323.8	364.6	408.1	14.3	22.7	31.8	54.3	2.5
United States	-31.9	-1.4	64.5	182.6	139.7	-26.7	-35.2	-93.2	-70.3	11.6
EUROPE	**6 518.4**	**9 208.6**	**9 780.9**	**8 551.6**	**7 496.8**	**1 189.7**	**1 703.0**	**1 759.4**	**2 033.0**	**1 211.0**
Bulgaria	-1.2	-0.7	0.8	-0.1	0.2	154.7	136.8	169.8	214.9	185.9
Croatia	-3.2	3.6	17.0	4.2	2.5	84.9	171.6	153.5	205.5	48.0
Cyprus	112.5	329.2	299.5	33.9	109.1	277.0	266.8	467.2	272.8	340.7
Malta	132.2	38.6	43.8	40.2	12.0	23.8	120.1	64.9	59.7	68.7
Montenegro	-	-	-	-	-	2.7	-0.2	8.5	15.5	11.4
Romania	15.0	5.4	-3.6	-20.1	-22.6	47.4	68.8	40.8	83.2	35.1
Russian Federation	8.8	14.2	-6.7	98.3	-38.7	39.7	48.3	59.5	87.7	55.1
Ukraine	-0.5	0.1	0.3	5.9	7.5	5.4	61.3	53.9	100.5	96.1
AFRICA	**319.4**	**281.3**	**158.0**	**164.1**	**149.4**	**13.4**	**3.7**	**-7.0**	**-5.5**	**-13.6**
Northern Africa	0.0	0.0	0.0	1.3	-4.0	-0.5	-0.6	-2.8	-0.3	-0.1
Algeria	-	-	-	-	-	-	-	-	-	-
Egypt	-	-	-	1.4	-4.0	.. c	.. c	.. c	.. c	-
Libya	-	-	-	-	-	-	-	-	-	-
Morocco	-	-	-	-	-	-	.. c	.. c	.. c	.. c
Tunisia	.. c	.. c	.. c	.. c	-	-	-	-	-	-
Other African countries	319.4	281.4	158.0	162.8	153.4	.. c	.. c	.. c	-5.1	-13.5
Nigeria	-	-	-	-	-	-	-	-	-	-
South Africa	.. c	.. c	.. c	.. c	.. c	.. c	.. c	.. c	.. c	.. c
AMERICA	**207.5**	**195.3**	**162.1**	**184.2**	**161.6**	**138.0**	**41.6**	**-30.5**	**-49.4**	**31.8**
Northern America	-2.0	37.2	74.5	182.0	138.5	-21.2	-30.1	-89.2	-67.0	12.5
Central America and Caribbean countries	209.6	157.8	88.0	12.1	32.9	83.0	18.4	15.8	-5.4	25.5
Bahamas	.. c	1.4	1.4	0.8	.. c	-	-	-	-	-
Bermuda	.. c	.. c	.. c	.. c	.. c	-	-	-	.. c	.. c
Cayman Islands	206.9	96.3	63.2	-1.0	-3.5	-	-	-	-	-
El Salvador	-	-	-	-	-	-	-	.. c	.. c	.. c
Guatemala	-	-	-	-	-	-	-	.. c	.. c	.. c
Honduras	-	-	-	-	-	-	-	-	-	-
Nicaragua	-	-	-	-	-	-	-	-	-	-
Panama	4.2	10.3	5.7	-1.2	-1.1	.. c	-	-	-	-
Virgin Islands, U.S.	-	-	-	-	-	-	-	-	-	-
South America	-0.1	0.2	-0.5	-9.9	-9.8	76.2	53.3	43.0	22.9	-6.2
Argentina	-	-	-	-	-	.. c	.. c	.. c	.. c	.. c
Bolivia	-	-	-	-	-	-	-	-	-	-
Brazil	.. c	.. c	-0.2	.. c	.. c	73.2	50.6	45.9	24.2	-3.5
Ecuador	-	-	-	-	-	-	-	-	-	-
Paraguay	-	-	-	-	-	-	-	-	-	-
Peru	-	-	-	-	-	-	-	-	-	-
Uruguay	.. c	.. c	.. c	.. c	.. c	-	-	-	-	-
Venezuela	-	-	-	-	-	-	-	-	-	-

Table 3. Foreign direct investment income by country *(cont.)*

Million US dollars

	Inward					Outward				
	2016	2017	2018	2019	2020	2016	2017	2018	2019	2020
ASIA	**344.5**	**414.2**	**437.8**	**307.0**	**413.4**	**481.1**	**400.2**	**162.6**	**222.3**	**197.8**
Near and Middle East	10.3	-15.9	-46.1	-54.6	-35.7	360.0	291.6	169.8	207.4	176.3
Gulf Arabian countries	2.1	-22.9	18.0	25.8	-14.1	39.2	24.8	28.6	32.0	19.1
Kuwait	-	-	-	-	-	.. c	-	-	-	-
Qatar	.. c	.. c	.. c	.. c	.. c	-	-	-	-	-
Saudi Arabia	-	.. c	-	-	-	-	-	-	-	-
United Arab Emirates	5.3	-18.6	25.4	32.9	-6.4	.. c	.. c	.. c	.. c	.. c
Other Near and Middle East	8.2	7.0	-64.1	-80.5	-21.6	320.8	266.8	141.2	175.4	157.2
Jordan	-	-	-	-	-	-	-	-	-	-
Other Asian countries	334.2	430.0	483.9	361.6	449.1	121.1	108.6	-7.2	14.9	21.5
China	46.4	55.3	71.0	37.7	37.5	3.3	-2.5	0.8	2.4	8.9
Hong Kong, China	6.9	23.2	92.4	52.3	22.8	.. c	-2.5	-46.9	1.5	0.4
India	1.9	5.6	5.8	-3.1	-0.1	0.6	1.3	1.7	1.0	0.7
Indonesia	-	-	-	-	-	-	-	-	.. c	.. c
Iran, Islamic Republic of	-	-	-	-	-	-	-	-	-	-
Malaysia	1.8	0.8	.. c	-0.2	.. c	.. c	-	-	.. c	.. c
Philippines	.. c	.. c	.. c	.. c	.. c	-	-	-	-	-
Singapore	19.7	26.2	28.7	38.1	47.1	3.7	7.0	31.5	2.5	4.1
Chinese Taipei	-	.. c	.. c	.. c	-	.. c	.. c	.. c	.. c	.. c
Thailand	.. c	.. c	.. c	.. c	.. c	-	-	-	-	-
Viet Nam	-	-	-	-	-	-	-	-	-	.. c
AUSTRALIA, OCEANIA AND POLAR REGIONS	**10.7**	**1.8**	**-5.7**	**4.6**	**7.9**	**.. c**	**0.8**	**9.2**	**8.8**	**2.6**
WORLD unallocated and confidential	**281.7**	**372.9**	**42.6**	**38.7**	**33.8**	**.. d**	**0.3**	**0.0**	**-**	**0.0**
European Union (since 01/02/2020)	**..**	**..**	**8 431.5**	**..**	**6 923.6**	**..**	**..**	**1 502.4**	**..**	**878.5**
G20 countries excl. European Union	**2 779.1**	**3 590.0**	**3 561.0**	**3 242.3**	**3 449.9**	**320.9**	**242.0**	**117.4**	**122.9**	**206.8**
G20 OECD countries	**2 722.2**	**3 515.0**	**3 491.2**	**3 108.7**	**3 450.5**	**187.4**	**137.2**	**14.6**	**11.5**	**158.2**
G20 Non-OECD countries	**56.9**	**75.0**	**69.7**	**133.6**	**-0.6**	**133.5**	**104.9**	**102.9**	**111.4**	**48.6**
MENA countries	**2.0**	**-22.9**	**18.0**	**28.0**	**-17.8**	**38.8**	**24.2**	**25.8**	**31.6**	**19.1**
ASEAN countries	**23.7**	**50.9**	**45.2**	**41.1**	**49.3**	**3.6**	**7.0**	**31.5**	**2.3**	**5.8**

- Nil; .. Not available; c Confidential data; d Secondary Confidentiality

Note: Data excludes resident Special Purpose Entities (SPEs). Detailed metadata at: *http://metalinks.oecd.org/idi/20220712/6d95*.

Source: OECD *International Direct Investment Statistics (database)*: *https://doi.org/10.1787/idi-data-en*

HUNGARY

Table 4. Foreign direct investment flows by industrial sector

Million US dollars

	Inward					Outward				
	2016	2017	2018	2019	2020	2016	2017	2018	2019	2020
All FDI activities	**-5 438.6**	**3 527.5**	**6 460.1**	**4 105.1**	**6 721.5**	**-8 272.2**	**1 221.6**	**3 363.5**	**3 238.2**	**4 286.3**
Agriculture, forestry and fishing	**10.5**	**43.6**	**-28.8**	**23.0**	**21.2**	**-0.1**	**-0.7**	**9.8**	**15.3**	**-1.4**
Mining and quarrying	**-19.0**	**0.7**	**87.0**	**-29.5**	**-26.8**	**22.6**	**143.4**	**-185.2**	**520.0**	**937.3**
Extraction activities	..	..	..	..	..	..	..	..	..	..
Manufacturing	**16 552.9**	**1 262.3**	**3 398.0**	**3 573.5**	**4 419.4**	**1 478.4**	**1 229.9**	**259.8**	**747.3**	**-216.2**
of which:										
Food products, beverages and tobacco	151.4	47.4	-484.9	51.3	156.6	5.6	7.7	29.4	6.3	22.2
Textiles, wood and paper products; printing	524.3	91.6	-18.8	301.3	-17.4	5.1	5.2	76.2	52.5	7.5
Chemical, rubber, plastic, non-metallic mineral products	964.6	1 269.4	1 329.6	423.0	2 714.5	825.6	189.4	200.0	-94.5	-251.3
Metal and machinery products, except electrical equipment	14 054.3	2 617.0	1 497.6	1 341.2	515.9	501.1	854.5	-88.1	698.8	104.1
Motor vehicles, trailers, semi-trailers, other transport equipment	548.2	-2 717.1	296.9	680.5	193.8	87.0	117.1	16.1	126.3	-100.3
Other manufacturing	310.1	-46.0	777.6	776.3	856.0	54.0	56.2	26.1	-42.3	1.6
Electricity, gas, steam and air conditioning supply	**-243.1**	**-455.5**	**-520.9**	**-271.0**	**-364.2**	**-18.0**	**23.9**	**-30.2**	**-30.6**	**-3.3**
Water supply; sewerage, waste management and remediation activities	**2.3**	**9.0**	**-6.5**	**3.2**	**3.1**	**0.6**	**1.6**	**1.3**	**2.3**	**-1.3**
Construction	**121.7**	**-53.3**	**120.1**	**62.0**	**-0.2**	**24.7**	**-4.4**	**3.2**	**21.9**	**52.0**
Services	**-22 150.2**	**2 373.5**	**3 047.6**	**375.8**	**2 418.2**	**-10 141.4**	**-608.8**	**2 381.1**	**1 326.0**	**3 570.5**
Wholesale and retail trade; repair of motor vehicles and motorcycles	-166.6	676.3	1 471.0	514.5	1 062.0	-153.8	206.8	160.2	-12.0	36.4
Transportation and storage	630.9	327.6	-131.6	1 049.2	-77.5	30.9	13.4	76.7	3.2	3.2
Accommodation and food service activities	60.5	64.4	-10.5	256.8	-154.9	-17.5	-71.1	-0.8	24.2	9.3
Information and communication	-340.0	-404.7	7.3	180.4	294.4	53.4	-50.1	-50.9	391.4	26.5
Financial and insurance activities	-9 860.4	27.1	562.3	132.5	856.5	596.2	-826.8	903.5	1 301.6	967.2
Activities of holding companies	-10 430.7	-64.5	286.9	-99.7	174.3	155.0	405.3	448.2	403.1	1 191.9
Real estate activities	-97.5	135.5	286.1	-673.6	-106.5	6.8	-1.6	33.7	477.5	258.5
Professional, scientific and technical activities	-3 715.1	78.7	920.6	92.0	655.1	221.6	57.1	-75.3	159.7	1 010.5
Administrative and support service activities	-8 754.4	1 390.5	-85.1	-1 205.9	-121.6	-10 887.7	58.8	1 336.3	-1 018.1	1 261.4
Public administration; activities of households and of extraterritorial organisations	-	0.0	0.0	0.0	-	-	-	-	-	-
Education	-0.4	3.3	11.5	8.0	2.3	1.2	0.1	0.7	0.0	-1.4
Human health and social work activities	9.8	9.1	10.3	28.9	1.8	2.0	1.0	0.7	1.3	1.1
Arts, entertainment and recreation	5.3	54.3	1.3	-3.7	5.9	2.8	2.6	-0.2	-0.8	-1.9
Other services	77.8	11.5	4.4	-3.2	0.8	2.7	1.0	-3.5	-2.1	-0.5
Not allocated and confidential	**0.0**	**0.0**	**0.0**	**0.0**	**-**	**0.0**	**0.0**	**0.3**	**0.0**	**0.0**
Private real estate activities	**286.2**	**347.3**	**363.5**	**368.0**	**250.9**	**361.1**	**436.5**	**923.4**	**635.9**	**-51.2**

- Nil; .. Not available

Note: Data excludes resident Special Purpose Entities (SPEs). Detailed metadata at: *http://metalinks.oecd.org/idi/20220712/6d95*.

Source: *OECD International Direct Investment Statistics (database)*: *https://doi.org/10.1787/idi-data-en*

HUNGARY

Table 5. Foreign direct investment positions by industrial sector
At year end

Million US dollars

	Inward					Outward				
	2016	2017	2018	2019	2020	2016	2017	2018	2019	2020
All FDI activities	**82 701.0**	**93 537.1**	**92 067.2**	**93 448.4**	**101 323.9**	**25 018.8**	**29 846.5**	**28 903.9**	**32 279.7**	**36 992.0**
Agriculture, forestry and fishing	**547.3**	**672.9**	**597.3**	**576.7**	**627.8**	**3.3**	**3.1**	**9.1**	**31.7**	**27.3**
Mining and quarrying	**229.0**	**377.9**	**423.2**	**382.5**	**353.4**	**2 887.1**	**3 273.1**	**2 896.5**	**3 381.0**	**4 000.7**
Extraction activities	..	..	..	..	..	..	..	..	..	..
Manufacturing	**24 494.8**	**39 236.7**	**37 850.8**	**39 787.2**	**45 397.6**	**7 846.0**	**9 979.7**	**9 960.1**	**10 703.2**	**9 640.8**
of which:										
Food products, beverages and tobacco	2 301.3	2 714.6	2 293.6	2 241.0	2 519.9	42.2	67.8	70.5	107.5	125.8
Textiles, wood and paper products; printing	1 805.7	2 198.9	1 962.2	2 070.4	1 882.5	70.0	83.2	150.9	201.4	217.9
Chemical, rubber, plastic, non-metallic mineral products	6 561.9	8 736.9	9 547.6	9 657.0	13 299.6	5 631.0	5 728.7	5 571.5	5 780.2	4 826.7
Metal and machinery products, except electrical equipment	4 686.8	7 689.3	8 348.7	9 539.1	10 301.7	1 391.7	2 611.5	2 817.6	3 081.4	3 474.9
Motor vehicles, trailers, semi-trailers, other transport equipment	5 089.6	13 404.9	11 011.9	11 045.9	11 314.6	295.3	992.7	858.2	1 076.2	513.6
Other manufacturing	4 049.6	4 492.1	4 686.7	5 233.8	6 079.4	415.8	495.7	491.3	456.6	481.9
Electricity, gas, steam and air conditioning supply	**2 392.4**	**2 275.4**	**1 475.2**	**1 277.4**	**1 267.1**	**23.5**	**41.6**	**10.4**	**8.5**	**14.9**
Water supply; sewerage, waste management and remediation activities	**62.7**	**88.1**	**75.7**	**77.0**	**85.6**	**16.6**	**17.9**	**15.9**	**16.3**	**18.2**
Construction	**931.3**	**1 100.6**	**1 177.7**	**1 197.9**	**1 185.0**	**15.2**	**25.6**	**28.8**	**154.5**	**240.1**
Services	**50 688.9**	**45 108.4**	**45 126.6**	**44 039.7**	**45 848.4**	**9 904.0**	**11 410.1**	**10 109.6**	**11 553.4**	**16 698.4**
Wholesale and retail trade; repair of motor vehicles and motorcycles	8 074.2	9 842.2	9 440.7	9 615.0	10 733.5	1 544.0	1 861.0	1 398.3	1 395.3	1 690.0
Transportation and storage	1 925.3	2 597.1	2 059.1	2 891.8	2 850.8	64.1	85.6	84.6	107.3	107.9
Accommodation and food service activities	695.1	902.6	913.3	1 169.5	929.2	137.6	77.3	76.0	64.4	72.4
Information and communication	5 117.6	4 951.7	4 608.2	4 781.6	4 856.0	470.9	256.9	209.2	633.1	725.5
Financial and insurance activities	6 459.3	7 901.6	8 161.6	8 430.7	9 223.8	7 065.1	8 292.9	6 422.7	8 022.5	9 350.1
Activities of holding companies	118.4	4.3	916.1	855.0	933.9	1 397.4	2 360.9	2 959.5	3 001.0	4 359.9
Real estate activities	5 743.4	6 967.5	8 169.3	7 694.5	7 819.4	98.4	141.4	163.8	512.1	768.9
Professional, scientific and technical activities	15 887.2	6 206.1	6 198.3	6 378.4	7 760.9	401.6	525.9	473.0	512.3	1 576.8
Administrative and support service activities	6 631.1	5 483.1	5 358.1	2 850.7	1 420.3	78.9	114.8	1 233.1	257.7	2 365.3
Public administration; activities of households and of extraterritorial organisations	-	0.2	0.0	0.0	-	-	-	-	-	-
Education	23.5	31.4	44.0	39.3	36.0	1.2	1.4	2.1	-0.6	-2.0
Human health and social work activities	61.2	81.0	82.8	107.5	100.1	4.4	7.1	7.4	8.5	10.2
Arts, entertainment and recreation	28.1	88.3	45.8	39.7	67.8	19.9	23.8	22.4	26.0	19.2
Other services	42.7	55.7	45.4	41.0	50.7	17.8	22.0	17.0	14.7	14.1
Not allocated and confidential	**0.0**	**0.0**	**-**	**0.0**	**0.0**	**0.3**	**0.4**	**0.3**	**-**	**-**
Private real estate activities	**3 354.5**	**4 677.0**	**5 340.7**	**6 110.0**	**6 558.9**	**4 322.7**	**5 095.0**	**5 873.2**	**6 431.2**	**6 351.7**

- Nil; .. Not available

Note: Data excludes resident Special Purpose Entities (SPEs). Detailed metadata at: *http://metalinks.oecd.org/idi/20220712/6d95*.

Source: *OECD International Direct Investment Statistics (database)*: *https://doi.org/10.1787/idi-data-en*

HUNGARY

Table 6. Foreign direct investment income by industrial sector

Million US dollars

	Inward					Outward				
	2016	2017	2018	2019	2020	2016	2017	2018	2019	2020
All FDI activities	**7 682.1**	**10 474.0**	**10 575.6**	**9 250.2**	**8 262.9**	**1 822.6**	**2 149.5**	**1 893.7**	**2 209.1**	**1 429.7**
Agriculture, forestry and fishing	**38.9**	**56.2**	**54.6**	**66.3**	**66.8**	**0.0**	**0.0**	**0.1**	**-0.4**	**0.3**
Mining and quarrying	**4.6**	**30.3**	**52.5**	**30.7**	**20.4**	**33.3**	**229.2**	**140.4**	**133.9**	**37.3**
Extraction activities	..	..	..	..	..	..	..	..	..	..
Manufacturing	**3 784.6**	**5 024.4**	**4 760.3**	**3 613.2**	**3 899.7**	**868.9**	**958.5**	**541.7**	**502.9**	**294.3**
of which:										
Food products, beverages and tobacco	336.8	249.9	294.6	217.1	296.4	1.8	15.1	-6.9	7.8	4.8
Textiles, wood and paper products; printing	171.8	155.5	180.3	238.8	170.1	10.1	12.2	3.3	11.1	14.9
Chemical, rubber, plastic, non-metallic mineral products	1 325.0	1 991.7	1 710.7	1 344.6	1 521.8	607.0	585.4	307.2	246.1	69.3
Metal and machinery products, except electrical equipment	712.9	1 037.8	1 151.9	795.7	602.1	188.0	259.9	247.5	220.5	82.7
Motor vehicles, trailers, semi-trailers, other transport equipment	749.0	1 045.5	909.5	605.1	788.9	27.9	31.2	-42.5	-9.4	104.1
Other manufacturing	489.1	543.9	513.3	411.8	520.3	34.1	54.7	33.1	26.8	18.4
Electricity, gas, steam and air conditioning supply	**156.7**	**116.1**	**111.8**	**157.9**	**62.5**	**-16.5**	**-7.1**	**0.5**	**0.6**	**0.9**
Water supply; sewerage, waste management and remediation activities	**7.5**	**11.0**	**9.8**	**13.6**	**12.4**	**2.6**	**3.2**	**1.4**	**1.0**	**-1.2**
Construction	**127.8**	**113.7**	**115.9**	**355.6**	**176.4**	**26.8**	**4.5**	**4.9**	**6.4**	**-12.7**
Services	**3 562.0**	**5 122.2**	**5 470.6**	**5 012.8**	**4 024.7**	**669.7**	**748.8**	**888.7**	**1 260.1**	**801.2**
Wholesale and retail trade; repair of motor vehicles and motorcycles	1 068.2	1 372.0	1 419.7	1 505.1	1 423.8	224.9	205.8	176.7	171.4	149.5
Transportation and storage	496.6	455.4	591.3	587.7	92.2	-12.9	-16.9	-19.8	-31.0	-30.6
Accommodation and food service activities	58.4	88.8	96.6	189.3	-83.0	7.7	4.8	-0.7	2.6	-6.6
Information and communication	531.6	511.3	656.1	728.7	605.7	16.7	11.4	3.5	49.5	55.3
Financial and insurance activities	560.9	1 077.4	1 002.4	789.4	825.8	379.9	502.7	624.3	913.9	619.4
Activities of holding companies	6.7	230.8	119.8	-39.5	53.3	112.7	206.7	330.3	325.9	90.2
Real estate activities	148.7	427.9	259.5	343.6	261.9	1.9	1.6	10.3	139.3	-19.9
Professional, scientific and technical activities	285.5	275.3	702.0	659.2	814.8	6.8	61.7	9.2	41.6	136.6
Administrative and support service activities	369.6	880.1	719.9	192.3	58.4	38.9	-26.5	86.9	-25.6	-99.9
Public administration; activities of households and of extraterritorial organisations	-	0.0	0.0	0.0	-	-	-	-	-	-
Education	1.7	5.0	7.1	3.6	4.3	-0.1	0.1	0.7	-0.2	-1.6
Human health and social work activities	9.3	11.0	6.7	6.8	8.9	0.9	1.0	0.7	1.3	1.1
Arts, entertainment and recreation	28.8	12.8	4.7	5.3	7.8	2.9	2.6	-0.2	-0.8	-1.7
Other services	2.7	5.1	4.7	1.7	4.1	1.9	0.4	-3.0	-1.9	-0.5
Not allocated and confidential	**0.0**	**0.0**	**0.0**	**0.0**	**0.0**	**0.0**	**0.0**	**0.0**	**0.0**	**0.0**
Private real estate activities	-	-	-	-	-	**237.8**	**212.4**	**316.1**	**304.5**	**309.6**

- Nil; .. Not available

Note: Data excludes resident Special Purpose Entities (SPEs). Detailed metadata at: *http://metalinks.oecd.org/idi/20220712/6d95*.

Source: *OECD International Direct Investment Statistics (database)*: *https://doi.org/10.1787/idi-data-en*

ICELAND

Table 1. Foreign direct investment flows by country

Million US dollars

	Inward					Outward				
	2016	2017	2018	2019	2020	2016	2017	2018	2019	2020
WORLD	**-427.2**	**-41.4**	**-381.6**	**-224.8**	**-1 026.8**	**-1 147.3**	**-208.3**	**76.0**	**478.7**	**-356.1**
OECD COUNTRIES	**-679.8**	**154.3**	**-432.6**	**-458.9**	**-1 076.2**	**-1 171.4**	**-291.8**	**51.2**	**382.4**	**-527.5**
Australia	-5.2	87.2	-0.8	-0.2	1.3	-3.8	-6.6	0.9	6.6	-6.0
Austria	1.8	-4.3	-6.4	2.3	-0.9	-	-	-	-	-
Belgium	36.7	-1.4	0.0	3.1	1.1	0.3	0.1	0.0	1.9	1.3
Canada	-134.7	44.9	0.3	-20.5	0.1	-44.5	-29.5	4.2	6.6	-0.1
Chile	-	-	-	-	-	4.6	6.1	-10.7	-0.8	-1.6
Colombia	-	-	-	-	-	-	-	0.0	-	-
Costa Rica	-	-	-	-	-	-	-	-	-	-
Czech Republic	5.2	-3.9	-3.0	0.6	-0.2	0.0	0.0	0.0	16.4	-40.4
Denmark	30.7	174.3	46.5	3.5	5.6	5.7	-3.5	-5.6	6.2	-6.1
Estonia	-	-	-	-	-	4.9	4.1	-15.0	4.2	4.5
Finland	5.8	21.5	3.1	-2.6	-2.3	-25.3	-2.1	-3.9	-18.7	-1.7
France	25.7	-75.8	0.0	18.1	0.4	0.0	-47.9	-6.0	-7.5	-20.7
Germany	-12.3	27.8	41.9	56.8	-20.5	21.2	8.0	24.5	13.0	-113.5
Greece	12.8	-12.3	-	-	0.0	0.0	0.0	0.0	0.0	0.0
Hungary	1.4	-2.5	0.0	0.0	-	-0.2	-1.9	0.1	-0.1	-2.3
Iceland	-	-	-	-	-	-	-	-	-	-
Ireland	69.1	-135.5	-69.8	-98.2	-7.7	0.9	0.9	18.2	3.2	2.0
Israel	-0.4	-0.3	0.3	1.9	-0.4	-	-	-	-	-
Italy	-26.5	-3.9	-10.0	-3.0	-7.7	0.0	0.0	0.0	0.0	0.0
Japan	-	-	-	-	-	0.0	-	-	0.4	0.4
Korea	-	-	204.3	-0.1	-8.8	0.0	0.0	-0.8	1.0	0.9
Latvia	0.9	2.1	9.3	2.1	4.9	1.3	15.8	-23.3	0.9	0.8
Lithuania	0.7	0.1	-	-	-	0.8	1.0	0.8	1.8	2.0
Luxembourg	-444.7	-553.2	-386.5	-301.4	-107.2	-3.9	25.3	30.9	17.8	-1.1
Mexico	-2.8	7.4	-	-	-	-0.3	0.3	-0.2	0.0	0.0
Netherlands	-506.8	-841.9	80.2	20.3	-554.6	20.7	-45.6	-127.0	232.6	-113.1
New Zealand	-	-	-	-	-	0.4	0.3	0.7	0.3	-0.8
Norway	85.5	-14.6	33.6	19.6	103.2	-41.1	-3.9	-80.5	15.7	-61.0
Poland	-	0.2	-0.4	0.2	0.1	0.1	0.3	0.3	0.9	-0.1
Portugal	-	-	-	-	-	0.0	-	0.2	0.4	1.2
Slovak Republic	2.8	-	-	-	-	0.3	-0.3	-0.6	-0.4	2.8
Slovenia	-	-	-	-	-	-	-	-	-	-
Spain	-1.8	-2.2	3.1	0.0	3.1	-207.7	-8.6	59.1	-2.4	3.7
Sweden	-4.5	-80.3	-44.8	-87.0	-13.4	-132.7	-160.8	42.0	-31.7	-7.1
Switzerland	151.9	-1 275.8	-301.6	32.8	-396.5	-6.5	-10.4	179.5	-124.9	2.5
Turkey	9.1	-0.1	0.8	-	-	3.0	0.1	0.2	0.1	-11.5
United Kingdom	116.6	-144.2	27.7	-85.6	-16.4	-771.2	-45.7	-66.7	55.1	-196.8
United States	-96.4	2 941.3	-60.5	-21.8	-59.2	2.3	13.7	30.2	183.8	34.3
EUROPE	**-211.4**	**-3 138.8**	**-560.9**	**-203.5**	**-1 005.3**	**-1 095.6**	**-246.4**	**9.5**	**181.5**	**-461.0**
Bulgaria	-5.0	-6.6	-1.2	-0.3	-2.5	-	-	-	-	-
Croatia	-0.1	2.6	-1.9	0.2	1.5	-	0.1	-	-	-
Cyprus	-3.2	-6.5	1.2	41.6	0.1	-38.9	11.4	13.2	-9.0	88.1
Malta	278.9	-207.5	-2.9	171.5	-3.5	0.1	-	-	-	-
Montenegro	-	-	-	-	-	-	-	-	-	-
Romania	-1.1	0.5	-0.8	1.8	-0.5	0.0	0.0	-0.1	-	-
Russian Federation	0.0	-1.2	19.2	0.1	-0.2	-2.0	-2.5	-1.8	2.3	-14.3
Ukraine	5.7	-	-	-	-	-	-	0.2	0.2	0.2
AFRICA	**0.1**	**1.5**	**0.2**	**10.4**	**0.5**	**-0.2**	**0.1**	**-0.3**	**4.0**	**0.8**
Northern Africa	-	-	-	-	-	-	-	-	0.0	0.0
Algeria	-	-	-	-	-	-	-	-	-	-
Egypt	-	-	-	-	-	-	-	-	-	-
Libya	-	-	-	-	-	-	-	-	-	-
Morocco	-	-	-	-	-	-	-	-	0.0	0.0
Tunisia	-	-	-	-	-	-	-	-	-	-
Other African countries	0.1	1.5	0.2	10.4	0.5	-0.2	0.1	-0.3	4.0	0.8
Nigeria	-	-	-	-	-	-	-	-	-	-
South Africa	0.1	0.4	0.2	10.6	0.7	-0.2	0.0	0.2	0.2	0.6
AMERICA	**-223.1**	**2 998.5**	**-60.8**	**-51.8**	**-30.1**	**-68.8**	**-10.4**	**17.4**	**189.7**	**33.3**
Northern America	-231.1	2 986.2	-60.3	-42.3	-59.1	-42.1	-15.8	34.5	190.4	34.2
Central America and Caribbean countries	-2.3	6.5	-0.5	-9.5	29.0	-30.9	-0.4	-6.8	-0.5	0.4
Bahamas	-	-	-	-	-	-	-	-	-	-
Bermuda	-0.7	1.3	-	-	-	0.7	-2.0	-3.0	0.1	0.1
Cayman Islands	-	-2.5	-0.1	-9.6	29.0	-31.2	0.9	-3.9	-0.9	0.0
El Salvador	-	-	-	-	-	-	-	-	-	-
Guatemala	-	-	-	-	-	-	-	-	-	-
Honduras	-	-	-	-	-	-	-	-	-	-
Nicaragua	-	-	-	-	-	-	-	-	-	-
Panama	-	-	-	-	-	-	-	-	-	-
Virgin Islands, U.S.	-	-	-	-	-	-	-	-	-	-
South America	10.2	5.8	0.0	-	-	4.3	5.8	-10.2	-0.1	-1.3
Argentina	-	-	-	-	-	-	-	-	-	-
Bolivia	-	-	-	-	-	-	-	-	-	-
Brazil	10.2	5.8	0.0	-	-	-0.2	-0.1	0.6	0.6	0.0
Ecuador	-	-	-	-	-	-	-	-	-	-
Paraguay	-	-	-	-	-	-	-	-	-	-
Peru	-	-	-	-	-	-	-	-	-	-
Uruguay	-	-	-	-	-	-0.1	-0.1	-0.1	0.0	0.3
Venezuela	-	-	-	-	-	-	-	-	-	-

Table 1. Foreign direct investment flows by country *(cont.)*

Million US dollars

	Inward					Outward				
	2016	2017	2018	2019	2020	2016	2017	2018	2019	2020
ASIA	**-1.5**	**6.4**	**243.3**	**19.5**	**7.3**	**5.8**	**6.7**	**2.8**	**51.9**	**57.8**
Near and Middle East	-3.6	6.4	0.3	1.9	-0.4	0.1	0.0	0.3	0.0	0.0
Gulf Arabian countries	-3.3	6.7	-	-	-	0.0	0.0	0.3	0.0	0.0
Kuwait	-	-	-	-	-	-	-	-	-	-
Qatar	-	-	-	-	-	-	-	-	-	-
Saudi Arabia	-	1.9	-	-	-	-	-	-	-	-
United Arab Emirates	-3.3	4.9	-	-	-	0.0	0.0	0.3	0.0	0.0
Other Near and Middle East	-0.4	-0.3	0.3	1.9	-0.4	0.1	0.0	-	-	-
Jordan	-	-	-	-	-	-	-	-	-	-
Other Asian countries	2.1	0.0	243.0	17.6	7.8	5.7	6.7	2.5	51.9	57.9
China	-2.0	-0.7	-1.2	-1.0	-1.0	3.1	6.1	2.8	50.6	56.1
Hong Kong, China	-6.4	-6.3	22.1	2.8	3.4	2.3	0.2	0.2	0.2	0.2
India	0.0	-	-	-0.7	-0.1	0.0	-	-	-	-
Indonesia	0.1	-	-	-	-	-	-	-	-	-
Iran, Islamic Republic of	-	-	-	-	-	-	-	-	-	-
Malaysia	-0.1	0.1	-	15.1	13.7	-	0.1	-0.1	-0.1	-0.1
Philippines	-	-	-	-	-	-	-	-	0.0	0.0
Singapore	3.0	4.5	17.6	1.1	0.3	0.1	0.0	-0.3	0.0	0.4
Chinese Taipei	-	0.0	-	-	0.0	-	-	-	-	-
Thailand	7.5	2.3	0.3	0.3	0.3	0.2	0.2	0.2	0.0	0.1
Viet Nam	-	-	-	-	-	-	0.0	0.4	-0.2	-0.1
AUSTRALIA, OCEANIA AND POLAR REGIONS	**-5.2**	**87.2**	**-0.8**	**-0.2**	**1.3**	**-3.4**	**-6.3**	**1.5**	**6.8**	**-6.7**
WORLD unallocated and confidential	**13.8**	**3.9**	**-2.5**	**0.8**	**-0.5**	**14.9**	**48.1**	**45.0**	**44.8**	**19.7**
European Union (since 01/02/2020)	**..**	**..**	**..**	**..**	**-704.3**	**..**	**..**	**..**	**..**	**-199.7**
G20 countries excl. European Union	**-117.9**	**2 890.7**	**221.9**	**-47.2**	**-111.4**	**-792.4**	**-104.2**	**-12.0**	**312.9**	**-270.6**
G20 OECD countries	**-126.3**	**2 884.5**	**203.7**	**-56.3**	**-110.8**	**-793.1**	**-107.7**	**-13.9**	**259.1**	**-313.0**
G20 Non-OECD countries	**8.5**	**6.2**	**18.1**	**9.1**	**-0.6**	**0.7**	**3.5**	**1.8**	**53.7**	**42.4**
MENA countries	**-3.3**	**6.7**	**-**	**-**	**-**	**0.0**	**0.0**	**0.3**	**0.0**	**0.0**
ASEAN countries	**10.5**	**6.9**	**17.9**	**16.5**	**14.3**	**0.3**	**0.4**	**0.3**	**-0.3**	**0.3**

- Nil; .. Not available

Note: Data excludes resident Special Purpose Entities (SPEs). Detailed metadata at: *http://metalinks.oecd.org/idi/20220712/6d95*.

Source: *OECD International Direct Investment Statistics (database)*: *https://doi.org/10.1787/idi-data-en*

Table 2. Foreign direct investment positions by country
At year end

Million US dollars

	Inward					Outward				
	2016	2017	2018	2019	2020	2016	2017	2018	2019	2020
WORLD	**9 841.0**	**10 129.9**	**8 750.7**	**8 415.4**	**7 536.0**	**6 058.2**	**5 268.6**	**5 229.4**	**5 346.3**	**5 420.1**
OECD COUNTRIES	**9 091.9**	**9 500.3**	**8 088.6**	**7 838.8**	**6 972.4**	**5 022.9**	**4 684.5**	**4 647.7**	**4 762.6**	**4 637.6**
Australia	-	-	0.0	-	-	240.1	-162.7	13.3	19.7	15.5
Austria	16.0	16.7	1.6	3.0	2.1	-	-	-	-	-
Belgium	4.9	5.3	4.8	13.8	13.1	0.1	17.1	16.4	38.8	44.1
Canada	195.4	190.2	196.4	5.5	5.1	35.6	12.0	15.4	22.2	22.6
Chile	-	-	-	-	-	32.6	39.2	41.7	41.5	39.7
Colombia	-	-	-	-	-	-	-	-	-	-
Costa Rica	-	-	-	-	-	-	-	-	-	-
Czech Republic	-	-	-	-	-	0.2	0.2	0.2	16.6	-
Denmark	424.6	467.8	475.1	496.3	534.0	84.8	109.1	62.1	58.2	70.8
Estonia	-	-	-	-	-	30.8	38.9	29.7	32.5	41.1
Finland	2.6	9.8	2.3	1.7	1.2	81.3	83.2	80.8	62.0	44.5
France	15.1	18.9	13.7	18.3	20.9	8.2	82.7	73.1	62.4	45.6
Germany	83.4	97.7	110.6	213.0	210.5	128.5	137.1	149.5	147.4	47.5
Greece	-	-	-	-	-	0.2	0.2	0.2	0.2	0.2
Hungary	-	-	-	-	-	1.5	1.0	3.2	3.1	0.7
Iceland	116.3	69.4	48.5	43.5	197.2	-	-	-	-	-
Ireland	57.7	63.2	58.1	79.7	66.4	9.1	12.4	19.7	22.0	26.5
Israel	2 788.6	2 789.5	2 328.0	2 099.9	1 356.9	-	-	-	-	-
Italy	6.0	5.6	4.9	4.7	5.1	0.0	0.0	0.0	0.0	0.0
Japan	-	-	-	-	-	5.6	5.8	6.0	11.0	12.0
Korea	-	-	188.4	213.1	203.2	8.2	8.2	8.0	8.8	9.8
Latvia	48.8	64.2	69.4	61.0	70.0	51.7	69.8	17.5	18.1	20.4
Lithuania	-	-	-	-	-	17.8	29.0	28.6	32.9	38.4
Luxembourg	568.5	329.2	226.2	197.7	286.8	290.2	158.1	158.1	-86.3	-82.2
Mexico	-	-	-	-	-	0.1	0.3	0.1	0.1	0.1
Netherlands	162.6	265.6	184.9	219.6	240.0	2 532.7	3 033.8	2 772.3	2 939.1	3 157.3
New Zealand	-	-	-	-	-	2.1	2.6	3.2	3.2	2.7
Norway	239.5	282.1	247.6	254.3	390.7	124.5	186.2	82.2	71.8	39.2
Poland	-	-	-	-	-	0.1	0.5	0.7	1.3	0.1
Portugal	-	-	-	-	-	-	-	0.5	2.4	4.0
Slovak Republic	-	-	-	-	-	6.2	-0.4	-1.0	-1.4	1.4
Slovenia	-	-	-	-	-	-	-	-	-	-
Spain	10.3	-1.7	0.8	7.7	6.9	47.1	45.8	51.1	40.2	48.6
Sweden	31.1	32.6	70.7	88.4	96.6	207.0	62.7	146.1	132.4	110.2
Switzerland	68.1	118.0	89.4	112.7	106.6	-7.0	-59.0	111.3	-16.6	-15.8
Turkey	-	-	-	-	-	4.9	11.3	11.0	10.9	-
United Kingdom	1 648.7	2 016.0	1 576.0	1 501.6	1 242.0	1 076.3	752.0	651.2	794.3	582.4
United States	2 603.7	2 660.1	2 191.3	2 203.3	1 917.2	20.4	36.4	95.7	273.9	310.0
EUROPE	**3 664.8**	**3 977.5**	**3 299.5**	**3 433.0**	**3 603.1**	**5 449.8**	**5 093.0**	**4 788.2**	**4 699.5**	**4 662.6**
Bulgaria	-	-	-	-	-	-	-	-	-	-
Croatia	-	-	-	-	-	-	0.1	0.1	-	-
Cyprus	76.2	29.9	40.5	12.1	16.6	526.1	109.6	85.9	81.8	174.4
Malta	53.1	54.6	44.9	70.2	62.3	0.1	0.1	0.1	-	-
Montenegro	-	-	-	-	-	-	-	-	-	-
Romania	-	-	-	-	-	0.5	0.6	-	-	-
Russian Federation	0.3	0.4	0.3	-	-	32.0	36.1	37.7	40.4	27.5
Ukraine	-	-	-	-	-	-	-	0.9	1.2	1.5
AFRICA	-	**2.4**	**2.6**	**2.7**	**3.2**	**1.0**	**1.7**	**0.4**	**2.9**	**3.8**
Northern Africa	-	-	-	-	-	-	-	-	0.4	0.4
Algeria	-	-	-	-	-	-	-	-	-	-
Egypt	-	-	-	-	-	-	-	-	-	-
Libya	-	-	-	-	-	-	-	-	-	-
Morocco	-	-	-	-	-	-	-	-	0.4	0.4
Tunisia	-	-	-	-	-	-	-	-	-	-
Other African countries	-	2.4	2.6	2.7	3.2	1.0	1.7	0.4	2.5	3.4
Nigeria	-	-	-	-	-	-	-	-	-	-
South Africa	-	1.3	1.6	2.4	3.1	1.0	1.0	0.9	1.2	1.7
AMERICA	**2 884.2**	**2 887.9**	**2 422.1**	**2 225.8**	**1 960.7**	**102.8**	**102.5**	**160.4**	**343.8**	**378.5**
Northern America	2 799.1	2 850.2	2 388.5	2 209.6	1 923.1	56.0	48.4	111.1	296.0	332.5
Central America and Caribbean countries	85.1	37.6	33.6	16.2	10.8	14.1	15.0	7.2	5.3	5.4
Bahamas	-	-	-	-	-	-	-	-	-	-
Bermuda	3.1	3.4	3.0	-	-	5.9	7.3	4.2	4.3	4.2
Cayman Islands	81.7	34.0	30.4	16.1	10.7	8.0	6.9	2.2	0.2	0.1
El Salvador	-	-	-	-	-	-	-	-	-	-
Guatemala	-	-	-	-	-	-	-	-	-	-
Honduras	-	-	-	-	-	-	-	-	-	-
Nicaragua	-	-	-	-	-	-	-	-	-	-
Panama	0.2	0.2	0.2	-	-	-	-	-	-	-
Virgin Islands, U.S.	-	-	-	-	-	-	-	-	-	-
South America	-	-	-	-	26.8	32.7	39.1	42.1	42.5	40.6
Argentina	-	-	-	-	-	-	-	-	-	-
Bolivia	-	-	-	-	-	-	-	-	-	-
Brazil	-	-	-	-	26.8	0.0	-0.1	0.4	1.0	0.6
Ecuador	-	-	-	-	-	-	-	-	-	-
Paraguay	-	-	-	-	-	-	-	-	-	-
Peru	-	-	-	-	-	-	-	-	-	-
Uruguay	-	-	-	-	-	0.1	0.0	0.0	0.0	0.3
Venezuela	-	-	-	-	-	-	-	-	-	-

Table 2. Foreign direct investment positions by country *(cont.)*

At year end

Million US dollars

	Inward					Outward				
	2016	2017	2018	2019	2020	2016	2017	2018	2019	2020
ASIA	**2 981.1**	**2 965.5**	**2 760.1**	**2 589.5**	**1 812.6**	**74.5**	**83.8**	**80.6**	**132.4**	**171.9**
Near and Middle East	2 788.6	2 791.4	2 329.7	2 101.5	1 358.5	0.8	0.0	0.3	0.3	0.3
Gulf Arabian countries	-	1.9	1.7	1.6	1.6	0.7	0.0	0.3	0.3	0.3
Kuwait	-	-	-	-	-	-	-	-	-	-
Qatar	-	-	-	-	-	-	-	-	-	-
Saudi Arabia	-	1.9	1.7	1.6	1.6	-	-	-	-	-
United Arab Emirates	-	-	-	-	-	0.7	0.0	0.3	0.3	0.3
Other Near and Middle East	2 788.6	2 789.5	2 328.0	2 099.9	1 356.9	0.1	0.0	-	-	-
Jordan	-	-	-	-	-	-	-	-	-	-
Other Asian countries	192.5	174.1	430.3	488.0	454.1	73.6	83.7	80.4	132.2	171.6
China	143.8	124.0	150.5	140.1	125.2	58.2	67.0	63.2	107.6	144.1
Hong Kong, China	29.4	23.7	33.7	46.3	52.4	0.7	0.9	1.2	2.8	3.0
India	-	-	-	-	-	0.0	-	-	-	-
Indonesia	-	-	-	-	-	-	-	-	-	-
Iran, Islamic Republic of	-	-	-	-	-	-	-	-	-	-
Malaysia	-	-	-	30.4	14.6	-	0.2	0.1	0.3	0.2
Philippines	-	-	-	-	-	-	-	-	0.0	0.0
Singapore	19.3	26.3	57.7	58.1	58.6	0.0	0.3	0.0	0.0	0.9
Chinese Taipei	-	-	-	-	-	-	-	-	-	-
Thailand	-	-	-	-	-	1.0	1.3	1.5	1.6	1.7
Viet Nam	-	-	-	-	-	-	0.0	0.4	0.1	0.0
AUSTRALIA, OCEANIA AND POLAR REGIONS	**-**	**-**	**0.0**	**-**	**-**	**242.2**	**-160.2**	**16.5**	**22.9**	**18.2**
WORLD unallocated and confidential	**310.9**	**296.7**	**266.4**	**164.4**	**156.5**	**188.0**	**147.7**	**183.4**	**144.8**	**185.2**
European Union (since 01/02/2020)	..	..	..	..	..	..	..	..	..	3 793.7
G20 countries excl. European Union	4 696.4	5 116.1	4 435.5	4 303.6	3 760.6	1 619.0	987.1	1 125.4	1 501.0	1 219.5
G20 OECD countries	4 552.3	4 988.5	4 281.3	4 159.4	3 603.9	1 527.9	883.2	1 023.2	1 350.7	1 045.6
G20 Non-OECD countries	144.2	127.6	154.1	144.1	156.7	91.1	104.0	102.2	150.2	173.9
MENA countries	-	1.9	1.7	1.6	1.6	0.7	0.0	0.3	0.7	0.6
ASEAN countries	19.3	26.3	57.7	88.5	73.2	1.0	1.8	2.0	2.0	2.7

- Nil; .. Not available

Note: Inward FDI positions are allocated according to the ultimate investing country. Data excludes resident Special Purpose Entities (SPEs). Detailed metadata at: *http://metalinks.oecd.org/idi/20220712/6d95*.

Source: *OECD International Direct Investment Statistics (database)*: *https://doi.org/10.1787/idi-data-en*

ICELAND

Table 3. Foreign direct investment income by country

Million US dollars

	Inward					Outward				
	2016	2017	2018	2019	2020	2016	2017	2018	2019	2020
WORLD	**-29.2**	**40.4**	**-42.4**	**-267.2**	**-364.7**	**435.8**	**302.1**	**363.9**	**324.2**	**245.0**
OECD COUNTRIES	**-18.5**	**49.1**	**-25.5**	**-262.0**	**-338.5**	**390.9**	**270.0**	**320.6**	**296.2**	**223.4**
Australia	-4.1	-1.7	-	-	-	-5.3	-0.2	0.8	2.0	0.2
Austria	3.1	6.1	9.1	-1.0	-0.9	-	-	-	-	-
Belgium	-0.1	0.3	0.3	1.3	1.2	0.3	0.1	0.1	1.8	1.8
Canada	-1.9	0.0	0.2	5.8	0.4	5.3	0.7	0.4	0.9	1.4
Chile	-	-	-	-	-	5.5	6.3	2.9	-2.1	-1.9
Colombia	-	-	-	-	-	-	-	-	-	-
Costa Rica	-	-	-	-	-	-	-	-	-	-
Czech Republic	-0.2	0.0	-	-	-	-	-	-	0.0	0.0
Denmark	13.1	12.1	4.7	17.4	10.4	24.4	22.4	16.9	16.0	13.7
Estonia	-	-	-	-	-	4.9	4.3	4.3	5.1	4.5
Finland	9.0	9.2	11.8	5.6	5.1	-0.8	0.9	1.1	3.0	2.8
France	-0.1	-0.1	0.0	-0.9	-0.8	0.1	2.2	2.0	1.9	1.7
Germany	0.6	-1.1	7.1	-10.0	-37.3	16.1	7.7	24.4	14.7	6.9
Greece	0.0	-	-	-	0.0	0.0	0.0	0.0	0.0	0.0
Hungary	0.0	0.0	-	-	-	-0.5	-1.2	-0.6	0.0	0.1
Iceland	-	-	-	-	-	-	-	-	-	-
Ireland	7.0	12.6	9.3	-7.5	-7.6	0.6	0.7	1.4	2.3	2.0
Israel	-	-	-	0.2	0.1	-	-	-	-	-
Italy	0.9	-3.1	-5.9	-5.4	-4.9	-	-	-	-	-
Japan	-	-	-	-	-	0.0	-	-	0.4	0.4
Korea	-	-	-0.7	-9.7	-8.8	0.0	0.0	-0.8	1.0	0.9
Latvia	3.2	2.9	10.6	5.4	4.9	7.4	11.2	1.1	0.9	0.8
Lithuania	-0.1	0.0	-	-	-	1.1	1.5	1.4	2.2	2.0
Luxembourg	134.6	-25.2	-50.9	-106.7	-138.8	16.9	24.3	30.9	17.8	-
Mexico	-0.5	-0.5	-	-	-	-	-	-	-	-
Netherlands	65.1	97.8	52.1	-21.2	-43.5	117.5	112.6	153.9	151.5	136.3
New Zealand	-	-	-	-	-	0.0	0.1	0.2	0.2	0.1
Norway	-0.5	7.9	9.5	-9.7	-10.7	3.5	31.9	16.5	2.4	2.3
Poland	-	-	-	-	-	0.0	0.0	0.0	0.6	0.1
Portugal	-	-	-	-	-	-	-	0.2	0.4	0.4
Slovak Republic	-0.1	-	-	-	-	0.4	-	-	-	-
Slovenia	-	-	-	-	-	-	-	-	-	-
Spain	-1.8	-3.8	-1.5	-1.6	-1.4	3.5	3.1	3.8	4.3	3.9
Sweden	-17.4	-49.7	-31.4	4.3	5.7	2.0	-1.7	10.0	-8.0	-2.5
Switzerland	-25.8	94.6	-11.9	-54.2	-64.7	0.1	0.2	1.2	1.9	0.4
Turkey	-0.9	-0.1	-0.2	-	-	3.0	0.1	0.2	0.1	-
United Kingdom	39.8	2.7	-5.8	1.9	9.0	181.5	37.1	46.7	70.9	39.4
United States	-241.5	-112.0	-32.0	-75.9	-55.8	4.6	7.3	1.6	4.1	5.8
EUROPE	**216.2**	**157.2**	**-5.1**	**-181.4**	**-273.6**	**418.0**	**278.5**	**354.8**	**319.6**	**237.7**
Bulgaria	-	-	-	-	-	-	-	-	-	-
Croatia	-	-	-	-	-	-	-	-	-	-
Cyprus	-1.5	-6.5	-7.7	0.8	0.7	11.0	-2.8	5.2	4.8	-1.8
Malta	-7.2	-1.0	-3.0	-2.1	-2.0	-	-	-	-	-
Montenegro	-	-	-	-	-	-	-	-	-	-
Romania	-	-	-	-	-	0.1	0.1	-0.1	-	-
Russian Federation	-2.5	-2.6	-0.6	-0.1	-0.1	-2.0	-2.5	-0.2	3.2	1.2
Ukraine	-0.2	-	-	-	-	-	-	0.2	0.2	0.2
AFRICA	-	**-0.3**	**0.2**	**0.6**	**0.5**	**-0.1**	**0.1**	**-0.5**	**-3.5**	**0.4**
Northern Africa	-	-	-	-	-	-	-	-	0.0	0.0
Algeria	-	-	-	-	-	-	-	-	-	-
Egypt	-	-	-	-	-	-	-	-	-	-
Libya	-	-	-	-	-	-	-	-	-	-
Morocco	-	-	-	-	-	-	-	-	0.0	0.0
Tunisia	-	-	-	-	-	-	-	-	-	-
Other African countries	-	-0.3	0.2	0.6	0.5	-0.1	0.1	-0.5	-3.5	0.4
Nigeria	-	-	-	-	-	-	-	-	-	-
South Africa	-	-0.3	0.2	0.8	0.7	-0.1	0.1	0.2	0.2	0.2
AMERICA	**-247.2**	**-115.5**	**-32.5**	**-79.7**	**-65.8**	**16.9**	**20.3**	**5.9**	**3.3**	**5.6**
Northern America	-243.4	-112.0	-32.0	-70.2	-55.4	9.8	8.0	2.0	5.1	7.2
Central America and Caribbean countries	-1.9	-2.8	-0.5	-9.5	-10.4	1.6	6.0	1.0	0.4	0.3
Bahamas	-	-	-	-	-	-	-	-	-	-
Bermuda	-1.4	0.4	-	-	-	0.7	0.5	0.0	0.1	0.1
Cayman Islands	-	-2.5	-0.1	-9.6	-10.4	0.9	5.4	0.7	0.0	0.0
El Salvador	-	-	-	-	-	-	-	-	-	-
Guatemala	-	-	-	-	-	-	-	-	-	-
Honduras	-	-	-	-	-	-	-	-	-	-
Nicaragua	-	-	-	-	-	-	-	-	-	-
Panama	0.0	0.0	0.0	-	-	-	-	-	-	-
Virgin Islands, U.S.	-	-	-	-	-	-	-	-	-	-
South America	-2.0	-0.7	-	-	-	5.5	6.3	2.9	-2.1	-1.9
Argentina	-	-	-	-	-	-	-	-	-	-
Bolivia	-	-	-	-	-	-	-	-	-	-
Brazil	-2.0	-0.7	-	-	-	-	-	-	-	-
Ecuador	-	-	-	-	-	-	-	-	-	-
Paraguay	-	-	-	-	-	-	-	-	-	-
Peru	-	-	-	-	-	-	-	-	-	-
Uruguay	-	-	-	-	-	-	-	-	-	-
Venezuela	-	-	-	-	-	-	-	-	-	-

Table 3. Foreign direct investment income by country *(cont.)*

Million US dollars

	Inward					Outward				
	2016	2017	2018	2019	2020	2016	2017	2018	2019	2020
ASIA	**-2.7**	**0.8**	**-5.0**	**-6.5**	**-25.7**	**3.5**	**1.6**	**2.8**	**2.6**	**0.9**
Near and Middle East	-0.1	-0.1	-	0.2	0.1	0.0	0.0	0.0	0.0	0.0
Gulf Arabian countries	-0.1	-0.1	-	-	-	0.0	0.0	0.0	0.0	0.0
Kuwait	-	-	-	-	-	-	-	-	-	-
Qatar	-	-	-	-	-	-	-	-	-	-
Saudi Arabia	-	-	-	-	-	-	-	-	-	-
United Arab Emirates	-0.1	-0.1	-	-	-	0.0	0.0	0.0	0.0	0.0
Other Near and Middle East	-	-	-	0.2	0.1	0.0	0.0	-	-	-
Jordan	-	-	-	-	-	-	-	-	-	-
Other Asian countries	-2.6	0.9	-5.0	-6.7	-25.8	3.5	1.6	2.8	2.6	0.9
China	-2.0	-0.7	-1.2	-1.1	-1.0	3.0	1.2	3.1	1.0	-0.6
Hong Kong, China	0.4	-1.1	-3.3	3.2	2.9	0.2	0.2	0.2	0.2	0.2
India	-	-	-	-	-	-	-	-	-	-
Indonesia	-	-	-	-	-	-	-	-	-	-
Iran, Islamic Republic of	-	-	-	-	-	-	-	-	-	-
Malaysia	0.0	0.0	-	0.0	-19.5	-	0.0	0.1	-0.1	-0.1
Philippines	-	-	-	-	-	-	-	-	-	-
Singapore	-1.2	2.4	-0.1	0.6	0.6	0.1	0.0	0.0	0.0	0.0
Chinese Taipei	-	-	-	-	-	-	-	-	-	-
Thailand	0.2	0.3	0.3	0.3	-	0.1	0.2	0.1	0.1	0.1
Viet Nam	-	-	-	-	-	-	-	-	-	-
AUSTRALIA, OCEANIA AND POLAR REGIONS	**-4.1**	**-1.7**	**-**	**-**	**-**	**-5.3**	**-0.1**	**1.0**	**2.2**	**0.3**
WORLD unallocated and confidential	**8.7**	**-0.1**	**0.0**	**-0.1**	**-0.1**	**2.8**	**1.7**	**0.0**	**0.0**	**0.0**
European Union (since 01/02/2020)	**..**	**..**	**..**	**..**	**-209.2**	**..**	**..**	**..**	**..**	**172.6**
G20 countries excl. European Union	**-214.1**	**-120.1**	**-38.9**	**-94.8**	**-98.6**	**206.1**	**53.6**	**78.3**	**100.5**	**57.5**
G20 OECD countries	**-207.6**	**-115.8**	**-37.3**	**-94.3**	**-98.1**	**205.2**	**54.8**	**75.3**	**96.1**	**56.6**
G20 Non-OECD countries	**-6.5**	**-4.2**	**-1.6**	**-0.5**	**-0.5**	**1.0**	**-1.2**	**3.0**	**4.4**	**0.9**
MENA countries	**-0.1**	**-0.1**	**-**	**-**	**-**	**0.0**	**0.0**	**0.0**	**0.0**	**0.0**
ASEAN countries	**-1.0**	**2.6**	**0.2**	**0.9**	**-18.9**	**0.2**	**0.2**	**0.2**	**0.0**	**0.0**

- Nil; .. Not available

Note: Data excludes resident Special Purpose Entities (SPEs). Detailed metadata at: *http://metalinks.oecd.org/idi/20220712/6d95*.

Source: *OECD International Direct Investment Statistics (database): https://doi.org/10.1787/idi-data-en*

ICELAND

Table 4. Foreign direct investment flows by industrial sector

Million US dollars

	Inward					Outward				
	2016	2017	2018	2019	2020	2016	2017	2018	2019	2020
All FDI activities	**-427.2**	**-41.4**	**-381.6**	**-224.8**	**-1 026.8**	**-1 147.3**	**-208.3**	**76.0**	**478.7**	**-356.1**
Agriculture, forestry and fishing	**40.4**	**10.1**	**13.5**	**27.7**	**9.4**	**-22.3**	**34.7**	**47.3**	**23.1**	**-162.8**
Mining and quarrying	**2.7**	**-0.9**	**46.0**	**48.5**	**-22.7**	**-**	**-**	**-**	**-**	**-**
Extraction activities	0.3	-0.9	42.5	48.5	-22.7	-	-	-	-	-
Manufacturing	**-96.3**	**98.3**	**175.7**	**-87.4**	**-236.6**	**97.5**	**3.3**	**119.4**	**285.3**	**-20.0**
of which:										
Food products, beverages and tobacco	-3.6	14.4	3.7	15.1	6.4	-26.6	1.3	-29.0	1.8	-8.9
Textiles, wood and paper products; printing	-	-	-	-0.3	-0.1	77.5	23.1	79.9	5.6	14.3
Chemical, rubber, plastic, non-metallic mineral products	-20.8	0.4	154.1	-118.3	-40.5	10.9	-6.6	2.8	-7.8	-15.5
Metal and machinery products, except electrical equipment	-95.4	-18.1	74.1	-12.9	-205.1	39.8	79.4	61.0	220.2	5.8
Motor vehicles, trailers, semi-trailers, other transport equipment	-	-	-	-	-	-0.7	-	-	-	-
Other manufacturing	23.5	101.7	-56.2	29.1	2.7	-3.4	-93.9	4.8	65.5	-15.8
Electricity, gas, steam and air conditioning supply	**1.8**	**-60.9**	**10.5**	**-73.0**	**-17.8**	**0.4**	**0.8**	**3.1**	**1.0**	**0.9**
Water supply; sewerage, waste management and remediation activities	**0.1**	**0.8**	**-23.6**	**-**	**-**	**-**	**-**	**-**	**-**	**-**
Construction	**15.1**	**8.6**	**-23.9**	**-6.8**	**1.6**	**-409.5**	**4.9**	**-1.7**	**-0.8**	**1.4**
Services	**-391.1**	**-98.0**	**-579.7**	**-133.5**	**-760.4**	**-825.8**	**-260.8**	**-95.0**	**171.9**	**-177.5**
Wholesale and retail trade; repair of motor vehicles and motorcycles	681.0	3 217.0	-279.7	241.3	-230.9	40.2	7.8	39.4	18.4	-25.0
Transportation and storage	1.6	-2.5	3.3	-12.0	-0.5	35.3	47.4	-34.2	11.6	14.5
Accommodation and food service activities	29.6	-3.4	34.7	19.5	15.0	-1.7	-17.8	-	-	-
Information and communication	18.7	136.7	78.6	9.1	17.8	-1.6	-33.9	-44.7	-6.0	1.3
Financial and insurance activities	-1 176.1	-3 460.0	-508.9	-375.1	-883.5	-411.0	-247.0	-87.7	59.3	-227.9
Activities of holding companies	-841.0	-3 446.5	-571.9	-430.1	-790.1	-407.2	-244.9	-86.9	46.4	-225.2
Real estate activities	15.3	8.1	-1.5	-12.2	122.0	-96.7	-5.3	37.8	35.1	-2.5
Professional, scientific and technical activities	35.3	11.3	76.7	-16.6	29.2	-236.0	-4.0	5.1	52.2	56.9
Administrative and support service activities	3.9	-4.9	17.1	12.5	170.5	-14.9	-8.5	-11.1	1.3	5.3
Public administration; activities of households and of extraterritorial organisations	-	-	-	-	-	-	-	-	-	-
Education	-0.5	-0.3	-	-	-	-	-	-	-	-
Human health and social work activities	-	-	-	-	-	-139.4	-	-	-	-
Arts, entertainment and recreation	-	0.0	-	-	-	-	0.4	0.5	0.1	0.1
Other services	-	-	-	-	-	-	-	-	-	-
Not allocated and confidential	**0.0**	**0.6**	**-0.2**	**-0.4**	**-0.4**	**12.3**	**8.9**	**2.9**	**-1.8**	**2.0**
Private real estate activities	**-**	**-**	**-**	**-**	**-**	**-**	**-**	**-**	**-**	**-**

- Nil

Note: Data excludes resident Special Purpose Entities (SPEs). Detailed metadata at: *http://metalinks.oecd.org/idi/20220712/6d95*.

Source: *OECD International Direct Investment Statistics (database): https://doi.org/10.1787/idi-data-en*

ICELAND

Table 5. Foreign direct investment positions by industrial sector

At year end

Million US dollars

	Inward					Outward				
	2016	2017	2018	2019	2020	2016	2017	2018	2019	2020
All FDI activities	**9 841.0**	**10 129.9**	**8 750.7**	**8 415.4**	**7 536.0**	**6 058.2**	**5 268.6**	**5 229.4**	**5 346.3**	**5 420.1**
Agriculture, forestry and fishing	**147.8**	**189.8**	**168.3**	**197.7**	**213.0**	**124.4**	**173.6**	**158.5**	**218.1**	**70.4**
Mining and quarrying	**39.8**	**39.8**	**67.7**	**133.9**	**113.6**	**-**	**-**	**-**	**-**	**-**
Extraction activities	27.4	39.8	55.0	133.9	113.6	-	-	-	-	-
Manufacturing	**1 238.4**	**1 243.8**	**1 311.9**	**1 288.8**	**1 160.3**	**1 573.7**	**821.0**	**1 091.2**	**1 345.1**	**1 417.4**
of which:										
Food products, beverages and tobacco	97.9	120.4	105.9	131.7	141.3	13.2	14.5	18.5	17.3	19.4
Textiles, wood and paper products; printing	-	-	-	5.6	5.4	144.7	156.5	225.2	232.9	271.7
Chemical, rubber, plastic, non-metallic mineral products	108.3	88.8	194.2	143.9	235.5	669.7	-150.0	64.0	55.0	44.4
Metal and machinery products, except electrical equipment	648.3	618.2	602.0	589.9	363.9	583.9	729.5	733.7	941.3	992.0
Motor vehicles, trailers, semi-trailers, other transport equipment	-	-	-	-	-	-	-	-	-	-
Other manufacturing	383.9	416.2	409.8	417.8	414.2	162.2	70.6	49.8	98.6	89.9
Electricity, gas, steam and air conditioning supply	**184.8**	**183.6**	**190.9**	**159.8**	**125.3**	**53.0**	**57.1**	**56.8**	**57.7**	**62.5**
Water supply; sewerage, waste management and remediation activities	**22.1**	**24.5**	**-**	**-**	**-**	**-**	**-**	**-**	**-**	**-**
Construction	**37.4**	**46.2**	**29.7**	**29.4**	**29.7**	**19.1**	**17.4**	**16.9**	**16.0**	**18.2**
Services	**7 991.8**	**8 193.8**	**6 848.9**	**6 602.5**	**5 891.3**	**4 054.0**	**3 999.0**	**3 756.1**	**3 648.4**	**3 788.9**
Wholesale and retail trade; repair of motor vehicles and motorcycles	734.3	1 419.8	1 086.9	939.2	827.3	673.6	666.4	638.0	687.6	679.0
Transportation and storage	31.3	35.0	36.0	43.8	43.4	263.5	303.5	290.6	270.1	302.7
Accommodation and food service activities	4.3	14.8	8.2	26.0	11.8	0.3	0.3	0.3	-	-
Information and communication	207.6	334.8	174.4	173.9	194.3	32.8	10.9	23.2	16.1	25.4
Financial and insurance activities	6 405.2	5 709.3	4 917.4	4 749.1	3 849.5	2 872.9	2 846.9	2 595.8	2 384.1	2 427.8
Activities of holding companies	6 046.8	5 004.5	4 219.6	3 864.9	2 982.1	2 834.2	2 804.3	2 556.0	2 315.4	2 359.7
Real estate activities	318.5	353.2	308.8	362.7	470.7	119.9	132.4	162.0	195.6	217.2
Professional, scientific and technical activities	151.9	179.0	232.9	224.2	244.8	59.7	6.2	13.0	57.1	92.1
Administrative and support service activities	133.6	142.9	80.0	83.7	249.6	31.2	30.9	31.4	36.3	42.7
Public administration; activities of households and of extraterritorial organisations	-	-	-	-	-	-	-	-	-	-
Education	5.0	5.1	4.4	-	-	-	-	-	-	-
Human health and social work activities	-	-	-	-	-	-	-	-	-	-
Arts, entertainment and recreation	-	0.0	0.0	-	-	-	1.4	1.8	1.6	1.8
Other services	-	-	-	-	-	-	-	-	-	-
Not allocated and confidential	**178.9**	**208.4**	**133.3**	**3.3**	**2.8**	**234.1**	**200.5**	**149.9**	**61.0**	**62.6**
Private real estate activities	**-**	**-**	**-**	**-**	**-**	**-**	**-**	**-**	**-**	**-**

- Nil

Note: Data excludes resident Special Purpose Entities (SPEs). Detailed metadata at: *http://metalinks.oecd.org/idi/20220712/6d95*.

Source: *OECD International Direct Investment Statistics (database): https://doi.org/10.1787/idi-data-en*

ICELAND

Table 6. Foreign direct investment income by industrial sector

Million US dollars

	Inward					Outward				
	2016	2017	2018	2019	2020	2016	2017	2018	2019	2020
All FDI activities	**-29.2**	**40.4**	**-42.4**	**-267.2**	**-364.7**	**435.8**	**302.1**	**363.9**	**324.2**	**245.0**
Agriculture, forestry and fishing	**-0.4**	**-3.3**	**-14.9**	**10.9**	**9.8**	**27.5**	**20.5**	**38.6**	**39.7**	**16.6**
Mining and quarrying	**-0.2**	**-0.9**	**5.6**	**-8.8**	**-36.2**	**-**	**-**	**-**	**-**	**-**
Extraction activities	-0.2	-0.9	5.4	-8.8	-36.2	-	-	-	-	-
Manufacturing	**-46.3**	**-73.5**	**-126.1**	**-196.6**	**-267.0**	**121.0**	**129.4**	**181.1**	**130.2**	**127.0**
of which:										
Food products, beverages and tobacco	-1.3	2.8	-4.5	7.9	7.2	1.4	1.3	2.3	1.5	0.6
Textiles, wood and paper products; printing	-	-	-	-0.1	-0.1	14.4	19.5	27.6	14.3	12.9
Chemical, rubber, plastic, non-metallic mineral products	-36.5	-92.8	-107.7	-114.7	-173.5	10.9	-0.4	2.8	-7.8	-3.9
Metal and machinery products, except electrical equipment	-33.1	-4.1	-29.6	-104.9	-108.0	76.9	111.0	147.9	119.4	115.0
Motor vehicles, trailers, semi-trailers, other transport equipment	-	-	-	-	-	-	-	-	-	-
Other manufacturing	24.5	20.6	15.8	15.2	7.5	17.3	-2.0	0.6	2.9	2.4
Electricity, gas, steam and air conditioning supply	**1.8**	**4.1**	**10.5**	**1.0**	**2.7**	**0.4**	**0.8**	**3.1**	**1.0**	**0.9**
Water supply; sewerage, waste management and remediation activities	**0.1**	**0.8**	**-**	**-**	**-**	**-**	**-**	**-**	**-**	**-**
Construction	**1.1**	**-14.3**	**-17.9**	**2.0**	**1.8**	**123.1**	**4.8**	**3.2**	**2.1**	**1.9**
Services	**14.7**	**130.2**	**100.6**	**-75.2**	**-75.4**	**161.5**	**144.0**	**135.0**	**151.1**	**98.5**
Wholesale and retail trade; repair of motor vehicles and motorcycles	-103.0	-119.1	12.8	16.7	9.1	31.3	26.5	32.2	40.9	26.1
Transportation and storage	1.1	-0.4	0.3	-0.5	-0.5	35.3	25.0	39.7	17.4	15.0
Accommodation and food service activities	-0.1	2.3	4.0	1.4	-18.2	-2.0	-	-	-	-
Information and communication	13.5	8.5	2.5	9.5	16.8	3.3	4.5	-10.3	8.4	7.7
Financial and insurance activities	76.5	209.6	75.6	-114.6	-82.0	92.0	90.4	80.6	78.8	45.5
Activities of holding companies	74.6	191.1	62.2	-103.5	-101.7	90.8	85.5	79.1	76.0	47.1
Real estate activities	6.2	7.3	-0.6	0.7	0.6	9.1	2.0	1.4	1.2	1.0
Professional, scientific and technical activities	4.7	11.4	4.5	-0.8	-12.2	1.8	0.4	-0.1	2.3	-2.5
Administrative and support service activities	16.2	10.8	1.5	12.5	10.9	-14.1	-5.1	-9.0	2.0	5.5
Public administration; activities of households and of extraterritorial organisations	-	-	-	-	-	-	-	-	-	-
Education	-0.5	-0.3	-	-	-	-	-	-	-	-
Human health and social work activities	-	-	-	-	-	4.8	-	-	-	-
Arts, entertainment and recreation	-	-	-	-	-	-	0.4	0.4	0.1	0.1
Other services	-	-	-	-	-	-	-	-	-	-
Not allocated and confidential	**0.0**	**-2.7**	**-0.2**	**-0.4**	**-0.4**	**2.3**	**2.4**	**2.9**	**0.2**	**0.2**
Private real estate activities	**-**	**-**	**-**	**-**	**-**	**-**	**-**	**-**	**-**	**-**

- Nil

Note: Data excludes resident Special Purpose Entities (SPEs). Detailed metadata at: *http://metalinks.oecd.org/idi/20220712/6d95*.

Source: *OECD International Direct Investment Statistics (database)*: *https://doi.org/10.1787/idi-data-en*

IRELAND

Table 1. Foreign direct investment flows by country

Million US dollars

	Inward					Outward				
	2016	2017	2018	2019	2020	2016	2017	2018	2019	2020
WORLD	**39 375.2**	**52 722.4**	**-12 009.9**	**149 429.1**	**80 687.2**	**30 056.4**	**-2 043.7**	**5 150.5**	**32 082.2**	**-44 894.6**
OECD COUNTRIES	**-51 120.2**	**37 331.8**	**-107 422.4 e**	**-68 905.2**	**69 267.2 e**	**11 446.4**	**-32 593.8**	**-54 681.9**	**66 233.1**	**-13 593.2**
Australia	-1 280.5	790.2	-396.6	245.2	67.2	-358.3	39.5	193.6	3.4	349.9
Austria	129.4	69.9	-99.1	.. c	176.6	-225.6	-126.3	254.9	104.1	77.5
Belgium	4 772.8	-1 586.1	12 947.0	2 485.2	486.6	-709.9	565.9	897.0	735.5	-1 924.8
Canada	-1 058.3	-1 867.9	-723.5	-285.5	.. c	118.3	326.9	-355.2	688.5	1 299.1
Chile	-57.5	-78.9	4.7	26.9	47.9	10.0	9.0	.. c	15.7	4.6
Colombia	-182.5	-16.9	-133.4	-48.1	.. c	.. c	.. c	.. c	.. c	-29.6
Costa Rica	.. c	38.3	.. c	31.3	-629.1	.. c	37.2	.. c	.. c	45.6
Czech Republic	-157.0	10.1	43.7	25.7	-13.7	.. c	22.5	363.5	-53.7	3.4
Denmark	-531.9	-466.7	-70.8	-282.1	690.6	.. c	101.5	338.7	961.6	.. c
Estonia	1.1	-	1.2	1.1	-	-	-	-11.8	.. c	.. c
Finland	-142.7	40.6	-64.9	2 099.0	305.4	.. c	-76.7	743.5	1 533.6	-18.2
France	1 866.6	2 790.0	5 627.3	1 408.3	2 240.5	418.0	1 406.8	-751.8	2 706.8	-404.6
Germany	2 813.2	-886.0	1 982.8	.. c	2 331.6	-1 073.8	-423.9	-961.9	1 550.4	-227.9
Greece	.. c	-158.9	132.2	.. c	.. c	7.7	.. c	-15.3	-38.1	.. c
Hungary	.. c	.. c	.. c	.. c	.. c	807.3	.. c	.. c	.. c	.. c
Iceland	.. c	.. c	.. c	.. c	.. c	.. c	.. c	.. c	.. c	.. c
Ireland	-	.. c	-	..	..	-154.8	-	-	-1 241.5	-441.0
Israel	14.4	33.8	63.7	19.0	44.4	119.4	158.9	240.8	209.3	387.5
Italy	2 306.8	1 856.6	1 700.7	2 270.2	1 825.6	-629.2	98.1	311.6	-30.2	-108.3
Japan	586.1	-2 614.1	4 563.9	2 508.7	.. c	428.0	-1 650.3	-272.6	35.8	95.7
Korea	.. c	164.6	-444.9	.. c	94.6	321.8	-6.8	.. c	80.6	-272.4
Latvia	.. c	3.4	.. c	.. c	-	.. c	.. c	.. c	.. c	.. c
Lithuania	.. c	.. c	.. c	-47.0	23.9	19.9	.. c	24.8	23.5	.. c
Luxembourg	-61 160.0	64 617.3	.. c	-67 880.9	8 235.9	-8 409.8	-91 038.2	31 718.4	65 498.7	-134 354.4
Mexico	-424.6	.. c	.. c	145.5	174.4	-125.0	189.4	41.3	.. c	8.0
Netherlands	7 410.2	26 319.5	.. c	125 253.6	-5 272.9	4 833.6	31 481.2	-85 836.2	-36 379.7	6 044.4
New Zealand	.. c	64.3	-102.7	39.2	17.1	6.6	-1.1	3.5	-1.1	2.3
Norway	186.9	20.3	479.2	712.0	-254.1	.. c	-38.3	-365.9	.. c	49.0
Poland	112.8	-32.7	60.2	-42.5	74.1	28.8	33.8	-62.6	-28.0	79.8
Portugal	183.6	251.4	4.7	70.5	2.3	-49.8	30.4	-234.9	-180.2	50.1
Slovak Republic	-55.3	-18.0	.. c	79.5	26.2	.. c	-18.0	.. c	-23.5	27.4
Slovenia	.. c	.. c	.. c	-1.1	4.6	-	-	.. c	.. c	1.1
Spain	-759.7	1 821.7	2 542.2	2 934.1	-515.1	67.5	-209.7	-542.9	-634.7	-208.5
Sweden	1 087.0	-426.1	-1 205.0	113.1	781.8	471.1	.. c	-98.0	-26.9	.. c
Switzerland	42 488.1	626.8	7 627.8	-1 810.1	-8 884.3	-3 384.9	1 821.7	.. c	.. c	-24 103.7
Turkey	-95.1	-147.7	.. c	-59.3	-157.3	-163.7	151.1	-123.9	409.7	66.1
United Kingdom	-17 207.8	5 254.2	-27 597.1	-11 838.1	2 781.8	12 006.0	2 265.8	4 275.9	7 251.8	-1 944.2
United States	-61 299.3	-59 817.4	87 638.4	-117 921.2	.. c	7 802.7	4 073.9	-5 970.7	19 584.7	.. c
EUROPE	**106 699.1**	**114 122.4**	**-182 831.3**	**76 050.6**	**10 804.6**	**591.6**	**-28 036.3**	**-12 797.1**	**19 661.9**	**-173 570.4**
Bulgaria	.. c	-3.4	2.4	7.8	-13.7	1.1	.. c	2.4	.. c	5.7
Croatia	-16.6	.. c	.. c	.. c	.. c	.. c	.. c	.. c	.. c	.. c
Cyprus	.. c	.. c	.. c	.. c	.. c	.. c	6.8	3.5	184.7	.. c
Malta	-165.9	.. c	-113.3	28.0	207.4	.. c	.. c	.. c	.. c	.. c
Montenegro	.. c	-	.. c	.. c	.. c	.. c	-	.. c	.. c	-
Romania	14.4	9.0	24.8	-61.6	.. c	-70.8	13.5	42.5	.. c	9.1
Russian Federation	1 090.3	127.4	185.3	-640.3	-288.3	182.5	7.9	-264.4	9.0	.. c
Ukraine	11.1	2.3	.. c	.. c	.. c	.. c	.. c	.. c	6.7	.. c
AFRICA	**-96.2**	**121.7**	**103.9**	**22.4**	**-43.3**	**.. c**	**45.1**	**.. c**	**.. c**	**.. c**
Northern Africa	.. c	68.8	-2.4	31.3	-9.1	.. c	-2.3	.. c	-4.5	.. c
Algeria	.. c	.. c	.. c	-2.2	.. c	-	.. c	-	.. c	.. c
Egypt	60.8	40.6	.. c	1.1	19.4	.. c	.. c	.. c	-4.5	4.6
Libya	.. c	.. c	.. c	.. c	.. c	-	-	-	-	-
Morocco	.. c	.. c	-13.0	17.9	-23.9	.. c	.. c	3.5	.. c	-4.6
Tunisia	.. c	-2.3	.. c	.. c	-1.1	.. c	.. c	.. c	.. c	.. c
Other African countries	.. c	53.0	106.2	-9.0	-34.2	.. c	47.3	.. c	.. c	.. c
Nigeria	45.3	11.3	1.2	10.1	.. c	.. c	-	.. c	.. c	-
South Africa	380.4	89.1	60.2	.. c	36.5	-22.1	40.6	48.4	45.9	5.7
AMERICA	**-55 142.1**	**-35 596.9**	**129 974.0**	**80 799.3**	**66 495.7**	**19 726.9**	**-5 317.3**	**-1 213.3**	**14 493.5**	**133 862.1**
Northern America	-62 357.6	-61 685.3	86 914.9	-118 206.7	52 242.7	7 921.0	4 400.9	-6 326.0	20 273.1	.. c
Central America and Caribbean countries	7 215.5	26 099.7	.. c	198 991.4	14 282.6	11 437.6	.. c	4 825.9	-5 966.6	-7 727.6
Bahamas	206.8	.. c	624.3	.. c	-	-	-	-	-	-
Bermuda	6 736.7	1 420.4	49 459.5	165 713.6	20 233.6	.. c	-4 191.2	.. c	-5 843.5	-11 132.8
Cayman Islands	1 781.5	.. c	-2 817.2	14 227.0	-6 771.5	588.3	-5 755.8	.. c	-825.0	.. c
El Salvador	.. c	.. c	.. c	-	-	-	-	-	-	.. c
Guatemala	.. c	-	-	-	.. c	-	-	-	-	-
Honduras	.. c	-	.. c	.. c	-	-	-	-	-	-
Nicaragua	.. c	.. c	-	-	-	-	-	-	-	-
Panama	103.9	36.1	.. c	-52.6	-2.3	-4.4	36.1	56.7	.. c	5.7
Virgin Islands, U.S.	-	.. c	1.2	.. c	-	-	-	-	.. c	-
South America	1.1	-13.5	.. c	14.6	-29.6	367.1	.. c	285.6	186.9	.. c
Argentina	23.2	-21.4	24.8	-9.0	1.1	29.9	31.6	51.9	5.6	.. c
Bolivia	.. c	.. c	.. c	-	-	-	-	-	-	-
Brazil	171.4	81.2	-200.6	43.7	-76.4	-86.3	-330.3	35.4	95.2	-74.1
Ecuador	.. c	6.8	.. c	3.4	.. c	.. c	-	-	.. c	-
Paraguay	.. c	.. c	-	.. c	.. c	-	-	-	-	-
Peru	-33.2	10.1	-80.3	.. c	.. c	.. c	.. c	.. c	-	-
Uruguay	-5.5	-	.. c	1.1	.. c	-	-	-	.. c	.. c
Venezuela	.. c	7.9	68.5	.. c	1.1	.. c	-	.. c	.. c	.. c

Table 1. Foreign direct investment flows by country *(cont.)*

Million US dollars

	Inward					Outward				
	2016	2017	2018	2019	2020	2016	2017	2018	2019	2020
ASIA	**-12 911.6**	**-1 615.4**	**23 259.8**	**-7 847.3**	**14 813.7**	**-2 007.1**	**.. c**	**5 594.2**	**1 277.3**	**-4 725.9**
Near and Middle East	-1 333.6	-395.7	-175.9	-566.4	-389.7	-59.7	137.5	1 173.1	.. c	.. c
Gulf Arabian countries	-909.0	-418.2	-251.4	-589.9	-506.0	-179.1	-19.2	.. c	.. c	.. c
Kuwait	.. c	3.4	.. c	.. c	.. c	.. c	-	-	.. c	-
Qatar	.. c	.. c	-17.7	.. c	.. c	.. c	.. c	-	.. c	.. c
Saudi Arabia	-161.5	.. c	-434.3	-823.9	-319.1	.. c	.. c	.. c	26.9	.. c
United Arab Emirates	-538.5	-248.0	203.0	204.9	-291.7	202.4	11.3	.. c	.. c	.. c
Other Near and Middle East	-423.5	24.8	75.5	23.5	116.2	118.3	157.8	.. c	209.3	.. c
Jordan	.. c	.. c	.. c	.. c	.. c	.. c	.. c	.. c	.. c	.. c
Other Asian countries	-11 576.9	-1 220.8	23 435.6	-7 280.9	15 204.6	-1 948.5	.. c	4 422.3	.. c	.. c
China	2 097.8	120.6	-21.2	2 129.2	2 086.6	.. c	.. c	.. c	.. c	.. c
Hong Kong, China	268.7	266.0	466.2	898.9	898.0	-479.9	.. c	441.4	-84.0	-9.1
India	-217.8	31.6	193.6	180.2	62.7	-10.0	9.0	48.4	-10.1	77.5
Indonesia	.. c	.. c	.. c	-2.2	-20.5	.. c	.. c	.. c	.. c	9.1
Iran, Islamic Republic of	.. c	-	-	-	-	-	-	-	-	-
Malaysia	6.6	11.3	16.5	-5.6	-28.5	.. c	1.1	.. c	-62.7	-53.6
Philippines	-61.9	-45.1	34.2	-6.7	.. c	.. c	.. c	.. c	-14.6	-5.7
Singapore	-14 155.7	962.7	.. c	.. c	1 388.0	248.8	.. c	-180.6	.. c	.. c
Chinese Taipei	2.2	-87.9	-158.1	.. c	.. c	25.4	31.6	.. c	153.4	325.9
Thailand	.. c	-18.0	.. c	-24.6	26.2	.. c	-6.8	.. c	.. c	1.1
Viet Nam	.. c	.. c	-1.2	-2.2	-	16.6	.. c	-13.0	4.5	-3.4
AUSTRALIA, OCEANIA AND POLAR REGIONS	**.. c**	**859.0**	**-504.0**	**285.5**	**85.5**	**-350.5**	**38.3**	**197.1**	**3.4**	**353.3**
WORLD unallocated and confidential	**.. d**	**-25 168.5**	**17 987.7**	**118.7**	**-11 468.9**	**.. d**	**32 711.1**	**13 321.1**	**25 591.6**	**-853.6**
European Union (since 01/02/2020)	..	..	..	..	**12 030.8**	..	..	..	..	**-134 189.2**
G20 countries excl. European Union	**.. d**	**.. d**	**.. d**	**.. d**	**.. d**	**.. d**	**.. d**	**.. d**	**.. d**	**.. d**
G20 OECD countries	**.. d**	**.. d**	**.. d**	**.. d**	**.. d**	**18 744.9**	**6 470.5**	**.. d**	**.. d**	**.. d**
G20 Non-OECD countries	**.. d**	**.. d**	**.. d**	**.. d**	**1 482.6**	**.. d**	**.. d**	**.. d**	**.. d**	**.. d**
MENA countries	**.. d**	**.. d**	**.. d**	**.. d**	**.. d**	**.. d**	**.. d**	**.. d**	**.. d**	**.. d**
ASEAN countries	**-14 402.3**	**.. c**	**18 858.7**	**.. c**	**1 437.0**	**-372.7**	**.. c**	**774.2**	**.. c**	**.. c**

- Nil; .. Not available; c Confidential data; d Secondary Confidentiality; e Estimated value

Note: Detailed metadata at: *http://metalinks.oecd.org/idi/20220712/6d95.*

Source: *OECD International Direct Investment Statistics (database): https://doi.org/10.1787/idi-data-en*

Table 2. Foreign direct investment positions by country
At year end

Million US dollars

	Inward					Outward				
	2016	2017	2018	2019	2020	2016	2017	2018	2019	2020
WORLD	**840 646.1**	**1 058 012.7**	**1 049 365.7**	**1 212 727.5**	**1 346 857.3**	**856 581.6**	**986 845.8**	**960 531.3**	**1 125 237.0**	**1 211 843.2**
OECD COUNTRIES	**639 685.9**	**870 374.2**	**764 448.1**	**722 316.3**	**851 851.8**	**711 684.4**	**798 833.1**	**715 748.8**	**883 218.4**	**933 617.6**
Australia	-731.5	403.0	424.8	657.2	784.1	.. c	1 364.8	649.2	1 062.7	3 178.3
Austria	448.0	480.9	389.3	.. c	510.5	.. c	-217.1	-49.2	74.1	211.1
Belgium	9 638.5	7 419.0	25 143.1	-16 343.5	-19 600.0	.. c	1 686.3	1 092.3	2 970.1	5 427.7
Canada	2 496.0	425.8	11 680.8	.. c	2 418.7	2 463.4	2 500.6	2 667.7	3 313.9	4 015.2
Chile	-161.3	-136.7	-121.4	-69.6	1.2	31.6	40.8	.. c	484.2	528.9
Colombia	.. c	254.3	113.4	64.0	27.0	.. c	.. c	.. c	104.5	62.6
Costa Rica	.. c	-70.8	-4.6	47.2	-22.1	.. c	105.5	37.8	11.2	61.4
Czech Republic	-132.8	12.0	73.3	102.2	89.6	.. c	-67.2	279.4	251.6	250.3
Denmark	506.0	130.7	-97.3	-374.1	481.0	.. c	-116.3	209.5	2 242.2	3 779.6
Estonia	1.1	1.2	1.1	2.2	2.5	.. c	.. c	.. c	.. c	.. c
Finland	-183.4	-101.9	-137.4	545.9	593.9	-763.2	-847.9	-87.0	1 667.0	1 682.4
France	20 509.1	23 816.3	24 112.7	24 646.1	27 591.1	3 319.3	5 361.0	7 155.9	.. c	3 544.0
Germany	4 759.1	7 140.8	7 452.5	7 046.7	9 333.7	3 725.1	3 871.4	1 183.9	3 018.4	3 636.0
Greece	.. c	.. c	234.7	249.4	251.6	100.1	-217.1	360.7	.. c	422.1
Hungary	.. c	.. c	.. c	.. c	279.8	.. c	.. c	.. c	.. c	.. c
Iceland	.. c	.. c	.. c	.. c	.. c	.. c	.. c	.. c	.. c	.. c
Ireland	-	.. c	-	-	-	.. c	.. c	-	10 450.5	11 005.0
Israel	128.6	151.1	-79.0	-55.0	17.2	.. c	.. c	.. c	1 482.8	1 740.1
Italy	8 216.5	10 142.7	10 124.8	10 650.4	12 184.3	549.2	682.4	1 947.6	1 859.1	2 107.0
Japan	2 539.3	421.0	4 914.1	.. c	.. c	6 232.7	3 882.2	3 620.3	3 549.8	3 552.6
Korea	4 837.1	5 111.5	656.1	12.4	110.4	.. c	758.0	983.5	.. c	764.5
Latvia	.. c	.. c	5.7	.. c	.. c	.. c	.. c	.. c	.. c	.. c
Lithuania	40.1	34.8	6.9	-48.3	-28.2	.. c	25.2	46.9	51.7	99.4
Luxembourg	.. c	268 463.7	200 470.6	126 253.7	146 414.3	423 202.3	339 971.2	377 783.4	521 925.4	454 423.9
Mexico	-321.5	.. c	-405.3	-228.0	-57.7	695.7	941.5	943.4	850.4	795.2
Netherlands	89 640.6	110 159.5	-5 804.9	153 292.5	163 798.0	57 785.4	181 039.8	82 761.6	69 346.2	71 634.6
New Zealand	80.1	139.1	34.3	61.8	.. c	.. c	353.8	.. c	.. c	.. c
Norway	591.3	813.1	1 683.1	2 351.2	2 244.4	.. c	.. c	113.4	.. c	.. c
Poland	24.2	-24.0	99.6	-18.0	46.6	.. c	375.4	709.9	685.2	816.1
Portugal	629.3	952.3	613.7	754.9	617.3	.. c	.. c	.. c	.. c	.. c
Slovak Republic	-47.4	-72.0	.. c	.. c	62.6	959.2	961.9	.. c	.. c	.. c
Slovenia	.. c	-6.0	-8.0	-11.2	.. c	.. c	.. c	14.9	.. c	16.0
Spain	8 403.1	11 107.0	12 586.4	15 074.1	11 895.9	.. c	.. c	10 573.6	.. c	.. c
Sweden	3 085.3	2 655.3	1 509.0	1 144.7	2 126.6	.. c	6 608.3	6 599.5	6 901.8	7 791.1
Switzerland	60 657.7	86 613.1	73 948.9	.. c	103 933.0	-18 538.0	-15 808.3	-242.7	13 411.6	-32 282.5
Turkey	.. c	.. c	-111.1	-184.2	-343.6	.. c	.. c	.. c	2 166.9	1 639.5
United Kingdom	78 050.0	70 197.9	58 450.9	42 286.0	46 101.4	99 266.4	106 291.7	98 329.5	107 598.3	116 054.7
United States	235 690.9	233 552.4	333 673.0	208 941.8	294 576.0	92 687.9	111 362.4	102 119.3	105 645.9	249 676.0
EUROPE	**497 426.0**	**729 005.8**	**529 992.0**	**630 848.1**	**673 483.9**	**630 141.2**	**708 088.3**	**664 244.3**	**807 090.5**	**738 088.1**
Bulgaria	-	-4.8	-	10.1	-1.2	.. c	.. c	.. c	47.2	62.6
Croatia	.. c	-4.8	.. c	10.1	46.6	.. c	.. c	.. c	.. c	.. c
Cyprus	.. c	.. c	.. c	.. c	19.6	.. c	844.3	869.0	1 085.1	1 343.7
Malta	.. c	467.7	336.6	261.7	463.9	.. c	.. c	.. c	.. c	-1 818.6
Montenegro	-	.. c	.. c	.. c	.. c	.. c	.. c	.. c	.. c	.. c
Romania	-8.4	2.4	29.8	-37.1	3.7	.. c	225.5	672.1	.. c	.. c
Russian Federation	2 422.3	2 680.5	2 687.2	1 894.0	1 844.4	.. c	604.5	382.4	404.4	478.6
Ukraine	-15.8	.. c	.. c	.. c	-17.2	.. c	.. c	.. c	.. c	.. c
AFRICA	**4.2**	**.. c**	**.. c**	**177.5**	**125.2**	**.. c**	**-227.9**	**-469.4**	**.. c**	**571.8**
Northern Africa	.. c	-4.8	-53.8	-6.7	-17.2	.. c	.. c	92.7	.. c	98.2
Algeria	-	.. c	-4.6	.. c	1.2	-	.. c	.. c	.. c	-
Egypt	44.3	-46.8	-29.8	-10.1	8.6	-	.. c	.. c	-3.4	1.2
Libya	.. c	.. c	.. c	.. c	.. c	-	-	-	-	-
Morocco	.. c	54.0	-6.9	7.9	-20.9	83.3	93.5	92.7	94.4	96.9
Tunisia	-	.. c	.. c	.. c	.. c	.. c	.. c	-	-	-
Other African countries	.. c	.. c	.. c	184.2	142.3	.. c	.. c	-562.2	.. c	473.7
Nigeria	24.2	-10.8	-9.2	.. c	.. c	.. c	.. c	.. c	.. c	.. c
South Africa	418.5	61.2	146.6	52.8	83.4	5.3	51.6	99.6	129.2	133.8
AMERICA	**308 094.2**	**320 768.8**	**473 152.0**	**518 393.6**	**604 232.4**	**170 419.5**	**181 131.0**	**175 628.6**	**185 319.0**	**304 590.7**
Northern America	238 187.0	233 977.0	345 353.8	207 998.2	296 996.0	95 151.3	113 863.0	104 787.0	108 959.8	253 690.0
Central America and Caribbean countries	70 498.6	86 959.7	128 262.0	310 757.1	307 559.2	74 008.6	66 319.3	69 681.7	75 080.9	49 671.1
Bahamas	.. c	.. c	11 920.1	.. c	6 786.1	-	-	-	-	-
Bermuda	48 187.0	29 124.5	74 603.8	228 403.7	253 108.4	53 506.9	50 314.2	54 484.8	53 334.1	23 636.0
Cayman Islands	12 142.9	45 767.6	41 228.5	.. c	47 031.5	.. c	.. c	13 442.9	.. c	23 871.6
El Salvador	.. c	-	.. c	.. c	.. c	-	-	-	-	.. c
Guatemala	-2.1	-2.4	-2.3	.. c	.. c	-	-	-	-	-
Honduras	.. c	.. c	.. c	.. c	.. c	-	-	-	-	-
Nicaragua	.. c	-	-	-	-	-	-	-	-	-
Panama	.. c	.. c	132.8	.. c	.. c	.. c	54.0	106.5	91.0	122.7
Virgin Islands, U.S.	-	.. c	.. c	.. c	.. c	-	-	-	-	-
South America	-591.3	-167.9	-463.7	-361.7	-322.7	1 260.7	948.7	1 159.8	1 278.4	1 229.6
Argentina	-47.4	-67.2	-38.9	-15.7	-13.5	.. c	.. c	213.0	210.1	265.1
Bolivia	.. c	.. c	-	-	-	-	-	-	-	-
Brazil	-131.8	-133.1	-327.5	.. c	-278.6	744.2	398.2	400.7	467.3	357.1
Ecuador	.. c	-	-8.0	.. c	-	.. c	.. c	.. c	.. c	.. c
Paraguay	.. c	.. c	.. c	.. c	.. c	-	-	-	-	-
Peru	.. c	-10.8	.. c	-61.8	-34.4	.. c	.. c	.. c	.. c	.. c
Uruguay	.. c	-8.4	-5.7	.. c	.. c	-	-	-	.. c	.. c
Venezuela	.. c	-63.6	17.2	.. c	.. c	.. c	.. c	.. c	.. c	-

Table 2. Foreign direct investment positions by country *(cont.)*

At year end

Million US dollars

	Inward					Outward				
	2016	2017	2018	2019	2020	2016	2017	2018	2019	2020
ASIA	**.. c**	**6 856.6**	**27 437.6**	**48 067.9**	**59 409.7**	**21 248.0**	**69 186.9**	**73 163.5**	**77 683.7**	**72 791.8**
Near and Middle East	.. c	-2 326.7	-1 336.2	-1 582.8	-1 866.5	1 414.6	1 602.3	1 790.7	.. c	-3 675.3
Gulf Arabian countries	-2 174.6	-2 485.0	-1 274.3	-1 555.8	-1 988.0	.. c	.. c	.. c	800.9	.. c
Kuwait	.. c	.. c	.. c	.. c	.. c	.. c	-	-	.. c	.. c
Qatar	.. c	.. c	.. c	.. c	-11.0	.. c	.. c	.. c	.. c	.. c
Saudi Arabia	.. c	.. c	.. c	.. c	.. c	.. c	7.2	56.1	64.0	.. c
United Arab Emirates	-462.7	-630.8	984.7	1 259.3	1 019.8	.. c	110.3	792.3	694.2	.. c
Other Near and Middle East	.. c	158.3	-61.8	-27.0	121.5	.. c	.. c	.. c	1 489.6	.. c
Jordan	.. c	.. c	.. c	.. c	-1.2	-	.. c	.. c	.. c	.. c
Other Asian countries	5 633.0	9 183.3	28 773.8	49 650.6	61 276.2	19 833.5	67 584.6	71 372.8	75 392.0	76 468.3
China	.. c	.. c	7 248.7	9 121.5	10 164.4	.. c	.. c	.. c	.. c	.. c
Hong Kong, China	634.6	855.1	1 812.5	2 766.8	3 404.1	5 621.4	.. c	.. c	.. c	.. c
India	-470.1	-796.4	-551.9	-399.9	-312.9	44.3	50.4	175.2	133.7	159.5
Indonesia	.. c	7.2	-2.3	-5.6	-27.0	.. c	.. c	.. c	.. c	.. c
Iran, Islamic Republic of	-	-	-	-	-	-	-	-	-	-
Malaysia	3.2	-39.6	-21.8	68.5	41.7	.. c	.. c	17.2	6.7	-43.0
Philippines	-41.1	8.4	41.2	35.9	105.5	.. c	.. c	304.6	.. c	.. c
Singapore	-4 653.7	-4 852.5	.. c	-994.2	1 422.3	1 219.6	.. c	.. c	.. c	.. c
Chinese Taipei	315.2	209.9	57.2	420.1	192.7	.. c	97.1	697.3	.. c	1 365.8
Thailand	-44.3	-	-87.0	-115.7	-96.9	.. c	.. c	12.6	.. c	11.0
Viet Nam	.. c	-	-	1.1	1.2	.. c	13.2	17.2	20.2	16.0
AUSTRALIA, OCEANIA AND POLAR REGIONS	**-653.5**	**544.5**	**456.8**	**717.8**	**863.9**	**.. c**	**1 718.6**	**1 162.1**	**1 847.9**	**4 303.6**
WORLD unallocated and confidential	**.. d**	**724.4**	**18 381.0**	**14 522.6**	**8 742.2**	**.. d**	**26 948.9**	**46 802.2**	**52 283.8**	**91 497.1**
European Union (since 01/02/2020)	**..**	**..**	**..**	**..**	**362 096.0**	**..**	**..**	**..**	**..**	**581 352.3**
G20 countries excl. European Union	**.. d**	**.. d**	**.. d**	**.. d**	**.. d**	**.. d**	**.. d**	**.. d**	**.. d**	**.. d**
G20 OECD countries	**.. d**	**.. d**	**.. d**	**.. d**	**.. d**	**.. d**	**.. d**	**.. d**	**.. d**	**388 963.1**
G20 Non-OECD countries	**.. d**	**.. d**	**.. d**	**.. d**	**.. d**	**.. d**	**.. d**	**.. d**	**.. d**	**.. d**
MENA countries	**.. d**	**.. d**	**.. d**	**.. d**	**.. d**	**.. d**	**.. d**	**.. d**	**.. d**	**.. d**
ASEAN countries	**.. c**	**.. c**	**13 630.6**	**-1 009.9**	**1 362.1**	**688.3**	**.. c**	**.. c**	**.. c**	**.. c**

\- Nil; .. Not available; c Confidential data; d Secondary Confidentiality

Note: Detailed metadata at: *http://metalinks.oecd.org/idi/20220712/6d95.*

Source: OECD *International Direct Investment Statistics (database): https://doi.org/10.1787/idi-data-en*

IRELAND

Table 3. Foreign direct investment income by country

Million US dollars

	Inward					Outward				
	2016	2017	2018	2019	2020	2016	2017	2018	2019	2020
WORLD	**61 827.9**	**75 764.9**	**92 976.5**	**94 832.6**	**105 622.8**	**14 638.9**	**17 361.1**	**19 827.7**	**17 405.1**	**16 705.4**
OECD COUNTRIES	**38 457.4**	**49 354.1**	**63 700.0**	**66 832.0**	**..**	**15 449.5**	**15 750.2**	**19 802.9 e**	**20 292.2**	**..**
Australia	.. c	22.5	-5.9	9.0	6.8	91.8	-12.4	-13.0	7.8	-61.5
Austria	12.2	4.5	5.9	9.0	9.1	15.5	-1.1	17.7	17.9	5.7
Belgium	1 217.5	2 008.8	4 028.1	2 580.3	1 784.6	79.6	39.5	64.9	-19.0	.. c
Canada	35.4	-48.5	-67.3	-191.4	-47.9	-25.4	4.5	-2.4	-38.1	9.1
Chile	-2.2	.. c	-1.2	.. c	-	-	-	-	.. c	1.1
Colombia	-	-	-	-	-	-	-	-	.. c	-
Costa Rica	.. c	.. c	-	-	-	4.4	.. c	-	-	-
Czech Republic	-	-	-	-	-	.. c	-11.3	-43.7	-38.1	.. c
Denmark	89.6	74.4	.. c	236.2	.. c	11.1	6.8	15.3	57.1	.. c
Estonia	-	-	-	-	-	-	-	-	-	-
Finland	13.3	11.3	9.4	3.4	.. c	-	.. c	.. c	.. c	-
France	2 255.9	2 437.2	2 778.2	2 786.3	2 010.3	142.7	140.9	50.7	275.4	194.9
Germany	758.6	352.8	935.9	-3 390.8	1 171.5	268.7	165.7	-133.4	90.7	80.9
Greece	-	.. c	.. c	.. c	.. c	.. c	.. c	.. c	.. c	.. c
Hungary	.. c	.. c	.. c	.. c	.. c	.. c	.. c	.. c	6.7	.. c
Iceland	-	.. c	-	.. c	-	-	-	-	-	-
Ireland	-	-	-	-	-	-	.. c	-	-	-
Israel	-	-	1.2	-	-5.7	.. c	.. c	.. c	.. c	221.1
Italy	1 659.8	1 652.6	1 645.2	2 265.8	1 876.9	67.5	16.9	53.1	25.7	-61.5
Japan	419.1	406.9	544.1	.. c	.. c	-11.1	-20.3	-38.9	.. c	9.1
Korea	85.1	67.6	5.9	15.7	.. c	.. c	.. c	.. c	.. c	.. c
Latvia	-	-	-	-	-	-	.. c	-	-	-
Lithuania	-	-	-	-	-	-	-	.. c	.. c	.. c
Luxembourg	4 598.0	11 272.7	14 676.0	17 331.2	9 023.4	10 401.4	9 696.8	10 668.0	12 260.2	12 507.1
Mexico	-1.1	-4.5	-5.9	-6.7	-2.3	45.3	.. c	27.1	.. c	55.8
Netherlands	12 987.9	7 436.6	7 692.7	10 753.4	10 689.5	2 981.3	4 123.5	5 734.7	5 102.4	2 376.1
New Zealand	-	4.5	1.2	1.1	-	.. c	.. c	.. c	.. c	.. c
Norway	.. c	-301.0	-14.2	79.5	-184.6	1.1	4.5	.. c	-10.1	2.3
Poland	-	-	-	1.1	2.3	1.1	19.2	7.1	16.8	16.0
Portugal	71.9	32.7	36.6	.. c	.. c	.. c	-6.8	.. c	-	.. c
Slovak Republic	-	-	-1.2	-1.1	-	.. c	.. c	.. c	.. c	.. c
Slovenia	-	-	-	-	-	-	-	-	-	-
Spain	246.6	558.0	535.8	363.8	469.5	45.3	-6.8	-8.3	-137.7	4.6
Sweden	188.0	181.5	190.0	110.8	-136.8	96.2	50.7	29.5	-124.3	-96.9
Switzerland	8 283.8	9 189.5	14 037.5	16 125.6	25 824.5	-1 003.0	.. c	173.5	49.3	-589.2
Turkey	-	.. c	.. c	.. c	.. c	26.5	.. c	.. c	.. c	9.1
United Kingdom	4 133.6	4 438.1	4 283.0	3 855.4	1 660.4	424.6	2 207.2	2 642.5	2 093.4	2 658.7
United States	684.5	8 332.8	11 980.4	10 846.3	8 055.8	498.7	-1 226.5	-272.6	423.2	3 324.2
EUROPE	**42 523.5**	**51 193.8**	**65 279.1**	**68 825.7**	**72 555.0**	**16 078.7**	**18 749.9**	**20 756.5**	**20 165.7**	**18 046.7**
Bulgaria	-	-	-	-	-	-	.. c	.. c	-	.. c
Croatia	-	-	.. c	-1.1	-	-	-	-	.. c	-
Cyprus	.. c	.. c	.. c	.. c	.. c	.. c	.. c	.. c	.. c	.. c
Malta	29.9	32.7	35.4	29.1	52.4	.. c	.. c	.. c	.. c	.. c
Montenegro	-	-	-	-	-	-	-	-	.. c	-
Romania	-	-	-	.. c	.. c	18.8	10.1	3.5	5.6	26.2
Russian Federation	.. c	.. c	1.2	-41.4	.. c	.. c	.. c	-41.3	.. c	.. c
Ukraine	-	-	-	-	-	.. c	.. c	.. c	.. c	.. c
AFRICA	**12.2**	**.. c**	**11.8**	**.. c**	**17.1**	**.. c**	**.. c**	**56.7**	**-21.3**	**10.3**
Northern Africa	-	-	-	-	-	-	.. c	.. c	-	-
Algeria	-	-	-	-	-	-	-	-	-	-
Egypt	-	-	-	-	-	-	-	-	-	-
Libya	-	-	-	-	-	-	-	-	-	-
Morocco	-	-	-	-	-	-	-	-	-	-
Tunisia	-	-	-	-	-	-	.. c	.. c	-	-
Other African countries	12.2	.. c	11.8	.. c	16.0	.. c	-	55.5	-21.3	9.1
Nigeria	-	-	-	-	-	.. c	.. c	-	.. c	-
South Africa	11.1	.. c	10.6	.. c	14.8	-	-	.. c	2.2	.. c
AMERICA	**18 402.1**	**22 968.1**	**25 531.7**	**21 277.3**	**27 980.6**	**3 290.9**	**2 165.5**	**2 748.7**	**948.2**	**1 916.8**
Northern America	721.0	8 283.2	11 913.1	10 654.9	8 008.0	473.3	-1 222.0	-275.0	385.1	3 333.3
Central America and Caribbean countries	17 685.5	14 686.1	13 622.1	.. c	19 972.7	2 729.2	3 270.2	2 902.2	.. c	-1 435.9
Bahamas	.. c	.. c	.. c	427.6	.. c	-	.. c	-	-	-
Bermuda	13 110.7	8 614.6	8 003.1	5 757.3	15 451.9	1 272.8	1 749.5	1 269.9	-582.1	-2 475.2
Cayman Islands	4 472.0	5 631.8	4 548.6	4 249.4	3 886.0	1 405.5	.. c	1 596.8	1 001.9	974.4
El Salvador	-	-	-	-	-	-	-	-	-	-
Guatemala	-	-	-	-	-	-	-	-	-	-
Honduras	-	-	-	-	-	-	-	-	-	-
Nicaragua	-	-	-	-	-	-	-	-	-	-
Panama	-11.1	-1.1	4.7	4.5	4.6	-	-	-	-	6.8
Virgin Islands, U.S.	-	-	-	-	-	-	-	-	-	-
South America	-4.4	-1.1	-3.5	.. c	-	88.5	117.2	121.6	.. c	18.2
Argentina	-	-	-	-	.. c	32.1	.. c	.. c	29.1	6.8
Bolivia	-	-	-	-	-	-	-	-	-	-
Brazil	.. c	-	.. c	-	-	54.2	.. c	94.4	14.6	9.1
Ecuador	-	-	-	-	-	-	-	-	-	-
Paraguay	-	.. c	-	.. c	-	-	-	-	-	-
Peru	-	-	-	-1.1	-1.1	-	.. c	-	-	-
Uruguay	-	-	-	-	-	-	-	-	-	-
Venezuela	-	-	-	-	-	-	.. c	-	-	-

IRELAND

Table 3. Foreign direct investment income by country *(cont.)*

Million US dollars

	Inward					Outward				
	2016	2017	2018	2019	2020	2016	2017	2018	2019	2020
ASIA	**677.9**	**1 139.7**	**1 999.3**	**4 578.5**	**4 809.1**	**.. c**	**.. c**	**.. c**	**.. c**	**.. c**
Near and Middle East	7.7	7.9	-26.0	108.6	21.7	.. c	.. c	514.6	189.2	85.5
Gulf Arabian countries	7.7	6.8	-27.1	.. c	26.2	.. c	.. c	.. c	.. c	-136.8
Kuwait	-	-	-	.. c	.. c	-	-	-	-	-
Qatar	-	-	-	-	-	-	-	-	.. c	.. c
Saudi Arabia	-	-	-	-1.1	-	.. c	-	.. c	.. c	.. c
United Arab Emirates	7.7	6.8	.. c	.. c	.. c	-	.. c	.. c	.. c	.. c
Other Near and Middle East	-	-	1.2	.. c	-4.6	.. c	.. c	.. c	.. c	221.1
Jordan	-	-	-	.. c	-	-	-	-	.. c	-
Other Asian countries	670.1	1 132.9	2 025.3	4 469.9	4 788.6	.. c	.. c	.. c	.. c	.. c
China	.. c	.. c	.. c	.. c	.. c	.. c	.. c	.. c	.. c	.. c
Hong Kong, China	.. c	.. c	.. c	487.0	467.2	2.2	-11.3	7.1	14.6	19.4
India	.. c	.. c	.. c	.. c	.. c	18.8	15.8	.. c	77.2	68.4
Indonesia	-	-	-	-	-	-	-	-	-	5.7
Iran, Islamic Republic of	-	-	-	-	-	-	-	-	-	-
Malaysia	-	-	-	.. c	.. c	-	-	-	.. c	.. c
Philippines	-	-	-	-	-	-	-	-	-	-
Singapore	99.5	138.7	.. c	.. c	151.6	.. c	11.3	7.1	.. c	.. c
Chinese Taipei	-	-	-	.. c	.. c	.. c	.. c	.. c	-	.. c
Thailand	-	-	.. c	.. c	.. c	-	-	-	-	-
Viet Nam	-	-	-	-	-	-	-	-	-	-
AUSTRALIA, OCEANIA AND POLAR REGIONS	**.. c**	**23.7**	**-4.7**	**10.1**	**6.8**	**99.5**	**-7.9**	**-18.9**	**7.8**	**-70.7**
WORLD unallocated and confidential	**.. d**	**439.6**	**159.3**	**141.1**	**254.1**	**.. d**	**-3 541.9**	**-4 205.1**	**-3 976.3**	**-3 385.8**
European Union (since 01/02/2020)	..	..	..	..	..	..	..	..	..	..
G20 countries excl. European Union	**.. d**	**.. d**	**..**	**.. d**	**..**	**.. d**	**.. d**	**..**	**.. d**	**..**
G20 OECD countries	**.. d**	**.. d**	**..**	**.. d**	**..**	**.. d**	**.. d**	**..**	**.. d**	**..**
G20 Non-OECD countries	**.. d**	**.. d**	**..**	**.. d**	**..**	**.. d**	**.. d**	**..**	**.. d**	**..**
MENA countries	**7.7**	**6.8**	**..**	**.. d**	**..**	**.. d**	**.. d**	**..**	**.. d**	**..**
ASEAN countries	**102.8**	**138.7**	**.. c**	**320.2**	**142.5**	**15.5**	**.. c**	**7.1**	**.. c**	**52.4**

- Nil; .. Not available; c Confidential data; d Secondary Confidentiality; e Estimated value

Note: Detailed metadata at: *http://metalinks.oecd.org/idi/20220712/6d95.*

Source: *OECD International Direct Investment Statistics (database): https://doi.org/10.1787/idi-data-en*

Table 4. Foreign direct investment flows by industrial sector

Million US dollars

	Inward					Outward				
	2016	2017	2018	2019	2020	2016	2017	2018	2019	2020
All FDI activities	**39 375.2**	**52 722.4**	**-12 009.9**	**149 429.1**	**80 687.2**	**30 056.4**	**-2 043.7**	**5 150.5**	**32 082.2**	**-44 894.6**
Agriculture, forestry and fishing	**.. c**	**.. c**	**.. c**	**.. c**	**.. c**	**-**	**-**	**-**	**-**	**-**
Mining and quarrying	**-**	**.. c**	**.. c**	**.. c**	**.. c**	**.. c**	**.. c**	**.. c**	**.. c**	**.. c**
Extraction activities	-	-	-	-	-	-	-	-	-	-
Manufacturing	**-3 059.8**	**-40 928.9**	**80 075.5**	**59 391.0**	**50 612.0**	**4 749.5**	**3 760.6**	**15 103.3**	**2 673.2**	**-39 144.2**
of which:										
Food products, beverages and tobacco	-410.3	-109.3	.. c	10 591.1	-903.7	358.3	.. c	626.7	3 759.1	.. c
Textiles, wood and paper products; printing	.. c	-	-	.. c	.. c	.. c	.. c	.. c	.. c	.. c
Chemical, rubber, plastic, non-metallic mineral products	12 029.2	-8 361.0	19 252.9	36 802.9	91 368.7	.. c	.. c	1 005.5	1 079.1	-24 768.1
Metal and machinery products, except electrical equipment	.. c	.. c	.. c	.. c	.. c	.. c	.. c	.. c	-1 893.0	.. c
Motor vehicles, trailers, semi-trailers, other transport equipment	.. c	.. c	.. c	-	-	.. c	.. c	.. c	.. c	.. c
Other manufacturing	1 066.0	1 938.9	19 623.5	.. c	-9 465.5	-97.3	16.9	3 472.2	.. c	.. c
Electricity, gas, steam and air conditioning supply	**.. c**	**.. c**	**.. c**	**.. c**	**.. c**	**.. c**	**.. c**	**.. c**	**.. c**	**.. c**
Water supply; sewerage, waste management and remediation activities	**-**	**-**	**-**	**-**	**-**	**-**	**-**	**-**	**-**	**-**
Construction	**-**	**-**	**-**	**1.1**	**1.1**	**-**	**-**	**-**	**-**	**-**
Services	**42 325.6**	**93 448.3**	**-92 960.0**	**90 017.9**	**30 019.4**	**23 942.3**	**-8 973.1**	**-11 752.6**	**27 882.0**	**-3 443.9**
Wholesale and retail trade; repair of motor vehicles and motorcycles	.. c	31 392.2	-3 121.7	5 348.7	-2 894.6	1 925.2	-1 792.4	-964.2	-687.3	-1 247.9
Transportation and storage	.. c	.. c	.. c	.. c	.. c	.. c	.. c	.. c	.. c	.. c
Accommodation and food service activities	-	-	-	-	-	-	-	-	-	-
Information and communication	7 806.0	90 701.2	-61 891.9	30 462.3	59 075.8	-1 297.1	.. c	.. c	.. c	3 981.8
Financial and insurance activities	6 564.2	5 056.9	-20 652.7	17 401.8	-380.6	14 734.0	8 090.4	-11 013.8	3 081.8	-3 457.6
Activities of holding companies	-1 812.5	1 630.0	-2 812.5	-2 805.3	39.9	-754.2	2 427.0	-9 645.9	753.4	2 926.5
Real estate activities	-	-	.. c	.. c	.. c	-	-	.. c	.. c	.. c
Professional, scientific and technical activities	18 794.6	.. c	-3 539.5	43 216.2	-13 865.5	2 079.0	-59 940.3	54 187.4	55 437.1	-10 453.6
Administrative and support service activities	1 533.8	-3 125.9	-4 233.4	-7 876.4	-12 311.1	797.3	.. c	3 602.0	.. c	-4 290.6
Public administration; activities of households and of extraterritorial organisations	-	-	-	-	-	-	-	-	-	-
Education	-	-	-	-	-	-	-	-	-	-
Human health and social work activities	-	-	-	-	-	-	-	-	-	-
Arts, entertainment and recreation	-	-	-	.. c	.. c	.. c	.. c	.. c	.. c	.. c
Other services	-	-	-	-	-	-	-	-	-	-
Not allocated and confidential	**.. c**	**.. c**	**.. c**	**.. c**	**.. c**	**.. c**	**.. c**	**.. c**	**.. c**	**.. c**
Private real estate activities	**-**	**-**	**-**	**-**	**-**	**-**	**-**	**-**	**-**	**-**

- Nil; c Confidential data

Note: Detailed metadata at: *http://metalinks.oecd.org/idi/20220712/6d95*.

Source: OECD *International Direct Investment Statistics (database)*: *https://doi.org/10.1787/idi-data-en*

IRELAND

Table 5. Foreign direct investment positions by industrial sector
At year end

Million US dollars

	Inward					Outward				
	2016	2017	2018	2019	2020	2016	2017	2018	2019	2020
All FDI activities	**840 646.1**	**1 058 012.7**	**1 049 365.7**	**1 212 727.5**	**1 346 857.3**	**856 581.6**	**986 845.8**	**960 531.3**	**1 125 237.0**	**1 211 843.2**
Agriculture, forestry and fishing	**.. c**	**.. c**	**.. c**	**.. c**	**.. c**	-	-	-	-	-
Mining and quarrying	**.. c**	**.. c**	**.. c**	**.. c**	**.. c**	**.. c**	**.. c**	**.. c**	**.. c**	**.. c**
Extraction activities	-	-	-	-	-	-	-	-	-	-
Manufacturing	**338 813.1**	**323 992.6**	**435 278.2**	**489 076.6**	**575 050.9**	**66 143.1**	**87 474.2**	**125 479.7**	**134 391.1**	**229 876.1**
of which:										
Food products, beverages and tobacco	5 640.4	5 044.4	.. c	.. c	.. c	20 756.8	.. c	37 648.3	.. c	.. c
Textiles, wood and paper products; printing	-	-	-	.. c	.. c	.. c	.. c	.. c	.. c	.. c
Chemical, rubber, plastic, non-metallic mineral products	75 389.5	88 749.1	118 797.8	163 057.7	282 683.8	.. c	.. c	.. c	2 101.8	80 569.4
Metal and machinery products, except electrical equipment	.. c	.. c	.. c	.. c	.. c	.. c	.. c	.. c	.. c	.. c
Motor vehicles, trailers, semi-trailers, other transport equipment	.. c	.. c	.. c	-	-	.. c	.. c	.. c	.. c	.. c
Other manufacturing	15 863.8	20 788.0	33 942.1	59 739.4	46 613.1	.. c	10 560.1	13 705.1	4 693.3	495.8
Electricity, gas, steam and air conditioning supply	**.. c**	**.. c**	**.. c**	**.. c**	**.. c**	**.. c**	**.. c**	**.. c**	**.. c**	**.. c**
Water supply; sewerage, waste management and remediation activities	-	-	-	-	-	-	-	-	-	-
Construction	-	-	-	-	-	-	-	-	-	-
Services	**500 819.0**	**732 762.1**	**612 933.4**	**722 506.2**	**770 611.1**	**758 951.2**	**865 181.1**	**809 029.1**	**954 272.1**	**946 344.3**
Wholesale and retail trade; repair of motor vehicles and motorcycles	18 194.4	52 753.7	33 220.7	33 717.1	35 720.9	16 775.6	19 342.8	12 215.5	11 878.2	11 749.9
Transportation and storage	.. c	.. c	.. c	.. c	.. c	.. c	.. c	.. c	.. c	.. c
Accommodation and food service activities	-	-	-	-	-	-	-	-	-	-
Information and communication	20 304.6	198 402.5	139 294.7	168 748.6	237 734.7	3 578.6	.. c	.. c	.. c	.. c
Financial and insurance activities	255 443.2	.. c	.. c	289 565.3	337 544.5	96 473.1	105 693.2	123 763.5	114 801.2	139 782.8
Activities of holding companies	22 537.2	24 346.4	24 362.3	23 737.4	25 162.6	7 573.5	9 648.6	29 192.8	36 127.8	46 127.1
Real estate activities	.. c	.. c	.. c	.. c	.. c	.. c	.. c	.. c	.. c	.. c
Professional, scientific and technical activities	137 960.4	121 421.2	84 113.8	150 597.6	85 619.1	555 569.7	507 453.8	516 360.2	677 266.9	594 809.2
Administrative and support service activities	67 058.1	75 790.4	78 844.7	72 154.6	64 949.1	43 842.1	42 764.5	28 568.8	52 584.8	41 773.2
Public administration; activities of households and of extraterritorial organisations	-	-	-	-	-	-	-	-	-	-
Education	-	-	-	-	-	-	-	-	-	-
Human health and social work activities	-	-	-	-	-	-	-	-	-	-
Arts, entertainment and recreation	-	-	-	.. c	.. c	.. c	.. c	.. c	.. c	.. c
Other services	-	-	-	-	-	-	-	-	-	-
Not allocated and confidential	**.. c**	**.. c**	**.. c**	**.. c**	**.. c**	**.. c**	**.. c**	**.. c**	**.. c**	**.. c**
Private real estate activities	-	-	-	-	-	-	-	-	-	-

- Nil; c Confidential data

Note: Detailed metadata at: *http://metalinks.oecd.org/idi/20220712/6d95*.

Source: *OECD International Direct Investment Statistics (database)*: *https://doi.org/10.1787/idi-data-en*

IRELAND

Table 6. Foreign direct investment income by industrial sector

Million US dollars

	Inward					Outward				
	2016	2017	2018	2019	2020	2016	2017	2018	2019	2020
All FDI activities	**61 827.9**	**75 764.9**	**92 976.5**	**94 832.6**	**105 622.8**	**14 638.9**	**17 361.1**	**19 827.7**	**17 405.1**	**16 705.4**
Agriculture, forestry and fishing	**.. c**	**.. c**	**.. c**	**.. c**	**.. c**	-	-	-	-	-
Mining and quarrying	**.. c**	**.. c**	**.. c**	**.. c**	**.. c**	**.. c**	**.. c**	**.. c**	**.. c**	**.. c**
Extraction activities	-	-	-	-	-	-	-	-	-	-
Manufacturing	**35 241.6**	**42 271.4**	**57 928.7**	**56 182.7**	**64 479.8**	**-3 473.4**	**-2 141.8**	**-2 052.4**	**-2 374.3**	**-4 520.8**
of which:										
Food products, beverages and tobacco	6 375.1	3 587.0	5 683.9	3 136.7	2 617.7	529.7	.. c	402.5	527.3	-784.0
Textiles, wood and paper products; printing	.. c	-	.. c	.. c	.. c	.. c	.. c	.. c	.. c	.. c
Chemical, rubber, plastic, non-metallic mineral products	16 080.9	21 823.9	31 629.9	31 112.7	39 802.8	.. c	-39.5	422.5	-116.4	-837.6
Metal and machinery products, except electrical equipment	8 734.9	12 636.7	17 035.3	18 151.8	21 441.6	.. c	.. c	.. c	.. c	.. c
Motor vehicles, trailers, semi-trailers, other transport equipment	.. c	.. c	.. c	-	-	.. c	.. c	.. c	.. c	.. c
Other manufacturing	4 035.2	.. c	3 556.0	3 743.4	608.5	-	-234.5	-23.6	.. c	-523.1
Electricity, gas, steam and air conditioning supply	**.. c**	**.. c**	**.. c**	**.. c**	**.. c**	**.. c**	**-83.4**	**.. c**	**.. c**	**.. c**
Water supply; sewerage, waste management and remediation activities	-	-	-	-	-	-	-	-	-	-
Construction	-	-	-	**1.1**	**1.1**	-	-	-	**.. c**	**.. c**
Services	**24 096.0**	**33 309.7**	**34 868.4**	**38 505.5**	**40 961.8**	**17 443.3**	**17 939.4**	**19 926.8**	**17 801.4**	**19 176.1**
Wholesale and retail trade; repair of motor vehicles and motorcycles	829.4	.. c	1 916.7	2 277.0	1 707.1	97.3	428.4	-87.3	-21.3	-155.0
Transportation and storage	.. c	.. c	.. c	.. c	.. c	-	.. c	-	-4.5	.. c
Accommodation and food service activities	-	-	-	-	-	-	-	-	-	-
Information and communication	8 431.9	12 257.9	19 118.4	21 968.0	28 668.9	-360.5	-130.8	-20.1	-938.1	909.4
Financial and insurance activities	7 267.5	7 559.5	5 977.8	4 952.4	4 740.7	893.5	1 122.8	1 210.9	145.5	-167.5
Activities of holding companies	914.5	1 105.9	368.2	172.4	296.3	686.7	976.2	1 089.3	.. c	.. c
Real estate activities	-	-	-	-	-	-	-	-	-	-
Professional, scientific and technical activities	3 626.0	2 839.6	3 311.7	5 542.4	4 374.9	16 497.8	15 956.5	18 341.8	18 476.4	18 470.7
Administrative and support service activities	4 021.9	7 782.7	4 683.1	3 609.1	1 693.4	274.2	273.9	243.1	17.9	-53.6
Public administration; activities of households and of extraterritorial organisations	-	-	-	-	-	-	-	-	-	-
Education	-	-	-	-	-	-	-	-	-	-
Human health and social work activities	-	-	-	-	-	-	-	-	-	-
Arts, entertainment and recreation	-	-	-	-	-	.. c	.. c	.. c	.. c	.. c
Other services	-	-	-	-	-	-	-	-	-	-
Not allocated and confidential	**120.5**	**.. c**	**.. c**	**.. c**	**.. c**	**1 352.4**	**.. c**	**.. c**	**.. c**	**.. c**
Private real estate activities	-	-	-	-	-	-	-	-	-	-

- Nil; c Confidential data

Note: Detailed metadata at: *http://metalinks.oecd.org/idi/20220712/6d95.*

Source: *OECD International Direct Investment Statistics (database): https://doi.org/10.1787/idi-data-en*

ISRAEL

Table 1. Foreign direct investment flows by country

Million US dollars

	Inward					Outward				
	2016	2017	2018	2019	2020	2016	2017	2018	2019	2020
WORLD	**11 988.0**	**16 893.0**	**21 515.0**	**17 363.0**	**24 283.0**	**14 579.0**	**7 624.0**	**6 087.0**	**8 690.0**	**6 375.0**
OECD COUNTRIES	**6 374.0**	**7 630.0**	**10 537.0**	**9 083.0**	**11 033.0**	**11 850.0**	**4 640.0**	**3 949.0**	**3 535.0**	**680.0**
Australia	-	.. c	.. c	.. c	.. c	79.0	76.0	41.0	.. d	.. d
Austria	-	..	..	-	-	-	..	..	-	-
Belgium	-22.0	.. d	-7.0	.. c	.. d	-	4.0	7.0	.. d	7.0
Canada	61.0	.. c	.. d	-	-	125.0	327.0	108.0	-	-
Chile	-	..	..	-	-	-	.. c	-	.. c	.. c
Colombia	-	..	..	-	-	-	1.0	.. c	.. c	.. c
Costa Rica	-	..	..	-	-	.. c	.. c	.. c	.. c	.. c
Czech Republic	-	..	..	-	-	-3.0	-1.0	.. d	.. c	.. c
Denmark	-	.. c	.. c	-	-	.. c	.. c	.. c	.. c	.. c
Estonia	-	..	..	-	-	-	..	..	-	-
Finland	-	..	..	-	-	10.0	.. c	.. c	.. c	.. c
France	114.0	.. d	-77.0	10.0	.. d	-20.0	-17.0	95.0	1.0	14.0
Germany	-5.0	30.0	27.0	806.0	.. d	115.0	266.0	.. d	33.0	156.0
Greece	-	..	..	-	-	2.0	-5.0	-1.0	4.0	-2.0
Hungary	.. c	.. c	.. c	.. c	.. c	-15.0	.. c	.. c	75.0	.. c
Iceland	.. c	.. c	.. c	-	.. c	-	.. c	..	-	-
Ireland	.. c	.. c	.. c	.. c	.. c	-	.. c	.. c	.. c	.. c
Israel	-	..	..	-	-	-	..	..	-	-
Italy	.. c	.. c	.. c	.. c	.. c	-8.0	13.0	19.0	.. d	15.0
Japan	137.0	573.0	152.0	.. c	.. c	96.0	.. d	1 369.0	102.0	104.0
Korea	-	..	..	.. c	-	19.0	19.0	17.0	.. d	.. c
Latvia	-	..	..	-	-	.. c	..	..	-	-
Lithuania	-	..	..	-	-	-	.. c	.. c	.. c	.. c
Luxembourg	672.0	-293.0	-344.0	485.0	56.0	178.0	76.0	34.0	.. c	-680.0
Mexico	34.0	.. c	1 595.0	.. c	.. c	-6.0	.. d	3.0	1.0	..
Netherlands	1 746.0	160.0	-94.0	2 413.0	-233.0	9 875.0	3 427.0	2 239.0	1 560.0	1 173.0
New Zealand	-	..	..	-	-	-	..	..	-	-
Norway	-	..	..	-	-	.. c	.. c	.. c	.. c	.. c
Poland	.. c	.. c	.. c	.. c	.. c	15.0	-34.0	.. d	5.0	.. c
Portugal	-	..	..	-	-	-	..	..	-	-
Slovak Republic	-	..	..	-	-	-	..	..	-	-
Slovenia	-	..	..	-	-	-	..	..	-	-
Spain	-	..	..	-	-	-47.0	8.0	92.0	28.0	-2.0
Sweden	65.0	-39.0	.. d	.. c	5.0	-5.0	.. c	.. c	.. c	.. c
Switzerland	26.0	-142.0	13.0	-79.0	41.0	85.0	51.0	-295.0	79.0	.. c
Turkey	.. c	.. c	.. c	.. c	-	6.0	12.0	8.0	9.0	5.0
United Kingdom	260.0	608.0	-190.0	150.0	.. d	-79.0	172.0	.. d	290.0	47.0
United States	2 818.0	.. d	.. d	4 699.0	11 647.0	1 407.0	144.0	707.0	1 150.0	-229.0
EUROPE	**3 371.0**	**7 124.0**	**-7.0**	**4 197.0**	**-546.0**	**10 213.0**	**4 670.0**	**1 820.0**	**2 873.0**	**668.0**
Bulgaria	-	..	..	-	-	26.0	21.0	.. c	.. c	-2.0
Croatia	-	..	..	-	-	-	..	..	-	-
Cyprus	-	.. c	.. c	.. c	75.0	-140.0	79.0	-9.0	20.0	.. d
Malta	-	..	..	-	-	-	..	..	-	-
Montenegro	-	..	..	-	-	.. c	..	..	-	-
Romania	-	..	..	-	-	-11.0	5.0	13.0	.. c	.. c
Russian Federation	-	..	..	-	-	70.0	46.0	26.0	.. d	22.0
Ukraine	-	..	..	-	-	55.0	47.0	.. c	.. c	.. c
AFRICA	**-**	**-**	**-**	**-**	**-**	**-23.0**	**-1.0**	**6.0**	**198.0**	**11.0**
Northern Africa	-	-	-	-	-	-	-	-	-	-
Algeria	-	..	..	-	-	-	..	..	-	-
Egypt	-	..	..	-	-	-	..	..	-	-
Libya	-	..	..	-	-	-	..	..	-	-
Morocco	-	..	..	-	-	-	..	..	-	-
Tunisia	-	..	..	-	-	-	..	..	-	-
Other African countries	-	-	-	-	-	-15.0	-1.0	6.0	198.0	11.0
Nigeria	-	..	..	-	-	-	.. c	.. c	.. c	.. c
South Africa	-	..	..	-	-	2.0	5.0	.. d	2.0	.. d
AMERICA	**2 726.0**	**2 109.0**	**12 219.0**	**5 265.0**	**12 306.0**	**1 973.0**	**656.0**	**1 146.0**	**1 506.0**	**10.0**
Northern America	2 879.0	844.0	9 207.0	4 699.0	11 647.0	1 532.0	471.0	815.0	1 150.0	-229.0
Central America and Caribbean countries	-159.0	1 255.0	3 002.0	265.0	618.0	333.0	174.0	158.0	205.0	57.0
Bahamas	-	..	..	-	-	-	..	..	-	-
Bermuda	15.0	.. c	.. c	.. c	.. c	.. c	..	..	-	-
Cayman Islands	-209.0	1 260.0	1 195.0	.. c	.. c	256.0	.. c	.. c	.. c	.. c
El Salvador	-	..	..	-	-	-	..	..	-	-
Guatemala	-	..	..	-	-	-	..	..	-	-
Honduras	-	..	..	-	-	-	..	..	-	-
Nicaragua	-	..	..	-	-	-	..	..	-	-
Panama	1.0	.. c	.. d	.. c	.. c	-	.. c	-	.. c	.. c
Virgin Islands, U.S.	-	.. c	..	.. c	-	75.0	.. c	.. c	.. c	.. c
South America	-	11.0	9.0	10.0	11.0	17.0	11.0	173.0	49.0	16.0
Argentina	-	..	..	-	-	-1.0	.. c	.. c	.. c	.. c
Bolivia	-	..	..	-	-	-	..	..	-	-
Brazil	-	..	..	-	-	18.0	14.0	174.0	45.0	7.0
Ecuador	-	..	..	-	-	-	.. c	.. c	.. c	.. c
Paraguay	-	..	..	-	-	-	..	..	-	-
Peru	-	..	..	-	-	-	.. c	.. c	.. c	.. c
Uruguay	.. c	.. c	.. c	.. c	.. c	-	..	..	-	-
Venezuela	-	..	..	-	-	-	..	..	-	-

Table 1. Foreign direct investment flows by country *(cont.)*

Million US dollars

	Inward					Outward				
	2016	2017	2018	2019	2020	2016	2017	2018	2019	2020
ASIA	**674.0**	**886.0**	**721.0**	**339.0**	**41.0**	**297.0**	**185.0**	**1 492.0**	**320.0**	**419.0**
Near and Middle East	-	-	-	25.0	-	-1.0	-	-	-	-1.0
Gulf Arabian countries	-	-	-	25.0	-	-	-	-	-	-
Kuwait	-	..	..	-	-	-	..	..	-	-
Qatar	-	..	..	-	-	-	..	..	-	-
Saudi Arabia	-	..	..	.. c	-	-	..	..	-	-
United Arab Emirates	-	..	..	.. c	-	-	..	..	-	-
Other Near and Middle East	-	-	-	-	-	-1.0	-	-	-	-1.0
Jordan	-	..	..	-	-	-	..	..	-	-
Other Asian countries	674.0	886.0	721.0	314.0	41.0	298.0	185.0	1 492.0	320.0	419.0
China	161.0	.. d	.. d	.. c	.. c	-2.0	.. d	.. d	117.0	77.0
Hong Kong, China	2.0	.. c	.. c	-	.. c	14.0	.. d	.. c	.. c	.. c
India	-	.. c	.. c	-	-	108.0	55.0	55.0	55.0	75.0
Indonesia	-	..	..	-	-	-	-	-	-	-
Iran, Islamic Republic of	-	..	..	-	-	-	..	..	-	-
Malaysia	-	..	..	-	-	-	.. c	.. c	.. c	.. c
Philippines	-	..	..	-	-	-	.. c	.. c	.. c	.. c
Singapore	374.0	204.0	33.0	31.0	-4.0	1.0	7.0	3.0	4.0	11.0
Chinese Taipei	-	..	..	.. c	-	24.0	.. c	.. c	.. c	.. c
Thailand	-	..	..	-	-	1.0	.. d	.. d	.. d	.. d
Viet Nam	-	..	..	-	-	12.0	.. c	.. c	.. c	.. c
AUSTRALIA, OCEANIA AND POLAR REGIONS	**-29.0**	**-10.0**	**-**	**-10.0**	**-9.0**	**81.0**	**76.0**	**41.0**	**62.0**	**48.0**
WORLD unallocated and confidential	**5 246.0**	**6 784.0**	**8 582.0**	**7 572.0**	**12 491.0**	**2 038.0**	**2 038.0**	**1 582.0**	**3 731.0**	**5 219.0**
European Union (since 01/02/2020)	**..**	**..**	**..**	**4 080.0**	**-823.0**	**..**	**..**	**..**	**1 760.0**	**676.0**
G20 countries excl. European Union	**3 645.0**	**2 121.0**	**11 195.0**	**6 131.0**	**11 034.0**	**1 929.0**	**1 179.0**	**2 030.0**	**2 055.0**	**519.0**
G20 OECD countries	**3 484.0**	**2 035.0**	**10 661.0**	**5 946.0**	**10 968.0**	**1 734.0**	**1 056.0**	**1 746.0**	**1 761.0**	**337.0**
G20 Non-OECD countries	**161.0**	**86.0**	**533.0**	**185.0**	**66.0**	**195.0**	**123.0**	**284.0**	**294.0**	**182.0**
MENA countries	**-**	**-**	**-**	**25.0**	**-**	**-**	**-**	**-**	**-**	**-**
ASEAN countries	**374.0**	**204.0**	**33.0**	**31.0**	**-4.0**	**14.0**	**15.0**	**29.0**	**17.0**	**21.0**

- Nil; .. Not available; c Confidential data; d Secondary Confidentiality

Note: Detailed metadata at: *http://metalinks.oecd.org/idi/20220712/6d95*.

Source: *OECD International Direct Investment Statistics (database)*: *https://doi.org/10.1787/idi-data-en*

Table 2. Foreign direct investment positions by country
At year end

Million US dollars

	Inward					Outward				
	2016	2017	2018	2019	2020	2016	2017	2018	2019	2020
WORLD	**107 483.0**	**127 161.0**	**143 971.0**	**161 397.0**	**185 188.0**	**94 633.0**	**101 540.0**	**104 879.0**	**105 097.0**	**110 210.0**
OECD COUNTRIES	**50 293.0**	**59 903.0**	**66 676.0**	**73 696.0**	**77 131.0**	**68 899.0**	**76 436.0**	**76 803.0**	**73 996.0**	**74 386.0**
Australia	-	.. c	.. c	.. c	.. c	822.0	849.0	.. d	740.0	717.0
Austria	-	..	..	-	-	-	..	..	.. c	.. c
Belgium	384.0	158.0	149.0	70.0	.. c	151.0	177.0	175.0	175.0	223.0
Canada	3 835.0	.. c	3 373.0	-	-	2 461.0	2 664.0	1 809.0	2 215.0	-
Chile	-	..	..	-	-	-	.. c	.. c	.. c	.. c
Colombia	-	..	..	-	-	-	..	.. c	3.0	3.0
Costa Rica	-	..	..	-	-	.. c	.. c	.. c	.. c	.. c
Czech Republic	-	..	..	-	-	32.0	.. c	.. c	.. c	.. c
Denmark	-	.. c	.. c	-	-	.. c	.. c	.. c	.. c	.. c
Estonia	-	..	..	-	-	-	..	..	-	-
Finland	-	..	..	-	-	.. c	.. c	.. c	.. c	.. c
France	853.0	824.0	707.0	743.0	756.0	46.0	23.0	185.0	-13.0	69.0
Germany	489.0	535.0	554.0	3 531.0	598.0	1 583.0	1 992.0	1 295.0	1 144.0	1 202.0
Greece	-	..	..	-	-	16.0	14.0	12.0	22.0	22.0
Hungary	.. c	.. c	.. c	.. c	.. c	73.0	.. c	.. c	140.0	153.0
Iceland	.. c	.. c	.. c	.. c	-	-	.. c	..	.. c	.. c
Ireland	.. c	.. c	.. c	.. c	.. c	.. c	.. c	.. c	.. c	.. c
Israel	-	..	..	-	-	-	..	..	-	-
Italy	.. c	.. c	.. c	.. c	.. c	115.0	139.0	101.0	121.0	153.0
Japan	359.0	1 409.0	1 517.0	428.0	360.0	1 763.0	1 759.0	3 028.0	2 929.0	2 807.0
Korea	-	..	..	.. c	-	237.0	239.0	209.0	198.0	185.0
Latvia	-	..	..	-	-	.. c	..	..	-	-
Lithuania	-	..	..	-	-	-	.. c	.. c	.. c	.. c
Luxembourg	3 522.0	3 343.0	3 270.0	3 191.0	3 377.0	1 349.0	1 727.0	1 461.0	960.0	233.0
Mexico	321.0	.. c	1 833.0	.. d	.. d	26.0	28.0	.. d	33.0	33.0
Netherlands	12 375.0	12 032.0	11 445.0	12 713.0	12 558.0	45 089.0	48 863.0	48 473.0	47 273.0	47 221.0
New Zealand	-	..	..	.. c	.. c	-	..	.. c	-	-
Norway	-	..	..	-	-	.. c	.. c	.. c	.. c	.. c
Poland	.. c	.. c	.. c	.. c	.. c	250.0	305.0	280.0	273.0	284.0
Portugal	-	..	..	-	-	-	..	.. c	.. c	.. c
Slovak Republic	-	..	..	-	-	-	..	..	-	-
Slovenia	-	..	..	-	-	-	..	..	-	-
Spain	-	..	..	-	-	-10.0	-3.0	109.0	85.0	81.0
Sweden	1 081.0	951.0	452.0	508.0	530.0	6.0	.. c	.. c	.. c	.. c
Switzerland	1 740.0	1 733.0	1 694.0	1 832.0	1 930.0	2 244.0	2 348.0	3 219.0	3 084.0	2 474.0
Turkey	.. c	.. c	.. c	.. c	.. c	711.0	864.0	584.0	668.0	797.0
United Kingdom	2 442.0	2 640.0	2 203.0	2 421.0	2 647.0	2 239.0	2 176.0	2 079.0	2 249.0	2 916.0
United States	18 680.0	.. d	29 734.0	30 971.0	37 575.0	10 517.0	11 133.0	12 017.0	11 380.0	10 573.0
EUROPE	**27 767.0**	**34 174.0**	**32 120.0**	**36 771.0**	**34 912.0**	**55 871.0**	**63 682.0**	**62 404.0**	**61 478.0**	**60 870.0**
Bulgaria	-	..	..	-	-	253.0	247.0	216.0	203.0	178.0
Croatia	-	..	..	-	-	-	..	..	.. c	.. c
Cyprus	-	-	.. c	.. c	.. c	230.0	367.0	293.0	348.0	235.0
Malta	-	..	..	-	-	-	..	..	-	-
Montenegro	-	..	..	-	-	.. c	..	..	-	-
Romania	-	..	..	-	-	75.0	71.0	.. c	55.0	65.0
Russian Federation	-	..	..	-	-	606.0	596.0	525.0	550.0	521.0
Ukraine	-	..	..	-	-	504.0	519.0	447.0	337.0	371.0
AFRICA	**-**	**-**	**-**	**-**	**-**	**-125.0**	**-129.0**	**-186.0**	**44.0**	**44.0**
Northern Africa	-	-	-	-	-	-	-	-	-	-
Algeria	-	..	..	-	-	-	..	..	-	-
Egypt	-	..	..	-	-	-	..	..	-	-
Libya	-	..	..	-	-	-	..	..	-	-
Morocco	-	..	..	-	-	-	..	..	-	.. c
Tunisia	-	..	..	-	-	-	..	..	-	-
Other African countries	-	-	-	-	-	-37.0	-129.0	-186.0	44.0	44.0
Nigeria	-	..	..	-	-	5.0	.. c	.. c	.. c	.. c
South Africa	-	..	..	-	-	13.0	19.0	19.0	22.0	21.0
AMERICA	**30 493.0**	**35 164.0**	**45 703.0**	**51 101.0**	**63 012.0**	**16 976.0**	**17 147.0**	**16 764.0**	**15 742.0**	**14 988.0**
Northern America	22 515.0	25 546.0	33 107.0	30 971.0	37 575.0	12 978.0	13 797.0	13 826.0	13 595.0	10 573.0
Central America and Caribbean countries	7 949.0	9 391.0	12 433.0	14 624.0	20 261.0	2 399.0	3 227.0	2 847.0	1 998.0	338.0
Bahamas	-	..	..	-	-	-	..	..	-	-
Bermuda	518.0	.. c	.. c	.. c	.. c	.. c	..	..	-	-
Cayman Islands	7 067.0	8 486.0	9 801.0	12 263.0	17 645.0	1 471.0	.. c	.. c	.. c	.. c
El Salvador	-	..	..	-	-	-	..	..	-	-
Guatemala	-	..	..	-	-	-	..	..	-	-
Honduras	-	..	..	-	-	-	..	..	-	-
Nicaragua	-	..	..	-	-	-	..	..	-	-
Panama	37.0	.. c	.. c	.. c	.. c	-	.. c	.. c	.. c	.. c
Virgin Islands, U.S.	6.0	..	..	-	-	369.0	.. c	.. c	.. c	.. c
South America	-	228.0	164.0	231.0	173.0	104.0	123.0	91.0	150.0	135.0
Argentina	-	..	..	-	-	-3.0	.. d	.. d	.. d	.. d
Bolivia	-	..	..	-	-	-	..	..	-	-
Brazil	-	..	..	-	-	107.0	108.0	91.0	132.0	117.0
Ecuador	-	..	..	-	-	.. c	.. c	.. c	.. c	.. c
Paraguay	-	..	..	-	-	-	..	..	-	-
Peru	-	..	..	-	-	.. c	.. c	.. c	.. c	.. c
Uruguay	.. c	.. c	.. c	.. c	.. c	-	..	..	-	-
Venezuela	-	..	..	-	-	-	..	..	-	-

Table 2. Foreign direct investment positions by country *(cont.)*

At year end

Million US dollars

	Inward					Outward				
	2016	2017	2018	2019	2020	2016	2017	2018	2019	2020
ASIA	**5 860.0**	**7 926.0**	**8 638.0**	**7 761.0**	**8 406.0**	**4 228.0**	**4 199.0**	**5 914.0**	**6 063.0**	**6 084.0**
Near and Middle East	-	-	-	39.0	99.0	21.0	21.0	19.0	18.0	18.0
Gulf Arabian countries	-	-	-	39.0	99.0	-	-	-	-	-
Kuwait	-	..	..	-	-	-	..	..	-	-
Qatar	-	..	..	-	-	-	..	..	-	-
Saudi Arabia	-	-	-	.. c	.. c	-	..	..	-	-
United Arab Emirates	-	..	..	.. c	.. c	-	..	..	-	-
Other Near and Middle East	-	-	-	-	-	21.0	21.0	19.0	18.0	18.0
Jordan	-	..	..	-	-	-	..	..	-	-
Other Asian countries	5 852.0	7 926.0	8 638.0	7 722.0	8 307.0	3 720.0	4 178.0	5 895.0	6 044.0	6 066.0
China	373.0	.. d	.. d	.. c	.. c	218.0	228.0	848.0	897.0	872.0
Hong Kong, China	30.0	.. c	.. c	.. c	.. c	308.0	333.0	306.0	-68.0	39.0
India	-	.. c	.. c	.. c	.. c	1 130.0	1 053.0	989.0	825.0	911.0
Indonesia	-	..	..	-	-	-	.. c	.. c	.. c	.. c
Iran, Islamic Republic of	-	..	..	-	-	-	..	..	-	-
Malaysia	-	..	..	-	-	-	.. c	.. c	.. c	.. c
Philippines	-	..	..	-	-	.. c	.. c	.. c	.. c	.. c
Singapore	5 090.0	2 891.0	2 809.0	3 214.0	3 717.0	30.0	39.0	41.0	801.0	806.0
Chinese Taipei	-	-	-	.. c	.. c	.. c	.. c	.. c	.. c	.. c
Thailand	-	..	..	-	-	15.0	21.0	5.0	7.0	8.0
Viet Nam	-	..	..	-	-	19.0	.. c	.. c	.. c	.. c
AUSTRALIA, OCEANIA AND POLAR REGIONS	-	**64.0**	**52.0**	**44.0**	**34.0**	**826.0**	**849.0**	**760.0**	**740.0**	**717.0**
WORLD unallocated and confidential	**43 363.0**	**49 833.0**	**57 458.0**	**65 720.0**	**78 824.0**	**16 857.0**	**15 792.0**	**19 223.0**	**21 030.0**	**27 507.0**
European Union (since 01/02/2020)	..	..	..	**31 079.0**	**28 747.0**	..	..	..	**51 742.0**	**51 020.0**
G20 countries excl. European Union	**27 732.0**	**35 286.0**	**44 490.0**	**49 560.0**	**53 222.0**	**22 591.0**	**23 867.0**	**24 564.0**	**24 091.0**	**25 837.0**
G20 OECD countries	**27 351.0**	**31 705.0**	**40 224.0**	**45 586.0**	**49 140.0**	**20 520.0**	**21 865.0**	**22 094.0**	**21 664.0**	**23 392.0**
G20 Non-OECD countries	**381.0**	**3 582.0**	**4 266.0**	**3 974.0**	**4 083.0**	**2 071.0**	**2 002.0**	**2 469.0**	**2 427.0**	**2 445.0**
MENA countries	-	-	-	**39.0**	**99.0**	-	-	-	-	-
ASEAN countries	**5 090.0**	**2 891.0**	**2 809.0**	**3 214.0**	**3 717.0**	**69.0**	**85.0**	**96.0**	**870.0**	**885.0**

- Nil; .. Not available; c Confidential data; d Secondary Confidentiality

Note: Detailed metadata at: *http://metalinks.oecd.org/idi/20220712/6d95.*

Source: *OECD International Direct Investment Statistics (database): https://doi.org/10.1787/idi-data-en*

Table 4. Foreign direct investment flows by industrial sector

Million US dollars

	Inward					Outward				
	2016	2017	2018	2019	2020	2016	2017	2018	2019	2020
All FDI activities	**11 988.0**	**16 893.0**	**21 515.0**	**17 363.0**	**24 283.0**	**14 579.0**	**7 624.0**	**6 087.0**	**8 690.0**	**6 375.0**
Agriculture, forestry and fishing	**-1.0**	**36.0**	**.. d**	**38.0**	**.. d**	**15.0**	**1.0**	**27.0**	**.. d**	**.. d**
Mining and quarrying	**-194.0**	**310.0**	**680.0**	**225.0**	**.. c**	**-200.0**	**.. d**	**.. d**	**.. c**	**.. c**
Extraction activities	-194.0	310.0	680.0	225.0	.. c	-200.0	10.0	9.0	.. c	.. c
Manufacturing	**2 870.0**	**2 189.0**	**5 059.0**	**3 630.0**	**11 314.0**	**12 136.0**	**4 295.0**	**3 385.0**	**2 527.0**	**1 902.0**
of which:										
Food products, beverages and tobacco	24.0	-8.0	22.0	.. d	-32.0	1.0	220.0	29.0	296.0	.. c
Textiles, wood and paper products; printing	27.0	64.0	21.0	.. d	76.0	147.0	66.0	203.0	108.0	.. c
Chemical, rubber, plastic, non-metallic mineral products	566.0	181.0	3 225.0	-221.0	725.0	11 403.0	3 689.0	3 300.0	1 950.0	1 690.0
Metal and machinery products, except electrical equipment	1 495.0	2 151.0	1 735.0	3 763.0	10 595.0	556.0	314.0	-158.0	158.0	126.0
Motor vehicles, trailers, semi-trailers, other transport equipment	33.0	7.0	24.0	-37.0	-3.0	9.0	-31.0	-3.0	.. c	.. c
Other manufacturing	725.0	-206.0	32.0	64.0	-47.0	20.0	37.0	14.0	.. d	106.0
Electricity, gas, steam and air conditioning supply	**46.0**	**.. d**	**.. d**	**-39.0**	**.. c**	**56.0**	**-69.0**	**13.0**	**.. c**	**.. c**
Water supply; sewerage, waste management and remediation activities	**3.0**	**.. d**	**-43.0**	**2.0**	**.. c**	**-3.0**	**.. c**	**.. d**	**-**	**-**
Construction	**115.0**	**20.0**	**30.0**	**38.0**	**34.0**	**-101.0**	**62.0**	**80.0**	**68.0**	**.. d**
Services	**6 319.0**	**11 276.0**	**16 149.0**	**10 447.0**	**10 551.0**	**1 299.0**	**3 778.0**	**4 846.0**	**4 708.0**	**1 473.0**
Wholesale and retail trade; repair of motor vehicles and motorcycles	284.0	138.0	79.0	172.0	213.0	51.0	568.0	64.0	9.0	.. d
Transportation and storage	-23.0	11.0	59.0	121.0	297.0	-12.0	34.0	.. d	7.0	117.0
Accommodation and food service activities	27.0	37.0	44.0	30.0	-6.0	36.0	323.0	.. d	204.0	.. d
Information and communication	2 847.0	2 362.0	3 605.0	5 246.0	7 493.0	71.0	75.0	151.0	58.0	.. d
Financial and insurance activities	1 132.0	680.0	8 642.0	2 108.0	-248.0	1 019.0	2 144.0	3 606.0	3 115.0	958.0
Activities of holding companies	..	1 004.0	8 702.0	2 021.0	-315.0	..	591.0	906.0	864.0	-1 031.0
Real estate activities	168.0	401.0	535.0	602.0	-240.0	125.0	509.0	726.0	1 077.0	417.0
Professional, scientific and technical activities	1 837.0	1 498.0	2 943.0	1 991.0	2 934.0	-11.0	85.0	223.0	233.0	110.0
Administrative and support service activities	-	.. d	199.0	132.0	63.0	-16.0	.. d	-13.0	.. c	.. c
Public administration; activities of households and of extraterritorial organisations	-	-	-	-	-	-	-	-	.. c	-
Education	2.0	.. d	14.0	24.0	29.0	11.0	4.0	1.0	5.0	13.0
Human health and social work activities	35.0	17.0	6.0	5.0	5.0	15.0	36.0	35.0	.. c	.. c
Arts, entertainment and recreation	4.0	..	22.0	15.0	6.0	8.0	.. d	2.0	.. c	-
Other services	6.0	3.0	1.0	1.0	5.0	2.0	1.0	7.0	.. c	.. c
Not allocated and confidential	**2 830.0**	**.. d**	**.. d**	**3 022.0**	**.. c**	**1 377.0**	**.. c**	**.. d**	**.. c**	**.. c**
Private real estate activities	-	..	..	-	-	-	..	..	-	-

- Nil; .. Not available; c Confidential data; d Secondary Confidentiality

Note: The statistical data for Israel are supplied by and under the responsibility of the relevant Israeli authorities. The use of such data by the OECD is without prejudice to the status of the Golan Heights, East Jerusalem and Israeli settlements in the West Bank under the terms of international law.

Note: Detailed metadata at: *http://metalinks.oecd.org/idi/20220712/6d95.*

Source: *OECD International Direct Investment Statistics (database): https://doi.org/10.1787/idi-data-en*

ISRAEL

Table 5. Foreign direct investment positions by industrial sector
At year end

Million US dollars

	Inward					Outward				
	2016	2017	2018	2019	2020	2016	2017	2018	2019	2020
All FDI activities	**107 483.0**	**127 161.0**	**143 971.0**	**161 397.0**	**185 188.0**	**94 633.0**	**101 540.0**	**104 879.0**	**105 097.0**	**110 210.0**
Agriculture, forestry and fishing	**260.0**	**308.0**	**286.0**	**299.0**	**316.0**	**25.0**	**96.0**	**119.0**	**69.0**	**78.0**
Mining and quarrying	**1 552.0**	**1 862.0**	**2 598.0**	**2 823.0**	**5 519.0**	**1 126.0**	**1 016.0**	**896.0**	**887.0**	**908.0**
Extraction activities	1 552.0	1 860.0	2 595.0	2 820.0	5 517.0	1 126.0	15.0	35.0	42.0	63.0
Manufacturing	**30 944.0**	**32 753.0**	**37 169.0**	**38 743.0**	**48 509.0**	**60 386.0**	**64 304.0**	**65 965.0**	**62 635.0**	**62 150.0**
of which:										
Food products, beverages and tobacco	1 611.0	1 671.0	1 625.0	1 707.0	1 720.0	749.0	1 503.0	1 199.0	1 385.0	1 493.0
Textiles, wood and paper products; printing	855.0	990.0	821.0	1 192.0	1 171.0	894.0	954.0	1 100.0	1 100.0	1 092.0
Chemical, rubber, plastic, non-metallic mineral products	5 540.0	5 599.0	8 546.0	7 260.0	6 968.0	52 970.0	56 203.0	58 055.0	55 991.0	54 515.0
Metal and machinery products, except electrical equipment	20 106.0	22 898.0	23 866.0	27 282.0	37 389.0	4 887.0	4 538.0	4 542.0	3 647.0	4 419.0
Motor vehicles, trailers, semi-trailers, other transport equipment	449.0	443.0	467.0	449.0	446.0	185.0	355.0	306.0	174.0	163.0
Other manufacturing	2 383.0	1 152.0	1 844.0	853.0	815.0	701.0	751.0	763.0	338.0	468.0
Electricity, gas, steam and air conditioning supply	**1 027.0**	**1 054.0**	**1 052.0**	**1 070.0**	**1 074.0**	**934.0**	**139.0**	**131.0**	**120.0**	**119.0**
Water supply; sewerage, waste management and remediation activities	**28.0**	**33.0**	**-11.0**	**-21.0**	**13.0**	**18.0**	**20.0**	**26.0**	**22.0**	**22.0**
Construction	**868.0**	**812.0**	**849.0**	**976.0**	**1 149.0**	**910.0**	**916.0**	**978.0**	**744.0**	**707.0**
Services	**62 242.0**	**76 830.0**	**88 946.0**	**100 059.0**	**108 548.0**	**19 906.0**	**24 914.0**	**26 800.0**	**28 716.0**	**30 139.0**
Wholesale and retail trade; repair of motor vehicles and motorcycles	2 939.0	2 285.0	2 409.0	2 496.0	2 681.0	310.0	393.0	480.0	107.0	126.0
Transportation and storage	151.0	179.0	289.0	410.0	766.0	-117.0	-91.0	-112.0	-123.0	..
Accommodation and food service activities	466.0	595.0	723.0	823.0	868.0	259.0	637.0	301.0	313.0	.. d
Information and communication	22 952.0	26 798.0	29 490.0	33 136.0	39 721.0	1 338.0	2 084.0	2 221.0	3 146.0	3 097.0
Financial and insurance activities	12 544.0	14 219.0	21 531.0	24 639.0	22 843.0	13 821.0	16 875.0	18 153.0	16 480.0	17 316.0
Activities of holding companies	..	10 743.0	18 172.0	21 065.0	19 132.0	..	13 097.0	11 636.0	8 111.0	6 714.0
Real estate activities	4 365.0	5 432.0	4 680.0	7 851.0	6 724.0	3 862.0	4 623.0	5 111.0	8 449.0	9 042.0
Professional, scientific and technical activities	16 971.0	19 635.0	21 865.0	23 024.0	27 107.0	292.0	320.0	523.0	232.0	377.0
Administrative and support service activities	1 471.0	7 267.0	7 509.0	7 255.0	7 319.0	-31.0	-18.0	-30.0	34.0	34.0
Public administration; activities of households and of extraterritorial organisations	-	.. c	.. c	.. c	.. c	-	.. c	.. c	.. c	.. c
Education	82.0	.. d	.. d	.. d	.. d	16.0	.. d	.. d	21.0	34.0
Human health and social work activities	164.0	177.0	181.0	135.0	186.0	7.0	34.0	70.0	.. d	-32.0
Arts, entertainment and recreation	64.0	78.0	89.0	96.0	104.0	46.0	40.0	58.0	83.0	83.0
Other services	73.0	70.0	70.0	70.0	76.0	103.0	1.0	8.0	5.0	5.0
Not allocated and confidential	**10 562.0**	**13 509.0**	**13 082.0**	**17 448.0**	**20 060.0**	**11 328.0**	**10 135.0**	**9 964.0**	**11 904.0**	**16 087.0**
Private real estate activities	-	..	..	-	-	-	..	..	-	-

- Nil; .. Not available; c Confidential data; d Secondary Confidentiality

Note: The statistical data for Israel are supplied by and under the responsibility of the relevant Israeli authorities. The use of such data by the OECD is without prejudice to the status of the Golan Heights, East Jerusalem and Israeli settlements in the West Bank under the terms of international law.

Note: Detailed metadata at: *http://metalinks.oecd.org/idi/20220712/6d95*.

Source: *OECD International Direct Investment Statistics (database): https://doi.org/10.1787/idi-data-en*

ITALY

Table 1. Foreign direct investment flows by country

Million US dollars

	Inward					Outward				
	2016	2017	2018	2019	2020	2016	2017	2018	2019	2020
WORLD	**28 440.8**	**23 995.9**	**37 658.7**	**18 145.4**	**-23 568.3**	**16 164.8**	**24 478.4**	**31 522.7**	**19 786.1**	**-1 851.8**
OECD COUNTRIES	**28 509.7**	**23 571.6**	**35 916.8**	**17 422.6**	**-23 349.7**	**4 114.4**	**13 985.5**	**17 842.6**	**8 984.0**	**-3 833.2**
Australia	66.2	34.4	89.3	65.0	35.3	45.8	177.4	196.2	-81.6	326.4
Austria	321.5	105.2	184.5	101.7	118.9	-9 176.9	709.2	320.6	850.0	-178.7
Belgium	-2 813.9	1 102.5	115.9	-1 188.3	1 753.1	2 926.1	-3 876.6	-2 326.4	2 458.2	535.1
Canada	-56.1	261.8	70.1	51.3	12.6	75.0	390.8	561.3	967.3	646.9
Chile	7.0	-246.8	-5.4	4.8	-30.9	-12.3	9 808.8	165.4	3 052.3	-81.2
Colombia	21.1	5.7	-0.9	4.2	4.3	81.0	90.7	36.7	7.2	59.3
Costa Rica	2.3	2.4	2.3	2.2	2.6	19.6	11.9	110.8	-182.3	-44.5
Czech Republic	55.2	75.9	-0.9	92.6	-323.6	3 459.4	10.5	-213.9	258.7	210.1
Denmark	-764.2	44.6	-104.6	222.3	-352.4	456.6	-181.0	-83.0	105.4	-321.5
Estonia	-29.2	-6.5	-49.0	-1.9	-4.5	-5.3	15.8	-2.5	0.4	-0.7
Finland	62.8	146.4	-320.5	301.5	-190.5	152.7	1.8	-198.6	-25.1	-63.8
France	18 029.3	-1 577.7	35 774.6	1 074.2	-685.4	1 009.7	1 107.6	2 086.3	1 669.1	-74.1
Germany	4 884.2	2 714.2	3 055.0	5 981.7	-1 181.2	-15.3	-2 132.3	2 458.5	193.0	-2 461.7
Greece	76.5	-140.6	-29.9	49.0	-42.3	150.3	80.9	544.5	182.4	8.2
Hungary	200.7	17.0	116.0	4.8	-77.6	142.4	-35.8	153.3	244.5	46.3
Iceland	18.6	28.3	0.2	0.2	-107.8	-11.2	-66.6	-10.6	-13.1	0.0
Ireland	70.0	1 940.2	78.2	-1 998.1	176.8	-336.2	-50.9	920.0	303.9	636.5
Israel	41.1	59.0	-21.9	44.8	-12.2	292.4	414.6	173.5	172.5	-335.2
Italy	-	-	-	-	-	-	-	-	-	-
Japan	278.8	163.4	176.6	-63.0	1 013.8	293.1	42.0	54.7	-96.8	98.9
Korea	-112.9	134.6	519.8	-290.0	357.0	133.5	36.7	280.2	106.1	140.8
Latvia	7.1	4.2	-1.8	-29.3	-39.6	48.2	3.2	2.6	-18.0	0.8
Lithuania	0.0	-1.3	3.6	-0.1	-0.2	-14.4	-1.9	0.4	-0.5	0.5
Luxembourg	-3 325.6	8 131.6	-9 968.8	10 310.1	-11 284.2	6 909.7	12 629.1	441.0	1 788.1	3 916.2
Mexico	98.9	-84.7	51.1	-2.2	-4.9	121.4	337.1	429.9	484.7	87.8
Netherlands	528.0	4 287.1	844.0	1 835.0	-5 678.1	-4 234.1	340.1	-405.8	-12 636.3	-9 222.4
New Zealand	0.6	-2.2	-2.2	2.1	2.8	34.7	14.1	12.3	15.3	27.4
Norway	403.7	121.2	384.8	126.0	83.4	1 420.1	180.8	285.4	318.5	-766.6
Poland	-14.6	-91.5	114.2	173.0	-210.6	-207.2	-2 207.3	-11.7	1 353.1	-220.8
Portugal	52.1	60.4	12.3	105.4	111.6	124.3	163.6	226.4	155.5	944.3
Slovak Republic	-17.0	-22.0	27.7	-4.7	5.2	-3 449.1	826.3	-89.3	-64.2	122.8
Slovenia	46.2	28.6	4.8	-0.1	3.1	332.2	12.4	118.2	209.1	-142.2
Spain	820.2	601.5	444.1	935.3	1 047.7	-387.1	-7 105.1	8 336.2	2 622.7	-3 012.9
Sweden	478.4	730.1	186.9	1 666.2	-388.2	87.4	-45.1	179.4	139.5	191.0
Switzerland	259.8	3 453.9	890.6	2 978.0	-1 371.3	-939.2	222.7	-741.9	2 192.3	399.0
Turkey	-317.2	-0.1	23.7	106.1	309.2	3 545.3	652.7	552.9	-29.6	218.9
United Kingdom	7 443.1	1 714.2	4 050.2	-4 472.5	-8 985.7	1 960.5	992.8	-392.9	480.9	2 568.7
United States	1 710.5	-216.5	-796.2	-758.0	2 586.6	-832.5	515.3	3 819.6	1 625.5	1 862.6
EUROPE	**25 794.9**	**24 274.1**	**35 293.0**	**18 838.5**	**-27 352.2**	**10 867.8**	**5 199.9**	**16 102.5**	**7 817.2**	**-4 460.1**
Bulgaria	23.6	-5.1	6.5	5.4	6.0	1 141.2	1 240.3	167.3	209.3	143.6
Croatia	39.5	24.9	35.5	24.1	-70.6	2 081.0	104.1	249.3	128.7	426.3
Cyprus	223.4	-245.3	-671.9	657.9	-52.8	-3.0	7.1	-2.6	0.8	-2.7
Malta	-617.6	314.2	120.6	-20.1	-250.6	35.2	-42.0	-66.3	26.4	69.9
Montenegro	0.3	0.4	0.4	0.4	0.4	-16.3	51.5	-79.2	-119.2	44.7
Romania	-26.9	103.8	-96.6	61.1	-27.0	788.5	501.8	3 333.9	382.3	65.2
Russian Federation	-437.2	415.2	-63.6	-322.8	299.7	2 424.6	938.8	667.8	1 756.3	295.8
Ukraine	-8.6	6.4	-6.5	15.8	30.3	-26.9	-206.7	-303.8	37.1	-7.3
AFRICA	**320.4**	**74.2**	**-42.8**	**90.9**	**241.3**	**2 687.1**	**2 711.1**	**3 326.9**	**1 555.7**	**-1 565.1**
Northern Africa	100.7	29.8	22.5	-66.1	281.1	1 279.7	2 130.5	1 937.3	1 514.4	-1 322.5
Algeria	64.1	16.2	68.1	46.6	320.7	920.0	981.0	1 059.8	808.0	-1 066.8
Egypt	28.2	-6.1	7.6	8.0	-8.2	236.1	794.3	277.1	723.5	175.8
Libya	-13.6	10.0	-52.7	-114.2	-33.1	-44.1	17.7	30.0	-43.3	11.4
Morocco	13.3	9.8	14.2	-9.1	-0.4	14.8	72.0	201.6	40.8	134.5
Tunisia	8.7	0.0	-14.7	2.5	2.1	153.0	265.4	368.8	-14.7	-577.3
Other African countries	219.7	44.4	-65.3	157.1	-39.8	1 407.4	580.6	1 389.6	41.3	-242.6
Nigeria	27.6	0.1	-0.3	0.4	1.8	346.5	279.5	670.4	-58.6	-85.3
South Africa	177.0	25.7	14.5	54.3	-24.0	485.3	231.4	102.6	-175.8	-98.7
AMERICA	**1 899.3**	**-537.1**	**241.3**	**-933.2**	**2 363.0**	**127.4**	**12 295.5**	**5 898.6**	**7 047.4**	**3 486.4**
Northern America	1 654.4	45.3	-726.1	-706.7	2 599.1	-757.5	906.1	4 381.0	2 592.9	2 509.5
Central America and Caribbean countries	21.7	-460.5	494.4	-82.9	-43.3	677.8	1 380.3	327.1	745.1	234.5
Bahamas	0.0	0.0	0.0	6.4	0.0	0.5	0.3	0.9	0.4	0.2
Bermuda	-0.3	-10.7	9.7	0.7	-0.1	-27.2	135.4	-5.1	3.7	-3.1
Cayman Islands	-241.7	-16.7	-15.0	-25.9	2.4	1.0	-23.5	-12.5	-44.2	83.2
El Salvador	0.0	0.0	29.9	0.0	0.0	1.0	-0.9	-0.2	0.0	0.0
Guatemala	0.5	0.4	0.5	0.5	0.4	22.3	-42.9	5.2	-15.1	-15.3
Honduras	0.0	0.0	0.0	0.0	0.0	-4.3	-0.8	-2.5	2.0	-7.4
Nicaragua	0.0	0.0	0.0	0.0	0.0	0.0	0.1	0.2	0.1	0.0
Panama	-8.2	0.3	2.3	1.4	-0.7	-34.6	109.5	-563.8	340.1	-5.5
Virgin Islands, U.S.	-	-	-	-	-	-	-	0.7	-3.6	-1.2
South America	223.2	-121.9	473.1	-143.6	-192.8	207.0	10 009.1	1 190.5	3 709.5	742.4
Argentina	129.9	81.8	121.1	57.0	44.0	-1 171.1	271.2	44.9	-28.7	169.7
Bolivia	2.7	4.4	3.1	3.0	3.0	2.9	3.1	4.3	-0.2	-20.2
Brazil	55.7	45.0	70.8	-118.9	-123.8	1 552.3	273.8	890.1	513.1	763.1
Ecuador	1.5	3.9	1.9	1.7	3.4	-11.2	5.5	3.5	1.0	-0.6
Paraguay	0.1	-0.3	0.2	0.7	0.4	0.2	0.3	0.5	-1.6	-0.8
Peru	24.5	9.3	10.4	0.4	-5.2	44.8	45.3	175.1	109.7	-12.6
Uruguay	88.5	-118.2	262.5	-96.1	-89.0	-1.8	4.4	-4.2	27.0	1.5
Venezuela	-107.6	93.3	9.5	-0.3	1.3	-262.2	-528.0	-156.0	2.0	-153.5

ITALY

Table 1. Foreign direct investment flows by country *(cont.)*

Million US dollars

	Inward					Outward				
	2016	2017	2018	2019	2020	2016	2017	2018	2019	2020
ASIA	**290.8**	**-64.4**	**2 128.3**	**4.9**	**1 060.3**	**2 450.9**	**3 914.4**	**6 280.4**	**3 256.2**	**310.0**
Near and Middle East	78.8	126.2	86.8	35.8	251.6	2 621.3	1 364.0	1 820.5	2 532.2	-518.7
Gulf Arabian countries	37.6	67.3	105.2	-12.6	278.8	2 211.8	724.0	1 237.5	2 059.2	-291.0
Kuwait	-1.3	1.7	-9.3	0.6	0.0	123.1	828.8	263.0	100.0	-122.3
Qatar	-26.1	27.6	16.2	-16.7	-63.2	107.9	283.6	-118.6	466.4	59.2
Saudi Arabia	6.9	72.3	2.7	3.4	1.5	-148.3	-487.8	-358.3	252.4	-493.5
United Arab Emirates	51.7	-33.7	114.8	1.9	347.9	1 831.4	309.0	1 152.3	969.3	193.3
Other Near and Middle East	41.2	58.9	-18.4	48.4	-27.1	409.5	639.9	583.0	473.0	-227.7
Jordan	0.4	-0.3	1.0	0.4	0.6	44.5	74.1	-132.8	-68.1	1.3
Other Asian countries	212.0	-190.6	2 041.4	-30.9	808.6	-170.4	2 550.4	4 459.8	724.0	828.7
China	-124.6	-400.7	1 303.4	70.4	-600.1	357.3	686.4	1 777.2	87.1	1 766.6
Hong Kong, China	57.4	-239.2	-31.5	48.2	25.5	-1 523.1	86.9	-55.6	-91.8	-2 045.9
India	-47.7	20.2	15.4	30.4	9.8	-18.3	291.5	189.6	-505.2	149.3
Indonesia	1.1	-1.2	1.0	9.5	-14.9	57.7	537.5	71.3	82.6	3.9
Iran, Islamic Republic of	34.9	1.0	2.6	0.8	-0.9	-123.9	-43.6	-179.9	150.8	23.0
Malaysia	6.4	16.9	-1.1	-3.3	0.8	223.7	722.9	438.7	179.2	168.2
Philippines	-0.1	0.7	2.3	1.2	2.3	3.2	9.3	474.2	238.3	68.5
Singapore	-10.7	118.6	-119.3	175.7	-205.0	103.1	101.4	369.7	112.2	249.7
Chinese Taipei	-79.6	-55.0	82.6	-66.6	195.4	-13.7	4.1	0.8	9.1	1.3
Thailand	11.3	-5.1	6.7	0.4	-25.0	-42.4	59.4	176.2	9.5	25.8
Viet Nam	-0.6	-1.6	-3.2	-4.3	-1.2	93.8	132.3	257.6	-18.8	257.9
AUSTRALIA, OCEANIA AND POLAR REGIONS	**67.1**	**32.3**	**86.8**	**67.2**	**38.2**	**40.5**	**355.5**	**209.7**	**54.6**	**399.3**
WORLD unallocated and confidential	**68.2**	**216.7**	**-47.8**	**77.0**	**81.1**	**-8.9**	**2.0**	**-295.4**	**55.0**	**-22.4**
European Union (since 01/02/2020)	..	..	..	..	..	..	..	..	..	..
G20 countries excl. European Union	**31 785.9**	**3 401.9**	**44 479.5**	**1 476.0**	**-6 950.5**	**9 875.9**	**4 862.7**	**13 432.0**	**7 300.6**	**5 971.4**
G20 OECD countries	**32 024.7**	**3 143.6**	**43 014.2**	**1 692.6**	**-6 542.6**	**6 336.5**	**2 120.0**	**10 046.8**	**5 318.7**	**3 415.1**
G20 Non-OECD countries	**-238.8**	**258.3**	**1 465.3**	**-216.6**	**-407.8**	**3 539.4**	**2 742.7**	**3 385.3**	**1 981.9**	**2 556.3**
MENA countries	**139.2**	**97.2**	**129.7**	**-75.7**	**557.4**	**3 556.1**	**2 886.7**	**2 945.0**	**3 506.9**	**-1 607.4**
ASEAN countries	**66.0**	**141.8**	**-107.6**	**180.0**	**-268.8**	**443.6**	**1 563.3**	**1 800.4**	**631.3**	**782.0**

- Nil; .. Not available

Note: Detailed metadata at: *http://metalinks.oecd.org/idi/20220712/6d95.*

Source: *OECD International Direct Investment Statistics (database)*: *https://doi.org/10.1787/idi-data-en*

Table 2. Foreign direct investment positions by country

At year end

Million US dollars

	Inward					Outward				
	2016	2017	2018	2019	2020	2016	2017	2018	2019	2020
WORLD	**352 626.2**	**424 743.1**	**434 624.3**	**443 531.9**	**469 293.6**	**456 380.4**	**547 577.5**	**554 359.7**	**558 577.7**	**586 800.4**
OECD COUNTRIES	**282 861.8**	**336 621.5**	**343 652.7**	**347 295.1**	**370 352.1**	**338 716.9**	**405 727.5**	**407 725.0**	**401 993.7**	**418 730.9**
Australia	587.2	3.9	7.0	27.8	46.9	2 246.0	2 844.8	2 687.4	2 602.5	3 412.0
Austria	3 960.9	4 163.6	4 243.6	4 229.2	4 887.6	18 268.5	20 986.6	20 032.0	19 942.8	21 080.7
Belgium	4 047.3	3 656.4	2 295.4	2 796.2	3 472.7	14 468.4	10 672.5	7 940.4	10 135.8	10 865.9
Canada	1 040.3	1 605.3	1 817.8	1 973.4	646.1	2 068.5	2 723.9	3 167.4	4 273.0	5 060.6
Chile	266.1	0.2	-115.9	-128.0	-151.7	1 794.0	13 467.1	11 077.0	13 096.0	10 841.9
Colombia	-	0.2	-	-	-	570.1	434.6	457.5	569.5	630.2
Costa Rica	-	-	-	-	-	362.9	240.3	377.5	167.6	273.9
Czech Republic	585.9	775.5	149.9	177.0	97.5	3 696.9	4 361.7	4 041.8	4 226.4	4 199.1
Denmark	2 661.3	2 560.0	2 062.7	2 457.5	1 290.1	1 971.0	2 104.7	2 158.1	2 152.6	2 087.2
Estonia	59.1	-	-	-	-	32.2	56.5	88.2	129.4	161.1
Finland	247.1	560.4	255.5	270.4	264.9	1 862.4	1 820.6	1 766.7	1 850.6	2 064.8
France	58 481.4	63 308.5	69 221.7	72 202.5	91 265.2	26 415.8	32 418.1	34 813.1	35 741.4	40 217.7
Germany	33 032.3	39 738.7	36 021.3	36 596.0	39 828.3	37 048.3	42 944.3	43 771.0	41 828.7	41 911.9
Greece	-	0.0	-	-	-	2 957.5	3 739.8	4 030.1	4 184.7	4 647.9
Hungary	111.7	151.3	275.4	273.3	191.0	2 572.0	1 593.8	2 815.6	2 794.6	2 970.0
Iceland	-	-	-	-	-	33.8	-31.4	-3.4	20.8	3.6
Ireland	1 387.5	3 557.0	2 051.8	1 685.2	3 994.2	9 351.2	9 745.4	8 835.8	8 785.8	10 144.6
Israel	156.5	252.5	217.2	133.3	361.8	1 602.2	2 279.4	1 767.0	1 873.3	1 706.6
Italy	33 128.2	32 382.3	41 280.6	49 495.5	35 242.6	-	-	-	-	-
Japan	4 646.9	11 113.6	8 600.8	8 039.2	10 061.4	1 507.7	1 859.9	2 139.0	2 128.8	2 126.0
Korea	596.3	1 225.2	1 500.3	1 155.9	2 035.5	1 183.0	1 444.7	1 719.1	1 937.3	2 190.2
Latvia	-	-	-	-	-	76.6	96.0	94.1	69.1	82.8
Lithuania	-	0.0	-	-	-	33.8	38.9	43.4	48.3	54.5
Luxembourg	25 704.5	25 893.6	24 855.9	26 984.1	24 708.3	25 480.2	46 329.0	44 685.8	35 792.5	42 108.0
Mexico	177.6	176.9	52.7	-82.8	295.6	1 784.7	2 183.3	2 449.4	3 159.0	3 359.5
Netherlands	19 368.6	17 535.7	12 803.3	13 260.1	18 522.4	59 628.1	64 437.8	64 283.5	51 529.0	42 599.5
New Zealand	-	782.4	281.3	314.8	213.7	44.4	64.1	51.2	65.7	89.6
Norway	532.0	616.8	477.9	546.8	762.3	978.0	1 224.8	1 435.9	1 707.1	1 160.6
Poland	101.0	-10.4	127.4	120.2	0.4	9 623.9	8 313.8	7 995.5	8 582.1	9 269.9
Portugal	307.0	330.0	318.4	283.0	166.7	2 098.3	2 526.4	2 820.8	2 927.9	2 909.9
Slovak Republic	-	0.0	-	-	-	646.6	1 586.8	1 372.9	1 233.8	1 369.2
Slovenia	51.8	0.7	1.1	1.2	1.9	1 303.8	1 268.3	1 411.5	1 608.1	1 905.7
Spain	4 967.1	5 289.2	5 355.2	5 752.7	9 208.3	33 982.5	35 783.5	41 624.2	45 784.3	44 678.7
Sweden	1 004.1	2 988.7	2 371.8	3 215.3	4 576.5	1 603.1	1 796.3	1 687.7	1 993.7	1 711.0
Switzerland	18 533.4	25 084.4	31 183.1	26 393.8	26 479.5	9 941.7	11 709.6	9 822.9	13 462.9	15 077.5
Turkey	-	1.3	13.3	49.4	387.0	8 283.1	8 527.9	7 708.9	5 932.4	6 070.3
United Kingdom	32 979.6	46 767.8	45 481.0	42 543.6	38 601.7	19 503.1	26 403.5	25 209.6	25 747.2	32 987.4
United States	34 139.1	46 109.7	50 445.1	46 528.4	52 894.0	34 659.3	38 444.0	42 181.3	44 645.8	46 974.9
EUROPE	**243 847.4**	**279 230.2**	**284 942.8**	**293 435.1**	**309 923.2**	**323 587.4**	**376 763.5**	**377 321.9**	**370 150.2**	**390 210.0**
Bulgaria	-	0.0	-	-	-	2 261.3	2 926.0	2 519.0	2 758.2	3 362.5
Croatia	-	-	-	-	-	3 138.5	3 353.8	3 673.7	3 888.1	4 330.7
Cyprus	517.2	344.9	253.9	238.8	644.9	141.5	160.2	148.4	146.6	157.9
Malta	-	7.5	143.2	97.5	136.0	530.6	568.7	428.0	585.1	892.8
Montenegro	-	-	-	-	-	243.0	369.3	336.8	218.7	288.8
Romania	-1.3	-8.4	55.3	74.5	-11.9	6 556.0	7 288.2	9 659.5	9 738.2	11 987.0
Russian Federation	478.3	2 219.6	1 694.9	1 884.2	3 248.0	11 514.0	13 238.5	12 167.1	14 081.0	14 125.8
Ukraine	-	592.1	582.1	806.8	1 210.2	684.6	586.0	314.6	435.2	425.2
AFRICA	**157.4**	**964.2**	**528.6**	**-9.7**	**2 099.1**	**22 576.5**	**27 942.1**	**29 469.4**	**30 848.8**	**32 172.4**
Northern Africa	151.1	183.5	110.1	225.9	2 011.3	18 780.7	23 400.9	24 186.7	25 164.0	25 896.6
Algeria	-	-	-	-	1 824.7	9 016.2	11 176.6	11 544.1	12 176.6	12 257.3
Egypt	-	-	-	-	-	7 380.2	9 155.9	8 955.4	9 420.8	10 299.5
Libya	146.2	177.9	104.5	220.4	181.7	263.6	317.5	331.8	357.6	394.7
Morocco	5.0	5.6	5.5	5.5	4.9	524.0	677.3	998.9	943.9	1 089.1
Tunisia	-	-	-	-	-	1 596.8	2 073.7	2 356.4	2 265.1	1 856.0
Other African countries	6.3	780.7	418.5	-235.6	87.8	3 795.8	4 541.2	5 282.7	5 684.8	6 275.8
Nigeria	-	-	-	-	-	837.8	1 239.0	1 814.9	1 723.3	2 063.7
South Africa	6.3	780.7	418.5	-235.6	87.8	1 634.1	2 014.9	2 035.1	2 218.2	2 170.6
AMERICA	**45 224.3**	**60 165.5**	**65 313.4**	**78 979.2**	**80 698.1**	**57 647.6**	**77 918.9**	**80 229.4**	**86 951.2**	**88 077.3**
Northern America	35 179.4	47 714.9	52 262.9	48 501.7	53 540.1	36 727.9	41 167.8	45 348.8	48 918.9	52 035.7
Central America and Caribbean countries	9 346.0	12 393.1	12 881.1	30 343.8	27 192.1	4 272.9	6 027.4	6 111.3	7 253.0	8 355.5
Bahamas	-	-	-	-	-	4.7	5.6	6.3	6.5	7.3
Bermuda	-	83.1	188.1	173.3	510.6	3.0	135.8	123.3	127.1	124.3
Cayman Islands	8 962.0	10 611.6	11 190.1	28 813.8	24 588.4	4.0	-20.5	-31.8	-75.5	7.2
El Salvador	-	-	-	-	-	7.8	7.0	6.7	6.7	6.7
Guatemala	-	-	-	-	-	162.5	484.2	489.5	488.0	496.8
Honduras	-	-	-	-	-	15.1	9.1	6.2	12.4	5.6
Nicaragua	-	-	-	-	-	0.6	0.8	0.9	1.0	1.1
Panama	8.7	65.5	21.3	-42.4	90.3	414.3	534.6	-18.3	512.4	735.1
Virgin Islands, U.S.	-	-	-	-	-	-	-	0.7	-3.0	-4.5
South America	698.9	57.5	169.3	133.6	-34.1	16 646.8	30 723.6	28 769.3	30 779.3	27 686.1
Argentina	92.3	49.6	28.1	-31.1	-	1 223.5	1 563.5	1 576.8	1 487.8	1 654.3
Bolivia	-	-	-	-	-	30.9	29.3	40.0	31.1	11.9
Brazil	337.2	3.0	253.6	289.2	113.9	10 969.9	13 269.7	13 281.9	13 153.7	12 069.6
Ecuador	-	-	-	-	-	35.9	44.0	48.9	45.9	51.3
Paraguay	-	0.1	-	-	-	8.0	8.9	10.7	6.9	6.5
Peru	-	0.2	-	-	-	374.8	537.9	684.4	778.4	797.0
Uruguay	3.2	4.2	3.6	3.5	3.7	48.5	59.5	59.2	88.3	97.2
Venezuela	-	-	-	-	-	1 612.9	1 297.5	1 493.3	1 456.1	1 433.4

ITALY

Table 2. Foreign direct investment positions by country *(cont.)*

At year end

Million US dollars

	Inward					Outward				
	2016	2017	2018	2019	2020	2016	2017	2018	2019	2020
ASIA	**13 249.1**	**25 274.1**	**22 547.8**	**20 803.3**	**25 809.5**	**50 028.5**	**61 585.3**	**64 448.5**	**67 639.1**	**72 460.3**
Near and Middle East	2 427.1	3 465.2	2 841.9	2 637.1	3 064.6	23 986.0	27 916.5	28 020.4	30 298.9	31 349.4
Gulf Arabian countries	2 270.6	2 965.7	2 643.4	2 331.2	2 702.8	20 413.9	23 154.0	23 496.1	25 329.7	26 166.7
Kuwait	455.7	537.8	681.8	519.3	567.3	1 699.5	2 503.1	2 648.8	2 708.1	2 798.4
Qatar	1 373.0	2 136.2	1 448.7	1 425.2	1 609.7	950.9	1 204.0	1 084.5	1 628.8	1 984.7
Saudi Arabia	145.8	238.5	453.1	264.3	507.1	5 831.4	5 810.2	5 300.7	5 490.9	5 465.7
United Arab Emirates	296.1	53.2	59.8	122.4	18.8	10 421.0	12 093.0	12 694.4	13 494.1	13 650.5
Other Near and Middle East	156.5	499.5	198.5	306.0	361.8	3 572.1	4 762.5	4 524.3	4 969.2	5 182.7
Jordan	-	-	-	-	-	981.1	1 191.9	1 013.7	981.1	1 073.5
Other Asian countries	10 822.0	21 809.0	19 705.9	18 166.1	22 744.9	26 042.5	33 668.8	36 428.1	37 340.1	41 111.0
China	3 556.6	5 791.0	5 551.5	5 317.1	6 039.0	8 480.6	10 858.2	11 637.0	11 756.9	14 058.1
Hong Kong, China	692.8	-56.5	13.3	4.8	9.2	2 842.6	4 067.4	4 285.8	4 062.5	3 215.6
India	364.4	909.2	863.6	737.6	459.7	6 106.2	7 373.6	6 959.3	6 724.9	6 916.5
Indonesia	-	-	-	-	-	262.9	808.1	854.7	910.7	1 008.5
Iran, Islamic Republic of	58.0	68.0	65.7	65.0	71.2	1 316.6	1 594.3	1 593.1	1 738.3	1 947.2
Malaysia	57.2	-	-	-	-0.8	1 059.3	1 987.0	2 299.9	2 428.4	2 855.9
Philippines	-	-	-	-	-	64.0	72.4	537.9	762.6	907.7
Singapore	190.7	1 646.6	1 638.7	1 613.4	2 122.0	689.1	745.8	944.0	1 127.8	1 508.2
Chinese Taipei	334.4	432.3	868.5	881.3	1 278.9	80.3	69.2	76.3	120.4	123.1
Thailand	1.3	33.5	-	-	148.9	317.0	346.8	461.2	429.3	414.5
Viet Nam	-	0.0	-	-	-	553.6	749.0	777.7	805.5	1 095.5
AUSTRALIA, OCEANIA AND POLAR REGIONS	**587.2**	**786.3**	**288.3**	**342.6**	**260.6**	**2 266.1**	**3 056.0**	**2 880.2**	**2 930.5**	**3 836.8**
WORLD unallocated and confidential	**49 560.8**	**58 322.7**	**61 003.5**	**49 981.4**	**50 503.1**	**274.3**	**311.6**	**10.3**	**57.9**	**43.8**
European Union (since 01/02/2020)	..	..	..	..	**238 487.5**	..	..	..	..	**307 770.9**
G20 countries excl. European Union	**203 789.7**	**252 424.9**	**263 704.8**	**266 754.5**	**281 759.8**	**180 722.1**	**214 731.2**	**219 658.8**	**223 820.4**	**241 779.8**
G20 OECD countries	**198 808.7**	**242 433.2**	**254 441.5**	**258 528.8**	**271 304.4**	**134 699.6**	**159 794.5**	**165 846.2**	**167 996.3**	**184 310.5**
G20 Non-OECD countries	**4 981.0**	**9 991.7**	**9 263.3**	**8 225.7**	**10 455.4**	**46 022.5**	**54 936.7**	**53 812.6**	**55 824.0**	**57 469.3**
MENA countries	**2 421.8**	**3 396.1**	**2 734.7**	**2 729.7**	**4 714.1**	**40 662.5**	**48 263.8**	**49 105.6**	**51 878.7**	**53 578.1**
ASEAN countries	**440.1**	**2 173.7**	**2 130.3**	**1 879.0**	**2 675.7**	**3 085.9**	**4 868.9**	**6 040.4**	**6 654.7**	**8 007.0**

- Nil; .. Not available

Note: Inward FDI positions are allocated according to the ultimate investing country. Detailed metadata at: *http://metalinks.oecd.org/idi/20220712/6d95*.

Source: *OECD International Direct Investment Statistics (database)*: *https://doi.org/10.1787/idi-data-en*

ITALY

Table 3. Foreign direct investment income by country

Million US dollars

	Inward					Outward				
	2016	2017	2018	2019	2020	2016	2017	2018	2019	2020
WORLD	**14 146.7**	**19 620.5**	**20 409.6**	**17 823.5**	**2 223.3**	**17 894.9**	**24 781.8**	**29 994.4**	**28 627.9**	**16 515.3**
OECD COUNTRIES	**14 015.2**	**19 607.3**	**20 383.7**	**17 613.2**	**2 227.2**	**15 165.6**	**20 785.8**	**25 314.9**	**23 525.7**	**14 330.7**
Australia	9.7	18.7	36.2	21.2	28.2	80.6	155.6	108.1	101.8	111.6
Austria	281.6	213.3	264.5	291.3	-33.4	874.8	926.8	938.9	1 085.5	447.5
Belgium	66.4	728.2	112.1	399.6	8.1	298.5	437.3	388.0	279.4	276.0
Canada	4.6	23.5	42.4	50.5	54.0	150.6	125.4	173.1	111.9	167.8
Chile	5.6	6.1	-0.1	-0.2	-0.1	12.9	524.9	734.1	1 621.0	893.8
Colombia	-0.4	-0.1	0.0	-0.1	-0.1	60.3	-8.8	-19.3	68.4	10.8
Costa Rica	0.0	0.0	-	0.0	0.0	18.8	1.1	2.0	-6.4	9.9
Czech Republic	28.4	49.6	47.2	194.6	225.4	770.7	381.2	347.5	505.0	226.3
Denmark	237.1	274.0	51.7	275.9	131.1	-11.6	9.2	15.4	8.1	29.2
Estonia	-30.6	-2.3	-1.8	-3.8	-2.9	1.3	0.9	1.6	1.2	1.7
Finland	11.6	-1.8	-0.4	20.2	31.8	170.8	170.4	73.2	78.8	-3.2
France	2 873.2	3 337.7	4 340.4	800.3	-150.4	1 606.3	1 294.6	1 626.0	1 528.3	1 092.2
Germany	1 773.7	2 181.4	1 425.3	1 209.9	-116.9	1 826.5	2 047.3	2 621.4	3 177.0	1 889.6
Greece	6.5	9.3	13.5	8.0	-4.7	67.0	91.8	78.7	42.1	37.0
Hungary	30.0	-32.4	11.5	11.4	67.5	85.6	83.6	150.1	278.1	241.8
Iceland	-1.1	-0.7	-	-	-	-41.8	1.3	0.3	-13.0	-
Ireland	6.9	87.6	62.3	73.1	39.6	1 245.0	1 482.7	1 676.6	1 505.1	1 507.5
Israel	-0.5	1.8	4.2	0.1	0.8	130.5	98.8	211.6	197.1	38.9
Italy	-	-	-	-	-	-	-	-	-	-
Japan	248.4	356.9	224.7	139.5	152.7	47.7	66.1	60.2	121.1	85.7
Korea	86.3	149.8	97.1	85.7	79.2	13.6	26.0	8.6	-29.6	6.2
Latvia	-0.1	0.0	0.1	0.0	-0.6	0.4	3.3	4.3	4.1	1.5
Lithuania	0.0	0.0	-0.1	0.0	0.0	1.5	1.4	1.7	0.7	2.2
Luxembourg	1 273.0	3 378.2	3 221.1	1 348.7	392.6	1 625.9	1 308.1	1 725.0	2 226.9	1 150.0
Mexico	-2.6	-0.5	-3.0	-1.2	-1.4	108.6	26.1	-38.2	100.9	81.2
Netherlands	4 379.8	4 197.2	6 244.2	8 474.7	1 485.9	1 874.7	4 085.7	7 844.9	4 349.8	-845.2
New Zealand	0.2	0.1	0.0	-0.1	-0.1	10.5	8.9	4.7	5.6	10.4
Norway	-15.9	-61.8	11.4	54.3	44.7	-13.7	44.1	18.5	36.9	-95.8
Poland	1.1	0.7	-2.0	0.3	3.7	1 134.0	795.3	590.6	612.9	474.8
Portugal	56.6	13.6	65.3	93.7	38.0	-11.0	113.7	128.4	202.9	226.4
Slovak Republic	0.9	0.5	-0.1	0.4	0.3	95.0	117.7	174.3	73.6	14.6
Slovenia	50.8	0.1	1.0	0.9	1.1	94.3	116.3	140.0	108.2	76.6
Spain	425.1	827.1	379.8	174.2	208.4	1 093.8	2 679.2	2 892.6	2 993.5	1 514.6
Sweden	188.1	144.5	292.8	244.8	282.9	120.5	64.7	107.2	163.3	14.8
Switzerland	615.9	1 619.3	1 033.9	1 121.8	682.9	290.0	235.1	616.6	481.3	578.8
Turkey	5.5	-2.3	-2.5	-2.2	1.6	471.5	667.7	473.7	145.2	309.8
United Kingdom	1 007.8	1 545.7	2 100.7	2 339.1	-1 243.5	1 120.2	1 677.0	695.4	745.3	2 248.6
United States	391.3	543.9	310.1	186.5	-179.0	-178.2	918.9	721.9	675.7	1 507.1
EUROPE	**13 385.7**	**18 490.0**	**19 863.7**	**17 192.7**	**2 068.8**	**16 041.7**	**20 709.4**	**25 254.3**	**22 558.5**	**12 953.7**
Bulgaria	10.3	0.3	0.6	-0.1	-1.4	225.2	237.0	252.4	323.5	134.4
Croatia	-0.5	-0.1	0.6	0.1	0.9	92.9	236.9	242.6	248.8	81.7
Cyprus	-1.0	3.3	5.2	10.3	-47.9	-0.8	-0.6	0.5	-0.5	-0.5
Malta	28.3	-8.1	10.4	-10.0	-5.5	-10.4	-25.9	-40.0	-34.7	12.3
Montenegro	-	0.0	-	-	-	6.0	8.1	10.1	0.5	4.4
Romania	-1.9	2.5	14.9	28.2	3.4	270.5	420.2	358.4	433.9	638.2
Russian Federation	7.6	-12.3	129.5	48.3	-22.5	475.6	811.4	914.0	781.3	540.8
Ukraine	0.1	-0.2	-0.1	-0.3	-0.1	11.8	-8.4	0.7	23.3	-0.4
AFRICA	**-14.7**	**-4.2**	**-31.4**	**-42.9**	**-34.7**	**495.5**	**736.8**	**905.9**	**767.9**	**695.2**
Northern Africa	-3.6	0.6	-30.1	-40.2	-33.4	236.4	324.3	335.9	450.4	709.5
Algeria	-0.6	-0.1	-0.8	-0.1	0.0	36.2	95.9	39.0	58.2	100.0
Egypt	-0.4	0.4	0.1	0.1	0.2	119.6	104.0	101.4	228.0	182.8
Libya	-1.8	0.8	-15.6	-28.2	-33.3	-0.3	-2.6	81.0	-1.2	-0.7
Morocco	-0.7	-0.5	-0.4	0.0	-0.3	42.8	73.6	50.6	80.2	72.4
Tunisia	-0.2	-0.1	-13.4	-12.0	0.0	38.2	53.3	63.9	85.2	355.0
Other African countries	-11.1	-4.8	-1.4	-2.7	-1.3	259.1	412.6	570.0	317.5	-14.3
Nigeria	-0.5	0.0	1.0	0.9	0.1	-37.1	33.4	22.4	48.8	63.1
South Africa	-6.7	-3.2	-2.9	-2.8	-1.7	70.0	67.2	21.8	75.0	-38.5
AMERICA	**383.9**	**564.2**	**210.1**	**413.7**	**-156.0**	**-690.1**	**1 063.7**	**1 565.2**	**3 267.9**	**2 631.6**
Northern America	395.9	567.3	352.5	237.0	-125.1	-27.6	1 044.3	895.0	787.6	1 674.9
Central America and Caribbean countries	-26.7	-25.5	-45.2	-23.7	2.1	64.3	111.0	28.8	148.9	140.6
Bahamas	-	-	-	-	0.2	-	-	-	-	-
Bermuda	-23.2	0.1	-0.3	0.0	0.0	-23.4	0.9	7.3	0.0	0.0
Cayman Islands	5.5	-22.3	-32.4	-27.1	0.0	-	-	-0.7	-0.8	-1.7
El Salvador	-	-	-	-	-	0.0	0.0	0.0	0.0	0.0
Guatemala	-	-	-	-	0.0	31.9	18.6	23.7	15.5	-0.1
Honduras	-	-	-	-	-	1.0	0.1	-5.8	0.1	0.1
Nicaragua	-	-	-	-	-	0.0	-	0.0	-	0.0
Panama	0.2	0.0	0.0	0.0	0.0	-96.4	33.4	29.1	11.9	-18.5
Virgin Islands, U.S.	-	-	-	-	-	-	-	-	-	-0.1
South America	14.7	22.3	-97.2	200.4	-33.0	-726.8	-91.6	641.4	2 331.5	816.2
Argentina	-2.8	-2.6	-2.5	-0.8	-1.1	179.1	119.7	93.9	119.6	152.0
Bolivia	0.0	-0.1	0.0	-	-	3.4	0.1	0.0	-0.2	0.0
Brazil	20.3	28.5	-84.9	203.4	-27.8	-714.0	-330.5	-3.1	484.7	-294.2
Ecuador	0.0	0.0	0.0	0.0	0.0	5.2	0.1	1.5	-0.6	0.5
Paraguay	-	0.0	0.0	0.0	0.0	-0.5	0.3	-0.2	-1.8	-0.9
Peru	-0.5	0.0	0.1	0.2	0.2	-7.9	-1.2	33.5	35.2	-6.6
Uruguay	-7.3	-5.4	-9.6	-2.0	-4.0	-1.3	-3.3	-10.1	-2.8	1.6
Venezuela	-0.1	-4.1	-0.4	0.0	0.0	-263.6	-392.0	-188.9	8.0	-7.7

Table 3. Foreign direct investment income by country *(cont.)*

Million US dollars

	Inward					Outward				
	2016	2017	2018	2019	2020	2016	2017	2018	2019	2020
ASIA	**383.5**	**553.0**	**330.9**	**238.7**	**317.0**	**1 956.7**	**2 108.4**	**2 155.3**	**1 923.2**	**110.0**
Near and Middle East	10.6	7.6	11.2	8.8	5.9	318.7	487.2	323.2	275.0	92.9
Gulf Arabian countries	11.1	5.9	7.1	8.7	5.0	187.1	397.9	47.5	65.5	30.9
Kuwait	0.0	0.0	1.6	1.1	3.4	0.1	294.4	1.9	30.7	1.0
Qatar	7.0	6.8	8.0	7.1	1.6	12.0	-19.4	-46.6	-45.0	-30.3
Saudi Arabia	-0.2	-0.2	0.0	-0.1	-0.2	137.9	53.4	31.4	43.1	11.6
United Arab Emirates	4.4	-0.7	-2.5	1.1	0.7	37.5	41.6	60.7	29.7	43.2
Other Near and Middle East	-0.5	1.8	4.1	0.1	0.8	131.6	89.3	275.7	209.5	62.0
Jordan	-	-	0.0	0.0	0.0	-0.2	-1.1	31.4	-2.0	0.6
Other Asian countries	372.9	545.3	319.7	229.9	311.1	1 638.0	1 621.1	1 832.1	1 648.2	17.2
China	2.7	-20.8	-12.3	-7.5	-10.4	809.5	1 010.9	962.2	899.4	1 370.5
Hong Kong, China	8.5	10.5	6.9	5.4	74.6	154.0	135.5	250.7	200.1	-2 003.7
India	-1.9	-2.9	-2.8	-0.5	0.1	221.5	209.2	237.6	175.4	246.6
Indonesia	-0.1	0.0	-0.1	-0.1	0.1	27.8	11.4	10.3	5.2	6.5
Iran, Islamic Republic of	0.4	0.3	1.6	0.5	-1.3	12.3	-93.5	-87.3	-15.3	37.6
Malaysia	-0.5	-0.6	-0.1	-0.1	-0.2	84.2	42.5	7.9	-7.2	-65.6
Philippines	0.0	-0.1	-0.1	-0.1	-0.1	0.3	2.4	2.4	2.7	-0.4
Singapore	12.2	45.5	1.1	-3.4	3.6	72.2	26.9	49.1	-12.2	35.7
Chinese Taipei	2.0	1.3	-0.8	2.1	-0.3	3.5	-0.8	1.4	7.3	2.5
Thailand	0.4	0.1	-0.2	0.6	0.5	23.6	76.6	54.3	30.8	75.9
Viet Nam	-0.1	-0.1	-0.2	-0.2	-0.3	121.1	53.1	83.7	38.1	88.8
AUSTRALIA, OCEANIA AND POLAR REGIONS	**9.8**	**18.9**	**36.3**	**21.1**	**28.1**	**91.1**	**163.5**	**112.8**	**107.4**	**121.8**
WORLD unallocated and confidential	**-1.6**	**-1.3**	**0.0**	**0.2**	**0.0**	**0.1**	**0.1**	**0.9**	**3.0**	**2.9**
European Union (since 01/02/2020)	..	..	..	..	..	..	..	..	..	..
G20 countries excl. European Union	**6 416.8**	**8 141.3**	**8 595.7**	**5 069.0**	**-1 439.0**	**6 454.8**	**8 957.4**	**8 718.5**	**9 261.2**	**9 495.0**
G20 OECD countries	**6 397.8**	**8 154.8**	**8 571.6**	**4 829.2**	**-1 375.6**	**5 247.4**	**7 004.6**	**6 450.2**	**6 677.6**	**7 499.7**
G20 Non-OECD countries	**19.0**	**-13.6**	**24.0**	**239.8**	**-63.4**	**1 207.4**	**1 952.8**	**2 268.2**	**2 583.6**	**1 995.4**
MENA countries	**7.5**	**6.4**	**-23.0**	**-31.5**	**-28.3**	**425.1**	**722.2**	**429.4**	**513.4**	**742.7**
ASEAN countries	**12.0**	**46.5**	**2.6**	**-1.5**	**5.4**	**329.3**	**213.0**	**207.8**	**57.4**	**140.9**

- Nil; .. Not available

Note: Detailed metadata at: *http://metalinks.oecd.org/idi/20220712/6d95.*

Source: *OECD International Direct Investment Statistics (database)*: *https://doi.org/10.1787/idi-data-en*

ITALY

Table 4. Foreign direct investment flows by industrial sector

Million US dollars

	Inward					Outward				
	2016	2017	2018	2019	2020	2016	2017	2018	2019	2020
All FDI activities	**28 440.8**	**23 995.9**	**37 658.7**	**18 145.4**	**-23 568.3**	**16 164.8**	**24 478.4**	**31 522.7**	**19 786.1**	**-1 851.8**
Agriculture, forestry and fishing	**448.3**	**408.0**	**67.9**	**289.0**	**-353.1**	**50.6**	**-73.7**	**59.8**	**-294.8**	**259.0**
Mining and quarrying	**-372.5**	**2 196.2**	**-148.2**	**157.0**	**-664.9**	**-3 407.4**	**2 068.5**	**-240.2**	**278.7**	**-2.5**
Extraction activities	-372.5	2 198.1	-148.2	157.0	-664.9	-3 380.1	2 068.1	-238.4	285.4	-17.9
Manufacturing	**5 184.9**	**9 130.0**	**8 480.8**	**2 695.2**	**-4 804.4**	**10 408.6**	**7 250.6**	**12 290.5**	**5 066.6**	**4 761.4**
of which:										
Food products, beverages and tobacco	1 721.0	-76.2	-315.4	-708.7	-275.7	339.8	831.6	524.1	624.9	-105.8
Textiles, wood and paper products; printing	-1 313.9	346.6	-469.3	-56.7	-1 172.7	-993.1	298.2	425.6	299.2	-140.1
Chemical, rubber, plastic, non-metallic mineral products	305.6	3 882.9	-167.8	-691.6	-245.7	631.4	1 092.6	3 620.7	560.2	5 631.4
Metal and machinery products, except electrical equipment	277.6	2 351.7	5 906.0	1 908.0	-1 163.5	4 827.0	5 549.7	4 889.0	3 579.6	2 462.9
Motor vehicles, trailers, semi-trailers, other transport equipment	-1 448.8	179.1	2 767.5	-1 969.9	-4 805.4	4 811.2	-200.2	738.4	688.7	140.2
Other manufacturing	5 643.4	2 445.8	759.8	4 214.1	2 858.6	792.4	-321.3	2 092.7	-686.0	-3 227.2
Electricity, gas, steam and air conditioning supply	**-983.3**	**-45.7**	**886.8**	**-121.8**	**-797.9**	**-3 158.1**	**1 551.2**	**3 104.9**	**341.9**	**583.9**
Water supply; sewerage, waste management and remediation activities	**-120.8**	**-20.8**	**-36.5**	**-21.8**	**-268.9**	**-3.3**	**29.5**	**-30.6**	**0.8**	**24.2**
Construction	**-847.8**	**137.9**	**111.4**	**-264.2**	**-187.1**	**2 636.5**	**3 765.0**	**8 623.1**	**4 039.6**	**-1 664.3**
Services	**23 288.9**	**10 311.5**	**26 329.4**	**13 538.2**	**-18 483.9**	**10 257.5**	**10 110.3**	**9 131.1**	**10 511.3**	**-5 266.0**
Wholesale and retail trade; repair of motor vehicles and motorcycles	3 673.6	3 717.7	-1 435.3	2 023.3	3 454.4	2 075.6	110.4	3 835.6	3 098.5	-1 325.6
Transportation and storage	225.0	-769.7	1 304.8	2 487.6	154.3	-293.0	807.3	-790.6	177.4	98.1
Accommodation and food service activities	657.5	-330.8	179.8	-463.4	-1 079.7	-30.7	-356.4	183.3	-660.6	25.7
Information and communication	509.6	182.4	-7.0	11 365.7	-5 194.4	-849.3	393.9	2 619.2	1 373.8	905.3
Financial and insurance activities	9 882.5	4 731.8	4 367.0	-6 557.4	-7 919.8	9 897.5	6 914.3	-3 714.3	-2 100.4	821.6
Activities of holding companies	-4 279.2	284.0	4 778.1	-312.4	289.1	3 014.9	325.5	-128.9	-4 125.8	591.7
Real estate activities	945.1	1 126.0	-391.7	1 248.8	-635.8	-241.0	254.0	383.7	14.2	577.6
Professional, scientific and technical activities	5 933.2	228.4	19 342.8	5 717.0	-10 001.1	1 815.2	1 100.2	2 679.2	8 271.4	-3 202.4
Administrative and support service activities	1 255.2	680.7	3 142.4	-2 222.2	3 158.7	-1 946.1	872.3	912.1	385.1	-604.8
Public administration; activities of households and of extraterritorial organisations	-	-	138.8	-0.4	46.3	57.4	-19.8	2 929.4	-297.7	-2 351.9
Education	-0.1	-	-	-	-	-2.2	-1.9	-7.3	1.7	-6.2
Human health and social work activities	19.4	18.1	30.0	17.5	-26.2	-39.4	-25.9	-72.0	96.7	2.8
Arts, entertainment and recreation	-118.0	686.4	-471.6	-118.7	-386.2	-187.6	55.2	172.7	145.4	-198.4
Other services	305.9	40.5	129.5	40.3	-54.6	1.3	6.7	0.1	5.9	-8.0
Not allocated and confidential	**0.0**	**0.0**	**0.0**	**8.0**	**92.5**	**0.0**	**0.0**	**0.0**	**0.0**	**10.4**
Private real estate activities	**1 843.1**	**1 878.8**	**1 967.1**	**1 865.8**	**1 899.4**	**-619.7**	**-222.9**	**-1 415.8**	**-158.1**	**-557.9**

- Nil

Note: Detailed metadata at: *http://metalinks.oecd.org/idi/20220712/6d95.*

Source: *OECD International Direct Investment Statistics (database): https://doi.org/10.1787/idi-data-en*

ITALY

Table 5. Foreign direct investment positions by industrial sector

At year end

Million US dollars

	Inward					Outward				
	2016	2017	2018	2019	2020	2016	2017	2018	2019	2020
All FDI activities	**352 626.2**	**424 743.1**	**434 624.3**	**443 531.9**	**469 293.6**	**456 380.4**	**547 577.5**	**554 359.7**	**558 577.7**	**586 800.4**
Agriculture, forestry and fishing	**1 254.4**	**2 164.8**	**1 686.4**	**1 936.2**	**1 748.4**	**541.8**	**531.2**	**703.0**	**399.6**	**904.8**
Mining and quarrying	**2 771.2**	**3 138.5**	**3 489.9**	**3 347.1**	**2 939.6**	**-3 435.0**	**3 665.2**	**5 888.1**	**10 374.3**	**2 959.6**
Extraction activities	2 771.2	3 138.5	3 489.9	3 347.1	2 939.6	-3 599.5	3 635.6	2 656.1	2 786.0	2 912.3
Manufacturing	**92 095.8**	**118 455.3**	**110 046.9**	**119 468.8**	**130 273.8**	**125 553.4**	**154 183.5**	**155 568.9**	**159 564.8**	**174 941.3**
of which:										
Food products, beverages and tobacco	17 642.0	19 755.0	15 718.5	18 429.3	16 555.4	9 274.3	11 370.0	9 711.2	10 426.1	10 267.3
Textiles, wood and paper products; printing	2 337.0	3 644.6	2 878.9	3 818.7	3 434.9	4 137.6	4 694.3	4 731.5	5 208.2	6 344.9
Chemical, rubber, plastic, non-metallic mineral products	23 144.1	30 069.6	24 246.2	25 884.5	28 767.9	18 255.5	20 485.5	22 927.6	23 961.8	32 141.5
Metal and machinery products, except electrical equipment	21 661.9	31 012.2	32 976.4	32 346.2	32 117.0	64 057.4	77 722.6	79 111.2	82 621.0	88 603.3
Motor vehicles, trailers, semi-trailers, other transport equipment	14 758.4	18 019.1	18 780.0	20 495.8	26 674.7	14 893.1	18 215.5	16 034.4	15 822.1	15 874.1
Other manufacturing	12 552.4	15 954.8	15 446.9	18 494.3	22 724.0	14 935.4	21 695.6	23 052.9	21 525.6	21 710.1
Electricity, gas, steam and air conditioning supply	**4 444.9**	**6 160.7**	**4 744.1**	**5 935.0**	**6 644.7**	**6 638.7**	**5 790.1**	**7 080.1**	**7 392.1**	**13 021.7**
Water supply; sewerage, waste management and remediation activities	**413.7**	**453.4**	**452.1**	**372.9**	**120.9**	**157.9**	**83.3**	**66.1**	**62.9**	**80.4**
Construction	**3 272.6**	**4 790.3**	**4 038.6**	**3 313.9**	**3 196.6**	**36 078.0**	**43 940.9**	**50 306.4**	**52 675.5**	**52 802.0**
Services	**223 761.4**	**259 574.3**	**279 609.4**	**277 302.4**	**287 993.2**	**269 361.2**	**314 669.1**	**311 367.9**	**303 474.5**	**316 591.9**
Wholesale and retail trade; repair of motor vehicles and motorcycles	34 988.9	42 779.8	50 174.9	44 027.6	48 589.7	33 006.2	33 939.0	40 516.2	43 670.0	45 627.9
Transportation and storage	11 172.3	13 318.6	12 471.4	16 021.7	16 924.2	4 930.8	6 610.3	6 623.7	7 143.4	5 235.2
Accommodation and food service activities	2 493.1	2 341.2	4 290.1	3 713.7	3 481.9	1 432.5	1 374.3	2 151.0	2 234.6	2 272.8
Information and communication	25 519.3	27 943.1	28 223.5	37 000.0	44 367.9	6 088.7	5 607.9	7 035.0	8 996.6	9 115.7
Financial and insurance activities	40 681.7	45 975.5	45 632.1	46 933.1	50 771.0	203 772.1	240 929.7	226 302.8	166 734.4	179 815.5
Activities of holding companies	4 226.3	3 883.0	8 692.6	8 665.0	10 352.9	125 687.5	125 777.7	122 369.1	78 397.7	87 812.5
Real estate activities	17 142.5	22 241.1	21 734.9	21 610.1	24 558.9	3 653.9	5 273.9	5 429.5	5 363.7	8 083.0
Professional, scientific and technical activities	77 692.3	87 400.4	97 977.2	91 337.5	78 318.4	14 409.8	17 420.2	16 530.3	62 851.8	61 769.4
Administrative and support service activities	12 224.2	14 409.7	15 631.0	12 710.4	16 828.6	-798.9	106.9	1 563.7	1 638.4	1 950.9
Public administration; activities of households and of extraterritorial organisations	-	-	135.9	133.3	198.6	425.9	324.4	3 017.6	2 568.3	277.9
Education	-	-	-	-	-	-2.5	-1.9	7.5	-19.1	28.0
Human health and social work activities	193.5	119.3	181.6	222.1	247.5	92.3	123.8	128.3	264.3	243.1
Arts, entertainment and recreation	539.0	1 427.3	1 389.9	1 874.3	1 941.0	2 255.8	2 752.8	1 727.9	1 759.2	1 881.5
Other services	1 114.9	1 618.4	1 766.9	1 718.6	1 765.5	94.7	207.9	334.7	268.6	291.1
Not allocated and confidential	**0.0**	**0.0**	**0.0**	**0.0**	**0.0**	**749.6**	**841.2**	**1 140.4**	**2 169.5**	**1 169.0**
Private real estate activities	**24 612.2**	**30 005.9**	**30 556.8**	**31 855.5**	**36 376.4**	**20 734.8**	**23 873.0**	**22 238.8**	**22 464.6**	**24 329.7**

\- Nil

Note: Detailed metadata at: *http://metalinks.oecd.org/idi/20220712/6d95*.

Source: *OECD International Direct Investment Statistics (database): https://doi.org/10.1787/idi-data-en*

ITALY

Table 6. Foreign direct investment income by industrial sector

Million US dollars

	Inward					Outward				
	2016	2017	2018	2019	2020	2016	2017	2018	2019	2020
All FDI activities	**14 146.7**	**19 620.5**	**20 409.6**	**17 823.5**	**2 223.3**	**17 894.9**	**24 781.8**	**29 994.4**	**28 627.9**	**16 515.3**
Agriculture, forestry and fishing	**-40.3**	**98.7**	**27.1**	**156.6**	**-13.0**	**2.8**	**34.6**	**-14.9**	**-23.4**	**12.3**
Mining and quarrying	**-184.7**	**-48.2**	**263.1**	**98.2**	**-261.1**	**70.1**	**42.9**	**560.2**	**132.8**	**-8.7**
Extraction activities	-184.7	-48.2	263.1	98.2	-261.1	69.7	42.6	562.6	140.9	-12.9
Manufacturing	**4 037.7**	**7 010.3**	**7 078.6**	**9 076.2**	**2 401.7**	**7 555.1**	**8 295.1**	**8 163.7**	**6 467.9**	**10 216.9**
of which:										
Food products, beverages and tobacco	831.5	879.6	1 064.8	523.2	673.2	679.5	805.8	640.0	987.0	721.0
Textiles, wood and paper products; printing	-31.8	-0.2	87.3	16.5	-657.9	307.7	232.4	199.4	306.5	139.7
Chemical, rubber, plastic, non-metallic mineral products	2 106.2	2 587.1	2 047.2	1 895.8	887.0	1 987.7	1 937.5	1 765.0	1 822.2	5 248.7
Metal and machinery products, except electrical equipment	883.4	1 897.8	1 767.6	2 013.5	1 372.3	2 232.0	2 284.9	2 450.9	1 300.3	1 583.2
Motor vehicles, trailers, semi-trailers, other transport equipment	-682.3	80.2	-678.1	471.0	-3 261.0	1 474.4	1 713.1	1 257.8	843.4	-201.6
Other manufacturing	930.7	1 565.8	2 789.7	4 156.1	3 388.1	873.8	1 321.4	1 850.7	1 208.5	2 725.8
Electricity, gas, steam and air conditioning supply	**-69.0**	**216.4**	**293.3**	**333.9**	**524.2**	**-252.6**	**75.1**	**27.0**	**121.3**	**476.8**
Water supply; sewerage, waste management and remediation activities	**-34.8**	**-16.5**	**-50.4**	**10.5**	**10.8**	**6.0**	**-2.0**	**2.4**	**6.4**	**3.6**
Construction	**38.9**	**24.6**	**-148.8**	**-104.8**	**36.5**	**-244.1**	**710.1**	**432.7**	**622.0**	**-122.6**
Services	**10 398.8**	**12 335.2**	**12 946.8**	**8 252.9**	**-475.9**	**10 757.6**	**15 626.1**	**20 823.2**	**21 300.9**	**5 937.0**
Wholesale and retail trade; repair of motor vehicles and motorcycles	2 352.1	3 654.4	4 057.7	4 061.8	1 835.2	1 077.4	1 404.3	1 990.3	2 039.3	-260.2
Transportation and storage	843.4	1 031.0	1 384.4	2 332.9	-1 124.5	273.3	287.0	36.6	231.1	352.6
Accommodation and food service activities	37.1	-74.4	-14.4	58.0	-240.8	210.0	215.2	180.8	128.0	-53.7
Information and communication	1 491.4	1 078.8	969.3	1 463.3	1 464.1	-343.2	192.8	66.1	323.3	193.0
Financial and insurance activities	2 885.8	2 731.6	1 386.0	-2 984.9	-3 462.9	8 407.7	12 865.0	17 330.3	15 099.0	7 947.0
Activities of holding companies	210.5	189.2	609.1	326.3	554.3	1 963.1	5 422.2	8 945.3	4 666.9	812.8
Real estate activities	1 129.1	128.8	1 576.9	883.5	-8.9	142.8	370.5	281.8	125.2	59.1
Professional, scientific and technical activities	1 069.1	2 996.4	2 796.5	1 573.7	676.9	861.2	169.8	632.3	3 071.0	-1 893.4
Administrative and support service activities	694.9	844.2	1 096.6	919.0	771.0	80.2	112.5	40.8	90.2	-175.8
Public administration; activities of households and of extraterritorial organisations	-	-	-1.0	1.9	-0.1	7.2	8.6	0.4	-6.0	-6.6
Education	-	-	-	-	-	0.6	-1.3	0.0	0.0	-5.8
Human health and social work activities	8.7	18.1	5.9	29.8	-16.1	-5.2	-9.4	-6.4	-12.5	-54.2
Arts, entertainment and recreation	-141.8	-88.3	-436.3	-176.2	-471.5	45.1	9.5	259.7	205.9	-160.0
Other services	28.9	14.4	125.1	90.0	101.7	0.6	1.4	10.5	6.5	-4.9
Not allocated and confidential	**0.0**	**0.0**	**0.0**	**0.0**	**0.0**	**0.0**	**0.0**	**0.0**	**0.0**	**0.0**
Private real estate activities	-	-	-	-	-	-	-	-	-	-

- Nil

Note: Detailed metadata at: *http://metalinks.oecd.org/idi/20220712/6d95.*

Source: *OECD International Direct Investment Statistics (database): https://doi.org/10.1787/idi-data-en*

JAPAN

Table 1. Foreign direct investment flows by country

Million US dollars

	Inward					Outward				
	2016	2017	2018	2019	2020	2016	2017	2018	2019	2020
WORLD	**17 749.5**	**9 354.2**	**9 961.4**	**13 723.6**	**10 254.9**	**151 287.1**	**164 563.0**	**144 962.9**	**232 723.3**	**115 716.0**
OECD COUNTRIES	**10 116.4**	**3 872.9**	**7 881.2**	**6 620.1**	**6 992.4**	**113 752.1**	**111 236.0**	**73 346.6**	**170 889.2**	**66 345.2**
Australia	442.2	307.6	101.6	163.9	47.8	4 399.5	4 549.6	2 094.5	10 191.8	17 646.3
Austria	11.5	35.6	8.5	1.9	-83.1	14.3	286.9	-40.0	10.1	2.3
Belgium	70.7	-136.2	367.2	-1 591.0	169.3	1 918.5	1 200.3	2 348.0	3 539.6	2 156.7
Canada	-52.4	61.4	75.2	102.0	74.0	676.2	937.5	2 919.7	3 930.7	2 747.2
Chile	1.5	2.2	3.5	2.2	2.3	-201.7	-57.3	328.4	1 313.9	1 676.5
Colombia	-	-	-	-	-	5.6	29.9	47.3	49.3	30.8
Costa Rica	-	-	-	-	-	-1.1	1.0	0.3	8.2	1.0
Czech Republic	-	-6.4	1.0	-	0.3	142.2	168.3	169.1	93.7	155.0
Denmark	91.2	11.3	60.6	-35.2	-42.0	-162.9	304.1	153.3	-20 396.5	1 392.1
Estonia	-	-	2.0	-	-	-	2.0	1.1	3.2	0.8
Finland	-21.1	35.9	-446.6	-28.8	-430.6	-4 089.1	831.3	584.1	-109.8	142.5
France	4 719.0	3 353.6	2 103.7	1 494.6	1 503.1	1 175.9	1 555.7	988.2	1 652.6	775.3
Germany	581.7	-1 127.1	-1 729.4	-479.8	-496.8	1 509.1	2 578.5	2 080.3	11 092.6	1 099.5
Greece	-	-	-	0.6	0.4	-0.4	-1.7	-3.6	0.0	-1.1
Hungary	0.4	27.0	-	-174.2	423.5	125.9	139.9	209.8	249.2	340.1
Iceland	-	-	1.2	-	-	-	7.3	-96.3	-	-
Ireland	511.0	-1 486.0	356.1	-64.9	75.6	2 572.1	2 070.9	6 574.7	57 537.3	-26 834.9
Israel	-64.5	35.6	1 234.3	-5.8	79.2	193.5	1 074.6	40.4	7.0	15.7
Italy	24.1	98.1	-60.3	-47.5	-85.0	454.7	-156.4	844.8	1 375.3	676.2
Japan	-	-	-	-	-	-	-	-	-	-
Korea	581.8	997.4	1 841.2	397.7	361.6	1 631.6	1 625.2	4 351.8	2 353.6	2 233.2
Latvia	-	-	-	-	-	0.7	0.4	-	-	-
Lithuania	-	-	-	-	-	-	-	-	-	-
Luxembourg	1 004.3	1 398.5	-867.9	-181.8	-411.6	1 020.6	6 111.6	-560.5	825.5	24 617.6
Mexico	-	-	2.0	0.7	-	1 886.6	1 308.7	1 313.6	620.9	833.7
Netherlands	-940.9	-1 363.1	-433.0	-2 515.7	270.9	3 585.0	14 266.4	8 069.6	3 267.0	13 997.5
New Zealand	-26.3	-17.4	8.1	14.8	20.1	400.0	369.0	323.3	241.3	473.4
Norway	-151.8	182.3	-150.5	-134.8	254.0	340.6	-102.4	433.9	582.5	183.4
Poland	-	0.3	-	-	-	144.6	72.5	18.0	113.2	17.0
Portugal	-6.2	-67.6	0.9	9.9	4.5	92.6	8.3	13.0	-6.3	1.7
Slovak Republic	0.9	-	2.0	-	-	48.4	16.6	17.7	-1.4	27.6
Slovenia	-	-	-	-	-	-0.2	-17.7	-39.4	0.3	0.5
Spain	2.0	33.1	-226.4	-46.7	41.5	800.4	317.0	4 332.7	510.4	1 347.3
Sweden	-87.4	267.3	195.7	156.3	-295.0	247.2	1 062.0	1 280.5	925.5	674.1
Switzerland	762.4	-2 499.9	-1 652.5	-2 980.4	-2 000.1	1 935.7	-1 543.3	222.7	36 948.1	11 292.7
Turkey	0.4	0.8	-	0.4	-	509.8	562.3	336.0	612.0	320.9
United Kingdom	-1 296.8	-104.5	1 344.0	-8.9	-34.5	41 413.2	25 876.0	17 104.9	6 722.5	-27 235.6
United States	3 958.8	3 832.9	5 739.1	12 570.5	7 542.9	50 967.7	45 812.3	16 932.3	46 683.2	35 539.2
EUROPE	**5 422.5**	**-1 338.3**	**-1 102.5**	**-6 463.7**	**-1 221.0**	**53 766.4**	**55 919.6**	**46 693.2**	**106 624.8**	**8 269.9**
Bulgaria	-	0.7	-	0.4	-	-63.0	74.8	-1.5	2.1	2.5
Croatia	-	-	-	-	-	-0.1	0.3	0.0	-0.1	-0.1
Cyprus	-0.4	0.4	2.4	2.5	-155.3	3.0	96.7	-6.7	54.7	139.9
Malta	1.1	0.8	0.9	-0.4	-2.5	-26.4	0.1	14.7	56.6	33.0
Montenegro	-	-	-	-	-	0.2	-0.2	-0.6	-1.1	-0.1
Romania	0.4	-	-	-	-	22.2	7.4	88.5	10.7	93.5
Russian Federation	2.7	3.6	1.4	3.6	0.4	108.1	240.6	468.7	415.9	489.5
Ukraine	-	-	-	-	-	28.4	24.7	16.9	11.9	26.4
AFRICA	**34.7**	**6.5**	**4.9**	**573.3**	**-44.1**	**-555.5**	**1 820.5**	**1 717.0**	**-1 140.4**	**-4 540.0**
Northern Africa	-	-	-	-	-	-15.9	140.5	51.7	109.7	20.0
Algeria	-	-	-	-	-	-	18.4	30.4	22.6	29.1
Egypt	-	-	-	-	-	-21.1	115.3	4.0	31.3	-12.7
Libya	-	-	-	-	-	-	-	5.1	34.1	-3.7
Morocco	-	-	-	-	-	5.3	6.8	11.8	21.7	7.3
Tunisia	-	-	-	-	-	-	-	0.5	-	0.0
Other African countries	34.7	6.5	4.9	573.3	-44.1	-539.6	1 680.0	1 665.2	-1 250.1	-4 560.0
Nigeria	-	-	-	-	-	7.3	2.0	5.7	4.1	4.3
South Africa	0.7	-3.1	-0.6	-0.5	-	928.2	1 107.4	1 460.8	-1 306.4	-4 530.2
AMERICA	**4 833.5**	**7 292.4**	**9 637.4**	**14 235.9**	**6 689.3**	**77 855.5**	**58 473.4**	**44 774.4**	**67 054.0**	**57 515.8**
Northern America	3 906.5	3 894.3	5 814.3	12 672.5	7 617.0	51 643.9	46 749.8	19 852.1	50 614.0	38 286.4
Central America and Caribbean countries	944.8	3 412.6	3 816.7	1 559.9	-913.4	25 455.0	12 755.2	22 243.6	11 949.0	13 957.7
Bahamas	-	2.3	-	1.9	-	-281.7	34.9	88.5	16.7	460.7
Bermuda	-18.2	20.7	-79.7	31.9	47.6	-315.2	7 278.9	309.4	413.6	4 263.3
Cayman Islands	748.6	3 315.7	3 451.2	1 374.6	-1 129.8	20 485.0	4 131.7	17 297.9	4 944.9	6 120.7
El Salvador	-	-	-	-	-	2.3	0.9	0.0	-0.5	-0.7
Guatemala	-	-	-	-	-	-	-	-	-	-
Honduras	-	-	-	-	-	-	-	-	-	-
Nicaragua	-	-	-	-	-	-	-	-	-	-
Panama	14.2	7.3	25.1	-5.8	-8.0	91.6	-226.5	124.6	374.6	-15.9
Virgin Islands, U.S.	1.8	-3.1	-	8.8	-	-2.1	-1.5	1.3	3.0	2.1
South America	-17.8	-14.4	6.5	3.5	-14.3	756.7	-1 031.6	2 678.7	4 491.0	5 271.7
Argentina	-19.2	-14.1	-5.3	1.3	0.9	122.4	583.1	438.7	129.9	36.2
Bolivia	-	-	-	-	-	-	-	-	-	-
Brazil	-	-2.6	8.2	-	-17.5	835.9	-1 618.9	1 802.2	2 375.0	2 899.7
Ecuador	-	-	-	-	-	-0.7	-	2.1	41.4	1.9
Paraguay	-	-	-	-	-	-7.4	30.0	-0.9	6.8	6.3
Peru	-	-	-	-	-	94.6	158.8	219.2	557.6	595.4
Uruguay	-	-	-	-	-	35.0	-113.2	-193.4	-8.2	13.5
Venezuela	-	-	-	-	-	-127.1	-44.0	34.9	25.3	11.3

Table 1. Foreign direct investment flows by country *(cont.)*

Million US dollars

	Inward					Outward				
	2016	2017	2018	2019	2020	2016	2017	2018	2019	2020
ASIA	**7 009.9**	**3 156.1**	**1 331.2**	**5 267.2**	**4 849.2**	**14 223.4**	**41 919.8**	**51 269.9**	**50 608.9**	**35 998.2**
Near and Middle East	43.1	112.8	1 390.8	189.2	185.3	682.2	1 959.1	820.1	-542.3	-379.3
Gulf Arabian countries	107.5	77.1	156.5	195.0	106.1	489.7	884.6	777.6	-551.4	-395.9
Kuwait	-	-	0.3	-	-	1.8	1.6	2.1	2.2	2.2
Qatar	-	-	-	-	-	40.0	72.5	14.1	15.0	0.9
Saudi Arabia	58.6	55.4	77.0	63.9	113.9	267.4	173.2	406.3	-910.0	-458.4
United Arab Emirates	48.9	17.1	76.7	131.1	-8.1	147.6	644.9	402.1	74.7	67.6
Other Near and Middle East	-64.5	35.6	1 234.3	-5.8	79.2	192.5	1 074.6	42.5	9.1	16.6
Jordan	-	-	-	-	-	-	-	-	-	-
Other Asian countries	6 966.9	3 043.3	-59.6	5 078.0	4 663.9	13 541.1	39 960.6	50 449.8	51 151.2	36 377.6
China	278.7	612.7	447.5	377.7	390.5	9 811.3	12 023.4	10 853.1	10 662.8	10 346.3
Hong Kong, China	1 226.8	-164.4	761.2	1 342.4	218.6	1 967.3	2 910.8	2 731.9	1 889.5	1 491.7
India	0.4	5.6	-4.6	35.3	41.2	4 104.3	1 619.8	3 145.6	4 145.4	1 906.7
Indonesia	38.9	195.8	-2.6	2.3	3.3	2 985.4	3 534.9	3 406.7	8 888.7	3 257.4
Iran, Islamic Republic of	-	-	-	-	-	2.7	-	2.5	-	1.2
Malaysia	15.7	38.1	18.5	73.3	-40.0	1 458.4	1 140.4	1 213.9	268.3	1 853.4
Philippines	-4.5	17.7	12.5	36.6	17.3	2 288.1	1 111.5	1 116.3	1 724.4	1 363.4
Singapore	2 450.3	484.6	-3 583.2	1 818.2	2 886.7	-18 361.5	6 910.5	13 710.8	14 083.7	6 321.1
Chinese Taipei	2 281.6	788.7	417.2	978.7	721.1	1 411.2	1 096.3	1 629.6	1 129.2	1 782.7
Thailand	102.1	72.9	47.4	23.0	36.1	4 085.4	5 455.7	5 659.5	3 359.8	3 516.1
Viet Nam	1.7	0.1	1.0	1.6	2.5	1 658.9	2 022.5	1 982.2	2 609.9	2 396.6
AUSTRALIA, OCEANIA AND POLAR REGIONS	**449.0**	**237.0**	**124.3**	**105.3**	**-18.6**	**5 998.5**	**5 456.6**	**443.1**	**9 481.9**	**18 394.0**
WORLD unallocated and confidential	**0.0**	**0.5**	**-33.9**	**5.6**	**-**	**-1.2**	**973.2**	**65.4**	**94.1**	**77.9**
European Union (since 01/02/2020)	..	..	..	..	..	..	..	..	..	..
G20 countries excl. European Union	**9 319.6**	**8 273.6**	**9 938.1**	**14 677.3**	**9 445.9**	**123 787.0**	**102 312.6**	**70 948.3**	**109 636.7**	**48 583.1**
G20 OECD countries	**8 958.8**	**7 420.3**	**9 417.0**	**14 193.6**	**8 913.2**	**104 624.1**	**84 649.3**	**48 966.2**	**85 235.4**	**34 635.9**
G20 Non-OECD countries	**360.7**	**853.3**	**521.0**	**483.7**	**532.7**	**19 162.9**	**17 663.3**	**21 982.1**	**24 401.3**	**13 947.2**
MENA countries	**107.5**	**77.1**	**156.5**	**195.0**	**106.1**	**473.8**	**1 025.1**	**830.9**	**-439.6**	**-375.1**
ASEAN countries	**2 605.7**	**809.2**	**-3 504.2**	**1 957.5**	**2 904.0**	**-5 621.8**	**20 469.8**	**27 594.2**	**30 753.7**	**18 501.3**

- Nil; .. Not available

Note: Detailed metadata at: *http://metalinks.oecd.org/idi/20220712/6d95.*

Source: *OECD International Direct Investment Statistics (database): https://doi.org/10.1787/idi-data-en*

Table 2. Foreign direct investment positions by country

At year end

Million US dollars

	Inward					Outward				
	2016	2017	2018	2019	2020	2016	2017	2018	2019	2020
WORLD	**196 613.9**	**202 441.1**	**204 523.6**	**223 809.7**	**232 313.5**	**1 315 221.1**	**1 497 525.0**	**1 568 765.7**	**1 780 245.8**	**1 837 075.4**
OECD COUNTRIES	..	..	..	..	..	**886 155.2**	**1 005 386.9**	**1 032 678.4**	**1 186 386.8**	**1 214 912.4**
Australia	..	667.9	919.3	928.2	776.3	65 442.8	68 041.5	65 321.2	71 084.8	87 724.2
Austria	..	..	..	..	..	..	..	..	..	..
Belgium	..	1 311.4	881.6	3 170.4	3 542.4	17 439.5	20 514.5	21 236.0	25 460.5	28 974.5
Canada	..	1 378.9	1 386.7	1 572.0	1 548.4	15 840.7	16 439.6	17 070.1	20 665.9	22 928.4
Chile	..	..	..	..	..	..	..	..	..	..
Colombia	..	..	..	..	..	..	..	..	..	..
Costa Rica	..	..	..	..	..	..	..	..	..	..
Czech Republic	..	..	..	..	..	..	..	..	..	..
Denmark	..	..	..	..	..	..	..	..	..	..
Estonia	..	..	..	..	..	..	..	..	..	..
Finland	..	..	..	..	..	..	..	..	..	..
France	..	39 072.7	44 718.6	45 679.4	41 747.3	12 799.6	15 330.6	15 516.2	16 242.7	15 485.9
Germany	..	8 109.0	10 385.3	10 940.6	9 427.8	18 057.7	23 074.2	22 467.0	33 979.8	37 275.9
Greece	..	..	..	..	..	..	..	..	..	..
Hungary	..	..	..	..	..	..	..	..	..	..
Iceland	..	..	..	..	..	..	..	..	..	..
Ireland	..	..	..	..	..	..	..	..	..	..
Israel	..	..	..	..	..	..	..	..	..	..
Italy	..	632.4	575.2	762.2	672.2	3 621.4	3 395.0	4 140.7	5 353.2	5 133.5
Japan	..	..	370.1	376.3	1 215.8	..	-	-	-	-
Korea	..	6 243.0	6 771.2	8 876.8	9 104.5	32 028.8	36 771.6	38 372.1	38 872.4	41 781.3
Latvia	..	..	..	..	..	..	..	..	..	..
Lithuania	..	..	..	..	..	..	..	..	..	..
Luxembourg	..	4 584.4	4 790.2	5 096.1	6 985.0	9 532.4	15 162.9	12 698.2	13 639.3	39 393.5
Mexico	..	234.6	259.8	259.2	283.1	8 794.5	10 377.8	11 913.7	13 311.0	13 640.6
Netherlands	..	8 130.9	6 573.9	6 998.0	4 527.0	94 713.0	114 317.0	116 814.4	119 301.4	134 492.1
New Zealand	..	338.8	342.2	264.5	281.5	3 396.2	3 730.2	3 909.9	3 808.0	4 240.2
Norway	..	..	..	..	..	..	..	..	..	..
Poland	..	..	..	..	..	..	..	..	..	..
Portugal	..	..	..	..	..	..	..	..	..	..
Slovak Republic	..	..	..	..	..	..	..	..	..	..
Slovenia	..	..	..	..	..	..	..	..	..	..
Spain	..	-182.5	-881.5	-152.4	-362.9	2 910.4	3 206.4	7 358.4	7 356.6	9 091.0
Sweden	..	425.4	495.4	660.7	-323.1	4 336.6	5 572.4	7 694.0	7 732.8	10 031.3
Switzerland	..	9 805.8	10 379.7	10 121.1	9 696.2	8 285.1	8 082.2	5 909.1	39 117.3	53 807.2
Turkey	..	..	..	..	..	..	..	..	..	..
United Kingdom	..	6 362.6	2 913.4	-2 600.8	6 273.2	118 135.2	151 633.6	154 551.4	163 617.1	131 674.8
United States	..	71 722.9	59 144.4	74 958.4	78 942.7	445 853.6	479 995.3	487 940.2	519 949.2	561 736.4
EUROPE	..	**83 039.9**	**87 743.7**	**85 956.0**	**86 878.3**	**312 439.5**	**387 489.8**	**408 444.3**	**522 530.1**	**487 635.2**
Bulgaria	..	..	..	..	..	..	..	..	..	..
Croatia	..	..	..	..	..	..	..	..	..	..
Cyprus	..	..	..	..	..	..	..	..	..	..
Malta	..	..	..	..	..	..	..	..	..	..
Montenegro	..	..	..	..	..	..	..	..	..	..
Romania	..	..	..	..	..	..	..	..	..	..
Russian Federation	..	51.4	52.7	55.1	58.5	1 503.9	1 576.5	1 523.4	2 194.5	2 388.8
Ukraine	..	..	..	..	..	..	..	..	..	..
AFRICA	..	**92.7**	**92.7**	**103.9**	**160.9**	**10 008.6**	**7 793.2**	**8 921.7**	**6 069.6**	**4 737.4**
Northern Africa	..	..	..	..	..	..	..	..	..	..
Algeria	..	..	..	..	..	..	..	..	..	..
Egypt	..	..	..	..	..	..	..	..	..	..
Libya	..	..	..	..	..	..	..	..	..	..
Morocco	..	..	..	..	..	..	..	..	..	..
Tunisia	..	..	..	..	..	..	..	..	..	..
Other African countries	..	..	..	..	..	..	..	..	..	..
Nigeria	..	..	..	..	..	..	..	..	..	..
South Africa	..	3.8	4.9	5.4	5.9	8 229.6	6 199.5	7 103.7	4 437.2	3 158.7
AMERICA	..	**78 573.0**	**67 867.3**	**83 631.2**	**86 497.8**	**549 724.5**	**596 208.4**	**618 796.8**	**664 238.5**	**710 497.1**
Northern America	..	73 101.8	60 531.1	76 530.4	80 491.1	461 694.3	496 434.9	505 010.3	540 615.1	584 664.8
Central America and Caribbean countries	..	..	..	..	..	..	..	..	..	..
Bahamas	..	..	..	..	..	..	..	..	..	..
Bermuda	..	..	..	..	..	..	..	..	..	..
Cayman Islands	..	5 423.7	9 012.1	7 994.2	6 186.1	31 340.5	35 222.3	46 565.8	46 033.7	42 443.1
El Salvador	..	..	..	..	..	..	..	..	..	..
Guatemala	..	..	..	..	..	..	..	..	..	..
Honduras	..	..	..	..	..	..	..	..	..	..
Nicaragua	..	..	..	..	..	..	..	..	..	..
Panama	..	..	..	..	..	..	..	..	..	..
Virgin Islands, U.S.	..	..	..	..	..	..	..	..	..	..
South America	..	..	..	..	..	..	..	..	..	..
Argentina	..	..	..	..	..	..	..	..	..	..
Bolivia	..	..	..	..	..	..	..	..	..	..
Brazil	..	-1 169.7	-3 147.8	-2 563.1	-2 847.1	24 467.1	21 659.2	21 265.6	22 903.7	21 371.5
Ecuador	..	..	..	..	..	..	..	..	..	..
Paraguay	..	..	..	..	..	..	..	..	..	..
Peru	..	..	..	..	..	..	..	..	..	..
Uruguay	..	..	..	..	..	..	..	..	..	..
Venezuela	..	..	..	..	..	..	..	..	..	..

JAPAN

Table 2. Foreign direct investment positions by country *(cont.)*
At year end

Million US dollars

	Inward					Outward				
	2016	2017	2018	2019	2020	2016	2017	2018	2019	2020
ASIA	..	**38 398.7**	**47 335.1**	**52 680.4**	**56 029.9**	**369 450.9**	**429 113.7**	**460 081.1**	**509 299.4**	**539 075.0**
Near and Middle East	..	1 290.4	-522.1	-160.8	-5 055.6	6 990.5	9 012.6	8 597.7	8 862.5	8 170.9
Gulf Arabian countries	..	..	..	..	..	..	..	..	..	..
Kuwait	..	..	..	..	..	..	..	..	..	..
Qatar	..	..	..	..	..	..	..	..	..	..
Saudi Arabia	..	-778.3	-3 159.2	-3 705.9	-5 646.1	4 850.9	4 897.0	5 202.8	4 725.4	4 522.8
United Arab Emirates	..	1 430.4	563.4	535.3	498.4	563.6	1 445.3	1 976.5	2 135.4	1 860.6
Other Near and Middle East	..	..	..	..	..	..	..	..	..	..
Jordan	..	..	..	..	..	..	..	..	..	..
Other Asian countries	..	37 108.3	47 857.3	52 841.2	61 085.5	362 460.4	420 101.1	451 483.4	500 436.8	530 904.1
China	..	1 593.8	2 339.1	2 677.8	2 538.3	108 230.4	117 568.0	121 165.3	126 733.1	138 566.3
Hong Kong, China	..	6 541.9	7 627.8	9 883.9	12 382.3	27 538.7	29 957.1	31 958.3	34 375.2	34 923.5
India	..	164.4	189.2	200.9	445.9	17 934.7	22 145.1	24 279.9	27 954.0	29 898.7
Indonesia	..	30.2	26.4	53.7	81.0	27 001.5	30 343.0	31 155.3	39 968.6	38 275.8
Iran, Islamic Republic of	..	..	..	..	..	8.8	9.1	11.8	12.0	13.8
Malaysia	..	292.3	306.5	226.9	384.0	12 618.5	14 096.4	16 335.4	16 954.3	18 226.3
Philippines	..	64.8	96.8	118.1	142.1	13 740.9	15 023.0	14 444.1	15 697.4	16 773.1
Singapore	..	13 939.3	21 031.3	20 344.1	24 488.6	39 563.3	59 361.9	71 573.3	84 369.9	92 886.0
Chinese Taipei	..	7 967.4	8 813.8	9 686.6	9 853.9	12 359.6	14 382.2	14 678.2	15 672.9	17 882.1
Thailand	..	135.0	121.6	176.2	203.8	53 797.8	61 409.8	66 729.9	75 105.2	74 697.4
Viet Nam	..	1.5	3.9	4.0	5.4	14 517.8	15 621.7	16 827.7	19 557.2	21 699.9
AUSTRALIA, OCEANIA AND POLAR REGIONS	..	**1 171.9**	**1 453.2**	**1 406.2**	**2 712.8**	**73 593.6**	**76 915.9**	**72 517.7**	**78 104.0**	**95 126.2**
WORLD unallocated and confidential	..	**1 164.8**	**31.6**	**32.1**	**33.8**	**4.0**	**4.1**	**4.2**	**4.2**	**4.5**
European Union (since 01/02/2020)	..	..	..	..	..	..	..	..	..	**286 110.9**
G20 countries excl. European Union	..	..	..	..	..	..	..	..	..	..
G20 OECD countries	..	..	..	..	..	..	..	..	..	..
G20 Non-OECD countries	..	..	..	..	..	..	..	..	..	..
MENA countries	..	..	..	..	..	..	..	..	..	..
ASEAN countries	..	..	..	..	..	**163 435.0**	**198 170.1**	**219 933.6**	**255 273.8**	**266 223.7**

- Nil; .. Not available

Note: Inward FDI positions are allocated according to the ultimate investing country. Inward FDI positions by immediate counterpart country are available for more geographic details and for 2014 in the OECD FDI database according to BMD4. Detailed metadata at: *http://metalinks.oecd.org/idi/20220712/6d95*.

Source: OECD *International Direct Investment Statistics (database): https://doi.org/10.1787/idi-data-en*

JAPAN

Table 3. Foreign direct investment income by country

Million US dollars

	Inward					Outward				
	2016	2017	2018	2019	2020	2016	2017	2018	2019	2020
WORLD	**32 634.0**	**33 301.9**	**34 927.6**	**33 504.3**	**30 212.3**	**105 867.5**	**120 205.2**	**130 294.6**	**136 709.4**	**134 544.7**
OECD COUNTRIES	**28 694.7**	**28 043.9**	**28 685.0**	**28 386.9**	**24 923.2**	**57 586.0**	**61 302.6**	**66 902.7**	**72 251.9**	**70 758.3**
Australia	93.4	106.5	55.3	130.6	109.0	3 452.5	7 919.0	8 249.0	8 743.0	7 229.8
Austria	..	..	..	..	..	..	..	..	..	..
Belgium	89.9	162.1	167.7	41.5	49.6	1 007.3	974.8	1 839.7	1 598.2	1 103.7
Canada	12.0	62.3	86.5	89.1	87.4	1 097.7	1 651.2	1 693.2	2 123.8	3 229.6
Chile	..	..	..	..	..	..	..	..	..	..
Colombia	..	..	..	..	..	..	..	..	..	..
Costa Rica	..	..	..	..	..	..	..	..	..	..
Czech Republic	..	..	..	..	..	..	..	..	..	..
Denmark	..	..	..	..	..	..	..	..	..	..
Estonia	..	..	..	..	..	..	..	..	..	..
Finland	..	..	..	..	..	..	..	..	..	..
France	5 341.1	5 318.0	4 564.1	3 264.8	2 022.3	605.5	672.8	798.6	859.0	754.9
Germany	1 124.8	1 852.4	1 324.6	935.0	439.5	941.5	2 180.2	2 048.0	2 124.4	628.1
Greece	..	..	..	..	..	..	..	..	..	..
Hungary	..	..	..	..	..	..	..	..	..	..
Iceland	..	..	..	..	..	..	..	..	..	..
Ireland	..	..	..	..	..	..	..	..	..	..
Israel	..	..	..	..	..	..	..	..	..	..
Italy	10.8	13.5	30.6	18.3	23.1	131.2	145.4	-86.9	75.8	188.1
Japan	..	-	-	-	-	..	-	-	-	-
Korea	492.1	705.5	621.0	257.1	262.6	2 639.0	2 738.8	2 668.2	3 436.3	3 888.1
Latvia	..	..	..	..	..	..	..	..	..	..
Lithuania	..	..	..	..	..	..	..	..	..	..
Luxembourg	980.0	720.3	1 159.9	1 102.8	723.0	384.2	539.7	430.3	317.9	363.9
Mexico	1.2	3.3	0.3	5.7	2.9	592.3	675.1	718.0	638.8	749.3
Netherlands	7 945.2	4 729.5	6 063.3	6 216.6	3 346.8	7 745.4	7 635.3	10 398.8	9 527.4	9 547.0
New Zealand	-2.8	-1.7	24.1	24.3	16.4	218.7	214.8	220.4	164.5	164.2
Norway	..	..	..	..	..	..	..	..	..	..
Poland	..	..	..	..	..	..	..	..	..	..
Portugal	..	..	..	..	..	..	..	..	..	..
Slovak Republic	..	..	..	..	..	..	..	..	..	..
Slovenia	..	..	..	..	..	..	..	..	..	..
Spain	3.3	3.0	6.5	0.8	1.8	186.3	297.7	348.4	375.1	469.7
Sweden	207.3	68.2	29.0	21.7	44.1	349.8	497.5	554.9	402.9	268.2
Switzerland	1 485.8	1 724.9	2 300.8	2 535.6	2 594.0	133.0	-3.7	1 425.0	1 205.4	503.4
Turkey	..	..	..	..	..	..	..	..	..	..
United Kingdom	1 078.5	855.1	1 214.5	1 031.0	1 246.5	5 201.1	6 197.7	6 566.1	8 237.4	7 993.8
United States	9 373.1	11 431.1	10 889.1	12 532.8	13 646.7	32 054.7	27 212.2	27 126.7	29 494.5	30 848.3
EUROPE	**18 785.6**	**15 714.8**	**17 032.2**	**15 431.8**	**10 807.1**	**17 927.9**	**21 306.9**	**26 831.6**	**28 611.5**	**25 526.4**
Bulgaria	..	..	..	..	..	..	..	..	..	..
Croatia	..	..	..	..	..	..	..	..	..	..
Cyprus	..	..	..	..	..	..	..	..	..	..
Malta	..	..	..	..	..	..	..	..	..	..
Montenegro	..	..	..	..	..	..	..	..	..	..
Romania	..	..	..	..	..	..	..	..	..	..
Russian Federation	1.0	-	0.3	-	-	36.4	353.8	507.3	688.8	477.1
Ukraine	..	..	..	..	..	..	..	..	..	..
AFRICA	**7.1**	**9.8**	**12.9**	**7.0**	**9.4**	**680.0**	**645.8**	**721.7**	**750.3**	**523.2**
Northern Africa	..	..	..	..	..	..	..	..	..	..
Algeria	..	..	..	..	..	..	..	..	..	..
Egypt	..	..	..	..	..	..	..	..	..	..
Libya	..	..	..	..	..	..	..	..	..	..
Morocco	..	..	..	..	..	..	..	..	..	..
Tunisia	..	..	..	..	..	..	..	..	..	..
Other African countries	..	..	..	..	..	..	..	..	..	..
Nigeria	..	..	..	..	..	..	..	..	..	..
South Africa	0.1	0.5	-	-	-	183.9	267.9	530.0	529.1	320.5
AMERICA	**10 324.9**	**12 240.1**	**11 863.6**	**12 094.2**	**12 960.0**	**38 256.8**	**36 834.0**	**38 373.4**	**43 979.2**	**46 646.0**
Northern America	9 385.1	11 493.4	10 975.6	12 621.8	13 734.1	33 152.4	28 863.5	28 819.9	31 618.3	34 077.9
Central America and Caribbean countries	..	..	..	..	..	..	..	..	..	..
Bahamas	..	..	..	..	..	..	..	..	..	..
Bermuda	..	..	..	..	..	..	..	..	..	..
Cayman Islands	748.2	474.3	198.9	-610.8	-825.7	3 835.4	4 198.5	4 561.7	6 878.9	7 144.0
El Salvador	..	..	..	..	..	..	..	..	..	..
Guatemala	..	..	..	..	..	..	..	..	..	..
Honduras	..	..	..	..	..	..	..	..	..	..
Nicaragua	..	..	..	..	..	..	..	..	..	..
Panama	..	..	..	..	..	..	..	..	..	..
Virgin Islands, U.S.	..	..	..	..	..	..	..	..	..	..
South America	..	..	..	..	..	..	..	..	..	..
Argentina	..	..	..	..	..	..	..	..	..	..
Bolivia	..	..	..	..	..	..	..	..	..	..
Brazil	-	-	-	-	-	-213.0	1 672.1	1 764.5	1 499.1	1 256.0
Ecuador	..	..	..	..	..	..	..	..	..	..
Paraguay	..	..	..	..	..	..	..	..	..	..
Peru	..	..	..	..	..	..	..	..	..	..
Uruguay	..	..	..	..	..	..	..	..	..	..
Venezuela	..	..	..	..	..	..	..	..	..	..

JAPAN

Table 3. Foreign direct investment income by country *(cont.)*

Million US dollars

	Inward					Outward				
	2016	2017	2018	2019	2020	2016	2017	2018	2019	2020
ASIA	**3 423.3**	**5 230.9**	**5 938.9**	**5 902.6**	**6 387.8**	**45 107.9**	**53 107.6**	**55 814.4**	**54 332.3**	**54 250.6**
Near and Middle East	-56.0	37.1	-7.1	4.5	3.2	1 127.4	1 348.4	1 294.5	615.7	-52.5
Gulf Arabian countries	..	..	..	..	..	..	..	..	..	..
Kuwait	..	..	..	..	..	..	..	..	..	..
Qatar	..	..	..	..	..	..	..	..	..	..
Saudi Arabia	-	-	-	-	-	611.1	697.0	1 039.7	318.7	-163.4
United Arab Emirates	0.8	7.1	8.1	0.6	2.6	511.5	761.3	282.7	288.6	174.0
Other Near and Middle East	..	..	..	..	..	..	..	..	..	..
Jordan	..	..	..	..	..	..	..	..	..	..
Other Asian countries	3 479.3	5 193.8	5 945.9	5 898.1	6 384.6	43 980.4	51 759.2	54 519.9	53 716.5	54 303.1
China	41.4	83.0	118.0	62.7	124.9	14 757.1	17 983.2	18 547.5	19 772.6	19 695.3
Hong Kong, China	771.2	950.7	1 066.1	1 018.4	667.9	3 180.8	3 981.0	3 072.2	3 315.5	3 936.0
India	5.0	16.9	-	32.9	33.4	1 421.3	2 152.4	2 216.3	1 328.2	910.0
Indonesia	58.8	6.5	1.9	1.7	1.4	2 210.6	3 072.5	3 051.1	3 574.9	3 453.7
Iran, Islamic Republic of	-	-	-	-	-	-	-	3.2	-	-
Malaysia	13.6	60.4	45.8	17.6	12.5	1 527.8	1 555.9	1 816.9	1 676.8	1 546.0
Philippines	0.4	-	0.0	8.6	0.5	1 403.5	1 474.1	1 706.0	1 618.6	1 285.2
Singapore	1 869.2	3 013.8	3 778.7	4 253.7	5 001.4	5 621.3	5 572.4	6 491.5	7 008.5	7 771.1
Chinese Taipei	188.8	336.2	283.2	213.0	220.8	1 770.8	2 366.2	3 284.3	1 644.9	2 053.2
Thailand	30.6	15.6	28.7	28.4	53.6	7 573.6	8 846.4	9 371.6	9 112.7	8 733.3
Viet Nam	3.1	1.7	2.2	3.6	3.9	1 635.4	1 744.9	1 998.5	1 827.6	1 991.8
AUSTRALIA, OCEANIA AND POLAR REGIONS	**93.0**	**106.3**	**79.9**	**68.8**	**48.0**	**3 894.9**	**8 310.9**	**8 553.5**	**9 036.1**	**7 598.5**
WORLD unallocated and confidential	**-**	**0.0**	**0.0**	**0.0**	**0.0**	**0.0**	**0.0**	**0.0**	**-**	**-**
European Union (since 01/02/2020)	..	..	..	..	..	..	..	..	..	..
G20 countries excl. European Union	..	..	..	..	..	..	..	..	..	..
G20 OECD countries	..	..	..	..	..	..	..	..	..	..
G20 Non-OECD countries	..	..	..	..	..	..	..	..	..	..
MENA countries	..	..	..	..	..	..	..	..	..	..
ASEAN countries	**1 980.4**	**3 101.3**	**3 857.2**	**4 314.0**	**5 075.0**	**19 978.1**	**22 293.5**	**24 548.1**	**24 105.3**	**23 745.2**

- Nil; .. Not available

Note: Detailed metadata at: *http://metalinks.oecd.org/idi/20220712/6d95.*

Source: *OECD International Direct Investment Statistics (database): https://doi.org/10.1787/idi-data-en*

JAPAN

Table 4. Foreign direct investment flows by industrial sector

Million US dollars

	Inward					Outward				
	2016	2017	2018	2019	2020	2016	2017	2018	2019	2020
All FDI activities	**17 749.5**	**9 354.2**	**9 961.4**	**13 723.6**	**10 254.9**	**151 287.1**	**164 563.0**	**144 962.9**	**232 723.3**	**115 716.0**
Agriculture, forestry and fishing	**0.6**	**12.5**	**49.3**	**12.7**	**14.2**	**53.1**	**-63.9**	**139.1**	**91.7**	**393.4**
Mining and quarrying	**15.9**	**164.6**	**29.9**	**38.7**	**14.5**	**4 045.9**	**1 105.5**	**9 622.0**	**9 721.4**	**7 208.0**
Extraction activities	..	..	..	..	..	..	..	..	..	..
Manufacturing	**11 219.7**	**9 062.1**	**10 762.1**	**5 620.7**	**326.6**	**52 899.4**	**55 355.3**	**57 642.0**	**103 846.7**	**68 006.0**
of which:										
Food products, beverages and tobacco	438.4	257.1	88.7	534.0	-254.4	2 976.9	10 141.3	594.8	5 437.6	14 798.6
Textiles, wood and paper products; printing	36.0	24.0	-34.6	46.4	46.8	2 757.8	1 215.9	3 227.2	1 924.0	3 112.2
Chemical, rubber, plastic, non-metallic mineral products	..	..	..	..	..	..	..	..	..	..
Metal and machinery products, except electrical equipment	..	..	..	..	..	..	..	..	..	..
Motor vehicles, trailers, semi-trailers, other transport equipment	3 750.2	3 230.0	1 632.3	2 237.2	1 865.7	12 508.4	8 441.3	11 043.8	22 486.8	18 171.2
Other manufacturing	..	..	..	..	..	..	..	..	..	..
Electricity, gas, steam and air conditioning supply	..	..	..	..	..	..	..	..	..	..
Water supply; sewerage, waste management and remediation activities	..	..	..	..	..	..	..	..	..	..
Construction	**136.0**	**30.6**	**-268.1**	**186.8**	**-7.2**	**1 630.1**	**1 547.2**	**2 339.3**	**1 851.1**	**1 630.2**
Services	**5 169.0**	**-881.5**	**-1 427.7**	**7 089.6**	**9 371.2**	**89 155.6**	**101 571.0**	**69 946.5**	**112 161.8**	**32 713.3**
Wholesale and retail trade; repair of motor vehicles and motorcycles	-2 411.8	-5 345.1	-5 164.5	-6 266.4	-3 750.5	18 768.1	28 472.2	13 660.6	58 140.7	10 643.7
Transportation and storage	1 520.7	767.2	50.7	210.4	239.6	2 291.3	1 187.9	2 194.5	2 188.4	1 949.9
Accommodation and food service activities	..	..	..	..	..	..	..	..	..	..
Information and communication	968.7	-667.8	-3 481.1	-300.1	-417.2	16 901.9	23 501.9	37 843.6	5 866.7	-22 177.7
Financial and insurance activities	3 313.8	1 525.6	6 357.5	11 851.0	11 656.7	8 502.0	32 908.7	25 592.9	37 035.8	34 853.2
Activities of holding companies	..	..	..	..	..	..	..	..	..	..
Real estate activities	308.5	425.8	714.5	299.9	-183.6	5 119.7	6 463.2	3 843.6	10 867.2	2 552.3
Professional, scientific and technical activities	..	..	..	..	..	..	..	..	..	..
Administrative and support service activities	..	..	..	..	..	..	..	..	..	..
Public administration; activities of households and of extraterritorial organisations	..	..	..	..	..	..	..	..	..	..
Education	..	..	..	..	..	..	..	..	..	..
Human health and social work activities	..	..	..	..	..	..	..	..	..	..
Arts, entertainment and recreation	..	..	..	..	..	..	..	..	..	..
Other services	..	..	..	..	..	..	..	..	..	..
Not allocated and confidential	**1 208.4**	**965.8**	**815.8**	**775.2**	**535.7**	**3 503.1**	**5 047.9**	**5 274.0**	**5 050.6**	**5 765.2**
Private real estate activities	..	..	..	..	..	..	..	..	..	..

.. Not available

Note: Detailed metadata at: *http://metalinks.oecd.org/idi/20220712/6d95*.

Source: *OECD International Direct Investment Statistics (database)*: *https://doi.org/10.1787/idi-data-en*

JAPAN

Table 5. Foreign direct investment positions by industrial sector
At year end

Million US dollars

	Inward					Outward				
	2016	2017	2018	2019	2020	2016	2017	2018	2019	2020
All FDI activities	**196 613.9**	**202 441.1**	**204 523.6**	**223 809.7**	**232 313.5**	**1 315 221.1**	**1 497 525.0**	**1 568 765.7**	**1 780 245.8**	**1 837 075.4**
Agriculture, forestry and fishing	**81.5**	**80.9**	**132.7**	**114.7**	**135.4**	**3 275.7**	**2 984.2**	**2 957.5**	**3 092.1**	**3 364.4**
Mining and quarrying	**117.6**	**274.3**	**160.0**	**212.2**	**227.5**	**83 214.4**	**77 565.0**	**77 989.6**	**83 533.9**	**85 134.2**
Extraction activities	..	..	..	..	..	..	..	..	..	..
Manufacturing	**81 159.7**	**88 042.3**	**79 672.7**	**89 435.2**	**86 397.2**	**554 005.7**	**617 584.7**	**625 112.9**	**729 083.6**	**751 478.9**
of which:										
Food products, beverages and tobacco	2 557.5	2 520.5	2 181.4	2 387.3	2 318.3	72 039.4	83 580.4	83 358.3	84 092.6	100 085.4
Textiles, wood and paper products; printing	467.2	479.2	453.2	475.7	597.7	17 042.1	17 714.1	20 138.0	21 416.0	22 153.6
Chemical, rubber, plastic, non-metallic mineral products	..	..	..	..	..	..	..	..	..	..
Metal and machinery products, except electrical equipment	..	..	..	..	..	..	..	..	..	..
Motor vehicles, trailers, semi-trailers, other transport equipment	26 011.5	29 057.8	31 181.1	33 236.6	31 612.3	114 617.1	125 618.1	127 091.6	139 167.4	157 521.9
Other manufacturing	..	..	..	..	..	..	..	..	..	..
Electricity, gas, steam and air conditioning supply	..	..	..	..	..	..	..	..	..	..
Water supply; sewerage, waste management and remediation activities	..	..	..	..	..	..	..	..	..	..
Construction	**780.1**	**579.4**	**161.9**	**569.3**	**299.1**	**6 898.9**	**7 760.8**	**9 096.2**	**7 696.9**	**8 703.0**
Services	**102 234.8**	**100 064.8**	**109 290.1**	**117 686.7**	**128 231.2**	**632 298.9**	**747 724.3**	**807 466.7**	**908 933.5**	**934 130.2**
Wholesale and retail trade; repair of motor vehicles and motorcycles	11 181.4	6 367.8	-179.9	-8 913.4	-10 488.0	182 152.0	210 584.8	226 319.3	275 818.8	283 093.1
Transportation and storage	3 693.8	3 563.3	3 949.8	3 738.2	4 067.7	18 025.5	16 791.5	18 247.6	20 375.9	19 858.4
Accommodation and food service activities	..	..	..	..	..	..	..	..	..	..
Information and communication	7 414.3	7 737.9	20 144.4	19 391.6	19 733.9	80 071.0	101 658.3	125 413.4	119 214.2	109 059.8
Financial and insurance activities	66 484.9	66 522.6	69 102.7	87 064.3	96 641.9	260 295.5	304 659.9	329 217.9	377 466.7	412 136.3
Activities of holding companies	..	..	..	..	..	..	..	..	..	..
Real estate activities	3 454.0	3 845.2	4 987.1	4 716.9	5 122.6	24 473.3	30 170.0	32 915.1	45 298.2	38 031.1
Professional, scientific and technical activities	..	..	..	..	..	..	..	..	..	..
Administrative and support service activities	..	..	..	..	..	..	..	..	..	..
Public administration; activities of households and of extraterritorial organisations	..	..	..	..	..	..	..	..	..	..
Education	..	..	..	..	..	..	..	..	..	..
Human health and social work activities	..	..	..	..	..	..	..	..	..	..
Arts, entertainment and recreation	..	..	..	..	..	..	..	..	..	..
Other services	..	..	..	..	..	..	..	..	..	..
Not allocated and confidential	**12 240.1**	**13 399.4**	**15 106.2**	**15 791.5**	**17 023.1**	**35 527.6**	**43 906.0**	**46 142.8**	**47 905.9**	**54 264.7**
Private real estate activities	..	..	..	..	..	..	..	..	..	..

.. Not available

Note: Detailed metadata at: *http://metalinks.oecd.org/idi/20220712/6d95.*

Source: OECD *International Direct Investment Statistics (database): https://doi.org/10.1787/idi-data-en*

JAPAN

Table 6. Foreign direct investment income by industrial sector

Million US dollars

	Inward					Outward				
	2016	2017	2018	2019	2020	2016	2017	2018	2019	2020
All FDI activities	**32 634.0**	**33 301.9**	**34 927.6**	**33 504.3**	**30 212.3**	**105 867.5**	**120 205.2**	**130 294.6**	**136 709.4**	**134 544.7**
Agriculture, forestry and fishing	**0.1**	**8.1**	**26.9**	**4.7**	**5.1**	**55.8**	**109.8**	**214.1**	**147.0**	**66.2**
Mining and quarrying	**4.9**	**31.9**	**15.1**	**12.2**	**4.5**	**2 637.9**	**9 063.8**	**10 864.9**	**12 632.6**	**10 506.4**
Extraction activities	..	..	..	..	..	..	..	..	..	..
Manufacturing	**12 640.5**	**11 770.7**	**11 653.9**	**7 823.3**	**5 386.7**	**51 807.8**	**57 379.4**	**61 743.3**	**57 446.6**	**57 365.4**
of which:										
Food products, beverages and tobacco	1 162.3	1 016.9	1 055.6	1 044.7	1 024.6	2 768.5	3 995.8	4 719.2	5 977.3	5 732.2
Textiles, wood and paper products; printing	36.0	43.9	27.7	36.0	61.5	763.5	1 135.0	1 411.7	1 535.7	1 145.5
Chemical, rubber, plastic, non-metallic mineral products	..	..	..	..	..	..	..	..	..	..
Metal and machinery products, except electrical equipment	..	..	..	..	..	..	..	..	..	..
Motor vehicles, trailers, semi-trailers, other transport equipment	4 215.1	3 738.0	3 189.2	1 796.9	904.2	16 820.8	16 809.4	16 315.5	18 215.5	19 170.5
Other manufacturing	..	..	..	..	..	..	..	..	..	..
Electricity, gas, steam and air conditioning supply	..	..	..	..	..	..	..	..	..	..
Water supply; sewerage, waste management and remediation activities	..	..	..	..	..	..	..	..	..	..
Construction	**86.4**	**95.6**	**98.5**	**15.8**	**18.0**	**547.2**	**456.1**	**540.4**	**580.1**	**483.4**
Services	**18 497.9**	**20 041.2**	**21 624.2**	**24 558.0**	**24 385.0**	**48 240.9**	**50 614.0**	**54 848.9**	**63 903.0**	**63 745.7**
Wholesale and retail trade; repair of motor vehicles and motorcycles	3 063.8	4 582.5	3 770.8	5 132.4	4 311.7	19 693.9	21 660.4	23 653.0	27 585.7	26 307.2
Transportation and storage	60.6	2 345.1	140.6	248.6	231.9	2 276.2	1 941.4	2 112.5	1 886.9	1 816.7
Accommodation and food service activities	..	..	..	..	..	..	..	..	..	..
Information and communication	4 345.9	3 447.2	1 526.2	1 394.0	1 705.9	2 942.7	5 496.5	3 503.0	7 161.3	8 829.6
Financial and insurance activities	9 282.3	8 401.3	14 689.3	15 189.9	16 827.7	18 151.0	16 361.9	18 575.8	22 268.0	23 831.1
Activities of holding companies	..	..	..	..	..	..	..	..	..	..
Real estate activities	274.3	239.8	143.6	187.6	95.8	729.2	1 007.4	794.2	1 258.9	1 367.4
Professional, scientific and technical activities	..	..	..	..	..	..	..	..	..	..
Administrative and support service activities	..	..	..	..	..	..	..	..	..	..
Public administration; activities of households and of extraterritorial organisations	..	..	..	..	..	..	..	..	..	..
Education	..	..	..	..	..	..	..	..	..	..
Human health and social work activities	..	..	..	..	..	..	..	..	..	..
Arts, entertainment and recreation	..	..	..	..	..	..	..	..	..	..
Other services	..	..	..	..	..	..	..	..	..	..
Not allocated and confidential	**1 404.2**	**1 354.3**	**1 509.0**	**1 090.4**	**413.0**	**2 577.9**	**2 582.1**	**2 083.0**	**2 000.0**	**2 377.6**
Private real estate activities	..	..	..	..	..	..	..	..	..	..

.. Not available

Note: Detailed metadata at: *http://metalinks.oecd.org/idi/20220712/6d95*.

Source: *OECD International Direct Investment Statistics (database): https://doi.org/10.1787/idi-data-en*

Table 1. Foreign direct investment flows by country

Million US dollars

	Inward					Outward				
	2016	2017	2018	2019	2020	2016	2017	2018	2019	2020
WORLD	**7 263.0**	**11 531.5**	**13 267.2**	**12 589.0**	**6 916.4**	**30 507.5**	**43 463.9**	**45 232.6**	**50 981.1**	**36 878.9**
OECD COUNTRIES	**4 619.0**	**6 407.4**	**7 131.6**	**8 746.8**	**2 469.3**	**12 486.8**	**20 259.0**	**19 455.3**	**21 501.1**	**18 618.9**
Australia	2.0	33.7	2 004.2	54.8	5.3	817.6	-715.4	485.9	233.5	47.3
Austria	118.0	5.0	-4.0	11.9	65.4	12.3	41.3	1 290.4	13.7	-9.9
Belgium	9.0	63.4	13.5	255.2	-200.5	43.2	122.9	262.6	141.2	880.7
Canada	153.0	124.2	-221.0	-48.5	1 051.1	293.9	-4.7	98.2	773.9	1 538.2
Chile	9.0	-	0.1	0.2	0.7	24.5	196.6	104.3	4.0	88.6
Colombia	-	-	-	-	-	.. c	5.8	-12.8	25.4	8.0
Costa Rica	-	-	-	-	0.2	.. c	-1.5	2.2	-9.0	8.4
Czech Republic	-	0.2	0.1	0.3	0.2	22.7	436.5	238.4	0.1	-43.4
Denmark	-13.0	-7.8	3.7	3.8	31.2	.. c	12.0	2.7	-5.7	0.3
Estonia	-	13.2	1.1	-7.1	-	-	-	0.0	.. c	.. c
Finland	27.0	12.5	-22.3	8.2	-33.8	.. c	36.5	-17.0	0.2	11.7
France	387.0	55.8	635.5	55.8	-83.0	-21.0	119.2	490.7	1 386.1	102.9
Germany	-3.0	704.7	-255.1	227.4	550.8	280.1	556.4	503.5	734.0	114.3
Greece	-	-	-	-	-	.. c	0.4	0.5	1.3	0.2
Hungary	27.0	3.7	-	315.4	-	125.8	432.0	378.9	784.9	880.3
Iceland	1.0	-0.2	-	1.0	-	.. c	0.0	189.3	.. c	.. c
Ireland	84.0	163.8	500.0	217.3	15.6	.. c	1 509.2	157.1	408.8	259.2
Israel	2.0	1.9	10.8	1.0	22.8	.. c	-0.3	26.1	22.8	1.7
Italy	68.0	60.9	8.4	-16.4	-20.9	-1.4	119.0	86.2	257.9	143.1
Japan	1 052.0	1 362.6	1 050.9	1 384.9	1 095.7	181.2	524.1	779.6	656.6	994.0
Korea	-	-	-	-	-	-	-	-	-	-
Latvia	-	-	1.2	0.3	-	.. c	0.2	-	0.0	-
Lithuania	-	0.2	0.1	0.1	-	-	-	0.0	.. c	.. c
Luxembourg	92.0	186.5	146.8	112.1	60.9	639.0	879.8	2 634.0	1 931.4	1 245.7
Mexico	24.0	-	10.1	12.7	4.1	-66.2	516.8	98.0	108.5	-179.5
Netherlands	616.0	1 113.7	133.1	2 306.7	-171.4	-377.0	35.8	464.4	-181.7	273.2
New Zealand	1.0	-2.6	-1.3	3.5	17.1	9.8	-13.4	23.1	-11.1	-2.8
Norway	107.0	46.7	1.1	89.5	35.5	.. c	27.5	2.3	2.9	-19.4
Poland	3.0	-	0.5	-0.3	-	-155.9	239.4	438.9	1 356.2	299.4
Portugal	13.0	0.4	-	-	-	.. c	48.7	15.6	21.4	17.4
Slovak Republic	-	0.1	0.1	-	-	197.2	-107.6	133.6	337.7	225.8
Slovenia	-	-	-	-	-	.. c	0.6	0.8	.. c	.. c
Spain	45.0	6.8	1 389.7	0.6	11.2	47.9	44.2	92.5	465.7	290.0
Sweden	190.0	2.2	-244.8	-26.2	-30.5	.. c	41.0	13.0	-42.1	74.5
Switzerland	401.0	185.8	26.3	201.4	94.7	94.1	65.6	135.9	104.3	249.9
Turkey	1.0	0.5	5.0	5.2	0.2	580.7	193.0	240.6	360.8	310.5
United Kingdom	153.0	1 151.8	-149.0	2 044.0	148.9	688.3	1 463.9	2 595.1	1 787.0	-428.0
United States	1 050.0	1 118.2	2 087.0	1 532.3	-202.2	9 100.3	13 437.9	7 490.7	9 832.8	11 246.4
EUROPE	**2 814.0**	**5 191.0**	**3 567.4**	**6 595.6**	**1 504.6**	**3 348.8**	**7 424.9**	**11 228.4**	**11 611.9**	**5 314.9**
Bulgaria	-	-	-	-	-	41.8	-21.7	-6.7	-2.0	0.9
Croatia	-	-	-	-	-	-	-	-	.. c	.. c
Cyprus	-	4.1	0.7	-	-0.1	.. c	-224.6	-83.5	.. c	.. c
Malta	427.0	1 405.1	1 370.2	782.5	1 027.5	-	-	14.2	.. c	.. c
Montenegro	-	-	-	-	-	-	-	-	-	-
Romania	-	-	-	0.7	-	.. c	84.5	3.8	-30.5	8.2
Russian Federation	-	2.0	5.7	4.1	2.5	687.4	513.3	461.6	581.5	259.5
Ukraine	-	10.1	0.0	-	0.1	.. c	0.3	2.9	6.0	-0.3
AFRICA	**-**	**11.2**	**5.5**	**-12.6**	**3.6**	**-453.8**	**232.2**	**65.3**	**300.6**	**-286.3**
Northern Africa	-	2.2	1.9	3.1	1.4	-350.2	69.4	60.6	79.2	19.7
Algeria	-	-	-	-	-	.. c	-0.7	1.8	1.9	1.1
Egypt	-	1.1	0.8	0.9	-0.1	.. c	36.1	23.1	77.1	40.8
Libya	-	0.9	0.9	2.1	1.4	.. c	4.8	2.1	2.8	-26.3
Morocco	-	0.2	0.2	0.1	0.0	.. c	25.5	29.6	-3.3	6.2
Tunisia	-	-	-	-	-	.. c	3.7	4.0	.. c	.. c
Other African countries	-	8.8	3.6	-15.7	2.2	-103.6	162.8	4.6	221.4	-306.0
Nigeria	-	0.3	0.9	0.4	0.2	.. c	217.2	37.6	-290.2	-12.3
South Africa	-	0.1	-	-	-	23.5	14.8	43.2	68.8	21.0
AMERICA	**2 103.0**	**2 342.2**	**3 152.1**	**2 545.4**	**1 646.4**	**13 441.6**	**19 126.8**	**13 699.1**	**16 690.7**	**16 144.4**
Northern America	1 203.0	1 242.3	1 866.0	1 483.8	848.9	9 394.2	13 433.2	7 588.9	10 606.7	12 784.7
Central America and Caribbean countries	891.0	1 098.2	1 285.7	1 061.4	796.7	2 471.8	3 755.1	5 005.7	5 801.6	2 075.8
Bahamas	2.0	14.3	-	-	-	-	-	38.2	.. c	.. c
Bermuda	330.0	747.9	133.4	113.7	37.7	.. c	2.2	-26.6	-106.9	-71.5
Cayman Islands	486.0	174.1	460.4	622.0	748.0	2 526.0	3 016.6	4 321.7	4 899.7	2 367.3
El Salvador	-	-	-	-	-	.. c	-0.6	0.4	10.7	2.4
Guatemala	-	-	-	-	-	.. c	13.9	2.0	2.1	-1.4
Honduras	-	-	-	-	-	.. c	-2.1	-6.2	-2.0	-7.3
Nicaragua	-	-	-	-	-	.. c	3.0	9.1	0.3	2.1
Panama	9.0	-4.5	0.7	-	0.2	-168.5	-194.5	18.4	176.3	12.6
Virgin Islands, U.S.	40.0	-	-	-	-	.. c	-	-	.. c	.. c
South America	9.0	1.2	0.4	0.2	0.8	1 575.6	1 938.5	1 104.5	282.4	1 283.9
Argentina	-	-	-	-	-	.. c	-1.0	337.1	2.0	1.3
Bolivia	-	-	-	-	-	.. c	51.1	-1.2	2.8	1.2
Brazil	-	1.1	-	-	-	1 308.2	1 571.0	439.0	122.3	914.1
Ecuador	-	-	-	-	0.1	.. c	6.0	0.0	0.0	0.0
Paraguay	-	-	0.1	-	-	.. c	0.2	0.5	1.2	0.2
Peru	-	0.1	0.3	-	-	182.4	108.8	237.7	124.7	270.5
Uruguay	-	-	-	-	-	.. c	-	-	.. c	-
Venezuela	-	-	-	-	-	.. c	0.0	-0.1	.. c	.. c

Table 1. Foreign direct investment flows by country *(cont.)*

Million US dollars

	Inward					Outward				
	2016	2017	2018	2019	2020	2016	2017	2018	2019	2020
ASIA	**2 291.0**	**3 946.5**	**4 543.5**	**3 399.3**	**3 738.1**	**13 199.5**	**17 362.6**	**19 638.1**	**22 122.8**	**15 629.0**
Near and Middle East	82.0	26.9	99.0	74.7	583.4	396.3	495.0	464.2	316.7	-33.1
Gulf Arabian countries	80.0	22.5	86.0	69.6	557.3	358.8	450.8	374.9	216.8	-61.4
Kuwait	-	-	1.3	-	471.9	.. c	1.3	-	-0.2	0.5
Qatar	-	0.1	-	-	-	0.6	0.2	0.0	1.7	-0.6
Saudi Arabia	86.0	-	4.4	25.5	10.1	373.0	176.8	476.1	216.8	-111.0
United Arab Emirates	-17.0	1.7	0.2	9.6	61.7	-79.3	234.9	-121.7	-3.9	52.1
Other Near and Middle East	2.0	4.3	13.0	5.2	26.1	37.5	44.1	89.3	100.0	28.3
Jordan	-	0.6	0.3	1.1	2.8	.. c	4.9	2.9	74.5	25.2
Other Asian countries	2 209.0	3 919.6	4 444.5	3 324.6	3 154.7	12 803.2	16 867.6	19 173.9	21 806.1	15 662.1
China	347.0	148.3	758.4	132.9	291.9	6 271.3	5 891.8	6 305.2	7 153.9	3 967.6
Hong Kong, China	313.0	1 194.6	931.5	713.4	99.0	-173.9	1 724.3	2 761.6	2 014.5	376.8
India	153.0	0.6	0.5	46.1	1.6	612.1	919.2	1 985.8	1 034.3	898.8
Indonesia	2.0	4.1	0.5	76.6	0.7	633.7	553.1	533.6	1 203.7	1 314.7
Iran, Islamic Republic of	-	0.1	1.9	-	0.1	.. c	-12.1	-47.3	-12.8	-30.8
Malaysia	-70.0	142.7	15.2	51.3	63.6	607.9	711.0	217.6	282.0	217.4
Philippines	-16.0	3.3	0.4	1.0	0.8	-187.3	486.8	-1 156.1	405.7	-386.2
Singapore	425.0	1 020.5	1 441.8	862.6	1 555.8	1 840.8	2 704.7	2 362.4	3 164.8	3 524.4
Chinese Taipei	3.0	26.1	228.3	13.0	37.4	17.2	104.2	178.4	95.5	-53.5
Thailand	-	5.3	3.1	7.2	0.9	233.4	84.4	345.8	230.0	146.9
Viet Nam	-	1.1	1.9	19.3	-0.3	2 295.6	3 339.7	4 353.6	5 030.5	2 937.6
AUSTRALIA, OCEANIA AND POLAR REGIONS	**4.0**	**40.6**	**1 998.7**	**61.9**	**23.7**	**971.5**	**-682.6**	**601.6**	**255.1**	**76.8**
WORLD unallocated and confidential	**51.0**	**0.0**	**0.0**	**-0.6**	**0.0**	**0.0**	**-**	**-**	**0.0**	**-**
European Union (since 01/02/2020)	..	..	..	..	**1 222.6**	..	..	..	..	**4 770.1**
G20 countries excl. European Union	**3 475.0**	**4 768.3**	**5 945.4**	**5 537.3**	**2 856.8**	**21 759.4**	**25 849.2**	**23 450.2**	**26 514.3**	**21 155.5**
G20 OECD countries	**2 887.0**	**4 612.2**	**5 176.0**	**5 252.1**	**2 550.1**	**11 853.5**	**16 210.2**	**12 868.6**	**16 131.0**	**13 889.3**
G20 Non-OECD countries	**588.0**	**156.2**	**769.5**	**285.2**	**306.8**	**9 906.0**	**9 639.0**	**10 581.6**	**10 383.3**	**7 266.2**
MENA countries	**80.0**	**27.1**	**90.2**	**76.9**	**561.8**	**12.5**	**525.1**	**438.4**	**370.5**	**-16.5**
ASEAN countries	**341.0**	**1 177.3**	**1 462.9**	**1 018.7**	**1 621.7**	**5 853.5**	**8 286.0**	**7 094.0**	**10 767.4**	**9 249.4**

- Nil; .. Not available; c Confidential data

Note: Data excludes resident Special Purpose Entities (SPEs). Detailed metadata at: *http://metalinks.oecd.org/idi/20220712/6d95*.

Source: *OECD International Direct Investment Statistics (database)*: *https://doi.org/10.1787/idi-data-en*

Table 2. Foreign direct investment positions by country
At year end

Million US dollars

	Inward					Outward				
	2016	2017	2018	2019	2020	2016	2017	2018	2019	2020
WORLD	**174 978.0**	**210 863.5**	**213 966.3**	**218 309.7**	**232 526.2**	**296 641.0**	**343 088.5**	**383 982.9**	**433 671.5**	**488 179.8**
OECD COUNTRIES	**135 601.7**	**157 266.9**	**161 400.1**	**165 090.1**	**174 624.7**	**126 418.8**	**148 737.9**	**166 676.3**	**190 948.3**	**218 250.1**
Australia	577.8	764.2	1 808.8	1 690.3	1 410.1	11 401.7	11 037.0	11 763.7	11 363.8	12 080.3
Austria	533.8	649.8	190.0	566.0	970.9	217.4	321.9	315.3	340.4	381.6
Belgium	359.3	602.5	595.0	795.1	1 354.0	1 482.1	1 777.6	1 956.4	2 041.4	3 187.8
Canada	2 201.9	2 344.7	1 842.4	2 652.3	3 662.4	3 735.1	3 883.0	4 135.4	4 891.0	5 884.2
Chile	24.9	15.7	-7.1	-9.6	-2.2	159.7	351.5	589.7	421.9	524.4
Colombia	0.1	0.1	-0.5	7.0	7.4	211.9	251.8	222.3	202.4	210.4
Costa Rica	0.1	0.1	0.1	0.0	-	34.4	27.4	44.2	35.6	43.8
Czech Republic	-2.6	1.1	-33.2	9.2	90.9	1 989.3	3 046.0	3 032.1	3 038.4	4 937.4
Denmark	549.2	223.5	406.9	379.2	364.0	30.8	39.6	35.6	28.0	32.4
Estonia	-	12.8	25.7	8.0	7.4	.. c	0.1	0.1	.. c	.. c
Finland	177.8	128.2	125.5	565.0	247.1	11.2	53.2	32.6	32.5	91.3
France	4 205.1	5 375.6	6 122.5	6 567.4	7 377.5	626.5	997.6	1 064.7	2 315.2	2 294.5
Germany	6 950.6	8 306.5	9 457.2	8 944.1	10 575.2	3 242.2	4 045.4	4 409.3	5 640.3	5 985.2
Greece	19.4	5.9	9.9	2.6	0.2	.. c	8.1	8.4	9.7	9.7
Hungary	3 589.3	3 582.3	3 759.6	3 669.0	4 081.0	344.3	1 836.2	1 858.3	2 760.3	4 203.4
Iceland	14.0	38.4	18.4	13.7	13.2	.. c	3.0	192.2	.. c	.. c
Ireland	823.6	-53.3	1 989.3	2 224.0	3 082.9	1 202.2	3 008.9	2 991.5	2 529.4	2 803.2
Israel	14.1	76.1	110.0	229.5	98.9	16.4	6.8	19.0	30.4	34.2
Italy	325.4	567.0	1 024.9	655.5	866.3	628.3	717.1	908.9	1 167.0	1 315.1
Japan	43 315.1	47 519.3	54 761.4	53 944.5	57 673.5	5 090.4	5 612.0	7 089.4	8 748.6	9 226.8
Korea	-	-	-	-	-	-	-	-	-	-
Latvia	-	-	1.2	1.5	-0.3	.. c	5.8	5.8	0.6	0.9
Lithuania	0.0	0.2	0.3	0.4	0.6	.. c	0.5	0.5	.. c	.. c
Luxembourg	1 296.9	1 804.4	1 229.6	1 489.3	1 628.3	3 791.2	4 893.8	6 183.1	7 967.3	11 632.2
Mexico	152.2	190.3	244.3	291.9	107.6	2 504.0	3 196.8	3 047.3	3 018.8	3 087.0
Netherlands	17 549.6	27 591.7	21 609.7	20 234.3	17 738.6	11 694.9	8 572.3	8 398.8	10 434.6	12 947.6
New Zealand	34.6	55.8	366.5	1 801.3	2 095.2	200.0	145.0	187.3	200.2	176.3
Norway	738.0	767.2	666.1	1 232.3	988.4	-270.0	11.8	13.2	22.5	1 307.1
Poland	9.4	9.6	9.1	15.8	9.4	828.8	1 209.9	1 677.0	2 819.8	3 391.4
Portugal	169.9	186.0	218.2	183.6	37.8	.. c	184.7	203.5	226.6	263.6
Slovak Republic	-0.9	-0.7	-18.6	-27.5	-4.6	2 437.7	2 613.5	2 605.0	2 936.2	3 444.0
Slovenia	5.4	5.3	13.0	12.6	10.9	.. c	9.0	8.8	.. c	.. c
Spain	510.6	428.8	520.6	535.6	507.4	826.1	987.6	955.3	1 389.0	1 682.2
Sweden	2 307.8	2 099.5	1 847.0	1 846.4	2 158.6	243.2	416.1	401.1	351.2	475.8
Switzerland	3 418.4	5 055.0	3 902.8	3 962.7	5 158.5	354.4	335.3	443.5	538.5	774.0
Turkey	27.4	34.8	-57.6	25.2	18.2	1 198.6	865.4	1 194.5	1 427.1	1 860.5
United Kingdom	13 952.0	14 941.4	16 209.0	15 481.0	17 245.7	4 888.5	7 627.9	10 352.4	11 700.5	10 963.3
United States	31 751.9	33 937.3	32 431.9	35 097.8	35 043.8	67 395.1	80 918.8	90 626.1	102 371.3	112 827.5
EUROPE	**63 544.6**	**82 239.7**	**79 191.3**	**77 751.6**	**83 675.6**	**43 031.6**	**52 276.5**	**57 277.2**	**69 790.9**	**85 106.7**
Bulgaria	1.0	1.0	1.0	0.1	0.1	235.3	141.8	135.1	67.6	73.3
Croatia	-	-	0.0	0.1	0.0	.. c	0.4	0.4	.. c	.. c
Cyprus	1.3	1.3	13.0	17.2	30.7	551.0	148.4	53.6	.. c	.. c
Malta	5 942.5	9 790.9	9 265.8	8 258.8	9 036.0	.. c	0.3	-9.7	.. c	.. c
Montenegro	0.1	0.1	-	-	-	-	-	-	-	-
Romania	-0.6	3.2	-1.5	0.1	0.6	197.4	610.8	113.5	76.4	26.4
Russian Federation	42.9	47.5	-8.8	40.0	30.7	2 482.6	2 617.5	3 051.6	3 959.4	3 764.0
Ukraine	1.3	1.4	1.4	1.5	1.4	158.4	203.4	162.4	168.9	167.8
AFRICA	**140.0**	**145.0**	**281.2**	**231.8**	**218.7**	**1 431.8**	**2 932.2**	**3 106.8**	**3 075.9**	**2 855.3**
Northern Africa	11.0	12.5	15.6	17.2	17.8	272.0	475.0	495.7	591.9	600.5
Algeria	0.1	0.1	0.1	-1.0	-1.0	4.4	2.6	62.5	65.4	66.4
Egypt	5.4	5.7	6.8	8.0	7.9	-128.6	-1.9	-2.6	93.0	118.1
Libya	5.0	6.0	7.2	8.5	9.4	383.0	393.0	369.3	373.3	349.9
Morocco	0.6	0.8	1.5	1.7	1.4	5.5	70.5	54.3	47.2	54.8
Tunisia	-0.1	0.0	0.0	-	0.0	.. c	10.7	12.2	.. c	.. c
Other African countries	128.8	132.3	265.5	214.6	200.1	1 159.9	2 454.5	2 612.8	2 485.8	2 256.1
Nigeria	7.4	8.3	18.0	17.9	18.6	43.1	450.1	476.2	195.9	188.7
South Africa	-1.7	0.5	1.0	-11.3	-8.5	202.9	214.9	223.4	253.2	272.0
AMERICA	**38 506.1**	**45 533.0**	**40 084.6**	**41 696.6**	**43 135.4**	**97 541.5**	**114 957.7**	**130 672.6**	**148 200.2**	**165 174.6**
Northern America	33 953.8	36 282.0	34 274.3	37 750.1	38 706.2	71 130.1	84 801.8	94 761.5	107 262.3	118 711.7
Central America and Caribbean countries	4 469.9	9 175.2	5 882.3	3 938.6	4 433.5	18 262.5	21 034.3	25 940.1	31 513.4	37 375.1
Bahamas	47.0	31.6	52.0	15.0	12.5	.. c	1.9	28.7	.. c	.. c
Bermuda	710.6	1 748.6	480.7	293.6	130.8	.. c	824.0	889.6	737.1	649.0
Cayman Islands	1 813.6	5 223.2	3 111.5	1 731.0	2 303.6	12 483.8	15 076.3	18 875.1	24 092.9	30 052.4
El Salvador	-	-	-	-	-	.. c	46.8	45.6	53.9	56.9
Guatemala	2.3	2.1	2.2	2.9	3.4	45.3	56.1	49.4	54.6	49.3
Honduras	-	-	-	0.3	-	20.8	21.0	14.8	12.8	3.0
Nicaragua	-	-	-	-	-	27.1	32.9	18.0	22.7	19.9
Panama	183.9	210.5	28.9	58.6	23.4	1 065.8	891.5	1 408.2	1 624.8	1 664.5
Virgin Islands, U.S.	-	-	-	-	-	.. c	0.4	0.4	.. c	.. c
South America	73.4	69.7	-76.5	5.2	-7.0	8 148.6	9 121.5	9 971.1	9 424.5	9 087.8
Argentina	2.9	4.9	-14.5	4.3	4.7	39.7	40.8	378.1	379.3	371.8
Bolivia	-	-	-	-	-	83.1	133.9	12.7	24.8	19.5
Brazil	44.0	47.7	-55.2	2.1	-17.9	5 656.4	6 141.1	6 274.0	5 811.2	5 102.9
Ecuador	-	-	0.0	0.0	0.1	15.2	36.8	36.8	6.0	6.0
Paraguay	0.8	0.7	0.9	0.8	0.4	.. c	3.8	6.6	7.6	7.7
Peru	0.6	0.4	0.7	0.6	0.5	1 970.0	2 132.2	2 421.1	2 544.4	2 814.4
Uruguay	0.1	0.1	-0.1	-	-	.. c	28.0	28.0	.. c	26.0
Venezuela	0.0	0.0	-0.6	0.0	0.0	.. c	1.4	1.8	.. c	.. c

Table 2. Foreign direct investment positions by country *(cont.)*

At year end

Million US dollars

	Inward					Outward				
	2016	2017	2018	2019	2020	2016	2017	2018	2019	2020
ASIA	**71 968.2**	**82 017.6**	**92 143.2**	**95 042.9**	**101 890.0**	**141 198.9**	**159 831.6**	**178 848.4**	**198 873.1**	**220 616.1**
Near and Middle East	2 193.0	3 155.9	2 398.6	3 001.3	4 283.4	1 590.2	2 476.9	2 600.9	2 357.9	2 394.0
Gulf Arabian countries	2 166.3	3 058.0	2 257.2	2 819.4	4 150.3	1 482.2	2 340.8	2 383.4	2 076.3	2 095.7
Kuwait	12.5	11.0	12.5	147.0	158.6	22.6	22.8	20.6	20.4	20.7
Qatar	0.1	0.1	0.2	0.4	2.5	12.1	10.3	14.2	24.0	23.4
Saudi Arabia	1 667.4	2 617.7	1 840.9	2 212.8	3 084.3	-472.2	95.7	210.2	84.7	67.3
United Arab Emirates	309.7	211.2	174.1	218.1	636.7	942.6	1 185.1	1 210.9	1 064.9	1 096.9
Other Near and Middle East	26.7	97.9	141.4	181.9	133.1	108.0	136.1	217.6	281.6	298.3
Jordan	6.8	12.8	11.6	12.7	14.5	15.0	19.1	17.4	84.7	94.0
Other Asian countries	69 771.6	78 858.4	89 740.5	92 037.6	97 602.7	139 604.8	157 350.9	176 243.6	196 511.4	218 218.3
China	5 576.7	5 661.1	8 147.7	8 684.3	8 608.6	69 240.6	77 477.5	77 603.8	79 469.7	87 869.1
Hong Kong, China	6 151.3	6 706.6	7 098.4	8 809.9	7 739.7	12 363.3	13 411.7	15 404.7	18 179.5	20 070.8
India	1 106.1	650.5	569.9	343.3	479.4	5 081.2	5 409.0	12 442.7	9 873.2	8 384.2
Indonesia	65.8	60.9	63.2	48.9	35.0	6 963.7	7 041.3	7 735.4	9 240.7	10 561.1
Iran, Islamic Republic of	68.6	80.1	80.0	73.5	74.3	22.4	-19.6	-27.8	-33.6	-37.3
Malaysia	1 318.0	1 730.7	2 285.9	2 339.2	2 287.3	4 184.0	5 110.6	5 474.4	6 335.0	6 068.7
Philippines	165.1	691.2	186.4	286.4	304.4	2 346.0	2 856.1	1 718.9	2 721.0	2 394.2
Singapore	11 585.3	15 034.3	15 437.3	16 254.6	18 619.5	10 843.1	13 938.5	16 181.9	20 638.9	25 380.0
Chinese Taipei	339.9	623.2	899.2	1 066.0	1 278.5	746.6	953.5	1 051.1	1 334.2	1 452.4
Thailand	-10.3	0.5	25.1	51.4	337.5	3 084.4	3 085.3	3 618.7	4 078.3	5 885.2
Viet Nam	-36.1	-26.6	7.6	-28.5	-42.7	12 555.8	15 705.7	20 377.0	27 631.4	31 183.3
AUSTRALIA, OCEANIA AND POLAR REGIONS	**803.2**	**911.3**	**2 266.1**	**3 581.9**	**3 602.9**	**13 437.3**	**13 090.6**	**14 078.0**	**13 731.4**	**14 427.1**
WORLD unallocated and confidential	**16.9**	**16.9**	**0.0**	**4.8**	**3.6**	**-**	**0.0**	**-**	**0.0**	**0.0**
European Union (since 01/02/2020)	..	..	..	..	**60 171.5**	..	..	..	..	**59 467.9**
G20 countries excl. European Union	**111 963.4**	**123 071.9**	**134 388.9**	**136 674.5**	**146 196.5**	**189 905.2**	**217 939.0**	**242 510.8**	**261 715.1**	**281 916.7**
G20 OECD countries	**103 459.4**	**113 981.1**	**123 844.7**	**125 350.0**	**133 980.2**	**100 710.4**	**118 901.1**	**134 591.7**	**152 643.6**	**165 524.4**
G20 Non-OECD countries	**8 504.0**	**9 090.8**	**10 544.2**	**11 324.4**	**12 216.2**	**89 194.8**	**99 037.9**	**107 919.1**	**109 071.5**	**116 392.4**
MENA countries	**2 189.7**	**3 092.1**	**2 362.1**	**2 924.6**	**4 260.2**	**1 777.5**	**2 835.6**	**2 904.6**	**2 746.5**	**2 786.1**
ASEAN countries	**13 105.0**	**17 501.5**	**18 023.7**	**18 968.7**	**21 558.4**	**44 390.6**	**52 463.1**	**60 325.3**	**76 546.4**	**88 672.5**

- Nil; .. Not available; c Confidential data

Note: Data excludes resident Special Purpose Entities (SPEs). Detailed metadata at: *http://metalinks.oecd.org/idi/20220712/6d95*.

Source: *OECD International Direct Investment Statistics (database): https://doi.org/10.1787/idi-data-en*

Table 3. Foreign direct investment income by country

Million US dollars

	Inward					Outward				
	2016	2017	2018	2019	2020	2016	2017	2018	2019	2020
WORLD	**3 997.0**	**3 615.4**	**4 402.0**	**3 443.0**	**2 474.9**	**9 054.5**	**10 090.4**	**9 629.2**	**9 062.9**	**6 870.2**
OECD COUNTRIES	**3 098.0**	**3 505.4**	**3 512.6**	**2 986.9**	**2 411.6**	**46.6**	**1 285.6**	**2 110.9**	**1 783.9**	**-27.1**
Australia	2.0	-	0.4	0.5	0.5	-359.5	-1 244.7	383.3	-171.8	217.6
Austria	86.0	0.1	0.0	9.9	7.0	.. c	8.4	37.1	-15.6	4.0
Belgium	1.0	8.0	4.2	244.3	137.6	.. c	68.4	36.6	82.8	337.4
Canada	78.0	4.3	-	4.6	2.5	-305.2	-85.0	-210.9	-2.9	-343.0
Chile	10.0	-	-	-	-	-12.6	12.2	-0.6	-24.3	24.0
Colombia	-	-	-	-	-	.. c	-1.0	-0.8	26.1	4.3
Costa Rica	-	-	-	-	-	.. c	-1.6	1.3	3.9	0.3
Czech Republic	-	-	-	-	-	406.5	410.7	354.6	356.5	113.7
Denmark	-1.0	5.6	2.3	0.1	12.4	.. c	1.7	2.2	-2.7	-0.7
Estonia	-	-	-	-	-	-	.. c	-	.. c	.. c
Finland	15.0	-	-	4.0	2.2	.. c	-0.1	-2.4	-0.8	-0.4
France	134.0	97.7	90.2	10.9	45.3	0.2	51.0	32.9	40.5	51.7
Germany	213.0	564.1	705.4	352.5	329.8	197.8	152.7	217.2	117.0	252.0
Greece	-	-	-	-	-	.. c	.. c	0.5	0.7	0.5
Hungary	12.0	8.6	-	3.6	-	.. c	419.5	-7.9	48.1	144.9
Iceland	-	-	-	1.0	-	.. c	.. c	-0.6	.. c	.. c
Ireland	66.0	0.0	231.2	80.2	1.4	.. c	-2.7	-3.9	-9.8	8.4
Israel	3.0	0.1	0.0	-0.3	-	.. c	-0.3	-6.0	-5.9	-5.1
Italy	10.0	2.5	56.0	-67.3	-64.9	55.8	54.4	48.8	57.2	68.9
Japan	643.0	1 041.1	575.3	1 122.3	1 051.6	64.1	141.3	85.3	-168.3	-372.7
Korea	-	-	-	-	-	-	-	-	-	-
Latvia	-	-	-	-	-	.. c	.. c	-	-	-
Lithuania	-	-	-	-	-	-	.. c	-	-	.. c
Luxembourg	83.0	0.1	-	7.3	1.1	-123.5	-13.2	401.9	343.5	186.5
Mexico	21.0	-	1.7	12.7	-1.9	-459.7	-99.0	-58.1	-195.7	-341.4
Netherlands	344.0	253.6	78.4	107.6	299.8	-158.9	89.3	150.1	375.1	244.5
New Zealand	2.0	2.8	-	-	-	.. c	0.4	16.5	1.8	-0.8
Norway	20.0	183.2	5.1	75.4	23.3	.. c	.. c	-4.4	0.4	-3.6
Poland	1.0	-	-	-0.2	-	60.5	38.9	-24.4	-225.8	-186.0
Portugal	3.0	-	-	-	-	.. c	9.8	15.2	15.1	14.0
Slovak Republic	-	-	-	-	-	382.8	367.6	399.5	476.3	214.3
Slovenia	-	-	-	-	-	.. c	.. c	0.2	.. c	.. c
Spain	36.0	-	0.9	1.7	1.2	40.7	59.7	16.1	103.5	41.5
Sweden	104.0	71.4	29.2	249.1	-26.5	.. c	29.5	30.8	43.2	34.0
Switzerland	249.0	59.9	30.9	90.8	81.5	.. c	9.5	8.0	1.0	32.6
Turkey	1.0	0.2	-	-	-	-122.1	86.4	69.2	170.5	258.2
United Kingdom	234.0	759.0	116.3	321.3	352.5	-31.3	323.9	345.1	183.6	-623.7
United States	728.0	443.1	1 585.0	355.1	155.2	464.8	367.9	-220.8	177.3	-401.0
EUROPE	**1 766.0**	**2 014.1**	**1 352.6**	**1 508.3**	**1 195.6**	**1 221.5**	**2 472.5**	**2 480.7**	**2 741.9**	**1 503.2**
Bulgaria	-	-	-	-	-	48.9	1.4	-3.6	5.8	6.7
Croatia	-	-	-	-	-	-	.. c	-	.. c	.. c
Cyprus	-	-	-	-	-	.. c	-213.0	-99.5	74.0	.. c
Malta	115.0	-	2.5	13.9	-7.9	-	.. c	-0.5	.. c	.. c
Montenegro	-	-	-	-	-	-	-	-	-	-
Romania	-	-	-	-	-	.. c	13.9	-10.9	-65.3	-1.4
Russian Federation	-	-	-	0.0	-	583.8	453.6	477.1	546.4	342.3
Ukraine	-	-	-	-	-	.. c	-	-0.2	-1.6	-0.5
AFRICA	**-**	**-**	**-**	**-**	**0.0**	**-562.4**	**-45.3**	**6.8**	**24.8**	**-579.1**
Northern Africa	-	-	-	-	-	-367.7	40.7	26.8	45.3	-1.2
Algeria	-	-	-	-	-	.. c	-0.7	-0.7	0.4	0.6
Egypt	-	-	-	-	-	.. c	37.4	22.2	44.3	33.2
Libya	-	-	-	-	-	.. c	-1.3	-0.6	-0.5	-28.3
Morocco	-	-	-	-	-	.. c	-0.1	-0.8	-3.7	-8.2
Tunisia	-	-	-	-	-	.. c	.. c	6.7	.. c	.. c
Other African countries	-	-	-	-	0.0	-194.8	-86.0	-20.0	-20.4	-578.0
Nigeria	-	-	-	-	-	.. c	-0.7	45.3	18.6	-13.0
South Africa	-	-	-	-	-	19.9	15.1	46.6	64.6	21.5
AMERICA	**804.0**	**447.7**	**1 598.8**	**500.2**	**-65.2**	**730.0**	**1 168.9**	**90.4**	**228.5**	**-456.0**
Northern America	806.0	447.3	1 585.0	359.7	157.7	159.6	282.9	-431.7	174.4	-744.0
Central America and Caribbean countries	-12.0	0.3	13.7	140.6	-222.9	-274.3	-163.0	61.2	-366.8	-635.7
Bahamas	2.0	-	-	-	-	-	.. c	15.0	.. c	.. c
Bermuda	-4.0	0.3	-	78.0	-	.. c	48.3	49.4	-58.3	-43.6
Cayman Islands	-46.0	0.0	12.0	0.8	-205.2	64.2	-103.7	19.8	-42.1	-17.1
El Salvador	-	-	-	-	-	.. c	.. c	2.6	5.4	2.4
Guatemala	-	-	-	-	-	.. c	0.1	0.5	0.1	-0.2
Honduras	-	-	-	-	-	.. c	-2.1	-7.2	-2.0	-7.3
Nicaragua	-	-	-	-	-	.. c	-2.2	-1.6	0.9	0.0
Panama	3.0	-	-	-	-	-40.1	1.7	41.1	34.6	-18.2
Virgin Islands, U.S.	12.0	-	-	-	-	-	.. c	-	.. c	.. c
South America	10.0	-	-	-	-	844.7	1 049.0	461.0	420.9	923.7
Argentina	-	-	-	-	-	.. c	0.3	-46.9	-4.4	0.0
Bolivia	-	-	-	-	-	.. c	1.1	-1.0	0.3	1.2
Brazil	-	-	-	-	-	859.8	1 040.8	516.2	420.9	892.9
Ecuador	-	-	-	-	-	.. c	-	-	-	-
Paraguay	-	-	-	-	-	.. c	.. c	-0.1	-0.3	-0.3
Peru	-	-	-	-	-	.. c	-4.3	-5.8	2.6	1.7
Uruguay	-	-	-	-	-	.. c	.. c	-	.. c	-
Venezuela	-	-	-	-	-	-	.. c	-	.. c	.. c

KOREA

Table 3. Foreign direct investment income by country *(cont.)*

Million US dollars

	Inward					Outward				
	2016	2017	2018	2019	2020	2016	2017	2018	2019	2020
ASIA	**1 389.0**	**1 150.8**	**1 450.2**	**1 434.0**	**1 343.8**	**8 035.5**	**7 709.2**	**6 608.8**	**6 221.9**	**6 304.6**
Near and Middle East	72.0	39.5	91.6	69.0	17.6	-550.3	-103.6	55.0	239.4	-96.5
Gulf Arabian countries	69.0	39.4	91.6	67.8	17.6	-552.6	-105.3	69.3	250.0	-104.2
Kuwait	-	-	-	-	7.3	.. c	-	-	0.0	0.1
Qatar	-	-	-	-	-	.. c	-	-	-	-
Saudi Arabia	51.0	-	-	31.0	10.0	-485.3	-182.1	131.5	268.2	-135.9
United Arab Emirates	8.0	0.1	-	9.4	0.2	-64.1	72.6	-64.4	-29.5	25.6
Other Near and Middle East	3.0	0.1	0.0	1.2	-	2.3	1.8	-14.4	-10.6	7.7
Jordan	-	-	-	-	-	.. c	5.5	-2.2	2.7	18.3
Other Asian countries	1 317.0	1 111.3	1 358.6	1 365.0	1 326.2	8 585.8	7 812.7	6 553.8	5 982.5	6 401.1
China	136.0	0.8	56.3	-20.0	78.6	6 111.4	4 235.5	3 730.7	2 020.4	2 899.9
Hong Kong, China	249.0	4.6	16.1	21.9	21.8	-141.5	-726.7	-443.9	-32.4	230.6
India	64.0	-	-	3.1	0.8	520.4	480.0	972.8	1 103.6	672.8
Indonesia	2.0	-	-	77.8	-	271.6	73.7	218.6	380.1	63.0
Iran, Islamic Republic of	-	-	-	-	-	.. c	-13.8	-47.3	-12.8	-31.2
Malaysia	21.0	0.3	-0.9	2.7	27.7	387.2	377.8	349.1	246.5	211.4
Philippines	-19.0	-	-	-	-	-342.0	-95.4	-1 295.7	518.8	93.3
Singapore	189.0	64.6	711.8	138.6	101.0	947.0	1 297.5	1 064.2	1 091.9	867.2
Chinese Taipei	32.0	-	-	1.5	45.1	15.1	78.9	101.0	81.7	97.0
Thailand	-	-	-	0.1	0.0	203.8	141.0	173.5	166.7	195.8
Viet Nam	-	-	-	17.1	-0.5	528.3	1 831.6	1 699.2	649.9	1 484.9
AUSTRALIA, OCEANIA AND POLAR REGIONS	**4.0**	**2.8**	**0.4**	**0.5**	**0.5**	**-370.1**	**-1 214.9**	**442.5**	**-154.1**	**97.6**
WORLD unallocated and confidential	**34.0**	**0.0**	**0.0**	**0.0**	**0.0**	**-**	**-**	**0.0**	**-**	**-**
European Union (since 01/02/2020)	..	..	..	..	**738.4**	..	..	..	..	**1 524.5**
G20 countries excl. European Union	**2 317.0**	**2 912.8**	**3 186.7**	**2 204.4**	**1 960.2**	**7 383.2**	**5 865.9**	**6 738.4**	**5 007.2**	**3 522.9**
G20 OECD countries	**2 064.0**	**2 912.0**	**3 130.4**	**2 112.5**	**1 870.7**	**-495.0**	**-251.1**	**691.8**	**207.4**	**-1 233.4**
G20 Non-OECD countries	**253.0**	**0.8**	**56.3**	**91.9**	**89.5**	**7 878.2**	**6 117.0**	**6 046.6**	**4 799.9**	**4 756.4**
MENA countries	**69.0**	**39.4**	**91.6**	**69.3**	**17.6**	**-918.1**	**-59.2**	**94.0**	**297.9**	**-87.1**
ASEAN countries	**193.0**	**64.9**	**710.9**	**236.2**	**128.2**	**1 994.9**	**3 605.3**	**2 147.1**	**2 961.1**	**2 884.6**

- Nil; .. Not available; c Confidential data

Note: Data excludes resident Special Purpose Entities (SPEs). Detailed metadata at: *http://metalinks.oecd.org/idi/20220712/6d95*.

Source: *OECD International Direct Investment Statistics (database)*: *https://doi.org/10.1787/idi-data-en*

Table 4. Foreign direct investment flows by industrial sector

Million US dollars

	Inward					Outward				
	2016	2017	2018	2019	2020	2016	2017	2018	2019	2020
All FDI activities	**7 263.0**	**11 531.5**	**13 267.2**	**12 589.0**	**6 916.4**	**30 507.5**	**43 463.9**	**45 232.6**	**50 981.1**	**36 878.9**
Agriculture, forestry and fishing	**2.0**	**5.0**	**-28.5**	**4.1**	**45.2**	**59.0**	**81.9**	**118.1**	**36.5**	**98.4**
Mining and quarrying	**13.0**	**0.1**	**1.6**	**2.4**	**-**	**-1 106.0**	**-1 126.1**	**873.2**	**336.8**	**-2 215.9**
Extraction activities	-	0.1	-	2.4	-	-1 029.0	-1 102.4	298.5	-511.8	-1 335.4
Manufacturing	**3 909.0**	**5 180.9**	**5 245.3**	**5 049.5**	**397.1**	**11 758.0**	**14 631.2**	**17 421.0**	**19 719.0**	**12 879.4**
of which:										
Food products, beverages and tobacco	154.0	150.3	142.6	524.4	-164.8	587.9	570.3	578.5	1 323.9	848.1
Textiles, wood and paper products; printing	111.0	73.5	30.4	74.9	23.5	489.0	411.4	178.8	459.9	450.8
Chemical, rubber, plastic, non-metallic mineral products	2 839.0	2 120.7	2 049.5	3 307.7	210.0	1 778.6	1 540.4	1 849.2	3 398.5	974.9
Metal and machinery products, except electrical equipment	-44.0	1 901.5	964.2	948.6	-197.9	5 578.1	7 756.9	10 163.9	8 042.7	6 887.2
Motor vehicles, trailers, semi-trailers, other transport equipment	-139.0	524.3	1 873.1	305.2	381.5	2 108.2	3 221.2	2 293.9	2 430.3	539.4
Other manufacturing	988.0	410.6	185.4	-111.1	144.8	1 216.3	1 131.0	2 356.7	4 063.7	3 179.0
Electricity, gas, steam and air conditioning supply	**50.0**	**-135.9**	**160.0**	**774.3**	**69.9**	**781.0**	**1 206.7**	**1 006.0**	**1 468.8**	**2 849.0**
Water supply; sewerage, waste management and remediation activities	**10.0**	**149.2**	**1.5**	**3.5**	**199.9**	**3.0**	**174.8**	**442.2**	**14.8**	**29.5**
Construction	**-33.0**	**11.8**	**14.7**	**26.6**	**16.5**	**778.0**	**638.1**	**885.8**	**502.1**	**829.7**
Services	**3 312.0**	**6 320.4**	**7 872.8**	**6 728.7**	**6 187.7**	**18 234.0**	**27 855.9**	**24 486.3**	**28 903.0**	**22 408.7**
Wholesale and retail trade; repair of motor vehicles and motorcycles	1 029.0	1 042.4	936.6	1 849.0	249.1	4 504.0	11 682.8	5 605.9	4 488.3	6 578.3
Transportation and storage	315.0	192.6	116.7	89.3	219.3	1 002.0	1 027.2	718.3	687.8	227.6
Accommodation and food service activities	770.0	808.3	281.1	341.5	-1.1	401.0	208.9	109.6	427.0	581.4
Information and communication	511.0	756.1	2 821.9	1 522.5	1 178.1	1 191.0	2 174.6	851.0	309.5	2 837.5
Financial and insurance activities	151.0	2 100.2	2 057.5	1 932.9	3 522.2	5 343.0	9 506.9	12 837.0	17 712.8	9 055.6
Activities of holding companies	580.0	76.4	656.6	482.1	1 737.8	479.3	1 105.3	1 648.6	1 179.3	729.4
Real estate activities	148.0	912.3	906.9	618.0	251.7	4 995.8	2 521.1	3 448.2	3 884.6	2 729.7
Professional, scientific and technical activities	309.0	400.6	128.3	249.3	471.2	519.0	458.5	948.7	809.6	615.0
Administrative and support service activities	-	72.2	377.7	49.5	97.1	176.9	-335.8	-203.7	112.8	-203.2
Public administration; activities of households and of extraterritorial organisations	-	-	-	-	-	-	258.0	-	0.1	0.2
Education	21.0	13.7	11.7	62.6	118.0	11.1	125.6	12.8	35.0	46.4
Human health and social work activities	-	-	-	0.1	16.1	68.9	175.4	181.5	120.0	15.9
Arts, entertainment and recreation	-14.0	16.0	233.3	30.5	48.6	9.0	5.4	-26.0	312.0	-84.3
Other services	72.0	5.8	1.1	-16.5	17.5	12.7	47.4	3.0	3.8	8.6
Not allocated and confidential	**-**	**0.0**	**0.0**	**0.0**	**0.0**	**0.1**	**1.3**	**-**	**0.0**	**0.0**
Private real estate activities	**-**	**-**	**-**	**-**	**-**	**-**	**-**	**-**	**-**	**-**

- Nil

Note: Data excludes resident Special Purpose Entities (SPEs). Detailed metadata at: *http://metalinks.oecd.org/idi/20220712/6d95*.

Source: *OECD International Direct Investment Statistics (database)*: *https://doi.org/10.1787/idi-data-en*

Table 5. Foreign direct investment positions by industrial sector

At year end

Million US dollars

	Inward					Outward				
	2016	2017	2018	2019	2020	2016	2017	2018	2019	2020
All FDI activities	**174 978.0**	**210 863.5**	**213 966.3**	**218 309.7**	**232 526.2**	**296 641.0**	**343 088.5**	**383 982.9**	**433 671.5**	**488 179.8**
Agriculture, forestry and fishing	**200.6**	**235.3**	**203.1**	**105.1**	**109.3**	**842.0**	**910.0**	**1 031.1**	**1 236.4**	**1 399.2**
Mining and quarrying	**11.1**	**44.8**	**42.8**	**42.7**	**40.4**	**35 209.0**	**34 055.1**	**33 676.6**	**34 734.5**	**32 445.0**
Extraction activities	3.0	44.8	2.9	2.9	2.9	26 806.4	25 601.9	24 678.8	26 666.5	24 192.6
Manufacturing	**66 721.2**	**79 861.6**	**82 015.7**	**80 728.3**	**85 127.6**	**110 985.0**	**135 266.9**	**135 519.5**	**162 087.1**	**178 835.6**
of which:										
Food products, beverages and tobacco	3 296.2	4 817.0	4 134.5	3 841.8	3 955.6	4 319.6	4 152.1	4 414.1	5 967.2	6 866.9
Textiles, wood and paper products; printing	1 606.6	1 359.0	2 538.0	1 785.0	1 612.7	5 729.7	6 424.2	5 536.3	6 413.0	7 003.6
Chemical, rubber, plastic, non-metallic mineral products	27 498.5	37 225.6	33 422.9	34 351.3	35 780.5	13 725.1	15 259.1	17 859.3	21 246.2	23 976.9
Metal and machinery products, except electrical equipment	18 067.2	20 369.9	23 757.8	23 012.2	25 136.0	50 536.8	60 291.8	65 102.0	71 742.6	79 415.0
Motor vehicles, trailers, semi-trailers, other transport equipment	8 216.7	7 099.0	8 347.5	8 252.5	8 547.2	25 735.6	37 816.9	28 616.6	38 267.6	40 203.6
Other manufacturing	8 036.1	8 991.1	9 815.0	9 485.5	10 095.7	10 938.4	11 322.7	13 991.3	18 450.6	21 369.6
Electricity, gas, steam and air conditioning supply	**1 002.9**	**1 053.8**	**1 139.1**	**1 071.8**	**1 655.3**	**5 013.0**	**6 391.2**	**7 258.2**	**8 580.8**	**10 214.8**
Water supply; sewerage, waste management and remediation activities	**146.3**	**194.0**	**245.2**	**123.9**	**221.7**	**18.0**	**166.2**	**612.0**	**803.8**	**842.6**
Construction	**1 306.1**	**1 801.4**	**1 635.7**	**1 748.1**	**1 931.3**	**1 813.0**	**2 987.7**	**3 578.6**	**4 566.5**	**5 558.1**
Services	**105 589.9**	**127 672.5**	**128 684.8**	**134 489.8**	**143 440.6**	**142 758.0**	**163 309.9**	**202 305.4**	**221 661.5**	**258 883.5**
Wholesale and retail trade; repair of motor vehicles and motorcycles	15 313.1	20 940.9	24 163.6	22 996.8	25 761.0	47 874.0	54 164.8	72 349.1	62 546.8	72 636.4
Transportation and storage	3 169.6	3 698.0	2 923.4	3 877.0	3 824.6	4 519.0	4 133.2	5 150.7	5 329.3	5 707.1
Accommodation and food service activities	14 584.0	17 937.6	15 987.5	14 865.7	13 069.4	2 351.0	3 048.4	2 574.5	3 650.4	4 400.1
Information and communication	4 579.9	7 382.6	7 689.8	8 409.2	10 330.7	5 495.0	6 366.3	6 403.3	8 462.5	10 021.7
Financial and insurance activities	54 129.8	61 630.1	60 792.7	66 133.4	72 935.4	54 265.0	68 982.9	84 638.0	105 205.8	125 223.9
Activities of holding companies	1.4	3 079.2	2 867.6	2 872.6	3 430.8	7 876.2	8 907.4	10 350.3	13 037.3	15 552.6
Real estate activities	6 858.3	8 658.4	10 578.0	11 114.6	10 007.0	15 477.1	17 270.3	21 094.7	24 435.6	28 344.0
Professional, scientific and technical activities	4 737.2	3 491.0	2 599.7	3 373.8	3 426.7	8 205.0	3 845.8	4 625.0	5 007.2	5 814.5
Administrative and support service activities	1 432.9	1 982.3	2 262.8	2 301.0	2 617.4	2 754.5	3 350.1	3 274.1	4 188.0	3 934.8
Public administration; activities of households and of extraterritorial organisations	-	-	0.1	-	-	17.7	17.7	17.7	17.7	3.1
Education	193.8	260.1	249.0	189.9	187.6	204.4	222.4	253.3	465.7	515.4
Human health and social work activities	12.0	12.0	1.9	1.6	17.3	426.7	611.0	674.0	873.4	889.9
Arts, entertainment and recreation	454.7	1 398.8	710.3	559.1	555.0	888.0	964.1	927.1	1 179.7	1 091.1
Other services	124.6	280.6	726.1	667.8	708.5	281.8	332.9	323.9	299.4	301.6
Not allocated and confidential	**0.1**	**0.1**	**0.0**	**0.0**	**0.0**	**2.7**	**1.3**	**1.3**	**1.1**	**1.1**
Private real estate activities	-	-	-	-	-	-	-	-	-	-

- Nil

Note: Data excludes resident Special Purpose Entities (SPEs). Detailed metadata at: *http://metalinks.oecd.org/idi/20220712/6d95*.

Source: *OECD International Direct Investment Statistics (database)*: *https://doi.org/10.1787/idi-data-en*

Table 6. Foreign direct investment income by industrial sector

Million US dollars

	Inward					Outward				
	2016	2017	2018	2019	2020	2016	2017	2018	2019	2020
All FDI activities	**3 997.0**	**3 615.4**	**4 402.0**	**3 443.0**	**2 474.9**	**9 054.5**	**10 090.4**	**9 629.2**	**9 062.9**	**6 870.2**
Agriculture, forestry and fishing	**3.0**	**4.5**	**-**	**3.0**	**6.1**	**0.3**	**13.6**	**6.9**	**-69.1**	**-11.4**
Mining and quarrying	**10.0**	**0.6**	**1.3**	**-**	**-**	**-2 267.0**	**-1 637.2**	**-18.3**	**-761.8**	**-2 692.5**
Extraction activities	-	0.6	-	-	-	-1 951.5	-1 717.3	-347.7	-405.4	-1 937.5
Manufacturing	**2 107.0**	**2 869.2**	**3 515.4**	**2 277.6**	**1 716.0**	**8 963.0**	**9 774.4**	**6 177.0**	**5 118.8**	**5 431.2**
of which:										
Food products, beverages and tobacco	144.0	147.4	155.3	309.3	188.7	224.1	0.1	8.2	-261.5	408.7
Textiles, wood and paper products; printing	118.0	22.4	81.8	54.9	8.9	27.4	73.6	-77.0	-127.3	-60.7
Chemical, rubber, plastic, non-metallic mineral products	661.0	1 860.1	2 169.2	1 012.2	881.7	834.5	734.4	238.0	473.2	-349.9
Metal and machinery products, except electrical equipment	305.0	587.4	732.5	729.8	540.7	5 109.3	6 913.9	5 792.3	2 953.7	5 205.8
Motor vehicles, trailers, semi-trailers, other transport equipment	760.0	104.4	61.9	116.5	28.9	2 204.1	1 544.1	-296.4	1 073.1	-939.9
Other manufacturing	119.0	146.8	314.7	54.9	67.1	563.7	508.3	511.9	1 007.7	1 167.3
Electricity, gas, steam and air conditioning supply	**51.0**	**52.4**	**96.3**	**29.5**	**3.5**	**161.3**	**378.2**	**311.4**	**334.0**	**319.4**
Water supply; sewerage, waste management and remediation activities	**-3.0**	**0.2**	**-**	**0.1**	**-0.6**	**13.5**	**11.7**	**19.2**	**4.4**	**9.8**
Construction	**50.0**	**5.5**	**-**	**10.6**	**-10.1**	**-532.0**	**-54.3**	**252.6**	**-95.5**	**134.4**
Services	**1 779.0**	**682.9**	**789.1**	**1 122.2**	**759.9**	**2 715.5**	**1 604.0**	**2 880.4**	**4 532.2**	**3 679.2**
Wholesale and retail trade; repair of motor vehicles and motorcycles	558.0	325.4	205.8	464.5	184.1	2 049.6	1 234.6	2 968.4	4 452.6	4 146.3
Transportation and storage	192.0	211.0	18.5	93.1	16.3	199.2	140.6	168.5	-4.2	242.0
Accommodation and food service activities	172.0	1.7	55.3	-50.4	-6.4	-12.9	-76.2	-181.8	-202.7	-231.1
Information and communication	305.0	5.3	2.4	23.0	4.7	52.8	-9.1	-278.3	-203.3	-612.1
Financial and insurance activities	325.0	81.9	475.5	460.0	516.8	-41.0	180.9	23.9	-158.0	52.0
Activities of holding companies	47.0	44.1	9.6	6.9	-17.7	-31.9	26.2	60.9	-194.3	-11.5
Real estate activities	96.0	1.0	25.8	42.7	-8.8	211.1	111.5	312.0	690.1	495.9
Professional, scientific and technical activities	129.0	44.5	1.4	72.6	53.0	286.5	6.7	-120.1	-46.2	-96.0
Administrative and support service activities	2.0	11.8	4.2	13.9	0.9	-24.9	124.6	29.1	49.2	-180.3
Public administration; activities of households and of extraterritorial organisations	-	-	-	-	-	-	-	-	-	-
Education	5.0	0.3	-	4.7	-	-8.5	-2.3	-19.4	-9.3	-9.6
Human health and social work activities	-	-	-	-	-	19.3	-1.9	68.5	-3.4	84.0
Arts, entertainment and recreation	-12.0	-	-	-4.0	-0.6	-15.0	-103.7	-86.7	-29.6	-209.4
Other services	7.0	-	-	2.0	-	-0.7	-1.7	-3.6	-2.9	-2.6
Not allocated and confidential	**-**	**0.0**	**0.0**	**0.0**	**0.0**	**0.1**	**0.0**	**-**	**-**	**-**
Private real estate activities	**-**	**-**	**-**	**-**	**-**	**-**	**-**	**-**	**-**	**-**

- Nil

Note: Data excludes resident Special Purpose Entities (SPEs). Detailed metadata at: *http://metalinks.oecd.org/idi/20220712/6d95*.

Source: OECD *International Direct Investment Statistics (database)*: *https://doi.org/10.1787/idi-data-en*

LATVIA

Table 1. Foreign direct investment flows by country

Million US dollars

	Inward					Outward				
	2016	2017	2018	2019	2020	2016	2017	2018	2019	2020
WORLD	**254.3**	**706.8**	**966.6**	**901.2**	**1 010.8**	**159.2**	**133.0**	**205.4**	**-103.0**	**265.5**
OECD COUNTRIES	**-69.7**	**409.2**	**574.8**	**673.9**	**859.3**	**98.4**	**65.4**	**53.1**	**-87.3**	**172.1**
Australia	-	-	-	-1.1	-1.1	-	-	-	-	-
Austria	108.4	-6.8	13.0	35.8	34.2	.. c	.. c	3.5	-	-
Belgium	-7.7	1.1	3.5	5.6	1.1	-	-	-	-	-
Canada	6.6	3.4	-	1.1	-	-	-	-	-	-
Chile	-	-	-	-	-	-	-	-	-	-
Colombia	-	-	-	-	-	-	-	-	-	-
Costa Rica	-	-	-	-	-	-	-	-	-	-
Czech Republic	1.1	-	-	62.7	3.4	.. c	.. c	-	-	-
Denmark	33.2	44.0	-30.7	4.5	53.6	.. c	11.3	13.0	-1.1	-1.1
Estonia	79.6	19.2	269.1	818.3	139.0	43.1	6.8	15.3	36.9	27.4
Finland	13.3	-25.9	-46.0	-6.7	-12.5	-	-6.8	5.9	-1.1	-5.7
France	7.7	16.9	15.3	2.2	-9.1	.. c	.. c	3.5	.. c	-2.3
Germany	-122.7	-9.0	22.4	404.1	136.8	1.1	-1.1	-9.4	-20.2	18.2
Greece	-	-	-	-	-	.. c	.. c	.. c	-	-
Hungary	-	1.1	-	-	-	-	-	.. c	-	-
Iceland	-6.6	22.5	-54.3	-11.2	3.4	.. c	-	.. c	20.2	3.4
Ireland	6.6	32.7	-30.7	32.5	-14.8	-	-	-	-	-
Israel	1.1	1.1	4.7	-	3.4	-	-	1.2	-	-
Italy	44.2	2.3	3.5	3.4	1.1	-	-	-	-	-
Japan	-	-	-	.. c	-	-	-	-	-	-
Korea	-7.7	-37.2	-2.4	22.4	-4.6	-	-	-	-	-
Latvia	-	-	-	-	-	-	-	-	-	-
Lithuania	61.9	110.5	26.0	88.4	233.6	37.6	53.0	41.3	-123.1	58.1
Luxembourg	210.1	71.0	232.5	-85.1	-148.1	1.1	-10.1	-3.5	19.0	-18.2
Mexico	-	.. c	-1.2	-	-	.. c	.. c	.. c	-	-
Netherlands	-8.8	2.3	-148.7	6.7	-80.9	-	-	-	-	1.1
New Zealand	-	-	-	-24.6	-	-	-	-	-	-
Norway	6.6	-325.8	3.5	-77.2	25.1	-	-	-	-	1.1
Poland	13.3	36.1	-	25.7	25.1	-15.5	-3.4	7.1	-4.5	6.8
Portugal	-	-	-	-	-	.. c	-	-	.. c	.. c
Slovak Republic	-	-1.1	-	-	-	.. c	.. c	-33.0	-6.7	21.7
Slovenia	-	-	-	-	-	-	-	-	-	-
Spain	-1.1	-	233.7	-249.6	9.1	6.6	4.5	1.2	-1.1	-6.8
Sweden	-456.7	597.5	211.3	-312.3	349.9	2.2	16.9	7.1	-4.5	49.0
Switzerland	71.9	-5.6	-4.7	-26.9	-18.2	17.7	-44.0	-24.8	25.7	2.3
Turkey	1.1	-1.1	3.5	3.4	1.1	-	-	-	-	-
United Kingdom	-60.8	-23.7	-139.3	-39.2	134.5	1.1	-6.8	-1.2	-11.2	5.7
United States	-3.3	-3.4	-7.1	-9.0	-5.7	17.7	42.8	33.0	-16.8	11.4
EUROPE	**105.1**	**662.8**	**834.4**	**547.4**	**837.6**	**109.5**	**71.0**	**112.1**	**-62.7**	**206.3**
Bulgaria	1.1	3.4	2.4	-2.2	1.1	.. c	.. c	1.2	.. c	.. c
Croatia	-	-	-	-	-	-	-	-	-	-
Cyprus	3.3	-82.3	-115.7	1.1	63.8	-3.3	-25.9	-34.2	-40.3	-4.6
Malta	-68.6	45.1	8.3	-42.5	-5.7	.. c	.. c	76.7	-1.1	-29.6
Montenegro	-	-	-	-	-	-	-	-	-	-
Romania	-	-3.4	4.7	2.2	5.7	.. c	1.1	.. c	2.2	4.6
Russian Federation	175.8	130.8	354.1	-82.8	-103.7	15.5	13.5	2.4	44.8	-16.0
Ukraine	17.7	12.4	5.9	6.7	1.1	-4.4	-4.5	18.9	-3.4	88.9
AFRICA	**7.7**	**5.6**	**1.2**	**-1.1**	**-**	**-**	**-**	**-**	**.. c**	**.. c**
Northern Africa	-	-	-	-	-	-	-	-	-	-
Algeria	-	-	-	-	-	-	-	-	-	-
Egypt	-	-	-	-	-	-	-	-	-	-
Libya	-	-	-	-	-	-	-	-	-	-
Morocco	-	-	-	-	-	-	-	-	-	-
Tunisia	-	-	-	-	-	-	-	-	-	-
Other African countries	7.7	5.6	1.2	-1.1	-	-	-	-	.. c	.. c
Nigeria	-	-	-	-	-	-	-	-	-	-
South Africa	-	-	-	-	-	-	-	-	-	-
AMERICA	**-23.2**	**-11.3**	**-13.0**	**58.2**	**16.0**	**37.6**	**45.1**	**24.8**	**-13.4**	**14.8**
Northern America	3.3	-	-7.1	-7.8	-5.7	17.7	42.8	33.0	-16.8	11.4
Central America and Caribbean countries	-26.5	-11.3	-5.9	64.9	21.7	19.9	1.1	-7.1	2.2	3.4
Bahamas	-	-	-	-	-	-	-	-	-	-
Bermuda	-	-	-	-	.. c	-	-	-	-	-
Cayman Islands	.. c	.. c	.. c	-4.5	.. c	-	-	-	-	-
El Salvador	-	-	-	-	-	-	-	-	-	-
Guatemala	-	-	-	-	-	-	-	-	-	-
Honduras	-	-	-	-	-	-	-	-	-	-
Nicaragua	-	-	-	-	-	-	-	-	-	-
Panama	-2.2	-3.4	-1.2	-	-	-	-	-	.. c	.. c
Virgin Islands, U.S.	-	-	-	-	-	-	-	-	-	-
South America	-	-	-	-	-	-	-	-	.. c	-
Argentina	-	-	-	-	-	-	-	-	-	-
Bolivia	-	-	-	-	-	-	-	-	-	-
Brazil	-	-	-	-	-	-	-	-	.. c	-
Ecuador	-	-	-	-	-	-	-	-	-	-
Paraguay	-	-	-	-	-	-	-	-	-	-
Peru	-	-	-	-	-	-	-	-	-	-
Uruguay	-	-	-	-	-	-	-	-	-	-
Venezuela	-	-	-	-	-	-	-	-	-	-

Table 1. Foreign direct investment flows by country *(cont.)*

Million US dollars

	Inward					Outward				
	2016	2017	2018	2019	2020	2016	2017	2018	2019	2020
ASIA	**48.7**	**-27.1**	**28.3**	**44.8**	**21.7**	**-**	**-12.4**	**11.8**	**-23.5**	**6.8**
Near and Middle East	29.9	-12.4	2.4	1.1	3.4	1.1	-13.5	13.0	-24.6	2.3
Gulf Arabian countries	2.2	-2.3	-1.2	3.4	2.3	.. c	.. c	.. c	.. c	-
Kuwait	-	-	-	-	-	-	-	-	-	-
Qatar	-	-	-	-	-	-	-	-	-	-
Saudi Arabia	-	.. c	-	-	-	-	-	-	-	-
United Arab Emirates	2.2	-1.1	-1.2	3.4	2.3	.. c	.. c	.. c	.. c	-
Other Near and Middle East	28.8	-9.0	2.4	-3.4	1.1	10.0	-	2.4	-4.5	2.3
Jordan	-	-	-	-	-	-	-	-	-	-
Other Asian countries	17.7	-14.7	26.0	43.7	18.2	-1.1	1.1	-	1.1	3.4
China	4.4	4.5	10.6	3.4	4.6	.. c	-	-	-	-
Hong Kong, China	-	-	2.4	2.2	44.4	-	-	-	-	-
India	-	-	-	5.6	-2.3	-	-	-	-	-
Indonesia	-	-	-	-	-	-	-	-	-	-
Iran, Islamic Republic of	-	-	-	-	-	-	-	-	-	-
Malaysia	-	-	-	-	-	.. c	-	-	-	-
Philippines	-	-	-	-	-	-	-	-	-	-
Singapore	5.5	4.5	1.2	3.4	-1.1	-	-	-	-	-
Chinese Taipei	-	-	-	-	-	-	-	-	-	-
Thailand	-	-	-	-	-	-	-	-	-	-
Viet Nam	12.2	5.6	5.9	5.6	-19.4	-	-	-	-	-
AUSTRALIA, OCEANIA AND POLAR REGIONS	**-**	**-1.1**	**-1.2**	**-25.7**	**-1.1**	**-**	**-**	**-**	**-**	**-**
WORLD unallocated and confidential	**116.1**	**77.8**	**116.8**	**277.6**	**136.8**	**12.2**	**29.3**	**56.7**	**.. d**	**.. d**
European Union (since 01/02/2020)	**..**	**..**	**..**	**..**	**792.0**	**..**	**..**	**..**	**..**	**120.8**
G20 countries excl. European Union	**46.4**	**81.2**	**257.3**	**313.4**	**150.4**	**47.6**	**53.0**	**15.3**	**-3.4**	**17.1**
G20 OECD countries	**-133.8**	**-53.0**	**-106.2**	**386.2**	**251.9**	**34.3**	**39.5**	**14.2**	**-50.4**	**31.9**
G20 Non-OECD countries	**180.3**	**134.1**	**364.7**	**-72.8**	**-101.4**	**13.3**	**13.5**	**1.2**	**45.9**	**-16.0**
MENA countries	**2.2**	**-2.3**	**-1.2**	**3.4**	**2.3**	**.. c**	**.. c**	**.. c**	**.. c**	**-**
ASEAN countries	**17.7**	**10.1**	**7.1**	**10.1**	**-20.5**	**.. c**	**-**	**-**	**-**	**-**

- Nil; .. Not available; c Confidential data; d Secondary Confidentiality

Note: Detailed metadata at: *http://metalinks.oecd.org/idi/20220712/6d95.*

Source: *OECD International Direct Investment Statistics (database): https://doi.org/10.1787/idi-data-en*

LATVIA

Table 2. Foreign direct investment positions by country

At year end

Million US dollars

	Inward					Outward				
	2016	2017	2018	2019	2020	2016	2017	2018	2019	2020
WORLD	**14 325.9**	**17 618.1**	**17 473.1**	**17 973.5**	**20 526.4**	**1 933.2**	**2 241.5**	**2 338.0**	**2 165.8**	**2 572.1**
OECD COUNTRIES	**9 380.2**	**11 565.1**	**12 687.2**	**13 135.3**	**15 123.3**	**889.6**	**1 069.8**	**1 511.3**	**1 416.5**	**1 718.0**
Australia	1.1	-	-	-	-1.2	-	-	-	-	-
Austria	215.0	235.1	239.3	276.3	321.5	14.8	16.8	18.3	15.7	14.7
Belgium	53.8	34.8	57.2	85.4	94.5	-	-	1.1	-	-
Canada	12.6	14.4	14.9	14.6	16.0	-	-	-	-	-
Chile	-	-	-	-	-	-	-	-	-	-
Colombia	-	-	-	-	-	-	-	-	-	-
Costa Rica	-	-	-	-	-	-	-	-	-	-
Czech Republic	14.8	13.2	20.6	77.5	90.8	8.4	12.0	11.5	9.0	8.6
Denmark	629.3	704.0	651.5	659.4	768.2	20.0	22.8	13.7	13.5	13.5
Estonia	1 011.9	1 563.9	1 739.2	2 435.4	2 784.4	234.0	253.1	230.1	268.5	316.6
Finland	433.2	452.1	471.7	550.4	590.3	14.8	19.2	14.9	20.2	17.2
France	95.9	115.1	169.5	142.7	148.5	22.1	27.6	22.9	28.1	29.5
Germany	643.0	784.4	869.0	1 151.4	1 441.9	22.1	43.2	55.0	56.2	79.8
Greece	-	2.4	-	1.1	1.2	-	13.2	14.9	15.7	18.4
Hungary	1.1	13.2	11.5	7.9	9.8	-	-	2.3	2.2	3.7
Iceland	102.2	103.1	49.2	49.4	57.7	-	-	1.1	28.1	6.1
Ireland	7.4	54.0	19.5	56.2	45.4	-	-	-	-	-
Israel	29.5	37.2	63.0	65.2	82.2	-	2.4	3.4	1.1	1.2
Italy	101.2	91.1	106.5	83.1	92.0	13.7	15.6	46.9	47.2	51.5
Japan	1.1	-	-	-	-	-	-	-	-	-
Korea	40.1	10.8	8.0	30.3	28.2	-	-	-	-	1.2
Latvia	-	-	-	-	-	-	-	-	-	-
Lithuania	754.7	1 103.4	1 075.1	1 185.1	1 538.8	363.7	485.7	565.6	425.7	554.7
Luxembourg	687.3	955.9	1 049.9	933.5	812.4	112.8	117.5	114.5	106.7	96.9
Mexico	-	1.2	-2.3	-3.4	-3.7	9.5	15.6	-	-	-
Netherlands	1 274.4	1 464.4	1 246.9	1 271.6	1 229.6	103.3	117.5	113.4	112.3	125.2
New Zealand	27.4	30.0	25.2	1.1	-	-	-	-	-	-
Norway	752.6	644.0	597.7	526.8	570.6	12.6	31.2	18.3	14.6	17.2
Poland	70.6	119.9	116.8	146.0	185.3	65.4	63.6	35.5	33.7	43.0
Portugal	-	-	-	-	-	6.3	7.2	6.9	9.0	11.0
Slovak Republic	2.1	1.2	3.4	1.1	1.2	20.0	67.2	34.3	27.0	54.0
Slovenia	-	-	-	-	-	2.1	3.6	3.4	3.4	4.9
Spain	2.1	9.6	226.7	11.2	27.0	9.5	10.8	12.6	13.5	13.5
Sweden	2 254.7	3 030.7	3 050.1	2 735.3	3 384.5	21.1	27.6	17.2	12.4	66.3
Switzerland	238.2	351.4	277.1	235.9	224.6	111.7	67.2	48.1	68.5	61.4
Turkey	30.6	34.8	16.0	15.7	17.2	-	-	2.3	-	1.2
United Kingdom	442.7	518.1	324.0	235.9	392.7	27.4	30.0	25.2	4.5	9.8
United States	205.5	173.9	188.9	152.8	170.6	36.9	85.2	80.1	77.5	95.7
EUROPE	**13 299.3**	**16 547.1**	**16 442.6**	**16 772.6**	**19 090.7**	**1 745.5**	**1 981.3**	**2 068.9**	**1 986.1**	**2 350.0**
Bulgaria	19.0	24.0	25.2	19.1	23.3	141.2	159.5	161.4	149.4	163.2
Croatia	-	-	-	-	-	-	-	-	-	-
Cyprus	1 347.1	1 448.8	1 235.4	1 351.4	1 535.2	131.8	93.5	87.0	116.8	99.4
Malta	398.4	542.1	512.9	392.0	447.9	7.4	4.8	88.2	91.0	71.2
Montenegro	-	-	-	-	-	10.5	12.0	11.5	-	-
Romania	-	-3.6	1.1	3.4	13.5	5.3	15.6	9.2	13.5	20.9
Russian Federation	1 392.4	1 841.0	1 947.6	1 809.7	1 838.3	134.9	121.1	115.6	135.9	127.6
Ukraine	150.7	158.3	154.6	160.6	207.4	19.0	20.4	52.7	24.7	121.5
AFRICA	**17.9**	**25.2**	**29.8**	**19.1**	**19.6**	**1.1**	**1.2**	**1.1**	**14.6**	**3.7**
Northern Africa	-	-	-	-	-	-	-	-	-	-
Algeria	-	-	-	-	-	-	-	-	-	-
Egypt	-	-	-	-	-	-	-	-	-	-
Libya	-	-	-	-	-	-	-	-	-	-
Morocco	-	-	-	-	-	-	-	-	-	-
Tunisia	-	-	-	-	-	-	-	-	-	-
Other African countries	17.9	25.2	28.6	19.1	19.6	1.1	-	1.1	14.6	3.7
Nigeria	-	-	-	-	-	-	-	-	-	-
South Africa	1.1	-	8.0	-	-	-	-	-	-	-
AMERICA	**345.7**	**308.2**	**373.3**	**356.1**	**385.3**	**68.5**	**125.9**	**108.8**	**86.5**	**103.1**
Northern America	218.2	188.3	203.8	167.4	186.5	36.9	85.2	80.1	77.5	95.7
Central America and Caribbean countries	127.5	119.9	168.3	187.6	197.6	30.6	39.6	28.6	7.9	6.1
Bahamas	-	-	-	-	-	1.1	1.2	1.1	1.1	1.2
Bermuda	17.9	10.8	10.3	13.5	12.3	-	-	-	-	-
Cayman Islands	6.3	10.8	18.3	10.1	8.6	-	-	-	-	-
El Salvador	-	-	-	-	-	-	-	-	-	-
Guatemala	-	-	-	-	-	-	-	-	-	-
Honduras	-	-	-	-	-	-	-	-	-	-
Nicaragua	-	-	-	-	-	-	-	-	-	-
Panama	9.5	4.8	3.4	16.9	18.4	-	-	-	2.2	-
Virgin Islands, U.S.	-	-	-	-	-	-	-	-	-	-
South America	-	-	1.1	1.1	1.2	1.1	1.2	-	1.1	1.2
Argentina	-	-	-	-	-	-	-	-	-	-
Bolivia	-	-	-	-	-	-	-	-	-	-
Brazil	-	-	-	-	-	1.1	1.2	-	1.1	1.2
Ecuador	-	-	-	-	-	-	-	-	-	-
Paraguay	-	-	-	-	-	-	-	-	-	-
Peru	-	-	1.1	1.1	1.2	-	-	-	-	-
Uruguay	-	-	-	-	-	-	-	-	-	-
Venezuela	-	-	-	-	-	-	-	-	-	-

LATVIA

Table 2. Foreign direct investment positions by country *(cont.)*

At year end

Million US dollars

	Inward					Outward				
	2016	2017	2018	2019	2020	2016	2017	2018	2019	2020
ASIA	**405.8**	**427.0**	**425.9**	**458.3**	**516.6**	**85.4**	**72.0**	**57.2**	**32.6**	**43.0**
Near and Middle East	121.2	131.9	166.0	170.7	195.1	61.1	55.2	37.8	9.0	13.5
Gulf Arabian countries	2.1	-	12.6	16.9	20.9	29.5	12.0	21.8	-	-
Kuwait	-	-	-	-	-	-	-	-	-	-
Qatar	-	-	-	-	-	-	-	-	-	-
Saudi Arabia	-	-2.4	-	-	-	-	-	-	-	-
United Arab Emirates	3.2	2.4	12.6	16.9	20.9	29.5	12.0	21.8	-	-
Other Near and Middle East	119.1	131.9	152.3	153.9	174.3	31.6	43.2	17.2	9.0	13.5
Jordan	-	-	-	-	-	-	-	-	-	-
Other Asian countries	283.5	293.8	261.0	287.6	321.5	24.2	16.8	18.3	22.5	30.7
China	69.6	74.4	43.5	30.3	27.0	-	-	-	-	-
Hong Kong, China	1.1	2.4	4.6	14.6	63.8	-	-	-	-	-
India	1.1	3.6	2.3	6.7	6.1	-	-	-	-	-
Indonesia	-	-	-	-	-	-	-	-	-	-
Iran, Islamic Republic of	-	-	-	-	-	-	-	-	-	-
Malaysia	-	-	-	-	-	1.1	1.2	1.1	1.1	1.2
Philippines	-	-	-	-	-	-	-	-	-	-
Singapore	65.4	79.2	74.4	68.5	71.2	-	-	-1.1	-1.1	-
Chinese Taipei	-	-	-	-	-	-	-	-	-	-
Thailand	-	-	-	-	-	-	2.4	5.7	3.4	3.7
Viet Nam	11.6	20.4	25.2	30.3	12.3	-	-	-	-	-
AUSTRALIA, OCEANIA AND POLAR REGIONS	**29.5**	**31.2**	**27.5**	**1.1**	**-**	**-**	**-**	**-**	**-**	**-**
WORLD unallocated and confidential	**227.7**	**279.4**	**174.0**	**366.2**	**514.2**	**32.7**	**61.2**	**101.9**	**46.1**	**72.4**
European Union (since 01/02/2020)	**..**	**..**	**..**	**..**	**15 649.8**	**..**	**..**	**..**	**..**	**1 878.8**
G20 countries excl. European Union	**3 037.8**	**3 662.7**	**3 697.0**	**3 672.2**	**4 173.5**	**267.7**	**339.4**	**349.2**	**351.6**	**398.8**
G20 OECD countries	**1 573.7**	**1 745.0**	**1 695.7**	**1 824.3**	**2 302.1**	**131.8**	**215.9**	**232.4**	**213.4**	**268.7**
G20 Non-OECD countries	**1 464.1**	**1 917.7**	**2 001.4**	**1 847.9**	**1 871.4**	**136.0**	**123.5**	**115.6**	**138.2**	**130.1**
MENA countries	**2.1**	**-**	**13.7**	**16.9**	**20.9**	**29.5**	**12.0**	**21.8**	**-**	**-**
ASEAN countries	**78.0**	**99.5**	**98.5**	**98.9**	**83.4**	**1.1**	**3.6**	**6.9**	**4.5**	**4.9**

- Nil; .. Not available

Note: Detailed metadata at: *http://metalinks.oecd.org/idi/20220712/6d95.*

Source: *OECD International Direct Investment Statistics (database): https://doi.org/10.1787/idi-data-en*

Table 3. Foreign direct investment income by country

Million US dollars

	Inward					Outward				
	2016	2017	2018	2019	2020	2016	2017	2018	2019	2020
WORLD	**1 188.8**	**1 389.9**	**1 861.2**	**1 624.3**	**1 108.8**	**117.2**	**216.4**	**157.0**	**114.2**	**115.1**
OECD COUNTRIES	**811.7**	**879.3**	**1 115.3**	**1 051.2**	**773.8**	**61.9**	**101.5**	**127.5**	**81.7**	**58.1**
Australia	-	-	-	-	-	-	-	-	-	-
Austria	18.8	24.8	29.5	30.2	21.7	.. c	-	-	-	-
Belgium	3.3	.. c	4.7	10.1	3.4	-	-	-	-	-
Canada	-	1.1	1.2	-	-	-	-	-	-	-
Chile	-	-	-	-	-	-	-	-	-	-
Colombia	-	-	-	-	-	-	-	-	-	-
Costa Rica	-	-	-	-	-	-	-	-	-	-
Czech Republic	6.6	-	9.4	6.7	.. c	.. c	.. c	-	.. c	-
Denmark	54.2	60.9	61.4	52.6	71.8	.. c	.. c	.. c	23.5	.. c
Estonia	89.6	112.7	146.3	169.0	133.3	-1.1	11.3	10.6	11.2	11.4
Finland	23.2	33.8	46.0	31.3	28.5	6.6	-	1.2	1.1	-
France	5.5	7.9	8.3	10.1	12.5	.. c	.. c	-	.. c	-
Germany	47.6	57.5	34.2	47.0	1.1	-	-1.1	-	-3.4	1.1
Greece	-	-	-	-	-	-	-	-	-	-
Hungary	-	-	-	-	-	-	-	-	-	-
Iceland	10.0	7.9	-	-5.6	-1.1	-	-	-	-	-
Ireland	-	5.6	1.2	1.1	-	-	-	-	-	-
Israel	-1.1	-	-1.2	-	-	-	-	-	-	-
Italy	6.6	10.1	7.1	10.1	3.4	-	-	-	-	-
Japan	-	-	-	-	-	-	-	-	-	-
Korea	6.6	.. c	-	-	-	-	-	-	-	-
Latvia	-	-	-	-	-	-	-	-	-	-
Lithuania	25.4	57.5	55.5	73.9	68.4	18.8	32.7	30.7	5.6	37.6
Luxembourg	48.7	120.6	81.4	110.8	38.7	.. c	.. c	-5.9	-6.7	-8.0
Mexico	-	-	-	-	-	-	-	-	-	-
Netherlands	54.2	82.3	102.7	113.1	76.4	-	-	.. c	.. c	-
New Zealand	-	-	-	-	-	-	-	-	-	-
Norway	91.8	81.2	62.6	51.5	20.5	-	-	-	-	-
Poland	6.6	9.0	15.3	23.5	27.4	26.5	27.1	35.4	-2.2	1.1
Portugal	-	-	-	-	-	-	-	-	-	-
Slovak Republic	-	-	-	-	-	.. c	.. c	.. c	1.1	.. c
Slovenia	-	-	-	-	-	-	-	-	-	-
Spain	2.2	1.1	11.8	3.4	-	5.5	.. c	-	12.3	-
Sweden	291.9	239.0	384.8	287.7	246.2	11.1	11.3	3.5	-	.. c
Switzerland	14.4	10.1	17.7	3.4	1.1	8.8	9.0	.. c	6.7	.. c
Turkey	-	3.4	4.7	3.4	-	-	-	-	-	-
United Kingdom	21.0	3.4	20.1	5.6	17.1	-3.3	1.1	.. c	6.7	-
United States	12.2	4.5	10.6	9.0	-	.. c	.. c	-	-	-
EUROPE	**1 046.1**	**1 192.7**	**1 480.0**	**1 286.2**	**875.2**	**88.5**	**140.9**	**132.2**	**99.6**	**93.4**
Bulgaria	.. c	2.3	1.2	.. c	.. c	-	-	-	-	-
Croatia	-	-	-	-	-	-	-	-	-	-
Cyprus	95.1	160.1	194.7	116.4	93.4	16.6	5.6	-1.2	1.1	14.8
Malta	33.2	34.9	34.2	13.4	20.5	.. c	-	-	1.1	-
Montenegro	-	-	-	-	-	-	-	-	-	-
Romania	-	-	-	-	.. c	-	-	-	.. c	-
Russian Federation	87.4	57.5	135.7	118.7	-22.8	-6.6	5.6	3.5	13.4	18.2
Ukraine	12.2	1.1	8.3	1.1	2.3	-5.5	-5.6	-	1.1	1.1
AFRICA	-	-	-	-	-	-	-	-	-	.. c
Northern Africa	-	-	-	-	-	-	-	-	-	-
Algeria	-	-	-	-	-	-	-	-	-	-
Egypt	-	-	-	-	-	-	-	-	-	-
Libya	-	-	-	-	-	-	-	-	-	-
Morocco	-	-	-	-	-	-	-	-	-	-
Tunisia	-	-	-	-	-	-	-	-	-	-
Other African countries	-	-	-	-	-	-	-	-	-	.. c
Nigeria	-	-	-	-	-	-	-	-	-	-
South Africa	-	-	-	-	-	-	-	-	-	-
AMERICA	**14.4**	**-11.3**	**-30.7**	**-34.7**	**19.4**	**1.1**	**2.3**	-	-	-
Northern America	12.2	5.6	10.6	9.0	-	.. c	.. c	-	-	-
Central America and Caribbean countries	2.2	-15.8	-41.3	-43.7	20.5	-	-	-	-	-
Bahamas	-	-	-	-	-	-	-	-	-	-
Bermuda	-	-	-	-	-	-	-	-	-	-
Cayman Islands	-	-	.. c	.. c	.. c	-	-	-	-	-
El Salvador	-	-	-	-	-	-	-	-	-	-
Guatemala	-	-	-	-	-	-	-	-	-	-
Honduras	-	-	-	-	-	-	-	-	-	-
Nicaragua	-	-	-	-	-	-	-	-	-	-
Panama	-	-	-	-	-	-	-	-	-	-
Virgin Islands, U.S.	-	-	-	-	-	-	-	-	-	-
South America	-	-	-	-	-	-	-	-	-	-
Argentina	-	-	-	-	-	-	-	-	-	-
Bolivia	-	-	-	-	-	-	-	-	-	-
Brazil	-	-	-	-	-	-	-	-	-	-
Ecuador	-	-	-	-	-	-	-	-	-	-
Paraguay	-	-	-	-	-	-	-	-	-	-
Peru	-	-	-	-	-	-	-	-	-	-
Uruguay	-	-	-	-	-	-	-	-	-	-
Venezuela	-	-	-	-	-	-	-	-	-	-

Table 3. Foreign direct investment income by country *(cont.)*

Million US dollars

	Inward					Outward				
	2016	2017	2018	2019	2020	2016	2017	2018	2019	2020
ASIA	**4.4**	**-**	**2.4**	**1.1**	**-**	**11.1**	**21.4**	**1.2**	**1.1**	**-**
Near and Middle East	-3.3	-3.4	-3.5	-3.4	-5.7	13.3	22.5	-	-	-
Gulf Arabian countries	-	1.1	3.5	2.2	-	.. c	.. c	.. c	-	-
Kuwait	-	-	-	-	-	-	-	-	-	-
Qatar	-	-	-	-	-	-	-	-	-	-
Saudi Arabia	-	-	-	-	-	-	-	-	-	-
United Arab Emirates	-	1.1	3.5	2.2	-	.. c	.. c	.. c	-	-
Other Near and Middle East	-3.3	-4.5	-7.1	-5.6	-5.7	11.1	21.4	-	-	-
Jordan	-	-	-	-	-	-	-	-	-	-
Other Asian countries	7.7	3.4	7.1	3.4	5.7	-2.2	-	1.2	1.1	-
China	-1.1	-	-	-	.. c	.. c	-	-	-	-
Hong Kong, China	-	-	-	-	-	-	-	-	-	-
India	-	-	-	-	-	-	-	-	-	-
Indonesia	-	-	-	-	-	-	-	-	-	-
Iran, Islamic Republic of	-	-	-	-	-	-	-	-	-	-
Malaysia	-	-	-	-	-	-	-	-	-	-
Philippines	-	-	-	-	-	-	-	-	-	-
Singapore	3.3	2.3	5.9	4.5	4.6	-	-	-	.. c	-
Chinese Taipei	-	-	-	-	-	-	-	-	-	-
Thailand	-	-	-	-	-	-	-	-	-	-
Viet Nam	-	-	-	-	-	-	-	-	-	-
AUSTRALIA, OCEANIA AND POLAR REGIONS	**-**	**-**	**-**	**-**	**-**	**-**	**-**	**-**	**-**	**-**
WORLD unallocated and confidential	**123.9**	**208.5**	**409.5**	**371.7**	**214.2**	**16.6**	**51.9**	**23.6**	**13.4**	**.. d**
European Union (since 01/02/2020)	**..**	**..**	**..**	**..**	**851.3**	**..**	**..**	**..**	**..**	**72.9**
G20 countries excl. European Union	**184.7**	**145.4**	**220.7**	**204.9**	**13.7**	**-16.6**	**9.0**	**4.7**	**24.6**	**19.4**
G20 OECD countries	**99.5**	**87.9**	**86.2**	**86.2**	**34.2**	**-7.7**	**3.4**	**1.2**	**11.2**	**1.1**
G20 Non-OECD countries	**86.3**	**57.5**	**135.7**	**118.7**	**-20.5**	**-7.7**	**5.6**	**3.5**	**13.4**	**18.2**
MENA countries	**-**	**1.1**	**3.5**	**2.2**	**-**	**.. c**	**.. c**	**.. c**	**-**	**-**
ASEAN countries	**3.3**	**2.3**	**5.9**	**4.5**	**4.6**	**-**	**-**	**-**	**.. c**	**-**

- Nil; .. Not available; c Confidential data; d Secondary Confidentiality

Note: Detailed metadata at: *http://metalinks.oecd.org/idi/20220712/6d95*.

Source: *OECD International Direct Investment Statistics (database)*: *https://doi.org/10.1787/idi-data-en*

Table 4. Foreign direct investment flows by industrial sector

Million US dollars

	Inward					Outward				
	2016	2017	2018	2019	2020	2016	2017	2018	2019	2020
All FDI activities	**254.3**	**706.8**	**966.6**	**901.2**	**1 010.8**	**159.2**	**133.0**	**205.4**	**-103.0**	**265.5**
Agriculture, forestry and fishing	**14.4**	**45.1**	**15.3**	**17.9**	**54.7**	**.. c**	**-**	**-**	**-**	**-**
Mining and quarrying	**1.1**	**12.4**	**-**	**13.4**	**13.7**	**-**	**-**	**-**	**-**	**-**
Extraction activities	1.1	12.4	-	13.4	13.7	-	-	-	-	-
Manufacturing	**22.1**	**32.7**	**159.3**	**115.3**	**129.9**	**73.0**	**25.9**	**10.6**	**3.4**	**5.7**
of which:										
Food products, beverages and tobacco	-16.6	-37.2	131.0	13.4	34.2	-	-	-	-	-
Textiles, wood and paper products; printing	22.1	58.6	2.4	31.3	30.8	56.4	9.0	16.5	-10.1	-10.3
Chemical, rubber, plastic, non-metallic mineral products	5.5	-20.3	48.4	3.4	11.4	.. c	-18.0	9.4	4.5	.. c
Metal and machinery products, except electrical equipment	4.4	14.7	11.8	12.3	18.2	-	-	.. c	-2.2	4.6
Motor vehicles, trailers, semi-trailers, other transport equipment	5.5	22.5	13.0	24.6	3.4	-	-	-	-	-
Other manufacturing	1.1	-6.8	-48.4	30.2	31.9	.. c	.. c	-16.5	.. c	4.6
Electricity, gas, steam and air conditioning supply	**24.3**	**-73.3**	**-24.8**	**1.1**	**-2.3**	**-1.1**	**.. c**	**.. c**	**.. c**	**.. c**
Water supply; sewerage, waste management and remediation activities	**-**	**-1.1**	**-1.2**	**-**	**.. c**	**-**	**-**	**-**	**-**	**-**
Construction	**15.5**	**72.1**	**64.9**	**-171.3**	**-1.1**	**29.9**	**.. c**	**3.5**	**-31.3**	**6.8**
Services	**87.4**	**485.9**	**546.4**	**600.0**	**577.8**	**39.8**	**83.4**	**119.2**	**-62.7**	**227.9**
Wholesale and retail trade; repair of motor vehicles and motorcycles	267.6	69.9	310.4	16.8	8.0	33.2	9.0	85.0	-5.6	23.9
Transportation and storage	66.4	51.9	30.7	11.2	-75.2	-	1.1	2.4	32.5	-16.0
Accommodation and food service activities	4.4	25.9	-22.4	-6.7	-11.4	-	-	-	-	-
Information and communication	33.2	-45.1	-2.4	31.3	72.9	4.4	-	8.3	19.0	-12.5
Financial and insurance activities	-205.7	310.0	186.5	154.5	325.9	-16.6	67.6	34.2	-99.6	116.2
Activities of holding companies	-6.6	18.0	44.8	10.1	109.4	-17.7	2.3	11.8	-82.8	86.6
Real estate activities	-66.4	129.6	182.9	364.9	101.4	8.8	.. c	9.4	1.1	29.6
Professional, scientific and technical activities	-21.0	-78.9	-178.2	35.8	143.6	14.4	5.6	-16.5	-10.1	27.4
Administrative and support service activities	-	13.5	3.5	-	-2.3	-	-1.1	3.5	1.1	-6.8
Public administration; activities of households and of extraterritorial organisations	-	-	-	-	-	-	-	-	-	-
Education	-	-	3.5	-	1.1	.. c	-	-	-	-
Human health and social work activities	4.4	-	1.2	2.2	-2.3	-	-	-	-	-
Arts, entertainment and recreation	5.5	9.0	29.5	-10.1	17.1	.. c	-	.. c	-	.. c
Other services	-	-	-	-	-	-	-	-	-	-
Not allocated and confidential	**.. c**	**.. c**	**.. c**	**.. c**	**.. c**	**.. c**	**.. c**	**.. c**	**.. c**	**.. c**
Private real estate activities	**.. c**	**.. c**	**.. c**	**.. c**	**.. c**	**14.4**	**11.3**	**15.3**	**16.8**	**9.1**

- Nil; c Confidential data

Note: Detailed metadata at: *http://metalinks.oecd.org/idi/20220712/6d95*.

Source: *OECD International Direct Investment Statistics (database): https://doi.org/10.1787/idi-data-en*

LATVIA

Table 5. Foreign direct investment positions by industrial sector
At year end

Million US dollars

	Inward					Outward				
	2016	2017	2018	2019	2020	2016	2017	2018	2019	2020
All FDI activities	**14 325.9**	**17 618.1**	**17 473.1**	**17 973.5**	**20 526.4**	**1 933.2**	**2 241.5**	**2 338.0**	**2 165.8**	**2 572.1**
Agriculture, forestry and fishing	**597.7**	**736.4**	**661.8**	**729.1**	**851.6**	**3.2**	**3.6**	**-**	**-**	**-**
Mining and quarrying	**121.2**	**148.7**	**167.2**	**140.4**	**166.9**	**-**	**-**	**-**	**-**	**-**
Extraction activities	121.2	148.7	167.2	140.4	166.9	-	-	-	-	-
Manufacturing	**1 690.7**	**1 978.9**	**2 039.2**	**2 111.9**	**2 388.0**	**205.5**	**248.3**	**206.1**	**216.8**	**246.7**
of which:										
Food products, beverages and tobacco	269.8	261.5	317.2	308.9	344.8	1.1	.. c	1.1	.. c	6.1
Textiles, wood and paper products; printing	529.1	629.6	706.4	718.9	803.8	113.8	133.1	140.8	129.2	130.1
Chemical, rubber, plastic, non-metallic mineral products	80.1	88.8	156.9	123.6	148.5	50.6	27.6	37.8	51.7	63.8
Metal and machinery products, except electrical equipment	171.8	244.7	198.1	229.2	272.4	4.2	3.6	5.7	4.5	9.8
Motor vehicles, trailers, semi-trailers, other transport equipment	98.0	124.7	132.8	159.5	149.7	-	-	-	-	-
Other manufacturing	541.8	629.6	527.8	571.8	668.8	35.8	82.8	21.8	31.5	39.3
Electricity, gas, steam and air conditioning supply	**521.8**	**686.0**	**636.6**	**596.5**	**677.4**	**10.5**	**9.6**	**22.9**	**12.4**	**22.1**
Water supply; sewerage, waste management and remediation activities	**11.6**	**4.8**	**6.9**	**10.1**	**12.3**	**-**	**-**	**-**	**-**	**-**
Construction	**647.2**	**663.2**	**724.8**	**533.6**	**539.9**	**43.2**	**49.2**	**53.8**	**25.8**	**34.4**
Services	**9 821.9**	**12 266.7**	**12 190.3**	**12 621.9**	**14 339.2**	**1 372.4**	**1 567.5**	**1 597.2**	**1 518.8**	**1 816.2**
Wholesale and retail trade; repair of motor vehicles and motorcycles	2 094.4	2 468.2	2 781.1	2 726.4	3 043.3	337.3	370.6	450.0	397.7	488.4
Transportation and storage	600.8	1 057.8	891.9	900.9	892.1	7.4	7.2	6.9	44.9	24.5
Accommodation and food service activities	148.6	235.1	182.0	288.7	308.0	-	-	-	-	-
Information and communication	457.5	594.9	557.6	596.5	733.8	5.3	6.0	6.9	22.5	11.0
Financial and insurance activities	3 730.4	4 218.0	4 194.0	4 281.1	4 979.8	841.2	940.3	899.9	803.2	900.7
Activities of holding companies	758.9	526.5	654.9	643.7	728.9	206.6	202.7	334.3	225.8	301.9
Real estate activities	1 917.4	2 620.5	2 788.0	3 062.2	3 385.7	40.1	48.0	41.2	61.8	101.9
Professional, scientific and technical activities	548.1	730.4	343.5	333.6	506.8	127.5	175.1	163.7	162.9	198.8
Administrative and support service activities	191.8	176.3	214.1	237.0	257.7	7.4	14.4	27.5	23.6	17.2
Public administration; activities of households and of extraterritorial organisations	-	-	-	-	-	-	-	-	-	-
Education	10.5	7.2	28.6	27.0	30.7	2.1	1.2	1.1	-	-
Human health and social work activities	10.5	7.2	9.2	9.0	7.4	-	-	-	-	-
Arts, entertainment and recreation	108.6	147.5	199.2	159.5	191.4	4.2	4.8	1.1	1.1	73.6
Other services	2.1	3.6	1.1	1.1	1.2	-	-	-	-	-
Not allocated and confidential	**183.4**	**247.1**	**176.3**	**362.8**	**564.5**	**-5.3**	**20.4**	**60.7**	**-12.4**	**-**
Private real estate activities	**730.5**	**886.3**	**870.2**	**867.2**	**986.6**	**303.6**	**343.0**	**397.3**	**404.4**	**452.8**

- Nil; c Confidential data

Note: Detailed metadata at: *http://metalinks.oecd.org/idi/20220712/6d95.*

Source: *OECD International Direct Investment Statistics (database): https://doi.org/10.1787/idi-data-en*

Table 6. Foreign direct investment income by industrial sector

Million US dollars

	Inward					Outward				
	2016	2017	2018	2019	2020	2016	2017	2018	2019	2020
All FDI activities	**1 188.8**	**1 389.9**	**1 861.2**	**1 624.3**	**1 108.8**	**117.2**	**216.4**	**157.0**	**114.2**	**115.1**
Agriculture, forestry and fishing	-	12.4	7.1	3.4	10.3	-	-	-	-	-
Mining and quarrying	**12.2**	**16.9**	**14.2**	**17.9**	**20.5**	-	-	-	-	-
Extraction activities	12.2	16.9	14.2	17.9	20.5	-	-	-	-	-
Manufacturing *of which:*	**139.3**	**228.8**	**246.7**	**192.5**	**241.6**	**1.1**	**6.8**	**2.4**	**1.1**	**2.3**
Food products, beverages and tobacco	8.8	30.4	36.6	30.2	35.3	-	-	-	-	-
Textiles, wood and paper products; printing	97.3	143.2	151.1	87.3	112.8	1.1	1.1	.. c	2.2	.. c
Chemical, rubber, plastic, non-metallic mineral products	1.1	1.1	8.3	3.4	12.5	-	.. c	-	-	-
Metal and machinery products, except electrical equipment	5.5	7.9	11.8	4.5	17.1	-	-	-	-	-
Motor vehicles, trailers, semi-trailers, other transport equipment	13.3	13.5	11.8	10.1	3.4	-	-	-	-	-
Other manufacturing	13.3	32.7	28.3	56.0	61.5	-	-	-	-	.. c
Electricity, gas, steam and air conditioning supply	**54.2**	**39.5**	**31.9**	**28.0**	**19.4**	**.. c**	**.. c**	-	-	-
Water supply; sewerage, waste management and remediation activities	-	-	-	-	-	-	-	-	-	-
Construction	**-2.2**	**1.1**	**-7.1**	**5.6**	**9.1**	**-1.1**	-	-	-	-
Services	**883.6**	**901.8**	**1 172.0**	**1 013.1**	**585.8**	**106.2**	**163.5**	**142.8**	**106.3**	**116.2**
Wholesale and retail trade; repair of motor vehicles and motorcycles	219.0	250.3	395.4	315.7	199.4	26.5	28.2	18.9	16.8	33.0
Transportation and storage	29.9	55.2	31.9	35.8	16.0	-	1.1	1.2	-	-
Accommodation and food service activities	1.1	10.1	-3.5	-1.1	-19.4	-	-	-	-	-
Information and communication	44.2	83.4	108.6	129.9	87.7	-	-	8.3	10.1	.. c
Financial and insurance activities	503.2	405.8	522.8	459.0	286.0	79.6	128.5	115.7	78.4	70.7
Activities of holding companies	36.5	39.5	66.1	61.6	31.9	2.2	19.2	8.3	17.9	8.0
Real estate activities	31.0	39.5	83.8	52.6	-27.4	-3.3	-	-1.2	-	-
Professional, scientific and technical activities	15.5	9.0	-26.0	-38.1	33.0	4.4	4.5	4.7	2.2	1.1
Administrative and support service activities	-1.1	14.7	10.6	15.7	6.8	-	-	-	-	-
Public administration; activities of households and of extraterritorial organisations	-	-	-	-	-	-	-	-	-	-
Education	-	-	-	-1.1	-	-	-	-	-	-
Human health and social work activities	-	-	-	-	-	-	-	-	-	-
Arts, entertainment and recreation	39.8	34.9	48.4	44.8	4.6	.. c	-	.. c	-	-
Other services	-	-	-	-	-	-	-	-	-	-
Not allocated and confidential	**101.7**	**189.4**	**396.6**	**363.8**	**222.2**	**.. c**	**.. c**	**11.8**	**6.7**	**-3.4**
Private real estate activities	-	-	-	-	-	-	-	-	-	-

- Nil; c Confidential data

Note: Detailed metadata at: *http://metalinks.oecd.org/idi/20220712/6d95*.

Source: *OECD International Direct Investment Statistics (database): https://doi.org/10.1787/idi-data-en*

LITHUANIA

Table 1. Foreign direct investment flows by country

Million US dollars

	Inward					Outward				
	2016	2017	2018	2019	2020	2016	2017	2018	2019	2020
WORLD	**302.3**	**1 018.6**	**976.0**	**3 021.6**	**3 484.4**	**43.1**	**80.1**	**703.8**	**1 746.5**	**2 867.8**
OECD COUNTRIES	**-185.1**	**1 082.4**	**583.1**	**2 601.6**	**2 721.5**	**-95.4**	**-163.2**	**610.3**	**1 639.0**	**2 544.6**
Australia	-3.3	0.1	8.0	-31.0	20.3	-	-	.. c	-	-
Austria	31.4	-42.5	20.9	-2.4	62.1	.. c	.. d	0.2	.. d	.. d
Belgium	-47.9	9.3	.. d	10.2	16.1	.. d	.. d	1.5	0.8	.. d
Canada	-0.4	19.1	.. d	-297.6	7.4	.. c	.. d	0.1	.. d	.. d
Chile	.. d	.. d	-	-0.1	0.2	-	-	-	-	-
Colombia	.. c	.. c	.. c	.. d	.. d	-	-	-	-	-
Costa Rica	.. c	.. c	-	.. c	.. c	-	-	-	-	-
Czech Republic	-1.7	0.8	-6.3	0.5	6.5	0.6	4.9	0.6	-0.3	1.8
Denmark	46.2	52.7	59.2	82.9	30.7	-2.1	-1.1	-0.1	0.2	1.0
Estonia	23.5	172.2	128.9	1 350.4	-56.8	-34.1	185.3	121.0	220.5	232.5
Finland	68.7	-36.3	-57.9	89.6	5.9	0.4	0.4	-0.4	0.0	8.1
France	19.5	157.7	-77.8	159.2	-23.8	1.9	0.3	-1.3	1.6	2.4
Germany	-144.3	15.6	239.3	1 430.1	3 448.1	5.2	4.2	-1.5	4.4	9.6
Greece	1.3	.. d	-0.9	0.1	-0.3	1.1	1.0	0.5	1.5	2.0
Hungary	2.9	-4.3	4.8	-1.4	-5.2	-1.0	-2.6	-0.2	0.0	19.5
Iceland	2.0	1.5	-0.7	8.0	-5.6	.. d	.. c	-	-	-
Ireland	5.0	20.2	16.8	60.6	39.3	.. d	143.5	-94.3	.. d	-9.0
Israel	15.3	13.7	16.9	6.2	3.6	.. c	-	.. c	-	.. d
Italy	18.7	4.6	8.9	-1.9	7.5	1.6	1.3	1.4	14.9	4.7
Japan	-0.6	0.3	-0.6	-4.1	3.6	-	-	-	.. c	-
Korea	-0.2	-0.1	-0.4	.. d	-0.3	-	-	.. c	.. c	.. c
Latvia	6.4	20.4	5.8	26.4	18.8	53.4	49.7	157.9	94.3	183.3
Lithuania	-	-	-	-	-	-	-	-	-	-
Luxembourg	-69.0	-23.0	134.3	662.7	-226.0	.. c	.. c	11.9	.. d	.. d
Mexico	-0.2	.. d	.. d	.. d	.. d	-	-	-	0.5	-0.8
Netherlands	560.1	154.2	130.5	67.2	-271.1	-81.7	-10.6	-31.0	17.7	-899.2
New Zealand	.. c	.. d	0.0	-0.1	0.2	-	-	.. c	.. c	-
Norway	90.1	-627.1	55.9	19.0	52.6	-0.1	1.3	-0.7	0.6	-1.0
Poland	287.0	-60.3	101.3	63.5	-97.7	4.1	18.7	194.2	-215.7	63.0
Portugal	0.8	0.3	0.4	.. d	11.2	-	.. c	0.2	.. d	.. d
Slovak Republic	.. d	2.2	.. d	0.2	0.9	1.3	0.1	-0.5	0.2	1.0
Slovenia	-1.4	3.9	-2.3	-4.4	.. d	0.3	-0.1	0.2	-0.3	1.5
Spain	7.7	7.8	20.2	-1.2	0.7	4.1	-1.6	0.4	-3.8	17.4
Sweden	-610.0	1 101.9	163.7	-939.8	227.7	-1.4	-11.4	246.8	5.9	-15.6
Switzerland	-276.8	40.6	72.8	89.9	-42.6	.. d	.. d	-0.2	.. d	.. d
Turkey	-0.1	-0.2	0.3	-1.6	2.7	0.6	.. c	-1.8	.. d	.. d
United Kingdom	-258.7	5.9	-338.4	-257.9	-544.0	1.3	-5.3	-4.1	2.7	-3.5
United States	41.4	71.7	.. d	15.0	41.6	2.7	0.3	10.9	1 490.6	2 917.6
EUROPE	**-16.1**	**749.2**	**1 160.9**	**3 006.1**	**2 783.7**	**21.7**	**48.9**	**687.8**	**256.9**	**-64.9**
Bulgaria	1.1	-0.8	2.9	-0.4	-1.2	-1.3	-22.4	-4.1	-9.4	48.1
Croatia	.. d	.. d	-0.5	.. d	-2.5	0.6	0.4	0.5	1.1	2.0
Cyprus	228.7	184.4	67.6	0.8	39.5	93.3	165.6	98.3	-52.1	274.2
Malta	-28.6	-432.7	340.8	-6.5	24.2	0.1	.. c	-47.0	.. d	.. d
Montenegro	-	-	-	0.2	-	-	-	-	-	-
Romania	1.0	1.2	28.3	3.8	0.3	4.7	7.7	-2.7	-5.2	4.6
Russian Federation	44.1	-15.2	-7.7	18.9	39.8	26.0	-3.6	17.9	21.8	-8.8
Ukraine	-7.3	13.8	24.2	22.9	-8.2	-19.6	26.9	25.0	91.1	17.9
AFRICA	**-0.5**	**-4.8**	**1.9**	**-14.8**	**2.4**	**.. d**	**.. d**	**0.3**	**0.9**	**1.6**
Northern Africa	-2.0	-2.7	0.0	-0.1	-0.2	-	-	-	-	-
Algeria	-	-	-	0.0	.. c	-	-	-	-	-
Egypt	-2.0	-2.8	-	.. d	.. d	-	-	-	-	-
Libya	-	0.0	0.1	-	- d	-	-	-	-	-
Morocco	-	-	-	.. c	.. c	-	-	-	-	-
Tunisia	-	-	0.0	-	-	-	-	-	-	-
Other African countries	1.5	-2.0	1.9	-14.7	2.7	.. d	.. d	0.3	0.9	1.6
Nigeria	.. c	.. c	0.2	-	-	-	.. c	.. c	-	.. c
South Africa	.. d	.. d	-0.7	-0.5	-0.9	-	-	-	-	.. c
AMERICA	**44.1**	**89.5**	**-419.7**	**-312.0**	**236.4**	**2.8**	**-0.8**	**11.3**	**1 490.1**	**2 922.4**
Northern America	41.1	90.8	-130.1	-282.6	49.0	2.7	0.4	11.0	1 490.7	2 922.0
Central America and Caribbean countries	2.9	-1.6	-289.6	-29.4	186.5	.. d	.. c	.. d	-0.6	0.4
Bahamas	.. c	-	-	-	-	-	-	-	-	-
Bermuda	.. d	.. d	.. c	.. d	.. d	-	-	-	- d	-
Cayman Islands	.. d	.. d	-0.7	.. c	0.4	-	-	-	-	-
El Salvador	-	-	-	-	-	-	-	-	-	-
Guatemala	-	-	-	-	-	-	-	-	-	-
Honduras	-	-	-	-	-	-	-	-	-	-
Nicaragua	-	-	-	-	-	-	-	-	-	-
Panama	.. d	-5.4	-1.3	-0.3	-1.0	-	-	.. c	.. c	.. c
Virgin Islands, U.S.	.. c	-	-	-	-	-	-	-	-	-
South America	0.1	0.3	0.0	0.1	0.8	-	.. c	.. c	-	-
Argentina	-	-	0.0	.. c	0.0	-	-	-	-	-
Bolivia	-	-	-	-	-	-	-	-	-	-
Brazil	.. d	.. d	.. d	0.3	0.2	-	-	-	-	-
Ecuador	-	-	0.0	0.0	-	-	-	-	-	-
Paraguay	-	-	-	-	-	-	-	-	-	-
Peru	.. c	.. d	-	-	.. c	-	-	-	-	-
Uruguay	-	-	-	0.0	-	-	.. c	.. c	-	-
Venezuela	0.0	-	-	-	-	-	-	-	-	-

Table 1. Foreign direct investment flows by country *(cont.)*

Million US dollars

	Inward					Outward				
	2016	2017	2018	2019	2020	2016	2017	2018	2019	2020
ASIA	**.. d**	**171.3**	**174.0**	**367.3**	**420.7**	**18.7**	**32.4**	**.. d**	**.. d**	**8.7**
Near and Middle East	17.3	16.3	19.4	68.3	9.9	2.7	4.7	1.7	5.3	3.2
Gulf Arabian countries	-0.1	1.1	1.6	65.5	2.1	.. d	.. d	1.0	.. d	.. d
Kuwait	-	-	-	-	-	-	-	-	-	-
Qatar	-	-	-	0.0	0.0	-	-	-	-	-
Saudi Arabia	-	-	-	.. d	.. d	-	-	-	-	-
United Arab Emirates	0.3	0.9	1.6	.. d	2.0	.. d	.. c	-0.4	.. d	.. d
Other Near and Middle East	17.5	15.2	17.8	2.8	7.7	.. d	.. d	0.7	.. d	.. d
Jordan	-	-	-	-	-	-	-	-	-	-
Other Asian countries	.. d	155.0	154.6	299.0	410.9	16.1	27.7	.. d	.. d	5.5
China	2.3	2.9	-2.2	2.2	-3.6	.. d	20.8	0.9	.. d	1.8
Hong Kong, China	311.1	144.5	195.3	254.6	453.5	-	-	.. d	.. d	.. c
India	0.0	-0.2	-0.6	11.8	-21.2	-	-	-	-	-
Indonesia	-	-	0.0	.. d	.. d	.. c	.. c	.. c	.. c	.. c
Iran, Islamic Republic of	-0.1	0.1	0.0	-	-	-	-	-	-	-
Malaysia	.. d	.. c	.. d	.. d	-5.8	-	-	-	-	-
Philippines	.. c	-0.1	0.1	-0.1	0.1	-	-	-	.. c	.. c
Singapore	-2.1	0.6	-28.6	35.5	-0.8	-	0.7	0.1	-	0.4
Chinese Taipei	0.0	0.1	-0.2	0.5	-0.1	-	-	-	-	-
Thailand	-61.1	4.8	.. d	.. d	-11.6	.. c	-	.. c	-	-0.5
Viet Nam	0.1	-	-	.. d	.. d	-	-	-	-	.. c
AUSTRALIA, OCEANIA AND POLAR REGIONS	**.. d**	**0.0**	**8.0**	**-31.2**	**20.5**	**-**	**-**	**.. c**	**.. c**	**-**
WORLD unallocated and confidential	**.. d**	**13.4**	**50.9**	**6.2**	**20.7**	**- d**	**- d**	**.. d**	**- d**	**0.0**
European Union (since 01/02/2020)	**..**	**..**	**..**	**..**	**..**	**..**	**..**	**..**	**..**	**..**
G20 countries excl. European Union	**-281.9**	**261.7**	**-302.2**	**1 049.3**	**2 975.0**	**55.5**	**21.7**	**23.7**	**1 527.7**	**2 930.3**
G20 OECD countries	**-328.2**	**274.4**	**-291.1**	**1 012.8**	**2 963.4**	**13.3**	**1.0**	**3.9**	**1 515.1**	**2 936.8**
G20 Non-OECD countries	**46.4**	**-12.7**	**-11.1**	**36.5**	**11.6**	**42.2**	**20.6**	**19.8**	**12.6**	**-6.5**
MENA countries	**-2.4**	**-1.9**	**1.6**	**65.4**	**1.9**	**.. d**	**.. d**	**.. d**	**.. d**	**.. d**
ASEAN countries	**-63.1**	**5.2**	**-36.7**	**33.1**	**-20.6**	**.. c**	**3.9**	**0.5**	**.. d**	**0.3**

- Nil; .. Not available; c Confidential data; d Secondary Confidentiality

Note: Detailed metadata at: *http://metalinks.oecd.org/idi/20220712/6d95*.

Source: *OECD International Direct Investment Statistics (database)*: *https://doi.org/10.1787/idi-data-en*

Table 2. Foreign direct investment positions by country

At year end

Million US dollars

	Inward					Outward				
	2016	2017	2018	2019	2020	2016	2017	2018	2019	2020
WORLD	**16 171.1**	**19 621.7**	**19 417.6**	**23 243.5**	**29 375.5**	**3 713.7**	**4 330.1**	**4 835.7**	**7 077.8**	**10 587.5**
OECD COUNTRIES	**13 645.5**	**15 509.2**	**16 230.8**	**19 790.0**	**25 549.0**	**2 822.2**	**3 077.7**	**3 553.6**	**5 690.5**	**8 824.2**
Australia	.. d	.. d	.. d	9.4	10.8	-	-	.. c	.. c	.. c
Austria	138.7	176.0	175.0	213.3	311.8	0.1	0.7	0.9	0.8	1.0
Belgium	278.2	365.1	278.0	120.0	149.6	1.3	4.5	6.2	6.8	9.4
Canada	.. d	465.5	377.0	151.9	211.6	0.6	0.8	.. d	0.9	5.8
Chile	0.0	0.1	0.0	0.0	0.1	-	-	-	-	-
Colombia	0.1	0.1	0.1	0.1	0.2	-	-	-	-	-
Costa Rica	-	-	-	-	-	-	-	-	-	-
Czech Republic	12.6	14.5	7.8	17.5	18.8	2.8	7.2	6.1	6.1	7.7
Denmark	808.4	911.9	914.2	933.9	1 089.4	1.4	2.0	-0.4	1.6	3.0
Estonia	859.7	1 087.3	1 063.1	1 135.0	1 216.1	406.3	665.0	764.6	986.2	1 309.2
Finland	570.8	689.4	626.2	778.4	900.7	3.2	5.0	4.5	5.5	15.7
France	441.0	476.0	460.6	673.8	686.2	9.4	11.4	10.0	34.1	40.9
Germany	1 090.2	1 324.1	1 299.2	1 624.7	1 960.1	12.3	22.9	21.5	28.1	36.2
Greece	0.7	1.1	1.1	3.6	2.3	6.3	8.3	8.4	10.3	14.1
Hungary	5.9	5.6	5.4	5.8	11.9	20.0	20.1	21.2	20.9	42.4
Iceland	38.1	44.0	32.9	38.1	48.1	0.2	0.3	0.3	0.1	0.2
Ireland	43.4	52.8	57.1	101.6	92.2	-49.4	96.5	0.6	1.6	-29.7
Israel	42.8	163.8	-180.5	-75.5	-106.2	.. c	.. c	.. d	-0.8	-0.5
Italy	43.6	61.5	63.9	63.3	78.5	9.2	12.2	13.1	30.2	38.8
Japan	23.2	19.8	21.4	18.4	20.5	.. c	.. c	.. c	.. c	-
Korea	0.1	0.1	-	0.5	0.6	-	-	.. c	.. c	.. c
Latvia	204.9	315.7	291.8	356.2	347.5	689.8	876.1	1 001.3	1 114.7	1 421.5
Lithuania	467.7	645.8	1 010.6	1 273.7	1 503.7	-	-	-	-	-
Luxembourg	144.9	179.1	189.1	616.1	692.5	511.5	-1.2	10.4	22.1	24.0
Mexico	.. d	.. d	.. d	.. d	.. d	-	-	-	0.6	0.2
Netherlands	929.5	1 261.3	1 442.0	1 290.8	1 174.1	766.2	852.9	808.0	1 264.5	372.4
New Zealand	.. d	.. d	.. d	.. d	.. d	-	-	.. c	-	-
Norway	1 047.5	469.4	443.4	483.6	504.8	4.3	7.0	6.0	6.6	4.8
Poland	696.6	873.4	965.5	874.5	964.2	323.2	382.3	549.4	309.5	398.2
Portugal	.. d	.. d	.. d	11.1	24.7	0.2	0.3	0.4	7.4	8.3
Slovak Republic	.. d	11.6	10.0	10.8	14.6	9.4	9.8	8.8	15.4	10.8
Slovenia	0.8	.. d	23.4	13.9	.. d	0.9	0.9	1.1	0.7	11.6
Spain	69.0	82.0	74.3	90.5	91.7	8.3	7.9	8.5	5.1	37.6
Sweden	3 124.1	3 360.4	3 368.8	3 694.0	4 614.4	38.6	36.0	250.8	255.4	212.5
Switzerland	426.9	429.1	439.9	604.1	643.0	0.7	1.1	0.9	1.0	1.8
Turkey	1.0	1.2	0.9	1.4	3.3	2.2	.. c	.. d	2.2	4.2
United Kingdom	1 501.6	1 648.8	1 983.2	2 156.6	2 397.8	34.6	31.7	26.7	31.1	17.6
United States	716.7	991.0	743.2	2 483.7	5 850.4	8.9	13.7	.. d	1 521.1	4 803.1
EUROPE	**14 354.0**	**17 139.4**	**17 510.7**	**19 914.7**	**22 266.0**	**3 692.2**	**4 268.0**	**4 760.7**	**5 502.0**	**5 701.8**
Bulgaria	3.9	1.0	1.8	2.2	2.6	89.7	78.2	74.1	73.2	126.7
Croatia	0.1	0.2	0.2	0.3	0.2	4.8	5.9	6.0	7.2	9.9
Cyprus	509.1	470.4	277.8	420.9	320.9	435.2	660.3	748.0	688.3	987.1
Malta	27.0	26.2	32.8	28.2	11.8	0.1	0.1	-45.3	1.0	1.9
Montenegro	0.1	0.1	0.0	0.2	0.3	-	-	-	-	-
Romania	0.8	1.8	2.3	7.3	8.6	19.2	31.8	20.0	14.7	14.4
Russian Federation	392.9	476.1	355.2	473.8	539.7	145.2	146.0	153.2	167.2	140.5
Ukraine	236.7	303.4	273.3	304.8	258.1	54.4	102.1	101.2	192.1	227.4
AFRICA	**16.2**	**.. d**	**.. d**	**3.3**	**.. d**	**0.3**	**-0.1**	**0.0**	**1.6**	**2.5**
Northern Africa	1.0	0.7	0.3	.. d	.. d	-	-	-	-	-
Algeria	-	-	-	0.0	0.1	-	-	-	-	-
Egypt	1.0	0.7	0.2	.. d	.. d	-	-	-	-	-
Libya	-	0.0	0.1	0.1	0.1	-	-	-	-	-
Morocco	-	-	-	-	-	-	-	-	-	-
Tunisia	0.0	0.0	-	-	-	-	-	-	-	-
Other African countries	15.2	.. d	.. d	.. d	4.8	0.3	-0.1	0.0	1.6	2.5
Nigeria	-	0.0	0.2	0.4	0.9	-	.. c	.. c	.. c	.. c
South Africa	.. d	.. d	.. d	0.2	.. d	-	-	-	.. c	.. c
AMERICA	**1 500.2**	**.. d**	**1 611.9**	**3 138.1**	**6 759.5**	**10.5**	**16.7**	**27.2**	**1 523.6**	**4 811.8**
Northern America	.. d	1 456.5	1 120.2	2 635.6	6 062.0	9.5	14.5	25.0	1 522.0	4 809.0
Central America and Caribbean countries	423.9	503.3	490.9	501.4	695.8	0.9	.. d	2.2	1.6	2.8
Bahamas	0.5	.. c	.. c	.. c	.. c	-	-	-	-	-
Bermuda	.. c	.. c	.. c	.. c	.. c	-	-	-	-	- d
Cayman Islands	331.8	.. c	.. c	.. c	.. d	-	-	-	-	-
El Salvador	0.1	0.1	0.0	0.0	0.0	-	-	-	-	-
Guatemala	-	-	-	-	-	-	-	-	-	-
Honduras	0.0	0.0	0.0	0.0	0.0	-	-	-	-	-
Nicaragua	-	-	-	-	-	-	-	-	-	-
Panama	.. d	.. d	.. d	.. d	.. d	.. c	.. c	.. c	.. c	.. c
Virgin Islands, U.S.	-	-	-	-	-	-	-	-	-	-
South America	.. d	.. d	0.8	1.1	1.8	-	.. c	-	-	-
Argentina	.. d	.. d	.. d	0.1	0.1	-	-	-	-	-
Bolivia	-	-	-	0.0	0.0	-	-	-	-	-
Brazil	0.2	0.2	.. d	0.9	1.2	-	-	-	-	-
Ecuador	-	-	-	-	-	-	-	-	-	-
Paraguay	-	-	-	-	-	-	-	-	-	-
Peru	0.1	0.1	0.0	0.0	0.0	-	-	-	-	-
Uruguay	-	-	-	-	-	-	.. c	-	-	-
Venezuela	-	-	-	-	-	-	-	-	-	-

Table 2. Foreign direct investment positions by country *(cont.)*

At year end

Million US dollars

	Inward					Outward				
	2016	2017	2018	2019	2020	2016	2017	2018	2019	2020
ASIA	**205.7**	**379.7**	**155.9**	**83.0**	**232.1**	**10.8**	**45.6**	**.. d**	**.. d**	**.. d**
Near and Middle East	58.9	183.6	-161.3	-52.8	63.8	9.9	15.2	16.1	21.2	27.5
Gulf Arabian countries	7.7	9.2	8.8	13.3	157.6	8.5	12.0	11.6	16.4	22.3
Kuwait	-	-	-	-	-	-	-	-	-	-
Qatar	-	-	-	0.1	0.0	-	-	-	-	-
Saudi Arabia	.. d	.. d	.. d	.. d	.. d	-	-	-	- d	- d
United Arab Emirates	.. d	.. d	5.6	.. d	.. d	8.5	12.0	11.2	13.9	17.0
Other Near and Middle East	51.1	174.4	-170.1	-66.0	-93.8	1.4	3.1	4.6	4.8	5.2
Jordan	0.1	0.1	.. d	0.4	.. d	-	-	-	-	-
Other Asian countries	146.9	196.2	317.2	135.8	168.3	0.9	30.5	.. d	.. d	.. d
China	21.7	40.5	47.3	30.1	34.7	25.9	52.1	50.6	43.5	48.5
Hong Kong, China	8.7	15.4	132.0	1.2	3.6	.. c	.. c	.. d	1.7	4.9
India	.. d	4.2	5.9	7.4	-2.1	-	-	-	-	-
Indonesia	-	.. c	.. c	10.8	14.7	.. c	.. c	.. c	.. c	.. c
Iran, Islamic Republic of	.. d	.. d	.. d	0.5	.. d	-	-	-	-	-
Malaysia	.. d	.. d	0.1	0.0	.. d	-	-	-	-	-
Philippines	-	-	-	0.0	0.0	-	-	-	.. c	.. c
Singapore	2.3	5.3	12.9	-16.0	17.7	.. c	-0.1	-0.1	-0.1	0.2
Chinese Taipei	0.1	0.1	.. d	.. d	.. d	-	-	-	-	-
Thailand	77.1	.. d	.. d	.. d	.. d	.. c	-28.4	.. d	-26.6	-29.6
Viet Nam	0.1	0.2	0.2	0.2	0.3	-	-	-	-	.. c
AUSTRALIA, OCEANIA AND POLAR REGIONS	**5.5**	**4.5**	**.. d**	**9.6**	**.. d**	**-**	**-**	**.. c**	**.. c**	**.. c**
WORLD unallocated and confidential	**89.5**	**.. d**	**.. d**	**94.8**	**.. d**	**-**	**-**	**- d**	**- d**	**- d**
European Union (since 01/02/2020)	**..**	**..**	**..**	**..**	**16 289.8**	**..**	**..**	**..**	**..**	**5 125.8**
G20 countries excl. European Union	**4 616.3**	**5 536.6**	**5 405.7**	**7 726.1**	**11 830.6**	**248.6**	**297.4**	**305.8**	**1 864.9**	**5 148.2**
G20 OECD countries	**4 193.0**	**5 006.6**	**4 983.6**	**7 199.0**	**11 237.6**	**77.3**	**95.3**	**97.3**	**1 648.8**	**4 948.1**
G20 Non-OECD countries	**423.3**	**530.0**	**422.1**	**527.1**	**593.0**	**171.4**	**202.1**	**208.6**	**216.0**	**200.1**
MENA countries	**10.5**	**12.1**	**12.1**	**15.5**	**161.5**	**8.5**	**12.0**	**11.6**	**16.4**	**22.3**
ASEAN countries	**79.6**	**103.2**	**101.4**	**67.5**	**99.3**	**-26.1**	**-24.6**	**-23.1**	**-21.8**	**-17.9**

- Nil; .. Not available; c Confidential data; d Secondary Confidentiality

Note: Inward FDI positions are allocated according to the ultimate investing country. Detailed metadata at: *http://metalinks.oecd.org/idi/20220712/6d95*.

Source: *OECD International Direct Investment Statistics (database): https://doi.org/10.1787/idi-data-en*

LITHUANIA

Table 3. Foreign direct investment income by country

Million US dollars

	Inward					Outward				
	2016	2017	2018	2019	2020	2016	2017	2018	2019	2020
WORLD	**1 678.3**	**1 944.2**	**2 193.0**	**2 317.9**	**2 229.2**	**145.9**	**165.7**	**303.1**	**229.8**	**319.4**
OECD COUNTRIES	**1 453.8**	**1 679.9**	**1 796.8**	**1 837.5**	**1 563.4**	**117.7**	**169.4**	**211.5**	**183.6**	**299.5**
Australia	-	0.1	0.1	-3.6	0.0	-	-	-	-	-
Austria	8.0	4.7	7.0	9.2	12.6	-	-	-	-0.1	0.2
Belgium	6.9	20.8	26.5	24.8	24.1	-1.2	3.9	1.2	2.0	2.6
Canada	4.8	-4.8	6.1	0.7	-10.9	0.0	0.0	-	-	-
Chile	-	-	-	-	-	-	-	-	-	-
Colombia	-	-	-	-	-	-	-	-	-	-
Costa Rica	-	-	-	-	-	-	-	-	-	-
Czech Republic	0.5	2.7	-2.6	0.7	7.1	0.7	4.6	4.9	0.0	1.9
Denmark	17.0	62.3	70.9	91.5	75.2	0.3	1.8	0.2	0.3	-1.1
Estonia	90.2	113.0	161.1	248.0	187.3	70.7	98.1	95.2	61.2	93.3
Finland	59.2	38.2	60.5	117.0	81.2	0.2	0.1	-0.4	0.2	0.0
France	20.2	58.1	45.1	59.5	8.1	2.3	1.3	1.6	3.5	4.4
Germany	82.6	113.0	130.1	156.2	167.2	1.2	1.1	0.6	1.3	9.0
Greece	-	.. c	.. c	0.0	0.0	0.3	0.1	0.4	-0.1	1.1
Hungary	0.9	1.2	1.4	1.2	2.6	-0.4	-2.5	2.8	0.3	19.6
Iceland	0.8	2.2	1.4	2.4	4.5	-	0.0	-	-	-
Ireland	4.1	4.0	-9.4	14.6	17.0	0.2	-0.2	-0.4	0.2	-1.7
Israel	2.7	1.8	.. d	4.4	2.9	-	-	0.0	-	0.1
Italy	3.7	4.6	3.8	3.5	3.8	0.0	-0.3	-	0.2	1.7
Japan	-	-	-	-	-	-	-	-	-	-
Korea	-	-	-	.. c	0.0	-	-	.. c	.. c	.. c
Latvia	51.2	53.0	42.4	38.8	59.6	19.9	27.7	65.0	58.4	108.8
Lithuania	-	-	-	-	-	-	-	-	-	-
Luxembourg	12.4	48.9	71.1	-23.5	91.6	.. c	0.0	0.8	6.0	4.0
Mexico	-	.. c	-	-	-	-	-	-	-0.2	0.1
Netherlands	213.4	248.2	260.2	290.7	250.7	19.0	28.4	31.0	9.0	11.1
New Zealand	-	-	-	-	-	-	-	-	-	-
Norway	61.1	93.2	80.1	72.4	71.9	0.4	0.3	-0.2	1.3	1.9
Poland	305.1	288.2	120.6	142.1	-144.1	-6.1	4.6	5.7	33.8	26.5
Portugal	0.5	0.1	0.1	0.0	-0.7	0.0	0.1	-	0.1	0.1
Slovak Republic	.. c	1.3	.. d	1.2	1.2	1.3	1.1	0.4	0.3	-0.3
Slovenia	1.9	1.8	-2.5	0.2	.. c	0.1	0.0	0.1	0.3	1.8
Spain	1.9	0.9	-2.5	9.8	1.3	0.2	-0.5	0.0	-0.3	-0.7
Sweden	401.8	396.4	518.8	449.6	447.5	0.8	-0.9	4.2	2.1	10.3
Switzerland	40.2	61.5	123.1	93.8	135.4	-	-	0.0	0.0	-
Turkey	-0.4	-0.3	-	0.1	0.1	0.6	.. c	-1.6	0.9	2.2
United Kingdom	19.4	26.2	42.3	-5.8	10.4	5.3	0.6	-0.9	1.4	1.2
United States	42.1	38.6	39.0	38.1	55.7	-1.2	-0.5	.. d	1.4	1.2
EUROPE	**1 560.5**	**1 786.5**	**1 935.0**	**1 984.6**	**1 713.3**	**147.2**	**165.6**	**301.0**	**224.3**	**313.0**
Bulgaria	-0.2	0.3	0.2	-0.1	0.1	6.2	0.1	3.6	-9.6	3.1
Croatia	.. c	.. c	.. c	.. c	-	0.1	-	0.0	0.4	0.7
Cyprus	85.7	70.9	94.2	111.6	101.3	-2.9	3.1	48.8	3.2	-15.2
Malta	17.7	11.0	8.6	1.9	1.2	-	.. c	-0.2	-0.2	-
Montenegro	-	-	-	-	-	-	-	-	-	-
Romania	-	.. c	.. c	0.0	0.1	1.4	-0.4	1.5	1.8	5.0
Russian Federation	16.3	6.3	13.6	20.7	47.1	14.4	-12.3	8.5	25.3	0.5
Ukraine	3.1	14.5	16.1	2.0	-14.0	1.8	-2.7	5.4	8.9	19.2
AFRICA	**1.8**	**-1.4**	**2.4**	**1.2**	**0.1**	**0.1**	**0.1**	**0.4**	**0.8**	**1.5**
Northern Africa	0.0	0.0	-	-	0.0	-	-	-	-	-
Algeria	-	-	-	-	.. c	-	-	-	-	-
Egypt	0.0	0.0	-	-	-	-	-	-	-	-
Libya	-	-	-	-	- d	-	-	-	-	-
Morocco	-	-	-	-	-	-	-	-	-	-
Tunisia	-	-	-	-	-	-	-	-	-	-
Other African countries	1.8	-1.4	2.4	1.2	0.0	0.1	0.1	0.4	0.8	1.5
Nigeria	-	-	-	-	-	-	-	-	-	-
South Africa	.. c	-	-	-	-	-	-	-	-	.. c
AMERICA	**45.4**	**33.4**	**43.6**	**38.5**	**44.5**	**-1.2**	**-1.5**	**0.9**	**1.2**	**1.3**
Northern America	46.9	33.8	45.1	38.9	44.8	-1.2	-0.5	0.9	1.4	1.2
Central America and Caribbean countries	-1.5	-0.4	-1.5	-0.4	-0.2	0.0	.. d	0.1	-0.2	0.0
Bahamas	-0.5	-	-	-	-	-	-	-	-	-
Bermuda	.. c	.. c	.. c	.. c	.. c	-	-	-	-	-
Cayman Islands	.. c	.. c	.. c	-	-	-	-	-	-	-
El Salvador	-	-	-	-	-	-	-	-	-	-
Guatemala	-	-	-	-	-	-	-	-	-	-
Honduras	-	-	-	-	-	-	-	-	-	-
Nicaragua	-	-	-	-	-	-	-	-	-	-
Panama	0.0	-1.1	-1.3	-0.3	-0.3	.. c	.. c	.. c	.. c	.. c
Virgin Islands, U.S.	-	-	-	-	-	-	-	-	-	-
South America	-	-	-	-	-	-	.. c	-	-	-
Argentina	-	-	-	-	-	-	-	-	-	-
Bolivia	-	-	-	-	-	-	-	-	-	-
Brazil	-	-	-	-	-	-	-	-	-	-
Ecuador	-	-	-	-	-	-	-	-	-	-
Paraguay	-	-	-	-	-	-	-	-	-	-
Peru	-	-	-	-	-	-	-	-	-	-
Uruguay	-	-	-	-	-	-	.. c	-	-	-
Venezuela	-	-	-	-	-	-	-	-	-	-

Table 3. Foreign direct investment income by country *(cont.)*

Million US dollars

	Inward					Outward				
	2016	2017	2018	2019	2020	2016	2017	2018	2019	2020
ASIA	**64.4**	**119.2**	**198.8**	**285.7**	**450.6**	**-0.2**	**1.5**	**0.7**	**3.4**	**3.6**
Near and Middle East	2.8	2.5	1.9	5.5	4.5	0.1	1.1	1.6	2.4	3.6
Gulf Arabian countries	0.3	0.1	-0.1	0.8	1.1	0.6	1.1	1.8	2.0	4.5
Kuwait	-	-	-	-	-	-	-	-	-	-
Qatar	-	-	-	-	-	-	-	-	-	-
Saudi Arabia	-	-	-	.. c	-	-	-	-	- d	- d
United Arab Emirates	0.3	0.1	.. d	.. d	1.1	0.3	0.4	.. d	0.4	0.6
Other Near and Middle East	2.5	2.4	2.0	4.7	3.5	-0.4	-	-0.2	0.4	-0.9
Jordan	-	-	-	-	-	-	-	-	-	-
Other Asian countries	61.6	116.6	196.9	280.2	446.1	-0.3	0.4	-0.9	1.0	0.1
China	0.4	0.5	-0.5	0.3	0.3	0.1	-0.5	-0.2	1.3	-0.1
Hong Kong, China	45.1	102.8	172.0	264.5	444.8	-	-	-	0.1	.. c
India	-0.6	0.0	0.3	0.3	-	-	-	-	-	-
Indonesia	-	-	-	-	.. c	-	.. c	.. c	.. c	.. c
Iran, Islamic Republic of	0.0	0.0	0.0	-0.1	-	-	-	-	-	-
Malaysia	-	-	-	.. c	-	-	-	-	-	-
Philippines	-	-	-	-	-	-	-	-	-	-
Singapore	-3.8	4.4	-1.0	5.9	2.3	.. c	0.7	0.1	0.0	0.3
Chinese Taipei	-	-	-	-	-	-	-	-	-	-
Thailand	18.0	9.8	26.2	9.9	-1.8	.. c	-1.0	.. c	-1.0	-1.0
Viet Nam	-	-	-	.. c	.. c	-	-	-	-	.. c
AUSTRALIA, OCEANIA AND POLAR REGIONS	**0.0**	**0.0**	**0.1**	**-3.7**	**0.0**	-	-	-	-	-
WORLD unallocated and confidential	**6.1**	**6.6**	**13.0**	**11.6**	**20.7**	-	**0.0**	-	-	**0.0**
European Union (since 01/02/2020)	..	..	..	..	..	..	..	..	..	..
G20 countries excl. European Union	**188.6**	**242.4**	**279.9**	**270.0**	**281.9**	**22.6**	**-10.1**	**9.0**	**35.3**	**20.5**
G20 OECD countries	**172.4**	**235.6**	**266.5**	**248.6**	**234.4**	**8.2**	**2.7**	**0.6**	**8.7**	**19.8**
G20 Non-OECD countries	**16.2**	**6.8**	**13.5**	**21.4**	**47.6**	**14.5**	**-12.7**	**8.4**	**26.6**	**0.6**
MENA countries	**0.1**	**-0.2**	**-0.2**	**0.8**	**1.1**	**0.6**	**1.1**	**1.8**	**2.0**	**4.5**
ASEAN countries	**14.2**	**14.3**	**25.2**	**15.7**	**0.8**	**-1.1**	**-0.5**	**-0.9**	**-1.0**	**-0.2**

- Nil; .. Not available; c Confidential data; d Secondary Confidentiality

Note: Detailed metadata at: *http://metalinks.oecd.org/idi/20220712/6d95*.

Source: *OECD International Direct Investment Statistics (database): https://doi.org/10.1787/idi-data-en*

Table 4. Foreign direct investment flows by industrial sector

Million US dollars

	Inward					Outward				
	2016	2017	2018	2019	2020	2016	2017	2018	2019	2020
All FDI activities	**302.3**	**1 018.6**	**976.0**	**3 021.6**	**3 484.4**	**43.1**	**80.1**	**703.8**	**1 746.5**	**2 867.8**
Agriculture, forestry and fishing	**65.6**	**61.9**	**-17.2**	**63.3**	**7.7**	**.. d**	**.. d**	**3.1**	**.. d**	**6.7**
Mining and quarrying	**-8.3**	**-13.1**	**1.4**	**29.8**	**-25.0**	**.. d**	**.. d**	**0.8**	**0.0**	**0.8**
Extraction activities	.. c	.. c	.. c	.. c	.. c	-	-	-	-	-
Manufacturing	**-494.7**	**529.4**	**4.2**	**328.8**	**-109.9**	**-36.7**	**1.2**	**21.2**	**-257.5**	**21.5**
of which:										
Food products, beverages and tobacco	-102.9	69.1	34.3	41.0	19.8	4.2	6.7	4.5	21.0	4.8
Textiles, wood and paper products; printing	-53.1	82.4	58.9	-21.8	-2.0	0.3	-5.1	-1.7	-0.1	-3.1
Chemical, rubber, plastic, non-metallic mineral products	-356.0	266.1	-220.7	138.1	-225.8	-51.9	-0.9	16.1	-278.7	22.3
Metal and machinery products, except electrical equipment	35.6	51.1	1.5	34.6	-10.0	5.6	6.9	-0.8	-0.8	0.2
Motor vehicles, trailers, semi-trailers, other transport equipment	-95.0	3.0	119.2	40.6	49.5	.. d	.. c	0.0	0.4	-1.0
Other manufacturing	76.8	57.7	11.0	96.3	58.7	.. d	.. d	3.0	0.7	-1.6
Electricity, gas, steam and air conditioning supply	**-7.6**	**11.9**	**.. d**	**.. d**	**-8.3**	**.. d**	**.. d**	**.. d**	**11.9**	**.. d**
Water supply; sewerage, waste management and remediation activities	**-8.5**	**7.5**	**.. d**	**.. d**	**3.6**	**.. d**	**.. d**	**.. d**	**.. d**	**.. d**
Construction	**-19.6**	**24.9**	**-151.8**	**39.7**	**29.3**	**33.0**	**7.3**	**5.9**	**12.4**	**17.8**
Services	**748.4**	**371.0**	**1 083.8**	**2 347.8**	**3 537.9**	**50.7**	**75.2**	**658.2**	**1 975.7**	**2 822.8**
Wholesale and retail trade; repair of motor vehicles and motorcycles	208.6	141.7	204.2	141.6	84.1	67.2	74.2	304.2	61.2	234.0
Transportation and storage	24.1	17.3	49.8	93.7	-3.3	7.0	39.1	56.6	16.6	26.4
Accommodation and food service activities	-9.3	14.2	-9.8	4.9	9.2	1.2	-2.5	1.9	-0.4	-2.4
Information and communication	51.9	7.7	26.2	52.6	17.7	8.9	-3.7	24.0	28.7	22.3
Financial and insurance activities	269.5	-100.7	149.5	1 634.0	3 491.7	29.5	57.0	-201.9	37.8	243.0
Activities of holding companies	.. d	-327.8	-45.3	1 653.2	3 137.6	43.6	-8.0	87.0	38.5	-65.3
Real estate activities	76.8	90.6	100.4	349.2	-210.5	-60.0	44.3	21.6	51.4	38.5
Professional, scientific and technical activities	107.8	191.2	520.3	23.8	127.9	-57.7	-161.7	473.8	1 736.8	2 221.5
Administrative and support service activities	15.9	1.0	44.5	49.5	14.0	39.4	26.1	-18.3	42.4	35.5
Public administration; activities of households and of extraterritorial organisations	-	-	-	- d	-	-	-	-	- d	- d
Education	-0.1	-0.2	0.1	.. d	1.0	.. d	1.6	-3.5	0.9	0.8
Human health and social work activities	-0.5	5.5	3.2	2.7	4.0	.. d	0.2	0.0	0.2	0.3
Arts, entertainment and recreation	2.7	2.7	-5.3	-4.0	0.9	.. d	0.7	.. d	.. d	3.0
Other services	1.0	-0.1	0.8	0.0	1.1	.. d	.. d	-0.5	.. d	.. d
Not allocated and confidential	**0.0**	**0.0**	**- d**	**- d**	**0.0**	**- d**	**- d**	**.. d**	**- d**	**.. d**
Private real estate activities	**27.0**	**25.1**	**47.9**	**69.3**	**49.1**	**2.4**	**3.7**	**-0.1**	**2.1**	**0.6**

- Nil; .. Not available; c Confidential data; d Secondary Confidentiality

Note: Detailed metadata at: *http://metalinks.oecd.org/idi/20220712/6d95.*

Source: *OECD International Direct Investment Statistics (database): https://doi.org/10.1787/idi-data-en*

LITHUANIA

Table 5. Foreign direct investment positions by industrial sector

At year end

Million US dollars

	Inward					Outward				
	2016	2017	2018	2019	2020	2016	2017	2018	2019	2020
All FDI activities	**16 171.1**	**19 621.7**	**19 417.6**	**23 243.5**	**29 375.5**	**3 713.7**	**4 330.1**	**4 835.7**	**7 077.8**	**10 587.5**
Agriculture, forestry and fishing	**264.4**	**368.1**	**339.1**	**404.7**	**456.5**	**28.5**	**32.3**	**34.1**	**36.3**	**47.1**
Mining and quarrying	**65.5**	**63.9**	**60.6**	**89.9**	**70.5**	**0.1**	**0.1**	**0.2**	**0.2**	**0.6**
Extraction activities	.. c	.. c	.. c	.. c	.. c	-	-	-	-	-
Manufacturing	**2 599.0**	**3 513.4**	**3 408.1**	**3 788.0**	**3 934.5**	**426.8**	**462.5**	**468.5**	**214.5**	**183.4**
of which:										
Food products, beverages and tobacco	520.1	654.3	639.8	738.5	817.2	29.1	27.2	44.6	70.0	77.6
Textiles, wood and paper products; printing	382.4	530.1	572.0	530.6	561.3	20.9	17.6	19.5	23.5	23.4
Chemical, rubber, plastic, non-metallic mineral products	980.1	1 377.2	1 086.8	1 208.1	1 024.9	328.6	358.0	341.0	58.5	41.0
Metal and machinery products, except electrical equipment	188.4	278.2	359.4	393.4	428.8	21.5	29.3	28.9	28.6	34.5
Motor vehicles, trailers, semi-trailers, other transport equipment	107.5	126.3	221.8	236.0	305.4	.. c	9.3	9.0	8.7	5.1
Other manufacturing	420.6	547.2	528.4	681.5	796.9	.. d	21.1	25.6	25.2	1.8
Electricity, gas, steam and air conditioning supply	**318.5**	**369.2**	**303.8**	**463.6**	**511.1**	**2.7**	**1.5**	**23.8**	**41.6**	**42.5**
Water supply; sewerage, waste management and remediation activities	**3.9**	**14.0**	**11.4**	**12.8**	**15.5**	**0.2**	**-2.2**	**-2.5**	**-1.1**	**-5.6**
Construction	**405.4**	**520.2**	**336.1**	**386.7**	**575.2**	**79.8**	**86.8**	**87.4**	**90.3**	**166.5**
Services	**12 126.5**	**14 288.1**	**14 525.3**	**17 420.2**	**23 020.6**	**3 081.0**	**3 637.6**	**4 118.0**	**6 539.8**	**9 980.0**
Wholesale and retail trade; repair of motor vehicles and motorcycles	1 981.1	2 366.6	2 325.2	2 611.1	2 915.5	642.8	833.2	1 088.0	1 172.3	1 457.5
Transportation and storage	417.0	465.5	459.5	589.9	653.3	32.7	87.5	134.4	136.6	183.5
Accommodation and food service activities	63.0	89.9	143.0	161.4	188.2	4.8	4.6	7.5	22.0	23.2
Information and communication	1 141.0	1 294.2	1 339.7	1 477.0	2 076.6	102.9	96.9	120.4	165.0	190.0
Financial and insurance activities	4 754.4	5 748.0	5 445.6	7 280.5	11 690.3	975.0	1 228.3	953.6	972.7	1 315.6
Activities of holding companies	1 217.0	1 410.9	1 324.0	2 944.3	6 612.9	296.3	378.0	435.6	458.6	411.9
Real estate activities	2 089.6	2 560.1	2 442.1	2 939.3	3 014.7	216.5	254.6	260.9	334.2	383.8
Professional, scientific and technical activities	1 072.1	1 394.4	1 928.5	1 873.9	1 910.2	966.4	961.1	1 416.0	3 550.6	6 198.0
Administrative and support service activities	556.6	295.4	378.4	406.8	469.4	120.8	147.1	119.8	165.2	198.8
Public administration; activities of households and of extraterritorial organisations	-	-	-	-	-	-	-	-	-	-
Education	0.8	1.1	1.2	1.4	8.1	14.4	17.8	12.0	14.1	17.2
Human health and social work activities	24.3	44.0	40.5	57.9	67.1	0.5	0.9	0.9	1.2	1.4
Arts, entertainment and recreation	23.0	25.6	18.4	17.6	21.0	3.7	5.3	4.5	5.8	10.8
Other services	3.5	3.3	3.3	3.4	6.1	0.4	0.4	0.1	0.1	0.1
Not allocated and confidential	**-**	**0.0**	**-**	**0.0**	**-**	**-**	**-**	**0.0**	**0.0**	**-**
Private real estate activities	**387.9**	**484.8**	**433.2**	**677.7**	**791.7**	**94.6**	**111.4**	**106.2**	**156.1**	**173.1**

- Nil; .. Not available; c Confidential data; d Secondary Confidentiality

Note: Detailed metadata at: *http://metalinks.oecd.org/idi/20220712/6d95*.

Source: *OECD International Direct Investment Statistics (database)*: *https://doi.org/10.1787/idi-data-en*

LITHUANIA

Table 6. Foreign direct investment income by industrial sector

Million US dollars

	Inward					Outward				
	2016	2017	2018	2019	2020	2016	2017	2018	2019	2020
All FDI activities	**1 678.3**	**1 944.2**	**2 193.0**	**2 317.9**	**2 229.2**	**145.9**	**165.7**	**303.1**	**229.8**	**319.4**
Agriculture, forestry and fishing	**5.6**	**16.2**	**-5.5**	**23.5**	**-0.1**	**-0.2**	**-0.1**	**2.5**	**0.2**	**6.4**
Mining and quarrying	**1.1**	**-6.1**	**8.5**	**4.7**	**-4.8**	**-0.4**	**-0.5**	**0.8**	**0.0**	**0.1**
Extraction activities	.. c	.. c	.. c	.. c	.. c	-	-	-	-	-
Manufacturing	**668.2**	**655.6**	**656.4**	**716.6**	**667.7**	**4.3**	**-7.2**	**16.5**	**7.2**	**26.7**
of which:										
Food products, beverages and tobacco	43.0	50.4	34.8	46.0	61.1	1.4	3.7	-1.6	3.9	3.2
Textiles, wood and paper products; printing	33.6	49.6	50.7	52.7	55.7	1.0	-1.9	-0.6	1.5	1.0
Chemical, rubber, plastic, non-metallic mineral products	495.8	455.3	457.1	515.5	393.0	0.7	-9.0	19.2	-0.7	20.3
Metal and machinery products, except electrical equipment	29.1	33.3	66.0	61.1	75.6	2.4	5.1	1.2	0.8	3.8
Motor vehicles, trailers, semi-trailers, other transport equipment	11.6	16.0	22.6	2.4	5.8	0.0	.. c	-0.1	-0.1	-0.9
Other manufacturing	55.1	51.0	25.2	38.9	76.4	-1.3	.. d	-1.6	1.9	-0.7
Electricity, gas, steam and air conditioning supply	**27.3**	**35.6**	**27.5**	**51.6**	**43.9**	**0.1**	**-0.3**	**-4.9**	**9.9**	**-0.5**
Water supply; sewerage, waste management and remediation activities	**0.9**	**3.0**	**1.2**	**1.2**	**3.6**	**1.9**	**1.1**	**0.9**	**0.5**	**-3.4**
Construction	**2.4**	**22.2**	**-13.5**	**18.2**	**28.2**	**7.3**	**1.5**	**6.9**	**15.3**	**0.4**
Services	**972.6**	**1 217.8**	**1 518.3**	**1 502.2**	**1 490.6**	**131.9**	**170.1**	**279.3**	**193.6**	**286.6**
Wholesale and retail trade; repair of motor vehicles and motorcycles	243.2	266.8	324.7	284.6	356.1	57.3	31.7	84.0	96.8	191.9
Transportation and storage	24.2	71.7	98.9	104.7	74.0	12.9	20.0	13.2	13.4	21.4
Accommodation and food service activities	8.1	15.1	9.3	15.1	2.7	-1.1	-2.0	0.1	2.5	-2.1
Information and communication	173.2	200.6	214.7	201.5	218.2	21.3	11.6	25.7	6.3	23.9
Financial and insurance activities	279.2	299.4	438.5	431.5	453.9	-4.9	1.9	6.9	-1.6	-8.0
Activities of holding companies	-2.0	0.4	26.8	21.4	81.0	3.3	2.9	15.9	9.9	-9.2
Real estate activities	123.3	159.0	175.5	218.2	169.4	0.1	21.8	35.7	3.1	8.1
Professional, scientific and technical activities	73.5	160.4	175.5	192.2	161.2	32.8	67.3	106.4	60.6	29.6
Administrative and support service activities	39.4	34.9	66.8	42.5	43.1	13.7	16.5	8.5	11.4	20.8
Public administration; activities of households and of extraterritorial organisations	-	-	-	-	-	-	-	-	-	-
Education	0.2	0.0	0.1	-0.1	0.6	.. c	1.6	0.2	0.9	0.4
Human health and social work activities	6.6	7.9	10.7	10.2	10.5	0.1	0.1	-	0.1	0.3
Arts, entertainment and recreation	0.8	2.0	1.9	1.8	1.1	-1.1	-0.1	-0.7	0.4	0.4
Other services	1.0	0.1	1.7	0.2	0.0	-0.2	-0.1	-0.6	-0.5	-
Not allocated and confidential	**-**	**-**	**-**	**-**	**-**	**-**	**0.0**	**-**	**0.0**	**0.0**
Private real estate activities	**-**	**-**	**-**	**-**	**-**	**1.0**	**1.2**	**1.1**	**3.0**	**3.1**

- Nil; .. Not available; c Confidential data; d Secondary Confidentiality

Note: Detailed metadata at: *http://metalinks.oecd.org/idi/20220712/6d95.*

Source: *OECD International Direct Investment Statistics (database)*: *https://doi.org/10.1787/idi-data-en*

LUXEMBOURG

Table 1. Foreign direct investment flows by country

Million US dollars

	Inward					Outward				
	2016	2017	2018	2019	2020	2016	2017	2018	2019	2020
WORLD	**132 572.2**	**12 403.3**	**-414 396.3**	**-174 244.9**	**-32 674.6**	**157 015.4**	**178 150.2**	**-439 301.3**	**-95 741.6**	**-17 012.0**
OECD COUNTRIES	**42 652.9**	**-256 006.1**	**-216 832.3**	**-96 839.8**	**-7 504.3**	**106 471.3**	**162 057.3**	**-415 922.3**	**-161 014.2**	**-11 492.9**
Australia	48.7	828.5	905.2	-2 782.9	-305.4	888.0	-510.7	-606.6	-1 491.1	683.8
Austria	206.8	1 081.1	90.9	-7 615.6	2 978.9	1 116.9	-225.5	3 257.4	1 298.6	1 212.5
Belgium	-4 030.7	40 516.3	32 944.6	-28 983.5	-1 336.8	6 010.2	9 101.6	22 493.8	-16 553.2	-13 657.0
Canada	26 942.4	16 404.0	6 474.7	-99 472.7	-30 382.9	1 471.9	2 988.4	9 142.0	3 550.9	-27 135.0
Chile	82.9	-144.3	3.5	-375.0	-1 564.7	197.9	-1 019.1	782.5	594.4	126.5
Colombia	..	..	..	..	..	..	..	..	..	..
Costa Rica	..	..	..	..	..	..	..	..	..	..
Czech Republic	-169.2	-581.7	-1 851.8	2 546.7	-2 224.5	1 983.9	4 701.8	-821.4	5 127.1	-4 532.2
Denmark	320.7	44.0	5 005.3	-5 136.0	155.0	1 799.2	640.3	1 513.0	2 477.3	-968.7
Estonia	26.5	10.1	-30.7	-14.6	5.7	25.4	-14.7	410.7	12.3	809.1
Finland	-207.9	-1 444.0	-118.0	302.3	5 475.8	9 499.1	1 853.2	2 339.2	324.6	933.3
France	-18 607.8	4 812.3	-1 523.7	6 217.4	7 551.0	4 090.5	1 958.1	22 171.6	2 109.0	6 128.8
Germany	1 697.4	20 108.2	6 336.6	18 319.7	-1 206.8	10 591.6	6 291.3	-808.5	36 346.1	20 137.9
Greece	61.9	36.1	44.8	-11.2	-1.1	-39.8	-91.3	238.4	364.9	70.7
Hungary	-15 049.2	-24 113.4	-40.1	4 107.2	-34 463.8	21 153.4	-4 170.9	-28 509.4	6 480.5	41 317.4
Iceland	2 828.7	-739.5	738.8	52.6	670.1	-3 239.0	16.9	1 588.6	-62.7	-144.7
Ireland	57 064.0	-70 062.0	-22 381.7	-31 924.3	-196 046.7	28 092.4	251 889.3	-83 425.0	-150 642.6	14 053.6
Israel	-925.6	-311.1	-563.0	1 020.9	-1 895.2	-141.5	257.0	1 174.3	1 467.6	131.1
Italy	27 412.4	9 809.5	-16 511.3	3 051.6	736.2	408.1	2 980.5	-7 924.0	11 576.2	-3 111.1
Japan	319.6	-647.1	902.9	6 790.6	-1 464.4	85.1	262.7	1 376.1	432.1	-817.1
Korea	222.3	156.7	-135.7	2 562.4	147.0	98.4	629.0	33.0	-77.2	-384.0
Latvia	-40.9	-37.2	40.1	25.7	53.6	92.9	-34.9	-10.6	-34.7	6.8
Lithuania	42.0	-1.1	-579.5	7.8	-1.1	7.7	-78.9	166.4	12.3	8.0
Luxembourg	-	-	-	-	-	-	-	-	-	-
Mexico	-952.1	-1 040.5	113.3	2 549.0	-585.8	-789.6	443.0	-558.2	-3 461.3	-2 419.4
Netherlands	26 364.0	-54 568.8	-115 116.3	-21 857.2	-49 153.3	76 903.7	67 118.7	-67 822.5	-82 696.7	-11 482.6
New Zealand	-270.9	-3 343.5	-820.3	49.3	-1 155.6	-591.6	-228.8	-35.4	109.7	-167.5
Norway	1 753.8	281.8	-958.3	-1 371.3	-110.5	368.2	100.3	-1 155.4	236.2	-3 325.4
Poland	-249.9	1 419.2	-1 299.4	-1 710.5	345.3	1 605.7	6 238.3	683.3	1 629.9	2 271.2
Portugal	-3.3	86.8	-612.5	1 835.9	91.2	3.3	-411.5	237.2	2 093.4	-2 924.2
Slovak Republic	-529.7	-137.5	-539.4	1 060.1	-204.0	-656.9	261.5	3.5	-227.2	-143.6
Slovenia	31.0	68.8	-8.3	88.4	-177.8	191.3	39.5	190.0	23.5	147.0
Spain	2 446.1	-2 174.5	-2 224.7	10 284.3	479.8	7 056.3	11 801.4	6 896.0	7 688.3	-5 973.8
Sweden	-1 791.4	-3 045.9	3 447.4	214.9	-3 290.0	4 937.5	-1 190.4	2 096.1	1 026.5	5 358.4
Switzerland	7 795.0	-13 261.2	-23 020.2	-40 398.5	-7 824.5	22 269.2	32 026.8	-6 654.1	65 919.6	-92 725.9
Turkey	52.0	-653.8	73.2	-905.6	-159.5	-645.8	-391.2	-145.2	-1 268.3	1 370.9
United Kingdom	-31 803.6	-21 605.2	-1 347.8	1 151.9	8 920.8	-33 427.0	56 702.7	-102 053.6	-13 867.7	14 127.6
United States	-38 391.0	-153 758.3	-84 271.2	83 480.4	298 495.7	-54 937.5	-287 956.3	-192 185.8	-41 532.5	50 077.5
EUROPE	**27 630.2**	**-125 992.6**	**-163 657.5**	**-46 540.9**	**-299 192.0**	**153 481.1**	**419 873.7**	**-235 404.2**	**-139 229.8**	**-20 634.8**
Bulgaria	44.2	-3.4	9.4	13.4	-47.9	69.7	98.1	472.1	-29.1	1 666.1
Croatia	-76.3	-1.1	-10.6	-11.2	115.1	-15.5	434.0	439.0	189.2	-38.7
Cyprus	-1 092.6	-1 340.3	3 596.1	-21.3	3 320.8	-3 989.8	-29 666.3	-383.6	16 415.5	4 631.3
Malta	2 900.6	937.9	-4 337.3	37 702.9	-17 356.1	-1 479.6	3 487.8	449.7	7 855.1	4 239.3
Montenegro	..	..	..	..	..	..	..	..	..	..
Romania	141.5	29.3	-123.9	180.2	75.2	276.5	515.2	-24.8	-223.9	80.9
Russian Federation	1 604.6	-3 585.8	8 167.1	4 502.4	1 921.4	-12.2	-8 801.7	-2 572.9	-6 863.3	675.8
Ukraine	..	..	..	..	..	..	..	..	..	..
AFRICA	**-2 929.3**	**1 056.3**	**475.6**	**980.6**	**2 674.6**	**-15 915.1**	**-3 463.0**	**2 231.8**	**-72.8**	**4 214.2**
Northern Africa	-25.4	-14.7	88.5	-22.4	1 985.2	456.7	-2 358.2	107.4	-15.7	3 555.6
Algeria	..	..	..	..	..	..	..	..	..	..
Egypt	-1.1	-14.7	5.9	-14.6	1 987.5	413.6	1 158.8	33.0	-41.4	-31.9
Libya	..	..	..	..	..	..	..	..	..	..
Morocco	22.1	-7.9	13.0	-14.6	-10.3	61.9	-3 516.0	56.7	5.6	3 571.5
Tunisia	..	..	..	..	..	..	..	..	..	..
Other African countries	-2 905.0	1 070.9	387.1	1 003.0	688.3	-16 371.8	-1 104.7	2 124.4	-57.1	658.7
Nigeria	-4.4	-	-18.9	-	13.7	5.5	5.6	16.5	5.6	17.1
South Africa	-390.4	-14.7	-1 921.4	1 129.5	-14.8	-15 799.0	-785.7	2 897.4	127.6	715.7
AMERICA	**47 778.4**	**120 828.5**	**-251 640.5**	**-144 277.4**	**229 074.6**	**-41 051.6**	**-311 799.1**	**-144 918.0**	**-84 149.8**	**26 700.9**
Northern America	-11 448.6	-137 355.4	-77 797.7	-15 992.4	268 112.8	-53 465.7	-284 967.9	-183 043.8	-37 981.6	22 941.3
Central America and Caribbean countries	57 880.1	260 164.6	-178 334.7	-125 483.0	-40 727.1	2 929.3	-31 033.7	38 891.8	-45 720.4	9 043.9
Bahamas	..	..	..	..	..	..	..	..	..	..
Bermuda	..	..	..	..	..	..	..	..	..	..
Cayman Islands	..	..	..	..	..	..	..	..	..	..
El Salvador	..	..	..	..	..	..	..	..	..	..
Guatemala	..	..	..	..	..	..	..	..	..	..
Honduras	..	..	..	..	..	..	..	..	..	..
Nicaragua	..	..	..	..	..	..	..	..	..	..
Panama	..	..	..	..	..	..	..	..	..	..
Virgin Islands, U.S.	..	..	..	..	..	..	..	..	..	..
South America	1 348.0	-1 981.7	4 490.7	-2 802.0	1 688.9	9 484.7	4 202.5	-764.8	-447.8	-5 285.5
Argentina	36.5	-24.8	-55.5	-13.4	-43.3	-461.1	395.7	-73.2	-673.9	-245.0
Bolivia	..	..	..	..	..	..	..	..	..	..
Brazil	1 244.1	-809.4	544.1	-935.9	5 466.7	8 165.4	6 523.5	-2 441.9	1 515.7	-6 373.8
Ecuador	..	..	..	..	..	..	..	..	..	..
Paraguay	..	..	..	..	..	..	..	..	..	..
Peru	..	..	..	..	..	..	..	..	..	..
Uruguay	-274.2	-1 671.7	4 281.8	-1 935.5	-2 606.3	-69.7	-294.2	246.7	-1 248.2	1 659.3
Venezuela	3.3	13.5	-	3.4	2.3	16.6	12.4	-55.5	4.5	1.1

LUXEMBOURG

Table 1. Foreign direct investment flows by country *(cont.)*

Million US dollars

	Inward					Outward				
	2016	2017	2018	2019	2020	2016	2017	2018	2019	2020
ASIA	**60 737.6**	**18 593.2**	**354.1**	**17 885.4**	**36 224.5**	**60 241.1**	**74 264.5**	**-60 448.5**	**129 046.2**	**-27 886.0**
Near and Middle East	-10 592.7	6 046.7	-1 638.1	32 888.2	23 327.6	900.1	5 489.8	-1 533.1	34 864.0	-31 956.7
Gulf Arabian countries	-9 698.1	5 410.9	-1 115.3	31 997.1	25 487.2	945.5	4 687.2	-3 192.5	33 180.3	-32 088.9
Kuwait	..	..	..	..	..	..	..	..	..	..
Qatar	..	..	..	..	..	..	..	..	..	..
Saudi Arabia	395.9	759.8	452.0	413.1	484.3	23.2	-67.6	28.3	43.7	-16.0
United Arab Emirates	..	..	..	..	..	..	..	..	..	..
Other Near and Middle East	-894.6	636.9	-521.7	891.1	-2 159.5	-45.3	802.6	1 659.4	1 682.5	132.2
Jordan	..	..	..	..	..	..	..	..	..	..
Other Asian countries	71 330.3	12 546.5	1 991.0	-15 002.8	12 895.7	59 340.9	68 774.7	-58 915.4	94 183.4	4 070.7
China	2 211.7	2 226.4	6 589.2	192.5	1 806.3	1 081.5	56.4	887.5	-2 179.6	778.3
Hong Kong, China	2 679.4	50 932.3	7 328.0	-10 136.6	-2 829.6	18 016.1	16 195.5	2 309.7	60 958.2	-3 335.6
India	1 273.9	-99.2	-38.9	56.0	-671.2	-785.1	249.1	113.3	-72.8	2 808.0
Indonesia	3 263.3	-44.0	96.8	-5.6	8.0	349.4	-59.7	96.8	92.9	6.8
Iran, Islamic Republic of	..	..	..	..	..	..	..	..	..	..
Malaysia	264.3	-20.3	460.3	-1 284.0	317.9	-1 421.0	-478.0	167.6	-1 314.2	341.9
Philippines	44.2	-5.6	10.6	-4.5	-36.5	-32.1	-22.5	-62.6	7.8	-1.1
Singapore	60 494.3	-39 805.0	-13 355.4	-13 462.4	16 183.5	41 565.9	50 700.0	-62 963.5	35 869.2	3 429.1
Chinese Taipei	-26.5	23.7	-89.7	236.2	-69.5	7.7	60.9	-7.1	455.6	61.5
Thailand	735.4	-137.5	259.6	72.8	-435.3	91.8	322.4	33.0	-73.9	47.9
Viet Nam	..	..	..	..	..	..	..	..	..	..
AUSTRALIA, OCEANIA AND POLAR REGIONS	**-644.7**	**-2 082.1**	**72.0**	**-2 292.6**	**-1 455.3**	**258.8**	**-727.1**	**-762.4**	**-1 336.6**	**593.7**
WORLD unallocated and confidential	**-**	**-**	**-**	**-**	**-1.1**	**1.1**	**1.1**	**-**	**1.1**	**-**
European Union (since 01/02/2020)	**76 909.2**	**-78 552.6**	**-115 794.9**	**..**	**-284 126.5**	**169 732.4**	**333 523.8**	**-125 674.5**	**..**	**60 243.9**
G20 countries excl. European Union	**-23 420.3**	**-127 177.3**	**-75 150.5**	**26 300.2**	**290 703.1**	**-79 604.1**	**-219 092.5**	**-272 623.6**	**-15 693.5**	**57 009.7**
G20 OECD countries	**-33 059.8**	**-125 585.6**	**-88 983.8**	**20 961.6**	**281 745.9**	**-72 166.3**	**-216 602.4**	**-271 559.1**	**-7 683.9**	**58 659.8**
G20 Non-OECD countries	**9 639.5**	**-1 591.7**	**13 833.4**	**5 338.6**	**8 957.3**	**-7 437.8**	**-2 490.1**	**-1 064.6**	**-8 009.6**	**-1 650.1**
MENA countries	**..**	**..**	**..**	**..**	**..**	**..**	**..**	**..**	**..**	**..**
ASEAN countries	**64 801.5**	**-40 083.4**	**-12 577.6**	**-14 711.7**	**16 043.3**	**40 988.6**	**51 420.4**	**-64 003.3**	**34 420.7**	**3 851.9**

- Nil; .. Not available

Note: Detailed metadata at: *http://metalinks.oecd.org/idi/20220712/6d95.*

Source: *OECD International Direct Investment Statistics (database): https://doi.org/10.1787/idi-data-en*

Table 2. Foreign direct investment positions by country

At year end

Million US dollars

	Inward					Outward				
	2016	2017	2018	2019	2020	2016	2017	2018	2019	2020
WORLD	**3 787 005.4**	**4 229 862.1**	**3 648 479.5**	**3 506 180.6**	**3 643 790.6**	**4 612 941.9**	**5 145 678.8**	**4 525 018.3**	**4 447 147.8**	**4 527 621.8**
OECD COUNTRIES	**2 860 980.3**	**2 849 018.9**	**2 563 911.2**	**2 516 955.7**	**2 631 305.7**	**4 099 803.9**	**4 549 183.3**	**4 040 684.7**	**3 903 273.4**	**3 978 990.1**
Australia	7 086.5	8 220.2	8 745.1	5 826.8	5 377.3	15 935.5	18 785.1	18 519.6	15 596.5	16 591.0
Austria	8 845.8	11 682.7	10 321.7	1 075.0	4 940.5	14 624.2	16 778.6	18 505.8	18 809.3	21 374.4
Belgium	89 725.9	137 066.4	166 894.9	133 025.2	139 372.9	130 886.5	155 780.8	160 784.3	145 303.3	141 059.0
Canada	208 789.9	230 052.8	244 676.0	162 374.7	135 716.0	94 240.5	98 606.4	98 310.1	113 698.0	87 067.1
Chile	209.8	66.0	71.0	-299.9	-1 121.6	1 367.1	931.9	1 665.9	2 096.2	2 288.6
Colombia	19.0	627.2	105.3	364.0	335.0	1 169.0	1 345.6	1 679.6	1 635.6	1 179.3
Costa Rica	-2.1	-3.6	-5.7	-7.9	13.5	390.0	393.4	1 317.8	1 358.1	315.4
Czech Republic	1 138.4	717.2	-1 082.0	1 505.3	-743.7	12 193.5	20 260.3	19 342.8	24 266.5	24 992.0
Denmark	1 258.6	1 096.2	5 178.6	7.9	581.7	15 023.7	17 528.2	17 596.7	20 610.0	21 660.3
Estonia	49.5	64.8	33.2	18.0	25.8	194.0	197.9	577.1	550.4	3 028.6
Finland	143.4	-1 229.3	-1 709.4	-1 359.2	3 733.0	12 406.5	15 286.6	17 814.3	18 572.2	20 552.2
France	71.7	5 399.4	-2 145.6	7 678.1	17 015.6	112 882.9	133 005.5	142 304.8	149 224.9	163 085.0
Germany	78 822.6	111 801.4	115 652.6	135 826.8	149 588.9	128 777.3	158 129.0	154 818.0	198 202.7	245 276.7
Greece	99.1	170.3	207.2	188.7	195.1	4 251.1	4 689.4	4 814.5	5 492.0	6 202.0
Hungary	25 245.1	686.0	634.3	2 500.6	-34 129.3	37 650.5	36 409.2	8 831.0	16 112.1	61 868.9
Iceland	-283.5	-1 099.8	-337.8	-280.8	-164.4	2 928.2	3 318.5	4 767.6	4 749.5	4 787.1
Ireland	478 078.4	479 269.6	469 752.7	438 900.2	256 841.3	361 062.5	612 727.3	537 236.1	377 481.5	381 228.4
Israel	870.7	604.5	56.1	1 340.1	-551.0	2 826.0	3 448.1	4 945.0	6 933.3	7 354.3
Italy	22 623.6	34 733.7	17 717.0	22 095.0	25 852.3	77 275.2	94 093.3	82 446.8	95 216.8	95 976.2
Japan	3 930.6	3 984.2	3 446.3	9 822.5	8 868.6	5 620.3	6 189.7	7 120.4	9 026.1	9 036.7
Korea	-1 429.3	-1 412.8	-1 604.1	872.8	948.6	980.3	1 709.0	2 473.1	2 711.8	3 496.1
Latvia	-44.3	-90.0	-35.5	3.4	58.9	214.0	205.1	194.6	151.7	192.7
Lithuania	512.3	581.7	-6.9	1.1	1.2	164.4	106.7	245.0	253.9	397.6
Luxembourg	-	-	-	-	-	-	-	-	-	-
Mexico	-6 185.3	-7 447.8	-7 323.1	-4 942.7	-5 301.3	17 035.9	18 337.7	16 894.9	13 663.2	10 148.5
Netherlands	483 397.3	467 619.3	344 564.9	353 422.8	316 895.3	764 343.8	893 253.8	793 702.8	709 602.3	620 578.0
New Zealand	5 440.1	3 268.2	2 812.0	2 820.7	1 999.0	634.6	386.2	303.4	399.9	211.1
Norway	5 681.5	6 746.2	5 469.4	3 885.6	4 183.3	13 075.8	14 168.9	12 989.5	12 689.3	9 734.9
Poland	2 177.7	3 592.0	1 465.5	23.6	382.9	16 984.3	24 206.0	24 826.0	27 290.5	32 352.4
Portugal	2 283.1	2 654.1	2 054.0	3 941.8	4 258.2	21 174.2	25 325.0	24 910.7	27 004.0	25 188.4
Slovak Republic	-820.1	-1 081.8	-1 556.0	-462.8	-725.2	3 651.3	4 400.3	4 418.4	3 840.7	3 914.6
Slovenia	-11.6	60.0	49.2	137.0	-41.7	785.3	921.1	1 065.9	1 080.7	1 321.6
Spain	-8 085.8	-10 066.0	-10 312.6	-872.8	1 589.2	56 109.4	71 109.4	81 115.2	88 337.5	88 052.5
Sweden	17 154.0	15 513.3	16 502.2	18 188.0	15 197.0	53 768.3	50 729.2	52 807.4	54 417.0	68 250.1
Switzerland	136 496.3	130 407.8	102 627.7	71 944.5	66 953.0	400 608.2	439 036.9	417 532.6	468 137.5	420 608.7
Turkey	362.6	-310.6	-218.7	-1 322.2	-1 492.2	9 045.0	11 845.8	6 218.2	4 868.6	6 105.0
United Kingdom	498 324.0	519 086.1	491 993.4	488 648.6	521 995.3	715 053.2	853 380.9	736 778.1	736 819.8	773 132.9
United States	799 534.1	697 194.8	579 317.6	660 421.3	992 673.9	996 194.8	744 002.2	563 808.1	530 064.0	600 699.5
EUROPE	**2 152 349.5**	**2 259 172.5**	**2 041 977.3**	**2 021 796.2**	**1 828 543.4**	**3 204 633.7**	**3 869 437.5**	**3 530 549.6**	**3 394 506.9**	**3 446 632.7**
Bulgaria	-10.5	-15.6	-5.7	7.9	-44.2	705.2	960.7	1 793.0	1 749.0	3 598.0
Croatia	-110.7	-128.3	-121.4	-130.3	-17.2	2 130.3	2 872.4	3 133.7	3 202.7	3 406.6
Cyprus	13 689.3	13 235.8	13 982.1	12 116.4	17 251.2	110 113.8	79 172.5	77 976.9	95 250.5	106 397.1
Malta	12 690.0	14 901.7	12 072.4	51 483.9	34 724.5	13 504.8	16 940.5	15 673.2	26 015.5	31 364.6
Montenegro	-2.1	-2.4	-2.3	-3.4	1.2	110.7	142.7	143.1	124.7	135.0
Romania	-13.7	15.6	-105.3	78.6	166.9	1 664.4	2 380.7	1 996.8	1 691.8	1 834.6
Russian Federation	-39 641.6	-39 076.5	-30 320.6	-25 923.4	-13 313.3	21 643.3	15 524.1	11 952.1	5 035.9	5 770.0
Ukraine	-42.2	-20.4	-81.3	-56.2	-39.3	561.8	707.6	557.6	711.1	1 169.5
AFRICA	**-1 167.9**	**472.5**	**440.8**	**1 230.1**	**4 034.9**	**11 857.3**	**12 609.7**	**14 763.0**	**14 406.9**	**15 746.7**
Northern Africa	303.6	301.0	381.3	359.5	2 302.1	859.1	1 779.8	2 088.4	2 325.3	2 786.8
Algeria	62.2	78.0	89.3	94.4	111.7	11.6	13.2	13.7	12.4	13.5
Egypt	114.9	100.7	106.5	94.4	2 008.8	561.8	1 578.3	1 510.2	1 458.1	821.0
Libya	-48.5	-55.2	-	-	-	-	-	-	11.2	17.2
Morocco	176.0	177.5	185.5	170.7	181.6	260.4	170.3	540.4	813.3	1 899.6
Tunisia	-1.1	-	-	-	-	24.2	18.0	24.0	30.3	35.6
Other African countries	-1 472.5	171.5	59.5	871.7	1 732.7	10 998.2	10 828.7	12 674.6	12 081.6	12 959.9
Nigeria	-13.7	-15.6	-35.5	-34.8	-22.1	178.1	183.5	192.4	194.3	208.6
South Africa	553.4	871.9	-1 530.8	-661.6	-551.0	6 215.9	5 825.1	8 029.5	8 028.5	9 172.9
AMERICA	**1 445 417.9**	**1 750 927.1**	**1 398 200.1**	**1 256 439.0**	**1 541 709.4**	**1 260 685.1**	**1 053 436.1**	**847 038.0**	**790 168.5**	**825 840.0**
Northern America	1 008 324.0	927 246.3	823 994.7	822 796.0	1 128 390.0	1 090 435.3	842 609.7	662 118.2	643 762.1	687 766.6
Central America and Caribbean countries	430 266.7	821 743.8	572 363.2	435 276.3	413 213.9	105 174.4	125 794.0	118 257.4	72 087.2	77 634.1
Bahamas	42 883.9	53 354.5	50 160.3	36 510.9	40 730.2	-984.5	611.7	3 259.7	-3 987.9	-4 503.6
Bermuda	239 692.2	443 737.1	305 973.2	140 853.7	140 760.8	57 266.8	75 443.8	56 212.5	10 434.7	12 230.9
Cayman Islands	90 259.3	244 844.1	144 705.7	137 379.2	120 555.9	20 217.1	17 619.3	22 967.7	21 972.6	27 002.1
El Salvador	82.2	-	55.0	-	229.5	159.2	26.4	-48.1	1.1	22.1
Guatemala	13.7	19.2	5.7	3.4	9.8	404.8	28.8	53.8	55.0	81.0
Honduras	-	-	-	-	-	25.3	32.4	32.1	32.6	25.8
Nicaragua	-2.1	-2.4	-	-	-	1.1	73.2	10.3	455.0	459.0
Panama	5 007.9	5 231.5	4 121.8	3 890.1	3 779.6	2 214.6	982.3	1 861.7	1 888.3	1 283.6
Virgin Islands, U.S.	-	-2.4	-17.2	-2.2	-2.5	207.7	502.5	3 179.5	7 052.3	7 025.4
South America	6 827.2	1 936.9	1 843.4	-1 634.5	105.5	65 076.4	85 033.6	66 662.5	74 319.3	60 439.3
Argentina	-48.5	-85.2	-142.0	-146.0	-164.4	3 548.0	4 870.5	4 093.2	3 574.5	2 638.4
Bolivia	-8.4	-3.6	-1.1	-1.1	337.5	76.9	48.0	63.0	74.1	78.5
Brazil	8 282.9	4 561.0	775.1	-783.0	4 686.5	52 088.1	71 968.1	52 643.7	60 683.0	46 834.0
Ecuador	-	-6.0	2.3	2.2	-1.2	45.3	103.1	431.6	1 854.6	1 518.0
Paraguay	-9.5	-9.6	-10.3	-10.1	-	175.0	279.4	81.3	22.5	330.1
Peru	109.6	206.3	419.1	639.2	770.6	3 377.3	2 880.8	3 220.7	3 043.1	2 595.4
Uruguay	-1 708.7	-3 415.7	627.4	-1 392.9	-4 730.6	3 193.8	2 145.6	2 356.3	952.6	2 607.7
Venezuela	-17.9	-4.8	-4.6	-7.9	-6.1	35.8	50.4	13.7	19.1	20.9

Table 2. Foreign direct investment positions by country *(cont.)*
At year end

Million US dollars

	Inward					Outward				
	2016	2017	2018	2019	2020	2016	2017	2018	2019	2020
ASIA	**177 634.7**	**207 192.4**	**196 203.3**	**217 918.4**	**261 937.7**	**118 632.9**	**190 323.8**	**113 226.5**	**231 442.4**	**221 811.3**
Near and Middle East	38 841.6	47 160.0	43 548.2	80 697.6	106 991.0	11 739.2	17 684.1	16 963.6	51 221.1	22 612.6
Gulf Arabian countries	36 999.1	44 529.9	41 550.3	77 598.3	105 961.5	7 085.5	11 891.3	9 698.9	41 862.5	13 135.4
Kuwait	-	-	-	-2.2	-7.4	-	-	-	-	-
Qatar	16 251.7	19 112.5	17 027.7	16 804.1	14 476.6	3.2	3.6	3.4	14.6	17.2
Saudi Arabia	2 629.9	4 252.8	4 153.9	5 880.7	6 676.9	126.5	134.3	142.0	186.5	1 007.5
United Arab Emirates	17 056.0	18 622.0	16 662.5	40 077.5	82 775.8	6 404.6	11 125.0	8 943.2	41 060.4	12 065.3
Other Near and Middle East	1 842.5	2 630.1	1 997.9	3 099.3	1 029.6	4 653.7	5 792.8	7 264.7	9 357.4	9 477.2
Jordan	-	-1.2	-	-	-	142.3	486.9	417.9	389.8	152.2
Other Asian countries	138 793.1	160 032.4	152 655.1	137 219.7	154 946.6	106 893.6	172 640.9	96 262.9	180 221.3	199 198.7
China	7 434.4	9 887.3	11 914.4	9 605.7	11 392.8	9 681.7	10 001.2	11 388.8	9 066.5	10 674.9
Hong Kong, China	36 693.4	92 210.4	94 986.3	83 622.8	83 199.2	17 726.4	29 948.4	24 772.2	86 512.0	83 394.3
India	-304.6	-419.8	-393.9	-346.0	-894.6	1 761.4	3 376.1	2 074.7	3 012.8	5 934.5
Indonesia	-186.6	-241.1	-139.7	-144.9	-137.4	956.0	869.5	880.5	988.5	825.9
Iran, Islamic Republic of	-	-	-	-	-	-	-	1.1	-	-
Malaysia	1 542.1	1 701.8	2 025.4	704.3	978.0	678.8	1 192.1	1 125.5	-200.0	-8.6
Philippines	20.0	14.4	25.2	20.2	-16.0	157.1	145.1	115.6	138.2	326.4
Singapore	89 291.7	52 161.2	39 978.2	30 417.9	48 004.7	67 088.6	115 273.4	43 982.1	65 906.5	81 397.7
Chinese Taipei	-25.3	-22.8	-111.1	104.5	478.6	327.8	383.8	346.9	821.2	860.2
Thailand	1 195.3	1 199.3	1 410.6	1 451.4	1 105.7	737.9	1 084.2	1 170.1	1 087.4	1 168.2
Viet Nam	-5.3	7.2	-11.5	-34.8	-23.3	1 189.0	2 390.3	1 141.5	1 048.1	1 078.7
AUSTRALIA, OCEANIA AND POLAR REGIONS	**12 771.2**	**12 098.8**	**11 657.9**	**8 795.8**	**7 565.3**	**17 134.0**	**19 871.7**	**19 441.3**	**16 624.4**	**17 588.7**
WORLD unallocated and confidential	**-**	**-1.2**	**-**	**1.1**	**-**	**-1.1**	**-**	**-**	**-1.1**	**2.5**
European Union (since 01/02/2020)	**1 228 909.0**	**1 288 250.2**	**1 160 001.1**	**..**	**952 969.7**	**1 952 543.5**	**2 437 471.8**	**2 248 931.8**	**..**	**2 173 152.5**
G20 countries excl. European Union	**1 590 650.4**	**1 581 051.8**	**1 434 572.9**	**1 474 783.2**	**1 858 938.5**	**2 269 061.9**	**2 250 653.6**	**1 920 896.5**	**1 959 668.6**	**2 093 472.8**
G20 OECD countries	**1 611 931.1**	**1 601 301.3**	**1 450 256.5**	**1 487 301.7**	**1 851 243.1**	**2 173 041.0**	**2 138 084.7**	**1 829 692.0**	**1 869 092.3**	**2 010 614.8**
G20 Non-OECD countries	**-21 280.7**	**-20 249.5**	**-15 683.5**	**-12 518.5**	**7 695.4**	**96 020.9**	**112 569.0**	**91 204.5**	**90 576.3**	**82 858.0**
MENA countries	**38 372.5**	**46 031.4**	**43 121.1**	**79 024.9**	**109 396.2**	**9 479.3**	**15 618.9**	**13 760.0**	**46 204.2**	**17 458.6**
ASEAN countries	**92 528.7**	**55 845.5**	**44 450.4**	**33 574.5**	**51 068.8**	**70 860.1**	**121 019.4**	**48 480.7**	**69 026.1**	**84 849.7**

- Nil; .. Not available

Note: Detailed metadata at: *http://metalinks.oecd.org/idi/20220712/6d95.*

Source: OECD *International Direct Investment Statistics (database): https://doi.org/10.1787/idi-data-en*

LUXEMBOURG

Table 3. Foreign direct investment income by country

Million US dollars

	Inward					Outward				
	2016	2017	2018	2019	2020	2016	2017	2018	2019	2020
WORLD	**137 071.8**	**127 024.0**	**129 407.5**	**115 408.0**	**131 404.0**	**155 930.6**	**151 768.7**	**155 642.6**	**143 648.3**	**147 002.8**
OECD COUNTRIES	**105 513.7**	**85 150.5**	**85 655.6**	**78 543.6**	**88 748.7**	**138 366.7**	**128 813.0**	**132 903.3**	**123 979.6**	**127 897.4**
Australia	-10.0	-24.8	60.2	-431.0	-208.5	341.7	450.9	1 805.7	1 492.2	974.4
Austria	196.8	-51.9	15.3	-12.3	39.9	1 103.6	731.6	1 679.5	1 324.3	1 167.0
Belgium	4 596.9	7 264.1	5 955.4	5 251.3	5 222.8	6 711.3	6 089.5	7 881.5	7 171.2	6 965.2
Canada	10 489.9	8 144.5	7 029.4	7 953.7	10 038.7	1 281.7	4 204.7	3 527.7	3 173.6	3 170.4
Chile	-	-6.8	-1.2	-57.1	-33.0	44.2	46.2	24.8	50.4	59.3
Colombia	-36.5	-41.7	-15.3	-24.6	-27.4	60.8	18.0	28.3	59.3	263.2
Costa Rica	-	-	-1.2	1.1	2.3	266.5	254.8	7.1	5.6	4.6
Czech Republic	3.3	19.2	-61.4	-89.6	-128.8	1 785.9	2 934.3	3 024.9	1 239.2	1 181.8
Denmark	-4.4	34.9	-2.4	13.4	92.3	888.0	292.0	357.6	350.4	414.8
Estonia	1.1	2.3	1.2	1.1	1.1	12.2	9.0	10.6	12.3	12.5
Finland	48.7	27.1	-69.6	-6.7	96.9	786.2	656.1	928.8	501.5	717.9
France	2 150.8	925.5	2 426.5	1 876.2	1 687.7	3 816.2	4 980.3	5 197.7	4 917.7	6 748.7
Germany	4 627.9	2 047.1	4 744.5	4 349.0	3 102.0	4 881.1	6 442.3	6 545.5	6 144.6	7 376.6
Greece	13.3	21.4	17.7	19.0	19.4	142.7	217.6	68.5	29.1	27.4
Hungary	1 572.5	506.1	8.3	-32.5	-1.1	380.4	86.8	854.5	645.9	1 667.2
Iceland	-	-4.5	-10.6	-1.1	-3.4	5.5	3.4	44.8	41.4	61.5
Ireland	28 995.9	7 467.0	6 323.6	6 106.6	4 493.4	25 472.7	15 375.9	10 440.2	12 000.4	9 729.9
Israel	17.7	39.5	56.7	28.0	6.8	-184.7	147.7	-73.2	-89.6	-49.0
Italy	676.8	793.6	1 501.2	1 869.5	1 507.7	2 385.3	2 388.7	2 898.6	2 696.7	3 000.6
Japan	-112.8	-66.5	107.4	126.5	136.8	453.4	521.9	594.8	790.3	1 192.0
Korea	-37.6	-157.8	-76.7	-33.6	177.8	116.1	99.2	151.1	236.2	360.1
Latvia	-1.1	-4.5	-8.3	9.0	12.5	-10.0	12.4	17.7	15.7	10.3
Lithuania	5.5	-	-	-2.2	-4.6	14.4	10.1	30.7	12.3	13.7
Luxembourg	..	..	..	..	..	..	..	..	..	..
Mexico	-305.2	-439.6	-521.7	-10.1	-521.9	606.0	709.1	1 365.5	1 226.9	1 263.8
Netherlands	6 775.4	14 077.3	13 201.9	15 344.2	13 026.8	21 452.0	19 759.9	22 879.7	20 785.9	22 681.5
New Zealand	127.2	197.3	66.1	51.5	65.0	76.3	41.7	50.7	41.4	58.1
Norway	31.0	48.5	28.3	-139.9	-273.5	199.0	404.7	590.1	347.0	396.6
Poland	17.7	25.9	76.7	101.9	70.7	1 164.4	1 641.3	1 593.3	945.9	1 033.6
Portugal	48.7	45.1	75.5	22.4	104.8	1 140.1	715.8	1 123.6	859.7	866.1
Slovak Republic	-11.1	-18.0	-34.2	-11.2	-8.0	779.6	480.2	834.4	532.9	127.6
Slovenia	-4.4	-1.1	1.2	2.2	5.7	47.6	33.8	57.8	57.1	54.7
Spain	158.1	372.0	-345.8	352.6	274.6	4 443.2	3 919.5	4 526.1	3 446.8	4 248.4
Sweden	610.4	145.4	1 097.6	961.6	1 133.9	2 708.2	2 422.5	1 680.6	2 603.8	2 158.4
Switzerland	6 202.6	5 291.4	5 733.5	4 936.8	4 973.2	15 815.5	15 877.6	13 062.7	18 864.9	17 751.6
Turkey	-	-34.9	-88.5	-178.0	-312.3	398.1	494.9	374.1	377.3	406.8
United Kingdom	11 372.3	16 287.9	14 870.8	9 926.1	16 723.6	17 281.9	17 917.9	22 856.1	21 697.1	22 420.5
United States	27 265.3	22 177.9	23 476.9	20 246.3	27 260.4	21 841.2	18 703.6	15 896.4	9 436.9	9 361.8
EUROPE	**79 366.4**	**70 019.2**	**65 993.2**	**61 066.8**	**65 871.2**	**119 459.3**	**111 694.3**	**116 727.3**	**115 761.8**	**119 669.5**
Bulgaria	-	-1.1	-	-	-	80.7	81.2	90.9	78.4	69.5
Croatia	-25.4	-5.6	-3.5	-3.4	-1.1	290.8	315.6	385.9	77.2	298.6
Cyprus	1 690.8	914.2	917.0	926.9	1 027.9	900.1	527.6	-28.3	1 543.7	1 244.4
Malta	1 219.7	347.2	224.2	154.5	345.3	259.9	383.3	516.9	1 354.5	3 032.5
Montenegro	-	-	-	-	-	16.6	2.3	1.2	4.5	5.7
Romania	-3.3	-3.4	-3.5	-4.5	-6.8	132.7	125.1	286.8	344.8	87.7
Russian Federation	955.4	210.8	113.3	286.6	813.7	617.1	2 539.7	2 014.6	904.5	565.2
Ukraine	-	-	-	-	-	71.9	87.9	68.5	71.6	126.5
AFRICA	**162.6**	**192.8**	**239.6**	**562.0**	**847.9**	**957.6**	**331.4**	**721.1**	**568.7**	**755.6**
Northern Africa	18.8	29.3	23.6	16.8	28.5	275.4	146.5	393.0	238.4	306.6
Algeria	-	-	-	-	-	2.2	-	-1.2	-	-
Egypt	-1.1	-	-	-1.1	9.1	225.6	109.3	94.4	-38.1	-37.6
Libya	-	-	-3.5	-	-	-	-	-	-	-
Morocco	21.0	29.3	27.1	17.9	18.2	42.0	27.1	284.4	265.3	331.6
Tunisia	-	-	-	-	-	6.6	10.1	14.2	11.2	11.4
Other African countries	143.8	164.6	216.0	545.2	819.4	682.3	184.9	328.1	330.2	449.0
Nigeria	-	-	-	-	-	21.0	21.4	23.6	22.4	16.0
South Africa	140.4	115.0	165.2	175.8	212.0	607.1	146.5	232.5	223.9	199.4
AMERICA	**52 346.6**	**50 932.3**	**53 792.0**	**44 461.0**	**53 951.0**	**30 713.3**	**31 468.8**	**29 688.4**	**19 922.8**	**18 410.3**
Northern America	37 755.2	30 322.4	30 506.3	28 199.9	37 299.1	23 124.0	22 908.4	19 424.1	12 610.5	12 532.2
Central America and Caribbean countries	11 721.8	18 578.5	23 264.5	16 212.9	16 575.5	4 622.4	4 396.3	7 179.3	4 885.3	2 615.4
Bahamas	97.3	780.1	1 680.6	1 450.8	591.5	-176.9	-171.3	-67.3	-176.9	-239.3
Bermuda	5 116.7	6 211.3	9 209.3	4 256.1	3 604.6	3 137.2	2 163.2	2 576.4	1 284.0	331.6
Cayman Islands	4 420.0	9 027.2	9 455.9	7 446.5	8 964.1	610.4	367.5	1 615.7	1 713.9	257.6
El Salvador	-	50.7	-	-	-	-2.2	3.4	2.4	-1.1	-
Guatemala	-	-	1.2	1.1	2.3	6.6	2.3	-2.4	1.1	2.3
Honduras	-	-	-	-	-	4.4	3.4	1.2	42.5	2.3
Nicaragua	-1.1	-	-	-	-	-	-	-	3.4	4.6
Panama	494.3	113.9	459.1	21.3	17.1	1.1	113.9	115.7	92.9	25.1
Virgin Islands, U.S.	-	-	-	-	-	-	5.6	773.0	15.7	21.7
South America	2 870.7	2 031.3	21.2	48.1	76.4	2 966.9	4 164.1	3 083.9	2 427.0	3 262.7
Argentina	-2.2	-	-7.1	-3.4	-9.1	445.6	178.1	385.9	260.8	100.3
Bolivia	-	-1.1	-	-	5.7	2.2	5.6	13.0	2.2	3.4
Brazil	2 918.3	2 076.4	-147.5	-207.1	-331.6	1 927.5	3 265.7	2 401.7	2 017.2	2 751.0
Ecuador	-	-	-	-	-	-	4.5	5.9	3.4	-1.1
Paraguay	-	-	-	-	-	7.7	12.4	-	-2.2	-
Peru	1.1	3.4	2.4	9.0	1.1	-14.4	143.2	90.9	-60.5	-60.4
Uruguay	-10.0	-	192.4	334.7	470.7	491.0	459.9	131.0	94.0	144.7
Venezuela	-	-	-	-3.4	-	2.2	-2.3	-	-	-

Table 3. Foreign direct investment income by country *(cont.)*

Million US dollars

	Inward					Outward				
	2016	2017	2018	2019	2020	2016	2017	2018	2019	2020
ASIA	**5 032.6**	**5 298.2**	**9 205.7**	**9 666.4**	**10 838.7**	**4 336.0**	**7 725.2**	**6 598.6**	**5 824.5**	**7 063.2**
Near and Middle East	2 090.0	1 915.2	2 098.4	2 347.5	3 197.7	164.8	742.9	662.1	259.7	368.1
Gulf Arabian countries	1 991.6	1 807.0	1 950.9	2 268.0	3 113.4	235.5	297.6	461.5	167.9	271.2
Kuwait	-	-	-	-	-	-	-	-	-	-
Qatar	837.1	828.5	626.7	660.5	714.5	-	-	-	-	1.1
Saudi Arabia	327.3	344.9	367.0	389.6	476.4	10.0	10.1	-20.1	-35.8	-38.7
United Arab Emirates	800.6	556.9	832.1	1 099.3	1 821.1	224.5	280.7	474.4	195.9	300.9
Other Near and Middle East	98.4	108.2	147.5	79.5	84.3	-71.9	445.3	199.5	92.9	96.9
Jordan	-	-	-	-	-	-	24.8	24.8	25.7	28.5
Other Asian countries	2 942.6	3 382.9	7 107.3	7 318.9	7 641.0	4 171.2	6 982.3	5 936.5	5 564.8	6 695.2
China	272.0	660.6	149.9	516.1	719.1	526.4	657.2	586.6	388.4	322.5
Hong Kong, China	945.5	1 644.7	2 734.6	2 669.9	3 182.9	413.6	1 456.4	1 698.3	1 857.2	2 445.6
India	-40.9	-19.2	-54.3	-87.3	-431.9	111.7	188.3	181.8	173.5	268.9
Indonesia	-102.8	-13.5	-7.1	-4.5	-6.8	103.9	138.7	164.1	119.8	129.9
Iran, Islamic Republic of	-	-	-	-	-	-	-	-	1.1	1.1
Malaysia	48.7	18.0	141.6	62.7	91.2	121.6	137.5	69.6	56.0	2.3
Philippines	-4.4	-	-	1.1	-	2.2	23.7	-	-	-
Singapore	1 960.6	1 203.9	3 923.1	3 905.7	3 753.8	2 136.5	3 456.2	2 116.1	1 627.7	1 629.6
Chinese Taipei	-	-2.3	-1.2	-13.4	-9.1	36.5	54.1	44.8	31.3	26.2
Thailand	16.6	31.6	27.1	28.0	26.2	74.1	72.1	69.6	75.0	84.3
Viet Nam	-	-	-	-1.1	-3.4	25.4	18.0	110.9	114.2	129.9
AUSTRALIA, OCEANIA AND POLAR REGIONS	**162.6**	**580.5**	**178.2**	**-348.1**	**-106.0**	**465.6**	**549.0**	**1 908.4**	**1 570.6**	**1 103.1**
WORLD unallocated and confidential	**1.1**	**1.1**	**-1.2**	**-**	**1.1**	**-1.1**	**-**	**-1.2**	**-**	**1.1**
European Union (since 01/02/2020)	**53 358.4**	**34 951.0**	**36 060.4**	**..**	**32 111.7**	**81 763.8**	**70 631.3**	**73 885.3**	**..**	**74 937.9**
G20 countries excl. European Union	**60 585.0**	**53 027.8**	**54 109.5**	**46 760.3**	**61 033.6**	**57 751.9**	**64 037.9**	**67 160.4**	**56 242.0**	**60 574.4**
G20 OECD countries	**56 117.4**	**49 652.8**	**53 530.0**	**45 694.6**	**59 592.0**	**53 402.6**	**56 913.5**	**61 213.3**	**52 189.6**	**56 275.8**
G20 Non-OECD countries	**4 467.5**	**3 375.0**	**579.5**	**1 065.7**	**1 441.6**	**4 349.2**	**7 124.3**	**5 947.1**	**4 052.4**	**4 298.6**
MENA countries	**2 093.3**	**1 910.7**	**2 066.6**	**2 339.6**	**3 200.0**	**645.8**	**692.1**	**1 087.0**	**567.6**	**707.7**
ASEAN countries	**1 918.6**	**1 318.9**	**4 240.5**	**4 135.2**	**3 862.1**	**2 466.0**	**3 847.4**	**2 528.0**	**1 990.4**	**1 973.8**

- Nil; .. Not available

Note: Detailed metadata at: *http://metalinks.oecd.org/idi/20220712/6d95.*

Source: *OECD International Direct Investment Statistics (database): https://doi.org/10.1787/idi-data-en*

LUXEMBOURG

Table 4. Foreign direct investment flows by industrial sector

Million US dollars

	Inward					Outward				
	2016	2017	2018	2019	2020	2016	2017	2018	2019	2020
All FDI activities	**132 572.2**	**12 403.3**	**-414 396.3**	**-174 244.9**	**-32 674.6**	**157 015.4**	**178 150.2**	**-439 301.3**	**-95 741.6**	**-17 012.0**
Agriculture, forestry and fishing	-	-	-	-	-	**-81.8**	**-166.8**	**31.9**	**9.0**	**8.0**
Mining and quarrying	**2.2**	**2.3**	**2.4**	**1.1**	**1.1**	**-7 159.1**	**-8 092.7**	**195.9**	**-1 291.8**	**2 370.4**
Extraction activities	-	-	-	-	-	-5 876.4	-5 626.2	-330.5	-917.9	1 595.4
Manufacturing	**1 363.5**	**785.7**	**-157.0**	**378.4**	**-335.0**	**6 678.1**	**-13 049.3**	**-1 430.4**	**-5 283.8**	**4 312.3**
of which:										
Food products, beverages and tobacco	-	-	-2.4	-1.1	-1.1	520.8	-7 338.5	-1 231.0	-619.1	-376.1
Textiles, wood and paper products; printing	639.2	989.7	-541.7	-1 220.2	33.0	-978.7	21.4	-107.4	-203.7	532.2
Chemical, rubber, plastic, non-metallic mineral products	1 147.8	-216.4	2.4	-64.9	-246.2	3 304.2	223.2	188.8	6.7	2 149.3
Metal and machinery products, except electrical equipment	-491.0	-13.5	348.2	1 624.3	-209.7	4 107.0	-1 214.1	2 928.1	-2 307.2	2 682.6
Motor vehicles, trailers, semi-trailers, other transport equipment	-6.6	16.9	-30.7	1.1	3.4	-411.4	-4 097.6	-2 480.8	-2 529.9	-1 415.4
Other manufacturing	74.1	7.9	66.1	40.3	86.6	136.0	-643.7	-729.4	370.5	739.6
Electricity, gas, steam and air conditioning supply	**-89.6**	**58.6**	**-106.2**	**-40.3**	**-3.4**	**-279.8**	**106.0**	**-415.4**	**-229.5**	**483.2**
Water supply; sewerage, waste management and remediation activities	**2.2**	**10.1**	**16.5**	**3.4**	**13.7**	**48.7**	**28.2**	**5.9**	**24.6**	**29.6**
Construction	**6.6**	**54.1**	**108.6**	**21.3**	**12.5**	**-784.0**	**-408.1**	**-17.7**	**60.5**	**161.8**
Services	**131 287.2**	**11 493.6**	**-414 259.4**	**-174 607.6**	**-32 362.4**	**157 688.8**	**198 692.4**	**-438 425.6**	**-89 780.6**	**-25 178.3**
Wholesale and retail trade; repair of motor vehicles and motorcycles	-3 309.7	-6 933.8	-39 072.3	24 087.1	-33 516.8	-23 453.5	-2 682.9	-8 155.3	2 778.5	18 379.5
Transportation and storage	48.7	-244.6	217.2	-208.2	69.5	-846.0	-1 007.8	1 022.1	463.5	899.1
Accommodation and food service activities	127.2	5 510.1	-5 282.7	-146.6	110.5	-311.8	-1 952.4	-60.2	-7.8	153.8
Information and communication	1 145.6	-5 568.7	5 194.1	-5 214.4	-1 171.5	3 638.2	-2 111.4	187.7	-5 705.8	1 043.9
Financial and insurance activities	138 606.7	30 795.9	-375 958.9	-184 155.4	-14 956.1	150 130.5	340 174.7	-349 421.7	-66 323.7	-79 205.7
Activities of holding companies	128 742.7	25 316.2	-387 771.7	-221 328.8	-26 429.6	155 095.7	341 240.0	-347 726.9	-67 357.0	-80 511.7
Real estate activities	-54.2	-3 243.2	-35.4	482.5	-286.0	1 968.4	-3 810.2	-56.7	-687.3	-37.6
Professional, scientific and technical activities	453.4	-10 984.1	297.4	-1 319.8	11 144.2	20 293.0	-131 504.9	-80 194.7	-18 693.6	16 034.2
Administrative and support service activities	-5 728.2	2 150.8	382.4	-8 133.9	6 242.7	6 150.6	1 331.3	-1 772.7	-1 788.9	17 494.0
Public administration; activities of households and of extraterritorial organisations	-	-	-	-	-	-	-	-	-	-
Education	-	-	-	-	-	-46.4	235.6	148.7	89.6	23.9
Human health and social work activities	-2.2	11.3	-1.2	1.1	1.1	47.6	-34.9	37.8	-21.3	-
Arts, entertainment and recreation	-	-	-	-	-	118.3	289.7	-152.2	124.3	42.2
Other services	-1.1	-	-	-	-	1.1	-234.5	-8.3	-7.8	-5.7
Not allocated and confidential	..	..	..	..	..	..	..	..	..	..
Private real estate activities	..	..	..	..	..	..	..	..	..	..

- Nil; .. Not available

Note: Detailed metadata at: *http://metalinks.oecd.org/idi/20220712/6d95*.

Source: *OECD International Direct Investment Statistics (database)*: *https://doi.org/10.1787/idi-data-en*

Table 5. Foreign direct investment positions by industrial sector

At year end

Million US dollars

	Inward					Outward				
	2016	2017	2018	2019	2020	2016	2017	2018	2019	2020
All FDI activities	**3 787 005.4**	**4 229 862.1**	**3 648 479.5**	**3 506 180.6**	**3 643 790.6**	**4 612 941.9**	**5 145 678.8**	**4 525 018.3**	**4 447 147.8**	**4 527 621.8**
Agriculture, forestry and fishing	-	-	-	-	-	**1 817.2**	**1 842.2**	**1 771.2**	**1 751.3**	**1 868.9**
Mining and quarrying	**5.3**	**7.2**	**8.0**	**7.9**	**9.8**	**18 641.3**	**11 391.2**	**10 591.9**	**9 449.6**	**10 613.6**
Extraction activities	-	-	-	-	-	12 828.1	8 037.9	7 288.8	6 569.3	7 465.9
Manufacturing	**3 853.7**	**5 849.1**	**5 115.6**	**5 470.7**	**5 479.2**	**135 676.2**	**134 654.6**	**123 310.1**	**116 562.6**	**113 854.5**
of which:										
Food products, beverages and tobacco	-44.3	-52.8	-46.9	-43.8	-44.2	17 021.2	10 504.9	8 863.1	7 990.3	7 506.4
Textiles, wood and paper products; printing	679.9	2 457.4	1 759.8	469.6	330.1	6 296.0	6 747.4	5 983.5	5 557.2	6 123.5
Chemical, rubber, plastic, non-metallic mineral products	2 934.5	3 247.8	2 946.0	2 887.0	2 926.7	39 587.9	43 540.4	40 693.8	39 566.4	43 357.5
Metal and machinery products, except electrical equipment	169.7	68.4	352.6	2 062.5	2 120.5	52 063.9	53 425.3	50 751.1	47 664.6	40 320.3
Motor vehicles, trailers, semi-trailers, other transport equipment	3.2	3.6	2.3	-	-	12 565.6	12 341.1	10 515.2	9 204.7	9 370.5
Other manufacturing	109.6	124.7	101.9	94.4	147.3	8 142.7	8 095.5	6 503.3	6 579.4	7 176.3
Electricity, gas, steam and air conditioning supply	**-113.8**	**-69.6**	**-170.6**	**-206.7**	**-228.2**	**5 108.0**	**5 485.7**	**4 147.0**	**3 591.3**	**3 940.4**
Water supply; sewerage, waste management and remediation activities	**13.7**	**18.0**	**21.8**	**23.6**	**28.2**	**290.9**	**320.2**	**275.9**	**260.6**	**277.3**
Construction	**156.0**	**190.7**	**261.0**	**255.0**	**273.7**	**4 937.3**	**5 098.3**	**4 887.8**	**4 878.7**	**5 398.2**
Services	**3 783 089.5**	**4 223 866.6**	**3 643 243.6**	**3 500 629.1**	**3 638 228.0**	**4 432 976.7**	**4 970 429.4**	**4 363 591.7**	**4 293 765.4**	**4 372 359.8**
Wholesale and retail trade; repair of motor vehicles and motorcycles	68 686.6	66 920.1	17 626.5	45 695.3	9 795.1	82 418.0	84 687.0	70 093.9	69 551.8	86 069.5
Transportation and storage	832.7	738.8	893.1	734.7	861.5	12 548.8	12 173.2	12 312.8	12 406.2	13 152.5
Accommodation and food service activities	223.5	6 145.4	707.6	463.9	27.0	1 938.4	107.9	58.4	109.0	157.1
Information and communication	3 330.9	738.8	4 880.9	12 197.3	-327.6	32 345.3	30 539.7	30 880.5	23 890.1	31 021.0
Financial and insurance activities	3 646 924.2	4 096 785.8	3 564 742.4	3 398 868.8	3 555 435.0	3 780 298.3	4 381 138.2	3 899 192.8	3 837 872.4	3 840 225.8
Activities of holding companies	3 638 463.2	4 074 719.4	3 536 011.0	3 405 575.2	3 518 526.2	3 706 418.3	4 305 225.5	3 827 528.1	3 754 077.7	3 764 092.5
Real estate activities	3 209.7	533.7	346.9	672.9	424.6	13 649.2	10 813.1	9 923.3	9 641.7	9 942.3
Professional, scientific and technical activities	36 552.1	25 575.7	27 767.3	22 922.9	40 644.3	479 639.5	416 996.9	310 933.1	311 733.3	344 817.8
Administrative and support service activities	23 241.3	26 321.7	26 175.9	18 968.8	31 249.2	28 735.1	32 155.2	28 418.8	26 618.7	44 814.1
Public administration; activities of households and of extraterritorial organisations	-	-	-	-	-	-	-	-	-	-
Education	-	-	-	-	-	104.4	367.0	478.6	566.2	640.6
Human health and social work activities	64.3	79.2	76.7	78.6	90.8	781.1	851.5	848.4	822.3	889.7
Arts, entertainment and recreation	24.2	27.6	26.3	25.8	28.2	286.7	576.9	427.1	528.0	596.4
Other services	-	-	-	-	-	231.9	22.8	24.0	27.0	31.9
Not allocated and confidential	**1.1**	-	-	**1.1**	-	-	**-2.4**	**-2.3**	**1.1**	-
Private real estate activities	-	-	-	-	-	**13 494.3**	**16 459.6**	**16 444.9**	**16 887.2**	**19 309.1**

- Nil

Note: Detailed metadata at: *http://metalinks.oecd.org/idi/20220712/6d95*.

Source: OECD *International Direct Investment Statistics (database)*: *https://doi.org/10.1787/idi-data-en*

LUXEMBOURG

Table 6. Foreign direct investment income by industrial sector

Million US dollars

	Inward					Outward				
	2016	2017	2018	2019	2020	2016	2017	2018	2019	2020
All FDI activities	**137 071.8**	**127 024.0**	**129 407.5**	**115 408.0**	**131 404.0**	**155 930.6**	**151 768.7**	**155 642.6**	**143 648.3**	**147 002.8**
Agriculture, forestry and fishing	-	-	-	-	-	**6.6**	**22.5**	**-7.1**	**9.0**	**10.3**
Mining and quarrying	**1.1**	**1.1**	**1.2**	**1.1**	**1.1**	**-1 394.4**	**-234.5**	**-185.3**	**-208.2**	**-263.2**
Extraction activities	-	-	-	-	-	-1 181.0	-423.9	-270.3	-367.2	-426.2
Manufacturing	**15.5**	**179.2**	**326.9**	**38.1**	**27.4**	**6 192.6**	**6 869.6**	**6 852.4**	**2 454.9**	**1 879.2**
of which:										
Food products, beverages and tobacco	5.5	4.5	-4.7	-3.4	-3.4	576.1	515.2	544.1	531.7	446.7
Textiles, wood and paper products; printing	279.8	13.5	105.0	53.7	53.6	519.7	503.9	345.8	257.5	243.9
Chemical, rubber, plastic, non-metallic mineral products	162.6	18.0	80.3	-2.2	-10.3	2 088.9	1 625.5	1 244.0	959.4	884.3
Metal and machinery products, except electrical equipment	-526.4	108.2	74.4	-69.4	-71.8	1 591.3	2 880.2	3 388.4	1 662.4	1 218.2
Motor vehicles, trailers, semi-trailers, other transport equipment	17.7	16.9	-29.5	3.4	3.4	628.1	571.5	728.2	-1 318.7	-1 307.1
Other manufacturing	76.3	18.0	101.5	56.0	55.8	788.5	774.4	601.9	362.7	392.0
Electricity, gas, steam and air conditioning supply	-	**3.4**	**2.4**	-	-	**232.2**	**234.5**	**289.2**	**270.9**	**264.4**
Water supply; sewerage, waste management and remediation activities	**4.4**	**11.3**	**13.0**	**3.4**	**14.8**	**45.3**	**96.9**	**37.8**	**36.9**	**37.6**
Construction	**37.6**	**65.4**	**46.0**	**44.8**	**42.2**	**142.7**	**74.4**	**108.6**	**52.6**	**57.0**
Services	**136 986.6**	**126 711.8**	**128 940.2**	**115 240.1**	**131 194.3**	**150 552.9**	**144 540.6**	**148 367.8**	**140 850.8**	**144 765.8**
Wholesale and retail trade; repair of motor vehicles and motorcycles	1 503.9	1 491.4	2 223.5	1 745.2	1 841.6	6 053.3	7 343.0	5 123.3	4 260.6	3 858.7
Transportation and storage	102.8	-4.5	141.6	16.8	10.3	677.9	1 313.3	866.3	1 013.1	854.7
Accommodation and food service activities	27.6	-19.2	47.2	92.9	94.6	1.1	-12.4	-4.7	12.3	5.7
Information and communication	92.9	-344.9	312.8	577.6	664.4	492.1	551.2	554.7	155.6	131.1
Financial and insurance activities	131 143.4	122 947.8	125 031.3	110 225.0	126 558.4	131 875.5	125 644.2	139 466.5	133 491.5	138 491.2
Activities of holding companies	124 927.6	118 941.5	120 498.1	104 911.0	120 655.3	129 203.8	122 159.8	136 288.2	131 843.7	136 784.0
Real estate activities	43.1	28.2	7.1	7.8	8.0	713.3	429.5	377.7	237.3	234.8
Professional, scientific and technical activities	3 351.8	2 272.6	1 076.4	2 485.2	1 979.5	10 733.2	8 560.5	1 603.9	1 443.0	947.0
Administrative and support service activities	709.9	325.8	88.5	80.6	27.4	-12.2	659.5	316.3	208.2	213.1
Public administration; activities of households and of extraterritorial organisations	-	-	-	-	-	-	-	-	-	-
Education	-	-	-	-	-	11.1	13.5	42.5	24.6	25.1
Human health and social work activities	6.6	9.0	5.9	3.4	4.6	-4.4	-	-10.6	-20.2	-20.5
Arts, entertainment and recreation	3.3	4.5	4.7	4.5	4.6	17.7	49.6	41.3	35.8	36.5
Other services	-1.1	-	-	-	-	-7.7	-10.1	-9.4	-10.1	-10.3
Not allocated and confidential	..	..	..	..	..	..	..	..	..	..
Private real estate activities	..	..	..	..	..	..	..	..	..	..

- Nil; .. Not available

Note: Detailed metadata at: *http://metalinks.oecd.org/idi/20220712/6d95.*

Source: *OECD International Direct Investment Statistics (database): https://doi.org/10.1787/idi-data-en*

MEXICO

Table 1. Foreign direct investment flows by country

Million US dollars

	Inward					Outward				
	2016	2017	2018	2019	2020	2016	2017	2018	2019	2020
WORLD	**31 066.9**	**34 200.2**	**33 740.3**	**34 075.6**	**..**	**159.6**	**3 987.9**	**8 364.7**	**10 639.5**	**2 644.0**
OECD COUNTRIES	**28 730.3**	**32 919.7**	**31 692.1**	**32 603.4**	**..**	**..**	**..**	**..**	**..**	**..**
Australia	97.1	1 378.9	608.4	767.7	..	..	..	..	..	..
Austria	50.1	95.5	115.0	173.7	..	..	..	..	..	..
Belgium	1 122.6	1 029.4	65.9	1 370.6	..	..	..	..	..	..
Canada	2 298.8	2 826.4	4 220.6	2 986.6	..	..	..	..	..	..
Chile	13.5	34.6	90.4	-30.6	..	..	..	..	..	..
Colombia	213.1	73.8	-2.9	223.6	..	..	..	..	..	..
Costa Rica	1.5	2.0	-1.4	-9.6	..	..	..	..	..	..
Czech Republic	0.3	0.1	1.9	0.1	..	..	..	..	..	..
Denmark	56.5	141.0	26.8	190.0	..	..	..	..	..	..
Estonia	-	0.0	0.1	0.2	..	..	..	..	..	..
Finland	-98.0	11.8	81.9	71.7	..	..	..	..	..	..
France	455.4	558.8	621.9	1 036.5	..	..	..	..	..	..
Germany	2 765.2	2 636.6	2 923.8	3 430.6	..	..	..	..	..	..
Greece	0.2	-	4.3	-	..	..	..	..	..	..
Hungary	4.5	5.4	-0.4	0.2	..	..	..	..	..	..
Iceland	-	0.0	0.0	-	..	..	..	..	..	..
Ireland	51.9	31.5	48.2	50.7	..	..	..	..	..	..
Israel	2 015.2	2.4	1.8	-2.8	..	..	..	..	..	..
Italy	806.3	1 864.7	1 530.9	1 498.8	..	..	..	..	..	..
Japan	1 963.0	2 440.6	2 277.8	1 479.7	..	..	..	..	..	..
Korea	1 122.8	257.3	702.6	170.7	..	..	..	..	..	..
Latvia	0.0	-	0.1	0.0	..	..	..	..	..	..
Lithuania	-	0.0	0.0	0.5	..	..	..	..	..	..
Luxembourg	17.3	4.5	310.6	14.5	..	..	..	..	..	..
Mexico	-	-	-	-	..	..	..	..	..	..
Netherlands	226.6	-207.5	751.7	909.9	..	..	..	..	..	..
New Zealand	1.1	-7.0	0.3	1.1	..	..	..	..	..	..
Norway	11.2	45.7	67.4	-2.9	..	..	..	..	..	..
Poland	0.4	0.6	-0.5	0.6	..	..	..	..	..	..
Portugal	7.3	11.5	26.9	26.3	..	..	..	..	..	..
Slovak Republic	0.0	0.9	0.2	0.3	..	..	..	..	..	..
Slovenia	-	0.2	0.1	5.5	..	..	..	..	..	..
Spain	3 567.3	3 373.2	4 167.3	4 056.0	..	..	..	..	..	..
Sweden	84.8	-40.6	161.7	83.2	..	..	..	..	..	..
Switzerland	582.3	300.4	631.1	721.7	..	..	..	..	..	..
Turkey	0.0	1.9	0.2	0.3	..	..	..	..	..	..
United Kingdom	455.8	500.6	630.1	788.0	..	..	..	..	..	..
United States	11 050.4	15 620.2	11 623.2	12 804.0	..	..	..	..	..	..
EUROPE	**10 187.0**	**10 395.3**	**12 240.9**	**14 487.6**	**..**	**..**	**..**	**..**	**..**	**..**
Bulgaria	0.0	0.1	1.4	1.9	..	..	..	..	..	..
Croatia	-	0.1	0.1	-	..	..	..	..	..	..
Cyprus	0.0	12.8	9.0	8.6	..	..	..	..	..	..
Malta	16.6	0.0	0.1	4.1	..	..	..	..	..	..
Montenegro	-	0.1	-	-	..	..	..	..	..	..
Romania	0.0	0.4	0.1	0.2	..	..	..	..	..	..
Russian Federation	1.9	14.9	63.0	44.7	..	..	..	..	..	..
Ukraine	0.3	0.7	0.2	0.7	..	..	..	..	..	..
AFRICA	**6.3**	**2.4**	**20.0**	**3.5**	**..**	**..**	**..**	**..**	**..**	**..**
Northern Africa	0.0	0.1	0.0	0.4	..	..	..	..	..	..
Algeria	-	0.1	-	0.1	..	..	..	..	..	..
Egypt	0.0	-	0.0	0.3	..	..	..	..	..	..
Libya	-	-	-	-	..	..	..	..	..	..
Morocco	0.0	-	-	0.0	..	..	..	..	..	..
Tunisia	-	-	-	-	..	..	..	..	..	..
Other African countries	6.3	2.3	20.0	3.1	..	..	..	..	..	..
Nigeria	-	-	0.0	-	..	..	..	..	..	..
South Africa	3.4	2.0	19.6	-1.0	..	..	..	..	..	..
AMERICA	**14 862.3**	**18 847.0**	**17 249.0**	**16 804.2**	**..**	**..**	**..**	**..**	**..**	**..**
Northern America	13 349.3	18 446.6	15 843.8	15 790.6	..	..	..	..	..	..
Central America and Caribbean countries	40.1	58.8	86.0	53.0	..	..	..	..	..	..
Bahamas	-	-	-	-	..	..	..	..	..	..
Bermuda	-	-	-	-	..	..	..	..	..	..
Cayman Islands	-	-	-	-	..	..	..	..	..	..
El Salvador	35.0	26.6	0.1	10.3	..	..	..	..	..	..
Guatemala	0.6	5.5	0.7	7.3	..	..	..	..	..	..
Honduras	0.3	0.8	0.5	1.2	..	..	..	..	..	..
Nicaragua	-	3.5	0.1	20.5	..	..	..	..	..	..
Panama	-1.3	16.6	34.8	21.1	..	..	..	..	..	..
Virgin Islands, U.S.	-	-	-	-	..	..	..	..	..	..
South America	1 473.0	341.6	1 317.7	960.6	..	..	..	..	..	..
Argentina	287.2	349.7	1 085.0	463.5	..	..	..	..	..	..
Bolivia	0.1	0.0	0.2	0.7	..	..	..	..	..	..
Brazil	912.6	-131.0	114.0	299.8	..	..	..	..	..	..
Ecuador	2.8	0.1	0.0	3.9	..	..	..	..	..	..
Paraguay	0.0	0.3	-	0.1	..	..	..	..	..	..
Peru	6.9	8.3	21.3	9.5	..	..	..	..	..	..
Uruguay	23.5	-1.2	28.2	26.1	..	..	..	..	..	..
Venezuela	13.3	7.1	-18.3	-36.0	..	..	..	..	..	..

Table 1. Foreign direct investment flows by country *(cont.)*

Million US dollars

	Inward					Outward				
	2016	2017	2018	2019	2020	2016	2017	2018	2019	2020
ASIA	**5 388.9**	**3 122.7**	**3 427.7**	**2 010.6**	..	..	..	..	..	..
Near and Middle East	2 017.7	2.5	-4.6	-2.8	..	..	..	..	..	..
Gulf Arabian countries	2.5	0.1	-6.3	-	..	..	..	..	..	..
Kuwait	-	-	-	-	..	..	..	..	..	..
Qatar	-	-	0.0	-	..	..	..	..	..	..
Saudi Arabia	-	0.1	-6.4	-	..	..	..	..	..	..
United Arab Emirates	2.5	-	0.1	-	..	..	..	..	..	..
Other Near and Middle East	2 015.2	2.4	1.8	-2.8	..	..	..	..	..	..
Jordan	-	-	-	0.0	..	..	..	..	..	..
Other Asian countries	3 371.2	3 120.2	3 432.3	2 013.5	..	..	..	..	..	..
China	68.6	203.5	260.5	85.5	..	..	..	..	..	..
Hong Kong, China	84.1	73.5	154.5	79.6	..	..	..	..	..	..
India	27.2	47.6	23.3	29.2	..	..	..	..	..	..
Indonesia	18.0	33.0	37.0	13.8	..	..	..	..	..	..
Iran, Islamic Republic of	-	-	-0.1	-	..	..	..	..	..	..
Malaysia	86.8	81.0	4.0	123.3	..	..	..	..	..	..
Philippines	-131.9	1.8	0.8	0.4	..	..	..	..	..	..
Singapore	93.8	13.4	34.9	11.0	..	..	..	..	..	..
Chinese Taipei	36.3	-33.0	-64.2	19.0	..	..	..	..	..	..
Thailand	-	0.1	0.1	1.4	..	..	..	..	..	..
Viet Nam	2.6	1.2	0.8	-	..	..	..	..	..	..
AUSTRALIA, OCEANIA AND POLAR REGIONS	**98.3**	**1 371.9**	**608.8**	**768.9**	..	..	..	..	..	..
WORLD unallocated and confidential	**524.0**	**460.9**	**193.9**	**0.8**	..	..	..	..	..	..
European Union (since 01/02/2020)	..	..	..	..	..	..	..	..	..	..
G20 countries excl. European Union	**22 333.8**	**28 605.9**	**26 735.5**	**25 898.3**	..	..	..	..	..	..
G20 OECD countries	**21 014.9**	**28 086.1**	**25 139.6**	**24 962.8**	..	..	..	..	..	..
G20 Non-OECD countries	**1 318.9**	**519.8**	**1 596.0**	**935.5**	..	..	..	..	..	..
MENA countries	**2.5**	**0.2**	**-6.3**	**0.4**	..	..	..	..	..	..
ASEAN countries	**69.3**	**130.5**	**77.6**	**149.8**	..	..	..	..	..	..

- Nil; .. Not available

Note: Data excludes resident Special Purpose Entities (SPEs). Detailed metadata at: *http://metalinks.oecd.org/idi/20220712/6d95*.

Source: *OECD International Direct Investment Statistics (database): https://doi.org/10.1787/idi-data-en*

Table 2. Foreign direct investment positions by country
At year end

Million US dollars

	Inward					Outward				
	2016	2017	2018	2019	2020	2016	2017	2018	2019	2020
WORLD	**432 742.4**	**497 296.9**	**516 647.0**	**567 781.8**	**545 611.6**	**149 645.1**	**181 664.0**	**160 279.7**	**175 633.1**	**189 535.6**
OECD COUNTRIES	**421 436.4**	**484 766.5**	**500 629.6**	**550 958.6**	**530 866.9**	**118 034.6**	**145 915.9**	**124 483.9**	**136 943.7**	**155 226.1**
Australia	473.2	522.0	614.1	604.1	615.6	.. c	.. c	.. c	.. c	-
Austria	651.8	817.1	1 059.8	1 277.1	1 159.1	.. c	.. c	.. c	.. c	-
Belgium	1 378.6	1 569.8	1 814.4	2 022.0	1 843.1	.. c	.. c	.. c	.. c	.. c
Canada	23 892.8	28 350.6	34 424.6	38 545.4	35 663.9	512.7	1 179.6	1 169.0	1 034.0	911.6
Chile	1 181.8	1 346.4	1 385.5	1 390.5	1 529.0	2 912.4	3 718.2	3 392.4	2 701.0	1 801.0
Colombia	804.7	941.0	1 061.2	1 145.6	1 078.9	887.4	4 639.1	4 689.6	5 332.4	4 103.2
Costa Rica	41.9	61.1	66.8	75.3	75.6	1 612.6	845.3	797.7	988.5	791.2
Czech Republic	16.5	21.5	21.6	22.1	24.0	.. c	.. c	.. c	.. c	.. c
Denmark	1 021.8	1 125.5	1 218.2	1 371.7	1 416.0	.. c	.. c	.. c	.. c	.. c
Estonia	0.1	0.1	0.3	0.5	2.3	-	-	-	-	-
Finland	58.2	59.5	60.1	76.8	60.0	-	-	-	-	-
France	3 744.4	4 711.4	5 427.5	6 381.8	6 127.8	.. c	.. c	.. c	.. c	.. c
Germany	10 750.4	15 222.1	16 323.8	19 310.2	19 661.9	-30.3	96.8	-127.5	947.0	1 314.3
Greece	1.5	1.6	1.8	1.8	1.6	-	-	-	-	-
Hungary	31.7	37.6	24.7	35.9	30.7	2 214.2	2 229.2	2 306.2	2 392.9	2 382.6
Iceland	4.9	5.0	5.0	4.9	5.0	-	-	-	-	-
Ireland	3 437.4	4 878.5	4 585.2	3 566.7	3 571.4	.. c	.. c	.. c	.. c	.. c
Israel	111.1	116.0	124.2	134.0	127.4	.. c	.. c	.. c	.. c	.. c
Italy	1 578.0	2 024.4	2 955.4	2 504.2	2 361.4	-	-	-	-	.. c
Japan	7 846.2	9 220.7	10 041.1	11 274.2	10 530.6	.. c	.. c	.. c	.. c	.. c
Korea	2 702.7	3 067.5	3 585.7	3 789.2	3 827.2	-	-	-	.. c	.. c
Latvia	.. c	.. c	0.1	0.2	0.1	.. c	.. c	.. c	-	-
Lithuania	0.3	0.3	0.4	0.9	1.1	-	-	-	-	-
Luxembourg	8 882.6	8 580.7	9 124.2	11 950.5	11 028.7	-	.. c	.. c	.. c	.. c
Mexico	-	-	-	-	-	-	-	-	-	-
Netherlands	74 723.3	107 329.0	103 522.2	115 670.0	112 656.6	30 371.0	32 175.0	26 265.9	25 922.2	8 908.1
New Zealand	173.1	200.8	217.5	306.5	263.8	-	-	-	-	-
Norway	209.8	219.3	211.8	261.6	333.5	-	-	-	-	-
Poland	19.5	30.9	21.3	22.5	21.9	.. c	.. c	.. c	.. c	.. c
Portugal	149.5	171.6	151.0	211.0	162.5	-	-	-	-	-
Slovak Republic	29.0	37.3	42.2	43.9	50.5	.. c	.. c	.. c	.. c	-
Slovenia	13.0	14.5	14.1	12.9	10.6	-	-	-	-	-
Spain	61 460.6	69 461.3	87 000.2	96 476.6	88 430.0	8 004.5	9 401.0	11 210.4	11 235.7	21 543.1
Sweden	2 304.9	2 466.0	2 564.7	2 903.7	2 888.2	-	-	-	-	-
Switzerland	12 996.7	14 572.5	13 505.0	14 944.0	15 024.8	1 080.0	471.8	465.3	1 404.3	393.8
Turkey	15.0	12.9	24.2	25.2	23.5	.. c	.. c	.. c	.. c	-
United Kingdom	21 609.0	24 407.9	21 712.6	23 519.2	25 423.4	16 809.1	19 569.2	13 364.9	12 732.7	17 162.6
United States	179 967.7	184 164.8	178 845.2	192 296.6	184 910.8	56 161.0	77 075.0	66 437.3	78 573.8	96 705.9
EUROPE	**205 321.9**	**258 066.0**	**271 714.4**	**303 017.6**	**292 713.4**	**61 114.7**	**66 678.9**	**55 167.7**	**56 655.0**	**53 463.6**
Bulgaria	1.6	1.7	3.1	5.1	4.7	-	-	-	-	-
Croatia	0.1	0.2	0.2	0.3	0.2	-	.. c	.. c	.. c	.. c
Cyprus	25.1	25.5	30.3	34.5	34.6	-	-	-	-	-
Malta	106.5	146.3	172.4	204.0	210.3	-	-	-	-	-
Montenegro	-	-	-	-	-	-	-	-	-	-
Romania	4.8	5.8	5.3	5.3	4.9	-	-	-	-	-
Russian Federation	16.7	17.4	17.5	18.3	15.4	-	.. c	.. c	.. c	-
Ukraine	1.2	2.0	2.4	3.3	3.1	-	-	-	-	-
AFRICA	**22.9**	**37.0**	**28.5**	**47.2**	**50.9**	**7.9**	**-**	**1.3**	**37.5**	**48.8**
Northern Africa	2.9	3.8	4.2	4.8	4.5	-	-	-	-	-
Algeria	2.3	2.6	3.0	3.2	3.1	-	-	-	-	-
Egypt	0.7	0.7	0.7	1.0	0.9	-	-	-	-	-
Libya	.. c	.. c	.. c	.. c	.. c	-	-	-	-	-
Morocco	.. c	0.5	0.5	0.6	0.5	-	-	-	-	-
Tunisia	0.0	.. c	.. c	.. c	.. c	-	-	-	-	-
Other African countries	10.4	26.3	14.2	29.5	33.8	-	-	-	-	-
Nigeria	0.5	0.5	0.5	0.5	0.6	-	-	-	-	-
South Africa	8.0	6.8	5.5	5.2	4.8	.. c	-	.. c	.. c	.. c
AMERICA	**212 027.9**	**221 508.9**	**225 084.5**	**243 397.7**	**232 742.1**	**87 200.7**	**114 793.8**	**104 149.4**	**117 770.0**	**134 752.4**
Northern America	203 860.5	212 515.4	213 269.8	230 842.0	220 574.7	56 673.7	78 254.6	67 606.3	79 607.8	97 617.5
Central America and Caribbean countries	3 760.1	4 228.4	4 686.4	5 306.8	5 136.0	11 338.5	11 804.6	12 061.2	14 499.4	14 363.3
Bahamas	194.4	215.9	231.0	238.3	306.0	.. c	.. c	.. c	-	-
Bermuda	158.4	144.3	152.2	142.6	128.3	.. c	.. c	.. c	.. c	.. c
Cayman Islands	648.1	477.6	537.9	549.7	600.2	-	-	.. c	.. c	.. c
El Salvador	8.9	9.2	9.2	8.1	11.4	1 189.6	674.0	870.2	962.7	1 013.6
Guatemala	77.8	101.4	179.6	179.0	126.2	1 611.9	811.0	773.6	1 094.7	1 181.4
Honduras	4.8	5.4	5.8	6.8	6.3	931.4	.. c	.. c	.. c	.. c
Nicaragua	33.2	40.1	44.7	48.9	47.7	781.9	203.2	314.7	1 027.3	1 076.4
Panama	1 295.4	1 554.1	1 560.8	1 706.6	1 464.8	345.6	473.0	399.3	750.2	604.0
Virgin Islands, U.S.	131.9	138.3	156.2	163.4	138.9	-	-	-	-	-
South America	4 383.1	4 738.3	7 100.0	7 211.6	6 996.7	18 860.8	24 004.5	23 573.8	23 121.3	22 279.4
Argentina	297.5	381.5	410.5	472.4	453.8	-766.3	936.5	1 630.2	1 311.6	946.0
Bolivia	.. c	.. c	.. c	.. c	.. c	.. c	.. c	.. c	.. c	.. c
Brazil	1 138.1	1 122.9	3 173.4	3 024.6	2 762.9	11 665.0	9 214.7	8 158.5	8 597.1	10 202.8
Ecuador	49.0	50.9	53.2	56.8	53.5	2 675.0	2 209.1	1 751.6	1 359.4	1 566.6
Paraguay	2.2	4.0	4.2	4.5	3.7	.. c	.. c	.. c	.. c	.. c
Peru	151.0	160.7	167.5	186.8	172.0	1 179.4	3 274.8	3 921.1	3 809.3	3 646.8
Uruguay	538.0	480.9	575.9	640.0	645.2	.. c	.. c	11.3	8.2	13.1
Venezuela	201.6	228.8	246.4	264.6	260.4	307.9	12.0	19.0	2.3	.. c

MEXICO

Table 2. Foreign direct investment positions by country *(cont.)*

At year end

Million US dollars

	Inward					Outward				
	2016	2017	2018	2019	2020	2016	2017	2018	2019	2020
ASIA	**12 914.3**	**15 059.8**	**16 895.1**	**18 701.8**	**17 647.3**	**849.5**	**173.8**	**805.2**	**1 119.2**	**1 266.1**
Near and Middle East	247.2	302.2	320.3	358.5	395.9	-	-	-	-	-
Gulf Arabian countries	135.3	185.2	195.0	223.4	267.6	-	-	-	-	-
Kuwait	-	-	-	-	-	-	-	-	-	-
Qatar	.. c	.. c	.. c	.. c	.. c	-	-	-	-	-
Saudi Arabia	5.4	6.0	4.1	4.4	4.0	-	-	-	-	-
United Arab Emirates	129.8	179.2	190.8	218.9	263.5	.. c	.. c	-	-	-
Other Near and Middle East	112.0	117.0	125.3	135.1	128.3	-	-	-	-	-
Jordan	0.0	0.0	0.0	0.0	0.0	-	-	-	-	-
Other Asian countries	12 663.4	14 753.3	16 429.5	18 198.0	17 246.2	213.8	105.4	134.1	182.2	324.6
China	620.9	698.8	849.0	1 005.0	873.5	25.5	-66.9	-46.2	-14.1	13.2
Hong Kong, China	211.5	204.4	228.5	258.1	230.5	-	-	-	-	-
India	423.6	500.5	505.6	478.0	495.2	188.3	172.2	180.4	196.3	311.4
Indonesia	0.8	0.7	0.6	0.6	0.6	-	-	-	.. c	.. c
Iran, Islamic Republic of	1.9	2.0	2.1	2.1	2.0	-	-	-	-	-
Malaysia	3.9	5.3	8.2	14.4	13.6	-	-	-	-	-
Philippines	1.6	1.9	2.8	3.5	3.5	.. c	.. c	.. c	.. c	.. c
Singapore	603.6	805.1	960.4	1 045.3	922.2	.. c	.. c	.. c	.. c	.. c
Chinese Taipei	229.3	228.0	222.2	286.8	305.7	.. c	.. c	.. c	.. c	.. c
Thailand	11.0	10.5	14.5	31.2	32.9	-	-	-	.. c	.. c
Viet Nam	2.9	4.4	5.4	5.8	5.5	-	-	-	-	-
AUSTRALIA, OCEANIA AND POLAR REGIONS	**719.6**	**802.4**	**910.4**	**985.7**	**954.0**	**4.3**	**13.9**	**-2.1**	**0.0**	**-**
WORLD unallocated and confidential	**1 735.8**	**1 822.9**	**2 014.0**	**1 631.8**	**1 503.9**	**468.1**	**3.7**	**158.1**	**51.3**	**4.7**
European Union (since 01/02/2020)	..	..	..	..	**251 764.3**	..	..	..	..	**34 148.1**
G20 countries excl. European Union	**255 090.3**	**274 438.9**	**278 920.4**	**303 258.7**	**293 756.6**	**84 565.0**	**108 177.2**	**90 766.6**	**103 378.5**	**127 567.8**
G20 OECD countries	**252 579.3**	**271 704.3**	**273 954.2**	**298 250.1**	**289 146.3**	**73 452.5**	**97 920.6**	**80 843.8**	**93 287.6**	**116 094.4**
G20 Non-OECD countries	**2 511.0**	**2 734.6**	**4 966.3**	**5 008.6**	**4 610.3**	**11 112.5**	**10 256.6**	**9 922.8**	**10 090.9**	**11 473.4**
MENA countries	**139.0**	**189.9**	**200.1**	**229.1**	**272.9**	-	-	-	-	-
ASEAN countries	**623.9**	**827.9**	**992.0**	**1 100.9**	**978.3**	-	-	-	-	-

- Nil; .. Not available; c Confidential data

Note: Data excludes resident Special Purpose Entities (SPEs). Detailed metadata at: *http://metalinks.oecd.org/idi/20220712/6d95*.

Source: *OECD International Direct Investment Statistics (database): https://doi.org/10.1787/idi-data-en*

Table 4. Foreign direct investment flows by industrial sector

Million US dollars

	Inward					Outward				
	2016	2017	2018	2019	2020	2016	2017	2018	2019	2020
All FDI activities	**31 066.9**	**34 200.2**	**33 740.3**	**34 075.6**	..	**159.6**	**3 987.9**	**8 364.7**	**10 639.5**	**2 644.0**
Agriculture, forestry and fishing	**98.3**	**141.1**	**-18.3**	**103.9**	..	..	..	..	..	..
Mining and quarrying	**929.6**	**1 380.2**	**1 655.5**	**1 920.1**	..	..	..	..	..	..
Extraction activities	231.7	673.0	992.7	1 242.9	..	..	..	..	..	..
Manufacturing	**18 039.9**	**15 522.3**	**15 560.1**	**15 964.4**	..	..	..	..	..	..
of which:										
Food products, beverages and tobacco	2 659.6	2 015.2	1 082.8	2 524.0	..	..	..	..	..	..
Textiles, wood and paper products; printing	821.6	435.6	426.5	250.5	..	..	..	..	..	..
Chemical, rubber, plastic, non-metallic mineral products	5 259.3	1 561.7	1 827.9	2 706.0	..	..	..	..	..	..
Metal and machinery products, except electrical equipment	2 789.1	2 526.3	4 210.0	1 413.2	..	..	..	..	..	..
Motor vehicles, trailers, semi-trailers, other transport equipment	5 482.2	7 848.7	6 595.4	7 405.0	..	..	..	..	..	..
Other manufacturing	1 028.0	1 134.9	1 417.6	1 665.7	..	..	..	..	..	..
Electricity, gas, steam and air conditioning supply	**1 293.8**	**2 099.7**	**4 971.3**	**1 236.8**	..	..	..	..	..	..
Water supply; sewerage, waste management and remediation activities	**8.5**	**10.4**	**-6.1**	**2.1**	..	..	..	..	..	..
Construction	**1 154.2**	**3 032.9**	**1 641.7**	**241.0**	..	..	..	..	..	..
Services	**9 542.7**	**12 013.6**	**9 936.2**	**14 607.1**	..	..	..	..	..	..
Wholesale and retail trade; repair of motor vehicles and motorcycles	1 919.9	3 116.0	2 898.0	3 244.9	..	..	..	..	..	..
Transportation and storage	1 869.7	3 374.8	1 330.6	870.5	..	..	..	..	..	..
Accommodation and food service activities	623.7	923.1	1 317.7	1 230.3	..	..	..	..	..	..
Information and communication	981.5	667.0	1 128.8	1 896.8	..	..	..	..	..	..
Financial and insurance activities	3 390.2	2 562.6	2 364.7	5 381.6	..	..	..	..	..	..
Activities of holding companies	-	-	-	-	..	..	..	..	..	..
Real estate activities	322.9	466.6	242.2	238.8	..	..	..	..	..	..
Professional, scientific and technical activities	206.8	328.9	328.9	456.2	..	..	..	..	..	..
Administrative and support service activities	155.1	349.3	216.3	1 189.2	..	..	..	..	..	..
Public administration; activities of households and of extraterritorial organisations	-	-	-	-	..	..	..	..	..	..
Education	0.0	30.2	63.7	-7.0	..	..	..	..	..	..
Human health and social work activities	11.9	10.4	6.6	21.2	..	..	..	..	..	..
Arts, entertainment and recreation	51.5	166.6	20.3	37.5	..	..	..	..	..	..
Other services	9.5	18.2	18.4	47.2	..	..	..	..	..	..
Not allocated and confidential	**0.0**	**0.0**	**0.0**	**0.0**	..	**159.6**	**3 987.9**	**8 364.7**	**10 639.5**	**2 644.0**
Private real estate activities	-	-	-	-	..	..	..	..	..	..

- Nil; .. Not available

Note: Data excludes resident Special Purpose Entities (SPEs). Detailed metadata at: *http://metalinks.oecd.org/idi/20220712/6d95*.

Source: *OECD International Direct Investment Statistics (database)*: *https://doi.org/10.1787/idi-data-en*

Table 5. Foreign direct investment positions by industrial sector

At year end

Million US dollars

	Inward					Outward				
	2016	2017	2018	2019	2020	2016	2017	2018	2019	2020
All FDI activities	**432 742.4**	**497 296.9**	**516 647.0**	**567 781.8**	**545 611.6**	**149 645.1**	**181 664.0**	**160 279.7**	**175 633.1**	**189 535.6**
Agriculture, forestry and fishing	..	..	..	..	..	..	..	..	..	..
Mining and quarrying	..	..	..	..	..	..	..	..	..	..
Extraction activities	..	..	..	..	..	..	..	..	..	..
Manufacturing	..	..	..	..	..	..	..	..	..	..
of which:										
Food products, beverages and tobacco	..	..	..	..	..	..	..	..	..	..
Textiles, wood and paper products; printing	..	..	..	..	..	..	..	..	..	..
Chemical, rubber, plastic, non-metallic mineral products	..	..	..	..	..	..	..	..	..	..
Metal and machinery products, except electrical equipment	..	..	..	..	..	..	..	..	..	..
Motor vehicles, trailers, semi-trailers, other transport equipment	..	..	..	..	..	..	..	..	..	..
Other manufacturing	..	..	..	..	..	..	..	..	..	..
Electricity, gas, steam and air conditioning supply	..	..	..	..	..	..	..	..	..	..
Water supply; sewerage, waste management and remediation activities	..	..	..	..	..	..	..	..	..	..
Construction	..	..	..	..	..	..	..	..	..	..
Services	..	..	..	..	..	..	..	..	..	..
Wholesale and retail trade; repair of motor vehicles and motorcycles	..	..	..	..	..	..	..	..	..	..
Transportation and storage	..	..	..	..	..	..	..	..	..	..
Accommodation and food service activities	..	..	..	..	..	..	..	..	..	..
Information and communication	..	..	..	..	..	..	..	..	..	..
Financial and insurance activities	..	..	..	..	..	..	..	..	..	..
Activities of holding companies	..	..	..	..	..	..	..	..	..	..
Real estate activities	..	..	..	..	..	..	..	..	..	..
Professional, scientific and technical activities	..	..	..	..	..	..	..	..	..	..
Administrative and support service activities	..	..	..	..	..	..	..	..	..	..
Public administration; activities of households and of extraterritorial organisations	..	..	..	..	..	..	..	..	..	..
Education	..	..	..	..	..	..	..	..	..	..
Human health and social work activities	..	..	..	..	..	..	..	..	..	..
Arts, entertainment and recreation	..	..	..	..	..	..	..	..	..	..
Other services	..	..	..	..	..	..	..	..	..	..
Not allocated and confidential	**432 742.4**	**497 296.9**	**516 647.0**	**567 781.8**	**545 611.6**	**149 645.1**	**181 664.0**	**160 279.7**	**175 633.1**	**189 535.6**
Private real estate activities	..	..	..	..	..	..	..	..	..	..

.. Not available

Note: Data excludes resident Special Purpose Entities (SPEs). Detailed metadata at: *http://metalinks.oecd.org/idi/20220712/6d95*.

Source: *OECD International Direct Investment Statistics (database): https://doi.org/10.1787/idi-data-en*

NETHERLANDS

Table 1. Foreign direct investment flows by country

Million US dollars

	Inward					Outward				
	2016	2017	2018	2019	2020	2016	2017	2018	2019	2020
WORLD	**55 430.7**	**9 285.3**	**87 862.6**	**-27 168.9**	**-69 170.4**	**186 165.0**	**21 031.5**	**-46 983.4**	**13 335.9**	**-119 396.0**
OECD COUNTRIES	**26 900.4**	**-23 753.8**	**93 235.0**	**1 944.5**	**-35 675.2**	**128 592.3**	**-2 074.2**	**-55 804.3**	**23 724.4**	**-108 539.0**
Australia	99.5	-68.8	74.4	-30.2	-86.6	3 051.0	1 220.8	6 720.2	-907.9	-4 412.5
Austria	5 325.7	2 091.1	1 482.4	-79.5	2 928.8	11 202.0	2 501.4	-1 644.0	2 583.7	-498.0
Belgium	-3 454.6	1 406.8	-2 533.9	6 788.3	1 023.4	-14 170.1	-25 069.3	-7 381.1	-23 390.8	3 081.5
Canada	458.9	129.6	214.8	-335.8	10 629.1	3 889.2	9 809.5	-2 223.5	2 972.1	-13 014.2
Chile	1.1	56.4	14.2	-5.6	3.4	-89.6	728.2	-121.6	743.3	-107.1
Colombia	-	125.1	830.9	59.3	-46.7	-266.5	698.9	13.0	-199.3	29.6
Costa Rica	-2.2	-7.9	27.1	-586.6	-550.4	-53.1	-372.0	-75.5	-1 814.6	-1 451.9
Czech Republic	202.4	21.4	41.3	-184.7	1 512.3	-288.6	-2 335.7	-234.9	649.3	4 300.9
Denmark	-190.2	519.7	473.3	-725.4	2 512.8	1 789.2	1 020.2	592.5	-1 594.1	1 986.3
Estonia	3.3	3.4	2.4	43.7	-22.8	-79.6	-55.2	44.8	29.1	-4.6
Finland	-275.4	-62.0	114.5	-815.0	-3 850.7	-766.3	529.8	-849.8	-64.9	972.1
France	2 850.8	16 665.5	14 632.4	-2 271.4	6 705.4	-7 318.4	19 626.9	2 133.8	-3 156.8	15 935.0
Germany	-27 619.2	-10 498.3	-1 332.5	19 935.1	-19 218.2	-5 114.5	16 797.4	2 177.5	8 482.0	-8 847.9
Greece	-1.1	7.9	-5.9	146.6	6.8	120.5	173.6	35.4	424.3	-394.3
Hungary	-8.8	22.5	17.7	10 416.4	1 887.2	-245.5	-994.3	-190.0	-466.8	-10 083.2
Iceland	-343.9	365.2	76.7	446.7	72.9	-13.3	-170.2	-5.9	67.2	550.4
Ireland	-6 280.0	1 113.7	12 349.8	6 699.9	-22 008.0	11 705.2	34 438.1	5 648.5	36 660.7	2 311.1
Israel	10 771.9	3 526.1	-168.8	57.1	-8 278.1	-1 017.4	1 727.0	408.4	2 413.5	1 467.8
Italy	-7 663.4	4 978.0	2 568.2	-848.5	-2 317.9	5 943.8	-6 431.1	3 839.3	-7 173.4	-11 053.0
Japan	242.2	2 217.3	1 128.3	-3 000.1	-2 310.0	-1 155.6	-674.1	-114.5	3 228.5	-951.6
Korea	-484.4	120.6	24.8	-368.3	1 063.2	-634.7	2 347.0	-712.9	-2 213.1	284.9
Latvia	-2.2	-2.3	-1.2	-5.6	-31.9	-119.4	160.1	187.7	15.7	-128.8
Lithuania	24.3	-2.3	-35.4	1.1	-10.3	15.5	64.3	7.1	-19.0	-62.7
Luxembourg	45 231.7	-1 284.0	-2 989.5	7 749.9	-19 724.2	-11 948.5	-10 369.7	-34 752.7	-5 571.5	-37 255.8
Mexico	6 360.7	-3.4	1 962.7	-1 032.1	-1 466.7	-1 082.6	2 155.3	2 905.7	221.7	-3 863.2
Netherlands	-	-	-	-	-	-	-	-	-	-
New Zealand	-5.5	-10.1	70.8	15.7	-325.9	-131.6	324.7	799.0	-1 538.1	-943.6
Norway	-397.0	1.1	1 771.5	-16.8	-1 010.8	671.2	-2 560.0	990.2	1 035.5	-155.0
Poland	-246.6	299.9	22.4	-342.6	84.3	477.7	843.2	419.0	314.6	921.9
Portugal	26.5	-47.3	-211.3	184.7	26.2	578.3	237.9	103.9	359.3	-202.8
Slovak Republic	39.8	-9.0	5.9	21.3	-37.6	-121.6	110.5	-295.1	-331.4	29.6
Slovenia	1.1	1.1	7.1	-19.0	-	94.0	49.6	48.4	-48.1	28.5
Spain	361.6	-258.1	527.6	4 194.6	-6 245.0	1 030.6	-30.4	1 759.7	8 857.0	4 568.7
Sweden	-675.7	2 977.1	826.2	-1 310.9	-3 589.7	5 217.3	906.3	2 838.4	-1 317.6	-2 892.3
Switzerland	14 676.5	-36 027.5	19 540.9	-14 792.3	-49 165.8	41 719.6	-57 096.2	57 331.5	-10 092.9	-52 529.9
Turkey	306.3	-25.9	-1 489.4	263.1	249.6	-110.6	766.5	343.4	-294.4	740.7
United Kingdom	-19 635.1	79 433.0	63 210.2	-24 715.1	103 878.1	121 321.5	45 091.9	-87 942.9	9 059.7	31 927.1
United States	7 223.3	-91 414.7	-19 157.3	-4 120.7	-28 511.7	-35 811.1	-37 853.7	-8 669.9	3 788.2	-30 274.6
EUROPE	**-4 588.1**	**61 968.2**	**110 493.3**	**10 935.9**	**-17 731.1**	**173 141.7**	**16 158.3**	**-53 155.9**	**15 252.4**	**-56 280.3**
Bulgaria	3.3	1.1	-	6.7	-25.1	120.5	152.2	23.6	-23.5	-19.4
Croatia	58.6	4.5	1.2	-33.6	36.5	267.6	-509.5	86.2	-62.7	78.6
Cyprus	-1 752.7	155.6	-1 554.3	718.7	-680.3	2 942.6	-456.5	-1 989.9	-1 422.8	-1 996.6
Malta	3.3	6.8	7.1	10.1	795.4	2 899.5	166.8	-1 405.6	-25.7	-295.2
Montenegro	-	-	-	20.2	-3.4	-13.3	-	-	-1.1	3.4
Romania	228.9	4.5	-3.5	-234.0	-87.7	319.6	732.7	620.8	-42.5	25.1
Russian Federation	-4 769.4	-1 331.3	980.8	-151.1	596.0	799.5	2 285.0	3 321.1	3 534.1	627.9
Ukraine	2.2	-1.1	2.4	-82.8	10.3	73.0	319.0	390.7	216.1	566.4
AFRICA	**32 641.8**	**-2 474.4**	**1 578.0**	**-24 954.7**	**-1 544.2**	**-4 970.7**	**-3 871.0**	**-2 930.5**	**-1 625.4**	**-2 022.8**
Northern Africa	29 557.7	-60.9	152.2	-39.2	-13.7	4 617.9	342.7	1 359.6	-1 222.4	-1 564.7
Algeria	29 565.4	-112.7	103.9	-31.3	69.5	1 005.2	-391.2	-56.7	120.9	-213.1
Egypt	-7.7	47.3	33.0	-11.2	-63.8	694.5	1 095.7	821.4	-1 441.8	-725.9
Libya	6.6	4.5	7.1	4.5	-2.3	2 989.1	-444.1	616.1	92.9	-1 013.1
Morocco	-5.5	-	5.9	-2.2	-21.7	21.0	33.8	14.2	-26.9	279.2
Tunisia	-1.1	-	2.4	-	5.7	-91.8	48.5	-35.4	31.3	109.4
Other African countries	3 084.2	-2 413.5	1 425.7	-24 914.4	-1 530.5	-9 588.6	-4 213.7	-4 290.1	-401.9	-458.1
Nigeria	-1 996.0	-11.3	10.6	-179.1	-	-760.8	2 244.4	-73.2	1 699.3	-313.4
South Africa	4 836.9	-2 333.4	-35.4	-28 120.5	-1 080.3	-11 680.9	1 042.7	-2 525.7	-351.5	-1 073.5
AMERICA	**15 750.3**	**-59 674.2**	**-30 755.3**	**-19 996.6**	**-32 549.3**	**16 871.6**	**-17 411.8**	**-2 104.3**	**-8 379.0**	**-18 129.9**
Northern America	7 682.2	-91 285.1	-18 942.5	-4 456.5	-17 883.8	-32 342.1	-28 038.6	-10 893.4	6 732.3	-43 324.2
Central America and Caribbean countries	15 038.2	20 324.7	-3 475.7	-6 846.5	-11 181.8	31 296.0	2 319.9	15 135.1	-13 437.8	20 730.5
Bahamas	190.2	-361.9	-	497.0	-1 637.6	837.1	-290.8	8 946.1	284.3	-8 876.4
Bermuda	20 863.7	6 955.2	-7 421.2	-6 056.2	-4 790.9	-1 747.2	-3 520.5	502.8	1 137.4	31 000.6
Cayman Islands	-451.2	1 341.5	1 293.5	-91.8	616.5	6 451.4	1 737.1	1 169.6	1 419.5	2 303.1
El Salvador	-	140.9	62.6	104.1	-20.5	-6.6	10.1	-5.9	2.2	-36.5
Guatemala	-	-	-	-1.1	-2.3	458.9	44.0	-110.9	-151.1	-30.8
Honduras	-	-	-	-1.1	-2.3	-11.1	92.4	10.6	49.3	-20.5
Nicaragua	-1.1	9.0	-9.4	28.0	-3.4	5.5	46.2	-50.7	-	-
Panama	-44.2	-24.8	-	-23.5	-131.1	-1 846.7	977.3	-83.8	208.2	-266.7
Virgin Islands, U.S.	-	-	-	4.5	-	5.5	-3.4	-51.9	-127.6	1 906.6
South America	-6 970.0	11 286.2	-8 337.1	-8 693.6	-3 483.8	17 917.7	8 306.8	-6 346.0	-1 673.6	4 463.8
Argentina	14.4	3.4	3.5	54.9	-111.7	795.1	1 560.1	262.0	1 623.2	39.9
Bolivia	1.1	-	406.0	40.3	128.8	-23.2	2.3	14.2	191.4	296.3
Brazil	-7 065.1	10 616.6	-9 780.5	-8 714.9	-6 676.9	17 553.9	4 670.3	-6 722.5	-2 760.6	-865.0
Ecuador	1.1	1.1	-1.2	-24.6	6.8	69.7	-55.2	44.8	-156.7	54.7
Paraguay	6.6	-	1.2	4.5	-6.8	-21.0	125.1	-8.3	6.7	-3.4
Peru	123.9	-168.0	139.3	145.5	-42.2	34.3	746.3	86.2	-429.9	167.5
Uruguay	3.3	665.1	-13.0	159.0	-564.1	-147.1	124.0	127.5	446.7	1 280.9
Venezuela	-63.0	-18.0	55.5	-200.4	-223.4	2.2	-302.1	-46.0	-854.1	-1 010.8

NETHERLANDS

Table 1. Foreign direct investment flows by country *(cont.)*

Million US dollars

	Inward					Outward				
	2016	2017	2018	2019	2020	2016	2017	2018	2019	2020
ASIA	**11 522.7**	**9 578.4**	**6 390.9**	**6 839.8**	**-16 980.1**	**-1 853.4**	**24 588.0**	**3 722.4**	**10 675.0**	**-37 659.3**
Near and Middle East	10 983.1	5 186.6	5 384.2	9 864.5	-12 031.9	2 452.7	3 274.7	2 076.0	-1 198.9	-10 121.9
Gulf Arabian countries	210.1	1 473.3	5 525.8	9 975.4	-3 814.2	3 052.1	1 175.7	1 570.9	-3 574.4	-11 694.6
Kuwait	3.3	5.6	203.0	-10.1	-6.8	-301.9	-19.2	27.1	126.5	-3 490.6
Qatar	-11.1	9.0	8.3	4.5	-37.6	263.2	197.3	-289.2	-138.8	-1 511.1
Saudi Arabia	48.7	1 924.2	3 867.6	9 937.3	-3 015.4	1 294.9	1 861.1	487.4	-1 771.0	722.5
United Arab Emirates	152.6	-512.9	1 510.7	154.5	-712.3	-310.7	-144.3	841.5	851.9	-1 012.0
Other Near and Middle East	10 773.0	3 713.2	-141.6	-110.8	-8 217.7	-599.4	2 099.0	505.1	2 375.5	1 572.7
Jordan	2.2	-	1.2	17.9	2.3	6.6	-9.0	35.4	-41.4	-12.5
Other Asian countries	539.6	4 391.8	1 006.7	-3 024.7	-4 948.1	-4 306.1	21 313.3	1 646.4	11 874.0	-27 537.3
China	225.6	-192.8	224.2	-89.6	585.8	986.4	875.9	573.6	1 230.3	805.7
Hong Kong, China	123.9	2 427.0	80.3	2 749.4	-4 157.3	-1 098.1	1 722.5	-547.6	10 802.6	-14 972.1
India	179.1	22.5	3.5	320.2	-70.7	-252.1	2 041.5	1 860.0	446.7	2 071.8
Indonesia	47.6	-11.3	100.3	96.3	-295.2	2 991.3	753.0	-378.9	-329.1	255.3
Iran, Islamic Republic of	1.1	1.1	-	-1.1	-3.4	232.2	-478.0	-4.7	-	-74.1
Malaysia	1.1	-316.8	-636.1	-1 632.2	-337.3	415.8	192.8	126.3	-535.1	-111.7
Philippines	27.6	-99.2	23.6	476.9	30.8	-149.3	-406.9	108.6	90.7	-1 464.4
Singapore	125.0	47.3	383.6	-1 398.2	121.9	-6 385.0	14 613.9	257.3	1 787.8	-3 977.2
Chinese Taipei	-25.4	204.0	-310.4	-16.8	-479.8	73.0	441.9	505.1	-122.0	-7 176.1
Thailand	16.6	4.5	-2.4	1.1	-217.7	-263.2	120.6	158.1	21.3	648.4
Viet Nam	1.1	-2.3	1.2	-131.0	727.1	402.5	179.2	113.3	-494.8	37.6
AUSTRALIA, OCEANIA AND POLAR REGIONS	**94.0**	**-78.9**	**145.2**	**-13.4**	**-395.4**	**2 951.5**	**1 559.0**	**7 481.4**	**-2 477.3**	**-5 262.7**
WORLD unallocated and confidential	**10.0**	**-33.8**	**10.6**	**20.2**	**29.6**	**24.3**	**9.0**	**3.5**	**-109.7**	**-41.0**
European Union (since 01/02/2020)	**6 188.2**	**18 120.8**	**24 414.0**	**..**	**-60 332.8**	**4 553.8**	**32 257.9**	**-28 174.2**	**..**	**-39 380.1**
G20 countries excl. European Union	**-44 342.6**	**10 231.1**	**57 200.5**	**-43 191.5**	**58 545.9**	**95 466.1**	**67 946.1**	**-84 666.6**	**15 628.6**	**-20 944.7**
G20 OECD countries	**-37 860.2**	**1 533.1**	**61 836.4**	**-16 524.1**	**68 614.2**	**82 978.0**	**52 856.5**	**-81 543.7**	**14 006.5**	**-23 529.3**
G20 Non-OECD countries	**-6 482.4**	**8 698.0**	**-4 635.9**	**-26 667.4**	**-10 068.4**	**12 488.1**	**15 089.6**	**-3 122.9**	**1 622.1**	**2 584.6**
MENA countries	**29 770.0**	**1 413.6**	**5 679.2**	**9 961.9**	**-3 818.8**	**7 675.6**	**1 513.9**	**2 965.9**	**-4 842.7**	**-13 268.4**
ASEAN countries	**223.4**	**-377.6**	**-76.7**	**-2 585.9**	**39.9**	**-3 093.0**	**15 740.1**	**441.4**	**511.6**	**-4 322.5**

- Nil; .. Not available

Note: Data excludes resident Special Purpose Entities (SPEs). Detailed metadata at: *http://metalinks.oecd.org/idi/20220712/6d95*.

Source: *OECD International Direct Investment Statistics (database)*: *https://doi.org/10.1787/idi-data-en*

NETHERLANDS

Table 2. Foreign direct investment positions by country

At year end

Million US dollars

	Inward					Outward				
	2016	2017	2018	2019	2020	2016	2017	2018	2019	2020
WORLD	**1 327 646.3**	**1 506 566.3**	**1 470 002.3**	**1 447 101.8**	**2 565 442.4**	**2 135 949.2**	**2 390 965.5**	**2 198 827.6**	**2 287 045.6**	**3 470 071.2**
OECD COUNTRIES	**1 145 216.6**	**1 280 823.9**	**1 298 527.6**	**1 281 761.4**	**2 221 864.0**	**1 728 834.2**	**1 912 946.8**	**1 747 523.5**	**1 678 326.2**	**2 916 371.3**
Australia	658.8	692.0	257.6	232.5	946.1	42 608.8	43 809.1	48 833.3	39 494.5	56 457.2
Austria	6 536.3	9 706.2	13 803.5	7 969.0	4 615.3	33 088.4	13 180.6	10 061.8	8 957.5	23 616.4
Belgium	75 421.1	86 102.2	73 473.8	53 119.5	213 790.6	88 038.4	91 213.7	88 231.1	52 596.0	90 150.9
Canada	2 510.8	2 097.6	3 256.2	2 930.8	39 995.1	36 711.3	46 253.3	45 289.7	54 211.4	118 953.2
Chile	30.6	137.9	76.7	-41.6	138.7	1 275.4	2 267.9	1 773.5	2 956.6	3 086.3
Colombia	7.4	243.5	1 422.0	1 246.9	2.5	601.9	1 468.0	1 323.6	945.9	2 152.4
Costa Rica	23.2	15.6	50.4	1 901.8	2 412.6	230.8	-235.1	-311.4	-116.8	99.4
Czech Republic	98.0	109.1	159.1	-501.0	17 527.3	7 307.9	7 088.0	6 396.8	6 322.2	35 292.7
Denmark	8 588.6	10 260.3	9 052.0	14 997.8	16 024.1	8 787.8	10 767.6	11 522.8	11 466.0	13 914.6
Estonia	44.3	20.4	92.7	29.2	43.0	73.8	14.4	65.3	80.9	265.1
Finland	2 890.3	2 656.5	2 231.5	1 340.1	23 648.3	4 815.0	6 462.0	4 747.0	3 236.4	11 868.9
France	47 670.5	68 071.5	77 684.9	87 360.1	127 321.1	69 423.4	113 303.0	89 827.1	73 421.7	127 666.0
Germany	109 315.9	113 070.3	135 034.3	153 066.7	256 789.8	89 638.5	131 505.2	123 240.2	122 728.6	255 581.1
Greece	163.4	167.9	162.6	-19.1	67.5	2 156.6	2 721.3	2 649.4	3 532.9	8 214.5
Hungary	175.0	221.9	239.3	1 129.0	16 964.0	8 041.5	7 558.2	5 606.8	4 728.2	8 518.8
Iceland	665.1	883.9	651.5	1 392.9	1 521.7	85.4	4.8	5.7	77.5	747.3
Ireland	21 598.0	23 496.0	42 875.0	52 213.0	77 762.9	23 415.2	60 311.8	63 663.8	69 290.0	87 880.7
Israel	34 649.5	53 502.0	55 082.4	37 837.6	32 865.4	10 906.5	11 202.9	10 154.6	22 902.7	32 996.7
Italy	48 646.6	53 108.7	63 256.2	64 978.7	20 814.8	107 808.6	127 964.7	111 087.7	87 667.9	115 722.2
Japan	16 385.6	18 741.9	19 694.3	29 694.5	79 506.7	14 119.3	16 237.7	17 312.8	17 107.4	38 133.5
Korea	1 141.6	1 796.6	934.3	3 270.1	4 898.8	10 726.3	13 576.4	12 602.5	10 447.1	16 922.3
Latvia	19.0	3.6	22.9	-1.1	12.3	-16.9	159.5	258.8	289.8	82.2
Lithuania	72.7	87.6	45.8	16.9	34.4	154.9	157.1	166.0	224.7	114.1
Luxembourg	257 861.3	250 506.1	238 423.4	236 135.7	261 434.5	153 952.8	126 192.1	103 935.2	93 812.6	206 485.5
Mexico	20 955.0	24 224.0	19 523.7	22 990.3	5 021.5	39 432.9	44 929.2	52 038.0	53 103.8	57 479.4
Netherlands	-	-	-	-	-	-	-	-	-	-
New Zealand	16.9	208.7	97.3	262.9	1 095.8	3 465.8	4 591.0	5 362.9	2 544.4	3 098.5
Norway	8 892.2	1 126.2	1 396.8	721.2	1 569.5	7 248.9	6 458.4	6 654.5	9 718.0	10 807.5
Poland	751.6	1 194.5	1 431.2	1 002.0	106.8	9 615.3	12 516.2	12 869.2	13 243.1	23 492.5
Portugal	2 247.3	2 694.9	2 768.5	2 227.6	1 083.6	5 055.3	5 967.9	6 575.5	7 169.2	6 595.9
Slovak Republic	-12.6	-20.4	17.2	-278.6	-295.7	1 596.9	1 944.1	1 719.7	1 544.6	1 746.2
Slovenia	7.4	3.6	14.9	46.1	58.9	578.7	710.0	670.9	556.1	765.7
Spain	18 914.3	24 628.2	23 248.2	31 002.0	15 021.5	32 531.9	37 125.2	33 191.0	40 267.4	74 863.2
Sweden	8 644.5	13 663.9	13 130.3	15 559.4	58 166.6	14 254.2	19 203.6	17 907.0	20 833.5	43 966.1
Switzerland	89 372.8	109 960.4	123 022.7	75 693.1	153 691.3	219 603.7	206 597.5	236 420.9	184 395.6	395 112.3
Turkey	10 403.7	8 860.6	6 417.4	6 006.5	3 977.2	9 929.4	10 548.1	9 432.1	9 740.5	14 233.6
United Kingdom	96 811.4	190 599.7	173 921.5	157 437.7	229 468.6	306 699.7	372 933.6	274 326.8	308 881.2	573 685.1
United States	253 142.2	208 326.9	197 027.7	221 940.0	556 173.8	365 857.5	357 627.7	332 923.1	340 776.2	455 702.5
EUROPE	**844 713.8**	**996 345.6**	**1 026 052.2**	**964 538.3**	**1 506 787.3**	**1 239 929.4**	**1 412 553.4**	**1 254 386.3**	**1 174 242.9**	**2 198 440.3**
Bulgaria	25.3	75.6	107.6	21.3	13.5	527.0	675.2	668.7	825.7	1 348.6
Croatia	13.7	3.6	3.4	-24.7	-139.9	1 717.1	1 886.5	573.6	569.5	2 089.8
Cyprus	10 890.7	6 983.7	3 417.7	1 344.6	1 892.3	8 512.7	8 962.6	6 356.8	7 843.2	8 202.2
Malta	40.1	91.1	104.2	25.8	1 340.0	2 506.6	2 981.5	652.6	652.7	1 174.4
Montenegro	-	-	-	-2.2	2.5	37.9	13.2	14.9	22.5	34.4
Romania	102.2	127.1	37.8	-50.6	3.7	3 836.8	5 022.8	5 439.7	5 448.2	7 933.5
Russian Federation	-172.9	-1 595.1	-131.7	-361.7	-1 284.8	13 708.2	15 928.3	14 048.5	18 424.0	30 970.7
Ukraine	101.2	10.8	164.9	130.3	133.8	1 184.8	1 501.6	1 925.8	3 339.7	9 504.2
AFRICA	**11 228.0**	**7 438.2**	**3 785.2**	**120 729.1**	**131 196.5**	**57 519.8**	**56 743.8**	**73 673.0**	**63 880.0**	**38 862.4**
Northern Africa	589.2	635.6	878.2	319.0	-71.2	14 887.7	18 408.5	45 365.2	41 510.9	-10 049.1
Algeria	372.1	302.2	453.4	342.6	93.3	-422.7	-467.7	-590.8	94.4	-1 237.0
Egypt	46.4	95.9	153.4	-94.4	-153.4	12 293.7	15 935.5	25 811.8	21 653.6	1 171.9
Libya	138.1	175.1	194.6	114.6	-	2 166.1	2 604.9	19 213.4	18 826.1	-10 488.4
Morocco	27.4	45.6	72.1	-50.6	-14.7	172.9	229.1	223.3	317.9	710.5
Tunisia	5.3	16.8	4.6	6.7	2.5	677.8	106.7	707.6	619.0	-207.4
Other African countries	10 638.8	6 802.6	2 907.0	120 410.0	131 268.9	42 632.0	38 335.3	28 307.8	22 369.1	48 912.8
Nigeria	214.0	90.0	135.1	-57.3	27.0	11 901.5	11 703.0	11 343.0	6 707.5	9 714.1
South Africa	9 835.6	6 084.2	28.6	115 468.4	126 651.1	22 642.6	21 204.1	11 580.0	11 009.9	18 812.1
AMERICA	**395 836.4**	**396 300.1**	**331 210.2**	**223 810.4**	**673 209.0**	**631 935.3**	**681 510.0**	**639 364.6**	**559 463.0**	**836 793.5**
Northern America	255 653.0	210 422.2	200 281.7	224 867.4	596 165.2	402 566.7	403 885.8	378 216.2	395 176.4	574 820.2
Central America and Caribbean countries	157 027.5	194 557.4	158 158.9	52 055.7	126 197.1	134 154.1	153 896.6	148 444.0	85 080.9	141 099.5
Bahamas	415.3	4.8	12.6	-10 999.8	-3 870.4	324.7	381.4	9 669.1	-412.3	-839.4
Bermuda	57 909.8	72 910.8	28 502.4	24 475.4	105 257.1	37 181.4	32 096.4	26 796.4	12 278.1	49 576.6
Cayman Islands	4 807.6	6 274.9	6 961.3	-416.8	1 529.0	16 343.4	14 294.8	11 309.8	8 006.1	5 810.5
El Salvador	-	248.3	308.0	378.6	3.7	50.6	61.2	45.8	28.1	4.9
Guatemala	1.1	1.2	2.3	11.2	16.0	704.1	706.4	556.4	466.2	88.4
Honduras	6.3	6.0	1.1	-1.1	-9.8	148.6	273.4	264.5	243.8	44.2
Nicaragua	1.1	18.0	1.1	42.7	-	10.5	74.4	12.6	10.1	3.7
Panama	43.2	61.2	58.4	67.4	-38.0	-366.8	891.1	730.5	847.0	834.5
Virgin Islands, U.S.	-	-	-	-	-	41.1	37.2	-4.6	368.5	1 704.5
South America	-16 844.1	-8 679.5	-27 230.4	-53 112.8	-49 154.5	95 214.5	123 727.5	112 704.4	79 205.8	120 872.5
Argentina	164.4	115.1	19.5	-100.0	-217.2	3 246.5	3 895.4	3 864.2	5 282.0	9 504.2
Bolivia	5.3	4.8	550.7	247.1	27.0	49.5	43.2	57.2	27.0	60.1
Brazil	-19 682.7	-12 933.6	-33 090.2	-59 338.4	-56 225.3	83 816.8	109 605.4	99 752.7	62 952.1	90 213.5
Ecuador	9.5	8.4	8.0	-28.1	-29.5	1 010.9	1 006.2	1 241.1	276.3	786.6
Paraguay	73.8	124.7	154.6	-	3.7	-3.2	159.5	113.4	111.2	498.2
Peru	2 269.4	2 329.1	2 020.8	1 576.1	-12.3	844.3	1 716.2	1 296.1	1 549.1	2 132.8
Uruguay	40.1	843.1	945.7	610.0	-220.9	1 379.8	1 095.0	2 356.3	2 539.9	3 930.5
Venezuela	123.3	95.9	166.0	102.2	148.5	2 945.1	2 402.3	856.4	777.4	2 111.9

Table 2. Foreign direct investment positions by country *(cont.)*

At year end

Million US dollars

	Inward					Outward				
	2016	2017	2018	2019	2020	2016	2017	2018	2019	2020
ASIA	**75 185.0**	**105 491.7**	**108 574.5**	**137 608.4**	**251 605.1**	**160 208.7**	**191 532.7**	**177 114.7**	**447 235.5**	**335 187.1**
Near and Middle East	42 657.3	64 042.9	71 963.6	74 964.1	80 904.4	25 751.0	28 055.9	28 375.3	266 224.4	60 425.8
Gulf Arabian countries	7 984.6	10 218.3	16 461.0	37 089.4	47 954.4	14 207.9	16 403.2	17 734.1	242 521.9	26 387.3
Kuwait	23.2	39.6	105.3	-16.9	-33.1	386.8	828.7	924.0	847.0	-379.2
Qatar	101.2	142.7	178.6	20.2	22.1	69.6	182.3	-75.6	1 313.2	1 066.4
Saudi Arabia	6 667.0	9 250.4	13 361.6	35 068.5	35 890.3	6 385.6	8 004.3	8 240.2	6 284.0	9 257.6
United Arab Emirates	1 045.6	544.5	2 634.5	1 987.2	12 053.0	2 374.8	2 018.5	2 755.9	219 114.8	10 473.7
Other Near and Middle East	34 672.7	53 824.7	55 502.6	37 874.6	32 950.1	11 543.2	11 652.7	10 641.2	23 702.5	34 038.5
Jordan	7.4	12.0	6.9	-7.9	57.7	86.4	100.7	85.9	341.5	474.9
Other Asian countries	32 527.7	41 448.8	36 610.9	62 644.4	170 700.7	134 457.7	163 476.9	148 739.4	181 011.0	274 761.3
China	1 583.2	759.2	1 135.8	-882.9	2 444.5	13 515.3	14 162.9	13 116.6	21 928.8	34 821.5
Hong Kong, China	9 764.9	15 058.8	10 219.8	27 087.2	52 224.8	12 352.7	14 834.5	13 162.4	35 329.1	18 603.5
India	658.8	88.8	91.6	-712.2	409.9	9 110.4	11 444.0	12 768.5	13 292.5	31 239.4
Indonesia	227.7	161.9	140.8	-91.0	1 175.6	4 373.4	5 526.5	5 208.4	6 843.4	9 095.6
Iran, Islamic Republic of	12.6	36.0	38.9	110.1	108.0	256.1	313.0	319.4	387.6	182.8
Malaysia	728.4	705.2	46.9	-845.9	2 294.8	1 893.1	2 038.9	2 158.2	4 418.1	14 193.2
Philippines	175.0	620.1	435.1	213.4	408.6	2 054.4	1 643.1	1 779.3	2 442.1	5 836.3
Singapore	893.9	1 706.6	2 603.6	6 789.5	15 897.7	30 785.3	47 486.2	31 232.0	28 611.5	50 063.8
Chinese Taipei	359.4	609.3	145.4	-548.2	9 325.1	5 206.1	6 161.0	13 257.4	12 665.7	16 662.2
Thailand	319.4	693.2	768.3	34.8	71.2	4 161.5	4 254.0	1 695.7	1 922.0	4 093.8
Viet Nam	32.7	38.4	2.3	-1 562.6	-687.2	2 190.4	2 474.2	2 531.5	1 364.9	1 641.9
AUSTRALIA, OCEANIA AND POLAR REGIONS	**685.1**	**1 003.8**	**388.1**	**494.3**	**2 030.9**	**46 329.7**	**48 594.4**	**54 300.4**	**42 179.3**	**60 833.2**
WORLD unallocated and confidential	**-2.1**	**-13.2**	**-8.0**	**-78.6**	**613.6**	**26.4**	**31.2**	**-11.5**	**44.9**	**-45.4**
European Union (since 01/02/2020)	**620 726.3**	**667 030.5**	**700 839.2**	**..**	**1 114 104.8**	**677 422.8**	**795 598.5**	**708 086.8**	**..**	**1 157 619.3**
G20 countries excl. European Union	**606 923.2**	**691 520.7**	**678 564.2**	**838 958.7**	**1 433 757.5**	**1 249 754.4**	**1 468 458.9**	**1 285 492.3**	**1 263 596.9**	**2 064 450.9**
G20 OECD countries	**607 642.0**	**689 589.8**	**697 008.2**	**749 907.9**	**1 324 913.5**	**1 092 955.6**	**1 278 687.9**	**1 116 913.2**	**1 117 580.3**	**1 830 536.3**
G20 Non-OECD countries	**-718.9**	**1 930.9**	**-18 444.0**	**89 050.8**	**108 844.0**	**156 798.8**	**189 770.9**	**168 579.1**	**146 016.6**	**233 914.6**
MENA countries	**8 592.8**	**10 879.1**	**17 364.3**	**37 401.7**	**47 943.3**	**29 241.1**	**34 967.6**	**63 233.3**	**284 508.0**	**16 955.5**
ASEAN countries	**2 412.8**	**3 963.8**	**4 118.4**	**4 547.3**	**19 181.5**	**47 131.9**	**65 194.3**	**46 243.4**	**45 876.2**	**85 565.1**

- Nil; .. Not available

Note: Data excludes resident Special Purpose Entities (SPEs). Detailed metadata at: *http://metalinks.oecd.org/idi/20220712/6d95.*

Source: OECD *International Direct Investment Statistics (database): https://doi.org/10.1787/idi-data-en*

NETHERLANDS

Table 3. Foreign direct investment income by country

Million US dollars

	Inward					Outward				
	2016	2017	2018	2019	2020	2016	2017	2018	2019	2020
WORLD	**69 279.0**	**64 182.2**	**87 001.1**	**73 890.1**	**126 908.3**	**87 923.3**	**104 257.7**	**132 888.0**	**107 192.4**	**123 032.5**
OECD COUNTRIES	**66 664.8**	**60 413.7**	**83 282.2**	**72 912.8**	**118 221.1**	**49 882.8**	**66 379.2**	**87 140.3**	**79 599.2**	**81 757.3**
Australia	7.7	6.8	7.1	1.1	-126.5	1 379.0	1 858.9	3 001.3	1 987.0	2 450.1
Austria	45.3	376.5	263.2	54.9	-4.6	1 343.6	1 782.2	2 463.1	2 432.6	2 004.6
Belgium	2 435.0	1 136.3	4 620.6	3 038.2	2 393.2	3 464.6	2 823.8	2 980.1	3 245.3	2 607.4
Canada	131.6	5.6	40.1	4.5	249.6	40.9	2 465.3	2 408.8	1 468.7	2 261.0
Chile	-	2.3	3.5	1.1	3.4	84.0	146.5	1 452.9	25.7	37.6
Colombia	-	5.6	50.7	79.5	5.7	8.8	72.1	149.9	25.7	52.4
Costa Rica	-	-	-	95.2	164.1	24.3	25.9	40.1	-21.3	-27.4
Czech Republic	2.2	2.3	2.4	-13.4	3 048.4	631.4	409.2	593.7	357.1	3 154.4
Denmark	201.3	83.4	96.8	-51.5	290.6	162.6	168.0	557.1	185.8	164.1
Estonia	-	-	-	-	-	-48.7	-53.0	5.9	4.5	41.0
Finland	395.9	400.2	570.0	287.7	732.8	133.8	51.9	1 620.4	869.8	280.3
France	2 013.7	7 536.9	1 625.2	2 256.8	2 450.1	4 128.1	3 938.7	3 904.2	2 928.5	4 818.2
Germany	3 387.2	5 740.1	10 382.4	13 880.0	21 107.7	3 258.9	3 634.3	4 722.1	4 630.0	5 621.7
Greece	1.1	4.5	8.3	9.0	31.9	52.0	131.9	94.4	71.6	208.5
Hungary	1.1	1.1	1.2	-1 119.4	286.0	182.5	187.1	384.8	296.7	428.5
Iceland	24.3	255.9	146.3	209.3	291.7	4.4	3.4	51.9	-1.1	-1.1
Ireland	635.9	749.6	660.9	3 090.8	6 230.2	1 407.7	2 276.0	2 772.3	1 267.2	2 953.8
Israel	-133.8	-11.3	11.8	1 281.8	337.3	31.0	329.2	40.1	17.9	-340.7
Italy	522.0	2 812.5	7 388.2	225.0	664.4	1 161.1	917.6	2 862.0	4 144.2	2 429.6
Japan	1 887.6	2 272.6	2 394.7	2 179.6	6 894.6	712.2	636.9	1 194.4	1 541.5	2 343.0
Korea	48.7	12.4	13.0	107.5	316.8	264.3	357.3	1 149.5	178.0	131.1
Latvia	-	-	-	-	-	-44.2	95.8	11.8	3.4	4.6
Lithuania	-	-	2.4	1.1	-	3.3	-	1.2	1.1	2.3
Luxembourg	31 675.3	6 550.6	8 966.1	11 627.7	17 230.8	2 163.0	9 206.4	4 487.2	2 480.7	1 597.7
Mexico	-272.0	1 988.5	1 836.4	982.9	-371.5	1 094.8	1 811.5	3 026.1	2 513.2	1 729.9
Netherlands	-	-	-	-	-	-	-	-	-	-
New Zealand	1.1	-	-1.2	-4.5	-2.3	60.8	341.6	453.2	43.7	276.9
Norway	633.6	-56.4	116.8	4.5	74.1	163.7	184.9	109.8	33.6	331.6
Poland	7.7	10.1	10.6	6.7	13.7	613.7	774.4	1 084.6	1 535.9	1 002.8
Portugal	-23.2	6.8	-9.4	3.4	316.8	458.9	368.6	457.9	302.3	160.7
Slovak Republic	1.1	-	-	-11.2	-6.8	94.0	89.1	153.4	107.5	109.4
Slovenia	-	-	-	-	1.1	23.2	21.4	47.2	17.9	29.6
Spain	1 278.3	2 017.8	3 818.0	1 474.3	3 038.2	1 014.0	1 559.0	1 291.2	1 690.4	1 891.7
Sweden	357.2	573.8	1 002.0	-67.2	2 970.9	1 071.5	959.3	2 204.7	444.4	1 229.6
Switzerland	3 976.6	9 646.0	7 531.0	6 411.1	14 469.5	12 378.6	11 789.0	13 448.6	24 452.0	21 685.5
Turkey	65.2	75.5	-208.9	45.9	59.3	331.7	193.9	264.4	451.1	541.3
United Kingdom	11 778.2	13 814.7	24 029.3	3 352.7	24 094.6	8 164.3	10 520.8	14 431.7	12 234.4	13 343.6
United States	5 578.9	4 398.6	7 953.5	23 642.7	11 129.3	3 901.4	6 398.4	13 408.5	7 636.9	6 174.4
EUROPE	**60 518.6**	**52 902.7**	**71 598.0**	**45 006.2**	**102 847.9**	**44 853.5**	**54 692.8**	**64 704.4**	**68 151.8**	**69 742.5**
Bulgaria	-	1.1	1.2	-	1.1	71.9	64.3	28.3	12.3	60.4
Croatia	-	-	-	-	1.1	25.4	16.9	34.2	11.2	12.5
Cyprus	495.4	109.3	-166.4	267.5	120.8	415.8	425.0	-342.3	-78.4	561.8
Malta	-	1.1	1.2	1.1	2.3	12.2	-24.8	11.8	11.2	3.4
Montenegro	-	-	-	-	-	35.4	3.4	3.5	1.1	2.3
Romania	1.1	-	2.4	1.1	3.4	234.4	242.4	382.4	279.9	542.5
Russian Federation	-92.9	286.3	-42.5	-9.0	26.2	1 048.3	1 054.0	2 650.8	3 474.8	1 546.4
Ukraine	1.1	1.1	1.2	1.1	-	151.5	324.7	406.0	419.8	78.6
AFRICA	**388.1**	**289.7**	**257.3**	**159.0**	**212.0**	**3 164.9**	**6 046.7**	**7 572.3**	**2 237.8**	**5 867.8**
Northern Africa	101.7	22.5	106.2	-	-1.1	948.8	3 071.8	3 197.2	695.2	2 096.9
Algeria	101.7	22.5	106.2	-	1.1	193.5	99.2	253.7	4.5	240.5
Egypt	-	-	-	-	-3.4	228.9	2 232.0	1 975.7	677.3	833.0
Libya	-	-	-	-	-	573.9	715.8	976.0	15.7	982.3
Morocco	-	-	-	-	1.1	6.6	2.3	-4.7	2.2	19.4
Tunisia	-	-	-	-	-	-54.2	22.5	-3.5	-4.5	21.7
Other African countries	286.4	267.2	151.1	159.0	213.1	2 216.1	2 974.9	4 375.1	1 542.6	3 770.9
Nigeria	6.6	2.3	3.5	2.2	10.3	1 093.7	2 394.3	1 147.2	759.0	1 680.9
South Africa	276.5	246.9	108.6	135.5	210.8	85.1	126.3	3 049.7	207.1	549.3
AMERICA	**5 593.3**	**8 084.8**	**11 421.0**	**23 541.9**	**12 543.6**	**22 876.3**	**24 361.4**	**38 315.8**	**19 623.9**	**18 684.9**
Northern America	5 710.5	4 404.2	7 993.6	23 648.3	11 380.1	3 934.5	8 861.5	15 817.3	9 106.7	8 436.5
Central America and Caribbean countries	1 632.2	4 737.9	4 501.4	2 696.7	4 429.6	9 704.7	7 964.2	9 228.1	7 995.1	4 751.0
Bahamas	2.2	-	1.2	-109.7	296.3	24.3	16.9	20.1	16.8	33.0
Bermuda	1 095.9	1 039.3	1 567.3	1 120.6	3 358.4	7 684.4	3 565.6	4 692.6	3 527.4	1 759.5
Cayman Islands	418.0	1 211.8	290.3	104.1	119.7	128.3	65.4	106.2	-35.8	-164.1
El Salvador	-	2.3	13.0	16.8	-	13.3	29.3	9.4	2.2	-
Guatemala	-	-	-	1.1	1.1	10.0	33.8	-60.2	16.8	6.8
Honduras	-	-	-	-	-	3.3	9.0	8.3	7.8	1.1
Nicaragua	-	-	1.2	1.1	-	2.2	2.3	-1.2	-	-
Panama	1.1	1.1	-	3.4	4.6	-23.2	14.7	8.3	-2.2	-14.8
Virgin Islands, U.S.	-	-	-	-	-	1.1	-1.1	-	-5.6	10.3
South America	-1 749.4	-1 057.4	-1 074.0	-2 802.0	-3 266.1	9 237.0	7 535.8	13 270.4	2 523.2	5 497.4
Argentina	-	-	2.4	-2.2	53.6	1.1	392.3	459.1	-29.1	-111.7
Bolivia	-	1.1	2.4	20.2	21.7	3.3	16.9	15.3	-9.0	230.2
Brazil	-1 751.6	-1 223.1	-1 176.7	-2 936.3	-3 365.2	9 021.3	6 499.8	10 524.0	2 512.0	4 887.7
Ecuador	-	-	-	-	-	24.3	62.0	457.9	21.3	12.5
Paraguay	-	-	-	-	-	18.8	33.8	29.5	-	23.9
Peru	-	130.8	14.2	3.4	8.0	-17.7	118.4	82.6	-23.5	67.2
Uruguay	-	22.5	27.1	28.0	-	59.7	63.1	174.7	12.3	12.5
Venezuela	-	1.1	-	2.2	3.4	19.9	120.6	-89.7	-15.7	282.6

Table 3. Foreign direct investment income by country *(cont.)*

Million US dollars

	Inward					Outward				
	2016	2017	2018	2019	2020	2016	2017	2018	2019	2020
ASIA	**2 760.1**	**2 891.4**	**3 704.7**	**5 180.8**	**11 438.2**	**15 583.3**	**16 957.5**	**18 796.2**	**15 127.1**	**25 968.1**
Near and Middle East	151.5	458.8	444.9	1 854.9	2 514.0	1 530.5	2 782.1	2 105.5	3 094.1	3 047.3
Gulf Arabian countries	285.3	467.8	426.1	565.3	2 176.6	988.6	2 061.8	1 996.9	3 072.9	3 315.1
Kuwait	-	1.1	-	1.1	3.4	219.0	390.0	1 135.4	368.3	2 413.7
Qatar	-15.5	1.1	2.4	2.2	-14.8	361.6	376.5	38.9	294.4	175.5
Saudi Arabia	291.9	453.2	349.3	553.0	1 056.4	40.9	128.5	80.3	58.2	199.4
United Arab Emirates	6.6	10.1	70.8	7.8	1 128.2	131.6	570.4	293.9	1 581.8	160.7
Other Near and Middle East	-133.8	-9.0	18.9	1 289.6	338.5	541.9	720.3	108.6	21.3	-266.7
Jordan	-	-	-	-	-	-10.0	2.3	10.6	1.1	41.0
Other Asian countries	2 608.6	2 432.6	3 259.8	3 325.9	8 923.1	14 052.9	14 175.4	16 690.7	12 032.9	22 919.7
China	55.3	63.1	70.8	19.0	485.5	1 931.9	1 898.3	2 327.4	2 100.1	3 072.4
Hong Kong, China	533.0	-12.4	241.9	1 166.5	903.7	1 419.9	1 321.2	1 653.5	642.6	1 531.6
India	-	1.1	-	-15.7	-753.3	207.9	671.9	166.4	175.8	2 128.8
Indonesia	4.4	3.4	3.5	2.2	781.8	951.0	541.1	819.1	19.0	891.2
Iran, Islamic Republic of	1.1	1.1	1.2	1.1	1.1	10.0	23.7	29.5	4.5	19.4
Malaysia	31.0	38.3	31.9	53.7	90.0	405.8	134.1	232.5	248.5	1 022.2
Philippines	1.1	-	5.9	-25.7	-99.1	567.3	341.6	605.5	262.0	166.4
Singapore	32.1	33.8	57.8	-104.1	687.2	6 173.8	6 344.3	5 632.0	6 315.9	10 046.7
Chinese Taipei	8.8	12.4	434.3	2.2	-485.5	248.8	355.1	488.6	133.2	257.6
Thailand	1.1	-1.1	-	-	1.1	384.8	317.9	324.6	88.4	437.6
Viet Nam	1.1	1.1	-	-63.8	-67.2	339.5	492.6	600.7	-265.3	487.7
AUSTRALIA, OCEANIA AND POLAR REGIONS	**7.7**	**6.8**	**7.1**	**-4.5**	**-129.9**	**1 457.5**	**2 208.3**	**3 519.4**	**2 039.6**	**2 769.2**
WORLD unallocated and confidential	**11.1**	**6.8**	**13.0**	**6.7**	**-3.4**	**-12.2**	**-9.0**	**-20.1**	**12.3**	**-**
European Union (since 01/02/2020)	**43 438.0**	**28 117.5**	**39 254.1**	**..**	**60 920.8**	**22 036.9**	**30 064.3**	**32 814.8**	**..**	**31 923.6**
G20 countries excl. European Union	**23 932.3**	**38 495.1**	**54 776.3**	**44 425.2**	**64 964.1**	**37 724.2**	**44 045.8**	**70 449.7**	**48 231.3**	**55 007.4**
G20 OECD countries	**25 148.7**	**38 664.2**	**55 460.9**	**46 678.6**	**66 468.4**	**24 436.6**	**32 733.6**	**50 372.9**	**39 713.4**	**41 843.9**
G20 Non-OECD countries	**-1 216.4**	**-169.1**	**-684.5**	**-2 253.4**	**-1 504.3**	**13 287.6**	**11 312.1**	**20 076.7**	**8 517.9**	**13 163.5**
MENA countries	**387.0**	**490.4**	**532.3**	**565.3**	**2 176.6**	**1 935.2**	**5 141.5**	**5 209.5**	**3 770.3**	**5 453.0**
ASEAN countries	**71.9**	**76.7**	**99.1**	**-136.6**	**1 394.9**	**8 885.3**	**8 205.4**	**8 243.8**	**6 674.1**	**13 226.2**

- Nil; .. Not available

Note: Data excludes resident Special Purpose Entities (SPEs). Detailed metadata at: *http://metalinks.oecd.org/idi/20220712/6d95*.

Source: *OECD International Direct Investment Statistics (database): https://doi.org/10.1787/idi-data-en*

Table 4. Foreign direct investment flows by industrial sector

Million US dollars

	Inward					Outward				
	2016	2017	2018	2019	2020	2016	2017	2018	2019	2020
All FDI activities	**55 430.7**	**9 285.3**	**87 862.6**	**-27 168.9**	**-69 170.4**	**186 165.0**	**21 031.5**	**-46 983.4**	**13 335.9**	**-119 396.0**
Agriculture, forestry and fishing	-	-	-	-	-	-	-	**-343.4**	**189.2**	-
Mining and quarrying	**7 339.4**	**-932.3**	**-2 406.5**	-	-	**-43 878.1**	**175 146.0**	**-69 825.3**	**41 190.0**	**-15 431.3**
Extraction activities	7 339.4	-932.3	-2 406.5	-	-	-43 878.1	175 146.0	-69 825.3	41 190.0	-15 431.3
Manufacturing	**6 207.0**	**63 691.8**	**17 387.0**	**51 547.1**	**-27 977.2**	**81 168.9**	**-87 251.7**	**-154 864.9**	**117 330.1**	**-92 719.1**
of which:										
Food products, beverages and tobacco	-2 920.5	51 445.2	6 630.5	-33 463.6	-23 268.4	-10 285.3	-23 452.8	-137 234.7	128.7	-3 642.2
Textiles, wood and paper products; printing	-11.1	-339.3	51.9	23 258.7	5 123.6	2 383.1	-870.3	3 083.9	22 365.4	-405.7
Chemical, rubber, plastic, non-metallic mineral products	-10 844.9	-1 406.8	5 800.8	4 191.2	-57 888.3	73 160.5	-49 429.6	-53 633.9	185 740.5	-71 855.3
Metal and machinery products, except electrical equipment	33 966.6	13 173.3	4 802.3	75 064.4	46 219.9	51 912.0	17 752.2	-44 246.4	151 707.2	-14 826.2
Motor vehicles, trailers, semi-trailers, other transport equipment	-14 049.5	358.5	-295.1	4 027.8	-966.4	-33 392.7	-7 760.1	-12 365.2	-270 436.6	-2 674.6
Other manufacturing	65.2	462.2	396.6	-21 531.4	2 801.1	-2 608.6	-23 492.3	89 531.5	27 823.8	684.9
Electricity, gas, steam and air conditioning supply	**-64.1**	**-6 751.2**	**-1 769.1**	**-4 355.8**	**15 964.7**	**1 309.3**	**-3 488.9**	**5 438.5**	**-2 729.2**	**26 267.8**
Water supply; sewerage, waste management and remediation activities	**-80.7**	**53.0**	**-46.0**	**-2 304.9**	**-202.8**	**3.3**	**-2.3**	**-79.1**	**-1.1**	**80.9**
Construction	**454.5**	**-558.0**	**-756.5**	**3 511.7**	**4 833.0**	**3 772.0**	**-5 399.6**	**-1 018.5**	**47 363.7**	**18 918.5**
Services	**41 570.3**	**-46 184.2**	**75 460.9**	**-75 503.2**	**-61 826.8**	**144 552.7**	**-63 495.7**	**77 887.4**	**-153 569.9**	**-57 035.9**
Wholesale and retail trade; repair of motor vehicles and motorcycles	6 759.9	16 951.9	9 753.3	8 095.8	-1 778.9	40 621.5	2 874.5	12 563.4	-254 236.0	16 272.4
Transportation and storage	3 916.8	2 223.0	2 687.4	11 656.8	-4 279.2	1 323.7	7 765.8	1 955.6	119 331.7	27 872.4
Accommodation and food service activities	-68.6	-66.5	-106.2	375.0	-1 131.6	-1 631.1	-5.6	83.8	89 564.5	-1 202.3
Information and communication	1 072.7	83.4	2 774.7	-36 460.3	15 154.4	80 306.3	12 002.0	-50 956.0	40 822.8	-14 474.1
Financial and insurance activities	28 375.5	-72 191.4	44 182.7	-7 639.1	-50 072.9	-37 263.1	-114 459.5	47 230.0	-109 659.7	-81 500.9
Activities of holding companies	67.5	-	-	-2 209.8	-108 279.2	5 335.6	-200 721.5	24 707.9	10 687.3	-104 518.5
Real estate activities	-687.8	5 439.1	14 345.6	2 902.7	2 028.5	-9 273.5	-3 415.6	1 393.8	4 542.7	4 925.4
Professional, scientific and technical activities	1 275.0	1.1	446.1	-17 605.5	-10 618.8	6 061.0	19 532.2	41 129.5	-45 293.9	-667.8
Administrative and support service activities	927.8	1 376.4	1 378.5	-34 269.6	-9 724.2	63 054.3	11 621.0	24 382.2	-9 245.5	-11 774.4
Public administration; activities of households and of extraterritorial organisations	-	-	-	-	-	-	-	-	-	-
Education	-	-	-	-	17.1	-	-	-	-	-
Human health and social work activities	-	-	-	-	-	-	-	49.6	12 825.5	899.1
Arts, entertainment and recreation	-	-	-	-2 560.2	-1 423.4	59.7	-	-8.3	581.0	1 989.7
Other services	-	-	-	1.1	3.4	1 292.7	588.4	63.7	-2 800.9	623.4
Not allocated and confidential	**4.4**	**-33.8**	**-7.1**	**-63.8**	**38.7**	**-829.4**	**5 406.4**	**95 774.8**	**-36 266.7**	**-729.3**
Private real estate activities	-	-	-	-	-	**66.4**	**117.2**	**47.2**	**-170.2**	**1 252.4**

- Nil

Note: Data excludes resident Special Purpose Entities (SPEs). Detailed metadata at: *http://metalinks.oecd.org/idi/20220712/6d95*.

Source: *OECD International Direct Investment Statistics (database)*: *https://doi.org/10.1787/idi-data-en*

Table 5. Foreign direct investment positions by industrial sector

At year end

Million US dollars

	Inward					Outward				
	2016	2017	2018	2019	2020	2016	2017	2018	2019	2020
All FDI activities	**1 327 646.3**	**1 506 566.3**	**1 470 002.3**	**1 447 101.8**	**2 565 442.4**	**2 135 949.2**	**2 390 965.5**	**2 198 827.6**	**2 287 045.6**	**3 470 071.2**
Agriculture, forestry and fishing	-	-	-	-	-	-	-	**98.5**	**-774.0**	-
Mining and quarrying	**13 588.1**	**12 770.4**	**7 608.2**	-	-	**141 288.1**	**152 953.9**	**161 798.7**	**-197 608.4**	**-157 751.9**
Extraction activities	13 588.1	12 770.4	7 608.2	-	-	141 288.1	152 953.9	161 798.7	-197 608.4	-157 751.9
Manufacturing	**390 460.6**	**546 904.5**	**418 265.4**	**2 176 563.7**	**1 880 060.1**	**1 143 562.8**	**1 274 984.4**	**1 156 391.1**	**1 003 037.5**	**1 081 511.8**
of which:										
Food products, beverages and tobacco	83 514.3	132 829.2	97 188.0	351 725.5	396 409.4	265 026.9	301 348.0	225 716.7	110 435.9	220 661.4
Textiles, wood and paper products; printing	722.0	322.6	297.7	45 724.6	42 730.4	17 756.9	19 023.7	30 700.7	66 774.9	68 548.3
Chemical, rubber, plastic, non-metallic mineral products	210 315.2	293 388.1	250 629.7	1 305 219.1	1 070 981.7	587 338.5	609 403.9	559 142.4	1 293 352.1	1 048 848.9
Metal and machinery products, except electrical equipment	87 549.3	109 661.8	61 641.9	313 872.2	222 980.7	206 813.5	252 112.0	222 444.5	-159 707.9	36 603.3
Motor vehicles, trailers, semi-trailers, other transport equipment	3 642.9	4 327.2	2 937.9	28 016.2	51 769.5	39 925.2	60 985.8	77 837.2	-113 977.8	-66 532.1
Other manufacturing	4 715.9	6 375.6	5 571.3	132 005.2	95 187.1	26 701.8	32 110.8	40 548.4	-193 839.6	-226 619.2
Electricity, gas, steam and air conditioning supply	**20 571.3**	**18 595.6**	**11 949.9**	**73 789.0**	**71 173.2**	**23 380.4**	**26 188.5**	**22 048.3**	**45 975.1**	**44 622.7**
Water supply; sewerage, waste management and remediation activities	**234.0**	**350.2**	**275.9**	**12 871.3**	**12 471.5**	**124.4**	**139.1**	**41.2**	**-315.7**	**88.4**
Construction	**5 843.8**	**5 717.2**	**2 689.5**	**71 740.1**	**88 650.1**	**4 884.6**	**7 591.7**	**6 227.4**	**138 656.5**	**145 998.3**
Services	**896 950.6**	**922 241.5**	**1 029 221.4**	**-891 453.6**	**507 500.3**	**807 135.0**	**906 746.2**	**825 002.3**	**1 303 963.2**	**2 409 663.8**
Wholesale and retail trade; repair of motor vehicles and motorcycles	106 255.9	109 321.2	97 347.1	623 112.8	627 084.3	236 408.8	225 000.0	202 857.8	795 103.3	631 762.2
Transportation and storage	38 247.1	44 150.9	32 089.5	283 399.2	193 690.0	31 876.3	48 362.9	44 583.2	297 484.8	328 088.1
Accommodation and food service activities	1 078.3	1 451.2	919.4	4 594.5	4 349.0	4 734.9	327.4	7 887.6	-756.0	2 138.9
Information and communication	29 711.2	29 347.6	24 791.6	199 068.7	336 346.8	164 115.1	154 736.1	128 058.2	-146 463.7	322 794.2
Financial and insurance activities	645 417.9	651 008.6	794 110.4	-2 226 087.4	-1 191 868.9	274 045.5	338 744.3	307 323.1	227 956.6	615 864.5
Activities of holding companies	-	-	-	57 418.6	702 887.5	39 641.6	55 567.3	43 315.8	-30 198.8	959 512.8
Real estate activities	49 055.6	56 007.4	61 033.9	38 656.5	50 527.7	8 682.4	11 132.2	16 606.4	-6 144.7	44 299.9
Professional, scientific and technical activities	13 454.2	14 198.8	3 639.8	60 085.4	202 639.6	42 911.4	56 337.3	42 221.2	71 530.0	309 657.6
Administrative and support service activities	13 731.4	16 754.6	15 290.8	109 565.3	272 659.2	44 342.8	71 861.4	63 218.5	50 105.6	145 042.3
Public administration; activities of households and of extraterritorial organisations	-	-	-	-	-	-	-	-	-	-
Education	-	-	-	-	1 902.1	-	-	-	-	1 245.6
Human health and social work activities	-	-	-	-	-	10.5	185.9	12 095.3	-997.5	-39.3
Arts, entertainment and recreation	-	-	-	16 134.6	10 157.1	27.4	2.4	69.8	17 277.0	11 115.5
Other services	-	-	-	18.0	13.5	-20.0	61.2	81.3	-1 132.3	-2 305.8
Not allocated and confidential	**-2.1**	**-13.2**	**-8.0**	**3 591.3**	**5 587.2**	**1 074.1**	**4 743.3**	**9 705.7**	**-26 027.9**	**-70 794.0**
Private real estate activities	-	-	-	-	-	**14 499.8**	**17 618.1**	**17 514.3**	**20 139.3**	**16 732.1**

- Nil

Note: Data excludes resident Special Purpose Entities (SPEs). National Bank of Netherlands note on the existence of a breaks in series between 2014 and 2015: *http://metalinks.oecd.org/idi/20220712/a3b2*

Detailed metadata at: *http://metalinks.oecd.org/idi/20220712/6d95.*

Source: *OECD International Direct Investment Statistics (database): https://doi.org/10.1787/idi-data-en*

NETHERLANDS

Table 6. Foreign direct investment income by industrial sector

Million US dollars

	Inward					Outward				
	2016	2017	2018	2019	2020	2016	2017	2018	2019	2020
All FDI activities	**69 279.0**	**64 182.2**	**87 001.1**	**73 890.1**	**126 908.3**	**87 923.3**	**104 257.7**	**132 888.0**	**107 192.4**	**123 032.5**
Agriculture, forestry and fishing	-	-	-	-	-	-	-	**13.0**	**-41.4**	-
Mining and quarrying	**164.8**	**307.7**	**-699.9**	-	-	**11 197.6**	**7 410.7**	**11 179.0**	**-1 657.9**	**-4 435.3**
Extraction activities	164.8	307.7	-699.9	-	-	11 197.6	7 410.7	11 179.0	-1 657.9	-4 435.3
Manufacturing	**14 368.0**	**18 775.8**	**16 440.5**	**3 267.7**	-	**38 849.9**	**60 121.7**	**71 914.3**	**-17 743.2**	**-24 958.4**
of which:										
Food products, beverages and tobacco	3 250.0	6 578.7	4 173.3	-	-	7 811.6	12 530.7	16 683.6	-2 013.9	-4 002.3
Textiles, wood and paper products; printing	19.9	28.2	-30.7	-	-	-5.5	328.0	1 226.2	14 293.1	-
Chemical, rubber, plastic, non-metallic mineral products	7 344.9	8 831.0	8 815.1	2 912.8	-	20 155.9	34 901.4	37 012.9	-306.7	-10 111.7
Metal and machinery products, except electrical equipment	2 006.0	1 387.7	1 223.9	-	-	5 331.2	8 193.0	8 415.0	-12 687.8	-5 669.5
Motor vehicles, trailers, semi-trailers, other transport equipment	1 005.2	556.9	480.3	-	-	1 611.2	634.7	4 441.2	-13 529.6	-4 025.1
Other manufacturing	743.1	1 393.3	1 778.6	356.0	-	3 946.7	3 536.2	4 137.9	-3 498.3	-1 149.9
Electricity, gas, steam and air conditioning supply	**2 149.7**	**552.4**	**-2 506.8**	-	-	**713.3**	**1 013.4**	**1 057.5**	**-1 279.5**	**-1 342.5**
Water supply; sewerage, waste management and remediation activities	**-70.8**	**-106.0**	**-40.1**	-	-	**1.1**	**-4.5**	**-5.9**	-	-
Construction	**446.8**	**128.5**	**-755.3**	-	-	**687.8**	**533.2**	**-267.9**	-	-
Services	**52 208.3**	**44 517.0**	**74 549.7**	**66 631.6**	**124 952.7**	**34 869.0**	**33 235.3**	**46 525.4**	**116 612.6**	**140 580.1**
Wholesale and retail trade; repair of motor vehicles and motorcycles	6 726.8	7 929.2	4 785.8	-	-	8 381.1	5 157.3	13 453.3	43 968.4	-3 063.2
Transportation and storage	4 373.5	467.8	1 744.4	-	-	2 418.4	1 166.7	1 467.0	-	6.8
Accommodation and food service activities	120.5	157.8	145.2	-	-	85.1	12.4	40.1	-2 909.4	-
Information and communication	1 589.1	1 994.1	2 575.2	1.1	-	5 975.9	4 886.7	6 929.1	-572.0	-163.0
Financial and insurance activities	33 413.7	24 590.2	56 179.6	66 248.7	122 808.0	14 320.5	15 884.3	18 471.6	75 438.3	135 931.6
Activities of holding companies	-	-	-	-	254 467.2	-81.8	373.1	838.0	-1 962.4	150 921.9
Real estate activities	1 764.9	3 898.1	3 141.7	144.4	-	967.6	724.8	541.7	-80.6	-
Professional, scientific and technical activities	74.1	86.8	16.5	-	2 145.9	1 508.3	1 582.7	1 186.1	5 355.4	8 663.2
Administrative and support service activities	4 146.9	5 392.9	5 962.5	237.3	-	1 184.3	3 815.8	4 423.5	-2 588.2	-794.3
Public administration; activities of households and of extraterritorial organisations	-	-	-	-	-	-1.1	-	-	-	-
Education	-	-	-	-	-	-	-	-	-	-
Human health and social work activities	-	-	-	-	-	-	-	2.4	-88.4	-
Arts, entertainment and recreation	-	-	-	-	-	26.5	-	8.3	-1 909.8	-
Other services	-	-	-	-	-	-	-	-	-	-
Not allocated and confidential	**12.2**	**6.8**	**13.0**	**3 990.8**	**1 955.6**	**1 604.6**	**1 947.9**	**2 472.6**	**11 301.9**	**13 188.6**
Private real estate activities	-	-	-	-	-	-	-	-	-	-

- Nil

Note: Data excludes resident Special Purpose Entities (SPEs). Detailed metadata at: *http://metalinks.oecd.org/idi/20220712/6d95*.

Source: *OECD International Direct Investment Statistics (database)*: *https://doi.org/10.1787/idi-data-en*

NEW ZEALAND

Table 1. Foreign direct investment flows by country

Million US dollars

	Inward					Outward				
	2016	2017	2018	2019	2020	2016	2017	2018	2019	2020
WORLD	**2 910.8**	**2 538.0**	**1 945.2**	**4 277.2**	**3 812.1**	**62.2**	**-222.5**	**424.9**	**-172.0**	**522.9**
OECD COUNTRIES	**.. c**	**2 320.2**	**811.0**	**2 132.8**	**..**	**.. c**	**-102.4**	**424.7**	**-455.1**	**..**
Australia	2 709.7	1 869.2	-460.0	2 408.8	2 504.2	7.9	205.2	456.2	303.9	439.1
Austria	.. c	.. c	.. c	.. c	.. c	..	..	.. c	.. c	.. c
Belgium	.. c	-13.8	.. c	-33.4	8.6	.. c	.. c	.. c	.. c	.. c
Canada	-1 033.0	223.2	-3.7	68.4	.. d	-33.5	-40.5	43.7	25.3	.. d
Chile	.. c	0.0	..	.. c	.. c	.. c	.. c	.. c	-427.7	.. c
Colombia	.. c	.. c	.. c	.. c	.. c	..	.. c	.. c	.. c	.. c
Costa Rica	..	..	..	..	..	..	..	..	..	..
Czech Republic	.. c	.. c	.. c	0.0	.. c	..	..	..	..	..
Denmark	.. c	1.2	.. c	.. c	.. c	..	..	..	..	..
Estonia	..	-	-	0.4	-0.4	..	..	..	..	..
Finland	.. c	1.0	.. c	.. c	.. c	0.2	-0.1	-7.1	..	..
France	35.1	-28.9	31.5	47.6	-0.6	8.8	17.8	-34.1	.. c	.. c
Germany	-49.0	779.8	-53.2	33.8	-31.3	20.8	-6.3	.. c	-19.6	.. c
Greece	..	..	..	.. c	.. c	..	..	..	..	..
Hungary	.. c	.. c	..	.. c	..	..	..	..	..	.. c
Iceland	..	..	..	..	..	..	..	..	..	..
Ireland	-41.1	-30.8	62.0	-15.1	.. d	.. c	1.0	-57.8	.. c	.. c
Israel	.. c	.. c	.. c	.. c	.. c	..	..	..	..	.. c
Italy	8.0	-0.2	.. c	0.7	0.3	.. c	.. c	.. c	.. c	.. c
Japan	280.9	194.9	265.7	87.7	349.0	6.1	8.3	0.0	-36.4	.. d
Korea	-13.8	5.7	5.3	0.6	1.6	0.2	-27.9	.. c	-0.4	.. c
Latvia	..	..	..	..	.. c	..	..	..	..	..
Lithuania	..	..	.. c	..	.. c	..	..	..	..	..
Luxembourg	-13.6	-8.0	177.8	.. c	.. d	.. c	.. c	..	..	..
Mexico	-0.1	.. c	.. c	.. c	.. c	14.4	.. c	.. c	.. c	.. c
Netherlands	28.8	-75.9	156.2	-66.5	.. d	-40.6	-107.0	.. c	.. c	.. c
New Zealand	-	0.0	-	-	-	-	0.0	-	-	-
Norway	.. c	.. c	.. c	.. c	.. c	..	..	..	..	..
Poland	0.0	0.0	.. c	0.3	.. c	..	..	..	..	..
Portugal	..	..	..	..	..	..	..	..	..	..
Slovak Republic	.. c	.. c	.. c	.. c	.. c	..	..	..	..	..
Slovenia	..	..	-	..	..	..	..	..	..	..
Spain	.. c	.. c	.. c	.. c	.. c	.. c	.. c	.. c	.. c	.. c
Sweden	-15.8	.. c	.. c	.. c	.. c	.. c	.. c	.. c	.. c	.. c
Switzerland	69.2	29.4	16.5	-21.4	4.8	0.0	0.1	..	..	.. c
Turkey	.. c	.. d	.. c	.. c	.. c	.. c	.. c	.. c	.. c	.. c
United Kingdom	112.0	-485.7	342.0	-1 041.0	.. d	48.4	9.8	-42.4	46.8	-89.0
United States	353.3	-106.4	-227.9	-76.5	28.8	-95.8	-282.6	-331.2	-332.8	113.9
EUROPE	**454.6**	**144.6**	**1 245.6**	**-339.5**	**76.4**	**106.8**	**29.1**	**-156.0**	**10.9**	**.. d**
Bulgaria	..	..	..	..	..	..	..	..	..	..
Croatia	..	-	0.0	0.0	0.0	..	..	..	..	..
Cyprus	..	..	..	..	.. c	..	..	..	..	..
Malta	.. c	.. c	..	..	..	..	..	..	..	..
Montenegro	..	..	..	..	..	..	..	..	..	..
Romania	.. c	.. c	.. c	.. c	.. c	..	..	..	..	..
Russian Federation	..	..	..	..	.. c	.. c	.. c	.. c	.. c	.. c
Ukraine	..	..	..	..	..	..	..	..	..	..
AFRICA	**.. c**	**.. c**	**.. c**	**1.2**	**.. c**	**.. c**	**0.6**	**-10.9**	**1.5**	**.. d**
Northern Africa	.. c	..	..	..	..	..	..	..	..	..
Algeria	..	..	..	..	..	..	..	..	..	..
Egypt	.. c	.. c	.. c	.. c	.. c	..	..	..	..	.. c
Libya	..	..	..	..	..	..	..	..	..	..
Morocco	..	..	..	..	..	..	..	..	..	..
Tunisia	..	..	..	..	..	..	..	..	..	..
Other African countries	.. c	..	..	..	..	.. c	..	..	..	..
Nigeria	..	..	..	..	..	..	..	..	..	..
South Africa	0.1	.. c	.. c	0.7	.. c	..	.. c	.. c	.. c	.. c
AMERICA	**.. c**	**.. d**	**.. d**	**379.2**	**.. d**	**.. c**	**-288.2**	**170.0**	**-120.5**	**112.3**
Northern America	..	..	..	..	..	..	..	..	..	..
Central America and Caribbean countries	.. c	..	..	..	..	..	..	..	..	..
Bahamas	.. c	.. c	.. c	.. c	.. c	..	..	..	..	..
Bermuda	24.0	52.3	.. c	.. c	.. d	0.5	27.2	13.8	476.9	-43.7
Cayman Islands	25.2	-248.7	-215.8	.. c	97.0	..	..	.. c	.. c	.. c
El Salvador	..	..	..	..	..	..	..	..	..	.. c
Guatemala	..	..	..	..	..	..	..	..	..	..
Honduras	..	..	..	..	..	..	..	..	..	..
Nicaragua	..	..	..	..	..	..	..	..	..	..
Panama	..	..	..	..	..	0.2	1.1	..	..	..
Virgin Islands, U.S.	..	..	..	..	..	..	..	..	..	..
South America	.. c	..	..	..	..	.. c	..	..	..	..
Argentina	.. c	-0.1	.. c	0.2	.. c	.. c	.. c	.. c	.. c	.. c
Bolivia	..	..	..	..	..	..	.. c	.. c	.. c	.. c
Brazil	.. c	0.0	.. c	.. c	.. c	.. c	.. c	3.1	-4.9	.. d
Ecuador	..	..	..	..	..	..	..	..	..	..
Paraguay	..	..	..	..	..	..	..	..	..	..
Peru	..	..	..	..	.. c	2.0	.. c	.. c	.. c	.. c
Uruguay	..	..	..	..	..	.. c	.. c	.. c	.. c	.. c
Venezuela	.. c	.. c	..	..	..	-1.1	0.1	-0.2	0.2	0.2

Table 1. Foreign direct investment flows by country *(cont.)*

Million US dollars

	Inward					Outward				
	2016	2017	2018	2019	2020	2016	2017	2018	2019	2020
ASIA	**402.4**	**607.4**	**1 056.7**	**1 826.3**	**1 367.9**	**-23.3**	**-117.3**	**-111.4**	**-374.7**	**.. d**
Near and Middle East	.. c	..	..	..	..	..	..	..	..	..
Gulf Arabian countries	.. c	..	..	..	..	..	..	..	..	..
Kuwait	..	..	..	..	..	..	..	..	..	..
Qatar	..	..	..	..	.. c	..	..	..	..	..
Saudi Arabia	..	..	-	..	..	-2.9	6.2	-12.8	1.3	.. c
United Arab Emirates	.. c	.. c	.. c	.. c	.. c	-9.4	.. c	-24.4	.. c	.. c
Other Near and Middle East	.. c	..	..	..	..	..	..	..	..	..
Jordan	-	..	..	..	..	..	..	..	..	..
Other Asian countries	.. c	..	..	..	..	.. c	..	..	..	..
China	33.7	128.9	4.9	28.1	58.7	-68.5	26.7	-21.1	3.3	15.5
Hong Kong, China	549.4	685.4	1 103.8	293.3	.. d	-22.7	131.6	144.9	-296.9	-102.4
India	0.9	.. d	0.3	.. d	4.1	.. c	.. c	.. c	.. c	.. c
Indonesia	.. c	0.2	0.4	-0.5	0.1	.. c	-21.9	-14.1	7.5	.. c
Iran, Islamic Republic of	..	..	..	..	..	..	..	..	..	..
Malaysia	.. c	-53.3	-24.9	.. c	.. d	0.3	-0.5	.. c	-24.0	.. c
Philippines	2.2	6.7	.. c	.. c	.. c	.. c	.. c	.. c	.. c	.. c
Singapore	-498.5	-338.6	-643.3	1 554.3	1 035.9	59.5	-164.7	-13.4	-41.4	.. d
Chinese Taipei	-0.6	0.4	.. c	.. c	.. c	-4.5	2.5	-0.8	2.4	.. d
Thailand	.. c	3.9	.. c	.. c	4.0	16.6	.. c	6.8	.. c	.. c
Viet Nam	.. c	2.1	.. c	-0.5	-0.3	-0.2	..	-6.9	.. c	.. c
AUSTRALIA, OCEANIA AND POLAR REGIONS	**2 708.3**	**1 864.0**	**-467.2**	**2 417.2**	**2 504.2**	**8.3**	**201.0**	**440.8**	**311.6**	**449.4**
WORLD unallocated and confidential	**-28.3**	**-29.5**	**686.2**	**-7.3**	**-262.2**	**77.9**	**-47.8**	**92.5**	**-0.9**	**147.0**
European Union (since 01/02/2020)	**..**	**..**	**..**	**..**	**.. d**	**..**	**..**	**..**	**..**	**.. d**
G20 countries excl. European Union	**2 437.0**	**2 582.3**	**-91.5**	**1 560.0**	**2 517.1**	**-134.2**	**-83.1**	**38.7**	**-20.3**	**607.8**
G20 OECD countries	**2 403.0**	**2 451.6**	**-100.5**	**1 530.2**	**2 460.0**	**-24.2**	**-102.5**	**77.5**	**-20.5**	**613.7**
G20 Non-OECD countries	**34.0**	**130.7**	**9.0**	**29.8**	**.. d**	**-110.0**	**19.4**	**-38.8**	**0.2**	**-5.9**
MENA countries	**-0.3**	**.. c**	**.. d**	**.. c**	**.. c**	**-12.2**	**.. c**	**-37.2**	**.. c**	**.. c**
ASEAN countries	**-448.5**	**-380.6**	**-324.6**	**1 427.2**	**1 057.4**	**76.5**	**-212.5**	**-204.7**	**-30.7**	**-60.2**

- Nil; .. Not available; c Confidential data; d Secondary Confidentiality

Note: Detailed metadata at: *http://metalinks.oecd.org/idi/20220712/6d95.*

Source: *OECD International Direct Investment Statistics (database): https://doi.org/10.1787/idi-data-en*

NEW ZEALAND

Table 2. Foreign direct investment positions by country
At year end

Million US dollars

	Inward					Outward				
	2016	2017	2018	2019	2020	2016	2017	2018	2019	2020
WORLD	**70 403.0**	**76 027.5**	**75 158.1**	**81 237.8**	**92 486.7**	**16 740.0**	**17 158.8**	**17 277.6**	**17 045.5**	**20 923.3**
OECD COUNTRIES	**.. c**	**60 092.1**	**58 702.8**	**62 514.4**	**..**	**.. c**	**13 252.2**	**13 655.4**	**13 067.7**	**..**
Australia	37 060.6	40 037.9	37 562.6	39 957.0	45 894.0	8 186.6	8 573.6	8 637.4	8 943.6	10 728.6
Austria	.. c	.. c	.. c	.. c	.. c	..	..	.. c	.. c	.. c
Belgium	.. c	427.8	72.8	-16.3	.. d	-6.2	.. c	.. c	.. c	.. c
Canada	1 877.4	2 563.8	2 952.4	3 511.4	3 208.4	112.0	57.2	103.7	133.3	287.0
Chile	.. c	..	..	.. c	.. c	.. c	.. c	435.5	.. c	.. d
Colombia	..	..	.. c	.. c	..	..	.. c	.. c	.. c	.. c
Costa Rica	..	..	..	..	..	..	..	..	..	..
Czech Republic	.. c	..	.. c	.. c	.. c	..	..	..	..	..
Denmark	.. c	1.1	0.7	.. c	.. c	..	..	..	..	..
Estonia	..	..	..	0.4	..	..	..	..	..	..
Finland	.. c	.. c	.. c	.. c	.. c	7.5	7.6	..	..	..
France	75.5	75.0	93.3	187.6	186.4	43.6	70.5	.. c	27.7	.. c
Germany	-184.2	539.4	451.9	514.6	450.0	46.8	44.0	.. c	12.4	.. c
Greece	..	..	..	.. c	..	..	..	..	..	..
Hungary	.. c	.. c	.. c	..	..	..	..	..	..	..
Iceland	..	..	..	..	..	..	..	..	..	..
Ireland	-56.0	-81.6	-2.0	-7.7	-89.0	.. c	58.8	.. c	.. c	.. c
Israel	.. c	.. c	.. c	.. c	.. c	..	..	..	..	..
Italy	.. c	.. c	0.4	1.1	1.4	.. c	.. c	.. c	.. c	.. c
Japan	3 639.5	3 937.7	3 781.1	3 829.7	4 779.4	-10.1	-1.0	73.8	.. c	.. d
Korea	.. c	.. c	.. c	.. c	.. c	.. c	.. c	.. c	.. c	.. c
Latvia	..	..	..	..	..	..	..	..	..	..
Lithuania	..	..	..	..	.. c	..	..	..	..	..
Luxembourg	226.4	335.8	483.9	445.1	414.3	.. c	.. c	.. c	.. c	..
Mexico	..	.. c	.. c	..	..	.. c	18.7	39.5	.. c	.. c
Netherlands	2 821.4	2 748.3	2 908.2	2 596.0	2 932.8	289.1	.. c	.. c	.. c	.. c
New Zealand	-	0.0	-	-	-	-	0.0	-	-	-
Norway	.. c	.. c	.. c	.. c	.. c	..	..	..	..	..
Poland	0.0	0.0	.. c	.. c	.. c	..	..	..	..	..
Portugal	..	..	..	..	..	..	..	..	..	..
Slovak Republic	.. c	..	.. c	.. c	.. c	..	..	..	..	..
Slovenia	..	..	..	..	..	..	..	..	..	..
Spain	.. c	.. c	.. c	.. c	.. c	.. c	.. c	.. c	.. c	.. c
Sweden	.. c	.. c	.. c	.. c	.. c	.. c	.. c	.. c	.. c	.. c
Switzerland	362.4	443.2	438.0	1 242.9	1 416.0	-0.1	..	..	..	.. c
Turkey	.. c	.. c	.. c	.. c	.. c	.. c	.. c	.. c	.. c	.. c
United Kingdom	3 735.6	3 334.0	4 311.2	3 262.8	4 145.8	850.3	951.2	885.0	818.6	702.0
United States	5 628.2	5 584.6	4 930.5	5 236.0	5 941.5	2 527.5	2 434.8	2 356.6	2 003.1	4 859.6
EUROPE	**8 147.4**	**8 624.7**	**10 096.2**	**10 099.5**	**10 879.7**	**1 967.3**	**2 161.9**	**2 005.2**	**1 907.4**	**1 261.6**
Bulgaria	..	..	..	..	..	..	..	..	..	..
Croatia	..	..	0.0	0.0	..	..	..	..	..	..
Cyprus	..	..	..	..	.. c	..	..	..	..	..
Malta	.. c	..	..	..	..	..	..	..	..	..
Montenegro	..	..	..	..	..	..	..	..	..	..
Romania	.. c	.. c	.. c	.. c	..	..	..	..	..	..
Russian Federation	..	..	..	..	.. c	.. c	.. c	.. c	.. c	.. c
Ukraine	..	..	..	..	..	..	..	..	..	..
AFRICA	**.. c**	**.. c**	**.. c**	**-0.1**	**.. c**	**.. c**	**.. c**	**.. c**	**.. c**	**.. c**
Northern Africa	.. c	..	..	..	..	..	..	..	..	..
Algeria	..	..	..	..	..	..	..	..	..	..
Egypt	.. c	.. c	.. c	.. c	.. c	..	..	..	..	..
Libya	..	..	..	..	..	..	..	..	..	..
Morocco	..	..	..	..	..	..	..	..	..	..
Tunisia	..	..	..	..	..	..	..	..	..	..
Other African countries	.. c	..	..	..	..	.. c	..	..	..	..
Nigeria	..	..	..	..	..	..	..	..	..	..
South Africa	-0.7	.. c	.. c	.. c	.. c	..	.. c	.. c	.. c	.. d
AMERICA	**.. c**	**10 511.5**	**.. d**	**12 657.6**	**.. d**	**.. c**	**.. d**	**.. d**	**3 222.4**	**.. d**
Northern America	..	..	..	..	..	..	..	..	..	..
Central America and Caribbean countries	.. c	..	..	..	..	.. c	..	..	..	..
Bahamas	.. c	.. c	.. c	.. c	.. c	..	..	..	..	..
Bermuda	.. c	.. c	.. c	.. c	.. c	203.2	207.7	210.0	.. c	712.8
Cayman Islands	715.5	829.3	897.1	1 686.0	1 914.1	..	..	.. c	.. c	.. c
El Salvador	..	..	..	..	..	..	..	..	..	..
Guatemala	..	..	..	..	..	..	..	..	..	..
Honduras	..	..	..	..	..	..	..	..	..	..
Nicaragua	..	..	..	..	..	..	..	..	..	..
Panama	..	..	..	..	..	-1.0	..	..	..	..
Virgin Islands, U.S.	..	..	..	..	..	..	..	..	..	..
South America	.. c	..	..	..	..	.. c	..	..	..	..
Argentina	.. c	.. c	.. c	.. c	.. c	.. c	.. c	.. c	.. c	.. c
Bolivia	..	..	..	..	..	..	.. c	.. c	.. c	.. c
Brazil	.. c	.. c	.. c	.. c	.. c	.. c	.. c	16.2	.. c	13.4
Ecuador	..	..	..	..	..	..	..	..	..	..
Paraguay	..	..	..	..	..	..	..	..	..	..
Peru	..	..	..	..	..	6.1	.. c	.. c	.. c	.. c
Uruguay	..	..	..	..	..	.. c	.. c	.. c	.. c	.. c
Venezuela	.. c	..	..	..	..	-0.8	-0.7	-0.8	.. c	-0.5

Table 2. Foreign direct investment positions by country *(cont.)*

At year end

Million US dollars

	Inward					Outward				
	2016	2017	2018	2019	2020	2016	2017	2018	2019	2020
ASIA	**12 296.1**	**13 481.6**	**14 947.4**	**15 859.7**	**19 189.6**	**3 256.0**	**3 259.7**	**3 006.3**	**2 680.8**	**2 320.7**
Near and Middle East	.. c	..	..	..	..	.. c	..	..	..	..
Gulf Arabian countries	.. c	..	..	..	..	.. c	..	..	..	..
Kuwait	..	..	..	..	..	..	..	..	..	..
Qatar	..	..	..	..	..	..	..	..	..	..
Saudi Arabia	..	..	..	..	..	.. c	-0.1	27.3	.. c	18.8
United Arab Emirates	.. c	.. c	.. c	.. c	.. c	.. c	.. d	34.4	.. c	.. c
Other Near and Middle East	.. c	..	..	..	..	..	..	..	..	..
Jordan	..	..	..	..	..	..	..	..	..	..
Other Asian countries	.. c	..	..	..	..	.. c	..	..	..	..
China	.. c	898.8	945.3	945.9	1 216.3	4.8	32.7	44.7	25.1	26.7
Hong Kong, China	3 983.2	5 095.3	7 433.1	6 611.0	7 109.6	1 425.8	1 559.6	1 608.5	.. c	1 286.1
India	.. c	.. c	.. c	.. c	127.0	.. c	.. c	.. c	.. c	.. c
Indonesia	.. c	.. c	.. c	.. c	.. c	.. c	.. c	.. c	.. c	16.8
Iran, Islamic Republic of	..	..	..	..	..	..	..	..	..	..
Malaysia	.. c	.. c	.. c	.. c	.. c	.. c	.. c	.. c	.. c	.. c
Philippines	.. c	.. c	.. c	.. c	.. c	.. c	0.3	.. c	.. c	.. d
Singapore	3 556.9	3 126.4	2 044.4	3 906.0	5 399.8	1 036.8	966.5	556.4	.. c	370.9
Chinese Taipei	-0.4	.. c	.. c	.. c	.. c	-1.3	1.6	10.7	.. c	.. d
Thailand	-0.3	3.6	.. c	.. c	.. c	.. c	-10.1	-0.8	.. c	.. c
Viet Nam	.. c	.. c	.. c	.. c	0.1	..	..	..	..	.. c
AUSTRALIA, OCEANIA AND POLAR REGIONS	**37 053.1**	**40 025.1**	**37 543.4**	**39 963.0**	**45 882.7**	**8 233.6**	**8 614.2**	**8 662.0**	**8 977.1**	**10 774.6**
WORLD unallocated and confidential	**2 531.7**	**3 384.7**	**2 614.4**	**2 658.1**	**4 244.7**	**431.4**	**399.9**	**219.3**	**.. d**	**697.7**
European Union (since 01/02/2020)	**..**	**..**	**..**	**..**	**5 083.3**	**..**	**..**	**..**	**..**	**.. d**
G20 countries excl. European Union	**52 668.0**	**57 071.0**	**55 136.9**	**57 563.5**	**65 990.7**	**11 835.7**	**12 220.7**	**12 298.5**	**12 139.0**	**16 981.2**
G20 OECD countries	**51 858.3**	**56 100.3**	**54 118.5**	**56 542.3**	**64 648.2**	**11 805.6**	**12 170.6**	**12 177.1**	**12 037.4**	**16 884.3**
G20 Non-OECD countries	**809.6**	**970.7**	**1 018.4**	**1 021.3**	**1 342.5**	**30.0**	**50.2**	**121.4**	**101.5**	**96.9**
MENA countries	**.. c**	**.. c**	**.. d**	**.. c**	**.. c**	**16.7**	**.. d**	**61.7**	**44.0**	**.. c**
ASEAN countries	**3 809.6**	**3 404.1**	**2 637.9**	**4 326.5**	**5 869.0**	**1 784.6**	**1 681.9**	**1 137.8**	**1 205.8**	**806.6**

- Nil; .. Not available; c Confidential data; d Secondary Confidentiality

Note: Detailed metadata at: *http://metalinks.oecd.org/idi/20220712/6d95*.

Source: *OECD International Direct Investment Statistics (database)*: *https://doi.org/10.1787/idi-data-en*

Table 3. Foreign direct investment income by country

Million US dollars

	Inward					Outward				
	2016	2017	2018	2019	2020	2016	2017	2018	2019	2020
WORLD	**5 437.8**	**7 091.6**	**6 951.9**	**5 891.4**	**4 841.0**	**741.9**	**522.7**	**372.1**	**604.8**	**535.1**
OECD COUNTRIES	**.. c**	**6 571.4**	**6 263.5**	**5 409.6**	**..**	**.. c**	**478.3**	**308.4**	**567.4**	**..**
Australia	4 201.4	5 062.1	4 918.2	4 273.3	3 725.4	387.8	265.9	244.3	287.7	308.7
Austria	.. c	.. c	.. c	.. c	.. c	..	-	..	.. c	.. c
Belgium	.. c	0.8	.. c	.. c	.. c	0.4	.. c	.. c	.. c	.. c
Canada	136.5	158.6	201.6	226.5	109.3	-25.8	-19.1	0.7	3.7	5.9
Chile	..	-	..	..	..	.. c	.. c	.. c	.. c	.. c
Colombia	..	-	..	..	..	..	.. c	.. c	.. c	.. c
Costa Rica	..	..	..	..	..	..	..	..	..	..
Czech Republic	..	..	..	..	..	..	..	..	..	..
Denmark	..	..	..	.. c	.. c	..	..	..	..	..
Estonia	..	..	..	..	..	..	..	..	..	..
Finland	.. c	.. c	.. c	.. c	.. c	0.0	0.0	0.0	..	..
France	22.5	30.5	12.2	.. d	32.2	-7.7	-0.7	-7.0	.. c	.. c
Germany	20.4	68.5	9.8	.. d	20.1	-0.8	0.5	.. c	.. c	5.6
Greece	..	..	..	..	..	..	..	..	..	..
Hungary	..	..	..	..	..	..	..	..	..	.. c
Iceland	..	..	..	..	..	..	..	..	..	..
Ireland	.. c	2.3	3.3	3.8	9.2	.. c	1.0	-0.1	.. c	.. c
Israel	..	..	..	..	..	..	..	..	..	.. c
Italy	..	-	..	..	..	.. c	.. c	.. c	.. c	.. c
Japan	125.8	174.4	167.1	70.8	107.1	.. c	.. c	.. c	.. c	3.1
Korea	.. c	17.6	17.7	18.1	8.1	4.0	2.5	.. c	.. c	2.0
Latvia	..	..	..	..	..	..	..	..	..	..
Lithuania	..	..	..	..	..	..	..	..	..	..
Luxembourg	-0.8	.. c	21.3	26.7	13.7	.. c	.. c	..	..	..
Mexico	..	-	..	..	..	2.8	.. c	.. c	.. c	1.6
Netherlands	167.6	241.6	224.5	177.4	161.6	0.2	.. c	.. c	.. c	.. c
New Zealand	-	-	-	-	-	-	-	-	-	-
Norway	.. c	.. c	.. c	.. c	.. c	..	-	..	..	..
Poland	..	..	..	..	..	..	..	..	..	..
Portugal	..	..	..	..	..	..	..	..	..	..
Slovak Republic	..	..	..	..	..	..	..	..	..	..
Slovenia	..	..	..	..	..	..	..	..	..	..
Spain	.. c	.. c	.. c	.. c	.. c	.. c	.. c	.. c	.. c	.. c
Sweden	.. c	.. c	.. c	.. c	.. c	.. c	.. c	.. c	.. c	.. c
Switzerland	52.7	.. c	41.7	33.4	27.9	..	0.0	..	..	.. c
Turkey	..	-	..	..	..	.. c	.. c	.. c	.. c	.. c
United Kingdom	158.8	351.5	363.2	252.0	84.4	32.7	-18.0	17.1	229.8	-19.8
United States	232.9	362.6	238.2	188.9	127.4	51.6	132.0	59.8	12.9	115.9
EUROPE	**539.5**	**828.8**	**750.0**	**663.9**	**439.3**	**150.5**	**96.1**	**16.3**	**260.0**	**10.7**
Bulgaria	..	..	..	..	..	..	..	..	..	..
Croatia	..	..	..	..	..	..	..	..	..	..
Cyprus	..	..	..	..	..	..	..	..	..	..
Malta	..	..	..	..	..	..	..	..	..	..
Montenegro	..	..	..	..	..	..	..	..	..	..
Romania	..	..	..	..	..	..	..	..	..	..
Russian Federation	..	..	..	..	..	.. c	.. c	.. c	.. c	.. c
Ukraine	..	..	..	..	..	..	..	..	..	..
AFRICA	**.. c**	**.. c**	**.. c**	**..**	**..**	**.. c**	**0.8**	**.. c**	**.. c**	**.. c**
Northern Africa	..	..	..	..	..	..	..	..	..	..
Algeria	..	..	..	..	..	..	..	..	..	..
Egypt	..	..	..	..	..	..	..	..	..	.. c
Libya	..	..	..	..	..	..	..	..	..	..
Morocco	..	..	..	..	..	..	..	..	..	..
Tunisia	..	..	..	..	..	..	..	..	..	..
Other African countries	.. c	..	..	..	..	.. c	..	..	..	..
Nigeria	..	..	..	..	..	..	..	..	..	..
South Africa	..	-	..	..	..	..	.. c	.. c	.. c	.. c
AMERICA	**.. c**	**.. d**	**.. d**	**425.9**	**320.4**	**.. c**	**151.6**	**.. d**	**.. d**	**110.2**
Northern America	..	..	..	..	..	..	..	..	..	..
Central America and Caribbean countries	.. c	..	..	..	..	..	..	..	..	..
Bahamas	.. c	.. c	.. c	.. c	.. c	..	-	..	..	..
Bermuda	18.9	65.0	88.1	-78.2	-40.2	46.9	40.6	14.1	9.3	-5.0
Cayman Islands	23.5	.. c	.. c	46.2	62.6	..	-	.. c	.. c	.. c
El Salvador	..	..	..	..	..	..	..	..	..	.. c
Guatemala	..	..	..	..	..	..	..	..	..	..
Honduras	..	..	..	..	..	..	..	..	..	..
Nicaragua	..	..	..	..	..	..	..	..	..	..
Panama	..	-	..	..	..	0.0	0.0	..	..	..
Virgin Islands, U.S.	..	..	..	..	..	..	..	..	..	..
South America	..	..	..	..	..	.. c	..	..	..	..
Argentina	..	-	..	..	..	.. c	.. c	.. c	.. c	.. c
Bolivia	..	-	..	..	..	..	.. c	.. c	..	.. c
Brazil	..	-	..	..	..	.. c	.. c	.. c	-1.0	-1.5
Ecuador	..	..	..	..	..	..	..	..	..	..
Paraguay	..	..	..	..	..	..	..	..	..	..
Peru	..	-	..	..	..	-0.4	.. c	.. c	.. c	.. c
Uruguay	..	-	..	..	..	.. c	.. c	.. c	.. c	.. c
Venezuela	..	-	..	..	..	0.0	0.0	0.0	0.0	0.0

Table 3. Foreign direct investment income by country *(cont.)*

Million US dollars

	Inward					Outward				
	2016	2017	2018	2019	2020	2016	2017	2018	2019	2020
ASIA	**269.7**	**555.9**	**690.7**	**528.3**	**355.9**	**121.0**	**5.7**	**30.7**	**46.3**	**99.6**
Near and Middle East	.. c	..	..	..	..	.. c	..	..	..	..
Gulf Arabian countries	.. c	..	..	..	..	.. c	..	..	..	..
Kuwait	..	..	..	..	..	..	..	..	..	..
Qatar	..	..	..	..	..	..	..	..	..	..
Saudi Arabia	..	-	..	..	..	0.0	-0.1	0.0	0.0	.. c
United Arab Emirates	.. c	.. c	.. c	.. c	.. c	.. c	17.1	.. c	.. c	.. c
Other Near and Middle East	..	..	..	..	..	..	..	..	..	..
Jordan	..	..	..	..	..	..	..	..	..	..
Other Asian countries	.. c	..	..	..	..	.. c	..	..	..	..
China	.. c	.. d	29.6	.. d	28.2	3.9	4.7	2.9	4.0	15.0
Hong Kong, China	153.3	269.7	288.4	306.7	156.1	-2.0	15.8	-5.3	-15.5	4.1
India	.. c	.. c	.. c	.. c	3.9	.. c	.. c	.. c	.. c	.. c
Indonesia	.. c	..	..	..	..	..	..	..	..	..
Iran, Islamic Republic of	..	..	..	..	..	..	..	..	..	..
Malaysia	.. c	.. c	.. c	.. c	.. c	.. c	0.4	-1.5	.. c	.. c
Philippines	.. c	.. c	.. c	.. c	.. c	.. c	.. c	.. c	..	.. c
Singapore	-41.3	76.9	189.6	152.0	53.4	85.4	.. c	.. c	45.2	37.6
Chinese Taipei	..	-	.. c	.. c	.. c	0.4	0.5	.. c	.. c	1.7
Thailand	..	-	..	..	..	.. c	0.3	.. c	.. c	.. c
Viet Nam	..	..	..	..	..	..	..	..	..	.. c
AUSTRALIA, OCEANIA AND POLAR REGIONS	**4 201.4**	**5 062.1**	**4 918.2**	**4 273.3**	**3 725.4**	**391.2**	**268.6**	**248.1**	**290.6**	**313.6**
WORLD unallocated and confidential	**-11.0**	**21.0**	**..**	**-**	**-**	**4.3**	**-**	**..**	**.. d**	**1.0**
European Union (since 01/02/2020)	**..**	**..**	**..**	**..**	**282.8**	**..**	**..**	**..**	**..**	**28.4**
G20 countries excl. European Union	**4 915.1**	**6 236.6**	**5 958.1**	**5 096.2**	**4 246.1**	**454.4**	**371.0**	**303.4**	**559.2**	**452.0**
G20 OECD countries	**4 913.8**	**6 225.9**	**5 928.0**	**5 085.0**	**4 214.0**	**447.3**	**365.7**	**299.9**	**556.8**	**430.0**
G20 Non-OECD countries	**1.3**	**10.7**	**.. d**	**11.1**	**32.1**	**7.1**	**5.3**	**3.5**	**2.4**	**21.9**
MENA countries	**.. c**	**.. c**	**.. c**	**.. c**	**.. c**	**.. c**	**17.0**	**.. c**	**.. c**	**-1.5**
ASEAN countries	**-26.9**	**82.9**	**185.5**	**121.8**	**52.0**	**86.6**	**-35.9**	**35.7**	**47.9**	**.. c**

- Nil; .. Not available; c Confidential data; d Secondary Confidentiality

Note: Detailed metadata at: *http://metalinks.oecd.org/idi/20220712/6d95.*

Source: *OECD International Direct Investment Statistics (database): https://doi.org/10.1787/idi-data-en*

NEW ZEALAND

Table 4. Foreign direct investment flows by industrial sector

Million US dollars

	Inward					Outward				
	2016	2017	2018	2019	2020	2016	2017	2018	2019	2020
All FDI activities	**2 910.8**	**2 538.0**	**1 945.2**	**4 277.2**	**3 812.1**	**62.2**	**-222.5**	**424.9**	**-172.0**	**522.9**
Agriculture, forestry and fishing	..	..	..	..	..	..	..	..	..	..
Mining and quarrying	..	..	..	..	..	..	..	..	..	..
Extraction activities	..	..	..	..	..	..	..	..	..	..
Manufacturing	..	..	..	..	..	..	..	..	..	..
of which:										
Food products, beverages and tobacco	..	..	..	..	..	..	..	..	..	..
Textiles, wood and paper products; printing	..	..	..	..	..	..	..	..	..	..
Chemical, rubber, plastic, non-metallic mineral products	..	..	..	..	..	..	..	..	..	..
Metal and machinery products, except electrical equipment	..	..	..	..	..	..	..	..	..	..
Motor vehicles, trailers, semi-trailers, other transport equipment	..	..	..	..	..	..	..	..	..	..
Other manufacturing	..	..	..	..	..	..	..	..	..	..
Electricity, gas, steam and air conditioning supply	..	..	..	..	..	..	..	..	..	..
Water supply; sewerage, waste management and remediation activities	..	..	..	..	..	..	..	..	..	..
Construction	..	..	..	..	..	..	..	..	..	..
Services	..	..	..	..	..	..	..	..	..	..
Wholesale and retail trade; repair of motor vehicles and motorcycles	..	..	..	..	..	..	..	..	..	..
Transportation and storage	..	..	..	..	..	..	..	..	..	..
Accommodation and food service activities	..	..	..	..	..	..	..	..	..	..
Information and communication	..	..	..	..	..	..	..	..	..	..
Financial and insurance activities	..	..	..	..	..	..	..	..	..	..
Activities of holding companies	..	..	..	..	..	..	..	..	..	..
Real estate activities	..	..	..	..	..	..	..	..	..	..
Professional, scientific and technical activities	..	..	..	..	..	..	..	..	..	..
Administrative and support service activities	..	..	..	..	..	..	..	..	..	..
Public administration; activities of households and of extraterritorial organisations	..	..	..	..	..	..	..	..	..	..
Education	..	..	..	..	..	..	..	..	..	..
Human health and social work activities	..	..	..	..	..	..	..	..	..	..
Arts, entertainment and recreation	..	..	..	..	..	..	..	..	..	..
Other services	..	..	..	..	..	..	..	..	..	..
Not allocated and confidential	..	**2 538.0**	**1 945.2**	**4 277.2**	**3 812.1**	..	**-222.5**	**424.9**	**-172.0**	**522.9**
Private real estate activities	..	..	..	..	..	..	..	..	..	..

.. Not available

Note: Detailed metadata at: *http://metalinks.oecd.org/idi/20220712/6d95*.

Source: OECD *International Direct Investment Statistics (database)*: *https://doi.org/10.1787/idi-data-en*

NEW ZEALAND

Table 5. Foreign direct investment positions by industrial sector

At year end

Million US dollars

	Inward					Outward				
	2016	2017	2018	2019	2020	2016	2017	2018	2019	2020
All FDI activities	**70 403.0**	**76 027.5**	**75 158.1**	**81 237.8**	**92 486.7**	**16 740.0**	**17 158.8**	**17 277.6**	**17 045.5**	**20 923.3**
Agriculture, forestry and fishing	**5 004.1**	**5 802.1**	**6 222.6**	**6 461.4**	**7 293.4**	**.. c**	**.. c**	**.. c**	**.. c**	**.. c**
Mining and quarrying	**504.2**	**380.8**	**1 507.1**	**1 269.5**	**1 467.5**	**.. c**	**.. c**	**.. c**	**.. c**	**.. c**
Extraction activities	..	..	..	..	..	..	..	..	..	..
Manufacturing	**10 848.0**	**10 995.0**	**10 988.6**	**11 358.4**	**12 236.4**	**6 260.4**	**6 543.6**	**6 772.8**	**6 700.0**	**6 443.4**
of which:										
Food products, beverages and tobacco	..	..	..	..	..	..	..	..	..	..
Textiles, wood and paper products; printing	..	..	..	..	..	..	..	..	..	..
Chemical, rubber, plastic, non-metallic mineral products	..	..	..	..	..	..	..	..	..	..
Metal and machinery products, except electrical equipment	..	..	..	..	..	..	..	..	..	..
Motor vehicles, trailers, semi-trailers, other transport equipment	..	..	..	..	..	..	..	..	..	..
Other manufacturing	..	..	..	..	..	..	..	..	..	..
Electricity, gas, steam and air conditioning supply	**1 804.7**	**1 880.9**	**1 793.6**	**1 828.0**	**..**	**.. c**	**.. c**	**.. c**	**.. c**	**.. c**
Water supply; sewerage, waste management and remediation activities	**..**	**..**	**..**	**..**	**..**	**..**	**..**	**..**	**..**	**..**
Construction	**374.9**	**432.8**	**428.0**	**654.8**	**429.1**	**.. c**	**.. c**	**.. c**	**.. c**	**.. c**
Services	**40 524.9**	**44 983.5**	**42 788.8**	**48 148.3**	**57 376.3**	**7 807.8**	**7 643.6**	**6 580.8**	**6 247.6**	**11 558.9**
Wholesale and retail trade; repair of motor vehicles and motorcycles	7 773.9	7 871.9	8 415.1	9 574.0	9 794.3	4 058.2	4 266.8	4 314.9	3 323.9	4 013.6
Transportation and storage	541.7	466.9	502.1	538.0	662.5	.. c	.. c	.. c	.. c	.. c
Accommodation and food service activities	566.4	801.5	846.6	1 831.3	..	.. c	.. c	.. c	.. c	.. c
Information and communication	1 657.9	1 605.4	1 462.2	1 479.4	1 722.9	.. c	.. c	.. c	.. c	.. c
Financial and insurance activities	24 833.9	27 777.9	25 933.6	28 909.6	35 606.5	1 743.2	1 269.1	.. c	1 502.9	.. c
Activities of holding companies	..	..	..	..	..	..	..	..	..	..
Real estate activities	2 307.9	2 447.5	2 555.9	2 748.7	3 184.1	.. c	.. c	.. c	.. c	.. c
Professional, scientific and technical activities	1 102.8	2 024.5	2 033.4	1 552.2	1 790.8	51.8	106.9	87.0	105.7	135.8
Administrative and support service activities	702.3	693.1	227.6	245.2	308.2	.. c	.. c	.. c	.. c	.. c
Public administration; activities of households and of extraterritorial organisations	.. c	.. c	.. c	..	.. c	..	-	..	..	..
Education	..	..	..	..	..	..	..	..	..	..
Human health and social work activities	842.6	1 061.4	1 094.9	1 710.7	..	.. c	.. c	.. c	.. c	.. c
Arts, entertainment and recreation	..	-	..	..	..	380.4	223.7	380.1	362.9	346.5
Other services	.. c	.. c	.. c	.. c	.. c	..	-	..	..	..
Not allocated and confidential	**11 537.8**	**11 552.4**	**11 429.3**	**11 517.5**	**13 684.2**	**10 479.6**	**2 971.6**	**.. c**	**.. c**	**.. c**
Private real estate activities	**..**	**..**	**..**	**..**	**..**	**..**	**..**	**..**	**..**	**..**

- Nil; .. Not available; c Confidential data

Note: Detailed metadata at: *http://metalinks.oecd.org/idi/20220712/6d95.*

Source: OECD *International Direct Investment Statistics (database): https://doi.org/10.1787/idi-data-en*

Table 6. Foreign direct investment income by industrial sector

Million US dollars

	Inward					Outward				
	2016	2017	2018	2019	2020	2016	2017	2018	2019	2020
All FDI activities	**5 437.8**	**7 091.6**	**6 951.9**	**5 891.4**	**4 841.0**	**741.9**	**522.7**	**372.1**	**604.8**	**535.1**
Agriculture, forestry and fishing	..	..	..	..	..	..	..	..	..	..
Mining and quarrying	..	..	..	..	..	..	..	..	..	..
Extraction activities	..	..	..	..	..	..	..	..	..	..
Manufacturing	..	..	..	..	..	..	..	..	..	..
of which:										
Food products, beverages and tobacco	..	..	..	..	..	..	..	..	..	..
Textiles, wood and paper products; printing	..	..	..	..	..	..	..	..	..	..
Chemical, rubber, plastic, non-metallic mineral products	..	..	..	..	..	..	..	..	..	..
Metal and machinery products, except electrical equipment	..	..	..	..	..	..	..	..	..	..
Motor vehicles, trailers, semi-trailers, other transport equipment	..	..	..	..	..	..	..	..	..	..
Other manufacturing	..	..	..	..	..	..	..	..	..	..
Electricity, gas, steam and air conditioning supply	..	..	..	..	..	..	..	..	..	..
Water supply; sewerage, waste management and remediation activities	..	..	..	..	..	..	..	..	..	..
Construction	..	..	..	..	..	..	..	..	..	..
Services	..	..	..	..	..	..	..	..	..	..
Wholesale and retail trade; repair of motor vehicles and motorcycles	..	..	..	..	..	..	..	..	..	..
Transportation and storage	..	..	..	..	..	..	..	..	..	..
Accommodation and food service activities	..	..	..	..	..	..	..	..	..	..
Information and communication	..	..	..	..	..	..	..	..	..	..
Financial and insurance activities	..	..	..	..	..	..	..	..	..	..
Activities of holding companies	..	..	..	..	..	..	..	..	..	..
Real estate activities	..	..	..	..	..	..	..	..	..	..
Professional, scientific and technical activities	..	..	..	..	..	..	..	..	..	..
Administrative and support service activities	..	..	..	..	..	..	..	..	..	..
Public administration; activities of households and of extraterritorial organisations	..	..	..	..	..	..	..	..	..	..
Education	..	..	..	..	..	..	..	..	..	..
Human health and social work activities	..	..	..	..	..	..	..	..	..	..
Arts, entertainment and recreation	..	..	..	..	..	..	..	..	..	..
Other services	..	..	..	..	..	..	..	..	..	..
Not allocated and confidential	..	**7 091.6**	**6 951.9**	**5 891.4**	**4 841.0**	..	**522.7**	**372.1**	**604.8**	**535.1**
Private real estate activities	..	..	..	..	..	..	..	..	..	..

.. Not available

Note: Detailed metadata at: *http://metalinks.oecd.org/idi/20220712/6d95.*

Source: *OECD International Direct Investment Statistics (database): https://doi.org/10.1787/idi-data-en*

NORWAY

Table 1. Foreign direct investment flows by country

Million US dollars

	Inward					Outward				
	2016	2017	2018	2019	2020	2016	2017	2018	2019	2020
WORLD	**-3 979.3**	**-5 758.3**	**-2 141.7**	**17 504.5**	**-5 002.6**	**2 329.3**	**-6 865.8**	**9 084.1**	**13 799.5**	**-1 740.0**
OECD COUNTRIES	**.. d**	**..**	**.. d**	**14 634.3**	**-4 426.0**	**.. d**	**..**	**.. d**	**7 488.5**	**-792.6**
Australia	..	..	.. d	258.8	-70.1	..	.. d	..	.. d	.. d
Austria	..	.. d	..	-183.2	-54.2	..	..	..	.. d	.. d
Belgium	..	..	..	-2 561.7	888.4	..	..	..	375.5	-82.5
Canada	..	..	..	.. d	783.0	..	..	..	739.3	123.3
Chile	.. d	..	.. d	.. d	.. d	..	..	.. d	494.9	.. d
Colombia	.. d	.. d	..	0.8	-0.2	.. d	.. d	.. d	16.8	.. d
Costa Rica	..	.. d	.. d	.. d	.. d	.. d	.. d	.. d	.. d	0.6
Czech Republic	.. d	..	..	-84.7	2.7	..	..	..	.. d	.. d
Denmark	..	..	..	.. d	.. d	..	..	..	.. d	1 217.2
Estonia	..	.. d	..	.. d	.. d	..	..	.. d	.. d	.. d
Finland	..	..	..	.. d	.. d	..	..	..	.. d	.. d
France	..	..	..	187.6	-1 936.6	..	..	..	.. d	.. d
Germany	..	..	..	1 834.7	-855.9	..	..	..	232.9	790.8
Greece	.. d	.. d	.. d	0.1	0.2	..	..	..	41.8	.. d
Hungary	..	..	..	1.0	-4.6	.. d	..	.. d	-4.7	.. d
Iceland	..	..	..	40.6	-50.9	..	..	..	.. d	380.1
Ireland	..	..	..	-421.4	-95.6	..	..	..	286.0	926.0
Israel	.. d	.. d	.. d	.. d	0.6	..	..	.. d	.. d	.. d
Italy	..	..	..	311.8	-132.3	.. d	.. d	..	-125.1	.. d
Japan	..	..	.. d	150.0	53.5	..	..	..	-1.1	1 036.1
Korea	..	..	..	5.6	-7.6	..	..	..	-7.7	143.0
Latvia	..	..	..	-0.1	0.4	..	..	.. d	-11.3	.. d
Lithuania	..	.. d	..	.. d	.. d	..	..	..	16.0	-69.9
Luxembourg	..	..	..	.. d	.. d	..	..	..	.. d	.. d
Mexico	..	..	..	-5.2	2.7	..	..	..	2.4	-38.9
Netherlands	..	..	..	3 453.3	-662.4	..	..	..	172.0	.. d
New Zealand	..	..	.. d	.. d	.. d	..	..	..	16.5	37.9
Norway	..	..	..	-	-	..	..	..	-	.. d
Poland	..	..	..	254.2	122.3	..	..	..	.. d	.. d
Portugal	..	..	..	17.3	-22.2	..	..	..	.. d	.. d
Slovak Republic	.. d	.. d	..	.. d	.. d	..	..	..	-51.5	-72.6
Slovenia	.. d	.. d	- d	- d	- d	.. d	.. d	.. d	.. d	.. d
Spain	..	..	..	533.2	-43.0	..	..	..	.. d	.. d
Sweden	..	..	..	1 462.1	.. d	..	..	..	34.4	-1 323.0
Switzerland	..	..	..	.. d	.. d	..	..	..	-486.0	80.1
Turkey	..	..	..	-2.6	7.4	..	..	..	-7.6	168.4
United Kingdom	..	..	..	.. d	.. d	..	..	..	85.2	-1 016.7
United States	..	..	..	.. d	.. d	..	..	..	.. d	-784.0
EUROPE	**..**	**..**	**..**	**11 477.3**	**-4 767.3**	**..**	**..**	**..**	**10 796.5**	**-1 738.5**
Bulgaria	..	..	- d	.. d	0.3	..	.. d	.. d	.. d	.. d
Croatia	..	.. d	.. d	.. d	.. d	..	.. d	.. d	.. d	.. d
Cyprus	..	..	..	.. d	.. d	..	..	..	.. d	.. d
Malta	.. d	.. d	.. d	-191.2	126.1	.. d	.. d	..	1 241.9	-765.6
Montenegro	.. d	- d	..	-	-	.. d	.. d	.. d	- d	.. d
Romania	.. d	.. d	.. d	-0.2	0.7	.. d	.. d	..	.. d	.. d
Russian Federation	..	..	..	-51.7	-13.5	..	..	..	170.8	349.8
Ukraine	.. d	..	..	.. d	.. d	..	.. d	..	-1.9	.. d
AFRICA	**..**	**..**	**..**	**.. d**	**-96.1**	**.. d**	**..**	**..**	**935.0**	**-1 395.2**
Northern Africa	..	..	..	.. d	.. d	..	..	..	.. d	72.9
Algeria	- d	.. d	.. d	.. d	.. d	.. d	.. d	.. d	.. d	.. d
Egypt	..	..	..	-1.3	4.2	..	..	..	0.7	4.8
Libya	.. d	..	- d	- d	- d	.. d	..	.. d	.. d	0.6
Morocco	.. d	.. d	.. d	.. d	.. d	.. d	..	..	.. d	.. d
Tunisia	- d	- d	- d	- d	- d	.. d	.. d	.. d	0.1	0.4
Other African countries	..	..	..	.. d	-91.9	.. d	..	..	.. d	-1 468.0
Nigeria	.. d	..	..	.. d	19.0	.. d	.. d	.. d	.. d	.. d
South Africa	..	..	..	-5.0	-0.4	.. d	.. d	.. d	.. d	.. d
AMERICA	**..**	**..**	**..**	**5 378.8**	**.. d**	**..**	**..**	**..**	**.. d**	**156.8**
Northern America	..	..	..	.. d	.. d	..	..	..	.. d	-633.7
Central America and Caribbean countries	..	..	..	.. d	.. d	..	..	..	.. d	.. d
Bahamas	.. d	.. d	..	.. d	.. d	..	.. d	.. d	.. d	.. d
Bermuda	..	..	..	.. d	.. d	.. d	.. d	.. d	.. d	.. d
Cayman Islands	..	..	..	114.7	-339.6	.. d	.. d	..	114.2	-67.5
El Salvador	..	..	..	-	-	..	..	- d	.. d	.. d
Guatemala	..	..	..	-	-	.. d	.. d	.. d	.. d	.. d
Honduras	..	.. d	.. d	- d	- d	.. d	.. d	.. d	.. d	.. d
Nicaragua	..	..	..	-	-	.. d	.. d	.. d	.. d	.. d
Panama	.. d	.. d	.. d	.. d	-28.4	.. d	.. d	..	55.7	87.0
Virgin Islands, U.S.	- d	- d	..	-	-	..	..	..	-	-
South America	..	..	..	433.1	-9.0	..	..	..	1 146.3	1 117.8
Argentina	.. d	..	.. d	1.5	0.1	..	.. d	.. d	.. d	.. d
Bolivia	- d	- d	- d	-0.5	0.4	.. d	.. d	.. d	.. d	.. d
Brazil	..	..	..	-16.0	43.0	..	..	..	640.0	783.3
Ecuador	..	.. d	.. d	.. d	.. d	.. d	..	.. d	.. d	.. d
Paraguay	.. d	.. d	.. d	.. d	.. d	..	..	..	-	-
Peru	.. d	.. d	.. d	.. d	.. d	.. d	.. d	.. d	.. d	.. d
Uruguay	.. d	.. d	.. d	.. d	.. d	.. d	.. d	.. d	1.6	.. d
Venezuela	.. d	- d	.. d	.. d	.. d	.. d	.. d	.. d	.. d	.. d

Table 1. Foreign direct investment flows by country *(cont.)*

Million US dollars

	Inward					Outward				
	2016	2017	2018	2019	2020	2016	2017	2018	2019	2020
ASIA	..	..	..	**.. d**	**.. d**	..	..	..	**2 654.5**	**.. d**
Near and Middle East	..	..	..	135.2	-76.3	..	..	.. d	.. d	242.3
Gulf Arabian countries	..	..	..	142.5	-81.0	..	..	..	.. d	31.4
Kuwait	.. d	.. d	.. d	.. d	.. d	.. d	.. d	..	-1.7	1.1
Qatar	.. d	.. d	..	6.9	.. d	.. d	..	.. d	1.6	.. d
Saudi Arabia	..	..	..	0.1	0.9	.. d	.. d	..	-16.7	.. d
United Arab Emirates	..	..	..	164.5	-13.4	..	..	..	.. d	-46.0
Other Near and Middle East	.. d	..	..	.. d	4.7	..	.. d	.. d	163.9	.. d
Jordan	..	- d	- d	-	-	.. d	.. d	.. d	.. d	.. d
Other Asian countries	..	..	..	.. d	.. d	..	..	..	.. d	.. d
China	..	..	..	508.4	-74.7	..	..	..	182.2	-52.3
Hong Kong, China	..	..	..	.. d	-0.7	..	..	..	-14.0	-14.2
India	.. d	..	..	-13.2	-6.7	..	..	..	-13.6	14.3
Indonesia	.. d	..	..	-11.3	10.1	..	.. d	..	51.7	95.6
Iran, Islamic Republic of	..	.. d	- d	- d	- d	.. d	..	..	-0.6	.. d
Malaysia	..	.. d	.. d	11.8	-19.2	.. d	..	..	-42.8	5.5
Philippines	..	..	..	3.0	-2.1	..	.. d	..	-0.6	5.4
Singapore	..	..	..	.. d	.. d	..	..	..	.. d	.. d
Chinese Taipei	.. d	.. d	.. d	2.7	-0.7	..	.. d	.. d	9.5	-7.0
Thailand	.. d	.. d	..	-2 700.9	4.2	..	..	.. d	323.7	-327.9
Viet Nam	..	..	..	4.4	-9.3	.. d	.. d	.. d	.. d	.. d
AUSTRALIA, OCEANIA AND POLAR REGIONS	..	..	..	**228.8**	**-319.8**	..	**.. d**	..	**.. d**	**.. d**
WORLD unallocated and confidential	..	..	..	**.. d**	**.. d**	**.. d**	**.. d**	..	**.. d**	**.. d**
European Union (since 01/02/2020)	..	..	..	..	**-5 546.3**	..	..	..	..	**-2 306.8**
G20 countries excl. European Union	..	..	..	**.. d**	**.. d**	..	..	..	**2 771.8**	**1 981.2**
G20 OECD countries	..	..	..	**.. d**	**.. d**	..	..	..	**1 643.4**	**752.8**
G20 Non-OECD countries	..	..	..	**412.8**	**-41.2**	..	..	..	**1 128.4**	**1 228.4**
MENA countries	..	..	..	**148.9**	**-85.2**	..	..	..	**.. d**	**99.8**
ASEAN countries	..	..	..	**.. d**	**.. d**	..	..	..	**.. d**	**.. d**

- Nil; .. Not available; d Secondary Confidentiality

Note: Data excludes resident Special Purpose Entities (SPEs). Detailed metadata at: *http://metalinks.oecd.org/idi/20220712/6d95.*

Source: *OECD International Direct Investment Statistics (database): https://doi.org/10.1787/idi-data-en*

NORWAY

Table 2. Foreign direct investment positions by country

At year end

Million US dollars

	Inward					Outward				
	2016	2017	2018	2019	2020	2016	2017	2018	2019	2020
WORLD	**147 524.4**	**145 487.8**	**153 178.3**	**169 293.5**	**169 440.6**	**192 013.0**	**200 887.5**	**200 999.2**	**214 389.5**	**209 741.1**
OECD COUNTRIES	**121 549.8**	**118 490.0**	**..**	**132 382.7**	**131 953.0**	**155 164.8**	**162 795.7**	**..**	**166 373.8**	**167 425.9**
Australia	113.9	-78.6	120.3	379.0	316.5	942.6	753.0	887.7	1 354.7	1 407.2
Austria	3 144.9	2 405.2	1 552.8	1 352.4	1 340.0	222.7	211.9	215.1	188.2	257.2
Belgium	7 263.2	7 344.3	3 912.1	1 288.7	2 308.2	5 357.7	-535.9	-386.9	8.3	447.8
Canada	1 191.4	4 717.7	-64.3	537.1	1 415.6	1 172.7	2 013.8	1 281.7	2 070.8	2 222.2
Chile	-5.7	4.1	.. c	.. c	.. c	1 294.0	1 217.1	649.3	1 078.0	903.5
Colombia	-0.3	.. c	-0.9	-0.1	-0.4	227.5	153.1	191.0	206.5	223.7
Costa Rica	-	.. c	.. c	-	.. c	.. c	16.2	13.9	23.6	20.5
Czech Republic	190.4	269.4	86.8	1.0	3.8	228.4	218.9	244.8	248.7	307.4
Denmark	5 906.3	8 161.4	7 292.6	6 914.2	6 268.3	11 599.2	13 278.0	13 207.3	15 794.3	17 104.8
Estonia	.. c	5.0	119.2	44.6	-90.0	658.9	486.4	218.8	187.8	204.2
Finland	3 279.1	2 451.3	6 307.6	7 561.5	8 472.8	1 435.4	1 783.9	1 590.1	5 626.4	6 589.1
France	7 331.1	6 638.4	5 226.5	5 364.0	3 494.3	2 750.2	4 606.3	4 905.3	8 795.6	9 338.0
Germany	8 057.8	6 461.5	6 099.7	7 876.2	7 274.7	2 111.8	2 533.3	2 958.5	3 339.4	3 806.7
Greece	.. c	0.2	-	0.1	0.4	10.7	28.7	35.4	72.2	52.2
Hungary	2.3	1.9	-1.8	-0.8	-5.4	416.6	1 461.6	200.1	185.8	164.7
Iceland	50.1	214.4	35.8	76.1	22.2	367.5	412.1	243.8	294.6	696.6
Ireland	-309.5	-59.4	918.6	487.6	410.6	2 180.9	2 201.9	2 037.3	2 301.7	2 841.9
Israel	.. c	.. c	.. c	1.9	2.7	2.1	-0.6	5.2	4.8	4.5
Italy	740.4	387.3	771.3	1 075.9	981.9	228.2	229.1	235.7	184.9	70.5
Japan	1 028.1	1 388.7	1 074.9	1 213.3	1 309.5	112.6	572.8	500.3	518.5	1 145.1
Korea	-259.7	-252.1	54.2	59.2	51.9	1 055.8	886.7	805.3	852.5	1 044.9
Latvia	-6.4	0.5	0.5	1.0	1.5	651.2	588.9	364.9	357.3	390.4
Lithuania	-20.3	76.6	4.0	-41.0	5.4	871.0	465.2	465.6	533.1	443.5
Luxembourg	13 070.7	12 330.2	14 122.6	15 420.5	14 432.8	.. c	.. c	7 535.3	4 952.4	4 387.5
Mexico	-19.5	-1.6	1.2	-4.0	-1.3	65.1	112.5	78.9	96.0	45.1
Netherlands	20 664.7	15 704.3	14 676.8	17 974.5	17 900.4	34 458.7	34 517.8	26 073.9	25 800.0	23 650.9
New Zealand	-22.9	-4.0	.. c	.. c	-10.4	6.5	23.6	47.3	62.4	89.4
Norway	-	-	-	-	-	-	-	-	-	.. c
Poland	488.2	652.4	537.6	787.9	901.5	948.1	1 567.4	1 462.5	1 523.6	1 621.0
Portugal	.. c	.. c	2.8	20.2	-4.3	21.3	31.9	73.6	74.1	15.5
Slovak Republic	-1.6	11.2	-0.3	-	2.5	170.5	184.5	190.2	157.3	117.5
Slovenia	.. c	.. c	-	0.1	.. c	-6.1	1.8	-9.7	-4.6	-3.9
Spain	456.0	306.5	640.3	1 168.5	1 153.7	7 912.1	7 241.8	7 578.5	8 317.9	9 279.7
Sweden	31 404.2	32 143.6	32 542.0	33 673.8	33 351.7	25 640.0	27 733.7	27 229.0	28 080.4	29 196.5
Switzerland	2 932.1	2 713.8	4 303.9	4 760.4	5 299.1	456.5	393.9	35.6	-280.0	-193.7
Turkey	17.5	6.2	1.5	-1.0	6.4	1 811.9	1 168.3	1 068.2	1 019.4	1 161.7
United Kingdom	7 269.5	7 360.4	10 077.3	11 491.1	12 255.2	12 983.9	18 532.3	14 951.8	15 677.2	14 774.3
United States	7 603.2	7 060.5	8 917.7	12 928.2	13 126.6	31 156.4	30 254.9	40 093.4	36 900.0	33 617.4
EUROPE	**116 565.9**	**110 452.4**	**114 780.8**	**125 134.7**	**124 116.5**	**123 598.1**	**131 532.9**	**117 669.5**	**130 017.5**	**132 579.7**
Bulgaria	-2.2	-2.6	-0.1	0.7	1.1	.. c	.. c	9.0	20.2	24.0
Croatia	-	.. c	-2.2	.. c	0.6	116.5	124.0	90.2	98.4	96.6
Cyprus	1 012.9	979.2	832.9	3 025.9	3 137.7	729.8	1 095.4	1 150.4	1 291.8	699.9
Malta	353.4	242.3	544.2	345.8	495.2	1 408.9	1 513.3	2 012.2	3 563.4	3 191.2
Montenegro	-	-	-	-	-	.. c	0.1	.. c	-	.. c
Romania	-216.8	48.2	0.8	0.5	1.2	110.6	116.8	241.4	179.8	335.6
Russian Federation	177.5	105.1	104.9	51.9	42.2	348.1	404.5	395.6	481.1	447.2
Ukraine	.. c	4.0	.. c	.. c	.. c	36.7	47.0	34.5	34.4	34.2
AFRICA	**-230.7**	**-125.1**	**-39.5**	**458.0**	**364.7**	**5 167.5**	**4 448.0**	**3 640.5**	**3 700.5**	**1 659.2**
Northern Africa	-17.1	-13.2	-3.3	3.0	-1.8	1 303.9	1 212.7	973.2	905.1	863.9
Algeria	.. c	-	.. c	-0.9	.. c	1 118.0	1 014.9	806.3	751.5	688.5
Egypt	-16.6	-12.8	-3.2	-4.6	-0.1	55.9	64.6	65.5	60.3	65.1
Libya	-	-	.. c	.. c	.. c	.. c	.. c	.. c	.. c	.. c
Morocco	.. c	-0.2	-	.. c	.. c	11.4	14.0	.. c	11.0	26.5
Tunisia	-0.1	.. c	.. c	.. c	.. c	.. c	.. c	.. c	.. c	2.9
Other African countries	-213.7	-111.9	-36.0	455.0	366.6	3 863.7	3 235.2	2 667.1	2 795.3	795.3
Nigeria	.. c	.. c	.. c	-23.7	-4.7	-1 063.3	.. c	-674.5	-532.6	-404.3
South Africa	4.3	-3.5	-4.6	-9.6	-10.1	83.6	85.1	135.7	147.3	109.6
AMERICA	**17 355.1**	**19 010.7**	**14 347.5**	**19 670.6**	**19 218.1**	**40 921.3**	**41 439.2**	**53 165.1**	**51 515.0**	**47 106.4**
Northern America	8 794.7	11 778.1	8 853.4	13 468.7	14 545.8	32 344.1	32 270.5	41 385.7	38 973.7	35 872.0
Central America and Caribbean countries	8 660.1	6 919.4	5 506.8	5 786.1	4 257.0	2 502.7	1 782.5	2 173.6	2 034.5	1 456.4
Bahamas	20.5	177.8	-10.8	20.2	.. c	.. c	.. c	34.1	18.8	20.6
Bermuda	4 241.5	3 308.9	3 329.5	3 433.3	2 691.2	2 153.2	1 418.3	1 760.4	1 349.2	671.5
Cayman Islands	3 514.6	2 541.5	1 247.2	1 355.9	1 003.8	222.2	154.8	200.9	349.5	313.5
El Salvador	-	-	-	-	-	-	-	.. c	.. c	.. c
Guatemala	-	-	-	-	-	.. c	.. c	.. c	.. c	.. c
Honduras	.. c	.. c	.. c	.. c	.. c	.. c	.. c	.. c	.. c	.. c
Nicaragua	-	-	-	-	-	.. c	.. c	.. c	.. c	.. c
Panama	-0.9	-0.7	-3.6	-2.8	-34.9	76.5	59.1	56.2	40.9	275.7
Virgin Islands, U.S.	.. c	-	-	-	-	-	-	-	-	-
South America	-99.5	313.4	-12.7	415.7	415.2	6 074.6	7 386.2	9 605.8	10 506.8	9 778.1
Argentina	-0.1	-0.7	0.2	1.7	1.9	149.2	140.4	169.9	214.4	248.2
Bolivia	.. c	.. c	-0.1	-0.6	-0.2	.. c	.. c	.. c	.. c	.. c
Brazil	-118.1	-94.5	-2.8	-18.9	22.5	4 176.5	5 660.5	8 310.2	8 802.8	8 062.5
Ecuador	-0.2	-2.7	-0.5	-0.2	.. c	.. c	.. c	.. c	1.6	2.1
Paraguay	.. c	.. c	.. c	.. c	.. c	-	-	-	-	-
Peru	.. c	.. c	.. c	.. c	.. c	216.1	190.1	280.3	208.2	341.3
Uruguay	12.5	8.3	.. c	.. c	.. c	.. c	8.9	-7.3	-5.6	-4.1
Venezuela	-	-	.. c	.. c	.. c	4.5	11.1	.. c	-2.4	.. c

NORWAY

Table 2. Foreign direct investment positions by country *(cont.)*

At year end

Million US dollars

	Inward					Outward				
	2016	2017	2018	2019	2020	2016	2017	2018	2019	2020
ASIA	**5 349.9**	**6 911.3**	**5 665.2**	**4 284.2**	**3 962.6**	**17 510.2**	**18 018.0**	**17 246.3**	**18 589.7**	**16 397.2**
Near and Middle East	-33.9	402.6	489.3	620.7	551.2	1 065.4	1 591.2	1 895.1	1 990.8	1 977.4
Gulf Arabian countries	-28.3	338.5	442.2	581.2	506.8	727.1	1 049.3	1 053.6	1 098.5	956.3
Kuwait	0.7	.. c	.. c	.. c	.. c	0.7	-0.1	2.2	0.7	.. c
Qatar	-0.2	.. c	13.7	20.5	12.3	5.3	2.2	2.8	3.9	35.9
Saudi Arabia	-1.7	-0.4	-0.9	-0.8	-	57.4	56.8	73.3	64.0	55.3
United Arab Emirates	-15.5	20.6	39.5	203.6	192.8	207.9	169.8	195.3	218.5	215.5
Other Near and Middle East	-5.6	64.2	47.0	39.6	44.4	338.3	541.9	841.5	892.3	1 021.1
Jordan	-	.. c	-	-	-	.. c	.. c	.. c	.. c	.. c
Other Asian countries	5 383.8	6 508.8	5 175.9	3 663.4	3 411.4	16 444.8	16 426.8	15 351.1	16 599.0	14 419.8
China	2 630.6	1 392.6	792.1	1 293.5	.. c	535.6	162.7	966.4	1 141.2	1 122.5
Hong Kong, China	-12.9	.. c	.. c	465.7	473.3	144.0	152.7	95.9	80.8	68.7
India	-13.7	31.9	30.3	16.9	9.1	189.2	213.6	351.4	376.8	413.1
Indonesia	0.3	-1.1	-1.6	-12.8	-2.3	120.8	158.5	139.4	182.5	172.9
Iran, Islamic Republic of	-	.. c	.. c	.. c	.. c	.. c	.. c	.. c	.. c	-19.2
Malaysia	702.8	619.6	37.6	49.3	29.7	223.1	275.8	236.7	201.1	219.0
Philippines	0.6	-1.3	-2.0	0.9	-1.3	26.1	33.1	34.9	33.8	36.8
Singapore	267.7	124.7	179.2	575.4	292.4	12 848.0	12 496.0	10 664.6	11 216.3	8 061.4
Chinese Taipei	0.3	0.1	-3.7	-1.0	.. c	10.4	16.0	4.3	14.0	7.0
Thailand	.. c	2 824.2	2 692.8	-6.0	-1.5	826.2	987.6	1 074.8	1 072.2	1 088.9
Viet Nam	.. c	36.7	7.9	12.2	2.9	97.9	118.8	85.7	126.5	181.6
AUSTRALIA, OCEANIA AND POLAR REGIONS	**471.9**	**492.9**	**303.3**	**529.5**	**199.3**	**1 124.5**	**794.2**	**969.9**	**1 446.2**	**1 587.1**
WORLD unallocated and confidential	**8 012.3**	**8 745.6**	**..**	**19 216.5**	**21 579.4**	**3 691.3**	**4 655.2**	**..**	**9 120.5**	**10 411.5**
European Union (since 01/02/2020)	**..**	**..**	**..**	**..**	**101 840.6**	**..**	**..**	**..**	**..**	**114 629.9**
G20 countries excl. European Union	**35 752.8**	**35 117.5**	**33 197.8**	**42 240.9**	**41 544.8**	**60 051.7**	**68 545.3**	**78 308.5**	**82 219.4**	**79 264.6**
G20 OECD countries	**33 073.7**	**33 688.2**	**32 280.2**	**40 919.1**	**40 231.5**	**54 391.3**	**61 663.1**	**67 766.7**	**70 809.2**	**68 633.1**
G20 Non-OECD countries	**2 679.2**	**1 429.4**	**917.6**	**1 321.8**	**1 313.2**	**5 660.6**	**6 882.2**	**10 541.8**	**11 410.1**	**10 631.5**
MENA countries	**-45.1**	**325.2**	**438.9**	**584.1**	**505.0**	**2 063.5**	**2 293.3**	**2 060.0**	**2 037.1**	**1 851.8**
ASEAN countries	**2 012.2**	**3 602.7**	**2 913.9**	**617.5**	**319.8**	**14 170.1**	**14 098.7**	**12 267.2**	**12 868.6**	**9 794.8**

- Nil; .. Not available; c Confidential data

Note: Data excludes resident Special Purpose Entities (SPEs). Detailed metadata at: *http://metalinks.oecd.org/idi/20220712/6d95*.

Source: *OECD International Direct Investment Statistics (database): https://doi.org/10.1787/idi-data-en*

NORWAY

Table 3. Foreign direct investment income by country

Million US dollars

	Inward					Outward				
	2016	2017	2018	2019	2020	2016	2017	2018	2019	2020
WORLD	**6 312.1**	**11 105.4**	**13 224.2**	**13 563.9**	**6 695.8**	**6 709.1**	**8 328.7**	**12 131.0**	**5 319.6**	**130.2**
OECD COUNTRIES	**6 268.1**	**11 101.1**	**..**	**14 383.4**	**6 234.5**	**5 698.7**	**6 079.8**	**..**	**3 760.7**	**-473.3**
Australia	-34.4	-10.4	2.1	2.0	26.2	-34.8	-24.4	-15.2	521.9	12.6
Austria	33.9	148.1	248.2	118.5	84.4	-30.5	-28.8	-15.9	26.3	-21.7
Belgium	188.6	165.9	115.6	130.8	69.8	261.1	-200.3	21.9	14.0	-145.6
Canada	-139.6	-102.6	36.9	47.7	28.5	153.6	306.4	113.8	108.7	-213.8
Chile	.. c	.. c	.. c	.. c	.. c	-81.5	96.2	157.6	33.6	39.4
Colombia	-	.. c	-	-	-	-16.2	-40.7	-25.4	4.5	23.7
Costa Rica	-	-	-	-	-	.. c	.. c	1.0	1.8	0.9
Czech Republic	14.2	35.2	.. c	-	-	45.8	21.9	20.4	12.3	21.5
Denmark	1 218.4	1 531.4	1 798.3	1 029.5	570.4	236.3	772.8	1 622.7	1 054.8	1 312.9
Estonia	-9.0	13.9	-1.8	.. c	1.4	35.4	88.4	29.6	53.2	36.9
Finland	150.1	-27.0	1 000.4	500.5	265.9	77.7	60.9	-103.0	41.6	62.0
France	531.3	922.3	1 041.0	730.8	414.8	114.4	175.2	406.5	118.7	92.1
Germany	584.7	494.3	333.9	388.4	443.6	952.0	101.1	214.8	-39.3	183.6
Greece	-	-	-	-	-	-0.1	0.6	0.4	7.0	6.9
Hungary	-	.. c	-	-	-	107.3	12.3	65.3	-56.6	-0.1
Iceland	4.5	.. c	3.7	6.4	-2.9	-2.0	5.9	28.9	-33.0	-17.2
Ireland	23.8	76.9	54.0	123.4	53.8	-15.6	29.5	323.5	52.4	-275.9
Israel	-	.. c	.. c	.. c	.. c	-1.8	.. c	.. c	.. c	.. c
Italy	-4.4	-108.2	8.9	-24.3	35.0	1.2	-12.8	6.1	6.7	-29.4
Japan	-4.2	34.0	66.1	8.5	105.2	0.4	3.5	3.0	33.3	-184.1
Korea	.. c	48.1	-3.9	.. c	-2.4	86.3	32.4	132.9	57.1	53.5
Latvia	-0.2	.. c	.. c	.. c	.. c	78.3	132.0	125.0	67.9	-16.8
Lithuania	-0.4	-0.2	.. c	.. c	-	50.0	53.7	86.3	58.9	26.8
Luxembourg	-52.0	534.5	360.7	295.3	335.2	-11.2	49.2	31.5	3.5	47.0
Mexico	.. c	.. c	.. c	-	.. c	6.1	-7.6	-3.0	7.4	5.0
Netherlands	452.8	1 519.6	1 349.8	5 473.9	653.6	1 813.1	2 081.0	773.6	264.6	-1 397.5
New Zealand	-2.5	.. c	.. c	.. c	.. c	7.4	9.7	16.4	14.5	25.2
Norway	-	-	-	-	-	-	-	-	-	-
Poland	-27.4	53.4	50.0	66.1	-37.1	62.0	13.3	94.7	84.8	69.2
Portugal	.. c	.. c	-0.2	9.0	.. c	0.8	1.1	1.6	0.7	1.2
Slovak Republic	.. c	.. c	-	-	-	-3.3	13.1	18.2	-29.8	-45.7
Slovenia	-	-	-	-	-	.. c	.. c	-1.7	0.7	.. c
Spain	18.2	78.5	162.5	207.5	35.3	-1.2	7.5	-223.9	17.2	9.7
Sweden	2 951.7	4 732.6	4 006.5	3 303.3	1 870.1	1 779.7	1 437.2	814.2	862.6	553.3
Switzerland	62.0	376.5	9.6	661.2	449.9	0.2	-18.0	13.0	-5.5	9.9
Turkey	.. c	.. c	.. c	.. c	-	28.8	-159.1	20.9	15.5	35.8
United Kingdom	26.9	-122.7	1 038.4	929.2	302.4	-54.3	512.0	2 895.6	300.6	-1 045.3
United States	396.4	651.2	830.4	387.7	529.3	88.3	566.3	561.5	83.9	292.4
EUROPE	**6 088.8**	**10 489.5**	**12 287.9**	**13 151.8**	**6 007.4**	**5 734.3**	**5 357.9**	**7 036.7**	**3 348.5**	**-703.7**
Bulgaria	.. c	-	-	-	-	.. c	.. c	.. c	2.2	2.3
Croatia	-	.. c	-	-	-	3.5	3.6	1.6	1.0	2.4
Cyprus	-13.7	-57.8	-12.7	-26.8	190.6	-58.7	-74.4	-383.8	2.3	-405.4
Malta	24.0	-4.4	.. c	59.9	14.3	160.2	25.0	-23.2	270.8	99.0
Montenegro	-	-	-	-	-	.. c	.. c	.. c	-	-
Romania	1.7	.. c	-	-	-	-0.5	11.6	6.4	18.3	9.3
Russian Federation	2.1	.. c	.. c	.. c	.. c	56.1	50.9	29.1	79.1	72.7
Ukraine	-	-	-	-	-	3.8	0.7	2.0	3.8	1.4
AFRICA	**5.7**	**-0.5**	**16.1**	**4.8**	**21.0**	**272.6**	**2 142.8**	**3 418.5**	**1 391.1**	**826.3**
Northern Africa	-	.. c	-	.. c	-	26.9	235.2	723.9	337.3	98.3
Algeria	-	-	-	-	-	45.8	203.2	618.2	273.8	92.0
Egypt	-	.. c	-	-	-	-11.3	9.6	6.9	6.5	10.0
Libya	-	-	-	-	-	-5.7	.. c	.. c	.. c	-2.0
Morocco	-	-	-	.. c	-	-1.5	.. c	.. c	-1.5	-1.6
Tunisia	-	-	-	-	-	.. c	.. c	.. c	-	.. c
Other African countries	5.7	-0.5	16.1	4.4	21.0	245.7	1 907.6	2 694.6	1 053.7	728.0
Nigeria	.. c	.. c	.. c	-	.. c	.. c	.. c	.. c	-8.4	.. c
South Africa	-	-	-	0.1	-	16.2	-8.3	25.0	3.4	-1.9
AMERICA	**594.2**	**46.1**	**829.5**	**508.9**	**528.0**	**-80.1**	**900.3**	**1 176.7**	**-544.0**	**-734.2**
Northern America	256.8	548.4	867.3	435.6	557.7	240.0	873.1	676.1	193.0	80.3
Central America and Caribbean countries	344.6	-507.4	-13.0	74.3	-35.2	28.2	-7.9	48.7	-636.8	191.3
Bahamas	.. c	-1.9	.. c	0.2	-	.. c	.. c	2.3	2.3	.. c
Bermuda	101.9	84.8	-49.2	87.2	118.3	46.3	-11.0	51.5	-882.2	-48.1
Cayman Islands	209.8	-613.7	-17.5	-52.2	-167.5	-36.8	-0.4	-21.3	14.0	35.3
El Salvador	-	-	-	-	-	-	-	.. c	.. c	.. c
Guatemala	-	-	-	-	-	.. c	.. c	.. c	.. c	.. c
Honduras	-	-	-	-	-	.. c	.. c	.. c	.. c	.. c
Nicaragua	-	-	-	-	-	.. c	.. c	.. c	.. c	.. c
Panama	-	-	.. c	-	.. c	3.8	6.9	7.9	5.1	-8.2
Virgin Islands, U.S.	-	-	-	-	-	-	-	-	-	-
South America	-7.3	5.1	-24.7	-0.9	5.4	-348.4	35.1	451.9	-100.1	-1 005.8
Argentina	.. c	.. c	-	-	-	21.1	23.9	18.4	7.7	-28.6
Bolivia	-	.. c	-	-	-	.. c	.. c	.. c	.. c	.. c
Brazil	-13.5	-0.4	1.1	-4.7	-0.3	-280.8	-49.9	285.4	-148.8	-1 028.7
Ecuador	-	-	-	-	-	.. c	-	.. c	.. c	.. c
Paraguay	-	-	-	.. c	.. c	-	-	-	-	-
Peru	-	.. c	.. c	.. c	.. c	1.2	-2.9	19.8	-	-12.1
Uruguay	.. c	.. c	.. c	.. c	.. c	.. c	0.1	-11.8	1.9	1.3
Venezuela	-	-	-	-	-	8.2	.. c	.. c	.. c	.. c

Table 3. Foreign direct investment income by country *(cont.)*

Million US dollars

	Inward					Outward				
	2016	2017	2018	2019	2020	2016	2017	2018	2019	2020
ASIA	**-396.4**	**503.4**	**-185.9**	**-112.7**	**76.0**	**860.6**	**-85.6**	**497.2**	**575.7**	**715.4**
Near and Middle East	-0.7	.. c	52.5	44.4	.. c	168.8	214.8	423.5	225.5	285.7
Gulf Arabian countries	-0.7	.. c	.. c	44.0	.. c	87.9	86.0	56.1	71.3	113.0
Kuwait	-	.. c	.. c	.. c	.. c	-	-	.. c	.. c	.. c
Qatar	-	.. c	-	.. c	.. c	-1.1	0.4	0.4	-0.3	9.9
Saudi Arabia	-	-	.. c	-	.. c	.. c	.. c	18.2	35.9	31.4
United Arab Emirates	-0.7	-3.5	-3.0	9.7	0.5	49.0	45.5	30.2	14.4	53.3
Other Near and Middle East	-	.. c	.. c	.. c	.. c	81.0	128.9	367.3	154.2	172.6
Jordan	-	-	-	-	-	.. c	.. c	.. c	.. c	.. c
Other Asian countries	-395.7	442.5	-238.2	-157.1	136.6	691.8	-300.4	73.9	350.2	429.6
China	46.3	47.9	26.8	43.0	73.3	23.6	79.6	258.6	172.2	130.6
Hong Kong, China	.. c	.. c	.. c	14.5	16.5	73.3	13.9	21.3	-0.3	38.2
India	-	.. c	.. c	.. c	.. c	19.6	5.9	21.8	28.6	-8.4
Indonesia	.. c	.. c	-	-	.. c	10.2	21.6	13.0	12.4	19.5
Iran, Islamic Republic of	-	-	-	-	-	-4.6	-0.6	1.0	-0.6	.. c
Malaysia	4.3	.. c	-6.1	4.5	.. c	41.0	-10.5	15.0	-52.2	-41.1
Philippines	.. c	.. c	.. c	-	.. c	2.4	0.7	1.1	2.6	-0.9
Singapore	-375.7	305.3	-373.1	-247.1	-57.4	87.5	-823.1	-912.1	-269.4	88.2
Chinese Taipei	.. c	.. c	.. c	-	-	.. c	1.6	2.1	2.4	1.2
Thailand	45.6	42.6	40.6	.. c	1.9	15.8	9.4	14.8	86.2	25.0
Viet Nam	.. c	.. c	.. c	.. c	-	18.8	24.8	30.5	21.7	.. c
AUSTRALIA, OCEANIA AND POLAR REGIONS	**12.1**	**31.9**	**-31.8**	**-24.7**	**23.6**	**-86.9**	**-14.3**	**1.1**	**545.2**	**37.4**
WORLD unallocated and confidential	**7.7**	**34.9**	**..**	**35.8**	**39.8**	**8.7**	**27.7**	**..**	**3.1**	**-10.9**
European Union (since 01/02/2020)	**..**	**..**	**..**	**..**	**5 004.8**	**..**	**..**	**..**	**..**	**197.0**
G20 countries excl. European Union	**1 284.7**	**1 885.3**	**3 421.1**	**2 522.9**	**1 970.1**	**1 233.7**	**1 640.2**	**5 006.4**	**1 405.3**	**-1 610.9**
G20 OECD countries	**1 249.6**	**1 806.1**	**3 353.5**	**2 472.7**	**1 882.6**	**1 341.8**	**1 492.8**	**4 336.9**	**1 214.5**	**-797.6**
G20 Non-OECD countries	**35.0**	**79.2**	**67.6**	**50.2**	**87.4**	**-108.1**	**147.4**	**669.5**	**190.8**	**-813.3**
MENA countries	**-0.7**	**.. c**	**.. c**	**44.3**	**.. c**	**116.0**	**323.2**	**782.3**	**410.9**	**210.3**
ASEAN countries	**-326.2**	**302.3**	**-338.9**	**-224.7**	**-55.8**	**182.3**	**-774.5**	**-838.1**	**-194.9**	**139.0**

- Nil; .. Not available; c Confidential data

Note: Data excludes resident Special Purpose Entities (SPEs). Detailed metadata at: *http://metalinks.oecd.org/idi/20220712/6d95*.

Source: *OECD International Direct Investment Statistics (database): https://doi.org/10.1787/idi-data-en*

NORWAY

Table 4. Foreign direct investment flows by industrial sector

Million US dollars

	Inward					Outward				
	2016	2017	2018	2019	2020	2016	2017	2018	2019	2020
All FDI activities	**-3 979.3**	**-5 758.3**	**-2 141.7**	**17 504.5**	**-5 002.6**	**2 329.3**	**-6 865.8**	**9 084.1**	**13 799.5**	**-1 740.0**
Agriculture, forestry and fishing	**.. d**	**..**	**..**	**.. d**	**-14.4**	**.. d**	**..**	**.. d**	**.. d**	**1 089.4**
Mining and quarrying	**..**	**..**	**..**	**1 092.8**	**-4 088.7**	**..**	**..**	**..**	**-1 606.6**	**-4 358.8**
Extraction activities	..	..	..	1 092.8	-4 088.7	..	..	..	-1 606.6	-4 358.8
Manufacturing	**..**	**..**	**..**	**982.4**	**-1 829.6**	**..**	**..**	**..**	**1 746.2**	**-1 568.6**
of which:										
Food products, beverages and tobacco	..	..	..	133.2	66.0	..	..	..	-90.1	-405.0
Textiles, wood and paper products; printing	..	..	.. d	57.2	-42.5	..	..	..	742.8	100.9
Chemical, rubber, plastic, non-metallic mineral products	..	..	..	-76.0	-791.3	..	.. d	.. d	1 582.5	-560.5
Metal and machinery products, except electrical equipment	..	..	..	306.6	-200.7	..	..	..	-823.5	-224.5
Motor vehicles, trailers, semi-trailers, other transport equipment	..	..	..	416.2	-569.9	..	..	..	-248.8	-175.7
Other manufacturing	..	..	..	145.4	-291.1	..	..	..	583.2	-304.0
Electricity, gas, steam and air conditioning supply	**..**	**..**	**..**	**476.6**	**-39.4**	**..**	**..**	**..**	**120.4**	**-529.4**
Water supply; sewerage, waste management and remediation activities	**..**	**..**	**.. d**	**120.7**	**-12.1**	**..**	**..**	**.. d**	**.. d**	**.. d**
Construction	**..**	**..**	**..**	**697.7**	**953.3**	**..**	**..**	**..**	**141.0**	**161.9**
Services	**..**	**..**	**..**	**7 847.0**	**-812.3**	**..**	**..**	**..**	**8 795.3**	**38.1**
Wholesale and retail trade; repair of motor vehicles and motorcycles	..	..	..	229.7	-125.0	..	..	..	280.6	105.8
Transportation and storage	..	..	..	-288.6	-2 099.3	..	..	..	777.7	1 631.3
Accommodation and food service activities	.. d	..	.. d	45.5	-83.2	..	.. d	.. d	.. d	.. d
Information and communication	..	..	..	1 138.6	695.6	..	..	..	2 916.0	219.4
Financial and insurance activities	..	..	..	3 163.9	210.7	..	..	..	5 893.1	10 298.5
Activities of holding companies	.. d	.. d	.. d	.. d	- d	..	..	.. d	238.9	.. d
Real estate activities	..	..	..	2 364.0	-168.3	..	..	..	442.8	1 222.9
Professional, scientific and technical activities	..	..	..	413.1	3 010.3	..	..	..	1 258.3	-561.2
Administrative and support service activities	..	..	..	738.1	-1 836.3	..	..	..	2 629.3	-2 778.5
Public administration; activities of households and of extraterritorial organisations	.. d	..	..	-	-	.. d	.. d	..	-6 360.7	-10 101.0
Education	..	..	.. d	.. d	.. d	.. d	.. d	.. d	.. d	-30.5
Human health and social work activities	..	..	..	20.9	-226.1	.. d	..	..	.. d	.. d
Arts, entertainment and recreation	..	.. d	.. d	.. d	-113.9	.. d	.. d	.. d	1.1	-3.7
Other services	..	.. d	.. d	6.7	-85.5	.. d	.. d	.. d	.. d	.. d
Not allocated and confidential	**.. d**	**.. d**	**.. d**	**.. d**	**.. d**	**.. d**	**..**	**.. d**	**.. d**	**.. d**
Private real estate activities	**.. d**	**.. d**	**.. d**	**.. d**	**.. d**	**..**	**..**	**..**	**1 337.4**	**3 362.9**

- Nil; .. Not available; d Secondary Confidentiality

Note: Data excludes resident Special Purpose Entities (SPEs). Detailed metadata at: *http://metalinks.oecd.org/idi/20220712/6d95*.

Source: *OECD International Direct Investment Statistics (database)*: *https://doi.org/10.1787/idi-data-en*

NORWAY

Table 5. Foreign direct investment positions by industrial sector

At year end

Million US dollars

	Inward					Outward				
	2016	2017	2018	2019	2020	2016	2017	2018	2019	2020
All FDI activities	**147 524.4**	**145 487.8**	**153 178.3**	**169 293.5**	**169 440.6**	**192 013.0**	**200 887.5**	**200 999.2**	**214 389.5**	**209 741.1**
Agriculture, forestry and fishing	**155.2**	**256.6**	**-509.4**	**529.3**	**524.6**	**2 147.1**	**2 157.7**	**1 180.1**	**2 489.3**	**3 590.7**
Mining and quarrying	**42 126.1**	**40 306.0**	**31 334.4**	**32 136.1**	**28 769.3**	**48 846.6**	**41 749.5**	**48 933.6**	**46 574.0**	**37 385.3**
Extraction activities	42 126.1	40 306.0	31 334.4	32 136.1	28 769.3	48 846.6	41 749.5	48 933.6	46 574.0	37 385.3
Manufacturing	**20 981.3**	**21 158.6**	**19 273.2**	**20 134.2**	**18 802.7**	**27 429.9**	**30 918.6**	**28 785.6**	**30 171.1**	**30 134.3**
of which:										
Food products, beverages and tobacco	2 892.5	2 879.8	2 272.6	2 380.3	2 534.9	2 625.1	3 050.9	2 772.7	2 689.7	2 481.8
Textiles, wood and paper products; printing	96.3	193.8	379.1	431.1	396.8	1 301.9	1 402.7	1 321.9	1 994.8	2 165.7
Chemical, rubber, plastic, non-metallic mineral products	9 560.1	10 370.8	9 257.2	9 084.4	8 479.0	9 490.4	10 545.2	9 891.5	11 363.1	11 076.4
Metal and machinery products, except electrical equipment	3 848.7	3 903.8	3 581.9	3 922.1	3 781.9	11 372.0	13 317.7	13 353.3	12 607.5	13 226.4
Motor vehicles, trailers, semi-trailers, other transport equipment	2 576.5	1 520.6	1 352.5	1 753.5	1 206.0	1 476.5	1 449.9	603.0	262.3	112.3
Other manufacturing	2 007.3	2 289.8	2 429.7	2 562.6	2 404.0	1 164.2	1 152.4	843.2	1 253.6	1 071.9
Electricity, gas, steam and air conditioning supply	**1 052.3**	**1 426.7**	**2 087.5**	**2 543.7**	**2 576.7**	**6 061.1**	**4 304.3**	**4 584.9**	**4 634.9**	**4 357.1**
Water supply; sewerage, waste management and remediation activities	**138.6**	**164.4**	**186.3**	**305.7**	**301.3**	**0.5**	**.. c**	**.. c**	**.. c**	**.. c**
Construction	**1 797.2**	**2 149.2**	**2 413.2**	**3 086.2**	**4 264.0**	**1 121.3**	**1 231.4**	**1 026.5**	**1 076.1**	**1 387.5**
Services	**69 383.9**	**67 789.4**	**76 518.5**	**83 652.6**	**85 604.9**	**81 890.7**	**93 976.6**	**88 875.6**	**98 850.0**	**97 864.1**
Wholesale and retail trade; repair of motor vehicles and motorcycles	12 247.8	12 957.1	14 814.7	14 888.7	15 278.5	4 496.2	4 714.4	4 926.0	5 169.9	5 569.3
Transportation and storage	8 922.4	10 352.0	10 966.1	10 567.1	8 761.1	10 227.4	11 244.5	9 047.8	11 076.2	10 828.0
Accommodation and food service activities	617.1	484.0	1 578.7	1 605.9	1 573.6	311.0	359.2	347.2	362.2	388.0
Information and communication	8 848.0	8 946.9	10 258.6	11 286.4	12 435.5	14 052.4	17 793.8	16 635.0	19 804.2	20 234.3
Financial and insurance activities	17 826.5	12 194.2	14 988.7	18 039.3	18 785.2	16 624.6	17 016.4	16 372.5	23 569.0	33 897.2
Activities of holding companies	.. c	.. c	.. c	.. c	.. c	481.7	.. c	-	146.8	272.5
Real estate activities	9 141.6	11 731.1	11 843.7	14 090.7	14 326.8	7 521.6	8 218.1	8 081.4	8 179.8	9 086.4
Professional, scientific and technical activities	5 653.8	3 889.5	3 376.1	3 773.9	7 202.1	5 620.8	5 838.6	5 896.7	7 132.2	6 710.7
Administrative and support service activities	4 960.9	5 939.8	6 982.6	7 665.0	5 916.2	4 141.5	3 241.0	5 104.4	6 729.3	4 540.1
Public administration; activities of households and of extraterritorial organisations	-	-	-	-	-	.. c	.. c	.. c	15 526.3	5 367.4
Education	29.4	.. c	12.3	23.7	33.9	15.1	24.5	33.9	34.4	.. c
Human health and social work activities	666.1	810.4	1 098.5	1 108.9	891.7	116.1	170.3	118.6	941.5	929.1
Arts, entertainment and recreation	326.2	385.4	416.2	415.6	302.2	12.4	.. c	.. c	53.6	51.9
Other services	144.0	72.1	182.4	187.4	98.1	139.2	159.8	.. c	.. c	.. c
Not allocated and confidential	**3 984.9**	**3 654.0**	**..**	**7 414.4**	**7 090.0**	**3 320.0**	**.. c**	**..**	**.. c**	**.. c**
Private real estate activities	**7 904.8**	**8 582.9**	**18 067.4**	**19 491.3**	**21 507.0**	**21 195.7**	**23 200.7**	**27 120.3**	**28 182.5**	**32 719.7**

- Nil; .. Not available; c Confidential data

Note: Data excludes resident Special Purpose Entities (SPEs). Detailed metadata at: *http://metalinks.oecd.org/idi/20220712/6d95*.

Source: *OECD International Direct Investment Statistics (database)*: *https://doi.org/10.1787/idi-data-en*

NORWAY

Table 6. Foreign direct investment income by industrial sector

Million US dollars

	Inward					Outward				
	2016	2017	2018	2019	2020	2016	2017	2018	2019	2020
All FDI activities	**6 312.1**	**11 105.4**	**13 224.2**	**13 563.9**	**6 695.8**	**6 709.1**	**8 328.7**	**12 131.0**	**5 319.6**	**130.2**
Agriculture, forestry and fishing	**9.5**	**32.5**	**95.8**	**90.2**	**76.0**	**127.0**	**56.8**	**74.6**	**55.4**	**-31.8**
Mining and quarrying	**945.5**	**4 062.5**	**5 044.5**	**6 041.6**	**685.3**	**143.7**	**2 190.1**	**4 889.4**	**1 016.8**	**-930.9**
Extraction activities	945.5	4 062.5	5 044.5	6 041.6	685.3	143.7	2 190.1	4 889.4	1 016.8	-930.9
Manufacturing	**1 110.8**	**683.6**	**1 829.4**	**1 403.1**	**1 276.1**	**2 588.3**	**2 957.7**	**1 735.6**	**1 335.2**	**61.2**
of which:										
Food products, beverages and tobacco	262.7	223.7	146.4	65.7	68.8	296.1	204.9	127.2	110.7	117.4
Textiles, wood and paper products; printing	-10.1	11.5	21.8	82.1	37.9	123.1	36.5	107.4	630.9	115.8
Chemical, rubber, plastic, non-metallic mineral products	1 255.1	1 404.5	1 773.0	1 163.3	498.4	977.5	1 822.5	1 047.7	160.6	-628.4
Metal and machinery products, except electrical equipment	-372.7	-159.0	-112.2	-32.6	206.4	1 122.1	578.5	559.7	418.5	462.9
Motor vehicles, trailers, semi-trailers, other transport equipment	-365.0	-1 099.7	-99.6	-228.0	281.7	-10.7	171.4	-189.9	-38.2	22.9
Other manufacturing	340.9	302.6	99.9	352.7	182.5	80.4	143.8	83.5	52.6	-29.4
Electricity, gas, steam and air conditioning supply	**-98.5**	**30.7**	**91.1**	**16.5**	**-18.8**	**217.7**	**-383.6**	**1 881.2**	**-98.4**	**-228.8**
Water supply; sewerage, waste management and remediation activities	**9.5**	**14.0**	**-14.5**	**18.1**	**5.8**	**0.8**	**.. c**	**.. c**	**-1.7**	**-**
Construction	**127.3**	**127.6**	**-18.9**	**145.0**	**350.0**	**108.6**	**104.7**	**-64.3**	**143.9**	**94.2**
Services	**4 144.8**	**6 129.2**	**5 693.3**	**5 788.3**	**4 175.8**	**3 354.9**	**3 416.2**	**3 615.2**	**2 851.8**	**1 197.6**
Wholesale and retail trade; repair of motor vehicles and motorcycles	1 441.5	1 679.2	1 157.9	1 265.9	1 153.2	326.4	494.4	335.3	529.3	568.8
Transportation and storage	-377.0	82.2	142.2	-392.9	-113.5	104.6	142.3	-151.8	-412.9	-850.5
Accommodation and food service activities	19.4	30.2	68.5	91.0	50.9	14.5	64.4	22.4	14.2	-89.3
Information and communication	437.6	1 279.0	957.0	1 207.0	849.6	1 673.9	1 378.2	1 598.0	1 577.9	1 295.2
Financial and insurance activities	2 305.7	1 929.2	2 162.2	2 262.1	1 424.9	479.8	346.5	583.7	-118.7	-340.1
Activities of holding companies	3.6	7.3	-	-	-	26.9	0.5	-	-19.8	11.8
Real estate activities	448.4	1 231.5	733.0	880.3	531.3	613.2	668.0	509.9	310.0	-9.3
Professional, scientific and technical activities	-266.9	17.9	235.3	166.8	159.2	-31.2	161.5	553.1	640.6	555.9
Administrative and support service activities	94.9	-179.5	170.0	140.9	131.0	155.7	123.2	101.0	218.8	96.7
Public administration; activities of households and of extraterritorial organisations	-	-	-	-	-	10.5	21.6	47.2	86.8	-49.8
Education	2.6	1.8	-	-0.6	-1.0	3.0	0.7	7.7	-1.6	-6.6
Human health and social work activities	13.8	8.5	32.5	14.5	-27.7	5.4	15.0	8.0	-11.3	21.9
Arts, entertainment and recreation	16.9	26.0	33.1	116.5	11.9	-0.7	.. c	.. c	.. c	1.3
Other services	8.0	23.3	2.0	36.7	6.2	-	-1.7	3.7	12.3	3.5
Not allocated and confidential	**63.2**	**25.3**	**..**	**61.0**	**145.5**	**168.1**	**.. c**	**..**	**16.7**	**-31.2**
Private real estate activities	**-**	**-**	**-**	**-**	**-**	**-**	**-**	**-**	**-**	**-**

- Nil; .. Not available; c Confidential data

Note: Data excludes resident Special Purpose Entities (SPEs). Detailed metadata at: *http://metalinks.oecd.org/idi/20220712/6d95*.

Source: *OECD International Direct Investment Statistics (database): https://doi.org/10.1787/idi-data-en*

POLAND

Table 1. Foreign direct investment flows by country

Million US dollars

	Inward					Outward				
	2016	2017	2018	2019	2020	2016	2017	2018	2019	2020
WORLD	**15 706.8**	**9 172.4**	**15 997.7**	**13 509.8**	**13 832.6**	**11 598.3**	**2 169.5**	**891.1**	**1 853.9**	**1 295.3**
OECD COUNTRIES	**15 111.8**	**7 065.9**	**13 008.5**	**13 197.8**	**12 251.8**	**12 059.8**	**3 491.4**	**82.2**	**1 389.5**	**606.8**
Australia	-1.7	-4.7	6.8	9.9	131.2	4.0	1.3	-6.9	-2.3	-1.4
Austria	1 115.1	1 311.2	1 885.7	363.1	889.7	7.0	67.7	0.6	16.7	2.9
Belgium	753.0	-99.6	92.4	938.9	546.2	16.7	31.8	58.7	-1.8	-27.6
Canada	-29.8	17.2	-5.5	30.5	-142.2	3 150.6	457.9	-1 558.0	147.7	12.0
Chile	0.9	-0.7	-8.3	7.6	-4.2	229.2	159.9	43.2	47.4	32.7
Colombia	-1.4	2.1	-2.7	1.3	0.4	-0.5	-0.4	47.1	96.9	10.2
Costa Rica	-0.4	-	-0.4	0.5	0.7	-	-	-	-	0.8
Czech Republic	104.6	754.2	616.9	289.4	542.6	113.8	-172.5	1 219.3	186.5	170.5
Denmark	-99.0	-34.0	170.8	358.1	662.4	283.1	50.7	-398.9	43.2	-50.0
Estonia	3.5	-5.0	-4.6	40.9	3.3	16.0	-23.3	64.3	-38.0	-1.3
Finland	-40.0	50.4	19.2	273.5	273.7	37.9	-1.3	6.7	86.2	14.7
France	1 652.8	-913.9	-133.1	323.5	-1 395.5	-28.4	-490.8	-352.0	-256.5	-119.3
Germany	3 624.3	3 763.9	2 072.7	3 312.7	2 157.5	295.7	226.8	101.2	438.9	164.4
Greece	8.8	-10.2	8.5	-2.1	3.1	6.3	6.4	0.8	2.6	15.9
Hungary	-89.3	1 000.7	-331.6	387.6	-345.7	927.9	173.2	241.6	-49.0	-347.9
Iceland	7.1	6.0	-0.3	-6.3	-0.9	-0.4	-0.3	0.0	0.3	0.2
Ireland	-577.5	225.5	-410.7	-213.6	521.7	-208.7	55.1	-12.7	-6.5	10.2
Israel	77.2	-134.1	52.6	50.3	42.7	8.2	-101.7	2.4	4.9	4.5
Italy	-468.6	-2 184.3	187.4	552.9	207.4	6.1	-67.9	24.5	-2.3	-16.5
Japan	97.5	183.1	122.1	55.0	9.1	0.5	-4.4	5.3	2.1	3.7
Korea	4.0	184.3	109.0	1 279.6	-118.3	-8.3	-15.3	3.2	-4.7	-8.0
Latvia	12.3	27.0	16.3	38.5	39.2	24.1	24.5	6.2	7.8	12.7
Lithuania	14.9	27.0	142.6	-205.0	39.3	239.8	1.1	61.5	289.1	-142.3
Luxembourg	2 140.1	2 159.1	1 817.5	1 951.6	2 316.8	5 724.4	627.9	1 823.4	-1 438.5	161.8
Mexico	-41.1	-12.7	11.7	1.8	5.2	5.5	-27.2	15.0	-3.4	-137.9
Netherlands	4 819.8	-1 739.1	9 077.8	3 478.1	3 542.0	296.4	39.0	-110.2	76.8	48.3
New Zealand	-0.1	0.5	0.1	0.5	-0.4	0.0	-0.1	-0.3	-	0.1
Norway	201.2	170.0	178.3	281.5	72.9	-116.2	258.7	206.0	139.3	64.8
Poland	-	-	-	-	-	-	-	-	-	-
Portugal	79.4	-6.5	226.1	73.4	54.4	1.3	-3.1	39.1	5.5	16.6
Slovak Republic	-35.1	102.3	164.2	78.4	49.3	83.3	68.3	133.0	94.3	60.3
Slovenia	-6.6	3.5	-10.2	-1.8	-2.2	5.9	1.8	5.8	13.5	-4.2
Spain	-203.6	498.1	-2 115.6	-77.4	334.8	80.8	130.3	154.4	281.5	-82.9
Sweden	13.2	622.8	-660.3	-330.8	203.2	984.8	1 927.6	-1 387.9	1 447.1	402.9
Switzerland	909.6	448.1	578.4	203.4	965.4	314.6	-55.9	-197.3	-61.7	73.1
Turkey	33.0	14.8	-7.4	-6.3	1.3	31.9	8.5	-2.2	5.2	23.2
United Kingdom	916.4	-63.2	-519.2	-1 060.8	483.5	-218.7	42.4	-24.4	57.3	156.1
United States	130.3	731.5	-341.9	720.4	163.0	-15.5	95.5	-83.0	-138.6	84.7
EUROPE	**15 537.7**	**8 046.7**	**15 814.3**	**11 095.7**	**13 743.5**	**8 091.2**	**1 403.2**	**2 601.5**	**1 619.5**	**1 050.6**
Bulgaria	62.3	-31.3	-10.8	-29.4	-60.9	139.3	-18.4	70.5	147.7	7.3
Croatia	18.6	-3.0	7.6	17.5	-17.4	114.0	54.0	5.8	29.7	-19.4
Cyprus	437.2	1 601.0	1 043.3	414.9	933.8	-1 616.2	-1 835.5	369.2	-296.7	293.7
Malta	46.1	290.2	1 693.7	53.4	620.2	182.2	-68.1	64.6	67.5	-6.1
Montenegro	-0.6	0.5	-0.1	-	2.2	1.0	2.4	1.2	-1.6	-1.8
Romania	12.7	0.8	-35.1	-15.1	19.0	132.0	102.6	228.1	193.8	15.7
Russian Federation	11.7	75.1	47.2	-237.3	48.6	17.0	74.5	3.9	38.5	67.2
Ukraine	-27.0	-7.6	-16.6	-151.8	4.6	57.3	122.3	139.4	113.8	55.1
AFRICA	**39.2**	**34.2**	**2.2**	**-67.2**	**19.7**	**67.2**	**52.5**	**-139.3**	**4.2**	**0.9**
Northern Africa	20.5	14.9	-3.6	-28.7	-8.6	4.2	10.9	1.6	-	2.3
Algeria	2.6	0.1	-0.5	0.5	-0.2	0.1	0.0	-	-	-
Egypt	19.2	9.2	6.7	1.3	-0.1	2.3	0.7	-0.1	1.0	-0.6
Libya	-	-	-	-	-	-	0.2	1.2	-0.5	-0.2
Morocco	0.8	2.6	-6.6	-26.6	-2.5	2.7	11.7	1.2	0.3	2.4
Tunisia	-2.1	3.0	-3.2	-3.9	-5.8	-0.9	-1.7	-0.7	-0.5	0.6
Other African countries	18.8	19.3	5.6	-38.3	28.3	63.0	41.7	-139.8	4.2	-1.4
Nigeria	-0.4	-0.1	-0.1	-0.5	-2.6	0.8	1.1	0.4	-0.5	-0.3
South Africa	-2.4	-1.6	-3.2	-4.9	7.0	65.4	37.4	-105.2	-2.1	-1.9
AMERICA	**14.5**	**785.6**	**-395.4**	**737.6**	**49.8**	**3 449.7**	**743.1**	**-1 535.6**	**126.6**	**-10.1**
Northern America	100.5	748.7	-347.3	750.6	20.8	3 135.1	553.4	-1 641.0	9.1	96.7
Central America and Caribbean countries	-90.9	35.9	-38.4	-12.0	26.0	93.4	8.8	17.3	-36.7	-121.4
Bahamas	-	-0.1	-1.8	1.8	-0.1	86.1	47.8	6.8	-32.8	19.3
Bermuda	-2.0	41.4	17.4	16.4	20.0	0.0	-	-	-	-
Cayman Islands	25.5	6.7	-48.2	-26.3	5.1	0.1	-1.0	-	-	0.8
El Salvador	0.0	0.0	-	-	0.1	-	-	-	-	-
Guatemala	-0.3	-	0.2	-	-	-	-	-	-	-
Honduras	-	-	-	-	-	0.1	-	-	-	-
Nicaragua	0.3	0.2	0.2	-1.8	-	-	-	-	-	-
Panama	-0.5	0.3	0.7	-0.8	-1.5	-0.4	-9.3	-3.9	-0.8	-0.6
Virgin Islands, U.S.	-	-	-	-	-	-	-	-	-	-
South America	4.9	1.1	-9.7	-1.0	2.9	221.2	179.3	88.1	154.2	14.6
Argentina	3.0	-2.6	7.5	-2.6	-0.1	0.3	2.5	0.4	1.3	0.5
Bolivia	-	0.1	-0.2	-	0.1	-	-	-	-	-
Brazil	3.5	0.6	-3.4	-6.5	7.5	-8.0	17.9	-2.4	7.8	-27.9
Ecuador	-	-	-0.1	-	-	-	-	-	-	-
Paraguay	-	-	-	-	0.0	-	-	-	-	-
Peru	-1.2	0.2	-0.3	-	0.6	0.1	-0.4	-0.3	0.5	-0.5
Uruguay	0.1	1.8	-2.6	-0.5	-1.4	0.1	-0.3	0.1	0.3	-0.3
Venezuela	0.1	-0.3	0.3	-	0.0	-	-	-	-	-

POLAND

Table 1. Foreign direct investment flows by country *(cont.)*

Million US dollars

	Inward					Outward				
	2016	2017	2018	2019	2020	2016	2017	2018	2019	2020
ASIA	**116.8**	**316.2**	**568.0**	**1 734.6**	**-115.7**	**-13.8**	**-30.5**	**-28.3**	**106.8**	**255.2**
Near and Middle East	59.0	-108.9	93.5	61.5	51.1	34.5	-77.9	59.0	46.9	91.9
Gulf Arabian countries	-15.2	25.6	40.2	9.6	9.6	24.9	25.3	53.2	42.2	86.2
Kuwait	1.2	-0.1	-0.8	4.2	-4.3	-	-	-	-	0.0
Qatar	0.2	-0.2	0.4	0.8	0.6	0.0	-	-	-	-
Saudi Arabia	-1.8	-1.4	24.1	-5.7	2.7	0.1	-0.4	-1.3	1.8	-0.9
United Arab Emirates	4.7	27.2	16.9	10.9	9.3	23.6	25.1	54.5	40.4	87.1
Other Near and Middle East	74.2	-134.5	53.3	51.8	41.4	9.6	-103.2	5.8	4.7	5.7
Jordan	-2.8	2.8	-0.5	0.5	-	-0.1	-	0.1	-	-
Other Asian countries	57.8	425.1	474.6	1 673.1	-166.8	-48.4	47.4	-87.3	59.9	163.3
China	13.8	56.9	93.4	146.6	15.6	9.8	-7.2	6.5	-18.5	13.1
Hong Kong, China	-79.6	-25.7	30.7	260.7	-130.2	0.5	7.2	16.2	-7.6	8.7
India	18.9	20.1	-12.7	21.1	8.5	4.9	22.4	21.9	93.2	9.3
Indonesia	-2.1	-0.2	-1.8	0.3	-2.2	-0.6	-0.4	4.0	-1.3	-0.5
Iran, Islamic Republic of	0.4	-0.2	-0.1	-	-0.2	-	4.2	2.2	0.8	0.2
Malaysia	-1.1	0.2	0.4	-2.9	5.2	-0.3	-4.4	2.0	-1.0	2.9
Philippines	1.0	-82.3	-29.9	-7.6	-6.8	-0.4	0.0	0.3	0.5	0.8
Singapore	-12.0	54.1	96.7	-67.7	74.8	-1.3	14.3	-137.8	4.9	-4.4
Chinese Taipei	-0.9	-1.4	19.9	3.9	1.9	-0.2	0.2	-0.2	0.3	-0.1
Thailand	-3.0	46.3	58.5	3.1	-2.2	6.2	-0.1	4.3	-3.9	131.7
Viet Nam	12.4	-11.2	-4.5	-1.3	6.3	-6.5	36.2	-0.8	2.3	-2.7
AUSTRALIA, OCEANIA AND POLAR REGIONS	**-1.5**	**-8.5**	**1.1**	**13.5**	**130.9**	**4.1**	**1.3**	**-7.2**	**-2.3**	**-1.4**
WORLD unallocated and confidential	**-**	**-1.7**	**7.5**	**-4.4**	**4.5**	**0.0**	**-0.1**	**0.1**	**-0.8**	**0.0**
European Union (since 01/02/2020)	..	..	..	..	**12 138.0**	..	..	..	..	**580.3**
G20 countries excl. European Union	**5 961.9**	**1 862.7**	**1 653.6**	**5 130.4**	**1 589.8**	**3 312.2**	**373.4**	**-1 949.3**	**364.1**	**219.9**
G20 OECD countries	5 917.2	1 715.8	1 502.5	5 219.2	1 502.2	3 223.4	226.7	-1 877.2	243.3	160.9
G20 Non-OECD countries	**44.7**	**146.8**	**151.1**	**-89.1**	**87.6**	**88.8**	**146.7**	**-72.1**	**120.8**	**58.9**
MENA countries	2.6	40.4	36.6	-17.7	0.9	29.0	36.1	54.8	42.7	88.7
ASEAN countries	**-2.7**	**6.7**	**117.9**	**-76.3**	**74.8**	**-3.8**	**42.3**	**-127.6**	**1.6**	**127.8**

- Nil; .. Not available

Note: Detailed metadata at: *http://metalinks.oecd.org/idi/20220712/6d95*.

Source: *OECD International Direct Investment Statistics (database): https://doi.org/10.1787/idi-data-en*

POLAND

Table 2. Foreign direct investment positions by country

At year end

Million US dollars

	Inward					Outward				
	2016	2017	2018	2019	2020	2016	2017	2018	2019	2020
WORLD	**188 760.6**	**240 382.2**	**229 527.2**	**240 586.4**	**249 723.3**	**27 876.2**	**29 190.3**	**24 618.3**	**26 939.5**	**28 136.2**
OECD COUNTRIES	**166 906.9**	**210 833.9**	**201 076.5**	**212 359.3**	**216 191.8**	**19 115.3**	**21 328.6**	**17 761.9**	**18 073.0**	**19 194.6**
Australia	341.8	424.4	722.7	967.5	1 026.0	7.6	5.4	-0.2	4.5	5.6
Austria	5 591.3	7 722.7	8 223.1	8 188.4	9 188.2	237.3	338.5	344.4	424.2	435.8
Belgium	1 810.1	2 961.0	2 999.2	3 100.5	3 480.3	-45.9	-150.7	-74.2	26.9	-2.1
Canada	1 627.5	2 078.3	2 009.3	2 363.7	2 629.3	1 960.6	1 862.3	-218.3	5.5	1 624.1
Chile	1.5	0.9	0.8	14.2	13.6	482.3	522.3	566.1	613.8	646.8
Colombia	-	-	-	-	-	-1.1	-1.4	45.4	142.7	153.8
Costa Rica	-	-	-	-	-	-	-	-	-	0.8
Czech Republic	917.0	1 279.1	1 428.9	1 328.1	1 465.0	2 038.3	3 495.6	2 788.4	2 994.2	3 201.6
Denmark	2 994.7	3 564.4	3 429.7	3 720.0	3 661.4	299.0	414.1	38.8	74.8	23.9
Estonia	11.2	18.4	21.1	45.0	69.3	9.8	-12.2	48.4	9.5	8.2
Finland	1 924.5	2 208.7	2 047.5	2 096.4	2 471.9	97.6	111.9	106.1	198.0	228.0
France	19 054.9	23 780.8	23 528.8	24 747.3	23 523.7	707.6	307.9	-11.9	63.7	-127.2
Germany	37 405.8	47 930.0	46 171.0	46 729.0	49 460.7	1 305.8	1 639.5	1 606.9	1 815.6	2 044.5
Greece	213.9	236.9	228.1	238.9	263.3	7.6	14.3	15.1	11.8	38.0
Hungary	149.9	269.6	294.1	514.5	732.1	1 366.7	1 659.4	2 009.6	1 529.6	1 241.2
Iceland	22.7	39.2	38.1	36.5	31.0	-0.4	-0.7	0.1	-0.3	-
Ireland	642.2	757.3	945.6	704.8	1 086.5	-178.9	80.7	11.7	-79.5	-71.6
Israel	792.8	943.2	1 087.6	1 336.0	1 381.6	269.8	152.8	137.8	264.6	332.1
Italy	7 641.2	4 916.3	5 167.7	5 173.3	5 364.8	107.1	138.8	152.8	117.2	120.5
Japan	4 118.6	6 167.7	5 286.4	6 354.2	7 043.7	-3.0	-6.5	-1.0	0.3	3.7
Korea	1 208.6	1 747.0	1 853.9	2 339.3	4 554.9	-7.7	-15.7	-17.8	-12.4	-22.1
Latvia	60.1	85.9	103.7	83.5	79.0	109.8	144.5	140.2	126.7	152.7
Lithuania	249.8	292.9	499.4	231.1	184.8	1 057.2	1 074.2	1 110.4	1 239.7	1 131.9
Luxembourg	1 824.6	2 338.2	2 276.4	2 597.6	1 994.5	7 656.0	6 259.6	6 264.1	5 163.1	4 267.0
Mexico	-5.1	-8.3	14.5	27.6	37.6	16.1	-6.2	6.5	1.3	-73.2
Netherlands	16 044.0	23 052.9	20 463.8	23 316.6	23 072.1	2 111.4	2 288.8	2 506.1	1 544.6	1 146.0
New Zealand	3.0	4.1	3.9	3.8	26.0	0.4	0.4	-	-	-
Norway	832.4	1 669.3	1 673.9	1 892.7	1 921.4	409.8	553.3	593.9	773.9	954.1
Poland	9 691.0	10 769.0	8 782.0	12 075.1	10 611.6	-	-	-	-	-
Portugal	2 236.6	2 949.5	2 844.2	2 522.3	2 413.7	47.5	60.7	73.3	68.2	78.8
Slovak Republic	264.5	658.9	659.7	773.7	635.6	419.5	562.3	799.9	709.9	736.8
Slovenia	66.9	71.4	74.5	74.2	73.8	15.9	18.6	26.4	33.2	40.4
Spain	8 476.1	11 721.2	10 510.2	10 346.6	8 326.4	70.8	-37.9	316.8	456.9	412.9
Sweden	3 647.5	4 625.5	4 952.5	5 403.7	5 659.0	-4 684.3	-3 312.8	-4 239.9	-2 482.8	-2 277.6
Switzerland	5 045.7	6 308.3	6 183.7	6 715.6	7 633.1	2 220.8	2 057.2	570.8	511.6	638.0
Turkey	85.0	111.7	106.4	123.4	95.6	273.3	271.4	260.9	262.8	269.5
United Kingdom	11 723.0	13 863.9	12 031.0	12 388.7	12 609.3	892.6	1 101.9	1 108.7	1 242.9	1 390.2
United States	20 441.6	25 566.4	24 413.1	23 785.4	23 371.0	894.3	809.1	721.0	359.4	441.9
EUROPE	**139 486.0**	**176 173.8**	**166 288.8**	**175 619.9**	**176 515.9**	**22 994.6**	**24 397.9**	**21 832.3**	**24 241.0**	**23 554.2**
Bulgaria	8.1	21.4	15.2	21.5	17.7	92.4	83.6	147.8	168.5	191.0
Croatia	44.8	59.8	75.3	81.2	53.5	148.4	223.0	218.1	217.0	211.3
Cyprus	-	-	-	-	-	3 643.9	1 854.0	1 646.4	3 497.4	3 534.2
Malta	-	-	-	-	-	815.8	822.6	791.2	785.2	829.9
Montenegro	-	-	-	-	-	28.6	35.7	36.0	33.7	34.3
Romania	-3.0	-8.4	-12.8	-24.2	-33.8	599.6	803.0	974.2	985.9	1 026.0
Russian Federation	841.4	991.1	775.5	802.2	787.0	720.7	913.1	738.3	831.8	760.7
Ukraine	-49.4	-230.3	-286.1	-476.3	-469.4	15.1	122.5	219.5	388.7	337.1
AFRICA	**1 173.4**	**544.7**	**637.8**	**693.9**	**615.7**	**280.9**	**311.6**	**212.9**	**210.9**	**222.4**
Northern Africa	5.9	10.7	8.2	2.6	-	57.2	73.5	73.5	68.7	76.6
Algeria	-	-	-	-	-	0.2	0.2	-	-	-
Egypt	-	-	-	-	-	2.8	1.6	0.7	1.8	1.1
Libya	-	-	-	-	-	-0.7	-0.6	0.5	0.3	-
Morocco	5.9	10.7	8.2	2.6	-	49.6	66.7	65.5	65.6	74.0
Tunisia	-	-	-	-	-	5.4	5.6	6.8	1.1	1.6
Other African countries	1 167.5	534.0	629.6	691.3	615.7	223.7	238.1	139.4	142.2	145.5
Nigeria	-	-	-	-	-	4.5	4.9	5.3	4.7	4.5
South Africa	1 167.5	534.0	629.8	688.9	614.5	64.1	117.5	7.7	5.5	4.0
AMERICA	**22 069.1**	**27 639.1**	**26 442.0**	**26 195.0**	**26 051.6**	**3 537.5**	**3 438.3**	**1 379.3**	**1 367.1**	**3 001.3**
Northern America	22 069.1	27 644.7	26 422.4	26 149.2	26 000.3	2 854.9	2 671.4	502.7	365.0	2 065.8
Central America and Caribbean countries	-3.7	-6.7	16.0	29.3	37.6	174.6	198.2	216.8	191.4	116.3
Bahamas	-	-	-	-	-	161.3	214.5	221.4	186.7	208.1
Bermuda	-	-	-	-	-	-	-	-	-	-
Cayman Islands	-	-	-	-	-	0.0	-	-	-	-3.2
El Salvador	-	-	-	-	-	-	-	-	-	-
Guatemala	-	-	-	-	-	-	-	-	-	-
Honduras	-	-	-	-	-	-	-	-	-	-
Nicaragua	-	-	-	-	-	-	-	-	-	-
Panama	-	-	-	-	-	10.5	4.2	3.7	3.7	3.7
Virgin Islands, U.S.	-	-	-	-	-	-	-	-	-	-
South America	3.7	1.0	3.6	16.5	13.6	508.0	569.3	659.8	810.8	819.0
Argentina	-	-	-	-	-	0.9	0.7	0.8	1.8	1.3
Bolivia	-	-	-	-	-	-	-	-	-	-
Brazil	0.0	0.1	-0.7	-0.9	-2.2	23.8	45.5	46.4	50.6	16.2
Ecuador	-	-	-	-	-	-	-	-	-	-
Paraguay	-	-	-	-	-	-	-	-	-	-
Peru	-	-	-	-	-	1.8	2.2	1.0	1.6	1.1
Uruguay	2.3	-	3.4	3.2	2.3	0.3	-	0.1	0.3	-
Venezuela	-	-	-	-	-	-	-	-	-	-

Table 2. Foreign direct investment positions by country *(cont.)*

At year end

Million US dollars

	Inward					Outward				
	2016	2017	2018	2019	2020	2016	2017	2018	2019	2020
ASIA	**8 323.8**	**11 571.6**	**11 384.5**	**13 817.5**	**16 806.0**	**1 055.1**	**1 036.7**	**1 194.6**	**1 117.3**	**1 355.1**
Near and Middle East	1 027.8	1 198.2	1 218.3	1 445.2	1 488.7	441.7	356.0	352.4	485.0	603.4
Gulf Arabian countries	213.3	230.7	106.6	97.1	92.3	169.2	201.6	209.0	215.7	265.3
Kuwait	46.5	49.9	43.6	42.6	37.5	0.0	0.0	0.0	-	-
Qatar	137.5	169.1	20.7	22.3	21.8	-	-	-	-	-
Saudi Arabia	25.1	1.0	16.8	22.4	21.9	0.9	0.5	0.1	1.8	1.1
United Arab Emirates	4.3	10.7	25.5	9.8	11.1	168.6	200.9	208.8	213.8	263.9
Other Near and Middle East	814.5	967.5	1 111.7	1 348.1	1 396.5	272.5	154.4	143.3	269.4	338.2
Jordan	-	-	-	-	-	-0.1	-0.1	-	-	-
Other Asian countries	7 296.0	10 373.4	10 166.2	12 372.3	15 317.3	613.4	680.7	842.1	632.2	751.9
China	707.2	847.8	935.4	1 222.5	1 240.5	87.5	83.9	239.5	226.5	247.4
Hong Kong, China	412.2	454.1	271.7	352.0	309.6	8.7	1.3	17.8	8.4	1.9
India	251.5	271.8	276.2	313.5	341.0	236.1	250.6	246.6	276.0	261.3
Indonesia	-	-	-	-	-	26.2	22.9	27.0	25.3	25.0
Iran, Islamic Republic of	5.9	12.6	-	-	-	-	6.0	8.8	8.4	9.3
Malaysia	259.2	246.3	728.0	570.3	644.2	28.2	26.3	33.4	31.6	35.9
Philippines	44.6	51.3	45.5	48.6	45.4	8.2	8.1	8.2	8.4	9.3
Singapore	24.4	235.1	427.3	844.0	869.7	122.7	126.3	118.4	-14.7	-34.3
Chinese Taipei	234.4	268.1	282.4	268.2	119.1	-0.1	0.4	0.1	-1.1	-0.8
Thailand	26.8	63.8	35.4	39.2	128.6	15.8	17.8	21.8	19.5	147.7
Viet Nam	2.5	2.2	18.3	20.1	20.4	0.1	44.8	18.9	19.0	18.6
AUSTRALIA, OCEANIA AND POLAR REGIONS	**344.8**	**428.5**	**726.4**	**971.0**	**1 052.0**	**8.1**	**5.9**	**-0.2**	**4.5**	**5.6**
WORLD unallocated and confidential	**18 353.6**	**25 134.1**	**24 047.7**	**23 835.4**	**29 250.4**	**0.0**	**0.0**	**-0.7**	**-1.3**	**-2.4**
European Union (since 01/02/2020)	**..**	**..**	**..**	**..**	**153 854.9**	**..**	**..**	**..**	**..**	**18 622.3**
G20 countries excl. European Union	**106 635.5**	**129 224.2**	**123 937.8**	**128 048.1**	**132 719.5**	**7 314.5**	**7 542.9**	**4 913.9**	**5 280.3**	**6 994.7**
G20 OECD countries	**103 643.0**	**126 578.4**	**121 304.8**	**124 999.6**	**129 716.7**	**6 154.3**	**6 108.1**	**3 607.4**	**3 860.8**	**5 677.7**
G20 Non-OECD countries	**2 992.6**	**2 645.8**	**2 633.0**	**3 048.5**	**3 002.8**	**1 160.2**	**1 434.8**	**1 306.4**	**1 419.5**	**1 317.1**
MENA countries	**235.1**	**257.0**	**129.4**	**101.1**	**95.0**	**226.5**	**275.0**	**282.6**	**284.1**	**341.9**
ASEAN countries	**357.6**	**598.7**	**1 254.5**	**1 522.3**	**1 708.3**	**201.2**	**242.6**	**228.0**	**89.3**	**201.9**

- Nil; .. Not available

Note: Inward FDI positions are allocated according to the ultimate investing country. Detailed metadata at: *http://metalinks.oecd.org/idi/20220712/6d95*.

Source: *OECD International Direct Investment Statistics (database): https://doi.org/10.1787/idi-data-en*

POLAND

Table 3. Foreign direct investment income by country

Million US dollars

	Inward					Outward				
	2016	2017	2018	2019	2020	2016	2017	2018	2019	2020
WORLD	**20 777.9**	**21 490.7**	**23 474.4**	**23 304.8**	**21 609.1**	**1 004.5**	**2 286.9**	**2 182.1**	**2 312.2**	**1 446.0**
OECD COUNTRIES	**20 062.0**	**20 394.5**	**22 780.7**	**22 838.3**	**20 559.1**	**421.2**	**1 495.3**	**1 492.7**	**1 654.8**	**551.0**
Australia	2.0	1.9	-1.6	-0.1	5.6	-2.0	-1.3	0.0	0.0	-0.2
Austria	503.1	795.3	637.0	453.1	359.8	6.5	-1.7	-4.2	-4.8	-4.5
Belgium	399.8	371.6	339.8	471.7	425.3	7.3	-2.4	-7.1	-3.2	7.8
Canada	29.2	25.3	23.1	26.4	-5.4	-1 722.5	552.5	28.7	73.2	55.4
Chile	0.0	-	-	-	-	31.5	39.3	47.5	47.3	33.3
Colombia	-	-	-	-	-	-0.2	-0.1	-1.1	4.5	5.8
Costa Rica	-	-	-	-	-	-	-	-	-	-
Czech Republic	116.8	94.8	131.4	111.2	255.5	170.1	234.7	224.4	216.4	177.2
Denmark	271.9	307.1	327.5	442.8	460.9	2.7	-1.1	-6.0	29.2	-5.9
Estonia	2.2	-8.3	-10.8	2.6	0.5	1.4	0.0	-0.6	-3.0	-3.0
Finland	168.4	221.4	290.8	252.3	244.9	11.1	8.8	4.3	4.7	2.4
France	1 672.3	1 991.5	1 859.1	1 903.5	1 546.5	6.7	2.9	-22.2	-71.3	-31.6
Germany	4 030.0	4 479.1	4 723.8	4 968.4	4 172.6	230.2	156.2	305.0	257.2	117.5
Greece	5.8	2.3	2.2	6.0	4.9	0.0	-0.5	0.3	0.4	-2.4
Hungary	28.1	79.0	38.2	67.1	36.3	58.5	93.7	249.6	214.5	-24.7
Iceland	-0.4	1.3	0.6	-0.2	-0.8	-	-	-	-	-
Ireland	134.9	129.9	143.7	102.6	181.2	-0.2	0.3	2.9	3.6	2.3
Israel	4.0	13.9	13.0	33.2	34.3	9.0	1.1	0.4	8.2	10.2
Italy	897.5	731.6	700.8	664.3	633.6	0.1	-85.5	-21.8	-4.1	-1.5
Japan	37.3	193.6	63.4	69.9	49.3	-	-	-	-	-
Korea	59.3	89.4	85.6	-133.2	-111.8	-0.1	-0.2	-1.3	-0.3	0.6
Latvia	27.3	50.3	48.1	58.2	51.4	9.6	13.0	16.7	18.3	23.4
Lithuania	6.8	17.8	-13.8	33.7	14.6	286.8	323.1	105.2	252.5	-122.3
Luxembourg	2 812.0	2 351.8	3 336.0	3 319.5	3 042.3	1 727.8	128.7	279.4	385.1	253.5
Mexico	0.1	0.4	1.2	0.8	1.7	-2.8	-0.4	3.3	2.6	-26.4
Netherlands	4 807.1	4 606.6	6 262.0	6 148.4	5 728.7	30.3	84.4	59.4	35.9	4.8
New Zealand	0.0	-0.1	-0.2	-0.1	-0.1	-	-	-	-	-
Norway	14.2	135.2	161.1	142.8	130.0	-10.8	213.9	208.6	118.8	-122.9
Poland	-	-	-	-	-	-	-	-	-	-
Portugal	116.0	117.6	139.0	113.3	42.2	6.9	1.1	1.6	2.5	2.5
Slovak Republic	17.2	13.2	27.3	48.1	32.6	58.5	69.0	104.2	127.7	138.8
Slovenia	7.2	7.6	7.1	8.5	10.0	3.0	1.9	1.4	3.1	1.2
Spain	736.7	821.4	812.3	689.8	416.1	19.0	10.8	18.9	7.1	-13.8
Sweden	661.7	360.1	422.8	454.3	520.5	-111.4	-82.8	-140.5	-70.7	-33.5
Switzerland	676.0	704.0	707.1	770.4	950.1	31.5	78.0	36.4	6.3	63.2
Turkey	0.6	-3.4	-2.6	-2.2	5.2	28.4	4.2	2.0	7.5	13.8
United Kingdom	902.6	1 197.5	1 047.9	1 011.4	857.7	-190.5	-4.3	0.1	12.4	2.7
United States	920.8	511.8	457.7	600.0	462.6	11.4	-18.8	-3.8	-22.4	27.2
EUROPE	**19 706.8**	**20 591.3**	**22 739.7**	**22 635.0**	**21 088.5**	**2 661.2**	**1 656.8**	**2 021.2**	**2 034.4**	**1 068.2**
Bulgaria	-4.8	-5.4	-4.7	2.8	1.3	3.1	15.7	19.9	152.5	5.4
Croatia	3.2	6.5	7.7	8.8	3.1	3.0	8.6	14.6	13.9	6.3
Cyprus	588.0	915.2	545.1	517.4	935.3	133.4	57.7	32.7	-138.2	315.6
Malta	58.6	95.7	51.4	-4.9	-9.4	22.4	82.4	224.9	86.0	58.1
Montenegro	-	-	-	-	0.1	3.1	6.7	3.7	2.3	-0.5
Romania	0.2	1.6	2.2	2.9	4.4	-30.7	51.6	80.8	168.8	97.9
Russian Federation	24.9	19.4	13.7	6.4	7.4	33.5	57.9	36.5	39.9	23.6
Ukraine	-14.1	-13.7	-14.6	-156.9	1.1	80.9	93.0	129.0	140.1	106.2
AFRICA	**1.2**	**2.2**	**3.4**	**3.6**	**7.2**	**-5.1**	**8.0**	**6.2**	**5.6**	**4.7**
Northern Africa	0.2	0.8	0.6	0.5	1.3	4.6	4.5	2.8	1.1	1.5
Algeria	-0.1	-	-	-	-	-	-	-	-	-
Egypt	-	-	-	-	-	2.3	0.7	0.0	0.5	-0.3
Libya	-	-	-	-	-	-0.1	0.1	0.4	-	-
Morocco	0.2	0.8	0.6	0.5	1.3	3.2	5.4	3.1	0.7	1.5
Tunisia	-	-	-	-	-	-0.8	-1.7	-0.7	-0.1	0.3
Other African countries	1.0	1.4	2.7	3.1	5.8	-9.7	3.5	3.5	4.5	3.2
Nigeria	-	-	-	-	-	0.0	0.1	0.2	0.2	0.1
South Africa	-	-	0.3	-	-0.2	-2.6	1.8	0.2	-0.5	-0.7
AMERICA	**912.8**	**544.3**	**503.6**	**646.8**	**479.3**	**-1 681.2**	**570.2**	**81.8**	**120.0**	**104.6**
Northern America	950.1	537.1	480.8	626.4	457.2	-1 711.1	533.7	24.9	50.8	82.6
Central America and Caribbean countries	-37.1	7.3	22.9	20.3	22.0	-2.8	-3.0	10.4	14.4	-19.6
Bahamas	-	1.6	-	-	-	0.9	7.4	10.6	12.7	7.9
Bermuda	-6.5	0.1	17.4	16.0	19.5	-	-	-	-	-
Cayman Islands	-33.5	-3.9	1.2	0.1	-	-	-0.9	-	-	-
El Salvador	-	-	-	-	-	-	-	-	-	-
Guatemala	-	-	-	-	-	-	-	-	-	-
Honduras	-	-	-	-	-	-	-	-	-	-
Nicaragua	0.1	0.2	0.2	0.0	-	-	-	-	-	-
Panama	0.3	-0.1	-0.1	-0.1	0.0	-0.5	-9.7	-3.5	-0.7	-0.6
Virgin Islands, U.S.	-	-	-	-	-	-	-	-	-	-
South America	-0.2	-	-0.2	0.1	0.0	32.7	39.5	46.5	54.9	41.6
Argentina	-	-	-	-	-	0.0	0.2	0.1	0.6	0.6
Bolivia	-	-	-	-	-	-	-	-	-	-
Brazil	-	-	-	-0.1	0.2	1.3	0.2	-	2.2	1.9
Ecuador	-	-	-	-	-	-	-	-	-	-
Paraguay	-	-	-	-	-	-	-	-	-	-
Peru	-	-	-	-	-	-0.1	-0.1	-0.1	0.2	-
Uruguay	-0.2	-	-0.2	0.2	-0.2	0.1	-0.1	-	-	-
Venezuela	-	-	-	-	-	-	-	-	-	-

Table 3. Foreign direct investment income by country *(cont.)*

Million US dollars

	Inward					Outward				
	2016	2017	2018	2019	2020	2016	2017	2018	2019	2020
ASIA	**155.0**	**352.9**	**229.7**	**19.6**	**28.6**	**31.6**	**53.4**	**73.1**	**152.2**	**268.6**
Near and Middle East	16.9	27.9	29.6	47.9	51.9	41.9	25.2	49.0	50.2	64.0
Gulf Arabian countries	12.7	17.0	17.4	15.2	17.7	33.1	24.1	48.5	41.9	53.8
Kuwait	1.0	1.9	0.9	0.9	0.9	-	-	-	-	-
Qatar	-	-	-	0.3	0.1	-	-	-	-	-
Saudi Arabia	-0.2	-0.3	-0.1	-0.2	-0.3	-	-0.1	-0.4	-0.2	0.4
United Arab Emirates	11.9	15.4	16.5	14.2	17.1	33.6	24.2	48.9	42.1	53.3
Other Near and Middle East	4.2	10.9	12.3	32.7	34.1	8.8	1.1	0.4	8.4	10.2
Jordan	-	-	-	-	-	-	-	-	-	-
Other Asian countries	138.1	325.0	200.1	-28.3	-23.2	-10.4	28.2	24.1	102.0	204.6
China	5.2	8.2	17.4	9.0	4.7	-4.4	-4.4	-5.4	5.8	12.8
Hong Kong, China	0.6	17.9	18.5	21.4	18.4	-0.6	-5.8	2.9	-0.1	-2.6
India	17.3	17.5	13.0	11.5	20.0	14.1	12.8	25.8	103.1	35.6
Indonesia	-	-	-2.5	-0.4	-0.1	-2.0	-1.0	0.6	1.2	-0.7
Iran, Islamic Republic of	0.3	-	-	-	-	-	0.0	0.1	0.3	0.3
Malaysia	0.9	-0.1	-0.4	-	0.0	-1.0	0.2	-0.7	-0.5	-0.1
Philippines	-0.1	-	0.1	-	0.1	0.6	0.1	0.0	0.4	0.4
Singapore	5.8	-3.0	3.7	-10.8	-5.2	10.5	29.1	9.1	2.1	3.2
Chinese Taipei	2.2	2.3	-1.6	-1.0	0.6	0.0	0.0	-	-0.2	-0.3
Thailand	-	0.4	4.8	6.9	0.6	2.0	-1.3	0.9	-2.6	165.2
Viet Nam	9.5	-1.1	-2.0	-1.6	-	-	0.2	3.2	2.6	-2.2
AUSTRALIA, OCEANIA AND POLAR REGIONS	**2.1**	**-0.5**	**-2.5**	**-1.9**	**5.5**	**-2.0**	**-1.3**	**0.0**	**0.0**	**-0.2**
WORLD unallocated and confidential	**-**	**0.5**	**0.6**	**1.6**	**0.0**	**0.0**	**-0.2**	**-0.3**	**-**	**0.0**
European Union (since 01/02/2020)	..	..	..	..	**19 115.2**	..	..	..	..	**971.6**
G20 countries excl. European Union	**8 599.2**	**9 263.2**	**9 000.2**	**9 135.3**	**7 649.6**	**-1 601.1**	**672.7**	**347.3**	**406.8**	**231.0**
G20 OECD countries	**8 551.9**	**9 218.6**	**8 958.4**	**9 109.1**	**7 617.7**	**-1 641.1**	**605.3**	**290.0**	**254.8**	**157.5**
G20 Non-OECD countries	**47.3**	**44.6**	**41.7**	**26.3**	**31.9**	**40.0**	**67.4**	**57.3**	**152.0**	**73.4**
MENA countries	**13.1**	**14.9**	**17.5**	**15.4**	**19.1**	**37.7**	**28.6**	**51.3**	**42.9**	**55.3**
ASEAN countries	**15.9**	**-3.8**	**3.8**	**-5.9**	**-4.5**	**10.1**	**24.1**	**13.5**	**2.9**	**165.8**

- Nil; .. Not available

Note: Detailed metadata at: *http://metalinks.oecd.org/idi/20220712/6d95*.

Source: *OECD International Direct Investment Statistics (database)*: *https://doi.org/10.1787/idi-data-en*

POLAND

Table 4. Foreign direct investment flows by industrial sector

Million US dollars

	Inward					Outward				
	2016	2017	2018	2019	2020	2016	2017	2018	2019	2020
All FDI activities	**15 706.8**	**9 172.4**	**15 997.7**	**13 509.8**	**13 832.6**	**11 598.3**	**2 169.5**	**891.1**	**1 853.9**	**1 295.3**
Agriculture, forestry and fishing	**67.6**	**142.5**	**-7.6**	**-56.3**	**-46.3**	**-13.1**	**-8.4**	**16.7**	**9.9**	**4.5**
Mining and quarrying	**43.1**	**86.8**	**170.6**	**-197.7**	**-21.1**	**3 287.1**	**918.4**	**-661.6**	**373.5**	**-24.7**
Extraction activities	-3.4	12.6	112.4	-18.5	3.6	466.0	323.7	208.4	75.3	-151.8
Manufacturing	**3 829.9**	**4 679.8**	**5 634.0**	**6 477.7**	**3 311.8**	**52.1**	**96.1**	**2 028.7**	**587.3**	**495.8**
of which:										
Food products, beverages and tobacco	1 102.8	606.4	493.9	405.5	350.3	-33.5	54.6	73.3	52.6	25.6
Textiles, wood and paper products; printing	-221.4	640.1	503.5	588.6	502.2	241.6	-44.5	27.1	74.0	-24.4
Chemical, rubber, plastic, non-metallic mineral products	-255.6	802.0	830.0	1 088.9	874.1	-238.2	-262.3	1 558.8	161.0	87.1
Metal and machinery products, except electrical equipment	1 222.8	947.6	1 467.9	1 061.1	362.0	283.7	244.7	525.8	145.9	328.0
Motor vehicles, trailers, semi-trailers, other transport equipment	1 258.7	1 052.2	933.3	1 540.6	1 255.7	-274.2	110.9	-214.4	123.7	57.1
Other manufacturing	722.7	631.5	1 405.5	1 792.9	-32.5	72.8	-7.2	58.1	30.2	22.5
Electricity, gas, steam and air conditioning supply	**-478.1**	**-1 382.1**	**293.4**	**810.5**	**635.5**	**1.9**	**524.5**	**-226.0**	**786.6**	**45.9**
Water supply; sewerage, waste management and remediation activities	**5.3**	**26.8**	**30.0**	**3.6**	**66.4**	**4.8**	**11.5**	**18.0**	**-0.3**	**12.6**
Construction	**889.2**	**953.6**	**1 060.8**	**542.8**	**-411.4**	**446.5**	**-12.8**	**51.6**	**294.8**	**-18.5**
Services	**12 067.6**	**5 310.5**	**7 471.1**	**5 552.0**	**10 258.1**	**7 691.5**	**836.9**	**135.5**	**-231.5**	**689.7**
Wholesale and retail trade; repair of motor vehicles and motorcycles	2 369.8	-1 434.0	3 820.0	1 723.7	1 651.8	1 153.5	515.4	128.0	756.3	107.1
Transportation and storage	-11.1	583.4	690.9	85.4	670.4	114.3	65.5	27.9	76.6	2.1
Accommodation and food service activities	2.1	89.1	227.8	737.1	139.7	154.1	103.6	40.6	97.1	-62.3
Information and communication	3 330.6	1 875.1	-1 699.7	-274.5	401.9	1 750.0	1 010.2	66.0	96.1	108.9
Financial and insurance activities	1 377.2	2 960.4	795.3	-616.7	2 138.4	-1 055.5	-455.6	432.5	-388.1	524.8
Activities of holding companies	854.9	4 159.7	307.6	-787.6	469.5	-225.6	-298.8	524.5	-1 118.9	321.5
Real estate activities	1 670.1	1 640.5	1 033.1	1 610.4	2 347.1	840.2	-150.5	-164.0	130.5	-58.4
Professional, scientific and technical activities	3 118.0	-822.2	2 065.2	1 817.7	2 404.4	2 816.1	-371.9	-71.8	-751.7	226.8
Administrative and support service activities	106.8	302.8	294.6	166.4	413.5	2 049.8	124.8	-326.9	-231.3	-189.3
Public administration; activities of households and of extraterritorial organisations	-	-	-	-	-	-	-4.2	-	-	-
Education	8.4	2.0	3.2	8.1	8.0	-17.1	-3.4	0.2	6.8	-
Human health and social work activities	51.9	46.9	83.6	201.6	106.9	-0.4	2.4	17.3	6.5	-19.9
Arts, entertainment and recreation	36.6	40.7	152.2	83.9	-59.4	2.9	2.7	-2.9	-17.7	0.9
Other services	7.0	25.8	5.3	8.9	35.3	-116.5	-2.1	-11.3	-12.2	49.1
Not allocated and confidential	**-717.7**	**-645.5**	**1 345.3**	**377.1**	**39.6**	**127.6**	**-196.7**	**-471.6**	**33.6**	**90.0**
Private real estate activities	-	-	-	-	-	-	-	-	-	-

\- Nil

Note: Detailed metadata at: *http://metalinks.oecd.org/idi/20220712/6d95.*

Source: *OECD International Direct Investment Statistics (database): https://doi.org/10.1787/idi-data-en*

POLAND

Table 5. Foreign direct investment positions by industrial sector

At year end

Million US dollars

	Inward					Outward				
	2016	2017	2018	2019	2020	2016	2017	2018	2019	2020
All FDI activities	**188 760.6**	**240 382.2**	**229 527.2**	**240 586.4**	**249 723.3**	**27 876.2**	**29 190.3**	**24 618.3**	**26 939.5**	**28 136.2**
Agriculture, forestry and fishing	**979.8**	**1 220.4**	**1 101.2**	**1 067.0**	**1 037.9**	**4.2**	**4.2**	**23.5**	**22.2**	..
Mining and quarrying	**512.5**	**592.1**	**772.1**	**549.0**	**532.7**	**2 903.6**	**2 937.0**	**1 673.4**	**1 874.2**	..
Extraction activities	70.4	95.9	224.8	201.4	207.0	1 012.3	1 306.7	1 241.7	1 066.2	..
Manufacturing	**59 236.6**	**77 743.9**	**72 799.0**	**79 351.7**	**82 008.0**	**4 213.9**	**5 382.8**	**5 224.1**	**4 611.7**	..
of which:										
Food products, beverages and tobacco	11 805.9	15 861.6	13 006.9	14 217.3	14 513.1	689.8	705.9	768.0	343.1	..
Textiles, wood and paper products; printing	5 937.7	7 479.9	7 000.7	6 838.9	7 593.7	366.3	308.8	278.5	358.4	..
Chemical, rubber, plastic, non-metallic mineral products	9 490.6	12 591.5	11 884.8	12 051.0	12 560.7	1 312.6	2 089.6	1 628.2	1 834.5	..
Metal and machinery products, except electrical equipment	10 902.1	14 251.4	14 037.4	14 997.5	15 322.2	1 063.9	1 387.2	1 790.9	1 849.0	..
Motor vehicles, trailers, semi-trailers, other transport equipment	11 594.5	14 940.1	14 964.5	16 156.4	16 887.5	497.0	589.3	469.6	389.0	..
Other manufacturing	9 505.8	12 619.3	11 904.7	15 090.2	15 130.6	284.4	302.1	289.0	-162.3	..
Electricity, gas, steam and air conditioning supply	**5 438.8**	**5 206.9**	**4 964.7**	**5 849.3**	**6 692.2**	**-1 329.4**	**-926.1**	**-1 040.0**	**-72.5**	..
Water supply; sewerage, waste management and remediation activities	**418.0**	**528.9**	**524.8**	**501.6**	**602.9**	**20.2**	**36.2**	**38.0**	**41.9**	..
Construction	**9 028.9**	**12 178.6**	**12 556.1**	**12 948.6**	**13 287.8**	**443.8**	**601.3**	**586.2**	**605.3**	..
Services	**114 115.0**	**145 042.2**	**136 932.4**	**137 460.8**	**143 475.7**	**21 557.4**	**21 164.4**	**17 745.5**	**17 851.8**	..
Wholesale and retail trade; repair of motor vehicles and motorcycles	28 387.8	33 784.8	33 825.1	36 941.6	37 662.3	2 786.1	3 513.9	3 585.5	3 316.7	..
Transportation and storage	2 184.1	3 097.5	3 891.8	3 274.1	3 925.6	620.0	724.0	668.7	782.3	..
Accommodation and food service activities	968.2	1 438.9	1 701.9	2 548.9	2 713.9	197.7	346.6	499.5	636.0	..
Information and communication	12 560.0	15 416.5	12 728.5	13 069.8	16 784.0	-25.1	640.5	665.4	814.5	..
Financial and insurance activities	34 432.9	49 361.0	41 991.6	35 520.2	31 008.7	9 756.5	9 075.4	6 250.8	5 462.5	..
Activities of holding companies	3 631.0	8 155.9	7 530.0	7 649.6	4 316.7	6 729.7	5 511.8	3 478.8	2 356.9	..
Real estate activities	16 680.8	21 103.9	22 478.5	24 552.2	26 852.9	787.2	466.7	582.2	907.0	..
Professional, scientific and technical activities	15 524.7	16 479.5	15 773.9	16 541.9	18 166.2	5 856.4	4 755.8	4 545.8	5 246.1	..
Administrative and support service activities	2 347.9	3 004.6	3 043.4	3 267.8	4 490.2	1 221.1	1 260.7	603.1	350.7	..
Public administration; activities of households and of extraterritorial organisations	-	-	-	-	-	0.6	0.7	0.7	0.7	..
Education	13.5	12.2	27.2	29.2	20.8	8.0	-3.7	-4.3	2.7	..
Human health and social work activities	764.6	970.4	970.0	1 174.4	1 263.6	4.7	-8.3	19.7	26.5	..
Arts, entertainment and recreation	137.9	202.3	348.7	383.7	389.3	37.0	45.2	38.2	20.0	..
Other services	112.6	170.7	151.8	157.2	198.0	307.2	346.7	290.2	286.1	..
Not allocated and confidential	**-968.9**	**-2 130.8**	**-123.2**	**2 858.3**	**2 086.0**	**493.5**	**415.3**	**367.6**	**485.8**	..
Private real estate activities	-	-	-	-	-	-	-	-	-	..

- Nil; .. Not available

Note: Detailed metadata at: *http://metalinks.oecd.org/idi/20220712/6d95.*

Source: *OECD International Direct Investment Statistics (database): https://doi.org/10.1787/idi-data-en*

Table 6. Foreign direct investment income by industrial sector

Million US dollars

	Inward					Outward				
	2016	2017	2018	2019	2020	2016	2017	2018	2019	2020
All FDI activities	**20 777.9**	**21 490.7**	**23 474.4**	**23 304.8**	**21 609.1**	**1 004.5**	**2 286.9**	**2 182.1**	**2 312.2**	**1 446.0**
Agriculture, forestry and fishing	**85.7**	**35.4**	**51.9**	**27.5**	**44.1**	**0.7**	**0.4**	**1.7**	**0.2**	**2.7**
Mining and quarrying	**-69.1**	**-41.4**	**34.4**	**-222.2**	**-37.1**	**-1 659.0**	**784.4**	**317.1**	**239.0**	**-52.4**
Extraction activities	-41.2	-41.3	4.2	8.2	-4.5	-20.7	193.0	198.3	101.4	-162.3
Manufacturing	**7 876.9**	**8 380.4**	**9 055.7**	**8 526.1**	**7 372.2**	**638.2**	**595.3**	**437.9**	**479.3**	**308.6**
of which:										
Food products, beverages and tobacco	1 303.0	1 392.7	1 478.3	1 547.0	1 564.4	49.1	42.6	28.4	32.1	61.3
Textiles, wood and paper products; printing	792.1	873.0	1 056.9	1 039.4	1 018.7	103.4	31.3	88.7	52.2	8.8
Chemical, rubber, plastic, non-metallic mineral products	1 300.9	1 432.7	1 561.9	1 668.2	1 724.1	325.8	392.6	117.6	133.2	24.2
Metal and machinery products, except electrical equipment	1 733.4	1 640.2	1 870.6	1 327.9	889.0	105.8	76.3	153.6	166.1	214.4
Motor vehicles, trailers, semi-trailers, other transport equipment	1 509.4	1 880.7	1 743.8	1 733.8	834.0	46.9	44.8	38.4	81.5	-10.2
Other manufacturing	1 238.0	1 161.0	1 344.0	1 209.7	1 342.1	7.0	7.7	11.2	14.1	10.1
Electricity, gas, steam and air conditioning supply	**-59.4**	**376.2**	**474.5**	**477.0**	**492.3**	**-46.3**	**-20.5**	**-26.9**	**-8.5**	**28.7**
Water supply; sewerage, waste management and remediation activities	**45.6**	**52.5**	**40.3**	**34.3**	**105.0**	**0.9**	**0.4**	**0.4**	**1.0**	**5.2**
Construction	**742.6**	**481.1**	**868.0**	**1 069.3**	**741.0**	**3.5**	**-38.3**	**18.4**	**296.1**	**11.7**
Services	**12 152.5**	**12 205.9**	**12 948.8**	**13 212.3**	**12 720.8**	**2 059.4**	**960.4**	**1 376.2**	**1 275.9**	**1 119.5**
Wholesale and retail trade; repair of motor vehicles and motorcycles	3 418.7	4 169.8	4 723.6	4 665.1	4 560.2	167.6	386.7	495.3	415.8	385.1
Transportation and storage	547.7	652.0	795.1	758.8	660.2	8.5	0.9	51.4	27.5	12.4
Accommodation and food service activities	87.2	96.8	90.9	257.7	-92.1	31.7	38.0	63.4	163.6	-78.5
Information and communication	1 482.2	2 096.5	656.5	1 119.2	1 813.3	37.4	43.0	98.5	120.0	152.6
Financial and insurance activities	2 514.3	2 435.6	3 162.5	3 361.9	2 436.4	-93.2	55.6	329.0	358.2	344.5
Activities of holding companies	94.4	283.1	282.5	857.7	645.4	-40.4	-48.6	172.1	147.1	176.0
Real estate activities	1 718.0	962.9	1 682.7	1 557.7	1 470.4	82.5	52.9	90.7	217.9	-77.5
Professional, scientific and technical activities	1 553.4	1 285.1	1 411.6	1 161.7	1 468.9	2.7	147.4	32.0	-128.2	284.6
Administrative and support service activities	778.0	441.6	330.0	255.7	298.2	1 814.2	191.1	162.2	31.0	55.1
Public administration; activities of households and of extraterritorial organisations	-	-	-	-	-	-	-	-	-	-
Education	5.6	-3.0	-2.3	4.9	5.6	2.4	-0.1	-0.3	-	-
Human health and social work activities	35.6	52.8	58.6	38.1	110.5	-1.1	0.6	1.8	-0.8	-0.9
Arts, entertainment and recreation	-11.7	-4.7	16.7	5.9	-43.0	2.7	1.5	0.0	-0.3	-0.7
Other services	23.6	20.7	22.8	25.6	32.1	3.9	42.9	52.3	71.2	42.9
Not allocated and confidential	**3.1**	**0.6**	**0.8**	**180.5**	**170.8**	**7.1**	**4.9**	**57.3**	**29.2**	**22.1**
Private real estate activities	-	-	-	-	-	-	-	-	-	-

- Nil

Note: Detailed metadata at: *http://metalinks.oecd.org/idi/20220712/6d95*.

Source: *OECD International Direct Investment Statistics (database)*: *https://doi.org/10.1787/idi-data-en*

PORTUGAL

Table 1. Foreign direct investment flows by country

Million US dollars

	Inward					Outward				
	2016	2017	2018	2019	2020	2016	2017	2018	2019	2020
WORLD	**5 682.8**	**6 913.5**	**7 176.9**	**12 251.2**	**7 565.8**	**878.0**	**-927.7**	**1 373.8**	**4 009.9**	**2 566.4**
OECD COUNTRIES	..	..	..	..	..	..	..	..	..	..
Australia	-6.6	4.5	-4.7	-3.4	-3.4	102.8	-27.1	-72.0	-13.4	-5.7
Austria	-31.0	801.5	233.7	-154.5	-13.7	5.5	-19.2	4.7	-6.7	8.0
Belgium	36.5	397.9	234.9	134.3	124.2	47.6	-12.4	-423.7	97.4	-17.1
Canada	10.0	-9.0	-	11.2	21.7	76.3	-5.6	-3.5	4.5	-34.2
Chile	-	10.1	14.2	-2.2	6.8	-	192.8	-8.3	209.3	61.5
Colombia	14.4	-2.3	-2.4	-	8.0	1.1	10.1	2.4	7.8	17.1
Costa Rica	1.1	-	1.2	1.1	-	-	-3.4	-	-	-
Czech Republic	3.3	-	-10.6	-14.6	1.1	-16.6	-21.4	23.6	-	4.6
Denmark	29.9	111.6	264.4	-28.0	-33.0	-8.8	6.8	5.9	-127.6	-26.2
Estonia	..	-	-	..	..	..	..	-	..	..
Finland	12.2	-44.0	10.6	13.4	-12.5	22.1	37.2	-73.2	9.0	2.3
France	109.5	746.3	611.4	1 076.9	2 103.7	-96.2	113.9	-88.5	266.4	41.0
Germany	495.4	-124.0	216.0	257.5	353.3	-228.9	-73.3	-37.8	-151.1	-238.2
Greece	..	..	..	..	..	-	..	..	..	..
Hungary	-1.1	-1.1	56.7	26.9	-1.1	-12.2	-22.5	69.6	45.9	-10.3
Iceland	-	-	-	-	..	-	-	-	-	-
Ireland	-296.4	13.5	-177.0	174.6	121.9	-251.0	-101.5	-4.7	53.7	240.5
Israel	..	..	..	..	..	..	..	..	..	..
Italy	-57.5	196.1	338.7	-23.5	147.0	-12.2	37.2	-93.2	4.5	51.3
Japan	-4.4	103.7	10.6	5.6	-9.1	-91.8	-192.8	8.3	1.1	103.7
Korea	15.5	55.2	27.1	26.9	19.4	-	-	-1.2	-	-1.1
Latvia	2.2	-	-	2.2	2.3	-	-	-	-	-
Lithuania	..	..	..	..	..	-	-	-	-	-
Luxembourg	2 060.2	2 379.7	164.1	2 424.7	-1 623.9	-1.1	-671.9	177.0	-100.8	-1 260.4
Mexico	15.5	7.9	-10.6	24.6	77.5	-12.2	7.9	21.2	16.8	-20.5
Netherlands	665.7	-51.9	809.6	-396.3	3 699.1	-162.6	-3 429.2	1 103.5	-802.6	2 021.7
New Zealand	1.1	-	4.7	1.1	-1.1	-	-	-	-	-
Norway	-14.4	4.5	8.3	1.1	3.4	-	3.4	8.3	5.6	-16.0
Poland	13.3	13.5	7.1	11.2	11.4	-21.0	-23.7	60.2	-9.0	-50.1
Portugal	-	-	-	-	-	-	-	-	-	-
Slovak Republic	-	..	..	..	..	..	..	..	-	-
Slovenia	-	-	-	..	..	-	-	-	-	-
Spain	788.5	210.8	1 982.8	5 002.8	2 053.6	609.3	1 437.3	566.5	4 359.1	1 649.0
Sweden	363.8	549.0	-37.8	218.3	135.6	11.1	34.9	-46.0	-53.7	26.2
Switzerland	276.5	414.8	-36.6	253.0	235.9	15.5	38.3	-64.9	144.4	-98.0
Turkey	4.4	81.2	-13.0	868.7	21.7	3.3	11.3	-17.7	-	28.5
United Kingdom	-82.9	-12.4	927.7	259.7	-570.9	258.8	184.9	125.1	173.5	234.8
United States	71.9	65.4	272.6	242.9	106.0	3.3	-480.2	-170.0	-324.6	21.7
EUROPE	**4 562.6**	**5 458.2**	**5 849.2**	**10 351.5**	**6 974.4**	**143.8**	**-2 422.5**	**1 222.7**	**3 882.2**	**2 661.0**
Bulgaria	-	2.3	-2.4	11.2	3.4	1.1	16.9	-14.2	1.1	-
Croatia	-	..	-	..	..	-	-	-	-	..
Cyprus	55.3	-19.2	72.0	76.1	29.6	-17.7	11.3	13.0	-3.4	9.1
Malta	-17.7	-245.7	131.0	97.4	103.7	7.7	20.3	26.0	6.7	-8.0
Montenegro	-	-	-	-	-	-	-	-	-	-
Romania	7.7	-4.5	-4.7	11.2	3.4	-10.0	3.4	-7.1	-19.0	75.2
Russian Federation	8.8	11.3	23.6	17.9	49.0	-	-45.1	-37.8	-	-1.1
Ukraine	3.3	-1.1	18.9	2.2	6.8	-7.7	-1.1	-	1.1	-
AFRICA	**-468.9**	**2.3**	**382.4**	**301.1**	**314.5**	**-118.3**	**1 264.8**	**605.5**	**348.1**	**35.3**
Northern Africa	16.6	31.6	15.3	57.1	43.3	89.6	308.9	319.8	370.5	-22.8
Algeria	8.8	4.5	2.4	10.1	4.6	-56.4	-23.7	-20.1	39.2	-71.8
Egypt	..	..	..	..	..	..	..	..	..	..
Libya	..	..	..	..	..	-	-	-	..	-
Morocco	8.8	-	8.3	12.3	10.3	-7.7	-9.0	80.3	13.4	-11.4
Tunisia	16.6	19.2	16.5	29.1	17.1	-8.8	7.9	-8.3	-4.5	-1.1
Other African countries	..	..	..	..	..	..	..	..	..	..
Nigeria	-215.6	1.1	1.2	7.8	3.4	-57.5	67.6	4.7	9.0	4.6
South Africa	11.1	-18.0	34.2	75.0	30.8	24.3	16.9	20.1	-241.8	-3.4
AMERICA	**640.3**	**293.1**	**-276.2**	**788.1**	**-631.3**	**765.2**	**558.0**	**-482.7**	**-288.8**	**14.8**
Northern America	81.8	56.4	272.6	254.1	127.6	79.6	-485.9	-173.5	-320.2	-12.5
Central America and Caribbean countries	325.1	140.9	-27.1	161.2	93.4	232.2	730.5	-500.4	59.3	-61.5
Bahamas	..	..	..	..	..	..	..	-	-	-
Bermuda	..	..	..	-	..	-	..	..	..	..
Cayman Islands	..	..	..	..	..	..	..	..	..	..
El Salvador	-	-	-	-	-	-	-	-	-	-
Guatemala	-	-	-	-	-	-	-	-	-	..
Honduras	-	..	-	-	-	-	-	..	-	-
Nicaragua	-	-	-	-	-	-	-	-	-	-
Panama	..	..	-	..	..	..	..	..	..	..
Virgin Islands, U.S.	-	-	-	-	..	-	-	-	-	-
South America	233.3	95.8	-522.8	372.8	-852.4	453.4	313.4	192.4	-28.0	88.9
Argentina	-1.1	-	1.2	-2.2	4.6	-1.1	6.8	-2.4	1.1	-13.7
Bolivia	..	-	-	..	-	..	-	..	..	..
Brazil	160.3	86.8	-558.2	386.2	-875.2	276.5	138.7	-86.2	-274.3	-120.8
Ecuador	..	-	..	-	..	-	-	-	..	-
Paraguay	-	..	..	-	-	..	..	-	..	..
Peru	-	-	..	..	..	..	..	..	..	..
Uruguay	-	2.3	3.5	1.1	3.4	6.6	1.1	-13.0	17.9	13.7
Venezuela	56.4	-	20.1	-4.5	-3.4	165.9	-40.6	136.9	-9.0	27.4

PORTUGAL

Table 1. Foreign direct investment flows by country *(cont.)*

Million US dollars

	Inward					Outward				
	2016	2017	2018	2019	2020	2016	2017	2018	2019	2020
ASIA	**956.5**	**1 155.5**	**1 220.3**	**813.8**	**912.8**	**-15.5**	**-301.0**	**101.5**	**84.0**	**-121.9**
Near and Middle East	..	..	..	..	..	..	..	..	..	..
Gulf Arabian countries	..	..	..	..	..	-	..	..	..	..
Kuwait	-1.1	7.9	4.7	9.0	5.7	-	-	22.4	-1.1	-5.7
Qatar	..	..	..	..	..	..	..	..	..	..
Saudi Arabia	..	..	..	..	..	..	..	..	-	..
United Arab Emirates	77.4	94.7	151.1	125.4	151.6	-5.5	-9.0	20.1	40.3	-315.7
Other Near and Middle East	..	..	..	..	..	..	..	..	..	..
Jordan	..	..	..	..	..	..	..	..	..	..
Other Asian countries	..	..	..	..	..	..	..	..	..	..
China	561.8	432.9	296.2	117.5	208.5	8.8	-6.8	-	-6.7	6.8
Hong Kong, China	-47.6	210.8	389.5	254.1	246.2	..	..	..	..	..
India	1.1	39.5	23.6	20.2	11.4	-11.1	12.4	-1.2	-4.5	1.1
Indonesia	..	..	..	..	..	..	..	..	..	..
Iran, Islamic Republic of	..	..	..	..	..	-	-	-	-	-
Malaysia	..	..	..	..	..	-	..	..	..	-
Philippines	-	..	..	..	..	-	-	-	-	-
Singapore	..	..	..	..	..	..	..	..	..	..
Chinese Taipei	..	-	..	-	..	-	-	-	-	-
Thailand	..	..	..	..	..	..	..	..	..	..
Viet Nam	..	..	..	..	..	-	..	..	..	..
AUSTRALIA, OCEANIA AND POLAR REGIONS	**-7.7**	**5.6**	**2.4**	**-1.1**	**-4.6**	**102.8**	**-27.1**	**-72.0**	**-12.3**	**-5.7**
WORLD unallocated and confidential	**-**	**-1.1**	**-1.2**	**-2.2**	**-**	**-**	**-**	**-1.2**	**-3.4**	**-17.1**
European Union (since 01/02/2020)	..	..	..	..	..	..	..	..	..	..
G20 countries excl. European Union	..	..	..	..	..	..	..	..	..	..
G20 OECD countries	..	..	..	..	..	..	..	..	..	..
G20 Non-OECD countries	..	..	..	..	..	..	..	..	..	..
MENA countries	..	..	..	..	..	..	..	..	..	..
ASEAN countries	..	..	..	..	..	..	..	..	..	..

- Nil; .. Not available

Note: Data excludes resident Special Purpose Entities (SPEs). Detailed metadata at: *http://metalinks.oecd.org/idi/20220712/6d95*.

Source: *OECD International Direct Investment Statistics (database)*: *https://doi.org/10.1787/idi-data-en*

PORTUGAL

Table 2. Foreign direct investment positions by country

At year end

Million US dollars

	Inward					Outward				
	2016	2017	2018	2019	2020	2016	2017	2018	2019	2020
WORLD	**122 725.8**	**152 169.6**	**147 826.9**	**157 837.6**	**171 325.3**	**57 777.0**	**62 672.1**	**52 522.3**	**56 177.3**	**57 264.7**
OECD COUNTRIES	..	..	..	..	..	..	..	..	..	..
Australia	7.4	16.8	11.5	5.6	2.5	..	266.3	194.6	179.7	192.7
Austria	541.8	2 477.8	2 123.9	1 894.0	474.9	..	152.3	147.7	138.2	158.3
Belgium	3 126.4	4 053.7	1 861.7	2 015.3	1 367.0	..	400.6	96.2	234.8	-257.7
Canada	682.0	762.8	729.3	732.4	823.4	..	40.8	40.1	43.8	19.6
Chile	6.3	22.8	38.9	30.3	41.7	..	219.5	221.0	424.6	463.9
Colombia	11.6	1.2	-	-	3.7	..	14.4	14.9	34.8	67.5
Costa Rica	2.1	2.4	3.4	4.5	4.9	..	6.0	5.7	5.6	6.1
Czech Republic	11.6	12.0	-3.4	-14.6	-19.6	..	57.6	64.1	40.4	57.7
Denmark	540.7	728.0	758.0	723.4	790.3	..	187.1	163.7	182.0	177.9
Estonia	..	..	..	..	..	..	..	..	..	..
Finland	89.6	49.2	83.6	101.1	88.4	..	36.0	-30.9	-18.0	-27.0
France	6 867.3	8 683.1	10 038.9	10 958.2	13 812.7	..	1 384.0	1 049.9	1 413.2	1 329.0
Germany	4 906.7	5 700.4	5 659.5	5 724.6	6 409.4	..	1 368.4	1 079.7	697.6	450.4
Greece	..	..	..	..	..	..	..	..	..	..
Hungary	27.4	30.0	588.5	29.2	18.4	..	135.5	692.7	98.9	123.9
Iceland	..	..	..	..	..	-	-	-	-	-
Ireland	1 853.1	2 169.6	1 788.4	1 824.3	1 563.4	..	1 138.2	893.1	752.6	483.5
Israel	..	..	..	..	..	..	..	..	..	..
Italy	845.4	1 162.1	1 473.6	1 273.9	1 801.4	..	668.0	493.5	563.9	595.2
Japan	326.8	510.9	474.0	486.4	521.5	..	130.7	123.7	126.9	240.5
Korea	122.3	187.1	193.5	206.7	233.2	..	-1.2	-3.4	-3.4	-6.1
Latvia	6.3	7.2	6.9	9.0	13.5	..	-	-	1.1	1.2
Lithuania	..	..	-	..	..	-	-	-	-	-
Luxembourg	20 836.9	26 974.1	25 970.9	28 663.2	29 533.7	..	3 249.0	2 439.9	2 434.3	1 062.7
Mexico	-2.1	6.0	87.0	110.1	298.2	..	58.8	80.1	125.8	96.9
Netherlands	31 140.5	37 041.3	32 080.4	34 146.3	36 016.7	..	14 541.9	10 772.8	12 702.8	14 552.7
New Zealand	7.4	46.8	49.2	48.3	50.3	-	-	-	-	1.2
Norway	136.0	190.7	139.7	138.2	162.0	..	16.8	6.9	15.7	6.1
Poland	..	66.0	48.1	60.7	14.7	1 263.8	2 074.8	1 986.5	1 392.9	946.1
Portugal	-	-	-	-	-	-	-	-	-	-
Slovak Republic	..	..	..	..	..	..	..	-	..	-
Slovenia	..	..	..	..	..	-	-	-	-	-
Spain	22 359.0	26 325.3	27 867.0	31 961.4	36 009.3	..	14 227.6	13 452.0	17 370.3	20 040.5
Sweden	..	1 776.2	1 740.3	1 890.6	2 354.9	205.5	160.7	125.9	47.2	24.5
Switzerland	2 439.1	3 150.6	3 020.4	3 262.2	3 785.7	..	109.1	-123.7	-10.1	-212.3
Turkey	..	137.9	120.2	198.8	217.2	63.2	63.6	55.0	50.6	54.0
United Kingdom	9 980.0	11 219.7	11 585.8	10 534.7	11 030.8	..	2 961.1	2 104.4	1 050.3	1 275.0
United States	..	1 766.6	2 003.7	2 028.8	2 098.4	1 575.8	1 036.2	1 452.9	1 112.1	1 131.4
EUROPE	**109 772.3**	**135 317.8**	**130 478.6**	**139 205.8**	**149 731.3**	..	**43 872.6**	**36 308.7**	**39 894.4**	**41 579.3**
Bulgaria	5.3	8.4	5.7	20.2	24.5	..	48.0	29.8	30.3	30.7
Croatia	..	..	..	..	..	-	-	-	-	..
Cyprus	605.0	665.6	756.8	832.4	915.5	..	16.8	29.8	22.5	20.9
Malta	1 267.0	1 321.7	1 407.1	1 533.4	1 570.7	..	410.2	356.1	341.5	374.3
Montenegro	-	-	-	-	-	-	-	-	-	-
Romania	..	-1.2	-11.5	1.1	1.2	194.0	220.7	207.2	173.0	203.7
Russian Federation	..	196.7	211.8	225.8	300.7	31.6	37.2	26.3	28.1	24.5
Ukraine	..	20.4	36.6	39.3	50.3	3.2	3.6	3.4	4.5	3.7
AFRICA	**1 976.4**	**2 931.2**	**3 059.3**	**3 155.5**	**3 459.3**	..	**9 966.4**	**8 392.5**	**8 306.0**	**8 096.7**
Northern Africa	109.6	176.3	199.2	258.4	282.2	..	1 656.3	2 074.7	2 395.0	2 348.8
Algeria	27.4	55.2	25.2	34.8	17.2	..	284.2	231.3	269.6	216.0
Egypt	..	..	..	..	..	..	..	..	..	..
Libya	..	..	..	..	..	..	..	..	..	..
Morocco	2.1	-	2.3	19.1	8.6	..	199.1	266.8	289.8	266.3
Tunisia	..	146.3	159.1	188.7	225.8	69.6	74.4	72.1	69.6	60.1
Other African countries	..	..	..	..	..	..	..	..	..	..
Nigeria	5.3	7.2	8.0	19.1	24.5	..	21.6	18.3	22.5	28.2
South Africa	..	146.3	182.0	248.3	305.6	249.8	287.8	267.9	87.6	88.4
AMERICA	**5 092.2**	**5 880.3**	**5 669.8**	**6 322.2**	**7 208.2**	..	**6 719.8**	**5 969.8**	**6 002.0**	**5 465.7**
Northern America	2 380.1	2 530.6	2 733.0	2 761.2	2 921.8	..	1 077.0	1 493.0	1 157.0	1 151.1
Central America and Caribbean countries	-110.7	73.2	219.8	425.7	327.6	..	1 224.5	698.4	751.5	411.1
Bahamas	..	..	..	..	..	..	..	..	..	..
Bermuda	..	..	..	..	..	..	..	..	..	..
Cayman Islands	..	..	..	..	..	..	..	..	..	..
El Salvador	-	-	-	-	-	-	-	-	-	-
Guatemala	-	-	-	..	-	..	..	..	..	-
Honduras	-	..	..	..	..	..	..	..	..	..
Nicaragua	-	-	-	-	-	-	-	-	-	-
Panama	..	..	..	..	..	..	..	..	..	..
Virgin Islands, U.S.	..	..	..	..	..	-	-	-	-	-
South America	2 822.8	3 276.6	2 715.8	3 135.3	3 958.8	..	4 418.3	3 778.3	4 093.5	3 903.5
Argentina	-1.1	-1.2	-1.1	-3.4	-	..	31.2	26.3	25.8	9.8
Bolivia	..	..	..	..	..	..	..	..	..	..
Brazil	2 764.8	3 202.2	2 604.8	3 048.8	3 847.1	..	3 749.1	3 150.9	3 212.8	2 840.8
Ecuador	-	-	..	..	..	..	..	..	-	..
Paraguay	..	-	..	..	..	..	..	..	..	..
Peru	..	..	..	..	..	..	..	..	..	..
Uruguay	..	6.0	9.2	11.2	16.0	25.3	28.8	18.3	37.1	52.8
Venezuela	..	37.2	55.0	46.1	43.0	294.1	279.4	104.2	78.6	109.2

Table 2. Foreign direct investment positions by country *(cont.)*

At year end

Million US dollars

	Inward					Outward				
	2016	2017	2018	2019	2020	2016	2017	2018	2019	2020
ASIA	**..**	**7 934.8**	**8 487.5**	**9 032.8**	**10 796.4**	**1 835.1**	**1 837.4**	**1 647.6**	**1 783.9**	**1 919.3**
Near and Middle East	..	..	..	..	..	..	..	..	..	..
Gulf Arabian countries	..	..	..	..	..	..	..	..	..	..
Kuwait	64.3	66.0	80.1	87.6	96.9	-	-	-	-	-11.0
Qatar	..	..	..	..	..	..	..	..	..	..
Saudi Arabia	..	..	..	..	..	..	..	..	..	..
United Arab Emirates	366.8	518.1	600.0	780.7	1 023.4	..	-	-4.6	34.8	56.4
Other Near and Middle East	..	..	..	..	..	..	..	..	..	..
Jordan	..	..	..	..	..	..	..	..	..	..
Other Asian countries	..	..	..	..	..	..	..	..	..	..
China	1 849.9	2 569.0	2 730.7	2 800.5	3 278.9	..	57.6	18.3	18.0	17.2
Hong Kong, China	2 224.1	2 764.5	2 845.2	2 870.1	3 437.2	..	..	..	..	..
India	-20.0	22.8	35.5	56.2	72.4	..	69.6	58.4	52.8	55.2
Indonesia	..	..	..	..	..	..	..	..	..	..
Iran, Islamic Republic of	..	..	..	..	..	..	..	..	..	..
Malaysia	..	..	..	..	..	..	..	..	-	-
Philippines	..	..	..	..	..	-	-	-	-	-
Singapore	..	..	..	..	..	..	..	..	..	..
Chinese Taipei	..	..	..	..	..	..	..	..	..	-
Thailand	..	..	..	..	..	..	..	..	..	..
Viet Nam	..	..	..	..	..	-	..	..	..	..
AUSTRALIA, OCEANIA AND POLAR REGIONS	**32.7**	**82.8**	**111.1**	**101.1**	**104.3**	**..**	**267.5**	**195.8**	**182.0**	**195.1**
WORLD unallocated and confidential	**..**	**22.8**	**20.6**	**20.2**	**25.8**	**..**	**8.4**	**8.0**	**9.0**	**8.6**
European Union (since 01/02/2020)	..	..	..	..	..	..	..	..	..	..
G20 countries excl. European Union	..	..	..	..	..	..	..	..	..	..
G20 OECD countries	..	..	..	..	..	..	..	..	..	..
G20 Non-OECD countries	..	..	..	..	..	..	..	..	..	..
MENA countries	..	..	..	..	..	..	..	..	..	..
ASEAN countries	..	..	..	..	..	..	..	..	..	..

- Nil; .. Not available

Note: Data excludes resident Special Purpose Entities (SPEs). Detailed metadata at: *http://metalinks.oecd.org/idi/20220712/6d95.*

Source: *OECD International Direct Investment Statistics (database): https://doi.org/10.1787/idi-data-en*

PORTUGAL

Table 3. Foreign direct investment income by country

Million US dollars

	Inward					Outward				
	2016	2017	2018	2019	2020	2016	2017	2018	2019	2020
WORLD	**5 700.5**	..	..	..	..	**2 516.9**	..	..	..	..
OECD COUNTRIES	..	..	..	..	..	..	..	..	..	..
Australia	-	..	..	-	-	..	..	..	..	..
Austria	..	..	..	..	..	..	..	..	..	..
Belgium	..	..	..	..	..	..	..	..	..	..
Canada	..	..	..	-	..	..	..	-	..	..
Chile	-	..	..	-	..	..	..	..	..	..
Colombia	-	-	-	-	-	..	..	..	..	..
Costa Rica	-	-	-	-	-	-	..	-	-	-
Czech Republic	-	-	..	..	..	..	..	..	..	..
Denmark	..	..	..	..	..	..	..	..	-	..
Estonia	-	..	-	..	..	..	-	-	..	..
Finland	..	..	..	..	..	-	-	-	..	..
France	..	..	..	..	..	..	..	..	..	..
Germany	..	..	..	..	..	..	..	..	..	..
Greece	-	-	..	..	..	-	-	..	..	-
Hungary	..	..	..	..	-	..	..	..	..	..
Iceland	-	-	-	-	-	-	-	-	-	-
Ireland	..	..	..	..	..	..	..	..	..	..
Israel	-	..	..	..	..	-	-	-	..	-
Italy	..	..	..	..	..	..	-	-	..	..
Japan	..	..	..	..	..	..	..	..	..	..
Korea	..	..	..	..	..	-	-	-	-	-
Latvia	-	-	-	-	..	-	-	-	..	-
Lithuania	-	-	-	-	-	-	-	-	-	-
Luxembourg	..	..	..	..	..	..	..	..	..	..
Mexico	-	-	-	-	..	..	..	..	..	..
Netherlands	..	..	..	..	..	..	..	..	..	..
New Zealand	-	-	..	..	..	-	-	-	-	-
Norway	..	..	..	-	..	-	..	..	-	..
Poland	..	-	..	..	..	..	..	..	..	..
Portugal	-	-	-	-	-	-	-	-	-	-
Slovak Republic	-	-	-	..	-	-	-	-	..	..
Slovenia	-	-	-	-	..	-	-	-	-	-
Spain	..	..	..	..	..	..	..	..	..	..
Sweden	..	..	..	..	..	..	..	..	..	..
Switzerland	..	..	..	..	..	..	..	..	..	..
Turkey	..	..	..	..	..	..	..	..	-	..
United Kingdom	..	..	..	..	..	..	..	..	..	..
United States	..	..	..	..	..	..	..	..	..	..
EUROPE	..	..	..	..	..	..	..	..	..	..
Bulgaria	..	-	..	..	-	-	..	..	..	..
Croatia	-	-	-	-	-	-	-	-	-	-
Cyprus	..	..	..	..	..	..	..	..	..	..
Malta	..	..	..	..	..	..	..	..	..	..
Montenegro	-	-	-	-	-	-	-	-	-	-
Romania	-	-	-	-	-	..	..	..	..	..
Russian Federation	-	-	-	-	..	-	..	..	-	-
Ukraine	-	-	-	-	..	-	-	-	..	..
AFRICA	..	..	..	..	..	..	..	..	..	..
Northern Africa	..	..	..	..	..	..	..	..	..	..
Algeria	-	..	-	-	-	..	..	..	..	..
Egypt	-	-	-	-	-	..	..	..	..	..
Libya	-	-	-	-	-	-	-	-	-	-
Morocco	-	..	..	..	..	..	..	..	..	..
Tunisia	..	..	..	..	..	..	..	..	..	..
Other African countries	..	..	..	..	..	..	..	..	..	..
Nigeria	-	-	-	-	..	..	..	..	..	..
South Africa	..	..	..	..	..	-	..	..	..	..
AMERICA	..	..	..	..	..	..	..	..	..	..
Northern America	..	..	..	..	..	..	..	..	..	..
Central America and Caribbean countries	..	..	..	..	..	..	..	..	..	..
Bahamas	..	..	..	..	-	-	..	-	-	-
Bermuda	-	-	-	-	-	-	-	..	-	-
Cayman Islands	..	-	-	..	-	..	..	..	-	..
El Salvador	-	-	-	-	-	-	-	-	-	-
Guatemala	-	-	-	-	-	-	-	-	-	-
Honduras	-	-	-	-	-	-	-	..	-	-
Nicaragua	-	-	-	-	-	-	-	-	-	-
Panama	..	..	..	..	..	..	..	..	..	..
Virgin Islands, U.S.	-	-	-	-	-	-	-	-	-	-
South America	..	..	..	..	..	..	..	..	..	..
Argentina	-	-	-	-	-	..	..	-	-	-
Bolivia	-	-	-	-	-	-	..	-	-	..
Brazil	..	..	..	..	-	..	..	..	..	..
Ecuador	-	-	-	-	-	-	-	-	..	-
Paraguay	-	-	-	-	-	-	-	-	..	..
Peru	-	-	-	-	-	..	..	..	..	..
Uruguay	..	-	-	-	-	..	..	..	..	..
Venezuela	-	-	-	-	-	..	..	..	..	..

Table 3. Foreign direct investment income by country *(cont.)*

Million US dollars

	Inward					Outward				
	2016	2017	2018	2019	2020	2016	2017	2018	2019	2020
ASIA	..	..	..	..	..	..	..	..	..	..
Near and Middle East	..	..	..	..	..	..	..	..	..	..
Gulf Arabian countries	..	..	..	..	..	..	..	..	..	..
Kuwait	..	..	..	-	-	-	-	-	-	-
Qatar	-	..	-	..	-	..	..	..	..	..
Saudi Arabia	..	-	-	..	..	..	..	..	..	..
United Arab Emirates	..	..	..	..	..	..	-	..	..	..
Other Near and Middle East	..	..	..	..	..	..	..	..	..	..
Jordan	-	-	-	-	-	-	-	-	-	-
Other Asian countries	..	..	..	..	..	..	..	..	..	..
China	..	..	..	..	-	..	..	..	-	..
Hong Kong, China	..	..	..	..	..	..	..	-	-	..
India	-	-	-	..	..	..	..	..	..	-
Indonesia	-	-	-	-	-	..	-	..	..	..
Iran, Islamic Republic of	-	-	-	-	-	-	-	-	-	-
Malaysia	-	-	-	-	-	-	-	-	-	-
Philippines	-	-	-	-	-	-	-	-	-	-
Singapore	..	..	..	..	..	-	-	..	-	..
Chinese Taipei	-	-	-	-	-	-	-	-	-	-
Thailand	-	-	-	..	..	..	-	-	-	-
Viet Nam	-	-	-	-	-	-	-	-	-	-
AUSTRALIA, OCEANIA AND POLAR REGIONS	..	..	..	..	..	..	..	..	..	..
WORLD unallocated and confidential	..	..	..	..	..	..	..	..	..	..
European Union (since 01/02/2020)	..	..	..	..	..	..	..	..	..	..
G20 countries excl. European Union	..	..	..	..	..	..	..	..	..	..
G20 OECD countries	..	..	..	..	..	..	..	..	..	..
G20 Non-OECD countries	..	..	..	..	..	..	..	..	..	..
MENA countries	..	..	..	..	..	..	..	..	..	..
ASEAN countries	..	..	..	..	..	..	-	..	..	..

- Nil; .. Not available

Note: Data excludes resident Special Purpose Entities (SPEs). Detailed metadata at: *http://metalinks.oecd.org/idi/20220712/6d95*.

Source: *OECD International Direct Investment Statistics (database)*: *https://doi.org/10.1787/idi-data-en*

PORTUGAL

Table 4. Foreign direct investment flows by industrial sector

Million US dollars

	Inward					Outward				
	2016	2017	2018	2019	2020	2016	2017	2018	2019	2020
All FDI activities	**5 682.8**	**6 913.5**	**7 176.9**	**12 251.2**	**7 565.8**	**878.0**	**-927.7**	**1 373.8**	**4 009.9**	**2 566.4**
Agriculture, forestry and fishing	..	..	..	..	..	..	..	-	..	..
Mining and quarrying	..	..	..	..	..	..	..	..	..	..
Extraction activities	-	-	-	-	-	-	-	-	-	-
Manufacturing	**233.3**	**232.2**	**553.5**	**3 174.7**	**931.1**	**-158.1**	**423.9**	**-541.7**	**2 896.0**	**-427.4**
of which:										
Food products, beverages and tobacco	..	..	..	..	..	..	..	..	..	..
Textiles, wood and paper products; printing	..	..	..	..	..	..	..	..	..	..
Chemical, rubber, plastic, non-metallic mineral products	..	..	..	..	..	..	..	..	..	..
Metal and machinery products, except electrical equipment	..	..	..	..	..	..	..	..	..	..
Motor vehicles, trailers, semi-trailers, other transport equipment	..	..	..	..	..	..	..	..	..	..
Other manufacturing	..	..	..	..	..	..	..	..	..	..
Electricity, gas, steam and air conditioning supply	..	..	..	..	..	..	..	..	..	..
Water supply; sewerage, waste management and remediation activities	..	..	..	..	..	..	..	..	..	..
Construction	**-328.4**	**284.1**	**-72.0**	**442.2**	**-30.8**	**-528.6**	**215.3**	**-62.6**	**17.9**	**-117.4**
Services	**3 235.7**	**4 805.5**	**4 152.0**	**5 670.0**	**1 856.4**	**256.6**	**520.8**	**219.5**	**-39.2**	**-474.1**
Wholesale and retail trade; repair of motor vehicles and motorcycles	566.2	821.8	-34.2	400.8	-155.0	544.1	-201.8	-496.9	132.1	441.0
Transportation and storage	..	..	..	..	..	..	..	..	..	..
Accommodation and food service activities	..	..	..	..	..	..	..	..	..	..
Information and communication	-91.8	-68.8	-311.6	147.8	-1 712.8	-123.9	-83.4	157.0	24.6	164.1
Financial and insurance activities	1 522.7	1 343.7	1 714.9	968.3	895.7	-468.9	-583.9	-480.3	-295.5	-429.6
Activities of holding companies	..	..	..	..	..	..	..	..	..	..
Real estate activities	672.3	943.5	1 053.9	2 141.5	887.7	807.3	107.1	-87.3	666.1	129.9
Professional, scientific and technical activities	454.5	926.6	1 137.7	1 421.7	2 004.6	-496.5	1 145.3	1 293.5	-60.5	-942.5
Administrative and support service activities	..	..	..	..	..	..	..	..	..	..
Public administration; activities of households and of extraterritorial organisations	-	-	-	-	-	-	-	-	-	-
Education	..	..	-	..	..	..	..	..	-	..
Human health and social work activities	..	..	..	..	..	..	..	..	..	..
Arts, entertainment and recreation	..	..	..	..	..	..	..	..	..	..
Other services	..	..	..	-	..	..	..	..	..	..
Not allocated and confidential	..	..	..	..	..	..	..	..	..	..
Private real estate activities	-	..	..	..	..	-	-	-	-	-

- Nil; .. Not available

Note: Data excludes resident Special Purpose Entities (SPEs). Detailed metadata at: *http://metalinks.oecd.org/idi/20220712/6d95*.

Source: *OECD International Direct Investment Statistics (database)*: *https://doi.org/10.1787/idi-data-en*

PORTUGAL

Table 5. Foreign direct investment positions by industrial sector

At year end

Million US dollars

	Inward					Outward				
	2016	2017	2018	2019	2020	2016	2017	2018	2019	2020
All FDI activities	**122 725.8**	**152 169.6**	**147 826.9**	**157 837.6**	**171 325.3**	**57 777.0**	**62 672.1**	**52 522.3**	**56 177.3**	**57 264.7**
Agriculture, forestry and fishing	..	..	..	..	..	..	..	..	..	..
Mining and quarrying	..	..	..	..	..	..	..	..	..	..
Extraction activities	-	-	-	-	-	-	-	-	-	-
Manufacturing	..	**9 338.0**	**9 253.5**	**12 145.6**	**13 146.4**	**3 262.4**	**3 487.6**	**2 681.5**	**5 566.2**	**4 328.1**
of which:										
Food products, beverages and tobacco	..	..	..	..	..	..	..	..	..	..
Textiles, wood and paper products; printing	..	..	..	..	..	..	..	..	..	..
Chemical, rubber, plastic, non-metallic mineral products	..	..	..	..	..	..	..	..	..	..
Metal and machinery products, except electrical equipment	..	..	..	..	..	..	..	..	..	..
Motor vehicles, trailers, semi-trailers, other transport equipment	..	..	..	..	..	..	..	..	..	..
Other manufacturing	..	..	..	..	..	..	..	..	..	..
Electricity, gas, steam and air conditioning supply	..	..	..	..	..	..	..	..	..	..
Water supply; sewerage, waste management and remediation activities	..	..	..	..	..	..	..	..	..	..
Construction	..	**3 370.1**	**2 735.3**	**3 173.4**	**2 947.6**	**3 286.6**	**4 167.7**	**3 113.1**	**2 980.2**	**3 097.3**
Services	..	**110 756.8**	**105 800.3**	**109 373.2**	**112 572.1**	**49 898.8**	**55 653.6**	**45 566.8**	**44 912.4**	**43 094.9**
Wholesale and retail trade; repair of motor vehicles and motorcycles	..	13 715.5	11 914.4	12 710.6	11 138.8	2 801.7	2 765.7	875.9	929.0	371.8
Transportation and storage	..	..	..	..	..	..	..	..	..	..
Accommodation and food service activities	..	..	..	..	..	..	..	..	..	..
Information and communication	..	8 011.5	1 267.5	7 084.9	5 905.0	-391.1	-199.1	-494.6	-441.5	-379.2
Financial and insurance activities	..	36 319.3	45 554.2	36 610.9	38 010.8	19 409.7	21 751.0	23 969.5	21 647.9	20 396.4
Activities of holding companies	..	..	..	..	..	..	..	..	..	..
Real estate activities	..	10 275.8	11 167.9	13 172.3	15 068.1	3 530.1	4 475.9	3 938.6	4 637.2	4 828.8
Professional, scientific and technical activities	..	31 953.7	25 114.5	28 118.4	30 370.6	22 412.8	25 101.9	15 965.2	17 155.7	17 321.1
Administrative and support service activities	..	..	..	..	..	..	..	..	..	..
Public administration; activities of households and of extraterritorial organisations	-	-	-	-	-	..	..	..	..	..
Education	..	..	..	..	..	..	..	..	..	..
Human health and social work activities	..	..	..	..	..	..	..	..	..	..
Arts, entertainment and recreation	..	..	..	..	..	..	..	..	..	..
Other services	..	..	..	..	..	..	..	..	..	..
Not allocated and confidential	..	..	..	..	..	..	..	..	..	..
Private real estate activities	-	..	..	..	..	-	..	..	..	..

- Nil; .. Not available

Note: Data excludes resident Special Purpose Entities (SPEs). Detailed metadata at: *http://metalinks.oecd.org/idi/20220712/6d95*.

Source: *OECD International Direct Investment Statistics (database): https://doi.org/10.1787/idi-data-en*

PORTUGAL

Table 6. Foreign direct investment income by industrial sector

Million US dollars

	Inward					Outward				
	2016	2017	2018	2019	2020	2016	2017	2018	2019	2020
All FDI activities	**5 700.5**	..	..	..	..	**2 516.9**	..	..	..	..
Agriculture, forestry and fishing	..	..	..	..	..	..	..	-	..	..
Mining and quarrying	..	..	..	..	..	..	..	..	..	..
Extraction activities	-	-	-	-	-	-	-	-	-	-
Manufacturing	..	..	..	..	..	..	..	..	..	..
of which:										
Food products, beverages and tobacco	..	..	..	..	..	..	..	..	..	..
Textiles, wood and paper products; printing	..	..	..	..	..	..	..	..	..	..
Chemical, rubber, plastic, non-metallic mineral products	..	..	..	..	..	..	..	..	..	..
Metal and machinery products, except electrical equipment	..	..	..	..	..	..	..	..	..	..
Motor vehicles, trailers, semi-trailers, other transport equipment	..	..	..	..	..	..	-	..	..	..
Other manufacturing	..	..	..	..	..	..	..	..	..	..
Electricity, gas, steam and air conditioning supply	..	..	..	..	..	..	..	..	..	..
Water supply; sewerage, waste management and remediation activities	..	..	..	..	..	..	..	..	..	..
Construction	..	..	..	..	..	..	..	..	..	..
Services	..	..	..	..	..	..	..	..	..	..
Wholesale and retail trade; repair of motor vehicles and motorcycles	..	..	..	..	..	..	..	..	..	..
Transportation and storage	..	..	..	..	..	..	..	..	..	..
Accommodation and food service activities	..	..	..	..	..	..	..	..	..	..
Information and communication	..	..	..	..	..	..	..	..	..	..
Financial and insurance activities	..	..	..	..	..	..	..	..	..	..
Activities of holding companies	..	..	..	..	..	..	..	..	..	..
Real estate activities	..	..	..	..	..	..	..	..	..	..
Professional, scientific and technical activities	..	..	..	..	..	..	..	..	..	..
Administrative and support service activities	..	..	..	..	..	-	..	..	..	..
Public administration; activities of households and of extraterritorial organisations	-	-	-	..	-	-	-	-	-	-
Education	-	..	-	..	..	-	-	..	-	-
Human health and social work activities	..	..	..	..	..	..	..	..	..	..
Arts, entertainment and recreation	..	..	..	..	..	..	..	..	..	..
Other services	..	..	..	..	-	..	..	..	..	-
Not allocated and confidential	..	..	..	..	..	..	..	..	..	..
Private real estate activities	-	-	-	-	-	-	-	-	-	-

- Nil; .. Not available

Note: Data excludes resident Special Purpose Entities (SPEs). Detailed metadata at: *http://metalinks.oecd.org/idi/20220712/6d95*.

Source: OECD *International Direct Investment Statistics (database)*: *https://doi.org/10.1787/idi-data-en*

SLOVAK REPUBLIC

Table 1. Foreign direct investment flows by country

Million US dollars

	Inward					Outward				
	2016	2017	2018	2019	2020	2016	2017	2018	2019	2020
WORLD	**805.1**	**4 008.2**	**1 674.0**	**2 510.6**	**-1 926.1**	**95.5**	**1 322.6**	**321.5**	**43.3**	**234.5**
OECD COUNTRIES	**1 407.7**	**4 534.0**	**1 707.4**	**3 204.4**	**-2 229.4**	**121.3**	**1 252.5**	**306.5**	**143.5**	**203.9**
Australia	.. c	1.2	-2.4	8.1	-14.6	.. c	.. c	.. c	.. c	.. c
Austria	163.0	-152.3	562.9	944.3	956.6	82.9	1.0	49.3	11.5	22.3
Belgium	38.4	342.5	280.2	-84.1	30.6	-	-	.. c	.. c	.. c
Canada	.. c	2.3	3.1	0.7	-18.4	.. c	.. c	.. c	.. c	.. c
Chile	.. c	-1.7	0.6	-0.8	0.5	.. c	.. c	.. c	.. c	.. c
Colombia	.. c	0.0	0.0	-0.7	0.9	-	-	-	.. c	-
Costa Rica	.. c	.. c	-0.1	0.2	0.0	-	-	-	-	-
Czech Republic	667.5	1 172.7	486.2	659.6	-194.0	-23.6	1 148.8	-51.1	58.4	175.8
Denmark	-82.4	76.7	26.3	5.3	-62.7	.. c	.. c	1.0	1.0	3.4
Estonia	.. c	2.8	3.1	2.1	-7.7	-	-	-	-	-
Finland	.. c	38.3	25.7	-1.7	34.2	.. c	.. c	.. c	.. c	.. c
France	-76.1	193.4	413.0	-88.3	-32.1	.. c	6.8	1.1	.. c	.. c
Germany	446.9	901.5	-295.3	934.6	-695.6	.. c	-1.5	2.2	10.3	-15.4
Greece	.. c	4.1	-5.8	0.9	4.7	-	-	-	.. c	.. c
Hungary	159.0	-13.4	-261.0	12.0	75.1	47.1	0.2	15.7	-20.7	2.2
Iceland	.. c	-0.2	-0.2	-0.2	0.1	.. c	.. c	.. c	.. c	.. c
Ireland	.. c	65.8	-109.9	-95.1	-86.1	.. c	-	.. c	1.0	.. c
Israel	.. c	22.1	11.8	-1.3	0.9	-	-	-	-	-
Italy	-864.4	179.7	154.1	236.8	439.0	.. c	2.0	0.9	-4.0	-14.3
Japan	.. c	36.6	9.5	-5.4	-0.1	-	-	.. c	.. c	.. c
Korea	-14.1	48.7	39.2	228.5	233.7	.. c	-	.. c	.. c	.. c
Latvia	.. c	0.6	19.8	-4.1	4.7	.. c	.. c	.. c	.. c	.. c
Lithuania	.. c	0.8	-0.7	-0.5	-0.3	.. c	.. c	.. c	.. c	.. c
Luxembourg	-408.2	322.9	-117.3	13.6	-471.5	.. c	-31.8	-15.7	-57.3	-0.8
Mexico	.. c	-2.1	-30.5	40.0	14.3	-	-	-	.. c	.. c
Netherlands	1 796.9	-798.9	-312.7	-102.9	-1 934.5	.. c	-98.9	49.0	14.1	-6.5
New Zealand	-11.4	-12.4	0.1	0.0	0.0	-	-	-	-	-
Norway	.. c	-20.9	-7.0	45.7	-6.8	.. c	.. c	.. c	.. c	.. c
Poland	21.4	158.1	16.4	38.8	-46.1	-51.8	109.0	142.8	43.4	-8.4
Portugal	.. c	0.8	-0.2	1.7	0.7	.. c	.. c	.. c	.. c	.. c
Slovak Republic	..	-	-	0.0	-	-	-	-	0.0	-
Slovenia	.. c	3.2	-3.7	-1.4	0.2	.. c	-0.6	0.6	-2.4	1.0
Spain	52.4	145.4	45.1	-5.9	-353.4	.. c	.. c	.. c	13.8	1.3
Sweden	119.0	689.6	79.5	33.1	12.1	-	-	-	0.0	-
Switzerland	-75.5	178.5	156.6	77.7	-122.4	.. c	-0.3	-0.9	0.0	-0.1
Turkey	.. c	20.1	1.3	-6.2	-5.1	.. c	.. c	5.5	3.8	13.9
United Kingdom	2.3	705.7	582.9	123.0	79.5	.. c	70.6	97.0	60.2	17.9
United States	-413.9	222.4	-63.4	195.7	-65.6	.. c	.. c	-0.2	12.5	0.7
EUROPE	**1 086.8**	**3 789.3**	**1 689.4**	**2 227.0**	**-2 040.9**	**88.6**	**1 275.5**	**304.7**	**12.5**	**224.8**
Bulgaria	.. c	-2.7	9.9	-5.3	5.3	.. c	-0.4	0.7	-0.7	0.5
Croatia	.. c	1.3	7.9	-11.1	5.3	.. c	2.2	5.2	-0.2	1.2
Cyprus	-182.2	-148.2	-17.9	-209.2	-518.6	-39.1	4.6	6.8	-124.8	8.5
Malta	.. c	31.4	142.4	-2.0	22.9	.. c	.. c	.. c	-	.. c
Montenegro	.. c	.. c	.. c	.. c	.. c	-	-	-	-	.. c
Romania	.. c	7.2	-45.9	-7.9	0.3	-9.2	2.3	-1.7	16.6	0.7
Russian Federation	.. c	10.8	48.9	-38.7	84.3	.. c	5.6	1.6	0.9	1.8
Ukraine	.. c	-1.0	-2.6	1.4	0.1	-3.1	-6.9	12.5	-6.6	-0.4
AFRICA	**.. c**	**-0.2**	**4.8**	**26.7**	**6.1**	**.. c**	**.. c**	**.. c**	**0.1**	**-1.2**
Northern Africa	.. c	2.4	7.0	19.2	-1.8	.. c	.. c	.. c	.. c	.. c
Algeria	-	-	-	-	-	-	-	-	-	-
Egypt	.. c	4.4	1.6	11.9	-7.3	-	-	-	-	-
Libya	-	-	-	-	-	-	-	-	-	-
Morocco	.. c	-3.4	3.1	4.4	3.0	.. c	.. c	.. c	.. c	.. c
Tunisia	.. c	1.5	2.3	2.9	2.5	.. c	-	-	-	-
Other African countries	.. c	-2.6	-2.2	7.5	8.0	.. c	.. c	.. c	0.6	-0.5
Nigeria	.. c	-0.1	-0.1	-1.1	0.0	.. c	.. c	.. c	.. c	.. c
South Africa	.. c	-3.7	2.7	.. c	-0.8	-	-	-	.. c	.. c
AMERICA	**-332.1**	**242.5**	**-71.3**	**169.5**	**-114.6**	**3.9**	**9.1**	**1.0**	**11.2**	**3.9**
Northern America	-405.6	224.7	-60.3	196.5	-83.9	-2.1	0.4	-0.3	13.0	0.7
Central America and Caribbean countries	81.4	16.4	-11.2	21.2	28.7	-	-	0.5	.. c	.. c
Bahamas	.. c	.. c	.. c	.. c	-	-	-	-	-	-
Bermuda	-	.. c	.. c	.. c	.. c	-	-	-	-	-
Cayman Islands	.. c	24.4	.. c	.. c	.. c	-	-	-	-	-
El Salvador	.. c	.. c	-	-	-	-	-	-	-	-
Guatemala	-	.. c	.. c	-	-	-	-	-	-	-
Honduras	-	-	-	-	-	-	-	-	-	-
Nicaragua	-	-	-	-	-	-	-	-	-	-
Panama	.. c	-0.2	.. c	-	.. c	-	-	-	-	-
Virgin Islands, U.S.	-	-	-	-	-	-	-	-	-	-
South America	-8.0	1.3	0.2	-48.1	-59.3	.. c	8.7	0.7	0.4	2.0
Argentina	0.7	-0.1	2.6	-50.6	-53.4	.. c	.. c	.. c	.. c	.. c
Bolivia	-	-	-	-	-	-	-	-	-	-
Brazil	.. c	3.0	-2.9	-1.7	3.5	.. c	.. c	0.3	.. c	1.5
Ecuador	.. c	0.0	0.0	-0.1	0.1	-	-	-	-	-
Paraguay	-	-	-	.. c	-	-	-	-	-	-
Peru	.. c	0.1	-0.1	-0.1	0.2	-	-	-	-	-
Uruguay	.. c	-	.. c	.. c	-11.0	-	-	-	-	-
Venezuela	-	.. c	.. c	.. c	0.0	-	-	-	-	-

Table 1. Foreign direct investment flows by country *(cont.)*

Million US dollars

	Inward					Outward				
	2016	2017	2018	2019	2020	2016	2017	2018	2019	2020
ASIA	**80.4**	**-12.0**	**52.1**	**79.3**	**237.9**	**.. c**	**37.5**	**15.6**	**18.2**	**6.5**
Near and Middle East	.. c	21.9	18.9	-3.7	-5.9	.. c	.. c	.. c	.. c	0.0
Gulf Arabian countries	.. c	0.1	7.2	-2.3	-6.9	-	-	-	.. c	.. c
Kuwait	.. c	.. c	.. c	-	.. c	-	-	-	-	-
Qatar	.. c	-0.9	0.9	-0.2	0.2	-	-	-	-	-
Saudi Arabia	.. c	-0.4	0.1	0.0	-3.0	-	-	-	-	-
United Arab Emirates	.. c	1.4	6.1	-2.0	-4.0	-	-	-	.. c	.. c
Other Near and Middle East	.. c	21.9	11.8	-1.4	1.0	.. c	.. c	.. c	.. c	.. c
Jordan	.. c	-0.1	0.0	0.0	-0.1	-	-	-	-	-
Other Asian countries	78.6	-34.0	33.2	83.1	243.8	.. c	37.3	15.4	18.0	6.5
China	.. c	6.4	-7.6	22.0	-30.1	.. c	31.4	7.7	3.4	3.2
Hong Kong, China	.. c	2.6	-14.0	2.1	-14.4	.. c	.. c	.. c	.. c	.. c
India	.. c	1.3	-4.7	0.5	7.7	.. c	.. c	1.0	.. c	0.9
Indonesia	.. c	-4.7	4.8	-2.7	-1.0	-	-	-	-	-
Iran, Islamic Republic of	.. c	.. c	.. c	-	-	-	-	-	-	-
Malaysia	.. c	-8.3	29.7	-75.3	1.2	-	-	0.0	-	-
Philippines	.. c	-	-0.2	0.6	0.2	-	-	-	-	-
Singapore	.. c	-65.2	-5.7	1.5	4.1	.. c	.. c	.. c	.. c	.. c
Chinese Taipei	.. c	-67.7	-22.6	10.6	32.8	-	-	-	-	-
Thailand	.. c	1.9	-0.9	-3.5	1.1	-	-	-	-	-
Viet Nam	.. c	14.5	4.4	.. c	8.5	.. c	.. c	-	14.2	.. c
AUSTRALIA, OCEANIA AND POLAR REGIONS	**-24.6**	**-11.3**	**-1.0**	**8.0**	**-14.7**	**.. c**	**.. c**	**.. c**	**.. c**	**.. c**
WORLD unallocated and confidential	**.. d**	**0.0**	**0.0**	**0.0**	**0.0**	**- d**	**.. d**	**- d**	**- d**	**.. d**
European Union (since 01/02/2020)	**..**	**..**	**..**	**..**	**-2 811.1**	**..**	**..**	**..**	**..**	**180.9**
G20 countries excl. European Union	**-892.6**	**2 322.2**	**855.4**	**1 600.0**	**-57.7**	**-8.7**	**128.1**	**118.8**	**93.1**	**18.0**
G20 OECD countries	**-858.0**	**2 309.6**	**811.5**	**1 667.7**	**-65.0**	**-28.2**	**80.1**	**108.2**	**88.9**	**10.5**
G20 Non-OECD countries	**-34.7**	**12.6**	**43.9**	**-67.7**	**7.2**	**19.5**	**48.0**	**10.6**	**4.2**	**7.5**
MENA countries	**2.6**	**2.4**	**14.1**	**16.9**	**-8.8**	**.. c**	**.. c**	**.. c**	**.. c**	**-0.6**
ASEAN countries	**31.2**	**-61.8**	**32.2**	**-175.7**	**14.0**	**.. c**	**.. c**	**.. c**	**.. c**	**.. c**

- Nil; .. Not available; c Confidential data; d Secondary Confidentiality

Note: Detailed metadata at: *http://metalinks.oecd.org/idi/20220712/6d95.*

Source: OECD *International Direct Investment Statistics (database): https://doi.org/10.1787/idi-data-en*

SLOVAK REPUBLIC

Table 2. Foreign direct investment positions by country

At year end

Million US dollars

	Inward					Outward				
	2016	2017	2018	2019	2020	2016	2017	2018	2019	2020
WORLD	**47 591.7**	**59 510.3**	**59 857.3**	**60 600.6**	**64 238.9**	**2 631.0**	**4 589.9**	**4 589.3**	**4 732.4**	**5 239.1**
OECD COUNTRIES	**46 192.4**	**58 505.6**	**58 871.4**	**59 986.0**	**63 139.9**	**2 199.9**	**4 045.3**	**4 050.1**	**4 261.0**	**4 663.8**
Australia	-3.4	-2.6	4.1	12.0	-2.1	1.3	.. c	.. c	.. c	.. c
Austria	6 860.6	7 651.6	7 703.8	7 683.3	9 489.1	124.1	168.9	205.5	331.6	364.7
Belgium	2 340.4	2 995.0	3 113.0	2 972.5	3 408.5	-	-	.. c	.. c	-
Canada	25.0	33.0	33.7	33.8	26.7	.. c	.. c	.. c	.. c	.. c
Chile	.. c	-1.6	-0.9	-1.7	-1.3	.. c	.. c	.. c	.. c	.. c
Colombia	-0.8	-0.9	-0.8	-1.6	-0.8	-	-	-	.. c	-
Costa Rica	.. c	.. c	-0.2	.. c	.. c	-	-	-	-	-
Czech Republic	5 423.3	7 731.1	8 164.0	8 594.9	9 122.6	900.1	2 388.7	2 247.9	2 370.9	2 510.7
Denmark	407.5	521.6	498.1	474.3	448.6	.. c	49.9	49.4	47.5	52.3
Estonia	15.6	16.7	15.5	17.2	1.0	-	-	-	-	-
Finland	107.7	155.7	231.2	171.6	222.2	.. c	.. c	.. c	.. c	.. c
France	881.9	817.5	1 295.7	1 202.6	1 250.0	64.7	73.4	70.3	.. c	.. c
Germany	2 666.1	4 558.9	4 159.3	4 972.5	4 708.1	40.5	41.4	41.7	54.7	36.9
Greece	-1.1	2.7	-1.2	-0.4	13.0	-	-	-	.. c	-
Hungary	2 597.3	2 999.6	2 611.9	2 566.5	2 679.7	135.1	162.3	168.7	177.7	189.3
Iceland	.. c	0.3	.. c	-0.7	-0.7	.. c	.. c	.. c	.. c	.. c
Ireland	421.4	547.5	301.1	68.3	-61.7	-	-	-	.. c	.. c
Israel	-1.0	5.3	16.3	14.5	13.7	-	-	-	-	-
Italy	2 311.4	2 791.2	2 907.5	3 024.4	3 800.9	26.4	31.9	32.0	27.2	11.2
Japan	72.1	127.9	102.8	61.6	76.1	-	-	.. c	.. c	.. c
Korea	3 060.2	3 446.1	3 263.9	3 475.3	4 023.8	-	-	.. c	.. c	-
Latvia	-0.1	-0.7	14.1	13.7	38.7	11.4	14.8	2.1	.. c	.. c
Lithuania	-2.2	-1.7	-2.3	-2.6	-3.2	.. c	.. c	5.2	.. c	.. c
Luxembourg	3 303.8	4 018.9	3 909.7	3 875.1	3 818.8	80.3	77.2	45.2	21.6	45.1
Mexico	-1.7	-4.8	-77.7	-36.2	-22.6	.. c	.. c	.. c	.. c	.. c
Netherlands	13 231.4	15 300.2	15 127.1	14 954.0	14 272.5	253.1	193.5	138.2	-44.9	160.1
New Zealand	5.7	-0.1	0.0	0.0	0.0	-	-	-	-	-
Norway	147.6	138.6	137.1	152.2	159.9	.. c	.. c	.. c	.. c	.. c
Poland	196.3	471.5	591.6	654.1	612.2	156.1	299.5	431.2	463.8	423.6
Portugal	-1.3	-0.8	-2.4	-1.0	0.1	.. c	.. c	.. c	.. c	.. c
Slovak Republic	..	-	-0.2	0.0	-	..	-	-0.2	0.0	-
Slovenia	8.8	11.9	6.1	4.5	7.6	17.1	18.9	18.5	17.1	18.1
Spain	650.9	837.8	869.5	891.9	596.3	.. c	.. c	.. c	26.5	28.2
Sweden	351.2	823.1	889.6	894.2	979.3	-	.. c	.. c	-	-
Switzerland	593.7	842.4	887.8	1 117.7	1 060.1	11.2	12.9	12.1	28.3	28.1
Turkey	-13.2	5.6	7.8	2.0	-3.5	146.1	164.5	159.7	160.4	174.1
United Kingdom	545.6	1 441.6	1 889.5	1 722.4	2 021.7	138.3	232.8	316.5	369.8	401.4
United States	-11.4	222.6	204.6	401.5	384.7	11.9	10.8	9.4	19.7	21.4
EUROPE	**43 701.0**	**54 881.7**	**55 537.8**	**56 016.3**	**59 096.6**	**2 517.4**	**4 423.3**	**4 418.9**	**4 545.9**	**5 035.4**
Bulgaria	22.7	22.9	31.3	25.4	33.5	4.4	4.9	5.3	4.9	5.0
Croatia	-1.5	-4.2	3.7	-7.4	-2.4	12.2	16.0	20.3	15.0	16.4
Cyprus	1 809.1	1 795.1	1 763.7	1 735.7	1 447.4	87.8	95.7	81.9	10.1	141.8
Malta	77.9	150.0	268.6	327.6	393.7	.. c	.. c	.. c	.. c	.. c
Montenegro	.. c	.. c	-	.. c	-	.. c	.. c	.. c	.. c	.. c
Romania	25.4	36.5	-10.0	-17.1	-17.2	7.5	11.4	10.1	29.3	16.8
Russian Federation	-225.4	-243.6	-191.3	-226.4	-156.3	35.3	45.9	40.2	42.4	39.0
Ukraine	-2.6	-3.4	-6.0	-4.4	-3.6	113.7	121.6	125.0	112.8	91.1
AFRICA	**31.8**	**48.7**	**53.1**	**82.1**	**98.6**	**.. c**	**.. c**	**.. c**	**4.0**	**1.5**
Northern Africa	-1.2	-0.5	5.4	23.3	23.6	.. c	.. c	.. c	.. c	.. c
Algeria	-	-	-	-	-	-	-	-	-	-
Egypt	-4.2	-0.3	0.4	11.0	4.2	-	-	-	-	-
Libya	-	-	-	-	-	-	-	-	-	-
Morocco	-0.7	-6.0	-2.8	1.7	5.0	.. c	.. c	.. c	.. c	.. c
Tunisia	3.7	5.8	7.8	10.6	14.4	-	-	-	-	-
Other African countries	33.0	49.2	47.7	58.8	75.0	.. c	.. c	.. c	1.1	0.7
Nigeria	0.0	-0.2	.. c	.. c	-1.5	.. c	.. c	.. c	.. c	.. c
South Africa	-9.8	-15.3	-7.5	-5.7	.. c	-	-	-	.. c	-
AMERICA	**322.4**	**671.8**	**487.1**	**674.9**	**641.0**	**52.2**	**66.2**	**64.9**	**73.1**	**80.0**
Northern America	13.6	255.6	238.3	435.2	411.4	12.2	11.9	10.4	21.4	22.9
Central America and Caribbean countries	123.0	209.7	63.7	106.5	148.0	.. c	.. c	.. c	.. c	.. c
Bahamas	.. c	.. c	.. c	-	-	-	-	-	-	-
Bermuda	-	.. c	.. c	.. c	.. c	-	-	-	-	-
Cayman Islands	.. c	82.5	.. c	.. c	.. c	-	-	-	-	-
El Salvador	.. c	-	-	-	-	-	-	-	-	-
Guatemala	-	.. c	-	-	-	-	-	-	-	-
Honduras	-	-	-	-	-	-	-	-	-	-
Nicaragua	-	-	-	-	-	-	-	-	-	-
Panama	1.8	73.1	.. c	.. c	.. c	-	-	-	-	-
Virgin Islands, U.S.	-	-	-	-	-	-	-	-	-	-
South America	185.8	206.4	185.1	133.1	81.6	26.2	38.6	37.3	37.0	40.9
Argentina	182.0	208.0	157.4	101.7	53.7	.. c	.. c	.. c	.. c	.. c
Bolivia	-	-	-	-	-	-	-	-	-	-
Brazil	4.9	1.0	-4.0	-5.7	-2.5	8.6	18.1	17.3	16.9	18.5
Ecuador	0.0	.. c	.. c	-0.1	0.0	-	-	-	-	-
Paraguay	-	-	-	.. c	-	-	-	-	-	-
Peru	.. c	0.0	.. c	-0.2	0.0	-	-	-	-	-
Uruguay	.. c	.. c	.. c	.. c	.. c	-	-	-	-	-
Venezuela	.. c	.. c	-	.. c	0.0	-	-	-	-	-

Table 2. Foreign direct investment positions by country *(cont.)*
At year end

Million US dollars

	Inward					Outward				
	2016	2017	2018	2019	2020	2016	2017	2018	2019	2020
ASIA	**3 534.1**	**3 910.9**	**3 775.8**	**3 815.2**	**4 404.8**	**54.7**	**93.1**	**99.6**	**106.2**	**118.4**
Near and Middle East	4.0	8.6	26.6	28.2	23.1	.. c	.. c	1.1	1.3	1.4
Gulf Arabian countries	2.4	0.5	7.7	11.2	6.5	-	-	.. c	.. c	.. c
Kuwait	.. c	.. c	-	-	.. c	-	-	-	-	-
Qatar	0.0	-1.0	-	-0.2	0.0	-	-	-	-	-
Saudi Arabia	.. c	10.8	10.5	10.3	7.9	-	-	-	-	-
United Arab Emirates	-9.1	-9.2	-2.7	1.3	-1.4	-	-	.. c	.. c	.. c
Other Near and Middle East	1.6	8.0	18.9	17.0	16.6	.. c	.. c	1.1	1.3	1.4
Jordan	.. c	-0.2	-0.2	.. c	.. c	-	-	-	-	-
Other Asian countries	3 530.1	3 902.3	3 749.1	3 787.1	4 381.8	54.2	92.3	98.5	104.9	117.0
China	26.7	36.1	25.1	41.2	14.1	23.9	52.6	56.5	55.8	60.0
Hong Kong, China	24.7	30.2	22.3	22.5	5.4	.. c	.. c	.. c	.. c	.. c
India	-3.4	-2.7	-6.7	-6.1	1.5	9.2	13.7	13.0	12.8	13.9
Indonesia	4.5	0.0	4.7	1.8	0.9	-	-	-	-	-
Iran, Islamic Republic of	-	-	-	.. c	.. c	-	-	-	-	-
Malaysia	76.1	77.0	100.5	24.1	26.6	.. c	.. c	-	-	-
Philippines	0.3	0.2	0.0	0.6	0.7	-	-	-	-	-
Singapore	103.1	51.2	122.3	141.3	158.6	.. c	.. c	.. c	.. c	.. c
Chinese Taipei	79.6	18.1	-4.8	6.0	.. c	-	-	-	-	-
Thailand	3.0	6.8	6.6	3.9	5.5	-	-	-	-	-
Viet Nam	81.0	112.0	111.8	13.5	.. c	.. c	.. c	.. c	.. c	.. c
AUSTRALIA, OCEANIA AND POLAR REGIONS	**2.3**	**-2.8**	**3.6**	**12.1**	**-2.2**	**1.3**	**.. c**	**.. c**	**.. c**	**.. c**
WORLD unallocated and confidential	**0.0**	**0.0**	**0.0**	**0.0**	**0.0**	**- d**	**.. d**	**.. d**	**- d**	**- d**
European Union (since 01/02/2020)	**..**	**..**	**..**	**..**	**57 259.1**	**..**	**..**	**..**	**..**	**4 188.2**
G20 countries excl. European Union	**9 523.7**	**13 431.5**	**13 779.6**	**14 783.0**	**16 178.1**	**520.4**	**703.6**	**774.2**	**848.3**	**873.7**
G20 OECD countries	**9 532.6**	**13 437.2**	**13 791.4**	**14 872.0**	**16 263.8**	**443.3**	**573.2**	**647.2**	**720.3**	**742.1**
G20 Non-OECD countries	**-8.9**	**-5.7**	**-11.9**	**-88.9**	**-85.8**	**77.0**	**130.4**	**127.0**	**128.0**	**131.6**
MENA countries	**.. c**	**3.0**	**15.9**	**37.2**	**32.9**	**.. c**	**.. c**	**.. c**	**.. c**	**0.8**
ASEAN countries	**267.9**	**247.2**	**345.9**	**185.1**	**218.3**	**17.9**	**23.2**	**23.0**	**29.5**	**31.4**

- Nil; .. Not available; c Confidential data; d Secondary Confidentiality

Note: Detailed metadata at: *http://metalinks.oecd.org/idi/20220712/6d95*.

Source: *OECD International Direct Investment Statistics (database)*: *https://doi.org/10.1787/idi-data-en*

SLOVAK REPUBLIC

Table 3. Foreign direct investment income by country

Million US dollars

	Inward					Outward				
	2016	2017	2018	2019	2020	2016	2017	2018	2019	2020
WORLD	**4 411.3**	**4 330.4**	**4 553.1**	**5 028.6**	**3 851.6**	**205.8**	**391.1**	**423.6**	**356.3**	**350.9**
OECD COUNTRIES	**4 485.3**	**4 421.3**	**4 522.3**	**5 046.2**	**3 890.6**	**167.3**	**354.9**	**377.0**	**295.7**	**310.8**
Australia	-	-	.. c	.. c	.. c	-	-	-	.. c	.. c
Austria	744.7	698.1	774.9	1 502.3	1 119.5	19.4	11.9	7.0	15.6	.. c
Belgium	223.8	211.8	197.8	183.9	127.5	-	-	.. c	.. c	.. c
Canada	2.8	.. c	.. c	.. c	.. c	0.1	0.2	.. c	.. c	.. c
Chile	-	-	-	-	-	0.4	.. c	.. c	.. c	.. c
Colombia	-	-	-	-	-	-	-	-	-	-
Costa Rica	-	-	-	-	-	-	-	-	-	-
Czech Republic	195.5	314.7	321.9	365.7	285.2	47.6	229.7	276.6	220.5	192.0
Denmark	46.0	61.6	56.3	45.0	33.6	3.0	.. c	2.4	2.4	.. c
Estonia	0.0	.. c	.. c	.. c	.. c	-	-	-	-	-
Finland	3.2	6.4	34.3	19.8	18.4	-	-	-	.. c	.. c
France	128.3	151.8	92.1	185.7	146.4	6.9	.. c	0.9	.. c	.. c
Germany	576.9	524.3	569.1	450.7	346.0	3.1	14.0	4.3	2.6	.. c
Greece	-	.. c	.. c	.. c	.. c	-	-	-	.. c	.. c
Hungary	247.1	182.9	155.4	58.9	41.8	20.7	-1.2	9.7	10.6	9.4
Iceland	0.1	-	-	-	-	-	-	-	-	.. c
Ireland	25.6	22.1	19.5	16.3	15.6	-	-	-	.. c	.. c
Israel	0.2	1.7	1.9	2.4	1.8	-	-	-	-	-
Italy	349.2	260.3	291.7	182.0	144.4	0.1	.. c	1.1	1.1	.. c
Japan	2.7	-19.5	-17.7	0.2	.. c	-	-	-	.. c	.. c
Korea	398.1	401.4	416.2	395.5	297.8	-0.8	-	-	-	-
Latvia	-	.. c	.. c	.. c	.. c	-	-	-	.. c	.. c
Lithuania	0.0	.. c	.. c	.. c	.. c	-	-	-	.. c	.. c
Luxembourg	283.3	257.2	367.6	581.9	452.9	-1.2	.. c	16.1	-2.5	.. c
Mexico	-	-	-	.. c	.. c	-	-	-	-	.. c
Netherlands	946.3	1 056.1	967.3	853.6	705.3	17.4	24.4	-4.1	-19.3	.. c
New Zealand	0.6	-	-	-	-	-	-	-	-	-
Norway	-1.5	15.3	3.3	1.2	1.0	-	-	-	0.0	.. c
Poland	29.6	21.5	20.5	28.4	.. c	4.0	34.8	30.1	30.0	28.9
Portugal	-	-	-	-	-	-	-	.. c	.. c	.. c
Slovak Republic	..	-	-	0.0	-	..	-	-	0.0	-
Slovenia	-0.4	-0.6	0.4	.. c	.. c	-	-	-	0.1	.. c
Spain	77.1	50.8	44.6	-19.9	-11.3	-	.. c	.. c	6.2	.. c
Sweden	24.4	33.0	23.3	38.6	27.2	-	-	-	-	-
Switzerland	43.6	104.6	43.4	45.4	34.8	-	-1.3	-1.6	2.8	2.8
Turkey	0.8	.. c	.. c	.. c	.. c	37.3	.. c	2.5	11.8	13.2
United Kingdom	139.6	80.5	99.1	111.1	85.3	9.2	.. c	.. c	9.2	1.5
United States	-2.6	-21.3	26.9	-8.1	0.0	-	1.6	0.4	2.2	0.5
EUROPE	**4 006.6**	**4 027.0**	**4 084.5**	**4 642.6**	**3 554.3**	**200.6**	**380.7**	**419.5**	**342.8**	**338.8**
Bulgaria	0.4	0.5	.. c	.. c	.. c	0.1	.. c	0.0	-0.3	0.3
Croatia	.. c	0.3	.. c	.. c	.. c	6.3	.. c	1.3	-0.6	.. c
Cyprus	-27.2	29.4	74.2	34.6	30.0	19.1	19.1	2.8	32.5	7.7
Malta	4.3	25.4	7.9	18.6	14.9	1.5	1.9	.. c	.. c	.. c
Montenegro	-	-	-	-	-	-	-	-	-	.. c
Romania	-	.. c	-0.5	.. c	.. c	0.0	.. c	0.8	1.0	.. c
Russian Federation	-2.6	-2.8	-2.1	-3.1	.. c	4.1	5.5	8.8	4.1	.. c
Ukraine	-0.4	-0.4	-0.6	-0.3	-0.2	0.7	0.4	29.5	9.7	.. c
AFRICA	**-0.8**	**6.9**	**-0.7**	**0.5**	**.. c**	**-**	**.. c**	**.. c**	**.. c**	**.. c**
Northern Africa	-	-	-	-	-	-	.. c	.. c	.. c	.. c
Algeria	-	-	-	-	-	-	-	-	-	-
Egypt	-	-	-	-	-	-	-	-	-	-
Libya	-	-	-	-	-	-	-	-	-	-
Morocco	-	-	-	-	-	-	.. c	.. c	.. c	.. c
Tunisia	-	-	-	-	-	-	-	-	-	-
Other African countries	-0.8	6.9	-0.7	0.5	.. c	-	-	-	0.0	.. c
Nigeria	-	-	-	-	-	-	-	-	0.0	.. c
South Africa	-	.. c	.. c	.. c	.. c	-	-	-	-	-
AMERICA	**-0.6**	**-21.1**	**27.5**	**-17.6**	**.. c**	**0.6**	**.. c**	**1.0**	**2.6**	**.. c**
Northern America	0.2	-21.6	29.0	-8.2	-0.1	0.1	1.8	0.4	2.2	0.6
Central America and Caribbean countries	-0.1	0.0	-1.7	4.1	.. c	-	-	-	-	.. c
Bahamas	-	-	-	-	-	-	-	-	-	-
Bermuda	-	.. c	.. c	.. c	.. c	-	-	-	-	-
Cayman Islands	-0.1	-0.1	.. c	.. c	.. c	-	-	-	-	-
El Salvador	-	-	-	-	-	-	-	-	-	-
Guatemala	-	-	-	-	-	-	-	-	-	-
Honduras	-	-	-	-	-	-	-	-	-	-
Nicaragua	-	-	-	-	-	-	-	-	-	-
Panama	-0.1	-0.1	.. c	-	-	-	-	-	-	-
Virgin Islands, U.S.	-	-	-	-	-	-	-	-	-	-
South America	-0.7	0.6	0.2	-13.5	-10.1	0.5	.. c	0.7	.. c	.. c
Argentina	0.5	0.5	0.5	-12.8	-9.7	-	-	-	-	-
Bolivia	-	-	-	-	-	-	-	-	-	-
Brazil	-1.2	0.1	-0.3	.. c	.. c	0.1	0.4	0.2	-	1.4
Ecuador	-	-	-	-	-	-	-	-	-	-
Paraguay	-	-	-	-	-	-	-	-	-	-
Peru	-	-	-	-	-	-	-	-	-	-
Uruguay	-	-	.. c	.. c	.. c	-	-	-	-	-
Venezuela	-	-	-	-	-	-	-	-	-	-

Table 3. Foreign direct investment income by country *(cont.)*

Million US dollars

	Inward					Outward				
	2016	2017	2018	2019	2020	2016	2017	2018	2019	2020
ASIA	**405.6**	**317.6**	**440.1**	**402.5**	**.. c**	**4.5**	**7.7**	**3.1**	**11.0**	**.. c**
Near and Middle East	-0.3	1.3	1.6	1.2	1.0	-	-	-	-	0.0
Gulf Arabian countries	-0.2	.. c	.. c	-0.9	.. c	-	-	-	-	.. c
Kuwait	-	-	-	-	-	-	-	-	-	-
Qatar	-	-	-	-	-	-	-	-	-	-
Saudi Arabia	-0.2	.. c	.. c	.. c	.. c	-	-	-	-	-
United Arab Emirates	-	-	-	.. c	.. c	-	-	-	-	.. c
Other Near and Middle East	-0.1	1.5	1.7	2.1	1.6	-	-	-	-	.. c
Jordan	-	-	-	-	-	-	-	-	-	-
Other Asian countries	405.9	316.3	438.5	401.3	.. c	4.5	7.7	3.1	11.0	.. c
China	-0.8	-1.2	0.4	-1.1	-1.5	5.0	8.0	2.2	2.8	4.5
Hong Kong, China	0.4	.. c	.. c	.. c	.. c	0.4	.. c	-	.. c	.. c
India	-	-	.. c	.. c	.. c	-	-0.3	1.1	-	1.0
Indonesia	-	-	-	-	-	-	-	-	-	-
Iran, Islamic Republic of	-	-	-	-	-	-	-	-	-	-
Malaysia	0.2	.. c	.. c	.. c	.. c	-	-	-	-	-
Philippines	-	-	-	-	-	-	-	-	-	-
Singapore	4.7	-66.2	7.3	2.5	.. c	-	-	-	0.0	.. c
Chinese Taipei	0.0	.. c	.. c	.. c	.. c	-	-	-	-	-
Thailand	0.1	.. c	.. c	.. c	.. c	-	-	-	-	-
Viet Nam	0.6	.. c	.. c	.. c	.. c	0.0	.. c	-	7.2	.. c
AUSTRALIA, OCEANIA AND POLAR REGIONS	**0.6**	**-**	**.. c**	**.. c**	**.. c**	**-**	**-**	**-**	**.. c**	**.. c**
WORLD unallocated and confidential	**-**	**0.0**	**.. d**	**- d**	**.. d**	**-**	**.. d**	**- d**	**.. d**	**- d**
European Union (since 01/02/2020)	**..**	**..**	**..**	**..**	**3 515.1**	**..**	**..**	**..**	**..**	**301.5**
G20 countries excl. European Union	**1 591.4**	**1 373.8**	**1 479.3**	**1 301.9**	**1 008.5**	**65.1**	**65.4**	**48.0**	**37.6**	**35.7**
G20 OECD countries	**1 595.8**	**1 377.4**	**1 480.8**	**1 315.9**	**1 019.7**	**56.0**	**51.8**	**35.7**	**30.8**	**26.4**
G20 Non-OECD countries	**-4.4**	**-3.6**	**-1.5**	**-14.0**	**-11.3**	**9.1**	**13.6**	**12.3**	**6.8**	**.. c**
MENA countries	**-0.5**	**.. c**	**.. c**	**-1.2**	**.. c**	**-**	**.. c**	**.. c**	**.. c**	**0.1**
ASEAN countries	**.. c**	**-64.9**	**38.2**	**3.6**	**.. c**	**0.0**	**.. c**	**-**	**7.2**	**.. c**

- Nil; .. Not available; c Confidential data; d Secondary Confidentiality

Note: Detailed metadata at: *http://metalinks.oecd.org/idi/20220712/6d95.*

Source: *OECD International Direct Investment Statistics (database): https://doi.org/10.1787/idi-data-en*

SLOVAK REPUBLIC

Table 4. Foreign direct investment flows by industrial sector

Million US dollars

	Inward					Outward				
	2016	2017	2018	2019	2020	2016	2017	2018	2019	2020
All FDI activities	**805.1**	**4 008.2**	**1 674.0**	**2 510.6**	**-1 926.1**	**95.5**	**1 322.6**	**321.5**	**43.3**	**234.5**
Agriculture, forestry and fishing	**-40.1**	**14.3**	**-1.1**	**13.1**	..	**.. c**	**.. c**	**.. c**	**-1.1**	..
Mining and quarrying	**-41.0**	**21.9**	**-18.7**	**39.3**	..	**0.3**	**243.5**	**167.2**	**.. c**	..
Extraction activities	49.5	12.2	-18.1	.. c	..	.. c	.. c	.. c	.. c	..
Manufacturing	**845.9**	**1 883.0**	**563.4**	**1 018.0**	..	**78.9**	**74.6**	**16.8**	**29.5**	..
of which:										
Food products, beverages and tobacco	-10.7	-13.0	-54.2	32.0	..	7.8	5.9	-11.3	-2.4	..
Textiles, wood and paper products; printing	93.9	62.7	-31.9	208.5	..	62.7	8.7	6.5	3.2	..
Chemical, rubber, plastic, non-metallic mineral products	257.3	132.1	-631.5	122.6	..	-0.4	8.4	3.9	-6.5	..
Metal and machinery products, except electrical equipment	-124.8	511.4	878.1	-15.2	..	-23.8	6.0	4.9	23.0	..
Motor vehicles, trailers, semi-trailers, other transport equipment	355.5	788.3	411.6	329.2	..	8.3	-2.2	2.1	11.9	..
Other manufacturing	274.7	401.5	-8.6	340.9	..	24.4	47.8	10.7	0.3	..
Electricity, gas, steam and air conditioning supply	**12.7**	**-106.1**	**474.9**	**178.3**	..	**4.7**	**0.2**	**22.9**	**-26.6**	..
Water supply; sewerage, waste management and remediation activities	**-2.5**	**17.5**	**16.4**	**11.5**	..	**.. c**	**2.0**	**6.3**	**.. c**	..
Construction	**12.5**	**46.8**	**1.8**	**121.6**	..	**-103.7**	**23.8**	**32.9**	**70.3**	..
Services	**17.6**	**2 130.8**	**637.6**	**1 128.8**	..	**106.4**	**980.1**	**73.0**	**11.2**	..
Wholesale and retail trade; repair of motor vehicles and motorcycles	292.9	141.5	199.9	367.7	..	47.4	44.6	1.0	5.2	..
Transportation and storage	54.7	83.4	95.1	-2.6	..	54.8	-4.3	1.9	3.7	..
Accommodation and food service activities	-38.3	-0.6	14.0	3.7	..	.. c	.. c	.. c	0.0	..
Information and communication	-202.1	189.3	164.5	164.5	..	33.0	127.1	56.7	-1.2	..
Financial and insurance activities	701.8	229.4	1 009.9	520.9	..	1.2	-98.3	34.0	-9.1	..
Activities of holding companies	3.4	-96.0	27.2	-17.3	..	3.7	-53.3	47.0	.. c	..
Real estate activities	-109.3	507.6	134.5	223.2	..	1.8	303.8	21.6	-13.3	..
Professional, scientific and technical activities	-132.5	1 173.0	-620.4	487.6	..	-114.4	137.0	123.1	1.5	..
Administrative and support service activities	-586.2	-339.8	-33.3	-578.8	..	.. c	6.7	-14.5	.. c	..
Public administration; activities of households and of extraterritorial organisations	-	-	-	-	..	-	.. c	.. c	21.3	..
Education	.. c	.. c	.. c	.. c	..	-	-	-	-	..
Human health and social work activities	-8.5	199.8	-339.9	-38.3	..	.. c	.. c	.. c	.. c	..
Arts, entertainment and recreation	81.3	-50.1	-4.3	-4.1	..	27.7	.. c	-58.2	.. c	..
Other services	-36.3	-2.7	.. c	-17.9	..	54.6	.. c	.. c	.. c	..
Not allocated and confidential	-	**0.0**	**-0.2**	**0.0**	**-1 926.1**	**.. c**	**.. c**	**.. c**	**.. c**	**234.5**
Private real estate activities	-	-	-	-	..	-	-	-	-	..

- Nil; .. Not available; c Confidential data

Note: Detailed metadata at: *http://metalinks.oecd.org/idi/20220712/6d95*.

Source: OECD *International Direct Investment Statistics (database): https://doi.org/10.1787/idi-data-en*

Table 5. Foreign direct investment positions by industrial sector

At year end

Million US dollars

	Inward					Outward				
	2016	2017	2018	2019	2020	2016	2017	2018	2019	2020
All FDI activities	**47 591.7**	**59 510.3**	**59 857.3**	**60 600.6**	**64 238.9**	**2 631.0**	**4 589.9**	**4 589.3**	**4 732.4**	**5 239.1**
Agriculture, forestry and fishing	**150.4**	**181.2**	**14.5**	**184.9**	..	**13.2**	**6.2**	.. c	**8.6**	..
Mining and quarrying	**94.5**	**76.1**	**-28.1**	**130.1**	..	**70.6**	**413.0**	**595.0**	**465.6**	..
Extraction activities	.. d	-18.8	-32.3	.. c	..	.. c	.. c	.. c	109.1	..
Manufacturing	**15 358.3**	**19 091.0**	**15 209.8**	**19 844.4**	..	**471.8**	**600.4**	**578.9**	**599.2**	..
of which:										
Food products, beverages and tobacco	637.7	670.5	1 152.3	636.0	..	35.9	48.0	37.4	39.1	..
Textiles, wood and paper products; printing	676.7	809.4	1 123.0	1 140.1	..	118.3	146.2	132.9	113.4	..
Chemical, rubber, plastic, non-metallic mineral products	3 587.1	4 115.7	2 657.8	3 833.4	..	61.5	76.6	64.2	71.1	..
Metal and machinery products, except electrical equipment	4 830.7	5 673.6	7 179.0	5 124.4	..	89.3	107.2	103.6	136.2	..
Motor vehicles, trailers, semi-trailers, other transport equipment	3 383.9	5 411.5	1 354.9	6 532.8	..	68.4	70.6	86.0	84.2	..
Other manufacturing	2 242.2	2 410.4	1 742.8	2 577.7	..	98.4	151.8	154.8	155.3	..
Electricity, gas, steam and air conditioning supply	**3 484.1**	**3 919.6**	**3 008.2**	**4 092.1**	..	**19.2**	**24.5**	**75.4**	**115.6**	..
Water supply; sewerage, waste management and remediation activities	**121.3**	**154.4**	**175.3**	**169.2**	..	**0.8**	**3.2**	**8.5**	**8.0**	..
Construction	**608.9**	**765.1**	**1 108.1**	**683.4**	..	**54.0**	**86.9**	**69.3**	**150.6**	..
Services	**27 774.2**	**35 322.9**	**40 369.5**	**35 496.4**	..	**2 001.4**	**3 455.8**	**3 255.4**	**3 384.9**	..
Wholesale and retail trade; repair of motor vehicles and motorcycles	4 344.0	5 091.3	7 170.7	4 777.7	..	485.8	603.8	546.3	675.8	..
Transportation and storage	1 833.5	2 149.4	3 318.8	2 048.1	..	133.1	153.7	113.4	164.9	..
Accommodation and food service activities	124.9	158.6	168.2	174.6	..	.. c	3.9	.. c	0.5	..
Information and communication	2 142.0	2 632.1	5 839.8	2 984.4	..	133.9	290.7	312.6	335.6	..
Financial and insurance activities	11 048.2	12 869.9	2 407.8	13 900.5	..	261.3	214.5	250.9	457.1	..
Activities of holding companies	-120.5	-541.8	-91.0	-20.2	..	.. d	80.7	161.0	123.8	..
Real estate activities	3 004.2	4 369.4	6 345.8	5 298.4	..	386.3	754.7	1 125.9	424.0	..
Professional, scientific and technical activities	1 636.3	3 315.4	12 877.4	1 906.7	..	381.6	598.1	678.6	637.6	..
Administrative and support service activities	3 158.4	4 019.4	464.4	3 778.4	..	.. d	23.3	195.7	2.5	..
Public administration; activities of households and of extraterritorial organisations	-	-	-	-	..	-	.. c	.. c	593.0	..
Education	.. c	.. c	1.0	17.3	..	-	-	-	-	..
Human health and social work activities	126.4	421.8	1 700.7	377.2	..	.. c	.. c	.. c	27.4	..
Arts, entertainment and recreation	252.0	181.2	61.0	136.5	..	49.8	57.7	.. c	76.5	..
Other services	103.3	113.2	14.0	96.6	..	.. c	.. c	.. c	-10.0	..
Not allocated and confidential	**0.0**	**0.0**	-	-	**64 238.9**	-	**0.0**	.. c	-	**5 239.1**
Private real estate activities	-	-	-	-	..	-	-	-	-	..

- Nil; .. Not available; c Confidential data; d Secondary Confidentiality

Note: Detailed metadata at: *http://metalinks.oecd.org/idi/20220712/6d95*.

Source: *OECD International Direct Investment Statistics (database)*: *https://doi.org/10.1787/idi-data-en*

Table 6. Foreign direct investment income by industrial sector

Million US dollars

	Inward					Outward				
	2016	2017	2018	2019	2020	2016	2017	2018	2019	2020
All FDI activities	**4 411.3**	**4 330.4**	**4 553.1**	**5 028.6**	**3 851.6**	**205.8**	**391.1**	**423.6**	**356.3**	**350.9**
Agriculture, forestry and fishing	**6.6**	**21.1**	**12.9**	**.. c**	**..**	**.. c**	**-3.5**	**.. c**	**-1.1**	**..**
Mining and quarrying	**40.7**	**40.2**	**82.5**	**42.0**	**..**	**.. c**	**-44.2**	**154.4**	**.. c**	**..**
Extraction activities	36.7	.. c	77.7	.. c	..	.. c	.. c	.. c	.. c	..
Manufacturing	**2 233.4**	**2 049.3**	**2 193.4**	**1 898.9**	**..**	**29.9**	**28.2**	**32.7**	**39.1**	**..**
of which:										
Food products, beverages and tobacco	89.0	49.1	19.6	63.8	..	.. c	0.2	0.9	.. c	..
Textiles, wood and paper products; printing	101.5	85.2	12.8	120.7	..	16.6	.. c	9.7	.. c	..
Chemical, rubber, plastic, non-metallic mineral products	616.1	530.5	-99.5	295.0	..	1.0	.. c	1.9	.. c	..
Metal and machinery products, except electrical equipment	601.1	505.7	1 670.1	288.4	..	0.3	5.1	13.4	23.3	..
Motor vehicles, trailers, semi-trailers, other transport equipment	664.1	688.0	434.8	917.3	..	3.3	.. c	3.2	0.0	..
Other manufacturing	161.5	190.7	155.6	213.8	..	8.2	11.7	3.6	.. c	..
Electricity, gas, steam and air conditioning supply	**81.0**	**30.1**	**101.7**	**61.6**	**..**	**0.9**	**2.6**	**1.3**	**.. c**	**..**
Water supply; sewerage, waste management and remediation activities	**5.0**	**15.0**	**32.1**	**16.7**	**..**	**0.1**	**0.3**	**1.9**	**.. c**	**..**
Construction	**21.0**	**63.6**	**35.8**	**61.4**	**..**	**3.7**	**25.2**	**4.0**	**.. c**	**..**
Services	**2 023.7**	**2 111.0**	**2 094.8**	**2 931.9**	**..**	**170.4**	**382.5**	**221.1**	**277.2**	**..**
Wholesale and retail trade; repair of motor vehicles and motorcycles	495.7	627.7	623.1	617.8	..	53.4	156.8	12.6	73.3	..
Transportation and storage	116.3	100.1	198.2	92.7	..	11.1	-5.6	4.2	-1.6	..
Accommodation and food service activities	-16.7	9.6	17.3	5.0	..	.. c	.. c	.. c	0.0	..
Information and communication	286.3	335.9	601.0	394.8	..	10.8	32.1	33.5	24.6	..
Financial and insurance activities	1 003.3	864.7	531.8	931.1	..	28.9	34.5	18.6	25.6	..
Activities of holding companies	-19.9	-30.8	-6.3	-21.4	..	8.6	10.7	6.0	.. c	..
Real estate activities	105.6	86.1	212.0	66.6	..	21.6	69.4	78.4	40.4	..
Professional, scientific and technical activities	74.9	-7.0	-261.9	795.8	..	33.0	34.0	46.0	83.7	..
Administrative and support service activities	-8.2	37.4	494.1	15.0	..	.. c	.. c	19.7	.. c	..
Public administration; activities of households and of extraterritorial organisations	-	-	-	-	..	-	.. c	.. c	.. c	..
Education	.. c	0.0	-	.. c	..	-	-	-	-	..
Human health and social work activities	0.9	-1.5	-327.9	.. c	..	.. c	.. c	.. c	.. c	..
Arts, entertainment and recreation	17.4	77.0	3.7	.. c	..	2.8	.. c	.. c	.. c	..
Other services	-51.9	.. c	.. c	.. c	..	.. c	.. c	.. c	.. c	..
Not allocated and confidential	**0.0**	**0.0**	**-**	**.. c**	**3 851.6**	**.. c**	**0.0**	**.. c**	**.. c**	**350.9**
Private real estate activities	**-**	**-**	**-**	**-**	**..**	**-**	**-**	**-**	**-**	**..**

- Nil; .. Not available; c Confidential data

Note: Detailed metadata at: *http://metalinks.oecd.org/idi/20220712/6d95.*

Source: *OECD International Direct Investment Statistics (database): https://doi.org/10.1787/idi-data-en*

SLOVENIA

Table 1. Foreign direct investment flows by country

Million US dollars

	Inward					Outward				
	2016	2017	2018	2019	2020	2016	2017	2018	2019	2020
WORLD	**1 244.7**	**895.8**	**1 383.3**	**1 462.9**	**205.2**	**289.6**	**337.7**	**280.7**	**609.7**	**508.3**
OECD COUNTRIES	**1 149.2**	**624.1**	**1 205.2**	**787.6**	**54.9**	**-11.7**	**195.9**	**44.4**	**-10.1**	**-156.5**
Australia	0.8	1.3	-15.2	-0.8	-1.0	2.7	3.1	-4.1	-2.4	2.8
Austria	148.6	435.0	267.0	172.8	130.9	-45.5	-4.6	9.8	-2.4	-44.8
Belgium	18.1	18.3	-17.8	-26.9	-37.8	-0.3	-0.3	0.4	1.3	0.3
Canada	-2.0	-1.1	-0.5	-1.1	0.1	2.4	-0.6	9.3	5.2	4.9
Chile	0.0	0.0	0.0	-3.2	2.1	1.0	2.3	2.2	-2.2	0.1
Colombia	0.0	0.0	0.0	0.0	0.0	0.4	0.1	-0.2	-0.1	-
Costa Rica	-	-0.1	-	-	0.0	-	-	-	-	-
Czech Republic	47.3	31.2	4.0	14.7	-4.5	19.7	-7.9	3.7	15.4	12.6
Denmark	-3.5	1.7	0.0	48.3	2.8	-4.9	1.1	3.3	-4.5	3.2
Estonia	-0.2	-0.1	-1.3	2.2	0.3	-	-	-	-	-
Finland	-10.9	3.9	-0.8	-2.3	7.6	-3.5	1.7	4.9	6.2	12.6
France	-22.6	63.1	-29.1	-103.6	-95.9	0.3	-7.4	1.6	-4.0	9.0
Germany	35.4	54.4	190.8	238.1	31.0	-21.2	129.2	21.2	-22.9	13.1
Greece	0.4	2.3	1.6	3.2	4.1	2.7	8.8	6.4	-13.4	1.3
Hungary	6.4	9.7	30.7	74.6	42.1	1.0	2.8	-2.3	4.7	1.3
Iceland	-	0.0	0.0	0.0	0.0	-	0.0	-	-	-
Ireland	31.6	-5.8	-0.7	-6.7	42.9	4.2	0.6	0.1	0.6	0.2
Israel	1.3	2.5	1.6	0.1	-0.9	-	-	-	0.0	0.0
Italy	91.2	-128.2	46.2	66.7	-21.4	13.6	39.0	-3.1	10.1	4.4
Japan	-0.9	-27.4	-28.2	-3.2	7.4	-0.9	-0.4	0.1	0.8	-0.3
Korea	1.0	1.3	-0.5	0.7	-2.0	0.1	-0.3	-0.7	-1.2	3.0
Latvia	0.5	0.3	0.3	-0.6	0.4	0.0	0.0	-0.1	-0.1	0.0
Lithuania	0.1	0.1	0.0	-0.1	-0.2	0.0	0.2	-0.2	-0.1	0.1
Luxembourg	469.8	-11.2	452.3	-14.6	37.2	3.7	-3.4	0.0	-1.2	-1.0
Mexico	-0.2	0.0	-0.7	2.7	-0.1	-3.7	1.7	-1.1	3.6	-3.2
Netherlands	135.8	54.4	91.6	223.2	-14.6	17.1	-8.2	27.4	-18.8	-246.2
New Zealand	0.0	0.0	-0.1	0.2	-0.3	0.0	0.1	-0.1	0.0	0.0
Norway	-0.6	1.0	-0.1	2.4	-2.1	-	0.0	-	0.0	-
Poland	8.5	-5.6	9.6	12.5	1.1	2.3	0.5	-3.0	17.8	2.5
Portugal	0.1	0.6	0.4	0.6	-0.7	-0.5	2.6	-1.7	1.9	-1.9
Slovak Republic	3.3	6.3	-1.4	5.1	20.1	-5.5	-0.1	-3.7	-0.8	2.9
Slovenia	-	-	-	-	-	-	-	-	-	-
Spain	1.9	2.3	-2.5	9.3	-8.0	16.9	9.3	1.2	-6.4	12.0
Sweden	81.8	7.8	-17.2	-188.9	-28.7	-1.5	7.9	1.1	18.1	-9.1
Switzerland	68.5	97.0	123.0	206.9	-35.8	-5.6	0.1	-1.3	4.6	-1.0
Turkey	-7.1	14.4	18.6	6.4	3.1	0.1	15.7	-3.6	1.0	2.1
United Kingdom	43.3	-0.1	16.9	63.8	-7.2	-11.5	-15.3	-0.8	-24.1	56.9
United States	1.8	-5.2	66.6	-15.1	-17.1	5.1	17.9	-22.4	3.2	5.4
EUROPE	**1 235.5**	**913.3**	**1 375.6**	**1 465.2**	**105.0**	**261.5**	**301.2**	**267.7**	**356.8**	**491.0**
Bulgaria	1.6	1.9	2.9	0.8	-1.8	-0.2	-0.1	-1.3	6.8	-8.1
Croatia	-27.2	62.3	35.6	58.0	4.8	105.6	176.5	139.7	277.7	53.6
Cyprus	15.0	-12.3	69.5	276.4	53.9	10.1	-9.6	1.5	7.9	15.4
Malta	51.6	11.3	6.7	-2.4	12.7	0.0	-0.5	0.4	0.5	0.7
Montenegro	2.6	6.5	3.5	3.3	-2.9	12.9	-11.5	6.8	6.7	9.1
Romania	-1.4	3.3	-4.4	2.4	-7.3	2.2	3.5	-10.8	5.2	-1.1
Russian Federation	6.8	116.8	16.4	22.9	-13.0	17.3	28.5	19.7	50.3	94.1
Ukraine	-1.8	-2.2	1.2	4.8	-0.4	4.5	7.9	3.4	7.3	-2.0
AFRICA	**-2.4**	**-0.4**	**1.6**	**-4.0**	**7.5**	**-11.1**	**-1.2**	**-4.4**	**3.8**	**-6.4**
Northern Africa	0.9	-0.6	2.3	-5.0	7.8	0.7	2.9	0.6	-4.8	2.4
Algeria	0.6	0.0	0.0	-	-	-	0.0	0.0	0.0	0.0
Egypt	0.0	-0.7	0.9	-7.8	6.4	-	-	-	-	-
Libya	0.0	-	-	-	-	0.7	2.3	0.5	-4.9	2.5
Morocco	0.3	0.0	1.6	2.7	1.5	0.0	0.6	0.0	0.1	-0.1
Tunisia	0.1	0.1	-0.3	0.1	-0.1	-	-	-	-	-
Other African countries	-3.3	0.3	-0.7	1.0	-0.3	-11.8	-4.1	-5.0	8.6	-8.8
Nigeria	-	-	-	-	-	-	-	-	-	-
South Africa	-0.2	0.2	-0.6	1.0	-0.4	1.0	-0.7	1.5	3.8	0.9
AMERICA	**3.5**	**-1.1**	**70.5**	**-24.9**	**-13.5**	**5.3**	**23.2**	**-9.5**	**220.6**	**9.1**
Northern America	-0.2	-6.3	66.1	-16.2	-17.0	7.5	17.3	-13.1	8.4	10.3
Central America and Caribbean countries	4.8	5.7	3.6	-4.2	0.2	-3.6	1.7	-1.1	209.5	-3.2
Bahamas	0.0	-	-	-	-	-	-	-	-	-
Bermuda	-	0.0	0.0	-	-	-	-	-	-	-
Cayman Islands	0.0	-	-	-	-	-	-	-	-	-
El Salvador	-	-	-	-	-	-	-	-	-	-
Guatemala	0.0	0.0	-	-	-	-	-	-	-	-
Honduras	-	-	-	-	-	-	-	-	-	-
Nicaragua	-	-	-	-	-	-	-	-	-	-
Panama	0.1	-2.2	-0.2	-2.6	-0.2	0.0	0.0	0.0	-	-
Virgin Islands, U.S.	-	-	-	-	0.0	-	-	-	-	-
South America	-1.1	-0.5	0.7	-4.5	3.3	1.5	4.1	4.8	2.7	2.0
Argentina	-0.6	-0.4	-0.1	-0.5	0.0	-	1.4	2.3	4.7	0.8
Bolivia	-	0.0	-	-	-	-	-	-	-	-
Brazil	-0.5	0.1	0.8	-0.3	-1.6	0.9	-1.9	0.3	-0.4	0.0
Ecuador	-	-	0.0	-	-	-1.1	0.0	0.0	-	0.8
Paraguay	0.0	-	-	-	-	-	-	-	-	-
Peru	-	0.0	0.0	-0.5	2.8	0.3	2.3	0.3	0.7	0.1
Uruguay	0.0	0.0	-	-	-	-	-	-	-	-
Venezuela	0.0	-0.1	-	-	-	-	-	-	-	-

SLOVENIA

Table 1. Foreign direct investment flows by country *(cont.)*

Million US dollars

	Inward					Outward				
	2016	2017	2018	2019	2020	2016	2017	2018	2019	2020
ASIA	**6.4**	**-13.3**	**-8.3**	**26.3**	**107.5**	**14.5**	**-1.9**	**16.0**	**15.8**	**-0.5**
Near and Middle East	13.0	21.0	14.9	2.5	-9.0	-0.8	-1.6	1.8	-5.5	-2.5
Gulf Arabian countries	11.7	18.7	13.9	1.9	-8.3	-0.8	-1.6	1.8	-5.5	-2.5
Kuwait	0.0	-0.1	-0.5	0.0	0.0	-	-	-	-	-
Qatar	-0.1	0.1	0.0	-0.1	-0.9	-	-	-	-	-
Saudi Arabia	0.4	0.5	0.4	-1.6	0.3	0.2	-0.1	0.0	-	-
United Arab Emirates	11.5	18.2	14.0	3.6	-7.7	-1.0	-1.5	1.7	-5.5	-2.5
Other Near and Middle East	1.3	2.3	1.0	0.7	-0.6	-	0.0	0.0	0.0	0.1
Jordan	0.0	-0.1	-0.5	0.6	0.2	-	-	-	-	-
Other Asian countries	-6.7	-34.3	-23.3	23.8	116.4	15.3	-0.3	14.3	21.3	2.0
China	6.2	2.2	0.2	-0.9	-2.7	11.8	1.0	14.4	21.9	6.7
Hong Kong, China	-7.1	-4.4	4.9	14.1	127.2	0.4	1.8	-2.9	-1.9	-4.7
India	2.3	-1.2	-3.3	14.8	-16.2	-0.4	0.2	0.2	0.1	0.1
Indonesia	-	-	0.0	0.7	-0.1	0.1	-0.1	0.0	0.0	0.0
Iran, Islamic Republic of	0.0	0.0	0.0	0.0	0.0	-0.1	-0.2	0.1	-	0.0
Malaysia	-0.7	-1.0	2.1	0.0	-0.2	0.1	0.1	0.1	0.2	-1.1
Philippines	0.0	0.0	0.0	0.1	0.2	-	-	-	-	-
Singapore	-5.2	-1.6	0.5	-2.2	2.0	0.1	-0.6	0.9	-0.7	-0.9
Chinese Taipei	0.0	0.0	0.0	0.0	0.0	-	0.0	-	-	0.0
Thailand	0.0	0.0	-0.5	0.7	-1.0	-	-0.1	-0.3	-0.1	0.8
Viet Nam	0.0	-	0.0	0.0	0.0	-	-	-	-	-
AUSTRALIA, OCEANIA AND POLAR REGIONS	**0.8**	**1.3**	**-15.3**	**-0.7**	**-1.3**	**2.7**	**3.1**	**-4.2**	**-2.4**	**2.8**
WORLD unallocated and confidential	**0.9**	**-4.0**	**-40.7**	**1.1**	**0.0**	**16.7**	**13.2**	**15.0**	**15.1**	**12.3**
European Union (since 01/02/2020)	..	..	..	..	..	..	..	..	..	..
G20 countries excl. European Union	**155.1**	**90.7**	**278.6**	**290.6**	**-136.6**	**17.7**	**211.1**	**34.9**	**49.8**	**200.9**
G20 OECD countries	**140.8**	**-27.5**	**264.9**	**254.6**	**-103.0**	**-13.1**	**182.7**	**-3.5**	**-30.8**	**98.4**
G20 Non-OECD countries	**14.4**	**118.1**	**13.7**	**35.9**	**-33.6**	**30.8**	**28.4**	**38.4**	**80.5**	**102.5**
MENA countries	**12.7**	**17.9**	**15.6**	**-2.6**	**-0.3**	**-0.1**	**1.3**	**2.3**	**-10.3**	**-0.1**
ASEAN countries	**-6.0**	**-2.6**	**2.1**	**-0.7**	**0.5**	**0.2**	**-0.7**	**0.7**	**-0.5**	**-1.2**

- Nil; .. Not available

Note: Detailed metadata at: *http://metalinks.oecd.org/idi/20220712/6d95*.

Source: *OECD International Direct Investment Statistics (database)*: *https://doi.org/10.1787/idi-data-en*

SLOVENIA

Table 2. Foreign direct investment positions by country

At year end

Million US dollars

	Inward					Outward				
	2016	2017	2018	2019	2020	2016	2017	2018	2019	2020
WORLD	**13 671.8**	**16 738.8**	**17 465.4**	**18 174.3**	**20 329.9**	**6 051.6**	**7 159.3**	**6 992.7**	**7 683.6**	**8 533.3**
OECD COUNTRIES	..	**14 011.5**	**13 711.3**	**14 544.9**	**16 326.9**	**924.9**	**1 245.2**	**1 248.0**	**1 242.4**	**1 131.1**
Australia	..	-	-	-	-	20.5	26.3	20.2	17.8	22.4
Austria	..	2 539.1	2 354.9	2 565.9	3 165.9	120.9	129.2	139.9	147.0	107.4
Belgium	..	142.1	115.2	126.3	92.4	2.7	2.8	3.0	4.3	5.0
Canada	..	-	-	-	-	8.6	8.6	17.0	22.3	27.6
Chile	..	-	-	-	-	1.0	3.4	5.4	3.1	3.3
Colombia	..	-	-	-	-	0.4	0.5	0.3	0.2	0.2
Costa Rica	..	-	-	-	-	-	-	-	-	-
Czech Republic	..	258.0	232.8	238.2	280.4	75.6	82.7	85.0	99.3	119.8
Denmark	..	-	-	-	-	10.5	13.1	15.6	10.9	15.4
Estonia	..	-	-	-	-	-	-	-	0.2	-
Finland	..	-	-	-	-	1.3	3.3	7.9	14.0	25.4
France	..	815.5	779.9	380.5	425.2	14.3	9.2	9.5	8.0	18.4
Germany	..	2 526.3	2 612.8	2 616.9	2 939.9	61.7	209.0	216.0	187.8	217.9
Greece	..	-	-	-	-	9.1	19.4	25.2	11.2	13.6
Hungary	..	-	-	499.9	605.0	24.4	25.8	31.9	36.3	41.0
Iceland	..	-	-	-	-	-	-	-	-	-
Ireland	..	-	-	-	-	5.2	6.2	6.0	6.4	6.0
Israel	..	-	-	-	-	-	-	-	0.0	-
Italy	..	1 568.4	1 512.2	1 691.6	1 801.7	79.3	127.4	117.8	128.3	142.1
Japan	..	409.0	392.1	397.0	445.0	1.6	1.3	1.4	2.2	2.0
Korea	..	-	-	-	-	4.8	5.1	4.7	3.4	7.0
Latvia	..	-	-	-	-	0.4	0.4	0.3	0.2	0.2
Lithuania	..	-	-	-	-	0.2	0.4	0.2	0.1	0.3
Luxembourg	..	313.9	275.0	509.9	357.2	5.6	3.8	3.6	4.3	1.1
Mexico	..	259.5	237.6	232.0	235.1	5.0	12.3	10.5	14.5	9.5
Netherlands	..	701.3	595.9	583.3	630.3	243.0	269.0	287.0	211.9	-41.5
New Zealand	..	-	-	-	-	0.0	0.1	0.0	0.0	0.0
Norway	..	-	-	-	-	-	0.0	0.0	-	-
Poland	..	81.4	33.7	41.3	45.9	70.0	89.7	82.8	100.7	108.2
Portugal	..	-	-	-	-	3.9	7.2	5.2	7.0	5.6
Slovak Republic	..	-	-	-	-	13.9	15.3	11.1	10.9	14.5
Slovenia	..	314.0	406.7	483.0	548.3	-	-	-	-	-
Spain	..	-	-	-	-	43.0	58.3	56.0	50.3	66.5
Sweden	..	165.7	181.3	215.2	203.4	9.9	12.9	13.3	31.5	25.0
Switzerland	..	1 335.1	1 405.2	1 473.8	1 621.8	20.3	15.7	13.3	22.2	22.8
Turkey	..	-	-	-	-	8.4	24.1	16.2	14.9	13.1
United Kingdom	..	438.0	877.7	943.1	1 029.3	14.6	-4.8	-5.8	11.8	69.6
United States	..	2 144.2	1 698.3	1 546.9	1 900.2	45.6	68.7	47.9	59.5	61.6
EUROPE	..	**12 841.8**	**13 197.4**	**14 425.4**	**16 064.7**	**5 524.1**	**6 533.9**	**6 468.2**	**6 886.6**	**7 658.9**
Bulgaria	..	-	-	-	-	12.5	13.0	10.7	17.3	12.8
Croatia	..	744.2	876.4	883.5	949.5	1 714.3	2 181.0	2 235.0	2 574.2	2 808.5
Cyprus	..	163.8	235.1	261.4	439.1	40.3	37.3	36.8	45.9	61.0
Malta	..	-	-	-	-	0.0	-0.5	-0.1	0.6	1.3
Montenegro	..	-	-	-	-	182.1	188.5	179.3	175.7	202.7
Romania	..	-	-	-	-	27.2	33.2	21.6	25.6	26.4
Russian Federation	..	599.7	541.1	489.7	481.0	413.2	465.6	408.3	508.0	521.8
Ukraine	..	-	-	-	-	32.4	46.5	49.2	59.4	54.5
AFRICA	..	-	-	-	-	**131.3**	**135.2**	**21.8**	**22.2**	**20.2**
Northern Africa	..	-	-	-	-	5.9	9.5	9.6	1.9	4.7
Algeria	..	-	-	-	-	0.0	0.0	0.0	-	0.0
Egypt	..	-	-	-	-	-	-	-	-	-
Libya	..	-	-	-	-	5.9	8.9	9.0	1.3	4.1
Morocco	..	-	-	-	-	0.0	0.6	0.6	0.7	0.6
Tunisia	..	-	-	-	-	-	-	-	-	-
Other African countries	..	-	-	-	-	125.4	125.7	12.2	20.3	15.5
Nigeria	..	-	-	-	-	-	-	-	-	-
South Africa	..	-	-	-	-	25.9	28.0	27.6	31.0	35.3
AMERICA	..	**2 403.7**	**1 935.9**	**1 779.0**	**2 135.3**	**65.2**	**100.3**	**90.7**	**320.6**	**345.4**
Northern America	..	2 144.2	1 698.3	1 546.9	1 900.2	54.3	77.3	64.9	81.8	89.2
Central America and Caribbean countries	..	259.5	237.6	232.0	235.1	7.6	15.3	13.5	224.0	238.4
Bahamas	..	-	-	-	-	-	-	-	-	-
Bermuda	..	-	-	-	-	-	-	-	-	-
Cayman Islands	..	-	-	-	-	-	-	-	-	-
El Salvador	..	-	-	-	-	-	-	-	-	-
Guatemala	..	-	-	-	-	-	-	-	-	-
Honduras	..	-	-	-	-	-	-	-	-	-
Nicaragua	..	-	-	-	-	-	-	-	-	-
Panama	..	-	-	-	-	2.6	0.8	0.8	0.8	0.9
Virgin Islands, U.S.	..	-	-	-	-	-	-	-	-	-
South America	..	-	-	-	-	3.3	7.7	12.3	14.8	17.7
Argentina	..	-	-	-	-	-	1.5	3.7	8.4	10.1
Bolivia	..	-	-	-	-	-	-	-	-	-
Brazil	..	-	-	-	-	2.5	0.5	0.7	0.3	0.4
Ecuador	..	-	-	-	-	-0.9	-0.9	-0.9	-0.9	0.0
Paraguay	..	-	-	-	-	-	-	-	-	-
Peru	..	-	-	-	-	0.3	2.7	3.0	3.7	3.8
Uruguay	..	-	-	-	-	-	-	-	-	-
Venezuela	..	-	-	-	-	-	-	-	-	-

SLOVENIA

Table 2. Foreign direct investment positions by country *(cont.)*

At year end

Million US dollars

	Inward					Outward				
	2016	2017	2018	2019	2020	2016	2017	2018	2019	2020
ASIA	..	**411.2**	**800.2**	**762.5**	**780.4**	**75.5**	**82.1**	**92.4**	**112.7**	**119.7**
Near and Middle East	..	-	-	-	-	3.6	2.3	2.5	1.4	-1.5
Gulf Arabian countries	..	-	-	-	-	3.5	2.2	2.5	1.4	-1.6
Kuwait	..	-	-	-	-	-	-	-	-	-
Qatar	..	-	-	-	-	-	-	-	-	-
Saudi Arabia	..	-	-	-	-	0.2	0.1	0.1	0.1	0.1
United Arab Emirates	..	-	-	-	-	3.3	2.1	2.3	1.3	-1.7
Other Near and Middle East	..	-	-	-	-	0.1	0.1	0.0	0.0	0.1
Jordan	..	-	-	-	-	-	-	-	-	-
Other Asian countries	..	411.2	800.2	762.5	780.4	72.0	79.8	89.9	111.3	121.3
China	..	2.2	408.1	365.6	335.4	46.1	53.9	64.0	84.6	98.8
Hong Kong, China	..	-	-	-	-	4.6	6.5	4.0	3.2	-1.5
India	..	-	-	-	-	-0.4	0.5	0.7	0.8	0.9
Indonesia	..	-	-	-	-	0.1	0.0	0.0	0.0	0.0
Iran, Islamic Republic of	..	-	-	-	-	-0.1	-0.3	-0.2	0.0	0.0
Malaysia	..	-	-	-	-	0.6	1.2	1.2	1.3	0.2
Philippines	..	-	-	-	-	-	-	-	-	-
Singapore	..	-	-	-	-	1.7	1.3	2.2	1.6	0.8
Chinese Taipei	..	-	-	-	-	-	-	-	0.0	-
Thailand	..	-	-	-	-	1.3	0.2	-0.1	0.3	0.0
Viet Nam	..	-	-	-	-	-	-	-	-	-
AUSTRALIA, OCEANIA AND POLAR REGIONS	..	-	-	-	-	**20.5**	**26.4**	**20.2**	**17.9**	**22.4**
WORLD unallocated and confidential	..	**1 082.1**	**1 531.9**	**1 207.4**	**1 349.5**	**234.9**	**281.4**	**299.4**	**323.6**	**366.8**
European Union (since 01/02/2020)	..	..	..	..	**12 484.1**	..	..	..	..	**3 801.9**
G20 countries excl. European Union	..	**8 762.8**	**9 059.7**	**8 663.3**	**9 592.8**	**751.9**	**1 037.4**	**960.7**	**1 103.8**	**1 258.8**
G20 OECD countries	..	**8 160.9**	**8 110.6**	**7 808.0**	**8 776.4**	**264.3**	**487.2**	**455.5**	**470.5**	**591.4**
G20 Non-OECD countries	..	**601.9**	**949.2**	**855.3**	**816.5**	**487.5**	**550.2**	**505.1**	**633.3**	**667.5**
MENA countries	..	-	-	-	-	**9.5**	**11.7**	**12.0**	**3.3**	**3.1**
ASEAN countries	..	-	-	-	-	**3.7**	**2.7**	**3.3**	**3.3**	**1.0**

- Nil; .. Not available

Note: Inward FDI positions are allocated according to the ultimate investing country. Inward FDI positions by immediate counterpart country are available for more years in the OECD FDI database according to BMD4.Detailed metadata at: *http://metalinks.oecd.org/idi/20220712/6d95*.

Source: *OECD International Direct Investment Statistics (database)*: *https://doi.org/10.1787/idi-data-en*

SLOVENIA

Table 3. Foreign direct investment income by country

Million US dollars

	Inward					Outward				
	2016	2017	2018	2019	2020	2016	2017	2018	2019	2020
WORLD	**1 252.3**	**1 254.8**	**1 565.6**	**1 618.1**	**1 182.6**	**176.5**	**219.7**	**357.3**	**376.4**	**278.8**
OECD COUNTRIES	**1 240.3**	**1 310.9**	**1 437.5**	**1 443.3**	**1 032.8**	**27.0**	**52.6**	**61.4**	**53.5**	**26.5**
Australia	0.1	1.2	-0.5	0.8	0.0	-4.7	-2.4	-1.8	-0.6	0.0
Austria	426.5	458.2	494.5	404.0	298.7	4.7	3.4	4.8	6.7	-3.0
Belgium	21.5	18.6	20.1	18.8	16.5	0.0	0.3	0.3	0.4	0.4
Canada	-0.1	-	-	-	-	0.0	0.5	-2.5	2.7	-0.3
Chile	-	-	-	-	-	-	0.0	0.0	-	-
Colombia	-	-	-	-	-	-	-	-	-	-
Costa Rica	-	-	-	-	-	-	-	-	-	-
Czech Republic	16.0	20.6	15.4	12.9	4.4	9.8	7.6	12.4	10.7	11.6
Denmark	20.6	15.4	18.8	14.9	16.1	0.7	0.7	1.3	1.5	1.1
Estonia	0.1	0.0	-	-0.7	-0.6	-	-	-	-	-
Finland	4.1	2.4	10.3	3.9	2.9	0.1	-0.4	0.1	0.3	2.0
France	103.5	105.7	138.0	56.9	22.3	0.2	-1.5	1.0	-0.1	0.1
Germany	172.6	180.0	172.7	151.8	130.0	7.3	13.3	2.3	8.6	-4.0
Greece	0.9	2.7	3.1	2.5	4.0	0.0	0.3	0.0	-0.6	0.2
Hungary	6.7	11.9	12.3	71.4	41.3	3.7	5.0	4.6	8.1	7.1
Iceland	-	-	-	-	-	-	-	-	-	-
Ireland	-6.9	-0.1	0.6	1.8	1.5	0.7	0.3	0.5	0.9	0.3
Israel	-0.1	0.0	0.2	0.2	1.2	-	-	-	-	-
Italy	96.1	60.9	104.2	100.9	74.1	0.4	11.6	3.4	-0.1	-0.5
Japan	4.0	0.2	3.0	3.4	5.7	-0.5	-0.1	0.0	0.2	0.0
Korea	0.0	-0.3	-0.2	-0.4	-0.1	0.8	0.8	-0.3	-1.0	0.1
Latvia	0.1	0.2	0.1	0.1	0.5	0.1	0.1	0.1	0.1	0.1
Lithuania	0.2	-	-	-	-	0.2	0.2	0.2	0.2	0.2
Luxembourg	102.9	62.0	6.4	111.7	18.6	-	0.5	-	-0.6	-
Mexico	-	-	-	0.2	0.1	-3.0	-1.3	-0.9	-1.7	-0.5
Netherlands	56.6	127.2	139.3	181.0	95.3	3.5	3.8	26.2	0.3	-0.2
New Zealand	0.0	-	-	-	-	-	-	-	-	-
Norway	0.2	1.2	1.0	0.9	1.0	-	-	0.0	-	-
Poland	4.9	3.7	3.3	3.6	0.3	7.0	9.5	10.2	11.8	10.5
Portugal	-	-	-	-	-	0.3	0.3	0.3	0.4	0.2
Slovak Republic	6.2	7.4	-0.6	6.8	6.2	-0.4	-0.7	0.0	0.1	0.7
Slovenia	-	-	-	-	-	-	-	-	-	-
Spain	0.0	1.7	1.1	1.8	-2.4	2.0	1.3	-0.4	1.3	0.8
Sweden	11.5	33.2	33.9	61.0	9.6	0.6	0.9	0.4	1.7	1.8
Switzerland	124.6	137.4	197.1	192.6	219.2	-3.3	0.0	0.6	4.4	2.3
Turkey	-0.3	0.5	0.3	0.0	-1.5	0.3	1.5	2.1	3.9	3.0
United Kingdom	50.3	48.2	39.6	43.9	60.3	-0.1	-0.3	2.6	0.8	3.2
United States	17.8	10.7	23.3	-3.5	7.6	-3.2	-2.1	-6.0	-7.1	-10.7
EUROPE	**1 236.4**	**1 246.7**	**1 523.0**	**1 615.0**	**1 170.5**	**184.1**	**223.0**	**374.5**	**374.6**	**295.6**
Bulgaria	1.0	0.1	0.6	0.3	0.7	1.0	-2.1	-0.3	0.7	0.2
Croatia	-29.7	-103.6	60.3	80.1	36.3	-13.7	35.1	86.1	100.2	54.3
Cyprus	14.7	5.9	4.6	29.1	58.7	9.1	-8.8	0.8	-1.4	0.2
Malta	11.7	11.9	9.2	-16.8	1.3	0.0	-0.5	0.4	0.6	0.7
Montenegro	3.7	2.2	0.5	2.4	2.3	12.8	10.2	13.4	10.1	6.6
Romania	0.1	-	0.2	-0.1	-0.2	1.4	1.0	1.3	0.9	1.9
Russian Federation	-3.5	-3.4	-2.2	1.9	-0.5	23.7	23.3	31.0	39.8	42.2
Ukraine	-0.9	0.2	0.0	0.7	-0.1	12.1	4.5	7.9	18.4	14.0
AFRICA	**-2.9**	**0.0**	**-0.1**	**-0.1**	**-**	**-11.2**	**-0.3**	**-4.2**	**9.6**	**-6.8**
Northern Africa	0.1	0.0	-0.1	-0.1	-	0.7	2.2	0.5	1.2	2.5
Algeria	0.0	-	-	-	-	-	0.0	0.0	0.0	0.0
Egypt	0.0	0.0	-0.1	-0.1	-	-	-	-	-	-
Libya	0.0	-	-	-	-	0.7	2.3	0.5	1.3	2.5
Morocco	0.3	-	-	-	-	0.0	-0.1	0.0	-0.1	-0.1
Tunisia	-0.1	-	-	-	-	-	-	-	-	-
Other African countries	-3.0	-	-	-	-	-11.9	-2.5	-4.7	8.4	-9.2
Nigeria	-	-	-	-	-	-	-	-	-	-
South Africa	0.0	-	-	-	-	0.8	-0.5	1.5	3.8	0.9
AMERICA	**17.9**	**7.4**	**26.5**	**-8.1**	**7.8**	**-7.4**	**-3.0**	**-9.4**	**-6.1**	**-11.5**
Northern America	17.7	10.7	23.3	-3.5	7.6	-3.3	-1.6	-8.4	-4.4	-11.1
Central America and Caribbean countries	0.2	-3.3	3.1	-4.6	0.3	-3.0	-1.3	-0.9	-1.7	-0.5
Bahamas	0.0	-	-	-	-	-	-	-	-	-
Bermuda	-	-	-	-	-	-	-	-	-	-
Cayman Islands	0.0	-	-	-	-	-	-	-	-	-
El Salvador	-	-	-	-	-	-	-	-	-	-
Guatemala	-	-	-	-	-	-	-	-	-	-
Honduras	-	-	-	-	-	-	-	-	-	-
Nicaragua	-	-	-	-	-	-	-	-	-	-
Panama	0.1	-2.2	-0.2	-0.7	-0.3	-	-	-	-	-
Virgin Islands, U.S.	-	-	-	-	-	-	-	-	-	-
South America	0.0	-	-	-	-	-1.2	-0.1	0.0	0.0	0.0
Argentina	0.0	-	-	-	-	-	0.0	0.0	0.0	0.0
Bolivia	-	-	-	-	-	-	-	-	-	-
Brazil	-	-	-	-	-	-0.1	-0.1	0.0	-	-
Ecuador	-	-	-	-	-	-1.0	0.0	-	-	-
Paraguay	-	-	-	-	-	-	-	-	-	-
Peru	-	-	-	-	-	-	0.0	0.0	-	-
Uruguay	-	-	-	-	-	-	-	-	-	-
Venezuela	-	-	-	-	-	-	-	-	-	-

Table 3. Foreign direct investment income by country *(cont.)*

Million US dollars

	Inward					Outward				
	2016	2017	2018	2019	2020	2016	2017	2018	2019	2020
ASIA	**0.0**	**-0.5**	**16.7**	**10.5**	**4.3**	**15.8**	**2.5**	**-1.8**	**-1.2**	**1.5**
Near and Middle East	2.8	0.8	14.5	8.5	5.1	1.3	-1.6	1.0	-1.3	-0.6
Gulf Arabian countries	3.0	0.8	14.3	8.2	3.9	1.3	-1.6	1.0	-1.3	-0.6
Kuwait	-0.1	0.0	0.0	0.0	0.0	-	-	-	-	-
Qatar	-	-	-	-	-	-	-	-	-	-
Saudi Arabia	0.4	0.9	0.4	0.4	0.1	-0.1	0.0	-	-	-
United Arab Emirates	2.7	-0.1	13.9	7.8	3.8	1.4	-1.6	1.0	-1.3	-0.6
Other Near and Middle East	-0.2	0.0	0.2	0.2	1.2	-	0.0	0.0	0.0	0.0
Jordan	0.0	-	-	-	-	-	-	-	-	-
Other Asian countries	-2.8	-1.3	2.2	2.1	-0.8	14.4	4.1	-2.9	0.2	2.2
China	0.2	-0.1	-0.7	-0.8	-4.8	9.1	1.8	-3.6	-0.5	1.1
Hong Kong, China	-6.9	-1.0	0.1	0.0	-1.1	4.3	1.3	1.3	0.8	0.8
India	0.0	0.0	0.0	-	-	-0.2	0.1	0.3	0.0	-
Indonesia	-	-	-	0.0	-0.1	-	-	-	-	-
Iran, Islamic Republic of	-	-	-	-	-	-0.1	-0.1	-	-	-
Malaysia	-	-	0.0	0.0	0.0	-	0.0	-	-	-0.1
Philippines	0.0	-	-	-	-	-	-	-	-	-
Singapore	0.0	0.0	0.1	-0.1	-0.1	0.0	0.0	0.0	0.0	0.1
Chinese Taipei	0.0	-	-	-	-	-	-	-	-	-
Thailand	0.0	-	-	-	-	-	-	-0.9	0.2	0.0
Viet Nam	-	-	-	-	-	-	-	-	-	-
AUSTRALIA, OCEANIA AND POLAR REGIONS	**0.1**	**1.2**	**-0.5**	**0.8**	**0.0**	**-4.7**	**-2.4**	**-1.8**	**-0.6**	**0.0**
WORLD unallocated and confidential	**0.8**	**0.1**	**-**	**0.0**	**0.0**	**0.0**	**0.0**	**0.0**	**-**	**0.0**
European Union (since 01/02/2020)	..	..	..	..	..	..	..	..	..	..
G20 countries excl. European Union	**441.1**	**404.4**	**478.0**	**355.5**	**293.2**	**30.9**	**44.4**	**29.1**	**48.7**	**34.6**
G20 OECD countries	**444.0**	**407.1**	**480.5**	**354.0**	**298.5**	**-2.5**	**19.9**	**-0.1**	**5.7**	**-9.7**
G20 Non-OECD countries	**-3.0**	**-2.7**	**-2.5**	**1.5**	**-5.3**	**33.3**	**24.5**	**29.2**	**43.0**	**44.3**
MENA countries	**3.1**	**0.8**	**14.2**	**8.1**	**3.9**	**2.0**	**0.5**	**1.5**	**-0.1**	**1.8**
ASEAN countries	**0.0**	**0.0**	**0.1**	**-0.1**	**-0.2**	**0.0**	**0.0**	**-0.9**	**0.2**	**0.0**

- Nil; .. Not available

Note: Detailed metadata at: *http://metalinks.oecd.org/idi/20220712/6d95*.

Source: *OECD International Direct Investment Statistics (database)*: *https://doi.org/10.1787/idi-data-en*

SLOVENIA

Table 4. Foreign direct investment flows by industrial sector

Million US dollars

	Inward					Outward				
	2016	2017	2018	2019	2020	2016	2017	2018	2019	2020
All FDI activities	**1 244.7**	**895.8**	**1 383.3**	**1 462.9**	**205.2**	**289.6**	**337.7**	**280.7**	**609.7**	**508.3**
Agriculture, forestry and fishing	**3.5**	**0.3**	**-0.1**	**0.6**	**2.8**	**3.7**	**2.4**	**1.1**	**2.6**	**7.3**
Mining and quarrying	**0.1**	**5.8**	**10.0**	**10.9**	**0.6**	**5.1**	**16.5**	**3.4**	**5.8**	**2.9**
Extraction activities	0.6	6.0	-1.6	7.2	-1.6	-	-	-	-	-
Manufacturing	**508.3**	**254.7**	**817.7**	**355.0**	**-11.8**	**120.3**	**244.9**	**53.0**	**142.7**	**171.1**
of which:										
Food products, beverages and tobacco	207.7	129.8	-1.3	253.6	8.3	6.1	16.5	4.5	18.8	0.9
Textiles, wood and paper products; printing	33.0	59.6	38.8	48.6	-31.6	1.3	0.6	-1.4	6.9	1.1
Chemical, rubber, plastic, non-metallic mineral products	140.6	11.4	125.4	43.0	40.7	41.4	124.7	57.4	66.7	112.4
Metal and machinery products, except electrical equipment	80.4	17.5	95.8	77.5	94.2	55.9	62.6	12.1	29.0	26.4
Motor vehicles, trailers, semi-trailers, other transport equipment	-20.0	-3.9	177.9	-42.7	-116.5	4.6	-14.6	0.5	17.9	-10.3
Other manufacturing	66.6	40.2	381.1	-24.9	-6.9	11.0	55.1	-20.2	3.5	40.7
Electricity, gas, steam and air conditioning supply	**-20.7**	**29.8**	**41.5**	**-3.3**	**71.7**	**14.0**	**40.3**	**27.5**	**11.1**	**17.3**
Water supply; sewerage, waste management and remediation activities	**-0.8**	**1.0**	**3.4**	**11.4**	**0.1**	**0.0**	**1.1**	**-0.4**	**-2.8**	**-0.6**
Construction	**28.7**	**45.4**	**-11.4**	**-13.8**	**30.2**	**6.5**	**6.1**	**-6.7**	**0.5**	**-2.3**
Services	**715.0**	**557.1**	**498.0**	**1 092.0**	**105.2**	**81.0**	**-47.5**	**120.8**	**370.7**	**276.9**
Wholesale and retail trade; repair of motor vehicles and motorcycles	31.6	85.8	220.1	33.1	15.5	68.8	23.1	22.6	100.4	-64.2
Transportation and storage	19.9	-6.8	4.4	-33.4	-1.5	-12.8	2.0	9.5	0.3	-0.7
Accommodation and food service activities	1.1	-11.5	-9.1	3.0	-13.1	-3.5	6.7	0.0	1.5	-1.6
Information and communication	38.2	27.4	55.5	58.1	64.5	13.4	-108.6	-3.3	-37.5	-39.0
Financial and insurance activities	445.9	255.2	114.2	689.2	16.7	21.2	25.3	74.4	207.5	400.5
Activities of holding companies	22.8	190.0	-7.2	130.8	36.2	4.6	-20.8	11.6	191.8	-130.5
Real estate activities	101.0	110.9	64.6	-156.4	68.6	4.9	5.6	4.5	94.0	12.0
Professional, scientific and technical activities	47.1	74.4	30.9	471.0	-33.7	-2.9	0.1	7.9	-2.8	-22.8
Administrative and support service activities	-15.6	17.8	14.7	10.3	-3.4	-10.0	-6.8	3.4	6.1	-12.4
Public administration; activities of households and of extraterritorial organisations	0.0	-	-	-	-	-	-	-	-	-
Education	-0.4	0.2	0.0	0.0	-0.2	0.0	0.0	0.0	0.0	0.0
Human health and social work activities	-0.2	1.1	1.6	13.3	-8.3	-	-	-0.3	-2.3	-0.1
Arts, entertainment and recreation	45.6	2.9	1.4	1.6	-1.2	0.5	1.1	-0.9	-0.4	-0.8
Other services	0.9	0.0	-0.3	2.1	1.4	1.4	4.1	2.9	4.0	5.8
Not allocated and confidential	**10.7**	**1.7**	**24.2**	**10.0**	**6.3**	**59.0**	**73.9**	**82.0**	**79.0**	**35.8**
Private real estate activities	-	-	-	-	-	-	-	-	-	-

- Nil

Note: Detailed metadata at: *http://metalinks.oecd.org/idi/20220712/6d95.*

Source: *OECD International Direct Investment Statistics (database): https://doi.org/10.1787/idi-data-en*

Table 5. Foreign direct investment positions by industrial sector

At year end

Million US dollars

	Inward					Outward				
	2016	2017	2018	2019	2020	2016	2017	2018	2019	2020
All FDI activities	**13 671.8**	**16 738.8**	**17 465.4**	**18 174.3**	**20 329.9**	**6 051.6**	**7 159.3**	**6 992.7**	**7 683.6**	**8 533.3**
Agriculture, forestry and fishing	**19.8**	**26.4**	**26.8**	**29.0**	**34.6**	**40.3**	**49.3**	**30.5**	**34.4**	**41.2**
Mining and quarrying	**46.0**	**61.9**	**68.4**	**61.2**	**66.2**	**26.0**	**42.5**	**45.1**	**49.9**	**57.1**
Extraction activities	33.7	44.8	41.1	34.7	36.1	-	-	-	-	-
Manufacturing	**4 446.8**	**5 567.8**	**6 253.7**	**6 239.0**	**6 805.0**	**1 509.5**	**1 903.6**	**1 914.1**	**2 034.0**	**2 388.4**
of which:										
Food products, beverages and tobacco	522.0	733.6	704.0	673.1	749.2	216.1	266.9	285.1	302.9	334.5
Textiles, wood and paper products; printing	446.3	552.9	536.8	523.6	559.2	6.5	11.6	10.8	13.2	18.8
Chemical, rubber, plastic, non-metallic mineral products	1 602.9	1 904.6	1 943.6	1 980.1	2 211.1	562.3	754.4	709.3	766.6	811.6
Metal and machinery products, except electrical equipment	639.3	852.3	941.0	998.9	1 155.6	183.3	324.2	336.2	352.9	494.6
Motor vehicles, trailers, semi-trailers, other transport equipment	393.5	451.6	583.5	642.6	577.9	161.6	81.9	115.1	135.5	74.5
Other manufacturing	842.9	1 073.0	1 544.9	1 420.8	1 552.0	379.8	464.6	457.7	463.0	654.4
Electricity, gas, steam and air conditioning supply	**350.6**	**439.5**	**447.6**	**448.8**	**569.1**	**143.4**	**198.6**	**248.4**	**250.5**	**229.7**
Water supply; sewerage, waste management and remediation activities	**61.3**	**69.9**	**92.5**	**101.7**	**108.4**	**12.4**	**16.2**	**15.0**	**11.0**	**10.3**
Construction	**162.3**	**262.3**	**230.4**	**197.8**	**262.5**	**62.0**	**109.6**	**38.6**	**41.4**	**67.0**
Services	**8 307.0**	**9 960.9**	**9 957.2**	**10 685.2**	**12 004.8**	**3 089.2**	**3 385.4**	**3 204.7**	**3 578.2**	**3 795.3**
Wholesale and retail trade; repair of motor vehicles and motorcycles	2 629.6	2 968.1	3 092.5	3 129.3	3 482.6	1 303.2	1 451.4	1 358.9	1 425.3	1 348.1
Transportation and storage	307.3	328.3	301.6	242.1	263.3	192.6	192.2	89.5	86.5	92.9
Accommodation and food service activities	102.9	122.7	138.1	158.6	133.0	41.0	53.3	50.7	44.2	46.4
Information and communication	790.1	945.4	976.0	1 027.4	1 143.0	171.9	213.0	182.5	172.9	135.5
Financial and insurance activities	3 080.7	3 682.9	3 379.1	3 905.2	4 564.2	1 016.0	1 050.8	1 123.9	1 357.8	1 763.3
Activities of holding companies	264.4	440.9	384.9	515.9	573.5	398.0	308.0	322.1	501.2	301.4
Real estate activities	834.8	1 089.7	1 203.5	1 122.1	1 296.3	311.8	328.9	316.2	373.9	331.1
Professional, scientific and technical activities	429.5	664.6	661.0	876.9	896.7	52.6	83.8	89.9	97.8	64.0
Administrative and support service activities	77.6	98.7	147.7	146.2	147.0	-41.2	-17.4	-46.2	-20.2	-28.3
Public administration; activities of households and of extraterritorial organisations	0.0	-	-	-	-	-	-	-	-	-
Education	-0.9	-	1.0	1.0	0.9	-0.2	-0.1	-0.1	0.0	0.0
Human health and social work activities	7.4	10.2	10.5	24.6	20.8	1.9	2.2	1.8	-0.6	-0.7
Arts, entertainment and recreation	27.7	27.7	25.5	29.3	30.9	10.4	-3.4	5.2	4.6	3.9
Other services	20.2	22.5	20.8	22.5	26.1	29.2	30.6	32.4	35.9	39.3
Not allocated and confidential	**278.0**	**350.0**	**388.8**	**411.6**	**479.3**	**1 168.8**	**1 454.0**	**1 496.2**	**1 684.3**	**1 944.4**
Private real estate activities	-	-	-	-	-	-	-	-	-	-

- Nil

Note: Detailed metadata at: *http://metalinks.oecd.org/idi/20220712/6d95.*

Source: *OECD International Direct Investment Statistics (database): https://doi.org/10.1787/idi-data-en*

SLOVENIA

Table 6. Foreign direct investment income by industrial sector

Million US dollars

	Inward					Outward				
	2016	2017	2018	2019	2020	2016	2017	2018	2019	2020
All FDI activities	**1 252.3**	**1 254.8**	**1 565.6**	**1 618.1**	**1 182.6**	**176.5**	**219.7**	**357.3**	**376.4**	**278.8**
Agriculture, forestry and fishing	**1.1**	**0.7**	**0.6**	**-1.3**	**-1.7**	**1.4**	**2.9**	**1.8**	**2.6**	**3.0**
Mining and quarrying	**0.0**	**-0.9**	**1.5**	**11.2**	**0.3**	**0.2**	**1.9**	**4.0**	**4.0**	**1.1**
Extraction activities	-1.1	-1.4	-1.9	6.9	-1.9	-	-	-	-	-
Manufacturing	**565.5**	**566.8**	**526.2**	**613.8**	**518.6**	**87.2**	**94.9**	**115.8**	**122.6**	**122.2**
of which:										
Food products, beverages and tobacco	46.7	59.7	74.8	102.4	89.6	21.6	25.1	29.8	25.0	28.1
Textiles, wood and paper products; printing	45.1	29.2	29.1	44.2	57.8	-0.4	0.8	0.5	0.2	1.9
Chemical, rubber, plastic, non-metallic mineral products	183.4	194.4	236.6	226.2	233.3	30.6	38.2	48.4	72.4	69.7
Metal and machinery products, except electrical equipment	92.4	42.3	96.4	80.0	42.2	20.9	38.1	32.6	29.5	25.5
Motor vehicles, trailers, semi-trailers, other transport equipment	62.6	90.9	78.6	36.4	-16.3	-1.1	-30.5	-9.5	-14.4	-25.1
Other manufacturing	135.3	150.3	10.5	124.6	111.9	15.6	23.2	14.0	9.9	22.1
Electricity, gas, steam and air conditioning supply	**-5.7**	**6.7**	**-1.9**	**8.3**	**7.0**	**4.4**	**2.3**	**8.4**	**11.8**	**5.8**
Water supply; sewerage, waste management and remediation activities	**7.2**	**8.1**	**9.7**	**10.2**	**11.4**	**0.3**	**1.1**	**0.2**	**-2.9**	**0.6**
Construction	**0.7**	**3.4**	**28.3**	**8.4**	**14.5**	**1.7**	**0.3**	**-1.7**	**0.1**	**5.8**
Services	**683.4**	**670.0**	**1 001.2**	**967.5**	**632.6**	**80.9**	**116.1**	**227.2**	**238.2**	**140.0**
Wholesale and retail trade; repair of motor vehicles and motorcycles	207.6	127.9	352.8	318.2	216.1	55.0	19.3	64.7	84.6	45.6
Transportation and storage	35.7	27.2	0.8	-13.5	18.9	-11.5	-2.2	-2.5	7.4	-2.1
Accommodation and food service activities	3.3	4.4	8.3	8.8	-14.4	-0.1	-0.2	1.7	2.2	-3.4
Information and communication	64.7	69.2	80.5	78.0	79.8	9.1	10.2	9.6	9.6	8.1
Financial and insurance activities	273.5	276.1	362.8	394.9	259.3	59.2	97.5	135.6	99.5	83.7
Activities of holding companies	21.4	-2.8	11.9	31.3	50.9	12.1	-6.7	27.0	1.9	-0.4
Real estate activities	65.6	89.5	101.6	118.3	26.6	-37.1	-12.6	5.2	31.9	9.5
Professional, scientific and technical activities	40.4	60.7	79.0	52.2	44.5	6.4	5.2	8.1	-4.3	2.0
Administrative and support service activities	-18.1	12.5	10.3	7.6	-0.4	-2.6	-5.7	2.0	5.1	-8.2
Public administration; activities of households and of extraterritorial organisations	0.0	-	-	-	-	-	-	-	-	-
Education	-0.4	-	0.0	0.0	-0.2	0.0	0.0	0.0	0.0	0.0
Human health and social work activities	0.7	1.1	1.6	2.1	2.1	-	-	-0.3	-2.5	-0.3
Arts, entertainment and recreation	8.6	-0.7	0.7	-1.1	-1.2	1.2	1.3	0.8	0.6	-0.9
Other services	1.7	2.2	2.7	2.1	1.4	1.3	3.2	2.4	4.1	6.0
Not allocated and confidential	**0.0**	**0.0**	**0.0**	**0.0**	**-**	**0.5**	**0.2**	**1.7**	**0.0**	**0.2**
Private real estate activities	-	-	-	-	-	-	-	-	-	-

- Nil

Note: Detailed metadata at: *http://metalinks.oecd.org/idi/20220712/6d95.*

Source: OECD *International Direct Investment Statistics (database): https://doi.org/10.1787/idi-data-en*

SPAIN

Table 1. Foreign direct investment flows by country

Million US dollars

	Inward					Outward				
	2016	2017	2018	2019	2020	2016	2017	2018	2019	2020
WORLD	**31 538.2**	**41 876.9**	**57 427.1**	**17 416.3**	**12 607.4**	**43 902.5**	**55 926.1**	**37 522.7**	**24 825.9**	**34 941.3**
OECD COUNTRIES	**29 570.9**	**40 210.8**	**51 711.3**	**18 553.7**	**11 723.1**	**31 354.6**	**46 263.1**	**23 820.4**	**14 879.7**	**25 631.9**
Australia	.. c	.. d	-106.2	119.8	-8.0	.. d	574.9	339.9	-40.3	650.7
Austria	.. c	125.1	-123.9	78.4	-458.1	.. d	688.8	-62.6	231.7	794.3
Belgium	-613.7	-812.8	1 271.1	1 294.1	2 021.7	496.5	1.1	79.1	831.7	299.7
Canada	.. d	48.5	-214.8	89.6	-455.8	.. d	.. d	-5 172.9	270.9	788.6
Chile	.. c	22.5	-5.9	84.0	-120.8	2 945.9	-9 475.8	764.8	1 525.8	-274.6
Colombia	.. d	165.7	466.2	-341.4	483.2	1 375.7	1 117.1	260.8	793.7	2 344.2
Costa Rica	.. c	.. d	389.5	-91.8	25.1	74.1	.. d	313.9	113.1	-912.8
Czech Republic	.. c	81.2	273.8	56.0	-45.6	.. d	103.7	101.5	106.3	96.9
Denmark	.. d	-308.9	238.4	-189.2	-180.1	.. d	.. d	206.5	-904.5	605.1
Estonia	.. c	-6.8	-2.4	-3.4	-	.. c	11.3	11.8	10.1	12.5
Finland	.. d	119.5	-8.3	-47.0	261.0	.. c	.. d	513.4	-164.6	180.1
France	3 236.8	2 427.0	3 066.2	-1 981.4	740.7	1 638.8	3 899.2	2 458.4	1 702.7	2 648.4
Germany	4 997.2	4 912.6	9 216.3	2 113.5	2 182.3	1 946.3	971.7	-1 725.5	-482.5	2 045.6
Greece	.. c	.. d	42.5	-358.2	29.6	.. d	-82.3	-31.9	-623.5	26.2
Hungary	-327.3	5.6	102.7	31.3	-13.7	.. c	90.2	198.3	-1 184.4	-5.7
Iceland	.. c	.. d	.. d	4.5	-1.1	.. c	-1.1	2.4	-1.1	-1.1
Ireland	125.0	5 622.8	-613.7	260.8	378.3	-2 992.4	2 769.7	370.6	4 530.4	586.9
Israel	.. c	.. d	3.5	6.7	4.6	.. c	22.5	362.3	31.3	18.2
Italy	273.1	-7 963.0	7 653.7	1 218.0	-4 109.4	1 299.3	1 254.7	-433.1	-787.0	1 252.4
Japan	.. d	.. d	4 620.6	672.8	597.2	.. c	24.8	-231.3	62.7	-2.3
Korea	56.4	.. d	88.5	445.5	86.6	.. d	.. d	1 410.4	34.7	-23.9
Latvia	.. c	.. c	- d	.. d	-1.1	.. c	.. c	7.1	-305.6	2.3
Lithuania	.. c	-	-	-	-	.. c	37.2	2.4	-36.9	-79.8
Luxembourg	3 083.0	5 993.7	16 377.9	6 507.3	-2 287.2	4 707.5	.. d	4 076.5	-624.7	3 326.5
Mexico	.. d	104.8	-177.0	-292.2	10 547.0	4 497.4	3 151.8	2 892.7	3 621.4	4 762.4
Netherlands	6 856.1	13 971.4	2 600.0	5 466.2	-17 873.5	-11 090.3	20.3	2 389.9	8 326.4	-2 988.0
New Zealand	.. c	15.8	-62.6	10.1	26.2	.. c	1.1	-	611.2	5.7
Norway	.. d	.. d	59.0	32.5	-19.4	.. d	269.4	394.2	255.2	304.3
Poland	.. d	84.5	3 014.3	54.9	-175.5	339.5	617.7	856.8	-70.5	290.6
Portugal	498.7	242.4	-155.8	3 468.0	-604.0	.. c	918.7	2 637.8	1 863.9	2 479.8
Slovak Republic	.. c	-3.4	-9.4	28.0	1.1	267.6	120.6	241.9	-23.5	123.1
Slovenia	.. c	1.1	-2.4	.. d	- d	.. c	2.3	2.4	1.1	3.4
Spain	-	-	-	..	..	-	-	-	..	..
Sweden	531.9	348.3	347.0	769.1	275.8	.. d	19.2	106.2	175.8	952.7
Switzerland	517.5	669.6	-1 018.5	162.3	12 948.1	.. c	-497.1	337.5	483.6	-116.2
Turkey	.. c	-18.0	-5.9	-66.0	.. d	.. d	3 079.7	1 354.9	1 169.8	813.7
United Kingdom	6 699.1	5 682.6	2 106.7	-427.6	8 480.9	.. d	21 733.7	5 445.5	-8 539.1	4 692.9
United States	.. d	8 480.4	3 132.3	-1 053.4	-1 029.1	14 355.9	14 821.3	3 912.4	2 822.1	-982.3
EUROPE	**26 952.3**	**30 695.5**	**44 451.8**	**19 503.0**	**1 682.1**	**9 039.0**	**35 746.8**	**20 234.9**	**4 633.4**	**18 975.5**
Bulgaria	.. c	-	1.2	1.1	-	.. c	.. d	11.8	-11.2	1.1
Croatia	.. c	-	1.2	-	-	.. c	23.7	-3.5	-12.3	33.0
Cyprus	.. c	240.1	-489.8	199.3	4.6	.. c	-50.7	-7.1	-7.8	-85.5
Malta	288.6	.. d	192.4	6.7	214.2	.. c	51.9	188.8	-79.5	-67.2
Montenegro	.. c	-	- d	-	-	.. c	.. d	-1.2	-4.5	-3.4
Romania	.. d	.. d	48.4	467.9	-70.7	.. c	-19.2	-30.7	49.3	17.1
Russian Federation	.. d	.. d	112.1	118.7	51.3	.. d	.. d	220.7	-2 643.0	158.4
Ukraine	.. c	-16.9	-82.6	6.7	222.2	.. c	-30.4	14.2	-192.5	-150.4
AFRICA	**.. d**	**.. d**	**-181.8**	**-50.4**	**101.4**	**426.8**	**.. d**	**-719.9**	**617.9**	**1 435.9**
Northern Africa	.. c	.. d	.. d	.. d	.. d	212.3	370.9	-1 043.3	509.3	723.6
Algeria	.. c	.. c	.. d	.. d	.. d	.. d	110.5	8.3	19.0	447.9
Egypt	.. c	.. d	.. d	.. d	.. d	.. c	.. d	69.6	26.9	34.2
Libya	.. c	.. c	.. d	.. d	.. d	.. c	.. c	-77.9	-32.5	153.8
Morocco	.. c	.. d	-28.3	-34.7	-21.7	.. d	296.5	-1 077.5	478.0	75.2
Tunisia	.. c	.. c	.. d	.. d	.. d	.. c	.. d	35.4	17.9	12.5
Other African countries	.. d	-30.4	.. d	- d	.. d	.. d	.. d	322.2	109.7	712.3
Nigeria	.. c	.. c	-24.8	-1.1	-6.8	.. c	1.1	4.7	3.4	21.7
South Africa	.. c	.. c	-153.4	17.9	42.2	.. c	156.7	85.0	2.2	-35.3
AMERICA	**2 522.4**	**9 342.8**	**-1 168.4**	**-3 473.6**	**7 017.7**	**.. d**	**17 761.2**	**13 783.8**	**17 639.1**	**10 549.3**
Northern America	308.5	8 528.9	2 916.3	-962.7	-1 484.9	14 870.1	16 992.4	-1 261.7	3 093.0	-192.6
Central America and Caribbean countries	2 995.7	-2 380.8	-1 194.4	-2 836.7	9 659.3	5 592.2	2 945.6	4 275.9	4 154.3	4 737.3
Bahamas	.. c	-15.8	-1.2	.. d	5.7	.. c	.. c	-2.4	56.0	12.5
Bermuda	.. c	.. d	-4.7	4.5	2.3	.. d	.. c	8.3	13.4	37.6
Cayman Islands	.. d	-2 765.2	348.2	-38.1	-28.5	.. d	.. d	-1 603.9	-38.1	240.5
El Salvador	.. c	-	-	4.5	-5.7	-60.8	.. d	53.1	218.3	175.5
Guatemala	.. c	-16.9	-2.4	9.0	.. d	.. d	.. d	250.2	63.8	37.6
Honduras	.. c	1.1	.. d	- d	8.0	.. c	-24.8	-5.9	61.6	-35.3
Nicaragua	.. c	-	- d	- d	- d	.. c	.. d	10.6	-392.9	-5.7
Panama	.. d	25.9	244.3	-1 629.9	-688.3	.. d	266.0	666.8	-267.5	201.7
Virgin Islands, U.S.	.. c	-	-	-	-	.. c	-	-	-	-
South America	.. d	3 194.7	-2 891.5	325.8	-1 157.8	12 134.2	-2 176.8	10 769.5	10 392.9	6 005.7
Argentina	801.7	92.4	2.4	69.4	43.3	.. d	1 701.0	3 033.2	1 918.7	365.8
Bolivia	.. c	-29.3	-3.5	-146.6	134.5	141.5	112.7	-28.3	199.3	-134.5
Brazil	-1 172.2	21.4	-3 452.1	310.1	-266.7	3 517.6	2 132.8	5 365.3	2 955.3	2 719.1
Ecuador	.. c	.. d	-	-9.0	-233.6	.. c	154.4	114.5	648.2	248.4
Paraguay	.. c	-	-22.4	21.3	-	.. c	.. d	-23.6	17.9	46.7
Peru	.. c	-91.3	109.8	34.7	-65.0	899.0	148.8	219.5	-219.4	274.6
Uruguay	.. d	2 673.9	-108.6	227.2	-1 359.5	.. d	2 628.8	702.2	1 243.7	-51.3
Venezuela	-219.0	.. c	123.9	76.1	226.8	.. d	-767.7	312.8	1 239.2	445.6

SPAIN

Table 1. Foreign direct investment flows by country *(cont.)*

Million US dollars

	Inward					Outward				
	2016	2017	2018	2019	2020	2016	2017	2018	2019	2020
ASIA	**.. d**	**1 704.4**	**14 182.7**	**1 019.8**	**3 646.7**	**2 088.9**	**1 387.7**	**3 888.8**	**1 434.0**	**3 195.4**
Near and Middle East	.. d	861.2	4 458.9	-756.7	1 702.6	90.7	.. d	2 225.9	901.2	1 087.2
Gulf Arabian countries	.. d	853.3	4 456.5	-803.8	1 678.6	98.4	361.9	1 881.3	860.9	1 066.7
Kuwait	.. c	18.0	.. d	.. d	.. d	.. c	.. d	51.9	-30.2	47.9
Qatar	.. c	.. c	3 759.0	-195.9	1 573.8	.. d	25.9	51.9	-25.7	-1.1
Saudi Arabia	.. c	.. d	-20.1	-49.3	-22.8	80.7	286.3	135.7	455.6	416.0
United Arab Emirates	.. d	1 099.1	755.3	-362.7	157.3	.. c	-15.8	1 635.8	450.0	511.7
Other Near and Middle East	.. c	.. d	2.4	47.0	23.9	.. c	67.6	344.6	40.3	20.5
Jordan	.. c	-	- d	- d	-	.. c	21.4	-1.2	3.4	2.3
Other Asian countries	.. d	844.3	9 723.8	1 776.6	1 944.2	.. d	.. d	1 662.9	532.9	2 108.3
China	.. d	-162.3	1 555.5	150.0	248.4	.. d	.. d	381.2	107.5	1 974.9
Hong Kong, China	.. c	524.2	568.9	156.7	804.6	.. d	-73.3	203.0	199.3	128.8
India	.. d	24.8	54.3	49.3	20.5	.. d	502.8	345.8	174.6	131.1
Indonesia	.. c	.. c	50.7	85.1	-9.1	.. c	.. d	40.1	17.9	-2.3
Iran, Islamic Republic of	.. c	-	-	-	-	.. c	-	9.4	-1.1	-1.1
Malaysia	.. c	.. d	-1.2	12.3	44.4	.. d	122.9	147.5	-174.6	-197.2
Philippines	.. c	-4.5	14.2	3.4	2.3	.. c	22.5	-715.2	20.2	6.8
Singapore	.. d	1.1	2 775.9	199.3	140.2	.. d	226.6	43.7	24.6	-63.8
Chinese Taipei	.. c	.. c	-	-	-	.. c	36.1	-17.7	45.9	62.7
Thailand	.. c	-	-4.7	5.6	4.6	.. c	14.7	10.6	4.5	34.2
Viet Nam	.. c	-	- d	-2.2	3.4	.. c	.. d	9.4	3.4	6.8
AUSTRALIA, OCEANIA AND POLAR REGIONS	**.. d**	**.. d**	**-167.6**	**129.9**	**19.4**	**.. d**	**563.6**	**367.0**	**557.5**	**656.4**
WORLD unallocated and confidential	**.. d**	**.. d**	**310.4**	**287.7**	**140.2**	**.. d**	**.. d**	**-31.9**	**-56.0**	**128.8**
European Union (since 01/02/2020)	..	..	..	..	..	..	..	..	..	..
G20 countries excl. European Union	**.. d**	**..**	**27 529.8**	**1 589.6**	**.. d**	**.. d**	**..**	**19 858.4**	**2 824.4**	**22 373.8**
G20 OECD countries	**.. d**	**..**	**29 380.4**	**838.5**	**.. d**	**.. d**	**..**	**10 251.4**	**-164.6**	**16 646.2**
G20 Non-OECD countries	**.. d**	**..**	**-1 850.6**	**751.1**	**107.1**	**.. d**	**..**	**9 607.0**	**2 988.9**	**5 727.6**
MENA countries	**.. d**	**..**	**.. d**	**.. d**	**.. d**	**.. d**	**..**	**834.4**	**1 378.0**	**1 799.4**
ASEAN countries	**-214.5**	**95.8**	**2 836.1**	**302.3**	**185.8**	**.. d**	**405.8**	**-463.8**	**-101.9**	**-215.4**

- Nil; .. Not available; c Confidential data; d Secondary Confidentiality

Note: Detailed metadata at: *http://metalinks.oecd.org/idi/20220712/6d95*.

Source: *OECD International Direct Investment Statistics (database)*: *https://doi.org/10.1787/idi-data-en*

SPAIN

Table 2. Foreign direct investment positions by country

At year end

Million US dollars

	Inward					Outward				
	2016	2017	2018	2019	2020	2016	2017	2018	2019	2020
WORLD	**591 525.2**	**717 944.4**	**751 615.5**	**769 238.4**	**865 741.8**	**539 109.3**	**623 869.0**	**600 090.5**	**620 147.2**	**626 168.9**
OECD COUNTRIES	..	**609 166.5**	**644 582.1**	**662 273.6**	..	**401 958.5**	**469 104.1**	**442 682.6**	**450 874.0**	**479 899.4**
Australia	..	4 501.1	7 891.0	7 915.1	..	908.6	1 555.5	1 491.9	1 464.8	2 345.1
Austria	..	1 017.0	1 181.6	1 270.5	..	741.0	1 851.8	1 630.4	1 471.6	2 190.5
Belgium	..	11 970.5	12 486.8	12 842.1	..	4 410.2	4 757.7	4 334.8	4 071.0	4 747.8
Canada	..	5 480.9	5 664.1	8 290.3	..	13 896.9	16 464.4	10 346.9	12 374.7	13 217.6
Chile	..	485.7	534.7	642.6	..	29 054.5	22 416.6	21 757.5	21 239.0	22 617.5
Colombia	..	3 966.2	3 820.7	3 073.5	..	6 965.3	8 563.2	8 502.4	9 524.8	11 805.1
Costa Rica	..	209.9	637.7	774.0	..	1 718.1	1 912.9	1 899.5	2 136.6	1 260.3
Czech Republic	..	133.1	41.2	44.9	..	855.9	1 092.6	1 173.6	1 184.0	1 373.2
Denmark	..	4 752.9	5 219.8	5 544.8	..	1 189.0	501.3	945.7	320.2	1 086.0
Estonia	..	-21.6	-21.8	-	..	22.1	28.8	29.8	31.5	47.9
Finland	..	563.7	593.1	524.6	..	138.1	84.0	523.2	332.5	558.4
France	..	85 638.0	85 254.2	85 943.6	..	15 324.1	22 541.4	24 414.9	27 978.0	31 400.2
Germany	..	76 871.0	81 475.8	84 293.4	..	22 639.4	28 000.7	26 022.4	23 917.1	26 949.3
Greece	..	376.6	312.6	302.2	..	809.5	782.0	708.7	863.9	1 142.5
Hungary	..	25.2	21.8	20.2	..	.. c	1 169.3	1 186.2	924.5	954.7
Iceland	..	30.0	29.8	31.5	..	6.3	6.0	8.0	7.9	7.4
Ireland	..	7 817.2	8 485.2	8 878.9	..	10 073.8	13 884.6	11 126.6	14 366.4	16 387.3
Israel	..	513.3	830.1	990.8	..	70.6	148.7	148.8	148.3	173.0
Italy	..	46 922.5	52 177.7	54 497.9	..	9 426.6	12 362.7	12 444.5	12 609.5	14 269.2
Japan	..	8 977.0	12 599.0	11 953.5	..	358.4	421.0	338.9	406.7	424.6
Korea	..	957.1	874.7	1 166.0	..	476.4	525.3	1 880.0	1 854.6	1 947.5
Latvia	..	7.2	17.2	24.7	..	3.2	237.5	234.7	6.7	9.8
Lithuania	..	3.6	4.6	10.1	..	15.8	54.0	52.7	30.3	-51.5
Luxembourg	..	22 146.8	19 026.8	21 413.2	..	7 972.0	9 068.1	10 151.1	10 520.1	15 206.8
Mexico	..	36 266.5	36 219.4	34 850.6	..	35 279.9	43 500.8	41 811.3	43 556.5	45 624.0
Netherlands	..	28 632.8	28 386.8	31 947.9	..	-2 862.9	-5 837.1	-7 636.8	6 834.4	726.5
New Zealand	..	791.6	703.0	82.0	..	.. d	30.0	29.8	122.4	137.4
Norway	..	6 393.6	6 700.3	6 901.8	..	2 430.7	3 129.0	3 226.5	3 783.4	4 238.6
Poland	..	232.7	507.2	378.6	..	7 766.4	11 214.9	10 851.8	8 971.0	7 069.6
Portugal	..	7 060.4	14 692.0	14 938.2	..	24 503.0	27 338.7	23 828.7	23 714.9	28 581.4
Slovak Republic	..	24.0	25.2	268.5	..	565.0	737.6	556.4	504.4	686.0
Slovenia	..	3.6	3.4	3.4	..	4.2	8.4	9.2	6.7	11.0
Spain	..	18 486.4	20 004.6	19 456.3	..	-	-	-	..	..
Sweden	..	12 417.8	12 373.5	13 653.1	..	1 165.8	1 165.7	1 181.6	1 268.3	2 542.6
Switzerland	..	24 035.7	22 262.4	23 459.9	..	14 659.0	14 866.9	12 610.5	11 701.9	8 705.4
Turkey	..	313.0	193.5	116.8	..	7 027.5	9 363.2	5 733.9	6 618.7	5 720.9
United Kingdom	..	110 229.1	110 180.9	104 323.7	..	91 625.4	124 690.6	122 176.6	106 667.0	109 501.8
United States	..	85 113.9	97 630.0	105 289.8	..	77 593.5	100 995.4	97 351.7	101 003.1	97 548.2
EUROPE	..	**481 892.5**	**501 599.5**	**507 337.7**	..	**249 828.2**	**289 936.4**	**273 516.1**	**275 543.7**	**290 603.8**
Bulgaria	..	-	-	3.4	..	407.9	706.4	680.1	649.3	711.7
Croatia	..	6.0	5.7	5.6	..	109.6	153.5	146.6	128.1	175.5
Cyprus	..	332.2	656.1	415.6	..	577.6	642.8	731.6	377.4	360.8
Malta	..	365.8	475.2	478.5	..	480.7	471.3	498.1	687.5	662.7
Montenegro	..	-	8.0	-	..	5.3	9.6	9.2	4.5	2.5
Romania	..	-7.2	-3.4	22.5	..	1 138.4	1 184.9	950.3	966.1	1 041.8
Russian Federation	..	3 663.9	3 777.2	4 477.6	..	952.9	1 409.2	1 025.9	632.4	725.2
Ukraine	..	27.6	26.3	11.2	..	71.7	67.2	80.1	59.5	60.1
AFRICA	..	**1 081.8**	**1 047.6**	**1 136.8**	..	**5 600.3**	**6 908.1**	**6 589.2**	**6 749.0**	**8 592.5**
Northern Africa	..	633.2	674.4	726.8	..	3 657.6	4 352.4	4 268.4	4 424.8	5 486.6
Algeria	..	52.8	77.9	125.8	..	247.7	376.6	348.1	202.2	689.7
Egypt	..	-	19.5	23.6	..	845.4	891.1	952.6	912.2	968.2
Libya	..	413.8	400.7	392.0	..	-26.4	183.5	400.7	180.9	381.6
Morocco	..	100.7	107.6	115.7	..	2 410.7	2 735.7	2 406.7	2 948.8	3 244.6
Tunisia	..	66.0	68.7	70.8	..	179.2	165.5	160.3	182.0	202.5
Other African countries	..	448.5	372.1	410.0	..	1 942.7	2 554.6	2 320.8	2 324.2	3 105.9
Nigeria	..	46.8	130.5	22.5	..	-	-	24.0	30.3	45.4
South Africa	..	349.0	172.9	344.9	..	1 078.3	1 277.3	1 206.8	1 222.2	1 116.7
AMERICA	..	**170 147.5**	**181 787.3**	**197 248.9**	..	**271 534.7**	**311 866.2**	**302 185.7**	**320 605.5**	**305 074.2**
Northern America	..	90 594.9	103 294.0	113 580.1	..	91 489.4	117 459.8	107 698.6	113 377.9	110 767.0
Central America and Caribbean countries	..	44 054.9	47 625.4	47 347.8	..	47 667.3	57 392.7	55 796.9	58 501.5	60 941.2
Bahamas	..	492.9	380.1	297.7	..	47.4	84.0	428.2	476.3	484.7
Bermuda	..	151.1	3 804.7	3 900.2	..	.. c	731.6	720.2	785.2	828.3
Cayman Islands	..	518.1	496.9	761.6	..	1 640.1	3 043.9	1 177.0	906.5	1 147.4
El Salvador	..	10.8	3.4	3.4	..	734.7	704.0	567.9	904.3	1 078.7
Guatemala	..	657.2	675.5	292.1	..	788.4	1 140.6	998.4	844.8	979.3
Honduras	..	8.4	10.3	11.2	..	145.5	110.3	105.3	129.2	96.9
Nicaragua	..	12.0	17.2	16.9	..	227.7	225.5	211.8	104.5	100.6
Panama	..	2 270.3	2 236.1	2 544.4	..	2 686.8	2 303.9	2 818.9	2 614.0	2 883.8
Virgin Islands, U.S.	..	-	4.6	10.1	..	-	-	-	-	-
South America	..	35 497.7	30 867.9	36 321.1	..	132 378.0	137 013.7	138 690.2	148 725.0	133 366.1
Argentina	..	7 691.3	7 602.5	9 264.2	..	17 112.9	21 825.4	25 042.4	23 853.1	18 430.5
Bolivia	..	30.0	18.3	16.9	..	2 052.3	2 236.7	2 032.3	2 390.5	2 288.6
Brazil	..	10 829.9	7 553.2	7 826.3	..	58 125.9	61 147.8	60 783.1	66 017.7	52 051.8
Ecuador	..	127.1	129.4	139.3	..	4 031.8	4 219.2	4 718.3	4 649.5	4 938.0
Paraguay	..	-	-	-	..	638.8	617.7	466.0	460.6	461.4
Peru	..	1 158.6	1 213.6	905.4	..	4 648.5	5 331.0	4 258.1	5 202.2	5 302.5
Uruguay	..	4 928.0	4 799.6	9 869.7	..	5 138.6	6 965.7	6 976.2	10 366.2	9 639.2
Venezuela	..	6 280.9	5 195.8	4 582.1	..	4 546.2	3 607.6	4 022.2	4 855.1	5 633.8

Table 2. Foreign direct investment positions by country *(cont.)*

At year end

Million US dollars

	Inward					Outward				
	2016	2017	2018	2019	2020	2016	2017	2018	2019	2020
ASIA	..	**47 085.6**	**48 146.3**	**45 130.3**	..	**11 204.8**	**13 625.6**	**16 362.5**	**15 806.6**	**19 435.5**
Near and Middle East	..	13 102.7	15 234.7	16 077.3	..	1 484.1	1 911.7	3 794.4	4 018.2	5 236.2
Gulf Arabian countries	..	11 947.7	13 742.8	14 914.6	..	1 397.7	1 698.2	3 615.8	3 832.8	5 017.8
Kuwait	..	845.5	722.5	439.2	..	51.7	135.5	258.8	248.3	311.7
Qatar	..	4 459.1	4 885.5	5 240.4	..	140.2	117.5	178.6	183.1	193.9
Saudi Arabia	..	835.9	699.6	669.5	..	796.9	1 007.4	1 065.9	802.1	1 208.7
United Arab Emirates	..	5 540.9	7 214.3	8 371.2	..	254.0	244.7	1 970.5	2 447.8	3 049.5
Other Near and Middle East	..	1 155.0	1 493.0	1 162.7	..	86.4	213.5	178.6	186.5	217.2
Jordan	..	-	-	-	..	-16.9	3.6	-	6.7	12.3
Other Asian countries	..	33 983.0	32 910.5	29 053.0	..	9 720.7	11 713.8	12 568.1	11 787.2	14 200.5
China	..	17 420.2	10 064.1	5 726.8	..	3 068.4	3 547.6	3 574.5	3 475.6	5 535.6
Hong Kong, China	..	907.9	2 375.8	1 809.7	..	2 308.4	2 610.9	2 284.2	1 914.2	1 907.0
India	..	296.2	371.0	424.6	..	1 361.9	1 778.6	2 041.4	1 533.4	1 841.9
Indonesia	..	15.6	18.3	19.1	..	42.2	105.5	83.6	158.4	155.8
Iran, Islamic Republic of	..	6.0	3.4	89.9	..	10.5	10.8	19.5	15.7	16.0
Malaysia	..	277.0	235.9	16.9	..	1 037.2	1 156.2	1 268.6	1 038.0	884.8
Philippines	..	682.4	957.2	679.6	..	.. c	704.0	95.0	96.6	106.8
Singapore	..	4 315.2	3 542.5	4 686.6	..	413.2	593.7	682.4	811.1	724.0
Chinese Taipei	..	7.2	9.2	92.1	..	25.3	60.0	65.3	131.4	208.6
Thailand	..	100.7	1 818.2	2 342.2	..	84.3	112.7	113.4	126.9	164.4
Viet Nam	..	-	-	-	..	12.6	12.0	26.3	28.1	36.8
AUSTRALIA, OCEANIA AND POLAR REGIONS	..	**5 393.4**	**8 684.5**	**8 136.4**	..	**.. d**	**1 583.1**	**1 518.2**	**1 581.7**	**2 477.6**
WORLD unallocated and confidential	..	**12 343.5**	**10 350.4**	**10 248.3**	..	**.. d**	**-50.4**	**-81.3**	**-139.3**	**-14.7**
European Union (since 01/02/2020)	..	**333 986.6**	**351 989.9**	..	..	..	**134 197.6**	**126 768.9**	..	**159 428.2**
G20 countries excl. European Union	..	**502 372.3**	**520 419.1**	**527 393.8**	..	..	**452 519.8**	**438 836.7**	**436 145.8**	**430 014.7**
G20 OECD countries	..	**461 270.1**	**490 160.3**	**498 640.8**	..	..	**360 421.0**	**344 013.1**	**338 450.9**	**348 948.3**
G20 Non-OECD countries	..	**41 102.2**	**30 258.8**	**28 753.1**	..	..	**92 098.8**	**94 823.7**	**97 694.9**	**81 066.4**
MENA countries	..	**13 223.8**	**15 079.0**	**15 814.4**	..	..	**6 077.0**	**7 902.5**	**8 286.9**	**10 544.9**
ASEAN countries	..	**5 391.0**	**6 570.9**	**7 745.5**	..	**2 039.6**	**2 685.3**	**2 271.6**	**2 261.3**	**2 075.1**

- Nil; .. Not available; c Confidential data; d Secondary Confidentiality

Note: Inward FDI positions are allocated according to the ultimate investing country. Inward FDI positions by immediate counterpart country are available for more years, including for the most recent year in the OECD FDI database according to BMD4.Detailed metadata at: *http://metalinks.oecd.org/idi/20220712/6d95*.

Source: *OECD International Direct Investment Statistics (database)*: *https://doi.org/10.1787/idi-data-en*

Table 3. Foreign direct investment income by country

Million US dollars

	Inward					Outward				
	2016	2017	2018	2019	2020	2016	2017	2018	2019	2020
WORLD	**23 652.5**	**28 808.5**	**32 970.6**	**32 175.1**	**26 825.1**	**33 708.9**	**36 231.5**	**43 159.4**	**42 329.6**	**34 151.6**
OECD COUNTRIES	**22 342.1**	**26 277.8**	**29 653.0**	**29 094.4**	**24 257.6**	**22 331.1**	**26 904.5**	**30 850.9**	**30 795.9**	**25 701.4**
Australia	.. c	-	5.9	-	1.1	.. d	94.7	75.5	52.6	65.0
Austria	.. d	154.4	211.3	166.8	185.8	.. d	.. d	-180.6	137.7	33.0
Belgium	.. d	.. d	411.9	456.7	420.5	.. d	299.9	367.0	287.7	241.6
Canada	.. c	.. d	217.2	54.9	72.9	.. d	295.3	188.8	197.0	127.6
Chile	.. c	1.1	20.1	20.2	.. d	.. d	1 370.8	1 526.0	990.7	1 091.7
Colombia	-108.4	.. d	-70.8	-26.9	-26.2	.. d	414.8	384.8	659.4	436.5
Costa Rica	.. c	.. d	-4.7	29.1	8.0	.. d	.. d	66.1	99.6	94.6
Czech Republic	.. c	.. d	8.3	9.0	4.6	.. d	115.0	92.1	92.9	101.4
Denmark	.. d	191.6	193.6	135.5	145.9	.. d	.. d	210.1	382.9	387.5
Estonia	.. c	.. c	.. c	2.2	-	.. c	2.3	.. c	3.4	3.4
Finland	.. d	.. d	61.4	50.4	54.7	.. c	7.9	13.0	4.5	4.6
France	.. d	4 470.7	5 180.0	4 743.1	3 929.3	.. d	1 262.5	1 448.1	1 419.5	1 136.2
Germany	.. d	2 500.3	3 651.6	3 127.7	2 797.7	.. d	378.8	919.4	911.2	808.0
Greece	.. c	.. d	22.4	12.3	25.1	.. d	.. d	60.2	38.1	28.5
Hungary	.. c	.. d	3.5	-9.0	2.3	.. c	233.3	152.2	80.6	82.1
Iceland	.. c	.. c	5.9	5.6	.. c	.. c	-	-	- d	- d
Ireland	.. d	250.3	306.9	398.5	393.2	549.6	437.4	22.4	510.5	604.0
Israel	.. c	-	9.4	9.0	8.0	.. c	.. d	13.0	12.3	12.5
Italy	.. d	2 475.5	1 502.4	2 134.8	1 570.4	.. d	804.9	899.3	783.6	702.0
Japan	.. d	195.0	276.2	634.7	378.3	.. c	-6.8	14.2	29.1	12.5
Korea	.. c	.. d	69.6	44.8	51.3	.. c	.. d	.. d	.. d	30.8
Latvia	.. c	.. c	1.2	- d	-	.. c	.. c	.. c	.. c	.. c
Lithuania	.. c	.. c	-	2.2	1.1	.. c	.. d	-	.. c	.. c
Luxembourg	723.2	3 287.1	4 051.7	4 531.5	3 720.8	.. c	452.0	454.4	89.6	321.4
Mexico	.. d	112.7	127.5	162.3	173.2	.. d	5 286.9	6 146.6	6 065.2	4 642.7
Netherlands	.. d	5 516.9	6 475.9	5 476.3	4 431.9	990.8	1 321.2	2 034.7	4 566.2	3 303.7
New Zealand	.. c	24.8	-47.2	6.7	8.0	.. c	.. d	7.1	4.5	5.7
Norway	.. d	.. d	56.7	69.4	34.2	.. d	444.1	483.9	419.8	322.5
Poland	.. d	-184.9	-142.8	-38.1	-20.5	.. d	541.1	670.4	433.2	287.2
Portugal	.. d	127.4	-16.5	277.6	315.7	.. d	1 916.4	2 567.0	1 889.6	1 548.7
Slovak Republic	.. c	.. c	.. c	3.4	1.1	56.4	75.5	57.8	16.8	25.1
Slovenia	.. c	.. c	.. c	.. c	.. c	.. c	.. c	1.2	1.1	.. c
Spain	..	..	..	..	..	..	..	..	..	..
Sweden	.. d	269.4	289.2	380.6	295.2	.. d	172.5	374.1	203.7	246.2
Switzerland	.. d	1 586.1	1 662.9	1 652.3	1 376.6	.. d	360.7	479.2	493.7	338.5
Turkey	.. c	12.4	-17.7	- d	.. d	.. d	.. d	1 528.4	1 146.3	792.0
United Kingdom	.. d	3 043.6	3 193.7	3 436.7	2 672.4	4 732.9	7 286.7	8 274.5	6 772.6	5 132.8
United States	.. d	.. d	1 860.0	1 140.7	1 196.6	.. d	2 225.2	1 913.1	2 715.8	2 817.1
EUROPE	**20 403.6**	**24 078.5**	**27 270.2**	**27 042.4**	**22 401.1**	**14 131.4**	**18 237.0**	**21 781.0**	**21 261.6**	**16 877.5**
Bulgaria	.. c	-	.. c	-	-	.. c	.. d	21.2	15.7	1.1
Croatia	.. c	-	.. c	1.1	-	.. c	.. d	9.4	23.5	13.7
Cyprus	.. c	-12.4	-54.3	-16.8	-33.0	.. c	75.5	-15.3	17.9	-27.4
Malta	.. c	.. d	152.2	-1.1	39.9	.. c	20.3	14.2	34.7	20.5
Montenegro	.. c	-	.. c	-	-	.. c	.. c	1.2	.. c	.. c
Romania	.. c	.. d	8.3	12.3	.. c	.. d	.. d	63.7	84.0	53.6
Russian Federation	.. c	.. d	15.3	25.7	8.0	.. d	202.9	433.1	75.0	132.2
Ukraine	.. c	.. d	-29.5	.. c	.. c	.. c	27.1	28.3	5.6	10.3
AFRICA	**.. d**	**96.9**	**145.2**	**101.9**	**101.4**	**.. d**	**654.9**	**603.1**	**463.5**	**511.7**
Northern Africa	.. d	86.8	93.2	71.6	68.4	.. d	.. d	486.3	415.3	447.9
Algeria	.. c	.. d	68.5	49.3	.. c	.. c	-1.1	.. d	-7.8	72.9
Egypt	.. c	-	.. d	.. d	.. d	.. c	.. d	.. d	.. d	.. d
Libya	.. c	.. c	.. c	.. c	.. c	.. c	.. c	.. c	.. c	.. c
Morocco	.. c	.. d	.. d	13.4	3.4	.. d	392.3	168.8	213.8	188.0
Tunisia	.. c	.. c	.. c	2.2	.. c	.. c	23.7	.. d	31.3	25.1
Other African countries	.. c	9.0	51.9	30.2	.. d	.. d	.. d	116.8	47.0	63.8
Nigeria	.. c	.. c	-	-	.. c	.. c	-	.. c	2.2	2.3
South Africa	.. c	-	.. c	.. c	.. c	.. d	71.0	61.4	31.3	51.3
AMERICA	**2 119.9**	**3 032.4**	**3 439.2**	**2 410.2**	**2 408.0**	**17 964.2**	**16 517.9**	**19 704.9**	**19 935.1**	**15 800.6**
Northern America	.. d	1 792.4	2 076.0	1 194.4	1 269.5	.. d	2 520.6	2 102.0	2 913.9	2 944.7
Central America and Caribbean countries	.. d	179.2	195.9	441.1	355.6	.. d	5 950.9	7 005.8	7 070.4	5 706.0
Bahamas	.. c	-7.9	-1.2	.. c	10.3	.. c	-	-1.2	.. c	.. c
Bermuda	.. c	.. c	.. c	.. c	.. c	.. c	.. c	.. c	13.4	.. c
Cayman Islands	.. c	.. d	-7.1	-6.7	-5.7	.. d	-66.5	263.2	95.2	133.3
El Salvador	.. c	-	.. c	.. c	-	.. d	.. d	109.8	108.6	110.5
Guatemala	.. c	2.3	-	.. c	.. c	.. c	83.4	105.0	76.1	93.4
Honduras	.. c	.. c	.. c	-	-	.. c	1.1	3.5	-4.5	-2.3
Nicaragua	.. c	-	.. c	.. c	.. c	.. c	.. d	28.3	1.1	-8.0
Panama	.. d	38.3	-14.2	98.5	67.2	.. d	.. d	161.7	142.2	197.2
Virgin Islands, U.S.	.. c	-	-	-	-	.. c	-	-	-	-
South America	188.0	1 058.5	1 164.9	773.5	782.9	.. d	8 046.4	10 597.2	9 950.7	7 149.9
Argentina	.. c	81.2	69.6	39.2	.. d	.. d	2 500.3	3 303.4	1 464.2	769.2
Bolivia	.. c	-	.. c	-1.1	.. c	.. c	.. d	66.1	207.1	83.2
Brazil	.. c	-122.9	241.9	-26.9	62.7	.. d	2 325.6	3 779.1	4 100.5	2 925.4
Ecuador	.. c	-3.4	.. c	-11.2	.. c	.. d	174.7	243.1	174.6	229.1
Paraguay	.. c	-	.. c	.. c	.. c	.. d	138.7	149.9	134.3	120.8
Peru	.. c	23.7	20.1	13.4	17.1	.. d	193.9	267.9	-73.9	194.9
Uruguay	.. d	667.3	579.5	523.9	542.5	.. c	.. d	612.5	925.8	668.9
Venezuela	.. c	.. c	.. c	.. c	108.3	.. d	289.7	220.7	1 307.5	584.6

Table 3. Foreign direct investment income by country *(cont.)*

Million US dollars

	Inward					Outward				
	2016	2017	2018	2019	2020	2016	2017	2018	2019	2020
ASIA	**.. d**	**1 565.8**	**2 144.5**	**2 601.6**	**1 892.9**	**.. d**	**712.4**	**973.7**	**615.7**	**893.4**
Near and Middle East	.. d	1 311.0	1 429.2	1 443.0	1 105.4	.. c	58.6	116.8	114.2	135.6
Gulf Arabian countries	.. d	.. d	1 421.0	1 391.5	1 079.2	.. c	38.3	103.9	105.2	121.9
Kuwait	.. c	21.4	.. c	.. c	.. c	.. c	1.1	-7.1	-23.5	-8.0
Qatar	.. c	.. c	.. c	.. c	.. c	.. c	.. d	22.4	-19.0	12.5
Saudi Arabia	.. c	-13.5	-16.5	-9.0	-11.4	.. d	21.4	41.3	58.2	93.4
United Arab Emirates	.. c	.. c	.. c	.. c	885.5	.. c	.. d	20.1	80.6	8.0
Other Near and Middle East	.. c	.. d	7.1	51.5	27.4	.. c	.. d	11.8	9.0	13.7
Jordan	.. c	-	- d	2.2	-	.. c	12.4	-2.4	-	2.3
Other Asian countries	.. d	252.5	712.9	1 157.5	782.9	.. d	653.8	856.8	501.5	757.8
China	.. c	.. d	81.4	73.9	57.0	.. d	.. d	321.0	275.4	323.6
Hong Kong, China	.. c	.. d	74.4	58.2	34.2	.. d	51.9	167.6	159.0	180.1
India	.. c	.. d	.. c	.. c	.. c	.. c	271.7	89.7	104.1	197.2
Indonesia	.. c	.. c	.. c	.. c	.. c	.. c	5.6	-4.7	-	-
Iran, Islamic Republic of	.. c	-	.. c	-	-	.. c	.. c	2.4	.. c	.. c
Malaysia	.. c	.. d	-2.4	- d	-2.3	.. c	.. d	178.2	-90.7	-29.6
Philippines	.. c	-	2.4	.. c	.. c	.. c	.. d	7.1	10.1	9.1
Singapore	.. c	37.2	179.4	311.2	230.2	.. c	-62.0	36.6	-56.0	-18.2
Chinese Taipei	.. c	-	-	-	-	.. c	3.4	.. c	.. c	-5.7
Thailand	.. c	-	1.2	1.1	- d	.. c	.. d	10.6	11.2	11.4
Viet Nam	.. c	-	.. c	.. c	.. c	.. c	2.3	-	1.1	2.3
AUSTRALIA, OCEANIA AND POLAR REGIONS	**.. c**	**.. d**	**-40.1**	**6.7**	**10.3**	**.. d**	**.. d**	**100.3**	**57.1**	**70.7**
WORLD unallocated and confidential	**.. d**	**.. d**	**11.8**	**12.3**	**11.4**	**.. d**	**.. d**	**-3.5**	**-3.4**	**-2.3**
European Union (since 01/02/2020)	..	..	..	..	..	..	..	..	..	..
G20 countries excl. European Union	**.. d**	..	**.. d**	**.. d**	**.. d**	**.. d**	..	**.. d**	**.. d**	**20 759.0**
G20 OECD countries	**.. d**	..	**16 066.3**	**.. d**	**.. d**	**.. d**	..	**.. d**	**.. d**	**16 266.7**
G20 Non-OECD countries	**.. d**	..	**.. d**	**.. d**	**.. d**	**.. d**	..	**8 024.3**	**6 108.8**	**4 492.3**
MENA countries	**.. d**	..	**.. d**	**.. d**	**.. d**	**.. d**	..	**.. d**	**.. d**	**.. d**
ASEAN countries	**.. c**	**.. d**	**175.9**	**311.2**	**231.3**	**.. c**	**-15.8**	**227.8**	**-125.4**	**-26.2**

- Nil; .. Not available; c Confidential data; d Secondary Confidentiality

Note: Detailed metadata at: *http://metalinks.oecd.org/idi/20220712/6d95*.

Source: *OECD International Direct Investment Statistics (database)*: *https://doi.org/10.1787/idi-data-en*

SPAIN

Table 4. Foreign direct investment flows by industrial sector

Million US dollars

	Inward					Outward				
	2016	2017	2018	2019	2020	2016	2017	2018	2019	2020
All FDI activities	**31 538.2**	**41 876.9**	**57 427.1**	**17 416.3**	**12 607.4**	**43 902.5**	**55 926.1**	**37 522.7**	**24 825.9**	**34 941.3**
Agriculture, forestry and fishing	**.. c**	**54.1**	**31.9**	**47.0**	**..**	**.. c**	**47.3**	**40.1**	**3.4**	**..**
Mining and quarrying	**-358.3**	**-1 484.6**	**-257.3**	**-24.6**	**..**	**266.5**	**1 907.3**	**-1 679.5**	**-180.2**	**..**
Extraction activities	.. c	-178.1	697.5	2.2	..	726.5	2 012.2	-1 236.9	216.1	..
Manufacturing	**-2 464.9**	**9 005.7**	**7 533.3**	**5 437.1**	**..**	**-748.6**	**-396.8**	**-688.1**	**-272.0**	**..**
of which:										
Food products, beverages and tobacco	-1 177.7	-705.7	-138.1	-378.4	..	633.6	-331.4	-550.0	-626.9	..
Textiles, wood and paper products; printing	295.3	110.5	116.8	2 830.0	..	231.1	-6.8	-30.7	598.9	..
Chemical, rubber, plastic, non-metallic mineral products	1 594.6	271.7	4 395.1	2 284.8	..	1 200.9	-1 743.9	-1 661.7	1 259.4	..
Metal and machinery products, except electrical equipment	-3 493.3	-2 699.8	-1 611.0	-941.5	..	-705.5	-1 783.3	-1 274.6	-2 149.3	..
Motor vehicles, trailers, semi-trailers, other transport equipment	-92.9	2 455.2	4 762.2	798.2	..	-2 930.4	1 963.7	3 052.0	408.6	..
Other manufacturing	409.2	9 573.9	7.1	845.2	..	821.6	1 504.9	-223.1	235.1	..
Electricity, gas, steam and air conditioning supply	**832.7**	**-11 812.6**	**-5 654.4**	**657.1**	**..**	**368.2**	**-7 827.8**	**-872.2**	**-405.2**	**..**
Water supply; sewerage, waste management and remediation activities	**.. c**	**-149.9**	**18.9**	**3.4**	**..**	**.. c**	**304.4**	**-28.3**	**640.3**	**..**
Construction	**295.3**	**196.1**	**2 116.1**	**-466.8**	**..**	**1 733.9**	**2 815.9**	**1 644.0**	**4 047.9**	**..**
Services	**29 775.5**	**41 418.1**	**51 295.9**	**9 646.3**	**..**	**42 472.6**	**58 866.0**	**38 658.1**	**19 425.7**	**..**
Wholesale and retail trade; repair of motor vehicles and motorcycles	13 212.4	-7 817.6	4 735.0	-4 037.8	..	10 753.1	6 029.8	-1 435.1	-6 684.2	..
Transportation and storage	2 358.7	661.7	946.5	405.2	..	4 328.2	5 386.1	1 743.2	1 102.7	..
Accommodation and food service activities	-1 012.9	-258.1	2 968.3	987.4	..	564.0	368.6	1 424.5	1 140.7	..
Information and communication	1 185.4	2 152.0	2 410.0	159.0	..	240.0	1 467.7	1 611.0	2 644.1	..
Financial and insurance activities	9 786.6	40 749.6	26 966.8	3 038.2	..	21 005.2	41 034.8	15 383.0	15 108.0	..
Activities of holding companies	10 160.3	42 316.5	23 834.5	5 441.6	..	12 830.9	31 249.0	3 179.5	7 773.4	..
Real estate activities	2 976.9	215.3	3 088.6	1 407.1	..	2 537.9	-927.7	2 266.0	166.8	..
Professional, scientific and technical activities	429.1	3 013.2	7 186.4	3 259.8	..	3 624.9	5 389.5	16 922.0	3 546.4	..
Administrative and support service activities	230.0	1 667.2	2 614.2	4 501.3	..	-776.3	-53.0	245.5	1 451.9	..
Public administration; activities of households and of extraterritorial organisations	.. c	-6.8	..	..	..	.. c	-	..	..	..
Education	.. c	-219.8	31.9	418.7	..	.. c	30.4	81.4	1 047.8	..
Human health and social work activities	.. c	157.8	282.1	-133.2	..	.. c	11.3	186.5	-210.5	..
Arts, entertainment and recreation	433.5	945.8	3.5	-493.7	..	-183.6	-	57.8	-10.1	..
Other services	.. c	160.1	62.6	133.2	..	164.8	126.3	172.3	120.9	..
Not allocated and confidential	**..**	**2 182.4**	**256.1**	**503.8**	**12 607.4**	**..**	**196.1**	**452.0**	**1 443.0**	**34 941.3**
Private real estate activities	**..**	**2 467.6**	**2 086.6**	**1 613.1**	**..**	**..**	**13.5**	**-3.5**	**123.1**	**..**

- Nil; .. Not available; c Confidential data

Note: Detailed metadata at: *http://metalinks.oecd.org/idi/20220712/6d95.*

Source: *OECD International Direct Investment Statistics (database)*: *https://doi.org/10.1787/idi-data-en*

SPAIN

Table 5. Foreign direct investment positions by industrial sector

At year end

Million US dollars

	Inward					Outward				
	2016	2017	2018	2019	2020	2016	2017	2018	2019	2020
All FDI activities	**591 525.2**	**717 944.4**	**751 615.5**	**769 238.4**	**865 741.8**	**539 109.3**	**623 869.0**	**600 090.5**	**620 147.2**	**626 168.9**
Agriculture, forestry and fishing	**1 190.1**	**1 496.8**	**1 531.9**	**1 799.6**	..	**450.1**	**478.5**	**580.5**	**576.3**	..
Mining and quarrying	**7 032.8**	**6 083.0**	**4 831.7**	**4 787.7**	..	**11 387.2**	**15 054.0**	**4 851.2**	**3 593.6**	..
Extraction activities	1 106.8	1 067.4	1 158.7	1 194.1	..	9 370.7	13 083.5	3 543.6	2 884.7	..
Manufacturing	**90 732.6**	**108 853.4**	**106 600.6**	**110 458.3**	..	**68 314.5**	**71 206.5**	**66 765.5**	**65 561.7**	..
of which:										
Food products, beverages and tobacco	18 247.1	19 875.3	18 330.7	17 830.8	..	9 002.8	9 376.3	8 738.3	8 585.7	..
Textiles, wood and paper products; printing	3 715.6	3 673.5	3 501.3	4 965.2	..	3 052.6	3 500.8	3 194.4	3 276.8	..
Chemical, rubber, plastic, non-metallic mineral products	30 816.9	33 237.0	35 162.6	35 907.7	..	25 072.2	24 261.2	21 352.2	22 067.0	..
Metal and machinery products, except electrical equipment	19 110.4	19 521.5	16 473.6	15 916.6	..	16 344.5	12 367.5	9 860.3	8 711.5	..
Motor vehicles, trailers, semi-trailers, other transport equipment	8 024.7	13 460.1	16 193.0	16 178.4	..	6 143.1	10 094.7	11 763.2	11 744.6	..
Other manufacturing	10 816.9	19 087.3	16 939.5	19 659.6	..	8 698.2	11 605.9	11 858.3	11 177.3	..
Electricity, gas, steam and air conditioning supply	**55 279.9**	**53 534.4**	**48 543.6**	**52 428.7**	..	**31 150.0**	**26 602.3**	**22 259.0**	**24 113.7**	..
Water supply; sewerage, waste management and remediation activities	**2 261.0**	**2 760.9**	**2 869.2**	**333.6**	..	**1 167.9**	**1 207.7**	**640.0**	**757.1**	..
Construction	**11 052.0**	**13 895.4**	**15 006.9**	**14 978.7**	..	**27 277.3**	**36 038.6**	**32 837.2**	**27 756.7**	..
Services	**285 978.7**	**359 948.4**	**399 144.7**	**401 323.3**	..	**373 591.2**	**442 921.6**	**442 342.6**	**465 084.3**	..
Wholesale and retail trade; repair of motor vehicles and motorcycles	53 550.1	53 257.4	56 343.0	56 428.9	..	37 303.7	40 213.5	36 866.3	43 083.6	..
Transportation and storage	13 088.4	17 722.5	16 649.9	14 130.5	..	11 492.6	10 752.0	10 492.3	17 824.1	..
Accommodation and food service activities	4 572.6	5 629.6	7 232.7	7 674.7	..	5 440.1	7 769.2	8 461.2	9 486.6	..
Information and communication	28 694.0	31 276.1	29 639.3	27 730.8	..	50 034.8	55 889.9	52 213.2	52 374.7	..
Financial and insurance activities	115 759.5	162 275.1	186 347.6	181 230.1	..	233 764.1	291 072.2	271 917.8	273 863.2	..
Activities of holding companies	69 739.6	110 959.5	134 037.1	135 930.1	..	70 967.6	92 918.0	90 775.1	98 117.3	..
Real estate activities	25 252.5	30 297.4	32 483.4	31 734.4	..	13 213.9	8 007.9	8 918.0	10 233.7	..
Professional, scientific and technical activities	18 830.0	25 106.7	34 384.0	41 298.6	..	17 165.6	24 239.6	46 321.3	47 954.4	..
Administrative and support service activities	21 109.9	27 006.5	28 591.7	34 099.1	..	3 737.7	3 127.8	3 638.7	6 414.3	..
Public administration; activities of households and of extraterritorial organisations	45.3	..	..	..	..	-	..	..	..	..
Education	.. c	2 294.3	2 303.6	2 707.3	..	.. c	879.1	1 324.7	2 218.6	..
Human health and social work activities	703.1	1 282.1	1 562.9	1 359.2	..	.. c	195.5	416.8	88.7	..
Arts, entertainment and recreation	2 044.9	3 054.7	2 878.4	2 199.5	..	-431.1	-476.1	608.0	550.4	..
Other services	.. d	725.6	707.6	716.7	..	878.0	1 250.9	1 164.4	991.9	..
Not allocated and confidential	**4 484.0**	**9 118.5**	**7 573.8**	**11 164.9**	**865 741.8**	**4 640.0**	**6 935.7**	**7 278.5**	**10 301.1**	**626 168.9**
Private real estate activities	**133 514.3**	**162 253.5**	**165 512.9**	**171 963.6**	..	**21 131.0**	**23 424.1**	**22 536.1**	**22 402.8**	..

- Nil; .. Not available; c Confidential data; d Secondary Confidentiality

Note: Detailed metadata at: *http://metalinks.oecd.org/idi/20220712/6d95*.

Source: *OECD International Direct Investment Statistics (database)*: *https://doi.org/10.1787/idi-data-en*

SPAIN

Table 6. Foreign direct investment income by industrial sector

Million US dollars

	Inward					Outward				
	2016	2017	2018	2019	2020	2016	2017	2018	2019	2020
All FDI activities	**23 652.5**	**28 808.5**	**32 970.6**	**32 175.1**	**26 825.1**	**33 708.9**	**36 231.5**	**43 159.4**	**42 329.6**	**34 151.6**
Agriculture, forestry and fishing	**.. c**	**37.2**	**30.7**	**41.4**	..	**.. c**	**28.2**	**38.9**	**29.1**	..
Mining and quarrying	**.. c**	**376.5**	**400.1**	**199.3**	..	**204.6**	**373.1**	**499.2**	**129.9**	..
Extraction activities	65.2	23.7	81.4	132.1	..	.. c	86.8	385.9	100.8	..
Manufacturing	**7 193.4**	**8 589.8**	**9 579.8**	**9 790.7**	..	**3 889.2**	**3 271.3**	**5 176.4**	**3 839.7**	..
of which:										
Food products, beverages and tobacco	1 038.4	892.8	791.9	810.5	..	498.7	509.5	420.2	353.7	..
Textiles, wood and paper products; printing	338.4	272.8	404.8	376.1	..	200.2	220.9	292.7	189.2	..
Chemical, rubber, plastic, non-metallic mineral products	3 777.5	3 814.7	4 801.1	4 325.5	..	1 353.5	893.9	2 113.8	1 350.1	..
Metal and machinery products, except electrical equipment	-299.7	1 227.6	1 285.3	1 252.7	..	731.0	676.4	1 064.6	616.8	..
Motor vehicles, trailers, semi-trailers, other transport equipment	1 639.9	1 510.5	1 535.5	2 065.4	..	434.6	92.4	439.0	206.0	..
Other manufacturing	697.8	871.4	762.4	959.4	..	671.2	878.1	846.2	1 123.9	..
Electricity, gas, steam and air conditioning supply	**1 967.3**	**2 414.6**	**1 180.2**	**2 208.7**	..	**1 954.0**	**1 649.2**	**1 353.7**	**1 826.9**	..
Water supply; sewerage, waste management and remediation activities	**.. c**	**48.5**	**24.8**	**10.1**	..	**257.7**	**277.3**	**30.7**	**22.4**	..
Construction	**.. c**	**120.6**	**459.1**	**535.1**	..	**-65.2**	**860.1**	**1 002.0**	**967.2**	..
Services	**12 222.7**	**15 665.7**	**19 476.0**	**17 639.1**	..	**27 612.5**	**29 403.7**	**34 594.6**	**33 193.8**	..
Wholesale and retail trade; repair of motor vehicles and motorcycles	3 728.9	3 357.0	6 153.7	4 758.8	..	3 333.0	4 259.9	4 172.1	3 535.2	..
Transportation and storage	442.3	794.7	834.4	996.3	..	1 433.2	3 313.0	2 725.1	2 017.2	..
Accommodation and food service activities	179.1	554.6	617.3	617.9	..	399.2	471.2	670.4	514.9	..
Information and communication	1 112.5	1 122.8	993.7	806.0	..	3 974.3	1 926.5	2 127.9	2 277.0	..
Financial and insurance activities	4 803.7	6 875.2	6 698.9	6 810.7	..	16 065.5	17 044.3	20 624.3	20 389.6	..
Activities of holding companies	2 276.9	3 979.3	3 440.3	3 859.8	..	3 442.4	2 866.6	3 402.6	4 665.8	..
Real estate activities	679.0	1 021.3	1 226.2	990.7	..	289.7	363.0	72.0	363.8	..
Professional, scientific and technical activities	253.2	825.2	1 428.1	1 591.9	..	1 683.1	1 792.4	3 666.9	3 528.5	..
Administrative and support service activities	948.8	873.6	1 249.9	795.9	..	384.8	287.5	302.1	331.4	..
Public administration; activities of households and of extraterritorial organisations	.. c	.. d	..	..	..	.. c	-	..	..	..
Education	.. c	29.3	22.4	11.2	..	.. c	-85.7	.. c	-10.1	..
Human health and social work activities	.. c	53.0	57.8	35.8	..	.. c	2.3	11.8	5.6	..
Arts, entertainment and recreation	.. c	4.5	57.8	50.4	..	-73.0	-38.3	-28.3	26.9	..
Other services	.. c	154.4	134.5	173.5	..	.. c	.. d	214.8	211.6	..
Not allocated and confidential	..	**71.0**	**166.4**	**239.6**	**26 825.1**	..	**163.5**	**212.4**	**2 107.9**	**34 151.6**
Private real estate activities	..	**1 484.6**	**1 653.5**	**1 511.3**	..	..	**205.2**	**251.4**	**212.7**	..

- Nil; .. Not available; c Confidential data; d Secondary Confidentiality

Note: Detailed metadata at: *http://metalinks.oecd.org/idi/20220712/6d95*.

Source: *OECD International Direct Investment Statistics (database): https://doi.org/10.1787/idi-data-en*

SWEDEN

Table 1. Foreign direct investment flows by country

Million US dollars

	Inward					Outward				
	2016	2017	2018	2019	2020	2016	2017	2018	2019	2020
WORLD	**19 153.0**	**12 511.4**	**3 806.7**	**9 110.6**	**18 798.1**	**4 702.5**	**27 368.7**	**17 833.8**	**16 104.4**	**23 906.6**
OECD COUNTRIES	**..**	**..**	**5 161.0**	**7 345.0**	**17 246.7**	**..**	**..**	**14 225.9**	**11 716.9**	**28 051.4**
Australia	.. c	-29.8	-177.3	24.2	107.2	112.0	-	242.2	112.7	149.1
Austria	20.7	758.2	144.8	140.5	225.0	76.2	183.5	76.2	42.1	15.4
Belgium	401.3	-394.8	-17.0	793.6	416.4	4 275.2	-13 934.7	-6 860.9	1 501.3	-441.5
Canada	104.7	-72.1	-11.2	-59.5	697.0	1 241.7	966.8	-44.1	452.3	203.9
Chile	.. c	-	.. c	.. c	.. c	-24.3	145.1	-3.7	431.2	-4.3
Colombia	.. c	-	-	.. c	-	38.8	53.8	-8.9	27.6	20.5
Costa Rica	-	-	-	-	-	2.7	-15.2	.. c	-0.8	-12.8
Czech Republic	1.4	2.8	-18.2	8.9	-22.5	1 781.1	-111.3	32.3	261.5	334.3
Denmark	809.2	1 585.2	3 172.6	-332.0	-2 076.7	-191.2	1 118.9	2 333.4	1 088.0	-2 539.7
Estonia	13.2	19.3	7.2	63.7	13.6	265.5	709.3	238.9	457.0	-15.0
Finland	1 149.9	302.4	1 693.4	723.6	-492.0	2 433.2	-900.0	880.1	-168.0	-890.9
France	112.3	2 543.6	326.8	88.2	-1 638.6	1 202.7	384.5	1 072.2	38.9	685.4
Germany	-424.1	-266.1	754.6	1 421.1	385.8	249.6	9 190.6	-6 381.1	1 125.9	883.1
Greece	.. c	-	-	.. c	.. c	-13.8	6.2	4.9	3.5	52.8
Hungary	.. c	1.2	-3.3	.. c	-9.3	113.2	-10.1	-70.3	101.6	-21.1
Iceland	-55.5	-3.0	-7.6	-	19.3	-0.6	-5.7	15.1	11.7	.. c
Ireland	-3 636.1	2 460.9	1 986.0	1 605.8	-1 113.1	670.6	3 269.0	11 414.1	-1 197.1	932.7
Israel	6.4	4.8	-	6.7	-39.4	40.1	17.4	74.1	475.9	-20.3
Italy	62.1	94.1	.. c	190.5	45.0	-2 255.5	651.5	1 838.4	124.3	266.7
Japan	352.4	920.2	1 072.1	132.4	295.7	231.6	214.7	379.7	-162.5	54.7
Korea	.. c	42.7	32.1	77.2	25.5	158.6	-258.6	-235.9	297.4	-64.3
Latvia	-7.9	.. c	-5.3	-30.2	7.4	-424.1	841.6	143.7	-354.6	356.6
Lithuania	3.3	.. c	.. c	14.2	-14.7	-371.1	1 159.8	392.3	-575.9	426.9
Luxembourg	164.0	33.8	-3 692.6	2 337.1	10 793.1	-6 890.9	-3 792.7	807.8	-2 534.3	-656.6
Mexico	.. c	-7.5	26.1	62.6	-26.6	1 681.1	-1 419.1	-432.8	97.7	280.9
Netherlands	9 550.5	-1 426.6	-4 003.8	-918.8	-2 329.3	-5 138.8	15 380.3	-5 988.6	2 225.4	1 184.9
New Zealand	.. c	-	0.2	.. c	60.3	3.6	28.0	17.7	54.4	5.8
Norway	-1 095.0	1 773.5	-149.4	-1 432.8	-3 029.1	1 644.1	4 665.1	4 604.9	2 481.6	1 159.5
Poland	.. c	760.7	60.3	1 126.2	219.8	1 196.4	440.3	-316.4	-50.7	440.0
Portugal	.. c	.. c	.. c	-81.5	104.2	119.3	119.2	103.2	53.7	97.6
Slovak Republic	3.9	.. c	-15.3	3.3	-6.4	324.8	205.1	-59.3	-63.6	-2.0
Slovenia	.. c	.. c	.. c	.. c	.. c	49.7	41.3	41.2	59.6	-56.6
Spain	37.2	-99.8	16.7	58.6	900.8	814.9	1 406.9	136.4	868.8	372.0
Sweden	-	-	-	-	-	-	-	-	-	-
Switzerland	364.9	3 199.6	-251.7	2 108.2	2 339.9	1 465.1	611.2	232.8	473.7	2 302.5
Turkey	1.9	1.6	-4.1	19.2	22.7	59.5	137.4	64.6	179.8	324.4
United Kingdom	3 813.2	6 012.6	914.0	2 093.3	1 564.7	-514.0	-378.7	4 584.0	1 789.7	4 450.4
United States	6 011.7	-3 668.2	2 373.3	-3 102.6	9 795.8	238.5	2 721.0	4 889.1	2 014.1	17 770.7
EUROPE	**11 686.2**	**16 975.1**	**-52.1**	**10 087.6**	**6 812.1**	**1 265.0**	**23 558.8**	**10 240.4**	**8 174.6**	**6 967.0**
Bulgaria	.. c	.. c	.. c	.. c	.. c	106.0	47.9	96.0	-181.1	57.9
Croatia	.. c	.. c	.. c	.. c	.. c	-58.9	50.8	31.1	47.3	-422.8
Cyprus	425.8	-480.8	.. c	-135.6	303.4	.. c	-19.9	79.5	158.8	-12.1
Malta	-98.4	.. c	109.4	20.2	277.1	-313.4	960.2	487.2	61.5	-631.8
Montenegro	-	-	-	-	-	-0.1	.. c	.. c	.. c	.. c
Romania	.. c	-	.. c	.. c	-2.3	145.4	34.5	38.7	95.8	74.5
Russian Federation	11.0	3.4	-19.2	28.9	-17.4	115.6	834.6	673.0	-257.5	-2 208.9
Ukraine	0.5	.. c	.. c	.. c	-	101.4	31.2	104.5	88.9	129.5
AFRICA	**.. c**	**5.9**	**2.6**	**.. c**	**.. c**	**-445.9**	**28.5**	**413.6**	**454.5**	**-27.6**
Northern Africa	.. c	1.4	-2.5	-0.4	0.4	-53.6	-20.5	26.5	21.3	10.4
Algeria	.. c	-	-	-	-0.8	-14.5	-2.5	12.8	-16.8	-19.1
Egypt	-1.3	1.4	-0.1	0.5	1.6	.. c	.. c	23.7	5.1	23.9
Libya	-	-	-2.5	-	-	-	-	4.6	-	-
Morocco	-	0.1	-	-1.0	.. c	7.6	-0.9	-17.5	29.9	0.2
Tunisia	-	-	-	-	-	.. c	0.1	2.9	3.0	5.5
Other African countries	.. c	4.4	5.2	.. c	.. c	-392.2	49.0	387.1	433.4	-38.0
Nigeria	1.5	0.5	-2.8	6.7	-0.9	.. c	-7.6	24.4	21.7	-41.5
South Africa	.. c	-0.8	7.9	.. c	.. c	94.7	400.4	184.3	276.7	-35.6
AMERICA	**6 334.5**	**-7 009.2**	**2 085.4**	**-1 648.0**	**8 937.6**	**3 530.6**	**2 614.7**	**5 761.0**	**3 766.5**	**17 227.1**
Northern America	6 116.4	-3 740.3	2 362.1	-3 162.2	10 492.7	1 478.1	3 687.5	4 848.6	2 423.0	17 974.9
Central America and Caribbean countries	421.1	.. c	-234.4	1 495.6	-1 569.4	1 682.8	-1 424.4	-256.8	23.5	-94.4
Bahamas	-0.5	-1.6	-	-	-	-	-0.8	0.8	4.2	-
Bermuda	.. c	59.7	9.0	.. c	-34.0	-3.6	26.0	.. c	34.8	.. c
Cayman Islands	.. c	.. c	.. c	-9.6	11.6	2.5	-31.6	27.8	-170.8	-44.0
El Salvador	-	-	-	.. c	-	.. c	.. c	.. c	.. c	0.4
Guatemala	-	-	-	-	-	4.6	-2.8	.. c	-4.8	-7.9
Honduras	-	-	-	-	-	.. c	.. c	.. c	1.6	.. c
Nicaragua	-	-	-	-	-	-	-	-	-	-
Panama	-	-	-	.. c	.. c	8.4	4.6	.. c	2.1	-2.9
Virgin Islands, U.S.	-	-	-	-	-	-	.. c	-	-	-
South America	.. c	2.7	.. c	18.7	14.3	369.8	351.7	1 169.2	1 320.0	-653.6
Argentina	.. c	-	-	.. c	.. c	136.3	180.4	245.6	77.1	88.7
Bolivia	-	-	-	.. c	.. c	-111.6	-172.1	253.0	-98.8	-313.5
Brazil	.. c	2.7	11.2	73.2	-1.8	222.3	94.4	591.0	810.4	-324.3
Ecuador	.. c	-	-	-	-	-	4.4	0.1	4.8	5.5
Paraguay	-	-	-	-	-	-0.1	-1.1	.. c	.. c	.. c
Peru	.. c	-	-	.. c	.. c	105.7	42.2	60.2	75.0	-76.4
Uruguay	.. c	-	.. c	.. c	.. c	13.8	-0.9	14.8	-13.4	-50.2
Venezuela	.. c	-	-	0.6	-	-14.5	5.4	17.4	3.1	2.4

Table 1. Foreign direct investment flows by country *(cont.)*

Million US dollars

	Inward					Outward				
	2016	2017	2018	2019	2020	2016	2017	2018	2019	2020
ASIA	**1 765.9**	**2 570.7**	**1 948.1**	**728.8**	**2 893.0**	**243.7**	**1 145.1**	**1 158.9**	**3 541.7**	**-414.6**
Near and Middle East	.. c	.. c	.. c	-10.9	-25.3	112.8	16.5	119.4	519.0	-53.7
Gulf Arabian countries	.. c	.. c	.. c	-17.4	13.5	75.0	4.4	43.0	17.2	-16.8
Kuwait	-	-	-	-	-	0.7	0.5	1.4	.. c	-0.2
Qatar	-	-	-	3.2	-1.1	-0.2	-0.2	-1.2	-14.0	-3.0
Saudi Arabia	.. c	.. c	.. c	.. c	13.6	19.4	8.2	-23.9	20.1	24.2
United Arab Emirates	-1.2	0.1	-0.3	5.1	1.0	56.2	-6.2	53.7	-4.9	-50.7
Other Near and Middle East	.. c	4.8	-	6.7	-38.8	37.6	12.1	76.4	501.8	-36.9
Jordan	-	-	-	-	-	0.2	0.4	0.1	0.1	0.3
Other Asian countries	1 930.0	2 670.3	2 040.8	739.6	2 918.3	131.0	1 128.6	1 039.4	3 022.7	-360.8
China	1 473.1	1 265.9	1 251.5	628.1	2 779.5	711.2	671.7	-26.4	592.2	964.6
Hong Kong, China	.. c	26.3	-291.4	-163.1	.. c	-864.0	343.4	210.6	2 159.0	-1 422.5
India	-0.1	16.8	0.2	11.0	-4.2	350.5	568.0	390.1	245.0	-138.9
Indonesia	.. c	-	-	.. c	.. c	33.7	7.6	36.5	53.4	-43.3
Iran, Islamic Republic of	-	-	1.8	-	-	.. c	.. c	-86.6	22.4	7.9
Malaysia	6.1	31.2	-12.0	19.6	.. c	96.8	34.4	24.9	2.5	-32.1
Philippines	.. c	-	-	.. c	.. c	77.7	-44.1	-67.3	20.9	.. c
Singapore	.. c	.. c	-11.9	50.7	26.3	-113.7	-583.8	126.1	-82.1	272.2
Chinese Taipei	-1.9	0.2	0.7	0.5	-5.8	-0.6	-19.2	-11.7	44.1	24.9
Thailand	.. c	0.5	-	.. c	-0.9	52.4	55.8	131.9	-14.6	-2.6
Viet Nam	3.6	1.1	-1.2	3.0	-8.9	5.0	9.5	18.6	19.2	-11.6
AUSTRALIA, OCEANIA AND POLAR REGIONS	**.. c**	**-29.8**	**-177.1**	**21.7**	**167.4**	**115.6**	**28.0**	**259.9**	**167.1**	**154.8**
WORLD unallocated and confidential	**.. d**	**-1.2**	**-0.2**	**.. d**	**.. d**	**-6.5**	**-6.4**	**0.1**	**-**	**-0.1**
European Union (since 01/02/2020)	**..**	**6 046.3**	**-606.0**	**..**	**6 001.7**	**..**	**17 404.7**	**622.8**	**..**	**717.4**
G20 countries excl. European Union	**11 198.5**	**6 755.1**	**7 253.6**	**1 578.3**	**14 032.5**	**4 089.5**	**14 975.2**	**8 046.5**	**7 887.5**	**23 331.6**
G20 OECD countries	**9 472.4**	**5 571.2**	**6 094.5**	**946.5**	**11 274.1**	**2 405.9**	**12 209.9**	**5 976.1**	**6 070.2**	**25 005.0**
G20 Non-OECD countries	**1 725.9**	**1 183.8**	**1 159.2**	**631.8**	**2 758.5**	**1 683.6**	**2 765.3**	**2 070.2**	**1 817.3**	**-1 673.5**
MENA countries	**.. c**	**.. c**	**.. c**	**-17.9**	**13.8**	**17.2**	**-23.4**	**67.1**	**59.5**	**-24.8**
ASEAN countries	**.. c**	**.. c**	**-25.1**	**53.9**	**23.0**	**167.5**	**-525.2**	**298.7**	**-1.3**	**182.1**

- Nil; .. Not available; c Confidential data; d Secondary Confidentiality

Note: Detailed metadata at: *http://metalinks.oecd.org/idi/20220712/6d95*.

Source: *OECD International Direct Investment Statistics (database)*: *https://doi.org/10.1787/idi-data-en*

SWEDEN

Table 2. Foreign direct investment positions by country

At year end

Million US dollars

	Inward					Outward				
	2016	2017	2018	2019	2020	2016	2017	2018	2019	2020
WORLD	**317 160.8**	**365 713.5**	**338 325.0**	**347 404.6**	**414 518.8**	**355 800.8**	**386 531.1**	**395 702.4**	**411 276.7**	**464 891.5**
OECD COUNTRIES	..	..	**318 031.9**	**325 055.3**	**390 652.8**	..	..	**342 783.5**	**354 001.6**	**405 777.3**
Australia	334.6	225.1	202.4	931.8	365.4	2 190.7	2 864.8	2 648.0	3 106.4	3 043.0
Austria	2 668.0	2 866.8	2 568.7	2 409.8	2 661.8	1 329.1	1 891.1	1 102.0	1 384.8	1 387.9
Belgium	1 976.7	4 714.5	1 027.0	1 351.6	3 004.8	18 130.1	-707.6	1 384.3	2 008.6	1 881.3
Canada	2 403.1	1 786.9	1 835.9	1 859.9	1 524.6	3 702.9	4 883.4	5 070.1	5 433.1	5 754.7
Chile	.. c	.. c	.. c	.. c	.. c	1 320.0	1 547.1	1 546.8	1 743.1	2 200.5
Colombia	-	-	-	-	-	229.2	288.7	240.1	247.4	296.6
Costa Rica	-	-	-	-	-	11.0	-4.1	-5.0	2.0	-2.4
Czech Republic	61.5	48.0	68.7	120.1	92.9	2 206.2	3 373.3	3 035.2	3 228.2	4 263.9
Denmark	23 463.7	24 358.1	25 320.9	25 019.1	26 778.6	21 135.7	21 306.4	23 952.1	26 061.4	26 541.5
Estonia	101.9	29.5	156.1	156.9	238.6	4 280.4	5 538.5	5 619.0	5 283.1	6 644.5
Finland	28 031.2	32 591.1	28 999.1	26 458.2	31 266.6	38 931.8	27 011.7	26 019.2	27 631.3	28 729.5
France	4 734.2	6 956.5	7 946.0	8 499.7	5 557.6	7 608.5	9 168.1	9 046.9	9 664.0	10 420.2
Germany	30 561.2	35 412.3	30 786.8	32 880.4	41 219.0	10 989.6	21 151.1	20 294.7	18 802.6	23 864.6
Greece	.. c	.. c	-2.6	.. c	.. c	175.7	182.5	133.7	132.6	334.2
Hungary	41.3	30.5	34.4	370.9	104.3	595.2	687.0	368.7	419.2	654.3
Iceland	.. c	.. c	.. c	.. c	.. c	37.3	88.8	259.9	276.4	.. c
Ireland	-1 888.2	1 212.5	4 761.1	10 294.2	11 421.4	2 211.1	11 977.6	10 682.8	11 552.9	12 756.0
Israel	.. c	.. c	.. c	.. c	.. c	654.8	523.1	434.1	756.4	367.2
Italy	966.4	1 130.0	1 553.6	2 320.8	2 234.0	5 694.5	7 472.1	8 369.4	8 002.3	8 644.3
Japan	2 991.3	4 590.9	5 133.1	4 353.2	5 656.3	3 414.1	3 671.1	3 909.6	3 779.7	3 659.3
Korea	187.7	.. c	.. c	.. c	.. c	2 566.0	2 525.0	2 689.9	2 881.6	3 097.3
Latvia	89.6	11.8	26.6	31.6	44.0	2 221.0	3 358.9	3 167.8	2 968.5	3 288.0
Lithuania	19.0	10.7	491.8	376.5	36.9	2 484.3	4 324.6	4 446.1	3 268.3	4 073.3
Luxembourg	46 425.5	52 702.0	42 240.1	46 093.5	59 401.1	18 691.7	15 251.5	13 551.7	12 561.8	12 825.2
Mexico	.. c	143.8	.. c	.. c	.. c	3 467.6	1 624.0	1 291.1	1 345.0	1 391.1
Netherlands	56 945.3	59 077.7	59 052.9	51 953.8	58 189.8	21 408.5	34 453.1	35 765.7	43 601.9	46 019.1
New Zealand	.. c	.. c	.. c	.. c	.. c	130.9	189.6	175.1	240.4	266.6
Norway	25 059.4	28 045.9	27 616.0	29 828.3	29 353.7	31 239.8	28 314.6	27 366.4	29 900.1	32 700.2
Poland	-3 138.9	-2 827.9	-4 399.3	-3 719.9	-2 653.1	6 247.4	8 396.7	6 905.5	5 764.8	7 126.8
Portugal	.. c	.. c	-24.3	-76.0	.. c	1 325.2	1 608.2	1 548.1	1 382.4	1 819.9
Slovak Republic	47.2	29.5	35.5	33.1	53.2	280.0	953.9	821.7	631.6	790.1
Slovenia	.. c	.. c	.. c	.. c	-	189.9	226.0	254.2	198.2	289.1
Spain	1 681.5	1 784.0	1 571.6	677.8	3 082.5	10 563.8	13 932.1	14 974.8	16 341.8	17 581.3
Sweden	-	-	-	-	-	-	-	-	-	-
Switzerland	8 140.0	8 797.4	7 509.7	8 300.5	10 058.8	10 130.4	11 839.4	11 076.0	10 520.6	11 680.5
Turkey	-7.6	-6.5	2.8	401.1	494.8	1 131.2	1 630.1	1 364.2	1 626.3	1 862.3
United Kingdom	37 130.2	50 735.7	48 107.8	48 874.8	50 825.5	20 680.1	24 270.7	29 513.3	29 976.0	33 310.9
United States	29 357.0	29 039.8	24 970.7	24 568.1	48 767.2	49 637.2	54 004.4	63 995.8	61 526.1	85 948.5
EUROPE	**272 543.1**	**319 233.9**	**296 264.8**	**303 632.7**	**345 976.3**	**258 545.3**	**280 081.9**	**281 449.4**	**294 144.4**	**323 021.3**
Bulgaria	.. c	.. c	.. c	.. c	-0.4	369.0	373.7	561.2	348.7	683.5
Croatia	.. c	.. c	.. c	.. c	.. c	336.9	392.9	627.2	553.7	415.4
Cyprus	6 509.0	8 470.4	.. c	6 158.0	6 865.9	1 543.0	1 505.4	1 501.0	1 237.1	1 214.1
Malta	285.5	514.1	607.7	1 115.2	.. c	762.4	1 573.5	1 339.4	1 722.1	720.9
Montenegro	-	-	-	-	-	.. c	.. c	.. c	.. c	.. c
Romania	.. c	.. c	.. c	.. c	.. c	662.6	756.9	619.7	833.9	1 146.6
Russian Federation	188.8	70.4	62.1	148.6	134.8	6 596.7	7 401.4	6 145.7	6 036.5	5 677.7
Ukraine	-	-	.. c	-	.. c	137.3	216.5	352.2	432.1	1 094.4
AFRICA	**97.8**	**32.7**	**96.5**	**-3.2**	**-47.8**	**4 336.9**	**4 536.7**	**4 358.5**	**4 497.5**	**4 708.9**
Northern Africa	-24.9	.. c	35.1	.. c	-46.6	697.2	546.8	355.2	403.5	693.3
Algeria	-	-	-	-	-	.. c	.. c	.. c	.. c	.. c
Egypt	-24.8	.. c	-	-	-46.7	246.9	.. c	.. c	.. c	339.5
Libya	-	-	35.1	-	-	-	-	-49.1	-	-
Morocco	.. c	.. c	-	.. c	.. c	383.5	.. c	244.0	236.4	294.2
Tunisia	-	-	-	-	-	.. c	.. c	.. c	.. c	.. c
Other African countries	122.8	33.3	61.4	-11.8	-1.2	3 639.7	3 989.9	4 003.3	4 094.0	4 015.7
Nigeria	87.0	-	92.7	.. c	-	34.8	.. c	-5.4	.. c	.. c
South Africa	.. c	-18.6	-19.3	.. c	-33.9	1 122.1	1 696.4	1 613.5	1 711.5	1 838.3
AMERICA	**34 778.9**	**32 794.0**	**28 575.1**	**29 885.7**	**51 532.7**	**65 408.5**	**69 980.8**	**79 604.9**	**78 528.4**	**102 918.0**
Northern America	31 760.1	30 826.8	26 806.7	26 428.0	50 291.8	53 357.0	58 964.3	69 142.6	66 992.8	91 741.1
Central America and Caribbean countries	2 821.7	1 679.0	1 650.9	3 354.6	.. c	4 115.8	2 253.4	1 529.4	2 147.8	2 068.4
Bahamas	.. c	.. c	.. c	-	-	.. c	.. c	.. c	.. c	-
Bermuda	.. c	.. c	580.9	380.4	310.1	.. c	.. c	-87.0	388.2	.. c
Cayman Islands	2 094.7	946.8	353.9	311.3	.. c	143.3	95.8	86.5	41.2	.. c
El Salvador	-	.. c	-	-	-	.. c	.. c	.. c	12.3	.. c
Guatemala	-	-	-	-	-	.. c	.. c	.. c	.. c	.. c
Honduras	-	-	-	-	-	.. c	.. c	.. c	.. c	.. c
Nicaragua	-	-	-	-	-	-	-	-	-	-
Panama	-	-	-	.. c	-	75.4	.. c	7.9	7.4	8.1
Virgin Islands, U.S.	-	-	-	-	-	.. c	.. c	.. c	.. c	.. c
South America	197.2	288.3	.. c	.. c	-40.1	7 935.7	8 762.9	8 932.8	9 387.8	9 108.5
Argentina	.. c	.. c	.. c	-	.. c	451.1	577.9	570.1	558.0	553.4
Bolivia	-	-	-	-	.. c	.. c	.. c	.. c	.. c	924.2
Brazil	.. c	.. c	.. c	.. c	-48.3	4 280.6	4 608.8	4 545.9	4 764.9	4 440.0
Ecuador	-	-	-	-	-	.. c	84.2	.. c	115.0	161.3
Paraguay	-	-	-	-	-	.. c	.. c	.. c	.. c	.. c
Peru	-	-	-	-	-	377.6	440.8	447.0	599.2	427.3
Uruguay	-	-	-	.. c	-	91.0	77.4	77.5	68.4	75.3
Venezuela	-	.. c	.. c	.. c	-	116.4	50.2	.. c	.. c	.. c

SWEDEN

Table 2. Foreign direct investment positions by country *(cont.)*

At year end

Million US dollars

	Inward					Outward				
	2016	2017	2018	2019	2020	2016	2017	2018	2019	2020
ASIA	**9 267.7**	**13 254.3**	**13 032.8**	**12 803.2**	**16 214.6**	**25 188.6**	**28 877.3**	**27 466.6**	**30 759.6**	**30 933.6**
Near and Middle East	336.1	.. c	.. c	236.5	284.9	1 190.7	1 002.8	1 029.1	1 496.3	950.9
Gulf Arabian countries	.. c	.. c	.. c	97.4	.. c	512.3	465.3	583.4	722.7	583.0
Kuwait	-	-	-	-	-	.. c	.. c	.. c	.. c	.. c
Qatar	-	-	-	-24.3	-	.. c	.. c	.. c	103.8	-10.6
Saudi Arabia	.. c	.. c	.. c	.. c	.. c	145.7	170.7	157.2	64.1	128.8
United Arab Emirates	-24.3	.. c	.. c	-37.1	.. c	284.3	228.7	354.7	473.6	367.2
Other Near and Middle East	.. c	.. c	.. c	.. c	.. c	678.3	537.5	445.6	773.6	367.9
Jordan	-	-	-	-	-	.. c	.. c	.. c	.. c	.. c
Other Asian countries	8 931.6	12 828.8	12 869.9	12 566.8	15 929.8	23 997.9	27 874.5	26 437.6	29 263.3	29 982.8
China	.. c	.. c	.. c	.. c	.. c	10 669.4	13 182.6	11 208.5	12 715.9	14 253.0
Hong Kong, China	.. c	564.0	392.4	227.0	.. c	508.8	511.3	1 121.5	2 852.3	1 138.5
India	102.3	104.7	-7.6	11.2	3.8	2 261.8	2 909.6	2 619.6	2 387.2	2 299.3
Indonesia	-	.. c	.. c	.. c	.. c	267.4	305.3	265.7	313.5	199.5
Iran, Islamic Republic of	-	-	.. c	.. c	.. c	.. c	.. c	.. c	.. c	.. c
Malaysia	.. c	.. c	-9.8	.. c	.. c	715.7	858.1	750.8	752.5	810.4
Philippines	.. c	.. c	.. c	.. c	.. c	359.8	296.3	151.3	157.4	184.7
Singapore	267.8	18.8	.. c	.. c	945.2	1 082.1	725.6	711.6	916.5	1 616.0
Chinese Taipei	29.1	24.6	.. c	34.7	36.8	204.8	239.9	335.7	261.6	249.4
Thailand	.. c	-21.8	-	-	.. c	1 414.7	1 888.4	1 820.0	1 877.8	2 122.2
Viet Nam	42.3	38.0	49.8	59.6	60.8	-5.2	0.9	7.1	20.0	17.9
AUSTRALIA, OCEANIA AND POLAR REGIONS	**334.5**	**222.7**	**192.6**	**917.5**	**397.4**	**2 321.5**	**3 054.3**	**2 823.0**	**3 346.8**	**3 309.6**
WORLD unallocated and confidential	**138.9**	**175.9**	**163.2**	**168.7**	**445.6**	**-**	**0.1**	**0.1**	**-0.1**	**0.1**
European Union (since 01/02/2020)	**..**	**230 675.7**	**211 356.5**	**..**	**252 251.6**	**..**	**205 213.0**	**204 802.0**	**..**	**235 926.5**
G20 countries excl. European Union	**114 665.0**	**138 039.8**	**127 664.9**	**132 661.5**	**167 499.9**	**136 877.1**	**164 117.4**	**175 319.2**	**174 694.8**	**210 386.3**
G20 OECD countries	**108 767.6**	**130 295.7**	**120 980.3**	**125 293.2**	**157 168.8**	**111 082.3**	**133 264.9**	**148 192.8**	**146 143.3**	**180 996.2**
G20 Non-OECD countries	**5 897.4**	**.. c**	**6 684.5**	**7 368.3**	**.. c**	**25 794.8**	**30 852.6**	**27 126.5**	**28 551.4**	**29 390.1**
MENA countries	**.. c**	**.. c**	**188.8**	**106.0**	**184.9**	**1 224.1**	**1 003.0**	**921.4**	**1 131.3**	**1 264.0**
ASEAN countries	**356.2**	**96.1**	**649.4**	**626.2**	**1 058.7**	**3 894.9**	**4 125.4**	**3 847.4**	**4 069.6**	**4 955.4**

- Nil; .. Not available; c Confidential data

Note: Detailed metadata at: *http://metalinks.oecd.org/idi/20220712/6d95*.

Source: *OECD International Direct Investment Statistics (database)*: *https://doi.org/10.1787/idi-data-en*

SWEDEN

Table 3. Foreign direct investment income by country

Million US dollars

	Inward					Outward				
	2016	2017	2018	2019	2020	2016	2017	2018	2019	2020
WORLD	**21 835.7**	**22 166.0**	**24 955.1**	**23 558.3**	**21 840.3**	**25 633.3**	**30 744.8**	**34 932.8**	**34 513.8**	**31 781.2**
OECD COUNTRIES	..	..	**23 318.8**	**22 349.3**	**20 668.2**	..	..	**28 654.6**	**28 454.5**	**25 206.9**
Australia	-0.9	-5.4	-7.5	48.2	-17.8	207.7	248.9	132.1	311.6	312.9
Austria	236.4	250.3	326.3	227.5	361.6	155.6	217.7	206.7	170.1	123.5
Belgium	309.1	246.3	-6.9	104.5	108.0	933.8	1 092.7	1 359.3	1 265.5	1 137.7
Canada	200.5	549.6	152.2	225.5	299.6	367.6	276.8	208.6	354.5	411.3
Chile	.. c	.. c	5.4	0.6	2.7	149.4	150.7	80.0	419.2	96.4
Colombia	.. c	-	-	.. c	-	11.7	-0.4	9.2	24.1	28.9
Costa Rica	-	-	-	-	-	-14.6	4.4	-3.7	-1.7	-6.9
Czech Republic	0.5	-	0.2	-5.5	0.5	242.5	302.9	217.6	301.2	-43.4
Denmark	1 582.7	1 378.5	1 515.8	1 304.3	514.5	1 690.3	1 680.1	1 701.1	1 358.0	676.6
Estonia	7.7	17.4	11.0	59.0	24.1	462.9	486.6	540.0	450.8	435.0
Finland	2 020.3	1 917.5	3 355.0	3 400.6	3 490.6	2 512.1	4 206.3	3 731.4	2 954.8	2 226.9
France	526.0	624.9	412.5	383.4	426.0	526.7	1 077.7	1 006.9	666.7	574.6
Germany	1 546.1	1 930.7	1 997.3	2 877.0	1 719.6	220.0	1 231.9	1 675.1	567.9	1 583.5
Greece	-	-	-	.. c	.. c	14.0	12.8	17.5	29.1	68.2
Hungary	.. c	.. c	.. c	10.9	.. c	41.6	93.5	77.7	50.1	127.4
Iceland	-55.5	-3.0	-7.6	-	19.7	0.6	-7.6	15.5	6.0	5.4
Ireland	-3.7	184.9	112.8	-174.0	276.6	199.4	296.4	431.2	472.5	365.9
Israel	6.4	4.8	-	6.7	-38.9	27.3	38.5	119.0	-14.9	-25.7
Italy	109.3	115.4	-58.7	161.6	74.3	327.4	435.4	310.6	430.7	265.2
Japan	511.7	456.9	535.2	214.2	418.6	425.4	277.5	209.1	148.8	408.7
Korea	14.0	41.3	35.4	69.5	33.8	124.4	408.9	305.6	449.9	203.6
Latvia	-9.5	.. c	-	-10.4	.. c	308.4	463.7	429.7	325.0	390.0
Lithuania	-	.. c	12.3	4.0	-	332.6	470.6	542.2	426.4	502.8
Luxembourg	959.3	1 317.1	2 215.1	1 578.2	757.4	1 145.9	636.8	135.6	265.8	-228.8
Mexico	.. c	-5.9	21.4	17.7	.. c	158.6	213.1	230.3	150.2	94.8
Netherlands	3 539.6	4 450.7	3 548.3	3 333.3	3 941.6	2 361.8	2 512.0	3 484.8	4 656.6	4 692.7
New Zealand	.. c	.. c	0.2	.. c	59.3	18.2	16.3	13.0	10.8	15.4
Norway	1 623.4	1 465.7	1 625.4	1 396.4	1 673.9	3 297.4	3 207.4	3 722.3	3 404.6	2 591.9
Poland	-65.2	-25.2	-51.4	-204.5	-281.1	462.3	267.8	332.9	341.6	421.3
Portugal	.. c	-	-	15.7	17.8	86.5	101.8	172.1	116.2	37.9
Slovak Republic	-	-	-	-	-	27.2	35.8	29.3	31.9	40.0
Slovenia	-	-	-	-	-	3.5	9.4	23.0	34.8	16.2
Spain	249.3	86.2	320.8	234.0	198.3	558.9	522.6	763.6	397.4	494.2
Sweden	-	-	-	-	..	-	-	-	-	..
Switzerland	811.5	802.4	1 005.0	713.4	785.3	1 701.0	1 137.7	1 213.2	1 437.3	1 094.3
Turkey	-	-	-	0.1	0.2	55.7	91.4	83.2	65.3	183.3
United Kingdom	3 934.0	2 963.6	4 156.2	4 230.9	3 729.2	259.7	296.4	2 179.0	2 022.5	1 642.3
United States	2 033.1	1 300.7	2 086.9	2 127.1	2 068.7	2 572.1	3 282.6	2 956.0	4 375.9	4 236.3
EUROPE	**17 594.6**	**18 078.4**	**20 937.9**	**19 782.6**	**18 120.8**	**19 026.2**	**22 210.8**	**25 891.3**	**23 651.5**	**20 976.9**
Bulgaria	-	-	-	-	-	51.7	48.0	41.3	40.2	57.0
Croatia	.. c	-	-	.. c	.. c	18.9	9.6	46.6	25.0	24.5
Cyprus	78.4	205.1	202.6	120.6	-9.7	78.4	89.6	117.9	108.0	124.4
Malta	103.0	80.6	219.1	20.6	277.3	156.4	181.0	196.7	233.9	423.4
Montenegro	-	-	-	-	-	0.6	0.6	0.1	-	0.3
Romania	.. c	.. c	.. c	.. c	-	34.7	32.9	71.8	61.3	35.6
Russian Federation	-1.2	-	-	1.8	.. c	511.3	763.5	807.2	748.2	636.9
Ukraine	-	-	-	-	-	85.2	32.8	91.4	71.3	147.7
AFRICA	**-3.3**	**4.8**	**.. c**	**.. c**	**-15.4**	**242.5**	**231.3**	**345.6**	**325.3**	**207.7**
Northern Africa	-	-	-	-	.. c	49.9	14.7	19.1	44.3	27.3
Algeria	-	-	-	-	-	4.2	-2.5	12.8	4.4	10.2
Egypt	-	-	-	-	-	28.2	3.0	11.9	7.7	10.8
Libya	-	-	-	-	-	-	-	-	-	-
Morocco	-	-	-	-	.. c	14.7	14.0	-8.5	29.2	0.9
Tunisia	-	-	-	-	-	2.8	0.1	2.9	3.0	5.4
Other African countries	-3.3	4.8	.. c	.. c	-15.4	192.6	216.5	326.3	281.0	180.5
Nigeria	-	-	-	.. c	.. c	-0.5	-7.0	19.3	28.9	20.3
South Africa	.. c	-	-	.. c	.. c	91.9	99.7	160.4	149.0	97.6
AMERICA	**2 579.9**	**2 234.2**	**2 251.5**	**2 112.3**	**2 040.1**	**3 791.2**	**4 671.5**	**4 728.6**	**6 345.5**	**5 777.4**
Northern America	2 233.6	1 850.2	2 239.3	2 352.7	2 368.3	2 941.5	3 559.1	3 168.2	4 728.3	4 647.8
Central America and Caribbean countries	371.2	378.8	-5.4	-270.4	-332.2	209.3	288.1	326.6	209.6	113.7
Bahamas	-0.5	-1.6	-	-	-	-	0.5	0.8	4.2	-
Bermuda	29.7	54.4	67.7	33.1	41.4	14.5	21.9	10.8	29.0	.. c
Cayman Islands	288.7	398.0	3.3	9.4	11.6	32.1	18.7	74.1	21.7	4.8
El Salvador	-	-	-	.. c	-	1.1	0.8	1.5	-	0.4
Guatemala	-	-	-	-	-	-7.9	14.3	-7.0	-4.8	-7.9
Honduras	-	-	-	-	-	0.9	0.2	0.7	1.6	-0.2
Nicaragua	-	-	-	-	-	-	-	-	-	-
Panama	-	-	-	.. c	.. c	7.1	4.8	-	0.4	0.3
Virgin Islands, U.S.	-	-	-	-	-	-	-	-	-	-
South America	-24.9	5.1	17.6	30.0	4.0	640.3	824.3	1 233.8	1 407.5	1 016.0
Argentina	.. c	-	-	.. c	.. c	180.0	184.0	170.8	137.2	119.4
Bolivia	-	-	-	.. c	.. c	204.2	218.1	452.8	222.0	126.4
Brazil	-20.9	4.7	12.1	28.7	1.7	7.6	200.0	462.1	525.9	619.1
Ecuador	.. c	-	-	-	-	-0.6	4.1	3.3	4.2	10.5
Paraguay	-	-	-	-	-	-1.2	-1.4	-1.2	0.7	.. c
Peru	.. c	.. c	.. c	.. c	.. c	79.1	40.7	40.3	55.4	14.7
Uruguay	.. c	-	-	.. c	.. c	25.8	22.5	-0.7	15.7	-2.2
Venezuela	.. c	-	-	0.6	-	-15.8	6.0	17.4	3.1	2.4

SWEDEN

Table 3. Foreign direct investment income by country *(cont.)*

Million US dollars

	Inward					Outward				
	2016	2017	2018	2019	2020	2016	2017	2018	2019	2020
ASIA	**1 664.1**	**1 853.4**	**1 772.3**	**1 626.1**	**1 651.8**	**2 347.5**	**3 366.1**	**3 822.4**	**3 869.3**	**4 490.8**
Near and Middle East	24.3	19.0	.. c	15.4	-15.6	107.9	76.8	196.0	49.9	-6.1
Gulf Arabian countries	.. c	.. c	.. c	.. c	.. c	66.4	37.8	69.8	59.9	30.5
Kuwait	-	-	-	-	-	2.0	1.2	1.4	0.8	0.9
Qatar	-	-	-	-	-	-0.2	-0.2	-1.2	-1.4	-3.9
Saudi Arabia	.. c	.. c	.. c	.. c	.. c	17.3	11.2	14.6	18.1	34.7
United Arab Emirates	-	-	.. c	-	-	33.5	15.2	42.6	19.5	-16.1
Other Near and Middle East	6.7	4.8	-	6.7	-38.9	41.5	38.8	126.1	-9.9	-36.6
Jordan	-	-	-	-	-	0.2	0.4	0.1	0.1	0.3
Other Asian countries	1 639.8	1 834.4	1 761.9	1 610.6	1 667.5	2 239.6	3 289.5	3 626.4	3 819.4	4 496.9
China	1 081.6	1 256.3	1 172.7	1 305.0	1 189.8	821.9	1 585.0	1 425.4	1 717.2	2 289.1
Hong Kong, China	-8.8	26.6	7.2	-2.2	1.7	229.9	182.9	668.0	631.9	777.1
India	1.1	14.6	1.6	1.5	-0.2	247.5	474.1	401.6	297.0	324.4
Indonesia	.. c	.. c	.. c	.. c	.. c	24.9	16.7	33.9	16.7	0.9
Iran, Islamic Republic of	-	-	-	-	-	15.3	-16.7	-69.5	22.4	7.9
Malaysia	7.0	35.2	-12.0	3.2	-0.8	65.1	75.6	80.5	94.9	50.1
Philippines	.. c	.. c	.. c	.. c	.. c	36.6	22.2	21.4	17.0	13.9
Singapore	26.1	4.1	21.5	20.7	25.5	3.4	-86.8	91.6	106.5	160.4
Chinese Taipei	.. c	-	.. c	.. c	.. c	32.7	62.0	89.8	66.4	78.3
Thailand	.. c	.. c	.. c	.. c	-0.1	99.5	154.3	164.0	148.1	83.7
Viet Nam	-	-	-	-	-	18.8	13.8	21.2	13.4	19.0
AUSTRALIA, OCEANIA AND POLAR REGIONS	**-0.2**	**-5.4**	**-7.2**	**47.8**	**41.5**	**225.9**	**265.1**	**145.1**	**322.3**	**328.3**
WORLD unallocated and confidential	**0.6**	**0.6**	**.. d**	**.. d**	**1.5**	**-**	**-**	**-0.1**	**-0.1**	**-**
European Union (since 01/02/2020)	**..**	**12 786.0**	**14 137.9**	**..**	**11 902.6**	**..**	**16 566.7**	**17 717.0**	**..**	**14 634.1**
G20 countries excl. European Union	**9 943.6**	**9 261.7**	**10 528.1**	**11 693.1**	**9 962.2**	**7 147.3**	**11 174.7**	**12 772.3**	**13 153.3**	**14 038.8**
G20 OECD countries	**8 875.1**	**7 971.8**	**9 331.0**	**10 355.2**	**8 756.7**	**5 245.0**	**7 840.4**	**9 296.2**	**9 543.9**	**9 916.5**
G20 Non-OECD countries	**1 068.3**	**1 289.9**	**1 197.1**	**1 338.0**	**1 205.4**	**1 902.3**	**3 334.3**	**3 476.0**	**3 609.4**	**4 122.3**
MENA countries	**.. c**	**.. c**	**.. c**	**.. c**	**.. c**	**116.1**	**48.0**	**85.5**	**108.0**	**45.9**
ASEAN countries	**29.5**	**39.4**	**9.7**	**23.2**	**23.9**	**261.4**	**198.0**	**458.1**	**395.9**	**335.4**

- Nil; .. Not available; c Confidential data; d Secondary Confidentiality

Note: Detailed metadata at: *http://metalinks.oecd.org/idi/20220712/6d95*.

Source: *OECD International Direct Investment Statistics (database): https://doi.org/10.1787/idi-data-en*

SWEDEN

Table 4. Foreign direct investment flows by industrial sector

Million US dollars

	Inward					Outward				
	2016	2017	2018	2019	2020	2016	2017	2018	2019	2020
All FDI activities	**19 153.0**	**12 511.4**	**3 806.7**	**9 110.6**	**18 798.1**	**4 702.5**	**27 368.7**	**17 833.8**	**16 104.4**	**23 906.6**
Agriculture, forestry and fishing	**30.3**	**3.7**	**2.8**	**33.9**	**-15.0**	**-0.5**	**5.4**	**8.4**	**-1.0**	**-1.8**
Mining and quarrying	**1 394.1**	**412.2**	**684.1**	**-1 437.5**	**574.2**	**1 562.7**	**544.3**	**177.0**	**699.4**	**-115.2**
Extraction activities	1 372.6	398.3	687.9	.. c	574.0	779.8	311.0	-18.0	430.6	-42.0
Manufacturing	**818.0**	**2 051.9**	**6 053.6**	**3 423.5**	**-6 350.5**	**4 417.3**	**13 203.5**	**15 666.7**	**7 223.4**	**5 766.3**
of which:										
Food products, beverages and tobacco	-128.8	441.6	756.2	588.9	124.9	.. c	679.7	471.7	-299.5	1 439.9
Textiles, wood and paper products; printing	-68.5	-504.6	245.1	1 656.7	629.4	321.4	.. c	.. c	.. c	-183.7
Chemical, rubber, plastic, non-metallic mineral products	511.9	1 995.2	-375.2	549.7	-8 698.4	-338.5	2 141.7	409.0	639.8	2 066.7
Metal and machinery products, except electrical equipment	422.7	1 576.1	3 747.8	-260.2	-310.7	323.6	5 261.6	11 431.9	1 513.7	3 633.0
Motor vehicles, trailers, semi-trailers, other transport equipment	397.0	-3 851.6	1 917.5	219.3	1 018.8	4 414.5	1 084.1	3 021.7	4 471.7	123.1
Other manufacturing	-316.3	2 395.3	-237.7	668.9	885.6	660.3	-912.5	-205.2	914.6	-1 312.7
Electricity, gas, steam and air conditioning supply	**105.4**	**-2 095.1**	**-667.7**	**460.7**	**-573.6**	**.. c**	**.. c**	**.. c**	**.. c**	**2 106.6**
Water supply; sewerage, waste management and remediation activities	**-23.3**	**15.2**	**33.6**	**-7.8**	**18.5**	**-134.6**	**76.4**	**46.7**	**-147.3**	**-61.5**
Construction	**370.6**	**134.0**	**-205.3**	**260.5**	**-39.6**	**-13.9**	**.. c**	**75.5**	**.. c**	**.. c**
Services	**16 489.8**	**10 364.3**	**2 550.7**	**1 634.6**	**25 572.2**	**-2 342.7**	**12 259.5**	**2 174.1**	**7 674.6**	**15 091.6**
Wholesale and retail trade; repair of motor vehicles and motorcycles	15 379.3	4 397.4	-3 378.1	1 310.7	4 478.5	-2 116.4	2 146.3	-1 262.9	2 541.5	2 310.9
Transportation and storage	285.2	38.8	464.1	-249.2	-628.5	-168.5	-1 200.9	394.5	-296.7	-1 235.1
Accommodation and food service activities	-254.5	105.5	10.5	-16.8	.. c	476.8	74.4	14.5	5.3	-77.3
Information and communication	-1 050.5	-612.5	-859.9	-728.5	-1 161.2	-1 722.4	-412.0	852.3	1 126.1	-2 495.0
Financial and insurance activities	3 348.7	2 743.3	-76.3	-680.8	19 567.8	-656.6	721.2	-2 262.6	851.6	15 619.7
Activities of holding companies	3 648.7	250.0	-1 446.3	-122.5	18 794.4	1 081.5	-31.2	-2 795.8	325.8	13 335.9
Real estate activities	-1 200.0	-956.7	1 232.7	502.1	1 128.4	288.0	2 243.6	1 638.4	-121.6	1 999.8
Professional, scientific and technical activities	-498.7	1 992.0	2 353.7	1 369.0	1 466.1	59.0	2 795.1	790.3	2 849.4	-1 827.6
Administrative and support service activities	573.7	2 748.2	1 791.4	40.7	583.6	1 345.6	5 377.8	1 775.8	909.3	717.2
Public administration; activities of households and of extraterritorial organisations	-	-	-	-	.. c	78.2	527.7	98.2	57.8	96.7
Education	0.2	8.4	8.5	0.1	6.9	0.6	5.3	18.9	9.8	11.2
Human health and social work activities	-119.2	-107.9	.. c	.. c	-248.7	80.6	156.9	131.8	-263.3	50.1
Arts, entertainment and recreation	-9.4	-7.4	24.2	-8.5	-2.6	-50.6	22.1	25.7	45.2	-26.3
Other services	35.3	15.1	2.0	-14.8	-	43.0	-198.0	-40.4	-39.9	-52.9
Not allocated and confidential	**-149.8**	**1 521.4**	**-4 961.7**	**4 150.1**	**-1 007.9**	**.. c**	**.. c**	**.. c**	**.. c**	**.. c**
Private real estate activities	**117.9**	**103.8**	**316.7**	**592.6**	**619.9**	**-54.9**	**.. c**	**127.7**	**575.4**	**466.9**

- Nil; c Confidential data

Note: Detailed metadata at: *http://metalinks.oecd.org/idi/20220712/6d95.*

Source: *OECD International Direct Investment Statistics (database): https://doi.org/10.1787/idi-data-en*

Table 5. Foreign direct investment positions by industrial sector

At year end

Million US dollars

	Inward					Outward				
	2016	2017	2018	2019	2020	2016	2017	2018	2019	2020
All FDI activities	**317 160.8**	**365 713.5**	**338 325.0**	**347 404.6**	**414 518.8**	**355 800.8**	**386 531.1**	**395 702.4**	**411 276.7**	**464 891.5**
Agriculture, forestry and fishing	**87.0**	**27.2**	**.. c**	**.. c**	**.. c**	**315.9**	**267.3**	**476.5**	**59.9**	**26.2**
Mining and quarrying	**1 400.2**	**1 696.9**	**1 577.9**	**1 210.0**	**1 866.2**	**3 560.5**	**3 596.7**	**3 953.5**	**6 182.8**	**4 128.1**
Extraction activities	959.3	.. c	1 236.0	701.9	1 857.7	.. c	.. c	1 608.6	.. c	.. c
Manufacturing	**126 855.4**	**141 303.6**	**130 286.3**	**129 015.8**	**143 329.9**	**143 849.8**	**159 329.1**	**166 549.3**	**165 670.0**	**175 465.1**
of which:										
Food products, beverages and tobacco	22 480.4	23 642.7	21 672.8	22 659.6	26 048.8	4 965.9	4 359.0	4 868.0	4 345.1	4 433.7
Textiles, wood and paper products; printing	14 300.8	15 442.4	14 368.3	16 766.6	18 993.5	11 869.2	.. c	.. c	.. c	16 412.3
Chemical, rubber, plastic, non-metallic mineral products	46 418.3	53 826.8	51 619.3	50 994.3	52 614.5	35 800.1	43 214.8	43 581.2	41 158.6	45 418.2
Metal and machinery products, except electrical equipment	13 125.1	16 100.0	16 179.1	14 437.0	16 493.9	46 384.3	47 357.7	50 055.9	50 807.5	55 874.1
Motor vehicles, trailers, semi-trailers, other transport equipment	20 459.8	19 708.6	16 953.4	16 057.4	18 253.4	35 884.1	38 412.3	40 956.3	44 320.6	43 622.5
Other manufacturing	10 071.0	12 583.1	9 493.4	8 100.9	10 925.7	8 946.2	10 120.2	12 429.3	9 634.5	9 704.1
Electricity, gas, steam and air conditioning supply	**22 630.4**	**24 152.0**	**20 934.4**	**21 809.2**	**26 321.6**	**.. c**	**.. c**	**.. c**	**.. c**	**.. c**
Water supply; sewerage, waste management and remediation activities	**768.6**	**875.2**	**855.3**	**1 121.7**	**752.3**	**586.7**	**664.7**	**674.7**	**588.6**	**.. c**
Construction	**1 823.4**	**2 306.9**	**1 372.1**	**1 192.0**	**1 024.9**	**3 772.2**	**4 089.2**	**4 651.4**	**5 230.7**	**5 205.8**
Services	**145 536.8**	**173 041.3**	**159 907.7**	**162 872.7**	**210 103.6**	**168 696.7**	**176 821.9**	**174 720.9**	**185 672.1**	**222 321.7**
Wholesale and retail trade; repair of motor vehicles and motorcycles	34 316.8	45 380.8	40 880.5	39 583.0	45 824.6	36 711.7	42 604.2	39 754.1	43 414.1	47 028.7
Transportation and storage	3 500.7	4 980.3	6 322.2	5 865.0	5 682.8	6 627.9	6 245.4	6 003.9	7 907.0	9 644.3
Accommodation and food service activities	897.5	1 697.2	529.7	188.1	459.4	2 402.6	585.2	.. c	.. c	.. c
Information and communication	13 554.8	15 140.6	13 435.9	11 895.2	13 818.5	17 386.6	23 408.4	28 671.1	23 618.0	21 829.2
Financial and insurance activities	59 826.0	65 339.4	61 429.2	64 814.1	92 529.2	74 760.7	57 176.2	45 318.6	48 914.8	68 695.9
Activities of holding companies	24 801.6	24 919.1	26 420.5	29 720.7	54 620.7	7 495.9	9 367.6	11 907.7	14 381.8	28 914.3
Real estate activities	17 034.6	19 253.7	17 178.4	22 465.7	30 332.3	11 045.6	16 808.1	18 596.6	24 678.0	30 451.3
Professional, scientific and technical activities	10 890.4	12 126.3	13 799.3	13 411.5	13 294.5	8 528.9	13 016.7	16 310.3	16 095.9	18 643.1
Administrative and support service activities	4 791.9	8 348.4	4 625.6	3 937.6	6 114.0	8 803.3	12 815.8	13 904.8	13 639.0	16 803.6
Public administration; activities of households and of extraterritorial organisations	-	-	-	.. c	-	.. c	.. c	2 163.8	.. c	.. c
Education	.. c	.. c	139.3	.. c	7.8	.. c	.. c	.. c	.. c	.. c
Human health and social work activities	282.4	.. c	1 095.3	.. c	1 492.7	1 162.3	2 479.9	2 760.4	2 566.4	1 638.5
Arts, entertainment and recreation	.. c	.. c	447.3	376.9	542.9	556.7	588.5	.. c	237.2	.. c
Other services	233.7	214.5	25.0	.. c	.. c	.. c	.. c	.. c	.. c	.. c
Not allocated and confidential	**5 438.7**	**7 187.0**	**.. c**	**.. c**	**.. c**	**.. c**	**.. c**	**.. c**	**.. c**	**.. c**
Private real estate activities	**12 620.3**	**15 123.3**	**14 196.1**	**14 696.9**	**17 278.7**	**20 236.9**	**25 655.1**	**24 175.2**	**25 651.9**	**31 658.5**

- Nil; c Confidential data

Note: Detailed metadata at: *http://metalinks.oecd.org/idi/20220712/6d95*.

Source: OECD *International Direct Investment Statistics (database): https://doi.org/10.1787/idi-data-en*

Table 6. Foreign direct investment income by industrial sector

Million US dollars

	Inward					Outward				
	2016	2017	2018	2019	2020	2016	2017	2018	2019	2020
All FDI activities	**21 835.7**	**22 166.0**	**24 955.1**	**23 558.3**	**21 840.3**	**25 633.3**	**30 744.8**	**34 932.8**	**34 513.8**	**31 781.2**
Agriculture, forestry and fishing	**30.3**	**3.7**	**2.8**	**38.4**	**-15.0**	**-0.5**	**5.4**	**8.9**	**-0.5**	**-**
Mining and quarrying	**363.0**	**463.6**	**329.6**	**-1.0**	**81.9**	**554.5**	**659.9**	**476.0**	**755.4**	**261.7**
Extraction activities	310.1	435.9	333.4	-0.1	82.0	297.0	304.9	140.6	533.8	-20.2
Manufacturing	**11 210.4**	**11 193.4**	**12 910.3**	**12 043.1**	**10 512.9**	**11 593.5**	**14 396.7**	**17 699.9**	**17 363.8**	**16 037.7**
of which:										
Food products, beverages and tobacco	962.3	661.9	1 129.1	1 299.9	1 007.4	1 325.8	832.9	814.3	742.7	1 262.0
Textiles, wood and paper products; printing	149.1	498.0	569.9	680.1	980.1	663.6	1 388.8	985.7	1 253.9	1 383.3
Chemical, rubber, plastic, non-metallic mineral products	5 323.7	4 225.3	5 868.4	5 138.1	4 787.6	159.3	1 426.9	2 348.0	2 843.5	1 656.4
Metal and machinery products, except electrical equipment	1 113.4	1 714.9	1 351.6	1 166.8	1 121.3	5 249.6	6 131.4	7 485.4	6 776.1	6 114.1
Motor vehicles, trailers, semi-trailers, other transport equipment	2 822.4	3 255.9	2 880.2	2 964.1	2 025.7	2 516.2	3 852.8	4 691.8	4 794.4	4 668.6
Other manufacturing	839.5	837.5	1 111.1	794.2	591.0	1 679.2	763.9	1 374.6	953.3	953.1
Electricity, gas, steam and air conditioning supply	**186.9**	**204.4**	**708.0**	**1 209.7**	**1 070.6**	**108.5**	**596.2**	**361.4**	**94.4**	**1 370.0**
Water supply; sewerage, waste management and remediation activities	**3.0**	**15.2**	**34.2**	**21.5**	**19.5**	**-32.8**	**77.8**	**60.6**	**9.4**	**10.6**
Construction	**162.6**	**458.5**	**115.2**	**113.3**	**-55.4**	**198.8**	**-59.9**	**115.3**	**323.3**	**556.2**
Services	**9 764.4**	**9 518.8**	**10 208.5**	**9 110.6**	**9 885.2**	**12 640.6**	**14 402.8**	**15 529.6**	**15 220.9**	**12 925.5**
Wholesale and retail trade; repair of motor vehicles and motorcycles	3 090.3	3 042.5	2 756.6	2 507.2	3 686.7	3 394.6	4 078.3	4 252.6	4 866.4	5 942.0
Transportation and storage	339.0	207.3	-138.2	173.0	-334.2	-20.9	57.4	-439.9	-39.9	-789.8
Accommodation and food service activities	37.7	132.1	60.3	-16.8	-134.1	126.3	99.9	18.1	5.3	-165.8
Information and communication	1 209.5	703.1	1 576.9	1 465.0	1 279.7	1 874.8	2 300.7	3 107.3	2 414.2	1 101.2
Financial and insurance activities	3 218.3	3 142.0	3 914.3	3 336.8	4 245.1	4 242.3	5 120.0	4 584.6	4 788.2	4 311.5
Activities of holding companies	642.4	264.0	390.2	1 051.9	869.4	314.1	197.8	295.3	444.5	599.6
Real estate activities	310.5	537.1	186.2	278.9	474.6	245.1	167.1	366.2	407.7	92.9
Professional, scientific and technical activities	1 119.1	1 219.6	1 330.2	895.7	560.0	1 283.8	941.5	1 630.1	827.0	788.5
Administrative and support service activities	484.0	541.4	446.1	435.5	332.8	1 114.2	1 201.0	1 682.9	1 611.0	1 444.6
Public administration; activities of households and of extraterritorial organisations	-	-	-	-	-	78.2	170.7	144.5	59.4	153.0
Education	0.2	8.4	8.5	0.1	6.9	0.6	5.3	18.9	9.8	11.2
Human health and social work activities	-77.0	-27.3	41.4	58.6	-233.5	89.3	79.8	-18.8	190.1	64.7
Arts, entertainment and recreation	-9.4	-7.4	24.2	-8.5	1.3	138.3	119.8	147.5	54.1	-26.3
Other services	42.0	19.8	2.0	-14.8	-	74.2	61.7	35.8	27.4	-2.1
Not allocated and confidential	**1.5**	**110.3**	**435.1**	**515.6**	**-212.7**	**426.5**	**428.7**	**491.2**	**532.5**	**458.1**
Private real estate activities	**113.6**	**198.1**	**211.5**	**507.2**	**553.2**	**144.2**	**237.2**	**189.9**	**214.7**	**161.5**

- Nil

Note: Detailed metadata at: *http://metalinks.oecd.org/idi/20220712/6d95*.

Source: *OECD International Direct Investment Statistics (database)*: *https://doi.org/10.1787/idi-data-en*

SWITZERLAND

Table 1. Foreign direct investment flows by country

Million US dollars

	Inward					Outward				
	2016	2017	2018	2019	2020	2016	2017	2018	2019	2020
WORLD	**150 285.4**	**111 199.5**	**-83 153.3**	**-105 797.1**	**-162 697.5**	**166 617.9**	**21 943.6**	**43 597.8**	**-56 168.5**	**-36 150.4**
OECD COUNTRIES	**143 363.7**	**63 961.9**	**-56 646.2**	**-122 411.4**	**.. c**	**190 460.6**	**-34 211.1**	**14 272.1**	**-52 794.0**	**.. c**
Australia	.. c	.. c	.. c	.. c	.. c	-489.1	-1 952.5	-8 743.5	-753.4	4 220.3
Austria	10 231.0	-1 124.1	3 540.1	170.3	7 276.9	248.7	-280.7	-214.7	1 767.3	-294.7
Belgium	-1 126.9	-1 168.5	-549.1	12 865.2	-1 645.6	-1 647.8	-4 342.3	-3 219.1	5 631.6	4 420.7
Canada	-137.6	2 989.8	50.7	-1 483.8	-1 360.4	-3 334.5	534.1	-6 876.9	8 423.1	-2 296.5
Chile	.. c	.. c	.. c	.. c	.. c	-467.5	-47.4	3 688.7	316.7	430.3
Colombia	.. c	.. c	.. c	.. c	.. c	11.0	301.7	3 544.2	631.8	41.4
Costa Rica	.. c	.. c	.. c	.. c	.. c	79.0	154.5	154.8	286.2	19.2
Czech Republic	.. c	.. c	.. c	.. c	.. c	-840.6	429.7	7.7	-325.7	27.5
Denmark	-371.5	1 483.2	245.8	-15 537.8	-2 180.8	-413.6	133.5	141.4	-110.5	26.6
Estonia	.. c	.. c	.. c	.. c	.. c	354.6	-328.1	18.9	44.3	103.0
Finland	.. c	.. c	.. c	.. c	.. c	171.9	-432.8	180.3	154.8	7.5
France	-2 933.5	531.0	10 623.5	3 483.1	622.5	2 932.7	-932.2	9 228.2	3 707.1	553.6
Germany	2 354.8	1 368.7	-8 955.4	-2 419.3	474.8	7 342.8	5 746.7	11 059.8	5 409.1	2 852.4
Greece	.. c	.. c	.. c	.. c	.. c	-382.7	187.5	-47.3	-53.3	-16.3
Hungary	4 529.9	2 553.2	-2 321.2	-1 075.8	-12 803.4	4 048.3	392.6	385.3	20 570.5	27 137.0
Iceland	.. c	.. c	.. c	.. c	.. c	.. c	.. c	.. c	.. c	.. c
Ireland	25 811.9	11 032.5	18 037.9	-64 024.9	12 351.1	36 712.1	-42 891.7	6 861.1	-36 968.3	-16 964.7
Israel	-200.0	-177.3	-26.1	54.2	-343.4	917.6	-152.8	42.6	-401.2	-71.4
Italy	535.4	25.7	-1 401.4	244.3	357.6	819.8	587.5	1 308.8	2 090.1	907.5
Japan	-441.9	-1 935.9	-656.7	17 442.0	12 081.9	2 281.6	4 507.7	2 488.8	905.0	760.5
Korea	.. c	.. c	.. c	.. c	.. c	-835.2	304.3	5.4	4 923.0	564.2
Latvia	.. c	.. c	.. c	.. c	.. c	4.1	96.2	37.5	45.4	-5.7
Lithuania	.. c	.. c	.. c	.. c	.. c	-0.4	-19.2	75.9	181.4	-37.4
Luxembourg	33 881.6	42 788.2	-29 313.6	-6 612.3	-110 213.8	26 771.8	-6 275.5	-3 371.4	-58 240.9	-24 155.7
Mexico	.. c	.. c	.. c	.. c	.. c	614.2	483.8	777.3	763.7	-225.8
Netherlands	51 810.0	47 461.0	-50 790.0	-18 672.7	-57 546.3	36 253.8	7 353.6	142.8	-10 566.4	-10 986.2
New Zealand	.. c	.. c	.. c	.. c	.. c	38.1	-18.9	41.0	117.6	-105.6
Norway	.. c	.. c	.. c	.. c	.. c	2 357.4	-364.8	-289.8	-3 547.6	493.0
Poland	.. c	.. c	.. c	.. c	.. c	356.8	669.0	528.0	525.7	942.4
Portugal	.. c	.. c	.. c	.. c	.. c	54.6	183.5	-6.0	-47.9	83.7
Slovak Republic	.. c	.. c	.. c	.. c	.. c	69.5	267.6	209.9	17.3	18.1
Slovenia	.. c	.. c	.. c	.. c	.. c	.. c	.. c	.. c	.. c	.. c
Spain	-563.5	-53.1	-248.5	-611.2	772.9	-225.4	330.1	1 142.2	1 533.5	3 306.9
Sweden	-103.7	800.5	587.4	288.0	1 531.2	-1 013.6	1 073.3	148.3	1 912.6	-388.2
Switzerland	-	-	-	-	-	-	-	-	-	-
Turkey	.. c	.. c	.. c	.. c	.. c	394.6	221.2	219.4	91.2	983.8
United Kingdom	6 064.1	-26 403.8	39 547.8	-6 434.2	-6 185.3	13 525.9	-14 770.5	12 733.6	5 946.8	4 928.0
United States	14 077.8	-16 805.0	-35 329.3	-40 872.5	19 823.4	63 742.3	15 167.0	-14 492.8	-6 961.8	17 124.3
EUROPE	**135 481.5**	**87 485.7**	**5 089.9**	**-100 572.8**	**-168 693.9**	**132 131.9**	**11 413.5**	**39 152.9**	**-53 489.9**	**-46 506.1**
Bulgaria	.. c	.. c	.. c	.. c	.. c	-15.4	36.9	-25.4	36.7	2 208.0
Croatia	.. c	.. c	.. c	.. c	.. c	17.6	56.5	-6.0	88.2	116.8
Cyprus	-487.9	1 298.6	-619.3	1 236.3	-495.0	-1 387.2	53 018.2	-501.0	-5.6	-45 250.7
Malta	.. c	.. c	.. c	.. c	.. c	.. c	.. c	.. c	.. c	.. c
Montenegro	.. c	.. c	.. c	.. c	.. c	.. c	.. c	.. c	.. c	.. c
Romania	.. c	.. c	.. c	.. c	.. c	-56.2	393.3	214.5	443.8	945.7
Russian Federation	.. c	.. c	.. c	.. c	.. c	1 068.9	4 602.2	2 668.9	3 929.5	974.8
Ukraine	.. c	.. c	.. c	.. c	.. c	-38.2	756.1	623.8	723.7	618.4
AFRICA	**.. c**	**.. c**	**.. c**	**.. c**	**.. c**	**359.0**	**-1 408.2**	**-632.9**	**3 233.0**	**2 381.9**
Northern Africa	.. c	.. c	.. c	.. c	.. c	-705.5	-98.6	-31.3	84.4	257.9
Algeria	.. c	.. c	.. c	.. c	.. c	.. c	.. c	.. c	.. c	.. c
Egypt	.. c	.. c	.. c	.. c	.. c	-415.5	-113.3	-72.0	86.7	234.8
Libya	.. c	.. c	.. c	.. c	.. c	.. c	.. c	.. c	.. c	.. c
Morocco	.. c	.. c	.. c	.. c	.. c	-333.4	-14.4	23.2	-14.4	28.7
Tunisia	.. c	.. c	.. c	.. c	.. c	2.4	12.7	15.4	27.7	9.5
Other African countries	.. c	.. c	.. c	.. c	.. c	1 064.5	-1 309.6	-601.6	3 148.6	2 124.0
Nigeria	.. c	.. c	.. c	.. c	.. c	162.8	35.0	-2.7	36.1	149.1
South Africa	.. c	.. c	.. c	.. c	.. c	861.8	-82.1	-365.7	2 307.0	58.3
AMERICA	**13 913.0**	**23 505.5**	**-89 321.4**	**-26 294.2**	**-10 930.7**	**38 004.8**	**5 314.0**	**7 591.7**	**-4 344.7**	**-10 524.0**
Northern America	13 940.2	-13 815.2	-35 278.4	-42 356.3	18 462.9	60 407.8	15 701.0	-21 369.7	1 461.4	14 827.8
Central America and Caribbean countries	.. c	.. c	.. c	.. c	.. c	-22 420.3	-11 089.7	20 270.0	-5 179.1	-28 952.5
Bahamas	.. c	.. c	.. c	.. c	.. c	.. c	.. c	.. c	.. c	.. c
Bermuda	.. c	.. c	.. c	.. c	.. c	-1 425.5	-12 754.8	26 034.8	-21 260.4	-2 029.9
Cayman Islands	.. c	.. c	.. c	.. c	.. c	.. c	.. c	.. c	.. c	.. c
El Salvador	.. c	.. c	.. c	.. c	.. c	.. c	.. c	.. c	.. c	.. c
Guatemala	.. c	.. c	.. c	.. c	.. c	17.6	-59.3	1.0	76.2	-46.7
Honduras	.. c	.. c	.. c	.. c	.. c	.. c	.. c	.. c	.. c	.. c
Nicaragua	.. c	.. c	.. c	.. c	.. c	.. c	.. c	.. c	.. c	.. c
Panama	.. c	.. c	.. c	.. c	.. c	-3 795.0	4 031.1	-221.9	137.9	-1 649.0
Virgin Islands, U.S.	.. c	.. c	.. c	.. c	.. c	.. c	.. c	.. c	.. c	.. c
South America	.. c	.. c	.. c	.. c	.. c	17.3	702.6	8 691.3	-626.9	3 600.7
Argentina	.. c	.. c	.. c	.. c	.. c	-514.5	51.2	244.3	228.4	466.3
Bolivia	.. c	.. c	.. c	.. c	.. c	-15.6	11.5	8.0	0.8	-4.5
Brazil	.. c	.. c	.. c	.. c	.. c	59.4	-184.8	1 251.9	1 012.8	-356.3
Ecuador	.. c	.. c	.. c	.. c	.. c	-15.2	37.0	81.7	0.4	4.1
Paraguay	.. c	.. c	.. c	.. c	.. c	.. c	.. c	.. c	.. c	.. c
Peru	.. c	.. c	.. c	.. c	.. c	-1.3	314.9	-217.6	-3 068.7	4 036.7
Uruguay	.. c	.. c	.. c	.. c	.. c	660.7	62.8	138.0	48.1	61.7
Venezuela	.. c	.. c	.. c	.. c	.. c	297.5	140.2	-38.7	180.2	-1 071.2

SWITZERLAND

Table 1. Foreign direct investment flows by country *(cont.)*

Million US dollars

	Inward					Outward				
	2016	2017	2018	2019	2020	2016	2017	2018	2019	2020
ASIA	**.. c**	**.. c**	**.. c**	**.. c**	**.. c**	**-2 927.7**	**9 137.4**	**7 438.7**	**332.0**	**14 451.7**
Near and Middle East	.. c	.. c	.. c	.. c	.. c	-3 273.7	-608.0	-2 815.9	-9 394.6	-2 718.2
Gulf Arabian countries	.. c	.. c	.. c	.. c	.. c	.. c	.. c	.. c	.. c	.. c
Kuwait	.. c	.. c	.. c	.. c	.. c	.. c	.. c	.. c	.. c	.. c
Qatar	.. c	.. c	.. c	.. c	.. c	-3.1	4.7	0.2	-35.8	344.7
Saudi Arabia	.. c	.. c	.. c	.. c	.. c	93.9	90.7	194.0	930.5	-856.3
United Arab Emirates	.. c	.. c	.. c	.. c	.. c	-3 869.3	-530.7	-3 397.1	-9 381.7	-2 375.9
Other Near and Middle East	.. c	.. c	.. c	.. c	.. c	.. c	.. c	.. c	.. c	.. c
Jordan	.. c	.. c	.. c	.. c	.. c	25.3	33.6	-3.5	14.7	-48.5
Other Asian countries	.. c	.. c	.. c	.. c	.. c	346.0	9 745.4	10 254.6	9 726.6	17 169.9
China	.. c	.. c	.. c	.. c	.. c	1 505.1	3 216.3	3 180.7	1 711.1	3 149.6
Hong Kong, China	.. c	.. c	.. c	.. c	.. c	-489.8	514.1	-271.4	405.8	849.2
India	.. c	.. c	.. c	.. c	.. c	164.6	1 050.7	895.6	248.9	-15.3
Indonesia	.. c	.. c	.. c	.. c	.. c	277.8	84.3	33.4	543.4	22.7
Iran, Islamic Republic of	.. c	.. c	.. c	.. c	.. c	.. c	.. c	.. c	.. c	.. c
Malaysia	.. c	.. c	.. c	.. c	.. c	162.4	618.5	-2 540.5	838.3	-30.8
Philippines	.. c	.. c	.. c	.. c	.. c	-18.1	770.3	-184.5	209.9	-338.9
Singapore	.. c	.. c	.. c	.. c	.. c	-2 517.6	-1 290.5	6 561.1	-4 593.7	11 679.1
Chinese Taipei	.. c	.. c	.. c	.. c	.. c	120.2	202.2	111.7	178.0	396.9
Thailand	.. c	.. c	.. c	.. c	.. c	-38.1	143.3	114.5	259.7	372.9
Viet Nam	.. c	.. c	.. c	.. c	.. c	83.9	73.2	-7.5	82.5	-19.8
AUSTRALIA, OCEANIA AND POLAR REGIONS	**.. c**	**.. c**	**.. c**	**.. c**	**.. c**	**-429.4**	**-1 874.1**	**-8 783.9**	**-523.8**	**4 028.8**
WORLD unallocated and confidential	**1 532.8**	**2 321.5**	**1 761.0**	**3 573.8**	**5 188.6**	**-520.7**	**-639.0**	**-1 168.5**	**-1 375.1**	**17.3**
European Union (since 01/02/2020)	..	..	..	..	..	..	..	..	..	..
G20 countries excl. European Union	**19 416.5**	**-34 636.9**	**135.1**	**-28 696.7**	**28 361.3**	**90 511.9**	**18 725.7**	**15 811.4**	**35 455.5**	**33 816.1**
G20 OECD countries	**.. c**	**.. c**	**.. c**	**.. c**	**.. c**	**86 994.9**	**9 897.2**	**7 708.1**	**24 544.0**	**30 372.3**
G20 Non-OECD countries	**.. c**	**.. c**	**.. c**	**.. c**	**.. c**	**3 517.0**	**8 828.5**	**8 103.2**	**10 911.5**	**3 443.9**
MENA countries	**.. c**	**.. c**	**.. c**	**.. c**	**.. c**	**-4 908.5**	**-549.3**	**-2 883.2**	**-8 919.3**	**-2 451.1**
ASEAN countries	**.. c**	**.. c**	**.. c**	**.. c**	**.. c**	**-2 059.1**	**399.6**	**4 046.6**	**-2 716.6**	**11 674.0**

- Nil; .. Not available; c Confidential data

Note: Detailed metadata at: *http://metalinks.oecd.org/idi/20220712/6d95.*

Source: *OECD International Direct Investment Statistics (database): https://doi.org/10.1787/idi-data-en*

SWITZERLAND

Table 2. Foreign direct investment positions by country

At year end

Million US dollars

	Inward					Outward				
	2016	2017	2018	2019	2020	2016	2017	2018	2019	2020
WORLD	**1 279 207.9**	**1 420 756.0**	**1 396 677.1**	**1 460 461.7**	**1 424 862.2**	**1 336 878.8**	**1 426 652.7**	**1 503 858.6**	**1 532 204.7**	**1 665 233.2**
OECD COUNTRIES	**1 130 455.9**	**1 236 448.6**	**1 192 511.0**	**1 236 402.1**	**.. c**	**1 049 556.7**	**1 083 693.9**	**1 135 333.5**	**1 144 540.9**	**.. c**
Australia	1 940.5	2 079.6	2 441.2	3 194.1	3 742.5	16 737.3	15 606.8	6 594.7	6 142.4	11 523.6
Austria	7 194.3	8 470.5	10 470.8	10 753.0	14 664.6	8 578.4	10 077.8	9 708.7	12 449.5	12 356.5
Belgium	5 524.9	4 921.4	3 632.7	17 342.4	22 224.6	15 313.8	13 607.9	8 644.0	13 878.8	20 154.3
Canada	34 915.7	37 968.4	30 538.7	30 308.4	29 112.0	43 371.2	37 235.3	28 583.3	38 587.6	36 146.1
Chile	.. c	.. c	.. c	.. c	.. c	-2 056.7	-2 018.7	1 828.3	1 873.0	2 298.7
Colombia	.. c	.. c	.. c	.. c	.. c	662.9	1 010.3	4 549.0	5 207.1	5 205.2
Costa Rica	.. c	.. c	.. c	.. c	.. c	770.4	927.1	1 061.9	1 327.9	1 390.7
Czech Republic	.. c	.. c	.. c	.. c	.. c	2 964.7	3 660.6	3 805.7	3 510.3	3 697.2
Denmark	2 447.4	4 075.3	4 337.8	5 540.8	2 327.4	1 547.2	1 672.6	1 581.4	1 453.4	1 583.1
Estonia	.. c	.. c	.. c	.. c	.. c	418.6	114.0	157.5	175.2	330.5
Finland	.. c	.. c	.. c	.. c	.. c	776.1	550.5	946.9	1 127.0	1 479.9
France	38 499.6	44 185.0	51 045.4	60 855.5	66 533.1	58 600.3	60 768.3	63 949.4	67 999.1	73 597.1
Germany	30 022.7	40 534.3	32 180.9	38 772.8	43 479.1	40 465.5	48 352.1	59 685.9	65 863.1	78 883.0
Greece	.. c	.. c	.. c	.. c	.. c	1 124.3	1 455.5	1 365.1	1 269.4	1 357.0
Hungary	1 029.8	2 158.6	1 219.9	872.5	-134.6	5 485.3	5 934.5	5 731.3	27 166.5	56 877.6
Iceland	.. c	.. c	.. c	.. c	.. c	.. c	.. c	.. c	.. c	.. c
Ireland	116 412.3	118 709.9	155 716.5	80 669.3	127 522.8	134 711.8	102 440.5	120 085.5	85 775.8	65 751.2
Israel	1 911.8	1 628.2	1 721.2	5 499.8	5 014.5	1 504.9	1 602.6	1 565.4	1 172.3	1 213.3
Italy	6 456.2	6 565.9	3 974.5	3 853.8	4 666.9	15 681.2	18 173.1	18 223.4	21 163.0	24 346.5
Japan	24 229.3	26 166.9	28 013.0	39 424.4	46 613.3	11 380.0	14 530.2	17 096.3	22 397.2	24 928.0
Korea	.. c	.. c	.. c	.. c	.. c	3 308.1	3 954.6	3 912.6	20 279.1	22 641.0
Latvia	.. c	.. c	.. c	.. c	.. c	39.2	141.4	170.0	214.7	225.7
Lithuania	.. c	.. c	.. c	.. c	.. c	392.6	397.6	468.7	678.4	798.1
Luxembourg	25 780.5	22 990.2	15 224.4	6 579.0	11 687.8	193 803.6	198 358.0	192 685.7	137 775.4	130 262.9
Mexico	12 901.1	12 632.0	11 259.8	10 265.1	8 654.6	4 575.7	4 859.8	6 016.3	6 809.1	6 338.9
Netherlands	75 748.2	70 679.7	55 682.5	63 866.9	73 452.0	141 337.6	160 574.3	165 797.7	180 698.4	180 444.3
New Zealand	.. c	.. c	.. c	.. c	.. c	604.3	392.5	379.3	947.1	897.0
Norway	.. c	.. c	.. c	.. c	.. c	4 830.8	4 441.0	4 605.8	2 661.6	3 433.5
Poland	.. c	.. c	.. c	.. c	.. c	5 264.7	6 842.7	6 872.8	6 900.4	8 286.8
Portugal	.. c	.. c	.. c	.. c	.. c	832.9	998.3	945.9	887.5	944.4
Slovak Republic	.. c	.. c	.. c	.. c	.. c	519.8	818.1	948.8	970.8	1 095.2
Slovenia	.. c	.. c	.. c	.. c	.. c	.. c	.. c	.. c	.. c	.. c
Spain	5 999.5	6 713.0	5 639.5	2 659.6	3 447.3	9 043.2	9 947.7	10 955.1	20 515.1	21 510.6
Sweden	10 116.7	12 231.3	12 743.2	12 692.8	14 558.0	6 218.9	7 754.5	8 436.1	12 404.5	12 973.0
Switzerland	34 985.1	36 804.9	56 511.9	74 473.3	59 589.8	-	-	-	-	-
Turkey	.. c	.. c	.. c	.. c	.. c	2 335.6	2 385.9	2 314.1	2 338.3	2 517.8
United Kingdom	52 712.7	70 859.9	71 110.9	68 282.8	34 125.7	55 003.5	54 254.6	81 841.0	85 518.7	101 503.9
United States	638 762.4	702 748.6	635 919.1	697 273.2	654 808.8	263 401.6	292 362.9	297 581.7	291 022.3	332 292.8
EUROPE	**463 813.1**	**503 324.7**	**553 490.7**	**520 956.8**	**536 563.7**	**757 177.9**	**816 731.6**	**872 795.1**	**869 922.1**	**929 468.9**
Bulgaria	.. c	.. c	.. c	.. c	.. c	280.2	338.7	243.0	332.5	3 292.9
Croatia	.. c	.. c	.. c	.. c	.. c	363.4	443.6	426.2	536.4	690.6
Cyprus	.. c	.. c	.. c	.. c	.. c	8 522.8	46 630.3	47 111.6	51 575.4	47 708.7
Malta	.. c	.. c	.. c	.. c	.. c	.. c	.. c	.. c	.. c	.. c
Montenegro	.. c	.. c	.. c	.. c	.. c	.. c	.. c	.. c	.. c	.. c
Romania	.. c	.. c	.. c	.. c	.. c	2 130.4	2 716.4	2 606.3	2 810.1	4 170.0
Russian Federation	21 016.8	28 394.1	18 895.9	17 255.4	18 107.2	17 512.2	21 936.1	23 308.4	29 341.6	31 560.3
Ukraine	.. c	.. c	.. c	.. c	.. c	589.7	1 522.0	2 026.6	3 015.7	3 454.8
AFRICA	**.. c**	**.. c**	**.. c**	**.. c**	**.. c**	**13 340.9**	**12 086.9**	**11 650.3**	**14 500.9**	**17 026.0**
Northern Africa	.. c	.. c	.. c	.. c	.. c	1 520.0	1 475.9	1 446.7	1 494.5	1 638.6
Algeria	.. c	.. c	.. c	.. c	.. c	.. c	.. c	.. c	.. c	.. c
Egypt	.. c	.. c	.. c	.. c	.. c	849.8	749.7	765.8	923.8	1 006.2
Libya	.. c	.. c	.. c	.. c	.. c	.. c	.. c	.. c	.. c	.. c
Morocco	.. c	.. c	.. c	.. c	.. c	405.7	429.0	478.9	372.4	434.3
Tunisia	.. c	.. c	.. c	.. c	.. c	34.7	41.0	47.1	47.0	52.4
Other African countries	.. c	.. c	.. c	.. c	.. c	11 820.9	10 611.0	10 203.6	13 006.4	15 387.4
Nigeria	.. c	.. c	.. c	.. c	.. c	478.5	448.9	437.6	307.1	404.5
South Africa	.. c	.. c	.. c	.. c	.. c	2 519.6	2 433.5	2 506.4	4 878.1	5 209.9
AMERICA	**740 323.0**	**825 785.6**	**749 744.7**	**823 668.5**	**754 277.2**	**442 200.7**	**462 333.0**	**488 377.5**	**488 589.5**	**532 185.7**
Northern America	673 678.1	740 716.8	666 457.7	727 581.5	683 920.8	306 772.9	329 598.2	326 165.0	329 609.9	368 438.8
Central America and Caribbean countries	.. c	.. c	.. c	.. c	.. c	118 269.8	114 166.5	136 998.5	134 936.7	137 771.4
Bahamas	.. c	.. c	.. c	.. c	.. c	.. c	.. c	.. c	.. c	.. c
Bermuda	.. c	.. c	.. c	.. c	.. c	42 611.1	46 895.4	74 654.9	46 735.8	68 849.9
Cayman Islands	.. c	.. c	.. c	.. c	.. c	.. c	.. c	.. c	.. c	.. c
El Salvador	.. c	.. c	.. c	.. c	.. c	.. c	.. c	.. c	.. c	.. c
Guatemala	.. c	.. c	.. c	.. c	.. c	181.9	167.3	182.0	258.8	204.6
Honduras	.. c	.. c	.. c	.. c	.. c	.. c	.. c	.. c	.. c	.. c
Nicaragua	.. c	.. c	.. c	.. c	.. c	.. c	.. c	.. c	.. c	.. c
Panama	.. c	.. c	.. c	.. c	.. c	260.1	4 017.1	3 331.8	3 588.8	2 453.8
Virgin Islands, U.S.	.. c	.. c	.. c	.. c	.. c	.. c	.. c	.. c	.. c	.. c
South America	.. c	.. c	.. c	.. c	.. c	17 158.0	18 568.3	25 214.0	24 042.9	25 975.4
Argentina	.. c	.. c	.. c	.. c	.. c	3 993.5	3 955.1	3 067.1	3 430.0	3 749.6
Bolivia	.. c	.. c	.. c	.. c	.. c	58.1	69.2	75.1	76.1	69.5
Brazil	.. c	.. c	.. c	.. c	.. c	10 430.1	10 712.5	10 502.2	11 166.0	9 196.3
Ecuador	.. c	.. c	.. c	.. c	.. c	214.4	240.1	325.5	307.7	320.8
Paraguay	.. c	.. c	.. c	.. c	.. c	.. c	.. c	.. c	.. c	.. c
Peru	.. c	.. c	.. c	.. c	.. c	655.5	329.8	24.2	-2 890.8	1 117.9
Uruguay	.. c	.. c	.. c	.. c	.. c	2 239.2	2 305.2	2 523.1	2 558.1	2 662.7
Venezuela	.. c	.. c	.. c	.. c	.. c	856.4	1 772.9	2 136.9	2 117.0	1 173.0

Table 2. Foreign direct investment positions by country *(cont.)*

At year end

Million US dollars

	Inward					Outward				
	2016	2017	2018	2019	2020	2016	2017	2018	2019	2020
ASIA	**.. c**	**.. c**	**.. c**	**.. c**	**.. c**	**103 408.4**	**114 882.6**	**118 564.4**	**145 289.6**	**166 783.6**
Near and Middle East	.. c	.. c	.. c	.. c	.. c	23 528.4	23 572.5	20 795.6	17 185.5	11 230.4
Gulf Arabian countries	.. c	.. c	.. c	.. c	.. c	.. c	.. c	.. c	.. c	.. c
Kuwait	.. c	.. c	.. c	.. c	.. c	.. c	.. c	.. c	.. c	.. c
Qatar	.. c	.. c	.. c	.. c	.. c	58.6	60.3	162.4	222.5	340.3
Saudi Arabia	.. c	.. c	.. c	.. c	.. c	900.0	983.0	1 135.1	2 247.7	1 317.2
United Arab Emirates	837.9	793.8	739.5	2 197.0	1 401.5	18 484.5	18 255.6	14 897.9	10 742.5	5 366.8
Other Near and Middle East	.. c	.. c	.. c	.. c	.. c	.. c	.. c	.. c	.. c	.. c
Jordan	.. c	.. c	.. c	.. c	.. c	240.9	283.1	263.9	257.7	170.7
Other Asian countries	.. c	.. c	.. c	.. c	.. c	79 880.1	91 310.1	97 768.8	128 104.1	155 553.2
China	7 228.0	17 357.5	17 092.9	16 044.2	18 039.0	19 644.5	22 690.5	22 628.5	24 254.5	28 606.6
Hong Kong, China	.. c	.. c	.. c	.. c	.. c	5 876.9	7 620.0	7 056.6	14 906.5	17 633.6
India	1 881.8	1 856.2	2 338.3	2 565.0	1 554.5	4 788.8	6 290.3	6 684.4	6 798.4	6 647.6
Indonesia	.. c	.. c	.. c	.. c	.. c	1 415.9	1 529.4	1 527.7	1 817.3	2 352.4
Iran, Islamic Republic of	.. c	.. c	.. c	.. c	.. c	.. c	.. c	.. c	.. c	.. c
Malaysia	.. c	.. c	.. c	.. c	.. c	5 921.5	6 212.3	4 152.3	4 702.0	4 473.0
Philippines	.. c	.. c	.. c	.. c	.. c	1 427.3	2 201.0	1 886.5	2 258.9	2 667.5
Singapore	.. c	.. c	.. c	.. c	.. c	18 331.3	18 474.4	25 370.6	22 159.2	36 931.7
Chinese Taipei	.. c	.. c	.. c	.. c	.. c	1 818.4	1 930.5	1 851.3	2 002.0	2 458.7
Thailand	.. c	.. c	.. c	.. c	.. c	2 465.7	2 710.5	3 010.2	3 314.1	3 660.5
Viet Nam	.. c	.. c	.. c	.. c	.. c	649.3	727.6	715.4	1 085.6	1 109.0
AUSTRALIA, OCEANIA AND POLAR REGIONS	**.. c**	**.. c**	**.. c**	**.. c**	**.. c**	**17 449.2**	**16 193.7**	**7 084.5**	**7 307.7**	**12 552.7**
WORLD unallocated and confidential	**37 042.6**	**41 763.6**	**41 095.5**	**46 911.9**	**57 656.2**	**3 301.8**	**4 424.9**	**5 386.7**	**6 595.0**	**7 216.3**
European Union (since 01/02/2020)	**.. c**	**.. c**	**.. c**	**.. c**	**394 796.1**	**.. c**	**.. c**	**.. c**	**.. c**	**754 785.8**
G20 countries excl. European Union	**901 374.6**	**1 015 100.9**	**929 583.0**	**1 007 012.5**	**953 281.0**	**576 064.4**	**623 013.9**	**657 158.2**	**712 053.5**	**803 358.5**
G20 OECD countries	**.. c**	**.. c**	**.. c**	**.. c**	**.. c**	**514 860.0**	**552 483.6**	**585 798.7**	**628 120.0**	**714 718.6**
G20 Non-OECD countries	**.. c**	**.. c**	**.. c**	**.. c**	**.. c**	**61 204.5**	**70 530.3**	**71 359.6**	**83 933.6**	**88 639.9**
MENA countries	**.. c**	**.. c**	**.. c**	**.. c**	**.. c**	**23 526.7**	**23 433.5**	**20 669.6**	**17 473.0**	**11 531.2**
ASEAN countries	**.. c**	**.. c**	**.. c**	**.. c**	**.. c**	**30 238.5**	**31 935.5**	**36 804.8**	**35 426.9**	**51 278.9**

- Nil; c Confidential data

Note: Inward FDI positions are allocated according to the ultimate investing country. Detailed metadata at: *http://metalinks.oecd.org/idi/20220712/6d95*.

Source: *OECD International Direct Investment Statistics (database): https://doi.org/10.1787/idi-data-en*

SWITZERLAND

Table 3. Foreign direct investment income by country

Million US dollars

	Inward					Outward				
	2016	2017	2018	2019	2020	2016	2017	2018	2019	2020
WORLD	**72 638.1**	**96 490.0**	**115 549.1**	**109 623.8**	**73 827.5**	**87 108.7**	**102 801.3**	**106 360.3**	**105 855.5**	**82 031.6**
OECD COUNTRIES	**61 032.6**	**80 127.9**	**105 129.4**	**96 625.9**	**.. c**	**58 154.0**	**68 157.5**	**70 897.5**	**73 108.7**	**.. c**
Australia	.. c	.. c	.. c	.. c	.. c	552.2	733.5	874.8	1 317.5	619.2
Austria	2 021.9	-2 714.7	2 816.4	622.8	757.1	1 267.8	1 119.0	1 133.3	2 069.4	575.4
Belgium	-22.0	54.8	-25.2	102.4	-1 418.5	-229.2	638.1	1 204.2	760.2	110.3
Canada	-2.4	-21.7	-20.1	-13.3	-50.7	-1 648.3	892.6	-533.5	-1 576.3	-1 906.4
Chile	.. c	.. c	.. c	.. c	.. c	34.7	117.6	138.3	148.3	128.1
Colombia	.. c	.. c	.. c	.. c	.. c	91.7	78.3	70.5	75.6	75.7
Costa Rica	.. c	.. c	.. c	.. c	.. c	127.2	165.3	188.2	157.1	144.6
Czech Republic	.. c	.. c	.. c	.. c	.. c	358.4	421.0	284.3	117.2	266.8
Denmark	1 826.1	1 595.4	1 164.6	3 288.3	2 227.2	80.1	87.9	97.6	147.4	690.9
Estonia	.. c	.. c	.. c	.. c	.. c	4.1	4.6	17.2	17.6	36.2
Finland	.. c	.. c	.. c	.. c	.. c	209.7	223.9	233.2	184.2	164.6
France	4 344.6	5 267.5	3 878.4	4 990.4	4 578.5	3 746.8	2 868.8	4 944.2	4 098.0	3 494.6
Germany	3 149.8	3 505.9	2 649.0	3 486.8	1 416.2	6 194.9	5 495.9	4 855.4	5 954.1	4 856.9
Greece	.. c	.. c	.. c	.. c	.. c	-59.8	74.4	147.4	126.7	-185.6
Hungary	1 391.3	1 357.1	844.3	1 168.7	413.7	640.9	643.6	485.6	262.2	411.4
Iceland	.. c	.. c	.. c	.. c	.. c	.. c	.. c	.. c	.. c	.. c
Ireland	-1 755.0	-2 331.5	9 351.1	5 032.2	5 277.3	4 165.8	788.6	-3 022.6	1 058.6	5 432.0
Israel	-124.1	-173.8	-303.2	-126.8	-74.7	138.3	125.4	125.9	155.1	178.4
Italy	210.6	39.2	306.0	151.2	101.5	948.9	1 378.9	1 629.1	1 938.4	288.0
Japan	113.6	-194.8	-40.3	40.1	-2 427.4	1 619.7	1 892.8	1 736.8	2 477.5	2 643.5
Korea	.. c	.. c	.. c	.. c	.. c	407.2	176.1	279.7	5 200.2	362.6
Latvia	.. c	.. c	.. c	.. c	.. c	5.1	8.4	10.6	15.3	14.4
Lithuania	.. c	.. c	.. c	.. c	.. c	13.0	19.9	72.8	46.0	40.6
Luxembourg	6 978.0	32 235.3	33 749.7	22 075.2	12 829.7	4 485.4	2 643.6	8 298.2	3 955.9	2 917.9
Mexico	.. c	.. c	.. c	.. c	.. c	542.9	514.0	632.8	546.8	389.1
Netherlands	26 819.5	38 517.7	34 135.9	43 745.2	27 482.6	11 879.3	20 447.3	14 606.3	13 982.2	6 027.2
New Zealand	.. c	.. c	.. c	.. c	.. c	64.8	65.9	75.2	89.1	72.6
Norway	.. c	.. c	.. c	.. c	.. c	36.3	93.5	116.2	-885.1	185.9
Poland	.. c	.. c	.. c	.. c	.. c	487.5	509.4	617.7	546.0	535.4
Portugal	.. c	.. c	.. c	.. c	.. c	34.0	110.7	75.3	105.2	118.3
Slovak Republic	.. c	.. c	.. c	.. c	.. c	40.2	44.5	92.7	63.9	72.2
Slovenia	.. c	.. c	.. c	.. c	.. c	.. c	.. c	.. c	.. c	.. c
Spain	30.2	-159.6	-71.7	-1.3	132.9	1 345.8	1 207.4	1 444.7	1 986.2	488.4
Sweden	722.9	1 367.3	689.6	787.0	874.6	448.2	1 503.7	1 306.4	1 616.6	786.1
Switzerland	-	-	-	-	-	-	-	-	-	-
Turkey	.. c	.. c	.. c	.. c	.. c	274.9	257.8	142.0	194.7	271.5
United Kingdom	2 824.2	3 238.6	7 535.7	6 077.0	8 941.4	967.5	1 928.3	2 237.0	2 216.4	36.1
United States	12 586.0	-1 510.7	8 421.1	5 370.4	8 816.2	19 085.6	21 036.6	26 403.7	24 088.6	19 751.5
EUROPE	**47 296.7**	**86 843.9**	**98 132.1**	**97 518.8**	**66 159.2**	**42 502.2**	**54 099.3**	**54 943.1**	**45 741.0**	**30 923.1**
Bulgaria	.. c	.. c	.. c	.. c	.. c	59.7	50.1	39.8	69.9	-49.6
Croatia	.. c	.. c	.. c	.. c	.. c	33.5	42.3	55.9	64.5	67.0
Cyprus	-21.0	309.2	9.8	1 527.5	-39.7	135.5	10 194.0	10 919.4	384.5	-119.9
Malta	.. c	.. c	.. c	.. c	.. c	.. c	.. c	.. c	.. c	.. c
Montenegro	.. c	.. c	.. c	.. c	.. c	.. c	.. c	.. c	.. c	.. c
Romania	.. c	.. c	.. c	.. c	.. c	72.0	70.6	207.2	71.1	86.8
Russian Federation	.. c	.. c	.. c	.. c	.. c	899.3	-10.5	2 113.7	2 827.0	960.9
Ukraine	.. c	.. c	.. c	.. c	.. c	-14.7	253.8	486.1	468.6	749.8
AFRICA	**.. c**	**.. c**	**.. c**	**.. c**	**.. c**	**166.5**	**359.0**	**93.4**	**442.2**	**629.6**
Northern Africa	.. c	.. c	.. c	.. c	.. c	-128.5	68.5	74.8	133.9	268.2
Algeria	.. c	.. c	.. c	.. c	.. c	.. c	.. c	.. c	.. c	.. c
Egypt	.. c	.. c	.. c	.. c	.. c	-152.9	22.5	41.4	137.5	257.1
Libya	..	..	..	..	..	.. c	.. c	.. c	.. c	.. c
Morocco	.. c	.. c	.. c	.. c	.. c	14.2	23.4	5.0	-31.9	-2.8
Tunisia	.. c	.. c	.. c	.. c	.. c	2.3	7.1	13.6	19.6	12.9
Other African countries	.. c	.. c	.. c	.. c	.. c	295.0	290.5	18.6	308.3	361.3
Nigeria	.. c	.. c	.. c	.. c	.. c	58.4	65.5	152.9	88.1	81.8
South Africa	.. c	.. c	.. c	.. c	.. c	-71.5	-49.4	-439.6	-12.4	63.0
AMERICA	**25 406.0**	**9 620.9**	**16 695.9**	**11 805.9**	**10 110.8**	**27 843.0**	**30 454.8**	**30 427.4**	**27 136.9**	**27 917.9**
Northern America	12 583.6	-1 532.3	8 401.1	5 357.2	8 765.4	17 437.3	21 929.2	25 870.2	22 512.2	17 845.1
Central America and Caribbean countries	.. c	.. c	.. c	.. c	.. c	8 718.6	7 881.8	3 617.4	3 868.4	9 526.0
Bahamas	.. c	.. c	.. c	.. c	.. c	.. c	.. c	.. c	.. c	.. c
Bermuda	.. c	.. c	.. c	.. c	.. c	6 025.1	6 734.5	4 747.2	5 902.0	4 527.0
Cayman Islands	.. c	.. c	.. c	.. c	.. c	.. c	.. c	.. c	.. c	.. c
El Salvador	.. c	.. c	.. c	.. c	.. c	.. c	.. c	.. c	.. c	.. c
Guatemala	.. c	.. c	.. c	.. c	.. c	10.3	18.7	32.1	27.9	21.6
Honduras	.. c	.. c	.. c	.. c	.. c	.. c	.. c	.. c	.. c	.. c
Nicaragua	.. c	.. c	.. c	.. c	.. c	.. c	.. c	.. c	.. c	.. c
Panama	.. c	.. c	.. c	.. c	.. c	344.9	566.5	422.0	368.2	256.5
Virgin Islands, U.S.	.. c	.. c	.. c	.. c	.. c	.. c	.. c	.. c	.. c	.. c
South America	.. c	.. c	.. c	.. c	.. c	1 687.2	643.7	939.8	756.3	546.8
Argentina	.. c	.. c	.. c	.. c	.. c	175.6	181.1	94.4	-76.8	446.0
Bolivia	.. c	.. c	.. c	.. c	.. c	5.0	5.7	7.7	0.7	1.9
Brazil	.. c	.. c	.. c	.. c	.. c	280.0	-36.8	573.3	726.5	-184.3
Ecuador	.. c	.. c	.. c	.. c	.. c	34.8	49.8	55.1	26.0	29.0
Paraguay	.. c	.. c	.. c	.. c	.. c	.. c	.. c	.. c	.. c	.. c
Peru	.. c	.. c	.. c	.. c	.. c	83.2	36.8	49.9	-109.9	-81.1
Uruguay	.. c	.. c	.. c	.. c	.. c	478.3	152.8	151.6	212.0	130.5
Venezuela	.. c	.. c	.. c	.. c	.. c	494.4	49.6	-212.7	-266.4	-17.3

SWITZERLAND

Table 3. Foreign direct investment income by country *(cont.)*

Million US dollars

	Inward					Outward				
	2016	2017	2018	2019	2020	2016	2017	2018	2019	2020
ASIA	**.. c**	**.. c**	**.. c**	**.. c**	**.. c**	**15 965.0**	**17 074.2**	**19 961.5**	**31 111.5**	**21 859.6**
Near and Middle East	.. c	.. c	.. c	.. c	.. c	3 121.3	2 687.5	1 231.4	-2 443.2	2 420.9
Gulf Arabian countries	.. c	.. c	.. c	.. c	.. c	.. c	.. c	.. c	.. c	.. c
Kuwait	.. c	.. c	.. c	.. c	.. c	.. c	.. c	.. c	.. c	.. c
Qatar	.. c	.. c	.. c	.. c	.. c	10.6	14.7	18.6	-22.8	312.4
Saudi Arabia	.. c	.. c	.. c	.. c	.. c	101.3	90.4	33.1	26.2	82.6
United Arab Emirates	.. c	.. c	.. c	.. c	.. c	2 674.8	2 124.3	838.8	-2 943.7	1 557.4
Other Near and Middle East	.. c	.. c	.. c	.. c	.. c	.. c	.. c	.. c	.. c	.. c
Jordan	.. c	.. c	.. c	.. c	.. c	43.4	46.9	44.7	38.3	-42.1
Other Asian countries	.. c	.. c	.. c	.. c	.. c	12 843.6	14 386.7	18 730.1	33 554.8	19 438.7
China	.. c	.. c	.. c	.. c	.. c	2 327.0	2 385.2	3 490.4	2 833.8	4 565.1
Hong Kong, China	.. c	.. c	.. c	.. c	.. c	1 052.8	1 950.4	2 104.0	2 217.0	3 315.4
India	.. c	.. c	.. c	.. c	.. c	359.5	778.2	694.7	646.4	515.8
Indonesia	.. c	.. c	.. c	.. c	.. c	193.8	215.5	194.2	222.8	284.0
Iran, Islamic Republic of	.. c	.. c	.. c	.. c	.. c	.. c	.. c	.. c	.. c	.. c
Malaysia	.. c	.. c	.. c	.. c	.. c	435.2	-33.2	971.9	899.1	509.8
Philippines	.. c	.. c	.. c	.. c	.. c	499.4	498.7	522.8	463.6	-49.4
Singapore	.. c	.. c	.. c	.. c	.. c	4 407.2	4 973.0	7 405.5	12 871.2	5 980.0
Chinese Taipei	.. c	.. c	.. c	.. c	.. c	423.6	463.3	451.5	403.2	439.5
Thailand	.. c	.. c	.. c	.. c	.. c	449.5	536.9	464.9	518.9	440.0
Viet Nam	.. c	.. c	.. c	.. c	.. c	166.0	174.2	198.1	198.4	179.6
AUSTRALIA, OCEANIA AND POLAR REGIONS	**.. c**	**.. c**	**.. c**	**.. c**	**.. c**	**631.9**	**814.0**	**934.9**	**1 423.9**	**701.5**
WORLD unallocated and confidential	**-54.0**	**393.7**	**1 064.6**	**385.9**	**59.5**	**0.0**	**0.1**	**0.0**	**0.0**	**0.0**
European Union (since 01/02/2020)	..	..	..	..	..	..	..	..	..	..
G20 countries excl. European Union	**22 939.3**	**9 355.7**	**22 746.7**	**19 962.0**	**20 799.2**	**36 957.5**	**40 729.1**	**49 956.1**	**53 649.2**	**37 539.7**
G20 OECD countries	**.. c**	**.. c**	**.. c**	**.. c**	**.. c**	**32 692.3**	**37 175.4**	**43 202.0**	**46 455.7**	**30 806.6**
G20 Non-OECD countries	**.. c**	**.. c**	**.. c**	**.. c**	**.. c**	**4 265.2**	**3 553.6**	**6 754.2**	**7 193.5**	**6 733.2**
MENA countries	**.. c**	**.. c**	**.. c**	**.. c**	**.. c**	**2 854.4**	**2 629.3**	**1 177.6**	**-2 467.2**	**2 506.5**
ASEAN countries	**.. c**	**.. c**	**.. c**	**.. c**	**.. c**	**6 158.4**	**6 378.1**	**9 767.9**	**15 189.9**	**7 350.6**

- Nil; .. Not available; c Confidential data

Note: Detailed metadata at: *http://metalinks.oecd.org/idi/20220712/6d95*.

Source: *OECD International Direct Investment Statistics (database): https://doi.org/10.1787/idi-data-en*

SWITZERLAND

Table 4. Foreign direct investment flows by industrial sector

Million US dollars

	Inward					Outward				
	2016	2017	2018	2019	2020	2016	2017	2018	2019	2020
All FDI activities	**150 285.4**	**111 199.5**	**-83 153.3**	**-105 797.1**	**-162 697.5**	**166 617.9**	**21 943.6**	**43 597.8**	**-56 168.5**	**-36 150.4**
Agriculture, forestry and fishing	..	..	..	..	..	.. c	.. c	.. c	.. c	.. c
Mining and quarrying	.. c	.. c	.. c	.. c	.. c	.. c	.. c	.. c	.. c	.. c
Extraction activities	.. c	.. c	.. c	.. c	.. c	.. c	.. c	.. c	.. c	.. c
Manufacturing	**5 158.7**	**58 295.5**	**-28 326.0**	**7 742.9**	**5 707.8**	**30 638.9**	**-8 586.1**	**13 228.2**	**25 472.8**	**1 369.5**
of which:										
Food products, beverages and tobacco	.. c	.. c	.. c	.. c	.. c	.. c	.. c	.. c	.. c	.. c
Textiles, wood and paper products; printing	.. c	.. c	.. c	.. c	.. c	.. c	.. c	.. c	.. c	.. c
Chemical, rubber, plastic, non-metallic mineral products	.. c	.. c	.. c	.. c	.. c	.. c	.. c	.. c	.. c	.. c
Metal and machinery products, except electrical equipment	.. c	.. c	.. c	.. c	.. c	.. c	.. c	.. c	.. c	.. c
Motor vehicles, trailers, semi-trailers, other transport equipment	.. c	.. c	.. c	.. c	.. c	.. c	.. c	.. c	.. c	.. c
Other manufacturing	.. c	.. c	.. c	.. c	.. c	.. c	.. c	.. c	.. c	.. c
Electricity, gas, steam and air conditioning supply	.. c	.. c	.. c	.. c	.. c	.. c	.. c	.. c	.. c	.. c
Water supply; sewerage, waste management and remediation activities	.. c	.. c	.. c	.. c	.. c	..	..	..	..	..
Construction	.. c	.. c	.. c	.. c	.. c	.. c	.. c	.. c	.. c	.. c
Services	**144 344.4**	**51 391.1**	**-54 146.2**	**-113 389.0**	**-168 720.3**	**137 786.1**	**30 820.8**	**30 795.1**	**-77 259.1**	**-37 520.2**
Wholesale and retail trade; repair of motor vehicles and motorcycles	12 995.0	11 816.3	16 709.3	-22 136.3	-8 210.4	14 510.7	-7 578.0	32 879.6	-31 277.1	13 080.9
Transportation and storage	771.7	1 500.9	313.4	3 976.2	-592.5	1 248.7	3 850.0	3 945.5	1 751.1	-691.8
Accommodation and food service activities	34.2	-273.9	-33.9	301.5	-3.6	-134.6	85.9	-48.6	169.6	-13.2
Information and communication	245.7	-703.9	-687.8	1 998.4	8 876.2	-218.5	-1 066.4	-95.7	-636.5	513.9
Financial and insurance activities	108 002.5	64 343.9	-55 257.9	-43 078.4	-193 638.1	109 268.4	53 051.0	10 504.0	-11 398.7	-49 183.7
Activities of holding companies	92 744.7	60 815.9	795.2	-29 764.1	-80 132.1	78 527.4	54 161.2	8 194.0	-31 475.0	-53 609.9
Real estate activities	.. c	.. c	.. c	.. c	.. c	.. c	.. c	.. c	.. c	.. c
Professional, scientific and technical activities	17 775.0	-24 892.8	-8 084.5	-53 766.7	24 796.3	8 244.2	-16 658.2	-14 019.1	-36 716.2	-1 133.7
Administrative and support service activities	.. c	.. c	.. c	.. c	.. c	.. c	.. c	.. c	.. c	.. c
Public administration; activities of households and of extraterritorial organisations	..	..	..	..	..	..	..	..	..	..
Education	.. c	.. c	.. c	.. c	.. c	..	..	..	..	..
Human health and social work activities	.. c	.. c	.. c	.. c	.. c	.. c	.. c	.. c	.. c	.. c
Arts, entertainment and recreation	.. c	.. c	.. c	.. c	.. c	.. c	.. c	.. c	.. c	.. c
Other services	.. c	.. c	.. c	.. c	.. c	.. c	.. c	.. c	.. c	.. c
Not allocated and confidential	.. c	.. c	.. c	.. c	.. c	.. c	.. c	.. c	.. c	.. c
Private real estate activities	**45.3**	**156.7**	**384.2**	**286.8**	**304.4**	**-520.4**	**-639.7**	**-1 168.5**	**-1 375.1**	**17.2**

.. Not available; c Confidential data

Note: Detailed metadata at: *http://metalinks.oecd.org/idi/20220712/6d95*.

Source: OECD *International Direct Investment Statistics (database)*: *https://doi.org/10.1787/idi-data-en*

SWITZERLAND

Table 5. Foreign direct investment positions by industrial sector
At year end

Million US dollars

	Inward					Outward				
	2016	2017	2018	2019	2020	2016	2017	2018	2019	2020
All FDI activities	**1 279 207.9**	**1 420 756.0**	**1 396 677.1**	**1 460 461.7**	**1 424 862.2**	**1 336 878.8**	**1 426 652.7**	**1 503 858.6**	**1 532 204.7**	**1 665 233.2**
Agriculture, forestry and fishing	..	..	..	..	..	**.. c**	**.. c**	**.. c**	**.. c**	**.. c**
Mining and quarrying	**.. c**	**.. c**	**.. c**	**.. c**	**.. c**	**.. c**	**.. c**	**.. c**	**.. c**	**.. c**
Extraction activities	.. c	.. c	.. c	.. c	.. c	.. c	.. c	.. c	.. c	.. c
Manufacturing	**131 951.7**	**167 016.4**	**171 250.1**	**178 635.5**	**187 349.8**	**402 990.1**	**418 449.5**	**440 799.8**	**470 277.4**	**498 708.8**
of which:										
Food products, beverages and tobacco	.. c	.. c	.. c	.. c	.. c	.. c	.. c	.. c	.. c	.. c
Textiles, wood and paper products; printing	.. c	.. c	.. c	.. c	.. c	.. c	.. c	.. c	.. c	.. c
Chemical, rubber, plastic, non-metallic mineral products	.. c	.. c	.. c	.. c	.. c	.. c	.. c	.. c	.. c	.. c
Metal and machinery products, except electrical equipment	.. c	.. c	.. c	.. c	.. c	.. c	.. c	.. c	.. c	.. c
Motor vehicles, trailers, semi-trailers, other transport equipment	.. c	.. c	.. c	.. c	.. c	.. c	.. c	.. c	.. c	.. c
Other manufacturing	.. c	.. c	.. c	.. c	.. c	.. c	.. c	.. c	.. c	.. c
Electricity, gas, steam and air conditioning supply	**.. c**	**.. c**	**.. c**	**.. c**	**.. c**	**.. c**	**.. c**	**.. c**	**.. c**	**.. c**
Water supply; sewerage, waste management and remediation activities	**.. c**	**.. c**	**.. c**	**.. c**	**.. c**	**.. c**	**.. c**	**.. c**	**.. c**	**.. c**
Construction	**.. c**	**.. c**	**.. c**	**.. c**	**.. c**	**.. c**	**.. c**	**.. c**	**.. c**	**.. c**
Services	**1 105 337.6**	**1 208 380.8**	**1 181 654.3**	**1 238 618.4**	**1 190 365.0**	**915 993.8**	**986 990.2**	**1 041 391.6**	**1 042 794.7**	**1 145 954.7**
Wholesale and retail trade; repair of motor vehicles and motorcycles	173 568.4	193 434.9	207 079.3	269 455.5	270 558.4	144 025.9	139 347.5	169 842.1	174 454.7	197 423.3
Transportation and storage	8 466.5	10 437.7	12 654.1	17 406.3	16 677.4	20 104.8	24 219.4	31 416.1	33 333.7	33 707.3
Accommodation and food service activities	2 859.0	2 943.4	2 877.1	3 197.4	3 511.7	996.8	1 195.0	1 222.6	1 284.7	1 283.7
Information and communication	15 596.9	14 574.4	14 317.5	12 680.2	24 068.0	9 368.5	10 383.8	10 483.2	10 020.8	11 749.5
Financial and insurance activities	609 657.1	703 533.3	688 460.0	707 196.0	590 872.1	521 631.4	588 444.6	613 636.5	643 613.3	674 735.6
Activities of holding companies	341 613.5	418 259.9	442 937.9	470 729.0	453 877.4	303 387.6	362 194.6	392 297.0	403 005.8	409 506.9
Real estate activities	.. c	.. c	.. c	.. c	.. c	.. c	.. c	.. c	.. c	.. c
Professional, scientific and technical activities	262 542.4	251 262.5	233 319.9	205 994.2	269 728.2	202 958.9	207 708.5	201 672.8	165 942.2	213 688.0
Administrative and support service activities	.. c	.. c	.. c	.. c	.. c	.. c	.. c	.. c	.. c	.. c
Public administration; activities of households and of extraterritorial organisations	.. c	.. c	.. c	.. c	.. c	.. c	.. c	.. c	.. c	.. c
Education	.. c	.. c	.. c	.. c	.. c	.. c	.. c	.. c	.. c	.. c
Human health and social work activities	.. c	.. c	.. c	.. c	.. c	.. c	.. c	.. c	.. c	.. c
Arts, entertainment and recreation	.. c	.. c	.. c	.. c	.. c	.. c	.. c	.. c	.. c	.. c
Other services	.. c	.. c	.. c	.. c	.. c	.. c	.. c	.. c	.. c	.. c
Not allocated and confidential	**.. c**	**.. c**	**.. c**	**.. c**	**.. c**	**.. c**	**.. c**	**.. c**	**.. c**	**.. c**
Private real estate activities	**37 130.3**	**38 800.6**	**38 485.3**	**39 285.5**	**43 623.0**	**3 302.1**	**4 424.9**	**5 386.7**	**6 595.0**	**7 216.3**

.. Not available; c Confidential data

Note: Detailed metadata at: *http://metalinks.oecd.org/idi/20220712/6d95.*

Source: *OECD International Direct Investment Statistics (database)*: *https://doi.org/10.1787/idi-data-en*

SWITZERLAND

Table 6. Foreign direct investment income by industrial sector

Million US dollars

	Inward					Outward				
	2016	2017	2018	2019	2020	2016	2017	2018	2019	2020
All FDI activities	**72 638.1**	**96 490.0**	**115 549.1**	**109 623.8**	**73 827.5**	**87 108.7**	**102 801.3**	**106 360.3**	**105 855.5**	**82 031.6**
Agriculture, forestry and fishing	..	..	..	..	..	.. c	.. c	.. c	.. c	.. c
Mining and quarrying	.. c	.. c	.. c	.. c	.. c	.. c	.. c	.. c	.. c	.. c
Extraction activities	.. c	.. c	.. c	.. c	.. c	.. c	.. c	.. c	.. c	.. c
Manufacturing	**14 936.6**	**16 480.9**	**15 320.7**	**21 133.8**	**17 253.1**	**37 184.4**	**37 123.5**	**46 234.7**	**41 562.1**	**38 106.8**
of which:										
Food products, beverages and tobacco	.. c	.. c	.. c	.. c	.. c	.. c	.. c	.. c	.. c	.. c
Textiles, wood and paper products; printing	.. c	.. c	.. c	.. c	.. c	.. c	.. c	.. c	.. c	.. c
Chemical, rubber, plastic, non-metallic mineral products	.. c	.. c	.. c	.. c	.. c	.. c	.. c	.. c	.. c	.. c
Metal and machinery products, except electrical equipment	.. c	.. c	.. c	.. c	.. c	.. c	.. c	.. c	.. c	.. c
Motor vehicles, trailers, semi-trailers, other transport equipment	.. c	.. c	.. c	.. c	.. c	.. c	.. c	.. c	.. c	.. c
Other manufacturing	.. c	.. c	.. c	.. c	.. c	.. c	.. c	.. c	.. c	.. c
Electricity, gas, steam and air conditioning supply	.. c	.. c	.. c	.. c	.. c	.. c	.. c	.. c	.. c	.. c
Water supply; sewerage, waste management and remediation activities	.. c	.. c	.. c	.. c	.. c	..	..	..	..	..
Construction	.. c	.. c	.. c	.. c	.. c	.. c	.. c	.. c	.. c	.. c
Services	**57 447.7**	**79 805.5**	**100 093.8**	**88 395.3**	**56 418.6**	**50 070.2**	**65 086.4**	**59 101.4**	**63 660.2**	**43 752.9**
Wholesale and retail trade; repair of motor vehicles and motorcycles	14 902.2	27 697.4	23 432.3	27 698.7	19 850.0	9 266.4	6 880.8	6 032.1	9 865.7	7 147.2
Transportation and storage	1 042.2	1 217.1	1 394.7	2 537.3	619.3	1 483.9	2 114.1	1 726.4	1 220.7	1 547.4
Accommodation and food service activities	165.1	72.5	46.5	-86.4	49.7	-146.7	80.5	69.6	87.0	12.5
Information and communication	3 339.2	3 541.7	2 159.4	2 725.9	2 856.6	179.4	621.1	184.0	-183.2	930.9
Financial and insurance activities	20 956.7	39 136.4	37 729.2	31 906.7	8 996.3	21 061.3	31 519.8	33 925.8	40 953.5	26 590.0
Activities of holding companies	1 581.5	18 211.1	24 669.8	18 816.4	3 812.9	7 015.3	21 291.2	19 675.9	24 111.2	9 842.1
Real estate activities	.. c	.. c	.. c	.. c	.. c	.. c	.. c	.. c	.. c	.. c
Professional, scientific and technical activities	16 610.4	11 945.6	36 937.5	23 099.4	23 128.7	16 760.7	22 388.3	16 495.1	10 430.1	7 722.1
Administrative and support service activities	.. c	.. c	.. c	.. c	.. c	.. c	.. c	.. c	.. c	.. c
Public administration; activities of households and of extraterritorial organisations	..	..	..	..	..	..	..	..	..	..
Education	.. c	.. c	.. c	.. c	.. c	..	..	..	..	..
Human health and social work activities	.. c	.. c	.. c	.. c	.. c	.. c	.. c	.. c	.. c	.. c
Arts, entertainment and recreation	.. c	.. c	.. c	.. c	.. c	.. c	.. c	.. c	.. c	.. c
Other services	.. c	.. c	.. c	.. c	.. c	.. c	.. c	.. c	.. c	.. c
Not allocated and confidential	.. c	.. c	.. c	.. c	.. c	.. c	.. c	.. c	.. c	.. c
Private real estate activities	..	..	..	..	..	..	..	..	..	..

.. Not available; c Confidential data

Note: Detailed metadata at: *http://metalinks.oecd.org/idi/20220712/6d95*.

Source: *OECD International Direct Investment Statistics (database): https://doi.org/10.1787/idi-data-en*

TURKEY

Table 1. Foreign direct investment flows by country

Million US dollars

	Inward					Outward				
	2016	2017	2018	2019	2020	2016	2017	2018	2019	2020
WORLD	**13 719.1**	**11 033.2**	**12 819.8**	**9 284.7**	**7 822.9**	**2 891.6**	**2 622.9**	**3 601.7**	**2 971.0**	**3 242.9**
OECD COUNTRIES	**6 939.7**	**4 192.7**	**5 601.6**	**2 827.0**	**2 954.9**	**2 180.2**	**1 908.1**	**3 201.5**	**2 342.0**	**2 279.1**
Australia	28.1	462.7	48.0	12.1	8.6	1.2	1.6	0.9	-0.5	1.6
Austria	364.4	-1 152.9	447.7	19.7	48.2	3.0	10.4	33.1	59.8	108.7
Belgium	406.7	213.9	144.9	-14.1	-48.1	2.8	11.2	19.8	39.1	4.8
Canada	117.9	41.7	33.6	35.8	-14.1	12.9	12.8	10.4	10.3	86.5
Chile	5.6	1.9	-	-	-0.1	0.1	0.1	-	4.4	-
Colombia	-	-	-	-	-	17.9	2.2	9.9	5.4	3.7
Costa Rica	-	-	-	-	-	-	-	-	-	-
Czech Republic	1.9	65.7	13.7	5.7	3.5	0.4	5.3	0.3	-0.4	-1.8
Denmark	63.6	31.0	216.6	26.7	25.2	1.8	0.7	0.4	0.6	1.2
Estonia	3.0	-	1.0	1.1	1.0	0.0	0.7	1.0	0.8	0.3
Finland	8.9	12.9	11.6	15.3	-123.3	0.4	3.6	4.3	47.2	0.1
France	-123.9	396.7	419.8	87.8	102.7	28.8	28.9	26.3	19.1	-8.9
Germany	644.7	374.6	229.1	8.2	211.9	13.3	178.0	111.7	340.8	176.8
Greece	7.0	1.3	20.1	10.1	8.3	2.4	19.0	21.5	11.0	12.2
Hungary	3.9	1.1	1.2	0.5	8.6	5.9	15.2	-14.6	11.3	22.6
Iceland	-	-	-	-1.0	-	-	-	-	-	-
Ireland	300.1	44.4	-165.8	189.7	372.1	-0.4	-0.9	0.9	0.5	6.3
Israel	5.2	3.2	36.7	36.2	30.5	1.0	1.2	6.6	4.4	0.4
Italy	209.0	43.6	393.8	60.5	-42.1	30.7	31.5	46.1	44.8	9.1
Japan	460.9	184.3	147.5	242.3	116.4	3.6	0.8	0.1	-0.5	0.5
Korea	132.5	34.2	185.6	55.1	81.8	15.7	0.3	-7.5	0.4	7.8
Latvia	3.2	0.0	1.2	2.4	-	1.2	8.6	0.9	1.2	1.6
Lithuania	1.0	1.0	1.0	1.1	1.0	-	0.1	1.1	0.7	0.2
Luxembourg	506.5	-265.9	444.2	-3.0	109.8	57.8	-389.4	42.7	17.6	-19.2
Mexico	-	-	-	1.1	2.1	1.1	4.1	3.9	3.5	0.3
Netherlands	1 634.9	1 647.9	1 107.8	329.2	322.1	716.2	697.8	1 609.1	679.3	886.6
New Zealand	-	4.8	2.0	2.0	2.0	0.1	-	0.2	0.1	-0.1
Norway	10.9	61.8	224.7	20.8	69.1	-4.0	0.9	0.4	-0.5	-0.1
Poland	1.5	8.0	7.9	4.6	1.0	1.5	3.0	6.8	2.2	1.9
Portugal	-0.5	1.1	1.3	0.7	1.0	2.3	49.5	13.8	4.8	-4.7
Slovak Republic	1.6	2.0	1.0	4.9	1.3	0.2	-1.2	1.0	1.1	0.7
Slovenia	0.0	6.6	-	0.2	0.7	1.0	11.8	2.3	12.3	2.9
Spain	293.8	1 403.2	219.4	289.9	7.2	6.6	9.6	21.1	36.4	12.6
Sweden	44.7	42.7	87.6	9.0	92.0	49.0	38.9	16.4	6.5	-45.6
Switzerland	343.9	11.6	150.0	289.1	125.3	54.7	23.2	107.1	99.0	85.7
Turkey	-	-	-	-	-	-	-	-	-	-
United Kingdom	952.5	275.1	670.6	734.4	587.1	337.8	334.9	338.0	289.7	130.5
United States	507.6	233.7	498.0	349.1	842.1	831.0	796.2	775.3	595.3	794.3
EUROPE	**8 535.1**	**6 353.3**	**7 060.7**	**3 848.5**	**2 927.8**	**1 473.8**	**1 175.9**	**2 612.5**	**2 016.1**	**1 589.6**
Bulgaria	13.2	4.8	21.5	10.8	8.9	4.1	43.7	8.9	25.6	13.3
Croatia	0.2	0.9	-	1.0	1.0	14.3	2.7	0.7	4.5	-64.3
Cyprus	5.3	-	-	-	-	-	-	-0.8	-	-
Malta	-39.7	0.9	21.1	31.1	2.6	19.8	15.6	30.9	15.6	0.2
Montenegro	-	-	1.0	1.0	1.0	10.4	3.1	22.7	13.7	2.8
Romania	4.0	1.0	7.1	3.5	9.3	53.1	12.3	21.8	38.1	110.7
Russian Federation	788.1	44.9	113.7	124.8	136.3	-59.2	30.9	20.1	97.6	47.9
Ukraine	35.1	18.0	53.2	33.5	30.6	12.2	-55.0	23.7	26.4	48.1
AFRICA	**86.2**	**124.2**	**239.2**	**402.3**	**320.6**	**91.1**	**105.2**	**64.6**	**43.8**	**96.1**
Northern Africa	72.4	59.4	188.8	297.0	218.2	60.6	78.3	44.6	18.2	84.8
Algeria	10.0	6.0	37.0	50.0	29.0	26.0	39.2	11.1	9.3	6.6
Egypt	36.0	32.2	71.8	99.0	79.2	24.9	30.8	3.8	7.4	7.7
Libya	22.6	20.0	66.0	124.0	93.0	-	-	0.4	0.4	-
Morocco	1.0	1.4	7.0	13.0	12.0	9.4	7.4	28.9	1.0	5.3
Tunisia	2.8	-0.2	7.0	11.0	5.0	0.4	1.0	0.5	0.2	65.3
Other African countries	13.8	64.9	50.5	105.2	102.4	30.4	26.9	20.0	25.5	11.3
Nigeria	-2.0	-	1.0	2.0	5.0	11.0	1.8	-	0.0	2.4
South Africa	0.0	1.0	3.8	11.0	7.6	0.0	0.1	7.0	5.6	2.3
AMERICA	**644.2**	**340.7**	**618.0**	**514.1**	**866.5**	**870.8**	**821.7**	**806.6**	**634.5**	**902.1**
Northern America	625.6	275.4	531.6	384.9	828.1	843.9	809.0	785.7	605.6	880.8
Central America and Caribbean countries	13.3	62.3	79.5	132.8	37.5	8.8	7.6	7.3	4.6	6.7
Bahamas	-	-	-	0.0	-	-	-	-	-	0.1
Bermuda	-	-	-	1.0	-	7.0	-	-	-	0.0
Cayman Islands	0.2	1.3	-	0.2	0.1	-	2.7	-	-	6.0
El Salvador	-	-	-	-	-	-	-	-	-	-
Guatemala	-	-	-	-	1.0	-	-	1.2	-0.2	-0.8
Honduras	-	-	-	-	-	-	-	-	-	-
Nicaragua	-	-	-	-	-	-	-	-	-	-
Panama	0.1	1.3	2.1	12.5	9.9	-	-	0.2	-	-
Virgin Islands, U.S.	-	7.0	0.3	1.5	-	0.3	-	-	-	-
South America	5.3	2.9	7.0	-3.5	0.9	18.0	5.1	13.5	24.3	14.5
Argentina	-	1.0	-	1.0	1.0	-	-	-	-	-
Bolivia	-	-	-	-	-	-	-	-	-	-
Brazil	-0.3	-	1.0	-4.5	-	0.1	0.8	1.1	3.9	0.4
Ecuador	-	-	-	-	-	-	2.0	2.5	-	9.0
Paraguay	-	-	-	-	-	-	-	-	-	-
Peru	-	-	-	-	-	-	0.0	0.1	10.5	1.5
Uruguay	-	-	-	-	-	-	-	-	-	-
Venezuela	-	-	6.0	-	-	-	-	-	-	-

Table 1. Foreign direct investment flows by country *(cont.)*

Million US dollars

	Inward					Outward				
	2016	2017	2018	2019	2020	2016	2017	2018	2019	2020
ASIA	**4 425.7**	**3 747.5**	**4 851.9**	**4 501.6**	**3 693.4**	**454.6**	**518.5**	**116.9**	**277.1**	**653.7**
Near and Middle East	3 257.0	3 087.5	3 136.5	2 985.9	1 687.2	313.6	402.8	27.6	164.5	457.4
Gulf Arabian countries	1 499.3	1 244.1	1 849.1	1 792.4	1 524.6	72.0	125.4	-14.2	29.4	359.7
Kuwait	258.2	197.7	343.0	177.1	142.7	-1.6	-0.1	-0.2	1.0	-0.1
Qatar	462.9	164.3	513.1	745.0	548.6	-4.7	-0.3	-3.0	0.0	-0.7
Saudi Arabia	372.3	525.2	432.4	254.7	76.4	0.3	5.3	-4.0	-0.4	-0.1
United Arab Emirates	291.3	135.1	106.6	42.0	131.0	38.8	52.6	-15.2	26.3	350.1
Other Near and Middle East	1 757.7	1 843.5	1 287.5	1 193.5	162.6	241.6	277.5	41.8	135.1	97.7
Jordan	39.3	37.1	138.9	172.2	104.6	-0.1	1.2	-0.3	0.2	0.0
Other Asian countries	1 168.7	660.0	1 715.3	1 515.7	2 006.2	141.0	115.7	89.3	112.6	196.3
China	346.1	146.9	81.2	85.4	253.2	33.0	10.3	26.9	3.2	21.0
Hong Kong, China	-53.0	17.2	178.5	191.4	337.1	0.3	0.1	0.8	-0.2	-1.2
India	-1.4	9.2	30.4	15.1	9.7	1.0	5.9	6.7	-8.7	2.8
Indonesia	-5.4	1.0	1.0	1.0	1.1	5.1	0.0	9.2	0.2	0.0
Iran, Islamic Republic of	95.2	55.0	425.4	518.0	665.0	0.1	-4.0	2.2	-	-
Malaysia	13.1	33.9	2.4	4.5	0.2	0.1	6.9	5.7	2.0	0.6
Philippines	-	-	0.0	1.0	2.0	-	-	0.1	0.6	0.0
Singapore	32.5	21.8	10.8	24.1	8.1	0.3	1.6	2.3	-0.2	3.1
Chinese Taipei	0.9	6.2	247.5	32.2	26.9	0.4	0.1	0.3	0.2	0.3
Thailand	-6.4	54.1	68.5	0.2	0.1	0.5	0.4	0.9	0.4	2.1
Viet Nam	0.4	-	-	-	1.0	20.4	1.3	1.9	1.0	0.2
AUSTRALIA, OCEANIA AND POLAR REGIONS	**28.1**	**467.4**	**50.0**	**18.3**	**14.6**	**1.4**	**1.6**	**1.2**	**-0.4**	**1.5**
WORLD unallocated and confidential	**0.0**	**0.0**	**0.0**	**0.0**	**0.0**	**0.0**	**0.0**	**0.0**	**0.0**	**0.0**
European Union (since 01/02/2020)	..	..	..	..	..	..	..	..	..	..
G20 countries excl. European Union	**4 428.6**	**2 775.7**	**3 289.4**	**2 074.6**	**2 381.9**	**1 256.5**	**1 442.4**	**1 372.0**	**1 404.1**	**1 272.7**
G20 OECD countries	**2 929.2**	**2 046.6**	**2 625.8**	**1 586.2**	**1 896.7**	**1 276.2**	**1 389.1**	**1 305.1**	**1 302.7**	**1 198.4**
G20 Non-OECD countries	**1 499.5**	**729.1**	**663.6**	**488.4**	**485.2**	**-19.8**	**53.3**	**66.8**	**101.4**	**74.3**
MENA countries	**1 761.0**	**1 379.3**	**2 288.0**	**2 462.4**	**2 005.3**	**132.8**	**205.6**	**31.3**	**46.9**	**443.2**
ASEAN countries	**34.2**	**110.8**	**82.7**	**30.8**	**14.5**	**26.4**	**10.1**	**20.1**	**3.9**	**6.3**

- Nil; .. Not available

Note: Detailed metadata at: *http://metalinks.oecd.org/idi/20220712/6d95*.

Source: *OECD International Direct Investment Statistics (database): https://doi.org/10.1787/idi-data-en*

Table 2. Foreign direct investment positions by country

At year end

Million US dollars

	Inward					Outward				
	2016	2017	2018	2019	2020	2016	2017	2018	2019	2020
WORLD	**148 428.2**	**196 877.4**	**145 261.7**	**164 899.9**	**233 923.8**	**38 368.6**	**45 583.4**	**44 557.4**	**48 679.3**	**50 725.6**
OECD COUNTRIES	**113 130.5**	**149 856.0**	**104 813.3**	**115 104.3**	**162 954.0**	**22 665.3**	**26 993.5**	**29 619.8**	**32 307.2**	**34 553.6**
Australia	69.3	27.4	13.0	18.9	60.6	-2.8	-7.5	-12.1	-17.0	-16.4
Austria	9 231.8	4 198.1	1 935.3	3 090.5	4 983.5	1 251.5	1 831.6	1 916.5	2 026.1	2 285.8
Belgium	3 191.7	3 367.1	2 477.0	2 664.5	3 473.5	213.7	205.9	353.5	696.5	855.7
Canada	879.7	1 687.2	1 369.4	1 261.8	1 147.3	18.5	20.6	15.5	13.8	1.5
Chile	11.8	..	-	-	-	7.1	8.1	-	8.0	0.2
Colombia	..	..	-	-	-	47.4	49.9	40.0	40.0	0.2
Costa Rica	..	..	-	-	-	-	-	-	-	-
Czech Republic	151.0	626.2	171.0	52.4	85.7	-0.2	-0.1	-0.8	-0.9	0.9
Denmark	541.8	896.2	693.8	885.8	1 236.8	0.0	-0.2	0.1	0.0	1.9
Estonia	0.2	0.3	-	0.1	0.1	-	-	-	-	0.1
Finland	2 440.4	2 375.3	1 358.8	1 295.4	159.5	0.4	1.8	2.7	18.6	0.2
France	6 174.8	8 571.0	4 580.2	5 384.9	8 765.7	106.6	137.4	98.4	187.6	65.5
Germany	15 383.4	20 431.9	13 187.2	16 325.9	22 998.3	1 356.5	1 777.8	1 788.9	1 846.5	2 560.3
Greece	152.9	180.7	77.3	78.1	122.9	26.3	42.0	41.3	50.5	64.7
Hungary	29.6	11.2	3.4	3.4	22.2	26.9	25.5	-0.2	26.8	42.0
Iceland	..	..	1.0	-	-	-	-	-	-	-
Ireland	728.4	788.3	751.7	938.8	1 449.7	647.7	659.0	584.7	543.1	618.9
Israel	944.0	1 262.3	880.5	1 010.4	1 310.5	114.1	124.5	143.4	142.2	119.1
Italy	4 207.3	5 117.2	2 787.1	7 942.2	10 423.0	144.4	155.3	140.1	172.1	126.9
Japan	3 041.5	5 252.1	2 695.4	4 278.0	7 598.1	0.2	0.6	2.3	3.4	3.9
Korea	1 796.3	2 323.5	1 902.6	1 453.6	1 760.8	6.7	0.6	2.2	18.0	0.3
Latvia	..	..	1.0	1.0	1.0	4.8	-12.9	-15.1	-17.2	-2.5
Lithuania	0.6	..	-	0.1	0.1	-	-	-	15.6	0.9
Luxembourg	9 110.5	13 148.3	6 178.3	8 063.5	12 362.6	1 846.6	511.2	534.7	636.7	343.4
Mexico	..	..	-	-	-	-8.0	7.9	-8.5	15.3	17.3
Netherlands	22 320.4	35 194.3	35 728.4	32 386.9	36 574.1	13 020.1	15 036.7	17 574.8	18 233.0	19 671.1
New Zealand	1.9	4.5	1.8	1.8	1.8	1.5	1.9	2.1	2.2	1.7
Norway	788.9	845.7	396.3	505.5	678.5	-	-	-	0.1	0.0
Poland	29.7	47.7	33.8	35.3	36.2	37.3	74.9	52.6	83.0	87.8
Portugal	39.4	45.5	4.0	4.4	4.7	5.3	6.3	13.7	16.8	19.6
Slovak Republic	..	27.3	21.5	41.7	118.9	-0.2	-2.2	-2.7	14.5	11.5
Slovenia	0.7	..	-	0.3	0.6	-0.1	1.6	12.4	20.4	17.5
Spain	7 448.1	10 618.3	5 741.0	6 456.5	6 548.3	273.4	250.7	205.9	74.9	124.9
Sweden	460.6	472.8	363.6	1 133.2	1 395.1	4.1	52.2	42.3	89.2	404.2
Switzerland	5 046.1	7 078.4	5 638.7	5 983.4	9 205.1	165.6	184.8	205.4	291.1	253.0
Turkey	91.1	..	150.3	114.9	262.1	-	-	-	-	-
United Kingdom	12 756.6	16 265.9	10 234.2	8 524.1	19 760.1	1 570.9	3 890.6	4 107.8	3 646.0	5 210.9
United States	6 058.8	8 814.8	5 435.3	5 167.3	10 406.7	1 826.6	2 007.0	1 817.7	3 450.5	1 660.8
EUROPE	**111 203.1**	**143 664.1**	**108 749.2**	**107 815.2**	**148 847.2**	**29 278.9**	**35 741.9**	**36 740.6**	**37 551.1**	**41 362.8**
Bulgaria	5.0	2.0	3.8	3.2	3.5	267.5	291.9	291.6	248.3	369.8
Croatia	0.0	0.0	-	33.9	49.0	157.2	139.8	157.3	209.4	161.0
Cyprus	..	..	-	-	-	-	-	-	-	-
Malta	132.8	107.2	27.3	53.9	49.5	1 754.4	2 050.6	1 760.4	1 898.0	2 007.0
Montenegro	..	..	-	-	-	-24.7	32.7	99.0	112.0	216.7
Romania	1.0	..	-	0.1	0.1	219.3	255.4	330.8	313.0	237.7
Russian Federation	10 415.2	12 732.4	16 071.5	5 665.8	7 897.6	467.5	428.7	696.0	864.8	914.7
Ukraine	7.5	..	-	-	-	124.7	115.3	176.7	263.2	294.2
AFRICA	**122.8**	**147.2**	**94.6**	**139.9**	**165.4**	**1 258.8**	**1 568.7**	**1 265.8**	**1 899.6**	**1 459.5**
Northern Africa	102.9	..	88.9	135.1	157.6	1 141.9	1 371.0	1 110.0	1 462.2	1 248.2
Algeria	..	..	-	-	-	632.3	1 174.1	908.2	1 238.3	1 029.8
Egypt	2.4	..	2.6	6.8	25.4	195.0	204.5	245.4	208.3	250.5
Libya	98.9	..	86.3	128.2	132.3	16.7	-119.4	-160.9	-113.4	-147.0
Morocco	1.6	..	-	-	-	247.9	72.3	88.5	106.2	149.6
Tunisia	0.0	..	-	-	-	50.1	39.4	28.8	22.8	-34.6
Other African countries	19.9	13.1	5.7	4.8	7.8	116.9	197.7	155.8	437.4	211.3
Nigeria	..	..	-	-	-	64.9	80.3	23.2	22.5	22.1
South Africa	2.2	..	-	-	-	7.8	14.8	8.3	9.3	3.6
AMERICA	**8 356.1**	**12 709.9**	**8 208.4**	**8 747.5**	**14 828.8**	**2 868.3**	**3 322.3**	**2 245.6**	**4 203.0**	**2 416.3**
Northern America	6 938.5	10 502.0	6 804.7	6 429.1	11 553.9	1 845.1	2 027.5	1 833.2	3 464.3	1 662.2
Central America and Caribbean countries	1 188.5	1 931.7	1 403.7	2 318.4	3 274.9	966.4	1 237.4	372.8	656.0	716.2
Bahamas	4.6	138.7	112.5	121.4	25.2	2.6	2.6	2.6	2.6	2.6
Bermuda	50.5	..	81.3	135.3	179.5	3.7	7.8	7.4	7.0	6.5
Cayman Islands	255.5	421.3	503.7	1 305.8	2 221.6	831.7	1 055.8	540.8	509.7	399.7
El Salvador	..	..	-	-	-	-	-	-	-	-
Guatemala	..	..	-	-	-	-	-	-	-	-
Honduras	..	..	-	-	-	-	-	-	-	-
Nicaragua	..	..	-	-	-	-	-	-	-	-
Panama	740.2	847.9	543.9	526.5	590.9	34.9	41.2	-261.5	3.9	268.1
Virgin Islands, U.S.	-	7.0	7.3	8.8	8.8	-	-	-	-	-
South America	229.1	..	-	-	-	56.8	57.4	39.6	82.7	37.9
Argentina	..	..	-	-	-	-	-	-	-	-
Bolivia	..	..	-	-	-	-	-	-	-	-
Brazil	217.3	..	-	-	-	-0.1	-0.6	-0.5	34.8	36.0
Ecuador	..	..	-	-	-	2.3	-	-	-	-
Paraguay	..	..	-	-	-	-	-	-	-	-
Peru	..	..	-	-	-	-	-	0.1	-0.1	1.5
Uruguay	..	..	-	-	-	-	-	-	-	-
Venezuela	..	..	-	-	-	-	-	-	-	-

TURKEY

Table 2. Foreign direct investment positions by country *(cont.)*

At year end

Million US dollars

	Inward					Outward				
	2016	2017	2018	2019	2020	2016	2017	2018	2019	2020
ASIA	**28 675.2**	**40 324.4**	**28 194.7**	**48 173.5**	**70 016.8**	**4 767.0**	**4 819.3**	**4 367.3**	**5 048.1**	**5 480.4**
Near and Middle East	21 226.3	27 940.2	20 414.1	38 409.5	54 599.2	2 526.8	2 467.3	2 622.6	2 123.6	2 611.7
Gulf Arabian countries	12 485.6	14 495.1	11 025.7	29 849.6	43 209.4	1 048.4	1 400.0	1 502.7	1 185.3	1 812.5
Kuwait	1 056.4	1 272.8	1 081.2	1 811.9	1 904.6	7.2	8.5	-83.0	-105.1	554.9
Qatar	4 940.6	..	6 427.2	22 094.6	33 120.8	110.0	-251.9	102.2	104.4	101.5
Saudi Arabia	3 888.3	..	2 004.2	804.8	863.8	-0.8	-49.7	-47.4	-59.9	29.9
United Arab Emirates	1 493.2	1 743.9	1 078.4	4 760.4	6 622.9	552.6	907.6	935.4	376.0	228.8
Other Near and Middle East	8 740.7	13 445.1	9 388.3	8 559.9	11 389.8	1 478.3	1 067.3	1 119.9	938.3	799.2
Jordan	70.4	83.5	21.4	11.4	52.1	22.6	13.7	13.2	16.7	13.5
Other Asian countries	7 448.9	12 384.2	7 780.7	9 764.0	15 417.6	2 240.3	2 352.0	1 744.7	2 924.4	2 868.7
China	492.4	1 566.8	1 155.0	1 426.9	1 866.4	181.1	260.9	190.8	60.6	161.5
Hong Kong, China	57.0	69.4	59.8	250.7	630.9	0.1	10.5	21.5	17.9	25.6
India	65.6	143.2	143.3	171.9	318.6	111.9	124.0	200.9	152.4	124.0
Indonesia	0.6	..	-	-	-	-48.2	-54.2	-49.0	138.7	120.2
Iran, Islamic Republic of	176.0	..	69.3	102.4	90.2	408.2	394.2	387.3	323.6	574.9
Malaysia	951.2	1 462.6	641.7	555.1	395.1	142.6	193.6	186.9	201.3	217.2
Philippines	..	..	-	-	-	-0.7	-0.6	-1.0	-1.1	-1.1
Singapore	193.5	274.2	213.4	267.5	465.9	17.5	24.4	32.5	11.6	9.4
Chinese Taipei	14.5	..	47.7	75.9	136.2	0.2	0.3	0.1	0.2	0.2
Thailand	493.7	..	745.7	1 080.2	2 069.7	104.0	91.6	128.9	120.3	116.8
Viet Nam	..	..	-	-	-	-	0.2	-	2.7	2.2
AUSTRALIA, OCEANIA AND POLAR REGIONS	**71.1**	**31.9**	**14.7**	**23.8**	**65.5**	**195.5**	**131.3**	**-61.9**	**-22.4**	**6.7**
WORLD unallocated and confidential	**0.0**	**0.0**	**0.0**	**0.0**	**0.0**	**-**	**0.0**	**0.0**	**0.0**	**0.0**
European Union (since 01/02/2020)	**..**	**..**	**..**	**..**	**110 864.7**	**..**	**..**	**..**	**..**	**30 076.6**
G20 countries excl. European Union	**65 540.5**	**87 550.0**	**61 728.8**	**58 540.8**	**94 128.9**	**5 738.9**	**8 714.0**	**8 951.3**	**10 536.8**	**11 020.6**
G20 OECD countries	**50 458.9**	**68 651.9**	**42 354.9**	**50 471.5**	**83 182.6**	**5 019.7**	**7 990.2**	**7 952.3**	**9 336.2**	**9 630.7**
G20 Non-OECD countries	**15 081.6**	**18 898.1**	**19 374.0**	**8 069.4**	**10 946.3**	**719.2**	**723.8**	**999.1**	**1 200.6**	**1 389.9**
MENA countries	**13 467.0**	**15 604.0**	**11 611.5**	**30 545.3**	**44 009.8**	**2 213.4**	**2 789.0**	**2 626.0**	**2 664.7**	**3 074.3**
ASEAN countries	**1 639.0**	**2 686.1**	**1 600.8**	**1 902.8**	**2 930.6**	**215.2**	**255.0**	**298.2**	**473.5**	**464.7**

- Nil; .. Not available

Note: Inward FDI positions are allocated according to the ultimate investing country. Inward FDI positions by immediate counterpart country are available for more years in the OECD FDI database according to BMD4.Detailed metadata at: *http://metalinks.oecd.org/idi/20220712/6d95*.

Source: *OECD International Direct Investment Statistics (database)*: *https://doi.org/10.1787/idi-data-en*

Table 3. Foreign direct investment income by country

Million US dollars

	Inward					Outward				
	2016	2017	2018	2019	2020	2016	2017	2018	2019	2020
WORLD	**3 137.5**	**3 280.3**	**3 200.6**	**3 500.8**	**1 789.3**	**201.5**	**297.4**	**957.1**	**812.5**	**1 100.5**
OECD COUNTRIES	**2 887.2**	**3 022.6**	**2 947.2**	**3 359.8**	**1 319.1**	**86.7**	**138.7**	**607.1**	**459.7**	**449.7**
Australia	0.4	0.6	0.7	0.8	-	-	0.1	0.1	0.2	0.0
Austria	88.1	9.5	15.1	42.0	11.7	-	-	1.3	0.8	35.7
Belgium	82.8	53.7	123.9	144.8	29.6	-	0.1	-	138.3	0.3
Canada	4.9	1.0	1.6	0.0	6.0	0.2	-	-	-	-
Chile	5.6	1.9	-	-	-	-	-	-	-	-
Colombia	-	-	-	-	-	0.0	-	-	-	-
Costa Rica	-	-	-	-	-	-	-	-	-	-
Czech Republic	16.5	0.0	10.4	22.6	-	-	-	0.1	-	-
Denmark	5.4	4.3	6.5	4.2	8.6	-	-	-	-	-
Estonia	-	-	0.2	-	0.2	-	-	-	-	-
Finland	12.3	1.0	55.9	7.5	2.6	-	-	-	-	-
France	178.1	208.9	207.7	172.2	44.5	2.0	0.2	0.1	-0.1	0.1
Germany	413.0	532.4	484.1	605.6	207.9	-2.4	10.0	19.0	10.7	70.3
Greece	0.8	8.7	14.9	13.4	2.0	-	-	0.0	0.7	1.9
Hungary	6.0	7.2	-	0.2	0.6	-0.1	-	-	-	-
Iceland	-	0.0	-	-	-	-	-	-	-	-
Ireland	11.5	1.0	5.9	13.1	8.0	0.0	-	-	0.2	0.1
Israel	9.8	5.7	15.9	0.0	-	-	-	-	0.6	0.4
Italy	75.3	62.8	69.0	74.3	77.2	-	-	2.0	0.1	0.0
Japan	148.0	13.0	39.2	26.6	9.4	2.6	-	-	-	-
Korea	20.8	34.5	37.6	64.8	16.2	-	4.4	-	-	-
Latvia	-	-	-	-	-	2.6	3.3	4.7	1.4	1.1
Lithuania	-	-	-	0.5	0.2	-	-	-	-	-
Luxembourg	90.2	242.2	310.6	309.7	69.3	0.1	13.0	23.7	10.0	3.5
Mexico	-	-	-	-	-	-	-	-	-	0.1
Netherlands	486.1	408.3	502.2	821.4	474.0	46.2	92.4	530.7	109.9	229.6
New Zealand	-	-	-	-	-	-	-	-	-	-
Norway	18.1	20.3	2.3	5.8	2.9	0.0	-	-	0.8	0.2
Poland	0.0	0.6	2.9	0.7	2.0	0.4	0.7	0.5	0.5	0.4
Portugal	7.3	5.1	4.2	-	0.3	-	-	-	-	0.2
Slovak Republic	18.8	13.9	1.3	0.6	0.1	0.0	-	-	1.5	0.7
Slovenia	-	-	-	-	-	-	-	-	-	-
Spain	211.9	127.9	195.3	170.8	42.3	-	0.0	11.3	6.0	0.2
Sweden	5.8	197.7	43.5	39.9	7.8	0.0	-	-	0.1	-
Switzerland	251.6	335.4	239.2	195.3	66.6	0.5	4.6	6.9	104.6	52.0
Turkey	-	-	-	-	-	-	-	-	-	-
United Kingdom	618.3	622.8	476.0	507.2	180.8	24.1	-0.1	2.6	45.5	39.9
United States	100.3	102.2	81.2	115.9	48.3	10.6	10.0	4.4	28.1	13.0
EUROPE	**2 614.5**	**2 867.3**	**2 779.9**	**3 159.4**	**1 251.5**	**77.9**	**143.1**	**697.4**	**503.3**	**531.5**
Bulgaria	0.6	0.1	1.1	0.3	0.2	0.1	0.4	8.3	3.4	0.0
Croatia	-	-	-	-	-	-	-	-	-	0.0
Cyprus	-	-	-	-	-	-	-	-	-	-
Malta	11.1	0.1	0.1	1.7	7.0	0.7	9.7	31.7	15.5	73.8
Montenegro	-	-	-	-	-	-	-0.2	-0.2	-0.2	-
Romania	0.0	-	-	0.7	0.5	-	-	0.2	0.2	4.1
Russian Federation	4.3	1.0	3.2	1.1	1.7	0.8	0.6	3.3	2.1	8.7
Ukraine	-	0.0	3.5	0.2	0.1	1.2	7.0	-	3.1	5.7
AFRICA	**5.5**	**0.5**	**69.5**	**0.9**	**0.7**	**3.2**	**5.5**	**3.3**	**8.3**	**38.8**
Northern Africa	5.5	0.5	68.7	0.4	0.6	3.1	5.5	3.3	8.3	38.3
Algeria	-	0.0	68.7	-	0.0	2.5	3.8	3.0	2.6	32.7
Egypt	0.1	0.1	-	0.1	0.0	0.6	1.7	0.4	5.6	4.1
Libya	5.3	-	-	-	-	-	-	-	-	-
Morocco	-	0.4	-	0.4	0.6	-	0.1	-	0.0	1.5
Tunisia	-	-	-	-	-	-	-	-	0.2	-
Other African countries	0.0	0.1	0.8	0.5	0.1	0.1	-	-	0.0	0.5
Nigeria	-	-	-	0.5	-	-	-	-	0.0	-
South Africa	-	-	0.8	-	0.1	-	-	-	-	-
AMERICA	**114.9**	**137.7**	**128.4**	**129.6**	**65.2**	**10.6**	**9.9**	**4.4**	**28.1**	**13.1**
Northern America	105.1	103.2	82.8	115.9	54.3	10.7	10.0	4.4	28.1	13.0
Central America and Caribbean countries	4.2	32.6	45.6	13.7	10.9	-0.1	-0.1	-	-	0.1
Bahamas	-	-	-	-	-	-	-	-	-	-
Bermuda	-	4.3	11.4	-	-	-	-	-	-	-
Cayman Islands	4.2	-	1.0	0.1	0.1	-	-	-	-	-
El Salvador	-	-	-	-	-	-	-	-	-	-
Guatemala	-	-	-	-	-	-	-	-	-	-
Honduras	-	-	-	-	-	-	-	-	-	-
Nicaragua	-	-	-	-	-	-	-	-	-	-
Panama	-	0.8	-	12.5	9.9	-	-	-	-	-
Virgin Islands, U.S.	-	-	-	-	-	-	-	-	-	-
South America	5.6	1.9	-	-	-	0.0	-	-	-	-
Argentina	-	-	-	-	-	-	-	-	-	-
Bolivia	-	-	-	-	-	-	-	-	-	-
Brazil	-	-	-	-	-	-	-	-	-	-
Ecuador	-	-	-	-	-	-	-	-	-	-
Paraguay	-	-	-	-	-	-	-	-	-	-
Peru	-	-	-	-	-	-	-	-	-	-
Uruguay	-	-	-	-	-	-	-	-	-	-
Venezuela	-	-	-	-	-	-	-	-	-	-

Table 3. Foreign direct investment income by country *(cont.)*

Million US dollars

	Inward					Outward				
	2016	2017	2018	2019	2020	2016	2017	2018	2019	2020
ASIA	**372.6**	**274.2**	**222.2**	**210.1**	**471.7**	**106.2**	**138.8**	**251.9**	**272.5**	**517.1**
Near and Middle East	153.5	156.7	86.8	78.6	424.2	83.3	95.1	209.0	242.6	433.4
Gulf Arabian countries	128.9	144.9	70.2	75.9	85.0	82.1	93.2	195.6	229.8	131.2
Kuwait	52.6	57.9	54.4	61.5	49.3	-	0.0	-	0.0	-
Qatar	43.3	52.4	0.4	0.0	-	-	-	-	4.6	0.9
Saudi Arabia	6.6	21.3	6.9	7.6	19.5	0.5	-	10.0	1.8	1.5
United Arab Emirates	26.4	10.9	7.7	6.8	16.2	0.3	0.1	0.7	4.4	15.1
Other Near and Middle East	24.6	11.8	16.7	2.6	339.2	1.2	1.9	13.4	12.8	302.2
Jordan	-	0.1	0.0	0.2	-1.5	-	0.0	-	-	-
Other Asian countries	219.2	117.5	135.4	131.6	47.5	22.9	43.8	42.9	29.9	83.7
China	2.6	2.4	22.1	0.1	1.7	0.8	18.1	0.1	0.2	0.0
Hong Kong, China	5.4	0.5	0.2	1.2	6.5	-	0.0	0.1	0.0	0.3
India	1.0	0.4	-	-	-	-	0.2	0.2	-	0.2
Indonesia	1.0	0.4	-	-	-	-	-	-	-	-
Iran, Islamic Republic of	-	-	-	-	-	-	0.2	26.0	0.2	-
Malaysia	8.5	4.0	5.2	-	-	-	-	0.1	0.1	13.3
Philippines	-	-	-	-	-	-	-	-	-	-
Singapore	27.5	32.2	27.7	37.4	12.1	2.4	0.5	-	0.0	0.6
Chinese Taipei	2.5	3.2	3.4	-	1.0	-	-	-	-	-
Thailand	1.0	26.7	-	-	-	-	-	-	-	-
Viet Nam	-	-	-	-	-	-	-	-	-	-
AUSTRALIA, OCEANIA AND POLAR REGIONS	**0.4**	**0.6**	**0.7**	**0.8**	**0.2**	**-**	**0.1**	**0.1**	**0.3**	**0.0**
WORLD unallocated and confidential	**0.0**	**0.0**	**0.0**	**0.0**	**0.0**	**-**	**0.0**	**0.0**	**0.0**	**0.0**
European Union (since 01/02/2020)	..	..	..	..	..	..	..	..	..	..
G20 countries excl. European Union	**1 574.4**	**1 603.7**	**1 430.0**	**1 576.0**	**613.2**	**39.1**	**43.5**	**41.7**	**88.5**	**133.7**
G20 OECD countries	**1 558.9**	**1 578.2**	**1 397.0**	**1 567.3**	**590.2**	**37.0**	**24.6**	**28.1**	**84.4**	**123.3**
G20 Non-OECD countries	**15.4**	**25.5**	**33.1**	**8.7**	**23.0**	**2.1**	**19.0**	**13.6**	**4.1**	**10.3**
MENA countries	**137.4**	**147.4**	**139.6**	**77.8**	**84.1**	**85.3**	**98.7**	**198.9**	**238.1**	**169.6**
ASEAN countries	**37.9**	**63.2**	**32.9**	**37.4**	**12.4**	**2.4**	**0.5**	**0.1**	**0.1**	**13.9**

- Nil; .. Not available

Note: Detailed metadata at: *http://metalinks.oecd.org/idi/20220712/6d95*.

Source: *OECD International Direct Investment Statistics (database): https://doi.org/10.1787/idi-data-en*

TURKEY

Table 4. Foreign direct investment flows by industrial sector

Million US dollars

	Inward					Outward				
	2016	2017	2018	2019	2020	2016	2017	2018	2019	2020
All FDI activities	**13 719.1**	**11 033.2**	**12 819.8**	**9 284.7**	**7 822.9**	**2 891.6**	**2 622.9**	**3 601.7**	**2 971.0**	**3 242.9**
Agriculture, forestry and fishing	**41.5**	**50.5**	**91.4**	**30.6**	**-27.8**	**7.2**	**20.2**	**17.3**	**11.1**	**3.0**
Mining and quarrying	**161.7**	**453.9**	**67.2**	**33.2**	**85.9**	**1 068.3**	**1 036.1**	**835.1**	**738.3**	**778.8**
Extraction activities	125.7	443.1	24.4	-19.6	-0.7	1 074.2	994.5	819.8	724.6	668.8
Manufacturing	**2 410.2**	**1 185.4**	**2 103.5**	**1 457.8**	**812.0**	**397.7**	**361.7**	**482.7**	**645.4**	**445.7**
of which:										
Food products, beverages and tobacco	728.1	363.3	475.8	172.8	64.7	41.5	25.7	63.1	-4.4	27.2
Textiles, wood and paper products; printing	168.0	137.3	179.7	33.6	57.6	71.6	126.1	195.0	138.6	71.4
Chemical, rubber, plastic, non-metallic mineral products	273.1	423.1	524.5	986.9	538.0	54.6	72.6	41.9	92.1	91.8
Metal and machinery products, except electrical equipment	721.7	118.7	114.7	171.2	151.8	60.7	22.5	43.8	125.7	58.9
Motor vehicles, trailers, semi-trailers, other transport equipment	168.6	30.7	350.5	183.4	-39.2	13.0	18.9	1.3	103.0	27.8
Other manufacturing	350.8	112.3	458.3	-90.2	39.1	156.3	95.9	137.7	190.3	168.5
Electricity, gas, steam and air conditioning supply	**629.5**	**-945.0**	**374.5**	**223.1**	**182.9**	**39.2**	**24.7**	**387.2**	**32.3**	**415.2**
Water supply; sewerage, waste management and remediation activities	**3.1**	**-5.3**	**4.0**	**2.1**	**-0.8**	**0.6**	**0.7**	**0.3**	**0.1**	**0.3**
Construction	**270.7**	**567.8**	**175.9**	**441.8**	**124.4**	**39.6**	**144.5**	**67.3**	**485.3**	**140.5**
Services	**6 312.4**	**5 083.0**	**4 088.3**	**2 117.3**	**2 244.3**	**1 339.0**	**1 034.7**	**1 811.9**	**1 058.6**	**1 459.4**
Wholesale and retail trade; repair of motor vehicles and motorcycles	932.9	1 262.2	1 244.2	870.4	577.3	78.4	118.2	62.3	109.8	107.7
Transportation and storage	1 553.1	1 926.5	877.0	419.4	103.9	139.5	108.5	37.3	170.3	-51.6
Accommodation and food service activities	258.2	91.2	422.0	126.0	99.7	47.9	123.7	-26.5	40.8	17.4
Information and communication	858.3	-173.8	207.5	552.3	1 013.9	84.7	38.8	17.1	-335.4	359.8
Financial and insurance activities	1 856.8	1 249.2	1 112.9	47.9	90.1	481.8	-79.7	1 152.1	407.6	618.9
Activities of holding companies	126.5	-2.2	83.1	266.9	22.7	257.3	191.5	886.4	265.1	515.3
Real estate activities	367.8	178.5	37.3	122.0	33.9	367.7	567.3	430.4	320.0	279.9
Professional, scientific and technical activities	105.1	70.2	-36.8	76.9	158.9	13.9	19.0	51.3	276.3	26.0
Administrative and support service activities	149.0	323.5	5.6	-221.5	-36.2	2.5	19.1	8.9	15.8	33.7
Public administration; activities of households and of extraterritorial organisations	0.1	0.4	2.0	-	-0.4	0.1	-0.8	-	0.1	0.2
Education	-74.1	-10.8	0.6	0.1	6.5	0.6	1.5	10.9	0.7	2.2
Human health and social work activities	315.0	126.2	91.2	89.8	71.0	85.3	4.3	4.1	10.0	11.4
Arts, entertainment and recreation	16.3	9.7	19.5	3.1	26.4	-0.6	2.6	1.2	1.1	0.8
Other services	-26.0	30.2	105.3	30.9	99.3	37.1	112.3	62.8	41.7	53.2
Not allocated and confidential	**-**	**0.0**	**0.0**	**0.0**	**0.0**	**0.0**	**0.3**	**0.0**	**-0.1**	**0.0**
Private real estate activities	**3 890.0**	**4 643.0**	**5 915.0**	**4 979.0**	**4 402.0**	..	..	..	..	..

- Nil; .. Not available

Note: Detailed metadata at: *http://metalinks.oecd.org/idi/20220712/6d95.*

Source: OECD *International Direct Investment Statistics (database)*: *https://doi.org/10.1787/idi-data-en*

TURKEY

Table 5. Foreign direct investment positions by industrial sector

At year end

Million US dollars

	Inward					Outward				
	2016	2017	2018	2019	2020	2016	2017	2018	2019	2020
All FDI activities	**148 428.2**	**196 877.4**	**145 261.7**	**164 899.9**	**233 923.8**	**38 368.6**	**45 583.4**	**44 557.4**	**48 679.3**	**50 725.6**
Agriculture, forestry and fishing	**748.0**	**1 399.7**	**483.6**	**904.9**	**1 463.3**	**8.8**	**29.6**	**32.2**	**21.7**	**14.1**
Mining and quarrying	**2 690.9**	**4 770.7**	**3 426.5**	**3 527.0**	**2 656.4**	**4 202.3**	**5 296.4**	**3 577.5**	**3 181.2**	**2 695.7**
Extraction activities	1 091.6	2 081.3	1 442.2	1 439.0	678.5	4 045.2	5 137.9	3 480.7	2 937.6	2 608.4
Manufacturing	**45 957.9**	**61 606.8**	**34 560.5**	**38 097.2**	**80 008.4**	**4 483.8**	**4 080.1**	**4 117.0**	**4 743.5**	**5 455.4**
of which:										
Food products, beverages and tobacco	9 858.9	12 305.4	6 273.5	7 805.6	20 627.9	2 051.6	709.2	787.9	1 062.2	1 281.6
Textiles, wood and paper products; printing	992.7	1 718.3	947.6	1 923.1	5 831.2	790.2	1 021.4	979.0	1 339.7	1 367.9
Chemical, rubber, plastic, non-metallic mineral products	13 787.1	19 168.4	12 872.4	11 955.9	23 807.6	641.6	819.5	652.3	652.3	904.5
Metal and machinery products, except electrical equipment	4 948.8	6 931.8	2 506.8	2 624.6	3 781.2	769.6	1 345.0	1 277.1	1 304.4	1 568.3
Motor vehicles, trailers, semi-trailers, other transport equipment	8 922.2	12 504.0	6 512.9	7 052.5	10 507.9	121.6	101.1	140.1	221.0	65.3
Other manufacturing	7 448.2	8 978.8	5 447.3	6 735.5	15 452.7	109.2	84.0	280.7	163.9	267.8
Electricity, gas, steam and air conditioning supply	**11 829.6**	**18 971.8**	**5 605.5**	**8 696.0**	**13 399.9**	**468.4**	**425.8**	**305.7**	**706.2**	**708.8**
Water supply; sewerage, waste management and remediation activities	**62.6**	**53.1**	**10.3**	**34.8**	**39.8**	**10.3**	**2.4**	**2.9**	**3.2**	**19.4**
Construction	**1 459.9**	**903.3**	**627.3**	**494.7**	**513.4**	**1 085.2**	**466.7**	**333.0**	**1 377.0**	**1 898.1**
Services	**85 679.5**	**109 172.1**	**100 548.1**	**113 145.4**	**135 842.7**	**28 109.9**	**35 282.4**	**36 189.1**	**38 646.6**	**39 934.2**
Wholesale and retail trade; repair of motor vehicles and motorcycles	32 069.7	40 345.8	44 979.6	42 487.9	53 873.4	1 574.7	2 057.6	2 760.8	2 115.4	1 921.4
Transportation and storage	3 359.9	7 086.5	4 629.9	3 456.4	2 953.4	1 433.2	2 826.7	1 399.5	1 598.5	1 212.0
Accommodation and food service activities	455.7	943.9	460.5	782.3	2 032.9	411.0	338.9	205.7	249.0	193.5
Information and communication	12 633.9	16 122.2	8 656.2	7 549.9	7 036.3	2 510.0	1 774.9	1 083.1	1 077.9	1 135.8
Financial and insurance activities	31 950.3	37 991.0	37 829.8	54 091.3	64 274.8	21 595.0	27 650.6	29 978.4	32 531.3	34 592.9
Activities of holding companies	3 999.7	5 187.8	3 019.2	4 462.6	3 321.4	13 266.3	18 980.4	21 067.0	23 118.1	24 540.4
Real estate activities	1 354.6	2 176.9	1 605.8	1 551.7	1 951.4	321.9	471.1	573.9	755.5	509.5
Professional, scientific and technical activities	315.8	686.3	313.2	318.6	471.1	45.4	53.6	6.3	39.0	25.6
Administrative and support service activities	1 569.8	2 103.3	1 376.2	1 372.8	1 490.6	60.4	12.2	27.9	27.3	11.5
Public administration; activities of households and of extraterritorial organisations	0.0	0.4	0.4	0.4	0.4	-	-0.8	-0.8	-0.8	-0.8
Education	11.6	13.6	6.8	0.5	7.4	5.6	4.8	2.5	-5.6	-6.6
Human health and social work activities	759.7	651.9	276.0	439.8	636.3	80.5	35.9	73.8	98.5	119.0
Arts, entertainment and recreation	572.4	129.1	74.7	69.1	94.4	24.6	26.2	59.8	47.6	50.6
Other services	626.2	921.2	339.0	1 024.9	1 020.4	47.6	30.6	18.1	113.0	169.9
Not allocated and confidential	**-0.1**	**-0.1**	**-0.1**	**-0.1**	**-0.1**	**-**	**0.0**	**0.0**	**0.0**	**0.0**
Private real estate activities	..	..	..	..	..	..	..	..	..	..

- Nil; .. Not available

Note: Detailed metadata at: *http://metalinks.oecd.org/idi/20220712/6d95*.

Source: *OECD International Direct Investment Statistics (database)*: *https://doi.org/10.1787/idi-data-en*

Table 6. Foreign direct investment income by industrial sector

Million US dollars

	Inward					Outward				
	2016	2017	2018	2019	2020	2016	2017	2018	2019	2020
All FDI activities	**3 137.5**	**3 280.3**	**3 200.6**	**3 500.8**	**1 789.3**	**201.5**	**297.4**	**957.1**	**812.5**	**1 100.5**
Agriculture, forestry and fishing	**22.9**	**12.7**	**13.3**	**3.6**	**3.1**	**0.2**	**-**	**0.1**	**0.6**	**1.4**
Mining and quarrying	**116.6**	**240.2**	**75.0**	**240.5**	**83.8**	**0.1**	**0.3**	**1.5**	**2.5**	**0.9**
Extraction activities	46.0	115.2	56.3	80.7	47.4	-	-	-	-	0.5
Manufacturing	**1 369.8**	**1 288.3**	**1 145.6**	**1 248.1**	**520.2**	**70.2**	**122.9**	**292.5**	**262.5**	**186.0**
of which:										
Food products, beverages and tobacco	496.8	483.4	337.9	255.2	50.0	13.3	23.6	24.4	171.9	83.5
Textiles, wood and paper products; printing	28.4	59.8	68.8	46.4	16.0	3.5	5.0	21.9	0.9	39.2
Chemical, rubber, plastic, non-metallic mineral products	350.2	196.2	168.5	170.6	132.6	29.3	34.4	30.8	32.8	32.5
Metal and machinery products, except electrical equipment	169.2	169.0	153.1	108.3	86.9	15.2	15.1	25.9	41.5	25.0
Motor vehicles, trailers, semi-trailers, other transport equipment	193.1	141.2	192.3	355.6	135.1	1.0	0.5	-	0.1	0.0
Other manufacturing	132.1	238.8	225.1	312.0	99.7	7.9	44.3	189.5	15.2	5.8
Electricity, gas, steam and air conditioning supply	**133.4**	**88.7**	**121.8**	**81.2**	**35.4**	**1.5**	**0.1**	**20.3**	**13.1**	**100.0**
Water supply; sewerage, waste management and remediation activities	**0.2**	**1.2**	**0.0**	**0.4**	**1.0**	**-**	**-**	**-**	**-**	**0.1**
Construction	**27.4**	**41.4**	**51.1**	**49.1**	**3.8**	**1.2**	**18.0**	**28.9**	**26.2**	**131.5**
Services	**1 467.1**	**1 607.9**	**1 793.9**	**1 878.0**	**1 142.1**	**128.3**	**157.2**	**613.8**	**507.6**	**680.7**
Wholesale and retail trade; repair of motor vehicles and motorcycles	517.0	456.0	363.9	285.6	165.9	4.5	5.2	14.9	37.4	14.4
Transportation and storage	313.2	193.5	358.0	438.4	317.3	0.1	4.9	11.2	7.2	9.5
Accommodation and food service activities	27.1	23.9	132.9	69.5	74.8	0.4	4.0	9.0	9.2	10.6
Information and communication	44.1	462.2	299.2	581.0	378.8	-0.2	19.3	2.2	4.5	292.1
Financial and insurance activities	319.4	308.3	484.4	336.0	146.9	121.2	104.3	519.1	406.1	296.2
Activities of holding companies	18.1	9.7	56.3	61.5	34.5	3.4	2.1	261.1	110.7	79.5
Real estate activities	35.9	13.0	19.5	15.6	5.8	-0.1	3.4	1.2	14.5	1.1
Professional, scientific and technical activities	123.0	62.5	30.9	43.2	12.9	0.4	4.8	4.6	4.4	47.1
Administrative and support service activities	35.4	20.8	32.4	56.8	28.4	0.7	9.9	1.1	0.1	2.7
Public administration; activities of households and of extraterritorial organisations	-	-	0.0	-	-	-	-	-	-	-
Education	0.0	0.0	0.4	0.6	0.2	0.1	0.0	-	-	-
Human health and social work activities	28.1	7.1	4.9	4.1	2.0	-	0.4	45.1	2.9	1.5
Arts, entertainment and recreation	7.2	5.0	6.4	25.2	0.8	0.4	-	3.1	-	0.0
Other services	16.7	55.6	61.0	22.0	8.3	0.9	1.1	2.4	21.4	5.6
Not allocated and confidential	**0.0**	**0.0**	**0.0**	**0.0**	**0.0**	**0.0**	**-1.0**	**0.0**	**0.0**	**0.0**
Private real estate activities	..	..	..	..	..	..	..	..	..	..

- Nil; .. Not available

Note: Detailed metadata at: *http://metalinks.oecd.org/idi/20220712/6d95*.

Source: *OECD International Direct Investment Statistics (database): https://doi.org/10.1787/idi-data-en*

UNITED KINGDOM

Table 1. Foreign direct investment flows by country

Million US dollars

	Inward					Outward				
	2016	2017	2018	2019	2020	2016	2017	2018	2019	2020
WORLD	**196 503.4**	**78 511.5**	**65 450.8**	**49 898.6**	**-1 493.6**	**-22 310.4**	**106 692.0**	**41 491.7**	**-35 355.4**	**-72 611.6**
OECD COUNTRIES	**152 390.0**	**51 399.7**	**.. d**	**58 391.0**	**-17 216.4**	**.. c**	**111 666.2**	**.. d**	**-41 305.6**	**-39 590.2**
Australia	-2 159.2	3 026.0	919.0	-4 546.9	1 222.9	1 215.9	-4 470.8	2 451.8	-667.1	-7 780.5
Austria	-101.2	-10.3	16.4	-158.5	-62.6	114.7	385.0	110.9	140.2	-209.9
Belgium	.. c	-2 818.7	1 191.8	1 002.9	978.8	.. c	.. c	.. c	.. c	3 495.7
Canada	155.2	.. d	.. d	.. d	.. d	-1 391.4	137.8	1 011.0	1 560.5	-989.7
Chile	-1.4	12.9	-7.4	4.3	-20.7	274.0	-42.5	109.8	.. c	-349.3
Colombia	-	.. c	0.9	-0.7	.. c	-167.3	.. c	38.0	-73.2	71.2
Costa Rica	-1.4	-	-0.3	-1.3	-	.. c	.. c	-23.3	-1.3	6.1
Czech Republic	-	-1.3	14.9	.. c	.. c	-66.1	218.9	90.3	166.6	-106.9
Denmark	36.4	534.4	443.9	6 247.2	143.3	1 063.4	-464.8	.. c	69.5	-26.1
Estonia	-	-	0.8	-2.8	18.0	-112.0	43.8	124.7	31.7	-35.3
Finland	-55.3	34.8	123.7	487.8	.. c	62.1	82.4	-37.6	.. c	.. c
France	618.1	7 700.2	-656.1	8 701.6	-2 136.8	697.7	-1 984.3	5 035.5	199.7	4 038.9
Germany	3 330.6	318.1	.. c	675.2	-3 761.3	-174.1	894.9	3 668.4	-1 584.6	1 681.4
Greece	12.1	-55.4	.. c	13.4	-1 292.9	.. c	148.1	109.7	-69.2	-46.4
Hungary	-13.5	43.8	-3.8	-0.1	-19.2	.. c	218.9	-34.5	190.8	-74.7
Iceland	56.7	-23.2	10.7	.. c	38.0	-1.4	2.6	.. c	55.3	551.6
Ireland	-948.7	673.4	.. c	-42.2	1 769.5	-7 641.0	13 060.8	-2 812.9	5 085.1	-940.9
Israel	25.6	.. d	1 153.6	1 281.1	108.5	125.5	230.5	91.9	41.5	.. c
Italy	-755.7	1 862.0	-278.0	1 366.6	696.5	430.5	-632.2	-837.6	-2 059.9	.. c
Japan	2 295.5	10 144.2	461.0	-13 649.5	.. c	-27.0	.. c	344.0	-223.8	-460.9
Korea	188.9	202.2	360.4	-23.1	-161.7	1 654.5	.. c	526.8	.. c	255.5
Latvia	1.4	7.7	10.1	3.3	2.7	-20.2	-	23.1	-187.5	66.9
Lithuania	1.4	.. c	0.4	7.6	6.3	-44.5	9.0	-28.2	-25.6	.. c
Luxembourg	29 121.5	5 499.6	.. c	8 328.3	-11 909.1	2 112.0	7 078.3	-736.5	-4 751.5	-1 161.8
Mexico	6.7	7.7	-9.5	.. c	.. c	569.5	1 129.3	1 882.8	648.2	-447.9
Netherlands	.. c	-2 319.1	-22 506.1	5 562.2	8 525.4	-17 797.6	.. c	8 098.4	-19 753.7	-7 308.7
New Zealand	55.3	-37.3	42.5	5.3	106.7	14.8	155.8	240.4	.. c	-322.7
Norway	.. c	461.0	.. c	1 235.5	401.1	1 376.5	.. c	-7 256.1	-966.8	-754.3
Poland	-1.4	67.0	7.8	84.1	16.6	-151.1	378.6	471.6	495.4	828.9
Portugal	8.1	-27.0	-0.8	235.7	23.8	-599.2	211.2	250.0	-83.4	-247.8
Slovak Republic	2.7	.. c	14.1	-8.0	9.4	-60.7	.. c	.. c	-25.2	-217.2
Slovenia	-	2.6	-1.4	-0.3	6.9	13.5	-25.8	43.8	51.6	-25.8
Spain	2 531.7	-797.1	5 079.3	-641.0	2 111.0	1 066.1	.. c	189.8	.. c	-519.9
Sweden	-13.5	1 070.0	-383.6	1 404.8	2 044.0	3 170.0	866.6	2 033.9	-110.9	609.3
Switzerland	1 144.4	5 114.6	1 857.8	-867.4	-2 771.4	-1 334.7	209.9	-3 409.9	-14 832.7	-3 005.3
Turkey	-10.8	39.9	-85.9	-35.7	-31.3	359.0	-316.8	506.8	-91.2	-16.6
United Kingdom	..	..	..	..	..	..	..	..	..	..
United States	25 049.9	20 392.7	53 328.1	38 509.5	11 816.3	982.5	92 951.3	5 712.3	-8 101.3	-14 448.9
EUROPE	**131 993.3**	**28 489.6**	**1 108.1**	**31 452.6**	**.. d**	**-34 803.0**	**13 574.6**	**3 572.8**	**-30 838.9**	**-16 484.7**
Bulgaria	-1.4	15.5	1.1	6.0	-48.0	-1.4	94.0	-9.0	17.7	7.3
Croatia	-	.. c	.. d	.. d	-24.9	-17.5	-32.2	.. d	-33.5	-34.0
Cyprus	103.9	.. c	536.0	-699.6	-679.0	.. c	-320.6	.. c	404.5	292.0
Malta	-44.5	-106.9	118.9	47.7	129.9	62.1	-1 344.3	-57.5	39.6	-554.1
Montenegro	-	-	.. d	.. d	-	.. d	.. d	.. d	.. d	1.1
Romania	2.7	.. d	-3.9	2.4	24.5	.. c	166.1	-32.3	-27.3	-113.3
Russian Federation	-64.8	-55.4	70.4	.. c	3.0	-583.0	-725.0	1 263.9	-16.6	-1 020.0
Ukraine	-2.7	11.6	1.7	2.6	1.3	-545.2	-83.7	-61.7	119.1	-162.9
AFRICA	**17.5**	**376.0**	**.. c**	**1 147.9**	**1 483.9**	**-8 461.5**	**.. c**	**13 328.1**	**5 114.6**	**-2 658.8**
Northern Africa	5.4	2.6	3.2	.. d	3.8	-1 596.5	.. c	.. c	.. d	-250.7
Algeria	-	.. c	0.1	.. c	.. c	.. c	.. c	.. c	.. c	.. c
Egypt	-	-1.3	1.2	2.2	7.5	-399.5	.. c	.. c	-230.3	.. c
Libya	5.4	.. c	-	-	.. c	.. c	.. c	4.0	0.6	.. c
Morocco	-	-1.3	2.0	0.4	.. d	-141.7	.. c	25.9	-50.8	.. c
Tunisia	-	.. c	-	-	-	-5.4	-	-2.7	-1.1	-19.6
Other African countries	12.1	373.4	.. c	.. d	1 480.1	-6 865.0	-5 973.5	.. d	.. d	-2 408.1
Nigeria	56.7	.. c	24.9	.. c	-23.3	746.3	330.9	-476.0	.. c	.. c
South Africa	-89.1	.. c	-341.1	.. c	1 437.6	.. c	423.6	3 333.0	-69.4	1 200.6
AMERICA	**28 348.2**	**28 581.0**	**60 739.8**	**28 850.3**	**23 772.2**	**2 657.2**	**99 262.2**	**9 859.0**	**-5 397.5**	**-17 994.7**
Northern America	25 203.8	.. d	.. d	.. d	.. d	-406.2	93 089.1	6 723.1	-6 555.7	-15 438.2
Central America and Caribbean countries	3 129.6	6 847.8	-229.3	-12 819.2	9 786.3	2 086.4	5 270.4	2 029.9	238.1	.. d
Bahamas	-78.3	33.5	204.3	-502.8	-542.8	93.1	.. c	-15.1	67.7	12.9
Bermuda	1 658.6	1 943.1	313.5	-786.9	421.8	-547.9	-157.1	-495.7	-458.6	-357.0
Cayman Islands	3 681.5	-16.7	-1 879.7	-5 921.8	1 271.3	.. c	3 427.8	.. c	848.1	.. c
El Salvador	-	-	-	-	-	.. c	.. c	.. c	-0.9	-2.6
Guatemala	44.5	158.4	15.2	-31.2	49.8	-20.2	101.7	-7.3	.. c	-34.1
Honduras	-	-	-	-	-	-4.0	.. c	.. c	.. c	-181.6
Nicaragua	-	-	-	-	-	-1.4	20.6	2.7	.. c	4.4
Panama	-2.7	6.4	-29.8	-7.9	14.1	12.1	.. c	.. c	8.6	-51.3
Virgin Islands, U.S.	2.7	.. c	9.1	.. c	0.7	1.4	-3.9	-0.3	2.7	.. d
South America	14.8	.. c	.. c	.. c	345.8	978.4	902.7	1 106.0	920.2	.. c
Argentina	-	-	-0.2	125.8	1.5	.. c	.. c	284.9	.. c	.. d
Bolivia	-	-	-	-	-	-	1.3	1.3	1.2	-16.8
Brazil	16.2	.. c	.. c	-47.6	.. c	466.9	261.4	706.1	274.0	.. c
Ecuador	-	.. c	-	-	-	.. c	18.0	.. c	16.4	-9.3
Paraguay	-	.. c	-	.. d	-	2.7	1.3	.. d	-0.4	.. d
Peru	-	-	-0.4	-0.2	0.9	29.7	61.8	35.4	70.5	-137.9
Uruguay	-	-	-	-	.. c	.. c	1.3	9.3	.. c	-43.7
Venezuela	-	-	-	-	.. c	43.2	94.0	-74.4	-25.8	.. c

Table 1. Foreign direct investment flows by country *(cont.)*

Million US dollars

	Inward					Outward				
	2016	2017	2018	2019	2020	2016	2017	2018	2019	2020
ASIA	**37 720.6**	**19 660.1**	**2 875.3**	**-7 005.7**	**.. c**	**16 969.0**	**.. c**	**11 430.0**	**-1 238.4**	**-25 311.7**
Near and Middle East	.. c	891.1	1 381.6	1 850.6	208.3	.. c	.. d	3 904.4	-2 075.7	.. d
Gulf Arabian countries	.. c	844.7	205.8	557.1	108.8	.. c	1 282.5	3 657.1	-3 527.0	-3 732.7
Kuwait	20.2	-9.0	5.7	14.5	20.2	8.1	.. c	1.5	.. c	.. c
Qatar	4.0	16.7	.. c	.. c	5.7	33.7	.. c	25.3	.. c	.. c
Saudi Arabia	-74.2	3.9	-4.4	86.8	194.0	653.2	696.6	424.2	-229.6	473.1
United Arab Emirates	.. c	645.1	52.5	338.1	-92.2	.. c	.. c	2 597.8	-3 003.3	-4 195.2
Other Near and Middle East	27.0	47.6	1 175.8	1 293.4	99.5	655.9	.. d	247.3	1 451.3	-270.5
Jordan	-	.. d	9.1	2.0	-16.0	.. c	.. c	.. c	4.7	0.3
Other Asian countries	.. d	18 769.0	1 493.7	-8 856.3	.. c	.. d	5 329.6	7 525.6	837.3	.. c
China	552.0	1 357.2	-112.0	1 032.2	-794.3	1 526.3	-330.9	1 999.3	-2 169.2	1 589.0
Hong Kong, China	.. c	2 724.7	1 539.7	3 069.1	1 712.6	3 859.6	2 978.4	5 396.3	-989.8	5 435.3
India	-792.2	1 874.8	-275.3	-26.7	-258.7	.. c	-441.7	116.1	1 016.8	-3 801.1
Indonesia	.. c	.. c	9.9	.. c	0.8	1 081.0	-614.2	-1 002.1	408.2	-1 079.0
Iran, Islamic Republic of	5.4	.. c	0.3	7.8	8.3	.. c	-1.3	0.1	0.0	3.8
Malaysia	-145.7	94.0	-0.6	154.6	15.1	902.8	535.7	456.0	.. c	.. d
Philippines	2.7	23.2	2.6	7.3	-2.0	43.2	65.7	139.5	218.6	.. d
Singapore	5 612.7	-664.4	404.3	-114.9	-40.7	.. c	-387.6	-2 796.2	4 117.8	-1 097.9
Chinese Taipei	-2.7	10.3	0.3	35.8	-11.1	483.1	337.4	97.5	.. c	199.4
Thailand	-4.0	38.6	.. c	92.8	63.6	790.8	-37.3	417.0	.. c	.. c
Viet Nam	.. c	-	-0.2	0.6	0.7	-54.0	.. c	360.5	792.5	-988.7
AUSTRALIA, OCEANIA AND POLAR REGIONS	**-1 576.2**	**1 406.1**	**962.7**	**-4 546.5**	**1 328.0**	**1 326.6**	**-4 567.3**	**3 301.8**	**-2 995.3**	**-10 161.6**
WORLD unallocated and confidential	**-**	**-1.3**	**.. d**	**0.0**	**.. d**	**1.4**	**-2 468.5**	**0.0**	**0.0**	**0.0**
European Union (since 01/02/2020)	**..**	**..**	**..**	**..**	**.. d**	**..**	**..**	**..**	**..**	**-12 391.8**
G20 countries excl. European Union	**.. d**	**.. d**	**.. d**	**.. d**	**.. d**	**.. d**	**.. d**	**27 427.1**	**.. d**	**.. d**
G20 OECD countries	**28 719.3**	**.. d**	**.. d**	**.. d**	**.. d**	**4 317.1**	**.. d**	**20 301.7**	**.. d**	**.. d**
G20 Non-OECD countries	**.. d**	**.. d**	**.. d**	**.. d**	**.. d**	**.. d**	**.. d**	**7 125.3**	**.. d**	**.. d**
MENA countries	**.. d**	**.. d**	**.. d**	**.. d**	**.. d**	**.. d**	**.. d**	**.. d**	**.. d**	**.. d**
ASEAN countries	**5 261.8**	**23.2**	**-477.7**	**663.0**	**41.0**	**-1 083.7**	**-283.3**	**-2 300.3**	**5 502.4**	**-24 239.4**

- Nil; .. Not available; c Confidential data; d Secondary Confidentiality

Note: Detailed metadata at: *http://metalinks.oecd.org/idi/20220712/6d95.*

Source: *OECD International Direct Investment Statistics (database): https://doi.org/10.1787/idi-data-en*

Table 2. Foreign direct investment positions by country

At year end

Million US dollars

	Inward					Outward				
	2016	2017	2018	2019	2020	2016	2017	2018	2019	2020
WORLD	**1 475 523.4**	**1 608 032.7**	**1 930 434.0**	**1 974 480.5**	**2 219 788.7**	**1 491 940.0**	**1 624 231.9**	**1 788 397.1**	**1 901 117.2**	**2 137 521.5**
OECD COUNTRIES	**1 199 040.5**	**1 302 699.6**	**.. d**	**1 619 943.9**	**1 796 331.6**	**1 082 914.3**	**1 228 098.9**	**.. d**	**1 434 946.1**	**1 633 413.5**
Australia	13 707.7	9 537.9	20 200.4	19 493.5	15 322.2	50 488.4	41 335.0	45 205.3	50 690.0	44 092.3
Austria	1 620.1	3 295.5	1 338.5	2 202.5	2 382.5	1 237.5	6 516.7	6 276.1	6 778.1	2 798.9
Belgium	32 478.8	21 928.1	119 796.1	121 472.3	160 505.1	18 363.9	16 087.0	19 078.8	31 328.2	51 783.1
Canada	.. d	25 777.6	.. d	.. d	35 150.1	25 920.8	30 636.4	36 465.3	.. d	36 857.3
Chile	64.0	177.0	.. c	45.1	255.0	1 504.5	1 364.7	1 414.7	1 618.3	1 888.3
Colombia	1.2	-	0.6	1.1	.. c	720.9	535.1	400.2	759.7	1 333.1
Costa Rica	-4.9	-	1.5	-1.2	-	264.5	56.7	7.5	24.3	.. c
Czech Republic	7.4	13.5	498.5	.. c	.. c	2 301.6	2 864.5	2 567.7	3 113.0	2 963.9
Denmark	8 335.6	9 085.3	7 467.8	8 304.3	10 888.0	8 488.1	6 949.1	7 633.4	8 511.6	8 358.8
Estonia	.. d	1.4	20.9	30.0	55.4	254.6	328.3	838.0	.. d	448.9
Finland	728.3	1 417.4	681.9	1 115.9	992.4	1 082.5	737.7	788.4	3 736.8	5 452.9
France	73 722.5	92 834.8	69 977.0	90 346.0	108 290.6	88 253.2	96 604.5	104 216.0	97 678.2	118 378.3
Germany	73 599.5	60 671.5	106 569.6	61 567.0	65 048.8	25 709.2	29 363.6	42 028.9	42 535.0	45 710.0
Greece	145.2	410.8	-1 396.9	277.2	-941.5	338.3	294.6	324.8	477.6	673.9
Hungary	-20.9	258.1	14.9	13.8	.. d	1 322.4	1 232.3	1 308.3	2 237.8	2 050.5
Iceland	.. d	320.2	.. d	.. d	.. d	.. c	9.5	60.9	-131.9	427.9
Ireland	14 128.4	18 897.4	18 870.5	30 460.0	46 189.8	59 292.7	87 562.5	67 402.6	65 276.8	105 596.8
Israel	585.6	702.6	15 806.7	1 790.6	.. c	.. d	1 299.8	.. d	1 068.6	1 783.6
Italy	6 223.4	11 594.4	7 624.5	6 896.3	9 694.5	15 318.0	13 023.9	19 196.8	18 253.5	23 977.3
Japan	57 189.1	66 968.0	113 216.0	109 081.5	99 474.7	5 411.5	7 213.9	9 307.0	7 188.9	6 147.1
Korea	2 278.3	3 025.3	2 674.6	2 027.3	2 003.2	7 549.5	8 779.9	7 242.3	5 093.0	5 190.5
Latvia	.. d	77.0	41.3	61.2	61.9	.. d	293.2	.. d	.. c	1 140.2
Lithuania	3.7	1.4	25.9	45.4	178.7	52.9	64.9	60.2	461.5	507.7
Luxembourg	141 221.6	157 273.3	141 472.9	155 449.4	151 070.0	138 730.5	138 135.4	148 187.9	146 667.5	146 107.0
Mexico	137.8	143.2	.. c	.. c	.. c	9 244.7	12 657.7	12 179.9	15 434.2	16 478.4
Netherlands	260 914.0	298 142.1	174 662.8	188 103.1	240 161.7	174 360.9	184 431.8	203 387.7	192 069.6	200 830.6
New Zealand	324.8	644.5	307.8	397.2	840.3	1 077.6	1 189.0	1 545.0	1 612.9	1 128.9
Norway	6 562.9	8 744.8	10 364.4	11 287.8	8 525.9	8 408.2	4 988.5	2 455.1	6 825.8	8 195.6
Poland	147.6	237.8	249.9	907.5	1 128.4	7 620.9	9 197.4	7 926.2	9 566.7	10 002.5
Portugal	513.0	936.4	316.2	690.3	490.6	4 139.5	4 961.5	5 575.3	5 615.5	6 374.4
Slovak Republic	13.5	-1.4	13.3	104.3	.. d	392.4	647.2	892.1	1 121.7	1 117.2
Slovenia	3.7	5.4	11.0	8.3	.. d	153.8	154.0	218.5	254.6	264.1
Spain	37 244.4	55 279.0	63 666.0	70 704.5	57 387.4	68 820.3	85 680.3	94 009.6	95 121.9	96 649.0
Sweden	9 070.0	13 673.8	12 014.5	9 775.8	12 685.2	22 833.1	26 604.5	26 053.0	28 497.0	41 713.0
Switzerland	55 736.3	61 018.8	85 602.5	100 180.8	101 914.9	27 217.4	38 721.8	62 093.7	74 171.0	55 023.4
Turkey	120.6	329.7	42.7	402.5	-9.3	9 554.7	9 256.9	7 737.7	9 377.0	10 354.8
United Kingdom	-	-	-	-	..	-	-	-	-	..
United States	379 012.2	379 278.5	528 959.2	603 643.9	642 728.8	296 443.6	358 975.8	374 599.9	466 462.0	571 613.5
EUROPE	**831 161.3**	**948 009.7**	**1 015 812.7**	**1 005 630.2**	**1 144 948.0**	**761 980.6**	**838 956.9**	**923 016.8**	**944 935.6**	**1 072 982.8**
Bulgaria	48.0	129.7	17.0	55.4	106.7	66.4	198.6	37.7	213.5	267.6
Croatia	-	-	0.2	.. d	75.8	294.0	-40.5	-8.1	427.4	425.4
Cyprus	5 212.2	5 080.4	9 809.2	5 374.6	4 278.6	3 973.4	3 026.6	.. c	6 401.6	3 336.4
Malta	830.4	968.8	1 345.4	1 138.0	1 518.2	.. c	1 871.4	682.0	1 059.9	944.3
Montenegro	.. d	-	-	.. d	-	-	.. d	7.9	.. d	10.3
Romania	7.4	8.1	3.7	7.5	213.7	1 216.6	824.2	586.3	724.8	685.8
Russian Federation	1 233.9	.. c	893.4	.. c	.. c	14 423.7	.. c	.. c	17 654.8	15 579.9
Ukraine	48.0	150.0	27.3	31.6	12.9	200.5	-448.6	-375.7	463.1	810.9
AFRICA	**2 405.0**	**4 437.2**	**2 441.0**	**4 058.9**	**7 821.8**	**55 471.8**	**44 658.8**	**49 148.6**	**43 953.6**	**36 555.9**
Northern Africa	253.4	.. c	278.1	.. c	.. c	.. c	.. c	.. c	.. c	9 559.3
Algeria	-	-	0.1	-	.. c	.. c	.. c	.. c	.. c	.. c
Egypt	22.1	35.1	36.9	44.9	32.9	.. c	.. c	.. c	.. c	.. c
Libya	228.8	.. c	231.1	.. c	.. c	-7.4	-8.1	.. c	-21.7	.. c
Morocco	1.2	-	10.0	5.8	-53.0	251.0	344.5	324.7	.. c	-4 091.4
Tunisia	1.2	.. c	-	-	-	9.8	-	-9.1	3.3	.. c
Other African countries	2 151.6	.. d	2 162.9	.. d	.. d	.. d	.. d	.. d	.. d	26 996.6
Nigeria	343.2	.. c	213.4	.. c	583.2	6 318.1	.. c	5 390.8	6 852.8	5 704.3
South Africa	1 283.1	2 995.5	1 238.8	1 753.6	5 961.1	16 511.3	12 221.3	14 292.8	5 820.4	13 446.6
AMERICA	**506 918.4**	**504 675.0**	**689 993.8**	**767 317.8**	**861 882.7**	**435 309.4**	**488 116.5**	**532 887.9**	**619 199.2**	**737 821.2**
Northern America	.. d	405 056.1	.. d	.. d	677 878.9	322 376.7	389 619.0	411 071.9	.. d	608 472.0
Central America and Caribbean countries	104 814.9	96 187.0	128 219.1	.. d	182 371.7	87 270.3	75 695.2	97 053.7	85 568.6	100 570.8
Bahamas	899.3	982.3	2 250.1	4 230.8	1 723.2	916.5	.. c	827.6	1 016.7	2 462.5
Bermuda	22 099.9	24 192.7	25 274.8	34 990.5	63 957.3	26 139.7	7 742.2	39 786.4	29 354.7	30 274.2
Cayman Islands	33 373.1	31 897.0	50 542.0	53 094.6	48 659.5	16 754.8	.. c	1 051.3	2 894.8	23 446.5
El Salvador	-	-	-	-	-	20.9	52.7	12.9	20.6	55.5
Guatemala	1 269.5	3 034.7	671.6	856.7	1 179.7	123.0	195.9	65.2	-24.8	331.6
Honduras	-	-	-	-	-	.. c	.. c	12.5	.. c	-388.3
Nicaragua	-	-	-	-	-	2.5	39.2	.. c	.. c	.. c
Panama	966.9	351.3	.. c	508.5	1 067.7	.. c	.. c	.. c	209.2	343.7
Virgin Islands, U.S.	11.1	.. c	0.8	-	14.9	1.2	-24.3	0.5	3.4	1.9
South America	.. d	3 432.0	.. d	.. d	1 632.1	25 663.7	22 802.3	24 762.2	.. d	28 778.4
Argentina	1.2	1.4	3.4	5.8	5.0	5 978.6	5 676.3	.. c	.. c	.. c
Bolivia	-	-	-	-	-	4.9	6.8	6.7	27.7	.. c
Brazil	.. c	.. c	.. c	2 183.9	983.9	16 604.7	14 784.5	11 636.7	18 139.2	13 070.8
Ecuador	-	.. c	-	-	-	32.0	58.1	124.6	129.8	153.6
Paraguay	-	.. c	-	.. d	-	.. d	10.8	24.6	37.3	.. d
Peru	1.2	2.7	0.7	1.5	1.1	220.2	143.2	.. c	758.0	948.8
Uruguay	-	-	-	-	.. c	40.6	63.5	88.6	132.5	44.6
Venezuela	-	-	-	-	.. c	479.8	156.7	.. c	29.4	73.1

Table 2. Foreign direct investment positions by country *(cont.)*

At year end

Million US dollars

	Inward					Outward				
	2016	2017	2018	2019	2020	2016	2017	2018	2019	2020
ASIA	**118 903.9**	**139 605.5**	**201 646.0**	**177 557.9**	**188 908.3**	**187 341.6**	**210 516.1**	**236 710.5**	**234 999.6**	**241 345.5**
Near and Middle East	8 028.0	9 832.5	25 456.2	13 548.3	29 547.4	29 862.2	48 280.0	43 249.6	52 961.5	42 953.7
Gulf Arabian countries	7 063.6	8 665.0	9 280.2	11 346.7	.. d	.. d	34 156.2	.. d	.. d	29 289.9
Kuwait	381.4	432.4	337.4	.. c	.. c	17.2	40.5	40.1	54.5	.. c
Qatar	62.7	145.9	421.1	.. c	.. c	200.5	.. c	189.3	.. c	.. c
Saudi Arabia	109.5	277.0	92.4	738.1	457.1	4 638.9	5 660.0	5 868.4	6 304.7	6 574.7
United Arab Emirates	5 274.9	6 481.6	7 052.7	7 538.6	7 667.0	6 256.6	8 308.3	16 785.1	13 854.0	5 345.5
Other Near and Middle East	963.2	1 167.4	16 176.0	2 201.6	.. c	.. c	14 123.8	.. c	.. c	13 663.8
Jordan	.. d	.. c	322.5	.. c	.. c	.. c	.. c	10.1	21.6	23.9
Other Asian countries	110 875.9	129 771.7	176 189.8	164 009.6	159 360.9	157 479.4	162 236.2	193 460.9	182 038.1	198 391.8
China	1 874.8	3 102.3	2 253.8	4 302.7	4 207.0	14 276.0	11 268.7	20 269.7	13 732.4	17 378.6
Hong Kong, China	.. c	27 569.2	29 250.7	23 526.6	28 269.5	75 429.9	.. c	91 193.6	91 132.3	102 406.4
India	1 830.5	10 772.9	14 359.9	11 828.4	12 133.9	16 223.4	17 726.0	18 597.1	20 615.1	23 681.0
Indonesia	.. c	-	1.2	0.7	15.8	7 229.7	6 170.8	5 738.8	7 806.3	6 676.7
Iran, Islamic Republic of	301.4	.. c	327.8	.. c	.. c	.. c	21.6	2.4	16.0	.. c
Malaysia	321.1	760.7	-307.2	968.7	999.2	4 215.8	4 514.3	3 680.0	4 831.1	4 909.9
Philippines	98.4	.. d	69.7	67.8	168.6	.. d	370.2	733.2	766.8	536.2
Singapore	22 418.5	12 241.6	9 959.6	10 717.1	10 595.9	13 125.8	8 882.6	14 408.0	21 205.7	18 211.1
Chinese Taipei	76.3	197.3	70.3	101.5	307.8	3 667.1	5 042.6	4 182.4	2 185.4	3 419.3
Thailand	152.5	471.6	.. c	860.9	536.8	2 973.3	2 968.5	4 409.5	3 125.4	4 632.2
Viet Nam	.. c	-	0.0	1.0	15.6	238.7	206.7	.. c	1 922.8	.. c
AUSTRALIA, OCEANIA AND POLAR REGIONS	**16 136.1**	**11 305.2**	**20 540.6**	**19 915.7**	**16 228.0**	**51 836.6**	**41 982.2**	**46 633.3**	**58 029.3**	**48 816.1**
WORLD unallocated and confidential	**-1.2**	**-**	**0.0**	**0.0**	**0.0**	**-**	**1.4**	**0.0**	**0.0**	**0.0**
European Union (since 01/02/2020)	..	..	..	..	**873 909.8**	..	..	..	..	**878 558.4**
G20 countries excl. European Union	.. d	.. d	.. d	.. d	.. d	**629 779.8**	.. d	.. d	.. d	.. d
G20 OECD countries	.. d	**650 160.8**	.. d	.. d	.. d	**533 893.5**	**607 847.6**	**658 179.2**	.. d	..
G20 Non-OECD countries	.. d	.. d	.. d	.. d	.. d	**95 886.3**	.. d	.. d	.. d	.. d
MENA countries	.. d	.. d	**9 927.5**	.. d	.. d	.. d	.. d	.. d	.. d	.. d
ASEAN countries	**24 397.8**	**14 764.2**	**13 757.9**	.. d	**12 352.3**	**29 233.6**	**25 014.2**	**31 456.7**	**41 169.3**	**38 931.3**

- Nil; .. Not available; c Confidential data; d Secondary Confidentiality

Note: Detailed metadata at: *http://metalinks.oecd.org/idi/20220712/6d95.*

Source: *OECD International Direct Investment Statistics (database): https://doi.org/10.1787/idi-data-en*

Table 3. Foreign direct investment income by country

Million US dollars

	Inward					Outward				
	2016	2017	2018	2019	2020	2016	2017	2018	2019	2020
WORLD	**70 274.0**	**67 481.3**	**96 922.4**	**70 636.2**	**49 327.0**	**68 005.4**	**95 923.3**	**125 459.4**	**100 945.2**	**65 915.5**
OECD COUNTRIES	**54 981.1**	**59 286.6**	**.. d**	**59 996.1**	**40 013.5**	**41 728.7**	**62 389.9**	**.. d**	**65 184.3**	**48 509.9**
Australia	-835.4	-288.4	-267.1	-76.4	500.9	2 580.3	5 269.1	5 222.0	1 928.6	-5 874.8
Austria	108.0	96.6	123.5	259.0	126.3	226.7	283.3	259.5	276.3	138.1
Belgium	2 807.0	2 356.4	3 719.4	1 934.7	2 103.4	1 944.7	1 551.6	1 907.6	2 846.9	.. c
Canada	1 503.4	-324.5	.. d	.. d	.. d	2 603.2	.. d	1 867.2	2 105.8	-480.2
Chile	6.7	5.2	-1.5	3.6	5.0	183.5	445.5	280.2	-10.8	-57.1
Colombia	-	.. c	0.4	-0.5	.. c	1.4	9.0	67.0	17.9	43.9
Costa Rica	-1.4	-	-0.4	0.4	-	13.5	.. c	-19.6	.. c	1.7
Czech Republic	-	-1.3	0.2	20.8	51.6	117.4	39.9	255.1	252.2	111.3
Denmark	1 013.5	149.4	804.3	841.9	577.4	782.7	1 201.4	506.9	621.4	.. c
Estonia	-	-	0.7	4.8	9.8	1.4	3.9	24.4	39.3	11.5
Finland	-10.8	59.2	112.4	383.0	90.6	136.3	70.8	161.1	35.6	.. c
France	-156.5	1 604.4	2 275.8	1 844.0	.. c	3 175.4	3 847.5	3 914.7	3 043.4	1 057.7
Germany	7 066.1	3 416.2	8 791.7	3 137.6	1 496.2	2 916.3	4 402.5	4 687.8	2 295.8	1 348.1
Greece	64.8	28.3	104.5	31.5	261.5	32.4	70.8	101.3	59.7	-24.6
Hungary	1.4	-18.0	1.0	-0.6	8.3	124.2	154.5	235.9	270.2	87.1
Iceland	.. d	.. d	.. d	22.5	.. d	1.4	-	.. c	.. c	326.6
Ireland	369.8	1 103.5	3 218.9	2 426.6	1 462.5	6 047.2	4 465.6	6 046.7	7 600.4	3 514.4
Israel	.. d	29.6	1 310.9	22.9	73.1	.. d	.. d	188.0	98.0	33.0
Italy	390.0	600.1	346.3	1 045.0	826.8	628.9	920.7	592.3	812.8	-307.1
Japan	4 247.0	8 593.9	6 800.3	3 029.6	5 777.6	1 346.8	819.0	535.7	675.1	352.3
Korea	133.6	212.5	404.4	172.7	41.3	620.8	892.4	1 049.0	895.1	504.9
Latvia	1.4	.. d	.. d	9.0	5.5	.. d	.. c	.. d	.. d	.. c
Lithuania	1.4	.. c	1.8	11.3	7.9	6.7	15.5	16.2	-66.6	-18.7
Luxembourg	1 638.3	2 259.9	4 456.2	4 159.0	1 755.3	.. c	3 274.5	2 179.7	95.3	2 412.0
Mexico	12.1	11.6	.. c	.. c	.. c	919.0	1 254.2	1 274.7	1 165.7	666.6
Netherlands	4 527.7	2 603.7	5 753.9	4 175.4	3 199.5	3 132.3	8 555.2	10 775.0	6 218.6	12 734.8
New Zealand	27.0	1.3	21.2	43.1	-243.6	287.4	338.7	351.4	208.6	68.1
Norway	35.1	140.4	-7.3	.. c	.. c	-242.9	631.0	874.0	98.1	62.2
Poland	5.4	11.6	17.6	41.7	45.2	642.4	920.7	727.5	901.4	972.4
Portugal	129.6	47.6	28.8	44.6	38.1	4.0	172.5	234.6	369.7	98.7
Slovak Republic	-	-	0.1	10.2	4.1	41.8	81.1	60.9	121.6	42.3
Slovenia	-	-	-0.1	0.5	.. d	18.9	15.5	19.1	40.4	-2.7
Spain	3 052.6	3 251.4	6 846.2	1 759.9	-1 405.6	1 450.7	1 813.0	2 147.8	2 094.3	726.0
Sweden	743.6	1 220.7	798.6	880.2	546.2	3 263.2	1 746.1	.. c	.. c	.. c
Switzerland	2 731.4	5 923.3	6 541.3	5 089.1	1 961.0	3 824.6	2 472.3	4 098.4	3 484.6	.. c
Turkey	8.1	7.7	37.1	28.1	63.0	6.7	197.0	385.7	211.7	-2.5
United Kingdom	-	-	-	-	..	-	-	-	-	..
United States	25 295.5	26 149.9	30 481.6	27 265.1	22 494.4	3 456.1	14 439.9	22 374.4	23 140.7	15 647.1
EUROPE	**29 561.4**	**28 839.8**	**47 740.0**	**30 611.5**	**12 926.0**	**33 303.6**	**41 867.1**	**52 586.0**	**44 293.7**	**42 771.6**
Bulgaria	4.0	-1.3	1.5	13.6	10.3	9.4	14.2	-3.1	23.9	8.1
Croatia	-	.. c	0.0	0.4	5.1	36.4	-5.2	.. d	.. d	-40.9
Cyprus	465.6	479.0	.. c	244.8	-163.4	-29.7	.. c	.. c	.. c	.. c
Malta	33.7	142.9	93.3	89.1	136.8	202.4	-33.5	-64.2	23.0	-46.1
Montenegro	.. d	.. d	-	.. d	-	.. d	-	.. d	.. d	0.9
Romania	-	.. d	0.1	-0.2	6.3	222.7	95.3	124.9	128.5	49.3
Russian Federation	-63.4	-18.0	118.9	.. c	44.6	1 047.2	1 035.3	.. c	.. c	-67.1
Ukraine	5.4	5.2	0.8	1.3	3.0	.. c	-12.9	69.0	111.3	.. c
AFRICA	**58.0**	**-240.8**	**-114.8**	**15.8**	**199.8**	**3 757.1**	**4 222.3**	**8 267.1**	**4 051.8**	**-1 311.9**
Northern Africa	6.7	5.2	1.6	.. d	13.8	.. d	.. d	.. d	.. d	-862.1
Algeria	-	.. c	0.0	.. c	-	.. c	.. c	.. c	.. c	.. c
Egypt	2.7	1.3	0.9	1.2	.. d	-36.4	-197.0	142.6	-505.1	-873.6
Libya	5.4	.. c	-	-	.. c	1.4	-	1.3	-2.2	-1.0
Morocco	-	-	0.7	0.4	13.8	-67.5	1.3	-6.5	-18.1	.. c
Tunisia	-	.. c	-	-	-	-1.4	-3.9	-1.3	-1.0	-1.0
Other African countries	51.3	-245.9	-116.4	.. d	186.0	.. d	.. d	.. d	.. d	-449.9
Nigeria	48.6	.. c	27.9	.. c	24.2	237.5	339.9	418.1	440.2	52.7
South Africa	-39.1	-279.4	-188.0	-104.5	78.6	2 261.8	2 868.9	3 607.5	677.1	.. c
AMERICA	**33 415.7**	**27 531.5**	**38 935.3**	**34 246.1**	**28 153.5**	**11 785.4**	**21 917.3**	**31 626.2**	**27 835.2**	**14 297.2**
Northern America	26 798.9	25 825.4	.. d	.. d	.. d	6 059.4	.. d	24 241.6	25 249.9	15 167.1
Central America and Caribbean countries	6 596.5	1 702.3	.. d	5 701.6	.. d	4 835.4	4 026.5	6 379.3	1 571.6	1 136.3
Bahamas	17.5	36.1	285.1	73.4	.. c	101.2	.. c	83.2	79.4	.. c
Bermuda	1 966.3	355.4	1 589.3	1 116.6	859.4	1 071.5	.. c	2 769.9	335.9	1 512.9
Cayman Islands	1 496.6	-21.9	1 878.1	1 655.4	2 671.5	1 504.7	1 568.4	-140.2	-381.8	-889.7
El Salvador	-	-	-	-	-	-	-1.3	0.3	1.1	3.1
Guatemala	95.8	81.1	18.0	62.0	75.8	-5.4	18.0	11.4	20.2	7.7
Honduras	-	-	-	-	-	-2.7	2.6	1.8	.. c	-208.9
Nicaragua	-	-	-	-	-	-2.7	1.3	0.1	-0.1	-0.1
Panama	33.7	-25.8	-45.3	15.2	-8.2	242.9	3.9	.. c	31.2	5.5
Virgin Islands, U.S.	-	.. c	8.7	.. c	0.1	1.4	-2.6	0.1	0.9	0.1
South America	18.9	5.2	.. c	.. c	.. c	889.3	.. d	1 005.2	1 013.7	-2 006.2
Argentina	-	-	0.3	0.9	1.9	.. d	.. d	.. d	174.1	-86.5
Bolivia	-	-	-	-	-	-	-	1.1	2.9	1.8
Brazil	12.1	-2.6	.. c	.. c	.. c	51.3	571.7	390.0	774.9	-1 836.2
Ecuador	-	.. c	-	-	-	5.4	5.2	0.9	2.5	-0.5
Paraguay	-	.. c	-	-	-	.. d	1.3	.. d	4.6	7.4
Peru	-	-	-0.1	0.1	0.6	79.6	86.3	61.8	60.4	-99.2
Uruguay	-	-	-	-	.. c	20.2	10.3	5.1	-4.1	9.4
Venezuela	-	-	-	-	.. c	9.4	42.5	-88.1	.. c	0.6

Table 3. Foreign direct investment income by country *(cont.)*

Million US dollars

	Inward					Outward				
	2016	2017	2018	2019	2020	2016	2017	2018	2019	2020
ASIA	**7 450.7**	**13 230.7**	**10 611.1**	**5 795.4**	**7 785.4**	**16 130.9**	**21 202.7**	**26 546.4**	**21 880.4**	**15 488.8**
Near and Middle East	187.6	206.0	1 729.9	596.9	346.2	1 673.4	3 423.9	4 345.6	4 725.7	3 213.1
Gulf Arabian countries	161.9	172.5	400.4	566.5	272.2	1 305.0	2 428.5	3 069.4	4 015.2	2 967.0
Kuwait	-5.4	1.3	11.3	19.6	3.8	.. c	.. c	.. c	.. c	.. c
Qatar	1.4	-2.6	.. c	.. c	.. c	33.7	.. c	16.8	.. c	.. c
Saudi Arabia	-2.7	-3.9	-2.4	18.9	24.1	686.9	913.0	687.7	953.8	566.0
United Arab Emirates	148.4	161.0	.. c	283.8	176.5	377.9	.. c	1 683.6	737.5	658.6
Other Near and Middle East	25.6	33.5	1 329.5	30.4	74.0	368.4	995.4	1 276.2	710.4	246.1
Jordan	.. d	1.3	9.7	.. d	.. d	.. d	3.9	0.3	3.7	2.2
Other Asian countries	7 263.2	13 026.0	8 881.2	5 198.5	7 439.2	14 457.5	17 780.1	22 200.8	17 154.8	12 275.8
China	5.4	-56.7	-265.7	67.5	96.1	2 615.4	2 017.8	2 473.0	847.7	2 071.9
Hong Kong, China	2 129.6	.. c	1 615.4	1 771.4	1 429.5	4 365.7	8 338.9	7 429.6	6 354.3	4 301.0
India	558.7	2 146.5	-124.0	12.7	-445.9	1 523.6	1 276.1	1 624.8	2 261.0	1 400.4
Indonesia	.. c	.. c	9.4	0.2	0.5	885.3	256.2	2 255.3	825.0	552.7
Iran, Islamic Republic of	1.4	.. c	1.4	10.1	5.1	.. c	-	0.1	1.2	4.2
Malaysia	-141.7	20.6	9.7	59.5	7.4	697.7	1 198.8	963.3	648.8	428.4
Philippines	.. d	5.2	5.4	7.5	7.7	207.8	153.2	187.9	167.1	21.3
Singapore	542.5	391.5	407.9	-15.9	541.0	310.4	834.4	2 185.7	2 651.6	862.8
Chinese Taipei	6.7	6.4	2.6	12.2	11.7	345.5	358.0	301.6	335.9	755.2
Thailand	8.1	6.4	6.6	36.6	-58.4	276.7	381.1	398.9	105.1	77.1
Viet Nam	.. c	-	0.0	0.1	0.9	233.5	279.4	245.4	181.1	245.4
AUSTRALIA, OCEANIA AND POLAR REGIONS	**-211.9**	**-1 880.0**	**-249.1**	**-32.6**	**262.4**	**3 028.3**	**6 712.6**	**6 433.8**	**2 884.0**	**-5 330.3**
WORLD unallocated and confidential	**-**	**-**	**0.0**	**..**	**0.0**	**-**	**1.3**	**0.0**	**..**	**0.0**
European Union (since 01/02/2020)	**..**	**..**	**..**	**..**	**9 018.0**	**..**	**..**	**..**	**..**	**30 296.8**
G20 countries excl. European Union	**.. d**	**.. d**	**.. d**	**.. d**	**.. d**	**.. d**	**.. d**	**.. d**	**.. d**	**.. d**
G20 OECD countries	**37 664.0**	**39 983.3**	**.. d**	**.. d**	**.. d**	**18 253.7**	**.. d**	**41 903.5**	**36 274.6**	**..**
G20 Non-OECD countries	**.. d**	**.. d**	**.. d**	**.. d**	**.. d**	**.. d**	**.. d**	**.. d**	**.. d**	**.. d**
MENA countries	**.. d**	**.. d**	**.. d**	**.. d**	**.. d**	**.. d**	**.. d**	**.. d**	**.. d**	**.. d**
ASEAN countries	**201.1**	**445.5**	**439.3**	**88.4**	**500.9**	**2 637.0**	**3 145.8**	**.. d**	**4 822.7**	**2 237.5**

- Nil; .. Not available; c Confidential data; d Secondary Confidentiality

Note: Detailed metadata at: *http://metalinks.oecd.org/idi/20220712/6d95.*

Source: OECD *International Direct Investment Statistics (database): https://doi.org/10.1787/idi-data-en*

UNITED KINGDOM

Table 4. Foreign direct investment flows by industrial sector

Million US dollars

	Inward					Outward				
	2016	2017	2018	2019	2020	2016	2017	2018	2019	2020
All FDI activities	**196 503.4**	**78 511.5**	**65 450.8**	**49 898.6**	**-1 493.6**	**-22 310.4**	**106 692.0**	**41 491.7**	**-35 355.4**	**-72 611.6**
Agriculture, forestry and fishing	**.. d**	**..**	**130.2**	**..**	**..**	**.. d**	**..**	**.. d**	**..**	**..**
Mining and quarrying	**-5 006.7**	**..**	**.. c**	**..**	**..**	**-10 352.2**	**..**	**-13 086.4**	**..**	**..**
Extraction activities	-5 363.0	..	.. c	..	..	-7 040.5	..	-18 271.1	..	..
Manufacturing	**.. c**	**..**	**3 368.9**	**..**	**..**	**-19 759.8**	**..**	**-12 568.4**	**..**	**..**
of which:										
Food products, beverages and tobacco	.. c	..	.. d	..	..	.. c	..	3 274.1	..	..
Textiles, wood and paper products; printing	-1 206.5	..	669.5	..	..	676.1	..	386.4	..	..
Chemical, rubber, plastic, non-metallic mineral products	4 753.0	..	2 308.1	..	..	-20 716.6	..	-17 124.5	..	..
Metal and machinery products, except electrical equipment	-3 666.7	..	405.6	..	..	-20.2	..	-1 527.5	..	..
Motor vehicles, trailers, semi-trailers, other transport equipment	190.3	..	1 125.6	..	..	.. c	..	1 262.9	..	..
Other manufacturing	.. c	..	.. c	..	..	-744.9	..	1 160.3	..	..
Electricity, gas, steam and air conditioning supply	**948.7**	**..**	**.. c**	**..**	**..**	**2 480.4**	**..**	**2 096.0**	**..**	**..**
Water supply; sewerage, waste management and remediation activities	**155.2**	**..**	**-35.7**	**..**	**..**	**232.1**	**..**	**290.7**	**..**	**..**
Construction	**632.9**	**..**	**973.7**	**..**	**..**	**228.1**	**..**	**308.9**	**..**	**..**
Services	**90 098.5**	**..**	**86 937.1**	**..**	**..**	**4 178.1**	**..**	**62 733.2**	**..**	**..**
Wholesale and retail trade; repair of motor vehicles and motorcycles	-776.0	..	-738.7	..	..	2 920.4	..	11 489.0	..	..
Transportation and storage	4 045.9	..	7 344.2	..	..	2 446.7	..	-312.4	..	..
Accommodation and food service activities	556.0	..	-4 422.2	..	..	3 863.7	..	3 311.0	..	..
Information and communication	6 530.4	..	50 533.2	..	..	-2 383.3	..	3 872.4	..	..
Financial and insurance activities	33 583.0	..	10 691.9	..	..	-2 970.3	..	38 088.7	..	..
Activities of holding companies	2 979.8	..	3 495.6	..	..	4 287.4	..	10 151.3	..	..
Real estate activities	691.0	..	1 380.9	..	..	.. c	..	-163.9	..	..
Professional, scientific and technical activities	40 257.8	..	7 963.9	..	..	1 052.6	..	5 146.8	..	..
Administrative and support service activities	5 153.8	..	16 491.2	..	..	414.3	..	765.7	..	..
Public administration; activities of households and of extraterritorial organisations	-5.4	..	-0.6	..	..	.. c	..	-6.0	..	..
Education	16.2	..	-358.1	..	..	577.6	..	385.4	..	..
Human health and social work activities	36.4	..	-1 489.9	..	..	.. c	..	-311.2	..	..
Arts, entertainment and recreation	484.5	..	-728.6	..	..	-17.5	..	456.2	..	..
Other services	-477.7	..	269.9	..	..	-18.9	..	11.4	..	..
Not allocated and confidential	**.. c**	**78 511.5**	**.. c**	**..**	**-1 493.6**	**.. d**	**106 692.0**	**.. d**	**..**	**-72 611.6**
Private real estate activities	**975.7**	**..**	**500.2**	**..**	**..**	**354.9**	**..**	**1 635.3**	**..**	**..**

.. Not available; c Confidential data; d Secondary Confidentiality

Note: Detailed metadata at: *http://metalinks.oecd.org/idi/20220712/6d95.*

Source: *OECD International Direct Investment Statistics (database): https://doi.org/10.1787/idi-data-en*

Table 5. Foreign direct investment positions by industrial sector

At year end

Million US dollars

	Inward					Outward				
	2016	2017	2018	2019	2020	2016	2017	2018	2019	2020
All FDI activities	**1 475 523.4**	**1 608 032.7**	**1 930 434.0**	**1 974 480.5**	**2 219 788.7**	**1 491 940.0**	**1 624 231.9**	**1 788 397.1**	**1 901 117.2**	**2 137 521.5**
Agriculture, forestry and fishing	**1 264.6**	..	**1 454.6**	..	..	**2 510.8**	..	**2 720.2**	..	..
Mining and quarrying	**132 329.9**	..	**79 600.3**	..	..	**202 806.0**	..	**182 543.9**	..	..
Extraction activities	130 880.8	..	78 890.1	..	..	212 398.8	..	178 582.0	..	..
Manufacturing	**334 730.0**	..	**323 151.7**	..	..	**258 536.1**	..	**295 432.4**	..	..
of which:										
Food products, beverages and tobacco	157 723.0	..	102 220.7	..	..	75 635.4	..	94 239.3	..	..
Textiles, wood and paper products; printing	6 014.3	..	4 970.2	..	..	3 001.6	..	3 234.9	..	..
Chemical, rubber, plastic, non-metallic mineral products	49 282.8	..	73 299.2	..	..	94 373.2	..	128 904.7	..	..
Metal and machinery products, except electrical equipment	54 824.7	..	59 513.6	..	..	22 262.3	..	26 439.1	..	..
Motor vehicles, trailers, semi-trailers, other transport equipment	18 538.6	..	39 036.6	..	..	18 020.7	..	20 014.2	..	..
Other manufacturing	48 346.7	..	44 111.5	..	..	45 243.0	..	22 600.2	..	..
Electricity, gas, steam and air conditioning supply	**54 853.0**	..	**60 078.9**	..	..	**.. c**	..	**23 358.1**	..	..
Water supply; sewerage, waste management and remediation activities	**3 333.7**	..	**5 264.0**	..	..	**1 987.9**	..	**4 801.7**	..	..
Construction	**11 789.9**	..	**12 460.8**	..	..	**1 732.1**	..	**.. c**	..	..
Services	**919 501.8**	..	**1 428 676.4**	..	..	**875 655.1**	..	**1 104 195.5**	..	..
Wholesale and retail trade; repair of motor vehicles and motorcycles	149 114.3	..	159 073.2	..	..	60 396.1	..	106 366.3	..	..
Transportation and storage	59 575.6	..	91 741.7	..	..	28 931.0	..	23 489.2	..	..
Accommodation and food service activities	26 292.3	..	150 487.7	..	..	34 191.2	..	41 514.7	..	..
Information and communication	98 525.0	..	178 615.1	..	..	151 643.5	..	152 071.2	..	..
Financial and insurance activities	443 907.0	..	556 534.0	..	..	518 002.2	..	641 559.4	..	..
Activities of holding companies	16.0	..	.. c	..	..	147 121.4	..	171 924.7	..	..
Real estate activities	7 582.7	..	9 964.9	..	..	12 874.9	..	13 873.5	..	..
Professional, scientific and technical activities	87 481.9	..	193 580.1	..	..	45 967.5	..	85 824.6	..	..
Administrative and support service activities	36 081.9	..	57 224.4	..	..	18 024.4	..	30 772.2	..	..
Public administration; activities of households and of extraterritorial organisations	1.2	..	4.4	..	..	.. c	..	-2 050.1	..	..
Education	2 409.9	..	3 089.9	..	..	5 345.1	..	1 284.0	..	..
Human health and social work activities	1 675.5	..	5 068.2	..	..	654.4	..	3 696.8	..	..
Arts, entertainment and recreation	5 553.0	..	20 959.9	..	..	1 614.0	..	5 490.6	..	..
Other services	1 301.5	..	2 333.1	..	..	.. d	..	303.2	..	..
Not allocated and confidential	**-**	**1 608 032.7**	**0.0**	..	**2 219 788.7**	**.. c**	**1 624 231.9**	**.. c**	..	**2 137 521.5**
Private real estate activities	**17 720.5**	..	**19 747.4**	..	..	**130 103.3**	..	**154 386.2**	..	..

- Nil; .. Not available; c Confidential data; d Secondary Confidentiality

Note: Detailed metadata at: *http://metalinks.oecd.org/idi/20220712/6d95.*

Source: *OECD International Direct Investment Statistics (database): https://doi.org/10.1787/idi-data-en*

Table 6. Foreign direct investment income by industrial sector

Million US dollars

	Inward					Outward				
	2016	2017	2018	2019	2020	2016	2017	2018	2019	2020
All FDI activities	**70 274.0**	**67 481.3**	**96 922.4**	**70 636.2**	**49 327.0**	**68 005.4**	**95 923.3**	**125 459.4**	**100 945.2**	**65 915.5**
Agriculture, forestry and fishing	**44.5**	..	**119.5**	..	..	.. d	..	**114.7**	..	..
Mining and quarrying	.. c	..	**2 384.4**	..	..	**940.6**	..	**24 738.5**	..	..
Extraction activities	.. c	..	2 356.8	..	..	-2 183.5	..	16 909.1	..	..
Manufacturing	**13 948.7**	..	**15 852.1**	..	..	**21 915.0**	..	**28 222.8**	..	..
of which:										
Food products, beverages and tobacco	2 179.5	..	3 115.2	..	..	5 726.0	..	11 141.9	..	..
Textiles, wood and paper products; printing	539.8	..	747.3	..	..	847.5	..	486.6	..	..
Chemical, rubber, plastic, non-metallic mineral products	3 040.5	..	4 327.7	..	..	10 425.1	..	9 998.8	..	..
Metal and machinery products, except electrical equipment	1 851.6	..	4 169.5	..	..	1 893.4	..	2 557.1	..	..
Motor vehicles, trailers, semi-trailers, other transport equipment	2 913.6	..	2 412.9	..	..	2 164.6	..	2 758.7	..	..
Other manufacturing	3 422.4	..	1 079.6	..	..	857.0	..	1 279.7	..	..
Electricity, gas, steam and air conditioning supply	**4 485.8**	..	**3 366.0**	..	..	**1 290.1**	..	.. c	..	..
Water supply; sewerage, waste management and remediation activities	.. c	..	**41.5**	..	..	**230.8**	..	**166.1**	..	..
Construction	**-570.9**	..	**722.1**	..	..	**256.4**	..	.. c	..	..
Services	**50 503.4**	..	**74 266.0**	..	..	**41 396.8**	..	**68 686.5**	..	..
Wholesale and retail trade; repair of motor vehicles and motorcycles	9 179.5	..	13 605.5	..	..	3 870.4	..	6 676.4	..	..
Transportation and storage	5 427.8	..	8 626.9	..	..	1 021.6	..	1 801.8	..	..
Accommodation and food service activities	.. c	..	.. c	..	..	6 897.4	..	7 991.4	..	..
Information and communication	2 956.8	..	8 050.7	..	..	4 124.2	..	4 511.4	..	..
Financial and insurance activities	28 310.4	..	35 366.2	..	..	19 581.6	..	39 138.4	..	..
Activities of holding companies	2 558.7	..	3 262.9	..	..	5 160.6	..	12 696.1	..	..
Real estate activities	193.0	..	157.4	..	..	689.6	..	571.5	..	..
Professional, scientific and technical activities	4 106.6	..	6 779.5	..	..	2 522.3	..	4 807.7	..	..
Administrative and support service activities	1 336.0	..	3 808.1	..	..	1 442.6	..	1 795.5	..	..
Public administration; activities of households and of extraterritorial organisations	.. d	..	.. d	..	..	.. c	..	.. c	..	..
Education	-64.8	..	-137.6	..	..	630.2	..	297.2	..	..
Human health and social work activities	8.1	..	-1 442.9	..	..	-1.4	..	-102.5	..	..
Arts, entertainment and recreation	20.2	..	666.4	..	..	161.9	..	406.1	..	..
Other services	78.3	..	-188.1	..	..	.. d	..	.. d	..	..
Not allocated and confidential	.. c	**67 481.3**	**0.0**	..	**49 327.0**	.. d	**95 923.3**	.. c	..	**65 915.5**
Private real estate activities	**147.1**	..	**170.7**	..	..	**1 662.6**	..	**1 678.0**	..	..

.. Not available; c Confidential data; d Secondary Confidentiality

Note: Detailed metadata at: *http://metalinks.oecd.org/idi/20220712/6d95*.

Source: *OECD International Direct Investment Statistics (database)*: *https://doi.org/10.1787/idi-data-en*

Table 1. Foreign direct investment flows by country

Million US dollars

	Inward					Outward				
	2016	2017	2018	2019	2020	2016	2017	2018	2019	2020
WORLD	**459 419.0**	**308 957.0**	**203 234.0**	**225 108.0**	**150 828.0**	**284 469.0**	**327 781.0**	**-157 407.0**	**28 596.0**	**234 919.0**
OECD COUNTRIES	**..**	**.. d**	**.. d**	**.. d**	**.. d**	**..**	**217 215.0**	**.. d**	**18 544.0**	**175 097.0**
Australia	5 660.0	-1 680.0	119.0	14 182.0	7 237.0	6 987.0	-621.0	-3 273.0	-3 806.0	3 745.0
Austria	3 496.0	2 417.0	-2 657.0	2 858.0	987.0	906.0	946.0	451.0	844.0	-1 173.0
Belgium	186.0	-2 201.0	2 505.0	1 746.0	3 992.0	2 727.0	1 481.0	9 801.0	4 553.0	4 358.0
Canada	65 140.0	71 025.0	29 132.0	33 189.0	18 208.0	12 589.0	16 356.0	15 944.0	34 406.0	16 299.0
Chile	116.0	-5.0	338.0	219.0	-33.0	287.0	-1 546.0	397.0	302.0	-952.0
Colombia	75.0	-31.0	-29.0	-53.0	-213.0	-170.0	13.0	846.0	117.0	-580.0
Costa Rica	82.0	-132.0	-72.0	26.0	97.0	51.0	197.0	234.0	254.0	201.0
Czech Republic	-1.0	22.0	-49.0	46.0	107.0	-262.0	243.0	1 181.0	95.0	201.0
Denmark	3 986.0	271.0	1 867.0	3 140.0	7 267.0	2 225.0	-222.0	-1 855.0	-1 035.0	1 068.0
Estonia	-	-4.0	-2.0	.. c	-1.0	-79.0	8.0	15.0	9.0	9.0
Finland	-73.0	666.0	1 457.0	248.0	650.0	2 196.0	-621.0	-597.0	747.0	564.0
France	28 553.0	15 406.0	992.0	13 498.0	14 005.0	357.0	3 708.0	1 242.0	6 360.0	-1 012.0
Germany	15 637.0	18 291.0	22 358.0	27 383.0	16 470.0	3 407.0	4 025.0	5 406.0	16 590.0	10 841.0
Greece	44.0	-51.0	-229.0	-28.0	40.0	40.0	80.0	149.0	-73.0	-136.0
Hungary	4 166.0	2 543.0	8 307.0	3 872.0	117.0	-604.0	541.0	1 284.0	-138.0	659.0
Iceland	.. c	-62.0	-29.0	-193.0	.. c	.. c	67.0	.. c	5.0	14.0
Ireland	8 645.0	31 039.0	67 432.0	-3 160.0	2 863.0	49 963.0	47 842.0	2 780.0	-82 222.0	21 990.0
Israel	90.0	112.0	1 631.0	619.0	1 279.0	683.0	1 235.0	701.0	3 586.0	7 068.0
Italy	737.0	1 206.0	1 489.0	1 489.0	1 604.0	298.0	388.0	7 468.0	1 905.0	1 642.0
Japan	33 732.0	45 520.0	20 817.0	35 283.0	23 139.0	-2 911.0	9 094.0	1 550.0	9 049.0	2 568.0
Korea	3 699.0	13 332.0	1 787.0	4 203.0	5 290.0	2 022.0	668.0	-1 664.0	2 365.0	-2 039.0
Latvia	-	.. c	.. c	.. c	.. c	11.0	10.0	8.0	8.0	7.0
Lithuania	.. c	.. c	.. c	.. c	.. c	4.0	16.0	18.0	-5.0	-
Luxembourg	49 203.0	29 121.0	-121 699.0	2 947.0	-5 528.0	31 153.0	39 283.0	31 538.0	12 413.0	17 554.0
Mexico	2 900.0	2 729.0	260.0	-263.0	1 846.0	5 837.0	5 907.0	6 456.0	6 530.0	3 456.0
Netherlands	43 143.0	24 644.0	78 306.0	3 409.0	29 027.0	33 363.0	22 491.0	-56 091.0	-11 433.0	27 908.0
New Zealand	-233.0	79.0	345.0	248.0	533.0	468.0	469.0	-160.0	299.0	523.0
Norway	-1 097.0	1 664.0	4 599.0	833.0	-1 601.0	-151.0	34.0	-375.0	-3 811.0	-1 714.0
Poland	170.0	411.0	17.0	-208.0	167.0	861.0	463.0	1 827.0	-428.0	297.0
Portugal	-5.0	71.0	-104.0	67.0	-21.0	402.0	120.0	217.0	-48.0	-515.0
Slovak Republic	2.0	-9.0	1.0	.. c	1.0	-280.0	289.0	-9.0	56.0	-18.0
Slovenia	.. c	1.0	7.0	.. c	-	16.0	8.0	-2.0	-22.0	-29.0
Spain	2 546.0	3 408.0	6 319.0	2 926.0	1 350.0	206.0	417.0	-2 422.0	3 993.0	1 633.0
Sweden	4 610.0	399.0	1 819.0	4 426.0	5 590.0	1 908.0	3 141.0	6 854.0	-1 940.0	2 136.0
Switzerland	46 595.0	-2 922.0	28 188.0	11 544.0	7 548.0	18 818.0	35 815.0	-16 449.0	627.0	16 692.0
Turkey	266.0	275.0	272.0	175.0	-55.0	379.0	506.0	721.0	226.0	2 392.0
United Kingdom	88 081.0	47 838.0	-2 796.0	15 679.0	2 126.0	42 027.0	24 590.0	12 369.0	18 537.0	39 641.0
United States	-	-	-	-	-	-	-	-	-	-
EUROPE	**.. c**	**.. c**	**.. c**	**93 069.0**	**87 329.0**	**.. c**	**.. c**	**.. c**	**.. c**	**149 731.0**
Bulgaria	-45.0	.. c	.. c	.. c	.. c	33.0	26.0	50.0	23.0	23.0
Croatia	.. c	.. c	.. c	.. c	.. c	10.0	30.0	-12.0	15.0	10.0
Cyprus	-607.0	-1 516.0	-137.0	18.0	51.0	-709.0	-524.0	-290.0	85.0	-304.0
Malta	601.0	341.0	-33.0	170.0	-36.0	-14.0	66.0	46.0	214.0	-188.0
Montenegro	-	-	-	-	-	-	-	-	-	-
Romania	.. c	-33.0	-39.0	.. c	.. c	100.0	-219.0	-153.0	104.0	194.0
Russian Federation	102.0	-119.0	185.0	-80.0	76.0	1 470.0	-1 149.0	1 208.0	-190.0	127.0
Ukraine	-2.0	4.0	-17.0	3.0	-	5.0	-54.0	10.0	31.0	-51.0
AFRICA	**-48.0**	**939.0**	**223.0**	**3 944.0**	**426.0**	**-2 660.0**	**534.0**	**-1 164.0**	**-3 393.0**	**2 079.0**
Northern Africa	.. c	.. c	.. c	.. c	80.0	-1 524.0	.. c	.. c	-180.0	31.0
Algeria	-3.0	.. c	.. c	.. c	3.0	-673.0	-105.0	-170.0	-212.0	111.0
Egypt	-39.0	75.0	-41.0	36.0	71.0	-465.0	-525.0	-516.0	13.0	-28.0
Libya	.. c	.. c	.. c	-	-	-332.0	.. c	.. c	39.0	-1.0
Morocco	.. c	-7.0	-3.0	1.0	-3.0	-74.0	-6.0	.. c	-14.0	58.0
Tunisia	-1.0	30.0	33.0	12.0	9.0	20.0	-23.0	-7.0	-6.0	-109.0
Other African countries	.. c	.. c	.. c	.. c	346.0	-1 136.0	.. c	.. c	-3 213.0	2 048.0
Nigeria	23.0	8.0	30.0	25.0	17.0	-156.0	1 354.0	-291.0	914.0	171.0
South Africa	88.0	569.0	12.0	-165.0	481.0	-86.0	429.0	201.0	451.0	-25.0
AMERICA	**95 795.0**	**66 942.0**	**.. c**	**65 728.0**	**24 546.0**	**71 334.0**	**91 495.0**	**-129 419.0**	**20 975.0**	**44 786.0**
Northern America	65 140.0	71 025.0	.. c	33 191.0	18 208.0	12 588.0	16 355.0	15 943.0	34 405.0	16 298.0
Central America and Caribbean countries	.. c	.. c	.. c	.. c	.. c	56 355.0	75 718.0	-141 433.0	-15 688.0	21 914.0
Bahamas	-460.0	179.0	349.0	555.0	111.0	1 163.0	-37.0	-10 922.0	755.0	1 140.0
Bermuda	23 222.0	-17 225.0	31 970.0	19 978.0	5 322.0	32 795.0	42 588.0	-149 490.0	-31 731.0	-4 189.0
Cayman Islands	3 082.0	7 541.0	5 102.0	7 415.0	-1 056.0	9 497.0	24 604.0	9 334.0	3 635.0	10 042.0
El Salvador	2.0	10.0	.. c	.. c	-1.0	325.0	15.0	-38.0	538.0	6.0
Guatemala	17.0	-11.0	-16.0	13.0	-6.0	-353.0	30.0	70.0	-7.0	-35.0
Honduras	17.0	-26.0	-27.0	-4.0	-3.0	9.0	24.0	-446.0	169.0	-258.0
Nicaragua	.. c	2.0	.. c	.. c	3.0	-35.0	-19.0	-43.0	-50.0	-81.0
Panama	89.0	-339.0	355.0	144.0	64.0	599.0	349.0	612.0	513.0	-139.0
Virgin Islands, U.S.	..	..	..	..	..	..	..	..	..	..
South America	.. c	.. c	.. c	.. c	149.0	2 381.0	-574.0	-3 932.0	2 253.0	6 558.0
Argentina	17.0	-22.0	-285.0	-311.0	-45.0	504.0	1 898.0	-4 412.0	1 169.0	.. c
Bolivia	.. c	29.0	-4.0	2.0	2.0	95.0	61.0	36.0	81.0	11.0
Brazil	-1 694.0	-524.0	2 986.0	2 668.0	417.0	3 336.0	2 351.0	557.0	-350.0	-3 562.0
Ecuador	-5.0	29.0	7.0	-	-6.0	30.0	-202.0	49.0	-34.0	-293.0
Paraguay	-	1.0	-7.0	.. c	-4.0	.. c	.. c	.. c	.. c	-12.0
Peru	23.0	4.0	4.0	-11.0	-2.0	-486.0	1 511.0	-421.0	1 444.0	1 054.0
Uruguay	68.0	-184.0	461.0	184.0	508.0	-58.0	-226.0	-130.0	-28.0	-148.0
Venezuela	369.0	-30.0	758.0	128.0	.. c	-1 295.0	-701.0	-963.0	-159.0	117.0

Table 1. Foreign direct investment flows by country *(cont.)*

Million US dollars

	Inward					Outward				
	2016	2017	2018	2019	2020	2016	2017	2018	2019	2020
ASIA	**.. c**	**.. c**	**.. c**	**.. c**	**.. c**	**.. c**	**.. c**	**.. c**	**.. c**	**.. c**
Near and Middle East	.. c	.. c	4 939.0	3 319.0	593.0	.. c	.. c	.. c	.. c	6 531.0
Gulf Arabian countries	569.0	.. c	.. c	.. c	.. c	.. c	.. c	.. c	.. c	-468.0
Kuwait	17.0	-10.0	158.0	-138.0	7.0	18.0	.. c	101.0	17.0	149.0
Qatar	178.0	261.0	.. c	.. c	.. c	700.0	1 237.0	.. c	682.0	54.0
Saudi Arabia	716.0	190.0	592.0	-479.0	.. c	744.0	519.0	243.0	210.0	359.0
United Arab Emirates	-432.0	4 265.0	3 450.0	3 024.0	-118.0	-2 335.0	3 386.0	946.0	-547.0	419.0
Other Near and Middle East	.. c	.. c	.. c	.. c	.. c	.. c	.. c	.. c	.. c	6 999.0
Jordan	-18.0	.. c	.. c	.. c	.. c	.. c	.. c	-44.0	-6.0	-26.0
Other Asian countries	.. c	.. c	.. c	.. c	.. c	25 299.0	.. c	.. c	.. c	.. c
China	18 004.0	2 211.0	320.0	4 315.0	-1 400.0	8 468.0	7 943.0	6 391.0	7 002.0	9 329.0
Hong Kong, China	1 720.0	786.0	3 309.0	592.0	796.0	583.0	1 093.0	611.0	5 066.0	1 733.0
India	-544.0	894.0	-1 072.0	-170.0	-179.0	4 854.0	3 623.0	656.0	2 581.0	881.0
Indonesia	-1 059.0	-233.0	32.0	54.0	45.0	-729.0	-861.0	-2 978.0	922.0	-332.0
Iran, Islamic Republic of	-	-	-	-	-	-	-	-	-	-
Malaysia	-172.0	499.0	448.0	-284.0	138.0	-1 191.0	1 342.0	-674.0	157.0	1 212.0
Philippines	-435.0	-87.0	-329.0	105.0	-13.0	756.0	562.0	238.0	236.0	19.0
Singapore	491.0	816.0	477.0	2 345.0	897.0	10 095.0	23 369.0	-39 799.0	15 279.0	14 609.0
Chinese Taipei	668.0	843.0	1 876.0	-1 746.0	1 661.0	548.0	680.0	339.0	1 113.0	-24.0
Thailand	711.0	-713.0	-298.0	-261.0	-56.0	1 772.0	1 041.0	1 317.0	1 178.0	324.0
Viet Nam	-1 123.0	-302.0	-61.0	-29.0	-114.0	171.0	36.0	154.0	-105.0	31.0
AUSTRALIA, OCEANIA AND POLAR REGIONS	**.. c**	**.. c**	**.. c**	**.. c**	**.. c**	**7 570.0**	**.. c**	**.. c**	**.. c**	**.. c**
WORLD unallocated and confidential	**3 033.0**	**350.0**	**-5 622.0**	**75.0**	**-21.0**	**-8 062.0**	**3 265.0**	**630.0**	**79.0**	**-108.0**
European Union (since 01/02/2020)	..	..	..	..	..	..	..	..	..	..
G20 countries excl. European Union	**260 035.0**	**216 908.0**	**77 200.0**	**150 650.0**	**.. d**	**89 553.0**	**79 374.0**	**48 085.0**	**103 957.0**	**.. d**
G20 OECD countries	**244 405.0**	**213 942.0**	**74 430.0**	**144 818.0**	**89 870.0**	**70 992.0**	**64 621.0**	**46 219.0**	**92 162.0**	**77 533.0**
G20 Non-OECD countries	**15 630.0**	**2 966.0**	**2 770.0**	**5 832.0**	**.. d**	**18 561.0**	**14 753.0**	**1 866.0**	**11 795.0**	**.. d**
MENA countries	**.. d**	**.. d**	**.. d**	**.. d**	**.. d**	**.. d**	**.. d**	**.. d**	**.. d**	**.. d**
ASEAN countries	**.. d**	**-18.0**	**279.0**	**.. d**	**.. d**	**.. d**	**25 503.0**	**.. d**	**.. d**	**.. d**

- Nil; .. Not available; c Confidential data; d Secondary Confidentiality

Note: Detailed metadata at: *http://metalinks.oecd.org/idi/20220712/6d95.*

Source: *OECD International Direct Investment Statistics (database)*: *https://doi.org/10.1787/idi-data-en*

UNITED STATES

Table 2. Foreign direct investment positions by country

At year end

Million US dollars

	Inward					Outward				
	2016	2017	2018	2019	2020	2016	2017	2018	2019	2020
WORLD	**3 561 808.0**	**3 952 314.0**	**4 179 984.0**	**4 439 255.0**	**4 626 452.0**	**5 518 644.0**	**6 097 690.0**	**5 792 290.0**	**5 907 424.0**	**6 152 301.0**
OECD COUNTRIES	**..**	**.. d**	**.. d**	**.. d**	**.. d**	**..**	**.. d**	**.. d**	**4 378 364.0**	**4 570 677.0**
Australia	73 526.0	80 891.0	78 788.0	93 451.0	101 594.0	167 791.0	169 749.0	166 269.0	161 200.0	163 466.0
Austria	3 507.0	11 527.0	12 792.0	13 548.0	17 184.0	7 566.0	7 987.0	6 848.0	6 921.0	4 947.0
Belgium	76 496.0	54 925.0	61 382.0	63 575.0	66 434.0	49 692.0	53 645.0	59 397.0	64 633.0	69 539.0
Canada	422 956.0	493 193.0	534 800.0	563 611.0	569 788.0	355 394.0	371 274.0	373 604.0	404 589.0	422 160.0
Chile	2 545.0	2 434.0	3 169.0	3 572.0	3 807.0	28 141.0	25 793.0	25 660.0	24 912.0	23 011.0
Colombia	2 428.0	2 574.0	3 223.0	4 066.0	4 080.0	7 884.0	7 669.0	7 236.0	7 286.0	7 767.0
Costa Rica	.. c	.. c	.. c	76.0	81.0	1 335.0	1 546.0	1 589.0	2 014.0	1 988.0
Czech Republic	2.0	39.0	41.0	44.0	45.0	4 896.0	4 844.0	5 253.0	5 456.0	5 629.0
Denmark	18 375.0	18 464.0	20 435.0	24 036.0	31 491.0	16 909.0	12 107.0	10 692.0	9 108.0	9 874.0
Estonia	-5.0	-4.0	-7.0	-9.0	-10.0	72.0	74.0	82.0	68.0	74.0
Finland	8 203.0	8 946.0	9 774.0	9 846.0	10 046.0	2 538.0	2 513.0	4 063.0	4 504.0	5 269.0
France	264 026.0	276 789.0	279 068.0	295 743.0	314 979.0	72 926.0	78 632.0	67 548.0	88 425.0	91 153.0
Germany	347 963.0	394 396.0	470 806.0	496 984.0	564 294.0	129 985.0	132 595.0	134 794.0	151 278.0	162 387.0
Greece	1 055.0	1 667.0	1 680.0	1 743.0	1 788.0	1 017.0	1 198.0	431.0	90.0	74.0
Hungary	62.0	56.0	41.0	48.0	89.0	7 392.0	6 672.0	5 283.0	12 166.0	13 295.0
Iceland	.. c	32.0	36.0	40.0	44.0	.. c	.. c	.. c	775.0	796.0
Ireland	234 899.0	275 664.0	351 891.0	379 474.0	296 425.0	399 885.0	457 301.0	444 037.0	398 749.0	390 274.0
Israel	56 198.0	39 063.0	37 939.0	33 811.0	29 181.0	11 615.0	28 160.0	28 997.0	32 984.0	40 437.0
Italy	34 583.0	30 371.0	33 286.0	37 110.0	37 871.0	30 573.0	27 617.0	32 842.0	28 270.0	31 093.0
Japan	431 555.0	498 893.0	522 315.0	663 400.0	679 000.0	124 039.0	117 134.0	108 933.0	128 539.0	131 643.0
Korea	41 129.0	54 109.0	56 783.0	54 778.0	62 401.0	39 278.0	40 237.0	37 282.0	38 476.0	33 888.0
Latvia	-	-	-	-	-	69.0	38.0	38.0	38.0	37.0
Lithuania	-	7.0	7.0	7.0	7.0	131.0	157.0	176.0	172.0	182.0
Luxembourg	28 851.0	30 730.0	32 519.0	33 567.0	39 609.0	646 508.0	703 066.0	720 628.0	751 657.0	759 360.0
Mexico	34 967.0	37 715.0	40 493.0	39 661.0	42 129.0	98 421.0	100 169.0	95 543.0	98 010.0	101 057.0
Netherlands	169 633.0	197 696.0	205 459.0	216 015.0	236 298.0	816 667.0	929 746.0	809 663.0	810 986.0	843 954.0
New Zealand	356.0	2 234.0	3 152.0	3 585.0	3 397.0	12 042.0	12 384.0	11 379.0	11 869.0	12 903.0
Norway	25 848.0	35 000.0	37 561.0	35 120.0	31 059.0	28 657.0	26 901.0	25 905.0	24 632.0	21 484.0
Poland	.. c	.. c	.. c	.. c	.. c	11 260.0	12 266.0	11 870.0	10 720.0	11 127.0
Portugal	.. c	.. c	.. c	.. c	.. c	2 288.0	2 372.0	2 504.0	2 437.0	2 538.0
Slovak Republic	-1.0	2.0	1.0	5.0	4.0	783.0	1 108.0	816.0	787.0	778.0
Slovenia	2.0	1.0	-	-	-1.0	353.0	337.0	307.0	285.0	265.0
Spain	70 766.0	83 196.0	88 354.0	90 534.0	88 660.0	36 651.0	35 482.0	31 916.0	35 787.0	38 533.0
Sweden	53 132.0	49 060.0	49 813.0	54 302.0	59 609.0	34 722.0	36 896.0	43 521.0	42 722.0	63 847.0
Switzerland	158 672.0	157 245.0	190 531.0	210 025.0	235 311.0	185 329.0	252 231.0	210 800.0	192 847.0	211 936.0
Turkey	2 147.0	2 327.0	2 548.0	2 623.0	2 539.0	3 726.0	4 074.0	4 193.0	3 834.0	5 814.0
United Kingdom	587 407.0	608 289.0	586 094.0	504 189.0	480 787.0	747 425.0	815 059.0	754 139.0	830 438.0	890 086.0
United States	70 891.0	94 487.0	78 932.0	89 683.0	183 859.0	-	-	-	-	-
EUROPE	**2 099 970.0**	**.. c**	**.. c**	**.. c**	**.. c**	**.. c**	**.. c**	**.. c**	**.. c**	**.. c**
Bulgaria	5.0	45.0	.. c	.. c	61.0	691.0	639.0	539.0	528.0	608.0
Croatia	4.0	7.0	8.0	8.0	9.0	197.0	225.0	209.0	184.0	192.0
Cyprus	.. c	-204.0	-526.0	-969.0	-1 299.0	4 903.0	4 340.0	5 090.0	5 165.0	4 860.0
Malta	8.0	40.0	66.0	63.0	60.0	547.0	597.0	1 442.0	1 637.0	1 471.0
Montenegro	-	1.0	-	-	-	5.0	5.0	5.0	5.0	5.0
Romania	-	-3.0	6.0	12.0	16.0	3 956.0	3 761.0	3 797.0	3 636.0	3 934.0
Russian Federation	4 265.0	3 903.0	3 686.0	3 579.0	3 521.0	14 357.0	13 786.0	12 779.0	13 597.0	12 538.0
Ukraine	3.0	-	-1.0	1.0	2.0	484.0	402.0	803.0	925.0	761.0
AFRICA	**4 484.0**	**4 995.0**	**5 184.0**	**5 059.0**	**5 477.0**	**49 926.0**	**50 403.0**	**48 069.0**	**46 053.0**	**47 500.0**
Northern Africa	.. c	.. c	.. c	.. c	.. c	15 176.0	15 160.0	15 506.0	14 790.0	14 215.0
Algeria	-	-	-	-	-	2 697.0	2 567.0	2 942.0	2 715.0	1 953.0
Egypt	-6.0	54.0	29.0	-4.0	-24.0	10 545.0	11 095.0	11 028.0	11 133.0	11 206.0
Libya	.. c	.. c	.. c	.. c	.. c	1 173.0	761.0	854.0	347.0	341.0
Morocco	-21.0	-29.0	-32.0	.. c	.. c	423.0	423.0	380.0	377.0	457.0
Tunisia	-	5.0	24.0	35.0	43.0	338.0	314.0	302.0	218.0	258.0
Other African countries	.. c	.. c	.. c	.. c	.. c	34 750.0	35 243.0	32 563.0	31 263.0	33 285.0
Nigeria	.. c	89.0	107.0	131.0	.. c	4 252.0	4 844.0	4 504.0	6 572.0	6 811.0
South Africa	3 880.0	4 037.0	4 225.0	4 051.0	4 443.0	7 398.0	8 058.0	9 088.0	9 167.0	10 023.0
AMERICA	**638 554.0**	**763 098.0**	**806 385.0**	**870 537.0**	**978 480.0**	**1 248 956.0**	**1 380 019.0**	**1 374 281.0**	**1 335 610.0**	**1 384 564.0**
Northern America	493 850.0	587 682.0	613 734.0	653 295.0	753 647.0	355 398.0	371 278.0	373 608.0	404 593.0	422 164.0
Central America and Caribbean countries	101 115.0	.. c	.. c	.. c	163 948.0	758 558.0	867 623.0	863 912.0	790 595.0	821 333.0
Bahamas	159.0	.. c	.. c	.. c	.. c	20 191.0	18 524.0	44 491.0	45 319.0	46 061.0
Bermuda	36 191.0	34 443.0	44 203.0	63 894.0	71 103.0	311 363.0	401 435.0	339 399.0	273 240.0	274 576.0
Cayman Islands	.. c	21 306.0	25 400.0	27 181.0	28 633.0	282 111.0	286 601.0	304 716.0	289 959.0	304 816.0
El Salvador	.. c	.. c	.. c	.. c	.. c	2 777.0	2 754.0	2 890.0	3 409.0	3 413.0
Guatemala	15.0	46.0	40.0	37.0	35.0	737.0	748.0	737.0	744.0	789.0
Honduras	2.0	2.0	2.0	2.0	2.0	1 283.0	1 330.0	1 202.0	1 362.0	1 111.0
Nicaragua	.. c	252.0	285.0	319.0	.. c	216.0	189.0	138.0	80.0	-3.0
Panama	728.0	662.0	722.0	799.0	811.0	4 472.0	4 821.0	5 206.0	5 785.0	4 583.0
Virgin Islands, U.S.	..	..	..	..	..	..	..	..	..	..
South America	43 589.0	.. c	.. c	.. c	60 884.0	134 485.0	140 609.0	136 247.0	140 070.0	140 700.0
Argentina	4 936.0	4 965.0	5 406.0	5 799.0	5 659.0	14 273.0	15 219.0	8 907.0	9 974.0	8 730.0
Bolivia	9.0	32.0	31.0	31.0	32.0	454.0	505.0	486.0	.. c	534.0
Brazil	31 266.0	48 617.0	47 461.0	48 319.0	44 676.0	67 922.0	77 486.0	78 963.0	80 864.0	70 742.0
Ecuador	-27.0	-14.0	3.0	20.0	24.0	981.0	715.0	781.0	681.0	29.0
Paraguay	-	-	-	-	-	189.0	168.0	145.0	210.0	197.0
Peru	246.0	.. c	.. c	.. c	498.0	4 541.0	5 700.0	5 455.0	6 470.0	7 394.0
Uruguay	354.0	322.0	337.0	346.0	378.0	2 149.0	1 087.0	1 080.0	998.0	.. c
Venezuela	1 830.0	1 899.0	1 886.0	1 934.0	1 671.0	5 113.0	3 174.0	2 338.0	2 168.0	1 647.0

Table 2. Foreign direct investment positions by country *(cont.)*

At year end

Million US dollars

	Inward					Outward				
	2016	2017	2018	2019	2020	2016	2017	2018	2019	2020
ASIA	**.. c**	**.. c**	**.. c**	**.. c**	**.. c**	**.. c**	**.. c**	**.. c**	**.. c**	**.. c**
Near and Middle East	99 663.0	.. c	.. c	.. c	.. c	.. c	.. c	.. c	.. c	.. c
Gulf Arabian countries	43 108.0	.. c	.. c	.. c	.. c	.. c	.. c	47 413.0	.. c	49 181.0
Kuwait	1 704.0	1 509.0	1 674.0	1 593.0	1 563.0	345.0	407.0	499.0	514.0	656.0
Qatar	2 988.0	3 109.0	2 619.0	3 561.0	3 854.0	7 992.0	13 008.0	14 124.0	14 905.0	15 494.0
Saudi Arabia	12 953.0	14 814.0	15 112.0	14 017.0	10 655.0	10 164.0	10 702.0	10 807.0	11 117.0	11 386.0
United Arab Emirates	24 904.0	30 463.0	33 350.0	35 220.0	44 725.0	13 699.0	16 881.0	18 055.0	18 441.0	19 468.0
Other Near and Middle East	56 555.0	.. c	.. c	.. c	.. c	.. c	.. c	.. c	.. c	.. c
Jordan	.. c	.. c	.. c	.. c	.. c	199.0	220.0	180.0	179.0	156.0
Other Asian countries	.. c	.. c	.. c	.. c	.. c	.. c	.. c	.. c	.. c	.. c
China	54 393.0	63 220.0	51 599.0	53 708.0	54 868.0	97 458.0	105 146.0	107 557.0	113 189.0	123 875.0
Hong Kong, China	15 167.0	16 166.0	17 321.0	18 627.0	18 337.0	69 287.0	79 048.0	81 215.0	89 346.0	92 487.0
India	8 445.0	6 669.0	6 274.0	12 755.0	12 698.0	40 121.0	45 160.0	42 197.0	41 982.0	41 904.0
Indonesia	516.0	560.0	658.0	679.0	837.0	15 049.0	13 866.0	19 886.0	19 324.0	18 715.0
Iran, Islamic Republic of	1.0	1.0	1.0	1.0	1.0	2.0	2.0	2.0	2.0	2.0
Malaysia	1 483.0	2 370.0	2 824.0	2 361.0	-92.0	10 069.0	11 767.0	10 385.0	12 139.0	13 529.0
Philippines	890.0	871.0	896.0	786.0	659.0	6 412.0	6 926.0	5 562.0	5 612.0	5 199.0
Singapore	77 885.0	98 412.0	64 658.0	65 428.0	65 207.0	243 165.0	293 452.0	232 940.0	260 642.0	270 807.0
Chinese Taipei	10 867.0	16 841.0	18 986.0	17 763.0	19 687.0	15 510.0	16 484.0	27 479.0	29 002.0	31 544.0
Thailand	2 132.0	2 349.0	2 253.0	1 847.0	1 809.0	18 386.0	15 578.0	16 415.0	17 628.0	17 450.0
Viet Nam	11.0	27.0	26.0	19.0	18.0	2 433.0	2 461.0	2 895.0	2 883.0	2 820.0
AUSTRALIA, OCEANIA AND POLAR REGIONS	**.. c**	**.. c**	**.. c**	**.. c**	**.. c**	**.. c**	**.. c**	**.. c**	**.. c**	**.. c**
WORLD unallocated and confidential	**771.0**	**10 544.0**	**12 679.0**	**..**	**..**	**20 749.0**	**25 553.0**	**-24 127.0**	**24 587.0**	**23 202.0**
European Union (since 01/02/2020)	..	..	..	..	..	..	..	..	..	..
G20 countries excl. European Union	..	**2 718 245.0**	**2 818 334.0**	**2 984 140.0**	**3 176 598.0**	**2 036 300.0**	**2 145 963.0**	**2 065 331.0**	**2 232 273.0**	**2 330 660.0**
G20 OECD countries	..	**2 571 460.0**	**2 683 913.0**	**2 841 233.0**	**3 039 241.0**	**1 769 558.0**	**1 856 540.0**	**1 775 147.0**	**1 933 059.0**	**2 032 747.0**
G20 Non-OECD countries	..	**146 785.0**	**134 421.0**	**142 907.0**	**137 357.0**	**266 742.0**	**289 423.0**	**290 184.0**	**299 214.0**	**297 913.0**
MENA countries	..	**.. d**	**.. d**	**.. d**	**.. d**	**.. d**	**.. d**	**.. d**	**.. d**	**.. d**
ASEAN countries	..	**.. d**	**71 722.0**	**71 572.0**	**.. d**	**295 689.0**	**344 239.0**	**.. d**	**.. d**	**.. d**

- Nil; .. Not available; c Confidential data; d Secondary Confidentiality

Note: Inward FDI positions are allocated according to the ultimate investing country. Detailed metadata at: *http://metalinks.oecd.org/idi/20220712/6d95*.

Source: OECD *International Direct Investment Statistics (database): https://doi.org/10.1787/idi-data-en*

UNITED STATES

Table 3. Foreign direct investment income by country

Million US dollars

	Inward					Outward				
	2016	2017	2018	2019	2020	2016	2017	2018	2019	2020
WORLD	**141 603.0**	**176 632.0**	**203 687.0**	**200 024.0**	**151 811.0**	**430 948.0**	**518 653.0**	**537 331.0**	**519 745.0**	**452 034.0**
OECD COUNTRIES	**..**	**.. d**	**.. d**	**.. d**	**.. d**	**..**	**349 249.0**	**343 199.0**	**350 382.0**	**294 228.0**
Australia	477.0	-833.0	2 206.0	2 421.0	2 158.0	6 123.0	8 025.0	10 245.0	9 081.0	7 348.0
Austria	569.0	884.0	1 196.0	976.0	1 065.0	391.0	346.0	670.0	664.0	284.0
Belgium	2 919.0	2 799.0	1 898.0	1 438.0	1 770.0	4 558.0	6 018.0	6 191.0	6 648.0	7 000.0
Canada	13 954.0	23 008.0	27 300.0	27 786.0	19 480.0	18 326.0	24 917.0	30 315.0	26 660.0	20 954.0
Chile	120.0	2.0	203.0	224.0	119.0	1 664.0	2 069.0	2 553.0	2 021.0	1 430.0
Colombia	21.0	2.0	12.0	19.0	6.0	404.0	831.0	1 130.0	857.0	332.0
Costa Rica	-1.0	2.0	-1.0	4.0	6.0	125.0	129.0	143.0	197.0	140.0
Czech Republic	1.0	.. c	.. c	.. c	-17.0	611.0	515.0	386.0	431.0	437.0
Denmark	1 093.0	1 437.0	1 739.0	1 824.0	2 103.0	658.0	451.0	-39.0	579.0	658.0
Estonia	-	.. c	-3.0	-1.0	.. c	3.0	9.0	15.0	9.0	10.0
Finland	472.0	322.0	821.0	1 053.0	1 342.0	47.0	85.0	139.0	121.0	420.0
France	12 751.0	11 033.0	12 208.0	11 340.0	13 497.0	2 716.0	3 202.0	1 153.0	2 855.0	1 598.0
Germany	12 397.0	20 869.0	22 623.0	20 421.0	18 252.0	4 805.0	6 649.0	5 358.0	7 171.0	5 502.0
Greece	.. c	60.0	60.0	52.0	31.0	125.0	134.0	177.0	79.0	123.0
Hungary	.. c	306.0	-885.0	1 581.0	1 660.0	447.0	532.0	470.0	238.0	611.0
Iceland	268.0	290.0	.. c	.. c	.. c	47.0	74.0	84.0	33.0	18.0
Ireland	7 153.0	9 677.0	9 023.0	8 209.0	7 988.0	54 310.0	62 276.0	58 430.0	62 692.0	55 982.0
Israel	229.0	369.0	186.0	100.0	364.0	837.0	814.0	803.0	1 036.0	515.0
Italy	550.0	781.0	1 539.0	1 354.0	983.0	1 620.0	1 521.0	1 559.0	1 784.0	1 131.0
Japan	18 107.0	27 183.0	26 215.0	27 000.0	20 542.0	12 872.0	12 456.0	12 633.0	12 121.0	14 899.0
Korea	1 086.0	1 674.0	1 654.0	1 691.0	1 922.0	2 638.0	1 924.0	2 791.0	2 638.0	2 513.0
Latvia	-	.. c	2.0	1.0	.. c	11.0	10.0	8.0	8.0	7.0
Lithuania	-	.. c	-	-	.. c	-1.0	3.0	-1.0	6.0	-2.0
Luxembourg	11 347.0	15 698.0	16 539.0	13 148.0	9 561.0	35 403.0	42 422.0	41 494.0	37 901.0	33 443.0
Mexico	1 372.0	1 341.0	1 388.0	1 649.0	2 505.0	6 846.0	8 733.0	9 111.0	9 600.0	6 508.0
Netherlands	11 849.0	13 503.0	20 721.0	19 753.0	10 813.0	70 098.0	79 489.0	83 119.0	82 678.0	65 859.0
New Zealand	-122.0	33.0	388.0	334.0	675.0	504.0	881.0	483.0	466.0	707.0
Norway	-254.0	700.0	2 466.0	1 218.0	-1 093.0	815.0	1 619.0	1 211.0	1 337.0	657.0
Poland	.. c	.. c	.. c	.. c	.. c	1 189.0	869.0	1 466.0	1 001.0	841.0
Portugal	-2.0	56.0	-15.0	46.0	33.0	167.0	190.0	150.0	177.0	124.0
Slovak Republic	-	.. c	-	-	.. c	-21.0	-1.0	29.0	-12.0	-7.0
Slovenia	-	.. c	-1.0	-	.. c	21.0	12.0	13.0	-	16.0
Spain	1 507.0	1 733.0	2 834.0	1 796.0	1 832.0	1 864.0	2 936.0	2 536.0	3 807.0	3 222.0
Sweden	3 292.0	2 682.0	3 701.0	3 472.0	3 667.0	1 841.0	3 043.0	1 293.0	3 399.0	1 844.0
Switzerland	18 291.0	13 779.0	20 295.0	19 615.0	11 134.0	29 971.0	29 532.0	21 477.0	21 856.0	17 681.0
Turkey	115.0	77.0	119.0	136.0	-19.0	260.0	622.0	605.0	466.0	324.0
United Kingdom	14 621.0	20 979.0	14 808.0	19 276.0	11 877.0	39 967.0	46 875.0	46 272.0	50 831.0	41 239.0
United States	-	-	-	-	-	-	-	-	-	-
EUROPE	**98 557.0**	**118 655.0**	**132 963.0**	**127 755.0**	**97 505.0**	**.. c**	**.. c**	**.. c**	**.. c**	**.. c**
Bulgaria	3.0	.. c	.. c	-	-	58.0	41.0	50.0	38.0	55.0
Croatia	-	.. c	1.0	1.0	.. c	10.0	11.0	11.0	12.0	9.0
Cyprus	125.0	-90.0	-105.0	-47.0	55.0	172.0	297.0	360.0	342.0	490.0
Malta	.. c	42.0	29.0	58.0	39.0	45.0	46.0	80.0	199.0	52.0
Montenegro	-	-	-	-	-	-	-	-	-	-
Romania	-	16.0	.. c	8.0	.. c	24.0	169.0	165.0	280.0	206.0
Russian Federation	-36.0	156.0	.. c	18.0	93.0	907.0	1 096.0	1 105.0	932.0	983.0
Ukraine	-	-4.0	-2.0	-1.0	-1.0	39.0	89.0	105.0	159.0	123.0
AFRICA	**4.0**	**105.0**	**204.0**	**327.0**	**544.0**	**2 040.0**	**2 485.0**	**3 561.0**	**3 784.0**	**1 758.0**
Northern Africa	.. c	.. c	.. c	.. c	-21.0	266.0	.. c	1 611.0	1 353.0	318.0
Algeria	-	-	-	-	-	254.0	391.0	436.0	487.0	38.0
Egypt	.. c	6.0	-44.0	-32.0	-28.0	180.0	581.0	1 105.0	794.0	269.0
Libya	-	-	-	-	-	-139.0	.. c	59.0	39.0	-2.0
Morocco	-	-2.0	-1.0	-	-	-43.0	1.0	-5.0	21.0	8.0
Tunisia	-	.. c	.. c	.. c	7.0	14.0	16.0	16.0	12.0	5.0
Other African countries	.. c	.. c	.. c	.. c	565.0	1 774.0	.. c	1 950.0	2 431.0	1 440.0
Nigeria	.. c	6.0	.. c	.. c	.. c	693.0	523.0	244.0	674.0	263.0
South Africa	17.0	-63.0	41.0	248.0	.. c	288.0	596.0	493.0	602.0	496.0
AMERICA	**20 658.0**	**26 599.0**	**34 456.0**	**36 419.0**	**27 000.0**	**102 227.0**	**127 557.0**	**136 587.0**	**128 272.0**	**110 405.0**
Northern America	13 954.0	23 008.0	27 300.0	27 786.0	19 480.0	18 325.0	24 916.0	30 314.0	26 659.0	20 953.0
Central America and Caribbean countries	.. c	.. c	6 107.0	6 995.0	7 249.0	78 687.0	93 038.0	96 858.0	93 182.0	84 589.0
Bahamas	-32.0	45.0	110.0	110.0	78.0	708.0	1 323.0	4 122.0	3 564.0	2 873.0
Bermuda	989.0	914.0	1 893.0	2 642.0	2 624.0	43 030.0	48 188.0	43 929.0	40 558.0	40 797.0
Cayman Islands	3 727.0	825.0	2 056.0	1 886.0	1 567.0	25 413.0	31 880.0	34 340.0	33 776.0	28 502.0
El Salvador	-	-	-	-	-	600.0	317.0	367.0	367.0	296.0
Guatemala	-	-12.0	-8.0	-4.0	-3.0	10.0	75.0	48.0	48.0	43.0
Honduras	-	-	-	-	-	114.0	74.0	96.0	282.0	54.0
Nicaragua	-	1.0	1.0	1.0	1.0	-23.0	-18.0	-24.0	-26.0	-29.0
Panama	117.0	-10.0	119.0	122.0	112.0	475.0	605.0	578.0	726.0	45.0
Virgin Islands, U.S.	..	..	..	..	..	..	..	..	..	..
South America	.. c	164.0	1 049.0	1 638.0	273.0	5 205.0	9 606.0	9 407.0	8 426.0	4 848.0
Argentina	-71.0	-136.0	3.0	-13.0	-29.0	1 698.0	1 811.0	1 077.0	344.0	-157.0
Bolivia	-	-1.0	-	-	-	108.0	84.0	70.0	78.0	32.0
Brazil	213.0	60.0	109.0	1 084.0	148.0	1 557.0	3 338.0	3 468.0	4 104.0	2 109.0
Ecuador	.. c	2.0	6.0	8.0	1.0	147.0	127.0	-54.0	139.0	65.0
Paraguay	-	-	-	-	-	21.0	.. c	.. c	44.0	11.0
Peru	.. c	-18.0	4.0	17.0	.. c	296.0	1 092.0	624.0	867.0	1 005.0
Uruguay	36.0	18.0	21.0	20.0	.. c	-54.0	111.0	124.0	61.0	4.0
Venezuela	73.0	236.0	.. c	.. c	.. c	-592.0	-225.0	50.0	-368.0	-158.0

Table 3. Foreign direct investment income by country *(cont.)*

Million US dollars

	Inward					Outward				
	2016	2017	2018	2019	2020	2016	2017	2018	2019	2020
ASIA	**20 177.0**	**.. c**	**.. c**	**.. c**	**.. c**	**.. c**	**.. c**	**.. c**	**.. c**	**.. c**
Near and Middle East	1 154.0	..	1 134.0	949.0	77.0	.. c	.. c	.. c	.. c	.. c
Gulf Arabian countries	928.0	.. c	.. c	.. c	.. c	..	8 174.0	9 562.0	.. c	.. c
Kuwait	30.0	-9.0	3.0	-122.0	.. c	69.0	57.0	77.0	45.0	139.0
Qatar	.. c	75.0	.. c	.. c	.. c	3 343.0	5 475.0	6 904.0	4 745.0	2 150.0
Saudi Arabia	.. c	.. c	.. c	76.0	.. c	1 097.0	1 165.0	969.0	872.0	618.0
United Arab Emirates	232.0	482.0	522.0	834.0	884.0	1 375.0	1 597.0	1 399.0	1 429.0	1 383.0
Other Near and Middle East	226.0	353.0	.. c	.. c	.. c	.. c	.. c	.. c	.. c	.. c
Jordan	-4.0	-5.0	.. c	.. c	-4.0	.. c	35.0	1.0	.. c	.. c
Other Asian countries	19 023.0	.. c	.. c	.. c	.. c	.. c	.. c	.. c	.. c	.. c
China	-745.0	209.0	1 271.0	1 197.0	115.0	12 330.0	13 634.0	12 970.0	11 023.0	10 714.0
Hong Kong, China	-202.0	-90.0	970.0	652.0	411.0	4 763.0	7 158.0	11 023.0	9 893.0	10 763.0
India	120.0	103.0	133.0	-212.0	122.0	4 094.0	4 351.0	3 889.0	3 689.0	3 594.0
Indonesia	29.0	59.0	27.0	36.0	32.0	1 031.0	1 542.0	3 129.0	573.0	1 050.0
Iran, Islamic Republic of	-	.. c	-	-	-	-	-	-	-	-
Malaysia	4.0	-31.0	-	-44.0	-95.0	862.0	1 349.0	1 412.0	1 420.0	1 317.0
Philippines	2.0	-38.0	-19.0	-11.0	-7.0	815.0	855.0	428.0	606.0	264.0
Singapore	166.0	688.0	1 309.0	852.0	480.0	23 810.0	29 955.0	40 981.0	34 866.0	34 309.0
Chinese Taipei	381.0	614.0	776.0	546.0	330.0	1 343.0	1 416.0	1 397.0	966.0	732.0
Thailand	89.0	-8.0	-58.0	11.0	-39.0	1 657.0	2 136.0	1 625.0	1 402.0	922.0
Viet Nam	-	-	-1.0	1.0	-1.0	136.0	77.0	161.0	302.0	209.0
AUSTRALIA, OCEANIA AND POLAR REGIONS	**405.0**	**.. c**	**.. c**	**.. c**	**.. c**	**..**	**..**	**10 802.0**	**9 686.0**	**..**
WORLD unallocated and confidential	**1 802.0**	**481.0**	**-605.0**	**103.0**	**42.0**	**-7 794.0**	**72.0**	**2 277.0**	**-7 652.0**	**4 778.0**
European Union (since 01/02/2020)	**..**	**..**	**..**	**..**	**..**	**..**	**..**	**..**	**..**	**..**
G20 countries excl. European Union	**.. d**	**.. d**	**.. d**	**115 508.0**	**.. d**	**119 175.0**	**142 457.0**	**147 142.0**	**145 346.0**	**121 423.0**
G20 OECD countries	**75 430.0**	**106 112.0**	**110 060.0**	**113 074.0**	**91 197.0**	**96 173.0**	**114 924.0**	**120 042.0**	**123 207.0**	**102 016.0**
G20 Non-OECD countries	**.. d**	**.. d**	**.. d**	**2 434.0**	**.. d**	**23 002.0**	**27 533.0**	**27 100.0**	**22 139.0**	**19 407.0**
MENA countries	**.. d**	**.. d**	**.. d**	**.. d**	**.. d**	**.. d**	**.. d**	**.. d**	**.. d**	**.. d**
ASEAN countries	**290.0**	**666.0**	**.. d**	**.. d**	**.. d**	**28 323.0**	**35 923.0**	**.. d**	**.. d**	**.. d**

- Nil; .. Not available; c Confidential data; d Secondary Confidentiality

Note: Detailed metadata at: *http://metalinks.oecd.org/idi/20220712/6d95*.

Source: *OECD International Direct Investment Statistics (database)*: *https://doi.org/10.1787/idi-data-en*

UNITED STATES

Table 4. Foreign direct investment flows by industrial sector

Million US dollars

	Inward					Outward				
	2016	2017	2018	2019	2020	2016	2017	2018	2019	2020
All FDI activities	**459 419.0**	**308 957.0**	**203 234.0**	**225 108.0**	**150 828.0**	**284 469.0**	**327 781.0**	**-157 407.0**	**28 596.0**	**234 919.0**
Agriculture, forestry and fishing	**-249.0**	**307.0**	**834.0**	**591.0**	**198.0**	**202.0**	**-79.0**	**133.0**	**-977.0**	**1 581.0**
Mining and quarrying	**19 935.0**	**3 274.0**	**-1 140.0**	**8 436.0**	**-4 369.0**	**-5 073.0**	**-11 233.0**	**-3 788.0**	**-6 282.0**	**1 954.0**
Extraction activities	19 755.0	2 831.0	-3 954.0	7 650.0	-4 295.0	-3 478.0	-11 059.0	-3 750.0	-8 919.0	-3 309.0
Manufacturing	**200 578.0**	**148 068.0**	**143 429.0**	**93 366.0**	**75 266.0**	**57 908.0**	**82 886.0**	**41 886.0**	**70 808.0**	**120 367.0**
of which:										
Food products, beverages and tobacco	24 265.0	28 938.0	36 029.0	4 998.0	-468.0	4 722.0	9 499.0	3 100.0	2 960.0	4 361.0
Textiles, wood and paper products; printing	2 056.0	2 917.0	3 993.0	-985.0	2 892.0	969.0	2 049.0	2 256.0	1 109.0	-350.0
Chemical, rubber, plastic, non-metallic mineral products	117 197.0	59 440.0	70 655.0	64 104.0	41 777.0	.. c	.. c	.. c	.. c	.. c
Metal and machinery products, except electrical equipment	32 684.0	47 769.0	23 733.0	18 560.0	25 880.0	23 406.0	43 940.0	18 416.0	23 114.0	21 657.0
Motor vehicles, trailers, semi-trailers, other transport equipment	23 903.0	8 219.0	7 666.0	7 516.0	4 670.0	7 697.0	7 995.0	6 053.0	4 365.0	-3 404.0
Other manufacturing	473.0	785.0	1 353.0	-828.0	514.0	.. c	.. c	.. c	.. c	.. c
Electricity, gas, steam and air conditioning supply	**.. c**	**.. c**	**.. c**	**.. c**	**4 906.0**	**1 558.0**	**153.0**	**-1 675.0**	**817.0**	**.. c**
Water supply; sewerage, waste management and remediation activities	**.. c**	**.. c**	**.. c**	**.. c**	**-133.0**	**-124.0**	**51.0**	**-40.0**	**-374.0**	**.. c**
Construction	**-72.0**	**2 598.0**	**-492.0**	**12 252.0**	**-841.0**	**1 008.0**	**-368.0**	**-61.0**	**-5.0**	**-99.0**
Services	**.. c**	**147 491.0**	**53 574.0**	**99 616.0**	**75 799.0**	**228 990.0**	**256 370.0**	**-193 864.0**	**-35 391.0**	**110 395.0**
Wholesale and retail trade; repair of motor vehicles and motorcycles	33 885.0	64 224.0	69 669.0	36 743.0	42 986.0	20 291.0	12 133.0	-15 988.0	22 754.0	2 494.0
Transportation and storage	14 495.0	8 038.0	-368.0	4 821.0	-326.0	3 539.0	3 560.0	-384.0	1 227.0	1 311.0
Accommodation and food service activities	1 889.0	9 950.0	-541.0	1 701.0	358.0	1 295.0	246.0	1 626.0	9 711.0	-1 655.0
Information and communication	19 035.0	3 392.0	12 061.0	36.0	965.0	21 466.0	16 316.0	55 847.0	9 626.0	5 803.0
Financial and insurance activities	.. c	24 271.0	46 370.0	31 925.0	25 255.0	151 306.0	201 972.0	-259 519.0	-104 549.0	63 861.0
Activities of holding companies	.. c	-8 599.0	2 606.0	15 020.0	-52.0	137 866.0	169 491.0	-355 894.0	-76 722.0	99 756.0
Real estate activities	13 110.0	8 551.0	23 972.0	7 627.0	9 013.0	402.0	4 219.0	163.0	733.0	303.0
Professional, scientific and technical activities	.. c	14 080.0	-97 940.0	14 777.0	1 943.0	14 473.0	-2 580.0	15 588.0	9 645.0	26 711.0
Administrative and support service activities	.. c	15 549.0	-637.0	-241.0	-2 532.0	14 178.0	11 436.0	7 011.0	13 164.0	11 077.0
Public administration; activities of households and of extraterritorial organisations	..	..	..	..	..	..	..	..	..	..
Education	1 533.0	-968.0	-265.0	-68.0	-345.0	-281.0	362.0	479.0	14.0	-356.0
Human health and social work activities	3 334.0	599.0	52.0	2 810.0	421.0	284.0	-958.0	256.0	156.0	2 074.0
Arts, entertainment and recreation	304.0	875.0	600.0	-1 002.0	-1 729.0	1 414.0	7 782.0	91.0	1 674.0	-834.0
Other services	1 928.0	-1 070.0	601.0	487.0	-210.0	623.0	1 882.0	966.0	454.0	-394.0
Not allocated and confidential	**65 383.0**	**7 219.0**	**7 029.0**	**10 847.0**	**2.0**	**-**	**1.0**	**2.0**	**-**	**721.0**
Private real estate activities	..	..	..	..	..	..	..	..	..	..

- Nil; .. Not available; c Confidential data

Note: Detailed metadata at: *http://metalinks.oecd.org/idi/20220712/6d95.*

Source: OECD *International Direct Investment Statistics (database): https://doi.org/10.1787/idi-data-en*

UNITED STATES

Table 5. Foreign direct investment positions by industrial sector
At year end

Million US dollars

	Inward					Outward				
	2016	2017	2018	2019	2020	2016	2017	2018	2019	2020
All FDI activities	**3 561 808.0**	**3 952 314.0**	**4 179 984.0**	**4 439 255.0**	**4 626 452.0**	**5 518 644.0**	**6 097 690.0**	**5 792 290.0**	**5 907 424.0**	**6 152 301.0**
Agriculture, forestry and fishing	**3 767.0**	**4 375.0**	**5 396.0**	**6 061.0**	**6 433.0**	**6 161.0**	**5 289.0**	**5 381.0**	**6 964.0**	**8 189.0**
Mining and quarrying	**93 054.0**	**101 822.0**	**97 982.0**	**105 050.0**	**89 361.0**	**163 529.0**	**162 908.0**	**165 305.0**	**160 105.0**	**154 291.0**
Extraction activities	68 070.0	76 683.0	62 191.0	69 350.0	53 692.0	124 240.0	124 952.0	123 153.0	118 509.0	107 289.0
Manufacturing	**1 476 461.0**	**1 595 788.0**	**1 719 274.0**	**1 805 020.0**	**1 866 756.0**	**687 625.0**	**806 448.0**	**738 377.0**	**857 510.0**	**956 176.0**
of which:										
Food products, beverages and tobacco	132 788.0	170 766.0	207 021.0	213 096.0	213 961.0	107 656.0	139 566.0	114 161.0	113 657.0	117 061.0
Textiles, wood and paper products; printing	20 851.0	21 439.0	25 331.0	26 333.0	29 070.0	19 213.0	20 409.0	21 909.0	22 159.0	21 857.0
Chemical, rubber, plastic, non-metallic mineral products	847 652.0	843 883.0	896 637.0	938 832.0	958 273.0	.. c	.. c	.. c	.. c	.. c
Metal and machinery products, except electrical equipment	325 841.0	417 651.0	438 402.0	463 904.0	495 621.0	252 649.0	327 841.0	287 919.0	340 591.0	365 553.0
Motor vehicles, trailers, semi-trailers, other transport equipment	137 494.0	128 352.0	136 869.0	149 471.0	155 341.0	75 646.0	87 292.0	83 444.0	87 195.0	83 137.0
Other manufacturing	11 836.0	13 697.0	15 014.0	13 385.0	14 490.0	.. c	.. c	.. c	.. c	.. c
Electricity, gas, steam and air conditioning supply	.. c	.. c	.. c	.. c	.. c	**15 839.0**	**21 102.0**	**13 395.0**	**14 161.0**	**14 909.0**
Water supply; sewerage, waste management and remediation activities	.. c	.. c	.. c	.. c	.. c	**746.0**	**908.0**	**1 749.0**	**1 300.0**	**1 245.0**
Construction	**25 807.0**	**30 818.0**	**29 532.0**	**41 568.0**	**40 711.0**	**6 477.0**	**6 444.0**	**6 607.0**	**6 043.0**	**6 227.0**
Services	**1 881 025.0**	.. c	**2 226 575.0**	**2 364 443.0**	**2 501 104.0**	**4 638 266.0**	**5 094 592.0**	**4 861 476.0**	**4 861 339.0**	**5 011 265.0**
Wholesale and retail trade; repair of motor vehicles and motorcycles	435 451.0	514 586.0	583 318.0	617 299.0	662 916.0	297 274.0	324 223.0	287 663.0	304 676.0	309 404.0
Transportation and storage	85 969.0	94 948.0	94 693.0	98 867.0	97 867.0	37 566.0	39 441.0	36 335.0	35 965.0	35 629.0
Accommodation and food service activities	22 388.0	30 197.0	25 817.0	27 659.0	28 060.0	25 067.0	25 048.0	41 331.0	50 891.0	51 331.0
Information and communication	171 474.0	197 266.0	208 932.0	216 525.0	243 163.0	218 343.0	240 143.0	292 489.0	292 274.0	299 826.0
Financial and insurance activities	822 612.0	898 998.0	909 202.0	970 945.0	1 032 607.0	3 694 843.0	4 074 718.0	3 815 640.0	3 771 837.0	3 869 448.0
Activities of holding companies	183 030.0	218 856.0	215 096.0	225 476.0	228 485.0	2 869 915.0	3 169 493.0	2 786 718.0	2 753 213.0	2 851 020.0
Real estate activities	74 839.0	90 944.0	116 771.0	124 453.0	133 926.0	40 719.0	43 810.0	43 056.0	43 123.0	42 258.0
Professional, scientific and technical activities	190 599.0	204 454.0	195 597.0	217 224.0	220 058.0	147 181.0	147 331.0	157 883.0	170 706.0	199 082.0
Administrative and support service activities	53 928.0	.. c	67 728.0	65 542.0	57 857.0	136 518.0	150 384.0	142 334.0	143 213.0	154 401.0
Public administration; activities of households and of extraterritorial organisations	..	..	..	..	..	..	..	..	..	..
Education	5 042.0	2 850.0	2 626.0	2 810.0	2 267.0	2 426.0	2 601.0	2 972.0	2 943.0	2 803.0
Human health and social work activities	12 181.0	13 057.0	13 862.0	16 806.0	17 270.0	8 251.0	6 236.0	5 102.0	5 393.0	7 521.0
Arts, entertainment and recreation	3 371.0	4 299.0	4 895.0	4 318.0	1 687.0	9 831.0	19 607.0	19 789.0	21 410.0	20 852.0
Other services	3 171.0	2 517.0	3 134.0	1 995.0	3 426.0	20 247.0	21 050.0	16 882.0	18 908.0	18 710.0
Not allocated and confidential	**81 694.0**	**120 167.0**	**101 225.0**	**117 113.0**	**122 087.0**	**1.0**	**-1.0**	**-**	**2.0**	**-1.0**
Private real estate activities	..	..	..	..	..	..	..	..	..	..

- Nil; .. Not available; c Confidential data

Note: Detailed metadata at: *http://metalinks.oecd.org/idi/20220712/6d95*.

Source: OECD *International Direct Investment Statistics (database)*: *https://doi.org/10.1787/idi-data-en*

UNITED STATES

Table 6. Foreign direct investment income by industrial sector

Million US dollars

	Inward					Outward				
	2016	2017	2018	2019	2020	2016	2017	2018	2019	2020
All FDI activities	**141 603.0**	**176 632.0**	**203 687.0**	**200 024.0**	**151 811.0**	**430 948.0**	**518 653.0**	**537 331.0**	**519 745.0**	**452 034.0**
Agriculture, forestry and fishing	**252.0**	**87.0**	**175.0**	**129.0**	**216.0**	**535.0**	**346.0**	**106.0**	**599.0**	**547.0**
Mining and quarrying	**-2 289.0**	**-1 325.0**	**2 999.0**	**2 195.0**	**-617.0**	**2 552.0**	**11 495.0**	**17 036.0**	**12 366.0**	**11 205.0**
Extraction activities	-3 491.0	-3 166.0	1 426.0	960.0	-1 683.0	-248.0	5 756.0	9 731.0	7 617.0	2 399.0
Manufacturing	**66 812.0**	**91 626.0**	**93 157.0**	**80 523.0**	**62 561.0**	**72 843.0**	**89 883.0**	**81 152.0**	**73 340.0**	**69 135.0**
of which:										
Food products, beverages and tobacco	7 885.0	11 621.0	10 788.0	10 162.0	10 301.0	6 761.0	10 006.0	7 660.0	7 109.0	6 644.0
Textiles, wood and paper products; printing	1 252.0	2 285.0	2 325.0	1 863.0	2 015.0	1 896.0	2 211.0	2 353.0	1 865.0	1 386.0
Chemical, rubber, plastic, non-metallic mineral products	29 525.0	46 043.0	43 501.0	41 559.0	26 776.0	28 543.0	30 537.0	28 659.0	28 332.0	28 310.0
Metal and machinery products, except electrical equipment	18 100.0	18 913.0	25 639.0	17 744.0	16 882.0	26 595.0	35 822.0	30 808.0	27 747.0	25 934.0
Motor vehicles, trailers, semi-trailers, other transport equipment	8 888.0	11 877.0	10 047.0	8 425.0	5 706.0	8 167.0	9 700.0	10 433.0	6 875.0	4 696.0
Other manufacturing	1 161.0	885.0	859.0	769.0	882.0	882.0	1 607.0	1 240.0	1 410.0	2 165.0
Electricity, gas, steam and air conditioning supply	**.. c**	**2 317.0**	**3 795.0**	**.. c**	**.. c**	**2 128.0**	**1 505.0**	**.. c**	**.. c**	**.. c**
Water supply; sewerage, waste management and remediation activities	**.. c**	**360.0**	**420.0**	**.. c**	**.. c**	**44.0**	**50.0**	**.. c**	**.. c**	**.. c**
Construction	**918.0**	**-734.0**	**-1 050.0**	**-51.0**	**738.0**	**264.0**	**-35.0**	**90.0**	**259.0**	**465.0**
Services	**.. c**	**84 300.0**	**104 189.0**	**112 315.0**	**85 469.0**	**352 583.0**	**415 410.0**	**437 872.0**	**432 056.0**	**369 859.0**
Wholesale and retail trade; repair of motor vehicles and motorcycles	14 403.0	23 729.0	32 505.0	32 558.0	26 321.0	27 382.0	27 137.0	32 450.0	32 077.0	30 795.0
Transportation and storage	3 218.0	4 869.0	5 539.0	5 528.0	4 622.0	4 334.0	4 249.0	3 713.0	4 380.0	2 733.0
Accommodation and food service activities	1 510.0	1 930.0	1 761.0	2 146.0	-262.0	2 687.0	3 464.0	4 378.0	4 617.0	882.0
Information and communication	2 119.0	5 047.0	7 581.0	8 240.0	5 384.0	17 128.0	15 043.0	20 994.0	19 532.0	13 463.0
Financial and insurance activities	40 281.0	37 362.0	45 837.0	50 994.0	41 061.0	266 748.0	325 615.0	345 038.0	328 193.0	287 161.0
Activities of holding companies	7 661.0	7 724.0	9 486.0	8 680.0	7 379.0	220 726.0	274 381.0	283 057.0	269 905.0	237 007.0
Real estate activities	3 630.0	2 058.0	1 155.0	2 887.0	2 459.0	1 386.0	2 446.0	1 915.0	1 331.0	1 768.0
Professional, scientific and technical activities	2 892.0	3 664.0	3 443.0	4 675.0	3 577.0	12 038.0	12 491.0	10 854.0	18 515.0	15 514.0
Administrative and support service activities	.. c	5 475.0	5 546.0	5 121.0	3 504.0	18 668.0	21 904.0	15 671.0	20 183.0	16 575.0
Public administration; activities of households and of extraterritorial organisations	..	..	..	..	..	..	..	..	..	..
Education	-174.0	-369.0	-292.0	-119.0	-326.0	236.0	195.0	585.0	800.0	726.0
Human health and social work activities	829.0	784.0	804.0	621.0	479.0	150.0	197.0	179.0	215.0	174.0
Arts, entertainment and recreation	-140.0	-146.0	139.0	-313.0	-1 500.0	724.0	1 095.0	1 036.0	1 349.0	-825.0
Other services	-80.0	-103.0	171.0	-23.0	150.0	1 102.0	1 574.0	1 059.0	864.0	893.0
Not allocated and confidential	**4 586.0**	**1.0**	**2.0**	**4 913.0**	**3 444.0**	**-1.0**	**-1.0**	**1 075.0**	**1 125.0**	**823.0**
Private real estate activities	..	..	..	..	..	..	..	..	..	..

.. Not available; c Confidential data

Note: Detailed metadata at: *http://metalinks.oecd.org/idi/20220712/6d95*.

Source: *OECD International Direct Investment Statistics (database): https://doi.org/10.1787/idi-data-en*

www.ingramcontent.com/pod-product-compliance
Lightning Source LLC
Chambersburg PA
CBHW061159240926
51846CB00006B/1062